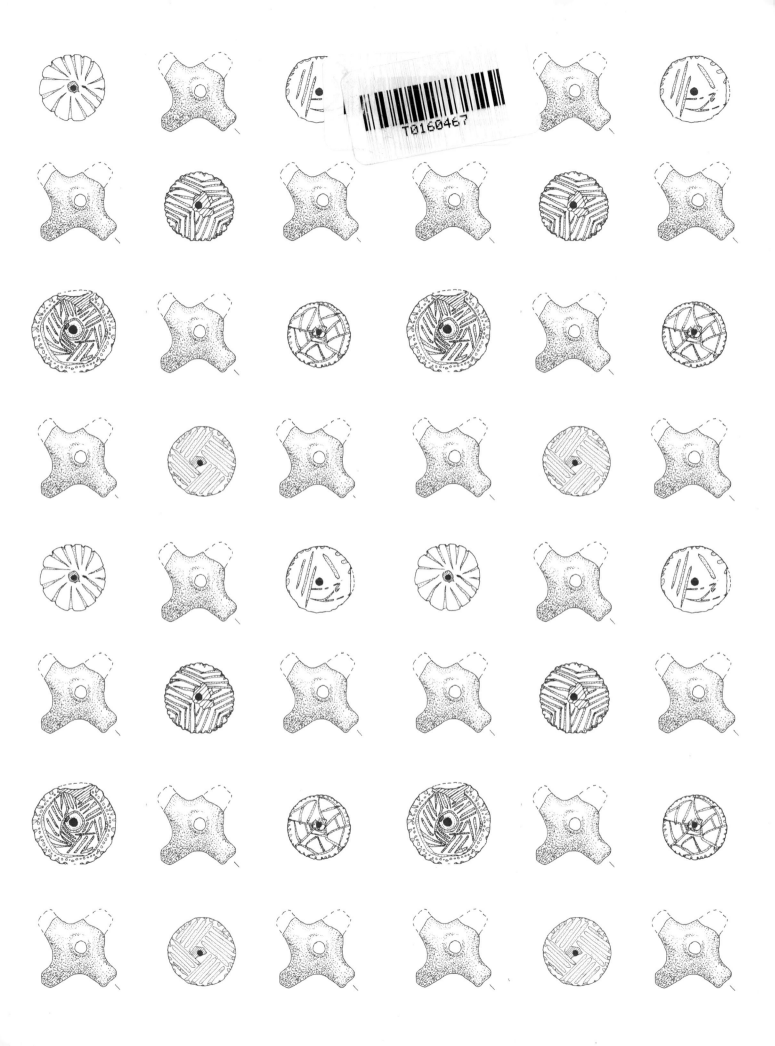

Monumenta Archaeologica

Volume 20

COTSEN INSTITUTE OF
ARCHAEOLOGY AT UCLA

Prehistoric Sitagroi:

Excavations in Northeast Greece, 1968–1970
Volume 2: The Final Report

Edited by

Ernestine S. Elster and Colin Renfrew

COTSEN INSTITUTE OF ARCHAEOLOGY
UNIVERSITY OF CALIFORNIA, LOS ANGELES
2003

Design and production: Leyba Associates, Santa Fe

Library of Congress Cataloging in Publication Data
    Prehistoric Sitagroi
    Monumenta Archaeologica: v. 20
    Bibliography: v2, p.
1. Sitagroi Site (Greece) 2. Excavations (Archaeology)—
Greece. 3. Neolithic period—Greece. 4. Copper age—Greece.
5. Greece—Antiquities. I. Renfrew, Colin, 1937– . II. Elster,
Ernestine S., 1925–. IV. Series: Monumenta Archaeologica (University
of California, Los Angeles. Cotsen Institute of Archaeology) ; v. 20

ISBN: 1-931745-02-1

Undertaken with the assistance of the Institute for Aegean Prehistory.
Additional support came from the Ahmanson Foundation and from the
National Endowment for the Humanities.

Contributors

J. M. ADOVASIO
Department of Anthropology and Mercyhurst Archaeological Institute, Mercyhurst College, Erie, Pennsylvania

MARTIN BISKOWSKI
Cotsen Institute of Archaeology at UCLA

SARANTIS DIMITRIADIS
Department of Mineralogy and Petrology, Aristotle University, Thessaloniki

JOHN DIXON
Department of Geology and Geophysics, University of Edinburgh

ERNESTINE S. ELSTER
Cotsen Institute of Archaeology at UCLA

ELIZABETH GARDNER
Independent Scholar, USA

DAVID HARDY
British School of Archaeology at Athens

J. S. ILLINGWORTH
Mercyhurst Archaeological Institute, Mercyhurst College, Erie, Pennsylvania

MICHELE MILLER
Archaeology Department, Boston University,

MARIANNA NIKOLAIDOU
Cotsen Institute of Archaeology at UCLA

COLIN RENFREW
Disney Professor of Archaeology and Director of the McDonald Institute for Archaeological Research in the University of Cambridge.

JANE M. RENFREW
Lucy Cavendish College, University of Cambridge

SIR NICHOLAS SHACKLETON, F.R.S.
Department of Earth Sciences, University of Cambridge

KATERINA SKOURTOPOULOU
Department of Archaeology, University of Cambridge

ELIZABETH SLATER
Professor of Archaeology, University of Liverpool

ZOFIA ANNA STOS
Research Laboratory for Archaeology and History of Art, University of Oxford

RUTH TRINGHAM
Department of Anthropology, University of California, Berkeley

Contents

List of Tables

List of Figures

List of Plates

Preface:
Overview and Acknowledgements

The task of publishing in detail and with full documentation the results and the finds from a major stratigraphic excavation is not a light one. The first volume reporting on the excavations at Sitagroi, undertaken from 1968 to 1970, appeared in 1986 (*Sitagroi* 1, referred to hereafter as volume 1). It contained an account of the excavations themselves, of the relative chronology resulting from the stratigraphic sequence, a detailed absolute chronology based on a long series of radiocarbon dates, and a full description of the pottery from each phase. Now, thirty years after the conclusion of the excavations, we are in a position to offer the second and final volume, detailing the remaining finds and materials unearthed at the site. Indeed, our goal has been to give due weight to each set of materials and, wherever possible, to follow along as crafts and technologies gave way to activities, thus shaping this volume with a character all its own.

Several factors were involved in this long task, not least other demands and the discharge of other responsibilities by the principal investigators and the various contributors. It is an undertaking which, we feel, would certainly have been better accomplished sooner. But as these words are written, fully thirty years after the conclusion of the fieldwork, we are above all content that the task is now completed and that the materials from Sitagroi are now fully available.

In this short preface we shall first recapitulate the aims of the enterprise, as initiated in 1968. It seems appropriate to indicate those objectives that were accomplished already in the first volume of the final report, and then we shall review synoptically the contributions offered here. The map (Preface figure 1) has been newly prepared and includes all of the sites referred to in both volumes of this Sitagroi report.

THE AIMS AND THE FIRST VOLUME

In the first volume of the final report (volume 1:477) the objectives of the enterprise were summarized as follows:

> The excavations at Sitagroi were conducted with two prime aims. The first of these was to investigate the environment and the material culture of the area in order better to understand the nature and the economic and social bases for the richness and diversity seen in the prehistoric remains. The second was to resolve, on the basis of a firm stratigraphy, the critical dispute over Balkan chronology, which was calling into question the entire development of the European early Bronze Age. Sitagroi was selected for excavation because of its key position at the northern limit of the Aegean basin and its contacts with the cultures of Balkan Europe, as surface finds initially indicated. The problem also involved the validity of applying radiocarbon dating to the prehistoric cultures of the Aegean and the rest of Europe.

The chronological aim was fully accomplished in the first volume. The stratigraphic sequence very clearly supported the view that the "copper age" (Chalcolithic) of the Balkans, the complex of cultures designated "Old Europe" by the late Marija Gimbutas, was contemporary with the later Neolithic of the Aegean, as we had earlier suggested (Renfrew 1971). The old link between the early Bronze Age of the Aegean, as represented by early Troy, and the copper age of the Balkans, as represented by Vinča and levels V and VI at Karanovo, was definitively broken. The radiocarbon chronology from Sitagroi was entirely consistent

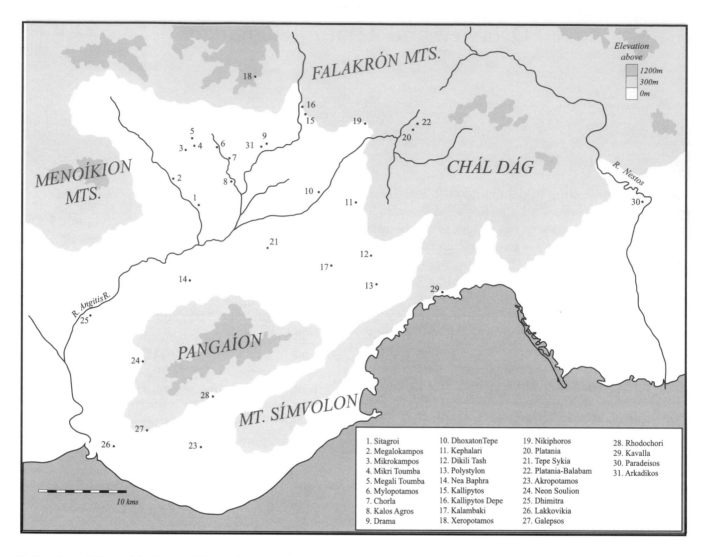

Preface Figure 1. Sites of the Drama Plain and surrounding region.

with the stratigraphy. The chronological controversy was effectively ended (despite some subsequent confusion raised by stratigraphic problems at the excavations at Pefkakia in Thessaly [Weisshaar 1989] and now fairly well settled [Andreou et al. 1996:597; Gallis 1987, 1994]). The implications of the "radiocarbon revolution" could be assimilated without further reservations about the efficacy of the method itself. All of that remains valid, and further implications are explored here in relation to the evidence of metallurgy at Sitagroi (see chapter 8).

In several chapters in the first volume, Colin Renfrew reported on the project, the excavations, the

radiocarbon chronology, and the site itself in relation to European prehistory at the time of its publication. Further, much of the environmental evidence that the project had gathered was presented by a number of archaeological scientists who joined the team: geomorphology (Donald Davidson and Barry Thomas), vegetational history (Judith Turner and James Greig, and Oliver Rackham); faunal remains (Sándor Bökönyi); avian evidence (D. Jánossy); development of the settlement pattern (Brian Blouet); and an analysis of site catchment (Eric Higgs and Claudio Vita-Finzi). The first volume also included the reports on the ceramics (Jenifer Marriott Keighley, Robert K.

Evans, and Andrew Sherratt) as well as a full account of the "mythical imagery"—the figurines—by the late Marija Gimbutas, and the "social ceramics"—the tripods, plastic vessels and stands—by Ernestine S. Elster.

The current volume includes numerous specialist studies that we feel very much enhance the various discussions. It should be noted however, that with the exception of Chapter 7 (Elizabeth Gardner) and Appendix 9.1 (Nicholas Shackleton), all final contributions were received within the last five years and/or benefited from a fairly recent update.

RECAPITULATION

The conduct of the excavation at Sitagroi was thoroughly discussed in volume 1, and the culture sequence and the chronology were fully presented there along with the relevant radiocarbon determinations. However, it may be to the convenience of readers using volume 2 who do not have volume 1 at hand that some of the basic and essential stratigraphic and chronological data are repeated here so that this volume can be read independently. In this short section, some of the information from volume 1 will be recapitulated. In each case a fuller discussion and description along with necessary documentation will be found in volume 1.

Sitagroi is of course a *tell* mound or *toumba*. In the first excavation season a key undertaking was to dig the deep sounding ZA from the summit of the mound down to the natural soil, a depth of some 10.5 meters. At the time a large area of 20 meters by 20 meters was opened nearby (squares PN, PO, QN, and QO) in which levels of the early Bronze Age were investigated, exposing the building episodes: the Bin Complex, the Long House, and the earlier Burnt House. A series of trenches of 1 meter width was opened running east-west down the toumba, namely OL, NL, ML, LL, KL, JL, and IL. These and other trenches are seen here as Preface figure 2. Other excavated areas are indicated on that axonometric diagram.

On the consistent basis of the stratigraphy, supplemented by the detailed study of the frequency of the ceramic fabrics recovered in each stratum during the pottery count undertaken for the materials from trench ZA, it was possible to divide the strata in

trench ZA into five phases, from phase I (the earliest settlement) to phase V, of the early Bronze Age. The very few finds of later date were not assigned a phase designation. These phases proved to be consistently valid for the site as a whole, although on the basis of the finds in the larger summit area (squares PN, PO, QN, and QO) it proved possible to subdivide phase V into an earlier phase, Va (associated with the Burnt House) and a later one, Vb (associated with the Long House and Bin Complex).

The pottery count was of course a quantitative one, based on the division of the Sitagroi ceramics into a number of pottery fabrics, in most cases determined on the basis of the decorative technique used, which in practice often involved the employment of paint. The pottery fabrics utilized for the ceramic count are listed here as Preface figure 3. In practice they cover almost the totality of the pottery found.

The consistency of the phasing was supported by the very satisfactory radiocarbon chronology which was obtained from twelve samples taken from trench ZA (plus five samples from the neighboring trench ZB to which it was linked stratigraphically) along with twelve additional samples from the other trenches. The impressive series of radiocarbon determinations is not repeated in detail here, but the outcome was a firm radiocarbon-based chronology expressed in Preface table 1 in both radiocarbon years and calendar years (calibration: Clark 1975).

Preface Table 1. Calibration of Radiocarbon Determinations

Phase	Duration (radiocarbon years bc)	Duration (calendar years BC)
Vb	2100–1800	2700–2200
Va	2400–2100	3100–2700
IV	2700–2400	3500–3100
III	3800–2700	4600–3500
II	4300–3800	5200–4600
I	4600–4300	5500–5200

Source: After *Sitagroi*, volume 1: 173, table 7.3.

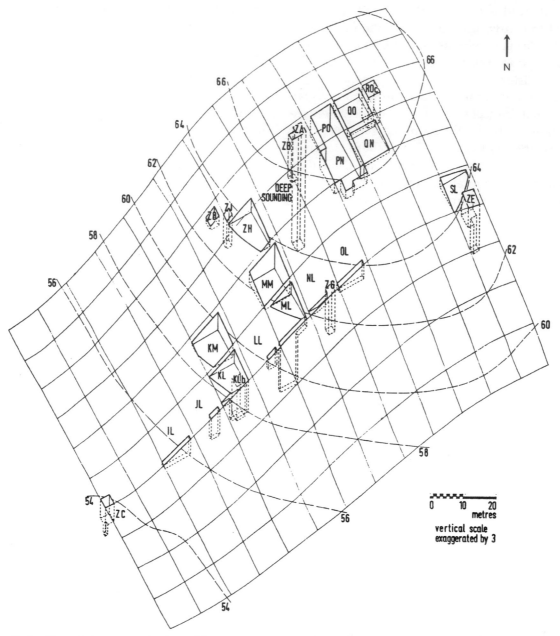

Preface Figure 2. Axonometric view of the excavation area at Sitagroi (after volume 1:18, figure 2.2).

The radiocarbon determinations for Sitagroi and the resulting chronology have been used subsequently by many authors to establish the basic chronology of the later Neolithic and early Bronze Age for much of northern Greece and the Balkans. As discussed in volume 1, they resolve several outstanding issues in Balkan prehistory, and of course they form the basis also for the chronological discussions in the present volume.

In order that the frequency of various categories of artifact might be assessed, the approximate volume of earth excavated for each phase in each excavated area was estimated (volume 1:222, table 8.1). These data are relevant in the same way to the finds reported in the present volume and are set out once again in Preface table 2.

Of course, these data quoted above are based on the detailed assignment of the successive strata in

Bl/R	=	Black-on-Red	I	=	Incised
Br/Bf	=	Brown-on-Buff	MBr/W	=	Matte Brown-on-White
Br/C	=	Brown-on-Cream	MR/Br	=	Matte Red-on-Brown
BT	=	Black Topped	O/O	=	Orange-on-Orange
Btx	=	Black Topped with	OP	=	Other Painted
		Differential Burnishing	Pi	=	Pithos
C	=	Coarse	PFP	=	Pale Fabric, Probably Painted
ClGvd	=	Clumsy Grooved	PlB	=	Pale Burnished
DB	=	Dark Burnished	R/Br	=	Red-on-Brown
Exc	=	Excised	Rp	=	Rippled
ExG	=	Excised-with-Graphite	Rrl	=	Rural
FBB	=	Fine Black Burnished	Rst	=	Rusticated
FIl	=	Fine Incised with Infillings	R/W	=	Red-on-White
GLC	=	Gray Lustre Channeled	Sm	=	Smooth
GR	=	Graphite-painted	Srd	=	Smeared
GrL	=	Gray Lustre	StP	=	Stamped Pointillé
Gvd	=	Grooved	W/R	=	White-on-Red

Preface Figure 3. Abbreviations of pottery fabrics (after volume 1:159, figure 7.10).

Preface Table 2. Volume (cu. m) of Soil Excavated

Trench	Phase I	Phase II	Phase III	Phase IV	Phase V	Total
ZA	10.8	22.5	19.8	13.5	24.3	90.9
IL	2	—	—	—	—	2
JL	7.5	—	—	—	—	7.5
KL	28.2	25.4	—	—	—	53.6
ML	7.2	7.2	18.2	—	—	32.6
MM	—	—	72.9	32.6	—	105.5
KM	—	40.5	—	—	—	40.5
ZE, SL	—	4	4	15	—	23
PN	—	—	—	—	89.1	89.1
QN	—	—	—	—	48.6	48.6
PO	—	—	—	—	100.4	100.4
QO	—	—	—	—	40.5	40.5
ZG	—	3.2	8	1.6	—	12.8
ZH	—	—	—	—	30	30
ZJ	—	4	3.6	3.2	—	10.8
ROc	—	—	—	25.6	20.4	46
Total	55.7	106.8	126.5	91.5	353.3	733.8
Approx. Total	60	110	130	90	350	740

Source: After volume 1:222, table 8.1.

the various excavated areas to the phases defined, as noted above. The assignment to phase for each excavated layer was undertaken on the basis of the pottery that each contained, in comparison with the frequencies noted for the basic stratigraphic sequence in trench ZA, and as supplemented by the ceramics of squares PN, PO, QN, and QO for phases Va and Vb. In this way every excavated layer could be assigned to a phase, with the exception of just a few where some mixing was noted, arising from stratigraphic disturbance, and a few others where the recovered sample size of potsherds was insufficient to permit secure attribution. These data were set out in volume 1 and are reported here as Preface table 3 so that the attribution to phase of any object whose stratigraphic context is noted may be established. The very complete consistency of the occurrence of ceramic fabrics by phase, and the repeated stratigraphic confirmation of the phase sequence, is supported by the consistency also of the radiocarbon determinations.

THE PRESENT WORK

In the present volume the two major outstanding goals of the Sitagroi enterprise are now brought to completion: the review of the environment and its utilization (the subsistence base), and the description of the material culture.

During the excavations at Sitagroi considerable emphasis was placed on the use of water flotation and water-sieving techniques (volume 1 {C. Renfrew 1986a]:21). The wet sieving (using a 3-mm mesh) proved particularly useful for the recovery of very small objects (for example, beads, chipped stone, fish bones, and dentine), frequently overlooked during the dry sieving, which employed a 3-cm mesh size. Another of the main objectives of the flotation recovery procedure was to obtain good samples of plant remains from every phase of the excavation. The result of these procedures was an unusually comprehensive sequence of samples of carbonized plant remains that allowed Jane Renfrew to give a

Preface Table 3. Periodization of Excavated Layers at Sitagroi

Trench	Phase I	Phase II	Phase III	Phase IV	Phase V
ZA	60–77	50–59	33–49	21–32	2–20 Va 15–20 + 11–13 Vb 2–10 + 14
IL	7, 9–11				
JL	(2)* 4–22 100–105				
KL	10–30 122 downward	(2, 3)* 4–8 (100–104)* 105–121			
ML	23–45	6, 7–21	(1, 2)* 3–5 100 downward		
MM*			11–54, 60–69 (less 13–15, 22–26 29, 30, 34, 39)	2–9, (10)** 13–15, 22–26, 29, 30, 34, 39	
KM		(2, 3)* 4–20			
ZE*		92 downward	84–90	7–83	
PN					All
QN					All
PO					All
QO					All
ZC	Mixed				
ZD				(3–9)*	
LL		4–11			
NL	Mixed				
OL	Mixed				
ZG		34–43, (45)*	13–33	(9–12)**	
ZHt				(1, 2)* (3–27)**	
ZJ		34–44, (45)*	23–33	(5–22)**	
ROc				53–73	2–52 Va 41–52+ 34 Vb 2–40
SL				(9–14)**	(7–8)**
ZB		131 downward	113–130	49–108	5–41

Note: ( )* indicates some mixing, contamination; ( )** attribution to phase uncertain.

Source: After volume 1: 172, table 7.1.

clear account of the principal features of agriculture and the consumption of plant foods at Sitagroi over a period of three millennia. These findings, which include the transition in the exploitation of wild grapes to domesticated grapes (with consequent implications for wine production) accord well with those from other sites which have now been excavated in the area—for example, *Dhimitra* (Foster 1997:217–219; J. Renfrew 1997: 220–226) and *Dikili Tash* (J. Renfrew, this volume, appendix 1.1).

With the publication of the plant remains from Sitagroi it becomes possible for scholars to compare the plant component of the diet with the animal component already fully described by Bökönyi in volume 1. Both may be related to the vegetational sequence (with its climatic implications) reported in the first volume by Judith Turner. These findings have to be considered, of course, in conjunction with those from other sites that have been studied in East Macedonia and indeed more widely in the Balkans. One particular feature of the Sitagroi findings that is likely to continue to prove useful is the very long stratigraphic sequence, with standardized recovery procedures in use, for the plant remains from the beginning of the middle Neolithic occupation of the site, ca. 5500 BC, to its abandonment toward the end of the early Bronze Age ca. 2200 BC.

Perhaps the most important and varied body of artifactual materials whose description was not undertaken in the first volume is the full range of tools and implements recovered. The bone tools form an important part of the material culture recovered from any site in the prehistoric Aegean, and again the long time span at Sitagroi allows the investigation (by Ernestine S. Elster) of changing patterns in utilization of species (and bone element) through time, and the comparison of these with those of other sites. Among the lithic materials, the chipped stone has been studied in detail by Ruth Tringham, pioneering, thirty years ago, a methodology of microscopic edge-wear study not then widely practiced and first introduced by the Soviet scholar Semenov (1964). Moreover, her work is important in offering detailed consideration for a site that spans the transition from Neolithic to early Bronze Age. Amplifying Tringham's chapter is appendix 3.1 by Sarantis Dimitriadis and Katerina Skourtopoulou, a petrographic study of the chipped stone raw material.

The report on the lithic petrology by John Dixon breaks new ground with the insight he offers into resource procurement. It is based not only on his detailed study of the artifacts themselves, undertaken during the excavation period of 1968 to 1970, but also on continuing studies, by himself and other petrologist colleagues, into the rather complicated geology of northern Greece. The outcome is a more detailed and circumstantial report than could have been presented in 1970. It is a report, moreover, that opens the way to further research in the area, which should ultimately give quite specific results concerning the source locations for a wide range of lithic materials. One such research project focusing on quarries in northeast Greece is now underway (Efstratiou and Fotiadis 1998)

The remaining lithic artifacts are presented by Ernestine S. Elster and range from agricultural implements and grinders in roughly shaped and/or ground stone to sophisticated polished stone artifacts that were evidently highly esteemed and of considerable social significance. Since Dixon identified the raw materials as local or nonlocal, we were able to interest Martin Biskowski, a specialist in the tools used in processing foodstuffs from Mesoamerica (Biskowski in press), in evaluating our assemblage from a comparative and economic perspective (appendix 5.1; and Biskowski in press). His appendix to Elster's chapter adds another dimension to her report of the material correlates to subsistence practice and resource utilization.

Together, these three studies—bone tools, chipped stone tools, and ground and polished stone tools—offer insights into the domestic or household economy through the artifacts themselves. Now these data may be compared and contrasted with the recovery of the food remains, leading to varying inferences about behavioral choice, activities, customs, patterns, and the like.

During the excavations at Sitagroi it was clear that various items, such as spindle whorls, loom weights, and other less obvious artifacts, pertained to the procedures of textile production. Indeed, the pot base bearing a cloth impression from Sitagroi phase I, discussed in chapter 6 by Elster and in appendix 6.1 by James Adovasio and Jeffrey Illingworth, is (at this writing) the earliest direct indication of a textile yet recovered in the Aegean world, to be set alongside the numerous basket impressions known from the early Neolithic onward. These materials have now been brought together by Ernestine S. Elster in what we believe is one of the more comprehensive studies of artifacts pertaining to spinning and weaving from any early prehistoric site in the Aegean. It offers support to the growing awareness of the importance of weaving in the prehistoric Aegean that has emerged after the pioneering work of Carington Smith (1975, 1977, and more recently, 2000), along with later, comprehensive studies by Barber (1991, 1994, 1997) and Burke (1998).

The chapter on ceramic technology by Elizabeth Gardner fulfills the aspiration expressed in the first volume that the excavations should make a contribution to the understanding of the evolution of pyrotechnology. The more recent retesting of the decorative paint on phase III pottery sherds (by Dr. Paul Doemeny), summarized by Colin Renfrew in a short note (appendix 7.2), reinforce our earlier information on this subject (Gardner 1979). Further documentation is presented by Colin Renfrew and Elizabeth Slater in the study of the evidence for metals and metallurgy at Sitagroi (and recent interpretation of lead isotope analysis [appendix 8.2]). In the thirty years since the excavations at Sitagroi first brought to light indications of copper working in the late Neolithic of the north Aegean, many finds in Greece have clarified the concept of a "copper age" or Chalcolithic phase during the later and final Neolithic of the area. The yet more abundant finds in the Balkans, such as those from the cemetery at Varna, have served to confirm the "autonomy of the south-east European copper age" (C. Renfrew 1969), and that is certainly the conclusion of the study presented here, although it remains the case that the prehistory of northwestern Anatolia for the period in question is only now becoming known.

The various small items made from a range of materials, which are found on prehistoric sites—beads, bangles, and bracelets—are rarely accorded the attention they deserve. This is in part because such finds are generally few in number unless careful recovery techniques are in operation, involving

the use of water sieving. At Sitagroi we were fortunate to host a sieving experiment conducted in Trench ZB by Sebastian Payne, which so effectively documented the importance of water sieving for the recovery of such materials (see Payne 1975). The chapter on these items of adornment (chapter 9) benefits from the contributions of three scholars, Marianna Nikolaidou (the chapter itself and the catalog, appendix 9.4), Nicholas Shackleton (appendix 9.1 on the molluscan remains and his catalog, appendix 9.2), and Michele Miller (appendix 9.3 on the technology of ornament production), and breaks new ground, both for the Aegean and for the Balkans, in according these small objects attention and comprehensive reporting. It is important for the reader to be aware that Shackleton's contribution dates from the 1970s while the other contributions were written in the 1990s. Thus this large assemblage is examined from several points of view, providing a broadened dimension to the study but also some duplication and differences of opinion. We do not find these divergences surprising since scholarship is frequently arguable but also because the time depth between excavation and publication inevitably leads to variances in methods of study and analysis.

The other small objects of clay, documented here in chapter 10 by C. Renfrew and in chapter 11 by Elster, Nikolaidou, and C. Renfrew, include many specific forms of interest. The "miniatures" and various rather enigmatic objects, including clay cylinders, pintaderas, and spheres, are a particular feature of the late Neolithic and copper age of "Old Europe," and it is hoped that their full publication here will be a step toward their more complete evaluation as comparable documentation becomes available from other sites throughout the southern Balkans (for example, *Karanovo* [Hiller and Nikolov 1997] and *Kovacevo* [Demoule and Lichardus-Itten 1994]) and northeast Greece (for example, *Servia*, [Ridley et al. 2000]; *Dhimitra* [Grammenos 1997], and *Arkadikos/Toumba Dramas* [Touloumis and Peristeri 1991]).

A valuable and useful addition, focusing on "context," is chapter 12, authored by Nikolaidou and Elster. Their contribution is to recontextualize artifacts and specific units representing each phase (as reported from both volumes 1 and 2) with the aim of assessing the various activities implied (and the actors so involved) as a first step in the analysis necessary for a discussion of cognition at Sitagroi.

The penultimate chapter is a brief report on the site survey carried out within and near the plain of Drama during the excavation period, mainly by David Hardy, often with the participation of Demetrios Chariskos of the Greek Archaeological Service. The distribution of these sites was analyzed and considered fully by Brian Blouet (see volume 1, chapter 6). Following the site survey associated with the Sitagroi project, many of these locations were visited and described by Grammenos (1991) in the course of his systematic work not only in the plain of Drama but in northern Greece more widely, contributing much to our understanding of settlement distributions. For the sake of completeness, the sites documented by us are concisely presented here (by Colin Renfrew and David Hardy), together with some of the principal surface finds recovered. Since plowing has continued at a number of these sites, many have suffered considerably during the subsequent thirty years; thus this documentation is relevant and necessary.

THE FUTURE

In the years since the completion of fieldwork at Sitagroi and the long preparation of *Sitagroi* volume 1, and then of this current volume, it has been increasingly evident to us that the work on one site is, in a sense, part of a continuum in the study of Aegean and Balkan prehistory. Before our work at Sitagroi began there were early enterprises in the north, notably Heurtley's *Prehistoric Macedonia* (Heurtley 1939), the excavations of R. J. Rodden at *Nea Nikomedeia* (published by Ken Wardle 1996), of Deshayes and Theocharis at *Dikili Tash* (1962), of Bakalakis and Sakellariou at *Paradimi* (1961), of Pontus Hellström at *Paradeisos* (1987), the site surveys of David French (1961, 1962, 1963), and of course the pioneering excavations of V. Mikov (1939, 1959) and G. I. Georgiev (1961, 1962) at *Karanovo* and then *Tell Azmak*. In recent years such work has continued (for example, at *Karanovo* by Hiller and Nikolov, [1997], at *Dikili Tash* by R. Treuil [1992], and at *Dhimitra* by Grammenos [1997]), and

it would certainly be possible to attempt here some new synthesis or overview, seeking to relate more recent discoveries to these earlier enterprises and to the findings of Sitagroi.

We have decided, however, that to delay the present volume further with the goal of producing some definitive synthesis would be a mistake because our research was neither intended nor designed to produce such a synthesis. Rather, the intention here is to complete the presentation of the Sitagroi findings as they arose from the project initiated in 1968. That project had clear goals and a well-defined project design. It was oriented toward the solution of specific chronological problems, then crucial to the development of the study of European prehistory, as well as to furthering the understanding of the relationships between material culture and environment in the plain of Drama and more widely in the Balkans. The first, more obvious and problem-oriented goal was rapidly achieved, and that objective saw its accomplishment with the publication of *Sitagroi* volume 1. Indeed, the chronological disputes of the 1960s and 1970s have receded into the distance now. The radiocarbon revolution is accomplished, and those earlier debates are now part of the history of the subject. The less focused yet more enduring objectives remain: the understanding of environment and culture, and of the dynamics of culture change.

It is already easy to see how future studies will be able to build on the work accomplished in east Macedonia in recent decades by a number of workers (see Andreou et al. 1996 for a broad review of research in northern Greece). The great range of ceramic styles, especially in Sitagroi phases II and III, cry out for more detailed analysis. Were some—for instance, the differing black-on-red painted styles—produced in specific prehistoric villages? What were the dynamics of personal interaction that resulted in the wide distribution of the graphite-painted wares of Sitagroi III, Dikili Tash, Karanovo VI, and the Gumelnitsa culture? It is clear that the observations noted on ceramic technology by Gardner and on lithic petrology by Dixon open the way to more detailed studies on interaction patterns. It would not be difficult to construct new theories in which the trade in *Spondylus* ornaments, in honey-brown flint, and now also perhaps in textiles (as in a model advanced by Elster in chapter 6), would play an important role.

For such enterprises as these, the basic data, for all the imperfections of recovery and of publication implicit in any practical field project, will be invaluable. Many of the Sitagroi finds, formerly housed in the Museum at Philippi, have now been transferred to the new Archaeological Museum of Drama, where materials from the site are on permanent exhibition. The site itself, which belongs to the Greek Archaeological Service, is well preserved and protected from plowing. It is evident, however, that those parts of the mound that were not acquired for the Archaeological Service prior to the excavations of 1968 have suffered considerable attrition. As noted earlier, the same is regrettably true of a number of other sites documented in the survey of chapter 13.

Future research will doubtless be undertaken in the plain of Drama, as indeed it has been in several projects since the excavations of 1968 to 1970. It is to be hoped that further work will be undertaken at Sitagroi itself. The level of phase Va associated with the Burnt House (volume 1 [C. Renfrew 1986b]: 190–203) probably extends more widely than the area already excavated, and there is the possibility of finding further well-preserved structures. Moreover, developments in excavation techniques, with the study of soil micromorphology and microstratigraphy through microscopic thin sections, may now make possible the solution of the problem of identifying house structures in unburnt strata—a problem we were not able to fully solve during the excavations of 1968 to 1970.

When further excavation is undertaken at Sitagroi there is one outstanding chronological problem that will be addressed—namely, the gap in the radiocarbon dates between those obtained for Sitagroi phase III and those from Sitagroi phase IV. Does this represent a real hiatus between phases III and IV? Or is it simply an aspect of sampling and the failure to recover radiocarbon samples for the later stages of phase III? These and many other questions—not least the explanation of the culture shift in the Balkans more widely from the final Neolithic to early Bronze Age—spring to mind. The task is an ongoing one. Yet, however problem-oriented the motivations for excavation and fieldwork, the answers in the long term will come from the documentation of the data and the secure preservation of the finds with the possibility of further study. We hope that is an objective well served by the present publication.

ACKNOWLEDGMENTS

Our first thanks are due to all those colleagues who have contributed to this volume, and also to those, mentioned by name in *Sitagroi* volume 1, who participated in or who contributed to the fieldwork at Sitagroi during the years 1968 to 1970. We have relied heavily on the notes and tabulations prepared in the field laboratory at Sitagroi by a number of colleagues, without whose careful documentation the accomplishment of the task of publication would not have been possible. The preliminary studies by John Hedges have been of value in a number of ways, and again we have benefited from the care given to the drawings by Gayle Wever, assisted by Daphne Hart, and to the photography by Peter Morley assisted by his wife, Zena Morley. The field notes prepared by David Hardy have naturally formed the essential basis of the account of the site survey, enhanced by the map (Preface figure 1) efficiently produced by Jenny Doole of the McDonald Institute, Cambridge, and further enhanced by Tara Carter of the Cotsen Institute of Archaeology at UCLA.

The major preparation of this, the second and final report, has been based at the Cotsen Institute of Archaeology at UCLA, coordinated by Ernestine S. Elster. Over the years so many have assisted in the various tasks that we refer to this group as "Team Sitagroi," and the editors are pleased to herewith name, honor, and thank them all (in alphabetical order). Notable among these were a group of organized, computer literate, patient, and hard-working archaeologists in various stages in their career: Dr. Brendan Burke, Ms. Tara Carter, Dr. Terisa Green, and Dr. Marianna Nikolaidou. Nikolaidou was with the Sitagroi project the longest and along the way moved with her young family to Europe, coauthored a paper inspired by Sitagroi data (Elster and Nikolaidou in press), and took on the responsibility of reporting on the ornaments (chapter 9), and with

Elster, on the *paralipómena* (chapter 11) and context (chapter 12). Brendan Burke recently served as an Assistant Professor at the American School of Classical Studies, Athens; and Terisa Green currently lectures in archaeology for UCLA's Department of Anthropology. Ms. Tara Carter, an anthropology graduate student and veteran of archaeological fieldwork in Iceland and Sicily, collected her M.A. as this is written, and is now studying for the doctorate; she provided continuity, great organizational ability, and a sure diplomatic touch. We salute these four Team Sitagroi members with respect and appreciation.

Further we note the inestimable contribution of the following archaeologists, students, scholars, avocational archaeologists, and loyal friends, all members at one time or another of the manuscript preparation and editing "Team Sitagroi": Nancy Bernard, Dr. Elizabeth DeMarrais, Josh Fiala, Beverly Godwin (for *both* volumes), Dr. Louise Hitchcock, Deborah Isaac, Hee Jin Lee, Patricia Oliansky (for *both* volumes), Robin Rosenfeld, Charles Sharp, Sheila Suniga, and Dr. Helen Wells. Some of these participants were supported under various grants received, others were volunteers; but the involvement of all was truly above and beyond the call of duty. All deserve a special *stilyassis*!

In addition, a number of scholars and professionals generously shared their expertise via discussion and consultation; we apologize to anyone whose name is inadvertently missing and are likewise pleased to recognize and thank one and all (in alphabetical order): Dr. Elizabeth Barber, Dr. Neil Brodie, Dr. Marilyn Beaudry-Corbett, Dr. Joan Carothers, Dr. Lloyd Cotsen (hons.), Dr. Mihalis Fotiadis, Dr. Kostas Gallis, Brenda Johnson-Grau, Dr. Ada Kalogirou, Dr. Katina Lillios, Dr. John Papadopoulos, Judy Porcasi, Dr. Judith Rasson, Dr. Nerissa Russell, Dr. James Sackett, Dr. Chris Scarre, Dr. John Schoenfelder, Dr. Rita Shepard, Dr. John Steinberg, and Dr. Tom Wake. The editors of this volume received strong encouragement from Dr. Charles Stanish, Director of the Cotsen Institute of Archaeology, UCLA and the former Directors under whom this manuscript began its journey to publication: Professors Giorgio Buccellati, Timothy

Earle, Richard Leventhal, Merrick Posnansky, and James Sackett.

We further appreciate the thoughtful queries, comments, and critique from the external (K. A. Wardle and Judith Rasson) and internal (John Papadopoulos and James Sackett) referees. The manuscript was a long one, and we thank them for their careful reading and suggestions.

Ms. Carol Leyba of Leyba Associates has been shepherding the work from manuscript stage to publication, exhibiting the same professionalism with which she tackled *Sitagroi* volume 1; we two editors were delighted that she could join Team Sitagroi for volume 2 and greatly appreciate her contribution.

We are particularly grateful to Dr. Chaido Koukouli-Chrysanthaki, Ephor of Antiquities for East Macedonia (retired), and now Director of the Thessaloniki Museum, for her continuing encouragement and support and indeed for her positive contributions to the project from the fieldwork of 1968 to 1970 until the present day. We have valued also the encouragement of friends from the village of Sitagroi including Mr. Eleutherios Adelphidis and family and Mr. Giannis Tzerzerlidis and family.

The Cotsen Institute of Archaeology at UCLA generously provided space, materials, and financial and technical support. Substantial financial assistance also came from the British Academy, the British School of Archaeology at Athens, the Archaeological Institute of America, INSTAP and its President Dr. Phillip Betancourt (who understood so well the need for emergency funds), and its benefactor, Dr. Malcom Wiener (hons.), the Ahmanson Foundation of Los Angeles, the Archaeological Institute of America, the Ernestine and Sandy Elster Philanthropic Fund of the Jewish Community Foundation of Los Angeles, and the NEH for Grant # RO-21741-88-00-1-0. We are especially pleased to single out the personal generosity of Ms. Ruth Baus, Dr. Lloyd Cotsen (hons.), the late Dr. Paul Gaebeline, Ms. Vita Tannenbaum Green, and our patron *extraordinaire*, Mr. Sandy Elster.

We have reserved for last the mention of Marija Gimbutas, whose death in 1994 deprived us of a warm and valued friend, and an energetic colleague.

One of the original initiators of the Sitagroi project, her enthusiasm for European prehistory, and especially that of "Old Europe" was a continuing inspiration. It is therefore to the memory of this good friend and devoted scholar, Marija Gimbutas, that this volume is respectfully and affectionately dedicated.

Ernestine S. Elster, Colin Renfrew
Los Angeles, November 2002

Prehistoric Sitagroi

Volume 2

1.

Grains, Seeds, and Fruits from Prehistoric Sitagroi

Jane M. Renfrew

INTRODUCTION

The aim of this analysis was to establish, as far as possible, the relative importance of the different species of plants represented in each phase, and to determine whether significant variations existed between phases. It was also hoped to establish whether the crop husbandry profile corresponded with that of other contemporaneous sites in Greece or with that of the southern Balkans. As all the work had to be done in the field, constraints were imposed on the amount of analysis that could be undertaken and the number of samples that could be examined fully. It was intended that at least forty samples should be analyzed from each occupation phase, deriving from as many different types of contexts as possible (see table 1.1).

The excavations yielded large quantities of carbonized grains and seeds from all phases of occupation. A total of 86,923 seeds were identified in 232 securely stratified seed samples. The seeds occurred in many different types of contexts: storage pits and pithoi, close to hearths, around postholes, inside and outside structures, in rubbish pits, and in almost every soil sample, showing that rubbish was widely spread throughout the site during all phases.

METHODOLOGY

The seeds were extracted from the soil by simple water flotation using buckets and 1.5-mm mesh flour sieves. The samples were first dried and then poured slowly and steadily into a bucket of water. The carbonized material, being lighter than the soil,

floated above the residue and was easily caught in collecting sieves. Some of the seeds floated to the surface, while others, notably the pulses, floated just above the mineral residue. Some specimens were not suitable for flotation, especially acorn cotyledons which exploded into a cloud of black dust upon contact with water. Once this disturbing phenomenon was observed, the rest of the sample was hand sorted. Following flotation, the seeds were dried on newspaper out of direct sunlight and stored for examination (J. M. Renfrew 1973b:21–23).

Some of the seed samples from square ZA were recovered by wet sieving large samples of deposit. This process yielded both carbonized and mineralized seeds and finds of all kinds. Although wet sieving was undoubtedly useful, it generally is not a recommended technique for botanical remains because the sample can be abraded and even destroyed by being shaken together with fragments of pottery and stone; indeed, the delicate seed material survived for thousands of years precisely because it had not been subjected to any sort of mechanical stress. The large volume of soil processed for each wet-sieved sample cut across more closely defined contexts and probably resulted in the mixing of seeds, giving a wider range of species in each sample than in those taken from specific features.

RESULTS

The results of the seed identifications for each phase are given in tables 1.2 through 1.6 which present the contents of each individual sample. The total number of seeds for each species found in the

1

samples from a phase of occupation is given at the end of each table, together with the number of samples in which each species occurs and the number of samples in which it is the chief component.

This chapter first presents a detailed analysis by phase of all the seed samples and then discusses the development of crop husbandry in east Macedonia in prehistoric times and how it relates to contemporary paleoethnobotanical finds from the rest of Greece and the southern Balkans.

Phase I
(4600–4300 radiocarbon years bc/5500–5200 calendar years BC)

The forty-seven samples yielding seeds and grains from phase I are given in table 1.2. A total of 1268 grains and seeds came from squares KL, ML, ZA, Klb, and sounding JL. Of these, four samples came from KL 21; six from JL 20/21 (probably from the same pit feature); eight samples came from JL 100 to 105, which may be a single deposit; one from a posthole in ZA 64; one from an oven in ML 42; and one seed from the contents of a pot from KL 10. The rest of the samples came from generalized contexts throughout the deposits of this phase.

As table 1.2 shows, the twin-grained form of einkorn wheat, *Triticum monococcum* L., was the most numerous of the cereal grains. It was present in thirty of the samples and formed the chief component of twenty of them; indeed, in nine samples it was the only species present. The largest sample of einkorn was found in pit 91 in JL 21, where 523 grains were associated with forty-nine grains of emmer wheat and ten seeds of wild grasses. Other large samples of einkorn wheat were found in ZA 63, 65, 66, and 67. In seventeen samples einkorn wheat occurred with emmer wheat, in five with barley, in seven with bitter vetch, in one with peas, in one with lentils, and in one with oats.

The next most frequently found cereal is emmer wheat, *Triticum dicoccum,* which was present in twenty-seven samples and formed the principal component of fifteen. It is notable that, unlike the finds of einkorn from this phase, which is also a hulled form of wheat but is solely represented by grains, the emmer wheat husks in the form of spikelet forks are represented in six of the samples, suggesting that the crop had not been completely threshed in these cases. Of these finds, three consist

only of spikelet forks and three contain both emmer wheat grains and spikelet forks. The largest sample was of fifty-four grains and a single spikelet fork from KL 21 (sample 40) which was associated with fourteen grains of einkorn, a single seed of Brome grass, three other grass seeds, and a seed of *Polygonum convolvulus,* black bindweed.

The only other sizable find was also from KL 21 (sample 39), which may well be part of the same deposit. Here, thirty-seven emmer grains and a spikelet fork were found with seven grains of einkorn, two grains of barley, two grains of oats, and a single seed each of vetch and *Polygonum convolvulus.* The quantities of emmer grains are small; only nine samples have more than five grains (eighteen samples have five or fewer emmer grains). Emmer forms the sole constituent of seven samples; in seventeen it occurs together with einkorn, in four with barley, in eight with vetch, in a single sample each with oats, peas, and lentils. Weed seeds are present in five samples with emmer and with grasses in three samples.

The most interesting find is from ML 42 (sample 121), where a fragment of an ear of emmer wheat with five spikelets on one side of the rachis and one on the other side were still articulated together, showing clearly that the ear had not been threshed. The only other form of wheat that may have been present at this time is bread wheat, *Triticum aestivum.* It is represented by a single grain found together with four grains of einkorn wheat and two grass seeds from KLb 143 (sample 155).

Barley grains of the hulled six-row form, *Hordeum vulgare,* were present in seven samples, yielding a total of twenty-two grains; only one sample had more than five grains (ML 39, sample 108). It occurred together with einkorn in five samples, with emmer in four samples, with vetch in three samples, and with oats in a single sample. Thus it does not appear to have been a major crop at this time. The same is true of oats, *Avena* sp., which is represented by only two grains from a single sample from KL 21 (sample 39); here it was associated with seven grains of einkorn, thirty-seven grains of emmer, two grains of hulled six-row barley, and a single seed each of vetch and black bindweed. There is no evidence that it was cultivated as a separate crop; the wild form is a common weed of cereal crops.

Of the pulse crops, bitter vetch, *Vicia ervilia*, is the most numerous: nineteen seeds were found in nine samples. It was the main component of one sample from ZA 76 (sample 72), where eight seeds were found together with a single emmer wheat grain. Peas, *Pisum sativum* var. *arvense*, are represented by only two seeds found in two different samples; in ZA 63 (wet sieving), a pea occurred with twenty-one einkorn grains, six emmer grains, and a single vetch seed. The other pea seed was found in a sample from JL 102 (sample 13), where it was associated with seven spikelet forks of emmer wheat and a single vetch seed. The only lentil seed, *Lens esculenta*, came from a pit in JL 21.

Grass seeds occurred in a number of samples. The distinctive boat-shaped seeds of brome grass, *Bromus* sp., were identified in two samples, and twenty seeds of other unspecified wild grasses were found in four samples. The largest find was from pit 91 in JL 21, where ten grass seeds were found with 523 einkorn grains and forty-nine emmer grains, suggesting that the weed seeds had not been thoroughly cleaned from these wheat crops. The other three finds were also associated with einkorn or emmer grains, or both.

The weed seeds are all typical of cultivated land. The most numerous were *Chenopodium album* which occurred in five samples from JL 100 through 105, yielding ninety-three seeds. Eight seeds of *Polygonum convolvulus*, black bindweed, were identified in samples from JL 100 and 104 and from KL 21. *Polygonum aviculare*, knot grass, was present as single seeds in two samples: from JL 105 and KLb 128. Speedwell, *Veronica hederaefolia*, was present in two samples: from JL 103 and JL 100 (a total of three seeds). Goosegrass, *Galium aparine*, was represented by a single seed in KLb 126, and dock, *Rumex crispus*, by a single seed in KLb 129. The samples with the largest number of weed seeds came from JL; those from 100, 102, and 103 were composed entirely of weed seeds and may represent the waste products of winnowing.

Wild fruit samples include one mineralized stone of *Cornus mas*, the cornelian cherry, found in the wet sieving of ZA 74s, and two carbonized nutlets of *Pistacia* cf. *atlantica* from KL 21 (sample 55; and one from a posthole in ZA 64). The carbonized shell of a wild almond, *Prunus amygdalus*, was found in KLb 125, sample 100.

The full results for each sample are presented in table 1.2. It is worth remarking that einkorn wheat and emmer wheat formed the chief components of twenty and fifteen samples, respectively, whereas hulled six-row barley formed the chief component of only one sample. Vetch was the only pulse to form a chief component of a sample and that was just in one case. Five samples consisting only of weed seed may represent the residues of crop processing. In two cases, pistachio nutlets formed the only seeds found in the sample.

Phase II
(4300–3800 radiocarbon years bc/5200–4600 calendar years BC)

Forty-five seed samples from phase II deposits yielded 5418 identified seeds and grains (table 1.3). They were found in KM (eighteen samples) levels 10, and 14 through 20. KL produced fifteen samples from levels 105, 107, 108, 110, 111, 112, 113, 115, and 117. Two samples came from ZA 52 and 58 (excluding the samples obtained by wet sieving). Wet sieving produced samples from ZA 51, 52 (three samples), and 53 through 58.

Samples with specific provenance include those from postholes in KM 10 (four grains of einkorn and two grains of emmer wheat) and in ZA 52 (two grains of emmer wheat and three grains of barley). Other finds came from hearths in KM 10 (three grains of einkorn and two vetch seeds) and KM 16 (three seeds of *Chenopodium album*, fat hen). Eleven grains of einkorn wheat were found under a pot from KM 17. From Feature A (dense carbon) in KL 108 came one grain of einkorn, three grains of emmer, one lentil, and two vetch seeds. Finds of weed seeds from KM 16 and 17, and from KL levels 106, 107, 111 and 115, suggest that these may be threshing residues.

Once again, einkorn wheat seems to have been the principal cereal crop. Some 2443 grains and eight spikelet forks were identified. Einkorn was present in thirty-one samples and formed the chief component of twenty of them (in nine samples it formed the only component). The spikelet forks were found only in sample 14 from KL 113, together with a single einkorn grain. The largest find was 1458 grains from the wet-sieving sample from ZA 53 where they were associated with fifty-one grains of emmer wheat, forty-one grains of club wheat, ninety-two grains of barley, sixteen lentil seeds, six vetch seeds, thirteen peas, and one cornelian cherry stone.

Three large samples of more than 100 einkorn grains each came from the wet-sieving samples from ZA 52, with 221, 130, and 296 grains, respectively. The wet-sieving sample from ZA 54 contained 105 einkorn grains. Seventeen samples contained more than five grains of einkorn; in fourteen samples, fewer than five einkorn grains were present. In twenty samples, einkorn occurs together with emmer wheat, in one with club wheat, in twelve with barley, in ten with lentils, in six with vetch, in five with peas, in one with chick pea, in four with grape pips, and in one with a cornelian cherry stone.

Emmer wheat was present in twenty-nine samples and formed the chief component of twelve of them. A total of 312 grains were found; in three cases, it was the only species present. Some sixty emmer spikelet forks occurred in eight samples: in five cases without any grains of emmer in the sample and in two cases just with weed seeds, which may suggest that they represent crop-cleaning residues. The largest find of emmer grains was from ZA 52 (wet sieving), where ninety-four grains were associated with 296 grains of einkorn, seventy-four grains of barley, twelve seeds of lentils, nine peas, and one grape pip. In twenty samples, emmer occurs with einkorn, in one sample with club wheat, in fourteen samples with barley, in eleven samples with lentils, in five samples with vetch, in six samples with peas, in one sample with chick pea, in four samples with grape pips, in one case each with almond and cornelian cherry stone, in one sample with grass seeds, and in three samples with weeds: *Chenopodium album*, *Galium aparine*, and *Veronica hederaefolia*. In only six samples were more than ten grains of emmer present; in twenty-one there were ten or fewer.

The only sample to yield seeds of the free-threshing, dense-headed club wheat, *Triticum compactum*, with its characteristic small, spherical grains, was from ZA 53 (wet sieving). Here, seeds were associated with grains of the hulled einkorn and emmer wheats, barley, peas, lentils, bitter vetch, and a cornelian cherry stone. No rachis segments were found.

Hulled six-row barley, *Hordeum vulgare*, was the other cereal crop found. It occurred in fourteen samples, yielding 251 grains. In every case, it was associated with emmer wheat, and in twelve cases with einkorn. In eight samples, it occurred with lentils, in three with vetch, in four with peas, in one with chick pea, in four with grape pips, and in one with a cornelian cherry stone.

Lentils, *Lens esculenta*, was the most frequently found pulse in phase II. A total of 132 seeds were recovered from eleven samples and were the chief component of one sample from ZA 56 (wet sieving) where seventy-two lentils were recovered. This sample also contained twenty-six grains of einkorn, forty-five grains of emmer wheat, three barley grains, one pea, and a goose grass (*Galium aparine*) seed. In all the samples, lentils occur with emmer wheat, in ten cases also with einkorn, and in eight cases with barley grains. In three samples, they occur with vetch seeds, in four instances with peas, and one with chick peas. In three cases, they were found with grape pips and once with a cornelian cherry stone. Some thirty-three peas, *Pisum sativum* var. *arvense*, were found in seven samples; in one case, they were associated with a single chick pea (*Cicer arietinum*) seed. The largest find was thirteen seeds from the wet-sieving sample from ZA 53, associated with 1458 grains of einkorn, fifty-one grains of emmer, forty-one grains of club wheat, ninety-two barley grains, sixteen lentils, six vetch seeds, and a cornelian cherry stone. Vetch, *Vicia* sp., occurs in seven samples, with a total of fourteen seeds.

One of the most interesting phase II samples consists of 1984 seeds of the common arable weed, *Polygonum aviculare*, knot grass, found in KM 17 sample 14 together with 106 seeds of fig, *Ficus carica*. It is possible that this collection represents either a hoard made by an insect such as an ant, or that it is a human refuse deposit. Of the other weed species present, *Chenopodium album* was found in four samples, *Polygonum convolvulus* in one sample, *Galium aparine* in one sample, and *Veronica hederaefolia* in two samples.

Besides the single find of 106 fig seeds from KM 17, the pips of wild grapes, *Vitis silvestris*, in ZA levels 51, 52 (two samples), and 54, all from wet sieving, are perhaps the most interesting fruit find from this level. As discussed in more detail later, Sitagroi is one of the few sites where it is possible to trace the development from wild to cultivated grapes through time. There are also two finds of wild almond shells from KL levels 113 and 115. Two *Pistacia atlantica* nutlets were recovered from the wet sieving of ZA 52, and one stone of *Cornus mas*, cornelian cherry, was found in the wet sieving of ZA 53 (see table 1.3).

Phase III
(3800–2700 radiocarbon years bc/4600–3500 calendar years BC)

Some forty-six seed samples were examined from phase III, and 3621 seeds were identified (table 1.4). The samples came from MM levels 11, 19 (two samples), 22, 29, 31, 40, 45, 49, 51, 52, 60, 60b, and 63. There were also samples from MMd 61 (two samples), 63, and 68; from ML 110 and 111 (two samples); from ZA 44 (five samples), 45, 46, 47, 48, 49, 50, and 51; from ZG 15, 16, 25, 30, 31, and 32 (two samples); and from ZJ 25, 29, 31 (two samples), and 33 (four samples). Two grape pips were found in column samples from ZB 130R and 131R.

Samples from specific contexts include the contents of pot 24 from ZA 44, which contained one seed of bitter vetch, and of pot A from MM 52, which contained six seeds of bitter vetch and five grains of einkorn. MM 19 feature 8, a wall, yielded two samples with a total of nineteen einkorn grains, five emmer grains, and a large vetch seed. Pot A in MM 22 contained three acorns; pit B in MM 29 contained eighteen acorns, and the hearth in MM 31 held 190 einkorn grains. Feature 5, a pit with very dark brown soil and carbonized wood (some of which was taken for radiocarbon dating) in MM 45, had one grain of einkorn, ten grains of emmer, three barley grains, one lentil, and three grape pips.

Once again, einkorn wheat was the most numerous cereal crop: 1739 grains were identified in thirty samples; it formed the major component of seventeen samples and was the only species present in five of them. The largest phase III find of einkorn grains was from ZA 50 (wet sieving), where 1190 were found together with thirty-six emmer wheat grains, 123 barley grains, sixteen lentils, twenty peas, and one grass seed. Einkorn grains were associated with emmer wheat in eighteen samples, with

six-row hulled barley in fourteen samples, with oats in one case, with lentils in ten samples, with vetch in seventeen samples, with peas in three samples, with grass seed in five samples, with the weed *Chenopodium album* in one case, with grape pips in two cases, with pistachio nutlets in three samples, and with cornelian cherry in one case.

Emmer wheat is represented by 190 grains and nine spikelet forks found in twenty-three samples. It was the chief component of three samples and the only species present in one of them. In two cases, emmer spikelet forks formed the only constituent of the sample. Emmer grains were associated with einkorn in eighteen samples, with barley in thirteen, with oats in one, with lentils in eight, with vetch in fifteen, with pea in three, with the weed *Chenopodium album* in one, with grape pips in two, with pistachio nutlets in three, and with cornelian cherry in one. The largest find was from ZA 44 (wet sieving), where fifty-six emmer grains were associated with thirteen einkorn grains, forty-eight hulled six-row barley grains, four lentils, 256 vetch seeds, three grape pips, and one pistachio nutlet.

Hulled six-row barley occurred in nineteen deposits, yielding 266 grains. It formed the major component of two samples and was the only component in one case. Barley grains occurred with einkorn and emmer wheat fourteen times; in one case it was associated with oats, in eleven with lentils, in thirteen with vetch, in four with peas, in one with *Chenopodium album*, in four with grass seed, in one with a grape pip, and in five samples with other fruits—three with pistachio, one with cornelian cherry, and one with acorn. The largest barley grain find came from ZA 50 (wet sieving), where 123 were associated with 1190 einkorn grains, thirty-six emmer grains, sixteen lentils, twenty peas, and one grass seed. Only one oat grain was recovered from ZA 49 (wet sieving); it probably represents a weed. The sample contained fifty-one einkorn grains, twenty-four emmer grains, six barley grains, twenty-two lentils, five vetch, five grass seeds, one *Chenopodium album* seed, and one cornelian cherry stone.

Lentils occurred in twelve samples, with a total of 112 seeds being identified. In no sample were they the dominant species. The largest number of lentils found in a single sample came from ZA 44 (dry sieving), where twenty-eight lentils were found with twenty-two einkorn grains, five emmer grains, ten barley grains, 546 seeds of bitter vetch, and eighteen seeds of grass peas. They were found in ten samples with einkorn wheat, in eight with emmer wheat, in eleven with barley, in one with oats, in nine with bitter vetch, in three with peas, in four with grass seed, in one with the weed *Chenopodium album*, in two with grape pips, in three samples with pistachio, and in one with cornelian cherry.

Vetch seeds were the most numerous pulses, with two types noted: the small seeded bitter vetch, *Vicia ervilia*, and the larger seeded *Vicia sativa*. Bitter vetch was the most numerous, with 1184 seeds identified, and twenty-four *Vicia sativa* seeds recovered. Vetch, found in twenty-four samples, formed the major component of ten and the only constituent of three samples. It was found in seventeen samples with einkorn, in fifteen with emmer, in thirteen with barley grains, in one with oats, in nine with lentils, in two with peas, and in four with grass seed. As noted above, bitter vetch was the only seed found inside specific pots from ZA 44 and MM 52.

Two types of peas were found in four samples: the small field pea, *Pisum sativum* var. *arvense*, and the larger seeded grass pea, *Lathyrus sativus*. A total of twenty-two field peas and twenty-four grass peas were identified; each type was found in two separate deposits. The largest field pea find was twenty seeds from ZA 50 (wet sieving), as detailed above. The largest grass pea sample was eighteen seeds found in ZA 44 (dry sieving). In three samples they were associated with einkorn, in three with emmer, in all four with barley, in three with lentils, in two with vetch, and in two with grass seed.

Apart from thirteen grass seeds found in six deposits and a single seed of *Chenopodium album* from ZA 49 (wet sieving), the phase III seed samples are notably short of weed seeds.

Of the fruits represented, wild grape pips were found in samples from ZA 44 (wet sieving) and MM 45 feature 5. Acorns are present in three samples: two are the sole contents of pits in MM 22 and MM 29, and the third was from ZG 32 where four acorns were associated with thirteen barley grains. The other fruits present include three *Pistacia atlantica* nutlets which occurred in three samples, from ZA 44, 47, and 48, where they were associated with einkorn, emmer, barley, lentils, and vetch. In the first case they are associated with wild grape pips and in the last case with grass seeds. A single almond shell was found in MM 11, and a single cornelian cherry stone came from ZA 49 (wet sieving). For a complete summary of the finds from phase III, see table 1.4.

Phase IV
(2700–2400 radiocarbon years bc/3500–3100 calendar years BC)

A total of forty-four samples containing 63,902 seeds were analyzed from phase IV contexts (table 1.5). The samples came from ZE 7 (four samples), 9 (two samples), 51, 54, 55, 56, and 57 (two samples), 58 (three samples), 59 (two samples), 60, 70 (two samples), and 76 (contents of pithos included 61,514 seeds). SL 7, 11 (three samples), 12, and 14 (two samples) contained seeds. Other seed finds came from ZJ 2, 3 (two samples), 6, 9, 13, 17, and 19, MM 34 (pit A); and ZA 26, 28 (two samples), 29 (two samples), and 32 floor 14.

Those found in special contexts include four acorns in pot 317 from ZE 7, and twenty-five acorns and two seeds of *Polygonum aviculare* (knotweed) found mixed with cockle shells in a pot in SL 11 (which might be the ingredients of some sort of seafood soup). The most striking find was of 61,300 barley grains and 213 acorns found in a pithos (pot 227) placed inside a larger pithos (pot 226) in ZE 76 (see volume 1: plate XXXVI, 2, figure 13.8). The site notebook records that a depression immediately beside the pithos was filled with a large quantity of acorns; it goes on to say, "the pithos and its contents and the acorns were found at the top of the steeply sloping destruction levels—they had fallen from the higher levels to the east in the collapse that accompanied the burning of the house to the east. The burnt acorns had fallen with them and above them as had much carbonized wood." On floor 14 in ZA 32, some seventy-five barley grains were found mixed with six grass seeds. The most striking feature of these seed samples is the large quantities of acorns found, particularly in ZE 7, 9, 51, 58, 59, and 70; and in ZA 28 and 29. The total number of cereal grains is 634, whereas the total number of acorns is 1435 (both figures exclude the exceptional find in the pithos in ZE 76).

Einkorn wheat is found in twelve samples, the largest find being from ZA 26 where 523 grains were associated with forty-nine grains of emmer wheat and ten grass seeds. No other find had more than four einkorn grains. Emmer wheat is even less well represented, with the find from ZA 26 being the largest of the fourteen samples in which it is present. The sample from ZJ 9 of thirteen grains is the only other one in which more than ten grains are present.

In contrast, hulled six-row barley occurs in eleven samples and is the major component in six of them. Most of the finds are of carbonized grains, but a single mineralized grain was found in SL 14. The most exceptional find came from the pithos in ZE 76; careful excavation showed that the grain was still in unthreshed ears when it was deposited in the pithos. Here the 61,300 barley grains were associated with 213 acorns and a wild grape pip; it seems that this was deliberate, as if the acorns were to be mixed with the barley grains in the preparation of foodstuffs, possibly bread or soup. It is most likely that these items were for human food rather than animal fodder (pigs would be sent to forage for acorns in the local woodland). It is sometimes the case that when harvests were poor, acorns were added to cereal grains to stretch out the flour supply.

Of the pulses, only two lentils were found: a single seed in each deposit from ZJ 17 and 19. In the find from ZJ 17, the seed was associated with a single grain of emmer wheat and five seeds of bitter vetch; in the find from ZJ 19, the lentil seed was found with two grains of einkorn, three grains of emmer, and two seeds of bitter vetch. Vetch was the only other pulse crop present. Two samples contained seeds of the larger seeded *Vicia sativa*: thirteen seeds were found in MM 34 pit A, and a single mineralized seed was found in SL 11, together with forty mineralized *Cornus mas* stones. Bitter vetch, *Vicia ervilia*, occurs in five samples, with a total of sixteen seeds.

Very few grass seeds and other weeds were found in samples from this phase. Of the twenty grass seeds, ten were found in a single sample from

ZA 26, which otherwise consisted entirely of einkorn and emmer wheat grains. The only weed seeds were two of *Polygonum aviculare* found with twenty-five acorns and some cockle shells in a pot from SL 11.

The most interesting finds are those of the acorn, *Quercus* sp.: 1648 were found in eighteen different samples. They occurred inside pots in ZE 7 (alone), SL 11 (with two seeds of *Polygonum aviculare*), and ZE 76 (pithos containing 213 acorns, a wild grape pip, and 61,300 barley grains). Most of the finds were of carbonized acorns, possibly charred when the bitter tannins were extracted. Mineralized acorns were found in ZE 7 (two samples), ZE 9, and ZA 28 and 29. In fifteen of the samples, they occur alone. The largest finds are from ZE 7, 9, 51, 58, 59, and 70; and ZA 28 and 29 (table 1.5).

The only other notable fruit found in phase 1V deposits was the cornelian cherry, *Cornus mas*, which was present in three samples. Cornelian cherry stones were found mineralized in one sample from SL 11, where forty stones were found with a single mineralized seed of *Vicia sativa*, common vetch. Another sample from the same level in SL contained seven carbonized cornelian cherry stones, together with a single einkorn grain and two grass seeds. The third find was from ZE 7 where a single carbonized cornelian cherry stone was associated with a single grain of einkorn and thirty-two acorns.

The overall impression of plant utilization in phase IV is of a switch from einkorn wheat to barley as the main cereal, supplemented by a considerable number of acorns. Einkorn and, to a lesser extent, emmer wheats were also present, as were bitter vetch, common vetch, a few lentils, and some cornelian cherry stones.

Phase V
(Phase Va 2400–2100 radiocarbon years bc/ 3100–2700 calendar years BC
Phase Vb 2100–1800 radiocarbon years bc/ 2700–2200 calendar years BC)

The fifty-one seed samples belonging to phase V contain 12,785 seeds (table 1.6). One sample came from the Burnt House, PO 158, of phase Va (see volume 1, chapter 8:190). The other samples attributable to phase Va came from ZA 16 and 19 (four samples). Two samples came from the Long House (see volume 1 [C. Renfrew 1986b]:189) found below the Bin Complex in PO/B 33 and PO/D 32 of phase Vb (see volume 1 [C. Renfrew 1986b]:187). Most of the seed samples belong to phase Vb and to the Bin Complex found in the upper levels of squares PN, PO, QN and QO. One sample from ROc 21 belongs to phase Vb; other phase V samples came from SL 3 and 5.

PHASE VA. The sample from the Burnt House in PO 158 came from inside oven 2 located in the apsidal end of the house. The site notebook describes the soil as being "gritty soil, porous burned daub, with some charcoal bits." The oven is shown in volume 1, plates XXX: 1, 2 and in XXX1: 1–4, and its location is shown on the plans of the Burnt House, in volume 1: figures 8.10, 8.11. The sample contained eight grains of einkorn wheat and twenty-seven of barley. Why the grains came to be inside the oven is not clear, although einkorn is easier to process after it has been lightly roasted; this is not necessarily the case with barley. It is true that all cereal grains are more palatable after being lightly toasted, before being ground to flour; and this task might have been happening when disaster struck the house.

The three samples from Hearth I in ZA 16 contained spikelet forks and grains of einkorn wheat, grains of emmer and club wheat, barley grains, small lentils, seeds of bitter vetch and common vetch, grass seeds of *Bromus sterilis* type, a goose-grass seed, grape pips, a juniper fruit, and eight acorns. It is difficult to imagine how these different sorts of seeds might have come together. It is quite possible that they were stray grains and seeds left on the floor after cooking and had been swept close to the fire for burning as rubbish.

The sample from ZA 19, which contained 1443 seeds and chaff fragments, appears to have been mainly residue from crop processing. The large numbers of spikelet forks of einkorn (495) and rachis fragments of club wheat (63) and rachis segments of barley (279), as well as the 367 grass seeds (mainly of *Bromus sterilis* and *Bromus mollis* types), support this view. The sample also contained sixty-two einkorn grains, twenty-two emmer grains, fourteen club wheat grains, eighty barley grains, twenty-two oat grains, a possible grain of millet, *Panicum miliaceum*,

four lentils, two bitter vetch seeds, eleven grape pips, and twenty-one grape stalks.

Since the phase Va finds came from so few and particular contexts, it is not possible to give an overall view of the relative importance of each species for this subphase, but just to note their presence in these levels. They are enumerated in table 1.6 together with the finds from phase Vb.

PHASE VB. Two samples were found associated with the Long House, which overlaid the Burnt House. One of them, consisting of fifteen acorns, was found in PO/B 33. The other, from PO/D 32, was the contents of pot 1, consisting of two grains of emmer wheat and an acorn.

The majority of the phase Vb grain samples came from the Bin Complex. They were found in PO 8 (six samples), PO 9 (three samples), PO 15 (one sample), QO 7 (three samples), QO 8 (nine samples), QO 9 (one sample), QN level 6 (two samples), QN 7 (two samples) and QN 8 (one sample). Single samples came from PN 6, 7, 8, 21, and 25, and three samples came from PN 15.

Of the finds from specific contexts in this complex, several deserve special notice. The three samples from PO 8 bin B give the widest range of species found in this level: twenty-four grains of einkorn, one grain of bread wheat, fifteen grains of barley, one seed of the small broad bean *Vicia faba*, thirty-five seeds of bitter vetch, four seeds of *Vicia sativa*, four seeds of *Euphorbia*, 635 seeds of *Polygonum aviculare*, fourteen seeds of *Polygonum convolvulus*, sixty-nine seeds of fig, and 116 acorns. Sample 687 from PO 8 appears to have come from the base of oven C and contained three grains of emmer wheat. From feature M, a ridge-backed hearth, in PO 9 came two samples with fifty-five lentils, seven seeds of bitter vetch, 175 seeds of the small broad bean *Vicia faba*, and four acorns. These features are shown in a plan (figure 1.1) with the finds detailed in table 1.7.

The clay-lined pit in QO 7 contained disappointingly few seeds—two einkorn grains, three emmer grains, two barley grains, and two *Polygonum convolvulus* seeds—suggesting that the pit may have been used to store cereals. The bulk of the QO 8 finds (figure 1.2) were located in the northeast corner of the square around the crushed whole pot 9. Samples from this spread of seeds consisted of 7911 seeds of bitter vetch mixed with three grains of emmer wheat, a single grain of barley, a single lentil, and four seeds of *Polygonum aviculare*. Four associated vessels (all referred to as "pot") also contained seeds of bitter vetch: pot 8 (SF 128; see volume 1: figure 13.20:5, a handled cup), pot 10 (SF 86; volume 1: figure 13.23:3), pot 12 (SF 85; volume 1: figure 13.24:1), and pot 13 (SF 139; volume 1: figure 13.24:4). In pot 10, the urn, they were mixed with twenty-one grains of einkorn, eight grains of emmer, a single barley grain, and eight grains of vetch. This find and the associated vessels are shown in the plan of figure 1.2 with the finds detailed in table 1.8. Perhaps it would be appropriate to include here the single find from the hearth in QO 9, which consisted of two grains of einkorn, twelve grains and a spikelet fork of emmer wheat, four seeds of bitter vetch, 120 seeds of *Polygonum aviculare*, one seed of *Brassica* sp., and thirty-seven seeds of fig. It is likely that this material is the remains of waste from crop cleaning which was being burnt on the fire.

The sample from a pit in QN 6 contained a single seed of bitter vetch, and the other grain sample from this level contained two acorns. The two samples from the same deposit in QN 7 consisted of ten grains of einkorn, six grains of barley, fourteen lentils, five small broad beans, ten seeds of bitter vetch, and eighty-two acorns. A sample of 123 mineralized acorns, collected by eye, were found in QN 8.

The most interesting finds from PN came from level 15 where three samples seem to have come from the same deposit. Together they contained five grains of einkorn, one grain of emmer, and 721 seeds of bitter vetch. The single hazelnut found in the hand of the skeleton in PN 21 probably belongs to a more recent period, perhaps Iron Age in date.

The overall picture of plant utilization in phase V shows that einkorn was the most numerous cereal. It occurred in nineteen samples, which contained 530 spikelet forks and 173 grains. It formed the major component of three samples, and the only component in one. The largest find was from ZA 19, where 495 spikelet forks and sixty-two grains were associated with twenty-two grains of

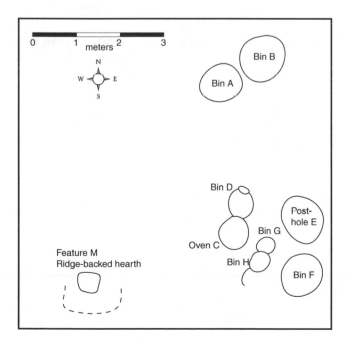

Figure 1.1. Plan of features: the Bin Complex in PO 8.

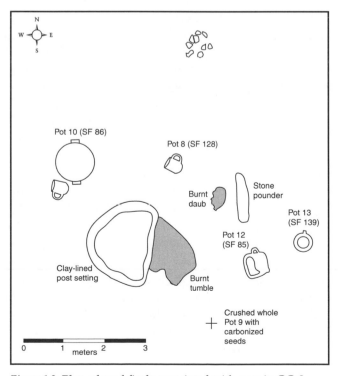

Figure 1.2. Plan of seed finds associated with pots in QO 8.

emmer, sixty-three rachis fragments and fourteen grains of bread wheat, 279 rachis segments and eighty grains of barley, twenty-two grains of oats, a possible seed of millet, four lentils, two seeds of bitter vetch, 367 grass seeds, eleven grape pips, and twenty-one grape stalks (pedicals) typical of cultivated vines.

Emmer wheat was present in thirteen samples: a total of 103 grains and a single spikelet fork were recovered. It formed the only component of two samples and the major component of none. The largest find was forty-three grains from a deposit in ZA 7 pit 1, which also contained twenty-three einkorn grains, two barley grains, seven lentils, 340 bitter vetch seeds, seven small broad beans, two grape pips, and twenty-one acorns. Bread wheat was represented in three samples, the largest find being of sixty-three rachis fragments and the fourteen grains in ZA 19 referred to above; the other two finds were of single grains from ZA 16 and PO 8 pit B.

Barley was present in fifteen samples, which contained 279 rachis segments and 141 grains. It formed the major component of two samples and was not the only component of any. The largest find was the 279 rachis segments and eighty grains from the sample in ZA 19. Oats were present in a single sample from ZA 19 which contained twenty-two oat grains associated with spikelet forks and grains of einkorn, grains of emmer wheat, rachis fragments and grains of bread wheat, rachis segments and grains of barley, a possible grain of millet, lentils, bitter vetch, grass seeds, and grape pips and stalks.

Pulses are chiefly represented by seeds of bitter vetch, *Vicia ervilia*: 9097 seeds were found in twenty-nine different samples. They form the only component of seven samples and the major component of nine. Another related species is *Vicia faba*, the small broad bean, which makes its first appearance in phase V. Some 228 seeds have been attributed to this species; they always occur in association with bitter vetch. The largest find came from PO 9 feature M (sample 10), where 175 seeds were found (including seven bitter vetch, fifty-four lentils, and four acorns).

Grass seeds were found in three samples, totaling 372 seeds. The largest find was of 367 seeds from ZA 19 where they were associated with spikelet forks and grains of einkorn, grains of emmer, rachis fragments and grains of bread wheat, rachis segments and grains of barley, oat grains, a possible seed of millet, lentils, bitter vetch, and pips and stalks of grapes. The most common weed seeds were *Polygonum aviculare*; some 761 were found in five samples. The largest quantity, 635 seeds, was found in pit B in PO 8 (sample 671), associated with five grains of einkorn, a single barley grain, nine seeds of *Polygonum convolvulus* (black bindweed), and two acorns. Other weed seeds recovered include one seed of *Galium aparine* (goosegrass); fourteen seeds of *Polygonum convolvulus* (black bindweed); one *Brassica* sp. (mustard family) and one *Euphorbia* sp.

Grape pips and stalks were found in several deposits from ZA 7 pit I, level 16 hearth I, and level 19. The largest find was from the latter sample and consisted of eleven pips and twenty-two stalks, all indicating the presence of cultivated grapes. Fig seeds were found in a couple of samples: sixty-nine in a sample from PO 8, together with four small broad beans and four bitter vetch, five seeds of black bindweed, and four seeds of *Euphorbia*. The other find was from QO 9, where they occurred with two grains of einkorn, twelve grains and a spikelet fork of emmer, four bitter vetch, 120 *Polygonum aviculare*, and a single *Brassica* seed. A single juniper fruit was found associated with the hearth in ZA 16, and a hazelnut came from the later grave in PN 21 (possibly Iron Age or later), where it was found in the hand of the skeleton.

Most notable are the finds of acorns, *Quercus* sp., which occur in nineteen of the samples, yielding 726 acorns. In thirteen samples they are the only species present. Two large finds were of 123 mineralized acorns found alone in QN 8, and 129 from PO 8 (sample 678). It is interesting to compare their presence with that of vetch, which occurred in twenty-nine samples. No vetch was found in fourteen of the acorn samples; they occur together in only four samples. In twenty-four of the vetch samples, no acorns were present.

Relationship of Prehistoric Farming at Sitagroi to Other Paleoethnobotanical Evidence for Early Agriculture in Northern Greece and the Southern Balkans

Prehistoric Farming at Sitagroi. The samples from Sitagroi vary widely in the number of seeds they contain, with the greater proportion of them having fewer than 100 seeds. Table 1.9 presents the frequency distribution of seed sample size by phase.

Samples consisting of more than 100 seeds are more numerous in phase V (thirteen) than in any other phase, with the smallest number (two) found in phase I. Since the preservation of the seeds is by no means random, it is difficult to get an idea of the relative importance of the different species in each phase. Indeed, in discussing the samples, the presence of a species must be treated as more important than its absence. This can clearly be seen in the following discussion of the larger seed samples: some species that are present in the smaller samples are not represented in the larger ones. Nonetheless, it seems sensible to use these larger samples to indicate the relative importance of the different species found in each phase. The actual figures for the composition of each sample of more than 100 seeds are given in table 1.10.

It is interesting to see that, with the single exception of an almond stone from phase I in Klb and another in phase III (MM level), all other species found on the site are represented in these larger samples. The results can be conveniently summarized by calculating for each phase the number of samples in which a species is present, and the number of samples in which it forms the major component (see the numbers shown in parentheses in table 1.11). The presence and dominance of species by phase in samples over 100 grains and seeds are presented in table 1.11.

Table 1.11 clearly shows that einkorn, *Triticum monococcum*, was the chief species of wheat grown in all phases, and it formed the chief component of two samples in phase I, five in phase II, four in phase III, and two in phase IV. Emmer wheat, *Triticum dicoccum*, was also present in all phases but did not form the chief component of any of these larger samples in any phase. Bread/club wheat, *Triticum aestivum/Triticum compactum*, was present only in

single samples in phases II and V and did not form a major component in either. Of the other cereals found, only hulled six-row barley, *Hordeum vulgare*, appears to have been important: it is present in the larger samples from phase II (six samples), phase III (six samples), phase IV (two samples, being the major component of one of them), and phase V (a single large sample). Barley is also present in a number of the smaller samples from phase I. Oats, *Avena* sp., and broomcorn millet, *Panicum miliaceum*, are present in single large samples from phase V as well as one in phase III. The pulse crops are represented by lentils, vetches, and peas. The lentils, *Lens esculenta*, are present in six large samples in phase II, forming the major component of one of them. (They are present only in a single small sample from phase I.) They are also found in six large samples in phase III, one in phase IV, and three in phase V.

The vetches, *Vicia ervilia* (bitter vetch) and *Vicia sativa* (common vetch), are present in the large samples from phase II onward (table 1.11), although they do occur in the small samples from phase I. In phase II, they occur in two large samples; in phase III in five samples, forming the major component of three of them; in phase IV in a single large sample; and in phase V in ten large samples, forming the major component of eight of them. Peas, *Pisum sativum* var. *arvense* and *Lathyrus sativus*, are found in five large samples from phase II and three large samples from phase III, but are not a major component of any of them. They also occur in small numbers in the small samples from phase I but not at all in phases IV and V. Grass seeds are found in one large sample from phase I, in four large samples from phase III, and in two large samples from phase IV; they probably represent weeds growing in the crops. Other weeds include knotgrass, *Polygonum aviculare*; black bindweed, *Polygonum convolvulus*; fat hen, *Chenopodium album*; and goose grass, *Galium aparine*. All of these occur in the larger samples: in phase II. *Galium aparine* occurs in one sample and *Polygonum aviculare* in another, of which it is the chief component. In phase III, *Chenopodium album* occurs in one large sample, and in phase V *Polygonum aviculare* occurs in four samples, in two of which it is the chief component. In two of these samples, it is associated with *Polygonum convolvulus*. In addition to these weed species, seeds of speedwell, *Veronica hederaefolia*, and dock, *Rumex crispus*, were found in the smaller samples from phase I.

Grapes occur in the large samples (see table 1.10) from phases II, III, and IV (wild grape pips); in phase V, cultivated vines are also represented. Acorns, *Quercus* sp., occur in phases IV and V: they are present in seven large samples in phase IV, forming the major component of six of them. In phase V, they are present in six samples forming the major component of three of them. Other fruits are found in phases II, III, and V: figs, *Ficus carica*; pistachio, *Pistacia atlantica*; and cornelian cherries, *Cornus mas*, are represented. *Cornus mas* is also present in phase IV in three of the smaller samples.

PREHISTORIC FARMING IN THE DRAMA REGION AND BEYOND. A comparison of seeds from prehistoric sites in Greece and southeast Europe with seeds recovered from Sitagroi is shown in tables 1.12 through 1.24. The finds from the comparison sites listed in these tables were recovered in different ways. Those dug before the 1960s did not use flotation to recover the seeds. The most recent excavations practiced flotation by hand or machine. In some cases, mineralized seeds were found (which do not float) and were recovered by eye/hand; in a few cases, grain impressions were in pottery, or silica skeletons of seeds occurred in mud daub.

The seed finds can be compared with those from other contemporary sites in east Macedonia. Seeds have been reported from Arkadikos, Drama (contemporary with Sitagroi I/II) (Valamoti 1998); Dikili Tash near Philippi (contemporary with phases III and IV at Sitagroi; the finds are summarized in appendix 1.1.1); Dhimitra in the Serres Basin (contemporary with phases III and IV at Sitagroi) (J. M. Renfrew 1997); Archontiko (contemporary with phase V at Sitagroi) (Valamoti 1997a); and Kastanas (Kroll 1991). The finds are compared in tables 1.12 through 1.18.

The close correspondence between the finds from the two middle Neolithic sites in the plain of Drama is interesting and not surprising. It is useful to have more than one site from a period in a region because the finds, where they differ, complement the range of species known. In this case, the finds from Arkadikos show that grass peas and flax were being cultivated, and *Pistacia terebinthus* and blackberries were being collected, whereas at Sitagroi, field peas and chickpeas were also being grown, and *Pistacia atlantica* nutlets, wild grapes, and wild almonds were being collected (table 1.12).

Of all the finds from these Late Neolithic samples, by far the most interesting are the grape pips. In this period we see in these northern Greek sites the first appearance of pips and fruit stalks from cultivated grapes, as well as pips from wild grapes. This find suggests that local wild grapes may have been coming into cultivation in this area at this time. The finds from Dhimitra show the best evidence for domestication (J. M. Renfrew 1995, 1997). The wild grape pips tend to be short, rounded, and squat in shape with short stalks and V-shaped grooves on the ventral side, whereas the cultivated grapes have elongated, pear-shaped pips with longer stalks and grooves running parallel to the ventral ridge. This difference can be better understood by comparing the measurements presented in tables 1.14–1.17.

The domestication of wild grapes, *Vitis silvestris*, to the cultivated *Vitis viniferea* appears to have taken place first in the area between the Caspian and the Black seas where wild grapes still grow abundantly. Early evidence of wine has been found in the residues in amphorae at Godin Tepe, Iraq, dating from around 3500 BC, suggesting that there may have been local domestication of wild grapes. These grapes were present from phase II (figure 1.3) and from phase III (figure 1.4) at Sitagroi, but the characteristic form of pips of cultivated grapes first appears in phase IV (figure 1.5) and together with fruit stalks (pedicals) in phase V (see table 1.6): the wild grapes have very robust stalks that do not fracture when a grape is removed from the bunch. This factor would put the appearance of domesticated grapes here at around 2400–1000 radiocarbon years bc/3100–2200 in calendar years BC. The finds from Dhimitra (J. M. Renfrew 1997) of cultivated grapes predate the finds from Sitagroi, as do those from Dikili Tash, being contemporary with Sitagroi III/IV, 3800–2400 bc radiocarbon years/4,600–3,100 calendar years BC. The grape pips from Sitagroi II through V are shown in figures 1.3 through 1.5, respectively.

Of the other late Neolithic finds at Sitagroi III, einkorn wheat was the principal cereal grown; at Dhimitra emmer wheat was the most common cereal, whereas in Sitagroi IV and at Dikili Tash, hulled six-row barley formed the principal cereal crop. The find of bread wheat from Dhimitra is also notable. The oat grains found at Sitagroi III and Dhimitra seem to represent weeds in the cereal crops rather than a crop in its own right. The pulse crops are represented by lentils at all three sites: at Sitagroi III they were fairly frequent (found in twelve samples), but only two seeds were found in Sitagroi IV; they occur in eleven samples at Dikili Tash and in twenty-one samples at Dhimitra. At all three sites they are less frequent than bitter vetch. Bitter vetch was particularly frequent in Sitagroi III, 1184 seeds being found in twenty-four samples; in Sitagroi IV, it occurs in only eight samples; at Dhimitra, too, it was by far the most numerous pulse, with 498 seeds being found in thirty-three samples. Some 1960 seeds were recovered from eleven samples at Dikili Tash. At Sitagroi III, six samples also

contained the larger seeds of *Vicia sativa*, and this species was also found in two samples from Sitagroi IV; it does not occur at the other sites. Field peas were found in Sitagroi III and at Dikili Tash but in very small numbers. The large-seeded grass peas, *Lathyrus sativus* and red vetchling, *Lathyrus cicera*, were found at all three sites and were clearly more important than field peas.

Apart from grapes, a wide range of fruits was collected. Present at Dikili Tash were figs, the small, round, wild pears, *Pyrus amygdaliformis*, and acorns. At Sitagroi, cornelian cherries, wild almonds, and *Pistacia atlantica* nutlets were found in addition to large quantities of acorns from 18 samples in Sitagroi IV. It has been suggested that these items may represent "famine food" collected to supplement poor harvests. Cornelian cherries and *Pistacia terebinthus* nutlets were collected at Dhimitra as well.

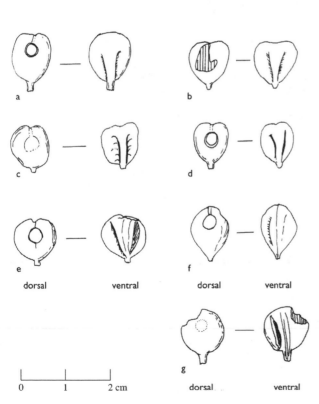

Figure 1.3. The grape pips from Sitagroi phase II in dorsal and ventral views: (a) ZA 51s; (b) ZA 51s; (c) ZA 52s; (d) ZA 52s; (e) ZA 54s; (f) ZA 52s; (g) ZA alpha, column sample.

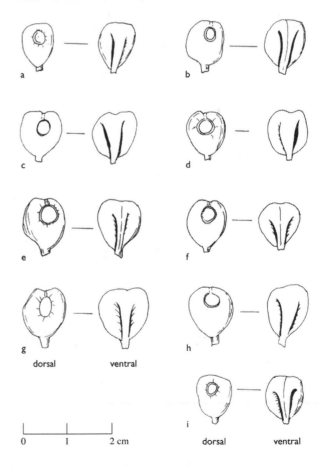

Figure 1.4. The grape pips from Sitagroi phase III in dorsal and ventral views: (a) ZA 45s; (b) ZA 45s; (c) MM 45; (d) ZA 48s; (e) ZA 48s; (f) ZA 48s; (g) ZB 131R, column sample; (h) ZB 130r, column sample; (i) ZA 49s.

The Early Bronze Age finds from Sitagroi V are compared in table 1.18 with those from Archontiko (Valamoti 1997a) and Kastanas (Kroll 1983, 1984) in northern Greece. New species appearing for the first time in the Early Bronze Age in north Greece include spelt wheat (not present at Sitagroi V where the hexaploid wheats are represented by the free-threshing bread and club wheats) and the small *Vicia faba* beans. The chief cereal at Sitagroi V continues to be einkorn wheat, closely followed by barley. Bitter vetch continues to be important at Sitagroi, with 9097 seeds found in twenty-nine samples. Acorns are also present in quantity in nineteen samples.

Cultivated and wild grapes are present at these Early Bronze Age sites, as they were throughout Greece at this time (J. M. Renfrew 1995).

Tables 1.19 through 1.24 compare the paleoethnobotany of Sitagroi with the major contemporary seed finds from the rest of Neolithic and Early Bronze Age Greece, and with paleoethnobotanical finds from Bulgaria and the former Yugoslavia in the southern Balkans.

It is notable that the importance of einkorn as the major Neolithic wheat crop at Sitagroi corresponds to its importance at other Neolithic sites such as Toumba Balomenou (Sarpaki 1995), whereas

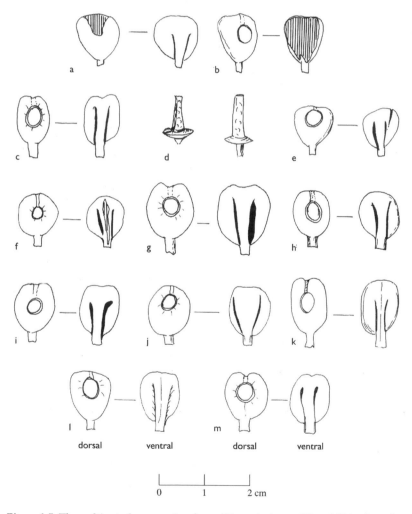

Figure 1.5. The cultivated grape pips from Sitagroi phases IV and V in dorsal and ventral views: (a) ZA 7, pit 1; (b) ZA 7, pit 1; (c) ZA 19, sample 8; (d) fruit stalks; (e) ZE 76, center of pithos (phase IV); (f) ZA 16, hearth 1; (g) ZA 19, sample 8; (h) ZA 19, sample 8; (i) ZA 19, sample 8; (j) ZA 16, hearth 1; (k) ZA 16, hearth 1; (l) ZA 16, hearth 1; (m) ZA 16, hearth 1.

Sesklo and other sites in Thessaly have a preponderance of emmer wheat during the Neolithic (J. M. Renfrew 1966). Emmer wheat at Sitagroi was present in all phases but does not appear to have been a dominant crop. The finds of hexaploid bread/club wheat in phases I, II, and V are interesting. Comparable finds from Dhimitra, Servia, and Kalythies suggest that bread wheat was being grown to a small extent in Neolithic Greece. The appearance of the hulled hexaploid, *Triticum spelta*, in the Early Bronze Age at Archontiko and Kastanas, as well as the free-threshing bread/club wheat at Tiryns, shows that hexaploid wheats were playing a role in the crop spectrum in the Early Bronze Age of Greece. In the former Yugoslavia, free-threshing hexaploid wheats are known from Vinča culture levels at Obre II, Butmir, and Medvednjak, and they occur in Veselinovo culture levels in Bulgaria at Kazanluk and in the subsequent Gumelnitsa culture levels at Bikovo and Unatcité.

All barley from Sitagroi is of the hulled six-row variety. No two-row barley grains were found, although they are known from other Neolithic sites in Greece.

The pulse crops are represented by lentils (found in all phases and found widely at other Greek Neolithic sites) and bitter vetch, which appears to have become increasingly important from phase III onward, with considerable amounts being recovered from phase V. Bitter vetch seems to have been widely important in the late Neolithic of Greece. It does not appear in Vinča culture sites, but is found in Bulgaria at four sites from the Veselinovo period and at seven sites of the Gumelnitsa culture.

Field peas and grass peas, found in smaller quantities at Sitagroi, are known from many middle and late Neolithic sites in Greece. Field peas are also found in Vinča culture sites and at a few contemporary sites in Bulgaria. It is interesting that they do not occur in the Early Bronze Age phase V at Sitagroi; instead, in these levels we find the small broad beans, *Vicia faba*, in a number of samples. This species, with finds at Sesklo and Dhimini, appears to have come into cultivation in Thessaly in the Late Neolithic and was widely grown in the Early Bronze Age.

The grape pip finds were discussed above. The widespread finds of wild grape pips at Neolithic sites in Greece is worth noting. Neither wild nor cultivated grapes appear to have been collected or grown farther north in the Balkans at this time. Figs were present at a number of Neolithic and Early Bronze Age sites in Greece, but only at Kazanluk II in the Balkans. Cornelian cherries seem to be typical of northern Greek Neolithic and Early Bronze Age sites, and also occur at Vinča and in Veselinovo levels at Kazanluk. The nutlets of *Pistacia atlantica* and *P. terebinthus* are often found at Neolithic sites in Greece and the eastern Mediterranean. Wild almonds occur in phases I and III; they also occur at a number of contemporary sites in Thessaly, Franchthi in the Argolid, and Knossos in Crete. The extraordinary finds of quantities of acorns in phases IV and V at Sitagroi suggest that crops may have failed and that acorns may have been gathered and processed to supplement cereals. Acorns are found at other Neolithic and Bronze Age sites in Greece, the former Yugoslavia, and Bulgaria.

Thus, the sequence of exploited plants at Sitagroi fits in well with finds from other sites in Greece and the southern Balkans. There is no evidence to suggest that the inhabitants of prehistoric Sitagroi practiced irrigation. Not all crops or fruits known from the adjacent areas were found at Sitagroi. Notable among these absences are flax, *Linum usitatissinum*, found at Arkadikos, and the small fruits of the wild pear, *Pyrus amygdaliformis*, so common at Dikili Tash. By taking a wide range of samples from different contexts in each phase, it seems likely that the picture obtained for the development of agriculture at Sitagroi is likely to be fairly comprehensive, given the nonrandom preservation of the seeds by carbonization. What is certain is that the alluvial plain on which Sitagroi stands supported a wide variety of cereals and pulses, while the surrounding hillsides provided wild fruits and nuts to supplement the cultivated crops.

Table 1.1. The Number of Seed Samples and the Total Number of Seeds Identified from Each Phase

Phase	No. of seed samples	Total no. of seeds
I	47	1,268
II	45	5,418
III	46	3,621
IV	43	63,902*
V	51	12,785

* A single sample from phase IV contained 61,513 seeds.

Table 1.2. Phase I Seeds

Seed sample*	Square	Layer	Remarks	Einkorn	Emmer	Bread/Club	Barley	Oats	Lentils	Vetch	Peas	Bromus	Grasses	Weeds	Cherry	Other	Total
2	KL	21	Sample 49 Feature B	1	11 5 sp. fks.		2			4		1	5				29
6	KL	21	Sample 39	7	37 1 sp. fk.		2	2		1				1 P.C.			51
7	KL	21	Sample 40	14	54 1 sp. fk.							1	3	1			74
13	KL	21	Sample 55													1 P. atl.	1
15	JL	21	Contents of pit 91	523	49								10				582
17	ML	24	Sample 36	1													1
24	JL	20	Pit dug into JL 21	5	1												6
50	JL	20	Pit dug into JL 21		1												1
51	JL	20	Sample 106	3	14												17
58	ZA	60	Sample 50	3													3
73	ZA	64	Posthole													1 P. atl.	1
85	ML	42	Sample 121		Part of one ear												1
91	ZA	76	Sample 72		1					8							9
114	ZA	74s	(M.S)	3											1		4
120	ZA	63	(M.S.)	5	3					1							9
125	ZA	63	Wet sieve	21	6					1	1						29
126	ZA	67	Wet sieve	163													163
137	ML	42	Sample 119	2													2
138	ML	42	Sample 112 (from oven)		1 sp. fk												1
139	ML	39	Sample 108		2 sp. fks.		9										11
160	JL	104	Sample 22	1	3									7 P.C.			11
124	JL	21	Contents of pit	6			3										9
136	JL	21	Contents of pit	4	1				1								6
161	JL	105	Sample 24		1												1
162	JL	104	Sample 19		5												5
166	JL	103	Sample 15											18			18
167	JL	102	Sample 10											3			3
168	JL	100	Sample 2											72			72
170	JL	102	Sample 13		7 sp. fks.					1	1						9
183	JL	105					2							3			5
189	ZA	66	Wet sieve	29	8												37
190	ZA	65	Wet sieve	28	2		3										33
211	KLb	128	Sample 104	1	2									1			4
213	KLb	126	Sample 102	1	4					1				1			7
214	KLb	125	Sample 99	3													3
215	KLb	124	Sample 97	1													1
216	KLb	129	Sample 106											1			1
217	KL	10	Pot contents	1													1
225	KLb	125	Sample 100	1	1											1 wild almond	3
228	KLb	121	Sample 95	7			1			1							9
267	KLb	135	Sample 125		1												1
268	KLb	142		1	2					1							4
269	KLb	140	Sample 143	1	12												13
271	KLb	132	Sample 115	3													3
273	KLb	139		5													5
283	KLb	145	Sample 162		2												2
284	KLb	143	Sample 155	4		1								2			7
Grand total for all samples				848	239	1	22	2	1	19	2	2	20	108	1	3	1268
Number of samples present				30	27	1	7	2	1	9	2	2	4	10	1	4	
No. of samples in which it is the major component				20	15	0	1	0	0	1	0	0	0	5	0	2	

*The 47 samples with 1268 grains and seeds identified came from squares KL, ML, JL, ZA, KLb.

Key: P. atl. *Pistacia atlantica* P.C. *Polygonum convolvulus* sp. fk. spikelet fork M. S. Mineralized seed

Table 1.3. Phase II Seeds

Seed sample*	Square	Layer	Remarks	Einkorn	Emmer	Bread/Club	Barley	Lentils	Vetch	Peas	Grasses	Weeds	Grapes	Other	Total
23	KM	10	Sample 6 ? hearth	3					1 large 1 small						5
29	KM	10	Sample 7 from posthole	4	2										6
42	KM	18		9											3
43	KM	17	Sample 11												9
44	ZA	52	Sample 37		2		3								5
45	KM	17	Sample 16	11											11
46	KM	17	Sample 12	7											7
59	KM	16	Sample 10		1					2					3
60	KM	17	Sample 14									1984 P.A.		106 fig	2090
61	KM	14	Sample 8	9	1		1								11
81	ZA	58	Wet sieve	17	10		1		1						29
103	KM	19	Sample 29	1	3 sp.fks. 2 grains			1 M.S.							7
104	KM	19	Sample 28		2					1					3
105	KM	20	Sample 32	10											10
106	KM	19	Sample 27	1											1
109	ZA	51	Wet sieve	41	28		7	7					2		85
110	ZA	52	Wet sieve	221	30		31	15	1	1 chick pea 6			4		308
111	ZA	54	Wet sieve	105	10		17	3		2			1		139
112	ZA	55	Wet sieve	34	1		1								36
113	ZA	57	Wet sieve	31 M.S.	4		3	3							41
115	ZA	52	Wet sieve	130	2		13	1							146
127	ZA	58		10	2		3								15
140	KM	20	Sample 35	1	1										2
141	KL	108	Feature A	1	3			1	2						7
142	KL	112	Sample 43		1sp.fk 2			1							4
144	KL	110		1	3										4
146	ZA	56	Wet sieve	26	45		3	72		1		1 G.A.			148
148	KL	105							1						1
149	KL	105								1		1 P.C.			2
150	KM	16	Sample 13 hearth									3 C.A.			3
151	KL	113	Sample 14	8 sp.fks. 1											9
152	KM	19	Sample 26	6	2 sp.fks. 14										22
153	ZA	53	Wet sieve	1458	51	41	92	16	6	13				1 C M	1678
154	KM	18	Sample 22	2											2
155	KL	113			1									1 wild almond	2
156	KL	108	Sample 15	1	1				1						3
157	KL	107			7 sp.fks.										7
158	KL	111	Sample 29		3 sp.fks.							4 C.A. 1 V.H.			8
159	KL	106	Sample 5									5 V.H.			5
164	KL	115	Sample 63		29 sp.fks.		2					2 C.A.			33
169	KM	20	Sample 35	1											1
173	KL	117	Sample 80	1	7 sp.fks.										8
177	KL	117	Sample 79	1								1 C.A.			2
178	KL	115	Sample 75		8 sp.fks.									1 almond	9
191	ZA	52	Wet sieve	296	94		74	12		9			1	2 P. alt.	488
Total for all samples				8 sp.fks. 2443 grains	60 sp. fks. 312 grains	41	251	142	14	33 1 chick pea	2	2002	8	106 fig 1 C.M. 2 almond 2 P. alt.	5418
Number of samples present				31	29	1	14	11	7	7	1	8	4	5	
No. of samples in which it is the major component				20	12	0	1	1	1	0	1	5	0	0	
No. of samples in which it is the only component				10	3	0	0	0	1	0	0	2	0	0	

*The 45 samples with 5418 seeds were identified from squares KL, KM, ZA, and JL.

Key

M.S.	Mineralized seed	G.A.	*Galium aparine*	V.H.	*Veronica hederaefolia*	P. alt.	*Pistacia altlantica*
P.A.	*Polygonum aviculare*	P.C.	*Polygonum convolvulus*	C.M.	*Cornus mas*	sp. fks.	Spikelet forks

Table 1.4. Phase III Seeds

Seed sample*	Square	Layer	Remarks	Einkorn	Emmer	Barley	Oats	Lentils	Vetch	Peas	Grasses	Weeds	Grapes	Acorns	Other	Total
8	MM	11	Sample 4												1 almond	1
34	MM	22	Contents of Pot A										3			3
49	MM	29	Pit B										18			18
52	ZA	44	Wet sieve	13	56	48	4		6 V. sat. 250 V. erv.			3			1 P. atl.	381
53	ZA	47	Dry sieve	22	3	3	6		5 V. sat. 33 V. erv.						1 P. atl.	73
55	ZA	48	Wet sieve	41	13	14		21	4 V. sat. 15 V. erv.	2					1 P. atl.	111
65	MM	31	Sample 21 Hearth	190												190
71	MM	40	Sample 29					1	1							2
78	ZA	44	Wet sieve		2	2			15							19
87	MM	51	Sample 49	2												2
88	MM	19	Wall	7	3											10
89	ML	111	Sample 9						3 V. erv.		1					4
92	MM	19	F.8 Wall	12	2				1 V. sat.							15
128	ZA	51	Wet sieve	13	5											18
130	ZA	49	Wet sieve	51	24	6	1	22	5 V.erv.		5	1 C.A.			1 C. mas	116
129	ZA	48	Wet sieve	23	2	2			2 V. erv.							29
132	ZA	45	Dry sieve	14		10		8	237 V. erv.	6 Lath.	3					278
131	ZA	50	Wet sieve	1190	36	123		16		20	1					1386
133	ZA	44	Dry sieve	22	5	10		28	546 V. erv.	18 Lath.						629
134	ZA	46		2		2			10 V. erv.							14
135	ML	110		12	2	1		3	2 V. erv.							20
163	ML	111	Sample 7		1	2				2						5
171	MM	52	Pot A	5					6 V. erv.							11
172	MM	49	Sample 44	2												2
227	ZA	44	Pot 24						1 V. erv							1
232	MMd	61	Sample 7	23	4											27
235	ZG	32	Sample 34	1	3 sp. fks. 1 grain				1 V erv.							6
238	MMd	68	Sample 22	6						1						8
239	ZG	25	Sample 24		4 sp. fks.											4
240	ZG	30	Sample 31		1 sp. fk.											1
241	MMb	61	Sample 9	15		1		1								17
242	MM	60	Sample 4	34	1 sp. fk. 4											39
253	ZG	32	Sample 35			13								4		17
254	ZG	15	Sample 12						1 V. erv.							1
255	ZJ	29	Sample 47			13		1	2 V. sat. 1 V. erv.							17
256	ZG	16	Sample 16			1										1
257	MM	45	Feature 5	1	10	3		1					3			18
270	ZG	31	Sample 32						1 V. erv.							1
274	ZJ	25	Sample 41	3					7 V. erv.							10
275	ZJ	33	Sample 54	4												4
278	ZJ	31	Sample 51	2	1				1 V. erv.							4
280	MM	60b	Sample 2	13		4			1 V. erv.							18
281	MM	63	Sample 18		1											1
282	MMd	63	Sample 13	2												2
285	ZA	44		12	14	8			6 V. sat. 44 V. erv							84
286	ZJ	31	Sample 50	2					1 V. erv.							3
Total for all samples				1739	9 sp. fks. 190 grains	266	1	112	24 V. sat. 1184 V. erv.	22 Pis 24 Lath	13	1	6	25	1 almond 3 P. atl. 1 C. mas	3621
Number of samples present				30	23	19	1	12	24	4	6	1	2	3	5	
Number of samples in which it is the major component				17	3	2	0	0	10	0	0	0	0	0	0	
Number of samples in which it is the only component				5	1	1	0	0	3	0	0	0	0	2	1 almond	

*The 46 samples with 3621 seeds identified came from squares ML, MM, ZA, ZG, and ZJ.

Key

V. sat.	*Vicia sativa*	Lath.	*Lathyrus sativus*	C. mas.	*Cornus mas*	Pis.	*Pisum sativum var arvense*
V. erv.	*Vicia ervilia*	P. atl.	*Pistacia atlantica*	C.A.	*Chenopodium album*	sp. fks.	Spikelet forks

Table 1.5. Phase IV Seeds

Seed sample*	Square	Layer	Remarks	Einkorn	Emmer	Barley	Lentils	Vetch	Grasses	Weeds	Acorns	Other	Total
27	ZE	7		1							32	1 C. mas	34
30	ZE	7	Seeds inside pot 317								4		4
31	ZE	7	Sample 316								140		140
32	ZE	7									26		26
33	ZE	9	Sample 8								55		55
54	ZE	9	Sample 9	4		9			1				14
62	MM	34						13 V. sat.					13
76	SL	7	Sample 13		2			2 V. erv.					4
79	SL	11	Sample 29					1 V. sat.				40 C. mas	41
90	SL	11	Sample 24	1					2			7 C. mas	10
93	SL	12	Sample 26			1							1
101	SL	14	Sample 41			1							1
118	SL	14	Sample 26								14		14
175	ZE	57	Sample 23	3		1							4
179	ZE	60	Sample 36	4	1								5
180	ZE	58	Sample 26	2	1	24							27
181	ZE	58	Sample 25		4	78							82
182	ZE	56	Sample 21								2		2
185	ZE	57	Sample 24	4									4
231	SL	11	Contents of pot							2 P.A.	25		27
234	ZJ	3	Sample 4	2 sp. fks. 1									3
236	ZJ	3	Sample 5	1	1	1							3
237	ZJ	6	Sample 9		1								1
244	ZE	76	Contents of pithos			61300					213	1 grape	61,514
246	ZE	70									106		106
249	ZE	70									104		104
259	ZE	51									100		100
258	ZJ	13	Sample 18		1			1 V. erv.					2
260	ZE	55	Sample 7		1	1							2
261	ZE	54	Sample 8		3	26							29
262	ZE	59			1								1
263	ZE	59									253		253
3	ZA	32	Floor 14			75			6				81
16	ZA	26	Sample 11	523	49				10				582
19	ZA	28	Sample 13								40		40
21	ZA	29	Sample 14								18		18
117	ZA	29	Sample 25								28		28
250	ZA	28									416		416
265	ZJ	19	Sample 32	2	3		1	2 V.erv.					8
266	ZJ	17			1		1	5 V. erv.					7
272	ZE	58	Sample 27								72		72
277	ZJ	2	Sample 36					6 V.erv.					6
279	ZJ	9	Sample 13	4	13				1				18
Total for all samples				552	82	61517	2	31	20	2 P.A.	1648	1 grape 47 C. mas	63,902
No. of samples present				12	14	11	2	8	4	1	18	3	
No. of samples in which it is the major component				5	2	6	1	1	0	0	1	2	
No. of samples in which it is the only component				2	1	0	0	1	0	0	17		

*The 44 Samples contained 63,881 seeds came from squares ZE, MM, SL, ZJ, and ZA.

Key

P.A.	*Polygonum aviculare*	V. sat.	*Vicia sativa*	V. erv.	*Vicia ervilia*	sp. fk.	*Spikelet fork*

Table 1.6. Phase V Seeds

Seed sample*	Square	Layer	Remarks	Einkorn	Emmer	Bread/Club	Barley	Oats	Millet	Lentils	Vetch	Weeds	Grapes	Acorns	Other	Total
35	PO	8	Sample 678											129		129
36	PO	8d												4		4
37	PO	8												18		18
38	SL	5	Sample 12	1						2						3
39	PO	7					3				1 V. erv.					4
41	PO	8	Pit B	19		1	14				1 V. faba / 31 V. erv.			114		180
47	PO	8	Sample 688								4 large V. / 4 V. erv.	5 P.C. / 4 Euph			69 fig	85
48	QO	7	Sample 662	1			2									3
56	PO	8	Sample 687		3											3
57	QO	7	Sample 664	1	3							2 P.C.				6
63	QN	7	Sample 9											63		63
64	SL	3												6		6
66	QN	6	Sample 6								1 V. erv.					1
67	PN	6	Sample 3				1									1
68	QN	7	Sample 9	10			6			14	5 V. faba / 10 V. erv			29		74
69	QO	7	Sample 5		2					3	1 V. faba / 3					9
70	PO	8	Sample 671	5			1					635 P.A. / 9 P.C.		2		652
72	QN	6	Sample 2											2		2
74	QO	8		9							27 V. faba / 28 V. erv.					64
75	PN	7	Sample 5				1				4 V. erv.					5
77	PO	9	Sample 8						1		7 V. erv.					8
80	PN	8	Sample 10											84		84
82	QO	8	Sample 20								411 V. erv.					411
83	QO	8	Sample 24				1		1		1500 V. erv.					1502
84	QO	8	Sample 25		3						2000 V. erv.	3 P.A.				2006
86	QO	8	Sample 26								4000 V. erv.	1 P.A.				4001
94	PN	15	Sample 16								530 V. erv.					530
95	QO	9	Sample 13 Hearth	2	1 sp. fk. / 12						4 V. erv.	120 P.A. / 1 Brass.			37 fig	176
96	PN	25	Layer 25											77		77
97	PO	15	Layer 19				2				19 V. faba / 7 V. erv.					28
98	PN	15	Sample 17	1	1						61 V. erv.					63
99	PN	15	Sample 15	4							130 V. erv.					134
100	QO	8	In pot 10	21	8		1				8 V. erv.					38
102	QN	8	Sample 17											123		123
107	PO	9	Sample 10						54		175 V. faba			4		233
108	PN	21	In hand of skeleton												1 hazelnut	1
22	ZA	16	Hearth 1											8		8
1	ZA	16	Hearth 1	35 sp. fks.			14				1 V. erv	4 grass / 1 G.A.	2			55
4	ZA	16	Hearth 1	*	*	*	*			*	*	*	*		1 juniper	Sample not counted
5	ZA	19	Sample 8	495 sp. fks. / 62 grains	22	63 rachis / 14 grain	279 rachis / 80	22	1	4	2 V. erv.	367 grass	11 pips / 21 stalks			1443
9	ZA	7	Pit I	23	43		2			7	340 V. erv.		2	21		447
20	ZA	5	Sample 3											18		18
22	ZA	16	Hearth 1											8		8
222	ZA	3	Contents of pot Layer 21	2	1						1 V. erv.					4
174	PO/B	33												15		15
184	ROc	21	Sample 23	2	2											4
218	PN	6	Contents of pot 44	2												2
219	POd	32	Contents of pot 1		2									1		3
220	QO	8	Contents of pot 14								11 V. erv.					11
221	QO	8	Contents of pot 13								2 V. erv.					2
226	PO	9	Contents of pot SF 10								1 V. erv.					1
230	QO	8	Contents of pot 8								2 V. erv.					2
247	PO	158		8			27									35
Total for all samples				530 sp. fks / 173 gr.	1 sp. fk / 103	63 rachis / 16	279 rachis / 141	22	1	86	228 V. faba / 9097 V. erv.	761 P.A. / 16 P.C. / 1 Brass. / 4 Euph. / 1 G.A.	36	726	106 fig / 1 hazelnut / 1 juniper	12,785
No. of samples present				19	13	3	15	1	1	9	29	7	3	19	3	
No. of samples in which it is the major component				3	0	0	2	0	0	0	9	2 P.A.	0	4	0	
No. of samples in which it is the only component				1	2	0	0	0	0	0	7	0	0	13	0	

*The 51 samples containing 12,990 seeds came from squares PO, QO, PN, QN, ZA, and SL.

Key

V. faba	*Vicia faba*	P.A.	*Polygonum aviculare*	Brass.	*Brassica sp.*	G.A.	*Galium aparine*	
V. erv.	*Vicia ervilia*	P.C.	*Polygonum convolvulus*	Euph.	*Euphorbia sp.*	sp. fk.	spikelet fork	

Table 1.7. Seeds from PO 8 Bin Complex

	Seed Sample	Einkorn	Emmer	Bread Wheat	Barley	Lentils	Bitter Vetch	Faba Beans	Weeds	Fig	Acorn
Pit B	41	19	-	1	14	-	31	1	-	-	114
	47	-	-	-	-	-	4, +4 layer	-	5 P.C. 4 Euph.	69	
	70	5	-	-	1	-	-	-	635 PA, 9 PC	-	2
	56	-	3	-	-	-	-	-	-	-	-
Oven C, Ridge-backed hearth	77	-	-	-	-	1	7	-	-	-	-
Feature M	107		-	-	-	54	-	175	-	-	4

Key: PA *Polygonum aviculare*   PC *Polygonum convolvulus*   Euph *Euphorbia* sp.

Table 1.8. Seed Finds Associated with Pots in QO 8

	Seed Sample	Einkorn	Emmer	Barely	Vetch	Lentils	*Polygonum aviculare*
Contents of crushed pot	82				411		
	83			1	1500	1	
	84		3		2000		3
	86				4000		1
Contents of pot 10 (SF86)	100	21	8	1	8		
Contents of pot 13 (SF139)	221				2		
Contents of pot 8 (SF128)	230				2		

Note: Two carbon 14 samples of carbonized bitter vetch from the crush pot yielded the following dates:
    (BM 653) = 1840 ± 78 bc   (Blu 781) = 2135 ± 150 bc

Table 1.9. Frequency Distribution of Seed Sample Size by Phase

Seeds per sample	I	II	II	IV	V	Total for each size category
1-10	31	30	22	21	19	123
11-20	5	3	12	5	4	29
21-30	2	2	2	5	1	12
31-40	2	3	1	2	2	10
41-50	1	1	0	2	0	4
51-60	0	0	0	2	0	2
61-70	0	0	0	0	3	3
71-80	2	0	1	1	2	6
81-90	0	1	1	2	2	6
91-100	0	0	0	1	0	1
101-200	1	3	3	3	5	15
201-1000	1	2	3	3	5	14
Over 1000	0	2	1	2	3	8
Total	45	47	46	49	46	233

Table 1.10. Composition of Samples of Over 100 Grains

Grain sample number	Square	Layer	Einkorn	Emmer	Bread/Club	Barley	Oats	Millet	Lentils	Vetch	Peas	Grass	Weeds	Grapes	Acorns	Other
Phase V																
107	PO	9							54	175 V. sat.					4	
102	QN	8													123	
99	PN	15	4							130 V. erv.						
95	QO	9 hearth	2	1 sp. fk 12						4 V. erv.			120 P. avic. 1 P.C.			37 fig
94	PN	15								530 V. erv.						
86	QO	8								4000 V. erv.			1 P. avic.			
84	QO	8		3						2000 V. erv.			3 P. avic.			
83	QO	8				1				1500 V. erv.						
82	QO	8							1	411 V. erv.						
70	PO	8	5			1							635 P. avic. 9 P.C.		2	
41	PO	8 pit B	19		1	14				1 V. sat. 31 V. erv.					114	
35	PO	8													129	
9, 10, 11, 12, 14	ZA	7 pit I	23	43		2			7	7 V. sat. 340 V. erv.				2	21	
Phase IV																
250	ZA	28													416	
16	ZA	26	523 495 sp. fks.	49	63 rachis	279 husks						10				
5	ZA	19	62	22	149	80	22	1	4	2		367		32		
263	ZE	59													253	
259	ZE	51													100	
249	ZE	70													104	
246	ZE	70													106	
244	ZE	76 pithos				61,300								1	213	
31	ZE	7													140	
Phase III																
133	ZA	44S	22	5		10			28	546	18 Lath.					
131	ZA	50R	1190	36		123			16		20	1				
132	ZA	45S	14			10			8	237 V. erv.	6 Lath.	3				
130	ZA	49R	51	24		6	1		22	5 V. erv.		5	1 C.A.			1 C. mas
65	MM	31 hearth	190													
55	ZA	48R	41	13		14			21	4 V. sat. 15 V. erv.		2				1 P. atl.
52	ZA	44R	13	56		48			4	6 V. sat. 250 V.erv.				3		
Phase II																
191	ZA	52R	296	94		74			12		9			1		2 P. atl.
153	ZA	53R	1458	51	41 C	92			16	6	13					1 C. mas
146	ZA	56R	26	45		3			72		1		1 G.A.			
115	ZA	52R	130	2		13			1							
111	ZA	54R	105	10		17			3		1 chick pea 2			1		
110	ZA	52R	221	30		31			15	1	6			4		
60	KM	17											1984 P. avic.			106 fig
Phase I																
15	JL	21 pit 91	523	49								10				
126	ZA	67 (WS)	163													

Key

V. sat.	*Vicia sativa*	P.C.	*Polygonum convolvulus*
V. erv.	*Vicia ervilla*	C. mas.	*Cornus mas*
C.A.	*Chenopodium album*	P. alt.	*Pistacia atlantica*
G.A.	*Galium aparine*	Lath.	*Lathyrus sativus*
P. avic.	*Polygonum aviculare*	sp. fk.	spikelet fork

Table 1.11. Presence and Dominance of Species by Phase in Samples of Over 100 Grains and Seeds

Phase	Total number of	Einkorn	Emmer	Bread/Club	Barley	Oats	Millet	Lentils	Vetch	Peas	Grass	Weeds	Grapes	Acorns	Other
V	13	5	3	1	1	1	1	3	10 (8)	0	0	4 (2)	1	6 (3)	1 (1 fig)
IV	9	2 (2)	1	0	2 (1)	0	0	1	1	0	2	0	0	7 (6)	0
III	7	7 (4)	5	0	6	1	0	6	5 (3)	3	4	1	1	0	3 (1 C. mas. 2 P. atl.)
II	7	6 (5)	6	1	6	0	0	6 (1)	2	5	0	2 (1)	3	0	3 (1 C. mas. 1 P. atl. 1 fig)
I	2	2 (2)	1	0	0	0	0	0	0	0	1	0	0	0	0

Note: Numbers in parenthesis indicate the number of samples in which the species forms the major component.
Key   C. mas. *Cornus mas*   P. atl.   *Pistacia atlantica*

Table 1.12. Comparison of Seed Finds from Arkadikos, Drama, and Sitagroi I/II

Species	Arkadikos*	Sitagroi I/II
Einkorn wheat	X	X
Emmer wheat	X	X
Barley	X	X
Bitter vetch	X	X
Lentil	X	X
Field pea		X
Grass pea	X	
Chickpea		X
Flax	X	
Fig	X	X
Wild grape		X
Pistacia terebinthus	X	
Pistacia atlantica		X
Cornelian cherry	X	X
Wild almond		X
Blackberry	X	

* Valamoti 1998

Table 1.13. Comparison of Seed Finds from Dikili Tash, Dhimitra, and Sitagroi III/IV

Species	Dikili Tash*	Dhimitra**	Sitagroi III/IV
Einkorn wheat	X	X	X
Emmer wheat	Wheat	X	X
Bread wheat		X	
Barley	X	X	X
Oats		X	X
Lentils	X	X	X
Bitter vetch	X	X	X
Common vetch			X
Field pea	X		X
Lathyrus sativus/cicera	X	X	X
Wild grapes	X	X	X
Cultivated grapes	X	X	
Cornelian cherry		X	X
Pistacia atlantica			X
Pistacia terebinthus		X	
Fig	X		
Wild pear	X		
Acorn	X		X
Wild almond			X

*The Dikili Tash seeds are reported in Appendix 1.1.
** Foster 1977

Table 1.14. Carbonized Wild Grape Pips from Dhimitra Compared with Wild Grape Pips from Sitagroi II and Sitagroi III (mm)

Parameter	Dhimitra (18 pips)	Sitagroi II (8 pips)	Sitagroi III (11 pips)
Pip length	3.0–5.0, average 4.2	4.0–4.9mm average 4.5mm	4.0–5.0mm average 4.5mm
Pip breadth	2.0–4.0, average 3.2		
Stalk length	0.5–1.0, average 0.9	0.3–1.0mm average 0.6mm	0.5–1.0mm average 0.7mm
Chalaza diameter	1.0–1.5, average 1.2	1.0–1.5mm average 1.2mm	1.0–1.5mm average 1.2mm
Breadth/length index	57–100, average 76	65–92, average 82	66–90, average 81

Table 1.15. Dimensions of Carbonized and Mineralized Cultivated Grape Pips from Late Neolithic Levels at Dhimitra (mm)

Parameter	Carbonized (86 pips)	Mineralized (20 pips)
Pip length	4.0–6.5, average 5.5	4.0–6.5mm average 5.6mm
Pip breadth	2.5–4.0, average 3.2	2.5–3.5mm average 3.1mm
Stalk length	1.0–2.0, average 1.23	
Chalaza diameter	1.0–2.0, average 1.3	1.0–1.5mm average 1.3mm
Breadth/length index	42–80, average 57	46–70 average 56

Note: It is interesting to compare these measurements with those of the cultivated grape pips from Dhimitra which were preserved both by carbonization and by mineral replacement.

Table 1.16. Two Sizes of Grape Pips from Dikili Tash (mm)

Parameter	Type A	Type B
Average length (and range)	4.6 (4.0–5.0)	5.3 (5.1–6.0)
Average breadth (and range)	3.7 (3.1–4.2)	3.8 (3.0–4.2)
Average length of stalk	0.6 (0.2–1.0)	0.8 (0.6–1.0)
Average Breadth/Length index	80	70

Note: The carbonized grape pips from contemporary levels at Dikili Tash belong to two size ranges (Logothetis 1970:36): the smaller type A are probably from wild grapes, while the larger type B pips might possibly come from cultivated vines. Some fruit stalks were found with them.

Table 1.17. Measurements of Grape Pips from Sitagroi V (mm)

Parameter	Pip size
Pip length	4.0–6.0, average 5.3
Stalk length	0.5–1.5, average 1.0
Chalaza diameter	1.0–2.0, average 1.8
Breadth/length index	50–90, average 71

Note: It is convenient to consider the dimensions of the 13 grape pips found in Sitagroi V, although they belong to the Early Bronze Age. They were found with a number of short berry stalks typical of cultivated grapes.

Table 1.18. Early Bronze Age Seeds From Sitagroi V, Archontiko, and Kastanas

Species	Sitagroi V	Archontiko	Kastanas
Einkorn	X	X	X
Emmer	X	X	X
Spelt wheat	—	X	X
Bread/club wheat	X	—	—
Hulled six-row barley	X	X	X
Oats	X	—	X
Millet	X	—	X
Lentils	X	X	X
Bitter vetch	X	—	X
Vicia faba beans	X	X	X
Grass peas	—	X	X
Field peas	—	—	X
Flax	—	—	X
Grapes	X	X	X
Figs	X	X	X
Cornelian cherry	—	X	X
Wild pear	—	—	X
Juniper	X	—	—
Hazelnut	X	—	—
Acorn	X	X	X
Blackberry	—	X	—
Elderberry	—	X	—
Brassica	X	—	—
Bilderdykia convolvulus	—	X	—
Camelina	—	—	X
Euphorbia	X	—	—
Fumaria	—	X	—
Goosegrass	X	X	—
Leucrium sp.	—	X	—
Lolium temulentum	—	X	—
Poppy	—	—	X
Polygonum aviculare	X	—	—
Polygonum convolvulus	X	—	—
Grasses	X	X	—

Table 1.19. Middle Neolithic Seeds from Greece (ca. 5500–4600 BC)*

	1. Franchthi	2. Athens	3. Achilleion	4. Otzaki	5. Servia	6. Arkadikos	7. Sitagroi I–II
Triticum monococcum	x	—	x	x	x	x	x
Triticum dicoccum	x	—	x	x	x	x	x
Triticum aestivum	—	—	—	—	x	—	x
Hordeum vulgare	—	—	x	x	x	x	x
Hordeum distichum	x	—	—	—	—	—	—
Avena sp.	—	—	x	x	—	—	x
Lens esculenta	x	—	—	x	x	x	x
Vicia sp.	x	x	—	x	—	x	x
Pisum sativum	—	x	x	x	x	—	x
Lathyrus sativus	—	—	—	—	x	x	—
Pistacia sp.	x	—	x	—	—	x	x
Cornus mas	—	—	—	—	—	x	x
Quercus sp.	—	—	x	—	—	—	x
Vitis silvestris	—	—	—	—	—	—	x
Polygonum aviculare	—	—	—	—	—	—	x
Prunus amygdalus	x	—	—	—	—	—	—
Pyrus amygdaliformis	x	—	—	—	—	—	—
Lithospermum arvense	x	—	x	—	—	—	—
Alcanna sp.	x	—	—	—	—	—	—
Anchusa sp.	x	—	—	—	—	—	—
Pyrus malus	—	—	x	—	—	—	—
Ficus carica	—	—	—	x	—	x	—
Rubus sp.	—	—	—	—	—	x	—

* See Preface table 1

References
1. Hansen 1991; J. Renfrew 1973c
2. Hopf 1971
3. J. Renfrew 1989
4. Kroll 1991
5. Heurtley 1939; Hubbard 1979
6. Valamoti 1998
7. J. Renfrew this volume; J. Renfrew 1973a, 1995

Table 1.20. Late Neolithic Seeds from Greece (ca. 4600–3500 BC)*

Seed	Macedonia					Thessaly						Argolid		Aegean Islands			
	1	2	3	4	5	6	7	8	9	10	11	12	13	14	15	16	17
	Dikili Tash	Dhimitra	Sitagroi III	Olynthos	Dhimini	Sesklo	Pefkakia	Pyrasos	Arapi	Visvikis	Rachmani	Lerna	Franchthi	Knossos	Saliagos	Kephala	Kalythies
Triticum monococcum	x	x	x	—	x	x	x	x	x	x	—	—	x	—	x	—	x
T. dicoccum	—	x	x		x	x	x	x	x	x	—	—	x	—	x	—	x
T. aestivum	—	x	—	wheat/millet	—	x	x	—	—	—	x	—	—	—	—	—	x
Avena	—	x	—	—	x	x	—	x	—	—							
Hordeum vulgare	x	x	x	—	x	barley	x	x	x						x	x	—
H. vulgare var. *nudum*	—	—	—	—	x	x	x	—		x							
Hordeum distichum	—	—	—	—	—	—	—	—	—	—	—	—	x				
Vicia faba	—	—	—	—	x	x											
Pisum sativum	x	—	—	—	x	x	x	x	x								
Lathyrus sativus	—	x	—	—	x	—	x									x	—
Lens esculenta	x	x	x	—	x	—	x	—	x	—	x	—	x				
Vicia ervilia	x	x	x	—	x	—	x	—	x								x
Vicia sp.	—	—	—	—	—	—	—					—	x				
Prunus amygdalus	—	—	x	—	x	x	x	—	x			—	x	x			
Pyrus amygdaliformis	x	—	—	—	x	—											
Ficus carica	x	—	—	x	x	x	x	—	x	—	x	x	—				
Vitus silvestris	x	x	x	—	x	x	x	—	x			—	x				
Quercus sp.	x	—	—	—	—	x	x										
Cornus mas	—	x	x	—	—	—	—										
Linum	—	—	v	—	—	x	x										
Camelina	—	—	—	—	—	—	x										
Pistacia	—	x	x	—	—	x	x	—				—	x				
Arbutus unedo	—	—	—	—	—	—	—	—	—	—	—	x	—				
Lithospermum arvense	—	—	—	—	—	—	—	—	—	—	—	—	x				
Alcanna	—	—	—	—	—	—	—	—	—	—	—	—	x				
Anchusa	—	—	—	—	—	—	—	—	—	—	—	—	x				

* See Preface table 1

References:
1. J. Renfrew 1969
2. J. Renfrew 1997
3. J. Renfrew, this chapter, 1973a
4. Mylonas 1929
5. Kroll 1979
6. Tsountas 1908; Wace and Thompson 1912; J. Renfrew 1966; Kroll 1991
7. Kroll 1991
8. J. Renfrew 1966
9. Kroll 1991
10. Bertsch and Bertsch 1949
11. Wace and Thompson 1912; J. Renfrew 1966
12. Hopf 1964
13. Hansen 1991; J. Renfrew 1973c
14. Evans 1921
15. J. Renfrew 1968
16. J. Renfrew 1977
17. Halstead and Jones 1987

Table 1.21. Early Bronze Age Seeds from Greece

Seed	1 Sitagroi V	2 Archontiko	3 Kastanas	4 Argissa	5 Lerna	6 Myrtos	7 Pefkakia	8 Sesklo	9 Tiryns
Einkorn	x	x	x	x	x	—	x	—	—
Emmer	x	x	x	x	x	—	x	x	x
Spelt Wheat	—	x	x	—	—	—	—	—	—
Bread/Club Wheat	x	—	—	—	—	—	—	—	x
Hulled 6-row barley	x	x	x	x	x	x	x	—	x
Naked 6-row barley	—	—	—	x	x	—	—	—	—
Oats	x	—	x	x	x	—	—	—	—
Millet	x	—	x	—	—	—	—	—	x
Lentils	x	x	x	x	x	—	x	—	x
Bitter vetch	x	—	x	x	x	—	—	—	x
Vicia faba beans	x	x	x	—	x	—	—	—	x
Grass pea	—	x	x	—	x	—	—	—	x
Field pea	—	—	x	—	x	—	—	—	x
Flax	—	—	x	x	x	—	—	—	—
Grape	x	x	x	x	x	x	—	—	x
Fig	x	x	x	x	x	—	x	—	x
Cornelian cherry	—	x	x	—	—	—	—	—	—
Wild pear	—	—	x	x	—	—	—	—	—
Prunus	—	—	—	—	x	—	—	—	x
Juniper	x	—	—	—	—	—	—	—	—
Hazelnut	x	—	—	—	—	—	—	—	—
Acorn	x	x	x	—	x	—	—	—	—
Blackberry	—	x	—	—	—	—	—	—	—
Elderberry	—	x	—	—	—	—	—	—	—
Olive	—	—	—	—	—	x	—	—	x
Onopordon	—	—	—	—	x	—	—	—	—

References:
1. J. Renfrew, this volume
2. Valamoti 1997a
3. Kroll 1991
4. Hopf 1962; Kroll 1983
5. Hopf 1962b
6. J. Renfrew 1972
7. Kroll 1991
8. J. Renfrew 1966
9. Kroll 1991

Table 1.22. Late Neolithic Crops in Yugoslavia, Vinča Culture (ca. 4500–3800 BC)*

Seed	1 Predionica	2 Anza IV	3 Gornja Tuzla	4 Lisicici	5 Lug	6 Obre II	7 Butmir	8 Vinča D	9 Medvednjak	10 Gomolava	11 Selevac	12 Valać
Triticum monococcum	—	x	x	x	x	x (+2)	x	x	x	x	x	—
Triticum dicoccum	x	x	x	x	x	—	—	x	x	x	—	—
Triticum	—	—	—	—	—	x	x	—	x	?	—	—
Hordeum vulgare	—	x	—	x	x	x	x	—	—	x	—	—
Avena sp.	—	—	—	—	—	—	—	x	—	x	—	—
Lens esculenta	—	x	—	—	—	x	x	—	—	x	x	—
Pisum sativum	—	x	—	—	—	x	x	—	—	x	—	x
Pyrus malus	—	—	—	—	—	—	x	—	—	—	—	—
Pyrus communis	—	—	—	—	—	—	x	—	—	—	—	—
Corylus avellana	—	—	—	—	—	—	x	—	—	—	—	—
Cornus mas	—	—	—	—	—	—	—	x	—	—	—	—
Quercus sp.	—	—	—	—	—	—	—	—	—	—	—	x
Tilia sp.	x	—	—	—	—	—	—	—	—	—	—	—
Galium aparine	—	—	—	—	—	x	—	—	—	—	—	—

(+2) = Twin-grained forms   *Compare with Sitagroi I/II

References
1. Hopf 1974
2. J. Renfrew 1976b
3. Hopf 1967, 1974
4. Hopf 1958
5. Hopf 1959
6. J. Renfrew 1976a
7. Schröter 1895; Hoops 1905
8. J. Renfrew unpublished, examination of carbonized seeds in Vinča Collection, Belgrade, 1966
9. J. Renfrew unpublished, examination of carbonized seeds for Dr. R. Galović
10. Van Zeist 1975; *Panicum miliaceum* and *Linum usitatissinum* were also found.
11. Hopf 1974
12. Hopf 1974

Table 1.23. Middle Neolithic Seeds from Bulgaria, Veselinovo Culture, Karanovo III (ca. 4400–4100 BC)*

Seed	1 Yassatepe	2 Karanovo	3 Azmak	4 Kazanluk	5 Veselinovo
Hordeum distichum	x	—	—	—	—
H. distichum var. *nudum*	x	—	—	—	—
Hordeum vulgare	—	—	—	x	—
H. vulgare var. *nudum*	—	x	—	x	—
Triticum dicoccum	—	x	x	x	x
Triticum monococcum	—	x	—	x (+2)	x
Triticum aestivum	—	—	—	x	—
Vicia ervilia	x	—	x	x	x
Lens esculenta	x	—	—	x	—
Pisum sativum	—	—	x	—	—
Pyrus sp.	—	—	x	—	—
Rubus sp.	—	—	—	x	—
Cornus mas	—	—	—	x	—

(+2) = Twin-grained forms   *Compare with Sitagroi I
References: 1. J. Renfrew 1969
                2. Kohl and Quitta 1966;
                  J. Renfrew 1969; Hopf 1973   4. J. Renfrew 1969; Hopf 1973
                3. J. Renfrew 1969; Hopf 1973   5. Arnaudov 1936–1937

Table 1.24. Eneolithic Seeds from S. Bulgaria, Gumelnitsa Culture (ca. 3890–2290 BC)*

Seed	1 Ezero	2 Azmak	3 Karanovo V-VI	4 Bikovo	5 Kapitan Dimitrievo III	6 Unatcité	7 Yassatepe II	8 Immamova Dubka	9 Meckur	10 Sveti Kyrillovo	11 Kazanluk
Triticum monococcum	—	x	x	x	x	x (+2)	—	—	x	—	x
Triticum dicoccum	—	x	x	x	x	x	—	—	—	—	x
Triticum aestivum	—	—	—	—	—	x	—	—	—	x	x
Triticum compactum	—	—	—	x	—	—	—	—	—	—	—
Hordeum vulgare	—	x	—	—	x	x	—	x	—	—	x
H. vulgare var. *nudum*	x	x	x	x	—	x	—	—	—	—	—
Lens esculenta	—	x	x	x	x	—	—	—	—	—	x
Vicia ervilia	—	x	x	x	x	x	x	—	—	—	x
Pisum sativum	—	x	—	—	—	—	—	—	—	—	—
Linum usitatissimum	—	—	—	—	x	—	—	—	—	—	—
Quercus sp.	—	—	—	—	—	—	—	—	x	—	—
Juglans sp.	—	—	—	—	—	—	—	—	x	—	x
Pyrus sp.	—	—	—	—	—	—	—	—	x	—	—
Rubus sp.	—	—	—	—	—	—	—	—	—	—	x
Vitis silvestris	—	—	—	—	—	—	—	—	—	—	x
Brassica sp.	—	—	—	—	—	—	—	x	—	—	—

(+2) = Twin-grained forms   *Compare with Sitagroi III

References:
 1. Hopf 1973
 2. J. Renfrew 1969; Hopf 1973; also Kohl and Quitta 1966
 3. Arnaudov 1939; 1937-1938; Kohl and Quitta 1966; J. Renfrew 1969; Hopf 1973
 4. J. Renfrew 1969; Hopf 1973
 5. J. Renfrew 1969; Hopf 1973; and Arnaudov 1937–1938
 6. Arnaudov 1940-1941; J. Renfrew 1969
 7. J. Renfrew 1969
 8. J. Renfrew 1969
 9. Arnaudov 1936, 1947-1948
10. Kazarow 1914 identifications by Professor St. Petkov, Sofia
11. Dennell 1978

Appendix 1.1
Seeds from Dikili Tash, 1967

Jane M. Renfrew

A total of twenty-three seed samples, containing 3337 seeds and fruits, were examined from Dr. D. Theocharis's excavations at Dikili Tash near Philippi and are summarized here. They came mainly from contexts corresponding to Sitagroi III/IV, and were found between September 7 and 16, 1967, in trench II (see table 1.1.1).

Hulled six-row barley is the principal cereal found in these samples, with a very small amount of hulled wheat. By far the most common pulse crop is bitter vetch, with lentils and grass peas also present in significant quantities, and a single field pea. The fruits include two types of grape pips: a larger and a smaller form, together with fruit stalks. There are also wild pears, figs, and a few acorns. All these seeds were recovered by visual inspection and not by flotation.

Table 1.1.1. Cereals, Pulses, and Fruits from Dikili Tash

Seed sample	Context	Date	Wheat	Barley	Lentil	Vetch	Grass pea	Field pea	Grape	Fig	Wild pear	Acorn
1	Z2	7/9/67	—	—	—	—	—	—	—	1	—	—
2	Z1 A	7/9/67	—	—	—	—	—	—	—	—	6	—
3	Z1 B	8/9/67	—	5	8	33	—	1	—	—	—	—
4	HI A	8/9/67	—	—	—	—	—	—	—	10	6	—
5	Z2 B	9/9/67	—	11	1	15	11	—	—	—	—	—
6	Z2 B	9/9/67	—	—	—	—	—	—	—	—	12	—
7	E2 B	9/9/67	—	—	—	—	—	—	—	10	—	—
8	Z2 B	11/9/67	—	7	12	37	23	—	—	—	—	—
9a	Q2 B	11/9/67	—	—	—	—	—	—	—	1	—	—
9b	Q2 B	11/9/67	—	—	—	—	—	—	23	—	—	—
10	Z1 A	12/9/67	—	—	—	—	—	—	—	—	14	—
11a	Z1 A	12/9/67	6	170	101	558	105	—	2	—	—	—
11b	Z1 A	14/9/67	—	171	197	655	154	—	—	1	1	—
12	H1 B	14/9/67	—	—	—	—	—	—	—	—	3	—
13	Q2 A	14/9/67	—	—	—	—	—	—	—	—	1	—
14	Q2 B	11/9/67	—	—	—	—	—	—	—	—	12	—
15	Z2 A-B	15/9/67	—	11	10	13	10	—	—	—	11	—
16	Z1 B	9/9/67	—	26	17	35	20	—	—	1	2	—
17	Z2 B	9/9/67	—	3	3	55	—	—	—	—	5	—
18	E2 B	9/9/67	—	13	7	30	8	—	1	—	—	3
19	Z2	16/9/67	1	30	12	300	—	—	9	—	—	—
20	D2	16/9/67	—	8	32	29	—	—	245	1	—	—
21	Z1	16/9/67	—	—	—	—	—	—	—	—	1	1
Totals			7	455	402	1960	331	1	280	25	72	4

2.

Bone Tools and Other Artifacts

Ernestine S. Elster

Archaeologists studying bone tools generally report the recurrent forms (presented as types), the skeletal parts selected for manufacture into implements and other artifacts, and the animal species represented. Much can be inferred about the behavior of toolmakers and users by identifying the animals kept or hunted and the environmental niche of each species. For example, red deer range in dense forests. The mature male sheds his rack in February, March, and early April, but only in particular areas of the forest (Choyke 1998:172). Only antler specimens with pedicle attached are clearly from hunted deer since naturally shed antlers have no pedicle. In Bökönyi's report of the refuse bone, red deer bone and antler represented 38% of the total wild bone recovered (volume 1 [Bökönyi 1986]:68–69). This suggests that Sitagroi villagers were familiar with the deer's habits and habitats and knew their way in the forests, successfully bringing back antler. Furthermore, skilled hunters acting within the social organization of the hunt, following whatever customs governed this activity, be they social, magical or religious, may account for the strong showing of red deer skeletal parts in the refuse bone of the settlement (Steele and Baker 1993:26).

Domesticates provided meat protein, fat, and secondary products such as milk, hide, hair, fleece, draft power, and the raw materials for tools. In exchange, the animals required food, pasture, and attendance—a relationship Bökönyi described as symbiotic. The wild animal contribution was similar, and was especially important when domestic herds were at risk, as during times of warfare or economic crisis (Bökönyi and Bartosiewicz 1997: 390).

The goals of this chapter are to present the species and elements used at Sitagroi, to describe and define the forms of the artifacts, to consider how toolmakers might have worked, and to discern some of the ways in which the pieces could have been used and by whom. I present some hypotheses about the Sitagroi villagers' preferences in selecting species and/or skeletal parts for specific tool forms over time based on cross-tabulations of various traits (tables 2.1–2.10). Although microscopic examination of the used surfaces of these artifacts was never undertaken at Sitagroi, observable use-wear was indicated by the draftspersons in the line drawings and on some of the inventory cards. I was not able to reexamine the bone tools before writing this chapter; therefore my work is based in the inventory cards, notebooks, and identification of taxa by Sándor Bökönyi, John Hedges, and Sebastian Payne.

METHODOLOGY AND DATA BASE

At the time of the Sitagroi excavation, 1968–1970, Semenov's (1964) seminal study of methods of microscopic use-wear analysis of lithics was being applied to the Sitagroi chipped stone (Tringham 1984, and this volume, chapter 3), but not to the bone tools, although he had experimented and reported on both. However, over the ensuing years, as with chipped stone, researchers explored microscopic edge-wear study, replication, and use of bone tools to identify bone working methods and wear patterns, with varying degrees of success (Campana 1989; LeMoine 1994; Maggi, Starnini, and Voytek 1997; Runnings, Bentley, and Gustafson 1989; Russell 1982; Smith and Poggenpoel 1988); the dissertation of Rosalia Christidou (1999) presents the most exhaustive recent study. Lately, hypotheses have been offered concerning the gender of the toolmaker and user (Spector 1991:388; Russell 1992). Experimenting with the formation of use-wear on bone tools, Russell applied her observations in a microscopic study of the bone artifacts from Neolithic Selevac, providing her with insight into manufacturing techniques and tool use (Russell 1990:522–548), albeit noting several limitations: (1) bone working on various softer organic materials left only undifferentiated polish, with the exception of pottery burnishing; thus the working traces did not always answer the question of use; (2) the softer surface of antler did not preserve microscopic evidence of edge wear as did bone. Nevertheless, Sitagroi bone tools and artifacts, stored in the new museum in Drama, are potentially a rich trove for the application of these current approaches of study.

The catalog (see appendix 2.1), produced as a first step to the writing of this report, was based on the data as codified in the bone notebook (the work of John Hedges), on the inventory cards, most of which I prepared serving as registrar during the field seasons of 1968 and 1969, and on the line drawings and plates. Identification of species and elements was the purview of Bökönyi, faunal specialist for the excavation. However, artifacts recovered during the fine-mesh water-sieving project were identified by Payne.

Young persons from the village were engaged to process the bone artifacts under supervision. Soil adhering to an artifact was brushed loose rather than washed. Not every artifact was sketched, illustrated, or photographed. The characteristics of a given artifact were tabulated whenever descriptive notes (in either the notebook or inventory cards) were specific (for example, "metapodial," "point," "chisel-end"). The artifacts listed in the tables come from Middle Neolithic phases I and II (abbreviated as "MN"), the Chalcolithic (or Late Neolithic) phase III (shortened to "C"), and the two Early Bronze Age phases IV and V, referred to as "EBA." In some tables data for the MN/C and EBA are condensed. There are several reasons for this: there is no interruption of settlement (and therefore chronological continuity) from phase I through III and likewise from phase IV to V, and thus they are treated each as a unit; furthermore, as others have noted, there is

very little change through time in the form of bone tools, and thus the units are not masking any typological differences; and finally, when presenting data describing the use of various taxa and elements through time, the phases are not combined in order to isolate whatever behavioral choice may be observable.

This report is based on 613 bone and antler artifacts representing 3000 years of herding, hunting, scavenging, and tool making. We can compare the size of this assemblage to those from other prehistoric Greek and Balkan sites: Russell (1990) worked with the Selevac sample of 1032 artifacts covering 1500 years; the count was 470 at Divostin (Lyneis 1988:301), 331 at Dhimitra (Christidou 1997:128), 100 at Dikili Tash (Séfériadès 1992b:99, 105, 110), and 318 at Karanovo (Hoglinger 1997:157). The UCLA section at Obre was trowelled systematically, yielding 826 tools (Sterud and Sterud 1974: 242–243). There is obviously much variation in the extent of recovery from site to site because of variability in site content, in excavation goals, and in methodology, leading to differences in recovery and the volume of earth displaced (see Preface table 2). These samples are comparable in a general chronological sense, but are they truly representative of the bone tool assemblage as a whole for each site? Answering that question requires that we compute the volume of earth moved at each excavation and evaluate the relative differences in methodology (sieved versus non-sieved) and site content. These are large questions that must be put on hold for another study.

A number of modified teeth and small artifacts were recovered and identified in the course of water sieving from test square ZB, an extension of the ZA sounding (see volume 1 [C. Renfrew 1986e]: 170). This project, designed by Sebastian Payne (1975), was undertaken to compare a fine-mesh-sieved recovery against then current field practice of hand recovery. The results added small artifacts plus teeth, bird, and fish bone (Payne 1975:11, 13). The latter findings, of fish bone, underscore the importance of the Angitis River as a source for food. The river, one of the environmental features of the site, may have led the first settlers to establish the site. In his environmental study of Dhimitra, also situated riverside, Fotiadis described the Angitis as "a copious perennial stream" (1997:71).

The bone tool assemblage was manufactured from skeletal elements of all five domesticated animals identified by Bökönyi in the refuse bone: cattle, sheep, goat, pig, and dog. Also utilized as raw material were elements from six of the twenty-nine wild animals: swine, red, fallow, and roe deer, aurochs, and tortoise (see volume 1 [Bökönyi 1986]: 68–69). Shell is treated in chapter 9 of this volume (see also appendixes 9.1, 9.2) along with all but five carapace specimens and the majority of perforated dentine. Although I discuss a few of the artifacts that we see as "elaborated," the majority of the items of adornment (for example, bone beads or pendants) are discussed in detail in chapter 9 along with the shell.

The refuse bone recovered from the excavations at Sitagroi totaled over 34,473 specimens (see volume 1 [Bökönyi 1986]:68–69). Of that number, 91% represented domesticates, with wild animals making up the remaining 9%. Table 2.1 is based on Bökönyi's tabulation of the refuse bone by phase. The six wild animals whose elements were used as raw material for the manufacture of artifacts represent 80% of the total of refuse wild bone, with red deer representing 38% of that number. As in many prehistoric sites of the Balkans and northeast Greece (Larje 1987:94; Séfériadès 1992b:99), the wild species provided raw material of considerable importance for artifacts. Although most tools were manufactured on bone elements from domesticated animals, we shall see that red deer antler was a special raw material with its own use trajectory. However, it must be noted that since antler is more easily recognized during excavation, its relative significance in the assemblage may reflect bias.

Table 2.1 presents the data of three millennia during which the mound *may* have held several separate and distinct episodes of occupation and temporary abandonment or relocation, with each episode's concomitant human activities of differing focus: house building, planting, herding, reaping, gathering, hunting, scavenging, cooking, tool making, tool using, and trading. Nevertheless, the general observation at Sitagroi is that the *forms* of bone artifacts change very little over time (also noted at

Table 2.1. Relative Percentage Over Time for Bone Specimen from Wild or Domesticated Taxa

Duration	% Domesticated	% Wild
Phase I (Middle Neolithic)	91.40	8.60
Phase II (Middle Neolithic)	96.53	3.47
Phase III (Chalcolithic)	91.88	8.12
Phase IV (Early Bronze Age)	82.33	17.67
Phase Va, b (Early Bronze Age)	93.48	6.55

Source: Based on Bökönyi 1986.

Selevac [Russell 1990:546]). This lack of change may be due in part to what lithic scholars refer to as "mechanical contingency": the properties of the raw material that knappers consider as they begin tool manufacture (Sackett 1966), such as shape, flaws, and size. In the same way, a long bone lends itself to being formed into a pointed tool, whereas the beam of an antler does not (Choyke 1998:171). Thus in the case of bone tools, function follows form. As we shall see, however, there was a change over time in species selection.

All faunal recovery has been reported as kitchen refuse (volume 1 [Bökönyi 1986]:65); thus meat protein came mainly from kept animals (see table 2.2), a pattern repeated at other Neolithic and EBA northern Greek sites (Yannouli 1994:330). Hunting and scavenging were not as important to subsistence but could have provided a special "treat," a traditional meal for a feast or celebration or, more practically, risk protection in times of herd failure as well as raw material for tools and other artifacts.

Bone artifacts total 452 and antler, 161. Because antler and bone properties are so different, I consider each group separately in evaluating taxa and element. Antler, seemingly much prized, is extremely resilient and absorbs shock without splitting. When the inner spongy core of a section of the rack is removed, the remaining sleeve provides a handle for holding another tool (Choyke 1998:171–172). Also, the number of artifacts that can be manufactured from an antler rack (figure 2.1) is potentially greater than from any other element: the multiple tines and basal, fork, or beam segments

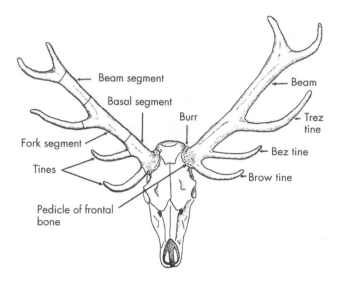

Figure 2.1. Red deer (*Cervus elaphus*) antler anatomy (after Lyneis 1988:302).

are all potentially useful. Antler at Sitagroi comes from three species: the large red deer (*Cervus elaphus*) and two smaller, more graceful species, roe deer (*Capreolus capreolus*) and, less frequently, fallow deer (*Dama dama*). If we can interpolate from modern hunter's reports, the roe deer was especially prized for its tasty meat.

The antler beams and subsidiary tines are a bony outgrowth of the male deer's brow, grown and shed annually. As a stag matures, his yearly antlers grow ever larger, along with the diameter of the beam and the number of tines; the latter are named in relation to their position closest to the burr: first "brow" tine, followed by "bez" and "trez" tines. A cross section of antler shows that the interior is composed of woven bone tissue, coarsely bundled together and surrounded by a compact surface or external layer that offers much more material for carving than do other types of bone (Choyke 1998:171). Because antler is stronger and more resilient than any other part of the deer, toolmakers selected, shaped, modified, and used various sections of beam and tine.

Well over half of the bone tool count (252 artifacts or 56%) is manufactured on elements from unidentifiable taxa (table 2.2). It is unfortunate that we cannot incorporate this large number of tools in all of the tabulations, since identification of even a

fraction of these could change the relative percentage of domestic versus wild raw material selected. Nevertheless, from the identifiable sample of 200 artifacts for a 3000-year period, almost two-thirds are from domesticates (130) and the balance from wild taxa (70). Even though these tabulations do not present a full picture, the data suggest that bone from wild taxa was especially important to the settlers as raw material for tool making, probably because elements from wild animals are stronger (Russell 1990:544, 548). The hunt also offered opportunities for participants to show their skill and for leaders to emerge (Rappaport 1968), and the artifacts made on bone elements of wild and/or trophy animals might well have taken on special significance.

Most tools were recovered from the combined MN/C (288 artifacts or 64%; phases I–III in table 2.2) rather than the EBA (164 tools, including four surface finds, or 36%; phases IV, V, and mixed contexts [X] in table 2.2). This count is affected by the richness of phase III levels and because the MN/C extends over the longest period of Sitagroi occupation (see Preface table 1). Lyneis (1988:318) commented on the contrast between bone assemblages for Divostin I (Early Neolithic Starčevo) and II (Middle Neolithic Vinča), particularly in the use of antler (very little in Divostin I and considerably more in Divostin II) and in the technology of bone working. No doubt a detailed microscopic study of the Sitagroi tools would also expose other differences in bone working and using.

TAXA AND ELEMENTS

Table 2.3 (MN/C) and table 2.4 (EBA) present the toolmaker's preference for skeletal elements. Results indicate that, for MN/C, caprovine metapodials, tibiae, ulnae, and astragali were preferred, the last possibly for use in gaming (Mellaart 1970: 162; Russell 1990:538–539) or, when pierced, as a pendant. From wild taxa, preference was for deer metapodials, and teeth from wild pig, generally pierced, but counts of identifiable taxa and elements were insignificant. Ribs were frequently used for tools, but clues as to taxa were often lost in the manufacturing process.

Table 2.2 Distribution of Bone Artifacts Over Time Manufactured from Domesticated or Wild Taxa

Taxon				Phases				
Domestic	I	II	III	IV	V	X*	Grand Total	%
Bos taurus L.	1	2	8	3	8	0	22	0.05
Caprovine	9	16	44	9	12	0	90	0.20
Sus scrofa dom. L.	2	3	5	0	4	1	15	0.03
Canis familiaris	0	1	1	1	0	0	3	0.00
TOTAL	12	22	58	13	24	1	130	0.29
Wild								
Bos primigenius	0	0	0	2	0	0	2	0.00
Cervus	0	2	3	9	1	1	16	0.04
Cervus elaphus L.	1	0	8	11	1	0	21	0.05
Dama sp.	0	0	0	0	1	0	1	0.00
Capreolus capreolus	0	1	6	1	0	0	8	0.02
Sus Scrofa fer. L.	0	4	7	3	3	0	17	0.04
Chelonia sp.	0	0	1	2	2	0	5	0.01
TOTAL	1	7	25	28	8	1	70	0.15
Unidentifiable	24	66	73	52	35	2	252	0.56
GRAND TOTAL	37	95	156	93	67	4	452	1.00
PERCENT	0.08	0.21	0.35	0.21	0.15	0.00	1.00	

* X indicates mixed or unknown contexts.

Table 2.3 Cross-tabulation of Bone Elements from Domesticated or Wild Taxa Used during the Middle Neolithic/Chalcolithic, Phases I–III

Taxon	Astragalus	Humerus	Jaw	Metapodial	Radius	Rib	Scapula	Shell	Skull	Tibia	Tooth	Ulna	Vertebra	Total	%
Domestic															
Bos taurus L.	1	0	1	1	1	1	0	0	1	0	0	5	0	11	0.07
Caprovine	11	3	0	41	0	0	0	0	0	9	0	5	0	69	0.46
Sus scrofa dom. L.	3	0	0	0	0	0	1	0	1	5	0	0	0	10	0.07
Canis familiaris	0	0	0	0	1	0	0	0	0	0	0	1	0	2	0.01
TOTAL	15	3	1	42	2	1	1	0	2	14	0	11	0	92	0.61
Wild															
Cervus	0	0	0	5	0	0	0	0	0	0	0	0	0	5	0.03
Cervus elaphus L.	1	0	0	8	0	0	0	0	0	0	0	0	0	9	0.06
Capreolus capreolus	0	0	0	6	0	0	0	0	0	1	0	0	0	7	0.05
Sus scrofa fer. L.	0	0	0	0	0	0	0	0	0	0	11	0	0	11	0.07
Chelonia sp.	0	0	0	0	0	0	0	1	0	0	0	0	0	1	0.00
TOTAL	1	0	0	19	0	0	0	1	0	1	11	0	0	33	0.22
Unidentifiable	0	0	0	2	0	21	0	0	0	1	2	0	0	26	0.17
GRAND TOTAL	16	3	1	63	2	22	1	1	2	16	13	11	0	151	1.00
PERCENT	0.11	0.02	0.00	0.42	0.01	0.15	0.00	0.00	0.01	0.11	0.09	0.07	0.00		1.00

During the EBA (table 2.4) caprovine metapodials and tibiae were again most important from domestics. Among wild taxa, preference continued for cervid metapodials. There were also canine teeth from wild pig; some of these were perforated, others were split, which occurs naturally (Judy Porcasi, personal communication, November 2001), and they could have been used in cutting (Russell 1990:531).

Table 2.5 presents the distribution of antler artifacts over time at Sitagroi. *Cervus elaphus* is the most frequently represented in phases I through IV. A few explanations for the importance of antler to the settlers at Sitagroi were given earlier, along with the admission that the significance of antler in the assemblage may reflect excavation bias. Choyke (1998:172) also considered this possibility, but because of the regularity of antler finds at many sites of the Great Hungarian Plain, she concluded that bias was not a significant factor.

As indicated in table 2.5, antler working increased through MN/C but dwindled beginning with the EBA, even though evidence of hunting is strong in the refuse bone of phase IV (see table 2.1, which shows that the highest percentage of wild animal bone recovery is in Phase IV). Indeed, the percentage of red deer increases over time: phase II: 1.4%; phase III: 3.7%; and phase IV: 6.6% (volume 1 [Bökönyi 1986]:68). Granted, the sample is small, and tables 2.2 and 2.5 suggest that there is no change in the *use* of wild animal elements for bone tool production from phase III to phase IV (twenty-five tools in III versus twenty-eight in IV). What is most significant is that the use of antler (table 2.5) decreases from 40% in phase III to 10% in phase IV. One interpretation is that while deer was being hunted and its skeletal elements used for tools, the EBA villagers were not as interested in producing antler artifacts.

A similar change was observed at the Yugoslavian Vinča sites, and this was explained in relation to agricultural practice. In the Selevac publication, Chapman (1990:24–25) and Tringham and Krstić (1990:593–594) noted that throughout the Neolithic and into the Chalcolithic, horticulture took place in

Table 2.4 Cross-tabulation of the Distribution of Bone Elements from Domesticated or Wild Taxa during the Early Bronze Age, Phases IV and V

	Fibula	Horn-core	Hyoid	Jaw	Metapodial	Radius	Rib	Scapula	Shell	Skull	Tibia	Tooth	Ulna	Vertebra	Total	%
Bos taurus L.	0	4	1	0	0	0	3	2	0	0	0	0	1	0	11	0.13
Caprovine	0	0	0	0	8	0	0	1	0	0	11	0	1	0	21	0.25
Sus scrofa dom. L.	3	0	0	0	0	0	0	0	0	1	0	0	0	0	4	0.05
Canis familiaris	0	0	0	0	0	0	0	0	0	0	0	1	0	0	1	0.01
TOTAL	3	4	1	0	8	0	3	3	0	1	11	1	2	0	37	
Wild																
Bos primigenius	0	0	0	0	0	0	0	2	0	0	0	0	0	0	2	0.02
Cervus	0	0	0	0	9	1	0	0	0	0	0	0	0	0	10	0.12
Cervus elaphus L.	0	0	0	0	12	0	0	0	0	0	0	0	0	0	12	0.14
Dama sp.	0	0	0	0	0	0	0	0	0	0	1	0	0	0	1	0.01
Capreolus capreolus	0	0	0	0	1	0	0	0	0	0	0	0	0	0	1	0.01
Sus scrofa fer. L.	0	0	0	1	0	0	0	0	0	0	0	5	0	0	6	0.07
Chelonia sp.	0	0	0	0	0	0	0	0	4	0	0	0	0	0	4	0.05
TOTAL	0	0	0	1	22	1	0	2	4	0	1	5	0	0	36	0.43
Unidentifiable	0	0	0	0	1	0	6	2	0	0	0	1	0	1	10	0.12
GRAND TOTAL	3	4	1	1	31	1	9	7	4	1	12	7	2	1	83	1.00
PERCENT	0.04	0.05	0.01	0.01	0.37	0.01	0.11	0.08	0.05	0.01	0.14	0.08	0.02	0.01	1.00	

Table 2.5 Distribution of Cervidae Antler Over Time

	Phase							
Taxon	I	II	III	IV	V	X*	Grand total	%
Capreolus capreolus	3	1	1	1	1	1	1	1
Cervus	8	8	7	4	4	4	4	4
Cervus elaphus L.	12	39	56	11	11	11	11	11
TOTAL	23	48	64	16	16	16	16	16
Unidentifiable	0	1	0	0	0	0	0	0
GRAND TOTAL	23	49	64	16	16	16	16	16
PERCENT	0.14	0.30	0.40	0.10	0.10	0.10	0.10	

* X indicates mixed or unknown contexts.

household plots. They surmised that as population increased and food requirements grew, this practice was replaced by the cultivation of new soils on "expandable land," no longer close to houses. Agriculturists replaced digging sticks of antler tine and hoes or mattocks from hollowed and shafted antler beams with the ard and simple plow.

Choyke (1998:157–178) saw an opposite development: more antler tools in the EBA compared with less in the Neolithic and Chalcolithic. She also explained this change in relation to agricultural practice, but her inference is that intensification of production and exploitation of new soils called for *more* antler tools, not fewer.

Another hypothesis that I might offer is that before the EBA, population had grown and some of the MN/C agriculturists had moved elsewhere. Over time, a new EBA group resettled or joined the remaining settlers on the mound, bringing a different practice of bone tool manufacture and use. In fact, we do see a change in the pattern of animal exploitation, which Bökönyi explains as responsive to a climatic change that began earlier than the beginning of the EBA (see volume 1 [Bökönyi 1986]: 70).

TYPES

Although the assemblage is divided into antler and other bone, the typology includes both materials, focusing on formal variation and modification. It is a challenge to design a bone typology, because the general form (for example, "point") may be the "type" but the configuration of the tip is a by-product of either the kind of material or intensity of use and generally varies considerably. Equally, the chisel end of a bone or an antler may have been used for the same task, but the elements vary. An ideal typology is extensive because it includes a focused, detailed, discrete, and comprehensive attribute system. Thus, unless the assemblage is large, the categories will represent such small numbers as to be without inferential power (see Russell 1990:526–527 for the Selevac attribute system). The line drawings and plates in this chapter give a sense of the variability in the assemblage (figures 2.2–2.20; plates 2.1–2.22). Table 2.6 (MN/C) and table 2.7 (EBA) compare the frequency of types as manufactured from bone elements of domestic or wild taxa; table 2.8 does the same for antler.

We can assume that various blades and flakes of chipped stone (this volume, chapter 3), or ground and polished edge tools and grinding stones (this volume, chapter 5) were used to form and shape bone artifacts. Lyneis (1988:317) reported on the bone and antler artifacts from Divostin, and her words regarding tools and methods for bone tool manufacture are appropriate for the Sitagroi assemblage: "Axes, adzes, sharp cutting blades and flakes, rotary drills and the thong-and-abrasive technique were available, in addition to grinding surfaces of sandstone or other rocks. Antler was chopped, whittled, hacked, adzed, cut with thong and abrasive . . . bone was grooved with a cutting tool, split, or broken along the grooves, polished to shape, and occasionally drilled" (1988: 317).

The artifacts reported here are very similar to those Lyneis describes and illustrates (1988:310,

Table 2.6 Cross-tabulation of Domesticated or Wild Bone Taxa and Types during the Middle Neolithic/Chalcolithic, Phases I and III

Taxon	Chisel end	Elab. piece	Flattened end	Misc. worked	Perforated	Pointed	Rounded end	Spatulate end	Total	%
Domestic										
Bos taurus L.	3	1	0	5	0	1	1	0	11	0.04
Caprovine	6	3	3	21	1	35	0	1	70	0.24
Sus scrofa dom. L.	2	2	2	4	0	0	0	0	10	0.03
Canis familiaris	0	0	2	0	0	0	0	0	2	0.00
TOTAL	11	6	7	30	1	36	1	1	93	0.32
Wild										
Cervus	0	0	0	2	0	3	0	0	5	0.02
Cervus elaphus L.	1	0	1	4	0	3	0	0	9	0.03
Capreolus capreolus	1	0	0	0	0	6	0	0	7	0.02
Sus scrofa fer. L.	0	2	0	9	0	0	0	0	11	0.04
Chelonia sp.	0	0	0	1	0	0	0	0	1	0.00
TOTAL	2	2	1	16	0	12	0	0	33	0.11
Unidentifiable	8	11	11	36	1	73	9	13	162	0.56
GRAND TOTAL	21	19	19	82	2	121	10	14	287	1.00
PERCENT	0.07	0.07	0.07	0.28	0.00	0.42	0.03	0.05	1.00	

Table 2.7 Cross-tabulation of Domesticated or Wild Bone Taxa and Types during the Early Bronze Age, Phases IV and V

Taxon	Chisel end	Elab. piece	Flattened end	Misc. worked	Pointed	Rounded end	Spatulate end	Total	%
Domestic									
Bos taurus L.	1	0	2	7	0	0	1	11	0.07
Caprovine	7	0	2	4	7	1	0	21	0.13
Sus scrofa dom. L.	0	2	0	1	1	0	0	4	0.03
Canis familiaris	0	1	0	0	0	0	0	1	0.00
TOTAL	8	3	4	12	8	1	1	37	0.23
Wild									
Bos primigenius	0	0	0	2	0	0	0	2	0.01
Cervus	2	0	0	3	5	0	0	10	0.06
Cervus elaphus L.	1	0	0	6	4	1	0	12	0.08
Dama sp.	1	0	0	0	0	0	0	1	0.00
Capreolus capreolus	0	0	0	0	1	0	0	1	0.00
Sus scrofa fer. L.	0	0	0	6	0	0	0	6	0.04
Chelonia sp.	0	3	0	1	0	0	0	4	0.03
TOTAL	4	3	0	18	10	1	0	36	0.23
Unidentifiable	4	9	2	25	39	3	5	87	0.54
GRAND TOTAL	16	15	6	55	57	5	6	160	1.00
PERCENT	0.10	0.09	0.04	0.34	0.37	0.03	0.04	1.00	

Table 2.8. Distribution of Cervidae Antler and Types

Taxon	Chisel end	Elab. piece	Flattened end	Misc. worked	Perforated	Pointed	Rounded end	Shaft-holed	Total	%
Cervus	1	0	2	20	0	0	5	0	28	0.17
Cervus elaphus L.	9	2	10	83	2	3	9	7	125	0.78
Capreolus capreolus	1	0	0	0	0	3	3	0	7	0.04
TOTAL	11	2	12	103	2	6	17	7	160	0.99
Unidentifiable	0	0	0	0	0	1	0	0	1	0.00
GRAND TOTAL	11	2	12	103	2	7	17	7	161	1. 00
PERCENT	0.07	0.01	0.08	0.64	0.01	0.04	0.11	0.04	1. 00	

311, 314, 315, 320–323; thus, lacking the opportunity to study the Sitagroi assemblage as did Lyneis at Divostin, I feel fairly comfortable assuming that these are the tools and techniques that were applied in producing the types described below. The types include the following:

POINTED PIECES (FIGURES 2.2–2.5; PLATES 2.1–2.3, 2.5; TABLES 2.9, 2.10). Pointed artifacts are the most numerous type in the assemblage (42% in MN/C; 37% in EBA). The several variations include tools on unidentifiable elements (figures 2.4c, 2.18a, plate 2.5d) or on long bones (figures 2.2, 2.3a, c, d, 2.4b, 2.5a, b; plates 2.1, 2.3c–g) or ribs (figures 2.3b, 2.5c; plate 2.2a–d, f) where the element is reduced by splitting and/or grinding with sides narrowed and smoothed. Antler fragments (figure 2.12c) including tine (figure 2.12a; plate 2.3a, b) were also used, as evidenced by wear observable on the pointed ends. One (see figures 2.2–2.4; plates 2.1, 2.2a–c) or both ends (figure 2.5a, b, d; plate 2.2d–f) converge to a point; these modified ends are the working surfaces. Termination can also appear transverse, angled, beveled, and/or chisel-like, as on several points manufactured of split rib, the tip worn down or broken, wear polish noted on the margin, and the opposite end used perhaps in scraping or burnishing (figures 2.3a, b; plate 2.2a–c). Many of these artifacts must have been multiple-use tools.

Although ribs were not as strong as metapodials, many more ribs were available as raw material. Nevertheless, metapodials, especially of caprovines and deer, were commonly selected and carefully made into points with the epiphyses ground, per-

haps for aesthetic reasons, or to operate more smoothly, perhaps with textiles (for example, figure 2.3c; plate 2.3e).

Some insight into the manufacturing process comes from the EBA Burnt House (volume 1 [C. Renfrew 1986b]:190–203; Elster 1997: pl. Vb) where a 30.3-cm-long red deer metapodial (figure 2.6; plate 2.4) was recovered from the floor of the "kitchen." It may be a preform because the tool-maker had already grooved it longitudinally (perhaps with a burin or a *pièce esquillée*) preparatory to splitting. A skillful worker could have produced a minimum of two tools and as many as four from a preform such as this, although the groove is not straight. A comparable long bone, with no evidence of working, was reported from the Arene Candide cave assemblage (Maggi, Starnini, and Voytek 1997: 517, 528, fig. 8:12).

If the goal is to produce a tool quickly, then it is quite effective to crack a long bone or rib with a hard stone and then select a splinter to be shaped by grinding and smoothing (Petrequin 1993:65). At least one artifact appears to illustrate this simplified method (figure 2.5c; plate 2.2d); it is probably unfinished since the rough parts along the long margin of the tool were not ground and smoothed away, although the tip was prepared and seems to have been used

This broad category includes objects often classified in the field as awl/penetration tool, some of which are heavy enough to work through rawhide or pierce the softer materials used in mat making (for example, figure 2.2c; plate 2.3d). The latter craft was practiced at Sitagroi as evidenced by impressions on

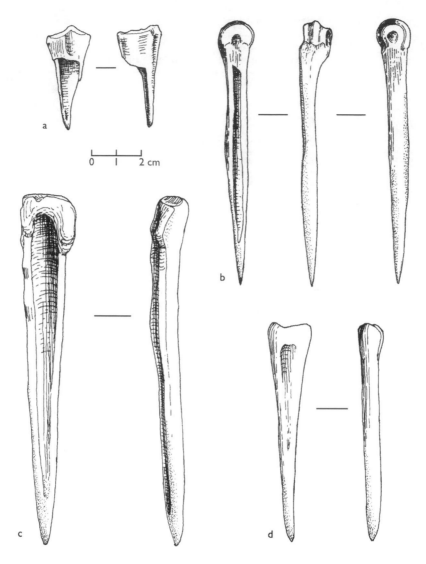

Figure 2.2. Pointed tools on metapodials; phase II: a, b; phase IV: c, d. (a) SF 3133, roe deer, plates 2.1f, 2.3c; (b) SF 3750, split distal metapodial, plate 2.1a; (c) SF 122, plate 2.3d; (d) SF 25, plate 2.1e.

sherds of both single and double weave (see this volume, chapter 6 and appendix 6.1; Elster 1992:45, fig. 6b, c). Russell also described "sharp awls needed to pierce and sew together the reeds in coiled basketry" from Selevac (1990:528). Other pointed tools are much lighter (figures 2.5a, b, d, 2.7a; plates 2.1g–k, 2.2e, 2.3g, 2.5a; see also in this volume, chapter 9, figure 9.27) and could have been used to pin up hair, or as a stylus to incise designs on spindle whorls (see this volume, chapter 6), figurines, and various types of ceramics (for examples of incisions, see volume 1, chapters 9, 10, 12, and 13). The

assemblage also includes a small, carefully made needle, about 6 cm long, with a fracture at the eyehole (figure 2.4d), one of the few artifacts whose use is not ambiguous. It is from phase III, where the evidence for spinning and weaving is strong (this volume, chapter 6; Elster 1997:29–35).

Pointed tools dominate many assemblages from prehistoric sites. At Selevac, over half of the total bone tool assemblage was pointed, and 57% of these were manufactured on ribs (Russell 1990:524). At Obre, more than a third were points (Sterud and Sterud 1974:244); at Arene Candide, the count of

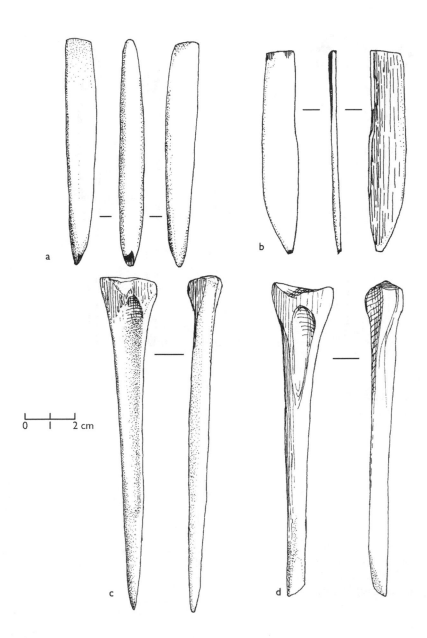

Figure 2.3. Multiple use bone tools; phase II: a, b; phase III: c; phase IV: d. Ends pointed, angled, and cross-cut on long bones (a, c, d) and rib (b): (a) SF 236, long bone with wear noted along ends and margin; (b) SF 3776, rib with wear along cross-cut and margin, plate 2.2c; (c) SF 1194, split long bone, ground diaphysis and wear noted along margin and tips, plate 2.3e; (d) SF 3709, split long bone, ground diaphysis and wear noted along tips, plate 2.3f.

awls, points, and needles exceeded 70% (Maggi, Starnini, and Voytek 1997:514, Tabla 1). A caution, especially concerning points, is that the identifying characteristics of specific taxa and elements are often lost in the manufacturing process. Therefore, although 42% of MN/C tools (table 2.6) were pointed (121 artifacts in all), more than half of these

(seventy-three artifacts) were from unidentifiable taxa. Nevertheless, when taxa and elements are identifiable in the MN/C assemblage of pointed tools (table 2.9), metapodials were most likely to have been used, first from caprovines, followed by roe deer, red deer, and unspecified deer. The tool count is smaller (table 2.10) for the EBA, but

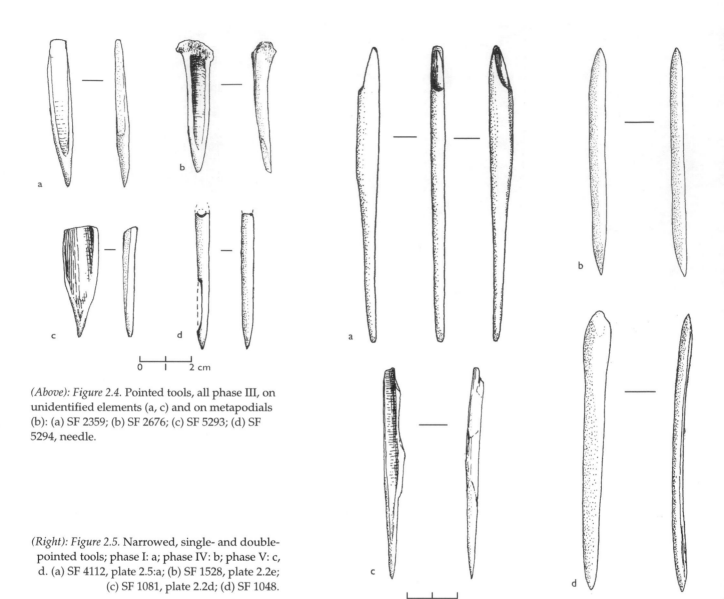

(Above): Figure 2.4. Pointed tools, all phase III, on unidentified elements (a, c) and on metapodials (b): (a) SF 2359; (b) SF 2676; (c) SF 5293; (d) SF 5294, needle.

(Right): Figure 2.5. Narrowed, single- and double-pointed tools; phase I: a; phase IV: b; phase V: c, d. (a) SF 4112, plate 2.5:a; (b) SF 1528, plate 2.2e; (c) SF 1081, plate 2.2d; (d) SF 1048.

caprovine and deer metapodials were most frequently chosen. Among the identifiable EBA pointed tools, we can determine that they were manufactured on a variety of elements from domesticated animals in addition to metapodials: tibiae, ulnae, and even humeri.

The mean length for pointed tools for which we have identification of *both* taxa and element indicates that the longest were manufactured on metapodials (tables 2.9, 2.10). During MN/C the range is 6.0 (*Bos taurus* L.) to 9.6 cm (*Cervus elaphus*).

The points from the EBA, range from 5.0 (*Capreolus capreolus*) to 10.2 cm (*Cervus elaphus*). Two deer metapodials from MN/C stand out for their greater length: 13.2 (figure 2.3c; plate 2.3e) and 11.2 cm (SF 3124). Not unexpectedly, the longer points in phase IV are also deer metapodials (figure 2.2c; plate 2.3d). One small, casually made point (it seems to have been snapped) is questionable regarding taxon; it is made on either roe deer or goat metapodial (figure 2.2a; plate 2.3c).

Table 2.9. Distribution of Pointed Bone Tools, Domesticated or Wild Taxa, and Elements for the Middle Neolithic-Chalcolithic, Phases I–III

Taxon	Element (Average Length cm)						
Domestic	Humerus	Metapodial	Rib	Tibia	Ulna	Total	%
Bos taurus L.	0	1 (6.0)	0	0	0	1	0.02
Caprovine	2 (3.1)	25 (6.3)	0	5 (6.3)	3 (3.9)	35	0.66
TOTAL	2	26	0	5	3	36	0.68
Wild							
Cervus	0	3 (9.3)	0	0	0	3	0.06
Cervus elaphus L.	0	3 (9.6)	0	0	0	3	0.06
Capreolus capreolus	0	6 (6.2)	0	0	0	6	0.11
TOTAL	0	12	0	0	0	12	0.23
Unidentifiable	0	1	4	0	0	5	0.09
GRAND TOTAL	2	39	4	5	3	53	1. 00
PERCENT	0.04	0.74	0.08	0.09	0.06	1. 00	

Table 2.10. Distribution of Pointed Bone Tools, Domesticated or Wild Taxa, and Elements from the Early Bronze Age, Phases IV and V

Taxon	Element						
Domestic	Fibula	Metapodial	Rib	Tibia	Ulna	Total	%
Caprovine	0	4 (7.2)	0	2 (5.8)	1 (5.8)	6	0.32
Sus scrofa dom L.	1 (7.3)	0	0	0	0	1	0.05
TOTAL	1	4	0	2	1	7	0.37
Wild							
Cervus	0	4 (7.2)	0	1 (4.3)	0	5	0.26
Cervus elaphus L.	0	4 (10.2)	0	0	0	4	0.21
Capreolus capreolus	0	1 (5.0)	0	0	0	1	0.05
TOTAL	0	9	0	1	0	10	0.53
Unidentifiable	0	1 (11.3)	1 (11.0)	0	0	2	0.11
GRAND TOTAL	1	14	1	3	1	19	1. 00
PERCENT	0.05	0.74	0.05	0.16	0.05	1. 00	

An interesting pointed artifact from phase I (figure 2.5a; plate 2.5a; see also figure 9.27) is carefully worked and smoothed, probably on a long bone, with wear polish noted from tip to tip along the left margin. The preserved length of this slim point is 11.7 cm (outside the range of MN points); the fracture is at the wider end. From the line drawing, Elizabeth Barber (personal communication, November 1995) proposed it as a weaver's "pin beater" used to "beat" or push the weft tight during the weaving process. It is described as smooth and thin and would have fit easily in the hand. But there are other possibilities for its use: as an awl, a pin, a burnisher, or to incise designs on ceramics.

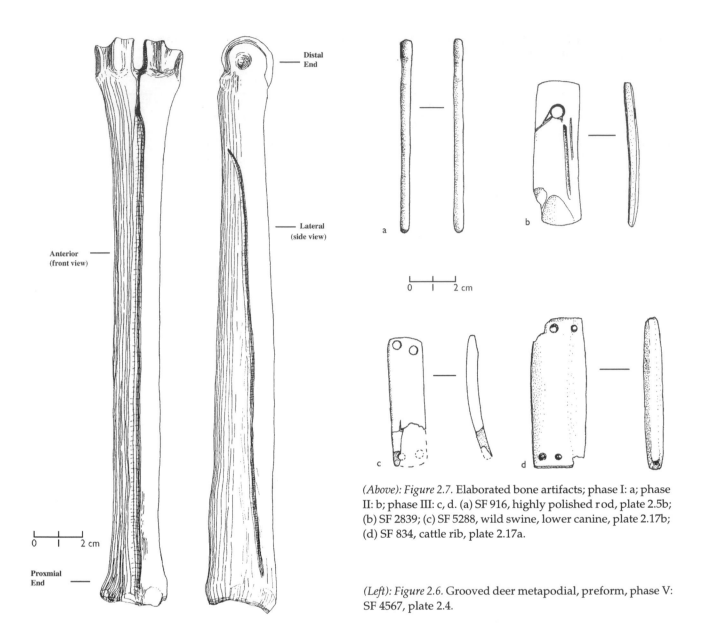

0   2 cm

(Above): Figure 2.7. Elaborated bone artifacts; phase I: a; phase II: b; phase III: c, d. (a) SF 916, highly polished rod, plate 2.5b; (b) SF 2839; (c) SF 5288, wild swine, lower canine, plate 2.17b; (d) SF 834, cattle rib, plate 2.17a.

(Left): Figure 2.6. Grooved deer metapodial, preform, phase V: SF 4567, plate 2.4.

BEVEL/CHISEL END. Tools of antler (figures 2.8a, b, 2.9a; plate 2.6a–c) and bone (figure 2.10; plate 2.7) are tabulated together because of the similarity of the modified ends. One method to produce this type with antler was to select a section of the beam (or tine), cut this longitudinally, and remove the spongy inside, ending up with hollow split halves. The edge of one end was then shaped into a bevel (figures 2.8a, b, 2.9a; plate 2.6a–c). Antler tine was also shaped at the tip into a chisel end (plate 2.6d). The bones illustrated in figure 2.10 and plate 2.7 exhibit an angled cross-cut that forms the working

edge. Taxa include a proximal caprovine metacarpal, perhaps originally sliced for marrow (figure 2.10a; plate 2.7a), a caprovine tibia from the Burnt House (figure 2.10b; plate 2.7b), and a subadult red deer tibia (figure 2.10c; plate 2.7d). These latter two tibia from a caprovine and red deer differ clearly, yet the fracture pattern of the modified end is virtually exact. I point these out because there must have been a corollary action used on both at different times and in various contexts. In terms of use, the beveled edges of both antler and bone could be used to scrape, gouge, and polish. However, the

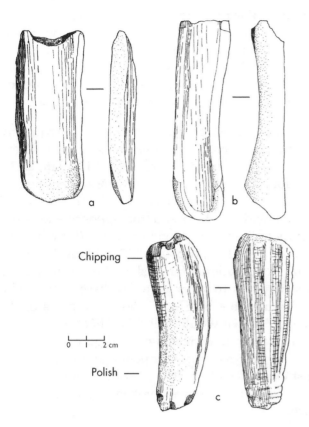

Chipping

Polish

Figure 2.8. Antler, phase II: a, c; phase IV: b. Split and inner core removed with wear at chisel end (a, b) and along sides (c): (a) SF 246, plate 2.6a; (b) SF 4645, plate 2.6c; (c) SF 4745, plate 2.11b.

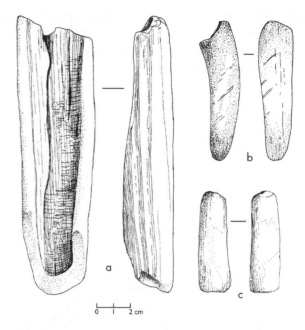

Figure 2.9. Antler, split with the core removed; phase I: b; phase II: a, c. (a) SF 5405, split antler with inner core removed and wear indicated on chisel end and along edge, plate 2.6b; (b) SF 111, red deer antler tine with rounded tip, plate 2.10b; (c) SF 447, antler punch, plate 2.11a.

antler halves are multifunctional since hollowed antler halves could be used as scoops or both halves could be tied around another tool forming a haft (Russell 1990:538).

ROUND END. Examples occur mainly on the naturally converging point of an antler tine (figures 2.9b, 2.11; plates 2.9, 2.10). The rounding at the tip may be a product of use, or caused by the stag rubbing his rack on a tree as he prepares for the shed (Russell, personal communication 1996). The toolmakers cut around and then break off the tine; this is referred to as the "cut and break" method (Lyneis 1988:303; Russell 1990:540). Sometimes this cut is observable at the wider end (plates 2.9, 2.10a, f). An antler with rosette and sharply pointed tine was recovered (figure 2.12a; plate 2.3a, b) and quite a few examples of waste (plate 2.10d–k) including one tine with a pathological bump (plate 2.10f). One split tine frag-

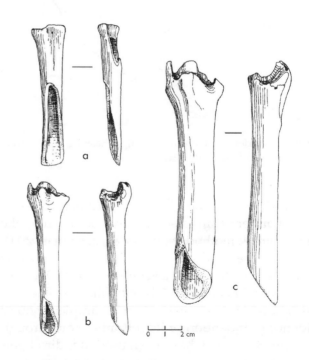

Figure 2.10. Sliced long bones with chisel and beveled end; phase IV: a, c; phase V: b. (a) SF 5427, metapodial with beveled edge of caprovine, plate 2.7a; (b) SF 4581, rounded tibia of caprovine, chisel end tibia of *Dama*, plate 2.7b; (c) SF 5410, red deer, plate 2.7d.

45

ment exhibits multiple use with wear polish along one margin and probably at the rounded end as well (figure 2.12c). This latter piece was also referred to in the discussion of pointed pieces.

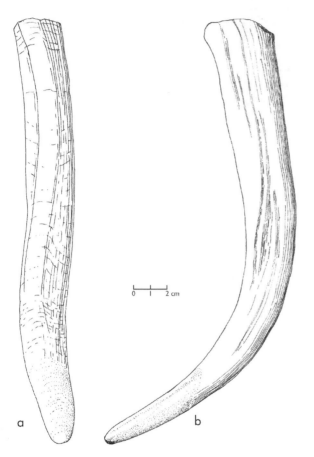

Figure 2.11. Antler tine with rounded tip, phase III. (a) SF 2916, plate 2.9; (b) SF 1249, plate 2.10e.

FLATTENED END. Generally these artifacts are sections of antler beams also probably obtained by the cut and break method (figures 2.8c, 2.9c; plate 2.11). On some, the worked end is flattened as if to be used as a punch (figure 2.9c; plate 2.11a). One artifact (figure 2.8c; plate 2.11b) exhibits possible animal gnawing and, like other examples, shows evidence of indention of its soft inner core through working. Some may have been used in indirect percussion as punches, a usage also inferred for antler tine. Tringham suggests such an application for antler in the production of blades (this volume, chapter 3).

SPATULAE. For these tools, ribs or antler have been split, cut, and shaped into a flat form which is rounded and wider at one end (figure 2.13b–d; plate 2.12a–d). The handle end would have resembled these fragments (plate 2.12e, f). A broken scoop of antler is also illustrated (plate 2.12g).

ANTLER SHAFT WITH HOLE AND SOCKET. Frequently and not surprisingly, sections of the large, resilient main beam was used (figures 2.14–2.17; plate 2.13a, 2.14) for this type of tool. Holes are round (figures 2.14, 2.16, 2.17; plates 2.8, 2.13a, b, 2.14), and placed near the wider or burr end; the opposite end is frequently hollowed to provide a socket (for example, figures 2.14–2.16 and plates 2.13–2.14) and exhibits wear. Examination of the shaft hole might offer some ideas as to what material these shafts held, and/or how the hole was made. The holes of the "mattocks" (we would call this a hoe), were more often circular than rectangular (figure 2.15; plate 2.13c, d, f for rectangular openings). In the case of most examples of shaft-hole antlers, the hollowed out or socketed end was broken and considerably worn.

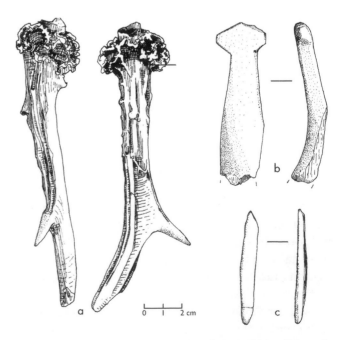

Figure 2.12. Antler: (a) Phase I, SF 3711, beam with pedicle and tine with wear at tip, plate 2.3a; (b) phase III, SF 4848, rough-out spoon from antler beam, plate 2.15a; (c) phase IV, SF 5108, tine fragment with wear noted along margin and tip.

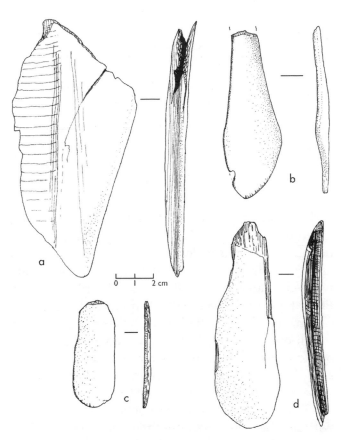

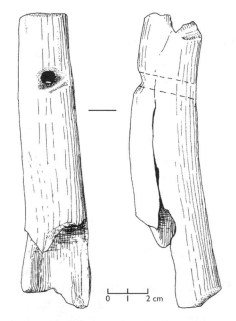

Figure 2.14. Perforated antler, fractured and hollowed out: phase II, SF 4522, plate 2.13a.

Figure 2.13. Worked scapula (a) and other elements ground to spatula shape; Phase III: b; phase IV: a; phase V: c, d. (a) SF 4660, plate 2.18b, (b) SF 501, plate 2.12d, (c) SF 4475, plate 2.12a; (d) SF 1558, plate 2.12b.

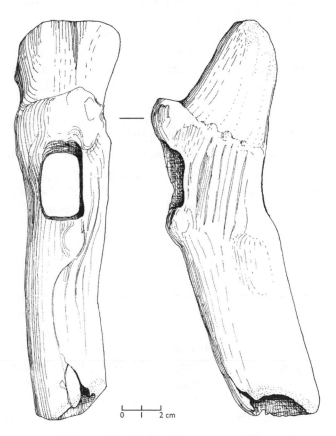

Figure 2.15. Antler beam with rectangular shaft hole: Phase III, SF 871, evidence of rosette and pedicle; wear at hollowed end and around pedicle, plate 2.13f.

Proposed uses of these tools vary. If the shafts were manufactured to hold a hammerhead, the working part was this missing shaft insert (for example, see figure 2.17; plate 2.14). If they were shafted punches, the shaft insert provided a handle and there were two (or three) working surfaces: the flattened cut where the brow tine was removed (figure 2.16) and the narrower fractured end where some of the spongy interior had been removed providing a socket into which a stone or wood tool could be fitted (figures 2.15, 2.16; plate 2.13b, f). Tines were occasionally drilled with holes (plate 2.8), but the narrower end is the working end and was probably used as a pick/digging stick. In the latter case, perhaps a wooden handle was fitted into the hole, although it is so small in the example above (diameter 0.8 cm) that the composite tool would have been rather lightweight. However, the

Table 2.11. Variation in Weight of Shaft-Hole Antler Tools

Small Find No.	Description	Phase	Weight (g)	Illustrations
4522	Beam section	II	90	plate 2.13a, figure 2.14
521	Beam with rosette and brow tine scar	III	240	plate 2.13b, figure 2.16
815	Beam section	III	120	plate 2.13c
871	Beam with worn pedicle and evidence of rosette	III	375	plate 2.13f, figure 2.15
1422	Beam section	III	65	plate 2.13d
310	Antler tine	V	47	plate 2.8

energy and time invested to produce a hole cannot be overlooked. This tine might have also functioned as the vehicle for indirect percussion used by a worker to produce, retouch, or shape edges of chipped stone blades. A fractured shaft hole antler tool (plate 2.22) was identified by Russell as shed antler, the burr area ground off and the densest, most compact, broad end used as a hammer. One fractured beam segment has unusual modifications (figure 2.14; plate 2.13a): a small perforation is near the narrower end, and much of the inner core was removed at the wider end. Russell (personal communication, 1996) pointed out that this is a common shape along the Adriatic, where it is thought to have been used in fishing and perhaps hung like a weight. Comparable examples include artifacts from Vinča (Bačkalov 1979:T. XXVI: 27, 28).

Some of the more complete antler shaft hole artifacts were weighed and the results appear in table 2.11. Considerable variation suggests quite clearly that these tools were put to various uses.

ELABORATED PIECES. This is a varied and interesting group of artifacts (see also chapter 9) that may not have required more time and energy to produce than the carefully modified points on metapodials (for example, figure 2.2) or the shaft-hole antler sleeves (for example, figures 2.15, 2.16), but they are certainly *not* expeditiously executed artifacts. The first settlers at the Sitagroi site (ca. 5400 BC) were familiar with the techniques of bone elaboration as demonstrated by a phase I spoon handle, carved on a long bone (figure 2.18a; plate 2.5d) and broken at the wider part where the indentation for the bowl begins. Particularly fine workmanship is observable in the way the handle was grooved, carved,

and smoothed (preserved length: 5.6 cm). Among the other artifacts which might also have functioned in the area of food serving or consumption are several from phase III, including an extensively worked antler beam (figure 2.12b; plate 2.15a). From the illustration, Russell (personal communication, 1996) identified this worked beam as a rough-out, thinned, but unfinished broken spoon or ladle. Since it represents considerable reduction and shaping, Russell's opinion was that it might have been prepared for use in ritual serving.

Two other phase III artifacts were elaborated with notches and probably made on split ribs. One of these (figure 2.18c; plate 2.16b) is slightly curved, with three notches on both margins and one on the preserved end. It was reduced by cutting, carving, grinding, and smoothing. It is 5.5 cm long and 1.4 cm wide. There appears to be widening at the break, so this may be the decorative handle of a spoon and comparable to one of those illustrated from Vinča (Bačkalov 1979: T. XXVII:11). Another smaller, narrower piece has double notches on both margins and an angled tip; stippling (drawings with clustered stippling or tiny dots indicating the representation of polish) suggests use polish along one side (figure 2.18d; plate 2.16a). Recovered from phase II is another artifact (figure 2.18e; plate 2.15b) with a notched flat "head," a rod-like body with broken, rough termination. It may be an unfinished artifact but its use is ambiguous, perhaps to pin up hair or clothing, or it could have been the long handle of a small spoon.

Functioning perhaps in a different realm is a narrowed, rounded, polished rod from phase I (figure 2.18b; plate 2.5c) with matching sets of four circling grooves at each end of the artifact. Barber

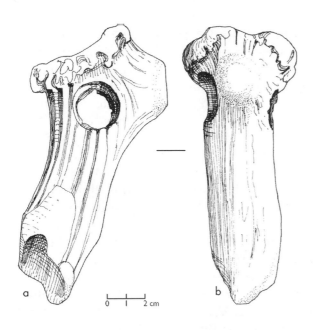

Figure 2.16. Multiple-use antler tool, phase III: round shaft hole in beam with rosette preserved, hammer surface at (a) cut brow tine, and opposite end (b); cut irregularly or worn with inner core removed: SF 521, plate 2.13b.

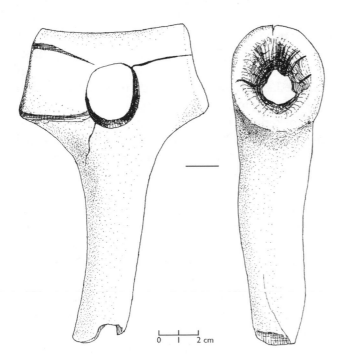

Figure 2.17. Antler with shaft hole, fork segment, phase II: SF 4798, plate 2.14.

(personal communication, November 1995) has suggested that this rod would have been useful as a net mending tool because string could be tied in one of its grooves, and the artifact would fit easily in hand as one maneuvered through the net. Spector's research (1991:396–401), from her excavation of a historic site in the American Midwest, offers an alternate interpretation. She excavated an engraved antler awl handle and learned that these artifacts were Native American women's tools and that the antler handles were engraved periodically to record accomplishments or stages as the owner grew from child to adult. The Sitagroi artifact with its grooves might well have signified something as important to its owner, and if so, carries a dimension beyond utility and, along with bone jewelry, suggests the symbolic side of Sitagroi life. Although I am not aware of analogous ethnographic literature pertaining to Greece and/or the Balkans, similarly incised,

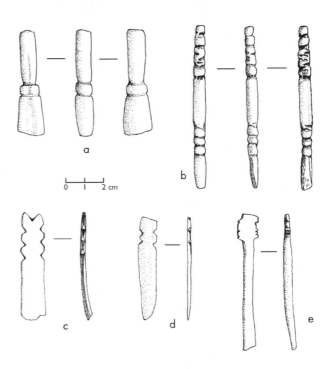

Figure 2.18. Elaborated bone artifacts. Phase I: a, b; phase II: c–e. (a) SF 106, shaped and grooved handle of spoon, plate 2.5d; (b) SF 3706, shaped rod with circling grooves at each end, plate 2.5c; (c) SF 3449, plate 2.16b; (d) SF 3111, probably split rib, shaped and notched, plate 2.16a (c, d), wear polish; (e) SF 4543, irregular notching at one end with narrowing below, evidence of wear polish on shank, plate 2.15b.

engraved bone artifacts from Obre II are described as "jewelry" (Benac 1973:104, pl. XXIV:3–5, 7).

Another extensively worked artifact looks very modest (figure 2.7a; plate 2.5b); it is a rod/pin, very smooth, round, and perfect in its own way. It might have been used to pin up a coil of hair or hold together a loosely woven textile.

The forms from later phases are sometimes unique and sometimes repeat. For example, animal teeth, especially from wild pig, are frequently perforated and were probably suspended as pendants, but they are discussed in chapter 9 of this volume. Elaborated pieces (see also chapter 9) include the perforated phase III "plaques," not unusual in southeast European sites of this time period. These

flattish, rectangular artifacts (figure 2.7b–d; plate 2.17a, b) were probably of cut and smoothed cattle ribs (although boar tusk is also suggested); single or multiple perforations are set along the narrower end, allowing them to be sewn on textiles, bound to leather, or strung on a multiple cord or leather thong. It has been suggested that they were used for card or tablet weaving, but these require only corner perforations (Barber 1991:534). One example (figure 2.7d) had six perforations, three bordering each narrow end; those at opposite corners were fractured, probably during use. These pieces are comparable to artifacts from Serbian Neolithic sites (Bačkalov 1979: T. XLV:16.5); also Selevac (Russell 1990:534), Arene Candide (Maggi, Starnini, and Voytek 1997:516, figs. 5–9), Dikili Tash (Karali-Yannacopoulos 1992:160, pls. 164, 206d, e), and Achilleion (Gimbutas 1989:252–253, fig. 8.4:1, 2).

MISCELLANEOUS WORKED ELEMENTS. Modified elements include scapulae, ulnae, and astragali. Two scapulae are illustrated: one fractured section (figure 2.13a; plate 2.18b) and the other, mended sections of auroch scapula (figure 2.19; plate 2.18a). Polish is noted on the line drawings along the ridge and on the flat surface. In Alaska, modified scapulae are used for fish scaling (Rita Shepard, personal communication, 2000). Russell thought they might have been used to polish pottery, although she observed no evidence for such use on the Selevac sheep-size scapulae (1990:539).

Worked ulnae from cattle and red deer are illustrated (figure 2.20a; plate 2.19a, b); wear polish is indicated along the longitudinal posterior edge and at the rounded point.

Astragali are reported frequently in archaeological reports (for example, Lyneis 1988:313–316, figure 10.3). Those illustrated here include a large example from red deer or cattle with ground lateral and medial faces (figure 2.20b; plate 2.20a). Three other examples from smaller animals are also ground; two of these (plates 2.20c, d; see also figure 9.22) were drilled and could have been suspended as pendants (see chapter 9), while the third was ground but not drilled (plate 2.20b). Russell reviewed the ethnographic and archaeological reports which pointed to the use of knucklebones in various games over time and worldwide, including

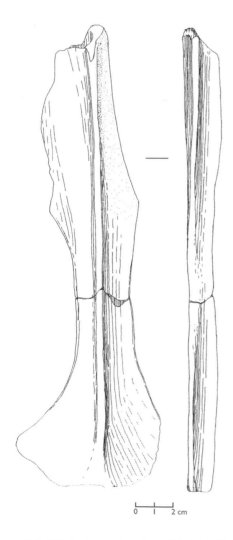

0   2 cm

Figure 2.19. Worked scapula, phase IV: SF 4617, spine ground and wear traces on upper surface, plate 2.18a.

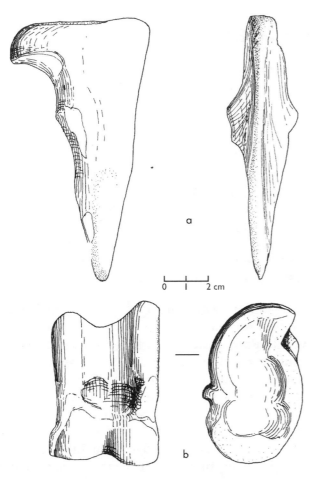

0   I   2 cm

Figure 2.20. Various worked elements, phase III: (a) SF 4693b, ulna of cattle or red deer with wear at straight edge and tip, plate 2.19; (b) SF 4698, large astragalus from cattle or red deer, ground on side, plate 2.20a.

neolithic Turkey, classical Gordion, ancient Rome, peasants in modern Iran, and children in Australia (1990:539). Lyneis came to no conclusion as to the function of the modified astragali at Divostin (1988:317). Probably these are multi-functional, playing roles in gaming, metrology, gambling, adornment or even divining.

Other modified and worked pieces of unidentifiable taxa and element are cataloged but have ambiguous function. Two pieces (plate 2.21) appear to have been worked considerably; these are either rib (plate 2.20a) or long bone (plate 2.20b). Worked teeth with perforations are discussed in chapter 9; a few are included in our tabulations as well (see figure 2.7c).

CONCLUSIONS

Sitagroi bone tool manufacturing must have involved anyone and everyone at some level. Herders, butchers, cooks, hunters, and scavengers all helped provide the raw materials. Some carvers, women, men, young, or old, took the time to elaborate the shapes beyond the dictates of utility, as demonstrated, for example, by the handles (figures 2.18a, c) and the rod (figure 2.18b). These shapes speak for an aesthetic sense and a symbolic vocabulary, qualities of Sitagroi life reflected in other aspects of the material culture and, like these bone artifacts, deserving of further study. Though fewer in number than stone tools, the bone tools allow us to imagine Sitagroi villagers making and using these objects: a child rubbing the sides of a bone splinter on sandstone to produce an awl, a youth digging up roots with an antler pick, or a potter burnishing her/his wares with a scapula. Bone and antler tools were the "green" artifacts of yesteryear: their manufacture recycled rubbish into objects of utility, adornment, and symbolism. It is not surprising that these raw materials would have a long history of use from prehistoric times and into the present day.

Appendix 2.1
Worked Bone Catalog
Ernestine S. Elster

Artifacts in this catalog are sorted first by phase; and within each phase, they are grouped by type and then sorted by small find (SF) number in numerical sequence. The context is given a lower-case "s" following the square and level to indicate that recovery of this artifact was from a sieve. Reference to illustrations (if illustrated) follows in order. Next is the description: animal, bone element (if identifiable), shape, observation of surface color and/or finish, and treatment of the ends of the tool (a slash [/] separates description of each end), and when available, measurements. Abbreviations for measurements are: L (length in cm), W (width in cm), D (diameter in cm), and Th (thickness in cm). Other abbreviations: "CS" indicates a sketch appears on the artifact inventory card; "NS" indicates no sketch is available on the card; "NI" indicates no information; "NR" indicates comments generously offered by Dr. Nerissa Russell.

Before creating this catalog, nine categories or types were defined and each artifact was so assigned based on the information in the field notebooks, notes and/or sketches on the inventory cards, and photographs. It must be stated again that complete data were not available for every artifact, but the field notebooks, inventory cards, etc. will all be deposited with the British School of Archaeology, Athens.

TYPE DEFINITIONS

SHAFT-HOLED ANTLER TOOLS. These were made either from the antler main beam and/or beam and fork. The shape of the hole is usually round and is near the wider or burr end; the opposite end is frequently hollowed to provide a socket and usually exhibits some wear. The antler may have been modified to accommodate various tools in the socket (for example, a mattock or hoe, a hammerhead, punch, or other stone tools). Beams with small holes may have been used as fishing weights. In any case, considerable energy and time were invested in modifying these antler tools.

CHISEL-ENDED TOOLS. One end of this tool type resembles the edge of a chisel and is sometimes beveled. Raw material includes antler or bone. Manufacturing these tools from antler requires cutting the element longitudinally and removing the spongy interior material, resulting in hollow split halves. These halves may be further modified by grinding or cutting one end with an angled cross-cut forming a chisel-like edge. Sometimes a tip of antler tine was prepared this way, although not necessarily split. The same is true of chisel ended tools made from long bones. This tool may have been used to scrape, gouge, and/or polish.

ELABORATED PIECES. These artifacts, made from both bone and antler, may not have required more time and labor to produce than some of the other tools, but certainly were not hastily shaped and finished. Included are a wide variety of shapes and forms with a variety of inferred functions. The assemblage is comprised of bone objects of both utility and ritual or ceremony. Some seem to be modified for use in food serving or food consumption, such as spoons. Other pieces are more ornamental, such as plaques and pins. Other pieces exhibit elaborate decorations, perhaps indicating a more symbolic meaning (see also in this volume, chapters 9 and 11).

FLAT-ENDED TOOLS. Bone or antler tools of this type exhibit at least one cross-cut and flattened end. The majority of these were made from antler, mostly beams. The "cut and break" technique in which the maker cuts around the antler and then breaks off the encircled end which is then flattened was probably used. Probable applications include use as a punch and for indirect percussion to produce blades.

MISCELLANEOUS WORKED PIECES. This category comprises bone artifacts modified in various ways, often with ambiguous function. Sometimes the taxa or the element may be unknown as well. These are often fragmentary pieces.

PERFORATED PIECES. A few artifacts are placed in this category (teeth or antler), but most are discussed either as elaborated pieces (for example, the plaques) or as teeth (this volume, chapter 9).

POINTED TOOLS. The type, of both antler and bone, includes tools in which one or both ends converge to a point. This tool type is made by reducing the element through splitting or grinding to produce narrowed and smoothed sides with the end or ends converging to a point. Some of the rib points were further modified at the wider end with a cross-cut. The modified ends, pointed or cross-cut, are the working surfaces. This tool type may be used in scraping, polishing, incising, and perforating. Pointed bone may also be in the form of a needle or as a pin used to fasten hair or garments.

ROUND-ENDED TOOLS. These tools exhibit one end with a rounded tip such as antler tine, naturally rounded and requiring no human modification. These tools were probably used as some sort of digging tool.

SPATULAE. These artifacts resemble a flat spatula. The raw material is either a rib bone or an antler. Manufacturing requires that the element be split, cut, and then shaped into a flat form, rounded and wider at one end. These types may have been used in food preparation, as a mixing spoon, in food distribution, or as a server.

PHASE I

Chisel-Ended

2850   JL 105; CS
Antler; *Cervus elaphus* L.
Surface: polish on tip and ends: rough/angled
L: 4.3; W: 1.4; Th: 0.8

2863   JL 105; CS
Antler; *Cervus elaphus* L.
Fragment, split middle
L: 10.7; W: 2.7; Th: 1.2

2867   JL 105; CS
Antler; *Cervus elaphus* L.
Tine; surface: rough; ends: cut/angled
L: 7.5; W: 2.6; Th: 1.3

4517   KL 133; CS
Metapodial; *Cervus elaphus* L.
Metatarsal; body: central longitudinal groove; surface: brown/gray; ends: rough/angled
L: 8.3; W: 2.1; Th: 1.6

4674   JL 105; CS
Tibia; caprovine
Fragment; ends: rough/angled
L: 6.9; W: 1.9; Th: 1.4

Elaborated Piece

106   IL 8; figure 2.18a; plate 2.5d
Unknown; unidentifiable
Possibly from a large animal; ground and grooved handle; body: widening toward fracture; surface: smooth, dark brown
L: 5.6; W: 1.6

120   ML 22; CS
Metapodial; caprovine
Bone; rod-shaped, tapering toward fractured end; surface: cream/brown at end
L: 5.7; W: 0.7; Th: 0.7

916   ZA 61; figure 2.7a; plate 2.5b
Unknown; unidentifiable
Probably a long bone; body: rod-shaped; ends: smoothed and rounded; surface: polished
L: 8.4; D: 0.6

923   ZA 77; CS
Unknown; unidentifiable
Plaque; fragment; body: rectangular, traces of perforation (?) near edge; surface: polished
L: 4.3; W: 1.3; Th: 0.7

3706   KLb 126; figure 2.18b; plate 2.5c
Unknown; Unidentifiable

Smoothed rod; with two sets of grooves circling
near both ends; fracture at one end; surface: polished, brownish yellow
L: 8.7; D: 0.7

Flat-Ended

2862   JL 105; CS
Antler; *Cervus*
Fragment, split; ends: rough/flat
L: 9.4; W: 3.2; Th: 1.3

4730   KL 151; CS
Tibia; *Sus scrofa* dom. L.
Fragmentary; ends: irregular
L: 6.4; W: 2.0; Th: 2.0

5306   ZA 63s; NS
Metapodial; caprovine
NI

Miscellaneous Worked

721   IL 5; CS
Rib; unidentifiable
Fragment; very tapered; surface: one face dark
brown, the other with extensive white deposits
L: 2.0; W: 0.8; Th: 0.3

3402   JL 103; CS
Rib; unidentifiable
Rectangular fragment; surface: polish light brown;
ends: cut/angled
L: 7.4; W: 2.0; Th: 0.3

4525   KL 125; CS
Antler; *Cervus elaphus* L.
Surface: yellow/cream with green/gray encrusta-
tion; honeycombed; coarse; split ends: cut/rounded
to point
L: 5.5; W: 2.1; Th: 1.1

4530   KL 124; CS
Antler, *Cervus*
Surface: yellowed; side honeycombed; split ends:
rough/rounded
L: 5.8; W: 2.6; Th: 0.9

4536   KL 130; CS
Unknown; unidentifiable
Body/section: roughly triangular; slightly curved;
surface: orange; ends: rough
L: 5.9; W: 1.0; Th: 0.7

4544   KL 151; CS
Antler; *Cervus*
Broken; surface: cream, one side coarse, the other
cut into indentation; ends: rough
L: 7.3; W: 3.1; Th: 1.0

4622   JL 104; CS
Antler, *Cervus*

Fragment; ends: rough/rounded
L: 6.5; W: 3.1; Th: 1.1

4630   ML 41; CS
Skull; *Bos taurus* L.
Fragmentary; shaved in places; surface: cream/
brown
L: 11.8; W: 2.2; Th: 0.9

4631   ML 41; CS
Skull; *Sus scrofa* dom. L.
Fragment; rough edges
L: 4.7; W: 4.0; Th: 0.9

4666   JL 102; CS
Antler; *Cervus elaphus* L.
Split, fragment; surface: coarse; ends: rough/
rounded
L: 7.0; W: 2.3; Th: 1.0

4667   JL 102; CS
Unknown; unidentifiable
Fragment; ends: tapering/rounded
L: 4.8; W: 0.8; Th: 0.5

4668   JL 102; CS
Antler; *Cervus elaphus* L.
Fragment; ends: cut, rounded, and worked
L: 9.1; W: 2.2; Th: 1.1

4672   JL 106; CS
Antler; *Cervus*
Fragment; surface: coarse; ends: rough
L: 5.4; W: 1.4; Th: 1.2

4673   JL 105; CS
Antler; *Cervus*
Fragment; rough edges
L: 7.2; W: 2.8; Th: 1.3

4675   JL 105; CS
Antler; *Cervus*
Fragment; split; rough edges; surface: spongy
L: 2.4; W: 2.4; Th: 1.4

4676   JL 105; CS
Antler; *Cervus elaphus* L.
Fragment; surface: coarse; ends: irregular
L: 5.8; W: 3.4; Th: 0.9

4677   JL 105; CS
Antler; *Cervus elaphus* L.
Fragment; surface: coarse; ends: irregular
L: 7.7; W: 2.5; Th: 0.9

4678   JL 105; CS
Antler; *Cervus elaphus* L.
Fragment; surface: coarse; ends: irregular
L: 6.0; W: 3.8; Th: 2.2

4686   JL 104; CS
Unknown; unidentifiable
Fragment; ends: irregular
L: 4.4; W: 1.4; Th: 0.5

4827 KL 10; NS
Antler; *Cervus elaphus* L.
Fragment

5359 ZA 55–76; NS
Unknown; unidentifiable
NI

5360 ZA 55–76; NS
Metapodial; caprovine
Metacarpal.

5361 ZA 55–76; NS
Metapodial; caprovine
Metacarpal

5362 ZA 55–76; NS
Metapodial; caprovine
Metatarsal

5363 ZA 55–76; NS
Unknown; unidentifiable
NI

5364 ZA 55–76; NS
Metapodial; caprovine
Metatarsal

5365 ZA 55–76; NS
Unknown; unidentifiable
NI

5366 ZA 55–76; NS
Unknown; unidentifiable
NI

5367 ZA 55–76; NS
Unknown; unidentifiable
NI

Pointed

132 JL 17; CS
Unknown; unidentifiable
Surface: light /dark brown
L: 3.2; W: 0.6; Th: 0.4

281 KL 14; CS
Unknown; unidentifiable
Body: pin shape; ends: converging/cut
L: 4.3

551 KL 14; CS
Unknown; unidentifiable
Fragment; probably a long bone; sharp at tip, some hollowing; surface: polished, light brown
L: 4.4; Th: 0.9

3707 KLb 125; CS
Unknown; unidentifiable
Tine (?); ends: rough
L: 2.6; W: 1.2

3708 KLb 124; plate 2.3b
Antler; *Capreolus capreolus* L.

Tine; surface: light tan ends: cut and break/converging to sharp point
L: 5.9; W: 2.5; Th: 0.7

3711 KLb 125; figure 2.12a; plate 2.3a
Antler; *Capreolus capreolus* L.
Rosette, beam, and tine; surface: orange
L: 14.2; W: 3.7

4112 KLb 137; figure 2.5a; plate 2.5a
Unknown; unidentifiable
Tapered with fractured end; surface: highly polished, yellow
L: 11.7; W: 1.0

4546 KL 131; CS
Unknown; unidentifiable
Splinter; surface: smooth, gray; ends: rounded/ tapered
L: 5.8; W: 0.9; Th: 0.4

4547 KL 134; CS
Tibia; caprovine
Split; surface: smooth, orange; ends: broken/tapering
L: 5.2; W: 1.4; Th: 0.8

4547 KL 134; CS
Tibia; caprovine
Split; surface: smooth, orange; ends: broken/tapering
L: 5.2; W: 1.4; Th: 0.8

4670 JL 103; CS
Antler; *Cervus elaphus* L.
Split; surface: coarse; ends: rough/tapering to a point
L: 16.2; W: 3.5; Th: 1.5

5304 ZA 63s; NS
Metapodial; caprovine
Fragment

Round-Ended

93 ZC 3; CS
Antler; *Capreolus capreolus* L.
Tine; surface: smooth, brown; ends: cut and ragged/converging
L: 4.8; W: 1.0

111 JL 11; figure 2.9b; plate 2.10a
Antler; *Cervus*
Tine; polished or smoothed near point
L: 8.2; D: 2.0

2861 JL 105; CS
Antler; *Cervus elaphus* L.
Tine, tip; surface: rough; ends: rough/tapering
L: 8.6; W: 4.1; Th: 3.1

Spatula-like

5305 ZA 63s; NS
Unknown; unidentifiable
NI

5352 ZA 71s; NS
Unknown; unidentifiable
NI

5414 ZA 63; plate 2.12g
Rib; unidentifiable
Split; ends: broken/rounded;
L: 4.4; W: 4.0; Th: 0.2; D: 4.0

5415 ZA 76; CS
Unknown; unidentifiable
Fragment
L: 2.5; W: 1.3; Th: 0.2

PHASE II

Chisel-Ended

246 ZA 52; figure 2.8a; plate 2.6a
Antler; *Cervus elaphus* L.
Surface: coarse; NR: hide scraping
L: 9.4; W: 2.8; Th: 1.0

913 ZA 58; CS
Unknown; unidentifiable
Shape: irregular, tapering toward angled end

1699 KM 20; CS
Tibia; *Capreolus capreolus* L.
Worked into flattened end; surface: polished
L: 6.4; W: 1.4; Th: 0.4

3710 ZG 40; CS
Unknown; unidentifiable
Narrowed and flattened; surface: pale yellow; ends:
rough/tapering

4519 KL 121; CS
Antler; *Cervus elaphus* L.
Surface: one side smooth, the other coarse, yellow/
brown; ends: broken/angled
L: 7.4; W: 4.1; Th: 1.5

4523 KL 118; CS
Unknown; unidentifiable
Surface: smooth, orange; ends: fractured/beveled
and rounded
L: 7.6; W: 2.3; Th: 1.4

4524 KL 118; CS
Antler; *Cervus*
Surface: orange, one side honeycombed, the other
coarse; ends: broken/flattened
L: 7.1; W: 2.5; Th: 1.3

4540 KL 110; CS
Tibia; caprovine

Split; surface: slightly burnished, dark brown; ends:
broken/beveled
L: 8.7; W: 1.4

4541 KL 110; CS
Tibia; *Sus scrofa* dom. L.
Split; surface: yellowish/brown; ends: broken/flat-
tened to a cutting edge
L: 7.2; W: 1.0; Th: 0.8

4550 KL 113; CS
Unknown; unidentifiable
Surface: smooth, orange; ends: broken/shaped to
flat, sharp end
L: 8.3; W: 1.8; Th: 0.7

4557 KL 117; CS
Metapodial; caprovine
Surface: buff/brown; ends: epiphysis/cut or bro-
ken obliquely
L: 5.3; W: 1.9; Th: 1.1

4707 ZG 40; CS
Unknown; unidentifiable
Sliced longitudinally; fragment; surface: polished;
ends: rounded/angled
L: 4.9; W: 1.7; Th: 0.9

4709 ZG 37; CS
Antler; *Cervus elaphus* L.
Split; ends: cut /angled
L: 7.5; W: 1.8; Th: 2.3

4716 ZG 43; CS
Radius; *Bos taurus* L.
Split fragment; ends: cut straight/angled
L: 8.2; W: 3.0; Th: 1.5

5405 ZA 51; figure 2.9a; plate 2.6b
Antler; *Cervus elaphus* L.
Split shaft fragment; surface: rough; ends: rough/
sliced
L: 16.5; W: 4.0; Th: 2.0

Elaborated Piece

447 KM 13; figure 2.9c; plate 2.11a
Antler; *Cervus elaphus* L.
Tine; cylindrical; surface: dull, gray/brown; ends:
flat and worked
L: 5.8; D: 1.7

1705 KM 20; see chapter 9: plate 9.27d
Rib; unidentifiable
Plaque; rectangular, flat; edges modified; perfora-
tions near shorter edge and centered along longer
edge
L: 3.7; W: 1.8; Th: 0.5

2839 KL 111; figure 2.7b
Canine?; unidentifiable

Pendant; rectangular; slightly curved; top and edges smoothed, one edge straight, the other, partly broken; perforation near the straight edge
L: 6.3; W: 2.1; Th: 0.5; D: 0.5

4443   ZJ 40; CS
Unknown; unidentifiable
Pin(?); surface: orange; ends: converging
L: 6.3; W: 0.6; Th: 0.4

4518   KL 121; CS
Antler; *Cervus*
Split; surface: yellow/brown; one side irregular, the other honeycombed; ends: rough/tapering to smooth end
L: 6.5; W: 2.5; Th: 1.2

5294   ZA 52s; figure 2.4d
Unknown; unidentifiable
Needle; ends: broken at "eye"/smoothed; converging; from sieve

Flat-Ended

4555   KL 117; CS
Ulna; *Canis familiaris* L.
Slightly tapering toward one end; surface: smooth, gray/yellow; ends: broken
L: 6.7; W: 0.8

4563   KL 114; CS
Unknown; unidentifiable
Surface: red/brown; ends: broken/flattened
L: 5.8; W: 2.2; Th: 0.5

4745   ZG 39; figure 2.8c; plate 2.11b
Antler; *Cervus elaphus* L.
Surface: rough; ends: broken tapering/flattened; probably used as a hammer
L: 9.2; W: 2.6; Th: 2.6

4845   KM 7; NI
Unknown; unidentifiable

5291   ZA 52s; NI
Unknown; unidentifiable
From sieve

5295   ZA 52; CS
Metapodial; caprovine
Metatarsal

5432   ML 19; CS
Antler; *Cervus elaphus* L.
Split fragment; surface: rough; ends: ragged/tapering
L: 7.0; W: 3.5; Th: 1.6

Miscellaneous Worked

3408   KL 117; CS
Unknown; unidentifiable

Fragment; oval in section; surface: burnished, black; ends: rough
L: 3.0; W: 1.5; Th: 0.9

3619   ZG 35; CS
Unknown; unidentifiable
Fragment; curved, hook-like
L: 0.3; W: 0.3

4000b   ZG 38s; CS
Fragment; irregular shape; from sieve
L: 2.4; W: 1.4

4338   KL 115; CS
Rib; unidentifiable
Split; surface: orange/brown, one side honeycombed; ends: cut and roughly rectangular
L: 4.1; W: 2.4; Th: 0.6

4339   KL 115; CS
Antler; *Cervus*
Inner porous section; one surface shaped; ends: cut/irregular
L: 5.5; W: 1.2

4526   KL 120; CS
Antler; *Cervus*
Split; surface: yellow/green/brown, one side coarse and honeycombed, the other cut into indentation; ends: broken
L: 7.8; W: 2.1; Th: 1.0

4531   ZE 100; CS
Antler; *Cervus elaphus* L.
Split; semi-circular section; surface: cream; ends: broken
L: 9.6; W: 3.3; Th: 1.7

4535   KL 107; CS
Antler; *Cervus elaphus* L.
Split; edges roughly parallel; surface: light brown, one side honeycombed, the other, cut indentation; ends: broken
L: 5.0; W: 1.8; Th: 0.8

4542   KL 110; CS
Unknown; unidentifiable
Split; surface: yellowish- orange; ends: broken/worked on one side
L: 7.7; W: 1.6; Th: 0.5

4549   KL 113; CS
Antler; *Cervus elaphus* L.
Surface: light brown, one side honeycombed, the other coarse; ends: broken/tapering
L: 5.9; W: 2.5; Th: 1.5

4551   KL 113; CS
Antler; *Cervus*
Oval-fragment; surface: one side honeycombed, the other coarse; ends: rounded/indented
L: 4.8; W: 2.4; Th: 1.2

4552 KL 117; CS
Antler; *Cervus elaphus* L.
Fragment; cylinder; surface: brown, one side
smooth, the other coarse; ends: broken
L: 8.6; W: 3.4; Th: 2.4

4553 KL 117; CS
Antler; *Cervus*
Fragment; surface: yellow/brown, one side porous;
ends: broken
L: 4.9; W: 4.1; Th: 0.5

4556 KL 117; CS
Antler; *Cervus*
Surface: yellowish/gray; porous area visible; ends:
both broken/slightly curved
L: 7.3; W: 3.2; Th: 1.2

4561 KL 117; CS
Metapodial; *Cervus*
Metatarsal; surface: gray/brown, polished side
smooth, shiny, the other bears an incised line; ends:
broken/socketed
L: 12.5; W: 1.8

4562 KL 114; CS
Unknown; unidentifiable
Surface: brown, one side honeycombed, the other
smooth; ends: cut/rough
L: 5.4; W: 2.0; Th: 0.3

4564 KL 114; CS
Metapodial; caprovine
Shaped; surface: smooth, yellow/orange; ends:
fractured/angled
L: 7.5; Th: 1.0

4648 ZJ 38; CS
Tibia; *Sus scrofa* dom. L.
Pottery polisher? (Cf. Russell 1990: 531, fig. 14.6);
surface: polished; ends: cut/tapering
L: 8.0; W: 2.0; Th: 0.5

4649 ZJ 38; CS
Unknown; unidentifiable
Fragment; ends: broken
L: 6.8; W: 1.2; Th: 0.5

4697 ZG 36; CS
Antler; *Cervus elaphus* L.
Split fragment; surface: rough; ends: broken
L: 8.4; W: 3.1; Th: 1.2

4701 ZG 40; CS
Antler; *Cervus elaphus* L.
Fragment; surface: rough; ends: broken
L: 18.1; W: 3.0; Th: 3.0

4702 ZG 40; CS
Antler; *Cervus elaphus* L.
Split fragment; surface: rough; ends: broken
L: 4.5; W: 3.9; Th: 1.1

4703 ZG 40; CS
Antler; *Cervus elaphus* L.
Split fragment; surface: rough; ends: broken
L: 4.8; W: 2.1; Th: 1.1

4708 ZG 37; CS
Antler; *Cervus elaphus* L.
Split fragment; surface: rough; ends: broken
L: 6.3; W: 2.4; Th: 1.1

4710 ZG 37; CS
Antler; *Cervus elaphus* L.
Split fragment
L: 6.3; W: 2.0; Th: 1.2

4722 ZJ 43; CS
Unknown; unidentifiable
Rod-like, slightly curved; smoothed; ends:
rounded/rough
L: 7.7; W: 1.1; Th: 1.1

4723 ZG 42; CS
Antler; *Cervus elaphus* L.
Split fragment; surface: rough; ends: rounded
L: 4.8; W: 2.0; Th: 0.9

4733 ZG 40; CS
Tibia; *Sus scrofa* dom. L.
Fragment
L: 4.6; W: 2.1; Th: 2.1

4819 KM 20; NS
Antler; *Cervus elaphus* L.
NI

4821 LL 2; NS
Antler; *Cervus elaphus* L.
NI

4823 KL 2; NS
Antler; Cervus elaphus L
NI

4824 KL 102; NS
Antler; *Cervus elaphus* L
NI

4826 KM 6; NS
Antler; *Cervus elaphus* L.
NI

4830 KL 4; NS
Antler; *Cervus elaphus* L.
NI

4837 ZA 54; NS
Antler; *Cervus elaphus* L.
NI

4843 ML 10; NS
Antler; *Cervus elaphus* L.
NI

4844 KM; NS
Antler; *Cervus elaphus* L.
NI

4853 KL 3; NS
Antler; *Cervus elaphus* L.
NI

4856 LL 4; NS
Antler; *Cervus elaphus* L.
NI

4859 ZA 52; NS
Antler; *Cervus elaphus* L.
NI

4871 KM 7; NS
Antler; *Cervus elaphus* L.
NI

4872 KM 7; NS
Antler; *Cervus elaphus* L.
NI

4901 KM 22; NS
Unknown; unidentifiable
NI

5299 ZA 55s; NS
Unknown; unidentifiable
From sieve

5301 ZA 55s; NS
Unknown; unidentifiable
From sieve

5355 ZΛ 54 33; NS
Rib; unidentifiable
From cleaning

5356 ZA 54–33; NS
Unknown; unidentifiable
From cleaning

5376 ML 15; NS
Unknown; unidentifiable
Fragment

5406 ZA 51; CS
Antler; *Cervus elaphus* L.
Split; ends: broken/cut
L: 10.4; W: 2.0; Th: 0.8

5408 KM 4; CS
Antler; *Cervus elaphus* L.
Split fragment; surface: smoothed; ends: broken
L: 5.0; W: 2.0; Th: 0.5

5409 ML 6; CS
Unknown; unidentifiable
Shaft fragment; ends: broken/slightly tapering
L: 9.0; W: 1.7; Th: 0.8

5431 KM 2; CS
Antler; *Cervus elaphus* L.
Split shaft fragment
L: 4.5; W: 1.3; Th: 0.5

5433 ML 19; CS
Unknown; unidentifiable

Fragment; surface: polished; ends: rough/polished
L: 8.5; W: 2.5; Th: 1.0

Perforated

4522 ZE 99; figure 2.14b; plate 2.13a
Antler *Cervus elaphus* L.
Cylindrical; hollowed out, horizontal; perforation near one end; surface: light brown/white; ends: both fractured
L: 14.5; W: 3.3; Th: 2.0; D: 0.8

5302a ZΛ 58; NS
Unknown; unidentifiable
From sieve

Pointed

236 ZA 50; figure 2.3a
Rib(?); unidentifiable
Square in section; one end worked to point, the other flattened and shaped into chisel; ends: irregular/wedge shape
L: 8.9; W: 1.2; Th: 0.9

247 ZA 52; CS
Unknown; unidentifiable
Pin(?); tapering; surface: polished; ends: converging/cut
L: 7.4; W: 0.8

434 KM 8; plate 2.10d
Antler; *Cervus elaphus* L.
Tine; ends: cut/tapering
L: 4.0; Th: 1.3

440 KM 13; plate 2.2b
Rib; unidentifiable
Section: flat triangular; surface: scratches near tip; ends: cut/tapering
L: 4.8; W: 1.3; Th: 0.4

472 ZA 52; CS
Pin-shaped, narrowed, straight; surface: polished; ends: converging/cut
L: 5.8; W: 0.6

967 KM 18; CS
Unknown; unidentifiable
Tapered fragment; surface: black/brown
L: 2.7; W: 0.7; Th: 0.4

983 KM 22; CS
Rib; unidentifiable
Flat splinter; ends: irregular/tapering
L: 5.5; W: 1.4; Th: 0.4

1107 ML 6; CS
Metapodial; *Bos taurus* L.
Thick, tapering to irregular tip; surface: polished
L: 6.0; W: 1.7; Th: 1.3

1448 KM 2; CS
Metapodial; caprovine
Metacarpal; surface: smooth, polished, gray/
brown; ends: epiphysis/tapering
L: 4.3; W: 1.4; Th: 1.0

1575 KM 16; CS
Antler; unidentifiable
Tine; partially worked at tip; petrified (?); surface:
smoothed
L: 5.3; W: 1.7; Th: 0.8

1700 KM 20; CS
Unknown; unidentifiable
Fragment; ends: rough /tapering
L: 5.4; W: 1.3; Th: 0.5

2359 KL 111; figure 2.4a
Unknown; unidentifiable
Ends: tapering/cut
L: 6.5; W: 0.4; Th: 0.4

2676 KLb 119; figure 2.4b
Metapodial; caprovine
Split; epiphysis present; tip broken; surface: pol-
ished
L: 5.9; W: 1.5; Th: 0.6

3133 ML 15; figure 2.2a; plates 2.3c, 2.1f
Proximal metapodial; roe deer; bone was not split
but base missing; surface: buff, with natural encrustation; ends: tapered/rough
L: 4.1; W: 1.7; D: 0.9

3738 ZG 37; CS
Unknown; unidentifiable
Split; surface: polished, light brown; ends: cut/
tapering
L: 7.1; W: 0.8; Th: 0.8

3750 KLb 114; figure 2.2b; plate 2.1a
Distal metapodial; *Cervus*
Split; casual finishing; ends: epiphysis/converging
L: 10.5; W: 1.5; Th: 0.9

3752 ZE 93; CS
Unknown; unidentifiable
Slender; surface: light brown; ends: tapering
L: 6.9; W: 0.7; Th: 0.7

3776 KLb 121; figure 2.3b; plate 2.2c
Rib; unidentifiable, flat, rectangular; edges: straight;
slightly curved toward tip; surface: light brown,
one side honeycombed; obverse smoothed; ends:
cut/angled to tip
L: 8.0; W: 1.5; Th: 0.3

4000a ZG 38s; CS
Ulna; caprovine
Split; surface: polished; ends: fractured/tapering;
from sieve
L: 5.0; W: 0.7

4000c ZG 38s; CS
Ulna; caprovine
Split; splinter; ends: irregular/converging
L: 2.1; W: 0.5

4006 ZG 42; CS
Tibia; caprovine
Split; splinter; ends: cut/converging
L: 6.0; Th: 0.8

4337 KL 115; CS
Unknown; unidentifiable
Split; surface: gray/brown; ends: cut/converging
L: 5.3; W: 1.0

4423 ZE 100; CS
Metapodial; caprovine
Shaped to converging end; surface: polished, dark
brown; ends: broken/rounded
L: 7.3; W: 0.9; Th: 0.5

4521 ZE 99; CS
Tibia; caprovine
Split; surface: slightly polished, brown; ends: frac-
tured/converging
L: 8.5; W: 1.1

4527 KL 106; CS
Metapodial; caprovine
Shaped to converging end; surface: polished,
smooth, gray; ends: cross-cut/rounded
L: 6.4; W: 1.0; Th: 0.8

4528 KL 106; CS
Unknown; unidentifiable
Edges run parallel, one side tapers sharply near the
tip; surface: gray/brown; ends: cut/angled tip
L: 5.2; W: 0.8; Th: 0.5

4532 KL 107; CS
Unknown; unidentifiable
Split; surface: yellowish; ends: cut/tapering
L: 5.0; W: 1.3; Th: 0.4

4533 KL 107; CS
Unknown; unidentifiable
Split; surface: brown; ends: broken/tapering
L: 6.2; W: 0.8

4548 KL 113; CS
Unknown; unidentifiable
Surface: smooth, brown; ends: cut/tapering
L: 5.6; W: 1.4

4558 KL 117; CS
Unknown; unidentifiable
Splinter; surface: gray; ends: broken/converging
L: 6.3; W: 1.0; Th: 0.5

4566 KL 114; CS
Unknown; unidentifiable
Surface: gray/yellow with encrustation; ends: bro-
ken/tapering to sharp tip
L: 8.1; W: 1.0; Th: 0.5

4571 ZA 53; CS
Unknown; unidentifiable
Surface: brown; ends: broken/shaped with pro-
truding tip
L: 4.5; W: 0.9; Th: 0.5

5290 ZA 52s; NS
Metapodial; caprovine
From sieve

5292 ZA 52s; NS
Metapodial; caprovine
From sieve
L: 4.9; D: 0.8

5293 ZA 52s; figure 2.4c
Unknown; unidentifiable
From sieve
L: 4.9; D: 1.3

5296 ZA 52s; NS
Unknown; unidentifiable
Fragment; from sieve

5298 ZA 55s; NS
Unknown; unidentifiable
From sieve

5300 ZA 55s; NS
Unknown; unidentifiable
Ends: converging/unknown; from sieve

5303 ZA 58; NS
Unknown; unidentifiable
From sieve

5445 ZA 52s; CS
Unknown; unidentifiable
Fragment; ends: converging/cut or broken; from
sieve
L: 1.1; W: 0.7

5552 ZA 52; CS
Unknown; unidentifiable
Fragment
L: 1.0; W: 0.4; Th: 0.1

Round-Ended

108 LL 4; plate 2.10b
Antler; *Cervus elaphus* L.
Tine; surface: polished through use; ends: irregular
L: 7.7; W: 2.0; Th: 1.6

1752 ZA 54; plate 2.10c
Antler; *Capreolus capreolus* L.
Tine fragment; surface: worn and polished through
use; ends: cut ragged/tapering
L: 7.6; W: 1.5; Th: 1.4

4410 ZJ 38; CS
Unknown; unidentifiable
Surface: orange/brown with encrustation; ends:
cut/tapering
L: 4.2; W: 0.9; Th: 0.3

4473 ZJ 44; CS
Rib; unidentifiable
Split; surface: smooth, brown; ends: angled/tapering
L: 5.6; W: 1.2; Th: 0.3

4534 KL 107; CS
Rib; unidentifiable
Surface: smooth, orange/brown; ends: broken/
tapering, rounded
L: 5.8; W: 1.1; Th: 0.6

4560 KL 117; CS
Antler; *Cervus*
Surface: light brown/cream, one side honey-
combed, the other irregular; ends: broken/tapering
L: 7.6; W: 3.5; Th: 1.5

4565 KL 114; CS
Rib; unidentifiable
Surface: slightly burnished, orange; ends: broken/
rounded and polished
L: 5.1; W: 1.0; Th: 0.6

5430 KM 2; CS
Unknown; unidentifiable
Fragment; includes joint area; rectangular in sec-
tion, tapering toward rounded tip
L: 8.5; W: 2.4; Th: 0.5

4711 ZG 37; CS
Antler; *Cervus elaphus* L.
Fragment; tip; surface: rough; ends: cut/converging
L: 5.8; W: 1.9; Th: 0.9

Spatula-like

2642 KL 109; CS
Rib; unidentifiable
Flat and thin tool; surface: polished; ends: irregu-
lar/flattened
L: 7.9; W: 0.8; Th: 0.6

4554 KL 117; plate 2.12g
Rib; unidentifiable
Split; surface: one side honeycombed, the other
smooth; ends: broken/flat and rounded
L: 4.0; W: 1.5; Th: 0.3

4568 KL 114; CS
Rib; unidentifiable
Surface: slightly burnished, polished, orange; ends:
broken/rounded
L: 5.1; W: 1.0; Th: 0.6

4847 KM 12; NS
Rib; unidentifiable
Split

5297b   ZA 52; NS
        Unknown; unidentifiable
        Fragment

5302b   ZA 58; NS
        Unknown; unidentifiable
        From sieve

Worked Tooth

1406   ML 21c; CS
        Canine; *Sus scrofa* fer. L.
        Tooth or tusk

5297a   ZA 52; NS
        Canine; *Sus scrofa* fer. L.
        Lower tooth

5400   KM 18; CS
        Canine; *Sus scrofa* fer. L.
        Lower tusk; two pieces joined
        L: 7.5; W: 2.0; Th: 0.5

5420   MM 11; CS
        Canine; *Sus scrofa* fer. L.
        Wild swine, lower canine; two pieces joined

Phase III

Chisel-Ended

222   ZA 93; CS
        Antler; *Capreolus capreolus* L.
        Split; ends: cut and break; ragged/angled
        L: 7.4; Th: 1.5

280   ZA 42; CS
        Tibia; unidentifiable
        Ends: ragged/angled
        L: 5.0; W: 1.8

3496   MMa 61s; CS
        Ulna; *Bos taurus* L.
        Cut and hollowed out; possible scoop; surface: polished; ends: ragged cut/tapering to beveled point; from sieve
        L: 9.0; W: 2.6; Th: 1.2

3673   MMa 63; CS
        Unknown; unidentifiable
        Split; surface: light brown; ends: flat cut, beveled/tapering; ragged
        L: 7.0; W: 2.0; Th: 1.1

3793   MMc 61; CS
        Rib; unidentifiable
        Surface: light brown; ends: flat cut/angled
        L: 7.5; W: 1.3; Th: 1.0

4417   ZG 30; CS
        Ulna; *Bos taurus* L.
        Surface: tan; ends: ragged/tapering irregularly toward rounded end

L: 11.8; W: 3.3; Th: 2.3

4427   ZG 22; CS
        Metapodial; caprovine
        Converging; Surface: light brown; ends: epiphysis ground/angled
        L: 4.6; W: 0.9

4646   ZJ 32; CS
        Ulna; caprovine
        Fragment; hollowed out; ends: angled/convex
        L: 4.9; W: 1.5; Th: 0.7

4681   MMd 63; CS
        Antler; *Cervus elaphus* L.
        Tine fragment; ends: broken, ragged/angled, flat
        L: 5.4; W: 1.6; Th: 0.7

4699   ZG 31; CS
        Metapodial; caprovine
        Ends: ragged/tapering; angled

4725   MM 65; CS
        Scapula; Sus scrofa dom. L
        Ends: converging at angle/cut; ragged
        L: 4.7; W: 1.9; Th: 0.7

Elaborated Piece

376   MM 20; CS
        Metapodial; caprovine
        Pin; surface: smooth, brown; decoration: clover leaf motif at broad end; ends: engraved end/tapering
        L: 6.5; Th: 1.0

834   MM 38; figure 2.7d; plates 2.17a, 9.27a
        Rib; *Bos taurus* L.
        Plaque; thin, rectangular in section; two perforations preserved at each end, traces of a third; ends: cut/partially broken at corners
        L: 6.7; W: 2.6; Th: 0.7

3111   ML 151; figure 2.18d; plate 2.16a
        Rib (?); unidentifiable
        Flat; ends: pointed/notched; two notches on each margin
        L: 5.4; W: 1.0; Th: 0.3

3449   MM 60s; figure 2.18c; plate 2.16b
        Unknown; unidentifiable
        Rib (?), flat fragment; rectangular; three notches on each long margin and one on top; opposite end broken (spoon handle?); from sieve
        L: 5.5; W: 1.4

3455   MMa 60s; CS
        Metapodial; caprovine
        Pin; split metatarsal; surface: one side polished; decoration: incised in cross design on head; ends: ground epiphysis/converging; from sieve
        L: 4.8

3770 ML 158; CS; plate 2.20d
Astragalus; *Sus scrofa* dom. L.
Pendant; perforated at one end
L: 2.7; W: 1.7; Th: 1.4

4543 ZE 87; figure 2.18e; plate 2.15b
Unknown; unidentifiable
Fragment; long bone or rib with wider, flat, notched "head"; surface: yellowish/gray; ends: cut, ragged/broken
L: 7.3; W: 0.5- 1.1; Th: 0.5

4802 ZA 47s; CS; figure 9.21; plates 2.20c, 9.16c
Astragalus; *Sus scrofa* dom. L.
Perforated; from sieve
L: 2.5; W: 1.7; Th: 0.9

4848 MM 12; figure 2.12b; plate 2.15a
Antler; *Cervus elaphus* L.
Ends: broken; slightly curved shaft/two horizontal angular protrusions, defined by two pairs of notches across the shaft; probably pre-form for spoon (NR)

5116 ZB 117r; NS
Canine; *Sus scrofa* fer. L.
Perforated; lower tooth

5288 ZA 48s; figure 2.7c; plates 2.17b, 9.27b
Canine; *Sus scrofa* fer. L.
Perforated; lower tooth fragment; from sieve

Flat-Ended

4683 MMd 61; CS
Unknown; unidentifiable
Fragment; ends: tapering/convex
L: 6.4; W: 1.9; Th:1.2

4712 ZG 32; CS
Tibia; caprovine
Ends: converging/cut on angle
L: 8.1; W: 1.2; Th: 0.4

4828 MM 36 NI; NS
Antler; *Cervus elaphus* L.

4850 MM 40 NI; NS
Antler; *Cervus elaphus* L.

4865 MM 21; NS
Unknown; unidentifiable
NI

4867 MM 21; NS
Antler; *Cervus elaphus* L.
NI

4869 ML 3; NS
Antler; *Cervus elaphus* L.
NI

4891 MM 40; NS
Unknown; unidentifiable
NI

5118 ZB 119r; NS
Antler; *Cervus elaphus* L.
NI

5120 ZB 120r; NS
Unknown; unidentifiable
NI

5280 ZA 46s; NS
Unknown; unidentifiable
From sieve

5282 ZA 47s; NS
Unknown; unidentifiable
From sieve

5284 ZA 48s; NS
Unknown; unidentifiable
From sieve

5285 ZA 48s; NS
Radius; *Canis familiaris* L.
From sieve

5287 ZA 48s; NS
Unknown; unidentifiable
From sieve

5373 ZA 49; NS
Tibia; *Sus scrofa* dom. L.
NI

5399 ZA 38; CS
Antler; *Cervus elaphus* L.
Shaft fragment; ends: tapering/ragged
L: 6.0; W: 3.5; Th: 0.9

5407 MM 40; CS
Metapodial; *Cervus elaphus* L.
Metatarsal; diaphysis split; ends: broken; two sides cut/tapering; flat
L: 7.2; W: 2.5; Th: 0.5

Miscellaneous Worked

800 ZA 47s; CS
Tibia; caprovine
Interior hollowed with gray deposits; surface: smooth, dark; ends: ragged/angled; from sieve
L: 5.6; Th: 1.9

1262 MM 50; CS
Metapodial; caprovine
Split; one side flat, the other with a central longitudinal groove; ends: ragged/cut
L: 4.1; W: 1.1; Th: 0.4

1449 MM 41; CS
Unknown; unidentifiable
Sliced bones; surface: smooth, yellow/brown; polished; ends: cut/worked into semicircle
L: 11.0; W: 2.8; Th: 0.7

3140 ML 154; CS
Antler; *Cervus*

Surface: roughly polished; ends: cut flat/broken;
pointed (?)
L: 6.3; D: 2.6

3542   MMd 65s; CS
Unknown; unidentifiable
curved; surface: polished, burned; ends: cut flat;
from sieve
L: 6.1; W: 0.7; Th: 0.6

3797   ZG 32; NS
Unknown; unidentifiable
Surface: brown
L: 6.0; W: 2.0; Th: 1.0

4616   MMd 68; CS
Metapodial; caprovine
Fragment; ends: broken; ragged
L: 1.6; W: 0.9; Th: 0.7

4621   MMd 66; CS
Astragalus; caprovine
L: 2.2; W: 1.3; Th: 1.1

4623   MMb 60; CS
Metapodial; *Cervus elaphus* L.
Split; surface: yellowish; ends: split epiphysis/broken cleanly
L: 6.5; W: 2.8; Th: 2.6

4624   MMb 60; CS
Unknown; unidentifiable
Fragment; wavy margin; ends: cut flat/tapering
L: 3.8; W: 2.3; Th: 1.0

4625   MMb 60; CS
Antler; *Cervus elaphus* L.
Tine fragment; ends: cut and break/cut
L: 4.1; W: 3.3; Th: 1.4

4626   MMb 60; CS
Antler; *Cervus elaphus* L.
Tine fragment; ends: converging/cut and break
L: 4.3; W: 3.4; Th: 1.4

4628   MMb 60; CS
Antler; *Cervus*
Tine fragment; ends: tapering/cut
L: 3.7; W: 2.7; Th: 0.8

4632   ZJ 32; plate 2.13e
Antler; *Cervus*
Tine fragment; ends: cut flat/converging
L: 14.8; W: 3.8; Th: 3.8

4653   MMd 66; CS
Astragalus; caprovine
L: 2.2; W: 1.2; Th: 1.3

4654   MMd 66; plate 2.20b
Astragalus; caprovine
Cartilage hollowed out and sides ground; surface:
orange
L: 2.5; W: 1.5; Th: 1.4

4664   MMd 63; CS
Metapodial; *Cervus*
Fragment; ends: tapering/epiphysis ground
L: 2.8; W: 1.2; Th: 0.8

4665   MMd 63; CS
Astragalus; caprovine
L: 2.2; W: 1.3; Th: 1.2

4679   MMd 63; CS
Rib; unidentifiable
Fragment; ends: cut flat and ragged/tapering
L: 4.9; W: 1.7; Th: 0.3

4680   MMd 63; CS
Antler; *Cervus*
Tine fragment; ends: cut flat/some tapering
L: 5.4; W: 1.2; Th: 0.8

4684   MMd 66
Astragalus; caprovine
Ends: cut
L: 2.3; W: 1.2; Th: 0.9

4685   MMd 68; CS
Unknown; unidentifiable
Fragment; ends: broken and ragged/tapering
L: 5.7; W: 2.6; Th: 0.2

4692   ZG 15; CS
Astragalus; *Cervus elaphus* L.
L: 4.9; W: 2.9; Th: 2.5

4693   ZG 31; figure 2.20a; plate 2.19b
Ulna; *Bos taurus* L.
Surface: polished; ends: cut flat/converging
L: 7.6; W: 6.0; Th: 1.5

4696   ZG 17; CS
Antler; *Cervus elaphus* L.
Ends: cut flat/tapering
L: 5.8; W: 1.8; Th: 0.7

4698   ZG 29; figure 2.20b; plate 2.20a
Astragalus; *Bos taurus* L.
Sides ground
L: 7.2; W: 4.7; Th: 3.2

4700   ZG 33; CS
Antler; *Cervus elaphus* L.
Ends: angled and blunt/tapering but ragged
L: 8.4; W: 3.1; Th: 0.7

4704   ZG 18; CS
Jaw; *Bos taurus* L.
Ends: cut and break/tapering to a point
L: 8.3; W: 1.8; Th: 1.3

4705   ZG 14; CS
Antler; *Cervus elaphus* L.
Fragment; ends: cut flat and rounded/ tapering
L: 2.9; W: 2.6; Th: 1.0

4706   ZG 14; CS
Antler; *Cervus elaphus* L.

Fragment; convex; ends: tapering/cut flat
L: 6.6; W: 2.1; Th: 0.8

4738   ZJ 26; CS
Antler; *Cervus elaphus* L.
Tine fragment; ends: cut and ragged
L: 3.8; W: 2.5; Th: 0.9

4739   ZJ 26; CS
Antler; *Cervus elaphus* L.
Tine fragment; ends: cut, ragged/broken
L: 3.4; W: 2.6; Th: 1.0

4740   ZJ 26; CS
Antler; *Cervus elaphus* L.
Ends: angled/cut flat
L: 4.2; W: 2.2; Th: 1.1

4741   ZJ 26; CS
Antler; *Cervus elaphus* L.
Tine; ends: tapering/cut flat
L: 3.9; W: 1.9; Th: 1.2

4820   MM 50; NS
Antler; *Cervus elaphus* L.
NI

4825   MM 21; NS
Antler; *Cervus elaphus* L.
NI

4832   ML 107; NS
Antler; *Cervus elaphus* L.
NI

4833   ML 3; NS
Antler; *Cervus elaphus* L.
NI

4835   ML 110; NS
Antler; *Cervus elaphus* L.
NI

4838   MM 16; NS
Antler; *Cervus elaphus* L.
NI

4839   MM 52; NS
Antler; *Cervus elaphus* L.
NI

4840   ML 119; NS
Astragalus; caprovine
NI

4841   MM 40; NS
Antler; *Cervus elaphus* L.
NI

4846   ZA 42; NS
Antler; *Cervus elaphus* L.
NI

4849   MM 48; NS
Antler; *Cervus elaphus* L.
NI

4851   MM 41; NS
Metapodial; *Cervus elaphus* L.
Metatarsal

4852   MM 27; NS
Antler; *Cervus elaphus* L.
NI

4866   MM 21; NS
Antler; *Cervus elaphus* L.
NI

4870   ML 110; NS
Antler; *Cervus elaphus* L.
NI

4875   MM 16; NS
Antler; *Cervus elaphus* L.
NI

4880   MM 48; NS
Antler; *Cervus elaphus* L.
NI

4881   MM 27; NS
Antler; *Cervus elaphus* L.
NI

4882   MM 27; NS
Unknown; unidentifiable
NI

4883   MM 27; NS
Antler; *Cervus elaphus* L.
NI

4884   MM 52; NS
Antler; *Cervus elaphus* L
NI

4886   MM 41; NS
Unknown; unidentifiable
NI

4887   MM 41; NS
Antler; *Cervus elaphus* L.
NI

4892   MM 40; NS
Antler; *Cervus elaphus* L.
NI

4893   MM 40; NS
Antler; *Cervus elaphus* L.
NI

4895   MM 12; NS
Astragalus; caprovine
NI

4896   MM 12; NS
Antler and skull; *Cervus elaphus* L.
Skull fragment and antler

5112   ZB 112r; NS
Unknown; unidentifiable
Metatarsal

5113a   ZB 112r; NS
Astragalus; caprovine
Pig astragalus

5115   ZB 117r; NS
Shell; *Chelonia* sp.
NI

5123   ZB 130r; NS
Astragalus; caprovine
NI

5274   ZA 44s; NS
Astragalus; caprovine
From sieve

5278   ZA 46s; NS
Astragalus; *Sus scrofa* dom. L.
From sieve

5279   ZA 46s; NS
Astragalus; caprovine
From sieve

5375   ZA 33; NS
Tibia; caprovine
NI

5403   MM 19; CS
Antler; *Cervus elaphus* L.
Split shaft fragment; ends: cut flat/tapering; ragged
L: 12.5; W: 3.2; Th: 1.0

5419   MM 11; CS
Antler; *Cervus elaphus* L.
Fragment; sawn; ends: ragged/converging
L: 7.5; W: 3.4; Th: 2.5

5436   MM 43; CS
Metapodial; *Cervus elaphus* L.
Fragment; diaphysis split; ends: cut flat/broken and ragged
L: 9.4; W: 2.2; Th: 1.2

5437   MM 41; CS
Antler; *Cervus elaphus* L.
Fragment; curved; ends: broken
L: 12.5; W: 6.5; Th: 3.0

5441   ZB 111r; CS
Unknown; unidentifiable
Fragment; narrow; ends: cut/broken; converging
L: 3.1; W: 0.4

5442   ZB 111r; CS
Canine; unidentifiable
Symmetrically grooved tooth
L: 2.1; W: 0.5

5614   MM 36; CS
Antler; *Cervus*
Surface: yellow/brown; ends: flattened
L: 4.0; W: 1.6

Perforated

2915   ZG 13; CS
Antler; *Cervus elaphus* L.
Mid-shaft section; worked to blunt end; shaft hole (?) near the middle; ends: cut and worked
L: 8.7; Th: 1.1; D: 3.2

5371   ZA 33; NS
Metapodial; caprovine
Metacarpal

Pointed

205   ZA 38; plate 2.1d
Metapodial; caprovine
Surface: faint vertical marks along one edge; ends: ragged/cut obliquely
L: 9.0

207   ZA 38; plate 2.1b
Distal metapodial; caprovine
Element not split but flake broken off near tip; surface: light, polish from the tip upward to mid-shaft; ends: epiphysis/converging
L: 9.2; Th: 2.1

798   ZA 47s; CS
Unknown; unidentifiable
Fragment; worked at one end; awl (?); ends: converging/ragged; from sieve
L: 7.3; W: 1.7; Th: 1.3

799   ZA 47; CS
Unknown; unidentifiable
Tip fragment; burned; ends: cut/converging
L: 0.7; Th: 0.3

807   MM 27; CS
Unknown; unidentifiable
Slightly and irregularly tapering; surface: brown, with lime deposits; ends: converging at tip/angled
L: 8.1; Th: 0.8

843   ML 107; CS
Metapodial; *Capreolus capreolus* L.
Ends: epiphysis/converging
L: 5.4; W: 1.8; Th: 1.4

863   MM 41; CS
Metapodial; caprovine
Surface: polished through use; ends: epiphysis/converging
L: 7.8; W: 1.0; Th: 0.9

883   MM 43; plate 2.1c
Metapodial; *Capreolus capreolus* L.
Metatarsal; surface: polished through use; ends: epiphysis/converging
L: 7.0; W: 1.5; Th: 0.9

1194   MM 12; figure 2.3c; plate 2.3e
Metapodial; *Cervus elaphus* L.

Metatarsal; surface: very smooth, yellow/brown; ends: epiphysis ground/converging
L: 12.9; W: 2.3; Th: 1.4

1253 MM 50; CS
Unknown; unidentifiable
Fragment; narrow; ends: ragged/converging
L: 7.9; W: 0.9; Th: 0.6

1258 MM 50; CS
Unknown; unidentifiable
Surface: highly polished, brown/dark brown, some deposits; ends: cut/tapering to blunt tip
L: 6.0; W: 1.3; Th: 0.9

1260 MM 50; CS
Unknown; unidentifiable
Fragment; narrow; surface: roughly polished; ends: cut/converging
L: 7.5; W: 0.8; Th: 0.4

1265 ML 113; CS
Unknown; unidentifiable
Fragment; small; ends: broken; ragged/broken; converging.
L: 3.1; W: 0.7; Th: 0.3

1268 MM 51; CS
Unknown; unidentifiable
Fragment; ends: broken/converging
L: 8.2; W: 0.9; Th: 0.5

1290 MM 52; CS
Metapodial; unidentifiable
Fragment; surface: polished; ends: broken/converging with tip worn
L: 9.9; W: 1.2; Th: 0.6

1447 MM 40; CS
Unknown; unidentifiable
Surface: highly polished, rich brown, some lime deposits; ends: cut and sharpened/converging
L: 4.8; W: 1.0; Th: 0.3

1454 ZA 47; CS
Unknown; unidentifiable
Split; ends: ragged/converging
L: 5.7; W: 1.1; Th: 0.9

1456b ZA 47s; CS
Humerus; caprovine
Small; narrow; ends: cut/converging; from sieve
L: 2.9; W: 0.4; Th: 0.2

1456c ZA 47s; CS
Humerus; caprovine
Small; narrow; ends: cut/converging; tip worn; from sieve
L: 3.3; W: 0.6; Th: 0.4

1523 MM 42; CS
Unknown; unidentifiable

Flattened; narrowed, polished; ends: cut/converging
L: 10.5; W: 0.9; Th: 0.3

1529 ZA 38; CS
Unknown; unidentifiable
Split; surface: smooth, brown; ends: converging toward fine tip/cut
L: 5.0; W: 0.5; Th: 0.7

1560 MM 43; CS
Metapodial; caprovine
Tapering with wavy margin; surface: polished, dark brown; ends: epiphysis/converging to sharp tip
L: 6.4; Th: 1.5

1569 ML 115; CS
Ulna; caprovine
Wide base, two protuberances at the other end, one of which is sharpened to long tip; surface: polished, gray/brown
L: 4.5; W: 2.1

1591 MM 50; CS
Metapodial; *Cervus elaphus* L.
Split; surface: finely polished; ends: ragged and broken
L: 6.3; W: 1.6; Th: 0.7

1703 MM 52; CS
Unknown; unidentifiable
Split fragment; triangular in section; two edges sharp, the third curved; ends: cut; angled/converging
L: 5.9; W: 1.5; Th: 0.6

2967 ZG 25s; CS
Unknown; unidentifiable
Section triangular; natural (?) groove down one side; ends: cut/converging with tip broken; from sieve
L: 4.5; W: 0.8; Th: 0.5

2985 ZG 28; CS
Unknown; unidentifiable
Split; narrowed; ends: cut flat/converging
L: 5.8; W: 0.7

2994 ZG 30s; CS
Metapodial; caprovine
Split, narrowed, tapering; surface: one side with polish; ends: ragged/converging with sharp tip
L: 8.2; W: 0.7; Th: 0.3

3121 ML 153; CS
Unknown; unidentifiable
Surface: pale brown; ends: cut/tapering
L: 5.3; Th: 0.6

3124 ML 151; plate 2.3g
Metapodial; *Cervus*
Split metatarsal; surface: polished; ends: ground epiphysis/converging
L: 11.2; W: 1.8; Th: 1.0

3136   ML 154; CS
Metapodial; caprovine
Split, tapering with wavy margin; fractured and repaired in lab; surface: light brown; ends: epiphysis/converging
L: 6.8; W: 1.3

3139   ML 154; CS
Metapodial; caprovine
Split, tapering; surface: polished, gray/yellow; ends: convex/converging
L: 5.3; W: 0.8

3413   MM 60b s; CS
Unknown; unidentifiable
Split; wavy margin; probably fragment; surface: yellowish; ends: cut/converging into a fairly sharp tip; from sieve
L: 7.0; W: 1.0

3420   MMc 60; CS
Unknown; unidentifiable
Surface: polished; ends: cut/tapering to broken tip
L: 8.0; W: 0.8

3480   MMc 61; CS
Metapodial; caprovine
Split, tapering; diaphysis trimmed; hollow; surface: polished; ends: cut flat with epiphysis/converging
L: 5.3; W: 1.0

3524   MMb 61; CS
Unknown; unidentifiable
Surface: polished; ends: cut/converging
L: 6.0; W: 1.1; Th: 0.5

3546   MMa 63; CS
Unknown; unidentifiable
Hollowed out; surface: black/brown; ends: broken and ragged/converging to broken tip
L: 2.6; W: 0.8; Th: 0.4

3549   MMd 65s; CS
Metapodial; *Cervus*
Split metatarsal; surface: polished on curved side; ends: rounded with epiphysis/converging; from sieve
L: 6.2; W: 1.6

3749   ZJ 29; CS
Unknown; unidentifiable
Surface: light brown; ends: cut/converging
L: 7.9; W: 0.9; Th: 0.5

3751   MMb 66; CS
Metapodial; caprovine
Tapering; surface: orange, one end polished; ends: rounded/cut; tapering with epiphysis
L: 7.1; W: 2.0

3781   ZG 17; CS
Tibia; caprovine

Surface: gray/brown; ends: cut/converging to fine tip
L: 6.8; W: 1.8; Th: 0.5

3788   MMt 61; CS
Unknown; unidentifiable
Surface: medium brown; ends: cut; one corner broken/converging
L: 3.3; W: 1.5; Th: 0.5

3843   MMd 65; plate 2.1h
Metapodial; caprovine
Split, tapering; surface: yellowish; ends: ground epiphysis/converging to very sharp tip
L: 4.6; W: 0.9

4724   MM 65; CS
Unknown; unidentifiable
Wavy margin; ends: tapering/cut
L: 3.5; W: 1.0; Th: 1.0

4864   MM 21; NS
Unknown; unidentifiable
NI

4873   ZA 42; NS
Metapodial; *Capreolus capreolus* L.
NI

4877   MM 48; NS
Unknown; unidentifiable
NI

4878   MM 48; NS
Unknown; unidentifiable
NI

4879   MM 48; NS
Metapodial; caprovine
NI

4889   MM 52; NS
Metapodial; *Capreolus capreolus* L.
Metatarsal

4890   MM 52; NS
Metapodial; *Capreolus capreolus* L.
Metatarsal

4897   MM 12; NS
Metapodial; caprovine
NI
L: 6.2; D: 0.9

5111   ZB 110r; NS
Unknown; unidentifiable
NI

5113b   ZB 112r; NS
Unknown; unidentifiable
NI

5117a   ZB 118r; NS
Metapodial; *Cervus elaphus* L.
NI

5117b   ZB 118r; NS
Unknown; unidentifiable
NI

5117d ZB 118r; NS
Unknown; unidentifiable
NI

5119 ZB 123r; NS
Unknown; unidentifiable
NI

5121a ZB 126r; NS
Unknown; unidentifiable
NI

5121b ZB 126r; NS
Unknown; unidentifiable
NI

5121c ZB 126r; NS
Unknown; unidentifiable
NI

5122 ZB 129; NS
Metapodial; *Capreolus capreolus* L.
NI

5272 ZA 44; NS
Unknown; unidentifiable
NI

5273 ZA 44s; NS
Unknown; unidentifiable
NI

5275 ZA 44s; NS
Metapodial; caprovine
Two fragments; from sieve

5276 ZA 44s; NS
Metapodial; caprovine
From sieve

5277 ZA 44s; NS
Unknown; unidentifiable
From sieve

5283 ZA 47s; NS
Unknown; unidentifiable
From sieve

5286 ZA 48s; NS
Metapodial; caprovine
Metatarsal; from sieve
L: 4.3; D: 0.7

5289 ZA 48s; NS
Unknown; unidentifiable
From sieve

5372 ZA 43; NS
Metapodial; caprovine
Metatarsal

5378 MM 53; NS
Metapodial; caprovine
Part of epiphysis

5418 MM 16; CS
Unknown; unidentifiable
Surface: one side incised; ends: cut at angle/converging
L: 7.5; W: 1.5; Th: 0.8

Round-Ended

388 MM 21; CS
Metapodial; unidentifiable
Triangular in section, carved to protruding blunted point; surface: one side of the point polished and smoothed through use; ends: ragged
L: 12.2; W: 3.2; Th: 0.8

765 ML 107; plate 2.10h
Antler; *Cervus elaphus* L.
Tine, cut and break; surface: some wear and polish; ends: ragged/rounded
L: 6.0; D: 2.3

1249 MM 50; figure 2.11b; plate 2.10e
Antler; *Cervus elaphus* L.
Tine; surface: one end polished; ends: cut and break/converging
L: 25.2; W: 2.5; Th: 1.3

2256 MM Clng; CS
Ulna; *Bos taurus* L.
Surface: encrustations; ends: ragged/tapers to thick, rounded tip
L: 8.1; W: 2.3; D: 2.1

2916 ZG 13; figure 2.11a; plate 2.9
Antler; *Cervus elaphus* L.
Tine; surface: possible marks of use on tip; ends: cut flat/converging
L: 20.0; D: 2.9

3132 ML 151; plate 2.10f
Antler; *Cervus elaphus* L.
Tine; surface: tip end scratched, polished; ends: ragged; broken/converging
L: 16.7; W: 3.3; Th: 2.4

3452 MMa 60s; plate 2.10i
Antler; *Cervus*
Fragment; surface: smooth, polished in places, tan; ends: broken; ragged/rounded; from sieve
L: 4.7; D: 1.5

3756 ZJ 29; plate 2.10g
Antler; *Cervus*
Split; surface: polished, light gray/brown; ends: broken/converging
L: 7.9; W: 1.6; Th: 1.4

4476 ZJ 32; CS
Unknown; unidentifiable
Surface: light brown; ends: cut/tapering to rounded point
L: 4.8; W: 0.8; Th: 0.5

5444   ZA 48s; CS
Unknown; unidentifiable
Ends: angled cut/rounded; from sieve
L: 1.5; W: 0.6

758   MM 20; CS
Antler; *Cervus elaphus* L.
Tine fragment; calcified; worked (?); ends: rounded
in use
L: 5.7; W: 1.3; D: 1.1

874   MM 41; plate 2.6d
Antler; *Cervus elaphus* L.
Tine; surface: polished and worn smooth along tip;
ends: smooth, flattened/tapering to a rounded tip
L: 11.9; W: 5.1; Th: 2.3

1263   ML 112; CS
Unknown; unidentifiable
Triangular in section up to the tip; polished; ends:
cut/tapering to rounded point
L: 6.0; W: 1.0; Th: 0.7

Shaft-Holed

521   MM 12; figure 2.16; plate 2.13b
Antler; *Cervus elaphus* L.
Beam with rosette; not petrified; one crack; with
perforation and socket, group of longitudinal paral-
lel grooves on one side; surface: light gray
L: 15.0; Th: 8.0

815   ML 107; plate 2.13c
Antler; *Cervus elaphus* L.
Shaft section; hollowed; indented; squarish hole
through center; surface: grooved, matt, yellow/
brown; ends: ragged/flattened
L: 13.8; W: 3.9; D: 3.9

871   MM 41; figure 2.15; plate 2.13f
Antler; *Cervus elaphus* L.
Beam with pedicle and rosette; rectangular hole
near the middle; ends: cut/hollowed for insertion
of stone or bone tool; extensive work; petrified
L: 20.0; W: 5.6; Th: 5.2

1422   MM 43; plate 2.13d
Antler; *Cervus elaphus* L.
Shaft section; squared hafting hole; surface: worn
smooth; ends: rounded
L: 10.1; D: 3.8

2945   ZG 18; plate 2.22
Antler; *Cervus elaphus* L.
Broken section; shaped like a mattock(?), perhaps
originally a squarish hole was cut for hafting; con-
siderable shaping and grinding
L: 12.7; W: 5.9; Th: 3.5

4798   MMb 61; figure 2.17; plate 2.14
Antler; *Cervus elaphus* L.

Beam and tine fragment; socketed; surface: light
orange; ends: flattened/cut and hollowed
L: 15.4; W: 2.6–9.6; Th: 4.2; D: 2.6

Spatula-like

501   MM 16; figure 2.13b; plate 2.12d
Unknown; unidentifiable
Ladle or pottery smoother; edges smoothed; ends:
narrow and ragged/rounded with indentation
L: 8.9; W: 3.2; Th: 0.3

1455   ZA 47s; CS
Unknown; unidentifiable
Probably a rib fragment; flat; roughly triangular;
ends: cut/rounded; from sieve
L: 7.4; W: 2.6; Th: 0.2

1456a   ZA 47s; CS
Humerus; caprovine
Small; narrow; possibly used as scoop; ends: cut/
converging; from sieve
L: 4.7; W: 1.5; Th: 0.5

3458   MMa 60; CS
Rib; unidentifiable
Flat fragment; ends: ragged/slightly tapering
L: 6.8; W: 2.0

Worked Tooth

1195   MM 20; CS
Canine; *Sus scrofa* fer. L.
One end broken; sharp point at the other end; one
side flat, the other curved; edges: sharp
L: 6.1; W: 0.9; Th: 0.4

1908   MM 54; CS
Canine; *Sus scrofa* fer. L.
Tooth forms 1/5 circle; carefully worked: polished
on outside, a few deposits on inside; severe crack-
ing; ends: ragged and broken
L: 6.95; W: 1.52–181; Th: 0.44

5421   MM 11; CS
Canine; *Sus scrofa* fer. L.
Splinter; lower tooth; surface: polished; ends: cut
and broken
L: 8.5; W: 1.8; Th: 0.4

5434   MM 43; CS
Canine; *Sus scrofa* fer. L.
Lower tooth
L: 4.0; W: 2.4; Th: 0.4

5442   ZB 111; CS
Unidentified
Symmetrically grooved canine
L: 2.1; W: 0.5

5443   ZB 126r; CS
Canine; *Sus scrofa* fer. L.

Fragment of lower tooth; cut
L: 1.7; W: 0.9

PHASE IV

Chisel-Ended

2740   ZE 64; CS
Tibia; caprovine
Hollowed; surface: polished; ends: beveled and angled/cut flat
L: 5.6; D: 1.3

3709   ZHt 22; figure 2.3d; plate 2.3f
Metapodial; *Cervus*
Metacarpal; surface: light brown, use-wear, polish on shade and ends; ends: cut/angled
L: 12.1; W: 2.5; Th: 1.6

4591   ZHt 26; CS
Rib; unidentifiable
Surface: yellowish; ends: broken, ragged/broken/angled
L: 11.8; W: 2.5; Th: 1.7

4644   ZHt 21; CS
Metapodial; *Cervus elaphus* L,
Surface: yellowish; ends: tapered; angled/cut
L: 13.1; W: 1.7; Th: 0.9

4645   ZHt 21; figure 2.8b; plate 2.6c
Antler; *Cervus elaphus* L.
Fragment; split; surface: polished; ends: angled/cut
L: 10.9; W: 2.9; Th: 1.3

4651   ZHt 19; CS
Tibia; caprovine
Fragment; surface: polished; ends: angled/tapered and rounded
L: 9.0; W: 1.4; Th: 0.4

4656   ZHt 7; CS
Unknown; unidentifiable
Fragment; ends: flat/broken or cut at angle
L: 6.0; W: 1.6; Th: 0.6

4736   ZHt 86; CS
Unknown; unidentifiable
Tapering; ends: cut/tapers to an angle
L: 5.8; W: 1.5; Th: 0.7

5427   MM 9; figure 2.10a; plate 2.7a
Metapodial; caprovine
Metacarpal; diaphysis split; ends; ground epiphysis/tapering to an angle
L: 8.0; W: 2.0; Th: 1.0

Elaborated Piece

2722   ZE 61; CS
Shell; *Chelonia* sp.
Pendant; body slightly curved, oblong plaque; surface: orange; decoration: fine parallel incisions near straight end, for suspension from string(?); ends: cut straight/rounded
L: 4.0; W: 1.3; Th: 0.3

4641   ZE 61; CS
Antler; *Cervus elaphus* L.
Pendant; split fragment; perforated near the middle edge; ends: broken and ragged/tapered and cut straight
L: 7.3; W: 1.7; Th: 1.0

4643   ZHt 24; CS
Unknown; unidentifiable
Fragment, rod-like, slightly tapering; surface: polished, yellowish; ends: cut
L: 4.6; W: 1.0; Th: 0.7

4734   ZHt 86; CS
Unknown; unidentifiable
Rod-like, slightly tapering; ends: broken
L: 6.3; W: 1.1; Th: 1.1

4735   ZHt 86; CS
Unknown; unidentifiable
Rod-like; rectangular in section; ends: broken/cut straight
L: 3.7; W: 0.6; Th: 0.6

5094   ZB 47s; NS
Shell; *Chelonia* sp.
Pendant; worked and pierced; from sieve

5124   ZB 101r
Canine; *Canis familiaris* L.
Tooth; perforated

Flat-Ended

4520   ZE 83; plate 2.19a
Ulna; *Bos taurus* L.
Fragmentary; one end fractured, the other smoothed; surface: yellow; ends: fractured/flattened, rounded, polished.
L: 12.0; W: 6.0; Th: 2.6

4876   MM 10; NS
Antler; *Cervus elaphus* L.
NI

5103   ZB 68r; NS
Tibia; caprovine
NI

5374   ZA 28; NS
Tibia; caprovine
NI

Miscellaneous Worked

25   ZA 25; figure 2.2d; plate 2.1e
Metapodial; *Cervus*

Metatarsal; diaphysis split; ends: ground epiphysis/converging
L: 8.6; W: 1.9

3029 ROc 59; CS
Unknown; unidentifiable
Two longitudinal grooves on one side; surface: polished, light tan/black; ends: cut
L: 5.3; W: 1.4; Th: 0.9

3563 ZE 60; CS
Metapodial; caprovine
Split; surface: polished; ends: broken/ground epiphysis
L: 3.9; W: 1.4; Th: 0.4

4529 ZE 61; CS
Unknown; unidentifiable
Split fragment; surface: light gray, one side honeycombed, the other smooth (wear?)
L: 3.3; W: 3.0; Th: 1.3

4584 ZHt 26; CS
Unknown; unidentifiable
Fragment; sides semicircular shape; flat; cut; surface: dark brown
L: 6.5; W: 3.3; Th: 0.8

4608 ZHt 26; CS
Scapula; *Bos primigenius Boj*
Fragment, scratched; surface: worked; orange/cream
L: 14.3; W: 6.6; Th: 3.3

4609 ZHt 26; CS
Unknown; unidentifiable
Fragment; one end smooth with traces of working and use; surface: yellowish; ends: converging/tapering with a point
L: 13.8; W: 2.0

4617 ZE 72; figure 2.19; plate 2.18a
Scapula; *Bos primigenius Boj*
Sides: shaped; rib: polished
L: 32.7; W: 4.2–10.1; Th: 1.2–2.4

4619 ZE 68; CS
Antler; *Cervus*
Fragment; split, shaped; ends: broken/tapering
L: 10.4; W: 5.9; Th: 2.6

4633 ZE 64; CS
Metapodial; *Cervus elaphus* L.
Diaphysis fragment; fire-hardened
L: 4.6; W: 2.6; Th: 1.0

4634 ZE 64; CS
Vertebra; unidentifiable
Fragment; surface: some polish observable
L: 4.8; W: 3.5

4637 ZHt 22; CS
Antler; *Cervus elaphus* L.
Split fragment; ends: ragged
L: 9.4; W: 3.0; Th: 0.9

4638 ZHt 22; CS
Antler; *Cervus*
Split fragment; ends: ragged
L: 7.0; W: 2.9; Th: 0.5

4639 ZHt 22; CS
Metapodial; *Cervus*
Split fragment; ends: cut
L: 5.1; W: 4.8; Th: 1.0

4640 ZE 61; CS
Antler; *Cervus*
Tine fragment; ends: ragged/converging
L: 8.7; W: 1.8; Th: 0.9

4642 ZHt 24; CS
Unknown; unidentifiable
Fragment; surface: polished; ends: cut flat/chiseled
L: 3.8; W: 0.9; Th: 0.9

4650 ZHt 19; CS
Metapodial; *Cervus elaphus* L.
Diaphysis split; epiphysis and one side pared down; surface: polished; ends: epiphysis/convex break
L: 6.9; W: 3.2; Th: 2.8

4655 ZHt 7; CS
Unknown; unidentifiable
Fragment; surface: polished, rounded; ends: cut/tapered
L: 4.8; W: 1.0; Th: 0.5

4658 ZHt 11; CS
Unknown; unidentifiable
Fragment; split; ends: tapering; ragged/cut
L: 7.6; W: 2.1; Th: 1.2

4660 ZHt 10; figure 2.13a; plate 2.18b
Scapula; *Bos taurus* L.
Fragment with ragged margin; some surface polish
L: 10.2; W: 6.6; Th: 0.8

4669 ZJ 2; CS
Metapodial; *Cervus elaphus* L.
Surface: some polish, dark brown, discolored; ends: ground epiphysis/tapering; broken (point or chisel?)
L: 4.4; W: 2.2; Th: 0.9

4690 ZG 7; CS
Antler; *Cervus elaphus* L.
Fragment; ends; ragged/cut
L: 3.1; W: 1.7; Th: 0.7

4691 ZG 7; CS
Antler; *Cervus elaphus* L.
Fragment; ends: ragged/cut
L: 4.5; W: 2.1; Th: 0.7

4695 ZG 11; CS
Scapula; caprovine
Fragment with ragged margins
L: 6.5; W: 3.0; Th: 0.6

4714 ROc 60; CS
Metapodial; *Cervus*
Ends: cut flat/angled
L: 4.0; W: 1.3; Th: 0.6

4715 ROc 60; CS
Metapodial; *Cervus*
Ends: rounded/rounded and ragged
L: 2.2; W: 1.2; Th: 1.1

4742 ZHt 86; CS
Scapula; *Bos taurus* L.
Fragment; some polish on surface; form: amorphous
L: 15.0; W: 5.0; Th: 0.7

4743 ZHt 86; CS
Antler; *Cervus elaphus* L.
Fragment; split; ends: rounded/ragged
L: 7.2; W: 3.0; Th: 0.8

4744 ZHt 86; CS
Metapodial; *Cervus elaphus* L.
Split; ends: rounded/tapering
L: 6.1; W: 2.2; Th: 1.0

4831 ZO 5; NS
Unknown; unidentifiable
NI

4834 MM 10; NS
Antler; *Cervus elaphus* L.
NI

4836 ZD 8; NS
Antler; *Cervus elaphus* L.
NI

4842 MM 2; NS
Antler; *Cervus elaphus* L.
NI

5102 ZB 64r; NS
Unknown; unidentifiable
NI

5105 ZB 72r; NS
Unknown; unidentifiable
NI

5106a ZB 74r; NS
Unknown; unidentifiable
NI

5106b ZB 74r; NS
Unknown; unidentifiable
NI

5106c ZB 74r; NS
Unknown; unidentifiable
NI

5109 ZB 105r; NS
Unknown; unidentifiable
Two pieces

5428 ZA 29; CS
Unknown; unidentifiable
Shaft fragment; strongly tapering; ends: cut; tapered/ragged
L: 7.5; W: 1.0

5429 ZE 6; CS
Metapodial; *Cervus elaphus* L.
Metatarsal; diaphysis split; surface: polished; ends: ground epiphysis/chiseled ended
L: 9.0; W: 2.8; Th: 1.0

5449 ZB 74r; CS
Unknown; unidentifiable
Body: tapering; ends: converging/cut straight
L: 1.7; W: 0.5

5550 ZB 74r; CS
Unknown; unidentifiable
Split; ends: rounded/tapering; flat
L: 2.3; W: 0.7

5551 ZB 105r; NS
Unknown; unidentifiable
NI
L: 1.3; W: 0.4

Pointed

122 ZA 29; figure 2.2c; plate 2.3d
Metapodial; *Cervus elaphus* L.
Diaphysis split; two ground flat sides, groove along the third one; surface: smooth, dark brown; ends: epiphysis cut/converging
L: 13.7; W: 2.2

128 ZA 32; CS
Metapodial; caprovine
Metacarpal; surface: mottled, light brown; ends: tapering/cut
L: 8.3; W: 1.8

165 MM 15; CS
Unknown; unidentifiable
Splinter; surface: tip polished through use; ends: converging/cut
L: 7.6

303 ZD 6; CS
Unknown; unidentifiable
Surface: encrustations; ends: cut flat/converging
L: 6.4; D: 0.9

321 ZE 7; CS
Unknown; unidentifiable
Surface: smooth, shiny, dark/light brown; ends: converging, sharp/broken
L: 12.8; D: 1.0

1528 ZA 32; figure 2.5b; plate 2.2e
Unknown; unidentifiable
Surface: polished, brown; ends: both ends converging
L: 9.1; D: 0.7

2704 ZE 51; CS
Unknown; unidentifiable
Surface: polished; ends: converging/broken
L: 4.8; D: 0.6

2759 ZE 68; CS
Unknown; unidentifiable
Split; surface: polished; ends: ragged/converging
L: 2.2; W: 1.2; Th: 1.3

2996 ZG 3s; CS
Metapodial; caprovine
Flat, partially split; ends: broken/tapering; broken; from sieve
L: 6.2; W: 0.9; Th: 0.8

3023 ROc 58; CS
Metapodial; unidentifiable
Metacarpal; epiphysis; diaphysis split; ends: epiphysis; perforated/converging; broken
L: 11.3; W: 3.0; Th: 2.1

3028 ROc 59s; CS
Unknown; unidentifiable
Surface: polished, dark discoloration; ends: converging: broken/cut and ragged; from sieve
L: 4.0; W: 1.6

3033 ROc 60; CS
Unknown; unidentifiable
Split; (glued); ends: cut/converging
L: 9.9; W: 1.1; Th: 0.6

3035 ROc 61; CS
Metapodial; *Cervus*
Metatarsal; surface: light tan; ends: ground epiphysis/converging
L: 9.4; W: 1.4; Th: 0.5

3236 ZHt 20; CS
Unknown; unidentifiable
Sliver; ends: both ends converging
L: 5.4; W: 0.7; Th: 0.6

3247 ZHt 24; CS
Metapodial; *Cervus*
Metacarpal; ends: epiphysis/converging
L: 8.4; W: 2.6; Th: 0.9

3255a ZHt 24; CS
Radius; *Cervus*
Surface: brown; ends: ground epiphysis/strongly converging; sharp
L: 8.5; W: 3.0

3687 ZJ 20; CS; plate 2.2a
Rib; unidentifiable

Surface: brown with white markings, one side honeycombed, the other smooth; wavy margin; ends: cut/converging
L: 11.0; W: 1.8; Th: 0.6

4585 ZE 73; CS
Metapodial; *Capreolus capreolus* L.
Metapodial; ends: thick, rounded tip with a tiny protuberance (possibly unworked or fractured?) at its end/angled, tapered; surface: pale orange
L: 5.0; W: 1.4; Th: 0.5

4620 ZE 64; CS
Unknown; unidentifiable
Fragment; surface: polished; ends: converging/angled
L: 8.2; W: 1.0; Th: 0.5

4636 ZHt 22; CS
Metapodial; *Cervus elaphus* L.
Diaphysis split; ends: ground epiphysis/tapered
L: 9.7; W: 3.1; Th: 1.6

4652 ZHt 17; CS
Unknown; unidentifiable
Split; ends: converging/broken
L: 5.4; W: 0.8; Th: 0.5

4659 ZJ 4; CS
Metapodial; *Cervus elaphus* L.
Surface: polished; ends: ground epiphysis/converging; tip broken
L: 7.1; W: 1.6; Th: 0.5

4661 ZHt 13; CS
Metapodial; *Cervus*
Fragment; diaphysis tapering; ends: converging/cut
L: 8.3; W: 3.3; Th: 1.4

4662 ZHt 13; CS
Unknown; unidentifiable
Fragment; ends: converging/angled
L: 9.0; W: 1.0; Th: 1.4

4726 ROc 61; CS
Unknown; unidentifiable
Ends: converging/ragged
L: 8.4; W: 2.0; Th: 0.9

4731 RO 55; plate 2.1g
Unknown; unidentifiable
Split; surface: polished; ends; converging/ragged
L: 9.3; W: 1.1; Th: 1.1

4732 ROc 72; plate 2.10j
Antler; *Cervus elaphus* L.
Semicircle in section; surface: multiple cuts; ends: converging/cut and ragged
L: 15.2; W: 2.6; Th: 1.9

5095 ZB 47s; NS
Unknown; unidentifiable
From sieve

5096 ZB 48r; NS
Unknown; unidentifiable
Probably a fishing implement

5097 ZB 49s; NS
Antler; *Capreolus capreolus* L.
From sieve

5099 ZB 58r; NS
Unknown; unidentifiable
NI

5104 ZB 70r; NS
Unknown; unidentifiable
NI

5107 ZB 76r +80r; NS
Metapodial; *Cervus elaphus* L.
NI

5108 ZB 104r; figure 2.12c
Unknown; unidentifiable

5110 ZB 107r; NS
Unknown; unidentifiable
NI

5353 ZA 31-32; NS
Unknown; unidentifiable
NI

5398 MM 30; CS
Unknown; unidentifiable
End: converging/broken
L: 7.8; W: 1.2; Th: 0.7

5402 MM 7; CS
Unknown; unidentifiable
Ends; tapering; tip cut and irregularly flattened/cut
L: 8.5; W: 1.2; Th: 0.6

Round-Ended

102 MM 2; plate 2.10k
Antler; *Cervus*
Fragment; surface: smooth, polished, dark brown;
ends: converging/broken
L: 4.3; Th: 1.0

4573 ZHt 26; CS
Metapodial; *Cervus elaphus* L.
Surface: highly polished; ends: ground epiphysis/
tapering
L: 4.9; W: 3.1; Th: 1.1

4592 ZHt 26; CS
Rib; unidentifiable
Surface: yellowish-brown; ends: broken/tapering
L: 5.8; W: 1.6; Th: 1.7

Spatula-like

4737 ZB 100g; CS
Unknown; unidentifiable

Semicircle in shape; tapered at ends; ends: converging/ragged
L: 10.1; W: 3.4; Th: 0.5

Worked Tooth

123 ZA 29; CS
Canine; *Sus scrofa* fer. L.
Irregular shaped fragment
Th: 3.0

4635 ZE 64; CS
Canine; *Sus scrofa* fer. L.
Tooth fragment
L: 8.2; W: 1.1; Th: 0.5

4857 MM 34; NS
Canine; *Sus scrofa* fer. L.
Lower tooth

PHASE V

Chisel-Ended

26 ZA 19; CS
Metapodial; *Cervus*
Metacarpal; diaphysis split; ends: ground epiphysis/angled
L: 6.4; W: 2.7; Th: 1.7

1340 PN 17; CS
Tibia; caprovine
Surface: polished through use; ends: broken and ragged/angled
L: 4.9; W: 1.6; Th: 1.5

1803 PO 23; CS
Tibia; caprovine
Surface: smooth, polished shiny, dark/light brown;
ends: worked to angle/broken
L: 6.8; D: 1.3

3331 PO 58; plate 2.21a
Rib; *Bos taurus* L.
Surface: polished, dark brown; semicircle in section;
ends: angled/broken and ragged
L: 22.0; W: 3.2; Th: 1.2

3778 ROc 12; CS
Tibia; caprovine
Split; surface: orange/brown; ends: angled/beveled cut
L: 7.0; W: 1.4; Th: 1.4

3779 ROc 13; plate 2.7c
Tibia; caprovine
Surface: polished, gray/brown; ends: angled, beveled/epiphysis broken
L: 8.5; W: 1.5; Th: 1.4

5410 QO 8; figure 2.10c; plate 2.7d
Tibia; *Dama* sp.

Surface: one end polished; ends: angled and beveled/epiphysis
L: 14.0; W: 2.4; Th: 1.5

5411   QO 8; CS
Unknown; unidentifiable
Fragment; ends: angled; converging/cut
L: 7.0; W: 1.5; Th: 0.5

Elaborated Piece

66   ZA 17; NS
Shell; *Chelonia* sp.
Pendant; suspension or string hole; margins have been worked
L: 4.0

654   PO 7; CS
Unknown; unidentifiable
Pin; surface: smoothed, dark brown with slight white deposits; ends: converging/cut
L: 5.0; Th: 0.4

655   PO 7; CS
Unknown; unidentifiable
Pin; one side slightly concave; surface: pale brown with slight, light gray deposits; ends: converging/angled
L: 7.0; W: 0.5

665   PO 8; CS
Unknown; unidentifiable
Pin; surface: smooth, pale brown/yellow; ends: converging; blunted tip/broken
L: 5.5; Th: 0.5

1031   QO 8s; CS
Unknown; unidentifiable
Cylindrical, slender; surface: highly polished; ends: broken/cut straight; from sieve
L: 6.2; D: 0.4

1048   QN 7; figure 2.5d
Unknown; unidentifiable
Pin; surface: some polishing, some deposits on underside, bright/light brown; ends: converging/tapered to point
L: 10.9; W: 0.4

1307   PN 10; CS
Fibula; *Sus scrofa* dom. L.
Pin; surface: shiny, yellow/brown; ends: converging to sharp tip/broken
L: 5.6; W: 0.6; Th: 0.4

1557   QN 7; CS
Fibula; *Sus scrofa* dom. L.
Pin; body: carefully tapered; surface: brown with lime deposits at thick end; ends: tapering/epiphysis split
L: 8.1; Th: 0.3

5089   ZB 37r (cf. chapter 9)
Tooth fragment; unidentifiable
Pierced
L: 7.0; W: 5.0

Flat-Ended

3790   POc 32; CS
Unknown; unidentifiable
Fragment; rounded edge; surface: polished, buff/orange; ends: flat; blunt/broken
L: 3.5; W: 2.2; Th: 0.7

4822   QN 6
Unknown; unidentifiable
NI

5088   ZB 16r; plate 2.21b
Long bone; *Bos taurus* L. (?)

Miscellaneous Worked

1598   ZA 9; CS
Jaw; *Sus scrofa* fer. L.
Fragment; one margin could have been used for carding wool; ends: cut, angled/serrated
L: 7.4; W: 3.5; Th: 1.4

1701   ZA 17; CS
Skull; *Sus scrofa* dom. L.
Fragment; flattened along two sides, forming a square edge
L: 8.4; W: 4.5; Th: 5.6

3574   POc 33; CS
Antler; *Cervus*
Curved; surface: two natural (?) irregular grooves on one side; ends: beam/cut at an angle
L: 4.9; D: 2.0

3697   PO 58; CS
Antler; *Cervus elaphus* L.
Fragment; surface: coarse; ends: flat/broken
L: 4.0; W: 4.5; Th: 3.5

4485   PNe 68; CS
Unknown; unidentifiable
Surface: black/orange; ends: converging/angled
L: 5.6; W: 1.4; Th: 1.0

4567   PO 159; figure 2.6; plate 2.4
Metapodial; *Cervus elaphus* L.
Metatarsal; vascular groove on one side and longitudinal groove on other side; surface: gray/yellow; ends: epiphysis/angled
L: 30.0; W: 4.3; Th: 3.0

4657   PNp 77; CS
Unknown; unidentifiable
Fragment; fire-hardened
L: 4.3; W: 2.8; Th: 0.6

4713 POd 35; CS
Antler; *Cervus elaphus* L.
Fragment; partly hollowed out; ends: broken and ragged/cut
L: 4.9; W: 2.3; Th: 2.3

4718 POc 125; CS
Horn-core; *Bos taurus* L.
Ends: cut straight/angled and ragged
L: 3.8; Th: 0.4

4719 POc 125; CS
Horn-core; *Bos taurus* L.
Split; fragment; shape: amorphous
L: 4.6; Th: 0.5

4720 POc 125; CS
Horn-core; *Bos taurus* L.
Ends: cut straight/angled
L: 4.1; Th: 0.5

4721 POc 125; CS
Horn-core; *Bos taurus* L.
Split fragment; shape: amorphous
L: 3.4; Th: 0.6

4727 ROc 4; CS
Antler; *Cervus elaphus* L.
Split fragment; ends: cut straight
L: 4.4; W: 2.4; Th: 0.4

4728 ROc 4; CS
Antler; *Cervus elaphus* L.
Split fragment; ends: ragged
L: 6.4; W: 3.0; Th: 0.4

4729 ROc 4; CS
Antler; *Cervus elaphus* L.
Split fragment; ends: cut straight/angled
L: 4.6; W: 1.7; Th: 0.4

5083 ZB 2r; NS
Antler; *Cervus elaphus* L.
Fragment

5084 ZB 3r; NS
Unknown; unidentifiable
NI

5086 ZB 9s; NS
Rib; unidentifiable
From sieve

5087 ZB 10r; NS
Unknown; unidentifiable
NI

5091 ZB 42r; NS
Hyoid; *Bos taurus* L.
NI

5092 ZB 44r; NS
Shell; *Chelonia* sp.
NI

5093 ZB 45s; NS
Metapodial; caprovine
Metatarsal; from sieve

5401 ZA 9; CS
Metapodial; caprovine
Polished, shaped; fragment; ends: converging/angled
L: 8.5; W: 1.0; Th: 0.3

5439 ZB 45s; CS
Unknown; unidentifiable
Fragment; shape: amorphous; from sieve
L: 2.7; W: 1.0

Pointed

76 ZA 2; CS
Tibia; caprovine
Surface: polished, burned; ends: converging/broken
L: 4.3; W: 0.9; Th: 0.5

1081 QN 8; figure 2.5c; plate 2.2d
Unknown; unidentifiable
Wavy margin; ends: converging/cut
L: 8.4; W: 0.9; Th: 0.5

1092 QN 8s; CS
Unknown; unidentifiable
Rectangular in section; surface: tip polished through use; ends: converging/cut; from sieve
L: 8.0; W: 1.4; Th: 1.0

1096 QO 8; CS
Unknown; unidentifiable
Split; ends: converging/cut
L: 4.1; W: 0.7; Th: 0.3

1099 QO 8; CS
Unknown; unidentifiable
Wavy margin; flat; ends: converging/broken
L: 4.3; W: 1.5; Th: 0.9

1568 PO 9; CS
Metapodial; caprovine
Surface: some polishing, mottled brown-gray; ends: beveled/converging with tip slightly broken
L: 6.6; W: 1.0; Th: 0.6

1620 PO 13; CS
Unknown; unidentifiable
Splinter; irregularly shaped; surface: few deposits; ends: both converging and sharp
L: 6.2; W: 0.5

1698 PO 18; CS
Ulna; caprovine
Fragment; wavy margin; ends: converging with tip broken/broken
L: 5.8; W: 0.8; Th: 0.4

1804 PO 23; plate 2.1i
Metapodial; split caprovine

Surface: polished along the shaft; ends: ground, epiphysis/converging.
L: 7.6; D: 0.5

1854 QN 8; plate 2.2f
Rib; *Sus scrofa* dom. L.
Surface: smooth, shiny, yellow/brown; ends: converging sharp tip/broken; probably a pin
L: 7.3; W: 0.9; Th: 0.5

2044 QOd 9; CS
Unknown; unidentifiable
Slender point; surface: polished, brown/yellow; ends: rounded/cut
L: 2.6; W: 0.5; Th: 0.3

2076 PNe 50; CS
Unknown; unidentifiable
Surface: polished, dark brown; ends: rounded/tapering
L: 5.7; W: 0.7; Th: 0.4

3357 PO 164; CS
Unknown; unidentifiable
Slender; ends: converging/cut
L: 4.6; W: 0.5

3774 PNc 80; CS
Unknown; unidentifiable
Finely sharpened; surface: light brown; wavy margin; ends: converging/cut
L: 5.3; W: 0.8; Th: 0.3

4401 PN ext S; CS
Unknown; unidentifiable
Surface: polished, yellow/brown; ends: converging to fine tip/cut

4432 PNc 87; CS; plate 2.1k
Tibia; caprovine
Surface: light brown; ends: converging to sharp tip/broken
L: 7.3; W: 1.5; Th: 0.5

4576 PN Clng D–C; CS
Unknown; unidentifiable
Surface: orange; wavy margin; ends: converging/broken
L: 6.0; W: 1.8; Th: 0.7

4671 PNf 54; CS
Unknown; unidentifiable
Splinter; curved; surface: dark, dirty, brown; ends: converging/cut
L: 5.3; W: 0.9; Th: 0.3

5090 ZB 40; NS
Unknown; unidentifiable
NI

5412 QO 8; CS
Unknown; unidentifiable
Split; ends: converging/broken
L: 5.0; W: 1.0; Th: 0.5

Round-Ended

4581 PO 160; figure 2.10b; plate 2.7b
Tibia; caprovine; surface: light brown; ends: epiphysis/tapering
L: 9.0; W: 2.5; Th: 1.1

4663 PNb 100; CS
Unknown; unidentifiable
Fragment; ends: round/broken
L: 8.9; W: 1.6; Th: 0.3

5440 ZB 2r; CS
Unknown; unidentifiable
Fragment; ends: tapered; round/broken; ragged
L: 1.5; W: 0.4

Shaft-Holed

310 PO 4; plate 2.8
Antler; *Cervus elaphus* L.
Tapering; probably a pick, perforated near larger end; ends: cut straight/converging
L: 13.6; Th: 1.9

Spatula-like

1558 QOa 8; figure 2.13d; plate 2.12b
Rib; *Bos taurus* L.
Not split; surface: smooth, light brown, scratched; ends: rounded/tapered; ragged; polisher (?)
L: 10.9; W: 3.6; Th: 0.9

4475 PNb 103; figure 2.13c; plate 2.12a
Split rib; unidentifiable
Rectangular; surface: brown; ends: rounded/tapered and rounded
L: 5.6; W: 2.2; Th: 0.3

4829 QO 4; plate 2.12c
Rib fragment, wear on wider end; unidentifiable

5354 ZA 4
Rib; unidentifiable

5413 ZA 14
Scapula; unidentifiable
Fragment; edges smoothed; surface: polished

Worked Tooth

4362 PN 68; CS
Canine; *Sus scrofa* fer. L.
Lower tooth; narrow, curved; surface: smooth, polished, white
L: 3., Th: 0.3

4717 PO 68; CS
Canine; *Sus scrofa* fer. L.
Lower tooth; surface: polished

Phase X (Unphased, Mixed)

Chisel-Ended

4516 Surface; CS
Tibia; *Sus scrofa* dom. L.
Split; surface: buff/gray; ends: angled and beveled/broken and ragged
L: 8.2; W: 2.1; Th: 0.5

4816 Surface; CS
Unknown; unidentifiable
Ends: angled and beveled/broken
L: 5.7; W: 2.2

Miscellaneous Worked

4610 Surface; CS
Unknown; unidentifiable

Hollow; surface: fire-hardened, highly polished; ends: tapered and angled beveled and cut
L: 4.6; W: 1.0

Pointed

3773 JL surface; CS
Unknown; unidentifiable
Wavy margin; depression on one side; surface: light gray; ends: converging/cut
L: 5.0; W: 0.8; Th: 0.5

4515 Surface; CS
Metapodial; *Cervus*
Roughly triangular; surface: buff/brown; ends: ground epiphysis/converging
L: 5.9; W: 1.8; Th: 0.8

Round-Ended

3200 ZH surface; CS
Antler; *Capreolus capreolus* L.
Tine fragment; surface: polished; ends: round/cut
L: 3.9; D: 0.8

3.

Flaked Stone

Ruth Tringham

The purpose of studying the cryptocrystalline rock artifacts from Sitagroi was to investigate the changing utilization of this resource through a 2500-year period in the prehistory of this area of southeast Europe. It was also intended that the study provide data concerning resource exploitation comparable to that from other Neolithic and Chalcolithic sites, such as Divostin (Tringham 1988), Obre (Sterud and Sterud 1974), Achilleion and Anzabegovo (Elster 1976, 1989), Franchthi (Perlès 1987, 1990), Vinča (Radovanovic et al. 1984), Gomolava (Kozlowski and Kaczanowska 1986), Selevac (Voytek 1990), and others. To this end, the artifacts were examined petrographically for the technique of reducing the nodules of raw material to usable edge tools, and for the mode of their utilization, breakage, maintenance, and discard (that is, their consumption). Microscopic examination of wear or contact traces was incorporated to help us study this latter aspect of resource utilization. All cryptocrystalline rock artifacts retrieved were examined both macroscopically and microscopically during the 1969 and 1970 field seasons.[1]

There are two points relevant to the conclusions drawn that bear mentioning here. These observations will supplement the distribution figures of artifacts retrieved from the occupational phases of Sitagroi in table 3.1. First, by far the largest part (80%) of the assemblage comes from phases II and III. Almost 80% of the lithic material from these phases was retrieved by wet sieving carried out in two trenches, ZA and ZB; an average of less than 20% was retrieved by troweling in the much larger exposed area. Not only does wet sieving bias the spatial distribution of the archaeological data, it also biases the kind of lithic data recovered. As Payne (1972) has pointed out, wet sieving with a

fine (3 mm) mesh increases the recovery of small chips of manufacturing debitage, which are entirely absent from the troweled samples. The troweled samples tend to give an exaggerated picture of the frequency of larger, finished, utilized, and retouched tools and cores. Dry sieving with a 1-cm^2 mesh tends to increase the overall occurrence of all classes of lithic material—cores, tools, and debitage—over the total retrieved by troweling. This bias is further complicated by the fact that the ratio of wet-sieved, dry-sieved, and unsieved earth excavated is not the same for all phases of occupation. It becomes especially important to take this bias into consideration when reaching conclusions concerning the changing ratio of utilized tools to debitage, of retouched to unretouched utilized tools, and of small to large tools.

The second point concerning retrieval of the assemblage is that the wet-sieved sample, which constitutes 75% of the lithic assemblage, came from trenches ZA and ZB, which were opened to control the stratigraphic observations of the larger exposures and to test the efficacy of the various retrieval techniques (Payne 1972). The greater part of the lithic assemblage, therefore, was retrieved without reference to architectural or other domestic features. Differences in the assemblage that might be caused by variable location in rubbish pits, within houses, in workshop areas, and from other contexts have unfortunately largely been omitted in this report. The sample retrieved from the Burnt House of phase Va is the most closely connected to a domestic feature.

The division between Sitagroi Va and Vb occupational phases has not been used in this report because the phase V sample is already small.

Table 3.1. Flaked Stone Assemblage and Retrieval Methods

| Phase | Retrieval method (N and %) | | | |
	Wet sieving (ZA, ZB 2-80r even, ZB 3-63r odd, ZB 101-131r)	Dry sieving (ZB 3-63s odd, MM)	Troweled trench recovery	Total pieces recovered
I	132	0	75	207
	63.7		36.2	3.9
II	1024	0	291	1315
	77.8		22.2	24.8
III	2288	197	409	2894
	79. 0	6.8	14.1	54.7
IV	355	24	155	534
	66.4	4.4	28.8	10. 0
V	172	72	96	340
	50.5	21.1	28.2	6.4
Total	3971	293	1026	5290
	75. 0	5.5	19.3	100

RAW MATERIALS OF THE FLAKED STONE INDUSTRY

Much of the discussion regarding production, redistribution, and consumption of resources rests on the identification of the raw materials, the location of their sources, and an understanding of their physical and chemical properties. The identification of cryptocrystalline rocks by petrographic means is notoriously difficult (Shepherd 1972). Chemical identification, using techniques such as neutron activation analysis, has met with more success, especially for locating obsidian sources. Such analysis is nevertheless limited in its ability to link specific mining areas with their hypothesized products (Aspinall and Feather 1972). Acknowledging these limitations, it is possible to locate a number of flint sources in southeast and central Europe (figure 3.1) within specific mountain ranges (Comsa 1967, 1971; Manolakkakis 1987, 1994; Nachev, Kovnurko, and Kunchev 1981; Nachev and Kunchev 1984; Vencl 1971; Voytek 1990). The available raw materials may be classified by the quality of their flaking properties in producing strong, regular, sharp, predictable edges.

The raw material identification of the Sitagroi lithic assemblage was carried out, in general, on the basis of macroscopic observations of color and structure. Six basic categories of raw materials were dis-

tinguished. A seventh category of "unidentifiable burned flint" has also been counted in the cross tabulations; this latter category had not been heat treated, but had burned during a house fire or through proximity to a hearth. The burned material is frequently patinated and crazed to such an extent that its original color and structure are unidentifiable. In addition, it had frequently been shattered by burning or by postdepositional (and postexcavation) mishaps. In spite of these deformations, however, microwear traces in the form of microflaking damage are observable on the flake edges.

The six raw material categories are obsidian, quartz, honey flint, opal, chert, and pebble flint.

Obsidian

Obsidian has a limited natural distribution and was highly prized in the past for its extremely fine, sharp edge and highly predictable fracture line. It has the obvious disadvantage that, although its edge is sharp, it is brittle and easily subject to fracture during use. Its use is thus limited to edges that must be sharp but not strong, unless the source of obsidian is nearby. The nearest sources of obsidian to Sitagroi are on the island of Melos (about 550 km to the south; see Torrence 1981) and in the Bükk mountains of northeast Hungary and related ranges in northwest Rumania and Slovakia (about 800 km to the north) (Nandris 1977). In the settlements in

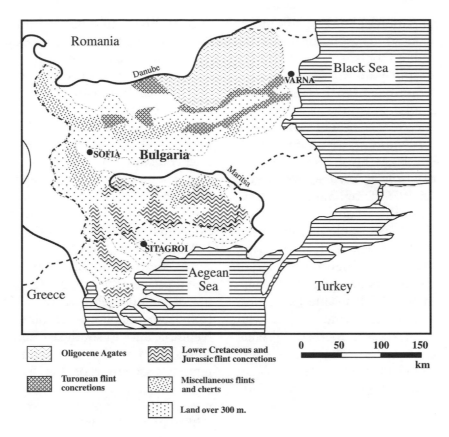

Figure 3.1. Source area map of southeastern Europe lithic resources.

the vicinity of the source area, obsidian makes up over 90% of the used tools (Barta 1960; Gabori 1950). At certain periods, for example, the end of the fifth millennium and the beginning of the fourth millennium BC, obsidian was an important source of flakable stone in all the settlements immediately north of the Danube River and west of the Carpathian Mountains (Chapman 1981).

In the prehistoric sites south of the Danube River, however, obsidian never played more than a minimal role in the flaked stone assemblages. It is present only in phases I and IV at Sitagroi. In phase I, it is represented by one used, unretouched blade. In phase IV, it is represented by one used, retouched blade accompanied by a tiny core and several waste flakes—a reflection of the entire manufacturing process.[2]

In spite of the clear "rational economic" unimportance of obsidian in the sites south of the Danube and east of the Carpathians, including Sita-

groi, it does occur in almost every lithic assemblage of the Neolithic and Chalcolithic sites as a minute proportion of the used tools. I am tempted to compare this situation with Gould's interpretation of the Western Desert Australian Aborigines' consistent, but limited, utilization of rocks from a specific source: flakes made only from these particular rocks could be used as special cutting tools in a specific initiation rite, even though their source might lie several hundred kilometers away (Gould 1978; Gould, Koster, and Sontz 1971).

Quartz and Rock Crystal

For the stone knapper, quartz and rock crystal are harsh, unyielding materials whose fracture line is usually extremely difficult to control. Rock crystal, like obsidian, will produce a sharp edge, but of limited length and extreme fragility. The poorer grades of quartz (that is, coarser grained) cannot produce a sharp edge. It is no wonder, then, that during most of the prehistoric occupation of Sitagroi, this group of raw materials played an insignificant role in the production of sharp-edged tools.

An exception to this pattern is the phase I assemblage in which quartz and rock crystal pieces make up 40% of the total. A similar occurrence of quartz has been noticed in a number of sites in southeast Europe contemporary with Sitagroi I, wherever these assemblages have been examined in any detail, as for example at Anzabegovo, Divostin I, and Banja (Elster 1976; Tringham 1988). However, in these sites, as in the Sitagroi I assemblage, the number of usable blanks (table 3.2) and used tools (table 3.3) is relatively small (15% and 11%, respectively, in Sitagroi I). The high percentage of debitage and unused flakes is unusual for the Sitagroi I assemblage, in which all usable flakes produced from other raw materials were worked.

Tools made from quartz and rock crystal were almost never modified by retouch (table 3.4) in any phase. The small number of used flakes were generally microblades (table 3.5) used to cut "soft" materials (table 3.6).

Sredna Gora "Honey" Flint

One of the finest quality flints in southeast Europe is found on the Danube platform of northeast Bulgaria and southeast Rumania, especially in the Sredna Gora mountain range (Manolakkakis 1994; Nachev, Kovnurko, and Kunchev 1981; Nachev and Kunchev 1984). This flint varies in color from a light honey to a dark brown and tends to be nearly or completely opaque. It is consistently of a high flaking quality with few irregularities. It was extracted from outcrops during the fifth to the mid-fourth millennium BC and may possibly have been systematically mined in the later part of this period. During the middle fifth and fourth millennium BC, this flint was distributed over a large area of southeastern Europe, including Sitagroi, by various mechanisms of exchange (Manolakkakis 1994; Sherratt 1976, 1984; Voytek 1990). Its exploitation played a crucial role in the changing pattern of lithic assemblages in prehistoric southeast Europe.

In the Sitagroi lithic assemblage, occurrence of this raw material increased from one-third of the utilized tools in phase I to two-thirds in phases II and III. Thereafter, its use gradually decreased to 30% in phase V. There is no doubt that the honey-brown flint was obtained from outcrop sources at least 200 km to the north, from the area that, in Sitagroi phases II and III, was inhabited by a society whose pottery represents a variant of the Maritsa/Gumelnitsa culture (Manolakkakis 1994; Todorova 1978, 1991). The climax of its usage in the source area coincides with the climax of its usage at Sitagroi. The reduction of its usage in phase V has also been observed in the early Bronze Age cultures of the source area in the late fourth and early third millennia BC (Pâunescu 1970; Sherratt 1972, 1976, 1983, 1984; Tringham 1991).

In comparison with their counterparts in subsequent phases, the inhabitants of phase I made less use of the honey-brown flint. However, they differ from the inhabitants of other early and middle Neolithic sites in southeast Europe outside the flint source area in that they had already established regular acquisition of this, the best-quality honey-brown flint from its distant outcrop source. The mechanism by which the material was obtained will only be elucidated when the lithic analysis is considered in the light of other data from Sitagroi and the source area (see Manolakkakis 1994). We can note, however, certain changes in the use of the honey-brown flint at Sitagroi.

The Sredna Gora flint was obtained in the form of cores that were probably already partially prepared—hence the lack of cortex on any flakes (table 3.7). The longest blades at Sitagroi, dating to phases II and III, rarely exceed 5 cm (figure 3.2). Only one blade approaches 15 cm in length, which is the usual length in this period for blades nearer the source area in Bulgaria and southern Rumania (Manolakkakis 1994; Pâunescu 1970). It seems likely, therefore, that even in the period of the greatest accessibility of the honey-brown flint, the cores were never as large as those nearer the source area. The blanks were struck from cores at Sitagroi and trimmed there. The wastage of blanks (see the section below on the ratio of usage to wastage) was highest, as one might expect, in the period of greatest availability of the flint (phases II through IV). In phases I and V, almost every blank flaked from a core of this material was used (see table 3.3). From

Table 3.2. Cross-Tabulation of Raw Material Category and Stage of Lithic Production

Raw material	Phase I				Phase II				Phase III				Phase IV				Phase V				Total
	C	B	D	T	C	B	D	T	C	B	D	T	C	B	D	T	C	B	D	T	
Obsidian No.	0	1	0	1	0	0	0	0	0	0	0	0	1	1	10	12	0	0	0	0	13
Row %				0.4									8.3	8.3	83.3	2.2					
Column %		1.7											2.5	0.5	3.2						0.0
Quartz No.	6	8	68	82	6	27	69	102	6	35	92	133	4	10	10	24	3	8	16	27	368
Row %	7.3	9.7	82.9	39.6	5.8	26.3	67.6	7.7	4.5	26.2	69.1	4.5	16.6	41.7	41.6	4.4	11.1	29.6	59.2	7.9	7.1
Column %	37.5	15.3	48.9		12	5.6	8.7		8.6	4.6	4.4		10.2	5.3	3.2		9	5.6	9.6		
Honey flint No.	2	18	27	47	30	336	598	964	29	386	1150	1565	9	71	83	163	7	31	29	67	2806
Row %	4.2	38.2	57.4	22.7	3	34.7	62	73.3	1.8	24.5	73.4	54	5.5	43.4	50.9	30.5	10.3	46	43.2	19.7	53.0
Column %	12.5	38.5	19.4		60	70.5	75		42	51.1	55.5		23	37.7	27		21.2	21.9	17.4		
Chalcedony No.	4	14	31	49	6	45	71	122	20	134	332	486	12	47	88	147	15	38	40	93	897
Row %	8.1	28.5	63.3	24.1	4.9	36.1	58	9.2	4.1	27.5	68.3	16.7	8	31.8	59.8	27.5	16.1	40.8	43	27.3	17.1
Column %	25	26.9	22.3		12	9.4	8.9		28.9	17.5	16		30.7	25	28.6		45.4	26.9	24		
Pebble flint No.	0	2	7	9	4	17	15	36	2	12	49	63	1	6	12	19	0	3	11	14	141
Row %		22	77.7	4.3	11	47.1	41.6	2.7	3.1	18.9	77.7	2.1	5.2	31.5	63.1	3.5		21.3	78.5	4.1	2.7
Column %		3.8	5		8	3.5	1.9		2.8	1.5	2.3		2.5	3.1	3.9			2.1	6.6		
Burned flint No.	1	3	0	4	0	13	26	39	5	97	268	370	1	16	71	88	5	30	46	81	582
Row %	25	75		1.9		33.1	66.6	2.9	1.3	26.2	72.4	12.7	1.1	18.1	80.6	16.4	6.1	36.9	56.7	23.8	11.0
Column %	6.2	5.7				2.7	3.2		7.2	14.1	12.9		2.5	8.5	23.1		15.1	21.2	27.7		
Chert No.	3	6	6	15	4	38	10	52	7	90	180	277	11	37	33	81	3	31	24	58	483
Row %	20	39.9	39.9	7.2	7.6	72.9	19.2	3.9	3.5	32.4	64.9	9.5	13.5	45.6	40.7	15.1	5.1	53.3	41.3	17	9.1
Column %	18.7	11.5	4.3		8	7.9	1.2		10.1	10.8	8.6		28.2	19.6	10.7		9	21.9	14.4		
Total No.	16	52	139	207	50	476	789	1315	69	754	2071	2894	39	188	307	534	33	141	166	340	5290
Row %	7.7	25.1	67.1	3.9	3.8	36.1	60	24.9	2.3	26	71.5	54.7	7.3	35.2	57.4	10.1	9.7	41.4	48.8	6.4	

C: Core
B: Blank
D: Debitage
T: Total

Table 3.3. Cross-Tabulation of Raw Material Category and Utilization of Blanks

Raw material	Phase I U	Phase I NU	Phase I T	Phase II U	Phase II NU	Phase II T	Phase III U	Phase III NU	Phase III T	Phase IV U	Phase IV NU	Phase IV T	Phase V U	Phase V NU	Phase V T	Total
Obsidian																
No.	1	0	1	0	0	0	0	0	0	1	0	1	0	0	0	2
Row %																
Column %	2.3									1		0.5				0.1
Quartz																
No.	5	3	8	7	20	27	10	25	35	0	10	10	0	8	8	88
Row %	62.5	37.5		25.9	74.1		28.6	71.4								
Column %	11.4	37.5	15.3	3.9	6.7	5.7	2.8	6.2	4.6		10.9	5.3		14	5.7	5.5
Honey flint																
No.	17	1	18	118	218	336	205	181	386	42	29	71	23	8	31	842
Row %	94.4	5.6		35.1	64.9		53.1	46.9		59.2	40.8		74.2	25.8		
Column %	38.6	12.5	34.6	66.3	73.2	70.6	58.2	45	51.2	43.8	31.5	37.8	27.4	14	21.9	52.3
Chalcedony																
No.	13	1	14	20	25	45	66	68	134	31	16	47	25	13	38	278
Row %	92.8	7.2		44.4	56.5		49.3	50.7		66	34		65.8	34.2		
Column %	29.5	12.5	26.9	11.2	8.4	9.5	18.8	16.9	17.8	32.3	17.4	25	29.8	22.8	26.9	17.3
Pebble flint																
No.	1	1	2	9	8	17	5	7	12	0	6	6	2	1	3	40
Row %	50.5	50		52.9	47.1		41.7	58.3					66.6	33.3		
Column %	2.3	12.5	3.8	5.1	2.7	3.6	1.4	1.7	1.6		6.5	3.2	2.4	1.7	2.1	2.5
Burned flint																
No.	1	2	3	5	8	13	20	77	97	8	8	16	16	14	30	159
Row %	33.3	66.6		38.5	61.5		20.6	79.4		50	50		53.3	46.7		
Column %	2.3	25	5.8	2.8	2.7	2.7	5.7	19.2	12.9	8.3	8.7	8.5	19	24.6	21.2	9.9
Chert																
No.	6	0	6	19	19	38	46	44	90	14	23	37	18	13	31	202
Row %		0		50	50		51.1	48.9		37.8	62.2		58	41.9		
Column %	13.6		11.5	10.7	6.4	8	13.1	10.9	11.9	14.6	25	19.7	21.4	22.8	22	12.5
Total																
No.	44	8	52	178	298	476	352	402	754	96	92	188	84	57	141	1611
Row %	84.6	15.4	3.2	37.4	62.6	29.5	46.7	53.3	46.8	51.1	48.9	11.7	59.5	40.4	8.8	

U: Used Blanks
NU: Not Used Blanks
T: Total

Table 3.4. Cross-Tabulation of Raw Material Category and Modification by Retouch

Raw Material		Phase I R	Phase I NR	Phase I T	Phase II R	Phase II NR	Phase II T	Phase III R	Phase III NR	Phase III T	Phase IV R	Phase IV NR	Phase IV T	Phase V R	Phase V NR	Phase V T	Total
Obsidian	No.	0	1	1	0	0	0	0	0	0	1	0	1	0	0	0	2
	Row %																
	Column %										2.3		1				0.0
Quartz	No.	1	4	5	0	7	7	3	7	10	0	0	0	0	0	0	22
	Row %	20.0	80.0					30.0	70.0								
	Column %	5.8	14.8	11.3		5.6	3.9	2.5	3.0	2.8							2.9
Honey flint	No.	9	8	17	40	78	118	77	129	206	18	24	42	10	13	23	406
	Row %	52.9	47.0		33.8	66.1		37.5	62.4		42.8	57.1		43.4	56.5		
	Column %	52.9	29.6	38.6	74.0	62.9	66.2	65.2	54.7	58.2	42.8	44.4	43.7	25.6	28.8	27.4	53.9
Chalcedony	No.	4	9	13	6	14	20	14	52	66	18	13	31	12	13	25	155
	Row %	30.7	69.2		30.0	70.0		26.9	73.0		58.0	42.0		48.0	52.0		
	Column %	23.5	33.3	29.5	11.1	11.2	11.2	11.8	22.2	18.7	42.8	24.0	32.3	30.7	28.8	29.7	20.5
Pebble flint	No.	0	1	1	3	6	9	0	5	5	0	0	0	0	2	2	17
	Row %				33.3	66.6											
	Column %		3.7	2.2	5.5	4.8	5.0		2.1	1.4					4.4	2.4	2.3
Burned flint	No.	0	1	1	1	4	5	5	15	20	2	6	8	11	5	16	50
	Row %				20.0	80.0		25.0	75.0		25.0	75.0		68.7	31.2		
	Column %		3.7	2.2	1.8	3.2	2.8	4.2	6.4	5.6	4.7	11.1	8.3	28.2	11.1	19.0	6.6
Chert	No.	3	3	6	4	15	19	19	27	46	3	11	14	6	12	18	103
	Row %	50.0	50.0		21.0	78.9		41.3	58.6		21.4	78.5		33.3	66.6		
	Column %	17.6	11.1	13.6	7.4	12.0	10.6	16.1	11.5	13.0	7.0	20.3	14.6	15.4	26.6	21.4	13.7
Total	No.	17	27	44	54	124	178	118	235	353	42	54	96	39	45	84	755
	Row %	38.6	61.3	5.8	30.3	69.6	23.6	33.5	66.5	46.8	43.7	56.2	12.7	46.4	53.5	11.1	

R: Retouch
NR: No Retouch
T: Total

this viewpoint, it is interesting that, in all phases of the settlement's occupation, the cores were extensively used in the manufacture of blanks, so that by the time they were discarded they could not have been used further; examples are illustrated from phases I to IV (figure 3.3a–e, g–n).

The blanks struck from honey-brown flint in the first three phases of the occupation at Sitagroi had been resharpened and especially shaped by retouch more so than the blanks manufactured from other lithic materials (see table 3.4). In phases IV and V, the occurrence of retouch on honey-brown flint blanks is equivalent to that of other materials.

Chalcedony, Opal

As a raw material for the manufacture of long, straight cutting edges, chalcedony is structurally inferior to the honey-brown flint from outcrop sources; it contains more impurities and occurs in smaller, more dispersed outcrops. This material is, however, local to the area of Sitagroi and is present in the lithic assemblages of all occupation phases. It became increasingly important as a source of raw material for cutting tools from phase IV to phase V, that is, when the use of honey-brown flint decreased. Thus, the pattern of its occurrence is very similar to that of chert (see below). This pattern may be explained in both cases by the increasing reliance during phases IV and especially V on local resources of lithic raw materials, perhaps as the source of the high-quality, but distant, honey-brown flint became less accessible. It should be noted that, in phase I, chalcedony is almost equally as important as honey-brown flint in the production of edge tools.

Throughout its utilization at Sitagroi, chalcedony was treated carefully, with very little being wasted. Compared with honey-brown flint and especially chert (see below), a higher percentage of blanks was used for edge tools (see table 3.3). From the point of view of modifying of the blanks' shape and the care taken in the tools' maintenance, chalcedony tools were not treated any differently until phase IV, the period of its increasing utilization. At this point, modification of the blank's shape by bulb truncation and retouch significantly increases (see table 3.4).

Chalcedony tools always tended to be small and narrow. They were used for a wide variety of purposes, especially on softer materials and those of medium resistance. In phase I, two-thirds of the sickle inserts were made of chalcedony (see table 3.6).

Cherts

The cherts have been distinguished from the various kinds of flint by their more crystalline structure, producing a less predictable line of fracture and blunter, less straight edges. Colors vary from gray to brown to black, and are completely opaque. It is uncertain whether they came from outcrop or derived sources, but probably these sources are not very far from Sitagroi. The pattern of chert occurrence is very similar to that of chalcedony, although cherts always occur in slightly lesser quantities than chalcedony. The pattern of chert utilization is, however, rather different from that of the other raw materials. More blanks were produced from chert for the amount of debitage retrieved than from other materials, which would suggest a difference in the technology of producing blanks of cherts, as well as a difference in the production sequence pattern (see table 3.2). In the first three phases, a higher-than-average number of blanks was utilized (see table 3.3). In phases IV and V, on the other hand, a lower-than-average percentage of these blanks was utilized, even though this is the period in which cherts were more favored or more available (according to the total numbers of chert pieces). This picture contrasts with that of chalcedony utilization during this period.

Overall, and especially during the period of their greatest abundance (phases IV and V), chert tools were much less frequently modified by retouch and bulb truncation than tools of chalcedony and honey-brown flint (see table 3.4). Also during this period, chert tools were used for a more limited set of tasks than those of honey-brown flint and chalcedony, and were used especially on "softer" materials (see table 3.6).

In general, I have the impression that the cherts were a local set of raw materials used with increasing frequency in the latter part of the occupation of Sitagroi in the production of "expedient" tools—

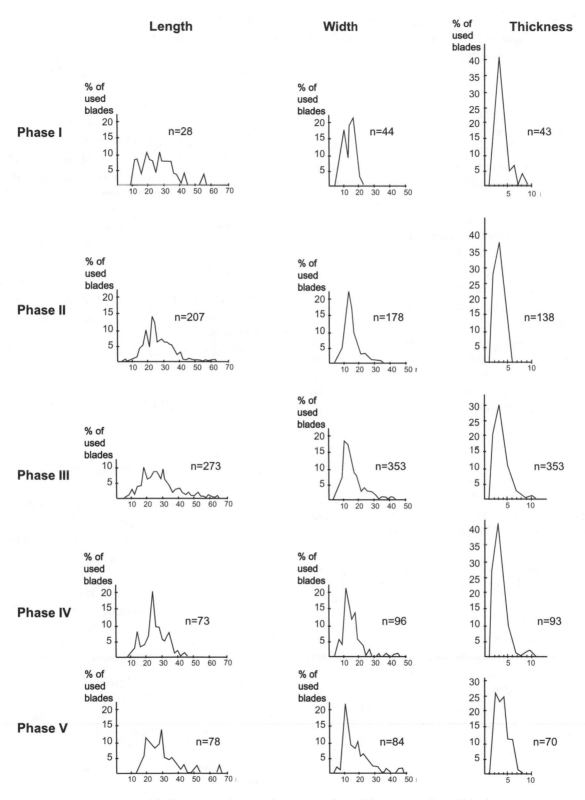

Figure 3.2. Dimensional range (length, width, and thickness) of used blanks.
Measurements are in mm.

that is, tools made with little preparation for a short-term task and needing no maintenance or prolonging of their use-life.

Pebble Flints

Included in this category are miscellaneous flints from derived sources, such as river gravels, presumably local to Sitagroi. In certain cases, these may have been brought downstream many miles from their original outcrop (Weide 1976). Flint from derived sources is characteristically eroded, has been broken into small nodules and pebbles, and has suffered from patination of its surface and other weakening processes. Such flint played an insignificant role in the lithic tool assemblage in all phases of occupation, never exceeding 5% of the total used tools (see table 3.3). In phase IV, tools made of these materials are absent.

In general, fewer cores and more debitage occur in this raw material category than in others (see table 3.2). A remarkable difference in the treatment of the pebble flints (which may be insignificant in light of their small numbers) can be observed in phase II. In this phase, when exploitation of the honey-brown flint was reaching its climax, one would expect a rejection of the poor-quality pebble flints; however, we see behavior quite to the contrary. More cores of pebble flint are found, a higher percentage of pebble flint blanks are used, and more tools of pebble flint in absolute terms (mostly used as sickle inserts) appear than in any other phase. This pattern is more to be expected in phase I because the early and middle Neolithic sites of much of southeast Europe contemporary with Sitagroi I are characterized by a dominating use of pebble flints for small edge tools. Sites such as Azmak 1, Lepenski Vir III, and Sitagroi phase I show, however, that outcrop sources of high-quality cryptocrystalline rocks in this period were already being exploited by the early agriculturalists, and the more easily accessible sources of low-quality derived flint were beginning to be rejected in their favor.

Summary

In phases II through IV, the lithic assemblage is characterized by an explosive increase in the utilization of high-quality honey-brown flint, which was brought to Sitagroi from distant outcrop sources in northeast Bulgaria when a variant of the Maritsa/Gumelnitsa culture flourished there. The assemblage is further characterized by an increasing reliance, during phases IV and V, on poorer quality materials, particularly chalcedony and chert, as honey-brown flint became less available. The possible reasons why honey-brown flint might have become less available, and the impact of this change on the production and consumption of tools of cryptocrystalline rocks, are discussed later in this chapter. Although it has not been demonstrated conclusively that chalcedony, chert, and other various jaspers, opals, and the like came from outcrops relatively close to Sitagroi, it is nevertheless hypothesized that the change reflects a decreasing reliance on raw materials obtained from far away by what was probably a set of complex exchange mechanisms and an increasing reliance on local raw materials (but see appendix to this chapter and chapter 4).

STRATEGIES OF FLAKED STONE TOOL PRODUCTION

All southeast and central European Neolithic lithic industries are based on the technology of producing flakes, otherwise known as blades, with roughly parallel edges and dorsal spines struck from prismatic cores. The assemblages from all occupation phases of Sitagroi are no exception. Blades never make up less than 80% of the total blanks in any phase and, more importantly, average 90% of the used tools. The production of blade tools has considerable advantages in the exploitation of cryptocrystalline rocks. At least two long straight edges are produced on every blank, and, with the help of secondary retouching, two additional edges of greater strength can be produced at the proximal and distal ends. Furthermore, the distinct dorsal spine of the blades provides an easy platform from which to resharpen the edges by retouch.

Irregularly shaped flakes were rarely used as tools (see table 3.5) and then almost always on less resistant materials, probably as expedient tools for temporary tasks (table 3.8). Most of the flakes were unused and may be counted as the debitage derived from blade production. In analyzing the debitage, flakes were divided arbitrarily into those above and those below 2 mm in width, based on the proposition that many flakes of the smaller category may be the result of secondary flaking of blanks for shaping and resharpening. To judge from the virtual absence of cortex on the surfaces of cores, blanks, and debitage of all raw material classes (see table 3.7), the initial preparation of nodules was carried out away from the site. This suggestion is strengthened by the fact that, among 5000 pieces of the Sitagroi assemblage, only 42 decortication flakes were found.

It is characteristic of the Sitagroi assemblages of all phases that all the cores were used as an available source of raw material until they were quite exhausted (see figure 3.3). Core fragments above 1.5 cm in length and width were used as blanks for tools (for example, see figure 3.3c–e). These two factors mean that not only is it difficult to reconstruct the process by which the cores were reduced and blanks produced, but it is impossible to reconstruct the primary form and size of the cores. However, one can obtain an impression of the techniques, precision, and relative care with which the striking platform and core were prepared before striking off the blank, by observing the character of the bulbar end, particularly the striking platform, of the blank itself (Semenov 1964). The presence of a faceted platform, which may be associated with soft-hammer percussion of striking and the production of more predictable fracture lines, reached its peak in phases II through IV, with a frequency curve similar to that of the long honey-brown flint blades. Faceted striking platforms, however, are virtually absent from the blanks of phase I, as they are in other early and middle Neolithic assemblages of southeast Europe.

Size Control in Artifact Production

There is a clear correlation between tool dimensions and standardization on the one hand and the nature of raw materials and the techniques used in tool manufacture on the other. For example, the maximum size of blanks made from derived pebble flints and volcanic rocks could never approach the maximum possible size of the long blades made from the honey-brown outcrop flint. One should not be too hasty in making such a correlation, however, because it is clear that other factors are involved: for example, the development and availability of equipment (antler or copper punches) and techniques (soft hammer and pressure flaking) which made the manufacture of longer blanks and standardization of size and shape possible, and the decision to use materials more frugally or more expansively. Elster (chapter 2) discusses the probable application of antler tools in the production of chipped stone tools (see figure 2.9c).

I previously remarked that, although blades frequently exceeded 15 cm in length in the Gumelnitza culture of Bulgaria near the source of the honey-brown flint, blades in the contemporary phases of Sitagroi (II and III) in this material exceed 6 cm in only three cases (one of which is 15 cm long) (figure 3.4a). The explanation for this lies in the difference in size of the available honey-brown flint cores. An additional factor, however, may be that the Sitagroi II and III knappers deliberately optimized and conserved their valuable honey-brown flint.

Although there is no obvious change in the overall size of the blanks throughout the occupation of Sitagroi, apart from a slight increase in width, thickness, and length in phases II and III, a definite tendency may be seen toward standardization of tool dimensions in phase II, and even more so in phases III and IV (see figures 3.2, 3.5). This is especially clear when information provided by microwear examination is added, demonstrating that blanks falling outside the standard width or length were generally not utilized. The size range of the utilized blanks is small: 15 to 40 mm in length, 8 to 25 mm in width, and 2 to 5 mm in thickness.

Standardization of shape and size was achieved using the following techniques:

- Skilled, initial flaking of the blank from the core. There is no doubt, as noted above, that a greater degree of skill is displayed by the phase II through IV knappers than by those earlier or later. In this, they were certainly helped by the adoption of antler (see chapter 2) and, perhaps, copper punches and hammers; by the soft-hammer percussion and pressure flaking techniques

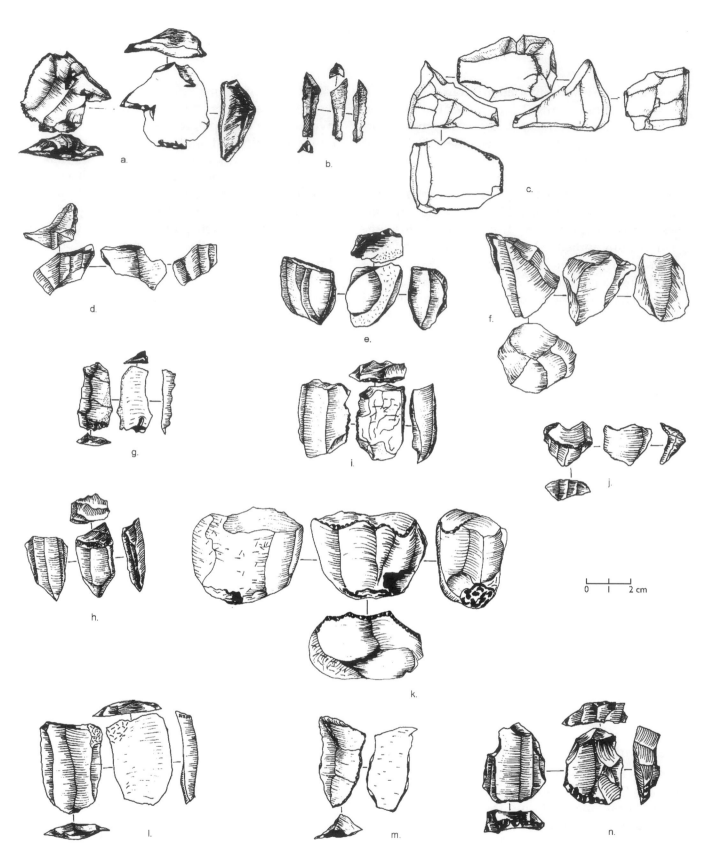

Figure 3.3. Examples of cores and core fragments from the lithic assemblage; phase I: a; phase II: b, c, n; phase III: d, e, j, l, m; phase IV: g, h, i, k; phase X (mixed): f. (a) ZA 63:3; (b) ZA 52:47; (c) ZA 52; (d) ZA 44:10; (e) SF 1734, ML 172; (f) SF 2919, ZG 3; (g) SF 3238, ZHe 20; (h) SF 2716, ZE 58; (i) SF 3237, ZHe 21; (j) ZA 47; (k) SF 3034, ROc 61; (l) ZA 44:32; (m) SF 889, MM 43; (n) ZA 50.

of striking; and by the superior flaking properties of their raw material. They were able, for example, to strike microblades less than 10 mm wide from microcores; the majority of microblades show no signs of use. This method of microblade production was a popular source of sharp edge tools in certain late Paleolithic, Epipaleolithic, and Mesolithic industries in the Mediterranean area and elsewhere (Kozlowski 1982; Kozlowski and Kozlowski 1987). It also occurs in certain late Neolithic and Neolithic assemblages of the Central Balkans and central Europe contemporary with Sitagroi III and IV—for example, at Divostin in Yugoslavia (McPherron and Gunn 1988; Tringham 1988). At Sitagroi, however, the production of microblades plays a minor role in the lithic industry; those few microblades that were used served as borers or piercers (for example, figure 3.6i–k; see tables 3.8, 3.9), as did those from sites such as Divostin. The majority of microblades found at Sitagroi were, in fact, part of the debitage resulting from the manufacture and trimming of blanks (see table 3.5; figure 3.7m, n).

- Selecting blanks of appropriate dimensions as they were struck from the core. This implies a willingness on the part of the consumers of lithic resources to reject as unusable (that is, to waste) those blanks that did not conform to the mean dimensions selected for specific tasks. This method was the dominant means of controlling and standardizing the dimensions and shape of flaked stone edge-tools in all phases at Sitagroi, and indeed in all the Neolithic and later assemblages of southeast and central Europe.

- Truncating the bulbar and distal ends of the blades to shorten the length of the blade while still retaining its mass and strength. The use of truncated blades whose snapped ends were further shaped by secondary trimming, giving the whole blank a geometric form, was important in the production of edge tools in many Mesolithic industries of Europe, including those of southeast Europe and the aceramic Neolithic industries of Thessaly (Kozlowski and Kozlowski 1987; Tringham 1968). The use of geometric-shaped truncated blades (trapezes, triangles,

Table 3.5. Cross-Tabulation of Category and Utilization of Blanks

Category	Phase I			Phase II			Phase III			Phase IV			Phase V			Total
	U	NU	T	U	NU	T	U	NU	T	U	NU	T	U	NU	T	
Blades and fragments																
No.	36	5	41	147	140	287	304	283	587	77	64	141	77	32	111	1026
Row %	87.8	12.2	78.8	51.2	48.7	60.2	51.7	48.2	77.7	54.6	45.3	75.0	69.3	30.6		
Column %	81.8	62.5	78.8	82.5	46.9	60.2	86.0	70.4	77.7	80.2	69.5	75.0	91.6	59.6	78.7	63.65
Flakes																
No.	4	3	7	18	21	39	29	49	78	13	20	33	5	19	24	181
Row %	57.1	42.9		46.1	53.8		37.1	62.8		39.3	60.6		20.8	79.1		
Column %	9.0	7.5	13.4	10.1	7.0	8.1	8.2	12.1	10.3	13.5	21.7	17.5	5.9	33.3	12.1	11.23
Microblades																
No.	4	0	4	13	137	150	20	70	90	6	8	14	2	4	6	264
Row %				8.6	91.3		22.2	77.7		42.8	57.1		33.3	66.6		
Column %	9.0		7.6	7.3	45.9	31.5	5.6	17.4	11.9	6.2	8.7	7.4	2.3	7.0	4.2	16.38
Total																
No.	44	8	52	178	298	476	353	402	755	96	92	188	84	57	141	1612
Row %	84.6	15.3	3.2	37.3	62.6	29.5	46.6	53.4	46.8	51.0	49.0	11.7	59.5	40.4	8.8	

U: Used Blanks
NU: Not Used Blanks
T: Total Number of Blanks

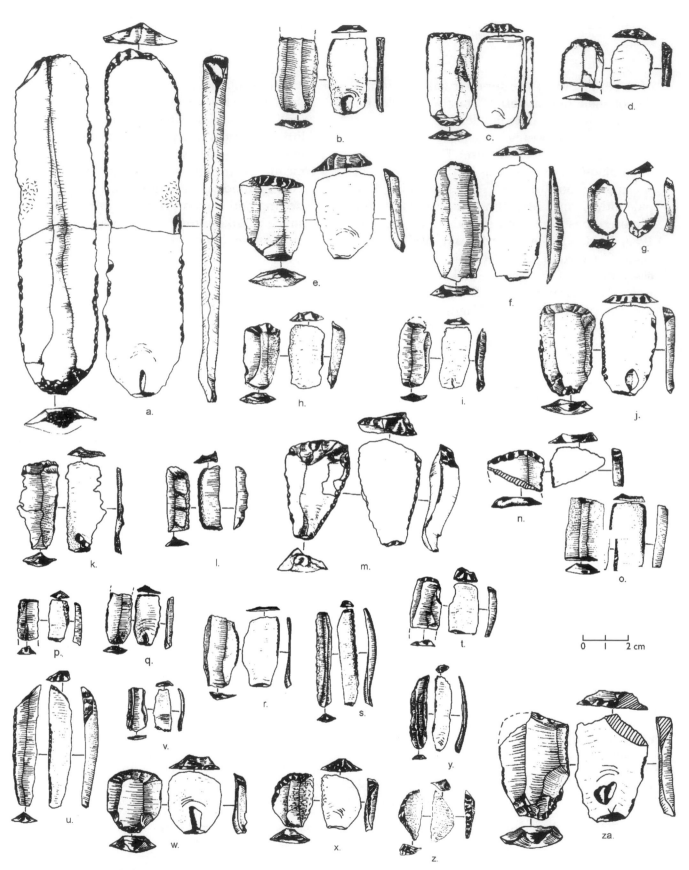

Figure 3.4. Examples of phase III lithic assemblage. (a) ZB 130:5; (b) ZB 130:1; (c) SF 2904, ZG 23; (d) ZB 125:5; (e) SF 1641, ML 4; (f) SF 1236, MM 49; (g) ZB 125:9; (h) SF 1237, ML 112; (i) ZB 121:3; (j) SF 1697, MM 41; (k) SF 91, ML 3; (l) SF 1764, ZJ 33; (m) SF 2957, ZG 22; (n) ZB 125:6; (o) SF 1244, MM 50; (p) ZB 123:2; (q) ZB 125:6; (r) SF 2936, ZG 25; (s) ZB 125:3; (t) ZB 122:1; (u) SF 1505, MM 19; (v) ZB 125:1; (w) SF 1293, MM 53; (x) ZB 102; (y) ZB 1 10; (z) SF 1143, MM 11; (za) SF 1404, MM 40.

crescents, and the like) is virtually absent from the Sitagroi assemblage, as it is from all the Neolithic and later flaked stone industries of southeast Europe (figure 3.8e–h; table 3.9).

Truncation of the bulbar end of the blades does occur, although infrequently. The bulbar end of the used tools is preserved or truncated in approximately equal numbers until phase V, when the bulbar end was truncated from a larger number of tools; these same tools also tended to be modified by retouch (table 3.10). This feature is very likely to be associated with the increasing use of carefully prepared hafts during this phase.

- Retouching or deliberately removing flakes from the surface or edge of a blank. Retouch made it possible to decrease the length, width, and thickness of a blank after it had been struck from the core; retouch in this way could change the overall shape of a blank. As with truncation of the bulbar end, retouch as a strategy to control the dimensions and shape of a tool is rare in the Neolithic and later assemblages of southeast and central Europe, and is restricted to certain task-specific tools.

The method of thinning a blank by removing flakes from its surface is extremely rare in these

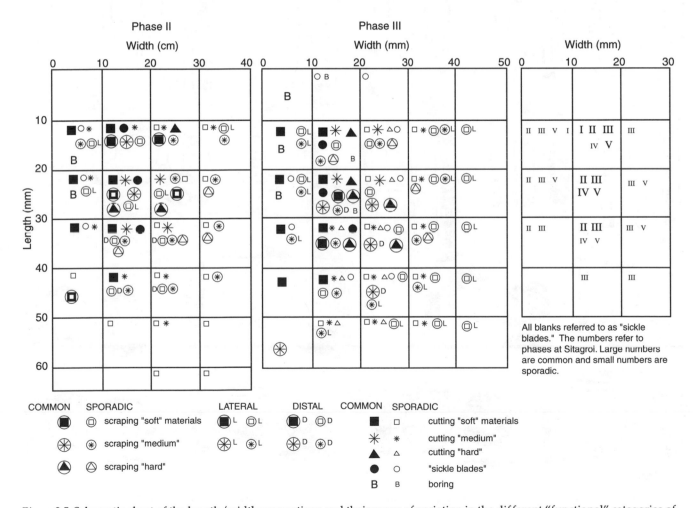

Figure 3.5. Schematic chart of the length/width proportions and their range of variation in the different "functional" categories of the lithic assemblage.

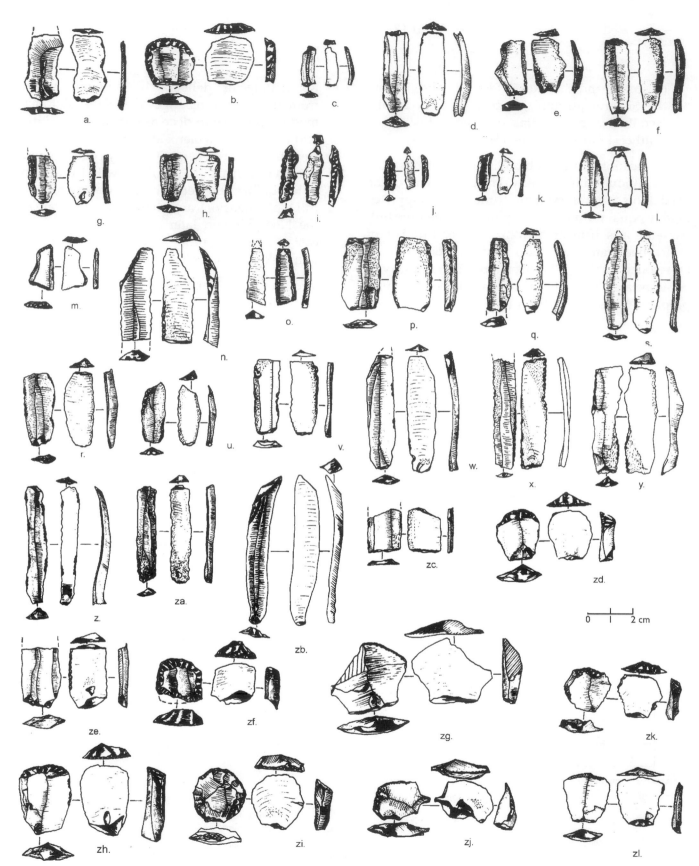

Figure 3.6. Examples of phase II lithic assemblage; from square ZA except for (t, u, x), and (zg) from ZB. (a) ZA 52:32; (b) ZA 55:3; (c) ZA 52:34; (d) ZA 52:1; (e) ZA 52:77; (f) ZA 52:12; (g) ZA 55:8; (h) ZA 52:11; (i) ZA 52:49; (j) ZA 52:39; (k) ZA 52:76; (l) ZA 52:38; (m) ZA 52:78; (n) ZA 55:907; (o) ZA 52:33; (p) ZA 52:54; (q) ZA 52:16; (r) ZA 52:83; (s) ZA 52:59; (t) ZB 131:4; (u) ZA 52:60; (v) ZA 52:69; (w) ZA 52:1193; (x) ZB131:7; (y) ZB 131:6; (z) ZA 52:14; (za) ZA 52:13; (zb) ZA 52:243; (zc) ZA 52:26; (zd) ZA 52:58; (ze) ZA 52:56; (zf) ZA 52:51; (zg) ZB 131:5; (zh) ZA 52:15; (zi) ZA 50; (zj) ZA 58:2; (zk) ZA 58:6; (zl) ZA 52:10.

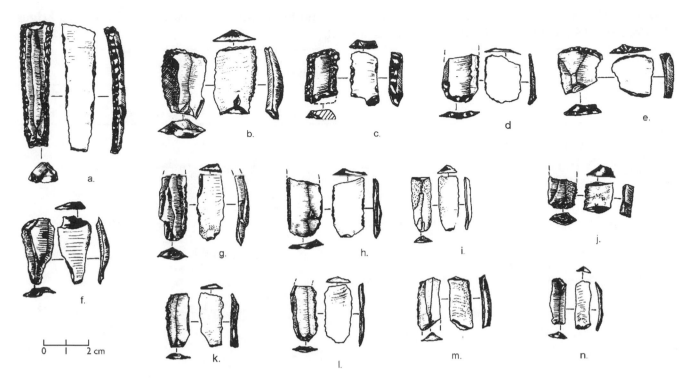

Figure 3.7. Examples of phase I (a–e, g, h, j, k) and II (f, i, l, n) lithic assemblages; all from ZA except (f) from ZB. (a) ZA 67:920; (b) ZA 63:1; (c) ZA 63:7; (d) ZA 65:1; (e) ZA 65:3; (f) ZB 131:3; (g) ZA 63:2; (h) ZA 63:4; (I) ZA 52:33; (j) ZA 65:2; (k) ZA 63:8; (l) ZA 58:4; (m) ZA 55:1; (n) ZA 52:52; (j) ZA 65:2; (k) ZA 63:8; (l) ZA 58:4; (m) ZA 55:1; (n) ZA 52:52.

assemblages, except on the projectile points of the Gumelnitsa and Tripolye cultures (Kunchev 1983; Pâunescu 1970). At Sitagroi, it occurs only in phase IV—for the purpose of manufacturing four triangular flat blades (see figure 3.8m–p). The removal of flakes from either the dorsal or ventral surface of a blade is quite a difficult task, one that requires particular skills (Crabtree 1968). It is, however, the most reliable way to eliminate the dorsal spine and to manufacture a flat, carefully balanced tool. It is thus one of the most successful ways to produce a balanced projectile head from cryptocrystalline rocks. For this reason, as well as because of their triangular shape, these blades, like their counterparts in Bulgaria and Rumania, have been interpreted as projectile points. The projectile points from Sitagroi, however, are smaller than those from Rumania and Bulgaria, being only about 2 cm long.

Calculating the frequency of retouch as a means of controlling the shape and size of a blade is complicated by the fact that not all flakes detached from the edges of a blank were removed during initial production of the tool. Flakes were also removed at a later point in the use-life of a tool to resharpen a dulled edge, repair a broken edge, change the position of the hafted edge, and so on.[3]

Identification of the retouch purpose, which was made on the basis of micro- and macro-observations of the Sitagroi assemblage, shows that such modification during initial manufacture is confined almost entirely to the edges of the tools, predominantly the distal end (especially in the first three occupation phases of the site; see table 3.4). The number of such tools never exceeds 20% of the total used blanks of any phase. Most of these retouched tools, especially in phases IV and V, were longer and wider blanks (for example, for phase III, see figures 3.4a, 3.9e; for phase IV: figures 3.10m, t).

UTILIZATION OF FLAKED STONE TOOLS

The ultimate aim in the analysis of microwear traces on the flaked stone assemblage at Sitagroi, as with that carried out on the Divostin assemblage

Table 3.6. Cross-Tabulation of Raw Material Category and Function Identification of Total Used Edges Against Soft (S), Medium (M), and Hard (H) Materials

Raw Material					Function						
	Cut				Scrape						
Phase I	S	M	H	Sickle	S	M	H	Borer	Groove	Projectile point	Edge
Obsidian											
No.	0	0	0	0	0	1	0	0	0	0	1
Row %											
Column %						33.3					1.6
Quartz											
No.	4	0	0	0	2	0	0	0	0	0	6
Row %	66.6				33.3						
Column %	33.3				33.3						9.7
Honey flint											
No.	4	1	2	3	3	2	8	2	0	0	25
Row %	16.0	4.0	8.0	12.0	12.0	8.0	32.0	8.0			
Column %	33.3	10.0	50.0	18.8	50.0	66.6					40.3
Chalcedony											
No.	2	4	0	10	1	0	0	0	1	0	18
Row %	11.1	22.2		55.5	5.6				5.6		
Column %	16.6	40		62.5	16.6						29.0
Pebble flint											
No.	0	2	0	0	0	0	0	0	0	0	2
Row %											
Column %		20.0									3.2
Burned flint											
No.	0	0	0	1	0	0	0	0	0	0	1
Row %											
Column %				6.3							1.6
Chert											
No.	2	3	2	2	0	0	0	0	0	0	9
Row %	22.2	33.3	22.2	22.2							
Column %	16.6	30.0	50.0	12.5							14.5
Total											
No.	12	10	4	16	6	3	8	2	1	0	62
Row %	19.4	16.1	6.4	25.8	9.7	4.8	12.9	3.2	1.6		

Continued on next page

and subsequently that carried out by Barbara Voytek at Selevac and Opovo, is to interpret these data in terms of the production, redistribution, and consumption of a particular resource—microcrystalline rocks. The reconstruction of specific tasks and work areas was less the goal of this study. The aim determines the kind of microwear analysis employed.

The methodology of microwear research has been discussed in detail in the literature, along with its potential and limitations in the study of the utilization of stone tools (Hayden, ed. 1979; Keeley 1980; Kozlowski and Kaczanowska 1986; Odell 1977; Tringham 1978, 1988; Voytek 1990; Yerkes and Kardulias 1993). In the microwear examination of the Sitagroi assemblage, a specific set of observations was chosen to help the large research investigation of the production and consumption of lithic resources. The observations provided information concerning the questions of wastage and conservation of lithic raw materials, the selection of specific raw materials and classes of preforms for specific tasks, the shaping of specific forms for specific tasks, the prolongation of the use-life of tools of different raw materials, and the pattern of discard and breakage of different materials. The concept of the

Table 3.6. Cross-Tabulation of Raw Material Category and Function Identification of Total Used Edges Against Soft (S), Medium (M), and Hard (H) Materials, cont.

Raw Material											
		Function									
	Cut				Scrape						
Phase II	S	M	H	Sickle	S	M	H	Borer	Groove	Projectile point	Edge
Quartz											
No.	3	1	0	3	0	0	0	0	1	0	8
Row %	37.5	12.5		37.5					12.5		
Column %	6.8	3.7		3.4					50.0		3.3
Honey flint											
No.	29	14	6	56	15	20	7	10	1	0	158
Row %	18.4	8.9	3.8	35.4	9.5	12.6	4.4	6.3	0.6		
Column %	65.9	51.9		63.6	75.0	62.5	70.0		50.0		66.1
Chalcedony											
No.	4	5	0	8	2	5	0	0	0	0	24
Row %	16.7	20.8		33.3	8.3	20.8					
Column %	9.0	18.5		9.1	10.0	15.6					10.0
Pebble flint											
No.	1	1	0	6	2	1	0	0	0	0	11
Row %	9.1	9.1		54.5	18.2	9.1					
Column %	2.3	3.7		6.8	10.0	3.1					4.6
Burned flint											
No.	1	2	0	3	0	2	1	0	0	0	9
Row %	11.1	22.2		33.3		22.2	11.1				
Column %	2.3	7.4		3.4		6.3	10				3.7
Chert											
No.	6	4	0	12	1	4	2	0	0	0	29
Row %	20.7	13.8		41.4	3.4	13.8	6.9				
Column %	13.6	14.8		13.6	5.0	12.5	10.0				12.1
Total											
No.	44	27	6	88	20	32	10	10	2	0	239
Row %	18.4	11.3	2.5	36.8	8.4	13.4	4.2	4.2	0.8		

Continued on next page

use-life of material culture plays an essential role (Schiffer 1987).

The microwear observations enabled an interpretation of the lithic assemblages in terms of the ratio of utilized to unused flakes; the fraction of a blank's perimeter utilized as an edge tool; and strategies to prolong the use-life of a tool before its final discard, such as resharpening a dull edge or repairing or reusing a broken tool.

In such a research program, it was necessary to be able to make observations regarding the entire assemblage rather than a selected sample. Thus, the strategy of microwear observation was chosen that would allow a large sample to be examined. The basis of the microwear identifications made on the Sitagroi assemblage is the variability of the location, size, and shape of the microflakes removed from the edges of the tool as a result of the tool's contact with other materials during its use-life. With the microwear examination carried out on the Sitagroi assemblage, it was possible to identify, with a good deal of confidence on this basis, which blanks had been used, which part of their periphery had been used, and with which predominant action.

Table 3.6. Cross-Tabulation of Raw Material Category and Function Identification of Total Used Edges Against Soft (S), Medium (M), and Hard (H) Materials, cont.

Raw Material	Function										
	Cut				Scrape						
Phase III	S	M	H	Sickle	S	M	H	Borer	Groove	Projectile point	Edge
Quartz											
No.	3	0	0	2	3	0	0	2	0	0	10
Row %	30.0			20.0	30.0			20.0			
Column %	4.0			1.3	8.8			4.0			1.9
Honey flint											
No.	45	50	22	73	22	39	24	30	4	0	309
Row %	14.6	16.1	7.1	23.6	7.1	12.6	7.7	9.7	1.3		
Column %	60.0	69.4	66.7	46.2	64.7	76.5	85.7	60.0			61.1
Chalcedony											
No.	17	12	3	40	4	5	1	11	0	0	93
Row %	18.3	12.9	3.2	43.0	4.3	5.3	1.1	11.8			
Column %	22.7	16.7	9.1	25.3	11.7	9.8	3.6	22.0			18.4
Pebble flint											
No.	3	0	0	1	0	0	0	2	0	0	6
Row %	50.0			16.7				33.3			
Column %	4.0			0.6				4.0			1.2
Burned flint											
No.	1	4	0	13	1	1	1	1	0	0	22
Row %	4.5	18.2		59.1	4.5	4.5	4.5	4.5			
Column %	1.3	5.6		8.2	2.9	2.0	3.6	2.0			4.4
Chert											
No.	6	6	8	29	4	6	2	4	0	0	65
Row %	9.2	9.2	12.3	44.6	6.2	9.2	3.1	6.2			
Column %	8.0	8.3	24.2	18.4	11.7	11.8	7.1	8.0			12.8
Total											
No.	75	72	33	158	34	51	28	50	4	0	505
Row %	14.9	14.3	6.5	31.3	6.7	10.1	5.5	10.0	0.7		
Phase IV											
Chalcedony											
No.	4	2	0	19	3	2	3	10	1	9	53
Row %	7.5	3.8		35.8	5.6	3.8	5.6	18.8	1.9	17.0	
Column %	25.0	28.6		36.5	17.6	20.0	60.0	71.4		90.0	36.7
Burned flint											
No.	0	0	2	5	1	2	1	0	0	0	11
Row %			18.2	45.5	9.1	18.2	9.1				
Column %			18.2	9.6	5.9	20.0	20.0				7.8
Chert											
No.	6	0	2	8	5	0	0	0	0	0	21
Row %	28.6		9.5	38.1	23.8						
Column %	37.5		18.2	15.4	29.4						14.8
Total											
No.	16	7	11	52	17	10	5	14	1	10	143
Row %	11.2	4.9	7.7	36.6	12.0	7.0	3.5	9.9	0.7	7.0	

Continued on next page

Table 3.6. Cross-Tabulation of Raw Material Category and Function Identification of Total Used Edges Against Soft (S), Medium (M), and Hard (H) Materials, cont.

Phase V	S	M	H	Sickle	S	M	H	Borer	Groove	Projectile point	Edge
Honey flint											
No.	3	10	2	7	3	5	0	0	0	2	32
Row %	9.4	31.2	6.2	21.9	9.4	15.6				6.2	
Column %	17.6	52.6	20.0	17.1	75.0	55.6					29.1
Chalcedony											
No.	7	1	6	12	1	2	2	4	1	0	36
Row %	19.4	2.8	16.7	33.3	2.8	5.6	5.6	11.1	2.8		
Column %	41.2	5.3	60.0	29.3	25.0	22.2	66.7				32.7
Pebble flint											
No.	0	1	0	1	0	0	0	0	0	0	2
Row %		50.0		50.0							
Column %		5.3		2.4							1.8
Burned flint											
No.	0	1	2	14	0	1	1	0	0	0	19
Row %		5.3	10.5	73.7		5.3	5.3				
Column %		5.3	20.0	34.1		11.1	33.3				17.3
Chert											
No.	7	6	0	7	0	1	0	0	0	0	21
Row %	33.3	28.6		33.3		4.8					
Column %	41.2	31.6		17.1		11.1					19.1
Total											
No.	17	19	10	41	4	9	3	4	1	2	110
Row %	15.5	17.3	9.1	37.3	3.6	8.2	2.7	3.6	0.9	1.8	

Table 3.7. Cross-Tabulation of Raw Material Category and Presence of Cortex

Raw material	Phase I C	NC	T	Phase II C	NC	T	Phase III C	NC	T	Phase IV C	NC	T	Phase V C	NC	T	Total
Obsidian																
No.	0	0	0	0	0	0	0	0	0	0	12	12	0	0	0	12
Row %																
Column											2.3	2.2				0.2
Quartz																
No.	12	70	82	1	101	102	2	131	133	1	23	24	2	25	27	368
Row %	14.6	85.3		1.0	99		2.2	97.7		4.1	95.8		7.4	92.5		
Column %	49.9	42.6	39.8	1.2	8.2	7.7	2.3	4.7	4.6	4.7	4.5	4.4	8.3	7.9	7.9	7.0
Honey flint																
No.	6	41	47	60	905	965	27	1538	1565	9	154	163	4	63	67	2807
Row %	12.7	87.2		6.2	93.7		1.4	98.5		5.5	94.4		5.9	94.0		
Column %	21.4	18.9	22.8	75.0	73.2	73.3	31.8	54.8	54.1	42.8	30.0	30.5	16.6	19.9	19.7	53.1
Chalcedony																
No.	9	40	49	11	111	122	40	446	486	10	137	147	9	84	93	897
Row %	18.3	81.6		15.4	84.5		8.2	91.7		6.8	93.1		9.6	90.3		
Column %	32.1	24.3	23.8	13.7	9.0	9.2	47.1	15.9	16.8	47.6	26.7	27.5	37.5	26.6	27.4	17.0
Pebble flint																
No.	0	9	9	4	32	36	4	59	63	1	18	19	1	13	14	141
Row %				11.1	88.8		6.1	93.8		5.2	94.7		7.1	92.8		
Column %		5.4	4.4	5.0	2.6	2.7	4.7	2.1	2.2	4.7	3.5	3.6	4.2	4.1	4.4	2.7
Burned flint																
No.	0	4	4	0	39	39	3	367	370	0	88	88	5	76	81	582
Row %													4.8	95.1		
Column %		2.2	1.9		3.1	2.9	3.5	13.1	12.8		17.2	16.5	20.8	24.1	23.8	11.0
Chert																
No.	1	14	15	4	48	52	9	268	277	0	81	81	3	55	58	483
Row %	6.6	93.3		7.6	92.3		3.2	96.7					5.1	94.8		
Column %	3.5	8.5	7.3	5.0	3.9	3.9	10.6	9.5	9.6		15.8	15.2	12.5	17.4	17.1	9.1
Total																
No.	28	178	206	80	1236	1316	85	2809	2894	21	513	534	24	316	340	5290
Row %	13.8	86.1	3.9	6.3	93.6	24.9	2.9	97.0	54.7	4.0	95.9	10.1	7.1	92.9	6.4	

C: Cortex   NC: No Cortex   T: Total

Table 3.8. Cross-Tabulation of Blank Category and Its Functional Identification

Category   Function

	Cut				Scrape						C/S			
Phase I	S	M	H	Sickle	S	M	H	Borer	Groove	Projectile point	S	M	H	Total
Blade														
No.	2	1	1	8	2	2	4	1	0	0	0	0	0	21
Row %	9.5	4.8	4.8	38.1	9.5	19.0	4.8							
Column %	22.2	20.0	50.0	61.5	33.3									47.7
Broken blade														
No.	3	4	0	4	3	0	0	0	0	0	0	1	0	15
Row %	20.0	26.7		26.7	20.0							6.7		
Column %	33.3	80.0		30.8	50.0									34.1
Flake														
No.	0	0	1	1	1	0	0	0	1	0	0	0	0	4
Row %			25.0	25.0	25.0				25.0					
Column %			50.0	7.6	16.6									9.1
Microblade														
No.	4	0	0	0	0	0	0	0	0	0	0	0	0	4
Row %	44.4													9.1
Total														
No.	9	5	2	13	6	2	4	1	1	0	0	1	0	44
Row %	20.5	11.4	4.5	29.5	13.6	4.5	9.1	2.3	2.3			2.3		
Phase II														
Blade														
No.	20(18)	18(14)	2	43(47)	8	11(13)	7	3	2	0	0	1	0	115
Row %	17.4	15.6	1.7	37.4	6.9	9.5	6.0	2.6	1.7			0.8		
Column %	64.5	90.0	40.0	68.2	44.4	50.0	87.5	37.5						64.6
Broken blade														
No.	4	1	2	17	0	7	0	1	0	0	0	0	0	32
Row %	12.5	3.1	6.2	53.1		21.9		3.1						
Column %	12.9	5.0	40.0	26.9		31.8		12.5						17.9
Flake														
No.	2	0	0	3	8	4	1	0	0	0	0	0	0	18
Row %	11.1			16.7	44.4	22.2	5.6							
Column %	6.4			4.8	44.4	18.1	12.5							10.1
Microblade														
No.	5	1	1	0	2	0	0	4	0	0	0	0	0	13
Row %	38.5	7.7	7.7		15.4			30.8						
Column %	16.1	5.0	20.0		11.1			50.0						7.3
Total														
No.	31(29)	20(16)	5	63(67)	18	22(24)	8	8	2	0	0	1	0	178
Row %	17.7	9.1	2.8	35.4	10.3	13.7	4.6	4.6	1.1			0.6		
Phase III														
Blade														
No.	29(30)	22(21)	9	70(69)	13(12)	13	10	4	0	0	2	9	7	188
Row %	15.5	11.8	4.8	37.4	7	7	5.3	2.1			1.1	4.3	3.7	
Column %	53.7	61.1	56.2	56.0	52.0	38.2	71.4	20.0			66.6	69.2	77.7	53.2
Broken blade														
No.	17(18)	11	7	52	5	12(11)	2	3	1	0	1	3	2	116
Row %	15.5	9.5	6.0	44.0	4.3	9.5	1.7	2.6	1.7		0.9	2.6	1.7	
Column %	31.5	30.5	43.7	40.8	20.0	35.2	14.3	5.0	33.3		33.3	33.3	22.2	32.8
Flake														
No.	5	3	0	3	5	8	2	1	1	0	0	1	0	29
Row %	17.2	10.3		10.3	17.2	27.6	6.9	3.4	3.4			3.4		
Column %	9.1	8.3		2.4	20.0	23.5	14.3	5.0	33.3			7.6		8.2

Continued on next page

Table 3.8. Cross-Tabulation of Blank Category and Its Functional Identification, cont.

Category							Function							
	Cut			Scrape							C/S			
Phase III	S	M	H	Sickle	S	M	H	Borer	Groove	Projectile point	S	M	H	Total
Microblade														
No.	3	0	0	1	2	1	0	12	1	0	0	0	0	20
Row %	15.0			5.0	10.0	5.0		60.0	5.0					
Column %	5.5			0.8	8.0	2.9		60.0	33.3					5.7
Total														
No.	54 (56)	36 (35)	16	126 (125)	25 (26)	34 (33)	14	20	3	0	3	13	9	353
Row %	15.2	10.1	4.5	35.7	7.0	9.6	3.9	5.6	0.8		0.8	3.9	2.5	
Phase IV														
Blade														
No.	6	0	4	25	5	3	0	1	0	2	0	1	1	48
Row %	12.5		8.3	52.1	10.4	6.2		2.1		4.2		2.1	2.1	
Column %	46.1		80.0	67.5	35.7	42.8		20.0		50.0				50.0
Broken blade														
No.	4	4	1	10	4	4	1	1	0	0	0	0	0	29
Row %	13.8	13.8	3.4	34.5	13.8	13.8	3.4	3.4						
Column %	30.7		20.0	27.0	28.5	57.1	25.0	20.0						30.2
Flake														
No.	2	0	0	1	5	0	2	0	1	2	0	0	0	13
Row %	15.4			7.7	38.5		15.4		7.7	15.4				
Column %	15.3			2.7	35.7		50.0			50.0				13.5
Microblade														
No.	1	0	0	1	0	0	1	3	0	0	0	0	0	6
Row %	16.7			16.7			16.7	50.0						
Column %	7.7			2.7			25.0	60.0						6.2
Total														
No.	13	4	5	37	14	7	4	5	1	4	0		1	96
Row %	13.3	4.1	5.1	37.8	14.3	7.1	4.1	7.1	1.0	4.1		1.0	1.0	
Phase V														
Blade														
No.	8	7	5(4)	21(22)	3	2	1	1	0	1	0	2	1	52
Row %	15.4	13.5	9.6	40.4	5.8	3.8	1.9	1.9		1.9		3.8	1.9	
Column %	53.3	63.6		60.0	75.0	40.0				50.0		66.6		61.9
Broken blade														
No.	7	1	0	12	0	3	0	0	1	0	0	1	0	25
Row %	28.0	4.0		48.0		12.0			4.0			4.0		
Column %	46.6	9.0		34.2		60.0						33.3		29.8
Flake														
No.	0	3	0	1	1	0	0	0	0	0	0	0	0	5
Row %		60.0		20.0	20.0									
Column %		27.3		2.9	25.0									6.0
Microblade														
No.	0	0	0	1	0	0	0	0	0	1	0	0	0	2
Row %				50.0						50.0				
Column %				2.9						50.0				2.4
Total														
No.	15	11	5(4)	35(36)	4	5	1	1	1	2	0	3	1	84
Row %	17.9	13.1	5.9	41.7	4.7	6.0	1.2	1.2	1.2	2.4		3.6	1.2	

S: Soft   M: Medium   H: Hard
C/S: Refers to multiple tools used for cutting and scraping the same material using different blade edges.
Figures in parentheses refer to the multiple tools used with the same action on different materials; they are counted only once in the totals.

Table 3.9. Macromorphological Classification of Blanks (following Pâunescu)

	Retouched blade	Sickle blade	Fine denticulate	Truncated blade	Borer/ piercer	Fiera point	Geo-metric	End scraper	Double end scraper	Arrow point	Total typed tools
Phase I											
No.	5	6	0	9	1	0	0	12	0	0	33
Row %	15.2	18.2		27.3	3			36.4			63.5
Column %	10.6	3.1		7.9	6.3			7.1			5.7
Phase II											
No.	16	55	0	30	4	4	0	37	2	0	148
Row %	10.8	37.2		20.3	2.7	2.7		25.0	1.4		48.4
Column %	34.0	28.6		26.3	25.0	23.5		21.9	28.6		25.5
Phase III											
No.	14	98	0	57	8	9	0	81	4	0	271
Row %	5.2	36.2		21.0	2.9	3.3		29.9	1.5		55.1
Column %	29.8	51.0		50.0	52.9		47.9	57.1			46.7
Phase IV											
No.	10	22	0	8	2	4	1	18	1	3	69
Row %	14.5	31.9		11.6	2.9	5.8	1.4	26.1	1.4	4.3	55.7
Column %	21.3	11.5		7.0	12.5	23.5	50.0	10.7	14.3		11.9
Phase V											
No.	2	11	13	10	1	0	1	21	0	0	59
Row %	3.4	18.6	22.0	16.9	1.7		1.7	35.6			58.4
Column %	4.3	5.7		8.8	6.3		50.0	12.4			10.2
Total											
No.	47	192	13	114	16	17	2	169	7	3	580
Row %	8.1	33.1	2.2	19.7	2.8	2.9	0.3	29.1	1.2	0.5	54.0

Table 3.10. Cross-Tabulation of Bulbar End Truncation and Functional Identification of Blanks

Bulbar end		Function												
		Cut				Scrape						C/S		
Phase I	S	M	H	Sickle	S	M	H	Borer	Groove	Projectile point	S	M	H	Total
Complete	4	2	1	6	0	0	1	0	1	0	0	0	0	15
Truncated	3	0	0	5	4	1	2	1	0	0	0	0	0	16
Broken	2	3	1	2	2	1	1	0	0	0	0	1	0	13
Total	9	5	2	13	6	2	4	1	1	0	0	1	0	44
Phase II														
Complete	11(9)	7(6)	1	21(23)	7	6(7)	2	1	0	0	0	1	0	58
Truncated	6	6(4)	1	13(15)	7	5	5	4	0	0	0	0	0	47
Broken	14	7	3	29	4	11	1	3	1	0	0	0	0	73
Total	31(29)	20(17)	5	63(67)	18	22(23)	8	8	2	0	0	1	0	178
Phase III														
Complete	19	9(8)	4	32	9	7	3	2	0	0	0	4	4	92
Truncated	11	8	2	34	7	8	5	10	2	0	1	3	1	92
Broken	24(26)	19	10	59(58)	9(10)	18	6	8	1	0	2	6(5)	4	168
Total	54(56)	36(35)	161	26(125)	25(26)	33	14	20	3	0	3	13(12)	9	352

Continued on next page

Table 3.10. Cross-Tabulation of Bulbar End Truncation and Functional Identification of Blanks, cont.

Bulbar end														
	Cut				Scrape						C/S			
Phase IV	S	M	H	Sickle	S	M	H	Borer	Groove	Projectile point	S	M	H	Total
Complete	6	1	0	16	6	1	1	2	0	2	0	0	0	35
Truncated	2	1	4	3	1	3	3	2	0	2	0	1	1	23
Broken	5	2	1	18	7	3	0	1	1					38
Total	13	4	5	37	14	7	4	5	1	4	0	1	1	96
Phase V														
Complete	2	4	1	4	0	1	1	0	0	2	0	0	0	15
Truncated	6	3	2	14	2	0	0	1						28
Broken	7	4	2(1)	17(18)	2	4	0	0	1	0	0	3	1	41
Total	15	11	5(4)	35(36)	4	5	1	1	1	2	0	3	1	84

S: Soft   M: Medium   H: Hard

C/S: Refers to multiple tools used for cutting and scraping the same material using different blade edges.

Figures in parentheses refer to the multiple tools used with the same action on different materials; they are counted only once in the totals.

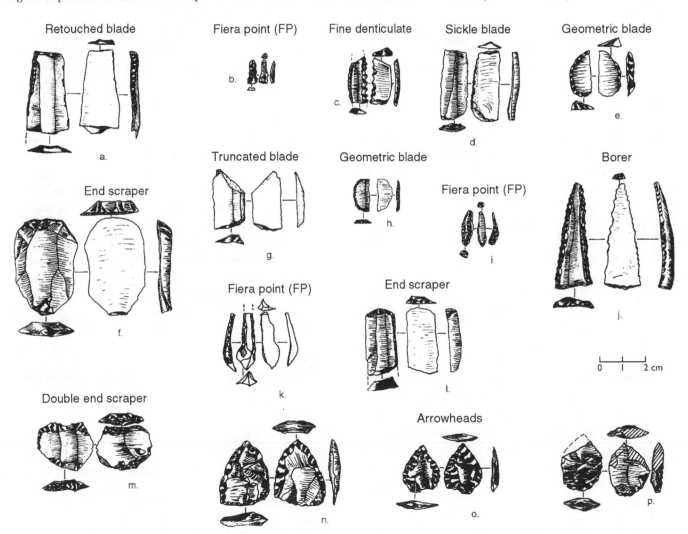

Figure 3.8. Examples of macromorphological types; phase I (a, j); phase II (b, d, e, g, k); phase III (f, h, i, l, m); phase IV (n–p). (a) ZA 63:6; (b) 52:44; (c) SF 2028, ROc 14; (d) ZB 128:1; (e) ZA 57; (f) ZA 42:216; (g) ZA 52:17; (h) ZB 116:2; (I) ZA 119:5; (j) ZA 63:5; (k) ZA 52:35; (l) ZA 44:35; (m) ZA 119:2; (n) SF 3257, ZHe 24; (o) ZA 107:6; (p) SF 2709, ZE 56.

Identification of the contacted (that is, worked) material was more doubtful. Rather than attempt to identify the actual contacted material, which would have necessitated a more time-consuming set of observations of gloss and abrasion under a high-power microscope (Keeley 1980), the hypothesized contacted materials were grouped according to classes of varying resistance: less resistant (meat, skin, leaves, and the like), medium resistant (wood), and more resistant (such as bone and antler). In addition, the high gloss recognized on a number of blades has long been interpreted more precisely as evidence of contact with organic materials containing a high degree of silica—such as grasses—including domestic grain crops and reeds (Anderson-Gerfaud 1982; Perlès and Vaughan 1983; Semenov 1964).

For convenience, the blanks of the Sitagroi assemblage were divided into four "edges": right, left, distal, and proximal. In subsequent analyses (for example, the Selevac and Divostin assemblages), the perimeter and its microwear were more accurately plotted and recorded by using polar-coordinate fields (Tringham 1988; Voytek 1990). In the analysis of the Sitagroi assemblage, utilization of the tool was examined by taking, as the basic unit of analysis, the blank itself and then each of its four edges, enabling a more thorough study of the multiple function of certain blanks and of the relationship of the utilized part of the perimeter with that part modified by retouch.

Utilization-Wastage Ratio

The relative wastage of blanks in the different raw material categories was discussed above. In general, a high proportion of unused blanks is characteristic of the late Neolithic and Chalcolithic assemblages of southeast Europe, including phases II and III at Sitagroi. As a corollary, a high proportion of used blanks is characteristic on the one hand of the early and middle Neolithic assemblages of southeast Europe (including, to a certain extent, Sitagroi phase I) and, on the other hand, the early Bronze Age assemblages of southeast Europe, including Sitagroi V.

The obvious interpretation of a high proportion of utilized to unutilized blanks is that of a con-

sumption strategy that would maximize, or at least optimize, the available raw materials. One would thus expect an increased wastefulness of resources as the outcrop flint became more available in large quantities in the late Neolithic/Chalcolithic periods. Part of the manifestation of "wastefulness" in this period (Sitagroi II through IV) is also bound up with the strategy of greater selectivity of blanks of particular sizes for specific tasks and the rejection of large numbers of flakes that did not conform to these size or shape requirements, or to both.

There is an interesting change through time observable in the attitude toward very thick or very thin blanks (see figure 3.2). In phases III and IV, these are regarded as viable potential tools. In phases II and V, there is a complete rejection of all blanks below 1 mm and above 6 mm in thickness for tool production. In fact, it is likely that the large number of rejected microblades (generally below 1 mm thick) in phase II has somewhat exaggerated the picture of outrageous wastefulness in this phase. The real picture is probably much closer to that of phase III.

If the basic unit of analysis is taken to each edge of a tool, much less extreme change is noticed through time from phases I–III (table 3.13). In this way, it is possible to observe changes in the frequency with which a blank is used on more than one edge (it is irrelevant at this point whether or not it is for the same purpose). Nevertheless during phases I–III, at least one-third of the blanks were used on more than one edge. In phase V, however, the number of blanks used on more than one edge decreased significantly to less than one-fourth (see table 3.11).

Reconstructing the strategy of consumption of a resource is more complicated than it may initially seem. The lack of wastage of whole blanks in phase V may be interpreted as a strategy to conserve dwindling supplies of high-quality imported honey-brown flint, and may be associated with a general decrease in the use of cryptocrystalline rocks as raw materials for edge tools. On the other hand, an examination of the utilization of the edges of the blanks themselves reveals a relatively "wasteful" strategy of using only a limited part of the blank's perimeter. This, however, is most probably explained by a change in the technique of hafting in phase V and in the increasingly specialized nature of the stone tools themselves (as is demonstrated below).

Identification of Utilization

The identification of the contacted material, the dynamics of that contact, and the subsequent inferences made as to the nature of the tasks the tools performed are of limited value in evaluating the economic importance of the tasks themselves. For example, it is difficult even with the microwear information to evaluate the importance or nature of harvesting with sickles without precise information concerning the spatial context of the tools. Identifying tool utilization is of much greater significance in understanding the variability in treatment of flaked stone tools from the point of view of, for example, selectivity of certain raw materials or dimensions or shapes for particular tasks, maintenance of the tools, and so on.

One of the most striking features of the flaked stone tool assemblage is the relative uniformity of tool utilization through time. This observation holds true whether the unit of analysis is the blank or the edge. In all phases, but especially phase V, tools (hereafter referred to as "sickle blades") identified as having been used for cutting silica-rich plants constitute by far the most numerous category, composing consistently more than one-third of the utilized blanks (see tables 3.6, 3.8, 3.9). Tools used on less resistant materials compose 25% of the utilized blanks, those used on materials of medium resistance compose 20%, and those used on materials of greater resistance compose only 8% of the utilized blanks. In addition, more blades were used for cutting than for scraping, or used as borers and projectiles. The latter constitute the rarest category, occurring only in phase IV.

Before the significance of these figures and their relative consistency throughout the occupation of Sitagroi can be considered, various factors must be examined. Most important is how long a blade was used in its particular task; second, how quickly an edge might be blunted while being used in a specific task; third, what attempts, if any, were made to pro-

long the tool's use-life; and, finally, where the tool was used and where it was discarded.

Selectivity and Standardization

Selection of different flakes and blades for particular tasks on the basis of their raw material properties or dimensions is as important a criterion of cultural variability as the modification of their shape and size by retouch.

The conclusions reached at the beginning of this report regarding the popularity of the different cryptocrystalline rocks through time at Sitagroi can be considerably enriched by the addition of microwear information on utilization. The overall importance of the honey-brown flint in phases II and III is associated with a complete absence of selectivity in the utilization of this material with a view to tasks. Honey-brown flint, along with the other cryptocrystalline rocks in phase III, is used for all tasks (see table 3.6). This is in contrast to phase IV, in which honey-brown flint is used for a more limited set of tasks, even though in phase IV honey-brown flint is still a plentiful raw material. In addition, in phases IV and V, greater selectivity is manifest in the choice of chalcedony predominantly for tasks involving work with more resistant materials, in the virtually complete rejection of quartz and pebble flints as raw materials for tools, and in the limited use of cherts for sickle blades.

A characteristic feature of the lithic assemblage throughout all phases is the importance of imported high-quality honey-brown flint. Until phase IV, it was practically the sole material used for edges in contact with more resistant materials, and throughout it was used exclusively in the manufacture of composite cutting-and-scraping tools.

In contrast to blades used on more resistant materials, which were made from fewer raw materials, sickle inserts and edges for use on less resistant materials were made from all categories of raw materials. Therefore, there is a discernible difference in the degree of selectivity of raw materials for particular tasks—for example, between phases II and III when little selectivity is discernible, and phases IV and V when raw materials are used more selectively.

Table 3.11. Cross-Tabulation of Raw Material Category, Functional Identification, and Multiple Utilization of Blanks

Raw material utilization					Function						
	Cut				Scrape						
Phase I	S	M	H	Sickle	S	M	H	Borer	Groove	Projectile point	Total
Obsidian											
Single	0	0	0	0	0	0	1	0	0	0	1
Quartz											
Single	2	0	0	0	2	0	0	0	0	0	4
Double	1	0	0	0	0	0	0	0	0	0	1
Honey flint											
Single	2	0	0	3	3	1	1	0	0	0	10
Double	1	0	1	0	0	0	3	1	0	0	6
Diff. Mat	0	1	0	0	1	0	0	0	0	0	2
Chalcedony											
Single	2	0	0	4	1	0	0	0	1	0	8
Double	0	2	0	3	0	0	0	0	0	0	5
Pebble flint											
Double	0	1	0	0	0	0	0	0	0	0	1
Burned flint											
Single	0	0	0	1	0	0	0	0	0	0	1
Chert											
Single	0	1	0	2	0	0	0	0	0	0	3
Double	1	1	1								
Total	9	6(5)	2	13	7	1(3)	5	1	1	0	45
Phase II											
Quartz											
Single	3	0	0	2	0	0	0	0	1	0	6
Diff. Act	0	1	0	1	0	0	0	0	0	0	2
Honey flint											
Single	10	6	4	29	11	8	3	6	1	0	78
Double	9	2	1	12	2	5	2	2	0	0	35
Diff. Act	1	2	0	3	0	0	0	0	0	0	6
Diff. Mat	0	1	0	0	0	1	0	0	0	0	2
Chalcedony											
Single	2	3	0	4	2	5	0	0	0	0	16
Double	1	1	0	2	0	0	0	0	0	0	4
Pebble flint											
Single	0	1	0	3	2	1	0	0	0	0	7
Double				1							1
Diff. Act	1	0	0	1	0	0	0	0	0	0	1
Burned flint											
Single	1	0	0	1	0	0	1	0	0	0	3
Double	0	1	0	1	0	1	0	0	0	0	3
Chert											
Single	0	0	0	3	1	3	2	0	0	0	9
Double	3	2	0	4	0	0	0	0	0	0	9
Diff. Act/Mat	0	0	1	0	1	0	0	0	0	1	3
Total	31(29)	20(16)	6	67	19	24(25)	8	8	2	1	186
Phase III											
Quartz											
Single	3	0	0	2	3	0	0	2	0	0	10
Honey flint											
Single	20	10	5	48	12	19	6	2	3	0	125
Double	11	12	3	12	3	4	4	7	1	0	57
Diff. Mat	(2)	11	9	0	2	(11)	(9)	0	0	0	22
Same Act	(1)	1	0	0	(1)	1	0	0	0	0	2
Diff. Act/Mat	(1)	(1)	0	0	1	0	0	0	0	0	1

Continued on next page

Table 3.11. Cross-Tabulation of Raw Material Category, Functional Identification, and Multiple Utilization of Blanks, cont.

Phase III	Cut S	M	H	Sickle	Scrape S	M	H	Borer	Groove	Projectile point	Total
Chalcedony											
Single	11	2	3	17	1	5	1	3	0	0	43
Double	2	5	0	11	1	0	0	2	0	0	21
Diff. Mat	(1)	0	0	0	1	0	0	0	0	0	1
Diff. Act	(1)	(0)	1	0	0	0	0	0	0	1	2
Pebble flint											
Single	1	0	0	1	0	0	0	2	0	0	4
Double	1	0	0	0	0	0	0	0	0	0	1
Burned flint											
Single	1	2	0	11	1	1	1	1	0	0	18
Double	0	1	0	1	0	0	0	0	0	0	2
Chert											
Single	2	2	2	15	2	4	2	0	0	0	29
Double	2	1	3	7	1	0	0	1	0	0	15
Diff. Mat	0	2	0	0	0	(2)	0	0	0	0	2
Total	54(59)	49(36)	16	125	28(25)	34(46)	14(23)	20	4	1	355
Phase IV											
Obsidian											
Single	0	0	0	0	0	0	0	0	0	1	1
Honey flint											
Single	4	3	1	8	8	5	0	0	1	0	30
Double	1	0	2	6	0	0	0	1	0	0	10
Diff. Mat	0	1	1	0	0	(1)	(1)	0	0	0	2
Chalcedony											
Single	4	0	0	5	3	0	3	2	0	0	17
Double	0	1	0	7	0	1	0	2	0	3	14
Burned flint											
Single	0	0	0	3	1	0	1	0	0	0	5
Double	0	0	1	1	0	1	0	0	0	0	3
Chert											
Single	2	0	0	6	0	0	0	0	0	0	8
Double	2	0	1	1	2	0	0	0	0	0	6
Total	13	5(4)	6(5)	37	14	7(8)	4(5)	5	1	4	96
Phase V											
Honey flint											
Single	3	2	0	3	3	2	0	0	0	2	15
Double	0	3	1	2	0	1					7
Diff. Mat	0	1	0	0	0	(1)	0	0	0	0	1
Chert											
Double	5	0	1	7	1	1	1	0	1	0	17
Diff. Mat	1	0	2	2	0	0	0	1	0	0	6
Diff. Act	0	1	0	0	0	(1)	0	0	0	0	1
Pebble flint											
Single	0	1	0	1	0	0	0	0	0	0	2
Burned flint											
Single	0	1	0	12	0	1	0	0	0	0	14
Double	0	0	0	1	0	0	0	0	0	0	1
Diff. Mat	0	0	1	0	0	0	(1)	0	0	0	1
Chert											
Single	5	4	0	7	0	0	0	0	0	0	16
Double	1	0	0	0	0	0	0	0	0	0	1
Diff. Mat	0	1	0	0	0	(1)	0	0	0	0	1
Total	15	14(11)	6(4)	35(36)	4	5(8)	1(2)	1	1	2	84

S: Soft; M: Medium; H: Hard
Diff. Mat: Tool used on different edges for different action on same material.
Diff. Act: Tools used on different edges for the same action on different materials.
Diff. Act/Mat: Tool used on different edges for different actions on different materials.
Single: Tool used on one edge only; Double: Tool used on two or more edges for the same action on the same material.
Figures in parentheses refer to the multiple tools used with the same action on different materials; they are counted only once in the totals.

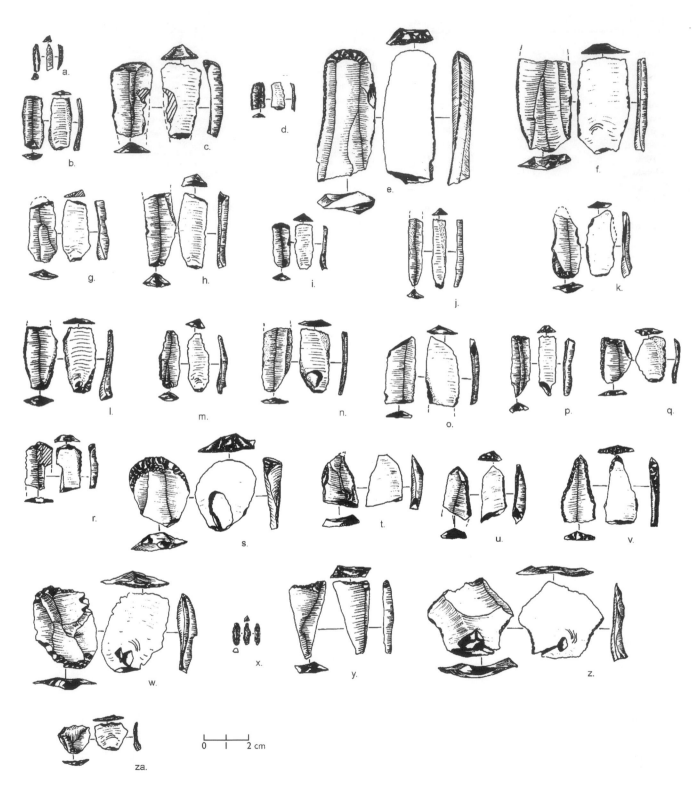

Figure 3.9. Examples of phase III lithic assemblage, all from ZA 39–48. (a) ZA 47:28; (b) ZA 47:7; (c) ZA 44:41; (d) ZA 48:6; (e) ZA 39:208; (f) ZA 41:214; (g) ZA 42:33; (h) ZA 47:50; (i) ZA 44:12; (j) ZA 44:11; (k) ZA 47:48; (l) ZA 47:38; (m) ZA 46:4; (n) ZA 46:3; (o) ZA 45:2; (p) ZA 44:13; (q) ZA 44:29; (r) ZA 42:34; (s) ZA 48:8; (t) ZA 47:3; (u) ZA 47:20; (v) ZA 47:43; (w) ZA 43:223; (x) ZA 44:18; (y) ZA 45:1; (z) ZA 47:19; (za) ZA 42:22.

With regard to selectivity from the point of view of the blank size thought to be appropriate for particular tasks, there is an observable increase in this phenomenon from phase II to phase III. In phase III, there is a remarkable coincidence of clusters of different functional categories and length/width clusters (see figure 3.5). Taking into consideration the higher frequency of retouch to control shape and dimensions in phase III, it seems likely that this coincidence was achieved by selecting the right size of blanks, aided by the production of blanks that were deliberately shaped to the right size by retouch (table 3.12). In phase II, on the other hand, the "correct" size was achieved in most cases by only selecting the blank, with very little modification of the size by retouch. The resulting coincidence of functional category and dimensional cluster in phase II is less spectacular than in phase III, but certainly greater than in phase I or IV.

In every phase but phase I, long, thin blades were used for cutting and short, broad blades for scraping. This is logical in terms of the optimal morphological efficiency of blades and flakes for particular tasks, as is discussed in the following section of this chapter. Tools used for scraping on their lateral edges are consistently narrower than those used for scraping on their distal and proximal edges, but they are nevertheless always shorter than those used for cutting. In phase III, among the scrapers used on their distal ends, two clusters are visible (see figure 3.5); one is composed of short, narrow tools, and the other of long, wide tools.

Various observations may be made about the selectivity of dimensions of blanks appropriate for optimal efficiency in working different materials. In general, the Sitagroi assemblage follows the logic of these expectations. Thus narrower, longer, thinner blanks tend to be used on less resistant materials, whereas shorter, wider, thicker blanks were used on more resistant materials. Some of the latter blades, especially in phase III, are almost as wide as they are long.

In contrast to their variation from the point of view of raw material, it is interesting to note that sickle blades display the greatest amount of consistency with regard to dimensions. Sickle blades rarely stray from the classic 2:1 blade proportions (see figure 3.5). As discussed below, this is very likely the result of sickle blades being fitted into slots of standard dimensions in hafts, unlike the majority of other flaked stone tools which were probably hand held. The only other tools with equally standardized dimensions are borers and scrapers used on more resistant materials, tasks also likely to require the use of a handle.

As mentioned above, four methods were used to standardize and control the dimensions of the blanks: truncation of the bulbar end, removal of flakes by retouch at the distal and proximal margins, careful preparation of the preform before striking the blank from the core, and strict selection among blanks for those that conformed to the required dimensions. On the basis of the ratio of utilized to nonutilized blanks and the dimensions of the different functional categories, a change in the strategy of controlling the size of blanks is observable. In phase II, control was carried out by selecting the right blank from among those struck relatively at random from the core, whereas in phase III, size was further controlled by bulb truncation and retouch (see tables 3.4, 3.10).

Bulb truncation and retouch were more important in the control of the size of tools used on more resistant materials, especially scrapers (see tables 3.10, 3.12). Much of this modification was not only to control the length of the tool, but also to enable the distal or proximal end to be used as a working edge. Conversely, those blanks used on less resistant materials exhibited the largest size range and were the least modified by retouch or bulb truncation. In phase V, however, when these latter tools have a more restricted size range, they were also more frequently subject to bulb truncation.

On the other hand, those tools with the narrowest dimensional range, the sickle blades, show a lower-than-average incidence of both bulb truncation and retouch. Their size control must have been by other means; for example, careful preparation before striking or selecting the appropriate blank. This situation is again different in phase V, when the bulbar end of sickle blades was frequently truncated.

Table 3.12. Cross-Tabulation of Modification by Retouch and Functional Identification of Blanks

Retouch modification	Function										
Phase I	Cut				Scrape					Projectile	
	S	M	H	Sickle	S	M	H	Borer	Groove	point	Total
Present											
No.	1	2	2	0	2	1	5	2	0	0	15
Row %	6.7	13.3	13.3		13.3	6.7	33.3	13.3			
Column %	8.3	20.0	50.0		33.3	33.3	62.5				24.2
Absent											
No.	11	8	2	16	4	2	3	0	1	0	47
Row %	23.4	17.0	4.3	34.0	8.5	4.3	6.4		2.1		
Column %	91.7	80.0	50.0		66.7	37.5					75.8
Total											
No.	12	10	4	16	6	3	8	2	1	0	62
Row %	19.3	16.1	6.5	25.8	9.7	4.8	12.9	3.2	1.6		
Phase II											
Present											
No.	0	7	3	5	10	20	7	5	0	0	57
Row %		12.3	5.3	8.8	17.5	35.1	12.3	8.8			
Column %		25.9	50.0	6.5	50.0	62.5	70.0	50.0			23.8
Absent											
No.	44	20	3	83	10	12	3	5	2	0	182
Row %	21.0	13.0	2.0	46.8	6.5	7.8	2.0	2.7	1.1		
Column %	24.1	74.1	50.0	53.9	50.0	37.5	30.0	50.0			76.1
Total											
No.	44	27	6	88	20	32	10	10	2	0	239
Row %	18.4	11.3	2.5	36.8	8.4	13.4	4.2	4.2	0.8		
Phase III											
Present											
No.	5	25	19	25	20	30	19	25	2	0	170
Row %	2.9	14.7	11.2	14.7	11.8	17.6	11.2	14.7	1.2		
Column %	6.7	34.7	57.6	15.8	58.8	58.8	67.9	50.0	50.0		33.7
Absent											
No.	70	47	14	133	14	21	9	25	2	0	335
Row %	20.9	14.0	4.2	39.7	4.2	6.3	2.7	7.5	0.6		
Column %	93.3	65.3	42.4	84.2	41.2	41.2	32.1	50.0	50.0		66.3
Total											
No.	75	72	33	158	34	51	28	50	4	0	505
Row %	14.9	14.3	6.5	31.3	6.7	10.1	5.5	9.9	0.8		
Phase IV											
Present											
No.	3	2	2	6	7	6	3	8	0	6	43
Row %	7.0	4.7	4.7	13.9	16.2	13.9	7.0	18.6		18.9	
Column %	18.8	28.6	18.2	11.5	41.2	60.0	60.0	57.1		60	30.1
Absent											
No.	13	5	9	46	10	4	2	6	1	4	100
Row %	3.0	5.0	9.0	46	10.0	4.0	2.0	6.6	1.0	4.0	
Column %	1.2	71.4	81.8	88.5	58.8	40.0	40.0	42.9	10.0	40.0	69.9
Total											
No.	16	7	11	52	17	10	5	14	1	10	143
Row %	11.2	4.9	7.7	36.4	11.9	7	3.5	9.8	0.7	7.0	

Continued on next page

Table 3.12. Cross-Tabulation of Modification by Retouch and Functional Identification of Blanks, cont.

Retouch modification	Function										
	Cut				Scrape					Projectile	
	S	M	H	Sickle	S	M	H	Borer	Groove	point	Total
Phase V											
Present											
No.	1	5	5	4	2	5	3	2	1	1	29
Row %	3.4	17.3	17.3	13.8	6.9	17.3	10.3	6.9	3.4	3.4	
Column %	5.9	26.3	50.0	9.8	50.0	55.6		50.0		50.0	26.3
Absent											
No.	16	14	5	37	2	4	0	2	0	1	81
Row %	19.7	17.2	5.0	45.6	2.5	5.0		2.5		1.3	
Column %	94.1	73.7	50.0	90.2	50.0	44.4		50.0		50.0	736
Total											
No.	17	19	10	41	4	9	3	4	1	2	110
Row %	15.5	17.3	9.1	37.3	3.6	8.2	2.7	3.6	0.9	1.8	

S: Soft   M: Medium   H: Hard

Note: Modification of the edge by retouch before utilization is identified by the non-convergence of used edge and retouched edge of lateral edges, and by retouch of the distal and proximal edges (used and unused) of the tool.

Prolonging Use-life

The two main strategies to prolong and maximize the use-life of a tool were multiple utilization and resharpening. Multiple utilization refers to the utilization of the perimeter of a blank either sequentially or synchronously for the same or different tasks. As might be expected, there are serious problems in recognizing synchronous and sequential utilization of the perimeter of a blank, even with the aid of microscopic examination (Tringham et al. 1974:192–193).[4]

The majority (60% to 66%) of blanks in all phases were used only on one edge (see table 3.13). Almost all the other blanks were used as double- or triple-edged tools; that is, they were used for the same purpose on different parts of their perimeter. A very few (up to 7%), mostly in phases III and V, were used as composite tools; that is, they were used as a cutting tool on one or both lateral edges, and as a scraper on the same contacted material usually at their distal and (more rarely) their proximal ends (from phase III, see figure 3.11). The remaining minute fraction were used as cutting tools on varying contacted materials on their two lateral margins, exclusively in phases II and III, or for cutting one material and scraping another (exclusively phase II) (table 3.13).

Almost all the double-edged tools are for cutting, although those for cutting more resistant materials were common until phase II. Double-edged sickle blades are, however, relatively rare (but some examples of those were merely reversed and thus exhibit silica gloss on both lateral margins [figures 3.6g, h, p, x, y, za; 3.9 b, n; 3.10f, n, o]). Edges used for scraping less resistant materials in all phases almost always occur as the single used edge of a blank. The tool category that occurs most frequently as a double-edged tool is the borer. Borers, however, never occur in combination with other actions. Thus, there were no tools of the morphological type referred to as "scraper-borers" (Pâunescu 1970).

Composite tools are confined almost exclusively to tools used for working (scraping and cutting) materials of medium and greater resistance, and occur mostly in phase III. These tools were made almost exclusively from honey-brown flint (in phase V they were also made of chalcedony). In addition to being of the best-quality materials, the composite tools were made of above-average-size blanks, were carefully shaped before utilization (unlike most other tools), and were almost all complete when excavated (figure 3.11). It seems that a good deal of time, energy, and care were invested in

Table 3.13. Cross-Tabulation of Multiple Utilization of Blanks and Their Functional Identification

	Function										
Utilization	Cut				Scrape					Projectile	
Phase I	S	M	H	Sickle	S	M	H	Borer	Groove	point	Total
One Edge Only											
No.	6	1	0	10	6	2	1	0	1	0	27
Row %	22.2	3.7		37	22.2	7.4	3.7		3.7		
Column %	66.7	16.7		76.9		66.7	25				61.3
2/More Same Function											
No.	3	4	2	3	0	0	3	1	0	0	16
Row %	18.8	25.0	12.5	18.8			18.8	6.2			
Column %	33.3	66.6		23.1			75.0				36.3
Diff. Mat											
No.	1	0	0	0	(1)	0	0	0	0	0	1
Row %	50.0				50.0						
Column %	16.7				33.3						2.2
Total											
No.	9	6(5)	2	13	6	2(3)	4	1	1	0	44
Row %	20.5	13.6	4.6	29.5	13.6	4.6	9.1	2.3	2.3		
Phase II											
One Edge Only											
No.	16	10	4	42	16	17	6	6	2	0	119
Row %	13.4	8.4	3.4	35.3	13.4	14.3	5	5	1.7		
Column %	51.6	50	80	66.7	88.9	73.9	75				66.8
2/More Same Function											
No.	13	6	1	20	2	6	2	2	0	0	52
Row %	25	11.5	1.9	38.5	3.8	11.5	3.8	3.8			
Column %	41.9	30	20	31.7	11.1	26.1	25	25			29.2
Diff. Act											
No.	2	3	0	(5)	0	0	0	0	0	0	5
Row %	40	60									
Column %	6.5	15									2.8
Diff. Mat											
No.		1(x2)	0	0	0	(1)	0	0	0	0	1
Row %		5									0.5
Diff. Act/ Diff. Mat											
No.	0	0	0	1	0	(1)	0	0	0	0	1
Row %				1.6							0.5
Total											
No.	31(29)	20(16)	5	63(67)	18	23(25)	8	8	2	0	178
Row %	17.5	11.3	2.8	35.6	10.2	13	4.5	4.5	0.6		
Phase III											
One Edge Only											
No.	38	16	10	94	19	29	10	10	2	0	228
Row %	16.7	7	4.4	41.2	8.3	12.7	4.4	4.4	0.9		
Column %	69.7	32	62.5	74.4	77.1	63.4	71.4	50	66.7		63.5
2/More Same Function											
No.	16	19	6	31	5	4	4	10	1	0	96
Row %	16.7	19.8	6.3	32.3	5.2	4.2	4.2	10.4	1		
Column %	27.6	38	37.5	24	18.7	8.7	28.6	50	33.3		26.7
Diff. Act/Diff Mat.											
No.	(2)	1	0	1	(1)	1	0	0	0	0	3
Row %	3.7	4		1.6	4.2	1.8					2.2

Continued on next page

Table 3.13. Cross-Tabulation of Multiple Utilization of Blanks and Their Functional Identification, cont.

Utilization	Function										
	Cut				Scrape					Projectile	
Phase III	S	M	H	Sickle	S	M	H	Borer	Groove	point	Total
Diff. Mat/Diff. Act (1)											
No.	(3)	13	9	0	3	(13)	(9)	0	0	0	25
Row %		52	36								
Column %	5.1	26	36		12.5	26.1	64.3				7
Diff. Mat/ Diff. Act (2)											
No.	0	(1)	0	0	1	0	0	0	0	0	1
Row %					4.2						0.7
Total											
No.	54(59)	49(36)	25(16)	126(125)	28(25)	34(46)	14(23)	20	3	0	353
Row %	15.6	14	7	35.3	7	12.8	3.9	5.6	0.8		

S: Soft   M: Medium   H: Hard

Diff. Act/Diff. Mat: Tool used on different edges for different actions on different materials.

Diff. Act/Diff. Mat (1): Tool used on different edges for different action on same material.

Diff. Mat/Diff. Act (2): Tool used on different edges for the same action on different materials.

Figures in parentheses refer to the multiple tools used with the same action on different materials; they are counted only once in the totals.

the manufacture and curation of these tools, which is very different from the general pattern of expediency observed in the flaked stone tool assemblages in southeast European prehistory (for example, see figure 3.10w).

The second major strategy to prolong a tool's use-life is resharpening dulled edges. Archaeologists analyzing lithic assemblages on the basis of macromorphological criteria alone suggest that the measurement of the angle of the retouched surface to the ventral surface of the flake would indicate the degree of resharpening or "reworking" of a scraper edge (Movius, David, and Bricker 1968:14–15). This deduction has subsequently been found to be accurate, provided one has determined that the retouched edge was utilized (Gould, Koster, and Sontz 1971).

As mentioned in note 1, the occurrence of resharpening defined as refreshing a dulled working edge and assumed to have been accomplished only by retouching (that is, the removal of small flakes from the edge) can be recognized by relating the location of retouch to that of utilization. Examples are clearest when the retouch is surrounded by silica gloss, evidence of earlier use in cutting grain (figure 3.12a, c, e, h, j). There is a spectacular change in the incidence of resharpened edges at Sitagroi, from a negligible count in phases I through III to an impressive increase in phases IV and V. This

increase in a strategy that prolongs the use-life of a tool, therefore, occurs at exactly the time when the availability of honey-brown flint started to decline. However, resharpening in phases IV and V not only occurs on this high-quality imported material, but also is observed most clearly in the sickle blades made from both high- and low-quality materials. In phase III, only 3.2% of the sickle blades were resharpened; in phase IV, 27% were resharpened; by phase V, 56% showed evidence of resharpening (figure 3.12, all phase V; table 3.14). The only other tools that were resharpened were distal scrapers, especially those used on medium and more resistant materials.

If we consider that a relative shortage of high-quality flint contributed to the increasing trend to prolong the use-life of tools toward the end of the occupation, then it is interesting to note that resharpening was virtually absent in phase I, when a shortage of this flint has also been suggested. In this phase, however, the strategy of maximizing the utilization of the available raw materials was to use every part of the perimeter of a blank.

Patterns of Breakage and Discard

This relatively new aspect of lithic analysis offers important information concerning the consumption of resources and site formation (Schiffer 1987). Unfortunately, information on this topic was generally not recorded in any detail in the analysis of the flaked stone assemblage at Sitagroi. It is possible, however, to make general statements that are pertinent to our conclusions.

There is a good correlation, for example, between flakes used only on one edge and their excavation in a broken state, and between flakes used as multiple tools and their excavation in an unbroken state. In phases IV and V, a higher proportion of tools of all categories is found broken, which may be a function of the area of the site being excavated in these phases. In connection with this observation, it should be noted that the projectile heads from phase IV (see figure 3.8n–p) were also complete upon excavation, which presumably reflects accidental discard. It is hardly likely that these tools, which represent considerable labor and skill in the execution of surface retouch, would have been deliberately discarded in a complete state.

The point of breakage is mostly at the bulbar end of the blade or flake, just above the bulb of percussion (looking toward the distal end) (see table 3.10). The distal end was broken off less frequently, and a fracture occurred very rarely down the length of a blade. This is to be expected in view of the mechanical properties of blades, and the fact that their greatest mass lies in the center. It is possible that what has been identified as accidental breakage is, in fact, the deliberate snapping off of the bulbar end. However, this ambiguity can be partially eliminated by observing whether wear traces were formed on the edge before or after the bulb was removed.

In general, little change is observed in the pattern of breakage during the different phases, at least on the basis of the rather superficial examination of this feature. It is unlikely, however, on the basis of other previously explored evidence, that the behavior associated with breakage and discard would remain unchanged during this period when such radical changes were observed in other aspects of the strategies of resource consumption. It is very likely that the calculations available regarding breakage and discard are biased by the fact that much of the phase V material comes from a house area, whereas that from phases II through IV is derived primarily from areas of secondary discard.

MACROMORPHOLOGICAL CLASSIFICATION

Variation in the strategy selected for achieving the final dimensions of a tool for particular tasks is one of the clearest indications of cultural variation. This fact has been recognized implicitly and intuitively in traditional analyses of flaked stone tools. Retouch of a surface or edge of a blank is the strategy in which variability in the end product is most obvious. Variability of location of retouch is, in fact, the main criterion used in the traditional macromorphological classifications of flaked stone tools.

Much of the information derived from microwear examination would support the intuitive conclusions about optimal morphological efficiency of the tools embodied in the traditional classifications. For example, tools requiring a greater mass, such as for scraping more resistant materials, are made on wider and shorter blanks, whereas those for cutting less resistant materials require less mass. Our ideas of optimal efficiency in tool shape for tool function do not, however, always coincide with the prehistoric view. Not all short, wide blanks are used for heavy tasks; not all tools used in heavy tasks are made from short, wide blanks.

Two major problems have to be taken into consideration before statements concerning the correlation between tool dimension and shape and tool function can be used as serious monitors of cultural change. First, it is essential to systematically test by experimentation the optimal efficiency of blade dimensions in different dynamic contact situations. Second, other factors have morphological requirements apart from the mechanics of contact of the tool's edge. For example, it may be hypothesized that the hafting requirements of a tool put stricter demands on its size and shape than did its edge-mechanics requirements.

Much greater problems, however, beset traditional analysts of stone tools. Their aim is to reconstruct cultural (or at least technological) change on the basis of change and variation in the location of retouch in relation to the bulb of percussion; yet this reconstruction is done without any empirical evidence for the location of the utilized and hafted/handled edges of the tools. Without this vital data, it is impossible (1) to know the purpose of the

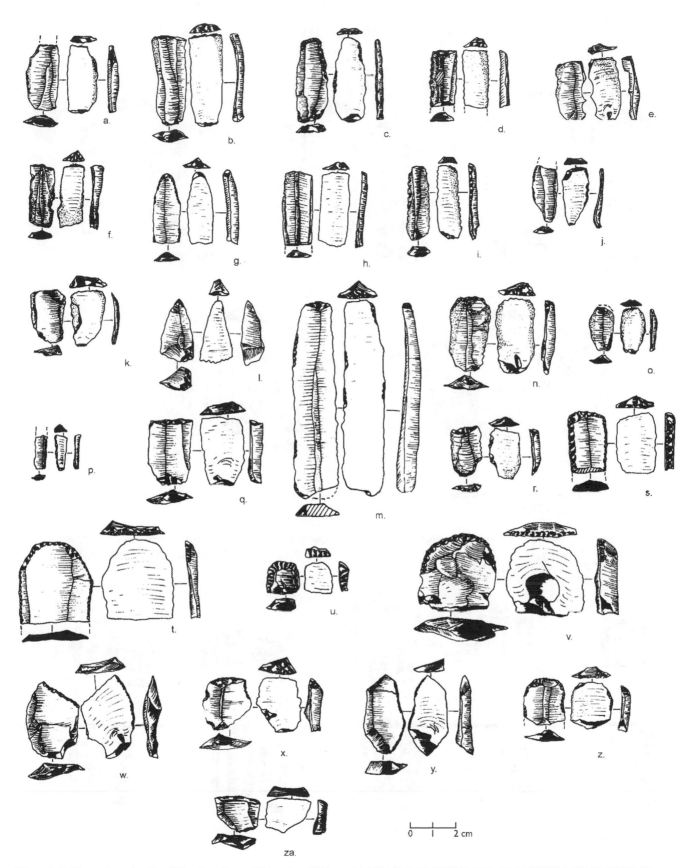

Figure 3.10. Examples of utilized blanks, phases IV (a–y) and V (z–za).(a) ZB 60:4; (b) SF 3042, ROc 65; (c) SF 2729, ZE 63; (d) ZB 58; (e) SF 3273, ZHe 28; (f) ZB 50; (g) SF 3250, ZHe 24; (h) SF 2714, ZE 56; (i) ZB 62; (j) ZB 60:6; (k) SF 2719, ZE 59; (l) SF 2755, ZE 67; (m) SF 3926, ZJ 22; (n) ZB 49; (o) SF 2761, ZE 68; (p) ZB 70; (q) SF 2777, ZE 71; (r) SF 2744, ZE 60; (s) SF 3208, ZHe 7; (t) SF 3405, ZHe 5; (u) SF 3239, ZHe 29; (v) SF 2913, ZG 12; (w) ZJ 4; (x) SF 3015 ROc 45; (y) SF 3329, PO/B; (z) SF 1604; (za) SF 2734, ZE 64.

117

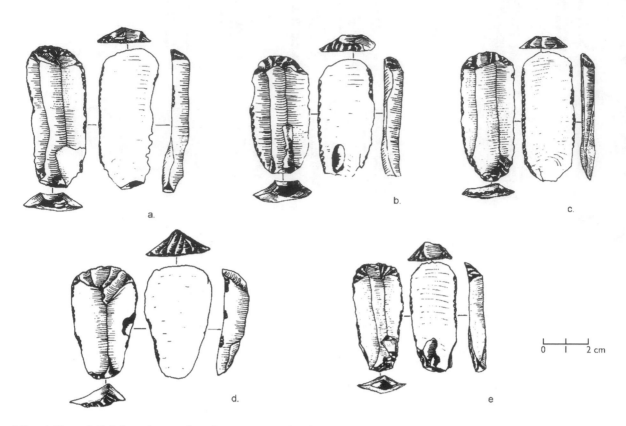

(Above): Figure 3.11. Selected examples of composite tools, phase III. (a) ZA 44:1; (b) SF 2949, ZG 19; (c) SF 1245, MM 50; (d) SF 1255, MM 50; (e) ZB 116:1.

(Below): Figure 3.12. Examples of phase V denticulate sickle blades. (a) SF 2305, ROc 14; (b) SF 4303, PN 264; (c) SF 3346, PO 128; (d) SF 2030, ROc 14; (e) SF 2449, PNc 82; (f) SF 1801, PO 19; (g) SF 1061, QN 7; (h) SF 1327, PN 13; (i) SF 3364, PN 77; (j) SF 2447, PM/F 55; (k) SF 1052, QN 7.

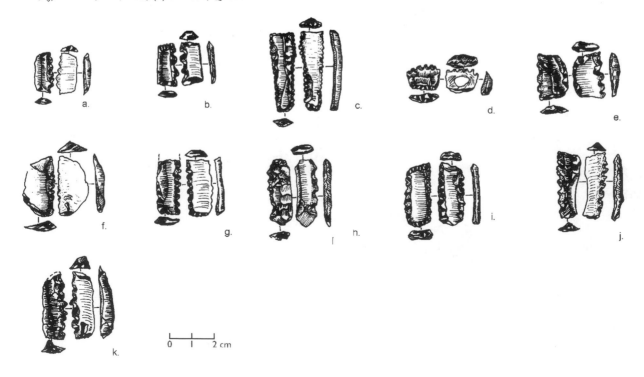

Table 3.14. Cross-Tabulation of Resharpening and Functional Identification of Blanks

Resharpening retouch					Function						
	Cut				Scrape					Projectile	
Phase I	S	M	H	Sickle	S	M	H	Borer	Groove	point	Total
Present											
No.	0	0	0	7	2	0	5	1	0	0	15
Row %				46.7	13.3		33.3	6.7			
Column %				43.8	33.3		62.5	50.0			24.2
Absent											
No.	12	10	4	9	4	3	3	1	1	0	47
Row %	25.5	21.3	8.5	19.1	8.5	6.4	6.4	2.1	2.1		
Column %				56.2	66.7		27.5	50.0	50.0		75.8
Total											
No.	12	10	4	16	6	3	8	2	1	0	62
Row %	19.3	16.1	6.5	25.8	9.7	4.8	12.9	3.2	1.6		
Phase II											
Present											
No.	0	0	0	10	9	15	6	0	0	0	40
Row %				25.0	22.5	37.5	15.0				
Column %				11.4	45.0	46.9	60.0				16.7
Absent											
No.	44	27	6	78	11	17	4	10	2	0	199
Row %	22.1	13.5	3.0	39.2	5.5	8.5	2.1	5.0	1.0		
Column %				88.6	55.0	53.1	40.0				83.3
Total											
No.	44	27	6	88	20	32	10	10	2	0	239
Row %	18.4	11.3	2.5	36.8	8.4	13.4	4.2	4.2	0.8		
Phase III											
Present											
No.	2	0	0	5	15	17	8	20	0	0	67
Row %	3.0			7.5	22.5	25.4	11.9	29.8			
Column %	2.7			3.2	44.1	33.3	28.6	40.0			13.3
Absent											
No.	73	72	33	153	19	34	20	30	4	0	438
Row %	16.7	16.4	7.5	34.9	4.3	7.8	4.6	6.9	0.9		
Column %	97.3			96.8	55.9	66.7	61.4	60.0			86.7
Total											
No.	75	72	33	158	34	51	28	50	4	0	505
Row %	14.9	14.3	6.5	31.3	6.7	10.1	5.5	10.0	0.7		
Phase IV											
Present											
No.	0	0	2	14	6	5	4	8	0	5	44
Row %			4.5	31.8	13.6	11.4	9.1	18.2		11.4	
Column %			18.2	26.9	35.3	50.0	80.0	57.1		50.0	30.7
Absent											
No.	16	7	9	38	11	5	1	6	1	5	99
Row %	16.2	7.1	9.1	38.4		5.0	1.0	6.1	1.0	5.0	
Column %			81.8	73.1	64.7	50.0	20.0	42.9		50.0	69.2
Total											
No.	16	7	11	52	17	10	5	14	1	10	143
Row %	11.2	4.9	7.7	36.4	11.9	7.0	3.5	9.8	0.6	7.0	

Continued on next page

Table 3.14. Cross-Tabulation of Resharpening and Functional Identification of Blanks, cont.

Resharpening retouch					Function						
	Cut				Scrape					Projectile	
	S	M	H	Sickle	S	M	H	Borer	Groove	point	Total
Phase V											
Present											
No.	0	0	2	23	3	3	3	2	0	0	36
Row %			5.6	63.9	8.3	8.3	8.3	5.6			
Column %			20.0	56.1	66.7	33.3		50.0			32.7
Absent											
No.	17	19	8	18	1	6	0	2	1	2	74
Row %	23.0	25.7	10.8	24.3	1.4	8.1		2.7	1.4	2.7	
Column %			80.0	43.9	33.3	66.7		50.0			67.3
Total											
No.	17	19	10	41	4	9	3	4	1	2	110
Row %	15.5	17.3	9.1	37.3	3.6	8.2	2.7	3.6	0.9	1.8	

S: Soft   M: Medium   H: Hard

Note: Resharpening of a utilized edge is identified by convergence of used edge and retouched edge of lateral, distal and proximal edges of the tool.

retouch (that is, was it to blunt, sharpen, or resharpen the edge; see note 3), (2) to explain the shaping strategy, and (3) most importantly, to be sure that the tools being compared as belonging to the same "type" are, in fact, comparable. For example, not all distally retouched blanks are used distally; retouch in the same location may be carried out before utilization on one tool and after utilization on another.

In addition, in restricting more detailed classification to retouched blades and flakes, and in lumping unretouched blades into much coarser categories, a great deal of information concerning the variation between form and function is lost. This is especially the case when dealing with the flaked stone assemblages of southeast Europe. I previously mentioned that at Sitagroi, as in all the Neolithic assemblages of southeast and central Europe, retouch was very rarely used to control the size and shape of blanks. By far the most common strategy was to select the appropriate blank after it was struck from the core without any subsequent retouching. Retouch used in these Neolithic assemblages of southeast and central Europe did not have the diversity of the European Upper and Late Paleolithic assemblages. This fact imposes severe limitations on the potential value of traditional tool typologies to monitor cultural or technological change in Neolithic central and southeast Europe.

To demonstrate these limitations in light of the information presented in this chapter, I have presented a macromorphological classification of the Sitagroi flaked stone assemblage (table 3.9), based on the traditional typologies offered by some southeast European archaeologists (Kaczanowska and Kozlowski 1990; Kozlowski and Kaczanowska 1986; Kunchev 1972; Kunchev 1983; Pâunescu 1970). This has a further purpose: making the material of Sitagroi more comparable with other more traditional analyses of Neolithic flaked stone tool assemblages in southeast and central Europe (Kozlowski 1982; Kozlowski and Kozlowski 1987).

Some of the types that form the basis of this classification have no functional connotations, such as "geometric" (figure 3.8e, h), "retouched blade" (figure 3.8a), "denticulate blade" (figure 3.8c), and "truncated blade" (figure 3.8g). Others, such as "end-scraper" (figure 3.8f, l), "borer" (figure 3.8j), and "sickle blade" (figure 3.8d) do have functional significance, at least subconsciously in the minds of the classifiers. In the case of end-scrapers (and double end-scrapers [figure 3.8m]) and borers, it is assumed that the retouched part of the tool coincides with the "active" edge (Pâunescu 1970). Thus, all those tools with a similar shaped active part (for example, a curved edge as opposed to a straight edge) are classified together. After microwear examination, however, it is clear that not all blades with the diagnostic criterion of end-scraper (retouch at the distal end) were used at their distal ends, or even for scraping. On the other hand, "borers," "Fiera points" (figure 3.8b, i, k) and "arrowheads" (figure 3.8n, o, p) do coincide with their identification on the basis of microwear examination.

Sickle blades constitute the one category that, in the traditional flaked stone tool typologies, is based not on the presence of retouch but on the presence of the by-product of tool utilization: the distinctive high gloss that forms the basis of my own identification of sickle blades. It is not surprising, therefore, that my functional identification agrees with this macromorphological type. It should be pointed out, however, that the telltale silica gloss is found in a large number of other morphological categories: end-scrapers, retouched blades, denticulate blades, and truncated blades.

In fact, the general conclusion that may be drawn from a traditional analysis of the assemblage agrees with the microwear examination. Results show that there is a great degree of similarity between the assemblages of phases II through IV, whereas the assemblages of phases I and V show marked differences from each other and the rest. Phases II through IV represent the period of occupation when the region had close contact with the Maritsa basin in south Bulgaria (see also Manolakkakis 1994). This fact could no doubt be used to explain this variability in the lithic assemblage. From the point of view of socioeconomic explanation of culture change, however, such an explanation of lithic variation is unsatisfactory and, moreover, is circular.

One of the features that draws together the assemblages of phases II through IV is the relatively large percentage of unretouched sickle blades (over 33%), end-scrapers (slightly less than 33%), and truncated blades (about 20%). Phases I and V, on the other hand, have fewer unretouched sickle blades (less than 20%). In phase V, end-scrapers and denticulate blades are by far the most important types. However, it should be remembered that all these denticulate blades and some of the end-scrapers in phase V are, in fact, sickle blades according to microwear examination, which immediately adds another dimension to the traditional information.

Are the denticulate and retouched sickle blades of phase V actually comparable to the unretouched sickle blades of phases II through IV? If so, what is the significance of the extra labor taken in their preparation? In other words, what is the nature of the change between the assemblages of phases IV and V?

These questions bring us very close to the conclusions concerning the cultural changes at Sitagroi as reflected in both microscopic and macroscopic observations made on the flaked stone tools. Thus, I move away from the traditional morphological typologies, but not from the relationship between the form and function of the tools.

SICKLE BLADES: A CASE STUDY

Sickle blades have been selected as that category of tools that best demonstrates the relationship between the form and function of flaked stone tools. It also demonstrates the explanations of shape and size standardization as well as of the strategies chosen to achieve such control of the flaked stone tools at Sitagroi.

Sickle blades contrast with all other functional categories by the great degree to which their size range was restricted. Not only do they conform to more standard dimensions, but they almost always conform to the classic 2:1 proportion of blade length to width. Such standardization was rarely achieved by retouching the distal end, but by the faster method of selecting the appropriate size of blank or by truncating the bulbar end. It is likely that in the Neolithic and Chalcolithic industries of southeast and central Europe, it was a common strategy to haft or insert the sickle blades and fix them with mastic in a groove prepared in a wooden or antler handle, in a way similar to actual examples found in the Chalcolithic levels of south Bulgarian sites (Behm-Blancke 1963; Georgiev 1958; Tringham 1971; Vaughan, Jarrige, and Anderson-Gerfaud 1987). Such a strategy would have demanded considerable standardization of blank size and shape. On the other hand, blades and flakes for cutting less resistant materials were not required to conform to such a narrow dimensional range because it is unlikely, based on current evidence, that they were fitted into any kind of handle or haft.

A large number of the sickle blades from the phase V assemblage have a radically different shape from those of the Neolithic and Chalcolithic assemblages of southeast Europe and from those of the preceding phases at Sitagroi. They are long, narrow, and blunted at their distal ends, and their edges are sharpened into a fine denticulate edge (see figure 3.12). These are the "fine denticulates" referred to in the traditional typologies (Pâunescu 1970).

On the basis of the microwear examination of these blades, the appearance of the denticulate edge does not signify a new style of flaked stone tool so much as a change in the strategy of production and consumption of flakes used to cut silica-containing plants. The appearance of the denticulate blades in phase V is unlikely to represent a new method of harvesting grain crops or reeds at Sitagroi, although this possibility cannot be entirely discounted. The material contacted and the dynamics of contact of the denticulate sickle blades are basically the same as the preceding and contemporary nondenticulate sickle blades (Vaughan, Jarrige, and Anderson-Gerfaud 1987). An important difference is that the area of gloss along the edge is parallel (see figure 3.12a, c, e–k) rather than diagonal (figure 3.13a) to the edge. But these changes are a function of the prehension of the tool rather than the behavioral activity of which the tool is a part. The shape of the denticulate blades and their edge blunting and resharpening may reflect more rigorous attention paid to placing and fixing the blades in their hafts. An alternative interpretation of the same features is that the sickle blades of phase V were held singly in the hand in contrast to the hafted nondenticulates.

Counting both denticulate and nondenticulate examples, sickle blades make up almost half of the utilized blanks in phase V. This does not reflect an increase in harvesting activities during the Early Bronze Age of southeast Europe, nor even in this phase at Sitagroi, but a narrowing of the range of tasks carried out with flaked stone edges. In fact, when compared with other Neolithic and Chalcolithic assemblages in southeast and central Europe, Sitagroi has a very high proportion of sickle blades in all phases of its occupation (at least 33%), in contrast to the early Neolithic site of Banja, Yugoslavia 8%) or the Chalcolithic phase of Divostin, Yugoslavia (13%) (Tringham 1988). It is clear that significant differences in behavior are being expressed, but these are unlikely to have anything to do with variation in the importance of the activities associated with these tools. No one would take seriously the suggestion that harvesting grain (always supposing that this was the activity with which the sickle blades were associated) was more important at Sitagroi than elsewhere.

Other explanations for the large number of sickle blades at Sitagroi may include the possibility that more blades were hafted compositely at Sitagroi than elsewhere to make a sickle. This seems unlikely because most of the Sitagroi sickle blades, especially in phase V, are larger than at other sites; so one would expect the reverse to be more likely. A second possible explanation is that sickle blades at Sitagroi may have been discarded more habitually at the settlement site rather than in the fields; this hypothesis is difficult to test in the absence of excavation of the fields. A third possible explanation is that all blades identified as sickle blades may well have been used to contact the same material—plants with a high silica content—but at Sitagroi they may have been hafted together to make a different kind of tool that required more flaked stone blades—for example, a form of threshing sledge. Microwear would tend to refute this hypothesis because, apart from the sickle blades of phase V, the location of the gloss that is diagnostic of the sickle blades is identical all over eastern Europe. A fourth possible explanation is that the sickle blades at Sitagroi may, in fact, have been used for a wider variety of tasks than in other parts of southeast Europe—for example, in cutting grasses and reeds in addition to harvesting grain. It seems likely, however, from the evidence for the use of hay, straw, and reeds as building materials throughout southeast Europe at this time, that we should not expect Sitagroi to demonstrate such a difference in the tools used to cut them.

Finally, the larger proportion of sickle blades at Sitagroi may be explained by the variability in the use-lives of the tools in the different parts of southeast Europe. For example, in phases II and III at

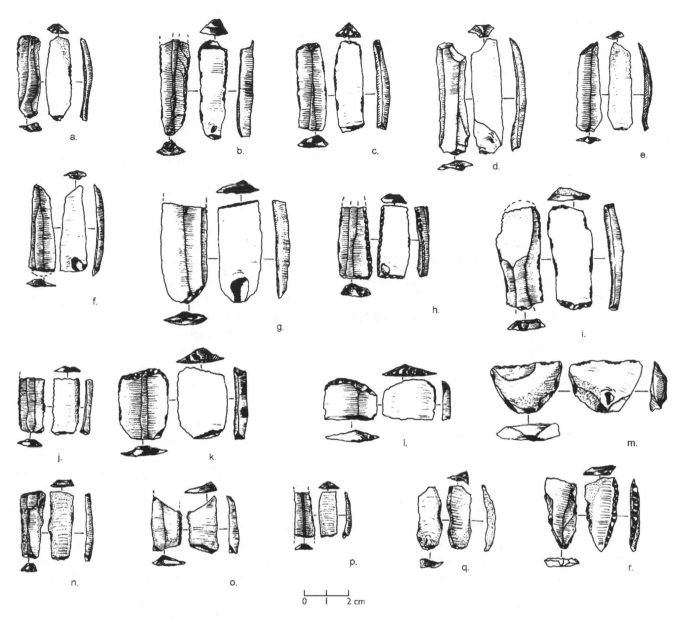

Figure 3.13. Examples of the utilized blanks of the phase V lithic assemblage. (a) SF 2094, PO/D 37; (b) SF 1617, PO 13; (c) SF 1415, QN 6; (d) SF 1601 (PN 14?); (e) SF 4503 (PO 23?); (f) SF 1329, PN 14; (g) SF 1055, PO 9; (h) SF 1602 (PN 14?); (i) SF 1605, PN 14; (j) SF 1608 (PN 14?); (k) SF 1805, PO 23; (l) SF 1606 (PN 14?); (m) SF 2844 PN; (n) SF 1603 (PN?); (o) SF 2060, PO/B 33; (p) SF 1607 (PN ?); (q) SF 1330, PN 14; (r) SF 3342, PM/F 56.

Sitagroi, sickle blades constitute a third of the utilized blanks, but no attempts were made to prolong the use-life of these tools. In phase V, on the other hand, sickle blades occur with a slightly higher frequency, but prolongation of the use-life by resharpening edges is a frequent feature. Given this fact, it seems very likely that, in the final phase of the occupation of Sitagroi, flaked stone blades were being used predominantly in association with the harvesting of silica-containing plants. This possibility becomes even greater when we remember that most of the sickle blades of phase V are likely to have been used singly. Thus, when we take into consideration the prolongation of the use-life of tools and the rate at which new tools were manufactured, used, and discarded, the frequency of the sickle blades in phases II and III (where sickle blades were consumed at a fast rate) is, in fact, probably not much greater than that of the sickle blades at Divostin. At this latter site, some resharpening of sickle blades occurs to prolong their use-life and slow their consumption rate (Tringham 1988). In this way, the assemblage of phase V at Sitagroi becomes outstanding because the sickle blades were consumed slowly and occur in large numbers as compared with blades used in other tasks.

CONCLUSION

The assemblages of the first occupational phase at Sitagroi displayed confidence, motivation, and knowledge of lithic resources. This is in contrast to the early assemblages of the west Balkans (that is, the Körös and Starčevo cultures). I suspect that the situation in the early Neolithic lithic assemblages of south Bulgaria closer to the source of the best stones would be very similar to that of phase I at Sitagroi.

The fluorescence of the flaked stone industry in the late fifth and fourth millennia BC in southeast and central Europe is mirrored in almost every other aspect of cultural behavior (Gimbutas 1991; C. Renfrew 1973a, 1986f; Sherratt 1972, 1976, 1984; Tringham 1971; Tringham and Krstić 1990). These aspects include increased population size and density, settlement nucleation and sedentism, accumulation of debris and increased rate of production and consumption of material resources, widened resource exploitation area through intersettlement exchange, and considerable development of technology—especially pyrotechnology (ceramics and metallurgy) (Chapman 1990; Tringham and Krstić 1990).

One way in which the range of utilized resources was broadened may be seen in the exploitation of outcrop sources of flint in the Balkans (Comsa 1967; Manolakkakis 1994) complemented by the development of technological equipment in the form of antler (and possibly copper) punches and hammers with which to manipulate these materials. This exploitation of outcrop flint sources must also have involved a more complex organization of the labor force in order to increase and intensify the production of the raw material, possibly mining the raw materials in the same way as the

contemporary copper mines in southeast Europe (Chernykh 1978b; Jovanović 1982) and the slightly later flint mines of northern Europe (Dzieduszycka-Machnikowa and Lech 1976; Weisberger 1980). The inhabitants of Sitagroi phases II through IV had developed access to sources of high-quality flint from central and northern Bulgaria. Relatively large quantities of this raw material were acquired through exchange and close contact with the Maritsa-Gumelnitsa and related culture settlements several hundred kilometers distance from Sitagroi (Manolakkakis 1994). There is no doubt that the strategies of resource consumption during this period have an "expansive" nature, reflected in how blanks were selected by size and shape appropriate for a particular job or otherwise were rejected as unusable (and therefore wasted) rather than retouched into the right shape and/or size. This period is also characterized by a lack of strategies to curate the material and prolong the use-life of the tools.

Significant changes can be seen between the assemblage of phase V and those preceding. Many of these changes began in the assemblage of phase IV. One example is the decrease in the utilization of the honey-brown flint imported from Bulgaria. In both phases IV and V, strategies to maximize resource consumption are visible; in phase IV these strategies comprise the resharpening of dulled edges and using a larger extent of the perimeter of each blank than in the preceding phases II and III. But in phase V, the strategy chosen was more complex than the mere maintenance and curation of tools: it appears to have been designed to conserve a dwindling resource—the honey-brown flint—by generally reducing its utilization to producing primarily sickle blades.

It might be argued that the role of cryptocrystalline rocks as a material for manufacturing sharp edge tools was being usurped at this time by another material, such as copper. This might have been more successfully argued for phases II and III when the use of copper tools can be demonstrated. However, for phase V there is no evidence of a material that could have been substituted for cryptocrystalline rocks. It is also possible that the use of wooden and antler handles and hafts for tools decreased in phase V, which would have been an important break in tradition with the preceding phases at Sitagroi.

The changes that are visible in the lithic assemblage beginning with phase IV and crystallizing in phase V reflect a pattern of significant socioeconomic change in the late fourth and early third millennia BC (Chapman 1990; Gimbutas 1991; Sherratt 1972, 1984; Tringham 1992; Tringham and Krstić 1990). These changes include a transformation of the settlement pattern; a decrease in pyrotechnological activities; and a withdrawal from the wide horizons of regular "international" exchange and from the expansive exploitation of a broad range of resources from a large area. These were the characteristics of the middle of the fifth through the middle fourth millennium BC and the period represented at Sitagroi by phases II and III and to a certain extent phase IV.

It is impossible on the basis of the lithic assemblage analysis alone, with or without microwear observations, to explain the changes observed in the Sitagroi assemblage. How are we to explain, for example, why the honey-brown flint was no longer utilized or available outside its immediate source area by the later fourth millennium BC? Was it the result of the more easily available outcrops becoming exhausted, as has been suggested to explain the sharp decrease in the use of copper oxide ores at this time? Or was it because the organization of procurement and redistribution in the source area was somehow disrupted? It is possible that the explanation lies not in the source area but in the consumption area, that is, in Sitagroi society itself. During phases IV and V, there may have been a growing lack of demand for an increasingly expensive commodity, so that there developed a change in the use-value of the honey-brown flint. But then one would have expected that the role of providing high-quality raw material for the production of edge tools would have been taken over by an equivalent material, a cheaper or more local cryptocrystalline rock, or a substitute material such as metal. In phase V, however, neither of these strategies is visible. On the other hand, what is visible in phase V is a strategy of conservation and small-scale use of existing lithic resources.

The exploitation of lithic resources and its changes are thus part of a more general picture of socioeconomic change in prehistoric southeast Europe. The pattern and explanation for these changes emerge from the various studies of material culture contained in the two volumes reporting the Sitagroi excavations and in conjunction with studies of the lithic and other data from other sites.

NOTES

[1] The chapter was written in it its final version in 1983. I am grateful that the editors allowed me to update it with more recent literature in 1994.

[2] Nine pieces of Carpathian obsidian were recovered from Late Neolithic levels and one from the Early Bronze Age site of Mandalo in northern Greece (Kilikoglou et al. 1996: 349). A single piece, from the Early Bronze Age, was sourced to Melos. Tests of four obsidian pieces from Sitagroi indicate a Melian source.

[3] Lithic analysts (e.g., (Movius, David, and Bricker. 1968:5–8) have argued that variation in the purpose of retouch can be reconstructed without having to resort to microwear observations, that is, without knowing which of the retouched edges were or were not used. There are many reasons why I disagree with this viewpoint. For example, there are numerous cases of two artifacts that manifest what is superficially the same form, but are instead the result of very different decisions during their use-lives. Distal retouch might, in one case, be to resharpen the distal end for use, and in another case to blunt the distal end to facilitate use of the lateral edge. The difference would become clear only after identifying the utilized edge.

Even with the aid of microwear observations, identification of the retouch purpose and the stage in the tool's use-life in which it was carried out still presents problems. The identifications in this study were made on the basis of the distribution of the retouch scars in relation to the damage resulting from either utilization or hafting/handling along the perimeter of a blank. The distinction between flake scars caused by the deliberate removal of flakes during retouching and those removed during utilization or by accidental contact has been discussed elsewhere (Tringham et al. 1974:181). In this study, it has been assumed that the lateral edge of a blade could have been used for any purpose without prior modification by retouch. Retouching of a lateral edge would not strengthen a cutting edge but would steepen and blunt the edge so that its use-life would be shortened before it began. Therefore, I am assuming that the coincidence of retouch scars with utilization traces on a lateral edge indicates that the purpose of the retouch was resharpening rather than shaping before utilization.

On the other hand, the proximal and distal ends of a blank are much more difficult to use without preparation and modification, unless the distal end of a core has been carefully prepared. For this reason, when retouch and utilization traces coincide at either the proximal or distal end, it has been assumed that, although the retouch is very likely to represent maintenance of the edge through resharpening, its original purpose was to make the distal or proximal end usable. Therefore it is necessary to take into account the possibility that the modification before use of distal and proximal ends has been overestimated. At this point it should be noted that in all phases of occupation at Sitagroi, the distal ends of some blades were usable immediately on being struck from the core, owing to careful core preparation.

In cases where the retouched edge, whether lateral or distal, has not been used, it is assumed (and in many cases this assumption is supported by microwear evidence) that the retouch served to shape and blunt the edge for hafting and handling by strengthening and thickening it and to remove protrusions.

[4] The least problem is incurred by those blanks—referred to as "double-" or "triple-edged" tools—that were used for the same action and on the same contact material on different parts of their perimeter. A much greater problem lies in interpreting tools used for different actions on the same or different contact materials, referred to as "composite tools." The bête noire of microwear studies is the specter of sequential use on the same edge. In this case, unless blessed by a fortunate accident, the microwear analyst is fairly helpless and must identify utilization on the basis of the evidence of the final task performed with that edge.

Appendix 3.1.
Petrographic Examination of Chipped Stone Materials

Sarantis Dimitriadis and Katerina Skourtopoulou

Our petrographic examination of the raw materials used for the manufacture of chipped stone tools is intended to complement Ruth Tringham's study while adding new evidence concerning the exploitation of the various resources. We focused on identifying possible provenance areas for the rock types used and have created a database that can be used to integrate any emerging activity patterns. Such patterns might include regional mobility or territorial exploitation of resources based on the information from the manufacture, maintenance, use, and discard of chipped stone.

SAMPLING STRATEGY AND CONSTRAINTS

The Sitagroi materials were examined within a broader research project involving the petrographic examination of the chipped stone resources during the Neolithic of northern Greece (Dimitriadis and Skourtopoulou 2001). Although we considered the variability of the raw materials macroscopically identified, we excluded two rock types from our examination: obsidian and quartz. Obsidian samples were not examined because they would have required us to apply expensive and time-consuming analytical techniques (see Kilikoglou et al. 1996). Quartz, although tabulated, was not petrographically analyzed because its simple structure would have revealed no particular source traits.

These obstacles constrained our achieving a more comprehensive sampling strategy that would have taken into consideration the production, use, and discard variability of chipped stone, as well as the microscale of intrasite contexts. Therefore, we have restricted our sampling to a broad temporal scale with regard to the chronological phases of the site and deliberately selected lithic samples from the stratigraphic trenches ZA and ZB (Sitagroi, volume 1 [C. Renfrew 1986e]:172) to represent all the occupational phases at Sitagroi. The resulting samples were equally divided between Middle and Late Neolithic and the Early Bronze Age (table 3.1.1). The fact that a large part (80%) of the chipped stone materials in these trenches (ZA and ZB) were retrieved by wet sieving (see Tringham, this volume [chapter 3], and 1984:257) increases the possibility that the sample is representative of the raw material variability.

Accordingly, an effort was made to cover all the most frequent macroscopic categories of siliceous materials. Seven categories (five of flint, one each of chalcedony and chert) were distinguished following macroscopic criteria, and samples were collected for petrographic analysis (table 3.1.2). To clarify the patterns in the material culture formed through the selection and exploitation of physical resources, we distinguished the technomorphological variability of the chipped stone assemblage as well. The identified modes of tool manufacture were numerous and reflect the multifaceted potential of human activities (Tringham 1984; see this volume, chapter 3). However, our fear of destroying useful archaeological evidence limited the amount of material available for petrographic analysis, so we thus restricted our sampling to the most common categories of materials produced (tool blanks, flakes, and blades) and ignored products such as exhausted and nonexhausted cores, large primary flakes, rejuvenation pieces, and undiagnostic waste.

Table 3.1.1. List of the Thin-Sectioned Samples by Phase and Context

ID	Context	Occupational phase	Rock description	Blank type
1	ZA 44 s	III	Honey-brown flint	Blade fragment
2	ZB 40 r	V	Possibly burnt chalcedony	Waste
3	ZA 17 s	Va	Honey-brown flint	Flake
4	ZB 131 r	II	Honey-brown flint	Flake
5	ZB 37 r	V	Chalcedony	Flake
6	ZB 11 s	V	Dark gray brown flint	Blade fragment
7	ZA 17 s	Va	Light beige cream flint	Waste
8	ZB 112 r	III/IV	Olive-brown flint	Waste
9	ZA 44 s	III	Dark purple jasper	Flake
10	ZB 131 r	II	Black flint	Flake
11	ZB 35 s	V	Honey-brown flint	Flake
12	ZA 44 s	III	Honey-brown flint	Flake
13	ZA 49 s	III	Honey-brown flint	Blade fragment
14	ZB 35 s	V	Honey-brown flint	Blade fragment
15	ZB 118 r	III	Honey-brown flint	Blade fragment
16	ZB 123 r	III	cream gray flint	Waste
17	ZA 44 s	III	Light gray flint	Flake
18	ZA 17 s	Va	Honey-brown flint	Blade
19	ZA 17 s	Va	Blue-light gray flint	Blade
20	ZB 2 r	Mixed	Chalcedony	Bladelet fragment
21	ZA 17 s	Va	Blue-light gray flint	Blade
22	ZA 44 s	III	Light beige gray flint	Blade
23	ZB 106 r	IV	Light gray-blue flint	Blade
24	ZA 17 s	Va	Honey-brown flint	Blade
25	ZB 5 s	V	Dark beige gray flint	Flake

THE PETROGRAPHIC ANALYSIS OF THE CHIPPED STONE ASSEMBLAGE

Given the above framework, we selected and thin-sectioned twenty-five samples of highly siliceous rocks to examine using a polarizing microscope. On the basis of the microstructures preserved in them, we were able to derive the following classifications (Dimitriadis and Skourtopoulou 2001):

1. *Recrystallized microgranular silica with poorly preserved remnants of silicified plant tissues or cellular structures.* Chalcedony spheroids usually line internal cavities in these rocks, which are probably volcanic tuffs within which plant fragments were incorporated during the period of volcanic explosion (plate 3.1.1). This class is represented by twelve of the twenty-five examined specimens. Apart from plant remnants (plate 3.1.2), ostracoid shells were also present in one specimen (plate 3.1.3).

2. *Silicified and/or devitrified acidic volcanic rocks with preserved porphyritic texture.* This class is represented by nine specimens (plate 3.1.4) of the twenty-five examined, and may be related to the first class in terms of its origin and source location.

The petrography of five other specimens did not permit definite characterization, but each one probably belongs to either of the first two classes, which together represent twenty-one of the total sample of twenty-five.

Each of the remaining four samples belongs to a different class, as follows:

a. *Silicified pelagic limestone* (plate 3.1.5).

b. *Radiolarian chert (recrystallized)* (plate 3.1.6).

c. *Extremely microgranular flint with rhombohedral dolomite crystals dispersed in it* (plate 3.1.7).

d. *A pure silica rock characterized by convoluted internal structures* which may be either inorganic or

Table 3.1.2. Macroscopically Distinguished Raw Material Categories

Raw material	Color*	Translucency	Texture	Knapping quality
Flint	Honey brown 7.5Y8/2–5/3, 5Y 8/3–4/3	Translucent at the edge, semi-translucent to opaque	Thin	High
Flint	Cream to gray beige to dark gray beige 10YR 8/3–7/2, 2.5Y 8/2–7/1	Opaque	Thin	High
Flint	Blue gray 5B 7/1–6/1	Opaque	Thin	High
Flint	Black N 3/ N 2.5/ –5Y2.5/1 2.5/2	Opaque	Thin to medium	High
Flint	Olive brown 5Y 5/1–4/4	Opaque	Thin	High
Chalcedony	White to grayish white N 8/ 2.5Y 8/1 5Y 8/1	Opaque	Medium to slightly coarse	Very good
Jasper or chert	Dark purple 2.5YR 2.5/2–2.5/4 10R 3/4	Opaque	Medium	High to very good to good

*The Munsell Color Charts code is only indicative.

may have been inherited and recrystallized fungal or algal structures (plates 3.1.8).

CORRELATING THE PETROGRAPHIC ANALYSIS WITH A WIDER GEOLOGICAL BACKGROUND

Identifying the exact geographical location of the lithic sources has been an archaeological goal for many decades. Its realization is still beset with difficulties, such as the lack of comparative material from geologically identified sources and the attribution of materials to only a few known sources, excluding alternative possibilities of geographical provenance. In an attempt to overcome these problems, we decided to integrate the petrographic variability recorded in the site samples with information on the regional geology that was obtained from geological maps and fieldwork. Our approach relied on the assumption that the availability of resources at the regional or local level plays a major role in the selection procedures followed by prehistoric people. The variability recognized among the lithic rock types used at a site should reflect the geological background surrounding the site. When major contradictions exist between the recognized background and the identified site samples, then long-distance mobility is the only plausible alternative to access resources. The spatio-temporal constraints inherent in this type of long-distance

movement (such as interterritorial boundaries, difficult landscape crossing, and time-consuming travel) lead to further implications concerning mechanisms of access involving intersite communication and exchange (see C. Renfrew 1968; Torrence 1986; Perlès 1990, 1992; Manolakkakis 1996).

Taking into consideration the petrographic variation of the raw materials, our research focused on pinpointing possible source areas with a geological profile allowing for the formation of flint rocks. Such areas can be located on the available geological maps, and this information was then tested by surveying potential source locations.

The geological information we collected provided a number of potential sources at various mobility scales. Since there are no acidic volcanic rocks or tuff exposed in the region of Sitagroi, the sources of at least the two main classes of the materials cannot be local. Exposures of similar volcanic rocks and tuff including plant fragments are known from Thrace, north of Alexandroupolis (area of Feres, Dadia) at a distance of 150 km or more from Sitagroi. Another potential area of outcrop locations is the southeastern Rhodope Plain where a number of open-air sites exist, attesting to human occupation dated at least to the Middle Paleolithic (Efstratiou 1992:649). Acidic rock exposures are also present in the Rhodope mountain range as near as 50 km from Sitagroi; thus this northern source is a second possibility.

Unfortunately, the Rhodope mountain range was not covered by our survey. There is strong evidence the range has resources, but the difficult terrain, with steep rocky relief and thick forest vegetation made a study of the area problematic. The range is also a boundary area, geographically divided between Bulgaria and Greece. Surveying this area would have required complicated formal processes, costly equipment, and a considerable time investment—options not possible at this juncture in our research.

The silicified pelagic limestone, radiolarian chert, and flint may all come from a single source (a sedimentary or meta-sedimentary sequence of undetermined age, on the available evidence) or from different sources, far from the Sitagroi region. Finally, it is interesting to note that on the basis of the specimens examined so far, it seems that the semi-translucent material macroscopically characterized as "honey-brown flint" (Tringham 1984:260, 263–264, and this volume, chapter. 3) corresponds mainly to class 1, being in fact recrystallized volcanic tuff including plant remnants. This suggests a procurement area, alternative to the distant sources in northern Bulgaria associated with the Maritsa-Gumelnitsa culture (ibid.).

CONCLUDING REMARKS

The petrographic study of the stone resources used for the production of chipped stone in Sitagroi has provided some interesting information on activity patterns related to lithic raw material exploitation and the possible routes of production and dispersion of stone tools. The two possible identified stone procurement areas, the Rhodope mountain range and the northern part of Greek Thrace, are differentiated in terms of their landscape, suggesting different community practices in relation to mobility and resource exploitation. The geographical and geomorphological factors characterizing these source areas, such as distance from the settlement, landscape relief, and vegetation type, can be translated into distinct mobility patterns for the people of Sitagroi, given the constraints present in each case. The lower siliceous rock exposures in the mountainous area of Rhodope appear close by, but are nevertheless restricted by the intervention of rough mountain passages. Thracian sources, on the other hand, are much farther to the east, requiring longer travel, and imply a mobility scheme with a broader geographical spread. At the same time, access to these Thracian sources, although more difficult in terms of distance, is easier because few landscape obstacles intervene.

This double landscape pattern of potential raw material procurement can be further discussed in terms of local practices and cultural communication. Different activities could have been combined with rock quarrying for each potential procurement itinerary. In the case of the Rhodope sources, short-term trips may have combined rock quarrying with other seasonal activities requiring forest or thick vegetation (such as summer animal grazing, hunting, and plant or wood collection). Trips crossing the Thracian Plain would have been more involved with agricultural activities. In addition, we would expect there to be greater cultural contacts in the thickly populated Thracian coastal and lowland areas than in the sparsely inhabited Rhodope forests (compare Theocharis 1971: fig. 7). The Thracian source might involve different territorial obstacles of owned or controlled land (for cultivated or grazing land, for instance), requiring the development of social ties between and among communities.

Observations on landscape variation, source location, and settlement dispersion for other areas of northern Greece and the Balkans during the time of the Sitagroi occupation have led us to wonder whether the Sitagroi inhabitants procured their materials directly or through various modes of exchange. A range of approaches has been advanced to identify variations in exchange as a community activity, stressing distance from source (Renfrew, Cann, and Dixon 1965; C. Renfrew 1975b, 1977; Torrence 1986; Perlès 1990) and varying with location and dispersion of total production (Perlès 1990, 1992, 1994). More clarified for certain areas than others, the picture that emerges is one in which various types of alliances are developed in accordance with subsistence practices and the need for intersocietal interaction (Perlès 1990, 1992; Perlès and Vitelli 1994, 1999; Demoule and Perlès 1993), sometimes with certain communities acting as intermediary sites of tool redistribution at various distance scales (Karimali 1995).

The participation of the community of Sitagroi in systems of chipped stone exchange is evidenced by the variability of stone resources attested at the site and the skill employed in tool production (Tringham 1984; see this volume, chapter 3). The suggested procurement sources offer different possibilities of community practices. On the one hand, systematic procurement from sources located in the Rhodope mountains, closer to the site, might have been a more culturally restricted and easily controlled community-centered practice. In contrast to this, long-distance procurement from Thracian or, alternatively, northern Bulgarian sources opens up possibilities of exchange rather than direct procurement observed elsewhere in northern Greece and the Balkans (Efstratiou and Fotiadis 1998).

As a means of understanding artifact mobility, recent researchers in these areas for the Middle and Late Neolithic have proposed a tripartite division into local, semi-distanced or regional, and distanced or interregional scales, defined on the basis of approximate calculations of walking or navigating distances (Perlès 1994:73; Manolakkakis 1996: 120). Information on stone procurement systems supports the development of regionalization, setting as a conventional limit a 20- to 50-km radius around the site or one to two days of walking (Manolakkakis 1996). Combinations of localized and intercommunal tool production and circulation are testified within this scale, while there is also evidence for the circulation of tools within much larger distances—surpassing 100 km (Manolak-kakis 1996; Voytek 1985; Perlès 1990, 1992, 1994; Dimitriadis and Skourtopoulou 2001).

Specifically, evidence available for sites in eastern Macedonia and Thrace demonstrates the existence of several different procurement systems, based on materials available regionally (Fotiadis 1984; Grammenos, ed. 1997:292-296; Kourtessi-Philippakis 1997; Dimitriadis and Skourtopoulou 2001; Skourtopoulou 1998). Provisional information on assemblages not yet published in detail also seems to support this inference (Touloumis and Peristeri 1991:364; Peristeri 1994:104; Koukouli-Chrysanthaki et al. 1997:550; Malamidou 1997:518; Triantafyllos 1986). Among the few materials for which a distant origin has been suggested, the only quantitatively significant one seems to be the "honey-brown flint" which, as mentioned earlier, has been generally attributed to sources in northern Bulgaria, specifically from the area of Dobrudja in the pre-balcanic platform in northern Bulgaria or the left bank of the Danube (Séfériadès 1992c:75). A second proposed location is the area of Smolin at the northeast edge of the Rhodopes where the intensively exploited Madara quarries are located (Chapman 1981). While our work offers an alternative to these suggestions, the location of a distinct source in the southern Rhodope range remains to be tested by future fieldwork. However, judging by the examined samples, the Sitagroi flint variety is volcanic in origin and not a sedimentary rock as is the Dobrudja region flint (Séfériadès 1992c:75).

Summing up the information from the few chronologically comparable excavated sites in this area, there are differences among the stone procurement strategies. While the use of rocks from sources both closer and farther away is noted at all sites, the degree to which inhabitants at each site rely on regionally available materials seems to vary at the site microscale. At some sites the settlers chose to rely largely on rocks available at sources more easily accessible with frequent routine trips; at other sites, the preference is for longer-distance sources involving planned traveling and the development of exchange relations and other cultural alliances. Based on the existing evidence, regional and local procurement seems to have been practiced for sites in the Serres Basin (survey data, Dhimitra I–III, Promachon-Topolnica, Kryoneri) (Fotiadis 1984; Kourtessi-Philippakis 1997; Koukouli-Chrysanthaki et al. 1997; Malamidou 1997) and the Thracian Plain (Makri II, Proskinites) (Dimitriadis and Skourtopoulou 2001; Skourtopoulou 1998; Triantafyllos 1986). In the Drama Plain, however, there seems to be more diversification, as the long-distance exchange networks (Sitagroi II–IV, Dikili Tash II) (Séfériadès 1992c; Tringham 1984, see this volume, chapter 3) appear to coexist with the use of regionally available materials (Arkadikos) (Peristeri 1994).

The patterns initially observed require further refinement in order to uncover the possible social strategies involved in stone procurement. The implications emerging from the present spatial patterning—for community alliances and cultural differentiation based on the choice of raw materials—

need to be further tested with future survey and excavation work. Survey work on the distribution of flint varieties for sites in the Serres Basin resulted in suggestions of site self-sufficiency for the individual communities (Fotiadis 1984; Grammenos, ed. 1997:292–296). This view can be further considered for the rest of eastern Macedonia and Thrace and compared with similar suggestions concerning Vinča culture and the Bulgarian Eneolithic (Voytek 1985; Manolakkakis 1996).

The correlation of information on strategies for stone procurement with those of tool-making and use, as well as other practices concerning the incorporation of the particular technical practice into the community routines, will shed further light on the issues discussed above. In this respect, one final point may be made concerning the contextualization of chipped stone evidence. While mobility involving resource procurement can be grouped into schemes of local, regional, and interregional scale, this type of perceived spatial division of activ-

ities often results in attributing exchange relationships between and within communities as a correlation of the distance from source. The understanding of intercommunal and intercultural relationships thus implied is largely based on boundary conditions of territoriality. However, the definition of this type of activity constraint is not always clear. Although it is generally based on the evaluation of economic and ecological factors (for example, Higgs and Vita Finzi 1972; Butzer 1982; compare Manolakkakis 1996:120), it more often than not relies on empirical implication rather than on the reconstruction of such factors, without paying particular attention to the totality of the organized community practices. As an alternative to drawing further inferences on exchange versus direct procurement, we might argue that a more comprehensive discourse is one that integrates strategies of tool production and use with information about other community practices involving extracommunal mobility.

4.

Lithic Petrology

John Dixon

GEOLOGICAL SETTING AND SOURCE IMPLICATIONS

This study was undertaken to clarify the stone sources exploited by the prehistoric Sitagroi settlers for the manufacture of grinding tools (pestles, rubbers, grinders, etc.), ground edge tools (axes, adzes, chisels, etc.), impactors (hammerstones, cobbles, etc.), and polished artifacts (bowls, maces). All of the sources referred to in the text are located on the lithic source map, figure 4.1. The preceding chapter 3, and especially its appendix 3.1, deal essentially with similar questions but focus, rather, on sources for stones used in the manufacturing of flaked stone tools. Subsequently, chapter 5 reports on the tools studied herein, but from the standpoint of manufacture, form, and use. Thus, chapters 3, 4, 5, and their appendices (appendix 5.1 is the catalog), provide an extensive database for research into the possible patterns of raw material acquisition, manufacture, use, trade, and exchange practiced by the Sitagroi settlers.

The site lies on an alluvial plain located in a Neogene fault-bounded basin. The plain is enclosed on three sides by upland metamorphic massifs composed of marbles, mica-schists, and amphibolites, which comprise the mountainous areas of Falakron, Menokion, Symvolon, and Pangaion (figure 4.1). These three "local" lithologies, together with quartz from the veins that cut the metamorphic terrain, dominate the lithic assemblages. Farther to the north in the higher ground toward the Nestos River and the Bulgarian frontier lie the structurally higher mylonitic gneisses, migmatites, and occasional amphibolites and relict high-grade metamorphic rocks of the Central Rhodope subgroup, also known as the Sidhironero Unit. If these rocks in the assemblages had been

used for tools, some of these latter lithologies would be distinctive enough to stand out from the rocks of the structurally lower units surrounding the plain. None of the latter has been recognized for certain; the amphibolites among them are not distinctive and could be present. Consequently no certain attributions to sources in the north have been made. "Local," therefore implies that a rock type most likely came from the immediately surrounding high ground, but possibly from farther north.

All of the metamorphic massifs have been intruded by granites (for example, the Kavala, Vrontou, and Skaloti-Echinos complexes), which are themselves variably deformed. Kavala Complex is closest to the site, but it is markedly foliated. The larger granites that are potential sources for unfoliated lithologies, such as Vrontou and Skaloti, while not particularly distant, are mostly drained by tributaries of the Strymon or Nestos and so do not contribute boulders and cobbles to the immediate vicinity of the site. Other granite masses of similar age and type are also present farther to the east in Thrace and farther north in Bulgaria. Granite and deformed granite are represented to a very minor degree in the assemblages and at present cannot be attributed to specific sources. "Probably local" would thus be a default attribution, considering that granites are not physically very distant. At least one thin-sectioned granite object is probably distinctive enough to be narrowed down to its source by someone with detailed knowledge.

Several other rock types discussed below are present in the assemblage of artifacts which, as far as is known, must come from farther afield. These rock types do not outcrop in the plain of Drama catchment or in the region to the north up to the Nestos. It is likely, however, that candidate sources and source areas exist for all of them within Greek

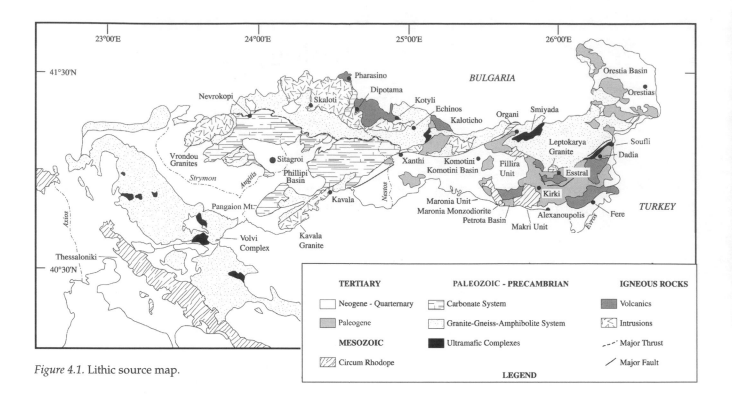

Figure 4.1. Lithic source map.

Macedonia and Thrace. For example, the sediments filling the basin of the plain of Drama are young and unconsolidated. As far as is known, they do not include equivalents of the few well-lithified sandstones and limestones found in the assemblages, which are more likely to have come from Early Tertiary basins farther east near Xanthi or Komotini. The same is true of the few volcanic rocks such as the porphyritic andesites in the collection, which are closely associated with these same basins.

Other relatively exotic rock types are metamorphosed or hydrothermally altered basaltic, doleritic, and gabbroic rocks that are unfoliated and thus are distinct texturally from the amphibolites found in the immediate hinterland. Possible sources exist both east (Soufli, Petrota) and west (Lake Volvi) of the site. The few ultramafic rocks in the collection (serpentinite and tremolite) are found in the same geological setting and probably came from the same general source areas.

There is an additional group of fine-grained, generally gray-green rocks (the FGGG group) that take a fine polish but are almost impossible to identify lithologically in hand specimens. These examples, when examined as thin-sections, include at least three different rock types that happen to converge on one another in both color and mechanical properties. They, too, can be attributed to geological contexts that exist in Thrace but which are not present in the Drama Plain hinterland.

The basic division of rocks is thus between local or Drama hinterland sources, which might extend into the upper Nestos valley, and nonlocal or exotic sources which the cumulative balance of probability would place in the hills surrounding the basins and plains to the east, in Thrace. There are no known lithologies that geological arguments would place right outside this region of northern Greece. It should be remembered that all the medium- and high-grade metamorphic massifs in this part of Greece are part of the so-called Rhodope Crystalline Complex that extends well into Bulgaria. Here, other mafic and ultramafic bodies and other Tertiary volcano-sedimentary basins occur with associations similar to those represented in the artifact suite.

LITHOLOGY AND USAGE

Represented within the artifacts are clear associations of particular lithologies with a function that can be related to mineralogy and texture (how the mineral grains are arranged). The capacities of a rock type to take and retain an edge, to withstand repeated impacts, and to take a wide, flat depression appear to be the three key factors that give rise to the different proportions of rock types used. These types include polished artifacts (axes, maceheads, etc.), impactors (pounders and hammerstones), and grinders (querns and rubbers). Polished artifacts appear to have the most severe criteria of acceptability, resulting in more of the sources being obtained outside the immediate plain of Drama catchment than is the case with pounders and ground stone, which have properties more easily met by the local marbles, schists, amphibolites, and vein quartz. To take an edge and retain it in use, a material must be either ultra-fine grained or glassy enough to fracture conchoidally, like obsidian or flint. Alternatively, if the material has to be ground and polished, rather than fractured, to form an edge, it must be composed entirely of individually hard, strong minerals well bonded together, as is the case in many hornfelses. Fineness of grain size and an interlocking or felted texture usually convey extra quality to the product, as, for example, with nephritic jade.

The main lithologies that satisfied the demand for polished, edged material were a range of compact amphibole-bearing rocks. These include well-crystalline foliated varieties that are probably local, and the group of nonschistose metamorphosed basalts, dolerites, and gabbros that are considered exotic, and the FGGG group, also inferred to be exotic. The serpentinites and tremolite rocks are also confined to the polished stone assemblage, as are almost all the metamorphosed basalts, dolerites, and gabbros and the majority of the amphibolites. The more straightforward rock types making up the ground stone assemblage and the impactors are described first, followed by the more distinctive lithologies in the polished assemblage.

GROUND STONE

The most abundant rock type from which querns of various designs were made throughout the site's occupation is a quartz-rich mica schist with essential sodic plagioclase feldspar, referred to as schist QFM (quartzo-feldspathic mica schist) in table 4.1. The mica is usually muscovite (white mica), but biotite (of various colors) is quite often present in addition. The schist is most commonly gray, occasionally pinkish where potassium feldspar is present, and usually has a planar foliation (that is, the constituent minerals are concentrated in specific plane layers) and schistose characteristics (meaning it will split along the micaceous foliation planes). The grain size is usually moderately coarse, with constituent minerals clearly visible to the naked eye. Compositionally, the rock type is a semi-pelite, a name given to a metamorphosed clay-rich sandstone, in this case one originally containing variable amounts of detrital feldspar and so termed *arkosic*. Where pink potassium feldspar is abundant. this rock may occur as porphyroblasts or augen, with the quartz-rich layers wrapped around them. If mica is less abundant, the rock is then reasonably termed a *gneiss*. The distinction is probably not significant;

Table 4.1. Raw Material of Ground Stone by Phase

Material	I + II	III	IV + V	Total
	N and %	N and %	N and %	N and %
QFM*	18	18	23	59
	75. 0	54.5	36.5	49.2
Gneiss	1	0	2	3
	4.2	0. 0	3.2	2.5
Marble	1	8	18	27
	4.2	24.2	28.6	22.5
Amphibolite	0	1	9	10
	0. 0	3. 0	14.3	8.3
Metadolerite	0	0	2	2
	0. 0	0. 0	3.2	1.7
Lst/Sst**	4	5	5	14
	16.7	15.2	7.9	11.7
Granite	0	1	2	3
	0. 0	3. 0	3.2	2.5
Vein Quartz	0	0	2	2
	0. 0	0. 0	3.2	1.7
No. of pieces	24	33	63	120
in each phase	20. 0	27.5	52.5	100

* Quartzo-feldspathic mica schist
**Limestone-sandstone

minor gneissic QFM rocks are probably scattered through the metasedimentary sequence among the schists and marbles.

The grade of metamorphism is not well characterized by the minerals present but is probably upper green schist to lower amphibolite facies. This closely related suite of rocks is typical of the metasediments interbedded with the marbles (metamorphosed limestones) of the immediately adjacent massifs of Pangaion, Symvolon, and Menokion, both as described in the literature and from the writer's own observations. A large number of the querns have clearly been fashioned from naturally flat cobbles bounded by micaceous foliation surfaces. These cobbles can be found in the local streambeds today. The typical microscopic structure of layers of quartz and feldspar separated by micaceous partings would make it easy to obtain a shallow depression by battering a foliation surface with a tougher hammerstone and grinding away the debris. With care, the mica partings will cushion the blows and prevent the stone from cracking across.

The sizes of the phase I and IV suites are small compared with those of II, III, and V, so that I and II are combined and IV is combined with V. In the analysis of usage patterns with time, there is thus a trade-off between stratigraphic resolution and statistical significance. In addition, there are the uncertainties attached to the classification of fragments and objects used for pounding and rubbing that may be refined through use. The changes in relative abundance of ground stone lithologies are plotted in figure 4.2, which shows the QFM+ gneiss association as the most abundant rock type in this group.

The next most abundant lithology is marble, but this material is common only from phase III onward, reaching about 30%, compared with 40% of QFMs by phase V. The marbles are typically light colored, pure, and well crystalline, most likely having formed from the metamorphic transformation of pure limestones. Occasionally, the marbles are micaceous. The marbles and QFM schists could have come from any of the immediately adjacent metamorphic terrains, most probably from the beds of streams that drain them and that dissect and rework alluvial fans containing cobbles deposited in earlier periods of higher rainfall.

Although such crystalline marbles are tough and well bonded, the calcite of which they are composed is a much softer mineral than quartz and feldspar and has three perfect cleavages. Controlled impacts will shatter the surface layer, allowing it to be ground away and hollowed out in a manner similar to schist but probably to a finer finish. One may speculate that more effort and skill are required to convert the average marble cobble into a flat or hollowed quern, but that the product is superior and affords less contaminated (perhaps better tasting?) food than is the case with a flat-sided slab of schist. This difference between the two might explain the relative increase in the use of marble over schist over time (although the rough surface of a coarse QFM quern is more valuable for certain tasks such as dehusking or grinding). Since both rock types would have remained freely available, perhaps the change reflects increasing diversity of use in food preparation.

The third local ground stone component is amphibolite, a metamorphic rock composed mostly of amphibole, a green, prismatic iron- and magnesium-bearing silicate, accompanied by feldspar, a white Na-Ca-Al silicate. In medium and high-grade amphibolites, these two minerals make up the bulk of the rock, with an opaque iron titanium oxide as an important accessory. In lower grade amphibolites, other minerals, such as epidote (yellowish Ca-Al-Fe silicate) and chlorite (green Fe-Mg-Al silicate), may occur, along with sphene (Ca-Ti silicate). In this study, the term *amphibolite* is reserved for

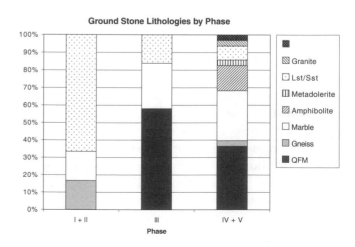

Figure 4.2. Ground stone lithologies by phase.

schistose or foliated rocks with this mineralogy. Amphibolites are the product of regional metamorphism of basic igneous rocks (basalts), which would originally have been lava flows, intrusive dikes, or tuffs and ashes, depending on the history of the terrain in question. Few regional metamorphic terrains are devoid of them, and the mineralogy and appearance of amphibolites to the naked eye is not always a reliable indicator of metamorphic grade, which might in this case distinguish local from more exotic sources. Medium- and high-grade amphibolites tend to be more coarsely crystalline and deep shiny green, while lower-grade variants are often duller green and finer grained. Intense deformation can, however, render these distinctions invalid, turning coarse rocks with clearly distinct green and white components into fine-grained, homogeneous dull green schistose rocks of indeterminate grade.

The two dominant minerals, green and white, reflect the fact that the original mineralogy of the parent basaltic rock was composed of a dark Fe-Mg mineral (pyroxene) and a light mineral (feldspar). Where the original rock was coarse grained, meriting the term *dolerite* or *gabbro*, the original two-tone texture can be inherited by the metamorphic daughter rock, provided that the rock has not been sheared during metamorphism. Large bodies of basic igneous rock in a terrain, tens or hundreds of meters thick, can be very resistant to deformation, and rocks that are mineralogically amphibolite but texturally still recognizably igneous can result. These rocks are described here as *metadolerites* and *metagabbros*.

In the case of the immediate hinterland adjacent to the site, the deformation is quite intense, becoming even more intense in the higher Sidhironero Unit. There are no known large basic bodies in this terrain, so it is probably unlikely that many, if any, of the amphibolites in the immediate hinterland have any preserved igneous texture. The igneous textured amphibolites in the artifact suite are considered exotic. The amphibolites that the author has seen and sampled in the field around and to the north of the site are all schistose to varying degrees and, from a provenance point of view, are not distinguishable from one another.

The amphibolites in the ground stone are a minor component, comprising only ten of the 114 pieces studied, nine of which are in phase V. As with those amphibolites (that is, metabasaltic rocks that lack a preserved igneous texture) in the polished stone, they are assumed to be local by default. It is argued, however, that the metadolerites and metagabbros are not local and, as local shearing will convert an unfoliated metadolerite into a thoroughgoing schistose amphibolite (although there is no way of going in the other direction), some of the amphibolites could have been imported with the metadolerites. Schistose amphibolites are likely to be found in close association with metadolerites, but the converse does not follow. Indeed, two objects in the phase IV+V group are identified as metadolerites. The metadolerite provenance question is discussed in the section "Polished Stone."

Three worked granite (*sensu lato*) pieces occur in the ground stone suite. One from phase III is a biotite aplite, a granitic rock poor in Fe-Mg silicates and typical of late-stage minor intrusions in granite complexes. Such intrusions occur between Paranestion and Skaloti and in the Vrontou complex. The two phase V pieces are an unfoliated granite and a foliated granite. Without thin-section confirmation, the correct petrological identification cannot be made. The foliated piece could be from the Kavala granite; the unfoliated piece is probably not Kavala, but is not attributable to any specific alternative source such as Vrontou, Skaloti-Echinos, or Xanthi (Jones et al. 1992). The distinctive monzodiorite SF 2424 (Petrology No. 81) was described on site as an unworked natural cobble. This somewhat unusual rock type of granitic affinity was not found in the Vrontou massif in the course of a recent investigation (Kolocotroni 1992). It may be present in the Skaloti-Echinos complex, but a more likely source is the Maronia monzodiorite south of Komotini (Kyriacopoulos 1987; Hague 1993). Although unworked, it is inferred to be an imported object.

The two remaining groups making up the ground stone assemblage are sandstone and limestone. The sandstones are well lithified and coarse grained. The limestones include a very fossiliferous variety rich in gastropod molds. The potential limestone source is the gastropod limestones of

Lutetian (Eocene) age among the Tertiary sediments of the Komotini Basin (Hague 1993). This attribution is speculative, however, without a paleontological identification. Sandstones occur in the same association. The lithification of these two rock types used as artifacts implies that they were from unmetamorphosed sedimentary beds old enough to have been buried and subsequently unroofed. In this part of Greece, that applies to the older Eocene marine sediments in the Tertiary basins of Xanthi, Komotini, and Kirki-Essimi, which seem to have been produced in an early phase of strike-slip-driven extension. Oligocene granites were subsequently intruded in locations controlled by the same tectonic regime. There is petrological evidence for the unroofing of several kilometers of granite, as in the case of Vrontou.

The younger Tertiary (Neogene) sediments of Miocene and Pliocene age, which subsequently filled the basins that were initiated in the earlier episode of extension, are poorly consolidated conglomerates of sands and marls that have not been buried and lithified. The inference is that major localized uplift and unroofing took place immediately post-Oligocene, while other areas continued to subside. The key implications for the provenance of these artifacts are that the only unmetamorphosed lithified sediments east of the Strymon are early Tertiary in age, and that they do not occur in and around the plain of Drama. Thin-section studies of the microfossils in the gastropod limestones might define the age precisely in order to locate the source with more confidence.

Ground Stone Lithology Use Over Time

Figure 4.2 summarizes the major ground stone lithologies in the I+II, III, and IV+V groupings. The sample contains twenty-four, thirty-three, and sixty-three pieces, respectively. Unphased material has been excluded, but objects from contexts described as uncertain or possibly mixed in phases II and III have been included. Local varieties at over 80% remain roughly constant as a proportion of the total. Two observations may be noted: (1) the selection of marble as an important raw material, at the expense, proportionally, of QFM schist from phase III onward, and (2) the incoming of a greater variety of lithologies largely in phase V: metadolerite (two

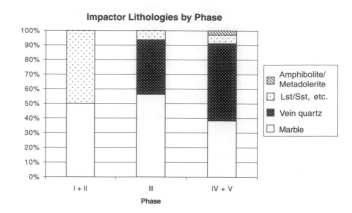

Figure 4.3. Impactor lithologies by phase.

pieces), granite (two pieces in phase V, and one in phase III), and vein quartz (two pieces). The last apparent trend should be evaluated with caution. The sample size is larger in IV+V than in the earlier periods combined. The number of objects made of rock types that appear only in phases IV and V is very small, and their inclusion in the data set obviously depends on the correctness of the classification. The trend toward greater diversity with time is less clear in the other categories of objects.

IMPACTORS

Lithologies and Sources

The examined suite of hammerstones and pounders comprises eight, sixteen, and thirty-four objects from the I+II, III and IV+V phase groupings, respectively (table 4.2; figure 4.3). The range of lithologies is very restricted: marble (twenty-three examples) and vein quartz (thirty examples) dominate; five other rock types are represented by one example each: limestone, sandstone, metamorphic quartzite, ironstone (hematite?), and amphibolite. The marble and vein quartz are local, as most probably are the amphibolite, but they are unsourceable in detail. The quartzite could be from the local metasedimentary sequence. The ironstone, likewise, could be from a very localized occurrence of vein-related mineralization within the metamorphic terrain. The limestone and sandstone are inferred to be imported from farther east for the reasons discussed in the preceding "Ground Stone" section.

Table 4.2. Raw Material of Stone Impacters by Phase

Material	I + II	III	IV + V	Total
	N and %	N and %	N and %	N and %
Marble	1	9	13	23
	12.5	56.3	38.2	39.7
Vein Quartz	6	6	18	30
	75.0	37.5	52.9	51.7
Lst/Sst, etc*	1	1	2	4
	12.5	6.3	5.9	6.9
Amph/Metadol**	0	0	1	1
	0.0	0.0	2.9	1.7
Totals	8	16	34	58
N and %	13.8	27.6	58.6	100

* Limestone-sandstone
** Amphibolite/metadolerite

Lithology and Usage

Why the inhabitants selected certain rock types is clear. A hammerstone needs to be tough, resistant to splitting, preferably dense, and unlikely to shed too much mineral debris during use. It must be available in, or at least fashionable into, handy-sized spherical or cylindrical lumps so that a decent mass can be lined up behind the impacting area. The local schists are ruled out because they split. Even if the schist is initially ellipsoidal as a cobble, it inevitably has the scholastically plane parallel to the elongation direction; impacts in the direction of the schistosity promote splitting. Foliated amphibolites, although tougher, have the same tendency to split. The individual amphibole crystals are not particularly resistant to crushing because they possess two good cleavages. Thus, even though an amphibolitic rock as a whole may resist cracking (because the crystals form an interlocking mass), impacts generate green crystalline powdered debris. Some unfoliated metadolerites with abundant feldspar undoubtedly make excellent impactors. If perfectly acceptable alternatives are readily available, however, why would anyone bother to seek out metadolerites when vein quartz meets all the criteria? Vein quartz, which does not tend to split, is essentially composed of intergrown, often large, crystals. It fractures conchoidally and generally unpredictably because defects and shear surfaces are generally present in large masses. Quartz is also resistant to chemical weathering. The net result is that alluvial and fluvial processes acting on a metamorphic terrain with abundant quartz veins will do an efficient job of destroying all unsuitable impactors, leaving rounded, coherent lumps of the strongest materials that are progressively overrepresented farther downstream from the source compared with their area of outcrop.

The use of marble for hammerstones presents more of a balance between advantage and disadvantage. The purest crystalline marbles are composed entirely of a three-dimensional mosaic of calcite grains, ranging from 0.5 to 10 mm or more in diameter. Unless the marble is extremely strongly deformed and platy, conditions in which the marble may well split, pure marbles are not schistose. The individual crystals, conversely, have three perfect cleavages and are quite soft (hardness 3: scratchable with steel or quartz and other silicates). Thus, crystalline marble is a tough rock in that fractures do not propagate through it easily, while on a grain scale it is soft and can be degraded by abrasion and impacts. One would not use a marble hammer to crush quartz grains or use it against a harder silicate surface, but a marble mortar and pestle set makes good sense for food preparation where a good smooth area of mutual contact is an advantage. This is still true 6000 years later.

Lithology: Distribution by Phase

The distribution by phase shown in table 4.2 is based on quite a small sample set of thirty-four pieces, so trends should be regarded with caution. In the sample only one piece in phases I+II is made of marble, compared with the six made of vein quartz; in phase III, however, marble outnumbers vein quartz by nine to six. This distribution seems to mirror the trend in ground stone utilization, with the balance favoring vein quartz in phases IV and V.

POLISHED STONE: AXES, ADZES, CHISELS, MACE-HEADS, AND SHAFTED OBJECTS

Lithologies and Sources

The polished stone objects evidently had to meet the exacting technical specifications of toughness, homogeneity, and nonfissile character, and they represent a considerable investment of time in their manufacture. Of the local rock types, only the amphibolites would have provided suitable material for usable tools, and many amphibolites would have been too schistose or too coarse to keep a sharp edge during use. The very fact that a wide range of lithologies was used and that many are clearly tougher and better able to take a lasting edge than amphibolite suggests that the criteria were ones of utility rather than appearance (figure 4.4). It would have been relatively easy, for example, to fashion axes from the fine-grained marbles and give them a high polish. They would have been short-lived as serious tools, however, and indeed marble represents only 6.6% of the total IV+V grouping. QFM does not meet the acceptability criterion at all. The net result is that local lithologies are represented least in the polished stone group: 27% in I+II, 16% in III, 46% in IV+V (table 4.3).

Amphibolite and Marble

Amphibolite and the few marbles are the local representatives. As metadolerite and metagabbro together are almost as abundant as amphibolite (thirty pieces compared with thirty-five amphibolites), some of the amphibolites are quite possibly imports. The amphibolite and marble objects have not been distinguished lithologically from their ground stone counterparts.

Metadolerite and Metagabbro

The metadolerites and metagabbros are a particularly interesting group. They share a recognizable igneous texture, most commonly characterized by rectangular white patches from 1 to 5 mm long. These patches represent the original magmatic feld-

Table 4.3. Raw Material of Polished Stone Tools by Phase

Material	I + II N and %	III N and %	IV + V N and %	Total N and %
Amphibolite	7	4	24	35
	26.9	10.8	39.3	28.2
Marble	0	2	4	6
	0.0	5.4	6.6	4.8
Metadolerite	6	12	12	30
	23.1	32.4	19.7	24.2
FGGG*	6	12	6	24
	23.1	32.4	9.8	19.4
Serpentine	4	5	3	12
	15.4	13.5	4.9	9.7
Lst**	1	0	3	4
	3.8	0.0	4.9	3.2
Sst***	2	1	6	9
	7.7	2.7	9.8	7.3
Volcanic	0	1	3	4
	0.0	2.7	4.9	3.2
Totals	26	37	61	124
N and %	21.0	29.8	49.1	

* Fine-grained, generally gray-green
** Limestone
*** Sandstone

spar crystals now replaced by an aggregate of one or more white metamorphic minerals, usually zoisite or clinozoisite intergrown with a secondary feldspar. In some, the primary feldspar is preserved. These white areas are set in a greenish or brownish groundmass that replaced the original pyroxenes or olivines or both. Some lithologies are weakly foliated, so that the white pseudomorphs after feldspar are slightly flattened but still recognizable. Texturally, the inferred parent rocks range from fine-grained microporphyritic basalts (possibly thin dikes originally) to medium-grained gabbros, the product of slower crystallization of larger bodies of basic magma.

Metadolerite (table 4.3) includes two variants: metadolerite-S (or metagabbro-S) and metadolerite/ gabbro-R. The S stands for saussuritized, the name given to the process of metamorphic transformation of original plagioclase feldspar into white aggregate of secondary minerals (mentioned above). This transformation is essentially isochemical at the scale of the whole rock; it needs water and the right pressure and temperature conditions acting on the original basaltic parent. The combination of zoisite or clinozoisite and intermediate or sodic plagioclase is stable over a wide range of medium- and low-grade

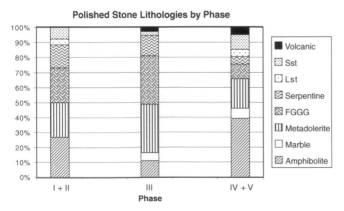

Figure 4.4. Polished stone lithologies by phase.

metamorphic conditions. The assemblage is not particularly susceptible to further degradation under surface weathering conditions. Saussuritization is an old, still useful term that essentially signifies a metamorphic transformation. This transformation has left the original disposition of chemical elements in the rock more or less unchanged, with the original light and dark minerals replaced by volumes of secondary light and dark minerals of roughly the same size and shape.

The R stands for rodingitized. Here the feldspar is replaced wholesale by one or more calcium aluminum silicates. In the case of an axe fragment, SF 1191 (Petrology No. 91, phase III), a thin-section analysis shows that the feldspar is replaced by prehnite. Rodingites are basaltic rocks (commonly gabbros) that have been metamorphosed and metasomatized (chemically transformed) by being in close proximity to ultramafic rocks undergoing serpentinization. The process can affect just the feldspar component, or it may alter the iron-magnesium silicates as well. The whole composition of the rock changes, and in extreme cases all the iron and magnesium is removed, leaving a completely white product; in SF 1191, the process is incomplete. The distinctive additional feature of SF 1191 is that the prehnite itself has clearly broken down under the action of groundwater to a soft, white, powdery mineral, as yet unidentified, but probably a zeolite. The result is that buried artifacts acquire a soft outer layer a few millimeters thick, which follows the surface profile. The darker iron- and magnesium-bearing minerals resist this decay and end up slightly proud on the surface. The soft exterior is clearly a postburial feature and in no way reflects the mechanical properties of the object when it was made.

Prehnite, when fresh, is a silicate mineral with the same hardness as feldspar. The thin-section of SF 1191 shows that prehnitization has not been complete: sharp transformation fronts cross the section, and unaltered feldspar is visible as gray translucent grains in hand specimens. So soft is the transformation product that the rock was mistaken in the field for a kaolinized granite, and the gray feldspar was misidentified as quartz. Using thin-section identification, objects that were clearly identified, such as SF 1191, can now be confidently placed in a rodingitized metagabbro-R or metadolerite-R category. SF

1191, and by inference the other members of this group, contain preserved igneous pyroxenes and may have been rodingitized at too low a temperature to develop amphibole. It is thus not strictly a metamorphic rock in the same sense as the amphibolites and saussuritized metadolerites. This distinction has implications for provenance.

PROVENANCE. The metadolerite/gabbro-S group comprises basic magmatic rocks that have been metamorphosed under green schist, epidote-amphibolite, or amphibolite facies conditions but without being significantly deformed in the process. Some were very fine-grained rocks to start with and so originally cooled rapidly as flows or thin-sheeted intrusions. In a regional metamorphic terrain in which deformation typically accompanies metamorphism, basic rocks are usually the most mechanically resistant to deformation. The ability to resist the imposition of a metamorphic schistosity, however, depends on the size of the body of the resistant rock. A metagabbro may have come from a body of gabbro that was originally large (tens of meters thick), and so deformation did not penetrate to its center. A microporphyritic, undeformed, otherwise fine-grained metadolerite, by inference, probably came from a large body of metabasaltic rock that was made up of many individually thin components.

Two types of closely related geological setting fit the metadolerite criterion: ophiolite complexes and metamorphosed ophiolite complexes. Ophiolites are tectonic slices of former oceanic crust caught up in orogenic belts, which preserve a more or less complete sequence from pillow lavas at the top, through a zone of 100% sheeted dikes, to gabbros, down to usually serpentinized ultramafic rocks at the base. If complete, the sequence is from 5 to 10 km thick. It is true that piles of thin lava flows unconnected to the sea floor generation, in a regional metamorphic terrain, might remain undeformed in their interior, and also that regional terrains, subject to a late-stage intrusive event (which escaped the deformation but not the heat and pressure) might also produce undeformed metadolerites. Nevertheless, the association of dolerites and gabbros strongly suggests derivation from a sheeted dike/gabbro complex. The eastern Mediterranean

141

region has many such examples (Dixon and Robertson 1984).

At this point, the characterization of the setting and the search for a matching provenance become more difficult. The process of sea floor spreading produces all the component igneous rock types, but also leads to a substantial proportion of them undergoing a postcrystallization reaction with hot, circulating sea water. The sheeted dike complexes in ophiolite complexes that have been sliced out of their parent ocean and dumped onto a continental margin are made of saussuritized metadolerite with an epidote-amphibolite facies mineralogy—that is, they are already low- to medium-grade metamorphic rocks. If this usually large mass of basic rock is subsequently buried and metamorphosed again, it may be reheated to something like the temperature it reached in its postmagmatic transformation and still remain undeformed because there is so much of it. It may reach a higher grade than before and become a regionally metamorphosed metadolerite or metagabbro while still retaining its parent's igneous texture although it is recognizably transformed from its former state on the ocean floor.

A third type of ophiolitic complex lies north of Lake Volvi in the Greek part of the Serbo-Macedonian zone, west of the Strymon Valley. It represents the deep roots of a very small oceanic rift that never came to maturity and was buried and metamorphosed essentially in situ (Dixon and Dimitriadis 1984). It has sheeted dikes and gabbros with well-preserved igneous textures but a clear metamorphic imprint that is not attributable to sea floor processes.

The rodingitization process requires feldspar-rich gabbro or dolerite to be physically close to ultramafic rock that is undergoing serpentinization (the transformation of mantle olivines and orthopyroxenes into hydrous serpentine) through the action of circulating water. The water, if at a high enough temperature, will promote the active reaction and transport of chemical constituents in and out of the adjacent gabbro. Again, these criteria are only readily met by ocean floor rocks in situ (rodingitized gabbros have been dredged from the present-day sea floor) or by disrupted tectonically juxtaposed gabbro-ultramafic associations derived from oceanic crust and then subjected to very low-grade metamorphism and fluid transport.

The thin-section and hand specimen appearance of the thirty metadolerite/gabbro objects is only consistent with derivation from one or more mafic-ultramafic associations of ophiolite type. Texturally, the axes of SF 486 (plate 5.9b; Petrology No. 93, phase III), SF 259 (plate 5.4b; Petrology No. 87, phase III), and hammerstone SF 2252 (Petrology No. 82, phase V) are thoroughly metamorphic in character and difficult to reconcile with the prehnitized but otherwise pristine metagabbro-R SF 1191. The simplest explanation is that at least two distinct sources are involved: one from an ophiolite complex incorporated in the regional metamorphic terrain of either the Serbo-Macedonian or Rhodope massifs, and the other from an ophiolite that preserves only ocean floor alteration or subsequent low-grade hydrothermal circulation, inducing rodingitization. None of these metadoleritic rocks can be matched by samples found covering the metamorphic terrain between Drama and the Skaloti-Echinos Complex to the north.

The Volvi Complex, from which the author has examined hundreds of thin-sections, is of the first or metamorphic type; indeed, all of the first three objects listed above could be matched with Volvi rocks. Conversely, the author is confident that the Volvi Complex does not contain rodingitized unmetamorphosed gabbros of the SF 1191 type. There are bodies of ophiolitic gabbro close to Thessaloniki and at various points northwest and southeast along the western margin of the Serbo-Macedonian Massif that are not metamorphosed. The author has visited most of them and is not aware of any with this distinctive rodingitization, although its presence is not ruled out.

To the east of the site, the most promising candidates are in eastern Thrace. One is the ophiolitic sequence of Soufli, 180 km east of the site: "one of the least known ophiolitic complexes of Greece [which contains] . . . serpentinized peridotites . . . metagabbros, gabbropegmatites, metadiabases [= metadolerites], amphibolites and chloritic schists" (Manganas and Economou 1988). The source reference (Maratos 1960) is a Greek-language geological survey publication, which the author has not yet been able to consult. Clearly, the right rock types are present. The Soufli Complex lies within the metamorphic rocks of the Rhodope Massif in the

Upper Sidhironero Unit, according to the map of Manganas and Economou (1988). It is a candidate for the metadolerite/gabbro-S suite source.

There is another ophiolitic body some 35 km to the west of Soufli, around Smiyada, which is shown on the regional sketch map in Manganas and Economou (1988) and on the source map in figure 4.1 (Dimadis and Zachos 1986), but about which nothing further is known. An additional small ultramafic complex is shown in figure 4.1 to the northeast of Xanthi. Nothing is known about that complex either.

Also in eastern Thrace, and more promising, is the Petrota Gabbro Complex (Hague 1993) southwest of Soufli which contains "a sequence of layered gabbros and gabbronorites ... [the] cumulate gabbros are frequently cut by finer grained doleritic dykes of similar composition...." (Hague 1993). The gabbros are not metamorphosed but "typically display a significant degree of alteration. This involves the saussuritization of plagioclase ... characteristic of low-grade metamorphism or late-stage hydrothermal alteration of basic igneous rocks and [is] particularly common in ophiolite complexes" (Hague 1993). Partly serpentinized ultramafic rocks were observed at one locality by Hague, and their presence supports the suggestion that the Petrota Complex is the disrupted lower part of an ophiolite. There is no specific mention of rodingitization, but the Petrota Complex is a possible (and accessible) source for unmetamorphosed ophiolitic basic rocks. The existence of an ultramafic, partly serpentinized component could be consistent with rodingites occurring somewhere within its confines. It has been dated as Jurassic and is probably related to the ophiolite complex exposed on Samothraki. Both lie in a region of Mesozoic rocks that have undergone low-grade metamorphism, the Circum-Rhodope Belt, the name of which conveys about as much as is known for certain about its tectonic significance.

The FGGG Group

The Fine-Grained Gray-Green (FGGG) group is, for the most part, exactly that. Some rocks show fine striping or discontinuous subparallel wisps of lighter and darker material. Their mineralogy is unresolvable to the naked eye, even with the aid of a magnifying glass. A number of igneous, metamorphic, and sedimentary rocks can fit this description. Five thin-sectioned specimens in this category fit broadly into two quite different types: calc-silicate hornfelses and volcaniclastics. Field identifications were not reliable. The specimens are a classic example of converging visual appearances; no amount of experience can ensure that the correct identification will be made from hand specimen alone. The provenance of the five sectioned rocks is discussed next, but it is just as impossible to assign any of the other FGGG objects to the correct petrological category as it was on site.

SF 54 AND SF 714.   SF 54 (Petrology No. 92, phase II, axe; figure 5.8; plate 5.11c) and SF 714 (Petrology No. 85, phase II, adze/axe; plate 5.2a) are calc-silicate hornfelses, impure calcareous sediments or muddy, sandy limestones thermally metamorphosed by an igneous intrusive body. SF 54 has granular-textured, fine-grained rocks with diopside, epidote (rodingite), and plagioclase feldspar. SF 714 has a possibly lower-grade assemblage of tremolite-diopside-calcite. Both are devoid of any schistosity, which implies that they were unmetamorphosed sediments prior to thermal metamorphism.

The only exposed intrusive igneous bodies in northern Greece that are not deformed and metamorphosed are the granites of Oligocene age previously mentioned as sources for the granite artifacts. The possible locations for an exposed contact between granite and older, but not metamorphosed sediment are very limited. The sedimentary rocks would have to be Eocene in age and come from one of the Tertiary basins in Thrace. The writer does not know of a specific instance, but the western margin of the Xanthi intrusion is possible, as is a small igneous body related to the Leptokarya Granite north of Essimi, which is shown as an outcropping within Eocene-Oligocene sediments (figure 4.1). It is not known whether the contact is intrusive or unconformable. The granites mainly outcrop in contact with older metamorphic rocks as they represent areas of post-Oligocene uplift and unroofing, whereas the basins represent regions of approximately contemporaneous subsidence. An intrusive/basin fill contact would imply tectonic inversion from subsidence to uplift, which is possible, but likely to be rare.

In this same context, SF 1060 (Petrology No. 98; plate 5.2d), an axe fragment from phase V, QO 8s, may be mentioned. It is a unique garnet-corundum-spinel-magnetite hornfels. It is not in the FGGG group, being dark and mottled, but requires in part the same geological setting as SF 54, an intrusive contact, and in this case, a contact with a laterite or bauxite-rich horizon (that is, an alumina- and iron-rich, silica- and calcium-poor layer such as is formed as a residual soil from the weathering of basalt lava or limestone that has not been subsequently deformed). The rock, high-grade hornfels, could have been derived from a parent that had already suffered low- or medium-grade regional metamorphism, of which no trace is retained in the completely recrystallized hornfels. The parent rock is rare, and the intrusive contact is an immensely unique circumstance. The Kavala Granite intrudes the marbles of Pangaion-Symvolon, but there is no record of bauxite horizons within the marbles in the accounts of Kronberg (1969) and Schenk (1970).

More promising are the low-grade metavolcano sedimentary units of the Circum-Rhodope group in eastern Thrace, which are intruded by the Maronia monzodiorite and which develop a contact aureole (Hague 1993), although no specific mention of metalaterites is made. This lithology is coincidentally similar to the Tievebulliagh metalaterite of Northern Ireland, which is a well-known raw material for axe manufacturing.

SF 176, SF 294, AND SF 3433. Three examples of axes —SF 176 (Petrology No. 90, phase III; plate 5.4d), SF 294 (Petrology No. 94, phase II; plate 5.11a), and SF 3433 (Petrology No. 95, surface find; plate 5.11e)— are fine-grained fragmentary volcanic rocks or ashes. SF 294 is the least metamorphosed and has a texture suggestive of an ignimbrite, with a welded ash-flow, and the original glassy fragments recrystallized to intergrown quartz and feldspar. It contains isolated pyroxene grains and recognizable lava fragments. SF 176 is a phyllite: a low-grade, weakly schistose metamorphic rock containing chlorite, clinozoisite, plagioclase, and quartz, which from the nature of the clasts was also a clastic volcanic rock prior to metamorphism. SF 3433 is a related rock, with abundant clasts of plagioclase feldspar of probable volcanic origin, deformed quartz ribbons, and metamorphic chlorite and epidote. It is inferred to have been a mixed volcani-clastic sediment with a crystal-rich ash component, as well as a quartz-rich nonvolcanic component.

Once again, the most probable source for these rocks is in eastern Thrace in the area of outcrop of the Circum-Rhodope Group, which includes green schist facies metavolcaniclastics (IGME: Maronia 1:50,000 sheet, quoted in Hague 1993). To the west, the nearest possible outcrops of low-grade metavolcanics are in the Paikon Massif west of the Vardar.

Serpentinite and Related Rocks

Serpentine and related rocks represent seventeen objects in the polished stone group, to which it is appropriate to add consideration of three objects classed as ornaments: one hammerstone, one rubber, and one natural pebble. Fifteen of these are variations of the typical green, partly translucent serpentine (strictly serpentinite), two are tentatively identified as such, while the remaining five are schistose ultramafic rocks, either antigorite schist (one specimen), which is a rock made of a metamorphic serpentine variety, or tremolite schist (four specimens), which is a product of the chemical modification of serpentinite during metamorphism.

Two phase V schistose axe specimens were sectioned: SF 1011 (Petrology No. 158; plate 5.12a) and SF 1347 (Petrology No. 156). SF 1011 is antigorite schist that has a dense interlocking texture of short antigorite flakes with minor components of talc and hematite. SF 1347 is a tremolite schist made of bundles and sheaves of fibrous tremolite crystals, forming a dense woven texture. The latter is essentially nephritic jade.

Potential source areas are essentially the same as those for the metadolerites and metagabbros. Serpentinite is a hydrated ultramafic peridotite, the rock of which the Earth's mantle is composed and which lies about 7 km beneath the sea floor. The detached slices of oceanic crust that form the ophiolite complexes, discussed as sources for the metadolerites, almost invariably have serpentinized ultramafic rock at their base. In a tectonic region like the eastern Mediterranean, ultramafic rock is by far the most common source of serpentinite and the rocks derived from it. There are ultramafic bodies at the eastern margin of the Serbo-Macedonian zone west of the Strymon, and there are four outcroppings in Thrace: Soufli, Smiyada, the body 20 km northeast of Xanthi, and the Petrota Complex. Other ultramafic bodies are exposed along the western margin of the Serbo-Macedonian zone, north and south of Thessaloniki, and in the major ophiolitic massifs of Vourinos, Pindos, and Othrys in central Greece.

The Soufli, Smiyada, and Xanthi bodies lie within the Rhodope Massif and are most probably metamorphosed. It is not known whether they include massive nonschistose serpentinite, which would polish up to the typical translucent form of the majority of the artifacts. Such an inclusion is not impossible if the ultramafic bodies are large. The schistose and tremolitic varieties almost certainly occur in all three, and they are the prime candidates for the source. If massive serpentine does occur in all three, there is unlikely to be any means of discriminating further among them.

Limestones and Sandstones

Four limestones, nine sandstones, one calcareous siltstone, and two quartzites are included in the polished stone group. While some of the limestones may be very fine-grained marble, and the two quartzites and one very well-cemented sandstone may be metamorphic, the majority of the sandstones and the calcareous siltstone (a fine-grained sandstone with carbonate fragments) are clearly unmetamorphosed but well-lithified sedimentary rocks. The same reasoning applies to the sandstones and limestones in the grinder and impactor categories. They are not local and most probably came from one of the Tertiary sedimentary basins east of Xanthi. They are not particularly distinctive rocks and probably could never be attributed to a specific source. The limestones, in general, offer greater potential, as they probably contain a datable microfauna that could constrain their source. Similar sedimentary basins of Tertiary age occur in Bulgaria.

Volcanics (Lavas)

Three pieces, two from phase V and one from phase III, are porphyritic basic or intermediate volcanics of a broadly andesitic type. One was sectioned (SF 1635, Petrology No. 88, phase III; plate 5.4c) and is a fresh two-pyroxene andesite or basaltic andesite

with phenocrysts of fresh clinopyroxene, glass inclusion-filled plagioclases, and hypersthenes, the last largely pseudomorphed by chlorite and clay minerals. The phenocrysts are set in a groundmass of plagioclase, clinopyroxene, and opaque oxide. The other two pieces are similar porphyritic volcanics: a probable biotite andesite (SF 3658, phase V) and a hornblende andesite (SF 656, phase V plate 5.12e). All three are consistent with having been derived from one of the outcroppings of Late Eocene to Late Oligocene calc-alkaline (andesitic) volcanics closely associated with the Tertiary sedimentary basins in eastern Macedonia and Thrace (Fytikas et al. 1984). Outcrops occur northeast of Xanthi, in the Petrota Basin, between Kirki and Essimi, and between Fere and Dadia south of Soufli. Hague (1993) describes two-pyroxene andesites from Petrota, but it is quite likely that any of the mapped occurrences will contain such lavas. More extensive outcrops of similar volcanics of the same age occur in Bulgaria southeast of Plovdiv.

Polished Stone Lithology Use Over Time

Remarkably little change occurred in the pattern of use of different lithologies over time (figure 4.4). With the exception of the lavas, all categories in IV+V are also represented in I+II. The lava sample size is small. The potentially local rock types are shown at the bottom of figure 4.4. It could be argued that phase III represents the period when imported material is at a maximum, with local components down to less than 20% of the total; this implies it is the period of greatest selectivity. Local supplies achieve over 40% market penetration by phase V. The FGGG, pieces that perhaps represent the most carefully selected group garnered from afar, fall from their peak of 30% in phase III to 8% in phase V.

GENERAL CONCLUSIONS CONCERNING SUPPLY AND PROVENANCE

Two broad themes run through the preceding analysis. The occupants of the site exploited the local metamorphic rocks when they clearly suited the task at hand. When they did not, as with the polished stone tools, their sources came from farther afield and encompassed a range of materials rather than a few much used products. The second point is that the geological arguments lead each time to the area of eastern Thrace as being the most likely location for all the nonlocal material. These arguments are independent of one another, and only at this stage is it appropriate to make the obvious additional point that the attributions are stronger because they are pointing to the same regions: the flows of knowledge or collectors to and from source and site will not be independent of one another for the different materials.

The writer is more familiar with the geology of northern Greece to the north and west of the site and has attempted to give full consideration to possible western sources for the exotic lithologies. The rodingitized gabbros, unmetamorphosed sandstones and limestones, fresh andesitic volcanics, hornfelsed non-metamorphic sediments, and undeformed monzo-diorite simply do not have obvious westerly sources until one passes well beyond the metamorphic belt running down the eastern edge of mainland Greece. Even then, there are no obvious sediments/granite contracts and no fresh andesitic volcanics until the Aegean arc is reached. The east has to be the source. Bulgaria is a different case. The mix of Thracian geology extends into Bulgaria, but details of lithologies and localities are harder to come by. Since a range of mountains is in the way, it seems logical to look for accessible sources as a criterion.

SUGGESTIONS FOR FUTURE WORK

The obvious thing is to carry out visual surveys of artifacts in the same three categories in collections from sites between Sitagroi and the Turkish frontier. The material from Soufli would be particularly interesting. One would expect some shifts in the usage patterns in the ground stone as the QFM source became replaced by a local equivalent. There should be some pattern to the use of specific polished lithologies in relation to the proximity of the source, once one approaches close to the sources themselves, assuming the overall inference is correct. If everything comes from deepest Bulgaria, then all that might happen is a shift to local equivalents of Sitagroi's local supplies and retention of the same mix of exotics.

The lithologies that might be traceable from a ground reconnaissance and input from local geological authorities are the volcanics, monzodiorite, rodingitized gabbros, and limestones, if the latter could be sampled for microfauna. A reconnaissance of the Soufli mafic/ultramafic complex would be a useful step, coupled with a data search via knowledgeable Greek authorities.

Appendix 4.1
Petrological Analysis
John Dixon

Phase	Context	SF No.	Pet. No.	Object	Ob. Cat.	Lithology	Field description	Thin-section description or comments	Source comments
I	ZA 67	919		Axe, flat-butt	P	Dolerite?	Dark gray, hard		
I	ML 45	984		Chisel	P	Quartzite	Gray, fine grained; mottled		Could be from local Rhodope metasedimentary sequence
I	ZA 66	1158		Saddle quern	G	Quartzo-feldspathic mica schist	Gray, micaceous; originally cobble	Quartzo-feldspathic mica schist. See SF 313 (Pet. No. 79), SF 1169 (Pet. No. 77), SF 1182 (Pet. No. 78) for petrography.	Local Drama catchment metasediments
I	ZA 65	1162	76	Saddle quern	G	Quartzo-feldspathic mica schist. See thin section description.	Off-white; originally cobble.	Coarse muscovite quartz schist with augen of potassium feldspar wrapped by quartz-albite and muscovite domains.	Almost certainly from local Rhodope metasediments interbedded with marbles, making up Pangaion, Falakro, and Menokion massifs
I	ML 22?	1179		?	?	Marble			Not distinctive; probably local.
I	KL 14	2397		Grindstone fragment	G	Sandstone			Not local; probably from Eocene sedimentary sequences in basins E of Xanthi, as for limestones
I	JL 102	2512		?	?	Amphibolite	Deep blackish green, fine/medium grained, weak foliation, hornblende and plagioclase distinguishable		Not distinctive; could be from Drama catchment metamorphics, i.e., local
I	JL 105	2543		Axe, large, asymmetric	P	Microgabbro	Good ophitic texture; slight foliation; no trace of metamorphism or alteration		
I	JL 105	2544		Chisel	P	Amphibolite/calc silicate?	Deep green, very fine grained	FGGG group.	Source or sources unknown
I	JL 104	2860		Axe flake	P	Amphibolite/calc silicate?	Grayish green, fine grained	FGGG group.	Source or sources unknown
I	KL 133	3681		Bracelet fragment?	O	Marble			Not distinctive; probably local
I	KLb 141	4116		Saddle quern	G	Quartzo-feldspathic mica schist		Quartzo-feldspathic mica schist. See SF 313 (Pet. No. 79), SF 1169 (Pet. No. 77), SF 1182 (Pet. No. 78) for petrography.	Local Drama catchment metasediments
I	KLb 141	4117		?	?	Limestone			

Key: SF No. = Catalog number (see chapter 5); Pet. No. = Petrology sample; Ob. Cat. (Object category) includes B, bowl fragment; G, ground stone; I, impactor; P, polished stone; and O, ornament fragment (see chapters 5, 9).

Phase	Context	SF No.	Pet. No.	Object	Ob. Cat.	Lithology	Field description	Thin-section description or comments	Source comments
I	KLb 141	4118		?	?	Gneiss	Foliated granitic gneiss		Possibly high-grade Rhodope metamorphics of the Sidhironero Unit (Central Rhodope Unit) N and NE of Drama Plain, or Kavala Granite; not very distinctive
I	ZA 65	4577		Flat grinder	G	Limestone	Pale buff		
I	ZA 65	4579		Hammer-stone, round	I	Marble	Moderately coarse		Not distinctive; probably local
II	KMa 1	54	92	Axe	P	Calc-silicate hornfels	Fine grained; FGGG group	Granular diopside-epidote-plagioclase rock. A contact metamorphosed impure limestone. One possible lithology in FGGG group.	Equigranular texture and mineralogy implies contact between marly sediment and an intrusive, probably granite; hence not Drama catchment but possibly Xanthi or Essimi area
II	LL 2	71		Axe fragment	P	Sandstone	Pale pink/buff. Coarse grained		Not local; probably from Eocene sedimentary sequences in basins E of Xanthi, as for limestones
II	LL 4	73		Axe fragment	P	Sandstone	Gray, coarse		Not local; probably from Eocene sedimentary sequences in basins E of Xanthi, as for limestones
II	ZA 52	249		Flat grinder fragment	G	Quartzo-feldspathic mica schist	Biotite bearing	Quartzo-feldspathic mica schist. See SF 313 (Pet. No. 79), SF 1169 (Pet. No. 77), SF 1182 (Pet. No. 78) for petrography.	Local Drama catchment metasediments
II	KL 4	262		?	?	Quartzo-feldspathic mica schist		Quartzo-feldspathic mica schist. See SF 313 (Pet. No. 79), SF 1169 (Pet. No. 77), SF 1182 (Pet. No. 78) for petrography.	Local Drama catchment metasediments
II	KL 2	294	94	Axe	P	Ash (volcani-clastic). See thin section description.	Green, fine grained; FGGG group	Fine-grained ashy volcaniclastic, possibly ignimbritic. Abundant plagioclase, isolated pyroxenes(?), minor lava fragments. Altered groundmass ex-glass(?).	Not Drama catchment; too low grade for Rhodope metamorphics; probably Circum-Rhodope Group, eastern Thrace
II	KM 8	436		Flat grinder ex-split cobble	G	Schist	Schistose biotite granite or gneiss.		Possibly high-grade Rhodope metamorphics of Sidhironero Unit (Central Rhodope Unit) N and NE of Drama plain, or Kavala Granite; not very distinctive
II	KM 13	448		Flat grinder ex-split cobble	G	Quartzo-feldspathic mica schist	Muscovitic	Quartzo-feldspathic mica schist. See SF 313 (Pet. No. 79), SF 1169 (Pet. No. 77), SF 1182 (Pet. No. 78) for petrography.	Local Drama catchment metasediments
II	KM 14	450		Axe ?	P	Limestone	Gray		Probably Thrace (see note for SF 2645; phase II)
II	KM 5	515		Ornament?, disk	O	Marble			Not distinctive; probably local

Phase	Context	SF No.	Pet. No.	Object	Ob. Cat.	Lithology	Field description	Thin-section description or comments	Source comments
II	KM 17	714	85	Adze, non-parallel; buttless	P	Calc-silicate hornfels. (See thin section description.)	Fine-grained mosaic of feathery white crystal aggs. in pale green waxy groundmass; FGGG group.	Tremolite-diopside-calcite low-grade hornfels. Probably from a granite/calcareous siltstone contact zone. Field identification as "altered dolerite or ash." FGGG type.	More likely Xanthi-Komotini Basin than Drama catchment
II	ZA 54	904		Axe, non-parallel, flat butt	P	Amphibolite	Deep green, finely mottled, fine grained	Very similar to SF 2309.	Not distinctive; probably local
II	ZA 52	926		Axe	P	Metadolerite-R	Patches of transparent brownish mineral in opaque white groundmass; Medium grained	Probably SF 1191 type, rodingitized dolerite.	
II	KM 14	951		Axe, parallel sided, flat butt	P	Metadolerite-R	Radiating sheaves of soft white crystals intergrown with more resistant pale green mineral; coarse grained.	Identical to 1191, rodingitized dolerite or gabbro. Soft white surface layer acquired after burial.	Metadolerite/gabbro, not known from Drama catchment; prehnitized rocks not known from Volvi, thus possibly Soufli or Petrota
II	KM 16	955		Bowl fragment	B	Marble			Not distinctive; probably local
II	KM 16	956		Chisel	P	Hornfels?	Very dark gray, fine grained with scattered white rect. phenocrysts andalusite?		
II	KL 104	966		Axe, non-parallel, flat butt	P	Amphibolite	Deep blackish green, fine/medium grained, weak foliation, hornblende and plagioclase distinguishable	SF 966, 2512, 2725, 2769, 3364 are all very similar.	Not distinctive; probably local
II	KM 19	968		Flat grinder	G	Quartzo-feldspathic mica schist		Quartzo-feldspathic mica schist. See SF 313 (Pet. No. 79), SF 1169 (Pet. No. 77), SF 1182 (Pet. No. 78) for petrography.	Local Drama catchment metasediments
II	KM 20	973		Axe, cone-shaped	P	Amphibolite	Dark blue/green.		Not distinctive; probably local
II	KM 22	987	86	Adze, non-parallel, flat butt	P	Amphibolite. See thin section description.	Deep brownish green; fine mesh texture of plagioclase latlithology	Epidote amphibolite retrograded from higher-grade garnet amphibolite. Now fine-grained intergrowth of amphibole and feldspar with relict garnet partly pseudomorphed by albite, plagioclase to epidote and rutile rimmed by sphene.	Distinctive texture; insufficient data to rule out a local origin.
II	ZA 52	1154		Saddle quern	G	Quartzo-feldspathic mica schist	Rusty buff; originally cobble	Quartzo-feldspathic mica schist. See SF 313 (Pet. No. 79), SF 1169 (Pet. No. 77), SF 1182 (Pet. No. 78) for petrography.	Local Drama catchment metasediments
II	ZA 50	1156		Saddle quern	G	Quartzo-feldspathic mica schist	Pinkish gray; originally cobble	Quartzo-feldspathic mica schist. See SF 313 (Pet. No. 79), SF 1169 (Pet. No. 77), SF 1182 (Pet. No. 78) for petrography.	Local Drama catchment metasediments

Phase	Context	SF No.	Pet. No.	Object	Ob. Cat.	Lithology	Field description	Thin-section description or comments	Source comments
II	ZA 50	1157		Saddle quern	G	Quartzo-feldspathic mica schist		Quartzo-feldspathic mica schist. See SF 313 (Pet. No. 79), SF 1169 (Pet. No. 77), SF 1182 (Pet. No. 78) for petrography.	Local Drama catchment metasediments
II	ZA 52	1159		Uniquern	G	Quartzo-feldspathic mica schist	Pinkish, ? potassium feldspar-rich	Quartzo-feldspathic mica schist. See SF 313 (Pet. No. 79), SF 1169 (Pet. No. 77), SF 1182 (Pet. No. 78) for petrography.	Local Drama catchment metasediments
II	ZA 52	1160		Hammerstone, round	I	Vein quartz			Not distinctive; local; common in virtually all metamorphic terrains
II	ZA 54	1164		Flat grinder	G	Quartzo-feldspathic mica schist		Quartzo-feldspathic mica schist. See SF 313 (Pet. No. 79), SF 1169 (Pet. No. 77), SF 1182 (Pet. No. 78) for petrography.	Local Drama catchment metasediments
II	ZA 54	1165		Flat grinder, ex-cobble; fractured	G	Quartzo-feldspathic mica schist	Gray	Quartzo-feldspathic mica schist. See SF 313 (Pet. No. 79), SF 1169 (Pet. No. 77), SF 1182 (Pet. No. 78) for petrography.	Local Drama catchment metasediments
II	ZA51	1169	77	Saddle quern	G	Quartzo-feldspathic mica schist. See thin section description.	Pale gray augen schist with potassium feldspar augen up to 2 x 3 cm; planar foliation with strong lineation; originally cobble	Potassium feldspar-bearing augen schist with quartz, albite, muscovite, and minor biotite.	Almost certainly from local Rhodope metasediments interbedded with marbles, making up Pangaion, Falakro, and Menokion massifs
II	ZA 51	1170		Flat quern ex-split cobble	G	Quartzo-feldspathic mica schist		Quartzo-feldspathic mica schist. See SF 313 (Pet. No. 79), SF 1169 (Pet. No. 77), SF 1182 (Pet. No. 78) for petrography.	Local Drama catchment metasediments
II	ML 16	1174		Uniquern	G	Limestone	Cream colored; fossiliferous, with external molds of gastropods concentrated in bands	Probably Tertiary. Same lithology as 1155, phase III.	Not Drama catchment; fossiliferous Eocene limestones occur in Petrota Basin and the northern edge of Komotini basin
II	ML 12	1179		Hammerstone, round	I	Vein quartz			Not distinctive; local; common in virtually all metamorphic terrains
II	KM 9	1182	78	Saddle quern	G	Quartzo-feldspathic mica schist	Gray; biotite bearing; originally cobble	Quartzo-feldspathic mica schist. See SF 313 (Pet. No. 79), SF 1169 (Pet. No. 77), SF 1182 (Pet. No. 78) for petrography.	Local Drama catchment metasediments
II	ZA 57	1419		Axe parallel-sided. D/E	P	Amphibolite, possibly hornfels	Brown (pale plus dark); strongly foliated, fine grained.		
II	KM 18	1755		Chisel, non-parallel flat butt	P	Serpentinite	Yellowish green, translucent with brownish patches		Not local; western Serbo-Macedonian Massif or eastern Rhodope, e.g., Soufli.
II	KL 106	2301		Ornament, pierced, shield shaped	O	Marble	White		Not distinctive; probably local

Phase	Context	SF No.	Pet. No.	Object	Ob. Cat.	Lithology	Field description	Thin-section description or comments	Source comments
II	KL 107	2309		Axe, non-parallel. C	P	Amphibolite	Fine grained, faintly mottled deep green		Not distinctive; probably local
II	KL 110	2335		Axe, broad, non-parallel	P	Serpentinite	Dark/medium green, blotchy' translucent in places		Not local; western Serbo-Macedonian massif or eastern Rhodope, e.g., Soufli.
II	KL 113	2377		Spheroid	I	Vein quartz			Not distinctive; local; common in virtually all metamorphic terrains.
II	KL 114	2390		Fragment, drilled	O	Marble	White		Not distinctive; probably local
II	KL 115	2634		Natural quartz single crystal fragment	N	Quartz			Not distinctive; probably local
II	KL 117	2645		Foot or leg	O	Limestone	Impure, argillaceous		If not marble, then not from Drama catchment. Limestones occur in Circum-Rhodope Group in Thrace and in Eocene of Komotini and Kirki-Essimi Basins. Not distinctive for provenance without petrographic or micro-paleo data.
II	KL 117	2648		Axe or chisel	P	Metadolerite-S?	White/pale yellow with broken porphyroblasts green amphibole(?); trace plagioclase lath texture; opaque oxide granules		Metadolerite group, thus not typical amphibolite of Drama catchment; probably meta-ophiolites of Volvi, Petrota, or Soufli.
II	KL 117	2661		?	?	Sandstone, micaceous			Not local; probably from Eocene sedimentary sequences in basins E of Xanthi, as for limestones
II	KLb 119	2679		Grinder	G	Limestone	Pale brick red, white on worked surface; recrystallized		
II	ZG 37	3637		Flat grinder ex-split cobble	G	Quartzo-feldspathic mica schist	Pale gray, muscovite bearing	Quartzo-feldspathic mica schist. See SF 313 (Pet. No. 79), SF 1169 (Pet. No. 77), SF 1182 (Pet. No. 78) for petrography.	Local Drama catchment metasediments
II	ZJ 34	3936		Axe fragment	P	Metadolerite			Metadolerite group, thus not typical amphibolite of Drama catchment; probably meta-ophiolites of Volvi, Petrota, or Soufli.
II	ZJ 36	3939		Axe, butt end	P	Metagabbro-R	Waxy green crystals in soft white matrix with translucent brownish plagioclase	Almost certainly SF 1191 type (Pet. No. 91 quartz vein) but richer in feldspar, and prehnite after feldspar.	Not local; ophiolite association but not Volvi; possibly Petrota or Soufli
II	ZJ 37	3941		Fragment	?	Siltstone	Fine grained, micaceous		Not local; probably from Eocene sedimentary sequences in basins E of Xanthi, as for limestones

Phase	Context	SF No.	Pet. No.	Object	Ob. Cat.	Lithology	Field description	Thin-section description or comments	Source comments
II	ZJ 38	3948		Hammer-stone, split fragment	I	Vein quartz			Not distinctive; local; common in virtually all metamorphic terrains
II	ZE 95	4219		Hammer-stone	I	Vein quartz			Not distinctive; local; common in virtually all metamorphic terrains
II	ZE 95	4220		Hammer-stone	I	Vein quartz			Not distinctive; local; common in virtually all metamorphic terrains
II	ZE 97	4222		Axe fragment, faceted blade	P	Serpentinite			Not local; western Serbo-Macedonian massif or eastern Rhodope, e.g., Soufli.
II	ZJ 44	4226		Bowl fragment	B	Marble			Not distinctive; probably local
II	ZJ 40	4254		Bowl fragment	B	Marble			Not distinctive; probably local
II	ZA 55	4572		Quern, doubly hollowed	G	Gneiss	Pink and green potassium feldspar-plagioclase-hornblende gneiss; angular block		Possibly high-grade Rhodope metamorphics of the Sidhironero Unit (Central Rhodope Unit) N and NE of Drama plain, or Kavala Granite; not very distinctive.
II	ZA 59	4578		Flat grinder	G	Marble	Banded		Not distinctive; probably local.
II mixed	KL 2	139		Saddle quern	G	Quartzo-feldspathic mica schist		Quartzo-feldspathic mica schist. See SF 313 (Pet. No. 79), SF 1169 (Pet. No. 77), SF 1182 (Pet. No. 78) for petrography.	Local Drama catchment metasediments
II mixed	KL 2	267		Axe non-parallel	P	Amphibolite	Alternating stripes of medium-grained amphibolite and very fine-grained grayish green material		Not distinctive; probably local
II mixed	KL 2	283		Hammer-stone, round	I	Chert			
II mixed	KL 2	299		Pendant?, pierced	O	Sandstone	Pinkish gray, medium-grained micaceous.		Not local; probably from Eocene sedimentary sequences in basins E of Xanthi, as for limestones
II mixed	KM 2	410		Axe/hammer, shafted, fragment	P	Serpentinite	Granular, green; resinous on polished surface		Not local; western Serbo-Macedonian massif or eastern Rhodope, e.g., Soufli.
II mixed	KL 2	451		Ring, bored, broken	O	Serpentinite	Talc rich		Not local; western Serbo-Macedonian massif or eastern Rhodope, e.g., Soufli
II mixed	KL 2	452		Bowl fragment	B	Marble			Not distinctive; probably local
II mixed	KL 102	716		Ring, bored, broken	O	Limestone			Probably Thrace (see note for SF 2645; phase II)
III	MLa 3	47		Rubber	G	Iron oxide	Black, possibly magnetite		Not distinctive

Phase	Context	SF No.	Pet. No.	Object	Ob. Cat.	Lithology	Field description	Thin-section description or comments	Source comments
III	MM 16	174		Axe fragment	P	Ash/phyllite/calc-silicate hornfels. FGGG group	Pale grayish green, foliated, possibly mylonitic	One of FGGG group, i.e., as Pet. No. 85, 89, 90, 92 or 94. (See text.)	Not local; identity not certain in lithology alone; fine-grained sediment/volcanic protolitlithology imply probable eastern Thrace Eocene or Circum-Rhodope source.
III	MM 16	176	90	Axe	P	Phyllite, low-grade meta-volcaniclastic. (See thin section description.)	Bottle green, finely banded, fine grained	Weakly metamorphosed chlorite-clinozoisite-plagioclase-quartz meta-volcaniclastic. Originally ashy sediment. One of FGGG group.	Not Drama catchment; too low grade for Rhodope metamorphics; probably Circum-Rhodope Group, eastern Thrace
III	ZA 38	259	87	Axe fragment	P	Metadolerite-S, foliated	Near black, fine/medium-grained mafic rock with dark mineral in probable ophitic texture	Zoisite-bearing amphibolitized meta-dolerite with relict pyroxene and two amphibole generations. "-S" signifies "saussuritization" or transformation of feldspars to pseudomorphlithology rich in Ca-Al silicate.	Metadolerite group, thus not typical amphibolite of Drama catchment; probably meta-ophiolites of Volvi, Petrota, or Soufli
III	MM 21	381		Hammer stone	I	Marble			Not distinctive; probably local
III	MM 21	393	89	Axe	P	Calcareous siltstone. (See thin section description.)	Mottled olive-green, gritty texture	Calcareous siltstone. Angular clasts of quartz and calcite in a carbonate and chlorite cement. Unmetamorphosed.	Not Drama catchment; most probably Tertiary sedimentary basins E of Xanthi
III	ZA 42	484		Grinder and/or rubber	G	Marble			Not distinctive; probably local
III	MM 12	718		Cone	?	Graphite	Small cone of metallic looking substance; hard. L.: 1.4 cm, W: 0.6 cm, Th: 1 cm		
III	MM 12	749		Rubber, spherical	G	Marble			Not distinctive; probably local
III	MM 27	802		Saddle or flat quern, both ends missing	G	Quartzo-feldspathic mica schist	Pinkish gray	Quartzo-feldspathic mica schist. See SF 313 (Pet. No. 79), SF 1169 (Pet. No. 77), SF 1182 (Pet. No. 78) for petrography.	Local Drama catchment metasediments
III	MM 27	811		Axe	P	Ash/phyllite/calc-silicate hornfels. FGGG group	Grayish green, fine gritty texture with scattered pale green inclusions	One of FGGG group, i.e., as Pet. No. 85, 89, 90, 92 or 94. (See text.)	Not local; identity not certain in lithology alone. Fine grained sediment/volcanic protolitlithology imply probable eastern Thrace Eocene or Circum-Rhodope source
III	ML 107	818		Wedge or chisel	P	Metagabbro-R?		SF 1191(?) type.	Not local; ophiolite association but not Volvi if unmetamorphosed and prehnitized; possibly Petrota or Soufli
III	ML 107	821		Axe	P	Metagabbro-R	As SF 1191 but foliation more pronounced		Not local; ophiolite association but not Volvi if unmetamorphosed and prehnitized; possibly Petrota or Soufli
III	MM	828		Fragment	?	Amphibolite/calc silicate?	Light grayish green; FGGG group	FGGG group.	Source or sources unknown

Phase	Context	SF No.	Pet. No.	Object	Ob. Cat.	Lithology	Field description	Thin-section description or comments	Source comments
III	MM 38	835			?	Vein quartz			Not distinctive; local; common in virtually all metamorphic terrains
III	MM 36	839		Hammerstone, spheroidal	I	Vein quartz			Not distinctive; local; common in virtually all metamorphic terrains
III	MM 27	840		Axe fragment?	P	Amphibolite/calc silicate?	Fine grained, greenish gray. FGGG group	FGGG group.	Source or sources unknown
III	MM 36	842		Adze, small	P	Serpentinite	Light/medium olive/grass green with white internal mottle; translucent to 5 mm; characteristic internal fractures		Not local; western Serbo-Macedonian massif or eastern Rhodope, e.g., Soufli
III	MM 40	845		Hammer stone	I	Marble			Not distinctive; probably local
III	MM 40	846		Axe	P	Ash/phyllite/calc-silicate hornfels. FGGG group	Pale gray, highly siliceous cherty rock with resinous green seams	One of FGGG group, i.e., as Pet. No. 85, 89, 90, 92 or 94. (See text.)	Not local; identity not certain in lithology alone; fine-grained sediment/volcanic protolitlithology imply probable eastern Thrace Eocene or Circum-Rhodope source
III	MM 43	879		Axe head	P	Metadolerite-S, foliated	Dark fine/medium-grained mafic rock with weak foliation	Probably very similar to SF 259.	Metadolerite group, thus not typical amphibolite of Drama catchment; probably meta-ophiolites of Volvi, Petrota, or Soufli
III	MM 43	891		Axe with side groove	P	Serpentinite?	Greenish gray with deeper green elongate, more translucent patches		Not local; western Serbo-Macedonian massif or eastern Rhodope, e.g.,.Soufli.
III	MM 44	899		Hammerstone, round	I	Vein quartz			Not distinctive; local; common in virtually all metamorphic terrains.
III	ML 107	1136		Hammerstone, broken	I	Vein quartz			Not distinctive; local; common in virtually all metamorphic terrains.
III	ZA 44	1155		Quern, doubly hollowed	G	Limestone	Cream colored; fossiliferous, with external molds of gastropods concentrated in bands.	Probably Tertiary. Same lithology as 1174, phase II.	Not Drama catchment; fossiliferous Eocene limestones occur in Petrota Basin and the northern edge of Komotini basin.
III	ZA 44	1161		Saddle quern	G	Marble	Medium-grained grayish buff; weathered block		Not distinctive; probably local
III	MM 18	1163		Hammerstone, round	I	Vein quartz			Not distinctive; local; common in virtually all metamorphic terrains.
III	ZA 34	1167		Hammerstone, round	I	Vein quartz			Not distinctive; local; common in virtually all metamorphic terrains.
III	ZA 38	1168		Flat grinder	G	Quartzo-feldspathic mica schist	White/gray striped; rare feldspar augen	Quartzo-feldspathic mica schist. See SF 313 (Pet. No. 79), SF 1169 (Pet. No. 77), SF 1182 (Pet. No. 78) for petrography.	Local Drama catchment metasediments

Phase	Context	SF No.	Pet. No.	Object	Ob. Cat.	Lithology	Field description	Thin-section description or comments	Source comments
III	ZA 41	1171		Saddle quern	G	Quartzo-feldspathic mica schist	Pink potassium feldspar, gray overall; quartz-feldspar-muscovite; originally cobble	Quartzo-feldspathic mica schist. See SF 313 (Pet. No. 79), SF 1169 (Pet. No. 77), SF 1182 (Pet. No. 78) for petrography.	Local Drama catchment metasediments
III	ZA 41	1172		Saddle quern	G	Quartzo-feldspathic mica schist	Pinkish-gray; quartz-feldspar-muscovite; originally cobble	Quartzo-feldspathic mica schist. See SF 313 (Pet. No. 79), SF 1169 (Pet. No. 77), SF 1182 (Pet. No. 78) for petrography.	Local Drama catchment metasediments
III	ZA 41	1173		Flat grinder, roughly rounded	G	Quartzo-feldspathic mica schist		Quartzo-feldspathic mica schist. See SF 313 (Pet. No. 79), SF 1169 (Pet. No. 77), SF 1182 (Pet. No. 78) for petrography.	Local Drama catchment metasediments
III	MM 12	1175		Saddle quern	G	Quartzo-feldspathic mica schist	Gray, pinkish streaks. trace biotite; originally cobble	Quartzo-feldspathic mica schist. See SF 313 (Pet. No. 79), SF 1169 (Pet. No. 77), SF 1182 (Pet. No. 78) for petrography.	Local Drama catchment metasediments
III	ZA 42	1177		Flat grinder, broken	G	Quartzo-feldspathic mica schist	Pinkish	Quartzo-feldspathic mica schist. See SF 313 (Pet. No. 79), SF 1169 (Pet. No. 77), SF 1182 (Pet. No. 78) for petrography.	Local Drama catchment metasediments
III	ZA 41	1178		Flat grinder, broken	G	Biotite aplite		Very feldspar- and quartz-rich granitic rock, commonly found as late intrusive sheets.	Not very distinctive but has to be one of Oligocene granite bodies, e.g., Symvolon, Skaloti, etc.
III	ZA 40	1183		Quern, doubly hollowed	G	Sandstone	Pale buff, coarse grained		Not local; probably from Eocene sedimentary sequences in basins E of Xanthi, as for limestones
III	ZA 38	1184		Saddle quern	G	Quartzo-feldspathic mica schist	Grayish; quartz-feldspar-muscovite; originally cobble	Quartzo-feldspathic mica schist. See SF 313 (Pet. No. 79), SF 1169 (Pet. No. 77), SF 1182 (Pet. No. 78) for petrography.	Local Drama catchment metasediments
III	ZA 41	1185		Hammerstone, round, flattened	I	Marble	White		Not distinctive; probably local
III	MM 40	1191	91	Axe? Fragment	P	Metagabbro-R (rodingitized gabbro)	Weakly foliated, coarse-grained, igneous-textured rock with gray translucent feldspar in opaque white groundmass with deep green opaque patches of a ferromagnesian mineral	Rodingitized gabbro. Fresh green clinopyroxene, with plagioclase partially replaced by radiating sheaves of prehnite, the latter showing 2–3 mm of surface alteration to opaque white zeolite or clay mineral. Soft outer layer is postburial.	Not local; distinctive; could be sourced ultimately; characteristic of ophiolitic gabbro/serpentinite association; not known from Volvi which is metamorphosed; possibly Petrota or Soufli
III	MM 47	1212		Hammerstone, round	I	Marble			Not distinctive; probably local
III	MM 47	1213		Flat grinder ex-split, flat cobble	G	Marble	Impure, micaceous, foliated		Not distinctive; probably local.

Phase	Context	SF No.	Pet. No.	Object	Ob. Cat.	Lithology	Field description	Thin-section description or comments	Source comments
III	MM 49	1226		Rubber?	G	Sandstone	Buff/orange, medium grained		Not local; probably from Eocene sedimentary sequences in basins E of Xanthi, as for limestones
III	MM 49	1228		Bowl fragment	B	Marble			Not distinctive; probably local
III	MM 49	1235		Axe	P	Ash/phyllite/calc-silicate hornfels. FGGG group	Pale gray with darker streaks and specks; scattered white rectangular grains; fine grained	One of FGGG group, i.e., as Pet. No. 85, 89, 90, 92 or 94. (See text.)	Not local; identity not certain in lithology alone; fine-grained sediment/volcanic protolitlithology imply probable eastern Thrace Eocene or Circum-Rhodope source
III	ML 112	1248		Axe? Fragment	P	Ash/phyllite/calc-silicate hornfels. FGGG group	Uniform waxy olive green	One of FGGG group, i.e., as Pet. No. 85, 89, 90, 92 or 94. (See text.)	Not local. Identity not certain in lithology alone. Fine grained sediment/volcanic protolitlithology imply probable eastern Thrace Eocene or Circum-Rhodope source.
III	MM 50	1269		Axe	P	Ash/phyllite/calc-silicate hornfels. FGGG group	Green, foliated, uniform color	One of FGGG group, i.e., as Pet.85, 89, 90, 92 or 94. (See text.)	Not local; identity not certain in lithology alone; fine-grained sediment/volcanic protolitlithology imply probable eastern Thrace Eocene or Circum-Rhodope source
III	MM 19	1277		Axe, parallel, flat butt	P	Tremolite?	Pale gray-green, foliated, lustrous matt of crystals.		Not known from Drama catchment metamorphics; more probably western Serbo-Macedonian massif or eastern Rhodope, Soufli area
III	MM 57	1281		Uniquern	G	Amphibolite	Foliated, feldspar rich; very little rounded, prismatic block		Not distinctive; probably local
III	MM 52	1289		Adze, non-parallel flat butt	P	Ash/phyllite/calc-silicate hornfels. FGGG group	Finely interbanded medium green and gray-green variants	One of FGGG group, i.e., as Pet. No. 85, 89, 90, 92 or 94. (See text.)	Not local; identity not certain in lithology alone; fine-grained sediment/volcanic protolitlithology imply probable eastern Thrace Eocene or Circum-Rhodope source
III	MM 53	1294		Saddle quern	G	Quartzo-feldspathic mica schist	Off-white; originally cobble	Quartzo-feldspathic mica schist. See SF 313 (Pet. No. 79), SF 1169 (Pet. No. 77), SF 1182 (Pet. No. 78) for petrography.	Local Drama catchment metasediments
III	MM 40	1405		Axe? Fragment	P	Feldspathic amphibolite	Greenish gray foliated amphibole-feldspar rock with rare hornblende-rich veins parallel to foliation		Not distinctive; probably local Drama catchment metamorphics
III	ZA 47	1413		Axe fragment	P	Ash/phyllite/calc-silicate hornfels. FGGG group	Grayish brown, fine-grained matrix with whitish 1 mm wisps	One of FGGG group, i.e., as Pet. No. 85, 89, 90, 92 or 94. (See text.)	Not local; identity not certain in lithology alone; fine-grained sediment/volcanic protolitlithology imply probable eastern Thrace Eocene or Circum-Rhodope source
III	MM 41	1421		Axe fragment	P	Serpentinite?	Pale greenish yellow, with mossy strings and oxide patches	Similar to more massive part of SF 891.	Not local; western Serbo-Macedonian massif or eastern Rhodope, e.g., Soufli

Phase	Context	SF No.	Pet. No.	Object	Ob. Cat.	Lithology	Field description	Thin-section description or comments	Source comments
III	MM 27	1506		Axe	P	Serpentinite	Dark/medium green, semi-translucent; typical serpentinous mottle; soft, good polish		Not local; western Serbo-Macedonian massif or eastern Rhodope, e.g., Soufli
III	MM 50	1539		Hammerstone	I	Marble			Not distinctive; probably local
III	ML 118	1563		Axe, flat butt	P	Metagabbro-R?	Soft opaque white powdery mineral, possibly kaolinite, with rare quartz(?)/feldspar strings	Almost certainly feldspathic variant of rodingitized gabbro suite as 1191. "Quartz" of lithology description probably plagioclase feldspar.	Metadolerite/gabbro, not known from Drama catchment; prehnitized rocks not known from Volvi, thus possibly Soufli or Petrota
III	ML 119	1588		Axe, parallel, flat butt	P	Metagabbro-R	Like SF 1191 except fibrous character of white phase clearer, feldspars larger, lower mafic content	Like 1191 but with slightly different mineral proportions.	Not local; ophiolite association but not Volvi if unmetamorphosed and prehnitized; Possibly Petrota or Soufli
III	MM 27	1635	88	Axe fragment (butt end)	P	Hypersthene andesite (See thin section description.)	Porphyritic basic volcanic	Hypersthene-cpx-plagioclase-phyric andesite or basaltic andesite. Prominent fresh phenocrysts of augite and glass-inclusion-filled plagioclase. Hypersthene relics in clay/chlorite pseudomorphed phenocrysts. Plagioclase-cpx-ore groundmass.	Not Drama catchment; most likely Petrota where two-pyroxene andesites occur, or Kirki-Essimi
III	MM 12	1757		Hammer stone	I	Marble			Not distinctive; probably local
III	ML 116	1901		Saddle quern	G	Quartzo-feldspathic mica schist		Quartzo-feldspathic mica schist. See SF 313 (Pet. No. 79), SF 1169 (Pet. No. 77), SF 1182 (Pet. No. 78) for petrography.	Local Drama catchment metasediments
III	MM 16	2827		Quern fragment	G	Quartzo-feldspathic mica schist		Quartzo-feldspathic mica schist. See SF 313 (Pet. No. 79), SF 1169 (Pet. No. 77), SF 1182 (Pet. No. 78) for petrography.	Local Drama catchment metasediments
III	ZG 14	2926		Saddle quern	G	Quartzo-feldspathic mica schist	Gray, muscovite bearing; some rounding of margins	Quartzo-feldspathic mica schist. See SF 313 (Pet. No. 79), SF 1169 (Pet. No. 77), SF 1182 (Pet. No. 78) for petrography.	Local Drama catchment metasediments
III	ZG 14	2928		?	?	Sandstone	Coarse-grained, angular quartz		Not local; probably from Eocene sedimentary sequences in basins E of Xanthi, as for limestones
III	ZG 15	2932		Ground fragment, fractured	G	Marble	Grayish, pale pink		Not distinctive; probably local
III	ZG 16	2941		Flat grinder	G	Quartzo-feldspathic mica schist	White, muscovitic	Quartzo-feldspathic mica schist. See SF 313 (Pet. No. 79), SF 1169 (Pet. No. 77), SF 1182 (Pet. No. 78) for petrography.	Local Drama catchment metasediments
III	ZG 17	2943		Hammerstone	I	Marble	Gray		Not distinctive; probably local

Phase	Context	SF No.	Pet. No.	Object	Ob. Cat.	Lithology	Field description	Thin-section description or comments	Source comments
III	ZG 21	2953		Flat grinder, ex-split cobble	G	Quartzo-feldspathic mica schist	Gray with quartz clots	Quartzo-feldspathic mica schist. See SF 313 (Pet. No. 79), SF 1169 (Pet. No. 77), SF 1182 (Pet. No. 78) for petrography.	Local Drama catchment metasediments
III	ZG 23	2959		Natural? angular fragment	N	Marble	White		Not distinctive; probably local
III	ZG 26	2968		Axe	P	Metagabbro-R	Waxy green crystals in soft white matrix with translucent brownish plagioclase	Almost certainly SF 1191–type quartz vein.	Not local; ophiolite association but not Volvi; possibly Petrota or Soufli
III	ZG 27	2975		Saddle quern	G	Quartzo-feldspathic mica schist	Off-white; quartz-feldspar-muscovite; originally cobble	Quartzo-feldspathic mica schist. See SF 313 (Pet. No. 79), SF 1169 (Pet. No. 77), SF 1182 (Pet. No. 78) for petrography.	Local Drama catchment metasediments
III	ZG 28	2984		Axe fragment	P	Marble			Not distinctive; probably local
III	ZG 30	2992		Hammerstone, spheroidal	I	Marble			Not distinctive; probably local
III	ML 150	3104		Pebble, round	N	Vein quartz?			Not distinctive; local; common in virtually all metamorphic terrains
III	ML 151	3122		Rubber	G	Marble			Not distinctive; probably local
III	ML 151	3129		Rubber	G	Marble			Not distinctive; probably local
III	ML 155	3142		Hammerstone, round	I	Vein quartz			Not distinctive; local; common in virtually all metamorphic terrains
III	ML 151	3411		Saddle quern	G	Quartzo-feldspathic mica schist		Quartzo-feldspathic mica schist. See SF 313 (Pet. No. 79), SF 1169 (Pet. No. 77), SF 1182 (Pet. No. 78) for petrography.	Local Drama catchment metasediments
III	MM 60b	3423		Flat grinder	G	Marble	White, micaceous		Not distinctive; probably local
III	ZG 14	3440		Axe fragment	P	Metagabbro-R?		Probably SF 1191–type quartz vein. Misidentified as "kaolinized granite" in field, as with others in this group.	Not local; ophiolite association but not Volvi if unmetamorphosed and prehnitized; possibly Petrota or Soufli
III	MMb 61	3447		Hammerstone, round, fractured	I	Quartzite, micaceous	Metamorphic quartzite		Could be from local Rhodope metasedimentary sequence
III	MMb 61	3448		Axe	P	Amphibolite/ calc silicate?	Greenish brown with whitish inclusions (feldspar?)	FGGG group.	Source or sources unknown
III	MMb 61	3450		Axe non-parallel	P	Serpentinite	Yellowish green; translucent		Not local; western Serbo-Macedonian massif or eastern Rhodope, e.g., Soufli

Phase	Context	SF No.	Pet. No.	Object	Ob. Cat.	Lithology	Field description	Thin-section description or comments	Source comments
III	MMd 61	3453		Worked pebble	P	Amphibolite	Striped, dark, coarse hornblende-rich layers alternating with lighter green fine-grained layers		Not distinctive; probably local
III	MMb 61	3457		Axe, butt end	P	Metadolerite-S	Coarse-grained, igneous texture well preserved		Metadolerite group, thus not typical amphibolite of Drama catchment; probably meta-ophiolites of Volvi, Petrota, or Soufli
III	MMc 61	3481		Flat grinder	G	Quartzo-feldspathic mica schist	Gray, muscovitic, weak foliation	Quartzo-feldspathic mica schist. See SF 313 (Pet. No. 79), SF 1169 (Pet. No. 77), SF 1182 (Pet. No. 78) for petrography.	Local Drama catchment metasediments
III	MMd 65	3529		Axe, now chisel, reworked, split, flat butt	P	Amphibolite	Green, fine/medium-grained, foliation not pronounced		Not distinctive; probably local
III	MMt 60	3560		Axe? flake fragment	P	Amphibolite/ calc silicate?	Pale gray-green	FGGG group.	Source or sources unknown
III	ZG 23	3599		Flat quern	G	Quartzo-feldspathic mica schist	Gray, weak foliation	Quartzo-feldspathic mica schist. See SF 313 (Pet. No. 79), SF 1169 (Pet. No. 77), SF 1182 (Pet. No. 78) for petrography.	Local Drama catchment metasediments
III	MMd 63	3628		Adze	P	Metagabbro-R?		SF 1191(?) type	Not local; ophiolite association but not Volvi if unmetamorphosed and prehnitized; possibly Petrota or Soufli
III	ML 153	3670		Mace head	P	Marble	Soft white on outside	Possibly fired and converted to lime, now hydrated, on outside.	Not distinctive; probably local
III	MMb 63	3824		Axe fragment	P	Amphibolite	Strongly flasered feldspathic amphibolite (sheared? metagabbro)		Not distinctive; probably local
III	MMc 65	3830		Saddle quern	G	Quartzo-feldspathic mica schist	Reddish, mottled; visible muscovite, chlorite(?) after biotite; originally cobble	Quartzo-feldspathic mica schist. See SF 313 (Pet. No. 79), SF 1169 (Pet. No. 77), SF 1182 (Pet. No. 78) for petrography.	Local Drama catchment metasediments
III	MMc 65?	3831		Hammerstone or pestle	I	Amphibolite	Deep grayish green, medium-grained		Not distinctive; probably local
III	ZA 41	4407		Hammerstone	I	Marble			Not distinctive; probably local
III	MM 66	4580		Hammerstone? rounded stone	I	Ironstone (hematite or goethite?)	Black		Not distinctive
III	ZG 16			Flat grinder	G	Limestone	Buff		Probably Thrace (see note for SF 2645; phase II)
III mixed	ML 2	94		Axe/ hammer, shafted, fragment	P	Metadolerite?			

Phase	Context	SF No.	Pet. No.	Object	Ob. Cat.	Lithology	Field description	Thin-section description or comments	Source comments
III mixed	ML 2	1045		?	?	Metadolerite			Metadolerite group, thus not typical amphibolite of Drama catchment; probably meta-ophiolites of Volvi, Petrota, or Soufli
IV	JL 12	113		Pendant ring fragment	O	Serpentinite	Light green, translucent		Not local; western Serbo-Macedonian massif or eastern Rhodope, e.g., Soufli
IV	ZA 32	129		Axe	P	Marble	White		Not distinctive; probably local
IV	SL 17	131		Spike	G	Marble			
IV	MM 34	895		Flat grinder ex-cobble, broken	G	Metadolerite			Metadolerite group, thus not typical amphibolite of Drama catchment; probably meta-ophiolites of Volvi, Petrota, or Soufli
IV	ZA 26	1473		Worked pebble	?	Amphibolite			Not distinctive; probably local
IV	ZA 26	1474		Flat grinder, rounded	G	Vein quartz			Not distinctive; local; common in virtually all metamorphic terrains
IV	MMb 1	1746		Axe, parallel	P	Amphibolite	Grayish green, fine grained		Not distinctive; probably local
IV	ZE 61	2720		Axe fragment	P	Amphibolite/ calc silicate?	Light gray-green, fine grained	FGGG group.	Source or sources unknown
IV	ZE 61	2724		Axe fragment	P	Amphibolite	Deep bluish green, medium grained.	·	Not distinctive; probably local
IV	ZE 61	2725		Adze	P	Amphibolite	Deep blackish green, fine/medium grained, weak foliation, hornblende and plagioclase distinguishable	966,2512, 2725, 2769, 3364 are all very similar.	Not distinctive; probably local
IV	ZE 64	2738		Hammerstone, round	I	Vein quartz			Not distinctive; local; common in virtually all metamorphic terrains
IV	ZE 64	2739	154	Axe/ hammer, shafted, fragment	P	Amphibolite, epidote-bearing. See thin section description.	Medium grained; non-schistose	Actinolite-albite-epidote-chlorite, with minor sphene after ilmenite. Chlorite replacing inferred former relict pyroxene in cores of larger amphiboles.	Possibly meta-ophiolite type, i.e., unfoliated, partly relict igneous texture suggests Volvi or possibly Soufli more likely than local Drama catchment metamorphics.
IV	ZE 67	2752		Axe	P	Amphibolite?	Grayish, greenish brown	FGGG group.	Source or sources unknown
IV	ZE 67	2754		Axe fragment	P	Limestone	Gray		Probably Thrace (see note for SF 2645; phase II)
IV	ZE 68	2760		Pebble, bashed	I	Marble			Not distinctive; probably local
IV	ZE 69	2769		Adze	P	Amphibolite	Deep blackish green, fine/medium grained, weak foliation, hornblende and plagioclase distinguishable	SF 966, 2512, 2725, 2769, 3364 are all very similar.	Not distinctive; probably local
IV	ZE 82	2789		Axe fragment	P	Amphibolite/ calc silicate?	Light grayish green	FGGG group.	Source or sources unknown
IV	ZHt 4s	2856		Chisel end, part drilled	P	Marble	White		Not distinctive; probably local

Phase	Context	SF No.	Pet. No.	Object	Ob. Cat.	Lithology	Field description	Thin-section description or comments	Source comments
IV	ZG 3	2900		Axe fragment	P	Amphibolite	Brown, fine grained, banded		Not distinctive; probably local
IV	ZG 6	2903		Bead or small rubber	O	Sandstone	Coarse grained		Not local; probably from Eocene sedimentary sequences in basins E of Xanthi, as for limestones for limestones
IV	ZG 7	2905		Flat grinder	G	Quartzo-feldspathic mica schist		Quartzo-feldspathic mica schist. See SF 313 (Pet. No. 79), SF 1169 (Pet. No. 77), SF 1182 (Pet. No. 78) for petrography.	Local Drama catchment metasediments
IV	ZE 58	3441		Axe fragment	P	Amphibolite	Deep bluish-green, medium-grained		Not distinctive; probably local
IV	ZE 61	3564		Fragment	?	Amphibolite	Medium grained, weak foliation		Not distinctive; probably local
IV	ZJ 4	3917		Hammerstone, broken	I	Vein quartz			Not distinctive; local; common in virtually all metamorphic terrains
IV?	SL 11	338		?	?	Amphibolite	Deep green hornblende, gray plagioclase; coarse, well foliated, streaky		Not distinctive; probably local
IV?	SL 11	341		Hammerstone, round	I	Sandstone			Not local; probably from Eocene sedimentary sequences in basins E of Xanthi, as for limestones for limestones
IV?	ZHt 6	3205		Pendant, pierced and grooved?	O	Serpentinized harzburgite?			Not local; western Serbo-Macedonian massif or eastern Rhodope, e.g., Soufli
IV?	ZHt 21	3240		Flat grinder	G	Marble	White, coarse grained		Not distinctive; probably local
IV?	ZHt 23	3712		Axe, flat	P	Metadolerite-S	Brown, foliated, resinous, sheared doleritic texture, probably amphibolitized	cf. 3704	Metadolerite group, thus not typical amphibolite of Drama catchment; probably meta-ophiolites of Volvi, Petrota, or Soufli.
IV?	ZHt 13	3714		Chisel	P	Amphibolite	Brown, weathered		Not distinctive; probably local
IV?	ZJ 22	3925		Chisel	P	Metagabbro-R	Waxy green crystals in soft white matrix with translucent brownish plagioclase	Almost certainly SF 1191–type quartz vein.	Not local; ophiolite association but not Volvi; possibly Petrota or Soufli
V	PO 5	313	79	Saddle quern	G	Quartzo-feldspathic mica schist. (See thin section description.)	Greenish gray; originally cobble	Quartz-albite-muscovite schist with minor biotite.	Almost certainly from local Rhodope metasediments interbedded with marbles, making up the Pangaion, Falakro, and Menokion massifs.
V	SL 3	327		Axe, round ended	P	Amphibolite/calc silicate?	Pale gray-green	FGGG group.	Source or sources unknown
V	SL 3	328		Spatula	P	Marble	White		Not distinctive; probably local

Phase	Context	SF No.	Pet. No.	Object	Ob. Cat.	Lithology	Field description	Thin-section description or comments	Source comments
V	PN 19	345		Axe, butt end	P	Sandstone			Not local; probably from Eocene sedimentary sequences in basins E of Xanthi, as for limestones for limestones
V	PO C/D 131	446		Pounder	I	Marble			Not distinctive; probably local
V	QO 2	486	93	Axe	P	Metadolerite-S	Relict igneous texture but sheared	Zoisite amphibolite derived from flaser gabbro. Meshwork of zoisite prisms after plagioclase. Interlocking masses of fine- grained amphibole after hornblende after original pyroxene. Patches of cummingtonite after probable orthopyroxene. Volvi type.	Metadolerite group, thus not typical amphibolite of Drama catchment; probably meta-ophiolites of Volvi, Petrota, or Soufli.
V	PO 5	494		?	?	Amphibolite	Feldspathic; medium coarse		Not distinctive; probably local
V	PO 8	656		Axe	P	Andesite, hornblende bearing.	Porphyritic, phenocrysts: large resinous plagioclase; hornblende(?)		Not Drama catchment. Most likely Petrota or Kirki-Essimi, Thrace.
V	PO 6	670		Hammerstone, spheroidal	I	Vein quartz			Not distinctive; local; common in virtually all metamorphic terrains
V	QN 5	692		Adze, parallel sided, flat butt	P	Metagabbro-R?	Soft white matrix with clear feldspar and green pyroxene	Probably SF 1191–type quartz vein. Misidentified as "kaolinized granite" in field, as with others in this group.	Not local; ophiolite association but not Volvi if unmetamorphosed and prehnitized; possibly Petrota or Soufli
V	QO 7	1011	158	Axe	P	Antigorite schist (serpentinite). (See thin section description.)	Fine grained, bluish green	Meshwork of short interlocking antigorite crystals, with minor talc and trace hematite. Metamorphosed serpentinite.	Not known from Drama catchment metamorphics. More probably western Serbo-Macedonian Massif or eastern Rhodope, Soufli area.
V	QN 6	1015		Cobble	N	Marble			Not distinctive; probably local
V	QN 6	1016		Hammerstone	I	Marble			Not distinctive; probably local
V	QN 6	1017		Hammerstone	I	Marble			Not distinctive; probably local
V	QN 6	1018		Hammerstone	I	Marble			Not distinctive; probably local
V	PN 6	1024		Saddle quern	G	Marble	White, medium-grained; broken rounded block		Not distinctive; probably local
V	QO 8	1039		Cobble	N	Biotite aplite		Very feldspar- and quartz-rich granitic rock, commonly found as late intrusive sheets.	Not very distinctive but has to be one of Oligocene granite bodies, e.g., Symvolon, Skaloti etc.
V	QO 8	1046		Pebble	N	Serpentinite	Brownish black		Not local; western Serbo-Macedonian massif or eastern Rhodope, e.g., Soufli

Phase	Context	SF No.	Pet. No.	Object	Ob. Cat.	Lithology	Field description	Thin-section description or comments	Source comments
V	QO 8s	1060	98	Axe	P	Hornfels. (See thin section description.)	Mottled, dark hornfels	Garnet-corundum-spinel-magnetite hornfels with diaspore(?). Contact metamorphosed laterite, possibly skarn-modified. Analogous to Tievebulliagh axe material.	Very distinctive rock type, by inference from an intrusive contact against an inter-lava soil horizon; possibly contact of eastern Thrace granite intruding Eocene volcanics, but could be more exotic.
V	QN 7	1067		Rubber	G	Marble			Not distinctive; probably local
V	QO 8	1069		Flat grinder	G	Marble	White, moderately coarse		Not distinctive; probably local
V	QN 7	1071		Axe	P	Limestone	Gray	Possibly fine-grained marble.	Local if marble, otherwise probably Thrace (see note for SF 2645; phase II)
V	QO 8	1079		Cobble	N	Marble			Not distinctive; probably local
V	QO 7	1088		Hammer-stone	I	Marble			Not distinctive; probably local
V	QO 8	1094		Hammer-stone, round	I	Vein quartz	Angular, some rounding		Not distinctive; local; common in virtually all metamorphic terrains
V	PN 5	1127		Axe/hammer, shafted, fragment	P	Amphibolite	Fine grained, weathered		Not distinctive; probably local
V	PN 16	1306		Hammer-stone, round, fractured	I	Marble	White, well crystalline, moderately coarse grained		Not distinctive; probably local
V	PN 12	1309		Hammer-stone, round, fractured	I	Vein quartz	Foliated outer surface		Not distinctive; local; common in virtually all metamorphic terrains
V	PN 11S	1311		Axe fragment	P	Amphibolite	Green, with brown-weathering feldspar; lineated amphibole; medium to coarse grained		Not distinctive; probably local
V	PN 12	1316		Rubber?	G	Marble	White		Not distinctive; probably local
V	PN 12	1318		Rubber	G	Amphibolite	Medium/fine grained		Not distinctive; probably local
V	PN 12	1319		Rubber	G	Amphibolite	Medium/fine grained		Not distinctive; probably local
V	PN 12	1320		Axe fragment	P	Amphibolite	Dark blackish green, hornblende-rich		Not distinctive; probably local
V	PN 11	1324	83	Flat grinder, fractured	G	Amphibolite. (See thin section description.)	Medium/fine grained, hornblende-rich, well foliated	Hornblende, plagioclase, opaque ore (probably ilmenite). Schistose. Classic equilibrated medium-grade amphibolite texture.	Not distinctive; probably local
V	PN 14	1325		Hammer-stone, round, fractured	I	Marble	White, well crystalline, moderately coarse grained		Not distinctive; probably local
V	PN 14	1326		Hammer stone	I	Marble			Not distinctive; probably local
V	PN 19	1343		Natural cobble	N	Marble			Not distinctive; probably local

Phase	Context	SF No.	Pet. No.	Object	Ob. Cat.	Lithology	Field description	Thin-section description or comments	Source comments
V	PN 18	1344		Mace head	P	Marble			Not distinctive; probably local
V	PN21 S	1347	156	Axe	P	Tremolite schist. See thin section description.	Bluish green, fine grained	Tremolite rock; bundles and sheaves of acicular tremolite crystals forming tough "woven" texture. Derived from ultramafic parent by metamorphism and metasomatism.	Not known from Drama catchment metamorphics; more probably western Serbo-Macedonian massif or eastern Rhodope, Soufli area
V	PN 26	1355		Hammer-stone, round	I	Vein quartz	Lineated surface, from concordant segregation in schist		Not distinctive; local; common in virtually all metamorphic terrains
V	PN 20?	1358		Ground fragment	G	Amphibolite	Hornblende schist		Not distinctive; probably local
V	PN 29	1365		Rubber	G	Marble	White		Not distinctive; probably local
V	QN 6	1416		Flat grinder, ex-split cobble	G	Quartzo-felds-pathic mica schist	Pinkish	Quartzo-feldspathic mica schist. See SF 313 (Pet. No. 79), SF 1169 (Pet. No. 77), SF 1182 (Pet. No. 78) for petrography.	Local Drama catchment metasediments
V	PO 9	1551		Axe, flat	P	Amphibolite	Deep lustrous black, faint mottle		Not distinctive; probably local
V	PO 16	1561		Axe	P	Amphibolite?	Grayish, very fine grained	FGGG group.	Source or sources unknown
V	PO 16	1564		Mace fragment	P	Micaceous sand-stone	Brick-red, fine grained		
V	PO 12	1570		Flat grinder	G	Amphibolite	Fine/medium grained, good planar foliation, strong lineation		Not distinctive; probably local
V	PO 18	1589		Hammer-stone, round	I	Vein quartz	Roughly rounded		Not distinctive; local; common in virtually all metamorphic terrains
V	PO 23	1590		Rubber	G	Amphibolite	Fine grained		Not distinctive; probably local
V	PN 28	1648		Axe butt	P	Amphibolite	Brown, medium grained		Not distinctive; probably local
V	PO 10	1650		Axe/ hammer, shafted, broken	P	Quartzite	Irregularly striped black/white; fine grained		Could be from local Rhodope metasedimentary sequence.
V	PO 10	1654		Axe frag-ment, blade end	P	Metadolerite-S	Porphyritic basaltic dike, amphibolitized	Probably Volvi type meta-morphosed porphyritic basaltic dike.	Metadolerite group, thus not typical amphibolite of Drama catchment; probably meta-ophiolites of Volvi, Petrota, or Soufli
V	PO 10	1691		Hammer-stone, round, fractured	I	Marble	White, well crystalline, moderately coarse grained		Not distinctive; probably local
V	PO 8	1732		?	?	Amphibolite	Schistose; feldspathic hornblende schist		Not distinctive; probably local
V	QN 8	1855		?	?	Schist tremolite?			Metamorphosed ultramafic; not known for certain in local Rhodope sequences Known from Western Serbo-Mace-donian and eastern Rhodope; Ultimately not sourceable

Phase	Context	SF No.	Pet. No.	Object	Ob. Cat.	Lithology	Field description	Thin-section description or comments	Source comments
V	QO 8	1862		Grooved stone	G	Sandstone	Coarse grained		Not local; probably from Eocene sedimentary sequences in basins E of Xanthi, as for limestones for limestones
V	PO/C 9	2013		Axe, rectangular	P	Altered volcanic?	Dark brown with dark quartz veins		
V	ROc 13	2025		Spheroid	G	Vein quartz			Not distinctive; local; common in virtually all metamorphic terrains
V	ROc 21	2038		Rubber	G	Sandstone			Not local; probably from Eocene sedimentary sequences in basins E of Xanthi, as for limestones for limestones
V	PO/D 37	2039		Rubber?	G	Marble	White		Not distinctive; probably local
V	ROc 23	2041		Ornament?, disk	O	Marble	White		Not distinctive; probably local
V	ROc 24	2042		Axe fragment	P	Amphibolite	Fine/medium-grained, no foliation; metamorphic texture		Not distinctive; probably local
V	QOd 9	2045		Hammerstone, round	I	Vein quartz	White; round pebble		Not distinctive; local; common in virtually all metamorphic terrains
V	QOd 9	2046		Hammerstone, round	I	Vein quartz	Pebble		Not distinctive; local; common in virtually all metamorphic terrains
V	QOd 9	2048		Axe fragment	P	Metadolerite-S	Plagioclase phenocrysts replaced by zoisite(?); hornblende developed in groundmass	Probably Volvi type metamorphosed porphyritic basaltic dike.	Metadolerite group, thus not typical amphibolite of Drama catchment; probably meta-ophiolites of Volvi, Petrota, or Soufli.
V	PO/C 25	2050		Axe	P	Metadolerite-S	Medium/coarse-grained igneous texture		Metadolerite group, thus not typical amphibolite of Drama catchment; probably meta-ophiolites of Volvi, Petrota, or Soufli
V	PO/C 29	2056		Axe/hammer, shafted, fragment	P	Sandstone	Buff, fine grained	May be low-grade metamorphic psammite.	Not local; probably from Circum-Rhodope sequence in E Thrace
V	PO/D 35	2069		Flat grinder, ex-flat cobble	G	Marble	Striped gray/white		Not distinctive; probably local
V	PO/D	2070		Flat grinder	G	Quartzo-feldspathic mica schist		Quartzo-feldspathic mica schist. See SF 313 (Pet. No. 79), SF 1169 (Pet. No. 77), SF 1182 (Pet. No. 78) for petrography.	Local Drama catchment metasediments
V	PO/D 34	2079		Hammerstone, round, fragment	I	Vein quartz, micaceous			Not distinctive; local; common in virtually all metamorphic terrains

Phase	Context	SF No.	Pet. No.	Object	Ob. Cat.	Lithology	Field description	Thin-section description or comments	Source comments
V	PO/D 34	2081	155	Axe	P	Metadolerite		Sub-ophitic fresh brownish cpx with included pseudomorphlithology of albite and epidote after intermediate plagioclase. Weak shear zones of albite+epidote+chlorite. Volvi type amphibolitized dolerite.	Metadolerite group, thus not typical amphibolite of Drama catchment; probably meta-ophiolites of Volvi, Petrota, or Soufli
V	PO/D 34	2085		Rubber	G	Marble	White		Not distinctive; probably local
V	PO/D 34	2088		Hammer-stone, round	I	Limestone	Grayish red		Probably Thrace (see note for SF 2645; phase II)
V	PO/D 35	2089		Rubber	G	Marble	White		Not distinctive; probably local
V	PO/D 37	2091		Rubber?	G	Marble	White		Not distinctive; probably local
V	PO A/C Balk	2096		Axe fragment	P	Amphibolite	Foliated, medium grained		Not distinctive; probably local
V	PO/C 32	2098		Rubber	G	Marble	White		Not distinctive; probably local
V	ZB 19	2109		Grinder and/or rubber	G	Marble			Not distinctive; probably local
V	PO/C 25	2214		Axe/rubber	P	Amphibolite	Medium/coarse grained		Not distinctive; probably local
V	PO/C 25	2215		Axe, split, square ended	P	Schist, actinolitic			Metamorphosed ultramafic; not known for certain in local Rhodope sequences Known from Western Serbo-Macedonian and Eastern Rhodope; ultimately not sourceable
V	PO/C 27	2220		Quern fragment	G	Quartzo-feldspathic mica schist	Pinkish	Quartzo-feldspathic mica schist. See SF 313 (Pet. No. 79), SF 1169 (Pet. No. 77), SF 1182 (Pet. No. 78) for petrography.	Local Drama catchment metasediments
V	PO 34	2225		Hammer-stone, round, fractured	I	Marble	White, well crystalline, moderately coarse grained		Not distinctive; probably local
V	PO/B 37	2231		Grinder, flat, fragment	G	Quartzo-feldspathic mica schist	White	Quartzo-feldspathic mica schist. See SF 313 (Pet. No. 79), SF 1169 (Pet. No. 77), SF 1182 (Pet. No. 78) for petrography.	Local Drama catchment metasediments
V	PO/B 33	2232	97	Polished fragment	P	Amphibolite	Light green; medium grained	Hornblende-epidote schist with very minor feldspar. Mafic layer in medium-grade amphibolite. Well crystalline, strong fabric.	Not distinctive; probably local
V	PO/B 33	2239		Flat grinder	G	Amphibolite	Feldspathic hornblende schist		Not distinctive; probably local

Phase	Context	SF No.	Pet. No.	Object	Ob. Cat.	Lithology	Field description	Thin-section description or comments	Source comments
V	PO/A 46	2247		Flat grinder	G	Quartzo-feldspathic mica schist	Gray, muscovitic	Quartzo-feldspathic mica schist. See SF 313 (Pet. No. 79), SF 1169 (Pet. No. 77), SF 1182 (Pet. No. 78) for petrography.	Local Drama catchment metasediments
V	PO/PN Balk	2249		Axe	P	Amphibolite	Brown, medium-grained		Not distinctive; probably local
V	PO/PN Balk	2252	82	Grinder/pounder, spherical	I	Metadolerite-S	Unfoliated, Volvi type; pyroxene partly transformed to brown hornblende; plagioclase saussuritized		Metadolerite group, thus not typical amphibolite of Drama catchment; probably meta-ophiolites of Volvi, Petrota, or Soufli
V	PO/A	2298		Ground fragment	G	Quartzo-feldspathic mica schist	Transitional to fine-grained granite gneiss	Quartzo-feldspathic mica schist. See SF 313 (Pet. No. 79), SF 1169 (Pet. No. 77), SF 1182 (Pet. No. 78) for petrography.	Local Drama catchment metasediments
V	PO/A ?	2299		Hammerstone, round	I	Vein quartz	Ex-pebble		Not distinctive; local; common in virtually all metamorphic terrains
V	PN/E 60	2400		Rubber	G	Marble	White		Not distinctive; probably local
V	PN/E 61	2404		Natural cobble	N	Quartzo-feldspathic mica schist		Quartzo-feldspathic mica schist. See SF 313 (Pet. No. 79), SF 1169 (Pet. No. 77), SF 1182 (Pet. No. 78) for petrography.	Local Drama catchment metasediments
V	PN/C 81	2414		Hammerstone, round	I	Vein quartz	Fractured pebble		Not distinctive; local; common in virtually all metamorphic terrains
V	PN/A 92	2422		Ground fragment	G	Quartzo-feldspathic mica schist	Off-white	Quartzo-feldspathic mica schist. See SF 313 (Pet. No. 79), SF 1169 (Pet. No. 77), SF 1182 (Pet. No. 78) for petrography.	Local Drama catchment metasediments
V	PN/A 92	2424	81	Natural cobble	N	Quartz monzo-diorite		Plag-px-hbl-bio-qz-kspar. Zoned euhedral intermediate plagioclase and hornblende are dominant. Pyroxene is scattered and partly amphibolitized. Minor biotite. Quartz and alkali feldspar are intergrown and interstitial. "Granite" sensu lato.	Probably a basic member of one of Oligocene granite complexes, e.g., Symvolon, Skaloti, or the Maronia Monzodiorite near Petrota
V	PN/A 92	2426		Pebble, broken	N	Amphibolite			Not distinctive; probably local
V	PN/A 92	2428		Hammerstone, round, fractured	I	Vein quartz	White		Not distinctive; local; common in virtually all metamorphic terrains
V	PN/B 100	2430		Hammerstone, round, fractured	I	Vein quartz			Not distinctive; local; common in virtually all metamorphic terrains

Phase	Context	SF No.	Pet. No.	Object	Ob. Cat.	Lithology	Field description	Thin-section description or comments	Source comments
V	?	2434		Saddle quern?	G	Quartzo-feldspathic mica schist	Gray, muscovite and biotite; broken block	Quartzo-feldspathic mica schist. See SF 313 (Pet. No. 79), SF 1169 (Pet. No. 77), SF 1182 (Pet. No. 78) for petrography.	Local Drama catchment metasediments
V	PN/E 62B	2434		Flat grinder, broken, roughly rounded	G	Quartzo-feldspathic mica schist		Quartzo-feldspathic mica schist. See SF 313 (Pet. No. 79), SF 1169 (Pet. No. 77), SF 1182 (Pet. No. 78) for petrography.	Local Drama catchment metasediments
V	PN/E 62B	2437		Flat grinder, square slab	G	Quartzo-feldspathic mica schist	Gray	Quartzo-feldspathic mica schist. See SF 313 (Pet. No. 79), SF 1169 (Pet. No. 77), SF 1182 (Pet. No. 78) for petrography.	Local Drama catchment metasediments
V	PN/C 62B	2438		Flat grinder	G	Quartzo-feldspathic mica schist	Includes calcite vein	Quartzo-feldspathic mica schist. See SF 313 (Pet. No. 79), SF 1169 (Pet. No. 77), SF 1182 (Pet. No. 78) for petrography.	Local Drama catchment metasediments
V	PN/E 63B	2440		Hammerstone, round, fractured	I	Vein quartz	Pinkish		Not distinctive; local; common in virtually all metamorphic terrains
V	PO/B 35	2800		Hammerstone, round, fractured	I	Vein quartz	Micaceous inclusions		Not distinctive; local; common in virtually all metamorphic terrains
V	QOc	2809		?	?	Amphibolite	Brown, fine/medium-grained, cream speckle		Not distinctive; probably local
V	ROc 26	3002		Rubber?	G	Sandstone			Not local; probably from Eocene sedimentary sequences in basins E of Xanthi, as for limestones for limestones
V	PN/CE 60 Balk	3306		Hammerstone, round	I	Vein quartz	Flattened, as derived from concordant segregation in schist		Not distinctive; local; common in virtually all metamorphic terrains
V	PO/A 48	3309		Flat grinder	G	Gneiss	Fine-grained granitic gneiss		Possibly high-grade Rhodope metamorphics of the Sidhironero Unit (Central Rhodope Unit) N and NE of the Drama plain, or Kavala Granite; not very distinctive.
V	PO/A 48	3311		Axe fragment?	P	Sandstone	Coarse grained		Not local; probably from Eocene sedimentary sequences in basins E of Xanthi, as for limestones for limestones
V	PO/A 48	3312		Flat grinder	G	Quartzo-feldspathic mica schist	Pink	Quartzo-feldspathic mica schist. See SF 313 (Pet. No. 79), SF 1169 (Pet. No. 77), SF 1182 (Pet. No. 78) for petrography.	Local Drama catchment metasediments
V	PO/B 43	3321		Uniquern	G	Limestone	Gray		Probably Thrace (see note for SF 2645; phase II)
V	PO C/D balk	3350		?	?	Amphibolite	Medium grained, weak foliation		Not distinctive; probably local

Phase	Context	SF No.	Pet. No.	Object	Ob. Cat.	Lithology	Field description	Thin-section description or comments	Source comments
V	PO 158	3360		Saddle quern	G	Quartzo-feldspathic mica schist	Yellowish gray, weathered	Quartzo-feldspathic mica schist. See SF 313 (Pet. No. 79), SF 1169 (Pet. No. 77), SF 1182 (Pet. No. 78) for petrography.	Local Drama catchment metasediments
V	PN/F 262B	3364		Rubber?, ex-broken axe	G	Amphibolite	Deep blackish green, fine/medium grained, weak foliation, hornblende and plagioclase distinguishable	966, 2512, 2725, 2769, 3364 are all very similar.	Not distinctive; probably local
V	PN/ D 77	3366		Axe, stumpy	P	Sandstone			Not local; probably from Eocene sedimentary sequences in basins E of Xanthi, as for limestones for limestones
V	PO/E 66	3371		Quern fragment	G	Quartzo-feldspathic mica schist		Quartzo-feldspathic mica schist. See SF 313 (Pet. No. 79), SF 1169 (Pet. No. 77), SF 1182 (Pet. No. 78) for petrography.	Local Drama catchment metasediments
V	PO/B 102	3389		Axe	P	Metadolerite?	White/buff, fine-grained, mottled texture resembling core texture of rodingitized gabbros; hard, not soft	Probably metadolerite with feldspar replaced by zoisite/clinozoisite; not subject to kaolinization on burial.	Metadolerite group, thus not typical amphibolite of Drama catchment; probably meta-ophiolites of Volvi, Petrota, or Soufli
V	PN/E 67	3390		Hammerstone	I	Marble	White		Not distinctive; probably local
V	PN/B 86	3392		Axe fragment	P	Amphibolite	Medium grained, unfoliated		Not distinctive; probably local
V	PN/ A 20	3567		Rubber	G	Amphibolite			Not distinctive; probably local
V	PN/ A 20	3568		Rubber?	G	Marble	White		Not distinctive; probably local
V	PO/B 36	3570		Quern fragment	G	Quartzo-feldspathic mica schist	Feldspar augen	Quartzo-feldspathic mica schist. See SF 313 (Pet. No. 79), SF 1169 (Pet. No. 77), SF 1182 (Pet. No. 78) for petrography.	Local Drama catchment metasediments
V	PN/ C 82	3572		Rubber	G	Marble	Buff on weathered surface		Not distinctive; probably local
V	PO/ C 31	3604		Hammerstone, round, split		Vein quartz?			Not distinctive; local; common in virtually all metamorphic terrains
V	PO 15	3606		Axe fragment	P	Limestone	Gray		Probably Thrace (see note for SF 2645; phase II)
V	PO/B 40?	3622		Mace head, shafted, or weight	P	Metadolerite-R?	White/buff altered foliated dolerite, soft surface	Saussuritized meta-dolerite, possibly partly prehnitized as in "R" or rodingitized type.	Metadolerite group, thus not typical amphibolite of Drama catchment; probably meta-ophiolites of Volvi, Petrota, or Soufli
V	PN Ex S, 50cm down	3658		Axe fragment	P	Biotite andesite?	Highly weathered (rotten) volcanic		Not Drama catchment. Most likely Petrota or Kirki-Essimi

Phase	Context	SF No.	Pet. No.	Object	Ob. Cat.	Lithology	Field description	Thin-section description or comments	Source comments
V	PO 159	3745		Axe fragment	P	Sandstone	Well-cemented olive-green orthoquartzite		Not local; probably from Eocene sedimentary sequences in basins E of Xanthi, as for limestones for limestones
V	PO 158	3785		Hammer stone	I	Marble			Not distinctive; probably local
V	PN Ext S	3799		Axe	P	Amphibolite	Deep black-brown green, with gray mottled feldspar; fine/medium grained; weak foliation		Not distinctive; probably local
V	PO/B 49	4269		Pebble, rounded	N	Amphibolite	Coarse grained, hornblendite in places	Axe raw material?	Not distinctive; probably local
V	PO/B 19	4272		Flat grinder	G	Quartzo-feldspathic mica schist	Reddish, Fe-stained	Quartzo-feldspathic mica schist. See SF 313 (Pet. No. 79), SF 1169 (Pet. No. 77), SF 1182 (Pet. No. 78) for petrography.	Local Drama catchment metasediments
V	PN/O 67	4273		Flat grinder, broken cobble	G	Quartzo-feldspathic mica schist	Feldspathic; transitional to fine-grained granite gneiss	Quartzo-feldspathic mica schist. See SF 313 (Pet. No. 79), SF 1169 (Pet. No. 77), SF 1182 (Pet. No. 78) for petrography.	Local Drama catchment metasediments
V	PN/D?	4274		Flat grinder, ex-cobble; fractured	G	Biotite granite			Not very distinctive but has to be one of Oligocene granite bodies, e.g., Symvolon, Skaloti, etc.
V	PN C/D Balk clearing	4304		Flat grinder, broken	G	Granite gneiss	Fine grained		Possibly high-grade Rhodope metamorphics of the Sidhironero Unit (Central Rhodope Unit) N and NE of Drama plain, or Kavala Granite. Not very distinctive
V	PO/C 136	4406		Flat grinder/rubber	G	Marble			Not distinctive; probably local
V	PN/D 79	4440		Rubber	G	Sandstone			Not local; probably from Eocene sedimentary sequences in basins E of Xanthi, as for limestones for limestones
V	PO/B 39	4454		Quern fragment	G	Quartzo-feldspathic mica schist	Pinkish white	Quartzo-feldspathic mica schist. See SF 313 (Pet. No. 79), SF 1169 (Pet. No. 77), SF 1182 (Pet. No. 78) for petrography.	Local Drama catchment metasediments
V	PN/F 62	4468		Axe or hammer fragment	P	Amphibolite	Deep green, fine/medium grained; foliation very poor	Similar to SF 966, 2512, 2725, 2769, 3364 but less clearly foliated.	Not distinctive; probably local
V	PN/A 95	4471		Hammerstone	I	Vein quartz			Not distinctive; local; common in virtually all metamorphic terrains
V	PO 17	4574		Saddle quern	G	Quartzo-feldspathic mica schist	Gray	Quartzo-feldspathic mica schist. See SF 313 (Pet. No. 79), SF 1169 (Pet. No. 77), SF 1182 (Pet. No. 78) for petrography.	Local Drama catchment metasediments

Phase	Context	SF No.	Pet. No.	Object	Ob. Cat.	Lithology	Field description	Thin-section description or comments	Source comments
V	PN/C 80	2411B		Flat grinder	G	Quartzo-feldspathic mica schist		Quartzo-feldspathic mica schist. See SF 313 (Pet. No. 79), SF 1169 (Pet. No. 77), SF 1182 (Pet. No. 78) for petrography.	Local Drama catchment metasediments
V	PN/A 92	2423?		Natural cobble	N	Quartzo-feldspathic mica schist	Rusty weathered; probably natural cobble	Quartzo-feldspathic mica schist. See SF 313 (Pet. No. 79), SF 1169 (Pet. No. 77), SF 1182 (Pet. No. 78) for petrography.	Local Drama catchment metasediments
V	PO 23	?		Flat grinder, slab, no rounding	G	Quartzo-feldspathic mica schist			
Va	ZA 12	1180		Ground fragment	G	Biotite granite	Weak foliation		Not very distinctive but has to be one of Oligocene granite bodies, e.g., Symvolon, Skaloti, etc.
Va	ROc 34	3008		Rubber?	G	Metagabbro-R?		Probably SF 1191–type quartz vein. Misidentified as "kaolinized granite" in field, as with others in this group.	Not local; ophiolite association but not Volvi if unmetamorphosed and prehnitized; possibly Petrota or Soufli
Va	ROc 34	3010		Quern fragment	G	Quartzo-feldspathic mica schist		Quartzo-feldspathic mica schist. See SF 313 (Pet. No. 79), SF 1169 (Pet. No. 77), SF 1182 (Pet. No. 78) for petrography.	Local Drama catchment metasediments
Vb	ZA 9	44		?	?	Amphibolite	Feldspathic; medium coarse		Not distinctive; probably local
Vb	ROc 2	2005		Axe	P	Amphibolite	Deep black-brown green, with gray mottled feldspar; medium-grained; weak foliation		Not distinctive; probably local
Vb	ROc 14	2029		Axe, broken	P	Metagabbro-S	Igneous textured fine-grained gabbro with brown/black ferromagnesian and white feldspar	Probably unfoliated metagabbro with feldspar replaced by zoisite/clinozoisite (i.e., saussuritized), not subject to kaolinization upon burial.	Not local; probably Volvi, Petrota, or Soufli
Vb	ROc 14	2034		Axe	P	Amphibolite	Grayish brown, fine/medium grained		Not distinctive; probably local
Vb	ROc 4	2217		Axe, triangular	P	Amphibolite	Greenish; brownish weathering; fine grained, schistose		Not distinctive; probably local
Vb	ROc 34	3012		Axe	P	Metagabbro-S	Igneous textured fine-grained gabbro with brown/black ferromagnesian and white feldspar	Probably unfoliated metagabbro with feldspar replaced by zoisite/clinozoisite (i.e., saussuritized), not subject to kaolinization upon burial.	Not local; probably Volvi, Petrota, or Soufli
Vb	ROc 51	3020		Fragment	?	Amphibolite	Pale grayish blue-green, fine grained; no feldspar separately distinguishable	Possibly lower-grade greenschist metabasite, cf. common amphibolite group.	Not distinctive. Probably local, but if low grade could be Circum-Rhodope Group (Thrace).
Vb	ROc 2	3660		Hone?	G	Marble			Not distinctive; probably local

Phase	Context	SF No.	Pet. No.	Object	Ob. Cat.	Lithology	Field description	Thin-section description or comments	Source comments
Vb	ROc 14	4478		Fragment	?	Amphibolite	Deep black-brown green, with gray mottled feldspar; medium-grained; unfoliated		Not distinctive; probably local
X	LKd 1 surface	9		Axe	P	Sandstone	Coarse grained		Not local; probably from Eocene sedimentary sequences in basins E of Xanthi, as for limestones for limestones
X	MNa 1	33		?	?	Amphibolite?	Grayish blue-green; coarsely tuffaceous texture		Source or sources unknown
X	NNa 1 surface	36		?	?	Amphibolite	Gray, foliated, fine grained		Not distinctive; probably local
X	KNd 1 surface	52		Axe	P	Amphibolite	Deep blackish green, fine/medium grained, banded		Not distinctive; probably local
X	MNb 1 surface	56		Fragment	?	Metadolerite-S	Visible ophitic dolerite texture; foliation weak	56, 276, 2205 could be the same rock.	Metadolerite group, thus not typical amphibolite of Drama catchment; probably meta-ophiolites of Volvi, Petrota, or Soufli
X	QR 1 surface	60		Axe/ hammer, shafted, fragment	P	Tremolite schist?		Metamorphosed ultramafic.	Not known from Drama catchment metamorphics; more probably western Serbo-Macedonian massif or Eastern Rhodope, Soufli area.
X	HLc 1 surface	273		Chisel	P	Metadolerite			
X	HLc 1 surface	274		Bowl fragment	B	Marble			Not distinctive; probably local
X	HNb 1 surface	276		Fragment	?	Metadolerite-S	Visible ophitic dolerite texture; foliation weak	SF 56, 276, 2205 could be the same rock.	Metadolerite group, thus not typical amphibolite of Drama catchment; probably meta-ophiolites of Volvi, Petrota, or Soufli.
X	Surface	471		Axe, broken	P	Amphibolite	Fine-grained, mottled deep green/grayish green		Not distinctive; probably local
X	none	830		Mace	G	Limestone	Gray, hard	Possibly fine-grained marble.	Local if marble, otherwise probably Thrace (see note for SF 2645; phase II)
X	LM 35	831		Adze, broken	P	Amphibolite/ calc silicate?	Irregularly banded streaks of fine grained, brownish green amphibolite and very fine-grained grayish green, more siliceous or feldspathic material	FGGG group.	Source or sources unknown
X	none	1104	96	Axe	P	Amphibolite	Dark green, gray mottle	Interlocking pale green actinolite prisms; minor feldspar; granular epidote, abundant opaque spinel.	Not distinctive; probably local
X	SNd 1	1184		Flat grinder	G	Limestone			Probably Thrace (see note for SF 2645; phase II)

Phase	Context	SF No.	Pet. No.	Object	Ob. Cat.	Lithology	Field description	Thin-section description or comments	Source comments
X	MNa 1	1187		Grinder/ pounder, spherical	I	Marble breccia		Probably fault breccia.	Not distinctive; probably local
X	KK 1	1683		Axe, broken	P	Amphibolite	Fine grained		Not distinctive; probably local
X	QNb 1	1709		Axe, triangular	P	Amphibolite?	Grayish brown, fine grained	FGGG group.	Source or sources unknown
X	QMd 1 surface	1719		Axe fragment	P	Amphibolite	Grayish blue-green, medium grained		Not distinctive; probably local
X	Surface	1725		Axe/ hammer, shafted, fragment	P	Amphibolite	Greenish black; fine/ medium grained		Not distinctive; probably local
X	KNc 1	1742		Axe/ hammer, shafted, fragment	P	Metagabbro-S? (olivine gabbro, serpentinized)	Gray-green with light green plagioclase.	Probably related to the metadolerite group; metamorphism minimal.	Metadolerite group, thus not typical amphibolite of Drama catchment; probably metaophiolites of Volvi, Petrota, or Soufli
X	ROc 1	2003		Axe	P	Amphibolite	Deep black-brown green, with gray mottled feldspar; medium grained; weak foliation		Not distinctive; probably local
X	OHb 1 surface	2205		Chisel? broken	P	Metadolerite-S	Visible ophitic dolerite texture; foliation weak	SF 56, 276, 2205 could be the same rock.	Metadolerite group, thus not typical amphibolite of Drama catchment; probably metaophiolites of Volvi, Petrota, or Soufli
X	OIb 1 surface	2207		Axe	P	Granite	Quartz, pink feldspar, hornblende(?)		Probably one of Oligocene granites, e.g., Vrontou, Skaloti, Symvolon
X	none	2210		Pebble, partly drilled	G	Quartz	Yellow	Unfinished axehead?	Not distinctive; probably local
X	surface	2248		Axe/ hammer, shafted, fragment	P	Serpentinite	Brown, veined dark brown; lizardite(?)		Not local; western Serbo-Macedonian massif or eastern Rhodope, e.g., Soufli
X	ML cleaning	2272		Fragment	?	Marble	White		Not distinctive; probably local
X	JL surface	2296		Axe fragment	P	Metadolerite-S	Medium/coarse-grained igneous texture		Metadolerite group, thus not typical amphibolite of Drama catchment; probably metaophiolites of Volvi, Petrota, or Soufli
X	JL surface	2507		Chisel, reused and reversed?	P	Amphibolite?	Faint greenish gray, foliated. possibly related to amphibole bearing hornfels; FGGG group	FGGG group.	Source or sources unknown
X	JL surface	2510		Chisel fragment	P	Metagabbro-R	Waxy green crystals in soft white matrix with translucent brownish plagioclase	Almost certainly SF 1191– type quartz vein.	Not local; ophiolite association but not Volvi; possibly Petrota or Soufli

Phase	Context	SF No.	Pet. No.	Object	Ob. Cat.	Lithology	Field description	Thin-section description or comments	Source comments
X	SL 105	2552		Saddle quern	G	Quartzo-feldspathic mica schist		Quartzo-feldspathic mica schist. See SF 313 (Pet. No. 79), SF 1169 (Pet. No. 77), SF 1182 (Pet. No. 78) for petrography.	Local Drama catchment metasediments
X	NQ 1 surface	2851		Axe/ hammer, shafted, fragment	P	Serpentinite	Lustrous bluish green with tight folds		Not local; western Serbo-Macedonian massif or eastern Rhodope, e.g., Soufli
X	JL surface	2865		Pebble, part drilled	G	Marble	Natural polish		Not distinctive; probably local
X	ZHt surface	3221		?	?	Amphibolite	Bluish green, medium grained		Not distinctive; probably local
X	ZHt surface	3226		Rubber?	G	Serpentinite			Not local; western Serbo-Macedonian massif or eastern Rhodope, e.g., Soufli
X	UJ 1	3433	95	Axe	P	Meta-volcaniclastic	Gray-green; medium grained; related to FGGG group	Greenschist facies metaclastic (crystal-rich tuff, possibly redeposited) with abundant plagioclase clasts, quartz micro-ribbons; metamorphic chlorite, epidote.	Not Drama catchment. Too low grade for Rhodope metamorphics. Probably Circum-Rhodope Group, eastern Thrace.
X	UF 1 surface	3434		Axe/ hammer, shafted, fragment	P	Serpentinite	Bottle green/deep yellowish green; faint mottling		Not local; western Serbo-Macedonian massif or eastern Rhodope, e.g., Soufli
X	Surface	3552		Axe with central groove	P	Metadolerite-S	Visible ophitic dolerite texture preserved but with variable weak foliation		Metadolerite group, thus not typical amphibolite of Drama catchment; probably meta-ophiolites of Volvi, Petrota, or Soufli
X	Surface	3553		Adze?	P	Amphibolite	Deep green, fine grained, faint gray mottle		Not distinctive; probably local
X	Surface	3558		Axe, broken	P	Amphibolite	Deep greenish brown, fine grained, no foliation evident		Not distinctive; probably local
X	Surface	3666		Axe protolith	P	Amphibolite	Bluish green, medium grained, foliated with marked lineation		Not distinctive; probably local
X	Surface	3690		Chisel	P	Amphibolite	Actinolite schist		Not distinctive; probably local
X	Surface	3691		Rubber	G	Iron oxide	Black, possibly magnetite		Not distinctive
X	ZK 2	3704		Axe	P	Metagabbro-(S?)	Deep resinous, slightly bluish green; serpentinized(?) olivine; 75% mafic		Not local; probably Volvi, Petrota, or Soufli

5.

Grindstones, Polished Edge-Tools, and Other Stone Artifacts

Ernestine S. Elster

Among the indestructible material correlates of prehistoric life, stone tools—polished and ground—offer a reliable source of information and impressions about the manufacturers and consumers of these tools. Patterns of raw material acquisition, tool manufacture and use, and changes in any or all of these variables through time are explored in this chapter. My goal is to offer observations inferred through this multivariate study about the courses of action that the Sitagroi settlers followed. Further, appendix 5.1 is a special report on the economic implications and grinding tools, by Martin Biskowski. Both he and I have relied on John Dixon's identifications of both raw material and likely sources (chapter 4, this volume). In every sense, chapters 3, 4, and 5 and their appendices provide the reader with as full a picture as may be offered (at this time) of these groupings of stone tools, all excavated more than three decades past.[1]

The database consists of over 500 ground and polished stone artifacts, some fragmentary, tabulated in three groupings or classes based on morphology and inferred function.[2] These groupings are defined as follows:

- Primary-use tools: Axe, adze, and chisel (all edged-tools), which I infer were used by the Sitagroi settlers directly against wood (and bark), bone, and antler to cut, chop, scrape, split, shape, and strip, or to dig in the earth, and hoe, as well as in stone working[3] (figures 5.1–5.6, 5.8–5.22; plates 5.1–5.15).

- Processors: Paired grinders, used one against the other, with the material to be processed in between, as well as several forms of impactors. This grouping includes quern, grinder, pounder, hammerstone, and impactor, which I

infer the householders at Sitagroi used in preparing and processing foodstuffs along with nonedible materials such as ochre and clays (plates 5.16–5.39).

- Presenters: I offer this category for the consideration of artifacts that are rarely found in large numbers but that nevertheless played a role in prehistoric society. This role is presently ambiguous, but because of their forms and raw material, I infer that these artifacts were employed in a social or symbolic sense, perhaps, to present or offer something, or to bestow something on another person. While potentially useful in the practical sense, these objects may also have represented an individual's (or a household's) status, position, or prestige at a particular time during the Sitagroi occupation. At Sitagroi these include fragments of marble bowls, maccheads, and a "scepter" (figures 5.23–5.34; plates 5.40–5.42). (Stone beads and pendants are separated from this grouping and are discussed fully in chapter 9 of this volume.) Certainly other tools (for example, axes) may have carried a social or symbolic meaning, but the regularity of these forms, such as the axes, warranted the traditional classification.

The distribution of these classes is examined over time (table 5.1), and formal variability is described along with a discussion of production and use history. I base my tabulation of the raw material as "local" or "not-local" on John Dixon's report (chapter 4) and his appendix 4.1, since comments in the field notebook or on the piece cards regarding raw material identification were essentially impressionistic. Martin Biskowski, whose research has focused broadly on grinding tools in

Mesoamerica (1997), contributed appendix 5.1 using the catalog, plates, and Dixon's report as a basis for his estimates of the working life of these processors, including the time involved to acquire the raw material and to produce the tools.

Over 40% of the recovered ground and polished stone artifacts came from the Early Bronze Age (EBA) occupation on the site in the context of the three building episodes of phase V: the Bin Complex, the Long House, and the Burnt House (see volume 1, chapter 8 [C. Renfrew 1986b]). A short discussion highlights this recovery.

The work of John Hedges, myself, and others during the three field seasons—including inventory cards, notebooks, and other archival material—provided the basis for this report. Close to one-third of the assemblage is illustrated; a catalog concludes this chapter.

DISCUSSION

These tools and artifacts represent the material correlates of prospecting, exchange, manufacture, use, and disposal—activities supported by a social network of miners and suppliers of raw material, and perhaps also by middlemen or women, stone workers and craftspeople, and finally consumers. Many of these artifacts were renewed, recycled, and curated—a testament to their long-term value. Lillios (1999:243) has suggested that stone axe amulets from late prehistoric sites in Western Europe may have been heirlooms, beginning their lives as larger functional tools, and over time (perhaps associated with ancestors of note), were transformed by further shaping and polishing. However, intrinsic value could have been calculated by any number of scales, which themselves changed over time (Bradley and Edmonds 1993:57). For example, value and significance could have been judged by the rarity and/or suitability of the stones; the ease or difficulty of the processes of extraction and acquisition of the raw material; or the workmanship, practicality, and/or desirability of the tool. It is also possible that the characteristics of the artifact's or tool's previous owner(s) conferred special status on each successive owner, as does an heirloom (see Lillios 1999).

In the following sections, all of the types in each class are defined and illustrated; cross-tabulations summarize (1) the temporal distribution of all classes (table 5.1); (2) of primary-use tools and local/not-local raw material over time (table 5.2); (3) of small, medium, and large celts over time (table 5.3); (4) and of processors and local/not-local raw material over time (tables 5.4, 5.5). Questions of terminology, manufacture, raw material, and the like are dealt with in turn as the discussion revolves around each of the three classes.

Table 5.1. Distribution of Classes of Stone Artifacts Over Time

Stone tool type	Phase I	II	III	IV	V	X*	Total
Presenters	0	14	3	0	5	5	27
Primary-use	9	31	34	20	48	29	171
Processors	10	38	71	23	152	11	305
Phase Total	19	83	108	43	205	45	503

* X indicates unphased or mixed contexts.

PRIMARY-USE TOOLS

I define primary-use tools as those that are applied singly and directly by the worker to his/her task—tree felling, antler shaping, turning soil—as opposed to the processing tools which are paired in the processing of another medium. Included in the primary-use category (N = 171) are formally shaped and edged axes, adzes, shaft-hole axes, hammer-axes, and chisels. Most were roughed out, given a ground edge or bit, and then polished; presumably they were used hafted but not necessarily. Their function in tilling the soil and in woodworking is generally accepted (see Dierckx 1992; Prinz 1988). Prinz (1988:270) concluded that the largest were deployed to fell trees and strip bark, while the smaller examples were operative in a variety of applications as are modern woodworkers' tools today. The smaller tools also could have begun life as larger artifacts, and reworked as they became damaged or worn. The various sizes might also have been used in agriculture and for many domestic chores: to chop or split wood, chisel, trim or shape antler and bone, in butchery or stone working, to renew the cutting edges of these same stone tools, and in shaping and forming the processors or presenters.

Axes and Adzes

In some reports, axes and adzes are referred to as "celts" without further distinction between the forms (Coleman 1977:5; Lamb 1936:178–193, fig. 55). Generally, however, scholars do attempt to discriminate between axes and adzes. For example, Sterud and Sterud (1974:223) wrote of the Obre tools, ". . . axes for brush clearance or adzes for tilling the soil." Following their interpretation of use—and this definition is repeated elsewhere (Sugaya 1993:444)—the expected difference might be that in section, the axe is symmetrical, as may be seen in the line drawings (figures 5.1, 5.2), and hafted on an angle to its handle, whereas the adze, viewed similarly, appears asymmetrical, and is hafted perpendicularly to its handle (figures 5.3, 5.4, 5.5).

Beth Prinz describes, in her edge-wear study of the assemblage from Divostin (1988:255–300), that the striations from wear were as expected, on angle to the bit of most axes and perpendicular to the adze bit. But some of her cases were not as straightforward; on occasion both axe and adze exhibited diagonal and perpendicular striations (Prinz 1988: 260, table 9.6). She also refers to an ethnographic case from New Guinea (Heider 1967:54, 55) where "[o]bjects with 'axe' symmetry are used as adzes and objects with 'adze' symmetry are used as axes . . ." (1988:260). Her point is that we cannot assume function from formal similarity to modern tools, unless the worked edge is studied for edge wear—and even then there is ambiguity. In fact, some of the Obre polished stone objects exhibited battered distal ends which the excavators hypothesized were caused by the percussive force of stone on stone; Sterud and Sterud's interpretation (1974: 232) was that these were being used as wedges to split wood and were not hafted at all. In fact, Rackham's analysis of charcoal samples from Sitagroi (volume 1, appendix A [Rackham 1986]:62) indicates that planks were split radially, which would have required both wedges and pounders since there is no evidence for saws. Furthermore, a number of Sitagroi tools were reported with butt damage, described as "very rough", "battered," and "hammered" (for example, from phase II [plate 5.2b] and from phase V [plate 5.10b]), presumably caused by percussive force. I expect that a tool used as a wedge would exhibit wear on the wedge edge as well as on the impacted surface and that evidence for such contact is identifiable.

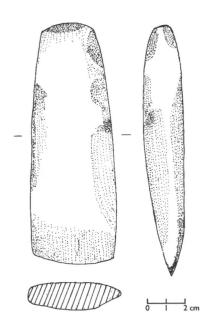

Figure 5.1. Axe, phase III: SF 393, matt, smooth, blue/green, plates 5.4a, 5.5b.

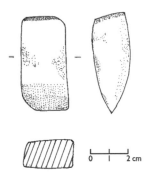

Figure 5.2. Axe, phase II: SF 951, mottled white with gray/ green, plate 5.3f.

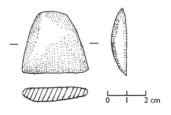

Figure 5.3. Adze, phase III: SF 842, matt, fine-grained, blue/ green, plate 5.7d.

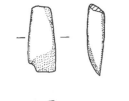

*(Right): Figure 5.4. Adze/chisel (?), phase II: SF 956, highly polished, fine-grained black, plate 5.3g.

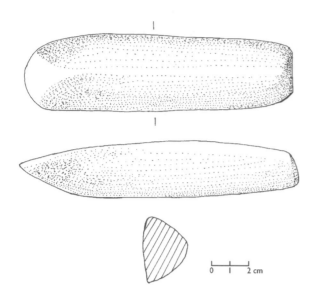

Figure 5.5. Adze, phase III: SF 818, white flecked with gray, plate 5.5c.

The majority of Sitagroi celts are axes (table 5.2), and although there is a distinction between adze and axe in application, the assemblage also includes examples that could be either. Occasionally the celt section-view suggests that a dulled bit was resharpened from the ventral side, thus changing adze into axe form. Perhaps a dark green celt from phase I (figure 5.6; plate 5.1a) underwent this process. Comments on wear marks on the inventory cards were essentially impressionistic, since systematic edge-wear study was not undertaken. Nevertheless, common sense indicates that artifacts with bits that clearly segregate as symmetrical or not might well have been used in different ways, although there was likely an easy shifting of application, perhaps more in line with need, with the size of the tool, and with the task at hand than with the morphology of the bit.

From a distance of thirty years I hesitate to change the original designation of adze or axe, but a number of tools might warrant a second look

Table 5.2. Distribution of Primary-Use Stone Tools of Local/Not Local Raw Material Over Time

Tool Type	Phase I	Phase II	Phase III	Phase IV	Phase V	Phase X*	Total
Adze							
Local	0	0	0	0	1	0	1
Not local	0	0	3	0	0	0	3
Not identified	0	1	1	0	1	0	3
Axe							
Local	2	4	4	9	13	7	39
Not local	0	10	19	2	15	9	55
Not identified	7	13	5	7	11	6	49
Chisel							
Local	0	0	0	0	1	0	1
Not local	0	0	1	0	0	0	1
Not identified	0	0	1	0	0	0	1
Other							
Local	0	0	0	0	2	0	2
Not local	0	1	0	0	0	1	2
Not identified	0	0	0	0	1	0	1
Shaft-hole axe							
Local	0	0	0	0	1	2	3
Not local	0	0	0	1	2	3	6
Not identified	0	2	0	1	0	1	4
Total							
Local	2	4	4	9	18	9	46
Not local	0	11	23	3	17	13	67
Not identified	7	16	7	8	13	7	58

* X indicates unphased or mixed contexts.

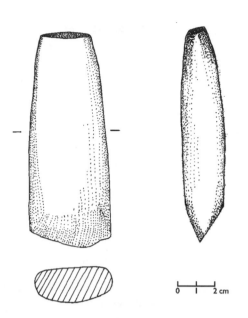

Figure 5.6. Axe, phase I: SF 970, highly polished, dark green, plate 5.1a.

Table 5.3. Distribution of Unbroken Small, Medium, and Large Celts Over Time

Length	Phase					Total
	I	II	III	IV	V	
Small	0	3	5	0	3	11
Medium	1	5	10	5	13	34
Large	1	1	4	1	0	7
Phase Total	2	9	19	6	16	52

Small: 3 to 4 cm in length
Medium: 5 to 8 cm in length
Large: 9 to 15 cm in length

because they are described as having an asymmetrical or, occasionally, a beveled bit but are designated as axes in the catalog (for example, SF 1506, phase III [figure 5.12; plate 5.7a]). Although Prinz points out that systematic micro-examination of the used edges can still produce ambiguous results, such research has been invaluable for providing traces of use history. For example, both Selevac (Spears 1990; Voytek 1990) and Divostin (Prinz 1988) demonstrate how the microscopic study of used edges indicated the intensity of use along with other observations such as manufacturing traces. In any case, questions of functional identification may still be posed; the Sitagroi stone assemblage will not suffer from the passage of time since all the contextual data are retained, and these artifacts offer an opportunity for profitable investigation by future scholars.

Axes are the largest grouping, comprising over 80% of primary-use tools; the phase distribution can be seen in table 5.3. As in other assemblages of material culture at Sitagroi, recovery is richest from the Chalcolithic, phase III, and also in phase V of the EBA.

As Dixon notes, nonlocal stones were selected for polished edge-tools, with the exception of the small grouping of local stone from phase I (see table 5.2). The recovery in phase IV also suggests a more local pattern of stone acquisition; but phases II and III reflect stone workers actively interested in and utilizing the best raw material for edge-tools—those that took a polish and held an edge. Stones with these qualities were not easily found in the Drama region, with the exception of marble and amphibolite. Dixon offers sources either to the east in the Xanthi Basin, or to the west and north around Lake Volvi (see this volume, chapter 4, figure 4.1). By phase III, and even more so in phase V, prospecting and trading in these raw materials must have been very active.

The scattergram of intact axes (figure 5.7) indicates that phases I–III (Middle Neolithic to Chalcolithic [MN/C]) saw the greatest size variation; size was more controlled during the EBA.[4] Large, intact axes range in length from 8.6 to 15.0 cm. Examples include the following: from phase I, an artifact 11.5 cm in length (figure 5.6; plate 5.1a); from phase II, an axe 8.6 cm in length (plate 5.3e); and from phase III, an axe of nonlocal stone (figure 5.1; plates 5.4a, 5.5b). Both the phase I and III examples are comparable to a Dikili Tash axe (Treuil 1992: pl. 118b). Another phase III axe (or "chisel or wedge" as named in appendix 4.1) is 15 cm in length, of nonlocal raw material (figure 5.5; plate 5.5c), and similar to a Divostin artifact (Prinz 1988: 295, pl. X: d).

Medium axes cluster between 5.0 and 7.0 in length. Illustrated examples of local stone include one from phase I (plate 5.1b) and several from phase II (plate 5.3a, d [figure 5.10]), as well as of nonlocal stone (figure 5.8 [plate 5.11c]; figure 5.9 [plate 5.3b]; and figure 5.2 [plate 5.3f]). Locally available amphibolite was used (figure 5.10; plate 5.3d); the latter form is comparable to a Dikili Tash artifact (Treuil 1992: pls. 123g, 118d, 119b). Over two dozen medium sized axes were recovered from phase III; one of these (figure 5.11; plate 5.6e) has been compared to a Dikili Tash tool (Treuil 1992: pl. 123b). Four others are also from phase III (plate 5.6a, c, d, f). Two are illustrated from phase IV: one of local and another of nonlocal stone (plate 5.9a, c); five are from phase V (plate 5.10a–e), all of nonlocal stone.

Small tools (shorter than about 4.0 cm) were recovered from throughout the sequence. Examples include a phase I artifact, perhaps a chisel (plate 5.1c); another possible chisel from phase II of local stone (plate 5.3g [figure. 5.4]); and a phase II axe of nonlocal rock (plate 5.3i). There are three from phase III, all of nonlocal raw material (figures 5.3, 5.12, 5.13; plate 5.7a, d, e), comparable to small axes from Dikili Tash (Treuil 1992: pls. 122a, 119e, 122b). A series from phase V are all of nonlocal material (plate 5.8a–f). The forms of these small tools seem not to have been affected by time; compare the examples from phases III, IV, and V (see figure 5.7). The function of these tiny axes is curious, since we do not know whether or not they were used. Prinz hypothesized that small tools were used for highly specialized wood-working because use-wear was observed on only one corner of the cutting edge (1988:261); a similar pattern may be observed on one Sitagroi artifact (figure 5.4; plate 5.3g). These objects may also have been used in pottery production as burnishers, polishers, or for incising designs on wet clay (for example, plate 5.8f). Alternately, Marija Gimbutas (Gimbutas, Winn, and Shimabuku 1989:333, 373, pl. 9.31:1, 2) held that the finely made, highly polished Achilleion greenstone axe miniatures, comparable to the Sitagroi finds, played a symbolic role and served in a ritual context, rather than being employed in a specific task.

Shaft-Hole or Hammer-Axes

This form is differentiated from the axes and defined by the hole drilled back from the bit, providing an opening or shaft in which a handle may

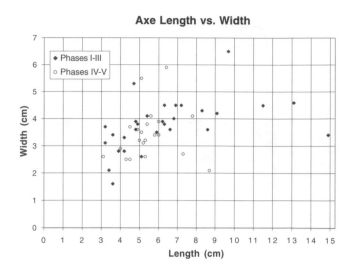

Figure 5.7. Scattergram for Middle Neolithic/Chalcolithic and Early Bronze Age axes: Length versus width.

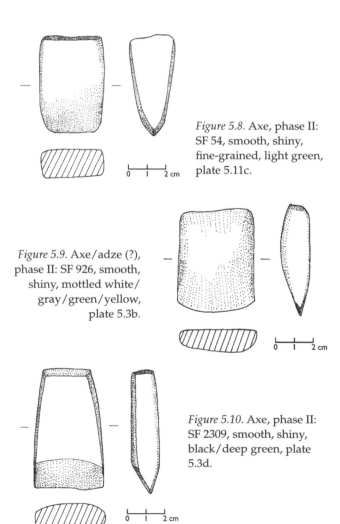

Figure 5.8. Axe, phase II: SF 54, smooth, shiny, fine-grained, light green, plate 5.11c.

Figure 5.9. Axe/adze (?), phase II: SF 926, smooth, shiny, mottled white/gray/green/yellow, plate 5.3b.

Figure 5.10. Axe, phase II: SF 2309, smooth, shiny, black/deep green, plate 5.3d.

180

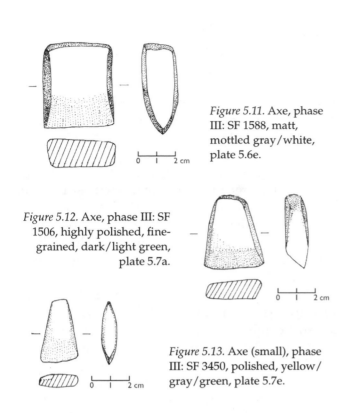

Figure 5.11. Axe, phase III: SF 1588, matt, mottled gray/white, plate 5.6e.

Figure 5.12. Axe, phase III: SF 1506, highly polished, fine-grained, dark/light green, plate 5.7a.

Figure 5.13. Axe (small), phase III: SF 3450, polished, yellow/gray/green, plate 5.7e.

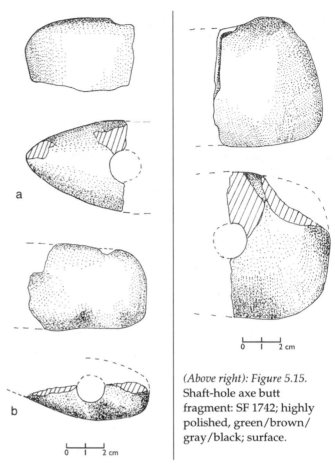

(Above right): Figure 5.15. Shaft-hole axe butt fragment: SF 1742; highly polished, green/brown/gray/black; surface.

(Above left): Figure 5.14. Shaft-hole axe: (a) Phase III, SF 410, granular green, bit fragment; (b) phase IV, SF 2739, medium grain, butt fragment.

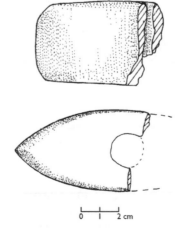

Figure 5.16. Shaft-hole axe bit fragment, phase V: SF 2851, polished, blue/green, plate 5.13b.

have been fitted. All thirteen examples in this group are fragments. At first this form seems to represent an improvement in terms of axe design, since once the handle is hafted into the hole and tied firmly, the tool should be better balanced, with less chance for the hafting to loosen. Yet all thirteen are broken at the shaft-hole, an observation Prinz made for all the Divostin hammer-axes (1988:274). Apparently, the drilling of the hole weakened the form. Balance was important if the shaft-hole axe was to be used for woodworking; it has been pointed out (Bradley and Edmonds 1993:189) that a perforation in the center of the blade will make the axe useless for woodworking.

Two of these quite sophisticated artifacts (figure 5.14a, b) of a nonlocal stone are comparable to Divostin tools (Prinz 1988:290, pl. V: b, c). Clearly, their manufacture requires considerably more skill than do the most highly polished celts (see, for example, figure 5.8; plate 5.1a). One characteristic is the squareness of the hammer end, noticeable in the surface find of gray-green, nonlocal raw material (figure 5.15) and comparable to another Divostin artifact (Prinz 1988:290, pl. V: d). Some of the hammer-axes have straight-cut or blocklike sides,

observable on two powerful-looking surface finds, one of dark brown nonlocal stone (plate 5.13a) and the other manufactured of nonlocal, blue-green serpentine (figure 5.16; plate 5.13b). These should be examined against those that are much narrower and might have been recycled celts, such as the surface finds in figures 5.17 and 5.18 [plate 5.14b, d], both of nonlocal raw material and similar again to Divostin artifacts (Prinz 1988:289, pl. IV:b; 290, pl. V:a).

A phase V unfinished hammer-axe (figure 5.19; plate 5.15) was manufactured of fine-grained quartzite partially shaped and polished. It was apparently broken during the course of manufacture; drilling for the shaft-hole had been initiated

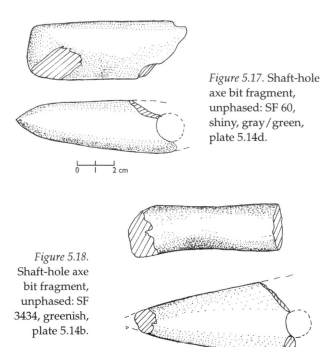

Figure 5.17. Shaft-hole axe bit fragment, unphased: SF 60, shiny, gray/green, plate 5.14d.

Figure 5.18. Shaft-hole axe bit fragment, unphased: SF 3434, greenish, plate 5.14b.

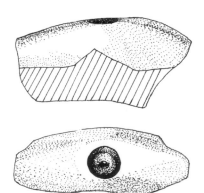

Figure 5.19. Unfinished shaft-hole axe fragment, phase V: SF 1650, dark blue with white striations, plate 5.15.

from both surfaces but was left unfinished. In the production of this hammer-axe, the hole was drilled after polishing, although I would have expected drilling to take place before polishing, as Prinz observed (1988:258) for similar axes from Divostin. Voytek, who examined a large assemblage of shaft-hole axes at Selevac (1990:451), proposed that the shaft was probably bored using a drill of bone or hardwood; Prinz (1988:258) suggested that a large bird bone, with sand as abrasive, was used. These ideas are problematic; nevertheless, the unfinished holes all seem to have been produced with a hollow drill, but no such drills of metal were recovered, nor were the presumably discarded central shafts.

The term "battle-axe" has been used, perhaps correctly, to refer to a form of shaft-hole axe from the Balkan Neolithic that widens and flares at the blade (Prinz 1988:274). None of the Sitagroi artifacts, however, have this characteristic; rather, the sides symmetrically converge at the cutting edge, which is also the case for several illustrated from Thermi (Lamb 1936:183, fig. 53). Benac refers to this form from Obre II as "ax-hammers" (1973:89, pl. XIII: 5). Moreover, as Doumas has pointed out (1998:158–162), the term "battle-axe" implies use as a weapon—an unproven inference, since axes placed as grave goods and not associated with other weapons could just as likely accompany a miner, woodman, mason, or carpenter as accompany a warrior (Doumas 1998:159). As to application, Doumas proposes that "hammer-axe" is a better term for a tool used in early metallurgy to hammer sheets and to crimp edges and joins. Their appearance in the third millennium of the EBA is thus congruent with the first hammered metal vessels in the Aegean (Doumas 1998:159). However, the evidence for metallurgy is not robust enough to support this application at Sitagroi (see chapter 8) nor, of course, is there any evidence for battles. I prefer the term hammer-axe for the Sitagroi artifacts since there were certainly many tasks for a percussive/cutting tool.

At any rate, five of the thirteen hammer-axes are from Early Bronze Age contexts, and six are from the surface and upper mixed levels. Probably the latter can be accepted as EBA, which was close to the surface (see volume 1, chapter 8 [C. Renfrew 1986b]).

Bradley and Edmonds (1993:189) viewed shaft-holes as a recycling technique undertaken to convert a woodworking tool into a mace-head. Further shaping and polishing of at least one butt fragment (figure 5.15) might have produced a roundish mace-head. In an interesting discussion, Bradley and Edmonds (1993:189, 204, 205) reported on the transformation of stone axes into mace-heads during the later Neolithic in England (3300 BC), along with a concomitant change in the status of these artifacts and the emergence of regional elites who monopolized prestige goods. The assessment of mace-heads as prestige goods during the later British Neolithic, including those mace-heads found deliberately smashed, has been supported by the contexts in which they surfaced: graves, river deposits, and ritual pits—the latter often correlated with rites of passage. None of this kind of evidence has been observed at Sitagroi. The few mace-heads found at Sitagroi are discussed with the other presenters.

Chisels

In this assemblage, chisels are narrower and sometimes smaller than axes or adzes, and asymmetrical in side view. Only a few artifacts are tabulated as chisels; these may have been recycled from a wider celt and provided with a beveled bit. An example of this tool, of nonlocal, green-gray stone from phase III (figure 5.20; plate 5.6g) is grooved along the side and comparable to a Dikili Tash piece (Treuil 1992: pl. 121d). Another is from phase IV (figure 5.21; plate 5.9e), similar to an artifact from Divostin (Prinz 1988:295, pl. X:d). Phase II yielded a small chisel (figure 5.4; plate 5.3g), comparable to a Dikili Tash piece (Treuil 1992: pl. 123f). Dierckx, writing of stone chisels from Bronze Age Crete, proposed that these were for the "dressing or beveling of planks, the shaping of pegs, and sculpture on wood" (1992:243). There are hundreds of small clay figurines from the MN/C that certainly can be viewed as sculpture (see volume 1, chapter 9 [Gimbutas 1986]), and there probably were artisans producing wood sculpture. The elaboration of bone, clay spindle whorls, and pottery in both shape and decoration may be read as further evidence of a Sitagroi aesthetic at work. No direct evidence of wood sculpture remains; nor do we find pegs which may

have been accessories to weaving (see this volume, chapter 6) and used for suspending hooks holding yarn and/or other items in a household. An inferred use of stone celts to dress wood and stone percussive tools to split logs is strongly supported by the horizontal impression of planking on the north wall of the EBA Burnt House (volume 1, chapter 7 [C. Renfrew 1986d]: 162).

Other axe bit fragments, presumably of shaft-hole tools, include examples of nonlocal stone (plates 5.14a, c; figure 5.22); comparanda include an axe from Dikili Tash (Séfériadès and Anagnosto-poulos 1992: pl. 124d).

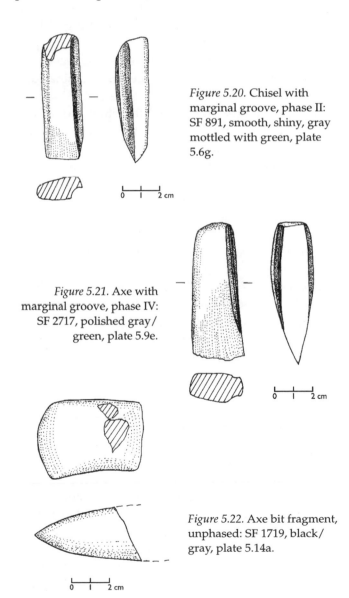

Figure 5.20. Chisel with marginal groove, phase II: SF 891, smooth, shiny, gray mottled with green, plate 5.6g.

Figure 5.21. Axe with marginal groove, phase IV: SF 2717, polished gray/green, plate 5.9e.

Figure 5.22. Axe bit fragment, unphased: SF 1719, black/gray, plate 5.14a.

Half a dozen fragments of worked stone were tabulated as "Other Polished Stone." These were modified purposely and/or through usage, but their forms are incomplete and the parent artifact ambiguous.

Manufacture

Prinz (1988:256–257) and Voytek (1990:451) concluded that in terms of Divostin and Selevac, celts were commonly made on large flakes. In Great Britain, Bradley and Edmonds (1993:88, 91–92) experimented with manufacturing axes from blocks or large flakes, and they found there was less waste when large flakes, rather than blocks, were reduced. They also observed that polishing did not require much skill but was time consuming. It appears that edge-tools took renewing easily—a pitted or dulled edge was replaced with a new edge through grinding against one of the slabby schists, using increasingly finer stones to obtain the surface polish. Voytek commented that the macrocrystalline rocks utilized at Selevac were easily reworked and recycled into a new tool; she cites worn adzes reused as pounders or reworked into a narrower form such as a chisel. There seems to be a general agreement that these tools were used over a long period, often in a recycled form, and that production techniques did not change much over time (Voytek 1990:451, 453). It has been pointed out (Prinz 1988:257) that the grinding and polishing needed to finish these tools often obliterates the evidence of manufacture; thus, production techniques can only be surmised or based on current replication experiments like the one referred to above.

Several formal characteristics of size and raw material were noted. For example, there are relatively long tools, manufactured with tapering sides and perhaps a slight widening at the contact edge (plate 5.1a [figure 5.6]; plate 5.3e; plate 5.4a [figure 5.1a]; plate 5.5b [figure 5.1b]; plate 5.5c [figure 5.5]; plate 5.9d). A few were regularly manufactured of a nonlocal, light colored stone, metagabbro (see chapter 4, this volume), with straight sides, almost squarish (perhaps broken), and occasionally with a beveled bit and edge (plate 5.2a; plate 5.3b [figure 5.9]; plates 5.4c, 5.5a; plate 5.6e [figure 5.11]; plate 5.6f; plate 5.6g [figure 5.20]; plate 5.10d, e; plate 5.11c [figure. 5.8]; plates 5.11d, e, 5.12a, b). Setting these two groupings aside, the remaining celts are similar in form, either medium or small (an exception is the tiny pointed artifact, plate 5.8f, which must have had a special use). The decision to produce one or the other general form must have been based on several criteria, such as whether or not hafting was a consideration or how the shape difference and raw material affected the ease, efficiency, and effectiveness of the tool in its application. In other words, bioenergetics played a role in making these small, medium, or large tools.

The cross-tabulation of the distribution of types (small to large) through time (table 5.3) indicates that the axe follows the pattern of almost all the other classes of artifacts at the site; it is represented at the onset of the settlement, increases in frequency during the Middle Neolithic phase II and Chalcolithic phase III; there is a drop in recovery during the onset of the EBA phase IV, and then it returns in strength in phase V.

Does this mean that the settlers of phase III were intensifying their subsistence base because of an increasing population with a need for cleared land and thus more axes? Or is the change in the distribution of these artifacts related only to the volume of earth moved for the different chronological phases?

The following is a hypothetical scenario to explain the EBA development. Phase II began the outward reach of the settlement as the population grew, its subsistence base in balance. By phase III, success could be seen in all aspects of material culture and expanding social networks. Artisan-like activity, production of prestige goods, and work of craft specialists would have been at their peak (for example, see volume 1, chapter 12 [R. Evans 1986]; also this volume, chapters 6, 8–11); clearly by phase III at Sitagroi, trading or exchange relationships had a considerable history, a history supported in this case by the use of nonlocal stone (also the case for chipped stone: see chapter 3). Nevertheless, change was inevitable, but not from invasions or from great climatic fluctuation. Rather, change was rooted in this long period of prosperity, which brought about an unchecked population growth and a depletion of soil (see this volume, chapter 1). Some of the population may have budded off (or moved to an unexplored [by the excavation team] part of the mound); evidence for this is a hiatus of radiocarbon determinations toward the end of phase III in the ZA stratigraphic sounding (see volume 1, chapter 8 [C. Renfrew 1986b]), although finds of refuse animal bone from ZA continued (sheep, goat, cattle, pig). Phase IV yielded noticeably fewer finds, which could also reflect the movement of people to the unexplored part of the Sitagroi mound. However, the alteration in material remains, especially the EBA pottery (see volume 1, chapter 7 [C. Renfrew 1986b: 158, figure 7.9]) does suggest the arrival of new settlers later in the EBA. Their arrival brought about a different subsistence pattern (see this volume and volume 1, chapter 5 [Bökönyi 1986]) and probably an alteration in social organization.

Change in the relationships among the people in the social network would inevitably have affected tool production. For example, if those involved in the raw material acquisition network had been relocated, all participants in the network would have been affected, from those who controlled the sources, to quarrymen, middlemen, craftsmen/women, and consumers. Partnerships may or may not have needed to be renegotiated, shifted, or ruptured. Others attempting to fill the vacuum would have sought a new set of linkages; one (out of many) possible changes might have been that more accessible stone would replace the nonlocal materials. and the production of stone tools would change, or new, different providers would enter the network with alternative choices for producers and consumers.

Raw Material

Various stones were selected for manufacture into axes, adzes, and other tools. One essential property of the raw material is its ability to take polish and an edge. Dixon recognized that the most popular of the "local" stones were probably from one of the three metamorphic massifs that frame the plain: Menokion, Symvolon, and Pangaion. Here might have been the sources for amphibolite, marble, mica-schist, and the specific stone that Dixon

described as coming from the veins that cut the metamorphic landscape. Amphibolite, often found as a shiny, dark-green stone, was used during all phases at Sitagroi and appears to have been the most frequently selected of the local stones for primary-use tools. Only locally available stones were used in phase I; but with phase II, stones sourced outside the Drama region are added: silicate hornfels (SF 714), serpentine (SF 2335), sandstone (SF 2661), volcanic ash (SF 294), and limestone (SF 2679). The use of these nonlocal stones continue in phase III, augmented by serpentinite (SF 1506), phyllite (SF 176), hypersthene andesite (SF 1635), calcareous siltstone (SF 393), and ash/phyllite/calc-silicate (A/P/C-S) hornfels (SF 811), all of which could have been traded in as part of some exchange. In contrast, during phase IV, the focus is almost entirely on local material; then with phase V, other new materials are introduced, which Dixon indicates could not have come from the local region because of its geological history. The most probable sources were the Xanthi Basin to the east, and around Lake Volvi to the west, both regions where rocks with many different geological histories can be found. Table 5.2 illustrates the distribution for 108 primary-use tools for which we have the identification "local" and "not local."

By the Chalcolithic period there were many settlement sites scattered across Macedonia and Thrace (Grammenos 1997:34; Andreou, Fotiadis, and Kotsakis 1996:563), and they were probably in contact with one another in some way. Trade and exchange of resources and products went along with information; and some form of ritual undoubtedly accompanied these activities, as ritual is always part of exchange (see Bradley and Edmonds 1993:92).

Many questions that are unanswered today should be resolvable with further research. For example: What are the exact sources of these raw materials? How hard are they to find, quarry, or mine? What were the route(s) for transporting the raw materials back to the site? Does acquisition involve a physical party going forth to the sources or quarries, the negotiation of a trading or exchange arrangement, or a combination of both? How was the ritual of exchange carried out?

Séfériadès and Anagnostopoulos (1992:84), reporting on the assemblage of polished stone tools recovered by the late J. Deshayes's team at Dikili Tash, also in the Drama Plain (see Preface, figure 1), write that the variety of raw material must represent a great medium of exchange. Because these two sites are no more than 20 km apart, it would be most interesting to eventually compare petrographic studies.

PROCESSORS

As defined earlier, processors (N = 307) include the many forms of grindstones used in pairs (with another material in between) for abrasive grinding (plate 5.16) and singly for percussion (plate 5.36). The stationary part of the processing pair includes querns with different forms of grinding surfaces: flat (plates 5.18–5.22), saddle shaped (plates 5.23, 5.24), hollowed (plates 5.17c, 5.25, 5.26), double-sided, both flat (plate 5.27) or both concave (plate 5.28), rimmed (plates 5.29, 5.30) and footed (plate 5.31). The variously shaped movable partner or hand mill included oval grinders (plate 5.34), flat ovals (plates 5.16a, 5.17b, 5.32) or round rubbers (plates 5.33, 5.37b), and pestles (plates 5.17a, 5.35a, b). The spherical or ball-shaped pebbles and cobbles (plates 5.38, 5.39), separated by size, were classed as pounders. Physical examination of these artifacts would have helped in deciding whether any of them were employed in "rubbing" as well.

The classification of "processor" is applied to millstones whose chief employment was either in readying foodstuffs for consumption or for processing nonedible materials. The former might have included grains, nuts, and other edibles. The nonedibles would have included minerals, dyes, salt, clay, tempering agents, and pigments such as hematite (which provided the red paint), or the mineral graphite (for the silver paint), both colors characteristic of phase III ceramic surface elaboration. A deposit of red ochre (see chapter 11) was identified inside a broken pot; it must have required some processing before use.

Querns

The flat and saddle quern forms, plus fragments thereof, are the most numerous in this grouping. Querns are modified stone slabs, set on the ground or floor and used with a hand-manipulated grinder, or rubber, for abrasive action. The grinding surface of the majority of querns is flat. Other querns were formed with an end ridge or "hill" which may have become developed by the grinding process over time; this characteristic would have prevented the grain from spilling off during grinding. However, it has been noted that greater productivity is achieved with a flat surface (see appendix 5.1 by Biskowski). The grinding surface of the saddle quern is characteristically concave, a form strongly represented in phase III; the flat form is more popular in phase V (see table 5.5). Hollowed stone slabs (mortars?) with a small round cavity were probably paired with a conical pestle which, with its rounded working end, could grind or crush whatever substance was held in the concavity of the mortar. However, the illustrated "pestles" are too large to have been used with the mortars described earlier (plates 5.17a, 5.35a, b).

Two broken slabs exhibited grinding surfaces on both sides of the stone. Biskowski noted that observable differences in the working surfaces of double or adjacent querns usually meant either that the different surfaces were used to grind different materials or that they were each used to produce different sizes of grain (personal communication, July 2000).

Some years ago Runnels examined many prehistoric querns from the Argolid, seeking evidence for manufacturing processes. He reported that the custom seemed to be to modify "a weathered boulder or slab of stone by a combination of flaking and pecking . . ." (1981:76). Although there was no organized study of manufacturing traces, we can assume that this was also the working pattern at Sitagroi. Some of the shapes of the grinders suggest the reduction process; for example, the flat slabs would have been shaped by chipping away on the perimeter, whereas the saddle querns and those with an end ridge or foot must have required more shaping, perhaps achieving their present form through use as well.

Raw Material

Dixon's study indicates that "gray slabby schist" was locally abundant; the majority of querns are manufactured of this easily available raw material.

Based on his report (chapter 4), table 5.4 summarizes the use of local and nonlocal raw materials for the different processors, by phase. Thirty-seven percent of processors from phases I through V are stationary grindstones; of these, 7% are manufactured of nonlocal raw materials (limestone, sandstone from well-lithified beds, and non-metamorphosed rock, probably from the Xanthi regions). The other 93% are manufactured of local gray slabby schist. A slightly higher percentage (10%) of movable processors, including the impactors, are manufactured of nonlocal, distinctive types (metagabbros, igneous rocks, limestones, sandstone), as is shown in table 5.4. All come from various distances afield (Dixon, personal communication, July 4, 2000). Biskowski discusses the economics inherent in acquisition of grinders manufactured of nonlocal raw material (see appendix 5.1).

Table 5.4. Distribution of Stationary/Movable Stone Processors of Local/Not Local Raw Material Over Time

Grinding tool type	Phase I	Phase II	Phase III	Phase IV	Phase V	Total
Stationary						
Local	8	17	31	0	44	100
Not local	0	0	3	0	5	8
Movable						
Local	0	21	33	22	91	167
Not local	2	0	4	1	12	19
Total						
Local	8	38	64	22	135	267
Not local	2	0	7	1	17	27

Table 5.5. Distribution of Stone Processing Types Over Time

Processor type	I	II	III	IV	V	X	Total
Ball/pounder	1	2	14	1	18	1	37
Conical pestle	1	2	0	0	5	0	8
Flat quern	2	7	10	3	37	2	61
Grooved/ whetstone	0	1	0	0	4	0	5
Hammer stone	1	1	4	1	22	0	29
Hollowed stone	0	2	1	0	1	0	4
Oval grinder/ rubber	3	12	20	14	52	5	106
Saddle quern	2	8	21	1	7	0	39
Other	0	3	1	3	6	3	16
Phase Total	10	38	71	23	152	11	305

All of the handmills, pestles, rubbers, and grinders, including oval flat and rounded/flat forms, were used stone on stone, with the materials to be processed in between. But the impactors—that is, the hammerstones (plate 5.36) and the variously sized spherical pebbles and cobbles (plates 5.38, 5.39)—could have been used directly against organic or nonorganic substances, with no need of a reciprocal slab. Microscopic study of wear traces should aid in differentiating among these various kinds of application. In any case, zones of battering on the butt ends of primary-use tools have been discussed earlier and were probably caused by percussive action.

There must have been various applications or multiple uses for any given tool; for example, the smaller end of a "pear"-shaped artifact might have functioned as a pestle, whereas the heavier, wider surface (plate 5. 37a) could have been employed to pound a wedge when splitting wood, or in butchery, or to pound one of the socketed shaft-hole antler tools (plate 2.14).

Cobbles and pebbles (plates 5.38, 5.39, all phase III) were probably collected from the nearby riverbed and perhaps used expediently in various ways. With similarly shaped artifacts from Selevac, Spears (1990:502) reported that evidence of battering can be identified in only one zone. It is also possible that some of these smaller spherical stones could have been hurled at a hunting target, rolled in gaming, or as one archaeologist suggested, served as a missile in combat (Kancev 1972:62). However, the zones of use on certain stones from Middle Neolithic and Chalcolithic levels at Dikili Tash (referred to as *molettes*) suggest impact or grinding, with the latter action altering the original spherical form of the cobble or pebble; all are described as reflecting use on one or several zones (Séfériadès and Anagnostopoulos 1992: 91, 95–97, pls. 177e, 179d, 181d, f). These have from one to four facets of use; raw materials include marble, quartz, and an unidentified hard stone. Blitzer described pebble or cobble size implements from Kommos; she inferred their use in crushing, hammering, and/or fracturing raw materials (1995:425–538). Winn and Shimabuku described "ordinary pebbles (from Achilleion) worn smooth by . . . the burnishing of ceramics . . . smoothed dorsally and ventrally . . ." (Winn and Shimabuku 1989b:272, pl. 9.4: 2–6).

Two grooved tools were earlier discussed with axes (figures 5.20, 5.21; plates 5.9e, 5.6g); these would have served in abrading, shaping, and/or polishing the edges of bone, shell, and wood artifacts, plus stone edge-tools (for example, chisels, axes, or adzes). In these cases the object being polished, shaped, or abraded is moved while the grooved stone or whetstone remains solidly in place, although with smaller tools, the abrader could have been moved during the process. Among the bone artifacts at Sitagroi is a finely polished bone rod (plate 2.7b), which could have been smoothed in such a groove. With experimentation Carol Spears (1990:502) produced grooves by grinding or abrading in the same location over time.

"Other" is the term applied to the grinding or percussive fragments employed in the various tasks proposed above and/or in various ways yet to be identified.

Presenters

Presenters (N = 27) include marble fragments (plate 5.40), mace-heads (plate 5.41), and a scepter (plate 5.42). As mentioned earlier, other tools used to cut down trees or till soil may have had an important social or symbolic role; for example, the nature of the stone and its qualities could have implied something about the status, relationships, or history of some of the owners, as Lillios (1997) found in her study of Chalcolithic tools in Portugal. Therefore, before examining this last set of artifacts, some cautionary words of introduction are in order. First, the name, "presenters," reflects a conscious decision to report these as artifacts embodying an extra dimension beyond the primary-use tools or processors. These objects either present something or are presented; as such, they allow for interpretation outside the realm of utility and the practical. They may have been expensive to make and/or represent a tradition, and thus were owned with pride, viewed with respect, or, when presented in exchange, formed and/or sealed alliances. However, social practice (Chapman 1981:71–77) can change or transform these perceptions. The prestige good of phase III was undoubtedly replaced by an entirely different set of material correlates over time.

Bowl Fragments

Although marble is not as hard as some stones, the process of shaping a block into a round form, removing the inside mass in order to produce a bowl with thin sides (less than 1.0 cm), and finishing the object by polishing, requires the investment of a significant amount of time and skill. Stocks (1993:596–603) reports on an experiment to reproduce a limestone vessel (the familiar barrel shape, 10.7 cm tall) using methods based on depictions in Egyptian tomb paintings and Mesopotamian finds of tools. Stocks used copper chisels and adzes to shape the outside, along with flint punches, chisels, scrapers, and sandstone rubbers; the core was removed with a tubular copper drill, a stone borer, and quartz sand abrasive. Stocks's work is of interest, although the Sitagroi fragments were all from open bowls (or plates), none judged deeper than 7.0 cm. Thus drilling would not have been essential, and plenty of stone tools were available to chip out the central mass.

The thirteen bowl fragments from Sitagroi allow us to make an interesting set of assumptions: first, there were reasons for artisans to make these bowls or plates and for them to be "consumed" as gifts or as special presenters; second, a specific set of tools was probably employed, and each craftsperson had his or her own set or had negotiated these from whomever controlled the Sitagroi polished and chipped stone inventory; and third, the raw material used was marble, available locally from the metamorphosed massifs probably no more than one to two hours' walk to the higher ground around the site (this volume, chapter 4; British Naval Intelligence 1945:135).The marble was not exotic, but its consistent use may have been controlled by tradition.

The bowls were open and rounded, probably with rounded bases (or perhaps the fragments represent shallow plates or even lids). Size variation (small, medium, and large), estimated from the line drawings of the rim fragments, ranges between 10.0 and 22.0 cm for the bowl opening; depth estimates range between 2.0 to 7.0 cm; and the walls are fairly thin, 0.04 to 1.0 cm. The bowl opening for the three largest, from phases II and III (figure 5.23

[plate 5.40e]; figure 5.24 [plate 5.40c]; figure 5.25 [plate 5.40b]), ranges between 18.0 and 22.0 cm, with bowl depth from 4.0 to 7.0 cm. and wall thickness between 0.06 and 0.07 cm, all with rounded rims. The middle sized examples include one from phase II with slightly more elaboration: a thick (1.0 cm) outcurving shoulder, and a rounded rim (figure 5.26, plate 5.40h); another example, with no phase attribution, has a cut rim (figure 5.27). The latter shape is comparable to a Saliagos example (Evans and Renfrew 1968:65, fig. 22:394). Similar fragments were recovered at Thermi (Lamb 1936: 178; fig. 51:30–46, 31–57). The estimated opening for both of these shallow bowls is 14.5 cm, with a depth of about 4.5 cm. The shallowest (figure 5.28; plate 5.40f), from phase II, with an estimated mouth diameter of 12.5 cm and a rounded rim, may have had a flatter base. Three others were illustrated; two of these smaller phase II artifacts had bowl openings estimated at 10.0 cm in diameter, rounded rims, wall thicknesses of 0.6 cm, and depths from 2.25 to 3.0 cm (figure 5.29 [plate 5.40g]; figure 5.30 [plate 5.40d]). The final example (figure 5.31, plate 5.40a), found close to the surface, is somewhat different because of the thickness of the wall (1.0 cm) and the sharp rim; the bowl opening is 10.5 cm and the depth is estimated at almost 5.0 cm. It could have been used with a pestle as a small mortar.

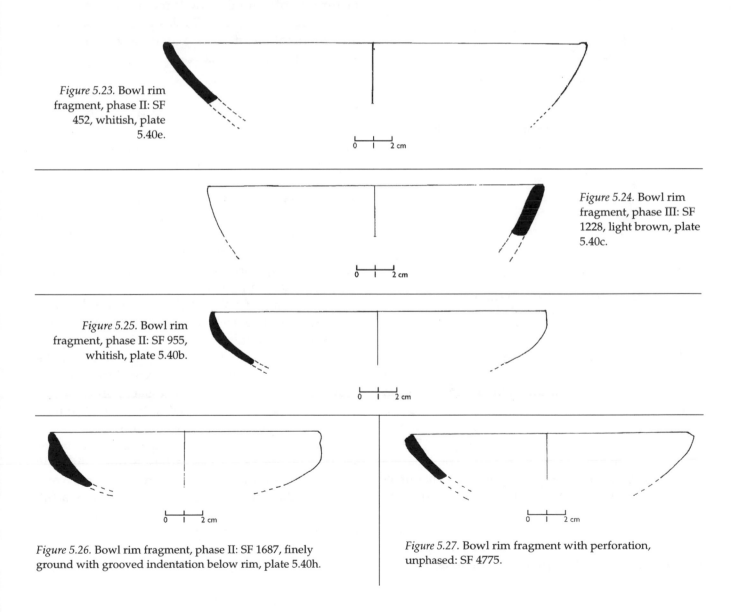

Figure 5.23. Bowl rim fragment, phase II: SF 452, whitish, plate 5.40e.

Figure 5.24. Bowl rim fragment, phase III: SF 1228, light brown, plate 5.40c.

Figure 5.25. Bowl rim fragment, phase II: SF 955, whitish, plate 5.40b.

Figure 5.26. Bowl rim fragment, phase II: SF 1687, finely ground with grooved indentation below rim, plate 5.40h.

Figure 5.27. Bowl rim fragment with perforation, unphased: SF 4775.

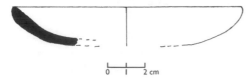

Figure 5.28. Bowl rim fragment, phase II:
SF 4254, whitish, plate 5.40f.

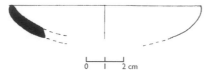

Figure 5.29. Bowl rim fragment, phase II:
SF 278, whitish, plate 5.40g.

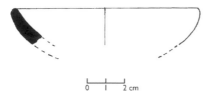

Figure 5.30. Bowl rim fragment, phase II:
SF 4266, whitish, plate 5.40d.

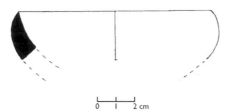

Figure 5.31. Bowl rim fragment, unphased:
SF 274, plate 5.40a.

Eight of the thirteen fragments are from phase II contexts; those from other phases may reflect curation. All are of a uniform shape: shallow, round, and of white marble—with one exception that is described as smooth, light brown stone, and is probably local marble (figure 5.24; plate 5.40c). These vessels may have been used for some particular service, as they seem purposefully manufactured in terms of form and selection of raw material.

The social significance of the eight marble fragments of phase II cannot be similarly assigned to the pieces recovered in phase V contexts. Indeed,

the marble pieces from the EBA contexts may have been curated, as we do with ancient objects such as Roman glass and coins. In other words, I do not know whether these are "presenters." In fact, the heavy querns made of sedimentary sandstone (perhaps from the Xanthi Basin) could have made a more expensive and valuable present at any point in time. Although we can propose the kinds of negotiations and activities that were needed to produce the marble bowls, the symbolic system or set of customs and beliefs that called for these artifacts remains obscure. However, the fragments of the carefully shaped and polished marble artifacts (which may include a mortar) demonstrate manufacturing skill, and the bowls themselves may have held various or combined roles in the presentation and preparation of food and treasures, as status symbols, or for exchange.

Mace-Heads

Polished spheres, with a centered shaft-hole (figures 5.32– 5.34; plate 5.41), were potentially powerful percussion tools as well as signifiers of importance. Kancev reported on all the ground and edge-tools from the EBA site of Ezero and describes the stone mace as a ". . . quite efficient aggressive weapon . . ." (1972:62), as does Benac for the Obre II examples (1973:87, pl. X:10). Probably the Sitagroi maces (N = 10) were not used literally as weapons, but perhaps symbolically, and just as effectively, to express force and power.

The drilling of a shaft-hole, such as for the hammer-axe but here in a round stone, might have given stability to the mace-head with the fitting of a handle into this shaft. But very importantly, the handle gave the artifact greater visibility. A mace-head must be visible, not necessarily in a crowd, but it must have the potential to be seen. The handle inserted in the shaft makes this possible.

Among the ten items cataloged as mace-heads, several are illustrated. The earliest is from phase III; line drawings indicate that two are between 6.5 and 7.0 cm in diameter. One phase V example is a full sphere of marble with the shaft perforation drilled from both sides (figure 5.32; plate 5.41b).

Two other half fragments show that the shaft-hole was drilled from one side only; one of these is

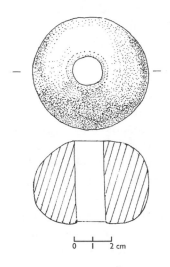

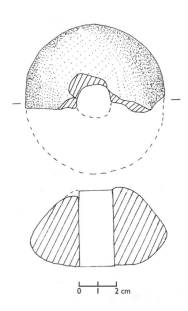

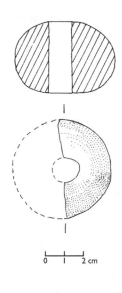

Figure 5.32. Mace, phase V: SF 1344, light gray, white blotches, plate 5.41b.

Figure 5.33. Mace fragment, phase III: SF 3670, powdery white, plate 5.41a.

Figure 5.34. Mace fragment, unphased: SF 830, matt blue/green with red patch, plate 5.41c.

from phase III, also of marble, with one flat and one domed surface (figure 5.33; plate 5.41a). The other fragment, without phase attribution, is of a blue-gray, possibly local stone, 5.25 cm in diameter, symmetrical in section, but the shaft-hole is off-center (figure 5.34; plate 5.41c). Comparanda include an unfinished mace-head from the Struma Valley site of Middle Neolithic Servia (Ridley, Wardle, and Mould 2000: 137 fig. 4.9, 138 pl. 4.6b, 139) reportedly manufactured of a "gypsum/alabaster?"; a mace-head in green stone from Poliochni, Blue Period (Brea 1964:605, Tav. C: 7, inv. no. 5009); and one from Rast (Dumitrescu 1980:23, pl. XII:15).

There are also a few fragmentary artifacts with drilled holes that were probably originally the butt section of an axe, adze, or hammer-axe. These could have been confused with a fragment of a round mace-head, but careful comparison showed clearly that these artifacts were not generated from a round stone, as were the true mace-heads. It is possible that these reflect the impulse to recycle or transform a tool into another type of artifact, as discussed earlier.

Scepter
Probably one of the most intriguing artifacts in this grouping was published earlier (volume 1 [C. Ren-

frew 1986b]:189, 264, 301, figure 8.4b, plate XXV); it is the broken, polished, zoomorphically carved shaft-hole scepter (plate 5.42) of black stone, recovered from the EBA Long House of phase Vb. The bit is fractured, but the complete butt section is a sculpture, carved into the natural likeness of a feline head with carefully incised eyes and mouth. Further incisions circle the neck, and two short lines of incised characters (proto-script or owner's mark?) are placed on the shoulder. Marija Gimbutas, writing about the "sculptural art" of Sitagroi (see volume 1 [Gimbutas 1986]:264) and the mythical imagery it represented, interpreted this as a lioness head and suggested that this animal reflected influence from the Near East. Supporting Gimbutas's animal identification are reports of lion bone remains from a northwestern Black Sea Eneolithic settlement (Bibikova 1973), also from prehistoric Bulgaria, and Neolithic Hungary, and the recovery of a lion tooth from Karanovo II (Bökönyi and Bartociewicz 1997:392–393). It seems to me that these citations negated, or at least neutralized, the need for a Near Eastern prototype. Gimbutas accepted this artifact as a scepter and identified it as a symbol for the EBA, phase Vb, "chieftain," or head of the Long House where this splendid artifact was found. Indeed, the scepter would have created a strong impression on the viewer, whether carried in a procession or kept stationary on display in the Long House, and it surely provided special status for its owner, his/her family, or clan.

John Chapman (1981:71–77) reflects on prestige and ritual in the Vinča communities, and his comments are appropriate here. He writes that the earlier Vinča sites in or around the Pannonian Basin were in an area of only fair agricultural potential,[5] and that their prestige items, including stone animal heads, mace-heads, imported *Spondylus*, and the like, provided the necessary exchange mechanism for whatever was desired. Concurrently, ritual activities were concentrated at specific sites or centers, such as at the type-site of Vinča and at Tordoš. Here excavators found hundreds of human and animal figurines, sometimes ritually broken. Chapman sees the entire social fabric as steeped in cult behavior and ritual that contributed continuously to "the perpetuation of cultural equilibrium"(1981:72). It is tempting to apply his analysis to Sitagroi, especially to the later Middle Neolithic and Chalcolithic periods, which are chronologically comparable to the Vinča sites and rich in artifacts that must have carried many and multilayered embedded messages. But if the Long House of the EBA phase V represented a chiefly structure, one would expect a social organization different from that in a small-scale egalitarian settlement. One significant difference is that in a chiefdom, exchange may be considered "redistribution" and centrally controlled (Chapman 1981:77). Applying this model to Sitagroi, the maces and presentable bowls might well have been among the prestigious items of exchange or redistribution, along with textiles, certain stones, and perhaps the knowledge and root stock for the domesticated grape. Jane Renfrew (see this volume, chapter 1) has shown that viticulture was in place by phase V, as supported by the repertoire of jugs, drinking cups, and pouring scoops that characterizes the ceramic assemblage of the EBA (see volume 1, chapter 13 [Sherratt 1986]). In any case, the scepter and the concepts that its presence suggests are congruent with the rising social stratification of the Bronze Age.

TOOLS IN CONTEXT: THE BURNT HOUSE

Uncovering a set of artifacts in situ, especially in relation to architectural and other features, offers enticing potential for "reading" the past. In this sense, exposure of levels attributed to the MN/C levels were not auspicious (see this volume, chapter 12), but those from the EBA revealed three context-rich building episodes (volume 1 [C. Renfrew 1986b]:184–203).

The processing tools recovered in contexts attributed to the phase Va Burnt House (BH) lend themselves especially to this discussion. Colin Renfrew has earlier published this exposure in detail (C. Renfrew 1970a; and volume 1 [1986b]:184–203), and I have considered craft and gender in relation to the BH construction and use (Elster 1997). The following short section specifically reviews the situation of the tools, equating the complex of tools, their implied use, and their context within a social group (the householders) in terms of the householders' actions and face-to-face interactions.

The plan of the house is reproduced (figure 5.35). It provided about 55 m^2 of space for its household of men, women, and children, with three distinct living and working spaces: the entry porch/courtyard in the south (5.3 x 3.7 m), a 5.3 m^2 all-purpose room (APR) separated from the entry porch by a presumed doorway; and an apsidal kitchen (AK) (5.3 x 2.8 m), entered from a door in the APR's north wall. I estimated that the BH could accommodate a family of six to eight (Elster 1997: 23; compare Naroll 1962:587–589).

Many processing tools were broken, either during or subsequent to usage, but even so, many of these heavy artifacts are not easily moved around or transportable. Nevertheless, site-formation processes probably did affect the condition, if not the find spots, of these tools. There seems to be logic to their placement in relation to the space and the associated artifacts in the two rooms, with the exception of two cases in the kitchen. Twenty-five grinding tools (many fragmentary) were reported from contexts in and around the Burnt House, but all could not be located on the plan. However, based on the field notebook and context, the following may be added to the thirteen specified on the plan and can be assumed to belong to the BH assemblage: SF 3360, 3390, 3745, 3785, 4307, 4308, 4406, 4493, 4507, 4512, 4586, 4604.

The female householder of the BH had considerable equipment in the kitchen: two clay-lined storage bins (figure 5.35: numbers 1 and 2) set in the floor, an oven platform (figure 5.35: number 3), a

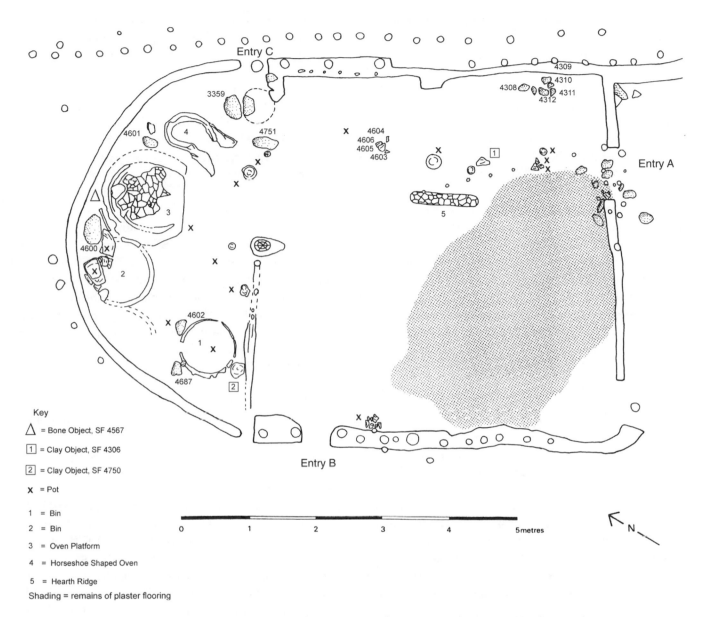

Figure 5.35. Plan of phase Va Burnt House with location of groups of grinding stones in four apsidal kitchen workstations: SF 4687 (plate 5.24), SF 4602; SF 4600 (plate 5.30); SF 4601 (plate 5.34); SF 3349, and three all-purpose room workstations: SF 4751 (plate 5.21); stone tools: SF 4603, 4606 (plate 5.26), 4604, and 4605; and SF 4308 (plate 5.32a), 4309 (plate 5.19), 4310 (plate 5.20), 431 1, and 4312.

small horseshoe-shaped oven structure (figure 5.35: number 4), many whole pots and fragments of pots in AK and APR (see volume 1, chapter 11 [Keighley 1986; Elster 1997) in various shapes, finishes, and sizes ("x" on figure 5.35). Scattered about were three bone tools (see this volume, chapter 2), seven clay spindle whorls and worked pottery sherds (see this

volume, chapter 6), other baked clay objects (see chapter 11), bone kitchen refuse (forty-three elements as reported in volume 1 [Bökönyi 1986:97–132]: cattle [6], sheep [10], goat [1], dog/wolf [3], red deer [4], roe deer [1], fallow deer [17], hare [1]), and the processing tools located on the plan (see figure 5.35) by individual small find (SF) numbers.

The first of the kitchen (AK) workstations is around storage bin number 1 and consists of a small saddle quern, SF 4687 (plate 5.24), and an irregular grinder, SF 4602. There is strong ethnographic evidence that women used these tools for grinding grains (Elster 1997; Murdock and Provost 1973). Jane Renfrew's study of the paleobotanical remains (see chapter 1) provides an inventory of harvested grains, thereby upholding my "reading" of a female working with these tools at this and other locations in the kitchen. The harvest would have been brought in by the action of men, women, and older children, but after this face-to-face interaction, it was the women who would have processed the grain into usable cereal (Murdock and Provost 1973: 207).

The second AK locale is occupied by a large flat quern, SF 4600 (plate 5.30), in a likely activity spot, near storage bin number 2 and the oven platform, and adjacent to a partially worked deer metapodial (SF 4567; plate 2.4). However, the working space is questionable, as it is here delimited by the projected apsidal "fence." Unless the fence was movable, this space was too cramped for a grinding station. Was this where unused equipment was stored? Either way, one can imagine two householders, together moving the fence or storing the quern for later use.

A third station is between the oven platform and oven structure number 4 and consists of a rubbing stone or grinder, SF 4601 (plate 5.34). Since the space is not generous, it may have been a place where children worked on polishing and shaping bone splinters, but close enough to communicate with other persons in the vicinity.

Following the curve of the apse brings us to the fourth kitchen station, consisting of a large quern, SF 3359, in association with what may have been the remains of a circular bin and near the fifth station. The latter is represented by a flat quern in three pieces, SF 4751 (plate 5.21), located in the "entry" between AK and APR. These last three stations could have allowed pre-adult and adult householders to communicate with one another as they made ready various foodstuffs or tools. All of these artifacts are from the same context, PO 159; those not on the plan include a broken grinder, SF 4602, and an axe fragment, pestle, or grinder, SF 3745. The raw material of this latter artifact was identified as nonlocal by Dixon (see chapter 4). Thus it is probably an axe fragment since processing tools were seldom manufactured of nonlocal stone.

Possible doorways are indicated on the plan (figure 5.35: Entry A, B, C) and, along with the hearth (figure 5.35:5), divide the APR into east and west halves. One half of the APR must have held sleeping equipment. Two more grinding stations are in the section north and south of the hearth. One group of processors was in the line of the doorways where the householders took good advantage of airy and light space. Here were found two broken querns, SF 4603 and SF 4606 (plate 5.26) plus two rubbers or grinders, SF 4604 and SF 4605—all with the exact excavation coordinates. Another station in the south corner of the house held five processors, mostly broken, including SF 4308 (plate 5.32a), SF 4309 (plate 5.19), SF 4310 (plate 5.20), SF 4311 and SF 4312. At these stations in the APR, we can imagine the young, adult, and older males and females of the BH household grinding clay, pigment, coarse salt, shaping thick shell, or polishing, sharpening, and shaping stone celts, bone awls, points, and other tools. All members of the BH household interacted with the processing tools in one way or another, negotiating space, work time, and materials.

The grinding tools and storage containers in the kitchen indicate that the women were processing grains on a regular basis. Moore (1975) and his team (Molleson 1994) have recently shown that deformations of the female skeletons excavated from the Neolithic Near Eastern site of Abu Hureyra demonstrated that some of the women had spent so many hours on their knees, bent over in grinding, that their toe bones, knee bones, and back vertebrae all exhibited trauma. We have no Early Bronze Age skeletons from Sitagroi, and so cannot be certain whose labor was involved; the inference is that it was women's work.

I've conservatively estimated storage for 80 kilos of dry foodstuffs based on the various storage vessels from the AK (see volume 1, plates CIII:1; CIV:1, 3; CV:3, 5) and the kitchen bins. There must have been a lot of processing going on, but even so, my estimate would be inadequate for twelve months for the Burnt House family, based on published estimates of minimum number of calories required per person per day (1,500 for men, 1,000 for women and children). However, they were also husbanding and hunting animals, and collecting wild foods (Elster and Nikolaidou, in press). When Kramer (1982:32) observed household practice in an Iranian village, she noted that each person consumed on average 160 kg of dry cereal annually; there, two small bins, or one large bin (one cubic meter in size), would have provided enough storage for a family of five or six for one year.

Both Runnels (1985) and Biskowski (2000) found that the task-specific properties of certain grinding stones caused them to be traded over wide distances. However, Dixon identified the raw material of those he examined from the BH as probably local (SF 3359, 3360, 3390, 3785, 4406). There were other nonlocal raw materials—for example, a broken *Spondylus* artifact (SF 4599; see chapter 9), a flint blade (see chapter 3), and the sandstone fragment (SF 3745). Thus the householders were involved in some sort of exchange, trade, and/or curation. Also two fragments (see this volume, chapters 8, 9) of copper or bronze represent the trading in of a rare raw material whose source is as yet unknown (see chapter 8).

The house itself and all combustibles were destroyed by the fire that preserved its imprint. What we exposed during excavation was probably only a skewed representation of the household goods, but still provided us with some ideas as to what the householders were doing. In addition to the artifacts referred to above, the householders left behind or unknowingly misplaced bone tools, spindle whorls, many vessels and pots, and other objects probably too cumbersome to carry. This assemblage provides evidence of householders in action and in face-to-face interactions: of harvesters and grinders of grain; of hunters and/or scavengers; of shepherds and consumers of lamb and wool; of traders with valuable goods, exchanging perhaps for the work of skillful weavers or potters.

Our picture is incomplete; we have some actors on the stage but not all their actions, and we must be satisfied for the moment because "[i]n archaeology all interpretations are provisional" (Bradley and Edmonds 1993:206).

NOTES

[1] This study was based on the inventory cards, field notebooks, drawings, photos, and notes from the Sitagroi excavations. The catalog (appendix 5.2), organized by phase (I–IV and unphased, or X), lists each type of tool, its context, measurements, and other characteristics. A study of the evidence of use-wear on each tool is a viable and future possibility, since all the tools with their documentation are stored in the new Drama Archaeological Museum in Greece.

[2] It would have been preferable to apply a classification system generated through use-wear analysis and morphology, but that was not possible; thus I have relied on the traditional method of inferring function from form.

[3] Katina Lillios kindly read this chapter in December 2001 and offered a number of important comments, including that axes can also double as weapons in addition to being useful tree-felling tools. Although we have no evidence for battles, Lillios reminds us of Lawrence Keeley's *War Before Civilization* (1996) which strongly suggests that we should not assume that ancient peoples did not engage in war! Still, at Sitagroi there were no signs or indications of battles.

[4] It should be kept in mind that the measurements reflect the last phase in the life of the tool. Thus size is the final size, and we can't know the original size of an artifact.

[5] Sitagroi's potential for agricultural productivity has been variously evaluated: as reflecting good agricultural potential (volume 1 [Blouet 1986]:133–143) and poor agricultural potential (volume 1 [Higgs and Vita-Finzi 1986]: 144-146). But Michael Fotiades' more recent intensive analysis of the environment of Dhimitra (1996:63–79), a chronologically comparable site, situated like Sitagroi, by the side of the Angista River, supports Blouet's positive evaluation. In addition, the recovery of fish bone and mussel shell from the excavation trenches at Dhimitra reflects a similar use of fish resources as at Sitagroi (see this volume, chapter 9, appendix 9.3). Clearly the availability of nearby riverine resources, terrace lands, and free draining alluvium provided the Dhimitra and Sitagroi settlers with a highly variable environment for exploitation.

Appendix 5.1.
Supplementary Report on the Sitagroi Groundstone Tools

Martin Biskowski

This appendix addresses some issues arising from the initial studies of the Sitagroi groundstone artifacts. The following analyses are not based on any direct examination of the artifacts, but instead rely on the artifact counts, photos, notes, and reports generated by the Sitagroi research project and the petrographic investigations and interpretations by John Dixon (chapter 4). Here we explore the significance of these results from a cross-cultural perspective and in particular contrast the Sitagroi grinding tools with comparable artifacts from Mesoamerica.

CHANGES IN FUNCTION OVER TIME

Grinding is only one of a number of different processing steps by which the nutritional or economic value of grain is enhanced. "Grinding" is often a composite activity with at least two distinct goals: milling (fractionation) and particle size reduction (comminuition). Milling separates and removes undesirable fractions of the grain. Typically, milling targets the elimination of highly fibrous fractions (bran, for example). Although fiber is valued in modern nutrition, this mainly reflects the adequacy of diets in the developed world. From a less advantaged perspective, fiber reduces the digestibility of important nutrients by physically obstructing the absorption of nutrients and speeding the transit of food through the intestines. Not surprisingly, fiber can reduce the availability of a wide variety of important nutrients, including starch (Snow and O'Dea 1981), proteins (Pedersen, Knudsen, and Eggum 1989:26), and minerals, particularly zinc (Reinhold et. al 1973; Solomons and Cousins 1984) calcium, and iron (Reinhold and Garcia-Lopez 1979, Reinhold, Garcia-Lopez, and Garzon 198 1). Mod-

ern commercial milling also targets the germ, but this is less typical of traditional milling. Retention of the germ is valuable because in most grains vitamins, minerals, and quality proteins are concentrated there. However, there can be disadvantages. In maize, the fats in the germ speed rancidity (see Gupta, Prakash, and Singh 1989). Also, the phytate levels in the germ can interfere chemically with the absorption of zinc and other minerals (O'Dell, Boland, and Koityonann 1972). The latter point can become especially significant in grain-dependent diets. Germ phytate levels have been shown to suppress zinc utilization in maize, barley, and rice (Pedersen and Eggum 1983a, 1983b, 1983c).

Particle size reduction provides two advantages. Smaller food particles speed the bioabsorption of important nutrients; for example, reduced particle size increases the intestinal hydrolysis of starch in most cereal grains (Snow and O'Dea 1981). Size reduction also affects cooking time. Physical and chemical transformations that depend on heating occur more quickly with smaller particles, and fine grinding has been suggested as one way by which populations in the American Southwest have adapted to the problem of conserving fuelwood (Christenson 1987).

Cooking is another processing step—one of the most primitive—associated with grinding. The application of heat breaks down complex molecules, enhances the availability of important nutrients, and sanitizes food. As might be suggested by the use of fine-grinding to conserve fuel, there is a generally inverse relationship between cooking intensity and grinding intensity, since both can be used to improve the availability of nutrients naturally present in grains.

Grinding is also associated with what we call "additive use," that is, the grinding tool itself has been shown to be an unintended but substantial source of minerals (Krause et al. 1993; Mbofung and Ndjouenkeu 1990; Kuhnlein and Calloway 1979). Naturally, the kind of mineral additives depends on the kind of stone material used in the grinding tool. Alkali additives, most notably wood ash and lime, contribute other minerals, but their common usage throughout the Americas (see Katz, Hediger, and Valleroy 1974) probably stems from their ability to help dissolve chemical bonds and separate the fibrous portions of maize kernels. Alkali processing also increases the availability of niacin, which otherwise might be bound in the kernel.

This discussion of grain processing is relevant to patterns of change in the form of Sitagroi querns over time (see table 5.1.1). During phases I and II, saddle and flat querns have approximately even frequencies, a point which probably reflects fairly unintensive grinding and a lack of clear differentiation in tool function. By phase III, saddle querns make up the majority, although flat querns are also present. Subsequently, in phases IV–V, saddle querns become much less common, and by phase V they account for only sixteen percent of the total. This transition probably reflects changing functional requirements in grinding associated with increasing dependence on plant foods. In particular, the decreased importance of grinding surface concavity implied by the transition from saddle to flat quern forms is consistent with several kinds of more intensive processing.

Grinding surface concavity often is assumed to be a byproduct of use. In individual artifacts, concavity that results from wear may be difficult to distinguish from concavity that is an intentional element of design. With the Sitagroi querns, however, it is possible to see this trait within the contexts of the whole assemblage and of the subsets of artifacts associated with specific phases, and it seems clear that the distinction between saddle and flat querns is both real and reflective of changes in the importance of concavity over time. Previous work in Mesoamerica suggests at least two reasons for the flattening of grinding surfaces in comparable artifacts.

First, concavity is valuable as a design element as a means of controlling spillage from loose ground matter, but certain changes in processing methods reduce the danger of spillage. Alkali processing, such as the lime treatment methodology applied to maize preparation in Mesoamerica, produces a compact mass of kernels, which are easily controlled, on the grinding surface of *metates* (the passive grinding tools used with the handheld *mano*). At Teotihuacan, the introduction of lime treatment and tortilla preparation at the beginning of the Classic Period (about AD 200) was accompanied by a clear flattening of metate grinding surfaces both longitudinally (in the direction of the grinding stroke) and laterally (Biskowski 1997). Thus, one explanation for the decrease in the frequency of saddle querns and the increase in frequency of flat querns by phase V is that some chemical processing regimen was used prior to grinding to facilitate milling or to introduce nutrient additives. A trend toward finer grinding also might yield a more compact grinding mass and less need to control spillage.

Table 5.1.1. Phase by Type of Quern

| Phase | Type | | |
	Flat	Saddle	Total
I	2	2	4
	2.04	2.04	4.08
	50.00	50.00	
	3.39	5.13	
II	7	8	15
	7.14	8.16	15.31
	46.67	53.33	
	11.86	20.51	
III	10	21	31
	10.20	21.43	31.63
	32.26	67.74	
	16.95	53.85	
IV	3	1	4
	3.06	1.02	4.08
	75.00	25.00	
	5.08	2.56	
V	37	7	44
	37.76	7.14	44.90
	84.09	15.91	
	62.71	17.95	
Total	59	39	98
	60.20	39.80	100.00

Note: Data are listed in the following order: Frequency, percent, row percent, and column percent.

Second, flattening facilitates a more complete use of the grinding surface. This is an important factor in intensive processing regimens, which emphasize fine-grinding. Flattening the grinding surface increases the amount of grinding work accomplished with each grinding stroke. In cases of extreme dependence on grain foods in the diet, household grinding with hand-operated stone tools can require hours of work. Increasing the efficiency of grinding becomes especially important in such cases to relieve the burden of grinding and to free labor and energy for other activities.

RESOURCE UTILIZATION

In order to consider issues involving stone procurement and grinding tool production at Sitagroi, once again it is helpful to utilize Mesoamerican research to establish a context for understanding the production and exchange of Sitagroi grinding tools. The fundamental similarities among simple hand-operated stone grinding tools create a number of common problems, which can be usefully addressed via a comparative approach.

Production and Transportability: A Theoretical Overview

A common perception about stone grinding tools is that the tools are so heavy and bulky, and the raw materials so generally available, that these artifacts should not have been traded over any substantial distance in prehistoric times without the assistance of pack animals, boats, or some other transportation device. At minimum, researchers hefting these heavy artifacts can readily come to believe that the lack of portability severely limited the movement of stone grinding tools through ancient exchange systems. Under such circumstances, the pattern of stone utilization should be less reflective of socioeconomic organization than of the availability of adequate stone materials.

In fact, several factors can justify their movement in long-distance exchange networks. Naturally, the absence of appropriate raw stone materials compelled considerable transportation effort when and where regular grain-grinding was essential to household well being. Rathje (1972) suggested that the system of long-distance exchange developed by the lowland Maya emerged in part from the effort to obtain a supply of igneous stone grinding tools from the southern Guatemalan highlands. In an extreme case from Baja California, vesicular basalt metates traveled to consumers 250 miles (400 km) away (Aschmann 1949:685).

However, scarcity of appropriate stone was not a problem to the people of Sitagroi; as Dixon notes (this volume, chapter 4), the kinds of stone used in most of the grinding tools were available in the local mountains and their drainages. Stone materials from more distant quarries may have been preferred for texture, durability, grittiness, or other, more subtle properties such as mineral content, but analyses so far have not identified a clear basis for preferring materials from more distant locations. Thus, we return to the initial problem: if the people of Sitagroi obtained their grinding tools mainly from local sources, does this indicate anything other than that the people of Sitagroi were not forced to go farther away to obtain these bulky but necessary tools?

One way of addressing this question is by examining the energetics of grinding tool manufacture and transport. Hayden (1987) studied the traditional process of manufacturing metates using stone tools and found that almost a week of skilled effort went into shaping and finishing a well-shaped metate (including procuring the manufacturing tools). In table 5.1.2, this information is incorporated into an earlier analysis of the energetics of the Mesoamerican obsidian and ceramic craft industries conducted by Sanders and Santley (1983). The work-time for manufacturing a metate is rounded up to seven days to reflect the accidental breakage of metates and the human down-time that inevitably results from prolonged pounding with heavy stone tools. A work-year of 300 days is used to maintain comparability with Sanders and Santley's original analyses (Biskowski 1990, 1997). The values in the rightmost column of table 5.1.2 represent the relative costs of producing various common household items. Such figures should be viewed cautiously, but they provide a sense of the qualitative differences in costs per item among typical household items. In particular, a well-made grinding tool represents a much larger investment of time and labor than other common domestic items. It should be noted here that the Sitagroi querns are much less thoroughly shaped than the highly finished, rectangular, footed metates whose production Hayden studied. If other production conditions were comparable—and here there are so many factors, including the relative availability of suitably sized boulders for the grinding tool blanks, the basic workability of the stone being shaped into a quern, and the availability of denser stone for the hammers, picks, and other manufacturing tools that the process of estimation is extremely crude and homogenizes variability between querns—then based on the shape alone, the overall manufacturing effort for a Sitagroi quern was perhaps one-third or less than what was invested in Hayden's metate. Still, even accounting for this lesser effort, the Sitagroi querns were costly tools.

Large grinding tools are similar to refrigerators in modern households. Both are important to daily food preparation; furthermore, both are costly, but the cost is bearable because both items have use-lives that can be measured in decades. Metates commonly are used for thirty years, and this use-life has implications for the size of the craft industry needed to maintain the supply of tools to a population. The figures for the *metatero* industry in table 5.1.3 are generated using thirty years as an average use-life and assuming five consumers per metate (Biskowski 1990, 1997). The rightmost column of table 5.1.3 reflects the supply capabilities of full-time craftsmen working 300 days in the year (or the equivalent effort by part-time craftsmen). Taken together, tables 5.1.2 and 5.1.3 reveal that metates have a high base cost per item, roughly equivalent to the cost of a family's entire ceramic needs for a year. However, because of the durability of these tools, the base cost per family per year for a metate is much cheaper and more comparable to the cost of obsidian tools.

Although there are no clear data on the durability of the Sitagroi querns, if the querns require only one-third as much effort to produce, the number of consumers supplied by the equivalent of a full-time craftsman is three times larger than the figure for the metatero—around 19,000 people. Again, it is necessary to view these figures cautiously, but they underscore the fundamental plasticity and small scale of grinding tool craft production. Setting aside the problem of transportability for the moment, a small number of part-time craftsmen might have supplied the Drama region, either working separately from several dispersed sources of stone or working in proximity to one another from a single source. Provided that appropriate stone is available, the economics of grinding tool manufacture place no significant constraint on the spatial or social organization of production. If transport costs also can be ignored, the organization of production implied by the pattern of stone utilization is likely to reflect specific social and economic relationships among the people of the region.

Table 5.1.2. Base Costs for Craft Items, Craftsmen

Type of specialist	Production output per craftsmen per year	Craftsman's total expenses (kg of maize per year)	Base cost per item (kg of maize)
Generalized lithic worker	150 cores (18,750 blades) and 4,800 bifaces	1,650	0.07
Generalized potter	923 vessels	1,650	1.79
Metatero	43 metates	1,650	38.37

Source: After Sanders and Santley 1983: table 11.4.

Table 5.1.3. Base Costs for Craft Items, Consumers

Type of specialist	Number of items used per family per year	Base cost per family per year (kd)	Number of consumers serviced per craftsmen
Generalized lithic worker	9 blades, 12 bifaces	1.47	5,607
Generalized potter	20 vessels	35.80	231
Metatero	0.033	1.27	6,450

Source: After Sanders and Santley 1983: table 11.4.

Sanders and Santley's (1983) work also aimed at comparing the transportability of obsidian goods and utilitarian ceramic vessels, and so it provides a particularly useful context for considering the transportability of stone grinding tools. By comparing the energetic costs of production and transportation, Sanders and Santley tried to explain a qualitative difference in the roles of obsidian and utilitarian ceramics in long-distance exchange. In Mesoamerica, the transportation of goods was almost completely limited to human burden-bearers. Beginning between 1000 and 500 BC, prehispanic peoples in Mesoamerica traded obsidian goods via long-distance exchange networks over hundreds of kilometers. Although Clark (1986) pointed out that the amount of obsidian transported from major prehispanic centers to extremely distant consumers was relatively small, substantially greater amounts traveled more modest distances. More importantly, the movement of obsidian through interregional exchange networks clearly surpassed the movement of simple utilitarian ceramics goods in both volume and distance.

In brief, Sanders and Santley estimated the direct transport costs by assigning an annual cost (in maize-kilograms) to a burden-bearer and assuming the burden-bearer could travel up to 30 km per day. The resultant transport-to-production cost ratios, plus new ratios for metates based on the assumption that a burden-bearer could carry a load of two metates, are presented in table 5.1.4. Since production costs remain fixed with respect to distance, these ratios show the linear increase in transport costs standardized by the production cost for each craft product. The low ratios associated with the transportation of obsidian are noteworthy; the relatively small costs of transporting finished obsidian goods make these craft products much more suitable for long-distance exchange than utilitarian ceramic vessels.

Viewed from the perspective that the cost of delivering a metate to a consumer 90 km away is slightly more than half of its production cost, metates cannot be considered particularly transportable. Nonetheless, well-made metates are inherently more transportable than utilitarian ceramic vessels. Depending on the availability of usable stone, various aspects of regional socioeconomic organization, and other factors, a reasonable distance limit on the human-borne transport of metates and comparable grinding tools should be 60 to 90 km. This matches ethnographic observations. For example, in highland Guatemala, at a time when human transport was still prevalent, McBryde (1947:72) observed that the supply zone around one metate production center was about 60 km; Horsfall (1987) lists many comparable cases.

Table 5.1.4. Ratios of Transport Costs to Production Costs as a Function of Distance

Distance (km)	Obsidian	Metates	Ceramics	Sitagroi Querns
30	0.028	0.189	0.404	0.567
60	0.056	0.378	0.808	1.134
90	0.083	0.567	1.213	1.701
120	0.111	0.756	1.617	2.268
150	0.139	0.945	2.021	2.835
180	0.167	1.134	2.425	3.402
210	0.194	1.323	2.829	3.969
300	0.278	1.890	4.042	5.670

The Source Analyses and the Sitagroi Querns

The Sitagroi querns required much less time and manufacturing effort than Hayden's metate. The absence of a standardized shape, finished borders, and supporting feet are some of the more important differences. The estimate advanced earlier—that a typical Sitagroi quern required about one-third the production effort of Hayden's metate—seems appropriate as a gross approximation based on the apparent shaping. Other factors, including the abundance of suitably sized boulders, the workability of the stone, and the availability of raw materials for tools, are less easily controlled. Furthermore, variability in materials and forms among the querns suggests that the amount of effort that went into these artifacts was not uniform. Still, for present purposes, one-third of the work that went into Hayden's metate, representing between two and three days of effort, provides a reasonable benchmark for evaluating the economic transportability of the Sitagroi querns. Reducing the contribution of production effort for metates in table 5.1.4 by one-third gives the transportation-to-production cost ratios for Sitagroi querns in the same table.

Clearly, if labor costs were a major consideration governing the production and exchange of the Sitagroi querns, these grinding tools were not likely to be carried by humans any great distance for exchange. Dixon's results bear this out: Out of fifty-seven querns analyzed, only eight (fourteen percent) could not be attributed to local sources. In addition, there is some evidence that the exchange of "exotic" querns into the Drama region was related in some way to differences in the production and use of querns. Flat querns are three times more likely to be made from nonlocal stone than saddle querns (table 5.1.5). Of course, the frequency of nonlocal querns is small, and this difference in source utilization between flat and saddle querns is not statistically significant (for a one-tailed Fisher's Exact Test, $p = 0.19$). On the other hand, the difference is improbable enough to warrant further examination.

When the flat querns are examined by themselves and considered by phase, the data in table 5.1.6 emerge. The difference in frequencies of nonlocal flat querns between the earlier and later phases is not statistically significant (for a one-tailed Fisher's Exact Test, $p = 0.18$), but again the frequencies are so small that only the most extreme differences can be expected to achieve statistical significance. Still the odd and focused nature of the use of nonlocal stone can be clarified in a couple of ways. In table 5.1.7, the flat querns from phases IV and V are combined not only with other flat querns but also with saddle querns, grinders, and grinder/pounders (rubbers are excluded for reasons which will be made clear below). Placed in this larger context, the association between phase IV–V flat querns and nonlocal materials stands out. Applying Fisher's Exact Test to the data in table 5.1.7 indicates that the probability of obtaining a configuration of table frequencies as or more extreme using the same row and column totals is $p = 0.042$ (both one-tailed and two-tailed tests).

Table 5.1.5. Contingency Table of Querns Submitted to Source Analysis

	Local	Not local	All sources
Flat querns	25	6	31
Saddle querns	24	2	26
All types	49	8	57

Table 5.1.6. Contingency Table of Flat Querns Submitted to Source Analysis

	Local	Not local	All sources
Phases I–III	12	1	13
Phases IV–V	13	5	18
All phases	25	6	31

Table 5.1.7. Frequencies and Row Percentages of Querns, Grinders, and Grinder/Pounders Submitted to Source Analysis

	Local	Not local	All sources
Flat querns, phases IV–V	13 (72.2%)	5 (27.8%)	18
All other querns, grinders, and grinder/pounders	89 (90.8%)	9 (9.2%)	98
All querns, grinders, and grinder/pounders	102 (87.9%)	14 (12.1%)	116

One point that is not clarified by this analysis is whether the increased use of nonlocal materials is a phenomenon associated with "late" flat querns or more generally inclusive of other grinding tools. Although none of the phase IV–V saddle querns were made from nonlocal materials, only four artifacts were analyzed. Correspondence analysis provides another way of examining the larger context of stone utilization over time and among different types of grinding tools (Bolviken et al. 1982; Madsen 1988). The two dimensions plotted in figure 5.1.1 provide about thirty-six percent of the total inertia in a multiple correspondence analysis of artifact types: time periods (phases I–II = Early, phase III = Middle, phases IV–V = Late), and source locality. This is not a large percentage, but for present purposes adding new dimensions is not especially helpful.

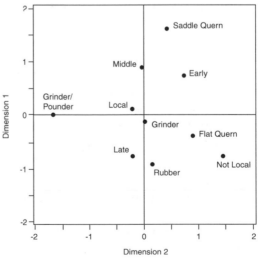

Figure 5.1.1. Multiple correspondence analysis of artifact types, time periods, and source locality.

The proximity of variable categories plotted in figure 5.1.1 indicates the degree of association. Dimension 1 is most easily interpreted; locations in the upper quadrants seem to be associated with the Early and Middle time periods (phases I–III), while the lower quadrants are associated with the Late time periods (phases IV–V). Unlike in the preceding analysis, rubbers are included in figure 5.1.1. Their close proximity to the Late time period (phases IV–V) underscores the fact that rubbers are much more abundant in later time contexts. Nonetheless, because only one in twenty-one rubbers was assigned to a nonlocal source, the Rubber category is not plotted close to the Not Local category.

DISCUSSION

Based on the data describing the Sitagroi grinding tools, two processes apparently began to influence the production, exchange, and use of querns during phases IV–V. The first process is the increased use of flat querns which probably reflects increasingly intensive processing of grains during the later time periods. This transformation matches Jane Renfrew's (chapter 1) observation of increasing dependence on grains during the same time periods. The second process is the importation of some flat querns from outside the Drama region.

Whether these processes were related is difficult to establish without direct examination of the artifacts. In a time period of increasing reliance on grains and intensification of food processing, imported flat querns might have been valued for several reasons. Although most querns continued to be made of local schists even in phases IV–V, Dixon (chapter 4) suggests that these schists were a source of contamination; imported querns may have been less gritty, and their value would have increased as people relied more on their output. Other properties—including texture, durability, and the sloughing of advantageous minerals—might have led the people of Sitagroi to prefer imported querns.

In addition, as grinding tools become an important focus of domestic activities, they become a vehicle for several kinds of symbolism. In Aztec culture, daily maize-grinding was prominently included in the invocation welcoming newborn females into life (Dibble and Anderson 1961:172–

173), and the hours spent on grinding helped the Aztecs differentiate themselves from less urbanized "barbaric" neighbors (Brumfiel 1994). Unsurprisingly, Mesoamerican metates were used to express socioeconomic status. For example, at the Mayan center of Copan the raw materials and morphology of metates were indicators of socioeconomic status (Spink 1982). Elsewhere, it was the quantity rather than the quality of grinding tools possessed by a household that conferred status and prestige (Hayden and Cannon 1984:66–82). In a different vein, Smith (1999) argues that symbolism related to ethnic origins promoted the importation of querns into a region of India.

The exact circumstances influencing the importation of querns at Sitagroi remains unclear. Still, in phases IV–V as the inhabitants depended increasingly on grains and grinding tools for their daily subsistence, it is reasonable to expect that the symbolic importance of these tools likewise expanded. As a result, the signs of increasing importation of querns are probably both valid, despite the small numbers of artifacts involved, and indicative that the Sitagroi querns played an increasingly important role communicating the status and prestige of some households.

FINAL COMMENTS

As noted earlier, these analyses examined recorded data, not the grinding tools themselves. The data are sufficient to suggest that the Sitagroi grain-grinding tools underwent substantial changes over time. Grain processing became more intensive, as might be expected with increased dependence on grain as a source of food. The incorporation of grinding tools into a system of regional exchange may further underscore their growing importance to household subsistence. Still, long-distance trade in these artifacts is not exceptional and is more indicative of general developments in the regional economy. A variety of additional analyses might be suggested for the Sitagroi grinding tools based on techniques archaeologists have developed in the past two decades: artifact attribute analyses, residue analyses, and geochemical analyses could contribute significant information not presently available.

Archaeologists studying grinding tools often must work under limitations similar to the ones encountered here. At present, these artifacts are not well understood. Usually they are infrequent in any given context, and generating a useful sample can be an unpredictable and time-consuming venture. Thus, even under the best of circumstances, analyses of grinding tools may occur very late in a research program, at a point where artifact or data collection cannot be revised. In addition, for many decades archaeologists have been inconsistent in collecting and curating these artifacts, and researchers working with such collections long afterward must be prepared to adapt their work to the materials that remain available.

More troubling, it has often been the case that archaeologists failed to collect these artifacts at all. This failure has many causes. In terms of research logistics, grinding tools are among the most problematic artifacts known to archaeology. They are heavy, bulky objects, and their value to a research project may be questioned when they must be added to bags of sherds carried on a survey or stored in a limited space. Studying them is also difficult. Even when a hundred or so are available for study, they cannot be poured out on a table like a similar number of sherds. Finally, archaeologists generally have recognized the most obvious function of grinding tools without appreciating the much wider significance of these tools in the lives of past peoples. Seeing grinding tools as an expensive source of little information, it is understandable that archaeologists sometimes avoid doing more than noting the presence of these artifacts.

In Mesoamerica, archaeologists are beginning to recognize the potential value of grinding tool research. Prior to the 1960s, manos and metates were rarely collected, and even in subsequent decades they were rarely collected and studied with consistency. This failing is particularly surprising given the long intertwined association between archaeology and anthropology in the region. Before the advent of mechanical milling, ethnographers recorded that 20th-century women still spent three to eight hours per day preparing tortillas (Isaac 1986; Lewis 1949:606-607; Foster 1967:52; Vogt 1970: 53; Chinas 1973:41). This degree of dependence has clear implications for many facets of household and community life. Nonetheless, for many years archaeologists continued to view these tools as little more than markers of household maize-processing. The recent transformation in attitudes can be linked to the conscientiousness of archaeologists collecting manos and metates on some projects (e.g., the Teotihuacan Mapping Project; Millon 1973; Millon, Drewitt, and Cowgill 1973) and the ethnographic and ethnoarchaeological work of Cook (1970, 1982), Hayden (1987); Hayden and Cannon (1984), and others highlighting the wider significance of these tools in modern households.

In many regions of the world, personal involvement in household grain-grinding is part of the distant past. In such regions, archaeologists may continue to overlook the potential value of grinding tool analyses without receiving corrective stimulus from ongoing ethnographic research. Consequently, it is hoped that this analysis of grinding tools at Sitagroi will provide a useful example of the possibilities inherent to this kind of research and promote further work.

Appendix 5.2.
Catalog of Grindstones, Polished Edge-Tools, and Other Stone Artifacts

Ernestine S. Elster

Artifacts are sorted in the following sequence: (1) by phase: I, II, III, IV, V, and unphased or mixed contexts); (2) by type, in alphabetical sequence: adze, axe, chisel, grinder, hammerstone, hollowed stone (mortar), impactor/pounder, mace, miscellaneous shape, pestle, quern, rubber, shaft-hole axe, spherical stone, vessel fragment, and whetstone; (3) by small find number in numerical sequence, followed by (if available); context; figure; plate, raw material ("JD" indicates lithology identification by John Dixon [see chapter 4]), description, and measurements (in cm). The final comment, "local" or "not local," refers to source, if noted in appendix 4.1.

PHASE I

Axes

919   ZA 67; plate 5.1b
Dolerite (?) (JD); section: shallow D-shape; cutting edge: symmetrical; sides: straight, tapering toward slightly rounded butt; butt: somewhat chipped, perhaps from accidental wear rather than deliberate striking; surface: smooth, polished, dark gray-green
L: 6.3; W: 4.5; Th: 1.6

970   ML 41; figure 5.6; plate 5.1a
Section: shallow D-shape; cutting edge: asymmetrical, no bevel; sides: slightly convex, tapering toward square-cut butt; surface: highly polished, dark green
L: 11.5; W: 4.5; Th: 2.4

984   ML 45; plate 5.1c
Quartzite (JD); fragment; section: symmetrical; cutting edge: flaked from one side, perhaps from wear; sides: straight, widening slightly from blade; surface: fine-grained, mottled, light gray; source: local
L: 3.5; W: 1.9; Th: 0.9

2512   JL 102
Amphibole (JD); surface: polished, fine- to medium-grained, black; source: local
L: 4.1; W: 2.1; Th: 1.2

2543   JL 105
Microgabbro (JD); ophitic texture
L: 8.5; W: 5.0; Th: 2.4

2544   JL 105
Amphibole (JD); fragment; sides: buff encrustation on one and two chips on the other; surface: smooth, polished, fine-grained, sea green/gray

2860   JL 104
Amphibole (JD); fragment; surface: polished, fine-grained, grayish green
L: 2.6; W: 3.1; Th: 0.5

5328   ZA 63s
Fragment; surface: polished, green/gray

Grinders

1179   ML 22
Marble (JD); rounded/flat; ovoid; source: local
L: 9.0; W: 6.7; Th: 3.9

Grinder/Pounders

4579   ZA 65
Marble (JD); spherical; one side slightly flatter than the other; surface: moderately coarse, whitish gray; source: local
L: 6.2; W: 5.5; Th: 4.4

Pestles

4118   KLb 141; plates 5.17a, 5.35a
Gneiss (JD); conical; one end battered; surface: foliated, gray with green and brown encrustation; source: not local
L: 12.0; W: 6.1; Th: 5.8

Pounders

1292 ML 22

Querns

1158 ZA 66
Saddle; schist (JD); fragment; surface: one side is smooth, light gray with green encrustation; the other has green patches and mica patches; source: local
L: 18.0; W: 13.0; Th: 5.5

2552 JL 105
Saddle; fragment; sides: both ground
L: 17.1; W: 15.6; Th: 4.4

4116 KLb 141
Schist (JD); fragment; flat; one side broken, rounded; the other smooth, flat; surface: light gray, with brown and green encrustation; source: local
L: 22.0; W: 16.7; Th: 8.7

4577 ZA 65
Limestone (JD); fragment; flat; one side smooth, flat, the other rounded; surface: pale cream with greenish tinges
L: 18.5; W: 13.3; Th: 6.5

Rubbers

1162 ZA 65
Schist (JD); fragment; flat; surface: whitish cream with slight green tinges; source: not local
L: 24.8; W: 11.0

4117 KLb 141; plate 5.17b
Oval; limestone (JD); one side broken; surface: gray with yellow/green encrustation; interior: micaceous
L: 11.5; W: 5.4; Th: 4.6

PHASE II

Axes

54 KMa 1; figure 5.8; plate 5.11c
Calc-silicate hornfels (JD petrology # 92); fragment; edges: sharp, one end broken; surface: smooth, polished, fine-grained, light green with matt, light brown patches; source: not local
L: 5.3; W: 3.5; Th: 2.9

71 LL 2
Sandstone (JD); fragment; ends broken; surface: smooth, matt, shades from pink/buff to light gray/brown; source: not local
L: 4.8; W: 4.6; Th: 1.7

73 LL 4
Sandstone (JD); fragment; ends broken; section: D-shaped; surface: coarse, light gray; interior: light brown; source: not local
L: 5.9; W: 3.3; Th: 2.4

143/ KL 2
1759 Two fragments; cutting edge: sharp; surface: smooth, polished, fine-grained, dark blue/gray; interior: matt, blue-gray
L: 4.0; W: 4.1; Th: 1.7

267 KL 2
Surface: gray-green
L: 4.8; W: 3.9; Th: 0.8

294 KL 2; plate 5.11a
Volcaniclastic ash (JD petrology # 94); fragment; edge: flaked through use; surface: polished, fine-grained, green; source: not local
L: 2.5; W: 3.7; Th: 1.1

450 KM 14
Limestone (JD); fragment; surface: dark gray; source: not local
L: 8.5; W: 4.4; Th: 1.2

478 KM 14; plate 5.3e
Section: symmetrical with straight edges; cutting edge: asymmetrical; sides: tapering toward small, rounded butt, badly worn; one side straight, the other slightly curved; surface: mottled gray, pink, and white; large flake missing from one corner
L: 8.6; W: 3.6; Th: 2.4

526 ZA 55
Fragment, blade broken; sides: one smooth, the other broken; surface: quartzite white/tan*
L: 4.8; W: 4.1; Th: 0.8

714 KM 17; plate 5.2a
Calc-silicate hornfels (JD petrology # 85); butt fragment; surface: fine-grained, greenish; source: not local
L: 3.4; W: 5.2

904 ZA 54; plate 5.3h
Amphibole (J.D); section: straight edges, slightly rounded near butt; cutting edge: asymmetrical; sides: straight with slight bevel, tapering toward square-cut butt; butt: several flakes; surface: smooth, polished, fine-grained, deep green/black; slight bevel on curved side and small bevel on the other, very close to the edge, as if sharpened on a whetstone; source: local
L: 4.2; W: 2.8; Th: 1.2

926 ZA 52s; figure 5.9; plate 5.3b
Metadolerite (J.D); section: D-shaped with well-defined edges; cutting edge: symmetrical, no bevel, evidence of wear; sides: straight; surface: smooth, polished, medium-grained, mottled in white/gray/green/yellow
L: 5.4; W: 4.1; Th: 1.5

951 KM 14; figure 5.2; plate 5.3f
Metadolerite (JD); section: straight sides, slightly
rounded edges; cutting edge: symmetrical, tiny
flakes along its length; sides: straight, parallel; butt:
flat, rough, square; surface: matt, coarse-grained,
white mottled with gray; edge and butt show signs
of wear; source: not local
L: 5.1; W: 2.6; Th: 2.0

966 KL 104
Amphibole (JD); fragment; surface: polished, fine- to
medium-grained, gray/green; source: not local
L: 6.5; W: 4.5; Th: 1.4

973 KM 20
Amphibole (JD); fragment; section: angular; edge
and butt: broken; surface: smooth, polished, dark
blue/green; source: local
L: 4.8; W: 2.6; Th: 2.0

987 KM 22; plate 5.2b
Amphibole (JD); section: D-shaped; cutting edge:
badly damaged, beveled; sides: straight; butt:
square-cut; surface: smooth, polished, fine-meshed
texture, dark gray/green; source: local (?)
L: 6.2; W: 3.9; Th: 1.3

1419 ZA 57
Amphibole (JD); fragment; section: D-shaped; cutting edge: sharp, broken; sides: rounded; surface:
smooth, fine-grained, dark gray with light gray
patches; interior: coarse, light gray
L: 3.9; W: 3.7; Th: 1.6

1755 KM 18
Serpentine (JD); fragment: butt; surface: green with
brown patches; source: not local
L: 3.6; W: 2.1; Th: 0.8

2309 KL 107; figure 5.10; plate 5.3d
Amphibole (JD); section: D-shaped; cutting edge:
fractured, symmetrical, beveled; sides: sharp,
slightly convex, tapering toward square-cut butt;
surface: smooth, polished, fine-grained, black; evidence of wear on butt; source: local
L: 6.3; W: 3.8; Th: 1.7

2335 KL 110; plate 5.3i
Serpentine (JD); section: D-shaped with rounded
sides; cutting edge: symmetrical, several tiny flakes;
sides: fairly straight, tapering markedly toward
slightly rounded butt; surface: smooth, highly polished, green-black; evidence of wear on butt and
sides; source: not local
L: 3.2; W: 3.7; Th: 1.2

2648 KL 117
Metadolerite-S (?) (JD); fragment; section: symmetrical; cutting edge: broken; sides: convex, tapering
toward broken butt; surface: volcanic, lath texture,
mottled green/white with yellow crystals
L: 6.3; W: 2.8; Th: 1.7

3936 ZJ 34
Fragment; surface: polished, gray
L: 2.1; W: 1.8; Th: 0.4

3939 ZJ 36
Fragment; butt: square-cut; surface: polished, mot-
tled white with greenish gray flecks
L: 2.8; W: 3.6; Th: 3.4

4222 ZE 97
Fragment; cutting edge: traces of bevel; surface: pol-
ished, greenish gray
L: 3.9; W: 3.4; Th: 1.4

5307 ZB 1009

5325 ZA 55s
Fragment; surface: matt, fine-grained, green/gray;
still exhibits grinding faces

5350 ZA 51s; plate 5.3a
Section: shallow D-shaped; cutting edge: asymmetrical; sides: straight, tapering toward convex butt; surface: polished, blue/gray
L: 7.2; W: 4.5; Th: 1.8

Chisels

956 KM 16; figure 5.4; plate 5.3g
Hornfels (?) (JD); section: subtrapezoidal; cutting
edge: asymmetrical, slight bevel on each side; sides:
slightly convex, tapering toward butt; butt: irregular,
square-cut, slightly flaked; surface: smooth, highly
polished, fine-grained, black
L: 3.6; W: 1.6; Th: 0.8

Grinders

283 KL 2
Rounded/flat
Diam: 6.6; Th: 3.3

515 KM 5
Grinder (?); marble (JD); narrow oval; surface:
smooth, matt, brown/light brown; edge ground into
undulations; source: local
L: 4.3; W: 1.3

1154 MM; plates 5.16a; 5.32b
Oval grinder

1160 ZA 52
Vein quartz (JD); rounded/flat; surface: cream,
orange; source: local
L: 6.1; W: 5.9; Th: 4.0

4219/ ZE 95
4220   Marble; vein quartz (JD); two fragments; rounded/ flat; surface: white with slight red veins, black at flattened end with brown encrustation; source: local
L: 6.4; W: 3.1; Th: 1.8

Grinder/Pounders

428   KL 101
Spherical; surface: smooth, light gray
L: 5.8; W: 6.1; Th: 5.9

1163   ZΛ 54
Vein quartz (JD); spherical; ends: slightly flattened; source: local
Diam: 6.7; Th: 4.5

Hammerstones

2377   KL 113
Vein quartz (JD); flattened sphere; battered; source: local
Diam: 4.6

Hollowed Stones

1156   ZA 50; plate 5.17:c
Schist (JD); fragment; indentation on top; base: flat; base surface: light pinkish gray/brown; source: local
L: 15.0; W: 14.0; Th: 6.0

1174   ML 16
Limestone (JD); rounded indentation on one side; edges straight; surface: cream; source: not local
L: 19.5; W: 16.0; Th: 6.5

Impactors

2679   KLb 119; plate 5.36
Limestone (JD); irregular square; small round ground depression in center of one side, surface: pale brick red
L: 20.5; W: 16.9; Th: 10.6

Maces

451   KL 2
Fragment; shaft hole broken; surface: grayish, polished
Th: 2.3

2390   KL 114
Fragment; circular; surface: white

Miscellaneous

249   ZA 52
Schist (JD); three steps cut into the material; one edge broken; surface: matt, gray/brown; interior: coarse, gray; source: local
L: 6.0; W: 5.4; Th: 3.4

2397   KL 114
Fragment; grooved; irregularly shaped, ground

3941   ZJ 37s
Siltstone (JD); fragment; surface: polished, fine-grained, dark gray

Pestles

5348   ZA 51s
Conical

5620   ZA 59
Conical

Querns

139   KL 2; plate 5.29
Rimmed (?) saddle; sides: one flat, the other slightly concave; edges: broken; surface: light gray/brown
L: 29.0; W: 16.5; Th: 2.0

436   KM 8; plate 5.18
Schist (JD); flat; both ends broken; sides: flat, matt, white; surface: coarse, white/gray; source: local
L: 25.0; W: 17.5; Th: 4.0

448   KM 13
Schist (JD); flat; sides: one flat, the other smooth, rounded; edges: broken; source: local
L: 21.5; W: 18.0; Th: 4.0

1157   ZA 50; plate 5.31
Footed; schist (JD); surface: matt, gray; source: local
L: 26.0; W: 16.0; Th: 5.0

1159   ZA 52; plate 5.16b
Schist (JD); flat; ends: one broken, the other rounded; one side is roughly concave; surface: light orange to pink; source: local
L: 18.0; W: 7.0; Th: 1.8

1164   ZA 54
Saddle; schist (JD); fragment; sides: flat; edges: one rounded, three broken; surface: light gray; interior: slightly micaceous; source: local
L: 5.6; W: 5.7; Th: 2.8

1169   ZA 51
Saddle; schist (JD); sides: one rounded, the other slightly concave with red marking; surface: light gray; source: local
L: 23.5; W: 11.0; Th: 4.0

1170   ZA 51
Schist (JD); flat; source: local

1182   KM 9
Saddle; schist (JD); fragment; sides: smooth, flat; surface: gray stone; interior: micaceous; source: local
L: 16.0; W: 11.0; Th: 4.0

3637   ZG 37
Saddle; schist (JD); sides: smooth; edges: broken;
surface: fawn/pale gray; source: local
L: 22.0; W: 15.5

4572   ZA 55
Saddle; gneiss (JD); fragment; roughly triangular;
sides: both concave; surface: gray; source: local
L: 22.0; W: 11.0; Th: 5.0

4578   ZA 59
Marble; flat; fragment; surface: pale, dusty, cream;
source: local
L: 18.5; W: 16.5; Th: 5.0

5330   ZA 55s
Flat

5332   ZA 52s
Flat

5349   ZA 51s
Saddle

Rubbers

262   KL 4
Schist (JD); oval, both ends broken; surface: gray;
shaped by grinding; source: local
L: 6.9; W: 4.9; Th: 2.5

659   KM 16
Sides: one sharp, the other smooth; surface: smooth,
polished, black
L: 3.6; W: 1.4; Th: 0.9

968   KM 19
Schist (JD); source: local

1165   ZA 54
Schist (JD); rectangular fragment; sides: smooth;
edges: coarse, light gray; surface: gray with dark
gray and green patches; source: local
L: 9.0; W: 7.0; Th: 4.0

1166   ZA 54; plate 5.32c
Oval; ends: one broken, the other rounded; sides flat;
surface: light gray/brown; interior: green encrustation
L: 16.0; W: 11.2; Th: 2.3

5331   ZA 52s
5333   ZA 58s
5347   ZA 51s

Shaft-Hole Axes

410   KM 2; figure 5.14a
Fragment; striking edge: symmetrical; sides: convex;
shaft hole: apparently drilled from one side, highly
polished; surface: dark green
L: 5.7; W: 4.6; Th: 3.7; Hole diam: 1.7

716   KL 102
Fragment; surface: matt, light gray/brown
L: 5.2; W: 2.2; Th: 1.9; Hole diam: 0.9

Vessel Fragment

278   KL 2; figure 5.29; plates 5.43a, 5.44a
Bowl rim fragment; marble; one edge curved; sur-
face: smoothly finished, opaque
W: 2.6; Th: 0.6; Diam: 10.1

452   KL 2; figure 5.23; plate 5.40e
Bowl rim fragment; marble; reground on adjacent
side and corner
L: 4.0; Th: 0.5; Diam: 22

464   ZA 51
Lid (?); carefully worked; sides flat
Diam: 15; Th: 1.6

955   KM 16; figure 5.25; plate 5.40b
Bowl rim fragment; marble; one edge: curved; three
edges: broken, rough, crystalline; surface: smooth,
shiny, white
L: 3.5; W: 2.5; Th: 0.5, Diam: 17.6

1687   KM 20; figure 5.26; plates 5.40h
Bowl rim fragment; marble; finely ground with
grooved indentation just below rim; three edges broken
L: 3.8; W: 3.7; Th: 0.4–0.8; Diam: 14.2

4254   ZJ 40; figure 5.28; plates 5.40f
Bowl rim fragment; marble; triangular; two edges
broken; surface: smooth, white
L: 4.0; W: 4.8; Th: 0.8; Diam: 12.2

4266   ZJ 44; figure 5.30; plate 5.40d
Bowl fragment; marble; three edges broken; slightly
curved; surface: smooth, white
L: 2.1; W: 2.9; Th: 0.7; Diam: 9.8

5326   ZA 58s
Bowl fragment; marble

PHASE III

Adzes

818   ML 107; figure 5.5; plate 5.5c
Metagabbro-R (?) (JD); section: D-shaped; cutting
edge: asymmetrical; sides: parallel, tapering toward
square-cut butt; surface: coarse, white flecked with
gray; source: not local
L: 14.9; W: 3.4; Th: 2.9

842   MM 36; figure 5.3; plate 5.7d
Serpentinite (JD); section: shallow; cutting edge:
signs of beveling, one or two flakes missing; sides:
straight, tapering toward butt; butt: sloped edge on
the same plane as cutting edge; surface: matt, fine-

grained, light to medium blue/green; source: not local
L: 3.6; W: 3.4; Th: 0.9

3448 MMb 61
Amphibole (JD); section: symmetrical, convex faces and rounded sides; cutting edge: asymmetrical, one face beveled; sides: convex, tapering toward rounded butt; surface: moderately polished, dark greenish brown/gray; flaked all over
L: 9.1; W: 4.2

3450 MM 61; figure 5.13; plate 5.17e
Serpentinite (JD); surface: polished, yellowish green, encrustation on one side; source: not local
L: 3.4; W: 2.1; Th: 0.9

3628 MMd 63s
Metagabbro-R (?) (JD); fragment: butt; surface: green/orange/white; source: not local
L: 5.6; W: 2.3; Th: 1.8

Axes

174 MM 16
Ash/phyllite/calc-silicate hornfels (JD); fragment; surface: grayish green; source: not local
L: 4.2

176 MM 16; plate 5.4d
Phyllite (JD); fragment; section: D-shaped; cutting edge: asymmetrical, well-defined bevel; sides: battered, one straight, the other convex; butt: slightly narrower than cutting edge, missing two large flakes; surface: highly polished, fine-grained, green; source: not local
L: 6.8; W: 4.0; Th: 1.8

259 ZA 38; plate 5.4b
Metadolerite (JD petrology # 90); fragment; surface: smooth, polished, fine-grained, dark gray; interior: matt; source: not local
L: 5.8; W: 2.5; Th: 2.4

393 MM 21; figure 5.1; plates 5.4a, 5.5b
Calcareous siltstone (JD petrology # 87); section: shallow D-shaped; cutting edge: symmetrical, sharp; sides: tapering toward square-cut butt, one fairly straight, the other slightly convex; surface: smooth, matt, gritty texture, mottled olive green/blue; source: not local
L: 13.1; W: 4.6; Th: 2.2

811 MM 27; plate 5.6:d
Ash/phyllite/calc-silicate hornfels (JD); section: D-shaped; cutting edge: symmetrical, sharp; sides: tapering toward slightly convex butt; one straight, the other convex; surface: smooth, matt, fine gritty texture, grayish green; source: not local
L: 6.6; W: 3.6; Th: 1.3

821 ML 107; plate 5.6f
Metagabbro-R (JD); section: symmetrical with vertical sides; cutting edge: symmetrical, flaked; sides: parallel, tapering toward square-cut butt; surface: smooth, matt, foliated, white flecked with gray; source: not local
L: 5.9; W: 3.5; Th: 2.3

828 MM no location
Amphibole/calc-silicate (?) (JD); fragment; surface: smooth, polished, fine-grained, light grayish green
L: 4.1; W: 3.9; Th: 1.5

840 MM 27
Amphibole/calc-silicate (?) (JD); fragment: blade; surface: smooth, polished, fine-grained, greenish gray; apparently flaked off during use
L: 3.3; W: 1.1; Th: 0.3

846 MM 40; plate 5.7c
Ash/phyllite/calc-silicate hornfels (JD); cutting edge: sharp; sides: rounded, smooth; surface: matt, fine-grained, pale gray to blue/green; source: not local
L: 4.2; W: 3.3; Th: 1.4

879 MM 43
Metadolerite-S (JD); section: D-shaped, squarish; cutting edge: symmetrical, beveled on one side; sides: straight, tapering toward slightly convex butt; surface: foliated, fine- to medium-grained, dark blue; source: not local
L: 4.8; W: 3.6; Th: 1.3

1191 MM 40
Metagabbro-R (JD petrology # 91); fragment; ends broken; sides: tapering; surface: foliated, coarse-grained, white mottled with gray and dark green; source: not local
L: 4.1; W: 2.8; Th: 1.6

1235 MM 49; plate 5.7b
Ash/phyllite/calc-silicate hornfels (JD); fragment; section: D-shaped, almost symmetrical; cutting edge: slightly asymmetrical, sharp, many scratches and long groove on one side from wear (?); sides: convex, tapering toward rounded butt; surface: fine-grained, gray/green; source: not local
L: 4.7; W: 5.3; Th: 1.2

1269 MM 50; plate 5.6a
Ash/phyllite/calc-silicate hornfels (JD); section: rectangular; cutting edge: asymmetrical, one edge: beveled; sides: convex, tapering toward rounded butt; surface: polished, foliated, fine-grained, dark gray to green; source: not local
L: 6.3; W: 4.5; Th: 1.3

1289   MM 52
Ash/phyllite/calc-silicate hornfels (JD); section: D-shaped; cutting edge: symmetrical, sharp, worn; sides: slightly convex, tapering toward rounded butt; surface: smooth, polished, blue-green with striations near cutting edge; source: not local
L: 4.8; W: 3.9; Th: 1.7

1405   MM 40
Feldspathic amphibolite (JD); fragment; section: symmetrical; cutting edge: symmetrical, broken, rough; surface: smooth, polished, crystalline, foliated, mottled blue/gray; source: local
L: 4.3; W: 6.2; Th: 2.8

1413   ZA 47
Ash/phyllite/calc-silicate hornfels (JD); fragment; cutting edge: sharp; one end: broken; sides: rounded; surface: smooth; fine grained, mottled dark/light gray to brown; interior: rough, light gray; source: not local
L: 3.1; W: 2.4; Th: 0.6

1421   MM 41
Double-bladed; serpentine (?) (JD); fragment; sides: one straight, the others broken; surface: smooth, polished, mottled white/yellow/green/brown; interior: crystalline; source: not local
L: 6.1; W: 3.0; Th: 1.5

1506   MM 27; figure 5.12; plate 5.7a
Serpentine (JD); section: trapezoidal; cutting edge: angled bevel; sides: straight, tapering toward rounded butt; surface: highly polished, dark/light green with light encrustation; interior: fine-grained; source: not local
L: 3.9; W: 2.8; Th: 1.1

1563   ML 118; plate 5.6b
Metagabbro-R (?) (JD); section: slightly asymmetrical, one edge straighter than the other; cutting edge: asymmetrical, sharp; sides: tapering toward square-cut butt, one convex, the other straight; small hole in one side; surface: matt, light brown with white patches; source: local
L: 8.3; W: 4.3; Th: 2.3

1588   ML 119; figure 5.11; plate 5.6e
Metagabbro-R (J.D); section: symmetrical; cutting edge: symmetrical, sharp; sides: parallel; butt: square-cut; surface: matt, mottled gray/white; source: not local
L: 4.9; W: 3.8; Th: 2.1

1635   MM 27; plate 5.4c
Hypersthene andesite (JD petrology # 88); butt fragment; section: D-shaped; sides: convex; butt: rounded; one end broken; surface: polished, blue-green; interior: crystalline with encrustation on one side; source: not local
L: 3.8; W: 4.8; Th: 2.5

2968   ZG 26; plate 5.6c
Metagabbro-R (JD); section: squarish D-shaped; cutting edge: asymmetrical, possibly from use; sides: slightly convex, tapering toward square-cut butt; surface: matt, mottled green/brown/white; source: not local
L: 6.9; W: 4.5; Th: 1.9

3348   MM 61
Section: symmetrical, convex edges and rounded sides; cutting edge: asymmetrical, one face beveled; sides: convex, one more so than the other, tapering toward rounded butt; surface: polished, dark gray/green; flaked all over
L: 9.2; W: 4.1; Th: 1.4

3529   MMd 65
Amphibole (JD); asymmetrical; surface: polished, fine-grained, dark green; source: local
L: 6.9; W: 2.6; Th: 2.1

3560   MMt 60
Amphibole/calc-silicate (?) (JD); fragment; sides: one ground, one smooth; surface: polished, light gray/green
L: 2.2; W: 1.4; Th: 0.3

3824   MMb 63; plate 5.5:a
Amphibole (JD); broken down one side; surface: greenish, glittering; ground to an edge; source: local
L: 9.7; W: 6.5; Th: 2.5

5320   ZA 44s; plate 5.6h
Fragment; section: symmetrical; cutting edge: symmetrical; sides: slightly convex; surface: gray
L: 3.5; W: 2.5; Th: 0.4

Chisels

891   MM 43; figure 5.20; plate 5.6g
Serpentinite? (JD); section: symmetrical; cutting edge: sharp; other edges: rounded; sides: parallel; surface: smooth, polished, gray mottled with green; object made by grooving and splitting a larger axe-head and polishing the break; source: not local
L: 6.6; W: 2.4; Th: 1.1

Grinders

484   ZA 42
Marble (JD); half-fragment; thick disc, rounded/flat; surface: white; source: local
L: 8.0; Th: 3.5

1757 MM 12
Marble (JD); quartzite; rounded/flat; flat side broken; small broken area near point; surface: white/light brown to dark brown, with encrustation; source: local
L: 8.9; W: 10.2; Th: 7.9

2827 MM 16
Schist (JD); fragment; rounded/flat; both sides ground; source: local
Diam: 16.2; Th: 4.0

2953 ZG 21
Schist (JD); fragment; rounded/flat; surface: gray; one side ground flat; source: local
L: 11.3; W: 11.5; Th: 4.0

2984 ZG 28
Marble (JD); fragment; surface: crystalline cream; three edges ground; source: local
L: 3.8; W: 3.0; Th: 2.5

3457 MMb 61
Metadolerite-S (JD); one side broken; surface: coarse-grained, igneous texture, black/gray with buff encrustation; source: not local
W: 5.3; Th: 4.0

4407 ZA 41; plate 5.37a
Marble (JD); oval; edges: round; surface: buff, brown; one side worked; source: local
L: 11.0; W: 7.8; Th: 5.3

4689 ZG 16
Spheroid; surface: pale yellowish gray; one side possibly ground/used
L: 5.4; W: 3.1

Hammerstones

2918 ZG 13
Quartzite (JD); one end and side battered
L: 9.2; W: 2.5; Th: 3.1

Hollowed Stones

1281 MM 57; plate 5.25
Amphibole (JD); thick block with central depression; foliated; source: local
L: 28.0; Th: 9.0

Impactor/Pounders

47 MLa 3
Iron oxide (JD); fragment; two sides broken, meeting at sharp edge; surface: smooth, polished, dark brown; interior: rough, black/dark brown
L: 7.0; W: 5.8; Th: 3.6

1177 ZA 42
Schist (JD); surface: pinkish; source: local

Maces

94 ML 2
Fragment; hole in center; surface: smooth, shiny, gray with light brown/yellow patches; shaft hole: matt, dark gray
Diam: 8.0

3670 ML 153; figure 5.33; plate 5.41a
Fragment; shaft hole; core: shell-like, very powdery white
Hole Diam: 1.9; Th: 4.2; Diam: 7.4

Miscellaneous

1248 ML 112
Ash/phyllite/calc-silicate hornfels (JD); fragment; surface: dark, waxy olive green; source: not local

5318 ZB 130r

Querns

802 MM 27
Saddle; schist (JD); fragment; edges: two flat, broken, the other curved; surface: light gray with light red patches, some small shiny flakes; interior: coarse, light gray/brown; source: local
L: 10.7; W: 10.5; Th: 3.3

1155 ZA 44; plate 5.28
Double-sided; limestone (JD); sides: both concave, with grinding hole on one; surface: smoothed, matt, light gray/brown; source: not local
L: 30.0; W: 15.0; Th: 12.0

1168 ZA 38
Schist (JD); fragment; flat; ends broken; surface: pale gray; interior: micaceous; source: local
L: 15.0; W: 13.5; Th: 3.0

1171 ZA 41
Saddle, schist (JD); surface: gray; source: local

1172 ZA 41
Saddle; schist (JD); surface: pinkish gray; source: local

1173 ZA 41
Schist (JD); flat; source: local

1175 MM 12; plate 5.20
Saddle; schist (JD); one side rounded, the other slightly concave; surface: light gray/brown with pinkish streaks; source: local
L: 31.0; W: 12.0; Th: 2.0

1176 ML 1
Saddle; fragment; edges: rough; surface: gray; interior: micaceous; both sides worked smooth
L: 24.0; Th: 3.0

1178   ZA 41
Biotite aplite (JD); fragment; flat; edges: two
rounded, two broken; flat sides; surface: reddish/
gray; source: not local
L: 10.0; W: 12.5; Th: 4.0

1183   ZA 40; plate 5.27
Double-sided; sandstone (JD); fragment; one side
flat, the other concave with three sloping edges;
surface: coarse-grained, light gray to pale buff;
source: not local
L: 20.0; W: 16.0; Th: 7.0

1211   MM 47
Saddle

1213   MM 47
Saddle; marble (JD); foliated; source: local

1294   MM 53
Saddle; schist (JD); fragment; surface: coarse, gray;
source: local
L: 23.0; W: 12.0; Th: 3.0

1901   ML 116
Saddle; schist (JD); surface: coarse, gray; one side
worked/ground; source: local
L: 18.5; Th: 4.0

2926   ZG 14
Saddle; schist (JD); fragment; surface: gray; source:
local
L: 26.5; W: 10.4; Th: 5.3

2932   ZG 15
Saddle; marble (JD); fragment; surface: gray/pale
pink; source: local
L: 8.1; W: 5.5; Th: 2.7

2941   ZG 16
Saddle; schist (JD); end fragment; surface: white;
source: local
L: 17.3; W: 9.9; Th: 4.1

2959   ZG 23
Saddle, marble (JD); surface: white; source: local

2975   ZG 27
Schist (JD); flat; broken; thickened at one end; sur-
face: off-white; both sides ground; source: local
L: 21.1; W: 11.9; Th: 3.2

3411   ML 151
Saddle; schist (JD); one side rounded; source: local
L: 21.4; W: 9.8; Th: 2.7

3423   MM 60b
Saddle; marble (JD); cobble fragment; one side
rounded; surface: white; source: local
L: 23.6; W: 11.0; Th: 4.5

3481   MMc 61
Schist (JD); fragment; flat; surface: weak foliation,
gray; both sides ground; source: local
L: 13.0; W: 12.0; Th: 4.6

3599   ZG 23
Schist (JD); fragment; flat; surface: weak foliation;
source: local
L: 15.0; W: 11.3; Th: 4.4

3830   MMc 65
Schist (JD); half-fragment; flat; surface: mottled, red-
dish; one side ground, partly broken; source: local
L: 21.5; W: 14.4; Th: 4.0

4580   MMd 66
Fragment; flat; heavy, dense; surface: black with
pink crystalline inclusions; two sides ground
L: 7.5; Th: 5.0

4769   ZA 42
Saddle; fragment; surface: pale gray; one side
ground
L: 20.0; W: 11.0; Th: 3.3

5315   ZB 123r
Saddle

5316   ZB 125r
Saddle

5317   ZB 126r
Flat

5319   ZB 117r
Flat

5329   ZA 45s
Saddle

Rubbers

741   MM 12
Surface: polished, dark brown; resembles calcified
antler
L: 8.2; W: 2.7; Th: 1.5

1161   ZA 44
Marble (JD); rectangular; edges: flat; surface:
medium-grained, grayish buff; source: local
L: 28.0; W: 16.0; Th: 7.0

1226   MM 49
Sandstone (JD); edges: sharp, squared; surface:
coarse, medium/rough-grained, light brown/
orange buff; source: not local

2928   ZG 14
Rubber (?); sandstone (JD); irregular fragment; surface: coarse-grained; one side ground smooth;
source: not local
L: 7.3; W: 6.0; Th: 5.2

3440   ZG 14
Metagabbro-R (?) (JD); fragment; one side curved;
the other side flat; surface: smooth, whitish with
green flecks; source: not local
L: 4.0; W: 1.3

3453 MMd 61
Amphibole (JD); surface: slightly polished, alternating layers of dark, coarse-grained and green fine-grained
L: 7.7; W: 4.3

4801 MM 20
One edge broken, one side curved, the other flat; surface: pale cream; both sides worked
L: 3.1; W: 3.8; Th: 2.3

5313 ZB 112r

Spherical Stones

381 MM 21; plate 5.39c
Marble (JD); surface: cream/gray; source: local
Diam: 3.0; Th: 3.1

749 MM 12; plate 5.39e
Marble (JD); surface: matt, light gray/light brown with white and yellow patches; source: local
Diam: 3.2

839 MM 36; plate 5.38k
Vein quartz (JD); asymmetrical with flattened edges; surface: white crystalline with red and pink patches; source: local
Diam: 4.9

845 MM 40; plate 5.38c
Marble (JD); spherical, flattened cobble; two edges broken; surface: matt, light gray/brown; source: local
Diam: 6.7; Th: 5.8

899 MM 44; plate 5.38e
Vein quartz (JD); cobble; spherical; slightly flattened; surface: pale cream/orange, crystalline; edges ground; source: local
Diam: 6.3; Th: 5.2

1136 ML 107; plate 5.38a
Vein quartz (JD); spherical, flattened; edges: curved; sides: smooth, flat opaque, red cortex; surface: coarse, red/gray with some crystalline inclusions; evidence of working; source: local.
Diam: 8.5; Th: 6.2

1167 ZA 34; plate 5.38f
Vein quartz (JD); spherical, flattened; surface: matt, cream/gray with red patches; source: local
Diam: 6.5; Th: 5.0

1185 ZA 41; plate 5.38d
Marble (JD); rounded/flat; surface: white; source: local
L: 8.6; W: 7.0; Th: 3.3

1212 MM 47; plate 5.38g
Marble (JD); spherical, flattened; source: local

L: 6.4; Th: 4.6

1539 MM 50; plate 5.39a
Marble (JD); spherical, flattened cobble; surface: one side cracked, smooth, dark gray/green; the other rough, light gray with light brown patches; source: local
Diam: 6.0; Th: 3.5

2943 ZG 17s; plate 5.39b
Marble (JD); spherical cobble; one side curved, the other broken; surface: coarse, gray; source: local
L: 5.4; W: 4.3; Th: 3.2

2992 ZG 30; plate 5.38j
Marble (JD); spherical; one side worn; surface: encrusted; source: local
L: 5.0; W: 5.5

3104 ML 150; plate 5.39d
Vein quartz? (JD); hard baked clay at one end; surface: cream with brown flecks; source: local
Diam: 3.3

3122 ML 151; plate 5.33a
Marble (JD); rounded/flat; both sides ground; source: local
Diam: 8.0; Th: 3.5

3129 ML 151; plate 5.38l
Marble (JD); rounded/flat cobble; surface: buff encrustation; source: local
L: 6.4; Th: 3.4

3142 ML 155; plate 5.38h
Vein quartz (JD); flattened sphere; surface: white; edges battered; source: local

3447 MMb 61; plate 5.38b
Quartzite (JD); rounded/flat cobble; flaked; one side flat, the other convex; surface: pale crystalline; source: local
Diam: 7.6

3831 MMc 65; plate 5.37b
Amphibole (JD); flattened; two pieces joined; surface: coarse, medium-grained, dark gray/green; two sides ground; source: local
L: 7.4; W: 6.5; Th: 4.6

314 ZB 112r; plate 5.38i
Spherical

Vessel Fragment

1228 MM 49; figure 5.24; plate 5.40c
Bowl rim fragment; stone; one edge curved, three edges broken, rough, light brown; surface: smooth, light brown
L: 2.9; W: 3.3; Th: 0.8; Diam: 17.5

PHASE IV

Adzes

3714 ZHt 13
Amphibole (JD); fragment; section: shallow D-shape; cutting edge: symmetrical, mostly missing; sides: parallel; butt: square-cut; surface: matt, dark gray/brown; source: local
L: 5.0; W: 3.2; Th: 1.0

Axes

129 ZA 32
Marble (JD); fragment, both ends broken; surface: gray/brown with white; pointed end has black spot; interior: crystalline; source: local
L: 13.2; W: 6.3; Th: 4.0

338 SL 11
Amphibole (JD); fragment, blade missing; section: D-shaped; sides: convex; surface: smooth, polished, coarse, foliated, dark gray; source: local
L: 6.7; W: 3.7; Th: 2.0

1277 MM 9; plate 5.7f
Section: symmetrical; cutting edge: symmetrical, slight beveling; sides: slightly convex, tapering toward square-cut butt; surface: smooth, matt, green mottled with white; interior: fine-grained
L: 3.2; W: 3.1; Th: 1.2

1746 MMb 1
Amphibole (JD); sides: one grooved; surface: polished, fine-grained, black/gray/green, with slight encrustation; source: local
L: 4.4; W: 3.3; Th: 1.2

2724 ZE 61
Amphibole (JD); fragment; surface: polished, fine-grained, deep bluish green; source: local
L: 7.2; W: 5.4

2725 ZE 61; plate 5.9a
Amphibole (JD); section: symmetrical; cutting edge: symmetrical, some flaking; sides: slightly convex, tapering toward rounded butt; surface: polished, fine- to medium-grained, with weak foliation, dark blue/gray; source: local
L: 6.0; W: 3.4; Th: 1.8

2752 ZE 67; plate 5.9c
Amphibole (?) (JD) or basalt; section: symmetrical; cutting edge: asymmetrical; sides: convex, tapering toward rounded butt, traces of two bevels on one side; butt: flaked; surface: polished, dark grayish greenish brown

L: 5.6; W: 4.1; Th: 1.5

2769 ZE 69; plate 5.9b
Amphibole (JD); section: D-shaped, vertical sides; cutting edge: asymmetrical, bevel on flat side; sides: straight, tapering toward rounded butt; surface: highly polished, fine-grained, weak foliation, dark gray/green; slightly worn; source: local
L: 4.9; W: 3.6; Th: 1.1

2789 ZE 82
Amphibole/calc-silicate (?) (JD); surface: polished, greenish gray
L: 3.8; W: 2.8; Th: 0.9

2809 ROc cleaning
Fragment; surface: black, caliche encrusted
L: 5.4; W: 4.3; Th: 2.0

2856 ZHt 4s
Marble (JD); fragment, ends and edges broken; partially drilled; surface: white; source: local

2900 ZG 3
Amphibole (JD); surface: smooth, polished, fine-grained, blue/gray/brown; source: local
L: 8.3; W: 4.0; Th: 2.9

3275 ZHt 28
Fragment; surface: black
L: 5.0; W: 5.0; Th: 2.8

3564 ZE 61
Fragment; section: D-shaped; cutting edge: asymmetrical; surface: polished, gray/blue
L: 3.9; W: 2.7; Th: 1.9

3712 ZHt 23s
Metadolerite-S (JD); fragment; surface: polished, dark/brown; source: not local

3925 ZJ 22; plate 5.9d
Metagabbro-R (JD); section: rectangular; cutting edge: slightly asymmetrical; sides: slightly convex, tapering toward rounded butt; butt: very rough, possibly from hammering; surface: polished, white/gray flecked with green; source: not local
L: 8.7; W: 2.1; Th: 1.9

Chisels

2717 ZE 58; figure 5.21; plate 5.9e
Igneous, rhyolite (?); fragment: broken and flaked; section: irregular rectangle; cutting edge: asymmetrical, irregular; sides: tapering toward slightly rounded butt; surface: coarse, moderately polished, gray/green; flakes indicate reuse of larger axe as chisel
L: 7.3; W: 2.7; Th: 1.5

Grinders

341 SL 11
Sandstone (JD); oval; surface: light gray/brown:
source: not local
L: 9.6; W: 7.2; Th: 5.6

1474 ZA 26
Vein quartz (JD); rounded/flat; sides: broken, one
rounded; ends: flat; surface: pink/cream; source:
local
L: 9.1; W: 6.4; Th: 5.7

2738 ZE 64
Vein quartz (JD); rounded/flat; sides: smooth;
source: local
L: 6.7; W: 4.3; Th: 5.1

3917 ZJ 4
Quartz; vein quartz (JD); half-fragment; oval; both
sides worked; source: local
L: 6.0; W: 3.5

4513 ZE 56
Rounded/flat; surface: smooth, buff, with slight
brown encrustation
L: 6.3; W: 4.9; Th: 3.8

5569 MM 2
Rounded/flat; D-shaped; surface: polished
L: 6.1; W: 3.7

Grinder/Pounders

2760 ZE 68
Marble (JD); spherical; slightly flattened; surface:
coarse, crystalline; source: local
L: 4.7; Th: 3.2

Hammerstones

5312 ZB 102r

Miscellaneous

895 MM 34
Metadolerite (JD); source: local

2720 ZE 61
Amphibole/calc silicate (?) (JD); D-shaped; both
sides and one end broken; surface: fine-grained,
green to light gray
Diam: 3.3; Th: 1.2

5309 ZB 58r

Querns

2905 ZG 7
Saddle; schist (JD); fragment; source: local.
L: 16.9; W: 10.5; Th: 10.9

3240 ZHt 21
Marble (JD); flat; ends broken; surface: smooth,
cream/brown; source: local
L: 15.5; W: 9.2; Th: 6.0

4752 ZA 31
Fragment; flat; surface: gray, micaceous; one side
worked
L: 13.5; W: 8.0; Th: 1.5

4761 ZA 29
Fragment; flat; surface: coarse, gray/pink, mica-
ceous
L: 9.0; Th: 4.6

Rubbers

1473 ZA 26
Amphibole (JD); triangular fragment; rounded
edges; sides: smooth, green/black; surface: matt,
medium-grained, weak foliation, gray/black;
source: local
L: 7.5; W: 6.0; Th: 4.5

3441 ZE 58
Amphibole (JD); fragment; surface: polished,
medium-grained, dark bluish green; partially
ground; source: local

4488 ZHt 24
Flat, triangular, thin; surface: light brown
L: 6.2; W: 5.2; Th: 0.6

4582 ZHt 23
Ends broken; sides flat; edges rounded; surface: dark
gray
L: 4.4; W: 2.5; Th: 0.8

4760 ZA 29
One side rounded, ground; surface: pinkish gray/
brown, with some mica inclusions
L: 6.0; Th: 3.5

4762 ZA 29
Sandstone; surface: pale honey/buff; four sides
worked
L: 8.0; Th: 4.1

5311 ZB 60r

Shaft-Hole Axes

2739 ZE 64; figure 5.14b
Amphibole (JD); fragment: butt; one end broken;
remaining edge: slightly waisted just behind shaft-
hole; butt: rounded; shaft hole: drilled from one side;
surface: polished, medium-grained, green; source:
not local
L: 6.3; W: 4.6; Th: 3.2; Hole Diam: 1.4

2754   ZE 67
Limestone (JD); fragment, part of shaft hole visible (?); surface: smooth, matt, gray
L: 5.9; W: 2.7; Th: 1.8

PHASE V

Adzes

2249   PO/PN back 180 E; plate 5.10a
Section: D-shaped; cutting edge: asymmetrical; sides: slightly convex, tapering toward square-cut butt; surface: smoothed, polished, dark gray, some encrustation
L: 7.8; W: 4.1; Th: 2.3

Axes

21   ZA 8; plate 5.8d
Section: shallow, D-shaped; cutting edge: symmetrical, sharp; sides: slightly convex, tapering toward rounded butt; surface: smooth, polished, dark blue; interior: fine-grained
L: 4.5; W: 3.7; Th: 1.3

327   SL 3
Amphibole/calc silicate (?) (JD); fragment; cutting edge: sharp; surface: smooth, matt, pale gray green; interior: fine-grained
L: 4.1; W: 2.9; Th: 1.4

328   SL 3
Marble (JD); sides: one flat, one curved with sharp edge; surface: matt, light gray/brown to dark brown; source: local
L: 10.0; W: 2.6; Th: 1.6

345   PN 19
Sandstone (JD); fragment; butt: rounded; surface: blue; source: not local

486   QO 2; plate 5.11b
Metadolerite-S (JD); fragment; surface: polished with black and pink flecks; source: not local
L: 3.6; W: 2.9; Th: 1.0

656   PO 8; plate 5.8e
Andesite (JD); section: D-shaped; cutting edge: symmetrical, sharp edges; sides: convex, tapering toward rounded butt; surface: smooth, polished, black/gray; interior: fine-grained; source: not local
L: 5.3; W: 2.6; Th: 1.8

676   PO 8
Fragment; curved side; surface: smooth, polished; black with light brown patches
L: 6.7; W: 4.8; Th: 3.3

692   QN 5; plate 5.8c
Metagabbro-R (?) (JD); section: very shallow, D-shaped; cutting edge: symmetrical, sharp; sides: straight, tapering toward slightly convex butt; surface: matt, white mottled with gray; source: not local
L: 5.1; W: 3.5; Th: 1.4

1011   QO 7; plate 5.8a
Antigorite schist (JD); section: symmetrical; cutting edge: asymmetrical, traces of wear; sides: slightly convex, tapering toward slightly convex butt, slight bevel on one face; surface: matt, blue-green; interior: fine-grained; source: not local
L: 5.4; W: 3.8; Th: 1.3

1060   QO 8s; plates 5.10e, 5.12b
Hornfels (JD); section: symmetrical; cutting edge: symmetrical; sides: tapering slightly toward square-cut butt, one straight, the other slightly convex; surface: smooth, polished, mottled, dark gray with light brown patches; source: not local
L: 6.4; W: 5.9; Th: 2.5

1071   QN 7
Limestone (JD); section: symmetrical; cutting edge: asymmetrical, sharp; sides: convex, rounded, tapering toward rounded butt; surface: matt, dark gray/blue; source: not local (local if marble)
L: 4.3; W: 2.5; Th: 1.2

1308   PN 11; plate 5.12c
Fragment; cutting edge: sharp, rough; surface: one side smooth, polished, black, the other rough
L: 4.7; W: 3.8; Th: 0.6

1311   PN 11s
Amphibole (JD); fragment; butt: rounded; surface: polished, medium- to coarse-grained, blue-gray; interior: crystalline; source: local
L: 3.6; W: 3.4; Th: 1.2

1320   PN 12
Amphibole (JD); fragment: split along axis; surface: black/green; source: local
L: 7.6; W: 3.3; Th: 1.6

1345   PN 19s
Fragment: butt; section: oval; sides: smooth, rounded; butt: rounded; surface: smooth, polished, dark blue/gray
L: 3.0; W: 2.6; Th: 2.5

1347   PN 21
Tremolite schist (JD); section: symmetrical; two cutting edges: both symmetrical; sides: parallel, rounded; surface: smooth, polished, fine- to coarse-grained, dark gray to bluish green; interior: fine-grained; source: not local
L: 3.1; W: 2.6; Th: 0.7

1551 PO 9
Amphibole (JD); fragment; section: asymmetrical, partly incomplete; cutting edge: missing; sides: one smooth, rounded; the other rough and badly flaked, but not from wear; both convex, tapering toward rounded butt; surface: polished; dark blue/gray; source: local
L: 7.0; W: 4.5; Th: 1.2

1561 PO 16; plate 5.8:b
Amphibole (JD); section: symmetrical; cutting edge: symmetrical; sides: parallel, rounded; butt: square-cut; surface: polished, very fine-grained, blue/dark gray; interior: fine-grained
L: 5.2; W: 3.1; Th: 1.6

1709 QNb 1
Triangular; section: ovoid; flaked on one side; surface: polished, dark gray/green
L: 3.6; W: 2.4; Th: 1.4

1732 PO 8
Amphibole (JD); fragment; sides: smooth, round; surface: matt, dark gray/green; interior: crystalline; source: local
L: 4.8; W: 6.9; Th: 2.3

2003 ROc 1
Fragment: one end broken; surface: black with white encrustation
L: 4.9; W: 3.5; Th: 1.8

2005 ROc 2
Amphibole (JD); cutting edge: unevenly blunted, flaked; surface: medium-grained, weak foliation, black with slight encrustation; source: local
L: 5.2; W: 4.4; Th: 1.7

2013 ROc 9; plate 5.10b
Altered volcanic (?) (JD); fragment; section: symmetrical; cutting edge: symmetrical; sides: parallel; butt: square-cut, battered, possibly from wear; surface: polished; dark gray/brown
L: 5.8; W: 3.4; Th: 1.5

2029 RO 14
Metagabbro- S (JD); fragment; section: asymmetrical; sides: convex, tapering toward rounded butt; surface: polished, fine-grained, blue/gray; source: not local
L: 6.7; W: 3.6; Th: 1.8

2034 ROc 14; plate 5.10c
Amphibole (JD); section: squarish, D-shaped; cutting edge: asymmetrical; sides: slightly convex, tapering toward square-cut butt; surface: polished, fine- to medium-grained, dark blue/gray; source: local
L: 6.0; W: 3.9; Th: 2.0

2042 ROc 24
Amphibole (JD); fragment; surface: polished, fine- to medium-grained, dark gray with light buff encrustation: source; local
L: 5.0; W: 2.5; Th: 2.9

2048 QOd 9
Metadolerite-S (JD); surface: one side smooth, the other rough, gray; source: local
L: 5.5; W: 4.5; Th: 3.1

2081 PO/D 34
Metadolerite (JD); trapezoid; section: symmetrical; cutting edge: symmetrical, beveled face; sides: slightly convex, tapering toward square butt; surface: greenish; source: not local
L: 5.3; W: 3.2; Th: 2.0

2217 RO 4; plate 5.8f
Amphibole (JD); section: symmetrical with vertical sides; cutting edge: symmetrical, blunted; sides: slightly convex, tapering to a point; surface: polished, fine-grained, dark blue/gray; source: local
L: 4.5; W: 2.5; Th: 1.0

2232 PO/B 33; plate 5.12a
Amphibole (JD); sides: both flat; surface: polished, medium-grained, green; source: local

3012 RO 34; plate 5.10d
Metagabbro-S (JD); section: symmetrical; cutting edge: asymmetrical; sides: slightly convex, tapering toward square-cut butt; surface: polished, fine-grained, igneous texture, dark blue/gray; source: not local
L: 5.1; W: 5.5; Th: 1.5

3020 ROc 51s
Amphibole (JD); fragment; one edge curved; surface: fine-grained, green/blue-black; source: local
L: 4.9; W: 3.8; Th: 1.4

3366 PNo 77
Sandstone (JD); asymmetrical; sides: inclined; butt: flat, hammered; surface: black/red; source: not local
L: 4.0; W: 2.9; Th: 1.4

3389 PO/B 102
Metadolerite (?) (JD); fragment; blade missing; section: symmetrical; cutting edge: broken; sides: convex; butt: rounded; surface: fine-grained, buff, gray mottled with brown; source: not local
L: 6.3; W: 3.8; Th: 2.3

3392 PN/L 86
Amphibole (JD); fragment; surface: polished, medium-grained, dark gray; source: local
L: 7.7; W: 4.1; Th: 2.0

3606 PO 15
Limestone (JD); fragment: butt; sides: straight; butt: square-cut; surface: blue/gray; source: not local
L: 3.9; W: 3.1; Th: 2.2

3658 PN extension
Blade fragment; biotite andesite (?) (JD); section: incomplete, probably symmetrical; cutting edge: symmetrical; surface: polished, brown; source: not local
L: 5.0; W: 4.4; Th: 1.9

3799 PN extension
Amphibole (JD); section: symmetrical; cutting edge: asymmetrical; sides: straight, tapering toward rounded butt; surface: polished, fine- to medium-grained, weak foliation, dark blue/gray, white encrustation; source: local
L: 5.2; W: 3.1; Th: 1.3

4355 PNe/f balk; sieve
Fragment; sides: two rounded to smooth curve, two broken; surface: polished, dark gray
L: 4.3; W: 4.0; Th: 3.1

4478 ROc 14
Amphibole (JD); fragment; sides: one smooth, one rough; surface: medium-grained, light gray; source: local
L: 5.2; W: 3.8; Th: 1.4

Chisels

2050 PO/C 25
Metadolerite-S (JD); surface: smooth, medium- to coarse-grained, black with light brown encrustation; source: local
L: 6.7; W: 2.4; Th: 2.0

Grinders

313 PO 5
Schist (JD); rounded/flat; edges: one rounded, two broken; sides: one flat, the other rounded; surface: slightly coarse, greenish gray; interior: micaceous; source: local
L: 20.5; W: 11.5; Th: 4.5

1039 QO 8
Biotite apetite (JD); rounded/flat; edges: rounded; surface: matt, white/gray; source: not local
Diam: 9.5; Th: 4.0

1053 QN 7
Cobble, oval; surface: smooth, with encrustation; edges ground
L: 6.9; W: 5.5

1343 PN 19
Marble (JD); rounded/flat; one side: defined, flat; surface: one side smooth; cream; source: local
L: 11.4; W: 8.3; Th: 4.7

2025 ROc 13
Vein quartz (JD); rounded/flat; evidence of probable wear/use; source: local
Diam: 5.0

2041 ROc 23
Marble (JD); rounded/flat; surface: ground smooth, white/beige; source: local
Diam: 5.1; Th: 1.6

2079 PO/D 34
Vein quartz (JD); fragment; side: one curved, ground; source: local
L: 3.5; W: 3.0; Th: 1.5

2109 ZB 19
Marble (JD); oval; sides: one smooth, flattened; surface: coarse; source: local
L: 9.0; W: 7.7

2119 ZB 19
Rounded/flat; surface: pale gray; possibly worked
Diam: 10.9; Th: 4.5

2225 PO 34
River cobble; marble (JD); oval; one side ground; surface: moderately coarse-grained, white; source: local
L: 8.9; W: 6.9; Th: 5.2

2400 PN/E 60
Marble (JD); oval; surface: white; one edge shows evidence of use; source: local
L: 4.9; Diam: 3.3

3008 ROc 34
Metagabbro-R (?) (JD); pebble; rounded/flat; sides: three sides ground flat; surface: white/gray; source: not local
L: 4.4; W: 2.7; Th: 2.0

3371 PO/E 66
Schist (JD); surface: brown/gray, micaceous with one patch of close flecks of mica; source: local
L: 5.9; W: 6.7; Th: 6.9

3390 PN/E 67
Cobble; marble (JD); rounded/flat; surface: white; source: local
L: 5.0; W: 6.2; Th: 5.3

4307 PN/D 80
Oval; surface: one side smoothed; white
L: 5.8; Th: 2.9

4406 PO/C 136
Marble (JD); ovoid; surface: smooth, brown/buff, with encrustation on one side; source: local
L: 8.3; W: 7.5; Th: 3.5

4440 PN/D 79
Sandstone (JD); edge: beveled; surface: brown/gray; source: not local
L: 5.6; W: 3.9; Th: 3.1

4462 PO/C/D balk
Rounded/flat; surface: coarse; possibly worked or used
L: 5.4; W: 6.2; Th: 4.6

4504 PN/E 261
Rounded/flat; surface: white with cream and black encrustation
L: 6.2; W: 5.6; Th: 3.8

4507 PO/A 52
Fragment; surface: coarse, pinkish gray
L: 5.4; W: 3.3

4601 PO 159; plate 5.34
Oval; surface: heavy crystalline
L: 23.0; Th: 8.7

4602 PO 159
Surface: coarse; one side ground
L: 21.0; Th: 9.9

4791 PO/A balk
Edges: beveled; one side broken; surface: light gray/green
L: 7.8; W: 5.9; Th: 1.3

Grinder/Pounders

670 PO 6
Vein quartz (JD); spherical; surface: coarse, indented, half light brown/half gray, some orange patches; source: local
Diam: 6.9

1018 QN 6
Marble (JD); spherical; flattened; one edge broken; surface: matt, white with light brown, gray patches; interior: rough, crystalline; battered; source: local
Diam: 8.0; Th: 5.3

1067 QN 7
Marble (JD); spherical; surface: smooth, light brown/gray; source: local
Diam: 5.3

1094 QO 8
Vein quartz (JD); spherical; flattened; surface: micaceous, quartz with pink patch; source: local
Diam: 7.4;Th: 5.6

1306 PN 16
Marble (JD); spherical; flattened sphere; surface: moderately coarse-grained, white; source: local
L: 11.5; W: 9.5; Th: 5.5

1309 PN 12
Vein quartz (JD); spherical; surface: foliated; source: local

1325 PN 14
Marble (JD); spherical; surface: moderately coarse, white; source: local
Diam: 6.4; Th: 4.7

1326 PN 14
Marble (JD); spherical; sides: both flattened with small indentations; surface: matt, one side white, the other light gray; source: local
Diam: 7.0; Th: 3.8

1354 PN 26
Spherical; large crack; surface: matt, cream/gray; interior: white

1589 PO 18
Vein quartz (JD); spherical; flattened; one side rounded; surface: pale gray/brown with encrustation; source: local
L: 6.8; W: 7.4; Th: 5.2

1691 PO 10
Marble (JD); spherical; surface: moderately coarse-grained, white; source: local

2045 QOd 9
River cobble; vein quartz (JD); spherical; flattened; surface: white; source: local
Diam: 6.6; Th: 5.5

2046 QOd 9
River cobble; vein quartz (JD); spherical; flattened; sides: battered with round indentation; source: local
Diam: 7.2; Th: 4.1

2252 PO/PN balk
Metadolerite-S (JD); spherical, irregular; surface: gray; wear area discernible; source: not local
Diam: 6.8

3604 PO/C 31
Vein quartz? (JD); spherical; partially broken; surface: quartz, creamy; source: local
L: 8.4; W: 6.4; Th: 2.6

4586 PN/F 264
Spherical

5308 ZB 35r
Spherical

Hammerstones

1015 QN 6
Marble (JD); ovoid; surface: pale cream, with encrustation; source: local
Diam: 5.7; Th: 7.0

1045 PO 8

2088 PO/D 34
Limestone (JD); section: roughly hemispherical; sides: both flaked and battered; one flat, the other rounded; surface: gray/red; source: not local
L: 6.5; W: 5.8; Th: 4.0

2299 PO/A no location
Cobble; vein quartz (JD); edge: battered; surface: white; source: local
Diam: 7.8; Th: 5.8

2414 PN/C 81
Vein quartz (JD); rounded; edges: battered, broken; source: local
Diam: 8.4; Th: 5.1

2424 PN/A 92
Large cobble; quartz monzodiorite (JD); ends: one broken, battered; source: not local
L: 13.5; W: 9.2; Th: 4.5

2428 PNa 92
Vein quartz (JD); flattened sphere; surface: white; evidence of battering and grinding; source: local
Diam: 6.8

2430 PN/B 100
Cobble; vein quartz (JD); half-fragment; flattened sphere; battered; source: local
L: 6.9; W: 4.0

2800 PO/B 35
Vein quartz (JD); cobble; edges: battered, broken; source: local
Diam: 7.8; Th: 3.1

3306 PN/C/E 60 balk
Vein quartz (JD); flattened sphere; edges: battered; sides: one flat, the other jagged; surface: heavy crystalline, discolored; source: local
Diam: 5.5; Th: 4.0

3311 PO/A 48
Hammerstone? (JD); sandstone; fragment; sides: two curved, ground, the others broken; surface: coarse-grained, pale gray; source: not local
L: 4.8; W: 3.6; Th: 3.6

Hollowed Stones

2434 PN/E 62B
Schist (JD); three fragments joined; surface: one side smoothed and pitted, the other irregular, gray/brown; source: local
L: 40.0; W: 18.0; Th: 7.5

Maces

1127 PN 5
Fragment; dark gray-blue stone; shaft hole: drilled from one side; large flake missing from surface, probably not from use
Th: 4.6

1344 PN 18s; figure 5.32; plate 5.41b
Two fragments joined; perforation made from both sides, but ridge not centered, as one side is worked more; surface: smooth, light gray with white blotches
Hole Diam: 1.6; H: 4.4; Diam: 6.1

1564 PO 16
Fragment; edges: broken, coarse, light gray/brown; surface: smooth, light gray; shaft hole: drilled from one side, smooth, gray
L: 4.2; W: 2.5

2409 PNc 80; plates 5.42
Fragment; shaft hole; one end broken; figure of feline animal head worked on other end; surface: polished, animal features incised; caliche encrusted
L: 8.3; W: 4.4; Th: 3.0

Miscellaneous

44 ZA 9
Fragment; edges broken; surface: smooth, dark gray/green with some crystalline areas; interior: rough, black/gray, crystalline
L: 7.3; W: 5.0; Th: 2.1

494 PO 5
Amphibole (JD); fragment; edges: one broken, sharp, pointed, the others rounded; surface: smooth, moderately coarse, dark gray/green, some encrustation; source: local
L: 4.3; W: 3.6

1046 QO 8
Serpentine (JD); surface: brownish black; source: not local

1365 PN 29s
Marble (JD); elongated, rounded edges; surface: matt, pink with red and light gray/white patches; source: local
L: 4.9; W: 3.3; Th: 3.1

1862   QO 8s
Sandstone (JD); fragment; grooved; ends: broken; one side curved with (natural?) groove; surface: coarse-grained, mottled, light gray/brown/yellow; interior: coarse, light gray/brown with red patches; source: not local
L: 5.0; W: 4.2; Th: 4.2

2232   PO/B 33; plate 5.17a
Amphibole (JD); sides: both flat; surface: polished, medium-grained, green; source: local

3205   ZHt 6
Fragment; one side with incised decoration; surface: black/brown
L: 7.7; W: 4.6; Th: 2.9

3308   PO/C 35
Calcite; surface: white with brownish stains
L: 6.7; W: 3.1; Th: 2.0

3364   PN/F 262b
Amphibole (JD); roughly triangular; surface: fine- to medium-grained, weak foliation, charcoal gray/green, white encrustation on one side; source: local
L: 5.5; W: 3.0; Th: 2.0

4310   PN/F 264
Fragment; ends: one blackened; sides: both blackened; surface: gray; possibly worked
L: 8.9; W: 6.9; Th: 3.8

Pestles

1855   QN 8
Schist(?) (JD) tremolite; conical; split along axis; edge: broken, fire-cracked; surface: smooth, unpolished, crystalline, dark veins, mottled gray, green/white
L: 5.2; W: 2.4; Th: 1.7

3002   ROc 26
Sandstone (JD); conical; edges: one convex, the other concave; surface: polished, fine-grained, red-brown; source: not local
L: 7.7; W: 3.8; Th: 2.7

3567   PN/A 20
Amphibole (JD); conical pestle; almost spindle-shaped; surface: one side ground smooth, black/cream, slight encrustation; source: local
L: 7.6; W: 2.6; Th: 2.3

3568   PN/A 20
Marble (JD); ovoid fragment; conical; broken end; sides: one worked flat, the other convex; surface: cream; source: local

4792   PN balk; plate 5.35b
Conical; ovoid; surface: smooth, very dark gray
L: 7.0; W: 2.6; Th: 4.1

Pounders

1016   QN 6
Marble (JD); river cobble; slight battering on one end; source: local
L: 8.5; W: 6.8

1017   QN 6
Marble (JD); river cobble (?); one end possibly battered; source: local
L: 8.5; W: 4.8; Th: 2.0

1079   QO 8
Marble (JD); ovoid; source: local
L: 15.0; Diam: 7.8

1355   PN 26
Vein quartz (JD); surface: smooth, black/white; source: local
L: 7.0; W: 6.0; Th: 4.5

2118   ZB 38
Quartz; surface: pale cream; one edge used for chopping

2425   PN/A 92
Quartzite; large core
Diam: 8.9; Th: 5.7

2426   PN/A 92
Amphibole (JD); cobble; broken; possibly ground; source: local
L: 7.6; W: 7.5; Th: 4.4

3745   PO 159
Sandstone (JD); surface: brownish/gray to olive green; source: not local
L: 8.5; W: 7.7; Th: 4.1

3785   PO 158
Marble (JD); surface: orange/pale brown, with gray encrustation; source: not local
L: 7.8; W: 8.1; Th: 4.0

4471   PN/A 95
Quartz; sides: one rounded, the other irregular; surface: gray, white
L: 5.9; W: 5.1; Th: 4.2

4754   PO 9
Irregular flattened sphere; surface: heavy, crystalline, white with some pinkish discoloration
L: 7.0; Th: 4.8

5310   ZB 36r

Querns

1024   PN 6
Marble (JD); fragment; flat; surface: medium- to coarse-grained, gray/white; two edges appear used; source: local
L: 11.0; W: 8.0

1180 ZA 12
Biotite granite (JD); flat; rough quadrant; straight-sided breaks; edges: rounded; surface: weak foliation; light gray; source: not local
L: 6.9;W: 5.8; Th: 6.7

1416 QN 6
Schist (JD); flat; base surface: gray, micaceous, with red patches; source: local
L: 12.5; W: 9.0; Th: 5.5

1648 PN 28
Amphibole (JD); fragment; flat; sides: two broken, one flat, one curved; surface: smooth, medium-grained, dark/brown; source: local
L: 6.7;W: 4.3

2247 PO/A 46; plate 5.22
Schist (JD); flat; two pieces joined; surface: gray; one side ground; source: local
L: 35.4; W: 24.5; Th: 5.7

2298 PO/A no location
Schist (JD); large fragment; flat; two sides possibly ground; source: local
L: 14.2; W: 8.1; Th: 8.4

2406 PN/D 74
Flat; possibly not worked
L: 15.0; W: 11.0; Th: 5.8

2411b PN/C 80
Schist (JD); fragment; flat; micaceous; source: local
L: 11.0; W: 14.5; Th: 4.9

2437 PN/E 62B
Schist (JD); fragment; flat; surface: gray; source: local
L: 20.0; W: 22.0; Th: 2.5

2801 PO/B 35
Flat; sides: one flat, the other irregular; surface: pale gray/green with mica
L: 6.5; W: 6.1; Th: 2.1

3010 ROc 34
Schist (JD); flat; sides: one ground flat, the other convex; surface: white/gray/red; source: local
L: 11.9; W: 5.5; Th: 3.2

3309 PO/A 48
Gneiss (JD); flat; almost complete; bottom rounded; surface: fine-grained; source: not local
L: 29.1; W: 19.9; Th: 6.7

3312 PO/A 48
Schist (JD); flat; cracked; surface: smooth, light brown/pink, micaceous; source: local
L: 28.0; W: 21.0; Th: 13.5

3321 PO/B 43
Limestone (JD); flat; one side flat; surface: coarse, gray; source: not local
L: 8.6; W: 8.0; Th: 4.5

3359 PO 159
Three fragments joined; flat; surface: coarse, gray, and partly discolored
L: 39.0; Th: 15.0

3360 PO 158
Saddle; schist (JD); fragment; surface: one side very smooth, the other partly coarse, buff/fawn to yellowish green; source: local
L: 34.0; W: 15.5; Th: 5.9

3570 PO/B 36
Schist (JD); fragment; flat; two edges broken; two sides ground; surface: pale; source: local
L: 7.8; W: 8.3; Th: 3.4

4271/ PO/B 49
4272 Schist (JD); two fragments; flat; one side rounded; edges: broken; surface: fairly smooth, gray/pink, with encrustation; interior: micaceous, pink striations; source: local
L: 12.5; W: 7.8; Th: 6.5

4273 PN/D 67
Saddle, schist (JD); edges: two smooth and rounded, two broken; surface: fine-grained, gray with white encrustation; interior: micaceous; source: local
L: 9.3; W: 9.2; Th: 7.8

4274 PN/D
Biotite granite (JD); flat; edges: one flat, the others rounded; surface: smooth, buff/gray, black encrustation on one edge; source: not local
L: 17.4; W: 14.6; Th: 8.2

4304 PN balk
Granite gneiss (JD); flat; roughly rectangular; sides: flat; edges: two broken straight, one curved; surface: fine-grained, light gray; source: not local
L: 24.0; W: 18.0; Th: 7.0

4309 PN/F 264; plate 5.19
Flat; both ends broken; surface: coarse, grayish

4310 PO/159; plate 5.20

Broken Quern Fragment

4311 PN/F 264
Flat; edges: broken, one rounded; surface: polished, two-tone buff and black
L: 8.9; W: 9.6; Th: 5.7

4312 PN/F 264
Flat; sides: one broken, the other rounded; edges: round; some fire blackening
L: 14.7; W: 9.7; Th: 4.4

4454 PO/B 39
Schist (JD); fragment; flat; one side split; surface: whitish cream/pink, micaceous; source: local
L: 9.4; W: 7.2; Th: 3.8

4493 PN/D 80
Flat; one side rounded; edges: broken; surface: one side smooth, light gray/orange
L: 8.9; W: 4.9; Th: 3.5

4512 PN/D 80
Fragment; flat; sides: one flat, the others broken; surface: smooth, gray/cream
L: 11.9; W: 8.3; Th: 5.1

4574 PO 17
Saddle; schist (JD); fragment; surface: gray; two sides worked; source: local
L: 23.0; W: 19.0; Th: 7.0

4600 PO 159; plate 5.30
Rimmed; source: local

4603 PO 159
Saddle; surface: crystalline, dark; one side curved, ground

4604 PO 159
Saddle; surface: one side ground smooth, coarse, pale gray
L: 13.7; Th: 7.7

4605 PO 159
Flat; surface: coarse, yellowish gray, one side smooth and blackened
L: 15.0; Th: 11.4

4606 PO 159; plate 5.26
Mortar; one edge broken; surface: coarse, pinkish gray
L: 29.0; Th: 12.2

4687 PO 159; plate 5.34
Saddle; heavy; crystalline
L: 31.0; W: 17.0; Th: 6.2

4688 PO 23
Fragment; flat; surface: micaceous
L: 25.0; W: 19.0

4751 PO 159; plate 5.21
Three fragments joined; flat; surface: coarse, gray
L: 27.0; Th: 5.0

4753 PO 9
Fragment; flat; surface: micaceous; both sides ground
L: 18.0; Th: 3.0

4755 PO 9
Fragment; flat; surface: fine-grained, pale cream; one side ground flatter than the other
L: 10.0; W: 10.0; Th: 2.2

4756 PO 9
Marble; fragment; flat; surface: pale cream/off-white
L: 10.0; Th: 3.3

4758 PO 9
Flat; one side broken; surface: dark, micaceous; one side ground
L: 14.0; W: 5.5

4759 PO 9
Fragment; flat; surface: coarse, gray, micaceous; one side ground
L: 11.0; W: 10.0; Th: 4.0

4789 PO/A balk
Fragment; flat; sides: one broken, the other flat; edges: beveled; surface: light gray/green
L: 9.6; W: 8.2; Th: 1.7

4790 PO/A 139 balk
Fragment; flat; sides: one broken, the other flat; edges: beveled; surface: light gray/green
L: 9.0; W: 6.6; Th: 1.5

4794 PO 23
Two fragments joined; flat; one side broken; surface: one side smoothed, buff, dark gray
L: 16.5; W: 11.0; Th: 3.0

Rubbers

1069 QO 8
Marble (JD); surface: moderately coarse, white; surface: local

1316 PN 12
Marble (JD); surface: mottled gray/white, encrustation on worked side; source: local
L: 7.2; W: 2.5; Th: 2.8

1318 PN 12
Amphibole (JD); edges: polished, black with light brown patches; surface: one side sloping, polished, black; the other flat, matt, fine- to medium-grained, light brown/gray; source: local
Diam: 4.5; Th: 2.8

1319 PN 12
Amphibole (JD); edges: rounded; surface: smooth, polished, fine- to medium-grained, dark gray; base: coarse; source: local
Diam: 5.1; Th: 4.0

1324 PN 14
Amphibole (JD); end: rounded; sides: smooth, black/green; surface: fine- to medium-grained, foliated
L: 9.0; W: 5.0; Th: 4.5

1358 PN 28 Clng
Amphibole (JD); both ends broken; four flat sides; edges: two sharp, two curved; surface: smooth, crystalline, dark green; source: local
L: 10.3; W: 3.0; Th: 1.6

1570   PO 12
Amphibole (JD); fragment; edges: unworked, one flat; surface: smooth, matt, fine- to medium-grained, planar foliation, black; three sides coarse
L: 10.0; W: 5.0; Th: 2.0

1590   PO 23
Amphibole (JD); surface: fine-grained; source: local

2069   PO/D 35
Marble (JD); lateral crack extends throughout; surface: smooth, striped gray/white; source: local
L: 18.3; W: 13.6; Th: 6.0

2070   PO/D 35
Schist (JD); surface: amber and brown deposits; source: local
L: 19.5; W: 17.7; Th: 10.0

2085   PO/D 34
Marble (JD); one side flat; surface: smooth, creamy/white; used for burnishing; source: local
L: 5.5; W: 2.2; Th: 2.0

2089   PO/B
Marble (JD); sides: both flat, one curved; surfaces: smooth, pale gray/white; used for burnishing (?); source: local
L: 6.0; W: 2.2

2091   PO/D 37
Marble (JD); surface: coarse, white; used on one or two sides (?); source: local
L: 5.6; W: 2.2; Th: 2.1

2093   PO/D 37
Fragment; surface: light brown/black with encrustation
L: 6.4; W: 2.9; Th: 1.9

2096   PO 25 balk
Amphibole (JD); fragment; surface: medium-grained, foliated, black with brown encrustation; source: local
L: 9.2; W: 7.6; Th: 2.4

2098a   PO/C 32
One edge slightly ground; surface: cream
L: 5.8; W: 3.3; Th: 2.6

2098b   PO/C 32
Surface: light brown; burnisher (?)
L: 4.2; W: 3.8; Th: 1.9

2214   PO/C 25
Amphibole (JD); large flake missing; some flaking; surface: smooth, medium- to coarse-grained, dark gray/mottled; source: local
L: 12.3; W: 5.2; Th: 2.4

2215   PO/C 25
Schist (JD); fragment; surface: gray, with slight encrustation
L: 8.6; W: 4.8; Th: 1.6

2231   PO/B 37
Limestone (JD); surface: light gray, micaceous; use-wear evident; source: not local
L: 6.2; W: 5.0; Th: 1.7

2239   PO/B 33
Amphibole (JD); sides: one flat, fractured; surface: black/gray, micaceous; source: local
W: 10.1; Th: 1.6

2404   PN/E 61
Schist (JD); two fragments joined; surface: gray; source: local
L: 11.4; W: 8.8; Th: 3.7

2422   PN/A 92
Schist (JD); surface: micaceous, off-white; one side possibly ground; source: local
L: 7.9; W: 11.1; Th: 6.3

3572   PN/C 82
Marble (JD); flattened on one side; buff on weathered surface; used as a polisher (?); source: local
L: 5.7; W: 3.2; Th: 3.0

3660   ROc 2
Marble (JD); triangular fragment; one side worked; used as a polisher (?); source: local

4308   PN/F 264; plate 5.32a
Long and narrow; found with burned bone attached
L: 17.0; W: 6.6; Th: 4.3

4757   PO 9
Roughly cylindrical; ends broken; surface: micaceous

4807   PO/C/D 126 balk
Oblong, flat; surface: smooth, blackish
L: 11.4; W: 9.0; Th: 4.0

Shaft-Hole Axes

1650   PO 10; figure 5.19; plate 5.15
Quartzite (JD); fragment; both ends broken; sides: rounded, smooth; perforation: incomplete; surface: matt, fine-grained, dark blue with white striations; source: local
L: 9.3; W: 4.5; Th: 3.5; Hole Diam: 1.7

1654   PO 10; plate 5.14c
Metadolerite-S (JD); fragment; one end broken; edges: rounded; surface: smooth, matt, dark green with light green flecks; source: not local
L: 3.8; W: 3.5; Th: 2.7

2056   PO 29
Sandstone (JD); fragment: butt; sides: convex; butt: rounded; shaft hole: drilled from both sides, not polished; surface: fine-grained, white/gray/light brown; source: not local
L: 5.3; W: 3.3; Th: 3.0

Spherical Stones

1088   QO 7
> Marble (JD); surface: matt, light gray; source: local
> Diam: 3.5

4359   PN/E/F balk
> Quartz pebble; round; surface: smooth, opaque, yellow
> L: 1.3; W: 1.1; Th: 0.7

Vessel Fragments

703   PO 7
> Small vase fragment

Whetstones

131   PO/C/D balk
> Marble (JD); surface: smooth, dark gray
> L: 9.8; W: 5.2; Th: 3.5

2038   ROc 21s
> Sandstone (JD); triangular; surface: smooth, buff/brown, white encrustation on one side; source: not local
> L: 4.7; Th: 2.3

3350   PO/C/D balk 131
> Amphibole (JD); fragment; surface: smooth, medium-grained, weak foliation, dark gray; source: local
> L: 9.8; W: 5.2; Th: 3.5

UNPHASED OR MIXED CONTEXTS

Adzes

831   LM 35
> Amphibole/calc-silicate (?) (JD); cutting edge: sharp; surface: smooth, polished, dark gray; interior: fine-grained
> L: 7.8; W: 2.8; Th: 1.1

Axes

9   LCD 1
> Sandstone (JD); fragment; weathered; surface: coarse-grained; source: not local
> L: 5.5; W: 4.0; Th: 1.0

36   NAn 1
> Amphibole (JD); fragment; sides: sharp; surface: smooth, polished, fine-grained, foliated, dark gray/blue stone; small area roughened; source: local
> L: 5.9; W: 2.6; Th: 2.5

52   KN 1
> Amphibole (JD); fragment, one end broken; surface: smooth, polished, fine- to medium-grained, dark gray with matt, light brown patches; interior: rough, light gray; source: local
> L: 7.6; W: 3.7; Th: 2.6

56   MOb 1
> Metadolerite-S (JD); fragment, ends broken; surface: smooth, polished, dark gray; interior: fine-grained, light gray; source: not local
> L: 5.0; W: 4.2; Th: 1.9

273   HLc 1
> Metadolerite (JD); fragment; section: rectangular; cutting edge: beveled
> L: 7.0; W: 2.9; Th: 2.8

276   HNb 1
> Metadolerite-S (JD); fragment; edges: sharp; cutting edge: missing; surface: smooth, polished, weak foliation, dark gray/green; interior: coarse; source: not local
> L: 3.3; W: 2.2; Th: 1.7

471   Surface; plate 5.3c
> Amphibole (JD); green stone; fragment; surface: fine-grained, mottled, dark greenish black stone; source: local
> L: 6.4; W: 3.5

1104   No location; plate 5.11d
> Amphibole (JD); fragment, one end broken; sides: rounded; surface: smooth, polished, black/gray mottled; interior: dark green; source: local
> L: 4.5; W: 3.4; Th: 2.1

1683   KK 1
> Amphibole (JD); fragment; edges: rounded; surface: smooth, polished, fine-grained, dark gray; source: local
> L: 5.7; W: 4.1; Th: 1.3

1719   QMd 1; figure 5.22; plate 5.14a
> Hammer-axe fragment: blade; sides: curved, one side indented; surface: polished, black, with encrustations on one side
> L: 5.5; W: 3.9; Th: 2.7

2205   OHb 1
> Metadolerite-S (JD); fragment, one end broken; surface: black volcanic (?) stone, weak foliation; source: not local
> L: 4.8; W: 3.5; Th: 1.4

2207   OIb 1
> Granite (JD); surface: smooth, dark gray; source: not local
> L: 6.0; W: 3.9; Th: 1.9

2507   JL surface
> Amphibole (?) (JD); fragment; ends: one broken, ground; surface: foliated, faint greenish gray
> L: 4.5; W: 2.2; Th: 1.3

2510   JL surface
Metagabbro-R (JD); fragment; surface: blue/gray flecks; source: not local
L: 2.1; W: 1.4; Th: 0.9

3433   UJ 1; plate 5.11e
Meta-volcaniclastic (JD petrology # 95); cutting edge: beveled; sides: flat, one tapering to cutting edge; surface: polished (?), medium-grained, gray green; source: not local
L: 5.3; W: 4.3

3552   Surface
Metadolerite-S (JD); cutting edge: flaked; surface: weak foliation, gray/white mottled, slight white encrustation; source: not local
L: 3.8; W: 3.5; Th: 1.4

3553   Surface
Amphibole (JD); sides: one flaked; butt: flaked; surface: fine-grained, faint gray mottle, deep green to black, with slight encrustation; source: local
L: 4.8; W: 3.6; Th: 1.4

3558   Surface
Amphibole (JD); cutting edge: shows evidence of use; sides: flaked; surface: fine-grained, deep greenish brown/black, with white encrustation; source: local
L: 4.0; W: 3.6; Th: 1.2

3704   ZK 2
Metagabbro-S (?) (JD); fragment; surface: medium-grained, greenish black; source: not local
L: 6.5; W: 4.1; Th: 1.5

4596   Surface
Fragment; green stone
L: 4.2; W: 2.0; Th: 1.0

4796   Surface
Fragment; sides: one broken; butt: thin, rounded; surface: dark green
L: 4.4; W: 3.4; Th: 1.5

4797   Surface
Fragment, broken diagonally; surface: polished, pale gray green with pale green veins

Grinders

3221   ZHt surface
Amphibole (JD); sides: one smooth, the other broken; surface: medium-grained, blue/gray; source: local
L: 9.1; W: 6.2; Th: 3.0

3666   Surface
Amphibole (JD); surface: medium-grained, foliated, bluish green crystalline; rounded end partially worked; source: local
L: 9.3; W: 5.4; Th: 3.1

4777   Surface
Three fragments joined

Grinder/Pounders

1187   MNa 1
Marble breccia (JD); spherical; conglomerate; surface: pink, with encrustations; source: local
Diam: 7

Maces

830   No location; figure 5.34; plate 5.41c
Fragment; semicircular; hole in center; fine-grained stone; ends broken, matt, blue/green with red patch; surface: matt, blue/gray
H: 4.0; Diam: 5.3

Miscellaneous

33   MNd 1
Amphibole? (JD); fragment; ends: broken; surface: smooth, polished, coarse, dark gray/green; interior: coarse, gray/green
L: 3.9; W: 4.1; Th: 2.8

2296   JL surface
Metadolerite-S (JD); fragment; sides: squared; two grooves; surface: polished, medium- to coarse-grained, igneous texture, gray; source: not local
L: 5.3; W: 3.3; Th: 3.5

3226   ZHt surface
Serpentinite (JD); fragment; surface: polished, black/green; source: not local
L: 5.7; W: 2.9; Th: 1.8

3690   Surface
Amphibole (JD); single groove on obverse; surface: green-gray; source: local
L: 9.7; W: 2.8; Th: 1.4

Querns

4783   Surface
Fragment; flat; surface: coarse; one side ground
L: 13.0; W: 16.0; Th: 8.7

4795   HNb 1
Flat; edges: three straight and broken, one rounded; surface: smooth, buff, pink
L: 10.7; W: 6.4; Th: 3.5

Rubbers

3691   Surface
Iron oxide (JD); one side flat; surface: smooth, black

4780   Surface
Polisher (?); marble; section: triangular; all sides ground
L: 5.8; W: 2.3

Shaft-Hole Axes

60 QR 1; figure 5.17; plate 5.14d
Tremolite-schist (?) (JD); section: symmetrical; cutting edge: symmetrical; shaft hole: incomplete, drilled from one side; surface: smooth, cracked, polished, gray/green, one end brown; interior: fine-grained; source: not local
L: 8.3; W: 3.1; Th: 2.6

1725 Surface
Amphibole (JD); fragment: butt; one side: steeply waisted, level with shaft hole; shaft hole: drilled from one side; butt: rounded; surface: fine- to medium-grained, dark green; source: local
L: 3.0; W: 2.8; Th: 4.4

1742 KNc 1; figure 5.15
Half fragment; edges: broken, gray/brown; surface: smooth, green/brown/ black with gray/brown rough areas; shaft hole: drilled from both sides, highly polished to remove the ridge, smooth, green/brown/gray/black; section: slightly asymmetrical
L: 7.6; W: 5.2; H: 6.9

2210 no location
Flint; quartz (JD); egg-shaped; incompletely drilled; surface: white/yellow, caliche on one side; source: local
L: 5.1; W: 3.9; Th: 2.0

2248 Surface; plate 5.13a
Serpentinite (JD); fragment; section: slightly asymmetrical; striking edge: symmetrical; sides: convex, narrow toward edge; surface: brown, patches of light brown, heavily veined in dark green; source: not local
L: 8.4; W: 4.5; Th: 4.8

2851 NQ 1; figure 5.16; plate 5.13b
Serpentinite (JD); fragment; one end broken; section: symmetrical; striking edge: flaked; sides: parallel, straight; shaft hole: drilled from one side, polished; surface: smooth, polished, greenish gray/blue; source: not local
L: 6.8; W: 4.2; Th: 4.3

3434 UF 1; figure 5.18; plate 5.14b
Serpentinite (JD); fragment; both ends broken; countersides: flattened; surface: polished, yellowish green; source: not local
L: 8.2; W: 3.9; Th: 2.5

Vessels

274 HLc 1; figure 5.31; plates 5.43a, 5.44a
Marble fragment; edges broken; surface: whitish
L: 2.6; W: 2.1; Th: 1.1; Diam: 10.4

2272 ML Clng
Bowl rim fragment; marble; triangular; two edges broken
L: 4.3

4775 Ofd 1; figure 5.27
Bowl fragment; marble; three edges broken; one perforation
L: 3.2; W: 4.3; Th: 0.7; Diam: 14.6

6.

Tools of the Spinner, Weaver, and Mat Maker [1]

Ernestine S. Elster

The artifacts discussed herein include complete and fragmentary clay spindle whorls (figures 6.1–6.15; plates 6.1–6.7a, b, e, f), loom weights (figures 6.18–6.23; plates 6.8–6.12), "spools" (figure 6.17; plate 6.7c, d, g, h), hooks (figures 6.24–6.27; plate 6.13a–d), and "anchor-hooks" (figures 6.28–6.30; plate 6.13e–p). Collateral evidence for spinning, weaving, and the making of perishable fiber products includes impressions of cloth, mat, and twine on fragments of baked clay (plates 6.14–6.19), auxiliary artifacts of bone (plates 2.4, 2.5a–c, 2.14) and shell (figure 9.17 [plate 9.14a]; figure 9.18 [plate 9.20b]); painted and incised designs on pottery resembling woven patterns (figure 6.31a); and figurines with depictions of clothing (figure 6.31b). All of these sets of direct and indirect evidence combine to reflect the active spinning, weaving, twining, basket and mat making of the Sitagroi settlers.

Since the termination of our fieldwork (1968–1970), a number of studies have appeared that examine the prehistory, history, and technology of spinning and weaving in the Greek archipelago (for example, Barber 1991, 1994; Burke 1998; Carington Smith 1975, 1977, 2000). Significant scholarship has also focused on the social, economic, and gender significance of textile production in various archaeological, ethnoarchaeological, and ethnological contexts (Campbell 1964; Costin 1993; Helms 1993; Kramer 1982; Murra 1962; Wiener and Schneider 1989). These useful forays into rich interpretive territory offer interesting ideas applicable to the householders of the Sitagroi settlement and their textile products.

During the excavation seasons of 1968 to 1970, when the Sitagroi team worked and lived in the eponymous village, we would regularly encounter the local women drawing wool from a distaff and spinning by hand using a wooden spindle and whorl. This activity seemed to go on whenever they were not involved in their many other domestic and economic tasks of sweeping, cleaning, washing, bread making, cooking, tending the vegetable garden, weaving, sewing, mending, and harvesting and stringing tobacco. A few women had looms in the main room of their house, where they produced the dowry rugs and linens brought to marriage. In one case, by necessity, a mother's textile production for her six daughters (!) was augmented by several aunts at *their* looms. Campbell (1964:59–69), studying a group of Sarakatsani shepherds and their families, described marriage customs in which wool and spinning held a symbolic role between the bride and groom. This was in addition to the importance of the woven goods included in the bride's dowry and those she presented to the groom's family. The life and economy of this group revolve around the flock and its products; thus there is a profound interrelationship of cloth and society.

Earlier (Murdock and Provost 1973:27) and recent research (Barber 1991:289; Elster 1997:28, nn. 72, 73) indicates that, cross-culturally, women are most often involved in cloth production. They are the spinners but not always the weavers. In her ethnographic study of a rural village in Iran, Kramer (1982) proposed archaeological correlates of domestic activities, including household size, subsistence, consumption practices, and spinning and weaving. She learned that the recognition of a weaver's skill (always female in these examples) was an important negotiating point in matrimonial discussions, an aspect not directly recognizable in the archaeological record (Kramer 1982:41). Schneider (1987), looking at cloth consumption and social identity, demonstrated how textiles used as gifts, in dowries, and/or for trade reinforce kinship ties and signify skill, wealth, power, and status. Elizabeth Barber[2] demonstrated that cloth was used in the Neolithic and the Bronze Age Mediterranean to record history and depict various ritual practices (1991:372–383). Others, focusing on modern cultures (for example, Kahlenberg 1977:28), have found that the importance of cloth and textile production has not changed over time: it swaddles the newborn, covers the marriage bed, and shrouds the dead.

While the evidence for textile production at Sitagroi is strong, it has been advanced that some of the artifacts may have been used for different purposes. These data sets, both direct (impressions) and indirect (artifacts, patterns, context), are ambiguous, not like a sickle blade with its telltale silica polish. Nevertheless, I am persuaded that many of the activities of Sitagroi spinners and weavers are reflected in this assemblage. My argument is that the clay whorls, weights, hook, and spool shapes represent part of a tool kit for the production of woven goods. Using this data I try to isolate changes in the tools for production of fiber perishables over time, changes that, along with the context of the textile equipment, should reflect certain aspects of social organization. Tables, figures, and plates illustrate the text and evaluate and compare the distribution of the artifacts and types through time and space. Comparanda and ethnographic parallels are presented throughout the discussion. Appendix 6.1 by J. Adovasio and J. Illingworth is a technological analysis of the fibers, yarns, and woven patterns based on the plates and line drawings of the impressions on pottery fragments. Appendix 6.2 is the catalog.

DISCUSSION

Raw Materials

The raw materials used for textiles in the Mediterranean were vegetable fibers from bast plants, such as flax and nettles, and fleece from sheep. Both bast and wool were spun into thread or yarn and then woven into cloth.

The processing of bast fibers from flax, hemp, or nettles is essentially the same, regardless of the raw material. Linen thread is obtained from the fibrous stalk of the bast plant, flax (*Linum usitatissinum*).[3] Ideally, these are planted close together to encourage height because taller stalks produce longer fibers. To obtain the finest thread, the plants are harvested while green, before the flax seeds ripen (Barber 1991:13). Then, the fibrous stalk or stem is washed and soaked until it softens and rots, in a process called *retting*. Next, the exterior casing is broken up by beating the stalks with a wood, antler (for example, plate 2.14), or stone (for example, plate 5.36) mallet or chopper. The fibers, separated from the casing by being drawn through a rigid comb, are ready to be spun into thread (Walton 1989:316). The result is a long, strong, but not particularly cohesive fiber that requires a fairly heavy whorl to spin, weighing 100 to 150 g (Barber 1991: 52). However, little pretreatment is necessary to make rope or cord from bast fibers.

The time involved in keeping and breeding woolly sheep makes the preparation of fleece for spinning into wool yarn perhaps more time consuming than obtaining bast fiber. Clipping with shears is reported as early as the late third millennium in Mesopotamia (Barber 1991:29) but certainly not at Sitagroi, since we have no evidence of shears. Plucking, the more likely method, would have taken place when the sheep were molting. Raw wool was washed, beaten, and carded (straightened) in preparation for spinning. Dyeing may have followed, with the scaly wool fibers absorbing color better than linen.

Different plant types (flax, hemp, nettles, reeds, grasses) produce either hard (leaf) or soft (bast) fibers for textile and mat making (Hurley 1979:3; Körber-Grohne 1991:93–94). Some of these were available to the Sitagroi villagers (Barber 1994:53; British Naval Intelligence 1944: fig. 66:113; this volume, chapter 1). They include *Linum usitatissinum*, whose seeds were edible, medicinal, and an oil source, and thus might not be preserved. Jane Renfrew (this volume, chapter 1) reported one specimen from the Sitagroi samples. However, she indicated that its presence is known, although not as a crop, from reports of the Greek sites, Sesklo, Argissa,

Pefkakia, and Kastanas, along with Kapitan Dimitrievo in Bulgaria. Recently Efstratiou et al. (1997) reported on their excavation of Neolithic Makri, located along the coast in Thrace. While Makri II yielded a few flax seeds, a real crop is reported from two late Neolithic sites, Arkadikos in the Drama Plain, and Makriyalos, close to the west coast of the Gulf of the Thérmai in Northern Piéria (Valamoti 1997b:50). I infer that both bast and leaf fibers were used at Sitagroi (see appendix 6.1).

THE TOOL KIT

Whorls

Whorls are used in spinning as partner to a slender rod, the spindle, which is slipped through the whorl's central perforation. We have no remaining spindles because they were probably of perishable wood (although possibly of bone [Hochstetter 1987: Taf. 36:1]), but the baked clay whorls, acting as flywheels to keep the spindle rotating, are preserved. The essential qualities of a whorl are its roundness and weight, of which the spinner makes good use.

From thread and mat impressions on clay we can distinguish between two types of spinning: S and Z.[4] The direction of the twist may be either clockwise or counterclockwise. Clockwise rotation produces a yarn in which the fibers lie in alignment to the middle stroke of the letter Z, called the Z-spun type. Its opposite, the counterclockwise spin, is the S type. Cord (or string) is made by twisting or plying two S (or Z) spun yarns in opposite directions (Walton 1989:317–318). Eight cord- or string-impressed body sherds from the EBA phase Va were published (see volume 1: plate XCVIII). Elizabeth Barber (personal communication, December 1995) and I agree that there is one Z twist (volume 1:

plate XCVIII: bottom, 1) and one questionable twist (volume 1: plate XCVIII: bottom, 4); the remaining six are S twists (volume 1: plate XCVIII, bottom: 2, 3, 5–8) with impressed knots observable on three sherds (volume 1: plate XCVIII, bottom: 2–4). The Z type indicates light cording that was probably produced from soft bast fibers since heavy cords or ropes were made from hard leaf fibers.

It is important that the whorl be matched to the kind of yarn spun; wool requires a medium weight while linen needs a heavier whorl. Carington Smith, who observed wooden whorls used in recent times by Greek women spinning wool, reports that these whorls ranged from 3.5 to 7 cm in diameter and weighed between 11 and 40 g (1975: 80). She concluded that the whorl must weigh at least 10 g and have a minimum diameter of 2 cm to be useful.

The 431 whorls (table 6.1) and 34 spools from Sitagroi are commonly of baked clay; they are products in themselves, modeled into several forms, three of which are further elaborated with incisions. If the whorl is a flat or shallow cone, its base may be (but not always) slightly concave. The top face refers to the surface extending from the top yarn hole to the carination or edge of the base. This "face" or surface may be flat, angled and deep, rounded, domed, pointed, truncated, or shallow and is the field for the elaboration of incised designs. Carination refers to the midsection of the biconical form and may be true, rounded, or flattened; a true bicone has two "faces."

The various forms are illustrated by drawings of section morphology (figures 6.1–6.4). The shapes grade into one another; thus the typology advanced is merely a construct and provides a method for sorting and tabulation. It may have had little relevance

Table 6.1. Distribution of Whorl Types Over Time

Type	Phase I	II	III	IV	V	X*	Total	%
Biconical	2	3	6	14	119	8	152	35
Conical	1	2	4	34	20	7	68	16
Flat	3	2	37	9	37	7	95	22
Reworked sherd	0	1	4	3	3	2	13	3
Shallow conical	2	7	51	10	11	4	85	20
Spherical, oval	0	2	1	10	1	0	14	3
Miscellaneous	0	0	1	0	2	1	4	1
Total	8	17	104	80	193	29	431	100
Percent	2	4	24	19	45	6	100	

* X indicates unphased or mixed contexts.

for the Sitagroi spinners or, perhaps happily, we may have isolated actual distinctions, such as the presence or absence of facial elaboration on specific forms over time, or a co-association of form and time (for example, shallow face/phase III and biconical/phase V). What these preferences might have meant and the percentage of the assemblage they constitute are discussed next.

Four main shapes—biconical (BC), conical with a flat base (C), flat (F), and shallow-faced, conical (SFC)—account for 93% of the whorls; the remaining 7% include spherical or oval (S-O), reworked sherds (RWS), and miscellaneous (M) shapes, some of which look like a degraded and squashed bicone. Incisions (facial elaborations) distinguish a group of conical, flat, or shallow-faced whorls from the plain ones. I think the addition of facial elaboration is important, and it will be discussed in detail.

- *Biconical* [BC] (35%): The idealized "type" is carinated around the middle (figure 6.1a, b), with faces angled from the yarn hole like a double cone (figure 6.5a–c [plate 6.1e, f]; plate 6.6). Carinated whorls with truncated top and base (fig-

ure 6.2a, b) were also tabulated, as were those with truncated top, base, and carination (figure 6.4a, b). The latter, very few in number, become almost rectangular in section (figure 6.4c, d) and may be a degraded form of the bicone. Bicones, both large and small (plate 6.6) and including a very few incised (plate 6.6d) and truncated forms, are associated with phase V.

- *Conical* [C] (16%): Forms with flat or slightly concave bases vary in the treatment of the truncation and/or the depth and shape of the face, as may be seen in the section drawings (figure 6.3a–f). In others, the cone is shallow (figure 6.6a, b [plate 6.3d], c–f; figure 6.7a [plate 6.3c], b–d [plate 6.2c], e [plate 6.2e], f; figure 6.8a–d [plate 6.1a], e [plate 6.1b]); and in some it is deep (figures 6.3a, b, c [plate 6.5a]). The tops of deep cones were sometimes truncated flat (figure 6.3c, d, e; plates 6.5f, g; 6.7a) or on an angle

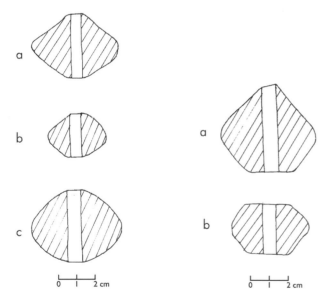

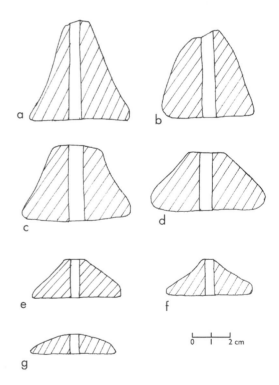

Figure 6.1. Whorl types, phase V: (a) SF 1631, biconical with carination; (b, c) with less pronounced carination. (b) SF 333; (c) SF 3336.

Figure 6.2. Whorls, phases IV (a) and V (b). (a) SF 3227, bicone with truncated base; (b) SF 1026, with truncated top and base.

Figure 6.3. Flat-based whorls, phase III (b, e, f); phase IV (a, c, d, g). Deep cones (a–d): (a) SF 3203; (b) SF 466; (c) SF 2742, plate 6.5a; (d) SF 3252, plate 6.5b. Shallow cones (e, f): (e) SF 2942; (f) SF1223; almost flat (g) SF 155.

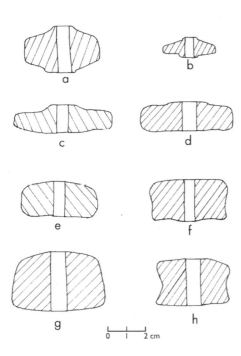

Figure 6.4. Whorls, various shapes, phases V (a, c–h) and III (b): (a) SF 2421b; (b) SF 5191; (c) SF 1338; (d) SF 15; (e) SF 1091; (f) SF 675; (g) SF 1065, plate 6.7a; (h) SF 659.

(figure 6.3a, b); only the shallow cones were incised. Distribution of the deep and/or truncated cone is tied to the EBA. The shallow incised cones are linked to phase III.

- *Flat* [F] (22%): Forms include flat perforated rondels, sometimes incised (figure 6.9a–d [plate 6.3b]; figure 6.10; figure 6.14b [plate 6.3h]; figure 6.14c; figure 6.14d [plate 6.1c]; plate 6.7b, f). The incised rondels exhibit a bimodal distribution (phases III and V), and there is a clear formal similarity with the incised cones noted above and the shallow-faced forms to be discussed. The distinctiveness of the facial incisions sets these groupings apart.

- *Shallow-faced cone* [SFC] (20%): Whorls are modeled with the top hole emphasized; the frequently incised face tapers to the base (figure 6.11c [plate 6.2b]; figure 6.11d [plate 6.2a]; figure 6.11e [plate 6.2d]; figure 6.12a [plate 6.3e], b–d [plate 6.3g]; figure 6.13a, b [plate 6.3f], c [plate 6.3a], d; figure 6.14a). These will occasionally be modeled with a concave or convex base (figure 6.14c; figure 6.14d [plate 6.1c]).

Undecorated examples of this form (plate 6.4a, b, e) are from phase IV.

- *Reworked sherds* [RS] (3%): Sherds seem to have been selected from discarded painted pottery and recycled as whorls by being shaped into an almost round form and then being perforating (figure 6.15a [plate 6.4g], b [plate 6.4d], c [plate 6.4c]).

- *Spherical and oval forms* [S/O] (3%): Forms include loaf-like (figure 6.4e), high-domed shapes (plates 6.4h, 6.5c).

- *Miscellaneous* [M] (1%): Pieces are not numerically significant but include some unusual shapes and a few drilled stones.

The use of the star-pointed stone artifact as a whorl (figure 6.16) is unlikely. It is heavier than the clay whorls; thus this artifact might have functioned as a flywheel for twisting twine. More likely, it was a pendant (see this volume, chapter 9) since it is rather large for a bead. Barber (1991:51) has noted that beads are usually less than 2 cm in diameter.

The minimum, maximum, and mean for height and diameter (cm), as well as for weight (g), are given in table 6.2, based on complete pieces only. All of the Sitagroi artifacts fall within Carington Smith's comments about size (1975:80). The biconical and discoid are more than twice as high as the flattest of the F type. SFC and F, both with facial elaboration, have large surface diameters, perhaps to provide the artisan with a larger area for incising. Variation in minimum diameter for each whorl type is not great, ranging from 2.4 to 2.9; the mean is 3.9 to 4.8, but the maximum diameters range more widely, from 6.1 to 9.4 cm.

The forty-eight F and SFC whorls weigh the least; more than half are between 20 and 60 g, with

Table 6.2. Dimensions of Whorl Types: Height, Diameter, Weight

Type	Height (cm)			Diameter (cm)			Weight (g)		
	Min.	Max.	Mean	Min.	Max.	Mean	Min.	Max.	Mean
Biconical	1.2	5.3	2.8	2.4	6.1	3.9	11	135	43
Discoid	2.1	5.3	3.3	2.8	6.4	4.3	23	185	78.5
Flat	0.5	2.6	1.6	2.9	9.4	4.8	7.5	—	—
Shallow conical	0.9	3.5	1.8	2.6	6.9	4.3	8.0	109.5	34.4

forty-three of them weighing less than 60 g. By contrast, half of the conical weigh 80 g or more, with one example being a hefty 185 g. Midway are the biconical, with eighty of the total 102 whorls weighing less than 60 g. Just over twenty weigh between 80 and 100 g, and five of them weigh between 100 and 138 g. Spinning varying thicknesses of woolen yarn or linen thread (or length of thread; see Papaefthymiou-Papanthimou and Pilali-Papasteriou 1998:187) may have called for differing whorl weights, and the changing whorl shape suggests that there was also considerable creative leeway for whomever made the whorls—the spinner (making them for herself) or the ceramist (making them for the spinner). This formal latitude must be especially true during phase V when all shapes are represented.

The percentage and number of whorls in phases I or II are low, but two phase I impressions, a faced weave (SF 1439; plate 6.19) and a finely woven mat (plate 6.17), are clear evidence that weaving was a practiced craft. There are diverse explanations for the low recovery of phase I and II whorls. Perhaps these Middle Neolithic excavation areas were not representative of the full range of activities. Equally, the majority of whorls used in phases I and II could have been manufactured from wood and thus are not preserved; or perhaps the spindle and whorl were not taken up in earnest until phase III. Spinning strictly by hand without a spindle is, of course, possible (Barber 1991:41, 42), but with a spindle and whorl the spinner can twist the bast or fleece fibers more tightly and quickly into strong linen or wool yarn. Nevertheless, this impression of a faced weave (SF 1439) is the earliest direct indication of a textile recovered at this writing in the Aegean world. As Elizabeth Barber wrote in the Coda to her important and exhaustive survey of textiles (1991:393), "Even the tiniest and humblest scraps of data were found to contribute serious information." And SF 1439, this small pottery sherd with its impression of a textile, does contribute a wealth of "serious information." It provides irrefutable documentation for experienced weaving already in phase I, and this evidence further implies the production of clothing, household goods, and, potentially, woven goods for ex-change/trade.

Probably it is reasonable to assume that woven goods held varying roles, some symbolic (as heirlooms, or for emblematic display and so forth), and certainly textiles represent gender and labor relations.

Almost one-fourth (104) of the whorl assemblage came from phase III contexts; of these, almost 40% are incised (41). Although incised examples are reported from all phases, incision is a significant attribute of the SF and F types of phase III.

What could account for the investment of time and effort to elaborate these whorls? Do the incisions convey a symbolic message, such as a mark of ownership, sisterhood, or "guild" membership? Each whorl is different, but, as discussed below, there are similarities among the incised patterns. The clustering of these whorls in phase III may reflect a newfound importance for the craft to which the whorls are attached and an economic significance to the value accorded to the end product, the woven good.

Flanking, radiating from, encircling, or framing the yarn hole and sometimes dividing the face into zones, are single, or sets of, or combinations of curving, linear, punctate, circling, spiraling, or serrating incisions which elaborate the face of the whorl in a lively fashion (see figures 6.5–6.14 and plates 6.1–6.3). About one-third of the Sitagroi examples (23) exhibit small incisions that serrate and encircle the whorl's edge (for example, figures 6.5c [plate 6.1f]; figure 6.6a [plate 6.2f]; figure 6.6d [plate 6.2g]; figure 6.6e, f; figure 6.7a [plate 6.3c]; figure 6.7b, d [plate 6.2c]; figure 6.8d [plate 6.1a]; figure 6.11c [plate 6.2b]; figure 6.11d [plate 6.2a]; figure 6.12d [plate 6.3g]). In one case (figure 6.8a) this serration is the single elaboration, since the face is unadorned. Another whorl, also singly elaborated but in this case strongly so, exhibits deep incisions curving and slashing from the string hole, across the whorl, cutting around the edge, and the whole design creates a sense of circular movement (figure 6.5a [plate 6.1e]).

Several impressions are derived from examining the drawings and plates of the incised whorls. An "alphabet" of incisions appears in repeated combinations, forming a design vocabulary. Skillful artisans were probably responsible for the carefully

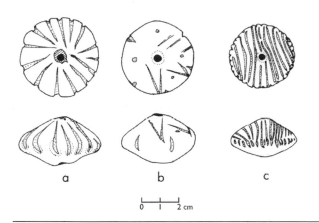

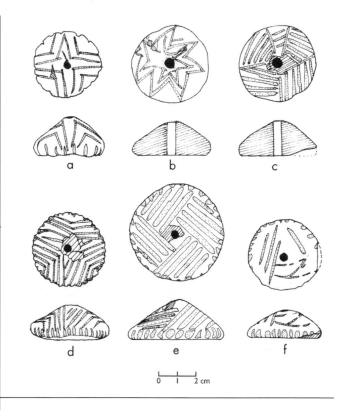

(Above): Figure 6.5. Whorls, phase III, incised bicones: (a) SF 4211, plate 6.1e; (b) SF 1288; (c) SF 2990, plate 6.1f.

(Above right): Figure 6.6. Whorls, incised cones, phases II (f) and III (a–e): (a) SF 3478, plate 6.2f; (b) SF 3488, plate 6.3d; (c) SF 841, plate 6.2h; (d) SF 5035, plate 6.2g; (e) SF 1266, plate 6.1g; (f) SF 3618.

(Below left): Figure 6.7. Whorls, incised shallow cones, phase III: (a) SF 183, plate 6.3c; (b) SF 229; (c) SF 2960; (d) SF 1543, plate 6.2c; (e) SF 1267, plate 6.2e; (f) SF 1275.

(Below right): Figure 6.8. Whorls, incised shallow cones, phase III: (a) SF 3421; (b) SF 3406; (c) SF 3419; (d) SF 5195, plate 6.1a; (e) SF 808, plate 6.1b.

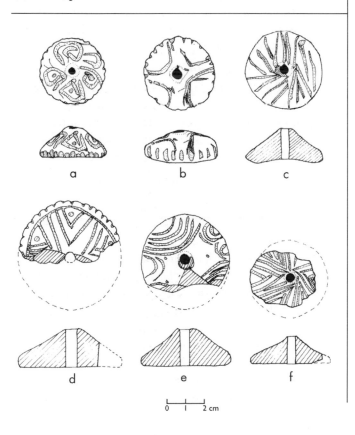

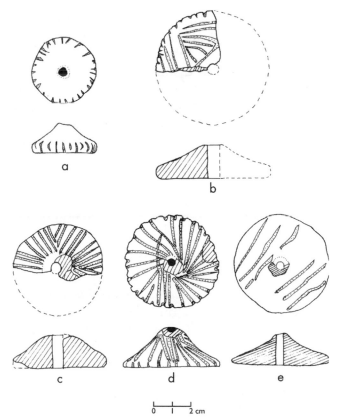

conceived, modeled, incised, and baked whorls. At the same time, other examples appear to have been casually produced (see figures 6.5b; 6.9a; 6.12a [plate 6.3e]; figure 6.14c). However, the full combination of incisions is unclear when a whorl is incomplete (for example, figure 6.14a, c, d). Many whorls reflect a clear relationship of design vocabulary to a circular field, similar to small Cretan seal stones wherein the artisan has curved the image to follow the shape of the field, although in the Sitagroi artifacts the motifs establish zones or registers for the circular field (also noted for Dikili Tash examples [Treuil 1992:127–128]). While the incisions *are* decorative, I think they may be read as conveying a self-conscious and symbolic message of pride, rightful pride in the tool that the adept spinner/weaver employs to practice her craft. The skillful hunter follows the same impulse in decorating his bow (Graburn, Lee, and Rousselot 1996:239).

The recurrent design elements which repeat and combine in varying ways may also represent a coherent vocabulary, or "symbolary," as understood by each (or more than one) whorl maker, or they may reflect artisans following another's lead or repeating themselves. Sometimes the elements are clear even in a fragment (for example, figure 6.11c [plate 6.2b]) but not always (see figures 6.13a [plate 6.3f]; 6.14a, c [plate 6.1c], and d). Because these whorls are so distinctive, it's instructive to note that the closest comparanda are from sites within the Drama Plain or close by (for example, Dikili Tash [Treuil 1992:124–130], Paradeisos [Hellström 1987:85–88], and Dhimitra [Grammenos 1997: PIN. 34, 36]). Examples of the elements and combinations with pertinent comparanda include:

1. *Radiating lines* (figure 6.5a [plate 6.1e]; figure 6.7 c; figure 6.8c, d [plate 6.1a]): Comparanda from Dikili Tash, M228 and M378 (Treuil 1992: pl. 201g [lower]); these have the added circling frame at the edge.

2. *Radiating lines combined with sets of angles dividing the face into zones* (figure 6.6a [plate 6.2f]; figure 6.6 d [plate 6.2g]; figure 6.7d [plate 6.2c]; figure 6.11 c [plate 6.2b]). Compare with whorls from Dikili Tash (Treuil 1992: pl. 201c, f) and Dhimitra (Grammenos 1997: PIN. 36:4); see also figure 6.11d [plate 6.2a], which is quite similar to Dikili

Tash M 644 (Treuil 1992:128 and pl. 202f) and to a whorl from Paradeisos (Hellström 1987:88, fig. 48:21).

3. *Radiating lines with ladder-like incisions placed in the interstices* (figure 6.6c [plate 6.2h]; figure 6.11b, figure 6.11e [plate 6.2d]; figure 6.13c; figure 6.14b [plate 6.3h]).

4. *Curving lines, single or nested sets, dividing the face into registers* (figure 6.7b, e [plate 6.2e]. Compare with Dikili Tash M162 and M 323 (Treuil 1992: pl. 202e), and with Dhimitra (Grammenos 1997: PIN. 37:1). I would consider figure 6.7a (plate 6.3c) in this grouping because the four spirals (and an additional arch) divide the face into registers and flank the yarn hole. A more elaborated example is M295 from Dikili Tash (Treuil 1992:128–130 and pls. 155d and 203a).

5. *Circling frames around the yarn hole and/or the edge* (figure 6.11a [plate 6.1h]). Parallel with Dikili Tash again (Treuil 1992: M 385, pl. 150c) and also comparable with a Dhimitra whorl also with punctate elements (Grammenos, ed. 1997: PIN. 34: 21).

6. *Multiple curving, circling, angled lines and punctate incisions* (figure 6.11a [plate 6.1g]; figure 6.13b [plate 6.3f]). Compare Dikili Tash M1853 and M385 (Treuil 1992: pl. 150b, c).

7. *Parallel lines crossing the face* (figure 6.5c [plate 6.1f]); or *randomly incised lines* (figure 6.6f, figure 6.8 e [plate 6.1b]); or, *in sets, en face* (figure 6.6e [plate 6.1g]. Compare with two virtually exact parallels from Dikili Tash, M 409 and M 190 (Treuil 1992: pl. 202e, upper and lower right).

8. *Random lines* (figures 6.5b, 6.6f, 6.9d [plate 6.3b]; figure 6.12a [plate 6.3e]; figure 6.14a).

Almost all excavation reports describe and illustrate some whorl examples; many of these formal shapes are reflected in the Sitagroi assemblage (figures 6.1–6.4). But especially striking is the similarity between specific Sitagroi artifacts and whorls from Dikili Tash as referred to above (Treuil 1992: 124–130, pls. 149–155, 201c–g, 203a); from Paradeisos (Hellström 1987:88, fig. 48:21); and from Dhimitra (Grammenos, ed. 1997: pl. 30:2, 5).

Hochstetter discussed whorls from Kastanas (1987:83–93), and many of the undecorated forms

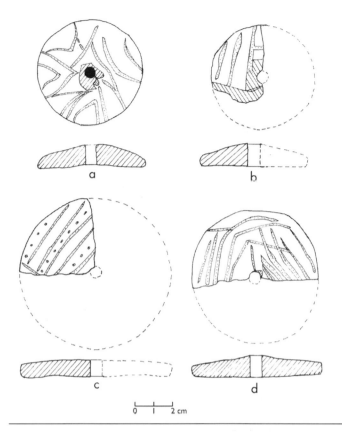

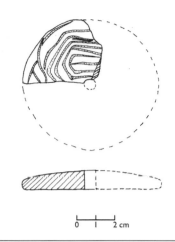

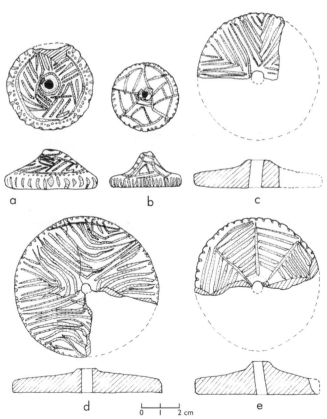

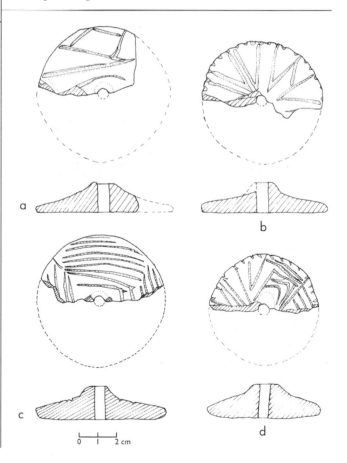

(Left): *Figure 6.9.* Whorls with flat faces, phases III (b–d) and IV: (a) SF 3924; (b) SF 747; (c) SF 1640; (d) SF 737, plate 6.3b.

(Above) *Figure 6.10.* Whorl, flat face, phase III: SF 1547.

(Below left): *Figure 6.11.* Whorls, flat and shallow faced, phase III: (a) SF 1222, plate 6.1h; (b) SF 1297; (c) SF 1254, plate 6.2b; (d) SF 1684, plate 6.2a; (e) SF 1440, plate 6.2d.

(Below right): *Figure 6.12.* Whorls, shallow faced, phase III: (a) SF 1423, plate 6.3e; (b) SF 3444; (c) SF 1437, plate 6.1d; (d) SF 3588, plate 6.3g.

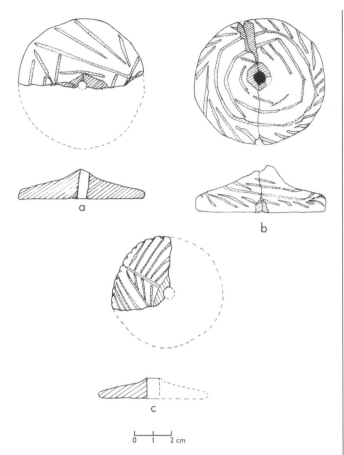

0   2 cm

Figure 6.13. Whorls with shallow and flat faces, phase III: (a) SF 862, plate 6.3f; (b) SF 739, plate 6.3a; (c) SF 1109.

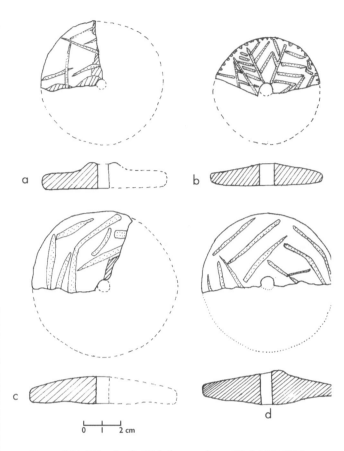

0   2 cm

Figure 6.14. Whorls, flattish faces, phase III: (a) SF 4904; (b) SF 2933, plate 6.3h; (c) SF 1548; (d) SF 2925, plate 6.1c.

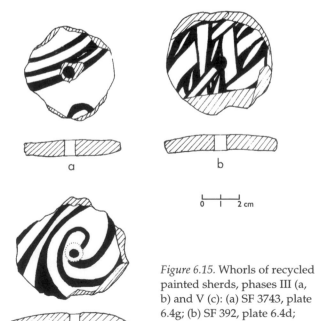

0   2 cm

Figure 6.15. Whorls of recycled painted sherds, phases III (a, b) and V (c): (a) SF 3743, plate 6.4g; (b) SF 392, plate 6.4d; (c) SF 22, plate 6.4c.

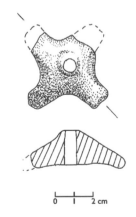

0   2 cm

Figure 6.16. Whorl (?), star-pointed, phase III: SF 159.

are comparable (Taf. 18:12–24, 20:1–7, 11–18); but the incised whorls differ because the incisions are placed on both faces of biconical shapes (Hochstetter 1987: Taf. 18:3–7, 9, 10), a pattern of incising also noted on whorls from Karanovo (Hiller and Nikolov 1997: Taf. 168:5, 6) but not at Sitagroi. The many whorls recovered from Bronze Age levels at Troy were recently discussed (Balfanz 1995:117–144), and a few of the incised patterns are somewhat comparable to Sitagroi examples although the formal shape differs (Balfanz 1995: Abb. 5: D7.255, D7.261 [from Troy III]; and Abb. 9 [Troy IV]). The many whorls from Professor Kostas Gallis's excavations at Plateia Magoula Zarkou (personal communication 1990) were undecorated, but again, the shapes (bicone, truncated, and shallow cone) are comparable.

My overall impression, based on the site reports cited above, plus Jill Carington Smith's article in the Servia report (2000:207-266) and several excavation reports in Thessaly (Pefkakia Magoula [Weisshaar 1989] and Achilleion [Gimbutas et al. 1989]), and in the Balkans (Divostin [McPherron and Srejovic 1988] and Selevac [Tringham and Krstić 1990]), is that these decorated whorls are very much representative of the Drama Plain and of Sitagroi phase III/Late Neolithic/Chalcolithic). Jill Carington Smith (2000:215), remarking on the paucity of whorls recovered from Servia compared with Dhimini and Sesklo (over 500) and Sitagroi (over 400), suggested that the Servia settlers of all periods were probably only spinning for their own needs. This comment is interesting in the light of my interpretation that incised, decorated whorls indicate the importance of the crafts of spinning and weaving and its product, textiles and, not incidentally, the women involved.

Spools

These clay artifacts (sometimes referred to as *bobbins*, *waisted weights*, or *whorls*) are convex or "waisted" between the flat top and base (for example, figure 6.17; plate 6.7c, d, g, h); they resemble a modern-day thread spool. The cross sections indicate the degree of similarity between some spools and spindle whorls (compare figure 6.4h with figure 6.17d), and perhaps some were used as whorls.

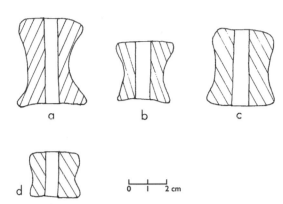

Figure 6.17. Spools, phase V: (a) SF 354; (b) SF 1003; (c) SF 371; (d) SF 366.

Phase V yielded twenty-nine of the thirty-four spools and a great many whorls; therefore I infer a separate use for the spools, perhaps related to weaving rather than to spinning. The spool diameter ranges from 2.6 to 6.9 cm; the mean weight is 24 g; and the height is from 1.1 to 4.6 cm, with a mean of 3.2 cm. All these artifacts have a central, longitudinal perforation.

Barber suggests that spools might have been used to hold supplies of different colored weft thread, such as would have been needed for weaving certain kinds of designs (1991:107, n. 17; 360). Carington Smith reminds us, however, that a length of cane or reed would have been equally suitable to hold various hues or thicknesses of weft thread (2000:228). If the spools held yarn, they might have been placed on a peg from which the yarn could be led to the loom. More recently, however, Barber reported observing spool shapes used by Japanese artisans for holding threads in a system of making cords (1997: 516, pl. CXCIIc). In her study of the Servia materials, Carington Smith (2000:227–232) reviews the various interpretations for the spool shape, some of which are not perforated, and concludes that the most reasonable application (especially as they are found in groups) might be as a simple loom weight.[5] If they were so used, the absence of a perforation would not matter as long as the spool was fairly convex, allowing the warp to be tied on securely. Comparanda are illustrated from Servia (Carington Smith 2000:229 [fig. 4.35]; 230 [pl. 4.19a, b]), Dhimitra (Grammenos: PIN. 34:17), Kastanas (Hochstetter 1987: Taf. 20:8, 23;

22: 1,2; 36:16, 17), and in many reports of Thessalian sites (for example, Achilleion [Gimbutas et al. 1989: fig. 8.6]).

Loom Weights

The recovery of fifty-eight loom weights, often fragmentary but in various shapes (table 6.3), is good evidence for the existence of the warp-weighted loom. This type of loom has an upper cross-beam from which the warp threads hang vertically; the loom weight keeps the warp threads taut (Barber 1991:91–113; Hoffman 1974:297–307; Rasson 1988:337).

Table 6.3. Distribution of Incised Whorls Over Time

Type	II	III	IV	V	Total
Shallow conical	1	40	2	4	47
Biconical	0	0	0	2	2
Flat	0	1	0	0	1
Phase total	1	41	2	6	50

According to ethnographic accounts (Hoffman 1974) and ancient representations of weaving (Barber 1991: fig. 130:307), loom weights are fastened at the bottom of the warp threads which have been divided usually into two alternating sets, forming a *shed*. One row of weights is fastened to the stationary part of the warp shed, hanging straight down from the header band. The alternating warp threads are attached to a horizontal shaft, called a *heddle*, that is moved backward and forward, behind and in front of the stationary warp threads as the shuttle with the weft passes through the warp. This group of warp threads also has a set of loom weights attached which sometimes clash together as the heddle bar is pulled to and fro.

It is assumed that the loom was made of wood: warp beams, side posts, shed and heddle bars, and various horizontal shafts necessary to separate the different warp threads. Barber, researching the evidence for the use of shed and heddle, concluded that the principle, although not the true shuttle, was well known by the Early Bronze Age (1991:109–113). Occasionally, an excavating team uncovered postholes and loom weights in an undisturbed context on a living floor, giving us a clear picture of the

width from posthole to posthole. One example is found at the Early Neolithic site of Tiszajeno, Hungary, where the row of loom weights extended 185 cm (Selmeczi 1969:17–23). Barber (1991:103) published estimates of widths between loom postholes from several sites—Late Neolithic Switzerland, 40 to 50 cm; Troy II, 110 cm; and Late Neolithic Gomolava, 120 cm—which demonstrates how differently the craft was practiced.

Weaving was very likely going on continuously throughout the life of the settlement, but the heaviness and shape of the weights vary perhaps in concert with the type and weight of the warp. For example, the average weight of a phase IV cylinder is 74 g (figure 6.19a), whereas the phase V pyramidal shape with rectangular base is 1370 g (figure 6.18 [plate 6.12a]). Wear traces were noted for some weights during the cataloging process; the line drawing suggests how the inside of the cylinder weight was worn down during use (figure 6.19a). It has also been reported that Scandinavian weavers working with a warp-weighted loom adjust the different sizes of weights used at the same time by tying more warp threads to heavier weights and fewer threads to lighter weights (Barber 1991:96, 97). Table 6.4 illustrates a bimodal distribution of loom weights. The cylindrical form (plate 6.9b, c) clusters in phase IV, and the pyramidal weights are linked to phase V; however, the overall sample size is too small for deriving serious inferences. With the exception of one stone example (SF 3622, figure 6.22b [plate 6.12e]) and a few coarsely shaped and perforated examples of rough, thick, pottery (figure 6.19b [plate 6.12g] and plate 6.12f), all loom weights are of baked clay. Characteristically for Neolithic loom weights, however, not all are modeled carefully.

The main loom weight shapes (see table 6.4) include:

- *Cylinder*, with lateral perforation (figure 6.19a). Of the fourteen cylinder weights, twelve were recovered from phase IV contexts and are of fairly uniform size (plates 6.9b, c, 6.10a, 6.11). Several are fractured (plate 6.9b, d). Length is 6 to 7.7 cm, diameter is 11.5 to 15.4 cm, and weight ranges from 600 to 950 g.

- *Bag, pear, and cone shape*, all with perforation at the top and a rounded base. There is great variation in the size of these weights; a small bag shape from phase III is 165 g (figure 6.20 [plate 6.8d]), while another, more conical example, from phase IV, weighs 1170 g (figure 6.21 [plate 6.9a]).

- *Pyramids* vary greatly in size (compare plate 6.12a–c with d and e); many are fragmentary (plate 6.11c, d). When complete, the form of the rectangular base and the top perforation is consistent (figures 6.18, 6.22a, b; plates 6.10b, 6.11a,

Table 6.4. Distribution of Loom Weights Over Time

Type	I	II	III	IV	V	X*	Total	%
Conical	0	0	0	1	0	1	2	3
Cylindrical	0	1	0	12	1	0	14	24
Discoid	0	0	0	3	2	1	6	10
Pear-shaped	1	0	1	1	1	1	5	9
Pyramidal	0	0	0	0	17	4	21	36
Ring-shaped	0	3	3	1	2	0	9	16
Unidentifiable	0	0	0	0	1	0	1	2
Phase total	1	4	4	18	24	7	58	100
Phase percent	2	7	7	31	41	12	100	

* X indicates unphased or mixed contexts.

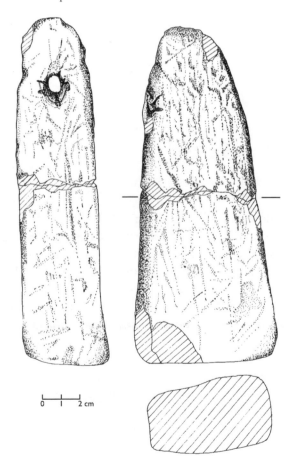

Figure 6.18. Loom weight, phase V: SF 1028, plate 6.12a.

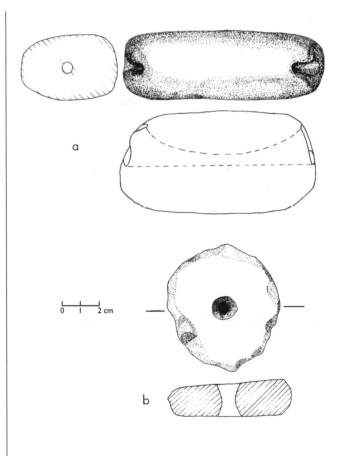

Figure 6.19. Loom weights: (a) Phase IV, SF 304b, cylinder with wear marks; (b) phase V, SF 372, sherd, shaped and perforated, plate 6.12g.

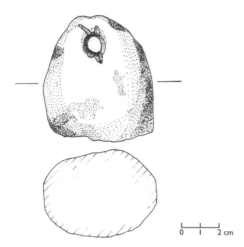

Figure 6.20. Loom weight, bag or pear shape, phase III: SF 492, plate 6.8d.

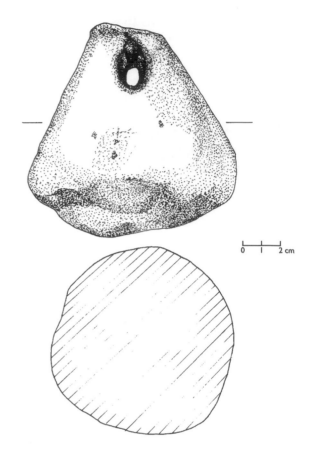

Figure 6.21. Loom weight, bag or pear shape, phase IV: SF 3060, plate 6.9a.

b, 6.12a–e). Twenty-one were found at Sitagroi, seventeen in secure contexts linked to phase V.

- *Ring weights* (figure 6.23 [plate 6.8a–c]), represented by nine examples, appear in phases II, IV, and V. External diameters range from 4.7 to 8.7 cm, internal diameters from 1.6 to 2.3 cm; all are carefully shaped and baked. This shape has also been described as a pot base. A type of pointed-base cup is part of the phase V pottery assemblage but not from earlier phases; thus we may be describing an artifact with multiple applications over time. A similar clay ring is published from Troy (Schliemann 1970:440, no. 630).

The site of Servia provides comparanda for two shapes, ring and pyramidal (Carington Smith 2000: 225, 239; pl. 4.20a, b); a bag or pear shape is illustrated from Karanovo (Hiller and Nikolov 1997: Taf. 68:5); Hochstetter published Kastanas cylinder and pyramidal forms (1987: Taf. 37:1, 5, 7); Rasson reported on the Divostin loom weights (1988: 337–338); and most recently Carington Smith reviewed many Greek and Balkan reports of these ubiquitous artifacts (2000:233–238). Weavers at EBA Archontiko used pyramidal shapes also of varying weights (150 g to 1050 g) which are very similar to the phase V EBA Sitagroi examples (figures 6.18, 6.22a) with top perforations (Papaefthymiou-Papanthimou and Pilali-Papasteriou 1998:187, fig. 5).

Anchors and Hooks

The baked clay "anchor" and hook assemblage is fragmentary for the most part (for example, plate 6.11e, f) and includes twenty-six hook forms (figures 6.24a [plate 6.13d]; figure 6.24b [plate 6.13a]; figure 6.25 [plate 6.13c]; figure 6.26 [plate 6.13b]; figure 6.27) and twenty-one anchor pieces (figures 6.28–6.30 [plate 6.13e–p]). The latter objects look something like an anchor and the term has been conventionally used (Carington Smith 2000:248–263; Weisshaar 1980), although any connection with sailing, ships, or the sea is highly unlikely. All examples were recovered from phase V or from disturbed contexts near the surface of the mound, as shown in table 6.5.

Although formally distinct, anchors and hooks have been frequently tabulated together as a group, possibly because they seem intuitively designed for the same general purpose of holding something.

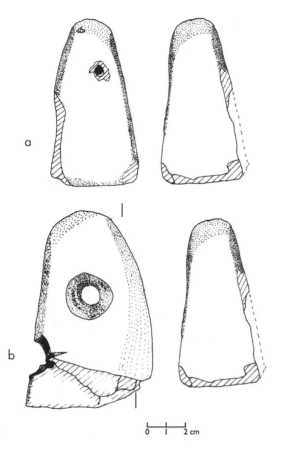

Figure 6.22. Loom weights, pyramid shape, phase V: SF 495, plate 6.12d; (b) SF 3622, plate 6.12e.

Both are modeled from a narrow length of clay, the shank, 1 to 3.5 cm thick and between 6.0 and 9.0 cm long. It is swung up to form the single arm of a hook, like a three-dimensional letter J, or is swung up both left and right to form the anchor. In section, the shank of both hook and anchor is more or less rectangular, although there are examples of round hook sections (figure 6.24 [plate 6.13d]; figure 6.27). The anchor has a single frontal piercing of its shorter, thicker shank (figure 6.30 [plate 6.13f]), while the hook has one (figure 6.24a [plate 6.13d]; figure 6.25 [plate 6.13c]) or two frontal piercings

Table 6.5. Distribution of Hooks and Anchors (All Phase V)

Type	Phase V	%
Hooks	26	55
Anchors	21	45
Total	47	100

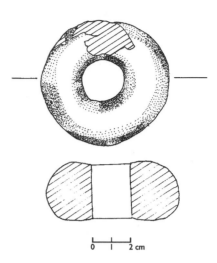

Figure 6.23. Loom weight, ring shape, phase III: SF 5017, plate 6.8a.

(figure 6.24b [plate 6.13a]; figure 6.26 [plate 6.13b]) near its double-pointed top. The fragments break with some regularity at two stress points: the hooks (figures 6.24–6.27 [plate 6.13a–d]) at the inner curve where the arm swings up (wear marks were observed in this hollow); the anchors (figures 6.28–6.30 [plate 6.13e–p]) at or just below the suspension hole and at the arm curve.

The tensile strength of these small baked clay artifacts was limited, and they could not be expected to withstand much pressure; thus only lightweight material could have been suspended. Both forms might have been used as auxiliary tools in the weaving process. It is not difficult to imagine the shank of these artifacts slipped over a peg or suspended by a string or thong from a post. The flattish back of the hook would fit against a surface, and its double shank perforation (figure 6.24b [plate 6.13a]; figure 6.26 [plate 6.13b]) suggests need for more secure support at times. The shorter, thicker anchor shank makes it more likely that it would have been suspended by a cord or thong slipped through the single hole. The high upswing of the arms suggests that these could have held supplementary weft threads, reeled off a spindle and then fed from the anchor to the loom. One preserved arm (figure 6.28b [plate 6.13e]) swings rather high, suggesting that archaeologists confronted with just an

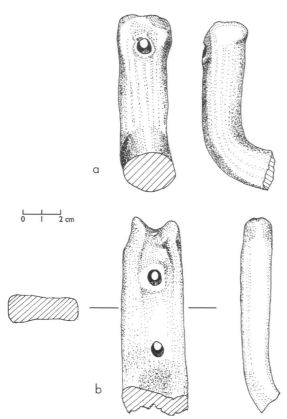

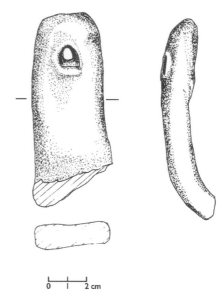

Figure 6.25. Hook/anchor shank, phase V: SF 539, plate 6.13c.

Figure 6.24. Hook/anchor shanks, phase V: (a) SF 57, plate 6.13d; (b) SF 529, plate 6.13a.

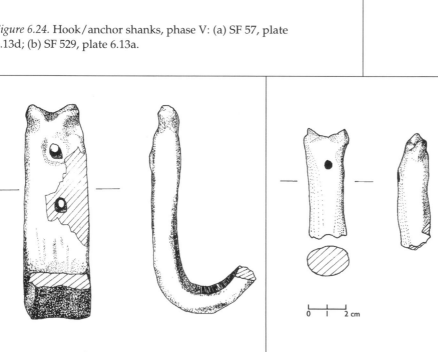

Figure 6.26. Hook shank, phase V: SF 538, plate 6.13b.

Figure 6.27. Hook/anchor shank, phase V: SF 1668.

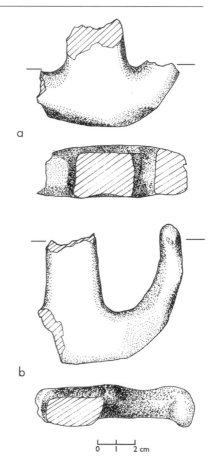

Figure 6.28. Anchor fragments, phase V: (a) SF 1334, plate 6.13n; (b) SF 1080, plate 6.13e.

244

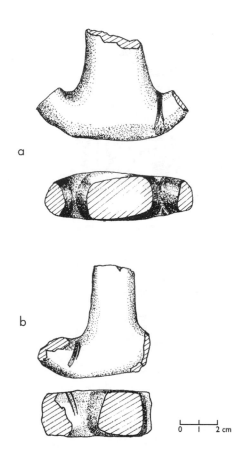

Figure 6.29. Anchor fragments, phase V: (a) SF 1681, plate 6.13g; (b) SF 5447, plate 6.13j.

cited above, studies of anchor and hook fragments from the archaic "blue" phase at Poliochni (Brea 1964) are comparable to the Sitagroi artifacts. Compare the lower portion of a Sitagroi anchor shank (figure 6.28b [plate 6.13e] to two Poliochni artifacts (Brea 1964: LXXXIII: b, e), both with the same high, upswinging arm.

Treuil (1992) published the findings from Deshayes' excavations (from 1961–1975) at Dikili Tash. There are many formal similarities between the two Drama Plain sites of Sitagroi and Dikili Tash in ceramics and other aspects of material culture. Unexpectedly, neither hooks nor anchors are much discussed by Treuil; however, it is possible that the record will change when the excavated materials from the years after 1975 are published. Nevertheless, one fragment from among the group of artifacts presented as "scoops" (Marangou 1992: 137–142, pl. 163f) is described as a handle having a half-moon or subtriangular section, dated with uncertainty to the Late Neolithic or Early Bronze Age. Because of the widening at the top end and the frontal perforation, this fragment seems comparable to Sitagroi hook shanks, all from the EBA.

arm fragment might interpret it, perhaps correctly, as part of a schematic figurine or a pot handle.

Drawings of anchors from Servia (Carington Smith 2000:261, 262) and Kritsana, Armenochori, and Saratsé, plus a horizontally pierced hook from Ayios Mamas (Heurtley 1939:203, fig. 67f–k) are comparable to the Sitagroi assemblage, and all are dated to the EBA. Weisshaar (1980:33–49, figs. 1:6–9, 2:3) sorted these and other examples (including pieces reported from sites including Saratsé, Mikhalitch, Argissa, Lerna, and Kastanas) into ten types based on the form found most frequently at certain sites. The Kirrha type had a horizontal perforation near the top of the shank, a characteristic never noted at Sitagroi. In addition to the examples

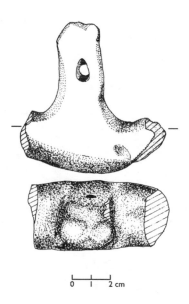

Figure 6.30. Anchor fragment, phase V: SF 2448, plate 6.13f.

COLLATERAL EVIDENCE

Impressions of Basketry, Mats, and Textiles on Clay

Sitagroi craftspeople, while preparing pottery for firing, unwittingly provided us with important evidence of fiber perishables. Freshly modeled pots were set on mats or cloth to dry, allowing the woven pattern to become impressed in the soft, unbaked clay. Firing baked the pot and preserved the impression. Discussion of these sherds is limited here, since appendix 6.1 is a report of the elements and techniques employed in producing fiber perishables at Sitagroi. The distribution of the impressions is provided in table 6.6.

Fifty-eight impressions, representing coiling and plaiting of mats and baskets plus faced plain-weave textiles, were recovered; the majority (44) came from phase III contexts. The phase I impression (SF1439; plate 6.19; figure 6.31a) was examined by several scholars, including Elizabeth Barber, who noted that it could represent a faced linen weave, in which the weaver chose to use a heavier yarn for either the weft or warp (Barber 1991:273). As noted earlier, it is an extremely important find, for it may be the first concrete example of textile production in prehistoric Greece. Carington Smith, who also examined the impression, wrote (personal correspondence) that it represented a high standard of weaving in the Middle Neolithic.

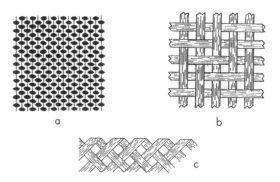

Figure 6.31. Impressions on clay, phase I (a), phase III (b, c). Schematic drawings: (a) weft-faced, plain-weave textile (for example, SF 1439 [plate 6.19]); (b) twill-plaited, 2x2–interval mat (for example, SF 1410 [plate 6.17], SF 1724 [figure 6.12; plate 6.15]); (c) mat edging, selvage technique (for example, SF 1639 [plate 6.18]).

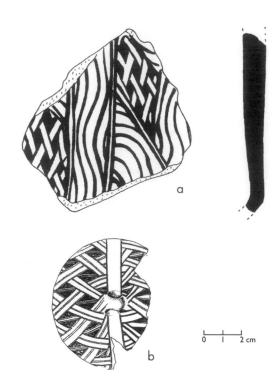

Figure 6.32. Painted designs of woven patterns on pottery, phase III: (a) Black paint on red burnished background, plain weave, SF 5583; (b) graphite-painted "webbing" on large lid, Pot 254 (see volume 1: figure 12.7:2; plate XLI:1).

Overall, the impressions show thin, finely prepared mats, not too practical as floor covering, but clearly selected by potters as surfaces on which their wares could dry. Rasson has also pointed out (personal communication, July 2001) that the impressions might have been deliberate, a form of decoration, since they could have been scraped off if the makers really didn't want them. A plain weave with double warp and weft, the so-called basket or double weave (Barber 1991:126–127), is the main type of pattern, based on a study of the inventory cards on which rubbings appear, and it accounts for the majority (88%) of the impressions (plates 6.15–6.18; figure 6.31b). Single plain weave (figure 6.31) is not strongly represented, less than 10%; there is one impression of coiling (SF 1542; plate 6.14). Mat makers wishing to produce a round mat would have selected this latter method. In the appendix to this chapter, Adovasio and Illingworth state that this technique is used to produce containers, hats, or bags. The impression of a plaited twill

Table 6.6. Distribution of Impressions on Clay

Type	I	II	III	IV	V	X*	Total	%
Cloth	1	0	1	0	0	0	2	3.5
Cord	0	0	0	0	6	2	8	14
Mat	1	0	41	2	2	0	46	79
Unidentifiable	0	0	2	0	0	0	2	3.5
Total	2	0	44	2	8	2	58	100
Percent	3.5	0	76	3	14	3.5	100	

* X indicates unphased or mixed contexts.

mat (SF 1639; figure 6.31d [plate 6.18]) shows how the maker wove in the end elements to finish off the edge of the mat, producing a self-edge or "selvage." Another impression shows the edge of another plaited twill mat, or the two-by-two twill, which was not woven back in (SF 5611; plate 6.16). Appendix 6.1 presents a discussion of the elements and techniques employed in producing fiber perishables at Sitagroi.

As for comparanda, sherds with textile or mat impressions have been recovered from virtually every site in Greece and the Balkans. Selected examples include, in Greece: Dhimitra (Grammenos 1997: PIN. 36:3), Achilleion (Winn and Shimabuku 1989a: figs. 4.18:1, 2; 4.31:4; 4.44; 4.45), and Servia (Carington Smith 2000:240–248); in Bulgaria, Karanovo (Hiller and Nikolov 1997: Taf. 96, 97); and in the former Republic of Yugoslavia, Divostin (Adovasio and Maslowski 1988:345–356) and Selevac (Tringham and Krstić 1990:670, pl. 10.1).

Painted and Incised Designs on Pottery

The weaving patterns on pottery probably indicate the borrowing of designs (or inspiration) back and forth, within the restrictions of each craft. It is not likely that we can determine the primacy of either craft. Still, Barber has observed that the narrow, stacked pictorial friezes on Greek geometric and earlier pottery provide occasional evidence for the quirks of producing cloth (1991:365–372 and 370, fn. 10), and that stacked registers are more natural in textiles. I am persuaded that certain designs on pottery described below also reflect textile patterns.

Regularly channeled, incised, excised, and painted geometric designs occur on pottery in groups of horizontal, vertical, and curving lines. Patterns similar to these can also be produced in textiles by weavers using threads of different colors

and textures. Simple angles and herringbone patterns in textiles are created by offsetting each line of weft; the centered dot and the edging triangles are made by supplementary weft. Barber refers to most of these patterns as weft designs (1991:293). Without textile remains these interpretations will always be questioned, but several graphite decorations on pottery look exceedingly like webbing (for example, figure 6.32a, b; also volume 1: figure 12.4). The weaving patterns can be identified on decorated sherds from the onset of the settlement, but examples, including almost whole vessels, are the most varied during phase III. A few examples from phases II and III are given here; the plates referenced are found in volume 1.

Phase II:
> White painted net: plate LXXXIV: bottom, 1
> Orange-on-orange paint (herringbone?): plate LXXXIV: top, 7

Phase III:
> Incised body fragment with centered dot: plate LXXIII: 2
> Graphite paint, checkerboard: plate LXXXIX: 6
> Graphite paint, net: plate LXXXVIII: top, 1b
> Black-on-red painted, net and dot: plate XCI: top, 2a
> Incised vessel and stand base: plate LXX: 2, 3
> Excised ware: plate XCII: top left: 6
> Graphite paint: plate LXXXVII: top: 14, 18, 19
> Graphite paint on lid, webbing: plate XLI: 1; on bowl: plate XLI: 3a, and this chapter, figure 6.32b.

Baked clay figurines dressed with painted aprons edged with triangles, and others with incised belts and skirts, depicted with hanging tassels, fringe, or string, provide a less ambiguous link between spinning and weaving and the fabrics used for clothing. Barber argues that the string skirt was a feature of women's wardrobes depicted in one way or another for 20,000 years. She proposes that this "peek-a-boo" garment was donned when the wearer wished to announce that she was sexually and socially available (1991:255–258). If valid for our Sitagroi material, it is a powerful argument for how textiles, including the use of string, potentially convey significant information (Gimbutas 1982: map 3, pls. 13, 21, fig. 8). Some examples from volume 1 (Gimbutas 1986:230–237) include naturalistically modeled figurines such as a seated torso with painted, tasseled, or fringed back aprons (volume 1: figure 9.14); a seated figurine fragment, including one leg with a painted front apron with triangle edging (volume 1: figure 9.20); and a figurine with incised lines circling the hip (belt?), from which a string (?) with tasseled ends hangs down and covers the body except the pubic area (volume 1: figure. 9.21).

Bone and Shell

A small group of artifacts of bone and shell are referred to here because of their likely association with textiles but are reported on in greater detail in chapter 2 (bone) and chapter 9 (shell). I discuss herein shell buttons and bone needles and smoothed, grooved, and/or pointed tools.

Among these artifacts of bone, only one can be surely identified as to use. This is a finely polished, small and pointed artifact from phase III with remnants of a smoothly made perforation at the now-fractured end (figure 2.4d); it was clearly a needle.

Two *Spondylus* shell buttons (this volume, chapter 9: figure 9.17 [plate 9.14a]; figure 9.18 [plate 9.20b]), both from phase III, are differentiated from beads by the V-shaped perforations on the back. These perforations allow the button to be affixed to a textile (or leather) by thread, yarn, string, or even a thin sinew.

Although the true shuttle was not invented (or needed) until sometime around the tenth century AD in the Mediterranean (Barber 1991:85 n. 3; 107), several of the bone artifacts from Sitagroi might have been used as weft shuttles with yarn hitched into the notch of these fairly smooth and slender tools. Potential weft shuttles include an unbroken, grooved deer metapodial (plate 2.4) recovered in

the EBA Burnt House but not in association with the spindle whorls. [6] Phase III yielded other bone artifacts, all fractured; thus we do not have the full length. One is notched (plate 2.5d). A possible notched net-mending tool may be found in the phase III assemblage (plate 2.5c). Other pointed pieces, fashioned from metapodials or rib splinters (plate 2.1), look like perforators, awls, or possibly pin beaters (plate 2.5a) for pushing down the weft threads on a loom.

Faunal Evidence

Earlier in this discussion I indicated that the phase III faunal evidence suggests the increased economic importance of wool-bearing sheep. This inference is based on Bökönyi's analysis of the refuse bone (volume 1, chapter 5:68–69) and illuminated by an interesting study of modern flock management that describes the differing strategies sheep managers use to obtain the maximum amount of meat, milk, or fleece (Payne 1973:281–303). Payne found that if subsistence was the desired end, the herd was composed of half mature and half immature animals. If the herd manager wanted wool production, however, mature sheep dominated the flock. These strategies can explain the changes observed in the archaeological faunal record.

Bökönyi reported that woolly sheep were among the domesticated animals (volume 1 [Bökönyi 1986]:76–81), and thus it appears that fleece was available. In his study, a quantitative sample of sheep bones was analyzed and the ratio of male to female and mature to immature animals was calculated (volume 1 [Bökönyi 1986]:80, table 5.8). The almost equal percentages of mature versus immature sheep bones during phases I and II indicate that sheep were kept for meat, milk, and wool. However, in the Late Neolithic/Chalcolithic phase III, animals were kept to obtain wool: the older, ostensibly larger animals provided more fleece. In phase IV, there is again mixed animal management, but the data from phase V suggest a renewed interest in the secondary product, wool. These statistics provide powerful evidence for economic decisions.

The amount of wool produced by the Sitagroi flocks can be estimated by reference to the remarkable archive of the Mycenaean palace economy at Knossos. The Mycenaean tablets provide detailed information regarding sheep, shepherds, flocks, fleece, wool, spinners, weavers, and dyers (Killen 1964:1–15; Burke 1998:107-110, 119–150). One unit of wool, "lana," is estimated as weighing 3 kg, which equals the fleece from four sheep (Melena 1975:13–15). The proposed allowance of 5 kg of wool per person for protection and warmth in the Aegean balances with Bronze Age Mesopotamian clothing rations (Halstead 1981:327). Scholars whose work has focused on the Knossos tablets indicate that, in the Late Bronze Age, the annual yield of wool was between 0.60 and 0.75 kg per sheep, with the higher figure representing wool from males.

Thus, a village of 40 to 100 persons, as estimated for Sitagroi (volume 1 [Blouet 1986]:142) would require something like 400 to 1000 sheep to provide the necessary wool. With the use of other grazing lands in summer, this number of sheep could be maintained in winter on 40 to 100 hectares of lowland. This is a rough estimate, since a number of issues have not been addressed, such as the number of males and females kept for breeding, the number of subadults for meat, and the number of castrated males (castrates grow larger and presumably give more wool).

SYNTHESIS: SPACE, TIME, AND FORM

The number, variability, and association of objects and features in space and through time offer provocative evidence for the practice and place of spinning, weaving, and mat making, specifically among the forms and distribution of artifacts in relation to phases III and V.

Recovery in phase III accounts for one-fourth of all whorls and more than three-fourths of all impressions. Most of the incised whorls were made during phase III. Weaving motifs were painted and incised on pottery, clothing was painted or incised on figurines, and sheep seem to have been kept for their fleece. I believe the importance of textile production is the connection among these four observations.

Isolation of architecture was ambiguous in phase III, and it was difficult to associate specific spaces with specific activities. Compensation is provided in part by a profusion of finds associated with hearths and artifact-rich destruction levels

from Square MM 16-50 (volume 1 [C. Renfrew 1986b]:212–215; see also this volume, chapter 12), allowing for interpretation of many activities, both domestic and extra-domestic in nature. Along with a great deal of building rubble (burnt daub), part of a hearth, and a destroyed square building, many classes of artifacts were recovered. Finds include clay figurines, tripods, pottery (see volume 1, chapters 9–12), miniature furniture (see this volume, chapter 11), tools for spinning and weaving[7] (dozens of whorls; see, for example, plates 6.1b, d, g; 6.2b, c, h; 6.3b, c, e, f; 6.4d, h; one weight [plate 6.8b]), many impressions (for example, plates 6.14, 6.16, 6.18), evidence for metalworking (sherds with splashes of copper or copper slag; see this volume, chapter 8), and imported raw materials (shell [see this volume, chapter 9], flint [see this volume, chapter 3], and stones for polished artifacts [see this volume, chapters 4 and 5]).

Rich evidence for spinning and weaving was also found in contexts of the EBA phase Va and Vb, from which half of all the whorls and loom weights, virtually all the spools, and all the hook and anchor shapes were recovered. Every whorl shape is represented, including a few incised examples; the most numerous are the biconical, truncated cone, and flat artifacts.

Two building episodes of particular interest were exposed in the excavation of the four contiguous 10-m squares, PN, PO, QN, QO (volume 1 [C. Renfrew 1986a]:19), placed at the summit of the mound (volume 1 [C. Renfrew 1986b]:184–203). These are referred to as the Burnt House (phase Va) and the Bin Complex (phase late Vb). The Burnt House (BH) has been discussed earlier in detail (volume 1 [C. Renfrew 1986b]:190–203; C. Renfrew 1970a; Elster 1997; this volume, chapter 5), but our interest here concerns the seven biconical whorls (two are illustrated; see figure 6.1c; plate 6.6a). Carington Smith (2000), discussing the Servia finds, writes that five or six whorls are the most to be expected in a family home since no spinner uses more than two or three. On this basis we can propose three spinners in the BH. That brief statement can only introduce the kinds of activities implied for the three householders and/or for others in the village: keeping sheep, managing the flock, acquiring wool or flax, preparing fleece or flax, making whorls and spindles, preparing the looms, setting up the yarn, negotiating weaving time, entering into trading associations, and so on.

The Bin Complex was very rich in sets of textile tools, exposed during the clearing of a series of floors, hearths, ill-defined walls, and clay-lined bins (volume 1 [C. Renfrew 1986b]:187–188; this volume, chapter 12). Because of the absence of postholes, Renfrew speculated that at least some of the area represented a courtyard associated with structures close to the surface of the mound and thus destroyed. Each discrete excavated unit (for example, QN 7) represented an observed or arbitrary stratum or layer. QN 7 (volume 1 [C. Renfrew 1986b]: 187) exposed a group of pyramidal weights (for example, plates 6.10b, 6.11a–d, 6.12b, c) near a wall and another nearby in an ash deposit associated with a feature that may have been a hearth.[8] The clustering of weights could indicate storage but probably indicates weaving and the presence of a loom. Several shapes of spindle whorls were found at the same level; most were biconical except for a domed one with a flat base (plate 6.5h), a truncated cone (figure 6.4g [plate 6.7a]), and a flat shape (unillustrated). Hook fragments were also exposed (plate 6.11e, f).

QN 8 includes a hearth, two clay-lined bins, a floor with two anchor fragments (SF 1690, 1737), four whorls (two biconical, one flat, and one spherical), and a loom weight.[9]

The deposit[10] in area QO 8 (volume 1 [C. Renfrew 1986b]:188) was exceedingly rich (pots, bone and stone tools, slag, etc.) in association with the tops of two fragmentary hooks, two anchors (plate 6.13e), several spools (for example, figure 6.17b), one weight, and many spindle whorls of various shapes (biconical, flat, truncated cone, and shallow-faced) all from the same level, plus a worked bone artifact that may have been used as a weft shuttle.

PN 7 (volume 1 [C. Renfrew 1986b]:187) yielded two loom weights, both reportedly found in one of the bins (the large pyramidal artifact is illustrated in figure 6.18 [plate 6.12a]). Other artifacts recovered included three hook fragments and two spindle whorls.[11]

Such a profusion of finds leads to some conclusions: the evidence is strong that textile production took place in several locations of a domestic nature: on the floor or near a wall of a house, and in or near a hearth. Alternately or additionally, spinning and weaving may have been practiced in an area outside of or between houses. Such a place might have first been selected because of the attractions of space, light, and fresh air and then became established by habit. The upright loom was easily movable by two people in case of inclement weather, just as the householders of modern Sitagroi village moved their drying racks of tobacco under shelter when rain struck. The regular co-association in the EBA of whorls and weights with anchors and hooks, artifacts whose usage is ambiguous, supports my interpretation that such tools are also associated with fiber working and formed part of the weaver's tool kit.

"Reading" these artifacts from the Chalcolithic and EBA leads to a picture of enormous liveliness and activity among craftspeople and artisans working in various media, negotiating space, raw materials, assistance, and the like. Production, consumption, gender roles, and site-formation processes are some of the topics that revolve around this complex recovery. A review and further analysis of these artifacts and their contexts appears in chapter 12.

The economic significance of woven goods in these prehistoric periods cannot be overemphasized, especially given what we know of the later Aegean cultures and the importance of textile production (Barber 1991, 1994; Burke 1998). As already noted, the Sitagroi trading network was wide: we know of three lithic sources, one supposedly close to the Bulgarian coast (chapter 2), one east in the Xanthi Basin, and one north of Lake Volvi (chapter 4); shell is known to have come from the south, from the Aegean coast (chapter 9). Sitagroi textiles undoubtedly played a significant role in this exchange system.

NOTES

[1] G. Ioannou (1987) published an old poem that captures the powerful metaphorical role of spinning and weaving for Greek society. It serves as a fitting introduction to this chapter: *Kokkini klosti demeni stin anemi tiligmeni dos' tis klotso na yirisei paramithi n' archinisei* (A red thread is tied

and wrapped around the spool. Give it a kick to turn and start telling a tale).

[2] Professor Elizabeth Barber served as consultant on this chapter. I very much appreciate her sharing with me an enormous wealth of knowledge. If I have gotten the history and technology right, it is due to her teaching; all mistakes are, of course, my own.

[3] Jane Renfrew discusses the dearth of flax seeds in the Sitagroi sample (chapter 1), although this plant was represented at other sites in the region (see table 1.12).

[4] Illustrated sherds impressed with string include two surface finds plus others from EBA phase V contexts (see volume 1: figure 13.13:6, 7; plate XCVIII, bottom: 1–8). For an analysis of Sitagroi textile, basket, and mat impressions on pot fragments, see this volume, appendix 6.1 by Adovasio and Illingworth.

[5] Early Neolithic Servia-Varytimides (Carington Smith 2000:227–232) yielded several dozen "spools"; only one is perforated, in this case, horizontally through the waist. Carington Smith provides a list of Neolithic comparanda from sites including Otzaki, Tsani, Achilleion, Elateia, Dhimini, Sesklo (see also Papaefthymiou-Papanthimou 1992: pl. 9,

perforated spools) and from the Bronze Age sites of Thermi, Tiryns, and Mycenae (Carington Smith 2000:227, 228). We are grateful to Ken Wardle for providing comparable information from Nea Nikomedia. At Nea Nikomedia, "spools" are distinguished from the approximately 100 "waisted weights" (Wardle 1996).

[6] Burnt House whorls: SF 3336, 3340, 3341, 3354, 3399, 4302, 4430.

[7] MM 16-50: 39 whorls, 20 impressions, 1 weight.

[8] Bin Complex QN 7 pyramidal weights: SF 1042, 1043, 1050, 1058; spindle whorls: SF 1022, 1049, 1059, 1063, 1064, 1065, 1068.

[9] Bin Complex QN8: anchor fragments SF 1690, 1737; spindle whorls: SF 1093, 1097, 1851, 1852; loom weight: SF 1087.

[10] Bin Complex QO 8: hooks: SF 1665, 1671; anchor fragments: SF 1080, 1085; spools: SF 1003, 1038, 1766; weight: SF 1029; whorls: SF 1030, 1033, 1040, 1047, 1051, 1072, 1073, 1077, 1082, 1084, 1090, 1718, 1856, 1858, 1859, 1861, 1863–1866.

[11] Bin Complex PN 7: weights: SF 1028 and 1032; hook fragments: SF 1729, 1730, 1731; whorls: SF 1025 and 130.

Appendix 6.1.
Basketry and Textile Impressions

J. M. ADOVASIO AND J. S. ILLINGWORTH

The basketry discussed in this appendix includes several distinct kinds of items, including rigid and semi-rigid containers (or baskets proper), matting, and bags. Matting includes two-dimensional or flat items, whereas baskets are more clearly three-dimensional. Bags may be viewed as intermediate forms because they are more or less two-dimensional when empty and three-dimensional when filled. As Driver (1961:159) points out, all of these artifacts can be analyzed in a similar fashion because the overall technique of manufacture is the same in all instances. Specifically, all forms of basketry are manually woven without frame or loom; thus, they technically constitute a class or variety of textile. In the present context, however, the term textile is restricted to fully or infinitely flexible materials, such as cloth or fabric, produced using a frame or loom.

Three major subclasses of basket weaves are usually viewed as mutually exclusive: twining, coiling, and plaiting. Twining denotes a subclass of basket weaves manufactured by passing moving (active) horizontal elements called wefts around stationary (passive) vertical elements called warps. Twining techniques may be employed to produce containers, mats, and bags, as well as fish traps, cradles, hats, clothing, and other "atypical" basketry forms. Coiling denotes a subclass of basket weaves manufactured by sewing stationary horizontal elements (the foundation) with moving vertical elements (stitches). Coiling techniques are used almost exclusively in the production of containers, hats, and, rarely, bags. Mats and other forms are seldom, if ever, produced by coiling. Plaiting denotes a subclass of basket weaves in which all elements pass over and under one another without meeting or engagement. For this reason, plaited basketry is technically described as unsewn. Plaiting may be used to make containers, bags, and mats, as well as a wide range of other nonstandard forms.

Coiling and plaiting, each represented by a single structural type, are represented at Sitagroi. A single textile type, faced plain weave, also occurs at the site.

ANALYTICAL PROCEDURES

Fifty-eight basketry or textile-impressed potsherds were recovered. High-resolution, scaled photographs of six sherds with their directly associated positive plasticine casts and rubbings of twenty specimens were received for analysis at the R. L. Andrews Center for Perishables Analysis, Mercyhurst Archaeological Institute, Erie, Pennsylvania. While the photographed specimens proved amenable to detailed attribute analysis following the protocols specified by Adovasio (1977), the rubbings were not sufficiently clear to permit such scrutiny. Nonetheless, as discussed below in the section called "Internal Correlations," the rubbings were useful in supplementing data obtained from the photographs.

All of the specimens in the photographs were measured using a Helios needle-nosed dial calipers and were corrected utilizing ratios derived from the centimeter scales in the photographs. The measurement error factor is approximately ±2.65%.

The radiocarbon determinations reflect information published in volume 1 (C. Renfrew [1986e]:172, table 7.1; 173, table 7.3) and Preface table 1 in this volume.

CRITERIA OF CLASSIFICATION

The six photographed positive impressions (plates 6.14–6.19) include one example of coiling, four of plaiting, and one probable textile. The coiled specimen was assigned to a single structural type based on the kind of basket wall or foundation technique used and the type of stitch employed. The specimen was also examined for the type of rim finish, method of starting, work direction, decorative patterns and mechanics, type and mechanics of mending, form, wear patterns, functions, method and preparation of foundation and sewing elements, raw material, and type of splice.

The four plaited specimens were assigned to one structural type based on the interval of element engagement. Plaited specimens were also examined for selvage treatment, shifts, method of preparation of elements, form, wear patterns, function, decorative patterns and mechanics, type and mechanics of mending, and raw material.

The lone textile fragment was assigned to a single structural type based on the interval of engagement and relative size of the warp and weft elements. The specimen was also examined for selvage treatment, floats or other warp/weft manipulations, proportion of warps and wefts, form, wear patterns, function, decorative patterns and mechanics, type and mechanics of mending, and raw material.

THE SITAGROI BASKETRY INDUSTRY

Coiling

Type I: Close coiling, bundle (?) foundation, split stitch on both (?) surfaces (figure 6.1.1; plate 6.14)
 Number of specimens: 1 (SF 1542)
 Type of specimen: Wall fragment
 Number of forms represented: 1
 Type of form represented: unknown
 Work direction: Right to left

TECHNIQUE AND COMMENTS. A foundation consisting of what appears to be a bundle of grasses or small-diameter reeds is sewn with intentionally split stitches that pierce the bundle. It is likely that stitches were intentionally split on both surfaces (see "Internal Correlations" below). The original

configuration of the work surface (that is, concave or convex) is unknown. The impression shows the non-work surface. No rim finish is apparent. Splices have moving ends bound under (compare Adovasio 1977: figs. 107b, 108b). The specimen appears to be somewhat irregularly sewn, but stitches are relatively closely packed. No decoration is apparent. The original specimen may have been watertight by virtue of the foundation type and relative tightness of the stitching. The configuration of the original vessel is unknown.

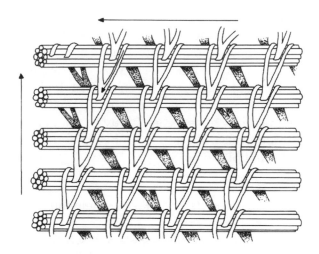

Figure 6.1.1. Schematic of type I basketry: Close coiling, bundle (?) foundation, split stitch on both (?) surfaces. The arrows indicate direction of work.

MEASUREMENTS
 Range in diameter of coils: 2.84– 3.06 mm
 Mean diameter of coils: 2.93 mm
 Range in width of stitches: 4.61–3.72 mm
 Mean width of stitches: 4.97 mm
 Range of gaps between stitches: 0.80–1.42 mm
 Mean of gaps between stitches: 1.17 mm
 Range and mean coils per centimeter: 2
 Range and mean stitches per centimeter: 2

RAW MATERIALS
 Bundle, unknown
 Stitches, unknown

Small Find	Context	Phase	Dates (calibrated)	Specimens
	MM 27			
1542	Level 27	III	4600–3500 BC	1

Plaiting

Type II: Twill plaiting, 2/2 interval (figure 6.1.2)

Number of specimens: 4 (SF 1724 [plate 6.15], SF 5611 [plate 6.16], SF 1410 [plate 6.17], SF 1639 [plate 6.18])

Type of specimens: Wall fragment with selvage, 1 (SF 1639); wall fragments without selvage, 3 (SF 1724, SF 5611, SF 1410)

Number of forms represented: 4

Type of forms represented: Mats

TECHNIQUE AND COMMENTS. Single elements pass over each other in a 2/2 interval. No shifts are present. One specimen (SF 1639 [plate 6.18]) exhibits a 90° selvage (Adovasio 1977: fig. 130). All specimens appear to be made of leaves that resemble bilaterally split *Yucca* sp. or reeds that look like either *Scirpus* sp. or *Typha* sp. The original specimens appear to have been lightly to moderately worn through use. All appear to be portions of flat mats or small placemats.

MEASUREMENTS

Range in diameter of plaiting elements: 0.82–14.39 mm

Mean diameter of plaiting elements: 8.18 mm

Range and mean angle of crossing of plaiting elements: 90°

RAW MATERIALS. Split reeds or leaves, genus/species unknown

Small Find	Context	Phase	Dates (calibrated)	Specimens
1410	ZA 63	I	5500–5200 BC	1
5611	MM 63	III	4600–3500 BC	2
1724	MM 47			
1639	MM 27	III	4600–3500 BC	1

Textile

Type III: Plain weave (figure 6.1.3; plate 6.19)

Number of specimens: 1 (SF 1439)

Type of specimen: Wall fragment without selvage

Number of individual forms represented: 1

Type of forms represented: Unknown

TECHNIQUE AND COMMENTS. Plain weave is the most elementary of all textile techniques and is the functional equivalent of simple plaiting, 1/1 interval in basketry. Single warps and wefts pass over and under each other in a 1/1 interval. Each weft element passes over and under successive warp units at a 90° angle, and each successive weft reverses the procedure of the one before it. In this impression, the warps and wefts are consistently of unequal size; hence, the specimen is not balanced. Without selvages, it is impossible to determine with certainty whether the larger diameter elements are warps or wefts. As a result, it is impossible to specify whether the specimen is warp faced or weft faced. In this situation, it is probably best to follow Barber (1991:127) and use the generic term "faced"

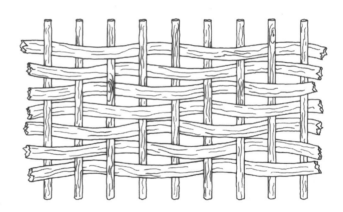

Figure 6.1.2. Schematic of type II basketry: Twill plaiting, 2x2 interval. This schematic depicts rigid plaiting elements as would be expected for a basketry construction—for example, plates 6.15–6.18.

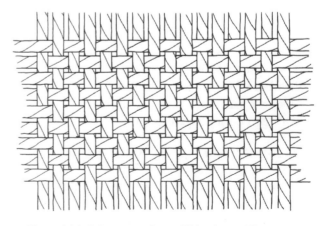

Figure 6.1.3. Schematic of type III basketry: Plain weave.

for this example of plain weave. In this regard, it should be noted that one section of the specimen exhibits what may be either V warp splices or, perhaps, more likely, weaving wedges (see Barber 1991:177, fig. 6.5). Weaving wedges are areas filled in from the selvage edge of a fabric with extra weft courses when the tension on the warps is uneven, producing a gap that must be closed. If these are weft wedges, then the fabric is warp faced. In any case, the warps and wefts appear to be fully flexible single-ply Z-spun or two-ply, S-spun, Z-twist elements. With the exception of the possible weft wedges which, if correctly identified, were clearly added for structural purposes, there are no warp/weft manipulations suggesting decorative devices. The original specimen, although it exhibits one small tear, appears lightly worn and apparently was part of a cloth or fabric of indeterminate configuration.

MEASUREMENTS

Range in diameter of smaller elements: 0.89–1.13 mm

Mean diameter of smaller elements: 0.98 mm

Range in diameter of larger elements: 1.24–1.74 mm

Mean diameter of larger elements: 1.44 mm

Range and mean of smaller elements per centimeter: 5

Range and mean of larger elements per centimeter: 4

RAW MATERIAL. *Linum* sp. (?)

Small Find	Context	Phase	Dates (calibrated)	Specimens
SF 1439	ZA 62	I	5500–5200 BC	1

INTERNAL CORRELATIONS

Technology

Despite the low frequency of fully analyzable specimens represented, a number of observations may be made about the basketry and textile industries at Sitagroi. First, it is clear that both of these interrelated but technologically distinct crafts are present in the Neolithic and later milieus of northeast Greece. Second, there is incontrovertible evidence in the Sitagroi assemblage for two of the three major subclasses of basketry (coiling and plaiting), as well as one structural type of textile (faced plain weave). Third, it is apparent that at least three functional kinds of items are represented: coiled containers or trays of indeterminate shape(s), mats, and cloth fabric of unknown configuration.

Fourth, it seems apparent that at least simple plaited matting was probably a common component of the basketry assemblage, based on its numerical preponderance in the photographed sample (four out of six specimens) and its high incidence (seven out of twenty specimens) in the rubbings. Plain-weave fabrics and coiled vessels may well have been equally (or more) common than plaited products, but direct evidence for their relative abundance is not available from the sherds themselves. In this regard, it should be stressed that the recovery of loom weights strongly suggests the extensive manufacture of plain weave and, perhaps, other varieties of textiles. Fifth, the recovery of a solitary piece of plain weave in conjunction with loom weights indicates the presumable use of heddle looms.

Sixth, it is unfortunate that the original sherds or positive impressions were not available for analysis, as more technological details would doubtlessly be available from first-hand scrutiny. This is especially true in the case of potential raw materials utilized by Sitagroi weavers. With the possible exception of the plain-weave fabric, which appears to be made of *Linum* sp., there are only indirect indications of the other plants exploited for perishable manufacture at Sitagroi. As discussed by Elster in chapter 6 and J. Renfrew in chapter 1, the evidence for flax is slim. However, *Linum* sp. was identified at nearby sites (table 1.20), and it is not surprising that the seeds are scarce since they have multiple uses, as food, oil, and medicine. As noted above, the foundation of the coiling may be a grass bundle or bunch of fluviatile reeds, while the source of the stitches is unknown. Similarly, although the plaited mats are clearly made of bilaterally split *Yucca* sp., *Scirpus* sp., or *Typha* sp.-like plants, their exact identification is impossible.

Chronology

Although it is very likely (see the section below, "External Correlations") that basketry and textiles were in continuous use at Sitagroi, no subclass or individual type of basketry is actually represented throughout the sequence. Type II (twill plaiting, 2/2 intervals) occurs in occupational phases I (5500–5200 BC), III (4600–3500 BC), and IV (3500–3100 BC). An unanalyzed rubbing (see below, "Analytical Procedures") indicates that Type II also occurs in occupational phase V (3100–2200 BC). Type III (plain weave) is restricted to phase I. The occurrence of Type I (close coiling, bundle (?) foundation, split stitch on both (?) surfaces) is limited to phase III. No basketry or textiles are directly documented for phase II (5200–4600 BC).

Given the obvious discontinuities in the temporal distribution of basketry and textile remains at Sitagroi, it is presently impossible to reconstruct even a skeletal outline for the development of these industries based solely on their impressions on clay. However, by combining these data with the study of changes in form and distribution through time for loom weights, spindle whorls, and other textile tools (this volume, chapter 6), it can be inferred that cloth production was maintained throughout the occupational phases at Sitagroi, although perhaps at different levels of intensity. Also, the faunal evidence from Sitagroi (volume 1, chapter 5) seems to indicate a growing focus on sheep-raising, which would have yielded progressively greater amounts of fleece.

EXTERNAL CORRELATIONS

As of this writing, the Sitagroi basketry and textile impressions are some of the oldest direct evidence for both of these industries in the Neolithic of northeast Greece, specifically, and southeastern Europe, generally. They are not, of course, the oldest examples of either craft in greater Europe or the contiguous Near East. Conclusive evidence now exists that plant fiber-based products such as cordage, basketry, netting, and even bona fide textiles were being produced in the Pavlovian variant of the Gravettian tradition in Central Europe by no later than 23,050 BC (25,000 BP) (Adovasio, Soffer, and Klíma 1996; Adovasio, Hyland, and Soffer

1997; Adovasio et al. 1998, 1999; Soffer et al. 1998a, 1998b; Soffer, Adovasio, and Hyland 2000). Similar materials are in evidence only a few thousand years later elsewhere in Upper Paleolithic Europe (Adovasio et al. 1992; Cheynier 1967; Leroi-Gourhan 1982; Leroi-Gourhan and Allain 1979) and in penecontemporaneous Near Eastern contexts (Nadel et al. 1994). Thereafter, the production of cordage, cordage by-products, basketry, and textiles is continuously, if episodically, documented through Mesolithic times in Europe (Clark 1952) and Epi-Paleolithic times in the Near East (Rimantiene 1979; Schick 1986).

Given the deep antiquity of perishable plant fiber–based artifacts in Europe and their ubiquity and abundance in ethnographically documented hunting and gathering, agricultural, and pastoral societies (see Adovasio et al. 1999; Soffer et al. 1998b), their occurrence in Neolithic and later contexts at Sitagroi is neither unprecedented nor unexpected. Indeed, plant fiber–based industries are probably as old in southeastern Europe as they are in the rest of the continent. Unfortunately, only limited evidence of earlier manifestations of these crafts currently exists in Greece. The documentation includes apparently numerous but incompletely described twill (?) plaited mat impressions from Achilleion, phases IIb (ca. 6100 BC [8050 BP]), IIIa–IIIb (approximately 6000 BC [7950 BP]), and IVa–IVb (ca. 5900–600 BC [7850-7550 BP]) in Thessaly (Gimbutas, Winn, and Shimabuku 1989). Additionally, there is evidence of twill plaited mat impressions at Anza I (6100–5800 BC [8050–7750 BP]), and Anza II (5800–5300 BC [7750–7250 BP]) (Gimbutas 1976b), and suspected spindle whorls from Nea Nikomedeia, also in early seventh millennium BC (ninth millennium BP) contexts (Rodden 1962, 1964a, 1965). Elster, in chapter 6, has presented comparanda, but we can add here a published Type III impression from Paradeisos (Johnson 1987: 76 [fig. 41:249]).

Despite the limited (but growing) data from mainland Greece or the Aegean, relatively abundant evidence of plant fiber–based crafts is nonetheless available from the contiguous Near East. As Barber (1991:127) notes, negative impressions of balanced plain weave and plain weave with double warps and wefts (that is, basket weave) are reported from Jarmo, Iraq, from ca. 7000 BC (8950 BP) (Adovasio 1975–1977:224; Adovasio 1983:425). Jarmo also produced impressions of the oldest coiling and twill plaiting currently known from the entire eastern circum-Mediterranean. Interestingly, although the Jarmo twill plaiting is literally indistinguishable from the Sitagroi material, the bundle foundation coiling from Jarmo is somewhat different. Specifically, while the Jarmo coiling employs a bundled fluviatile reed foundation, it is sewn with noninterlocking stitches in a left-to-right work direction, the exact opposite of the pattern at Sitagroi (Adovasio 1983:426).

By ca. 6500–6000 BC (8950–7950 BP), actual basketry, textiles, cordage, and netting exist in both preceramic sites such as Nahal Hemar in the Judean Desert (Schick 1986) and Neolithic Çatalhöyük on the Anatolian plateau (Burnham 1965). While space precludes an extended discussion of these assemblages, it is significant that the Çatalhöyük materials include balanced and faced plain weaves as well as twill plaited and bundle foundation coiled basketry. Interestingly, although twined textiles are represented at both Çatalhöyük and Nahal Hemar, no early twining is currently known from the Greek mainland.

Within the next thousand years, basketry manufacture and textile production are so widely documented in the Near East that it is tempting to interpret the appearance of textiles and basketry in southeastern Europe as a prime example of diffusion. In this scenario, the techniques of plain weave, twill plaiting, and bundle foundation coiling are but the artifactual signatures of the imported "package" of Near Eastern domesticates and/or their makers. As satisfying as this picture may still be to some researchers, it is much more prudent to view these crafts as local expressions of a very ancient and wholly indigenous European weaving tradition rather than a phenomenon derived—part, parcel, wheat, and sheep—from the Near East.

Whatever their ultimate ancestry, the basketry and textile impressions from Sitagroi not only provide additional direct and incontrovertible evidence of these industries in early Neolithic Greece, but also—to paraphrase O. Soffer—inform us of an all too often ignored aspect of Paleolithic and Neolithic economies, the labor of women.

ACKNOWLEDGMENTS

The authors wish to express their deep and profound thanks to the Sixteen Men of Tain as well as to Booker Noe for their untiring support throughout the production of this chapter. This appendix was edited by J. Jones and D. R. Pedler, Mercyhurst Archaeological Institute.

Appendix 6.2.
Catalog of the Tools of the Spinner, Weaver, and Mat Maker

Ernestine S. Elster

The catalog is first sorted by phase: I, II, III, IV, V, and Mixed Contexts. Under each phase the artifacts are registered in numerical order in this sequence: hook-anchor, impression, loom weight, whorl/spool. For each artifact, information follows this order: Small Find number; context; published illustrations, if any; description: this may include but will not always include whether complete or incomplete; surface decoration: presence/absence, location, color, finish; and measurements: weight (Wt) in grams (g), the following in cm: diameter (D), height (H), width (W), and string hole diameter (HD). All available information and measurements are included.

PHASE I

Impressions

1410 ZA 63; figure 6.1.2; plate 6.17
Twill plaiting or double weave without selvage; mat (?); vessel base fragment; impression on underside
L: 10.5; W: 1.3

1439 ZA 62; figure 6.1.3; plate 6.19
Faced plain or single weave; cloth; vessel base fragment; impression on underside; surface: black.
L: 6.1; W: 4.0; Th: 0.8

Loom Weights

64 IL 6
Pear shaped; half fragment, broken at end, crack across the whole object; surface: light gray
L: 6.8; W: 6.0

Whorls

77 OL 7
Biconical; surface: smooth, matt, red/light gray; core: light gray
H: 2.0;D: 3.4; HD: 0.5

114 KL 13
Flat; slightly raised upper face; surface: coarse, porous, light brown
H: 0.6; D: 3.0; HD: 0.2

263 OL 2
Flat; approximately 2/3 preserved
H: 1.6; D: 5.1; HD: 0.8

277 JL 16
Biconical; approximately 1/2 preserved; surface: light gray/brown
H: 3.4; D: 5.8; HD: 1.25; Wt: 101

535 ML 22
Shallow conical; approximately 1/2 preserved; surface: matt, black/dark brown; core: coarse, light gray/brown
H: 2.0; D: 5.3; HD: 0.8

JL 105
Shallow conical incised zigzags around edge; surface: dark gray encrustations on all around; micaceous inclusion in core
H: 3.1; D: 5.9; HD: 0.9

2502 JLs
Shallow conical; hole not completely pierced
H: 2.0;D: 4.0; HD: 0.4

2522 JL 103
Deep conical; truncated cone with slightly concave sides; surface: slightly burnished, beige; core: beige
H: 3.3; D: 3.1; HD: 0.5

2541 JL 105
Flat; surface: dark gray encrustations; core: micaceous inclusions; decoration: incised zigzags around edge
H: 1.1; D: 5.9; HD: 0.9

PHASE II

Loom Weights

756 ZA 55
Cylindrical; approximately 1/2 preserved; surface: coarse, light gray
W: 113.0; H: 4.1; D: 6.0; HD: 1.3

2347 KL 111
Ring shaped; approximately 1/2 preserved; surface: matt, gray; core: coarse temper
W: 145.0; H: 3.4; D: 6.3; HD: 1.5

2393 KL 114
Ring shaped; approximately 2/5 preserved
H: 1.4;D: 5.1

2667 KL 117
Ring shaped; approximately 1/4 preserved; burned
W: 120.0; H: 3.8; D: 6.2; HD: 1.3

Whorls

145 KL 2
Flat; approximately 2/3 preserved
H: 1.1; D: 6.0; HD: 0.8

403 KM 2
Biconical; core: gray
H: 4.1; D: 5.0; HD: 0.9

413 KM 2
Shallow conical; decoration: three pairs of parallel incisions on top
H: 1.2; D: 4.0; HD: 0.6

421 KM 2
Shallow conical; one large chip
H: 1.2; D: 3.8; HD: 0.6

424 KL 2
Shallow conical; decoration: angular incisions on top form a network pattern
H: 2.5; D: 4.5; HD: 0.5

509a ML 8
Shallow conical
W: 22.0; H: 1.2; D: 4.6; HD: 0.5

534 LL 2
Deep conical; truncated cone; approximately 1/2 preserved; surface: smooth, red; underside: flat, matt, dark gray; core: red with dark gray edges
H: 2.9; D: 5.6; HD: 0.8

809 ML 8
Shallow conical; surface: matt, red with some light brown patches
W: 22.0; H: 1.2; D: 5.0; HD: 0.5

1546 ML 8
Shallow conical; surface: matt, gray, edge: red/gray, underside: matt, red/gray
W: 29.5; H: 2.2; D: 4.5; HD: 0.5

1549 ML 8
Deep conical; approximately 1/2 preserved, including entire base; surface: smooth, shiny, light brown/gray; core: coarse, dark brown
H: 5.0; D 4.2; HD: 0.9

1611 ML 7
Flat; approximately 2/5 preserved; surface: smooth, shiny, light brown, edges: dark brown; core: light gray with brown patches
H: 1.3; D: 5.8; HD: 0.5

2619 KL 115
Spherical; ovoid; approximately 1/4 preserved; surface: matt, gray
H: 3.7; D: 7.0

2659 KL 117
Spherical; approximately 1/3 preserved; surface: matt, gray; core: red; poorly fired
H: 3.4; D: 5.0

3618 ZG 34; figure 6.6f
Shallow conical; decoration: incised lines on top; serrated edges
W: 18.5; H: 1.5; D: 3.9; HD: 0.5

5025 ZB 131
Reworked sherd
W: 8.5; H: 1.1; D: 2.5; HD: 0.5

5200 ZA 55s
Biconical

5351 ZA 59s
Biconical; incomplete

Phase III

Impressions

481 ZA 42
Double weave; baked clay fragment; surface: coarse, gray
L: 7.0; W: 3.0

1409 MM 40
Cloth; vessel base fragment; impression on the underside
L: 10.5; W: 9.7; Th: 1.5

1457 MM 43
Double weave; vessel base fragment; impression on the underside; surface: buff/pink with much encrustation
L: 6.8; W: 3.6; Th: 4.6

1470 MM 19
Double weave; surface: brick red, with encrustation
L: 6.7; W: 7.5; Th: 6.5

1471 MM 23
Unidentifiable; vessel fragment: base and side; impression on the underside
L: 5.5; W: 5.9; Th: 2.3

1481 MM 20
Double weave; baked clay; surface: dark gray with lighter patches
L: 8.0; W: 6.5; Th: 1.5

1487   MM 50
Double weave; triangular clay fragment, impressions on one side; surface: red.
L: 7.3; W: 4.8; Th: 1.7

1489   MM 20
Double weave; clay fragment; surface: red with black discoloration
L: 5.9; W: 4.9; Th: 3.5

1490   MM 19
Unidentifiable; clay fragment; underside: impressions; evidence of burning; surface: red
L: 9.0; W: 6.8; Th: 2.3

1491   MM 19
Double weave; vessel base fragment
L: 8.5; W: 7.8; Th: 1.4

1509   MM 27
Double weave; vessel base; surface: brown with black discoloration
L: 12.1; W: 4.3

1541   MM 27
Double weave; vessel base fragment, impressions on underside; surface: red/orange deep
L: 5.4; W: 3.5

1542   MM 27; figure 6.1.1; plate 6.14
Coil; clay fragment; surface: matt, pale red
L: 5.8; W: 3.7; Th: 1.6

1571   ML 115
Double weave; baked clay fragment; surface: matt, reddish/black
L: 8.8; W: 2.4; Th: 2.3

1586   MM 41
Double weave; baked clay fragment; surface: black; core: lighter
L: 4.5; W: 2.8; Th: 1.1

1597   MM 52
Double weave; clay fragment with different impression on each side; surface: light brown
L: 6.5; W: 4.0; Th: 1.5

1600   MM 21
Double weave; vessel fragment; surface: light brown
L: 4.5; W: 2.5; Th: 1.0

1630   MM 27
Double weave; vessel fragment; surface: light brown
L: 4.5; W: 3.5; Th: 0.7

1634   ML 107
Double weave; vessel fragment: base and side; surface: reddish; impression on the underside
L: 6.5; W: 5.0; Th: 1.5

1639   MM 27; figure 6.1.2; plate 6.18
Twill plaiting or single weave with selvage of flat mat; vessel fragment: base and side, impression on the underside; surface: reddish
L: 4.5; W: 5.4; Th: 1.0

1644   MM 53
Double weave; vessel fragment: base and side; impression on underside
L: 6.0; W: 5.3; Th: 1.3

1655   ML 105
Double weave; baked clay fragment; surface: light brown with black burnt traces; core: reddish
L: 7.6; W: 3.0; Th: 2.4

1724   ZA 47; figure 6.1.2; plate 6.15
Twill plaiting or double weave without selvage; baked clay fragment; surface: brown

1744   ZA 40
Double weave; vessel fragment: base and side; impression on the underside; surface: unburnished, black; core: light brown
L: 11.4; W: 9.5; Th: 1.9

1762   ZA 42
Double weave; vessel fragment: base and side; surface: unburnished, light red/light brown.
W: 13.2; Th: 1.5; H: 3.3

1763   ZA 43
Double weave; vessel fragment: base and side, impression on the underside; surface: unburnished, light red/light brown
L: 5.9; W: 1.4; H: 5.4

1764   ZA 41
Double weave; vessel fragment: base and side; surface: coarse, light red/gray/brown/black
W: 20.5; Th: 1.0; H: 8.4

3561   MMc 61
Double weave; vessel fragment: base and side; impression on the underside
L: 9.6; W: 9.0; Th: 2.0

3571   MMc 61
Single weave; baked clay fragment; surface: red
L: 5.0; W: 2.7; Th: 1.1

3602   ML 155
Double weave; vessel base, impressions on the underside
L: 10.3; W: 9.3; Th: 1.8

3721   ZJ 23
Double weave; baked clay fragment; surface: dark gray with brown encrustation
L: 5.2; W: 4.3; Th: 1.6

3740   ZJ 23
Double weave; baked clay fragment
L: 8.7; W: 6.1

3766 ZE 90
Double weave; baked clay fragment; surface: black
with encrustation
L: 5.2; W: 3.4; Th: 1.5

3768 ZG 21/22
Single weave; baked clay fragment; surface: light
gray
L: 8.6; W: 6.8; Th: 1.5

4422 ZG 30
Single weave; baked clay fragment; surface: gray,
impressions filled with buff encrustation
L: 3.3; W: 3.0; Th: 1.4

4810 ZG 33
Double weave; baked clay fragment
L: 4.5; Th: 1.2

4815 ZG 29
Single weave; baked clay fragment; surface: coarse,
red, possibly burned, impressions are slightly
blackened
H: 6.6; L: 3.6; W: 1.5

4908 MM 41
Double weave

5382 MM 27
Double weave; vessel base; surface: red

5383 MM 43
Double weave; vessel base; surface: black
L: 14.5; W: 11.5; Th: 1.5

5384 MM 40
Double weave; vessel base; surface: red
ZA 42; figure 6.32a
Red baked clay; surface: black on red paint with
weaving pattern
L: 10.0; W: 7.5; Th: 0.65–1.15

5611 MMc 63; figure 6.1.2; plate 6.16
Twill plaiting or double weave without selvage;
baked clay fragment
H: 7.2; L: 6.0; W: 1.5

5612 MMa 61
Double weave; baked clay fragment; surface: black
L: 7.4; W: 6.0; Th: 1.5

5617b ML 3
Double weave; baked clay fragment; surface: black
L: 7.1; W: 5.3; Th: 1–1.8

Loom Weights

220 ZA 42; plate 6.8c
Ring shaped; surface: coarse
D: 4.7; HD: 2.0

492 ZA 49; figure 6.20; plate 6.8d
Pear shaped
H: 4.0-4.5; W: 6.0; Th: 6.6; HD: 0.8; Wt: 165

1520 MM 36; plate 6.8b
Ring shaped; surface: smooth, dark gray, smudges
of burn marks
D: 5.7; HD: 2.1

5017 ZB 119; figure 6.23; plate 6.8a
Ring shaped
D: 6.8; HD: 2.2

Whorls

130 ZA 34
Deep conical; approximately 1/2 preserved; sur-
face: smooth, shiny, black; core: coarse, light brown
H: 3.5; D: 5.6; HD: 0.7; Wt: 95.0

159 MM 11; figure 6.16
Miscellaneous; four branches project in cruciform
shape; two branches broken; surface: grayish/red;
core: black
H: 1.9; L: 4.8; HD: 0.7

175 MM 17
Flat; slightly curved upper surface; one large chip;
surface: smooth, red with black areas; core: coarse,
red/light gray
H: 1.6; D: 4.9; HD: 0.6

179 MM 16
Shallow conical; concave base; surface: matt, light
brown
H: 1.5; D: 4.5; HD: 0.5; Wt: 27.5

182 MM 18
Deep conical; truncated cone; chipped: side, one on
top; surface: matt, red; underside: gray patches
H: 2.1; D: 4.0; HD: 0.6; Wt: 24.0

183 MM 19; figure 6.7a; plate 6.3c
Shallow conical; surface: light brown; decoration:
incised spirals radiating from center on top, serrated edge
H: 1.7; D: 3.5; HD: 0.4; Wt: 17.0

201 ZA 35
Shallow conical; approximately 2/5 preserved; surface: matt, black; underside: matt, light gray; core:
coarse, dark gray; decoration: incised radiating
chevrons and dots on top
H: 1.8; D: 7.6; HD: 1.0

219 ZA 42
Biconical; surface: smooth, black with brown
patches
H: 1.7; D: 2.5; HD: 0.5; Wt: 11.0

229 ZA 44; figure 6.7b
Shallow conical; surface: dark gray; decoration: ser-
rated edges
H: 1.7; D: 3.8; HD: 0.6; Wt: 26.0

231 ZA 47
Flat; loaf shaped, slightly raised toward hole;
approximately 1/3 preserved; surface: matt, black;
core: coarse, light gray
H: 1.6; D: 4.8; HD: 0.6

256 MLa 2
Flat; loaf shaped; approximately 1/2 preserved;
surface: matt, light brown with red patches; core:
coarse, light brown/gray
H: 1.4; D: 6.9; HD: 0.7

391 MM 21
Spherical; biconvex shallow, incompletely perfo-
rated; stone; surface: gray
H: 2.4; D: 4.1; HD: 0.9

392 MM 21; figure 6.15b; plate 6.4d
Reworked sherd; surface: matt, red; decoration:
painted black on red linear pattern on both faces
H: 0.8; D: 5.7; HD: 0.7; Wt: 35.0

466 ML 3; figure 6.3b
Deep conical; approximately 1/2 preserved; sur-
face: smooth, pinkish-yellow
H: 4.6; D: 4.9; HD: 0.8; Wt: 108.0

543 ML 2
Shallow conical; pinched on top; approximately 1/
2 preserved; surface: matt, black; core: coarse, black
H: 2.5;D: 6.2; HD: 0.9

737 MM 16; figure 6.9d; plate 6.3b
Flat; approximately 1/2 preserved; surface: matt,
red/gray; decoration: short incised lines on top
H: 1.2; D: 6.8; HD: 0.7; Wt: 63.0

739 MM 12,29; figure 6.13b; plate 6.3a
Shallow conical; two halves (joined with SF1659);
surface: matt, light brown/gray; underside: matt,
gray; core: light gray; decoration: incised concentric
circles on top, short radiating lines around edges
H: 2.5; D: 6.9; HD: 0.7; Wt: 77.0

740 MM 12
Flat; approximately 1/3 preserved; surface: matt,
light gray/brown
L: 4.1; H: 1.0; HD: 0.8

742 MM 12
Flat; approximately 1/3 preserved; surface: matt,
light gray/brown
H: 1.1; D: 6.6; HD: 0.6

746 MM 11
Shallow conical; approximately 1/3 preserved; sur-
face: coarse, black with light brown patches
H: 1.9; D: 4.5; HD: 0.5

747 MM 16; figure 6.9b
Flat, loaf shaped; approximately 1/4 preserved;
surface: coarse, light brown; decoration: incised
parallel and vertical lines on top
H: 1.3; D: 5.6; HD: 0.7; Wt: 63.0

777 ZA 47s
Shallow conical; surface: matt, red; decoration: on
top, sets of parallel incisions in a chevron-pattern
H: 1.5; D: 3.7; HD: 0.4; Wt: 17.5

808 MM 2z; figure 6.8e; plate 6.1b
Shallow conical; surface: coarse, porous, brown;
decoration: incised parallel lines on top
H: 1.8; D: 5.0; HD: 0.5; Wt: 32.5

841 MM 36; figure 6.6c; plate 6.2h
Shallow conical; surface: matt, dark gray; underside: dark gray; decoration: sets of parallel incisions
on top
H: 1.9; D: 4.1; HD: 0.6; Wt: 26.0

850 MM 40
Shallow conical; surface: matt, red-brown
H: 1.5; D: 4.6; HD: 0.6; Wt: 30.8

862 MM 41; figure 6.13a; plate 6.3f
Shallow conical; approximately 1/2 preserved; surface: matt, dark gray; decoration: incised network
pattern on top
H: 1.7; D: 6.9; HD: 0.6; Wt: 53.0

887 MM 43
Shallow conical; pinched on top; large chip; sur-
face: matt, light brown/gray
H: 2.1; D: 6.3; HD: 0.6; Wt: 70.0

890 MM 43
Shallow conical; pinched on top; surface: matt, light
brown
H: 1.3; D: 3.4; HD: 0.5; Wt: 14.0

1109 ML 107; figure 6.13c
Flat, slightly curved top; approximately 1/3 preserved; surface: matt, light brown decoration: sets
of parallel incisions on top, serrated edge
H: 1.1; D: 5.9; HD: 0.7

1126 ML 104
Flat; slightly curved top, slightly concave base;
approximately 1/2 preserved; surface: smooth,
light brown; core: coarse, light brown
H: 1.4; D: 6.3; HD: 0.6; Wt: 50.0

1222 ML 112; figure 6.11a; plate 6.1h
Shallow conical; one large chip off edge; decoration: sets of parallel angled incisions on top, surrounded by an incised circle and dot border,
serrated edge
H: 2.1; D: 4.6; HD: 0.5; Wt: 35.5

1223   MM 49; figure 6.3f
Shallow conical; surface: matt, light brown; underside: matt, dark gray
H: 2.0; D: 4.5; HD: 0.5; Wt: 32.5

1242   ML 112
Shallow conical; approximately 1/2 preserved; surface: matt, light brown, underside: matt, black
H: 1.1; D: 4.9; HD: 0.8

1250   MM 43
Shallow conical; approximately 2/5 preserved; surface: coarse, black; core: light brown patches
H: 1.8; D: 6.4; HD: 0.6

1254   MM 50; figure 6.11c; plate 6.2b
Flat; slightly raised around hole; approximately 1/3 preserved; surface: matt, black; core: matt, dark gray; decoration: incised radiating chevrons on top; serrated edge
H: 1.5; D: 6.6; HD: 0.7

1261   MM 50
Biconical; surface: matt, light gray/brown
H: 1.5; D: 3.5; HD: 0.5; Wt: 15.8

1266   MM 51; figure 6.6e; plate 6.1
Shallow conical; surface: gray; decoration: four sets of parallel incisions form a kind of net work pattern on top; serrated edge
H: 2.2; D: 5.1; HD: 0.5; Wt: 44.0

1267   MM 51; figure 6.7e; plate 6.2e
Shallow conical; approximately 5/6 preserved; surface: gray/brown; decoration: sets of incised concentric arcs around edges
H: 1.9; D: 4.7; HD: 0.6; Wt: 37.0

1275   ML 112; figure 6.7 f
Shallow conical; approximately 5/6 preserved; surface: matt, dark brown; decoration: incised radiating chevrons on top
H: 1.5; D: 4.2; HD: 0.5

1288   MM 52; figure 6.5 b
Biconical; surface: worn, matt, reddish brown/gray; decoration: incised angular elements and dots on top
H: 2.6; D: 3.9; HD: 0.5; Wt: 32.5

1297   MM 53; figure 6.11b
Shallow conical; concave faces; surface: reddish-brown; underside: smooth, dark gray; decoration: incised web-like pattern on top, serrated edge
H: 1.9; D: 3.6; HD: 0.4; Wt: 17.0

1423   MM 43; figure 6.12a; plate 6.3e
Flat; slightly raised upper surface, raised more strongly around hole; ca.1/3 preserved; decoration: incised pattern on top consisting of parallel lines and a rectangular element attached to one of them
H: 1.7; D: 7.0; HD: 0.6; Wt: 70.0

1431   MM 43
Shallow conical; approximately 5/6 preserved; surface: matt, dark gray with red and yellow-green patches
H: 1.7; D: 6.1; HD: 0.4

1437   MM 40; figure 6.12c; plate 6.1d
Shallow conical; approximately 2/5 preserved; surface: matt, red; core: light gray with red and black patches; underside: matt, red/light gray; decoration: incised chevrons and parallel lines on top
H: 1.9; D: 6.9; HD: 0.6

1440   MM 43; figure 6.11e; plate 6.2d
Flat; raised around hole; approximately 1/2 preserved; surface: matt, dark brown; underside: dark gray; decoration: incised web-like pattern on top, serrated edges
H: 1.8; D: 6.8; HD: 0.7; Wt: 78.0

1452   MM 41
Flat; approximately 1/3 preserved; surface: light brown/dark brown; edge: light brown
H: 1.1; L: 6

1458   ML 110
Shallow conical; approximately 1/3 preserved; surface: matt, light brown/red, underside: light gray; decoration: incised radiating chevrons on top, serrated edges
H: 1.6; D: 6.0; HD: 0.8

1462   MM 43
Flat; approximately 1/2 preserved; surface: matt, black/dark brown; core: coarse, black with brown edges
H: 1.0; D: 6.0; HD: 0.6

1468   MM 19
Shallow conical; approximately 1/2 preserved; surface: coarse, red/dark brown patches; underside: red/black
H: 1.9; D: 6.2; HD: 0.6

1484   MM 20
Flat; very slightly curved top; approximately 2/5 preserved; surface: light gray with red and black patches; core: coarse, red/light gray; underside: matt, dark gray/brown
H: 1.4; D: 6.0; HD: 0.9

1540   MM 50; plate 6.4 h
Reworked sherd; broken; coarse edges; surface: burnished, brown, underside: light brown
H: 0.8; D: 3.8; HD: 0.4; Wt: 14.0;

1543   MM 57; figure 6.7d; plate 6.2c
Shallow conical; approximately 1/3 preserved; surface: black/light brown; core: coarse, black; underside: light/dark brown; decoration: incised radiating chevrons and dots on top, serrated edges
H: 2.0; D: 5.6; HD: 0.7

1544 MM 50
Flat; top raised slightly toward the hole; approximately 1/4 preserved; surface: matt, dark brown/gray; decoration: incised chevrons (?) on top
H: 1.4; D: 6.8

1545 MM 21
Flat; approximately 1/2 preserved; surface: matt, brown
H: 0.8; D: 5.0; HD: 0.6; Wt: 26.5

1547 MM 21; figure 6.10
Flat; approximately 1/4 preserved; surface: matt, gray/brown; underside: dark gray/red; core: red; decoration: incised web-like pattern on top
H: 1.0; D: 7.2; HD: 0.7

1548 MM 21; figure 6.14c
Flat, slightly curved top; approximately 1/3 preserved; surface: matt, brown, underside: matt, red; core: light brown with a red lower edge; decoration: incised lines on top
H: 1.5; D: 7.8; HD: 0.7

1567 ML 116
Shallow conical; approximately 3/4 preserved; two fragments (joined with SF1576); surface: matt, brown; underside: brown; decoration: incised web-like pattern on top, serrated edges
H: 1.3; D: 6.6; HD: 0.4; Wt: 54.0

1627 ML 105
Shallow conical; approximately 1/2 preserved; surface: matt, light gray/brown; underside: red/brown; core: red/brown
H: 2.1; D: 5.3; HD: 0.5; Wt: 40.0

1629 ML 115
Flat; surface: matt, light/dark brown with shiny flecks; edge: coarse, light brown. W: 7.5; H: 0.5; D: 3.1; HD: 0.5

1636 MM 27
Flat, loaf shaped; approximately 1/2 preserved; surface: matt, light brown; decoration: incised radiating chevrons with connecting lines on top
H: 0.9; D: 6.2; HD: 0.6; Wt: 31.0

1640 MM 27; figure 6.9c
Flat; approximately 1/4 preserved; surface: matt, brown; decoration: incised concentric bands on top with punched dots between
H: 0.9; D: 8.1; HD: 0.7

1658 MM 27
Shallow conical; approximately 1/4 preserved; surface: matt, light gray; decoration: serrated edges
H: 1.5; D: 5.4; HD: 0.6

1684 MM 54; figure 6.11d; plate 6.2a
Flat; raised around the hole; approximately 3/4 preserved in three fragments (joined with SF1739,

SF4766); surface: matt, black; underside: matt, dark gray; decoration: incised chevrons and groups of lines on top, serrated edges
H: 1.4; D: 7.8; HD: 0.6; Wt: 76.0

1696 M 53
Flat; approximately 1/3 preserved; surface: matt, black; core: brown/light gray
H: 0.8; D: 6.8

1708 ZA 35
Flat; slightly raised toward hole; approximately 1/3 preserved; surface: smooth, shiny, dark brown; edges: smooth, red/dark brown
H: 1.3; D: 8.6; HD: 0.7

2925 ZG 14; figure 6.14d; plate 6.1c
Flat; approximately 1/2 preserved; core: gray with micaceous specks; decoration: incised parallel lines on top
H: 1.7; D: 7.1; HD: 0.7; Wt: 76.0

2933 ZG 15, figure 6.14b; plate 6.3h
Flat; very slightly curved faces; approximately 2/5 preserved; surface: black/pink; decoration: incised radiating chevrons between radiating lines on top, serrated edge
H: 1.2; D: 5.8; HD: 0.7

2942 ZG 16; figure 6.3e
Deep conical; truncated cone; surface: chipped, light brown
H: 2.1; Top D: 1.2; D: 4.7; HD: 0.6; Wt: 39.5

2946 ZG 18; plate 6.4a
Flat; raised very slightly toward hole; surface: gray
H: 1.3; D: 5.3; HD: 0.6; Wt: 42.0

2960 ZG 22; figure 6.7c
Shallow conical; slightly concave base; surface: light brown; decoration: incised sets of parallel lines on top
H: 1.7; D: 4.1; HD: 0.5; Wt: 26.3

2966 ZG 25
Flat; white marble; approximately 1/2 preserved; decoration: serrated edges
H: 0.6; D: 4.8; HD: 0.2; Wt: 27.0

2990 ZG 30, figure 6.5c; plate 6.1f
Biconical; decoration: incised parallel lines on top and around edges
H: 2; D: 3.5; HD: 0.4; Wt: 17.5

2991 ZG 30; plate 6.4e
Shallow conical; surface: matt, tan, with fingerprint impressions
H: 1.9; D: 4.0; HD: 0.4; Wt: 22.0

3128 ML 151; plate 6.4f
Shallow conical; concave base; surface: dark gray with light brown encrustation
H: 1.6; D: 4.2; HD: 0.6; Wt: 23.0

3145   ML 157
Shallow conical; surface: brown
H: 1.3; D: 5.9; HD: 0.8; Wt: 52.0

3406   ZG 15; figure 6.8b
Shallow conical; approximately 1/4 preserved; surface: tan; decoration: incisions on top, serrated edges
H: 1.8; D: 6.2; HD: 0.7

3419   MMc 60; figure 6.8c
Shallow conical; approximately 1/2 preserved; decoration: incised radiating lines on top and underside
H: 1.8; D: 4.8; HD: 0.6

3421   MM 60c; figure 6.8a
Shallow conical; decoration: serrated edges
H: 1.6; D: 3.5; HD: 0.5; Wt: 16.5

3424   MMc 60
Flat; raised slightly toward hole; approximately 1/4 preserved; surface: reddish
H: 1.5; D: 6.0; HD: 0.4

3444   ZG 20; figure 6.12b
Flat; raised strongly around hole; approximately 1/2 preserved; surface: orange; decoration: incised radiating lines on top
H: 1.6; D: 6.4; HD: 0.6; Wt: 45.0

3478   MMc 61; figure 6.6a; plate 6.2f
Shallow conical; decoration: incised radiating chevrons on top, serrated edges
H: 2.0; D: 3.8; HD: 0.5; Wt: 26.0

3488   MMa 61; figure 6.6b; plate 6.3d
Shallow conical; surface: dark gray; decoration: incised star-like pattern on top
H: 1.8; D: 4.2; HD: 0.6; Wt: 24.5

3541   MMd 65
Flat; approximately 1/3 preserved
H: 1.1; D: 7.0; HD: 0.8

3573   MMb 60
Flat; approximately 1/3 preserved; surface: matt, gray; core: tan
H: 1.1; D: 5.8; HD: 0.4

3588   ZG 23; figure 6.12d; plate 6.3g
Shallow conical; approximately 1/2 preserved; surface: matt, tan/gray; decoration: incised web-like pattern on top, serrated edges
H: 1.9; D: 5.8; HD: 0.6; Wt: 48.5

3589   MMd 67; plate 6.4b
Shallow conical; surface: matt, brown
H: 2.0; D: 4.5; HD: 0.4; Wt: 34.5

3732   ZJ 27
Flat; raised slightly toward hole; approximately 1/2 preserved; surface: dark
H: 1.8; D: 4.2; HD: 0.2; Wt: 29.0

3743   ZJ 26; figure 6.15a; plate 6.4g
Reworked sherd; chipped edges; surface: red; decoration: graphite painted curved lines
H: 0.9; D: 4.8; HD: 0.6; Wt: 22.0

4202   ZE 86
Flat; top slightly concave, raised around hole; approximately 1/2 preserved; surface: burnished, black
H: 1.6; D: 6.0; HD: 0.5; Wt: 64.0

4211   ZE 90; figure 6.5a; plate 6.1e
Biconical, decoration: incised radiating lines, originating at top and continuing to the edge
H: 2.4; D: 4.4; HD: 0.4; Wt: 35.5

4904   MM 41; figure 6.14a
Flat; slightly raised around hole; decoration: incised web-like pattern on top
H: 1.4; D: 6.7; HD: 0.6

4905   MM 43
Shallow conical

4907   MM 40
Shallow conical

5026   ZB 126r
Shallow conical; decoration: incised groups of concentric arcs on top

5027   ZB 126r
Shallow conical; decoration: incised groups of concentric arcs on top

5035   ZB 123r; figure 6.6d; plate 6.2g
Shallow conical; decoration: incised groups of chevrons on top, radiating from hole
H: 1.9; D: 3.8; HD: 0.4; Wt: 28.0

5191   ZA 44s; figure 6.4b
Flat; slightly raised around hole on both sides
H: 1.2; D: 2.9; HD: 0.5; Wt: 11.0

5195   ZA 46s; figure 6.8d; plate 6.1a
Shallow conical; decoration: on top incised lines, radiating from hole in a whirl-like pattern
H: 2.2; D: 5.1; HD: 0.4; Wt: 36.5

5196   ZA 48s
Biconical
H: 1.6; D: 3.7; HD: 0.4; Wt: 25.0

5554   MM 41
Shallow conical

5578   MM 20
Shallow conical; approximately 1/4 preserved; decoration: incised chevrons (?) and parallel lines on top, serrated edge
D: 5.4; HD: 0.5

5609   MM 60
Shallow conical; approximately 1/3 preserved; decoration: incised web-like pattern on top
H: 2.0; D: 6.4

5617a ML 155
Shallow conical; approximately 1/2 preserved
H: 1.5; D: 6.0

PHASE IV

Impressions

1140 MM 39
Double weave; vessel fragment: base and side;
impression on the underside; surface: reddish
L: 0.18; W: 0.7; Th: 2

3735 ZJ 20
Double weave; baked clay; vessel fragment: base
and side; impression located on the underside.
L: 12.7; W: 7.2

Loom Weights

125 ZA 31
Cylindrical, irregular; broken at one end; surface:
very coarse, dark gray/brown; unbaked.
Wt: 600

304 a ZD 6
Cylindrical; section: oval; top and underside: bro-
ken; surface: very coarse, brown/gray; unbaked
L: 14.0; D: 4.7–6.9; HD: 0.8; Wt: 765

304 b ZD 6; figure 6.19a
Cylindrical; oval in section with eccentric perfora-
tion; surface: fairly smooth, light gray-brown
L: 13.9; D: 5.1–7.3; HD: 0.9; Wt: 675

344 SL 14
Cylindrical; broken down all sides but one; surface:
coarse, gray; unbaked
L: 7.1; W: 5.2; Th: 4

346 SL 14
Cylindrical; surface: orange, coarse
L: 13; W: 7.6; Th: 1.5; Wt: 905

347 SL 11
Discoid; stone
D: 14.0; HD: 1.8; Wt: 805

476 ZE 8
Cylindrical; one side broken
L: 14.3; W: 7.4; Th: 5.7; Wt: 880

1346 SL 14
Cylindrical; slightly irregular in shape, eccentric
perforation; surface: coarse, reddish-brown; poorly
fired
L: 13.9; W: 7.8

2703 ZE 51; plate 6.10a
Cylindrical
H: 13.5; D: 6.5; HD: 1.3–1.6; Wt: 785

2778 ZE 72
Cylindrical; split asymmetrically, one face broken;
surface: slightly burnished, dark; core: dark gray
L: 8.1; D: 5.8

3057 ROc 73; plate 6.9b
Cylindrical; broken; surface: orange
L: 12; D: 6.3; Wt: 600

3058 ROc 73; plate 6.9c
Cylindrical; surface: pinkish-gray
L: 10.8; D: 6.2; HD: 0.8; Wt: 720

3059 ROc 73; plate 6.9d
Cylindrical; broken; surface: orange
L: 9.2; W: 7.1

3060 ROc 73; figure 6.21; plate 6.9a
Conical
L: 10.0; W: 9.8; HD: 0.7–1.0; Wt: 1170

5011 ZB 57
Discoid; pierced sherd; incomplete

5014 ZB 64
Ring shaped; incomplete

5448 ZHt 28
Discoid; pierced sherd
Th: 2.3; D: 9.2; HD: 0.5

Whorls

126 ZA 30
Deep conical; chipped on top; surface: smooth, red-
pink
H: 3.7; D: 5.2; HD: 0.8; Wt: 112.0

136 ZA 27
Biconical; approximately 1/4 preserved; surface:
matt, black; core: dark, brown; poorly baked
H: 3.5; D: 5.2; HD: 0.6

152 MM 7
Shallow conical; surface: light brown/gray; decoration: sets of incised parallel lines on top form a net
like pattern around hole
H: 1.2; D: 2.6; HD: 0.2; Wt: 8.0

155 MM 9; figure 6.3g
Shallow face; surface: smooth, black/light brown
H: 1.1; D: 4.5; HD: 0.6; Wt: 21.0

257 MM 10
Flat; chipped edges; surface: smooth, brown; core:
black.
H: 0.8; D: 5.2; HD: 0.5; Wt: 30.8

258 MM 10
Reworked sherd; chipped edges; surface: smooth,
light gray; core: gray
H: 1.1; D: 5.2; HD: 0.5; Wt: 35.8

305 ZD 7
Biconical; biconvex shallow; surface: matt, black, rubbed away in some areas; core: light brown
H: 1.2; D: 3.0; HD: 0.5; Wt: 13.5

319 ZE 7
Deep conical; slightly damaged round hole at top; surface: smooth, dark gray.
H: 5.1; D: 4.7; HD: 1.1

320 ZE 8
Deep conical; approximately 1/5 preserved; surface: smooth, shiny, black; core: light gray
H: 1.3; D: 4.0

343 SL 13
Deep conical; truncated cone; badly chipped all around; surface: smooth, shiny, light brown; core: coarse, light brown
H: 2.5; D: 5.4;Top D: 2.3; HD: 0.8; Wt: 75.0

345 SL 14
Shallow conical; approximately 1/2 preserved; surface: matt, red brown/black; core: light brown/gray
H: 2.2; D: 5.0; HD: 0.8; Wt: 68.0

348 SL 15
Shallow conical; hole not completely drilled through; surface: matt, dark brown/light brown, underside: dark brown
H: 1.6; D: 2.9; HD: 0.4

469 MM 2
Biconical; biconvex; surface: matt, black/light gray with red patches
H: 2.7; D: 3.4; HD: 0.7

542 MM 10
Flat; approximately 1/2 preserved; surface: smooth, light brown/red; edges: black/brown
H: 0.8; D: 6.4; HD: 0.9

712 MM 10
Flat; approximately 1/2 preserved; surfaces: one dark brown, the other light brown; core: light brown
H: 1.0; D: 5.8; HD: 0.4–0.7; Wt: 48.0

734 MM 13
Deep conical; approximately 2/5 preserved; surface: smooth, shiny, dark brown; hole surface: matt, black; core: coarse, brown
H: 3.8; D: 4.8; HD: 0.8; Wt: 65.0

893 MM 34
Deep conical; incomplete; surface: smooth, light brown/gray; core: black/dark gray
H: 3.9; D: 2.9; HD: 0.5

1129 ZE 8
Flat, loaf shaped; approximately 1/3 preserved; surface: matt, black; core: light brown
H: 0.8; D: 5.0; HD: 0.5

1131 ZE 9
Deep conical; approximately 1/3 preserved; surface: red/light gray with shiny flecks; core: black with red edges
H: 3.2; D: 5.0; HD: 0.5

1132 MM 2
Spool; bases broken off; surface: burnished at spots, pale gray
H: 3.5; D: 3.0; Top D: 2.8; Middle D: 2.6; Wt: 34

1144 MM 2
Spool
H: 2.5; D: 3.3; Top D: 3.2; Middle D: 2.9; HD: 1.1

1647 SL 11
Deep conical; approximately 3/5 preserved; four fragments joined; surface: smooth, gray
H: 4.2; D: 4.9; HD: 1.1

1749 MMb
Biconical; surface: light brown
H: 2.2; D: 3.0; HD: 1.1; Wt: 23.0

2111 ZB 100b
Biconical; surface: matt, gray
H: 3.2; D: 3.6; HD: 0.5

2112 ZB 101
Flat; surface: matt, red/orange
H: 1.7; D: 4.4; HD: 1.0

2708 ZE 55
Deep conical; approximately 1/2 preserved; surface: matt, gray; core: gray
H: 4.5; D: 4.4; HD: 0.6

2711 ZE 56
Deep conical; approximately 1/2 preserved; surface: matt, red; core: gray
H: 4.0; D: 4.9; HD: 1.0; Wt: 101.0

2721 ZE 61
Deep conical; approximately 1/3 preserved; surface: matt, gray; core: gray; poorly fired
H: 3.5; D: 4.8; HD: 0.7

2742 ZE 63; figure 6.3c; plate 6.5a
Deep conical; truncated top, slightly concave faces; surface: dark gray; burned
H: 4.0; D: 5.8; Top D: 2.6; HD: 0.9; Wt: 88.0

2753 ZE 67
Flat; stone: mica schist
H: 1.2; D: 9.4; Wt: 222.5

2757 ZE 68
Deep conical; approximately 1/2 preserved; surface: burnished, slightly blackened
H: 4.5; D: 5.7; HD: 0.7; Wt: 185.0

2765 ZE 69; plate 6.5e
Deep conical; eccentric hole; surface: matt, gray; core: reddish
H: 3.7; D: 5.4; HD: 0.9; Wt: 90.0

2770 ZE 69
Biconical; approximately 1/2 preserved
H: 3.5; D: 5.3; HD: 0.7; Wt: 74.0

2787 ZE 80
Shallow conical; approximately 1/2 preserved; surface: dark gray
H: 2.6; D: 4.7; HD: 0.7; Wt: 80.0

3043 ROc 65
Deep conical; approximately 1/2 preserved; surface: yellow/gray
H: 3.2; D: 5.1

3049 ROc 65
Biconical; chipped; light gray/light brown
H: 2

3203 ZHt 5; figure 6.3a
Deep conical; approximately 3/4 preserved; surface: matt, gray; core: gray
H: 5.2; D: 5.3; HD: 0.8; Wt: 110.0

3206 ZHt 5; plate 6.5f
Deep conical; truncated cone; surface: gray with slight natural encrustation
H: 3.8; D: 4.0; Top D: 1.8; HD: 0.6; Wt: 60.5

3224 ZHt 24
Biconical
H: 3.2; D: 5.9; HD: 0.7; Wt: 106.5

3227 ZHt 17; figure 6.2a
Biconical with flat base; approximately 1/2 preserved
H: 4.6; D: 5.0; HD: 0.8; Wt: 113.0

3231 ZHt 18
Flat; surface: matt, red/gray
H: 1.7; D: 4.6

3232 Zht surface
Biconical; approximately 1/2 preserved; surface: matt, gray; core: gray
H: 1.9; D: 2.8; HD: 0.5

3234 ZHt 20
Deep conical; truncated cone; approximately 1/2 preserved
H: 4.1; D: 5.5; Top D: 3.0; HD: 1.3; Wt: 120.0

3242 ZHt 22
Deep conical; asymmetric; approximately 1/2 preserved; surface: gray
H: 4.0; D: 4.5

3244 ZHt 24
Deep conical; truncated cone; surface: light brown, blackened in parts
H: 3.2; D: 5.9; HD: 0.7; Wt: 106.5

3248 ZHt 24
Deep conical; approximately 1/2 preserved; surface: dark gray
H: 5.4; D: 4.6; HD: 0.7; Wt: 122.0

3249 ZHt 24
Deep conical; approximately 1/2 preserved; surface: dark gray; core: large pink inclusions
H: 6.0; D: 4.7; HD: 0.8

3252 ZHt 24; figure 6.3d; plate 6.5b
Deep conical; truncated cone; surface: pale yellow/gray
H: 3.5; D: 6.0; Top D: 2.0; HD: 0.8; Wt: 105.5

3253 ZHt 24
Shallow conical; top broken off; surface: black; decoration: serrated edge
H: 3.2; D: 5.9; HD: 0.8; Wt: 109.5

3621 ZHt surface
Biconical; approximately 1/2 preserved; surface: matt, pinkish-gray
H: 4.2; D: 5.1; HD: 0.8

3682 ZHt 23
Reworked sherd; chipped edges; surface: dark gray
H: 1.0; D: 5.5; HD: 0.8; Wt: 36.0

3703 ZHt 22
Biconical; approximately 1/3 preserved; surface: slightly burnished, dark
H: 2.2; D: 4.6; HD: 1.0

3713 ZHt 13
Deep conical; incomplete; surface: matt, dark
H: 4.4; D: 1.0

3723 ZHt 22
Biconical; approximately 1/2 preserved
H: 3.8; D: 5.5; HD: 0.7

3783 ZHt 24
Deep conical; approximately 1/2 preserved; surface: orange/brown with buff encrustation
H: 4.2; D: 3.3

3901 ZJ 1
Deep conical; approximately 1/2 preserved; surface: matt, reddish/gray
H: 3.1; D: 6.0; HD: 0.7

3902 ZJ 1
Deep conical; truncated cone with slightly concave faces; top chipped
H: 3.2; D: 5.5; HD: 1.0

3903 ZJ 1
Shallow conical; approximately 1/2 preserved; surface: matt, pale gray
H: 3.4; D: 5.6; HD: 0.6

3909   ZJ 3
Deep conical, dome shaped; approximately 1/2 preserved; surface: matt, dark
H: 3.2; D: 5.9; HD: 1.1; Wt: 87.0

3914   ZJ 3
Deep conical; approximately 1/2 preserved; surface: matt, dark
H: 3.6; D: 4.9; HD: 1.0

3921   ZJ 18
Shallow conical; curved sides, concave base
H: 1.4; D: 4.4; HD: 0.8; Wt: 28.5

3924   ZJ 20; figure 6.9a
Flat; slightly domed top; concave base; surface: matt, gray
H: 1.1; D: 5.6; HD: 0.7; Wt: 37.5

4451   ZHt 11
Deep conical; approximately 1/2 preserved; surface: light brown
H: 4.1; D: 4.0

4545   ZHt surface
Shallow conical; chipped; surface: dark gray; core: large chips of grit
H: 3.5; D: 4.8; HD: 0.9

4593   ZHt 27
Reworked sherd; edges badly chipped; surface: buff
Th: 1.0; D: 5.0-5.5; HD: 0.5; Wt: 34.5

4594   ZHt 27
Deep conical; chipped sides and top; surface: buff
H: 2.1; D: 4.0; HD: 0.5

5006   ZB 57r
Deep conical; incomplete

5008   ZB 47s
Flat; incomplete
H: 0.8; D: 6.8; HD: 0.5; Wt: 58.0

5016   ZB 104r
Deep conical; incomplete

5021   ZB 106r
Shallow conical; incomplete
H: 0.9; D: 4.5; HD: 0.4; Wt: 27.0

5438   ZHt 23
Deep conical; incomplete

5446   ZHt 52
Biconical; incomplete; surface: red

PHASE V

Hooks and "Anchors"

57   ZA 4; figure 6.24a; plate 6.13d
Hook; fragment; perforated; surface: smooth, shiny, black; core: coarse, black; well fired
H: 8.4; W: 2.9; Th: 2.0; HD: 0.9

496   QO 5
Hook; top; surface: smooth, black; core: coarse, gray
H: 5.7; W: 2.0; Th: 1.7; HD: 0.8

529   QO 6; figure 6.24b; plate 6.13a
Hook; top (joins with SF 2211); surface: smooth, black; core: coarse, light gray
H: 10.1; W: 3.8; Th: 1.6; HD: 0.9

538   QO 6; figure 6.26; plate 6.13b
Hook; perforated with two holes; surface: smooth, burnished, black; core: coarse, gray
H: 10.8; W: 3.6; Th: 1.3; HD: 0.8

539   QO 6; figure 6.25; plate 6.13c
Hook; top; surface: lightly burnished, brown; coarse paste and temper.
H: 10.7; W: 4.0; Th: 1.8; HD: 1.2

706   PO 7
Hook; top; surface: pink/gray; well fired
H: 4.1; W: 3.2; Th: 1.8

1080   QO 8; figure 6.28b; plate 6.13e
Anchor; lower part preserved; surface: burnished, brown; medium fine paste and temper; well fired
H: 6.5; W: 8.0; Th: 1.5

1085   QO 8
Hook; top; perforated; surface: smooth, light brown/light gray; core: coarse, light brown; well fired
H: 5.0; W: 1.5; Th: 1.1

1334   PN 15/26; figure 6.28a; plate 6.13n
Anchor; fragment; surface: smooth, black, core: coarse, light gray
H: 5.7; W: 8.0; Th: 2.4

1336   PN 15/26; plate 6.13l
Anchor; fragment; surface: smooth, gray with some black patches; core: coarse; hard-fired
H: 5.8; W: 5.5; Th: 1.5

1352   PN 26
Anchor; end; surface: coarse, porous, red; coarse paste and temper; low fired
H: 5.7; W: 2.0; Th: 1.6

1361   PN 15/26; plate 6.13o
Anchor; fragment; surface: once burnished, brown; medium coarse paste and temper; well fired
H: 3.0; W: 9.0; Th: 1.8

1552   PO 9; plate 6.13k
Anchor; fragment; surface: smooth, dark gray, smudges of burn marks; unevenly fired
H: 3.0; W: 8.0; Th: 2.1

1649   PN 15/26; plate 6.13h
Anchor; fragment; surface: smooth, light red-brown; core: coarse, light red/light gray; well fired
H: 5.8; W: 5.8; Th: 2.3

1665 QO 8
Hook; top; perforated; surface: matt, light brown/gray; core: coarse, light gray
H: 5.9; W: 3.9; Th: 1.5; HD: 0.7

1668 PN 12; figure 6.27
Hook; top; surface: coarse, gray/red
H: 5.5; W: 2.3; Th: 1.6; HD: 0.5

1670 QN 7, BC; plate 6.11e
Hook; top; perforated; surface: coarse, black; core: coarse, red
H: 3.1; W: 2.3; Th: 1.9; HD: 0.7

1671 QO 8
Hook; top; surface: matt, black; core: coarse, light gray
H: 5.5; W: 3.1; Th: 1.4

1674 QN 7, BC; plate 6.11f
Hook; top; perforated; surface: smooth, dark brown; core: black/light gray
H: 5.7; W: 2.0; Th: 1.6

1681 PO 9; figure 6.29a; plate 6.13g
Anchor; fragment; surface: matt, black; core: coarse, light gray
H: 5.8; W: 7.8; Th: 2.1

1690 QN 8
Anchor; top; perforated; surface: matt, light brown/light gray; core: coarse; hard fired
H: 3.9; W: 1.9; Th: 1.7

1720 Surface
Hook; top; perforated; surface: matt, pink/gray stripes; coarse temper
H: 5.7; W: 1.9; Th: 1.9

1728 PN 5; plate 6.13i
Anchor; fragment; flat surfaces: matt, light gray/brown/black; curved underside: light gray/orange; core: coarse, black/gray
H: 5.1; W: 4.3; Th: 2

1729 PN 7
Hook; top; perforated; surface: matt, gray; medium temper
H: 5.3; W: 2.5; Th: 2.1

1730 PN 7
Hook; top; perforated; surface: matt, gray with brown stripe; medium coarse temper
H: 7.1; W: 2.4; Th: 2

1731 PN 7
Hook; middle; surface: coarse, matt, brown; coarse temper
H: 8.4; W: 3.2; Th: 2

1737 QN 8
Anchor; end; surface: matt, gray/brown; coarse temper
H: 5.4; W: 2.9; Th: 1.4

2031 ROc 15
Hook; top; perforated; surface: brown/black; coarse, heavy temper
H: 4.3; W: 3.0; Th: 2.2

2201 ROc 15
Anchor; middle
H: 3.5; W: 3.1; Th: 1.1

2224 PO 3
Anchor; end; surface: coarse, brick red with extensive gray deposits
H: 4.7; W: 3.1; Th: 1.7

2263 PO 17
Hook; middle; surface: brown/gray; coarse temper
H: 3.0; W: 2.8; Th: 2.0

2264 PO 16
Anchor; end; surface: matt, tan
H: 4.4; W: 2.0; Th: 1

2265 PO 8
Hook; middle; remains of hole visible; surface: matt, red/gray; core: gray
H: 4.4; W: 2.8; Th: 1.8

2266 PO 8
Hook; middle; surface: matt, gray; core: gray; coarse to medium temper
H: 4.5; W: 2.6; Th: 1

2287 PN/A 1
Hook; top; perforated, roughly modeled; surface: coarse; heavily tempered
H: 3.4; W: 2.5; Th: 1.8

2402 PN/E 61
Anchor; end; surface: black, burnished; medium temper
L.: 4.8; W: 1.6; Th: 1.5

2448 PN/D 76; figure 6.30; plate 6.13f
Anchor; both tips broken off; perforated
H: 7.8; W: 7.3; Th: 3.0, HD: 0.7–1.3

2868 PO 23
Anchor; end; surface: matt, beige; core: light gray
L: 4.5; W: 2.2; Th: 1.7

2869 PO 19
Anchor; middle; surface: matt, gray, core: gray; decoration: dotted
L: 7.2; W: 3.4; Th: 1.6

3605 PO 3
Hook; middle; perforated
H: 3.9; W: 2.6; Th: 0.8

4404 PN Ext; plate 6.13m
Anchor; fragment end; surface: black; core: black
H: 8.0; W: 3.0; Th: 2.1

4419 ROc 7
Hook; top; perforated; surface: black
H: 4.9; W: 1.8; Th: 2.0

4472 PN/B 103
Hook; end; surface: brown/red
L: 5.6; W: 1.8; Th: 1.7

4477 ROc 13
Hook; middle; roughly rectangular in section; surface: brown/gray
H: 4.1; W: 2.1; Th: 1

4480 ROc 21
Hook; middle; roughly rectangular in section; surface: cracked, gray.
H: 3.7; W: 2.3; Th: 2.3

4779 ROc 34; plate 6.13p
Anchor; middle; surface: matt, dark
H: 4.3; W: 5.2; Th: 2.1

5447 PO/A/C balk; figure 6.29b; plate 6.13j
Anchor; fragment; surface: black
H: 3.7; W: 4.0; Th: 1.8

Impressions

3370 PO/E 65
Double weave; mat; vessel fragment: base and side, impression on underside; surface: red/gray
L: 4.3; W: 3.4; H: 2

5002 ZB 41s
Double weave; mat

Loom Weights

330 SL 4
Cylindrical; fragment; surface: smooth, gray
H: 7.8; W: 5.7; Th: 3.4

357 QO 2; plate 6.12f
Discoid; pierced sherd; surface: red
H: 2.7; D: 7.7

372 QO 5; figure 6.19b; plate 6.12g
Discoid; pierced sherd; surface: brick red
H: 2.7; D: 8.5; HD: 0.9

495 PO 6; figure 6.22a; plate 6.12d
Pyramidal; surface: dark gray; unbaked
H: 8.8; W: 4.2; HD: 0.7

707 PO 7
Ring shaped; fragment; surface: matt, black; core: coarse, light gray
Th: 1.3; D: 7

1028 PN 7, BC; figure 6.18; plate 6.12a
Pyramidal; broken at height 10.8; perforated at top; surface: coarse, brown/gray
H: 22.9; W: 5.8; Wt: 1510

1029 QO 8, BC
Pyramidal; rectangular in section, corners missing; surface: very coarse, gray; unbaked
H: 14.0; W: 6.0; Th: 9.0

1042 QN 7, BC; plates 6.11a, 6.12b
Pyramidal; trapezoid in section; two fragments; coarse temper; poorly baked
H: 19.5; W: 9.6; Th: 5.9; Wt: 1285.0

1043 QN 7, BC; plates 6.10b, 6.11b, 6.12c
Pyramidal; triangular in section; two holes on top; surface: coarse, pinkish-gray; unbaked

1050 QN 7, BC; plate 6.11d
Pyramidal; four fragments, three of unidentifiable shape, the other with curved side; shredded grass temper; poorly fired
H: 10.8; W: 7.9; Th: 4

1058 QN 7, BC; plate 6.11c
Pyramidal; roughly rectangular in section; core: orange/black
H: 14.0; W: 8.3; Th: 5.9

1087 QN 8
Unidentifiable

1111 SL 2
Pear shaped; hole pierced through at an angle; fragment; surface: smooth, light gray
H: 3.0; W: 3.7; Th: 2.5

1305 PN 8
Pyramidal; rectangular in section; fragment; organic temper; unbaked
H: 6.0; W: 7.2; Th: 1

1331 PN 15/26
Pyramidal; rectangular in section, perforated on top; shredded grass and straw temper
H: 9.4; W: 8.0; Th: 5.7

1411 Surface
Pyramidal; trapezoidal in section; top: perforated; fragment; temper contains shell
H: 9.0; W: 8.2; Th: 7.0

1502 PO 16
Pyramidal; trapezoidal in shape; surface: extremely coarse, gray; unbaked
H: 20.0; W: 9.3; Th: 5.9

1562 PO 16
Pyramidal

1646 PN 12
Pear shaped; perforated on top; surface: very coarse, gray; unbaked

1748 QN 7
Ring shaped; incomplete; surface: black/light brown; core: light brown
H: 2.1; D: 6.2; HD: 1.0

2213 Surface
Pyramidal; very irregular surface: one side smooth
H: 10.3; W: 3.5; Th: 3.0

2223 OCb 1
Pyramidal; slightly broken on top; surface: coarse, brick red with extensive gray deposits
H: 7.6; W: 4.8

3032 LO surface
Pyramidal; perforated on top; surface: tan with some discoloration
H: 7.5; W: 4.6; Th: 3.8

3622 PO/B 40; figure 6.22b; plate 6.12e
Pyramidal; stone; irregular fragment; drilled perforation; preserved, rounded end, grooved and partially drilled across its straight side
H: 9.9; W: 6.0; Th: 3.8; HD: 1.1

4763a QN
Pyramidal; rough lumps; unbaked
H: 7.0; W: 5.5; Th: 6.0

4763b QN
Pyramidal; rough lump, perforated; unbaked
H: 12.0; W: 5.0; Th: 7.0

4784 PO/C 33
Pyramidal; fragment; surface: orange/gray
H: 9.8; W: 6.5

5552 PN/C 38
Pyramidal; fragment
H: 16.0; W: 9.0; Th: 6.0

5553 PN/C 83
Pyramidal; top fragment; perforated
H: 6.0; W: 6.0; Th: 5.0

Whorls

15 ZA 7; figure 6.4d
Flat
I I: 1.6; W: 1.6; D: 5.0; HD: 0.8; Wt: 50.5

19 ZA 8
Shallow conical; surface: light gray/brown; decoration: short incised slashes on top, serrated edge
H: 1.3; D: 3.7; HD: 0.4; Wt: 13.5

22 ZA 17; figure 6.15c; plate 6.4c
Flat; reworked sherd; edges: coarse, broken; decoration: painted, black on red spiral pattern
H: 1.0; D: 5.5; HD: 0.6; Wt: 30.5

23 ZA 2
Flat; approximately 1/2 preserved; surface: matt, red, underside: matt, black
Th: 1.3; D: 5.8; HD: 1.8

34 ZA 4
Deep conical; truncated cone; approximately 1/2 preserved; surface: matt, light brown/gray; hole surface: red; core: coarse, black
H: 4.2; Top D: 2.6; D: 5.1; HD: 1.1; Wt: 100.0

46 ZA 16
Flat; reworked sherd; hole not completely drilled through; surface: light brown/black; edges: coarse, brown
H: 1.0; D: 5.1; HD: 0.8; Wt: 41.0

285 PO 3
Flat; incomplete; edges: smooth; surface: pinkish-gray
D: 4.1; HD: 0.8; Th: 0.9; Wt: 40

308 PO 3
Biconical; fracture at string hole; surface: smooth
H: 2.8; D: 3.5; HD: 0.7; Wt: 29.0

312 PO 4
Spherical; surface: smooth
H: 2.8; D: 3.3; HD: 0.6; Wt: 32.5

315 PO 6
Flat; surface: smooth
Th: 1.4; D: 4.8; HD: 0.7; Wt: 40.0

316 PO 6
Biconical; surface: smooth, red-brown
H: 3.3; D: 4.5; HD: 0.6; Wt: 35.0

318 PO 6
Flat; surface: smooth, grayish-pink
H: 1.5; D: 4.5; HD: 0.6; Wt: 27.8

332 SL 6
Spool
H: 4.6; Top D: 4.2; Middle D: 3.7; D: 4.8; HD: 0.7

333 SL 7; figure 6.1b
Biconical; surface: matt, light gray/brown
H: 2.4; D: 3.2; HD: 0.7; Wt: 24

352 PN 2
Shallow conical; curved; fracture on side; surface: smooth
H: 2.2; D: 3.8; HD: 0.9; Wt: 31.5

354 PN 2; figure 6.17a
Spool
H: 4.6; Top D: 3.2; Middle D: 2.3; D: 3.8, HD: 0.8; Wt: 51.0

356 PN 2
Deep conical; truncated cone; surface: smooth, reddish
H: 2.8;Top D: 3.2; D: 3.8; HD: 0.8; Wt: 40.8

361 QO 3
Deep conical; truncated cone; incomplete; surface: smooth, red/dark gray, underside: black/red; core: light gray
H: 3.4; Top D: 2.5; D: 4.8; HD: 0.7

363 QO 3
Spool
H: 2.4; D: 3.2; HD: 0.6

364 QO 3; plate 6.5g
Spool or whorl
H: 2.8; Top D: 2.5; Middle D: 2.8; D: 3.7; HD: 0.6; Wt: 42.5

366 QO 4; figure 6.17d
Spool
H: 2.5; Top D: 2.6; Middle D: 2.3; D: 2.7; HD: 0.7; Wt: 28

368 QO 5
Spool
H: 4.0; Top D: 3.3; Middle D: 2.4; D: 3.3; HD: 0.8; Wt: 40.5

371 QO 5; figure 6.17c
Spool.
H: 4.1; Top D: 3.3; Middle D: 2.8; D: 3.6; HD: 0.9; Wt: 67

373 PN 4; plate 6.7h
Spool
H: 2.0; Top D: 2.6; Middle D: 2.2; D: 2.8; HD: 0.8; Wt: 21.0

465 ZA 9
Biconical; approximately 1/3 preserved; surface: smooth, dark brown; core: black with brown edges
H: 1.3; D: 3.7; HD: 0.8

468 ZA 16
Deep conical; approximately 1/2 preserved; surface: smooth, red; core: coarse, dark gray
H: 3.9; D: 5.2; HD: 0.5–0.8

477 QO 7
Shallow conical; curved
H: 2.5; D: 5.1; HD: 0.6; Wt: 18.0

491 PO 5
Biconical; slightly convex
H: 3.1; D: 4.2; HD: 0.7; Wt: 55.5

509b PN 4
Flat; incomplete; surface: matt, red/gray; hole surface: matt, red
H: 1.6; D: 10.6; HD: 0.9-2.0

608 PO 8; plate 6.6g
Biconical; surface: matt, light brown
H: 2.0; D: 3.0; HD: 0.6; Wt: 16.5

652 QO 7
Biconical; sides slightly concave; incomplete; surface: cracked, matt, black with red patches; core: coarse, black with red around the edge
H: 3.4; D: 3.8; HD: 0.8

653 PO 7
Spool
H: 4.0; Top D: 3.7; Middle D: 3.2; D: 3.7; HD: 0.7; Wt: 54

657 PO; figure 6.4h
Spool; or cylindrical whorl, slightly waisted
H: 2.5; Top D: 3.9; Middle D: 3.5; D: 4.0; HD: 0.8; Wt: 52.5

658 PO 8; plate 6.5d
Deep conical; dome shaped; top surface: matt, dark gray with light brown patches; underside: matt, light brown
H: 2.5; D: 4.8; HD: 0.8; Wt: 52.5

659 PO 8
Biconical; flattened, irregularly modeled; surface: matt, black
H: 2.2; D: 4.4; HD: 0.7; Wt: 33.3

660 PO 8
Biconical; sides slightly curved; surface: matt, light gray/brown; core: coarse, brown
H: 3.4; D: 3.8; HD: 0.7; Wt: 47.0

673 PO 8
Spool
H: 3.0; Top D: 3.0; Middle D: 2.7; D: 2.9; HD: 0.8; Wt: 30.0

674 PO 8
Biconical; fracture at string hole; surface: shiny, black/dark brown with patches of light brown
H: 3.6; D: 4.2; HD: 0.8; Wt: 46.0

675 QO 7; figure 6.4f
Spool or cylindrical whorl; slightly waisted
H: 2.3; Top D: 4.0; Middle D: 3.9; D: 4.0; HD: 0.8

677 PO 8
Biconical; with asymmetric hole; surface: matt, light gray/light brown
H: 3.3; D: 4.7; HD: 0.7; Wt: 59.0

682 QN 5
Spool
H: 3.1; Middle D: 2.3; D: 2.8; HD: 0.5

684 QN 5
Biconical; slightly concave; surface: matt, patches of black/red/light brown
H: 2.9; D: 3.6; HD: 0.8; Wt: 31.3

689 PO 8
Flat; surface: black/dark gray with patches of red ochre
Th: 1.7; D: 4.8; HD: 0.8; Wt: 50.0

690 PO 8
Biconical; slightly concave sides; incomplete; surface: matt, dark gray with light brown patches; core: light brown
H: 2.2; D: 2.8; HD: 0.7; Wt: 15.5

693 QN 5
Biconical; incomplete; straight; surface: matt, black; core: black with light brown patches
H: 2.5; D: 3.7; HD: 0.8; Wt: 46.0

694 QO/C 8
Shallow conical; slightly concave base; surface: matt, light brown with light gray patches
H: 1.3; D: 3.6; HD: 0.5; Wt: 18.0

697   PN 5
Flat; slightly raised around hole on both faces; surface: matt, black/dark brown
H: 2.4; D: 5.2; HD: 1.2; Wt: 73.0

701   PO 8
Flat; incomplete; surface: smooth, brown; hole surface: gray; core: brown
H: 1.4; D: 4.4; HD: 0.9

702   PO 8
Spool
H: 4.0; Top D: 3.4; Middle D: 3.1; D: 3.9; HD: 0.8; Wt: 57.0

1003   QO/C 8; figure 6.17b
Spool
H: 3.2; Top D: 3.0; Middle D: 2.1; D: 2.8; HD: 0.8; Wt: 41.0

1010   QN 6
Biconical; surface: smooth, dark gray/light brown
H: 3.4; D: 4.1; HD: 0.8; Wt: 50.5

1012   QO 7
Biconical; surface: matt, black with light brown patches
H: 2.6; D: 4.0; HD: 0.8; Wt: 40.0

1013   QO 7; plate 6.6c
Biconical; surface: matt, black/dark gray with light gray patches
H: 3.2; D: 4.0; HD: 0.6; Wt: 45.0

1014   PO 9; plate 6.6d
Biconical; fracture at string hole; decoration: incised groups of parallel lines on top
H: 2.1; D: 4.2; HD: 0.6; Wt: 32.3

1020   PO 9
Biconical; one side concave; fracture at string hole; surface: matt, black; core: light gray
H: 3.3; D: 3.3; HD: 0.7; Wt: 27.0

1022   QN 7
Biconical; surface: matt, red/light gray
H: 2.5; D: 3.8; HD: 0.5

1025   PN 7
Biconical; one side slightly concave; surface: matt, light/dark brown
H: 3.2; D: 4.0; HD: 0.6; Wt: 43.0

1026   PO 9; figure 6.2b
Biconical with truncated top and base; surface: matt, light brown with a few dark brown and red patches
H: 2.7; D: 4.1; HD: 0.7; Wt: 46.5

1030   QO 8
Biconical; surface: smooth, black; core: light gray
H: 2.6; D: 3.3; HD: 0.6; Wt: 30.0

1033   QO 8
Biconical; surface: matt, black with light gray and brown patches
H: 3.0; D: 3.6; HD: 0.7; Wt: 29.5

1034   QN 7
Shallow conical; small fracture on top; decoration: incised lines radiating from the hole on top, straight and angular lines arranged in different directions elsewhere
H: 1.8; D: 3.9; HD: 0.5; Wt: 20.0

1038   QO 8
Spool
H: 2.7; Top D: 2.8; Middle D: 2.2; D: 2.8; HD: 0.7; Wt: 2.8

1040   QO 8
Biconical; incomplete; surface: cracked, matt, light gray; core: black/dark brown
H: 3.1; D: 3.8; HD: 0.6; Wt: 31.3

1047   QO 8
Biconical; flattened, small protuberance near hole; surface: smooth, red/black
H: 1.8; D: 4.2; HD: 0.8; Wt: 35.0

1049   QN 7; plate 6.5h
Dome shaped; surface: black/dark brown
H: 2.2; D: 3.4; HD: 0.8; Wt: 26.0

1051   QO 8
Flat; surface: shiny, black with yellow/green patches
H: 1.8; D: 5.2; HD: 0.8; Wt: 55.0

1054   PO 9
Deep conical; truncated cone; surface: matt, red/dark gray
H: 3.0; Top D: 2.4; D: 3.5; HD: 0.7; Wt: 37.0

1057   PO 9
Biconical; incomplete; surface: matt, dark brown; hole surface: smooth; core: coarse, dark brown
H: 3.6; D: 3.7; HD: 0.9; Wt: 44.0

1059   QN 7
Flat; surface: matt, black/dark brown
H: 1.6; D: 5.0; HD: 0.8; Wt: 54.5

1063   QN 7
Biconical; biconvex; eccentric hole; surface: coarse, light brown with dark brown/black patches
H: 3.2; D: 4.3; HD: 0.6; Wt: 62.0

1064   QN 7
Biconical; surface: matt, red/dark gray
H: 2.0; D: 3.0; HD: 0.7; Wt: 18.5

1065   QN 7; figure 6.4g; plate 6.7a
Cylindrical with concave top, flat base; surface: matt, reddish-gray
H: 3.1; Top D: 4.1; D: 5.0; HD: 1.0; Wt: 90.0

1068 QN 7
Shallow conical; truncated cone; surface: coarse, dark brown; underside: matt, black
H: 1.9; Top D: 3.9; D: 4.8; HD: 0.8; Wt: 45.5

1072 QO 8
Biconical; straight; surface: matt, black; core: light brown/gray
H: 2.7; D: 3.8; HD: 0.7; Wt: 36.0

1073 QO 8
Biconical; sides slightly curved; incomplete; surface: matt, black with light gray patches; core: light gray
H: 1.3; D: 3.7; HD: 1.0

1075 QN 8
Biconical; incomplete; surface: smooth, shiny, black; core: light brown
H: 2.3; D: 4.8; HD: 0.8

1077 QO 8
Biconical; incomplete; surface: matt, black/dark brown; core: light/dark brown
H: 2.1; D: 3.7; HD: 0.7

1078 QN 8
Biconical; incomplete; surface: matt, black/dark brown; core: black/dark gray
H: 3.1; D: 4.8; HD: 0.6; Wt: 56.0

1082 QO 8
Flat; incomplete; surface: crumbly, red/light gray; poorly fired
H: 2.5; D: 3.5; HD: 0.8; Wt: 23.5

1084 QO 8
Biconical; incomplete; surface: matt, black with light brown patches; core: light gray
H: 3.0; D: 4.8; HD: 0.6; Wt: 60.0

1090 QO 8
Flat; surface: matt, one side dark gray, the other light gray/red
H: 1.8; D: 5.5; HD: 0.8; Wt: 64.5

1091 QO 8; figure 6.4e
Flat; concave top like a "bread loaf"; surface: matt, with light gray/black patches
H: 1.9; D: 4.0; HD: 0.7; Wt: 37.8

1093 QN 8
Flat; loaf shaped; surface: matt, black, with red/light brown patches
H: 2.2; D: 4.7; HD: 0.8; Wt: 55.0

1097 QN 8
Biconical; asymmetrical; surface: one cone black, the other light brown/gray
H: 2.4; D: 3.6; HD: 0.6; Wt: 30.0

1100 QO 8
Biconical; surface: matt, brown/light gray/black/red
H: 2.7; D: 3.3; HD: 0.5; Wt: 26.5

1117 SL 2
Spherical; approximately 1/4 preserved; surface: matt, brown/gray; core: dark gray
H: 3.1; D: 3.8; HD: 0.6-0.9

1125 SL 3
Deep conical; approximately 1/4 preserved; surface: matt, black/dark brown; core: black/dark brown
H: 4.3; D: 4.2; HD: 0.7

1138 QN 6
Biconical; one cone is curved and bulbous, the other strongly concave and more slender; incomplete; surface: matt, black
H: 2.3; D: 2.4; HD: 0.8

1139 QN 6
Flat; eccentric hole; incomplete; surface: matt, dark gray
H: 2.2; D: 4.1; HD: 1.0; Wt: 50.0

1147 PN 6
Deep conical; truncated cone; incomplete; surface: matt, gray; core: coarse, gray; temper: rather coarse
H: 2.8; Top D: 1.6; D: 3.8; HD: 0.7; Wt: 35.3

1302 PN 7
Biconical; surface: matt, brown/gray
H: 2.0; D: 2.7; HD: 0.7; Wt: 13.8

1310 PN 12
Deep conical; truncated cone; incomplete; surface: matt, light gray/brown; underside: matt, dark gray, hole surface: red
H: 3.6; D: 3.4; HD: 0. 6; Wt: 41.3

1314 PN 12
Shallow conical; surface: coarse, gray with black shiny patches
H: 2.1; D: 4.5; HD: 0.9; Wt: 46.5

1315 PN 12
Spool
H: 2.9; Top D: 3.1; Middle D: 2.2; D: 3.2; HD: 0.6, Wt: 32.0

1317 PN 12; plate 6.7c
Spool
H: 4.2; Top D: 3.6; Middle D: 2.6; D: 3.7; HD: 0.6; Wt: 60.8

1323 PN 14
Shallow conical; dome shaped; surface: matt, brown with light gray patches
H: 1.5; D: 3.6; HD: 0.5; Wt: 23.0

1335 PN 16
Biconical; surface: matt, brown/dark gray
H: 2.4; D: 4.1; HD: 0.7; Wt: 39.5

1338 PN 18; figure 6.4c
Flat; one face very slightly curved, the other slightly raised around hole; surface: matt, black with light brown patches
H: 1.5; D: 5.2; HD: 0.7; Wt: 38.0

1342 PN 19s
Biconical; sides slightly curved; surface: matt, gray/dark gray; coarse temper
H: 2.4; D: 3.5; HD: 0.7; Wt: 35.5

1356 PN 26s
Biconical; incomplete; surface: matt, black with dark brown and light gray patches; core: light gray with dark patches
H: 3.5; D: 3.9; HD: 0.7; Wt: 51.0

1359 PN 28; plate 6.6e
Biconical; slightly eccentric yarn hole; surface: matt, pink/gray
H: 2.5; D: 5.3; HD: 0.8; Wt: 56.5

1360 PN 28
Flat; slightly domed; surface: red/gray; coarse temper
H: 1.7; D: 4.8; HD: 0.7; Wt: 45.5

1363 PN 28
Spool
H: 3.3; Top D: 3.7; Middle D: 2.7; D: 3.7; HD: 0.8; Wt: 50.5

1364 PN 28
Biconical; slightly concave sides; surface: matt, black with light brown patches
H: 2.4; D: 3.9; HD: 0.7; Wt: 34.5

1507 PO 8
Spool
H: 3.7; Top D: 3.8; Middle D: 3.3; D: 3.6; HD: 0.8; Wt: 61.0

1565 PO 17
Spool
H: 3.2; Top D: 3.3; Middle D: 2.9; D: 3.3; HD: 0.8; Wt: 43.5

1579 PO 9
Biconical; one cone is curved; surface: matt, black/dark brown with light gray patches
H: 3.7; D: 2.8; HD: 0.7; Wt: 36.0

1585 PO 3
Spool
H: 2.5; Middle D: 2.0; D: 3.0; HD: 0.5

1593 PO
Biconical; asymmetrical, sides slightly concave; fracture at string hole; surface: coarse, dark/light brown; core: dark brown with red patches
H: 2.0; D: 2.4; HD: 0.5

1610 PO 9; plate 6.7e
Flat; one side raised very slightly around the hole; surface: crumbly, one side black and shiny, the other light brown/gray, hole surface: brown; poorly fired or in a fire
H: 1.4; D: 5.2; HD: 0.8; Wt: 45.0

1618 PO 12
Biconical; straight, shallow; surface: matt, dark gray with light brown and yellow patches
H: 2.4; D: 3.9; HD: 0.7; Wt: 32.5

1623 PO 13
Flat; surface: matt, black on one side, black with light gray patches on the other
H: 2.3; D: 3.8; HD: 0.8; Wt: 39.0

1631 PO 10; figure 6.1a
Biconical; slightly concave sides; surface: matt, light gray/light brown with dark brown and black patches
H: 3.4; D: 4.7; HD: 0.7; Wt: 71.0

1633 ZA 13
Biconical; dark gray/brown
H: 3.5; D: 3.1; HD: 0.4; Wt: 36.0

1651 PN 19; plate 6.6f
Spherical; surface: matt, brown/light brown with light gray patches
H: 3.4; D: 3.9; HD: 0.8; Wt: 52.0

1653 PN 28; plate 6.7d
Spool
H: 2.8; Top D: 3.5; Middle D: 2.6; D: 3.7; HD: 0.7; Wt: 49.5

1656 PO 10
Biconical; biconvex; surface: matt, tan/dark gray; well fired
H: 2.0; D: 3.0; HD: 0.7; Wt: 17.3
QO 8

1671 QO 8

1679 PN 26
Biconical; incomplete; surface: matt, black with light brown patches; core: coarse
H: 1.3; D: 3.7; HD: 0.6

1688 PN 25
Spherical; incomplete; flattened sphere; surface: matt, light gray/red; core: black with red edges
H: 2.3; D: 3.6; HD: 0.6; Wt: 29.0

1711 PO 8
Biconical; one cone straight, the other curved; surface: badly cracked, matt, light gray-brown/black; poorly fired
H: 3.2; D: 4.4; HD: 0.8; Wt: 45.0

1717 QO/B 1
Spherical; slightly irregular; approximately 1/3 preserved; surface: dark brown/red; hole surface: matt, red
H: 2.7; D: 2.8; HD: 0.4

1718 QO 8
Shallow conical; curved sides; incomplete; surface: matt, light brown, underside: brown/gray; core: brown; decoration: incised chevrons on top
H: 2.2; D: 4.0

1721 PN 7
Biconical; surface: smooth, shiny, light brown
H: 2.0; D: 3.5; HD: 0.6; Wt: 23.3

1733 PN 12
Shallow conical; incomplete; surface: matt, gray;
coarse temper
H: 2.5; D: 4.3; HD: 0.8

1765 QO
Biconical; surface: gray/light brown
H: 2.4; D: 3.5; HD: 0.7; Wt: 25.0

1766 QO 8
Spool.
H: 3.0; Top D: 3.8; Middle D: 3.4; D: 4.1; HD: 0.7; Wt:
58.5

1802 PO 23
Flat; slightly raised toward hole; surface: matt,
gray; core: dark gray
H: 2.1; D: 4.5; HD: 0.7; Wt: 53.75

1806 PO 23
Biconical; one cone is concave; surface: slightly
eroded, one cone matt, medium gray, the other
matt, medium/dark gray
H: 3.1; D: 3.9; HD: 0.9; Wt: 40.5

1851 QN 8
Spherical; flattened sphere; surface: matt, gray
H: 2.2; D: 3.3; HD: 0.7; Wt: 31.0

1852 QN 8

1853 QN 8
Biconical; slightly asymmetrical; incomplete; sur-
face: smooth, dark gray; core: coarse, dark gray
H: 2.4; D: 4.1; HD: 0.6; Wt: 40.0

1856 QO 8
Biconical; almost octagonal in shape; surface: matt,
gray/brown
H: 3.0; D: 3.4; HD: 0.6; Wt: 31.5

1858 QO 8
Biconical; sides curved, slightly asymmetrical, with
eccentric hole; surface: matt, brown/gray
H: 2.7; D: 3.3; HD: 0.6; Wt: 27.0

1859 QO 8
Deep conical; truncated cone; incomplete; surface:
smooth, gray/dark brown; underside: dark gray;
core: gray
H: 2.7; Top D: 3.3; D: 3.7; HD: 0.8

1860 QN 8
Biconical; biconvex; surface: smooth, matt, gray;
core: coarse, gray
H: 2.5; D: 4.8; HD: 0.9; Wt: 62.0

1861 QO 8
Flat; loaf shaped; surface: matt, light gray/light
brown
H: 2.0; D: 5.0; HD: 0.8; Wt: 45.5

1863 QO 8
Biconical; surface: matt, light gray/dark gray
H: 2.7; D: 3.4; HD: 0.5; Wt: 25.8

1864 QO 8
Biconical; incomplete; surface: matt, medium gray;
core: coarse, light gray
H: 2.9; D: 3.5; HD: 0.8; Wt: 45.0

1865 QO 8
Biconical; incomplete; surface: matt, light gray/
brown; core: black/light gray
H: 2.8; D: 2.6; HD: 0.7; Wt: 24.0

1866 QO 8
Flat; incomplete; surface: matt, dark gray/light
brown with yellow and red patches; core: dark gray
H: 2.0; D: 4.0; HD: 0.9

1867 QO 9
Biconical; surface: matt, black with gray and yel-
low/green patches
H: 2.4; D: 2.7; HD: 0.7; W: 16.5

2000 ROc 1
Deep conical; dome shaped; chipped, slight localized cracking on top; surface: smooth, with gray
deposits
H: 3.3; D: 4.8; HD: 0.8

2002 ROc 1
Biconical; chipped at widest circumference; surface:
light brick with white deposits
H: 2.4; D: 4.2; HD: 1.1

2004 ROc 1
Deep conical; dome shaped; slight chipping at base
and apex; surface: gray with white deposits
H: 2.5; D: 3.6; HD: 0.4

2010 ROc 7
Biconical; surface: red/black/light brown
H: 3.0; D: 4.1; HD: 0.7; Wt: 41.5

2012 ROc 9
Biconical; chipped base; surface: fairly smooth,
dark gray/brown
H: 3.4; D: 4.2; HD: 0.8; Wt: 54.5

2014 ROc 9; plate 6.7f
Flat; surface: smooth, red-brown, burnt on one side
H: 1.9; D: 4.0; HD: 0. 6; Wt: 39.0

2016 ROc 9
Biconical; slightly broken at both ends; surface:
smooth with a few encrustations
H: 4.0; D: 3.8; HD: 0.8; Wt: 29.0

2021 ROc 13
Flat; loaf shaped; surface: smooth, reddish
H: 1.7; D: 4.3; HD: 0.6; Wt: 42.0

2024 ROc 13; plate 6.7b
Flat; surface: smooth, reddish
H: 1.5; D: 4.9; HD: 0.8; Wt: 46.5

2027 ROc13
Biconical; surface: matt, gray; hole surface: reddish
H: 2.2; D: 3.1; HD: 0.6; Wt: 19.5

2036 ROc 19
Flat; surface: matt, light brown/gray
H: 2.4; D: 4.5; HD: 0.9; Wt: 61.5

2039 ROc 22
Biconical; chipped; surface: light gray with dark
gray patches; core: contains grit
H: 2.5; D: 3.7; HD: 0

2040 ROc 21
Biconical; badly chipped; surface: dark gray with
white stains
H: 3.7; D: 4.1; HD: 0.9; Wt: 51.0

2043 QO/D 9; plate 6.6h
Biconical
H: 2.8; D: 3.3; HD: 0.8; Wt: 25.5

2051 PO/C 25
Biconical; worn at base; surface: smooth, dark
gray/light brown
H: 1.8; D: 3.2; HD: 0.6; Wt: 20.0

2052 PO/C 27
Spool; rather small
H: 2.5; D: 2.0; HD: 0.7; Wt: 12.0

2053 PO/C 27
Flat; slightly raised central part; surface: red/black
H: 2.4; D: 3.9; HD: 0.8; Wt: 38.5

2055 PO/C 29
Biconical; surface: brown with black deposits
H: 2.8; D: 3.6; HD: 0.6; Wt: 32.0

2058 PO/B 33
Spool
H: 4.0; Top D: 3.9; Middle D: 3.2; D: 4.4; HD: 0.9; Wt:
68.0

2061 PO/A Clng
Spherical; flattened sphere; irregular in shape,
eccentric hole; incomplete; chipped surface
H: 2.3; D: 3.1; HD: 0.5

2063 PO/B 35
Biconical; surface: dark gray/black
H: 3.0; D: 3.6; HD: 0.7; Wt: 33.0

2068 PO/A 45; plate 6.7g
Spool
H: 2.7; Top D: 2.7; Middle D: 2.3; D: 2.9; HD: 0.5; Wt:
27.0

2071 PO/A 46
Spherical; surface: black; poorly fired
H: 2.7; D: 2.6; HD: 0.7; Wt: 21.5

2072 PO/A 46
Biconical; surface: smooth, gray/brown
H: 2.4; D: 3.5; HD: 0.5; Wt: 27.5

2073 PO/A 46
Biconical; surface: smooth, light brown
H: 2.1; D: 4.0; HD: 0.4; Wt: 31.5

2087 PO/D 39
Shallow conical; incomplete; surface: gray with red-
dish tinges
H: 1.8; D: 5.0

2099 PO/C 33
Biconical; surface: matt, pale
H: 3.2; D: 4.3; HD: 0.7; Wt: 53.5

2108 ZB 19
Biconical; incomplete; surface: gray
H: 3.8; D: 4.8; HD: 1.2; Wt: 86.0

2110 ZB 23
Spool
H: 4.1; Top D: 3.4; Middle D: 3.2; D: 3.6; HD: 0.8; Wt:
68.0

2114 ZB 37
Biconical; asymmetrical, one cone is convex and
bulbous, the other concave and slender; incomplete; surface: matt, dark
H: 1.9; D: 3.6; HD: 1.5; Wt: 19.5

2203 PO/C 27
Biconical; incomplete; surface: gray; decoration:
incised linear elements
H: 3.7; D: 3.8; HD: 0.6; Wt: 48.0

2208 PO Clng
Flat; approximately 1/2 preserved
H: 1.7; D: 5.0; HD: 0.7

2229 PO/B 33
Biconical; incomplete; surface: matt, gray
H: 3.3; D: 4.3; HD: 0.7; Wt: 47.5

2250 QO Clng
Flat; incomplete; surface: dark gray, with slight
encrustation
H: 1.8; D: 5.0

2251 PN/F
Biconical; surface: coarse, pinkish-yellow
H: 3.9; D: 4.5; HD: 0.8

2282 PN/A 91
Biconical; incomplete; surface: matt, gray/beige;
core: dark gray
H: 3.3; D: 4.7; HD: 0.7; Wt: 31.0

2291 PN/B 100
Deep conical; incomplete; surface: matt, gray
H: 3.8; D: 4.5; HD: 0.8; Wt: 74.0

2403 PN/E 61
Biconical; incomplete; surface: gray/charcoal;
coarse temper
H: 1.3; D: 3.7

2405 PN/E 62
Deep conical; truncated cone; incomplete; surface:
wet smoothed, buff/gray
H: 2.8; Top D: 2.5; D: 3.7; HD: 1.2

2408 PN/E 62
Spool; small
H: 2.6; D: 2.8; HD: 0.8; Wt: 28.5

2421a PN/A 92
Spherical; flattened sphere; surface: buff/gray
H: 2.8; D: 4.1; HD: 0.7; Wt: 46.5

2421b PN/A 92; figure 6.4a
Flat; slightly raised toward hole on both faces; sur-
face: buff with smudge marks; orange temper
H: 2.6; D: 4.0; HD: 0.7; Wt: 36.0

2421c PN/A 92
Flat; loaf shaped; surface: black, burned
H: 2.2; D: 3.5; HD: 0.7; Wt: 32.0

2436 PN/E 63B
Reworked sherd; surface: buff with white encrusta-
tion
H: 0.8; D: 4.2; HD: 0.4; Wt: 22.0

2810 QO Clng
Deep conical; truncated cone; incomplete; surface:
matt, gray; core: brown
H: 3.3; D: 2.8

3007 ROc 21
Biconical; badly chipped; surface: dark brown
H: 2.6; D: 3.7; HD: 0.8

3009 ROc 34
Biconical; surface: gray, with one burnished, brown
area
H: 2.8; D: 3.7; HD: 0.6; Wt: 34.5

3303 PN/A/C balk 90
Flat; incomplete; surface: matt, black/brown
H: 2.3; D: 4.5; HD: 0.8; Wt: 59.0

3304 PN/A/C balk; plate 6.5c
Dome shaped; incomplete; surface: gray
H: 4.0; D: 3.6; HD: 0.7; Wt: 63.5

3305 PN/A/C balk 92
Biconical; asymmetrical, one cone is convex, the
other concave; incomplete; surface: black/light
brown
H: 2.3; D: 4.1; HD: 0.7; Wt: 37.5

3307 PO/C 35
Biconical; incomplete; surface: matt, gray, core:
gray
H: 4.3; D: 5.9; HD: 0.8

3314 PO/A 49
Biconical; incomplete; surface: coarse, gray
H: 2.5; D: 4.6; HD: 0.9

3317 PO/A/C 25
Biconical; surface: gray
H: 2.7; D: 3.4; HD: 0.8; Wt: 24.0

3322 PO/B 44
Biconical; surface: matt, red; core: red
H: 3.4; D: 4.5; HD: 0.8; Wt: 53.5

3323 PO/B 45
Biconical; incomplete; surface: matt, gray/tan; core:
gray
H: 1.3; D: 3.7

3334 PO/B/D 58
Spherical; flattened sphere; surface: slightly bur-
nished
H: 2.8; D: 4.2; HD: 0.8; Wt: 41.5

3336 PO/C 136 figure 6.1c
Biconical; surface: matt, heavy dark
H: 3.8; D: 4.9; HD: 0.8; Wt: 84.0

3340 PO/A 54
Biconical; surface: matt, gray with black discoloration
H: 3.3; D: 4.9; HD: 0.7; Wt: 64.0

3341 PO/A 54
Biconical
H: 3.5; D: 4.6; HD: 0.7; Wt: 57.0

3347 PO/C/D 129
Biconical; incomplete; surface: matt, gray
H: 3.2; D: 4.1; HD: 0.6

3354 PO 159; plate 6.6a
Biconical; surface: burnished, black
H: 4.0; D: 5.1; HD: 0.8; Wt: 83.5

3362 PN/F 262B
Deep conical; truncated cone; incomplete; surface:
light brown/dark brown
H: 3.2; D: 4.8; HD: 0.8; Wt: 77.5

3363 PN/F 262B
Biconical; surface: orange on one cone, black on the
other
H: 5.3; D: 6.1; HD: 0.9; Wt: 135.0

3391 PN/C 86
Flat; slightly raised toward hole; surface: gray/
brown
H: 1.3; D: 3.7; HD: 0.5

3398 PN/C 86
Biconical; incomplete; surface: gray; core: contains
stone
H: 2.4; D: 4.0; HD: 0.7

3399 PN/E 68
Biconical; surface: gray
H: 3.7; D: 4.5; HD: 0.7; Wt: 76.5

3400 PO/D 32
Spool
H: 2.9; Middle D: 2.4; D: 3.6; HD: 0.9

3630   PO 10
Biconical; surface: matt, black with light gray/brown patches
H: 1.6; D: 3.5; HD: 0.7; Wt: 24.5

3655   PN
Biconical; approximately 1/4 preserved; surface: dark
H: 2.8; D: 2.4

3694   PN 20
Flat; very slightly raised toward hole on both surfaces; incomplete; surface: gray
H: 1.6; D: 4.7; HD: 0.9

4300   PN balk
Biconical; incomplete
H: 3.0; D: 3.8

4302   PN/D 80
Biconical; incomplete; surface: burnished, black
H: 3

4305   PN balk Clng
Reworked sherd; hole not completed; incomplete; surface: dark gray
H: 1.1; D: 5.7; HD: 0.5

4350   PN/PO balk
Biconical; surface: brown/dark gray
H: 3.0; D: 4.1; HD: 0.6

4364   PN/C 88
Biconical; incomplete; surface: light brown; core: dark gray patches
H: 3.6; D: 4.4; HD: 0.7; Wt: 71.0

4402   PN/D 78
Spool; exceptionally small
H: 2.3; Top D: 2.1; Middle D: 1.7; D: 2.3; HD: 0.4; Wt: 28.0

4403   PN Ext
Biconical; incomplete
H: 2.3; D: 3.7; HD: 0.5

4405   PN Ext South
Biconical; surface: brown
H: 3.2; D: 3.9; HD: 0.7; Wt: 41.0

4426   PN Ext
Reworked sherd; hole incomplete; surface: orange
H: 1.0; D: 5.1; HD: 0.7; Wt: 22.0

4428   PN/A 95
Biconical; biconvex; surface: gray/pink
H: 2.1; D: 2.8; HD: 0.6; Wt: 19.5

4430   PN/C 89
Biconical; incomplete; decoration: slashed incisions around edge; surface: dark gray
H: 5.0; D: 4.2

4433   PN/C 87
Biconical; incomplete; surface: gray/buff
H: 2.0; D: 5.1; HD: 0.7; Wt: 65.0

4435   PN/C 87 or 81; plate 6.6b
Biconical; surface: orange/black
H: 4.3; D: 5.5; HD: 0.9; Wt: 120.0

4436   PN/C 86
Biconical; incomplete; surface: dark brown on one side, orange on the other
H: 3.8; D: 4.6; HD: 0.8; Wt: 67.0

4447   ROc 50
Biconical; approximately 1/2 preserved; surface: dark gray
H: 3

4474   PN/F 262
Biconical; incomplete; surface: light gray
H: 3.9; D: 5.1; HD: 0.8; Wt: 85.0

4509   PN/E/F balk
Biconical; approximately 1/2 preserved; surface: coarse, dark
H: 3.3; D: 5.0; HD: 0.7

4583   PN/C 88
Biconical; incomplete; surface: pink/gray
H: 1.5; HD: 0.7

4590   PO/D 33
Deep conical; truncated cone with slightly concave sides; incomplete; surface: burnished, pinkish-gray
H: 3.8; Top D: 1.8; D: 3.3; HD: 0.6

5007   ZB 37
Biconical; incomplete
H: 1.3; D: 3.7

5012   ZB 10r
Biconical
H: 2.0; D: 2.4; HD: 0.6; Wt: 13.0

5555   PO/A 48
Miscellaneous: unidentifiable shape.
H: 1.3; D: 3.7

MIXED CONTEXTS

Impressions

?   NM 1 surface; volume 1:plate XCVIII: bottom, 4
Cord

186   NL 1 surface; volume 1:figure 13.137, plate XCVIII: bottom, 3
Cord

Whorls

4   LNc 1
Shallow conical; decoration: incised radial chevrons on top
H: 1.9; D: 3.4; HD: 0.7

31 NOa 1
Flat; chipped edges; surface: smooth, one side light brown, the other black
H: 1.9; D: 5.5; HD: 0.7

58 HNd 1 X1
Shallow conical; surface: matt, red/light gray
H: 2.0; D: 4.5; HD: 0.4

282 Surface
Spool
H: 3.4; Top D: 3.2; D: 4.7; HD: 0.8

336 SM 2
Deep conical; top rounded; surface: smooth, pinkish-gray, groove down one side
H: 5.3; D: 4.4; HD: 0.9

735 Surface
Deep conical; slightly chipped around base; surface: smooth, black
H: 4.0; D: 5.9; HD: 1.0

1280 LM 2
Deep conical; dome shaped; surface: smooth, matt, brown
H: 2.6; D: 4.3; HD: 0.7

1614 Surface
Miscellaneous; crescent-shaped; approximately 1/2 preserved; surface: smooth, dark brown in center, light brown near edges; core: light gray
H: 1.7; D: 6.4; HD: 0.9

1615 Surface
Deep conical; truncated cone; approximately 1/3 preserved; surface: smooth, light gray with red and green patches; underside: dark gray; core: dark gray
H: 3.5; D: 4.2; HD: 0.7

1747 NNd 1
Flat; surface: one side light brown, the other light brown/black
H: 1.4; D: 4.8; HD: 0.7

1753 LOd 1
Deep conical; dome shaped; approximately 1/2 preserved; surface: light brown/black/red brown; core: red brown/gray/black gray
H: 3.8; D: 5.2; HD: 0.9

1760 RLd 1
Biconical; surface: light brown/grayish brown
H: 2.6; D: 3.8

1761 NLa 1
Flat; loaf shaped; approximately 1/3 preserved; surface: red-gray/black-gray; core: black/red/gray
H: 1.8; D: 6.0; HD: 0.8

2206 Surface
Biconical; one chip off one end
H: 3.2; D: 3.7; HD: 0.7

2209 OGc 1
Flat; stone; chipped; surface: pink/gray with white veins
H: 0.8; D: 3.4; HD: 0.5

2222 OCg 1
Biconical; approximately 4/5 preserved; surface: smooth, dark gray/red brown
H: 2.5; D: 3.5; HD: 0.4

2233 PCa 1
Shallow conical; surface: red/brown; decoration: 4 incised lines, radiating from hole on top, alternate with 4 large incised dots
H: 1.7; D: 3.3; HD: 0.5

2804 PEx 1
Flat; slightly domed upper top; large chip on one side; surface: buff with gray staining; decoration: incised chevrons around edge with alternating rows of punctates
H: 1.6; D: 5.0; HD: 0.5

2848 Surface
Reworked sherd; approximately 1/2 preserved; surface: one side orange, the other gray
H: 1.2; D: 8.4; HD: 0.8

3445 Surface
Deep conical; surface: black/brown
H: 4.4; D: 5.0; HD: 0.8

3661 Surface
Biconical
H: 2.8; D: 4.5; HD: 0.8

3662 Surface
Spherical; biconvex; asymmetric; surface: pale gray
H: 2.6; D: 3.7; HD: 0.6

3663 Surface
Flat; approximately 1/2 preserved; surface: dark gray
H: 1.7; D: 4.7; HD: 0.8

3688 Surface
Biconical; approximately 3/4 preserved; pale gray
H: 3.6; D: 5.2; HD: 0.9

3689 Surface
Biconical; surface: red
H: 2.6; D: 3.0; HD: 0.6

3757 ZL 15
Flat; approximately 1/2 preserved; surface: dark gray on one side, light brown on the other; core: orange
H: 1.5; D: 5.0; HD: 0.7

3763 ZL 19
Biconical; surface: black
H: 2.5; D: 3.9; HD: 0.7

4765 OJb 1
Shallow conical; approximately 1/2 preserved; surface: matt, gray
H: 3.0; D: 4.5; HD: 0.9

4772 OGb 1
Reworked sherd; approximately 1/2 preserved; hole not completely pierced through; surface: matt, gray
H: 1.1; D: 6.7; HD: 0.5

4782 PJc 1
Deep conical; truncated cone; chipped; surface: pinkish
H: 3.3; Top D: 2.8; D: 4.1; HD: 0.8

Loom Weights

100 OL 4
Pear shaped; perforated in the center; surface: smooth, gray/pink

L: 4.0; W: 4.85

2241 PFc
Conical; vertically barred, large chip missing from base; surface: brick red
H: 5.4; D: 4.1

2246 U
Biconical; surface: smooth, black
H: 4.3; D: 5.7; HD: 0.7

2847 Surface
Discoid; pierced sherd; approximately 3/4 preserved; three fragments joined; badly chipped; surface: orange; core: dark gray
H: 1.3; D: 10.8; HD: 0.9

7.

Technical Analysis of the Ceramics

Elizabeth Gardner

This technological study of early ceramics was conducted to describe the manufacturing techniques used during each occupation period at Sitagroi and to determine whether this technology became increasingly complex in the Chalcolithic levels. A most important question was whether Sitagroi artisans understood metallurgical technology and applied this technology to the ceramic production *before* metalworking became a specialty. As Forbes (1950) and Tylecote (1962) have indicated, it is impossible to smelt pure metals from their oxides and sulfides without knowing how to control the atmosphere during firing and to produce high firing temperatures. It was necessary, therefore, to look for these variables during the analysis of the materials; this evidence is a very important addition to our knowledge of the site.

METHODS

This study represents considerable laboratory time but has not benefited from recent revision. Nevertheless, it serves as a useful companion to chapters 11, 12, and 13 in volume 1, in which the quantitative study of the pottery sherds followed a strict stratigraphic sequence, forming the basis of the Sitagroi chronology (see volume 1 [C. Renfrew 1986e]:147–174; and this volume, Preface table 3). Sherd samples were collected from the deep sounding (ZA) that penetrated the full depth of the mound. It was felt that a fully representative sample of wares from every period could be found there, and many samples of each type were selected from every level. "Ware" is the general term used for the more-than thirty ceramic fabrics listed (see Preface figure 3) and defined earlier (see volume 1 [C. Renfrew 1986e]:155–160).

The Greek Archaeological Service consented to moving the samples to the Laboratory of Old World Archaeology at the University of California at Los Angeles (UCLA), where the materials were inspected and analyzed under controlled conditions. The ceramics laboratory had equipment to facilitate accurate analyses, including a Lindberg Hevi-Duty muffle kiln and pyrometer, a Lindberg Hevi-Duty tunnel kiln with pyrometer, a Nikon stereo zoom microscope (40 X), and a Bausch and Lomb petrographic microscope.

The purpose was to describe the sherds fully, determine their hardness using the Mohs' Scale (Shepard 1965:115), and then determine firing temperatures and the atmosphere of the original firing. Other tests were also performed to determine the varieties of black pigment that were used. Shepard has described many of these tests (1965:172–178); others were devised by Dr. Eleanor Siebert of the UCLA Department of Chemistry.

SHERD DESCRIPTION

The surface of a sherd was inspected for the following variables: slip; paint; color and color variation; additions before and after firing; method of decoration such as use of infill, hematite, graphite paint or wash; and techniques such as channeling, rippling, punctation, fingernail impression, gouging, incising, burnishing (light, medium, or heavy), and nonplastic inclusions. The core was examined for temper and color changes (for example, carbon coring). Fresh breaks in a sherd often aided in the recognition of slip (self-slip or coating) and also showed a coil outline, indicating that the coil manufacturing technique was used. The interior surface of the sherd was examined to determine its treatment: painting, smudging, smoothing, or burnishing.

DETERMINATION OF THE FIRING TEMPERATURES

An approximation of the original firing temperature and kiln atmosphere conditions, consistent with standard pyrometric cones, can be obtained using approximately 1.0 to 1.5 g samples. A small chip of sherd is broken off and ground in a mortar; the resulting powder is mixed with any polyvinyl acetate adhesive to the consistency of cookie dough. This material is packed tightly into a 1- to 2-cm section of an ordinary plastic drinking straw. The samples are labeled and allowed to dry thoroughly (up to two days). When the material is dry, the cylinders are placed on fired stoneware plaques and fired rapidly (10° to 20° C per minute) in a pyrometer-controlled muffle kiln for oxidized firings or a tunnel kiln equipped with a methane torch to reduce the air intake for reduction firings. A target temperature is selected, usually around 900° C, and initially one cone of each sample is fired to that temperature. The firing temperature is determined by the amount of glass formed in the cone and comparative color change. The cylinder is inspected with a hand lens (10 X) to determine the amount of glass present. It must be noted whether or not the sample is just formed or is not holding together, or if the sample has sintered, meaning that a glass lattice can be observed. If the sample appears to shine, it is vitrified and overfired. Ideally, the sample should be sintered. With an unknown sample fired in an oxidizing atmosphere, one can begin firing at 900° C and then raise or lower the temperature of succeeding firings by 25° C increments. At the end of each firing, color change and glass formation should be compared with those of previous firings. This is a rough comparative technique based on the premise that fusible clays containing about 3% iron exhibit definite changes in response to heat and atmosphere (Frierman, Elster, and Gardner 1971).

Wares fired at low temperatures (phases I and II) are shown on plate 7.1. Those fired at high temperatures (phases III–V) are shown on plate 7.2. All the wares were described and defined in volume 1 (chapter 7 [C. Renfrew 1986e]:155–160).

PHASE I CERAMICS

Phase I is characterized by wares that have been smudged in firing or incompletely oxidized, either of which demonstrates poor atmosphere control. The Brown-on-Buff ware sherds indicate, if they are not intrusive, that a completely oxidizing atmosphere could be produced at this time. A true graphite wash appears on a ware with a well-levigated clay and no intentional temper; it was well and thoroughly fired in an incompletely oxidizing atmosphere with a smoky reduction at the end. The graphite had been very finely crushed, even to a powdery consistency, and disappeared completely upon oxidation. Decoration is simple: fingernail impression and pinching are most prominent, with an interesting treatment of buff- or red-slipped wares that are reduced at the rim. Black topping was probably accomplished by inverting the vessel and placing the rim in the ashes of the fire, which would reduce that area resulting in a black rim or "top" while oxidizing the rest of the pot. Analysis of the Barbotine ware showed that fine river sand was intentionally ground before being added to the clay slip. Microscopic inspection revealed sharp fractions in the quartz grains, whereas the quartz of ordinary sand temper is always rounded and smooth. Technically, this was an uncomplicated phase. A description of the ware types follows. The core and interior of individual sherds may differ from the standard defined in volume 1 (chapter 7 [C. Renfrew 1986e]:155–160).

Phase I Wares

Fine Black Burnished

Exterior:	Black slipped; heavily burnished, mirrorlike surface; thin walled
Mohs' test:	3.0
Core:	Well-levigated, buff, micaceous clay body with high iron content; thoroughly fired
Mohs' test:	3.0
Temper:	None
Interior:	Lightly burnished; charcoal color
Mohs' test:	3.0
Firing:	Initial oxidized atmosphere, reduced and smoky at sintering point, sintered at 975° C

Gray Lustre and Gray Lustre Channeled

Exterior:	Black slipped with flecks of muscovite; medium burnish; graphite wash on all surfaces
Mohs' test:	3.5
Core:	Black carbon core; not thoroughly fired; buff clay body when reoxidized
Mohs' test:	4.0
Temper:	Not intentional; flecks of quartz and mica
Interior:	Some samples had a buff slip; all lightly burnished
Mohs' test:	3.5
Firing:	Smoky reduction of oxidized paste, sintered at 1000° C

Rural

Exterior:	Thick, coarse ware; gray, buff or light brown color; some samples wet smoothed, others roughly smoothed; grain and straw impressions on some samples
Mohs' test:	3.5
Core:	Micaceous clay body; some pieces with carbon coring, others thoroughly fired
Mohs' test:	3.5
Temper:	Heavily tempered with river sand; large, medium, and fine grains of quartz; traces of lime and feldspar; one sample tempered with chopped straw (monocotyledon)
Interior:	Lightly burnished; some smoothed
Mohs' test:	3.5
Firing:	Incompletely oxidized; a few samples show light carbonization; sintered at 1050° C

Rusticated

Exterior:	Thick, coarse ware in gray, brown, and reddish colors; decorated by wet smoothing; fingernail impressions or pinching on surface distinguishes this from "Rural"
Mohs' test:	4.0
Core:	Well-fired, colored cores with very little carbon coring; brick red clay body upon reoxidation
Mohs' test:	4.0
Temper:	Moderate amount of fine river sand with occasional large quartz inclusions
Interior:	Wet smoothed; same colors as exterior
Mohs' test:	4.0
Firing:	Primarily oxidized; some samples not fully oxidized; sintered at 1050° C

Smeared

Exterior:	Painted or slipped ware; unevenly burnished while still wet, resulting in a smeared effect;

some samples streaked. In all cases, heavy burnishing produced smooth surfaces.

Pale Fabric, Probably Painted

This is a large category of wares in gray, buff, light brown, and light orange. Their clear, light colors demonstrate oxidizing conditions of firing. Most of the samples exhibit a carbon core. All have been burnished or smoothed and probably painted.

Brown-on-Buff

Exterior:	Thin-walled fine ware; highly burnished, buff clay body painted with matt brown plus flecks of mica
Mohs' test:	3.5
Core:	Orange to buff well-levigated clay with flecks of lime and mica; well-fired
Mohs' test:	3.5
Temper:	No intentional temper
Interior:	Smoothed or lightly burnished
Mohs' test:	2.5
Firing:	Oxidizing atmosphere; sintered at 950° C

Black Topped

Exterior:	Slipped with buff, gray, or red; black rim band definitely painted on, probably with an organic substance, then reduced. Some samples streak-burnished, others with medium burnish.
Mohs' test:	3.5
Core:	Well-levigated buff on orange clay body
Mohs' test:	3.5
Temper:	None; unintentional flecks of lime and mica
Interior:	Smoothed; usually charcoal colored
Mohs' test:	3.5
Firing:	Body fired under oxidizing conditions; rim reduced, probably by inverting the vessel and placing it in sand for firing

Coarse

Exterior:	A heavy, very coarse, roughly worked ware of the pithos type; roughly smoothed, large quartz pebbles visible; colors are gray, charcoal, and light brown
Mohs' test:	3.5
Core:	Large areas of carbon coring
Mohs' test:	4.0
Temper:	Heavily tempered; large, medium, and small quartz grains and pebbles with traces of feldspar, lime, and flecks of mica
Interior:	Smoothed more than exterior

Mohs' test: 3.5
Firing: Colors indicate smoky firings with oxidation at the beginning

Smooth

Exterior: This large category has no any distinctive qualities other than burnishing. Colors range from buff to charcoal to orange-red; some samples show spalling where crushed limestone inclusions have burned out. This is utilitarian pottery; the majority of samples are incompletely oxidized.

Dark Burnished

Exterior: Not a distinctive group; contains all dark wares, excluding fine black-burnished ware. Colors are brown, dark brown, charcoal, and dark red, all fired as smoky reductions of an oxidized paste. Most samples exhibit carbon coring.

Pale Burnished

Exterior: This group contains all of the nondistinctive light-colored wares: grays, buffs, creams, and light oranges. All have medium burnish and usually no temper. Samples ran from oxidized to incompletely oxidized. Most exhibit carbon coring.

PHASE II CERAMICS

Some smoked wares continue unchanged from phase I: Black Burnished, Gray Lustre and Gray Lustre Channeled, Rural, Rusticated, and Coarse. In phase II, however, we see a great proliferation of painted wares indicating technical innovation in the firing method. Clay fabrics and temper remain the same, but the change comes in the use of clear iron oxide paint colorants and control of oxidation. Several varieties of painted ware have the lowest firing temperatures on the site, which suggests that, even though the firing method provided better atmosphere control, it did not fully utilize the updraft principle and therefore could not be considered in terms of a beehive kiln.

The dominant paint colors of this phase are brown, orange, red, cream, and buff, all produced by iron oxide impurities in the clay. These are the preferred early clay paints on pottery: they are less refractory than pure iron oxides and form a good bond when fired at low temperatures. The majority of white paints are pure kaolins or a mixture of clay and calcite. They usually become powdery after firing because they are much more refractory than a clay body, making them difficult to work with. This property may be the reason why no definite white-painted ware was found in this phase. The two sherds in the White-on-Red sample were decorated with faint white lines that resemble oxidized graphite painting. No white pigment was visible upon microscopic examination (40 X). A few crystals of graphite indicate, however, that these sherds were once painted with graphite. A mistake in firing or a reoxidation removed all but a few traces of the paint. This ceramic could have been an early experiment preceding the establishment of the graphite-painted wares of phase III. A description of these ware types follows.

Phase II Wares

Brown-on-Orange

Exterior: Decoration of matt brown paint on orange micaceous clay body; medium burnish; rare (tabulated with Other Painted (OP) on Preface figure 3)
Mohs' test: 4.0
Core: Thoroughly fired; well-levigated, orange clay body with mica and lime flecks
Mohs' test: 3.5
Temper: None
Interior: Lightly smoothed, pitted
Mohs' test: 3.5
Firing: Oxidized; sintering at 1000° C

Orange-on-Orange

Exterior: Decoration of dark orange painted lines on a lighter brick-orange micaceous clay body; fine fabric; light to medium burnish; fairly rare
Mohs' test: 2.5
Core: Thoroughly fired, well-levigated, brick-orange clay body
Mohs' test: 3.0
Temper: None
Interior: Light burnishing; same brick-orange color
Firing: Oxidized; sintering at 1000° C

Orange Burnished

Exterior: This rare group contains samples that are bright brick-orange in color, highly burnished, and very porous; orange paste is micaceous and well levigated (tabulated with Pale Burnished (PLB) on Preface figure 3).

Mohs' test: 3.0
Core: Brick-orange core; thicker samples exhibit carbon coring
Mohs' test: 2.5
Temper: None
Interior: All samples show medium burnishing
Mohs' test: 2.5
Firing: Bright orange indicates oxidation; sintering at 1000° C

Red Slipped

Exterior: Burnished surface; reddish-brown slip color; one sample heavily pitted; rare
Mohs' test: 3.0
Core: Carbon coring; not well fired
Mohs' test: 3.0
Temper: Some samples have fine sand temper; one sample has chipped straw and fine shell or limestone tempering (calcium carbonate), and flecks of mica
Interior: Red slipped; smoothed, with spalling
Mohs' test: 2.5
Firing: Low oxidized firing; sintered at 975° C

Red-on-Buff

Exterior: Brownish-red paint on buff clay body; medium burnish; micaceous and very porous (tabulated with Red-on-White (R/W) on Preface figure 3)
Mohs' test: 3.0
Core: Most samples exhibit carbon coring
Mohs' test: 3.0
Temper: None; flecks of mica
Interior: Rough smoothed
Mohs' test: 3.0
Firing: Oxidized; sintered at 950° C

Brown-on-Red

Exterior: Brownish-red slip; decorated with chocolate brown slip paint, heavy over burnish (rare; included with Other Painted [OP] on Preface figure 3)
Mohs' test: 2.5
Core: Thicker samples all exhibit carbon coring
Mohs' test: 2.5
Temper: Very fine river sand, lime and mica flecks
Interior: Medium burnish; very porous
Mohs' test: 2.5
Firing: Low, oxidized, sintered at 975° C

White-on-Red

Exterior: Maroon red slip over brick-red clay body; on the samples available there is no white pigment visible; white lines are made by oxidized graphite paint; some crystals are still visible (40 X); micaceous clay, medium burnish
Mohs' test: 2.5
Core: Very thick carbon core
Mohs' test: 2.5
Temper: Large amount of very fine river sand
Interior: Medium burnish; also painted with graphite that has burned off
Mohs' test: 2.5
Firing: Low, oxidized, sintered at 950° C

Brown-on-Cream

Exterior: A very fine thin ware with high burnish; some samples are matt painted; paint is cream and chocolate brown with mica flecks
Mohs' test: 3.0
Core: All samples exhibit carbon coring
Mohs' test: 3.0
Temper: None
Interior: Wet, smoothed, with flecks of mica
Mohs' test: 2.5
Firing: Low, oxidized, sintered at 950° C

Brown-on-Buff (see also same ware described earlier with phase I)

Exterior: Buff slipped and painted with a chocolate matt (that is, non-shiny) brown color; medium burnish.
Mohs' test: 3.5
Core: Micaceous, well-levigated, orange clay body; thick carbon core
Mohs' test: 3.5
Temper: None
Interior: Buff-on-charcoal slipped; medium burnish
Mohs' test: 3.5
Firing: Low, oxidized, sintered at 975° C

Black Topped

Exterior: Buff- or red-slipped clay body with charcoal shoulder or rim; heavy burnish, flecks of mica
Mohs' test: 3.5
Core: A few samples are well fired; most have carbon core
Mohs' test: 3.5
Temper: None
Interior: Black painted and/or smoked; medium burnish
Mohs' test: 3.5

Comment: Upon oxidation, the black rim disappeared, indicating either a black organic paint or smudging, or both

Firing: Oxidizing, except for rim and interior; vessel was probably turned upside down with rim covered by sand or ashes during firing

Incised Types

(1) Pithos:

Exterior: Thick ware; buff-slipped, red clay body; heavy burnish and deep grooves with white limestone infill

Mohs' test: 4.5

Core: Well tempered with river sand, flecks of limestone

Mohs' test: 4.0

Interior: 4.0

Firing: Oxidized, well-fired; not yet sintered at 1100° C

(2) Pithos Type same as above but with shallow grooves and no infill

(3) Pithos Type same as above but thinner fabric with very shallow grooves

(4) Pithos Type like above, but very fine black ware and very fine incising with white limestone infill (Maritsa type); smudged during firing

Black Burnished (continues from phase I)

Exterior: Black-smudged ware with heavy, mirrorlike burnish; micaceous

Mohs' test: 4.5

Core: A few red, oxidized cores but most samples have carbon coring

Mohs' test: 4.0

Temper: None; very fine, well-levigated clay

Interior: Black smudged; medium burnish; micaceous

Mohs' test: 4.0

Firing: Short smudging of oxidized paste, sintered at 975° C

Rippled

Exterior: Fabric is same as for Black Burnished Ware, except that surface has a fine shallow rippled effect

Firing: Sintered at 975° C

Gray Lustre and Gray Lustre Channelled (continues from phase I)

Exterior: Black slipped with graphite wash

Mohs' test: 3.5

Core: Brick-red or light gray

Mohs' Test: 3.0

Temper: Lightly tempered with sand; some medium-size quartz inclusions visible and lime flecks

Interior: Black smudged with graphite wash

Mohs' test: 3.0

Firing: Short smudging of oxidized paste; sintered at 1000° C

Rural

Exactly the same ware as in phase I.

Rusticated

Exactly the same ware as in phase I.

Coarse

Utilitarian ware; plentiful, coarse, thick, heavy, dark fabric, with large amounts of sand temper. Most samples are incompletely oxidized; a few are smoked.

Pale Burnished

This is an undistinguished group with pale colors: buff cream, light brown, and orange. Smoothed or lightly burnished; not tempered, but thoroughly oxidized clay bodies of well-levigated clay.

Dark Burnished

This group includes brown, reddish-brown, black, and gray-colored sherds. All have been lightly burnished but are not distinguished in any other way. Clays may or may not be tempered with moderate amounts of river sand. Most samples are incompletely oxidized; some are smoked.

PHASE III CERAMICS

The most interesting ceramics appeared during phase III. They developed with the use of higher firing temperatures, and surface decoration of graphite paint, and white infill. Certain utilitarian wares and some of the painted pottery from phase II (Brown-on-Cream and Orange-on-Orange) continued unchanged from earlier periods. True white pigment appeared for the first time on the Red-on-White ware. The fabric is very thin, well levigated, and has a thoroughly fired orange-red core. The white paint was applied as a very thin coat, and it was absorbed into the porous fabric, as was the red, producing a matt effect. The new Black-on-Red ware is particularly distinctive. The samples are all of a well-levigated, nontempered fabric of varying thickness. All have an orange-red or brownish-red slip with black manganese paint decoration, and an overall heavy burnishing causes the black to have a shiny appearance. The Red-on-White and the Black-on-Red wares are the only ceramics fired under controlled oxidation conditions. Other wares continue to be incompletely oxidized or smoked.

A second distinctive group of ceramics is the Graphite-Painted ware. This fabric varies in thickness and contains moderate to heavy river-sand tempering. The samples are heavily burnished, and then painted with graphite. The variously colored cores indicate that the pottery was initially oxidized or incompletely oxidized up to a temperature of 730° C, at which point graphite becomes fugitive. Some samples had been subjected to a smoky firing that deposited carbon and blackened the iron clay impurities.

An earlier determination of graphite on Gumelnitsa-type ware was carried out in 1968 at the UCLA Geology Museum using a Norelco standard x-ray defracto-meter, with a copper K alpha source, at a one-per-minute scan rate (see appendix 7.2 for report of more recent testing). The standard for comparison was a pure graphite crystal from Ceylon: UCLA mineral specimen, MS 128. Further tests revealed that the graphite was unevenly crushed, combined with a binder, and painted on the pottery. Upon oxidation to 730° C and above, the powdery soft carbon particles disappeared, leaving crystals, the largest of which remained even at temperatures up to 1200° C. Graphite also occurs in a refractory form, accounting for the results after refiring. These firing temperatures are significant in answering the question posed in the introduction and are discussed in further detail in the summary to this chapter.

The remaining wares were decorated by grooving or incising. The Grooved wares displayed clear oxidizing colors, while the large carbon cores demonstrated incomplete firing. The Incised wares generally had clear orange-red cores, but other colors in the smoky range indicated short smudging of oxidized pastes. White calcium carbonate infill was applied to many wares after firing; bands of graph-

ite were painted on others. A few samples displayed red iron oxide, a soft, powdery, easily rubbed-off material that was applied after firing.

Phase III Wares

Certain wares carry through from the earlier phases without change: Rippled, Rusticated, Rural, Black Topped, Brown-on-Buff, Brown-on-Cream, and Orange-on-Orange.

Grooved

Exterior:	Fairly coarse fabric of brown, orange, or buff color burnished moderately; grooves vary from rather wide and shallow to marked and heavy rippling; some grooves are gouged into leather hard clay body with a resulting rough appearance
Mohs' test:	4.0
Core:	Most samples have large carbon cores
Mohs' test:	4.0
Temper:	None, but lime and mica flecks noted
Interior:	Wet smoothed or lightly burnished
Mohs' test:	4.0
Firing:	Oxidation atmosphere, sintered by 1050° C

Incised without Infill

Exterior:	A thick-walled fabric with deep incisions; colors are black, brown, and reddish-brown, with light to medium burnish
Mohs' test:	3.5
Core:	All samples had well-oxidized orange or buff cores
Mohs' test:	3.5
Temper:	A few samples were lightly tempered with river sand, while others were heavily tempered with large quartz inclusions and lime flecks
Interior:	All samples wet smoothed with traces of finger marks
Mohs' test:	3.5
Firing:	Primarily oxidizing atmosphere, with some incomplete oxidation; a few samples were smoked; sintered at 1000° C

Incised with Infill

Exterior:	All samples are 1.5 cm or thicker; colors are brown, reddish-brown, charcoal, and gray; some samples show traces of graphite and red ocher paint; medium to high burnish; incised lines range from very fine shallow incision (Maritsa type) to deep, broad incisions, all with infill

Mohs' range: 3.0–4.0

Core: Very little carbon coring; most samples show a well-fired brick-orange-red interior

Mohs' range: 3.0–4.0

Temper: A few samples have no temper; thicker sherds show large amounts of sandy temper and medium and large quartz pebbles

Interior: Light to medium burnishing

Mohs' range: 3.0–4.0

Firing: Oxidation atmosphere; occasional smudging of oxidized paste; Maritsa type; sintered at 1100° C

Red-on-White

Exterior: Thin fine ware; matt reddish-brown painted stripes on white background, without burnish on porous, well-levigated, orange-red paste

Mohs' test: 4.5

Core: Thoroughly oxidized; red clay core

Mohs' test: 4.0

Temper: None

Interior: Wet smoothed orange-red clay body; marks of burnishing utensil visible

Mohs' test: 4.0

Firing: Oxidation atmosphere, 975° C

White-on-Red

The available samples are not a true ware. A red-slipped vessel painted with graphite was reoxidized, thus leaving pale white stripes where the graphite had been. Under the microscope (40 X), white pigment is not visible, but a few graphite crystals are.

Graphite Painted

Exterior: A highly decorative, distinct ware, with background colors of black, brown, red, or caramel slip, all burnished and with graphite painted designs. The majority of samples are thick: 1.0 to 1.5 cm and more.

Mohs' test: 4.5

Core: Few samples have carbon coring; most show a thoroughly oxidized orange-red clay body

Mohs' test: 3.0

Temper: Moderate to heavy amounts of river sand with medium to large quartz pebbles included in the larger samples

Interior: Most samples are black slipped and lightly burnished

Mohs' test: 3.0

Firing: Oxidized firing with final smudging of the oxidized paste; sintered at 1100° C

Black-on-Red

Exterior: All samples of this fine decorated ware show a highly burnished brick-orange-red clay body painted with a black manganese paint

Mohs' test: 4.5

Core: Thoroughly fired brick-orange-red cores

Mohs' test: 4.5

Temper: None; well-levigated clay

Interior: Usually moderately burnished with manganese black-painted design

Mohs' test: 4.5

Firing: Oxidation atmosphere; sintered at just over 1000° C

Pale

Not a distinctive group; colors are buff, cream, and light orange with light to medium burnish with no decoration; oxidized.

Black Burnished

Exterior: Black-slipped surface with medium to heavy mirrorlike burnish

Mohs' test: 2.5

Core: Samples have either light gray color and are thoroughly fired or have a black carbon core

Mohs' test: 2.5

Temper: Well-levigated paste with no temper

Interior: Light to medium burnish over black slip

Firing: Smudged firing of oxidized paste, sintered at 1050° C

PHASE IV CERAMICS

In the EBA levels, the ceramics reflect a "culture" change. Gone are the oxidized painted and graphite decorated wares. Phase IV sherds display carbon cores and evidence of long smoky firings, with only a few samples exhibiting the brick-red cores of oxidation. Painted decoration is no longer used; incision, grooving, and punctation are more commonly found. Black-burnished wares become popular again, but they are more highly fired. Decoration is distinctive by the addition of lugs or a raised thumbprint chain. The remaining wares are coarse and utilitarian, clearly showing that potters no longer displayed the same interest in decorative pottery.

Phase IV Wares

Fine Incised with White Infill

Exterior: Charcoal color; thick, deeply incised design with a white carbonate infill; heavy burnish
Mohs' test: 4.5
Core: Thick areas of carbon coring
Mohs' test: 4.0
Temper: Moderate amounts of river sand, mica, and lime flecks visible
Interior: Lightly burnished; charcoal color
Mohs' test: 4.0
Firing: Not completely oxidized; sintered at 1050° C

Incised

Exterior: Very distinctive ware of charcoal color; body decorated with very fine, shallow, straight and short lines arranged parallel in pattern or in chevron design; heavy burnish
Mohs' test: 5.0
Core: Thoroughly fired; same charcoal color as surface
Mohs' test: 4.5
Temper: Lightly tempered with river sand; various sized quartz inclusions visible
Interior: Lightly burnished; same color as exterior
Mohs' test: 4.5
Firing: Incomplete oxidation; some samples lightly smoked, not quite sintered at 1100° C

Grooved

Exterior: Buff- or charcoal-colored, medium burnish; decoration of wide, shallow grooves (rippled effect) or thin, narrow, deeper grooves; micaceous, thicker ware (0.8 to 1.0 cm)
Mohs' test: 4.5
Core: Large areas of carbon coring
Mohs' test: 4.0
Temper: Moderate amounts of river sand; many mica flecks
Interior: Wet smoothed
Mohs' test: 4.0
Firing: Not completely oxidized; sintered at 1050° C for fine-grooved ware and 1100° C for regular wide-grooved ware

Stamped Pointillé

Exterior: Charcoal or gray color with very light burnish; surface design of stamped, fine punctation infilled with white substance
Mohs' test: 4.5
Core: Thoroughly fired cores

Mohs' test: 4.5
Temper: No temper in some samples; others moderately tempered with river sand; medium to large quartz inclusions
Interior: Lightly burnished; always the same color as the exterior
Mohs' test: 4.5
Firing: Smoky firing of oxidized paste; just beginning to sinter at 1100° C

Black Burnished

This ware is a continuation from phase III; however, the decoration is distinctive for phase IV (legs and thumbprint chain decoration)

Exterior: Heavily burnished black surface; crude burnishing strokes visible
Mohs' test: 4.5
Core: Thoroughly fired black core
Mohs' test: 3.0
Temper: Moderate amounts of very fine river sand
Interior: Lightly burnished, pin-prick spalling where inclusion has burned away; very porous
Mohs' test: 3.0
Firing: Long smoky firing, sintered at 1050° C

Rusticated

This ware is greatly abundant in this phase. Clays are not well levigated or wedged (layers show up on section); a crude, rough utilitarian ware.

Exterior: Black, charcoal, or dark brown; surface embedded with river sand, mica, quartz pebbles, and lime flecks; very rough spalling
Mohs' test: 3.5
Core: Thoroughly fired
Mohs' test: 3.0
Temper: Heavily tempered with coarse gravel
Interior: Roughly smoothed; embedded with coarse gravel; same color as surface
Mohs' test: 3.0
Firing: Smoky, firing of oxidized paste, sintered at 1000° C

Others

Some wares continue unchanged from the preceding periods: Black-on-Red, Graphite Painted, Pale Burnished, and Dark Burnished.

PHASE V CERAMICS

Most wares continue unchanged from earlier phases, including Pointillé, Grooved, and Pale Burnished.

Incised wares, however, are very distinctive. The incisions become extremely thin and deep as if done with a pin and are arranged as chevrons, slashes, triangles, and lozenges. Some contain white infill applied after firing. Barbotine ware appears again, but its character is more coarse and the fabric is less well made, crumbling when fractured. The most common wares are dark burnished, brown and charcoal colored, smudged, and carelessly constructed. The temper includes quartz grains of all sizes, but more grains are larger than those observed earlier. Technically, the wares are well and highly fired, but the artistic or aesthetic expression of the earlier phases is missing.

Phase V Wares

Incised

	Distinctive for this period.
Exterior:	Colors are gray, buff, and light brown, decorated with very thin, deep incisions (as if done with a pin); some samples have white infill in the thin incisions; decorations are chevron, slashes, triangles, and lozenges; all samples are of a thicker ware (1.0 to 1.5 cm), with medium to heavy burnish
Mohs' test:	4.5
Core:	Most samples are thoroughly fired; some have brick-orange-red cores, others show black coring
Mohs' test:	4.0
Temper:	Small quantity of fine to medium river sand
Interior:	Medium burnish; same colors as exterior
Mohs' test:	4.0
Firing:	Short smudging of oxidized paste, sintered at 1100° C

Pointillé

Exterior:	Colors are brown or charcoal; medium burnish; decoration of very fine, infilled punctate; micaceous clay body
Mohs' test:	4.5
Core:	Thoroughly fired gray clay body of poor quality; not well levigated
Mohs' test:	4.0
Temper:	Lightly tempered with river sand
Interior:	Roughly smoothed
Mohs' test:	4.0
Firing:	Smudging of oxidized paste, sintering at 1100° C

Barbotine

Exterior:	Charcoal color; coarse fabric; slip contains fine particles of ground river sand which gives the vessel surface a sandy effect; slip trailed across vessel surface by fingers
Mohs' test:	3.5
Core:	Thoroughly fired gray cores
Mohs' test:	3.0
Temper:	Moderate amounts of river sand; clay body flakes easily
Interior:	Lightly burnished
Mohs' test:	3.0
Firing:	Incomplete oxidation; smoky firing, sintered at 1050° C

Pale Burnished

	This is not a distinctive type, but a group of wares colored light brown, light buff, and light orange. All samples show medium burnishing. Fabric contains a large amount of fine river sand temper and seems rather fugitive, as it flakes easily. All samples are thoroughly fired, and cores are generally the same color as the exterior. Clay is not well prepared and contains quartz inclusions, as well as mica and lime, and some samples show evidence of burned out organic material.
Mohs' test:	3.0–4.0

Dark Burnished

	These samples are brown and charcoal-colored smudged wares. Burnishing is light and careless with large quantities of sand temper present and many quartz pebble inclusions of all sizes. Cores are thoroughly fired and generally the same color as the exterior. These samples were all of a hard quality.
Mohs' test:	4.0–4.5

Dark Burnished with Gouging

Exterior:	Black color; heavy burnish; decoration made by gouging with a pointed tool; some samples have a white calcium carbonate infill
Mohs' test:	5.0
Core:	Most samples exhibit gray or black coring
Temper:	Moderate amounts of fine river sand; all particles are small and uniform
Firing:	Incomplete oxidation followed by a smoky firing, sintered at 1050° C

Some wares continue unchanged from previous periods: Grooved, Black Burnished, and Coarse.

A sample of Roman wheel-made black ware from the surface was included in the testing, but only for interest.

Roman Black Wheel-Made (Surface Find)

Exterior:	Black slip; highly micaceous, very smooth matt surface; surface trailings indicate wheel-made ware
Core:	Thoroughly fired, brick-orange-red clay body
Temper:	None
Interior:	Matt, black slip; smooth, with wheel trailings
Mohs' test:	3.5
Firing:	Oxidized, sintered by 1000° C

SUMMARY

The Sitagroi ceramics are similar to those found in sites throughout Macedonia for the same period, displaying affinities with Thessaly and the Gumelnitsa culture of Bulgaria, where pottery had reached a high degree of sophistication.

Sitagroi potters capably manufactured a wide range of ceramic products, from coarse utility wares to more artistic and ritual varieties. Careful analysis demonstrates that these wares were thoroughly fired at relatively high temperatures. The potters' complete control of an oxidation atmosphere produced clear and brightly painted ceramics, as well as the usual range of smoky wares found on most sites.

The two questions immediately of interest were: (1) Do the ceramics demonstrate firing temperatures high enough to expect melting or smelting of metals from their ores, and (2) do the ceramics demonstrate positive evidence for controlled reduction firing? These are the issues, first outlined in the introduction, and that I have attempted to answer.

The firing temperatures of these vessels range from approximately 750° C to 1100° C, with a few samples not yet sintered at the highest temperature. According to the literature (Wertime 1964: 264–1265), it is possible to reduce copper, lead, and even iron from pure oxide minerals by contact with charcoal at 600° C or even lower, but this method is not practical for iron because it will still contain rocky impurities. Although iron working is really not relevant in this discussion, I will mention that the common early slags for all metals are composed of iron silicates or calcium-iron silicates that melt at around 1200° C. Copper, tin, and lead melt below the temperature of fusion of these slags, but iron does not. If it is pure, iron melts at 1537° C. If a dull red heat is produced, iron can be reduced to a metallic sponge that can then be consolidated by hammering the particles together. From this evidence it is possible that Sitagroi technicians managed to produce heat sufficient for the melting and smelting of metallic oxide ores. However, smelting of sulfide ores seems to be a process too complex for the level of technology demonstrated by the ceramics and ovens.

Since black or smoky-colored pottery is usually taken as an indication of reducing conditions, it was felt that a thorough analysis of the black-burnished and black-painted sherds would resolve the question of atmospheric conditions during firings for all periods, as well as determine positively the nature of the black color. The smoky or smudged wares were produced by the same techniques used for centuries among past as well as modern potters. Smudging is a method by which the carbon and products of combustion are deposited on the surface of the vessel. It can be accomplished in several ways: the most common is to smother the fire by adding green wood, sawdust, or manure at the peak or end of firing. The sooty smoke settles into the pottery pores, turning the pot permanently black. Present-day Pueblo potters of the Rio Grande Valley still smudge pots by smothering the fire at its maximum temperature (700° to 750° C) with very fine, loose manure, and then shutting off the draft and leaving the pots to sit in the smoke from fifteen to twenty minutes before removing them (Shepard 1965:88–89). A second method of blackening pots is by partially closing off the draft so that the gases of combustion cannot combine with oxygen. This method works well with clays that contain large amounts of organic impurities or iron oxides, producing a vessel that looks carbonaceous throughout. A third method is to paint the vessel with a black pigment, such as manganese, that will remain under oxidizing conditions. Two methods require a controlled reduction firing: painting the pot with an organic substance and painting with an iron oxide pigment.

To begin the tests, the black ware sherds were refired in an oxidizing atmosphere to 5000° C. The carbon easily burned away, and the sherd color turned to orange, light buff, or tan. Many sherds exhibited the light cores of well-oxidized pottery, and in this case it was determined that the largest percentage of sherds were indeed subjected to smoke during firing. A few sherds with carbon cores must have been treated the same way, except that they were not completely oxidized before the smoking commenced. It remained to be determined whether the Black-on-Red sherds contained iron oxide in the paint or another mineral; this would be final proof for or against the use of reduction firing. Upon refiring in an oxidation atmosphere, the red and black colors were as clear and bright as before, indicating that the black was not iron oxide, which converts to red ferric oxide during this test. The application of several chemicals proved the black pigment to be manganese.

The common oxides and hydroxides of manganese are black or brownish-black and retain their color when fired in an oxidizing atmosphere. Manganese ores are available to potters in many forms, the chief sources being nodules, concretions, and bog ores. Manganese paints do not demonstrate evidence of physical (sintering) or chemical change (fluxing) during firing. They are soft and can be easily scraped from the sherd surfaces. They have been relatively permanent on prehistoric wares, however, as a result of vigorous burnishing, which compacts the pigment and presses it into the clay. A second factor in securing permanence is adding manganese to a well-levigated fine clay slip containing silica which, when fired, acts like a glaze.

The analysis produced no proof of true controlled reduction in this sample but demonstrated that smoking was a viable technique and, supported by concrete examples, is an important contribution (rather than mere speculation) to our understanding of Sitagroi pottery technology. The definition of reduction firing is understood by potters to mean a prolonged firing using insufficient oxygen, where the carbon monoxide formed unites with oxygen from the clay body to form carbon dioxide, producing color changes in coloring oxides (Nelson 1966:319). These true chemical and physical changes are far different from the incomplete combustion or carbon deposition demonstrated on the Sitagroi sherds.

At this point it is necessary to make some observations about the pyrotechnology at Sitagroi. At this writing, literature on the Neolithic to Early Bronze Age periods in Greece is sadly lacking in good descriptive evidence for kilns and ovens, particularly for the early periods. In his survey of the Neolithic, Weinberg (1965:27) stated that firing was probably done without a kiln, merely in a pit or hearth. In fact, hearths are present in all stages, but ovens are sporadic until the Bronze Age. The descriptions available about ovens are less than complete, making it difficult to decide which are suitable as kilns. Dumitrescu (1966:171), in describing recent excavations at the prehistoric site of Gumelnitsa (with levels contemporary with Sitagroi III), stated that even though the site abounds in locally made graphite-painted and polychrome pottery, no kiln has ever been found.

It is surprising that, when an updraft kiln is so easy to construct and so efficient, we find so little evidence for it in the archaeological record so far. The ovens of Sitagroi are not well known: very little evidence for them still exists. A possible technological reason could be that the ceramics were fired on the floor-level hearths or in pits, which were found in abundance. In the absence of a permanent kiln, potters can either fire in a pit or surround the pottery with fuel above ground, raising the pottery on rocks or a grate. When a pit is used, either fuel is stacked around the pottery or a large fire is built first; in the latter case, the fuel is allowed to burn to coals and then the pottery is placed in the hot "oven" with the coals raked around and over it. With these two methods it is possible to produce the smoky and clear-colored oxidized wares that were found. If the pots are not to be smoked, they may or may not be covered with other sherds to protect them from direct contact with the fire. Then the fuel burns down at the end of the firing until the coals are sufficient to burn away the sooted areas. Modern potters wait until white ash is formed before drawing out the pottery, for it must be remembered that the last effect of the firing is the result we see on the pottery.

Simple ovens like the semi-cylindrical model found in phase III (see volume 1: figure 8.20b [plate XL:2]) are usually located inside houses, as in the house model (see volume 1: figure 8.20a), or directly beside them. They are not ideally suited for firing pottery, as such a process requires intense heat—a good reason for placing these furnaces out in the open. Bread ovens simply have too much of their surface open to the air and heat is lost. Beehive ovens utilize an updraft, allowing for higher firing temperatures and good atmosphere control. In phase III the one oven excavated (see volume 1: plate XXXVIII) had several drafts opening onto the floor, just less than a foot of curved baked clay wall, and no fire box. It was not possible to state definitely that this was a beehive oven. Ghirshman, in his description of the evolution of pottery furnaces at Sialk (1938:38–40), describes this kind of oven as the next step after the hearth and fire pit, establishing it as the first distinct furnace: a dome of earth with draft holes in the lower part, one or more openings in the upper part, and no fire box. Draft regulation is antiquated, but a better control of oxidation is obtained. Since little is known about ovens in pre-historic sites, including the evidence available from Sitagroi, it seems likely that most of the pottery at Sitagroi was fired on hearths or in pits.

Finally, students of early metallurgy have noted that the roasting and smelting of ores can be accomplished by using the simple hearths and pits just described. Metallic oxides are placed in clay crucibles, which are then set upon a hot fire; the crucible and its contents are covered with charcoal, and the fire is boosted by the wind or an artificial blast of air until the ore melts. The surface of the liquid is then skimmed to rid it of the charcoal and surface scum, after which the metal is ready to pour (Coghlan 1962:70–71). The result of this simplistic operation is not always the best, but many cultures have used this method through time. It works both for firing pottery and for smelting metallic oxides.

It would seem then that there is some interrelationship and corresponding development between the specialties of ceramics and metallurgy, for only later in Greece does the development of a true reverberatory furnace precede or perhaps coincide with the introduction of smelting sulfide ores and the alloying of complex metals.

Appendix 7.1.
Graphite Painted Pottery

Elizabeth Gardner

Since writing the original paper on the Sitagroi ceramics, further study on the graphite painted pottery has been conducted (Gardner 1979) and is reflected here. During the Copper Age (5000–3500 BC), Sitagroi was apparently linked to the Balkans rather than to the Aegean, and the technology of the graphite-painted ceramics makes this relationship even more apparent.

The Neolithic and Copper Age ceramics housed in major and provincial museums of Bulgaria and Romania were studied firsthand. The Graphite ware that abounds in these collections looks surprisingly different from the Sitagroi examples. The graphite paint on the Sitagroi ceramics has a sparkling crystalline quality, somewhat like grains of sugar, and it looks fresh and brand new. The ceramic artifacts in the National Museum at Bucharest from the Gumelnitsa site in Romania were dismal in comparison. The graphite paint could hardly be seen, and in some instances it had disappeared entirely or left a white residue. The very smooth, even greasy, quality of the paint gave a gray or tarnished effect to the objects decorated with it.

All of these wares, sparkling or dull, had been grouped together into the same ceramic category by archaeologists because of their graphite content. From a technological point of view, however, they are quite different. To illustrate various characteristics of graphite ware, it was necessary to determine exactly how the Sitagroi painted ware was manufactured. The results of this study revealed a complex process of pottery decoration, indicating a sophisticated Copper Age technology, perhaps leading ultimately to the development of the more complicated process of metalworking. In fact, artifacts made of copper were found at Sitagroi in the Late Neolithic levels, together with a type of pottery that had an overall graphite wash producing a metallic sheen. Such a wash suggests early interest in the use of metal.

The graphite-painted ceramics of Bulgaria and Romania are typically found with a black background, although red and buff are known. Many of the sherd samples also appeared dark in the cross section, indicating that carbon remained in the fabric as a result of incomplete firing or smudging. Smudging is produced by firing in a smoky atmosphere, where partial reduction allows carbon deposits to remain in the pores of the fabric. When there is a lack of oxygen in the reduction, the iron oxide constituent of the earthenware clay remains in its ferrous or black state. Only when oxygen freely combines with the clay does the iron oxide content turn red or to ferric oxide. Nearly every sample of graphite-painted ware from Sitagroi was oxidized. Red and buff backgrounds were common, and those with black backgrounds had a red interior, indicating the use of a black paint. Only in thick-walled samples does a carbon core appear, implying that these Copper Age ceramics are most commonly oxidized. At present writing, kilns have not been identified for this period; therefore controlled reduction is not a possibility. These ceramics were probably fired in pits. At Sitagroi massive pits several meters deep were found containing large amounts of carbon debris.

The graphite-painted ware from Sitagroi was intensively analyzed in the ceramics laboratory of the UCLA Art Department and the laboratories of the Materials Department of the School of Engineering, UCLA. A Norelco x-ray diffractometer was used to detect trace elements, both in the paint and on the surface of the sherds. An electron probe and scanning electron microscope provided detailed information concerning the crystal structure and changes of these elements. Atomic absorption analysis, using an acid digestion bomb, was performed on the graphite paint in the United States Customs Laboratory at San Pedro, California, to determine the percentage of its constituents, particularly the trace elements.

These tests were conducted to learn more about the composition of the paint, firing temperatures, and chemical changes in the fabric resulting from manufacturing techniques. Two types of Graphite ware were identified for the Gumelnitsa complex (chronologically phase III). So far the first variety has been found mainly north of the Rhodope Mountains in Bulgaria and Romania, with only occasional samples located in northern Greece. The paint is usually shadowy and thinly applied in the form of spiral or geometric designs on a black, red, or buff background. Often there is little paint on the sample, and it can be easily rubbed or scraped off. It burns away on a secondary experimental firing under oxidizing conditions. The sherd samples are usually thin walled and black in section, although some clear orange-red clay fabrics were found in this category. Firing techniques included smudging for the thoroughly fired black wares and oxidation for the red fabrics.

Pit firing under these conditions does not harm the graphite because the carbon it contains helps to keep out oxygen during the firing, and the ash impurity of the graphite contains silica, which helps bond the paint to the vessel. Natural graphite, which can be easily found throughout the mountainous areas of the Balkans, was applied by rubbing it directly onto the ceramic fabric, accounting for the smooth quality of the paint. Small cones of this natural graphite have been found in the Copper Age levels of the Karanovo mound in Bulgaria. These cones are very pointed, much like the lead in a pencil, indicating the method of use. This variety should not be considered unusual in any way because the technology is in line with the level of pottery manufacture found everywhere else for this period.

The second type of graphite ware is found south of the Rhodope Mountains in sites throughout the plain of Drama in Greece. In contrast to the first variety, the paint is thickly applied and has a very grainy or crystalline appearance. It is found on vessels with various colored backgrounds, and all samples have a brick-red interior indicating oxidation firing. The silver-colored paint is well bonded, difficult to remove, and seldom disappears on refiring, even at temperatures exceeding 1000° C. I could not reproduce this technique in the laboratory, perhaps due to trace elements not yet identified. X-ray diffraction shows the main constituent to be graphite. The scanning electron microscope has defined silica crystals in various stages of formation, indicating transformation through ascending and high temperatures, possible only under oxidizing conditions. It seems that the carbon in the graphite caused local reduction of the paint only, and the high ash content of the graphite provides, in some samples, up to 75% of the silica available for crystallization and bonding to the sherd surface like glass. In fact, the sharp outlines of some silica crystals seen under the microscope indicate that the graphite was originally crushed and mixed with some medium for painting onto the sherd surface. This condition accounts for the greater amount of silica present and explains the more permanent bonding of this variety of paint.

The revelation of this research is best seen in the unusual x-ray diffraction patterns. The peaks on the readout strips definitely indicate the formation of iron carbide and carbon iron between the surface of the sherd and the paint. In the case of the graphite-painted pottery, the high iron content of the clay reacts with the high carbon content of the natural graphite in the appropriate temperature range to produce iron. Iron carbide is a simple compound of iron and carbon, and while carbon iron is the simplest form of all varieties of iron, it can be formed at relatively low temperatures when iron oxides are present as a flux.

The production of Sitagroi graphite-painted ware is unique because it was regularly manufactured for over 1000 years under the conditions required for earthenware clays, fired in the lower temperature ranges without a kiln. The result is probably unintentional and only a variation of the main northern type of pottery. This technique worked and continued to be popular, although Copper Age potters may not have been aware of what was truly happening. Nevertheless, the Sitagroi potters' experiments with the elements advanced metallurgy: they demonstrated how impure ingredients can combine. Copper Age potters were learning how to reduce locally or fully by means of a chemical process that allowed the carbon to extract oxygen from the product or the atmosphere. The temperatures required for either pottery manufacture or smelting are not as significant as the reduction process itself, because impurities always contain ingredients that lower the actual temperature needed to produce the results.

In this case, the study of how graphite was applied to pottery is just as significant as analyzing shapes and decoration. The technologies revealed are another satisfying way to appreciate the inventiveness and creativity of the prehistoric potters of southeastern Europe.

Appendix 7.2.
The Occurrence of Graphite-Painted Surface Decoration on Pottery from Sitagroi Phase III

Colin Renfrew

In view of the special interest of the so-called graphite-painted pottery commonly found in strata of phase III at Sitagroi (and at most other sites of the Balkan Gumelnitsa culture to which Sitagroi phase III is linked), two well-stratified Sitagroi potsherds were selected for more recent study, with the approval of the Greek Archaeological Service. I thank Sarah Kennington, Chief Registrar, the Fowler Museum of Cultural History, UCLA, in whose care the sherds reside, for releasing them for this noninvasive test, and my co-editor, Ernestine S. Elster, for initiating this testing program. Finally, I thank Dr. Paul Doemeny of the U.S. Customs Service, Long Beach, California.

The sherds selected for study are:

- Sample X70.1480D, from MM, layer 19: A rim sherd with curving graphite lines on a light buff/brown burnished surface (plate 7.2.1).

- Sample X70.1483D, from ZA, layer 32: A body sherd with parallel graphite lines on a black burnished surface (plate 7.2.2).

The analysis worksheet (laboratory number 95-21206) of the U.S. Customs Service, dated the 20 November 1995, reads:

> X-Ray Fluorescence analysis (kevex) by M. Samarin: Sherd no. 2 placed on sample holder with gray area exposed and tan area covered followed by the reverse of tan and gray areas. No differences were found in elemental content.

> Scanning Electron Microscope analysis performed by M. Samarin and P. Quiming: Sherds no. 1 and no. 2 were chosen because of the greater amount of gray lines. Sherd no. 2: gray surface particles (plate-like) removed for analysis (2 separate analyses).

> PGT X-Ray Analysis shows high silicon and low aluminum for both gray particles. Tan particles removed for analysis resulting in the same results; high silicon and low aluminum. Sherd no. 1 was analyzed in the same manner as sherd no. 2 resulting in identical results.

> Carbon analysis by R. Boglin: Sherd no. 1 used for analysis. Gray particles analyzed showed 27% carbon, and a blank of tan particles showed 2.8% carbon.

> CONCLUSION: The samples, gray colored lines on sherds no. 1 and no. 2 are composed of carbon (graphite).

On the basis of the examination, Dr. Doemeny reached the following conclusions:

> Carbon analysis of the gray lines showed them to be carbon. No carbon was found in the area outside the gray lines. X-Ray Fluorescence Analysis using scanning electron microscopy of the gray lines did not show any different composition in relation to an area outside the gray lines. What was seen was calcium, aluminum, trace iron and a large amount of silicon. This is a calcium aluminum silicate clay. Since no element was seen at a higher level and both surfaces showed calcium aluminum silicate, and the carbon content of the gray area is essentially carbon, I would conclude that the gray lines are carbon or graphite.

In addition, SF 718, recovered in contexts of phase III (noted in appendix 4.1), is a piece of graphite worked into an approximately conical shape. Although included among the artifacts, its principal significance may have been as a raw material.[1] Already in phase I, graphite was likely used to give an overall wash effect (volume 1, chapter 11 [Keighley 1986]:346) to the Gray Lustre ware. It is possible, therefore, that this cone (SF 718) may have been used in the process of ceramic decoration, in which case it might reasonably be claimed as the world's earliest pencil.

The conclusion noted above in the analysis worksheet is an important result, confirming perhaps for the first time what has been widely assumed, namely that the gray lines seen on the so-called graphite painted ware are indeed composed of carbon and presumably of graphite. The conventional designation for this ceramic fabric is well founded. The broader technical inferences in the field of pyrotechnology based upon the identification of this decoration as graphite are thus supported.

NOTE

[1] Small graphite cones and pieces were earlier reported from the settlement tell in the eastern outskirts of the city of Ruse, northeastern Bulgaria, along with vessels decorated with graphite paint (Georgiev and Angelov 1957:54–57, 77: fig. 38:1, 2).

8.

Metal Artifacts and Metallurgy

Colin Renfrew and Elizabeth A. Slater

INTRODUCTION

A principal objective of the excavations at Sitagroi was to elucidate a central problem crucial to European prehistory: the chronological relationship between the southeast European Copper Age and the Early Bronze Age of the Aegean. The traditional and at that time generally accepted view of Childe, Milojčić (1949), and Garašanin (1958) was that the two ages were contemporary, and that the significant developments in the Late Neolithic of the Balkans, such as the inception of copper metallurgy, were due to civilizing influences from the Early Bronze Age Aegean. The alternative view, prompted in part by the early application of radiocarbon dating, was that the Balkan Copper Age occurred far earlier than the Aegean Early Bronze Age, and that copper metallurgy in the Balkans was probably a product of local invention (C. Renfrew 1969).

The site of Sitagroi, because of its Aegean location, was chosen specifically to cast light upon these relationships, yet surface finds from the site suggested links with the Veselinovo and Gumelnitsa cultures of the Balkans. The early stratigraphic and chronological position of finds related to the later Neolithic of the Balkans (notably Sitagroi phase I related to the Veselinovo culture) and those of the Copper Age (Sitagroi phase III related to the Gumelnitsa culture) was confirmed. The metal objects found in Sitagroi phases II and III strata were recognized as being among the earliest yet found in the Aegean world (C. Renfrew 1970b, 1971).

The general validity of these claims is now widely recognized (Andreou, Fotiadis, and Kotsakis 1996; Chernykh 1992; Demoule 1994; Demoule and Perlès 1993; Séfériadès 1992a). The claims have been supported by analogous findings from Dikili Tash (Treuil 1992) and other sites in the northern Aegean and are indeed amplified by significant new metal finds from the southern Aegean (Phelps, Varouphakis, and Jones 1979; Zachos 1996b).

The long stratigraphy at Sitagroi allows the chronological contexts of the metal finds to be reliably established. Despite the relatively modest nature of the individual metal objects, their abundance and the coherent picture they present offer new insights into the origins of Aegean metallurgy. Appendix 8.1 presents a full description of the metal finds; appendix 8.2 describes the crucible fragments and sherds with evidence of metalworking. Tables 8.1 through 8.4 provide the results of various analyses: electron microprobe, lead isotope, and X-ray fluorescence. The first three sections in this chapter are by Elizabeth Slater (ES), and the subsequent extensive discussion is by Colin Renfrew (CR).

METALLURGICAL OBSERVATIONS (ES)

The 130 samples were drawn from metal objects and those nonmetallic finds that possibly relate to metal technology. Many of the samples are fragments of ceramic slag and are not discussed here. A complete cross section was removed from each metal find examined. Since many of the samples were extensively corroded, the sections were mounted and analyzed on the Microscan V Microprobe Analyzer. The analysis was conducted by focusing the electron beam on a spot of 0.5 micron in diameter and then examining the small remaining area of uncorroded metal. Although this method is not very accurate due to the high limits of detection, the samples could not have been subjected to other types of analysis without the risk of including some corrosion product. However accurate the analysis, there is no certainty that the

301

present constitution of the metal is that which it was originally. The nonmetallic samples obtained in 1968 were sparked on a large quartz spectrograph; the phases represented were subsequently determined using the microprobe analyzer. The nonmetallic samples collected in 1969 were analyzed using the spectrograph, and X-ray powder photographs were taken to identify the phases. These observations can be summarized as follows:

1. Phase I: Five nonmetallic samples; no evidence of metalworking.

2. Phase II: Four metal objects, two completely corroded (figure 8.1a; plate 8.1b); no intentional alloying in the object analyzed. Eight nonmetallic samples; no evidence of on-site smelting.

3. Phase III: This was the most interesting phase because it contained sherds with copper deposits, eleven copper objects (for example, figure 8.1b [plate 8.2c], figure 8.1c, figure 8.1d [plate 8.3a], figure 8.1f [plate 8.2a], and figure 8.1g [plates 8.2f, 8.9a], and a gold bead (figure 8.1e [plate 8.4]). Three objects contained tin, but not in percentages as high as those normally associated with deliberate alloying. Two objects contained lead, but the amounts were less than those found in objects from later periods.

   Nonmetallic samples: Twenty-four; one of copper slag from ML 111 and a possible sample of one from ML 114.

4. Phase IV: Six metal objects (for example, figure 8.2; plate 8.5). The fishhook (SF 335; figure 8.2b; plate 8.5:c) is a larger object than those found in the earlier occupation levels. While not sampled, it may be of copper. Three other objects have a lead content exceeding 2%, and one (SF 5625; plate 8.9e) has a tin content of 5.96%.

   Nonmetallic samples: Twenty-one; no evidence of smelting.

5. Phase V: Fourteen metal objects (for example, figure 8.3; plates 8.6–8.8). SF 317 (figure 8.3d) is a tin bronze. Two others (SF 3005 [plate 8.7] and SF 5339, shown in figures 8.3b and c, respectively), both corroded, contain higher concentra-

tions of tin than those associated with unalloyed copper. Six objects contain appreciable lead.

Nonmetallic samples: Thirty-five; no evidence of on-site smelting. None of the structures excavated appear to be concerned with metal technology. Several ovens and hearths, generally found in a domestic situation (for example, the oven in PO 158, part of the "Burnt House" [see figure 5.35]) during phase Va, do not seem to have been used for a metallurgical purpose.

FURTHER OBSERVATIONS ON THE ANALYSES (ES)

While there is an increasing amount of data concerning the chemical composition of native coppers (for example, Rapp et al. 1980), which suggests that native material can be distinguished from materials with the high levels of impurities expected from the products of primary sulfide ores, there is still considerable dispute regarding the validity of using composition alone as a fundamental criterion to distinguish native from smelted material (for example, Maddin, Wheeler, and Muhly 1980). For the Sitagroi material, this issue is further compounded because the initial analyses were conducted in the later 1960s using a first-generation microprobe analyzer that had neither the levels of precision nor the sensitivity that current systems provide. Only tentative conclusions are therefore possible, and neither the analytical nor lead isotope data points to any known source for the raw materials.

Although discoveries in the last decade have vastly increased the number of mines and copper ore deposits known to have been worked in Europe during the Bronze Age and the Balkan Copper Age, there is a paucity of smelting sites and direct information concerning the processes involved. Attention has therefore increasingly turned to the possibility of small-scale smelting systems based on crucible smelting that would not have left direct evidence in the form of furnaces, for instance. Some examples of crucible smelting are known for both copper (for example, Glumac and Todd 1991; Hook et al. 1991) and tin ores, but such smelting is not suggested for the Sitagroi material.

SHERDS WITH COPPER DEPOSITS (ES)

Forty sherds have a deposit of copper, or copper corrosion product, on their surfaces (figure 8.4; plates 8.10–8.11). All but four are from phase III, but unfortunately most are not connected with working areas. Those from MM 61 and ZJ 4 were found near ovens. Two are illustrated from MM 20: SF 5564 (figure 8.4c; plate 8.11a) and SF 5584 (figure 8.4i; plate 8.10); these, along with MM 21, were some distance east of the MM oven. Another sherd (SF 5628, analyzed on table 8.4) from ZG 22 was beside a hearth; the others were from ordinary occupation levels. The position of the deposit on the sherd is of interest: seventeen have an internal deposit: two on the rim only, three on the inside and rim, two on two sides and the rim, ten on the broken edge and one side. Two have deposits on the outside, and four have a deposit only on the broken edge. The sherds have a slight curvature in two directions which, together with the rough nature of the pottery and a reconstruction made from several fragments, suggests that they were portions of vessels used in crucible smelting. Such use would account for the rim deposits, as any metal would have been poured out. With the exception of two pieces from ZA 46s, all pieces with a deposit on the broken edge came from different locations and were of varying thicknesses, which would seem to preclude the idea that they came from a few broken vessels.

Adding sherds to the melt would serve no useful purpose, but the broken pieces may have been used to hold back dross upon pouring to give a clean casting or to remove the dross before pouring. The radius of curvature of some of the pieces is too large for them to be considered part of a vessel. One such piece, from ZG 30, was removed for further study. It has a deposit of hydrated copper oxide on the concave side with some copper and copper carbonate on the rim; the deposit ends abruptly on the convex side at a sharp raised edge. This context suggests that the sherd was part of a lid.

These vessels could have been used to remelt and cast imported smelted copper. Some copper objects from phase III contained traces of sulfur, indicating production from sulfide ores with incomplete oxidation during the matt blowing stage. There is one sample of copper slag from this phase but few other indications of on-site copper

smelting. Eleven copper objects were recovered from this phase but, as in the rest of the site, they are small, and there is no other evidence of the extensive metal technology that would be expected with the discovery of the forty sherds. That liquid metal had been produced in this period was indicated by the discovery of three small pieces of corroded copper and particles of copper carbonate in the soil, possibly the result of metal being splashed upon pouring.

The conclusion reached is that the sherds were connected with metalworking, but there is a surprising lack of other evidence (for example, bun ingots and slag) to indicate whether metalworking was conducted on a large scale.

DISCUSSION (CR)

Stratigraphic Observations

In general, stratigraphic control during the excavations at Sitagroi was good. The full sequence for the site was observed in the deep sounding ZA (along with the adjoining sounding ZB); that sequence is fully documented in chapter 7 of volume 1 [C. Renfrew 1986e]. Extensive areas of the strata assigned to phase V were investigated in the Main Area at the summit of the mound, including squares PO, PN, and QN. Regarding phase III finds, the areas investigated to the west of the mound summit, designated MM and ML, are particularly important. The level diagram for square MM is shown in figure 8.18 of volume 1. The position of sounding ZG, from which several significant finds were made from phase III, is seen in figure 2.2 of volume 1. Sounding ZG is some 15 m southeast of square MM.

It should be noted that the metal objects and small fragments were almost invariably recovered from the sieves. As noted in chapter 2 in volume 1 [C. Renfrew 1986a], all the soil excavated from the site (except that selected for wet sieving) was passed through a coarse 3-cm mesh sieve (see volume 1 [C. Renfrew 1986a]:21). In addition, material from sounding ZB was water sieved using a 3-mm mesh sieve. It is therefore no coincidence that a significant proportion of the smaller objects was recovered from ZB. At the time of the excavation, such recovery procedures were not generally used on prehistoric sites in Greece, and it may well be that the abundance of metal finds from Sitagroi owes as much to the recovery procedures as to any especially high frequency of metal objects at the site.

In general it proved difficult to recognize buildings and other structures at Sitagroi unless they had been burned, as in the case of the Burnt House of phase Va. The consequence is that, while the various finds may be regarded as coming from secure stratigraphic contexts, the precise contextual circumstances of deposition were generally unclear. Finds were not generally assignable to a well-defined functional context (but see chapter 12 for discussion of contextual association). As noted below, there was a marked concentration of sherds with copper encrustation in square MM layer 20 and adjacent levels, but no metal finds discovered at the site came from a recognizable in situ context of use. The occurrence of these sherds in and near square MM layer 20 is discussed further below.

The Range of Artifact Types

The metal finds from prehistoric Sitagroi are in themselves modest (table 8.1). As inspection of figure 8.1 indicates, the finds of phases II and III (assignable to the Copper Age or Chalcolithic) include a copper pin, an awl, and beads (see chapter 9 for discussion of these artifacts as items of adornment). There is also a gold bead (SF 4803; figure 8.1e; plate 8.4). No objects comprising any substantial thickness of metal, such as flat axes, were found; each artifact recovered contains only a small amount of metal, at most a few grams. And, of course, there are none of the shaft-hole axes and axe-adzes that are a common feature of Balkan

Copper Age metallurgy, as documented in the lands to the north, although they are not in fact commonly found on settlement sites.

Broadly comparable finds have been made at Dikili Tash (Séfériadès 1992a), where a small copper bead (M 1760) from Dikili Tash I (Séfériadès 1992a: pl. 146a), contemporary with the finds from Sitagroi phase II, was found. From Dikili Tash II, contemporary with Sitagroi III, came nine copper awls (Séfériadès 1992a: pl. 146b), the only category of metal find represented, although it may be surmised that water sieving would have also yielded beads and small copper fragments. The other copper finds from Dikili Tash are unfortunately unstratified. The Chalcolithic levels at Paradeisos, farther to the east, yielded two copper needles (Hellström, ed. 1987: figs. 48, 18, 19), alternatively described as awls (Papathanassopoulos, ed. 1996: no. 185).

The artifacts at Sitagroi and those from northern Aegean settlements can be closely paralleled at the various settlement sites of the Gumelnitsa and Karanovo V/VI periods in Romania and Bulgaria (Todorova 1978; Chernykh 1978a). Those of Sitagroi phase V (Early Bronze Age) are sometimes thicker, up to 0.8 cm, but the technology is the same. They are, in effect, cast metal rods that were subjected to both hot and cold working to give them their final form as awls, pins, and fishhooks. With Dikili Tash phase IIIB, the equivalent of Sitagroi phase V, came an awl and a knife, and then a dagger from the later Bronze Age; none of the finds analyzed is of tin bronze. Lead fragments were also found in Dikili Tash III levels. The artifact types from the Plain of

Table 8.1. X-Ray Fluorescence Analyses

| SF no./Phase | Artifact | Metal | | | | | | | | | |
		Cu	Sn	Pb	Ag	As	Sb	Fe	Zn	Ni	Co
Phase II											
234	Copper fragment	88.1	1.4	<0.1	<0.1	<0.3	1.7	8.7	<0.3	<0.1	–
Phase III											
880	Awl	98.6	<0.3	<0.1	0.1	–	<0.3	0.1	1.3	<0.1	–
782	Copper lump	93.0	<0.3	<0.1	<0.1	1.3	0.63	1.2	<0.3	<0.1	–
MM 20		96.8	<0.3	0.4	<0.1	0.33	1.1	1.4	<0.3	<0.1	–
Phase Vb											
2057	Awl	98.1	0.31	0.25	0.26	0.71	<0.3	0.2	<0.3	0.1	–
3005	Awl	95.5	<0.3	0.3	0.7	1.6	1	0.9	<0.3	<0.12	–

Source: From McGeehan-Liritzis and Gale 1988.

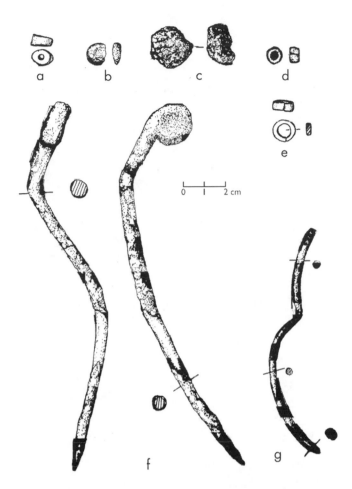

Figure 8.1. Phase II (a) and III (b–g) metal objects: (a) SF 5336, copper bead, plate 8.1b; (b) SF 781, small copper disk, plate 8.2c; (c) SF 782, small lump of copper; (d) SF 783, copper bead; (e) SF 4803, gold bead, plate 8.4; (f) SF 880, copper r oll-headed pin, plate 8.2a; (g) SF 1238, copper awl or fi shhook, plates 8.2f, 8.9a.

Drama are thus comparable with those from such Bulgarian sites as Ezero (Georgiev et al. 1979).

Evidence of Pyrotechnology and Metallurgy

The use of copper is already attested in phase II by a flat piece of copper some 1.2 cm long (SF 2999; plate 8.1a) and by two beads. As noted above, the stratigraphic position is secure. Moreover, the volume of material excavated and sieved from phase I (see volume 1 [C. Renfrew 1986a]:22) did not produce copper finds, suggesting that copper was not used (or at the least was very infrequently used) during that phase.

Examination has revealed that the more numerous finds from phase III in some cases show clear evidence of casting. In several cases (for example, SF 3439: plate 8.9b; and SF 5621), the "as-cast" dendritic microstructure is seen, obviously implying that copper was already being melted and cast at this time. Such a procedure does not necessarily imply that the copper was already being smelted from its ores, however; native copper might well have been employed in some cases. Other specimens show evidence of cold working and annealing (for example, SF 1238: figure 8.1g, plate 8.9a; SF 5622: plate 8.9c).

Examination by Moesta (1989) of a copper awl from a contemporary site in south Bulgaria shows the awl was formed by melting together smaller pieces of native copper, as indicated by the presence of small silver particles. The very low concentration of impurities in some specimens from Sitagroi, shown in table 8.2, might permit the hypothesis that native copper was sometimes used there. Other Copper Age specimens at Sitagroi show much higher impurity levels, and these may well be the product of smelting. There is doubt, however, as to whether composition alone can be used to distinguish native from smelted copper (see Maddin, Wheeler, and Muhly 1980). So while we may probably assume that much of the copper used was the product of smelting, some native copper may also have been used.

Activities on Site

A number of the Copper Age artifacts from Sitagroi show evidence of casting, and others of cold working and annealing. As noted previously, it would seem that some of the copper was the product of smelting from copper ores, while native copper may also have been used. The question therefore arises as to where these activities took place.

No molds were recognized at Sitagroi. Such finds are in fact very rare, not only in the Balkans but at more widely distributed Copper Age and Early Bronze Age sites. Indeed, convincing evidence from settlement sites for the on-site practice of metallurgy is very rare. Moreover, although there is good evidence for the extraction of copper and copper ore from such Copper Age mining sites

Table 8.2. Electron Microprobe Analyses

SF no./ Phase	Artifact	Metal										
		Cu	Sn	Pb	Ag	As	Sb	S	Si	Fe	Zn	Ni
Phase II												
2999	Copper fragment	90.8	–	0.4	0.41	–	–	–	–	0.02	–	–
Phase III												
880	Awl	92.0	–	–	0.5	–	–	–	3.0	–	–	–
1238	Awl	94.4	0.56	–	–	0.6	0.4	–	0.0	–	0.0	–
3439	Fragment	93.2	–	–	–	–	–	–	–	0.04	–	–
5334	Bead	98.7	–	0.04	0.28	–	–	–	–	–	–	–
5340	Bead	97.5	0.32	0.01	–	–	–	0.06	–	–	0.14	–
5621	Copper fragment	94.8	0.82	–	–	–	–	–	–	0.002	0.03	–
5622	Metal fragment	96.1	0.21	–	–	–	–	0.01	–	–	–	–
5623	Copper fragment	92.4	0.07	–	–	–	–	–	–	–	–	–
Phase IV												
30	Pin	96.05	0.69	–	–	0.36	0.48	–	–	–	0.088	–
3229	Pin	97.8	–	–	–	–	–	–	–	0.02	–	–
5341	Ring	62.4	–	–	–	0.1	–	–	–	0.21	–	–
5624	Metal fragment	93.2	3.2	2.1	–	–	–	–	–	–	0.4	–
5625	Metal fragment	90.0	5.9	4.1	–	–	–	–	–	0.06	–	–
5626	Copper fragment	96.2	0.12	2.4	–	0.4	–	–	–	–	0.02	–
Phase Va												
3017	Pin	91.2	0.9	–	–	–	–	0.06	–	–	2.34	–
Phase Vb												
317	Awl	72.3	8.14	0.29	–	–	–	0.42	3.6	–	0.05	–
1041	Nail	89.5	0.56	1.45	–	0.7	–	0.43	0.24	–	–	–
2084	Copper fragment	94.9	0.006	3.75	–	–	–	–	–	–	–	–
2086	Copper awl	90.3	–	4.31	0.02	2.25	–	–	–	0.65	–	–
3005	Awl	81.2	2.3	0.1	–	–	–	–	–	–	0.23	–
3313	Point	92.8	–	1.78	3.89	–	–	–	–	0.049	–	–
5337	Hook	97.0	–	1.39	–	1.4	–	0.01	–	–	–	0.027
5339	Metal fragment	93.2	3.42	0.03	0.13	–	–	–	–	–	0.002	–
Phase V												
331	Awl	88.4	0.74	6.12	–	0.81	–	–	–	–	0.158	–
5627	Metal fragment	99.2	–	0.64	–	0.05	–	–	–	–	–	–

Source: From this volume (C. Renfrew and Slater, appendix 8.1).

as Ai Bunar in Bulgaria (Chernykh 1978b) and Rudna Glava in Yugoslavia (Jovanović 1986), evidence for the actual working of the raw material through smelting and then casting is virtually nonexistent in the Balkans. Workshops or other appropriate installations for smelting and casting have not been found in the vicinity of the quarries.

In these circumstances the recovery from phase III levels of some thirty-six sherds or crucible fragments with copper deposits adhering to them is of considerable interest. Since there is no reason to think that these pieces were imported in this condition to the site, they are evidence of at least the melting of copper and therefore presumably the casting of copper on the site. We see below that, while such evidence might also be taken as indicating the on-site smelting of copper from its ores, smelting does not in fact seem to be represented.

Nine of the sherds came from level 20 of square MM and may be regarded as forming an association: the product of a single phase of activity. To these, the six from layers 50 to 21 and the one from layer 11 in that square should probably be added. On the other hand, the four sherds with copper deposits from square MM layers 61 and 60 probably belong to an earlier context. The sherds from level 20 and the adjoining levels of square MM were found mainly in the eastern half of this 9 x 9 m square and within 5 or 6 m of a structure (see volume 1: figure 8.19; plate XXXVII:2) that seems to have been a hearth enclosed on three sides by pisé walls. These sherds formed part of a rich debris, including much pottery (for example, pot 67; see volume 1: plate XLI:3), many figurine fragments (for example, SF 377; see volume 1: plate LI:1), a broken clay axe (SF 375), a worked bone pin (SF 376), a flint blade (SF 374), and a shell bead (SF 379), to mention only some of the small finds recovered during the excavation of level MM 20. Other items were recovered from the sieve. Adjoining levels (see the levels diagram in volume 1: figure 8.18) provided abundant additional finds, including the two copper objects recovered from layer 43: the roll-headed pin (SF 880: figure 8.1f, plate 8.2a) and the awl or bent fishhook, SF 1238 (figure 8.1g; plate 8.2b).

The structure in question enclosed a baked clay area, interpreted as a hearth. This was not, however, one of the very carefully constructed ovens, of which a good example was excavated in the lower levels of the adjoining square ML (see volume 1: plate XXXVIII), because it did not have the deep make-up of the stones and sherds clearly seen in volume 1, plate XXXVIII:3. But there was a baked clay surface, seen in the lower part of plate XXX-VII:2 in volume 1. This baked surface was surrounded on three sides by a pisé wall, preserved through heating or burning, and open to the east. This was an exceptional installation. Its similarity to and difference from other pyrotechnological installations are discussed below.

Sherds with copper encrustation of a nature comparable to those from square MM were found in other contexts on the site. The first of these contexts, as noted above, is layers 61 and 60 of square MM, from which four such sherds came; this should be regarded as a separate and earlier context from that discussed above. Four other like sherds came from layers 30 and 29 of sounding ZG (with three from later layers), three from sounding ZJ, and others from the deep sounding ZA (with

ZB). Thus we have what might be regarded as five separate contexts, of which three were soundings; only in square MM were such sherds found in the course of a larger area excavation. As we have seen, while one may not feel able to claim an in situ functional association, there may well be a relationship with the structure enclosing a hearth in that square. Four sherds were found in the phase IV levels of squares ZE and ZH. These sherds may suggest a continuation into phase IV of the technology that the finds of phase III represent.

One of the most complete of these finds, SF 5584 from MM layer 20 (figure 8.4i; plate 8.10) is clearly a crucible, apparently of oval shape, some 9 x 6 cm. The fabric was very coarse, with large grit and a wall thickness of up to 1.7 cm. Traces of copper were evident on the rim and may be discerned in a color photograph (C. Renfrew 1973d: pl. 127:1). Other fragments were from similar small crucibles (see figure 8.4; plate 8.6). But, as noted, some of the pieces, although fragmentary, seem to have a large radius of internal curvature, suggesting they may have been flat in form, possibly lids. In just a few cases, however (for example, the sherds from ZB 112r), the ware was finer; these may be sherds from preexisting ceramic vessels, not from crucibles.

It is abundantly clear that these sherds are indications of on-site crucible melting of copper, presumably for casting. The absence of any appreciable quantities of slag from the layers in which these sherds were found (or indeed from elsewhere on the site) seems a reasonably clear sign that copper ores were not being brought to the site for smelting. One concludes, therefore, that the copper was smelted elsewhere and brought to the site in metallic form, perhaps in small ingots (of which none have been found).

Pyrotechnological Installations

Three principal forms of pyrotechnological installation were found at Sitagroi. The first is the hearth ridge seen in phase IV (see volume 1: plate XXXVI:1) and phase V (see volume 1: plate XXIX:3) levels. It consists simply of a low ridge of baked clay some 70 cm long and 4 or 5 cm high, with a slightly raised part of the baked clay area level with the floor forming the hearth.

The second installation is the oven, open at the front, with a very carefully prepared floor and a low dome superstructure. It is most clearly seen in two miniature clay models, both from the layers close to layer 20 of square MM and forming part of the same context: the oven model, SF 813 from MM layer 27 (see volume 1: figure 8.20b, plate XL:2), and the house model, SF 755, from MM layer 16 (see volume 1: figure 8.20a, plate XLI:1). As noted above, a comparable structure was found in layer 151 of square ML, although the dome was not preserved. A similar structure was found in the Burnt House of phase Va (see volume 1: figure 8.12; this volume, figure 5.35), seen on the right in plate XXX:1 and the upper right in plate XXX:2 of volume 1. It is a form of a single-chamber bread oven, well known ethnographically. A fire was lit within it and the embers encouraged to reach a red glow. The ample sherds and stones forming the platform beneath retained the heat. The embers were then raked out, and the bread to be baked was placed in the aperture. Many comparable examples were found at Dikili Tash (Deshayes 1974).

The third type of heating installation was found in a single example in the Burnt House of phase Va: oven 2 (see volume 1: figure 8.17, plate XXXI; this volume, figure 5.35). Several samples were removed and subjected to careful scrutiny. Several samples were taken from the 5175 grams of slag found inside this oven and from other nonmetallic finds in level 158 of square PO. They were found to be a mixture of calcium, aluminum, and sodium silicates containing no other metallic elements. Six soil samples were also taken from three positions: from the mouth, the interior, and the lateral opening of the installation. They were sieved for any metal or slag particles greater than 1 mm in diameter. Ten grams of each sample were then covered with aqua-regia and left for three days so that any metal present would leach out. The liquids were then analyzed on a large quartz spectrograph; no copper, tin, lead, or zinc was present.

When discovered, the oven was full of slag. When this was removed, the oven floor was found to be hemispherical, with a raised side opposite a hole in the oven wall 5 cm above floor level. This hole could possibly have served as an air inlet, the blast being deflected by the raised floor. If the hole,

which was above floor level, had been used to drain liquid from the oven, a residue would have been left. Conversely, if it had been used to draw, for example, slag from the liquid surface, the hole would have been rather low in the wall. The material around the hole showed no sign that a liquid as hot as 1000° C had passed through it, and there were no metal particles on the walls or in the outside area near the hole. The oven was in a house near a domestic area, and it appears unlikely that it was used for a metallurgical purpose.

The question remains, then, as to what kind of installation did in fact produce the temperature exceeding the 1000° C required for on-site crucible melting. So far we have no clear indication of installations for the melting or smelting of copper from the Aegean Copper Age. None has been claimed among the hearths and ovens of Dikili Tash (Deshayes 1974). Crucible fragments are not reported as being associated with these features, which are probably bread ovens. One potter's kiln or oven was indeed found in Dikili Tash I levels, contemporary with Sitagroi's phase II. Although the account given of this find is tantalizingly brief (Treuil 1992:43), the structure may be compared with a potter's kiln from Galabovci in Bulgaria (Petkov 1964). Indeed, metallurgical installations are not well documented from the Copper Age Balkans in general (Todorova 1978:71) nor from the Bronze Age Aegean in the succeeding millennium. To generalize further, it is fair to say that direct in situ indications of early casting are scanty in Copper Age and Early Bronze Age Europe as a whole (Bognar-Kutzian 1976; Glumac and Todd 1991), with some of the best evidence coming from Chalcolithic Iberia (Hook et al. 1991; Craddock 1995: 133). Craddock (1995:100) illustrates a simple hemispherical hearth in North America in which crucible melting might have taken place, as well as crucible furnaces for smelting (1995:203) from Late Bronze Age Timna in the Levant. There are suggestions that casting can be carried out in open hearths (1995:125); although in such cases one might expect the use of blowpipes or bellows from which clay or terra-cotta tuyères might be found.

Is it perhaps possible that crucible melting was carried out in this way at Sitagroi, perhaps in the installation already briefly described from the phase

III levels in square MM? In that connection it is worth noting that figurine fragments were abundant in phase III squares ML and MM. Their production would, of course, not require as high a temperature as that needed to cast copper, but it would involve a baking process, and it is possible that there could be an association. Some years ago Frierman (1969) suggested that the reducing conditions and perhaps the temperature required to produce graphite ware, a common feature of Sitagroi phase III, might approach those needed for copper metallurgy, although further work (Kingery and Frierman 1974; this volume, chapter 7) showed that, in fact, such pottery was made at a temperature well below 1100° C. One concludes, therefore, that crucible melting did indeed take place at Sitagroi during phase III, although the smelting process was probably undertaken at or near the mines or quarries from which the copper ore was obtained.

Sherds with an encrustation of copper similar to those of Sitagroi have been reported from Late or Final Neolithic Giali near Nisyros (Sampson 1988), from the Alepotrypa Cave at Diros in the Mani (Zachos 1996b:142, 228), and from Mandalo in western Macedonia (Andreou, Fotiadis, and Kotsakis 1996:572, n. 256). It may be that similar melting procedures were carried out at these sites. At Sitagroi the evidence is sufficiently abundant to lead to a definite conclusion.

COPPER SOURCES (CR)

The trace element analyses undertaken for the metal objects found at Sitagroi are not likely to lead to any clear ascription as to the copper's origin. Despite earlier optimism, there is now a generally cautious attitude about the prospects of characterizing metal sources on the basis of a straightforward trace element analysis.

Of course, it would be possible to look to the now well-studied mines of Rudna Glava in Yugoslavia, even if recent work (Pernicka et al. 1993) suggests that many of the Copper Age artifacts of the Vinča culture did not come from this source. The mines at Ai Bunar in Bulgaria might give rise to a similar proposal, but again they have not been found to be as influential in the local supply of copper as had first been assumed (Chernykh 1978b).

The work of Noel Gale and his colleagues at Oxford on lead isotope analyses has certainly opened up new avenues of investigation into the characterization of metals (Gale et al. 1991). These investigators have analyzed a number of samples from Sitagroi (see tables 8.3, 8.4; SF 1238: figure 8.1g, plates 8.2b, 8.9a; SF 3439: plate 8.9b; SF 3229: figure 8.2c, plates 8.5a, 8.9d; SF 2084: plate 8.9f; SF 880: figure 8.1f, plate 8.2a; SF 3017: figure 8.3a, plate 8.8; SF 1041: figure 8.3g, plate 8.6a; SF 2057: figure 8.3f, plate 8.6c; SF 2086: figure 8.3j, plate 8.6d; SF 331: figure 8.3i, plate 8.6f; SF 3005: figure 8.3b, plate 8.7). A preliminary study (McGeehan-Liritzis and Gale 1988: figs. 4, 5) shows that analyses of the Sitagroi samples may be used to distinguish these samples from those of both the Laurion field in Attica, which became such an important source in Early Bronze Age times, and from Cyprus, which became a major supplier later in the Bronze Age. Instead, the Sitagroi examples are likened to specimens analyzed from Early Bronze III to Middle Bronze from Sesklo in Thessaly (figure 8.5). The authors conclude:

Table 8.3. Lead Isotope Analyses

SF no./ Phase	Artifact	Inv. no.*	$^{208}Pb/^{206}Pb$	$^{207}Pb/^{206}Pb$	$^{206}Pb/^{204}Pb$
Phase III					
88	Awl	8			
1238	Awl	7	2.07892	0.83972	18.697
782	Copper lump	3	2.06830	0.83829	18.635
MM 20		5	2.06402	0.83449	18.677
Phase IV					
3229	Pin	9	2.06902	0.83274	18.871
Phase Va					
3017	Pin	31	2.06402	0.83274	18.871
Phase Vb					
2086	Copper awl	13	2.06504	0.83380	18.823
2057	Awl	14	2.07291	0.83480	18.808
1041	Nail	12	2.07174	0.83982	18.631
3005**	Awl	11	2.07010	0.83546	18.713
3005	Awl	33	2.07160	0.83592	18.796

Source: From McGeehan-Liritzis and Gale 1988.

* McGeehan-Liritzis and Gale (1988)

** Note that at an earlier stage two samples (numbers 11 and 33) have in error been designated with the same Small Find number (SF 3005) and context.

Table 8.4. Electron Microprobe Analyses

| | | Metal | | | | | | | | | | | |
SF no./Phase	Artifact	Cu	Sn	Pb	Ag	As	Sb	Fe	Zn	Ni	Au	Bi	Co
Phase III													
1238	Awl	99.3	–	0.2	0.03	0.38	0.03	–	0.01	–	–	–	–
5628	Sherd	97.1	–	<0.1	0.18	0.22	0.03	0.01	–	0.04	0.17	–	–
Phase Vb													
2084	Copper fragment	94.9	–	3.7	–	–	–	–	–	–	–	–	–
Phase V													
331	Awl	98.6	–	0.3	0.09	2.95	–	–	0.06	0.14	–	–	–

Source: From McGeehan-Liritzis and Gale 1988.

If the presumption of a single copper source is correct, then we are able to say that, wherever the source was located, it was known from Thessaly to northern Greece and was exploited from the late neolithic (evidence from Sitagroi III and Dhimini) until the beginning of the middle bronze age (Sesklo). (1988:212)

They go on to propose Skouries in Chalkidiki as a strong contender, but observe:

At present we cannot exclude the possibility that Balkan copper sources may have supplied Sitagroi. We must emphasise at this point that we have no evidence to exclude the possibility that several different copper sources may have supplied Sesklo, Sitagroi and Petromagoula. (1988:214)

More recent work now inclines them toward the latter solution, and Dr. Gale has recently written:

We have now looked into comparisons between new analyses of copper deposits in northern Greece and the published lead isotope analyses of copper-based artifacts from Sitagroi. Many of the Sitagroi objects overlap with the mixed sulfide ore deposits, containing copper ores, of Kirki (Treis Vrises), Essimi and Virini which occur north of Alexandroupolis. One of the two early bronze age Sitagroi objects overlap with copper-containing ores in the Chalkidiki region. (personal communication, December 1996)

Very tentatively, Gale has proposed the following ascriptions based on his lead isotope analyses:

- Associated with mines north of Alexandroupolis: Sitagroi SF 782 (figure 8.1c), 1238 (figure 8.1g), 3005 (figure 8.3b), 1041 (figure 8.3g), and 2057 (figure 8.3f).

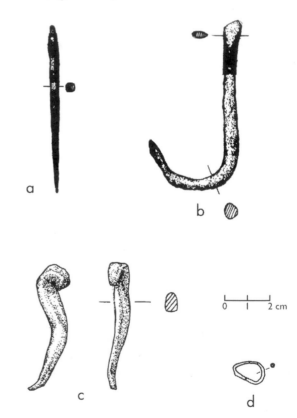

Figure 8.2. Phase IV metal objects: (a) SF 30, copper pin, plate 8.5b; (b) SF 335, copper fishhook, plate 8.5c; (c) SF 3229, copper pin, plates 8.5a, 8.9d; (d) SF 5341, copper ring.

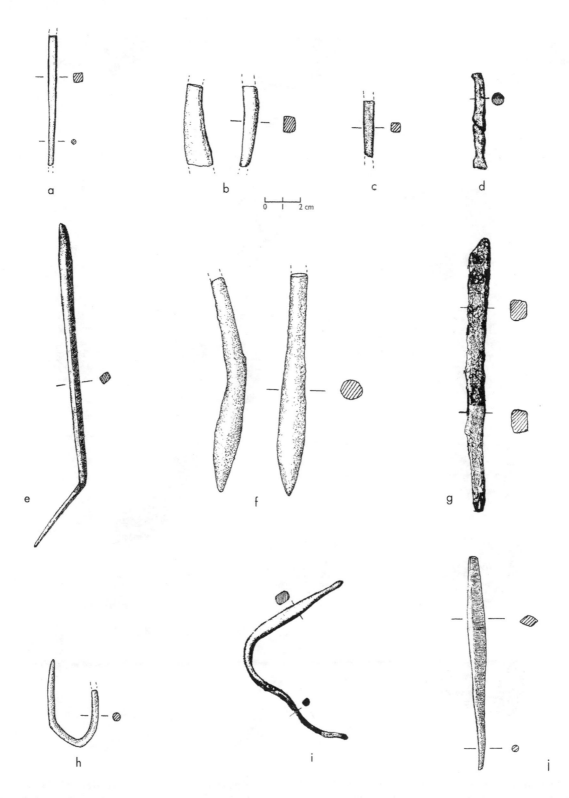

Figure 8.3. Metal objects from phase V (i), Va (a, e), and Vb (b–d, f–h, j): (a) SF 3017, copper pin, plate 8.8; (b) SF 3005, copper awl, plate 8.7; (c) SF 5339, bronze (?), probably part of awl or pin; (d) SF 317, bronze awl; (e) SF 3313, copper point, plate 8.6b; (f) SF 2057, copper awl, plate 8.6c; (g) SF1041, large copper nail, plate 8.6a; (h) SF 5337, copper fishhook, plate 8.6e; (i) SF 331, copper awl, plate 8.6f; (j) SF 2086, copper awl, plate 8.6d.

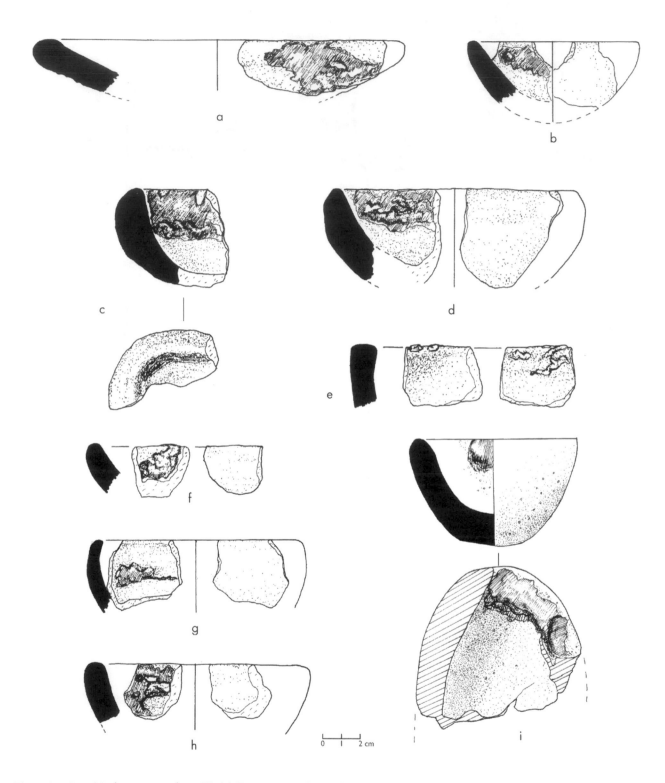

Figure 8.4. Crucible fragments, phase III: (a) SF 5565, rim sherd; (b) SF 5562, rim sherd, plate 8.11c; (c) SF 5564, rim sherd, plate 8.11a; (d) SF 4906, sherd, plate 8.11b; (e) SF 5561, rim sherd; (f) SF 5563, rim sherd; (g) SF 5566, rim sherd, plate 8.11d; (h) SF 5567, rim sherd; (i) SF 5584, base and rim fragment, plate 8.10.

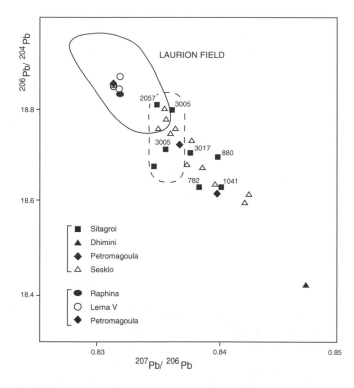

Figure 8.5. Lead isotope analyses graph (after McGeehan-Liritzis and Gale 1988:211).

- Associated with mines in the Chalkidiki area: one of the sherds with copper from MM layer 20 (SF number not available) analyzed by McGeehan-Liritzis and Gale (1988); also SF 2086 (figure 8.3j)

- Perhaps associated with the Pontokerasia mine north of the Chalkidiki area: SF 9.

- Perhaps associated with the Nikisiani mine in Pangaion: SF 3017 (figure 8.3a). Gale stresses that he and his colleagues have not yet had the opportunity to visit these sources, and they do not know if there is any evidence for early mining there.

Since these observations were contributed by Dr. Gale, further work at Oxford has permitted the new Appendix 8.3 by Zofia Anna Stos. Here she develops further the interesting and important suggestion that the copper used at Sitagroi came from a wide variety of sources. Of the ten samples listed in her table 8.3.2, four have a suggested provenance from possible Bulgarian sources near Burgas, three may come from the Cycladic Islands, one from

Lavrion (likewise in the southern Aegean), one from the southeast Rhodope Mountains, and one from Anatolia. At this relatively early stage of characterization research, it is probably wise to treat these specific ascriptions with a good deal of caution. There are several very local copper sources, one very close to Sitagroi itself on Mount Pangaion (see the map in Preface figure 1), and further work would be needed to exclude their use.

At the same time, however, there is the strong suggestion here of a wider perspective, with copper reaching the site, no doubt at different times, from a very wide variety of sources. And although the sample size is small, it is suggestive that the earlier samples (of phase III) are assigned sources to the north, in what is now Bulgaria, while all the samples for which a southern Aegean source is suggested are from the Bronze Age levels at Sitagroi. The likelihood of a northern origin for the earliest metallurgical practices at Sitagroi was proposed above on other grounds, and these findings would harmonize with it.

It is too early yet to base firm conclusions upon these suggestions. But they certainly do indicate avenues for further research.

THE USE OF TIN BRONZE (CR)

Several of the electron microprobe analyses undertaken (table 8.2) show the presence of appreciable quantities of tin. But it must be stressed that the analyses, carried out in the late 1960s using one of the first-generation microprobe analyzers, are not precise.

One should view with caution the percentages of tin reported from the analysis of SF 5624 (3.2% Sn) and SF 5625 (5.9% Sn). That small quantities of tin should be present naturally in the smelted copper need not occasion surprise, and these two analyses should not be regarded as proof of deliberate admixture to produce the alloy bronze. This conclusion is at variance with that offered by McGeehan-Liritzis and Gale (1988:220). Observations from Sitagroi suggest, however, that it would not be wise to place too much weight upon the analyses, especially since the two pieces might then achieve the status of the earliest tin bronzes known from the Aegean at a time when alloying with tin to make bronze was not yet practiced in the Balkans. Such a claim would require more definitive evidence.

A fragment of an awl (SF 317; figure 8.3d) from phase Vb was analyzed and found to contain 8.1% tin. This item is indeed regarded as a tin bronze and the product of deliberate alloying. It was produced at a time, broadly contemporary with Troy II, when tin bronze was coming into use in the Aegean, even if it was not yet produced in the Balkans. Although the metallurgical industry of Sitagroi III was precocious, as seen in Aegean terms, that of Sitagroi phase Vb was not, and this find is not a remarkable one when viewed in a broader Aegean context.

SITAGROI AND THE ORIGINS OF AEGEAN METALLURGY (CR)

The Aegean and the Balkans

The excavations at Sitagroi provide evidence that could at once be recognized as confirming the chronological picture that sets the Balkan Copper Age well before the Aegean Early Bronze Age (C. Renfrew 1971). It was possible to recognize that, while the initial impetus in the Aegean toward copper metallurgy experienced during the Aegean Late Neolithic came from the north, the Aegean development of pyrotechnology and indeed the social developments of the day favored the developing craft specialization (C. Renfrew 1973c). The rhythm of development was established primarily by internal factors. Several major developments in our understanding of early metallurgy in southeast Europe confirm and extend those early observations.

In the first place, the wide extent of copper mining in the Balkans has come to be much better understood. The copper mines at Rudna Glava in Yugoslavia have been well excavated and published (Jovanović 1971), and the important quarries at Ai Bunar have also been well studied (Chernykh 1978b). It should be noted, however, that the metallurgical analyses undertaken suggest that much of the copper used in the Balkans at this time came from sources other than these sites (Jovanović 1986; Pernicka et al. 1993). Eleven early mining sites are now known (Greeves 1982:538).

Second, a number of studies have cast new light on the origin and development of copper metallurgy in the Balkans. Chapman and Tylecote (1983) have noted the very early occurrences of copper fragments and trinkets in the Balkans, some of them from the early Neolithic, well before the Copper Age. Finds from the late Neolithic and the early stages of the Copper Age have been reviewed by Comsa (1991a, 1991b) and Jovanović (1991). It becomes permissible to wonder whether a very early acquaintance with copper, possibly in its native form, and the very simplest working, first cold and then with annealing, might not be expected in any area where copper or its ores are fairly abundant. Of course, trinkets of cold-worked and annealed copper are known still earlier from Anatolia, notably from Çayönü (Maddin, Stech, and Muhly 1991). But there is little reason to doubt that so simple a technology might be hit upon locally in favorable circumstances.

The place of the Bulgarian and Yugoslav discoveries within a wider geographical frame have been investigated and reviewed by Chernykh (1978a, 1992; see also Greeves 1982). Chernykh recognizes a Copper Age Balkan-Carpathian metallurgical province that has chronological priority over other copper working in Europe or elsewhere in the (former) USSR, including the Caucasus.

It is clear that the metalworking technology (and in many cases the copper) in the Tripolye culture of the Ukraine (including the Karbuna hoard) derives from that of the Gumelnitsa culture of Bulgaria and Romania and its neighbors. In the Gumelnitsa area proper, there is a predominance of shaft-hole axe-hammers, but relatively few shaft-hole axe-adzes, which are more frequent in the Middle Danube and Transylvania to the west and north, respectively. Greeves, following Chernykh (1978a), summarizes some important points:

> The Gumelnitsa focal area, besides covering the territory of the eponymous culture, also includes the Kodjadermen and Karanovo VI cultures. . . . There is evidence of a class of highly skilled professional craftsmen using two- and even three-piece open molds at the end of the fifth millennium BC. These may well be the oldest molds of this type in the Old World, though the finds from Sialk III and IV in central Iran may be contemporary. Equally unexpected is the fact that the scale of metal production at this time was not

paralleled again until the Late Bronze Age. . . . Contemporary Anatolian sites of the fifth and fourth millennia BC have relatively little copper. . . . In general the eneolithic in Bulgaria is characterized by the large-scale production of heavy shaft-hole axe-adzes, axe-hammers and chisels. Awls too, are widespread. Ornaments represent only five percent of the total assemblage. Interestingly molds are practically unknown, which contrasts with the Early and Middle Bronze Ages, when the scale of metal production was less. . . . Chernykh begins the Early Bronze Age at circa 3500 BC and draws attention to the gap of some 300 to 500 years between the end of the eneolithic and the beginning of the Bronze Age. (1982:539)

In light of these observations, it seems permissible to see Sitagroi in phases II and III (and Dikili Tash at that time) as being on the periphery of this Balkan-Carpathian metallurgical province. The graphite painted pottery, the figurines, and other finds from both sites show how closely the material assemblage as a whole is related to Gumelnitsa-Kodjadermen and Karanovo V and VI. But compared with the recovery from the latter complexes, the quantity of metal finds at Sitagroi and Dikili Tash is relatively small, and the copper shaft-hole tools so common in the Balkans at this time are simply not found in Greece. Awls and similar objects do constitute the main copper finds on settlements in both areas, and as noted earlier, molds are generally absent. The contrast between the precocity of the Balkans during the Copper Age in metallurgical matters and the slow start of the Balkan Bronze Age should also be noted.

The third discovery, already heralded by the small gold hoard from Chotnica in Bulgaria (Angelov 1958:389) is, of course, the great wealth of the gold finds from the Varna Cemetery, which may be recognized as the earliest substantial find of golden objects anywhere (C. Renfrew 1978a). Occasional gold artifacts are not rare in the Balkans at this time (Makkay 1991), but they are simply not seen in Anatolia or elsewhere in the Circumpontic area (Chernykh 1991) at this early date.

In this context the modest bead from phase III at Sitagroi (SF 4803; figure 8.1e) may again seem a shade peripheral. This find is amplified by the important small group of gold objects from Aravissos near Pella in northern Greece (Grammenos 1991:109, pls. 29, 30; Papathanassopoulos, ed. 1996: nos. 301–303). There are also two pendants of hammered sheet gold analogous in form to finds from Varna and Sesklo, as well as to a more recently discovered example from Platomagoules (Papathanassopoulos, ed. 1996: no. 299). The pendants were accompanied by two hammered sheets with perforations, closely paralleled in the Varna Cemetery but so far unknown elsewhere in the Neolithic or Copper Age Aegean, with the single exception of an interesting find from the late Neolithic levels at the Cave of Zas in Naxos (Zachos 1990:34; Papathanassopoulos, ed. 1996: no. 304): a fine ring of sheet gold.

In some ways these finds are even more indicative than those of copper because of their ultimately Balkan inspiration. The golden pendants clearly fall within the wider Balkan distribution of this type, and the rectangular strips with pairs of perforations at the ends correspond closely to those used at Varna as human facial decorations. This is a very specific form, and it is interesting to observe it occurring not only in north Greece in the important Aravissos find, but also in the south at the Cave of Zas in the Cycladic Islands.

Finds relating to the actual working of metal are still rather rare for the Aegean Neolithic, and they do not at present contradict the emerging picture. In addition to several copper artifacts from Neolithic Kephala on Kea in the Cycladic Islands, there are several crucible fragments and pieces of slag (Coleman 1977:4, 114). The status of the slag finds (which are unstratified specimens from the surface) was, however, questioned by Cooke (Cooke, Nielsen, and Nielsen 1978) and also by Coleman (1977:114) who concluded that "it is possible that some of the slags were not so old as is suggested" and therefore the evidence for smelting, as opposed to melting, should perhaps be discounted. The crucible fragments are broadly analogous to those of Sitagroi. The picture that emerges is thus related: crucible melting for the purposes of casting, with no clear evidence for on-site smelting nor any indication of a furnace to produce the temperature required for melting.

Similar conclusions may be tentatively offered for the finds from Mandalo (Andreou, Fotiadis, and

Kotsakis 1996:572) and Giali (Sampson 1988:218, 253; the crucible fragments are illustrated in color in Papathanassopoulos, ed. 1996:291, no. 186). On the basis of two small amorphous lumps of copper found in the vicinity of a large hearth-pyre, the claim has also been made that copper was being melted at the Alepotrypa Cave in the Mani (Papathanassopoulos, ed. 1996:228). Crucible sherds have not been reported, however, and this claim cannot yet be considered well documented.

Aegean Developments

The foregoing discussion makes little reference to Anatolia for the simple reason that little is known of the development of metallurgy there, after the very early origins at Çatalhöyük and Çayönü, until the striking growth of the developed Early Bronze Age as documented at Troy, Horosztepe, and Alaça Hüyük. The rich tombs of the Maikop culture of the northern Caucasus, classified in Anatolian terminology to the beginning of the Early Bronze Age, are perhaps too distant to be relevant. At the same time, however, we should bear in mind that occasional finds, like those of the Chalcolithic level XXXIV at Beycesultan (Lloyd and Mellaart 1962: 281, pl. XXXIV) may be only the tip of an as yet undiscovered iceberg (for east Anatolia, see also Yener, Geçkinli, and Özbal 1996). These finds amount to "a typical household collection of small metal objects," including awls and needles, but also a fragment that Stronach identifies as the top of a dagger blade (1996:281, figs. 8, 14).

While one should not forget the Chalcolithic finds from Mersin in southeast Anatolia, including the occurrence there of what de Jesus (1980:133) regards as tin bronze already in the Late Chalcolithic, it may be appropriate to follow him in imagining a Balkan origin for the earliest metallurgy of the Aegean coast, as documented at Troy:

> Even though Troy I metallurgy may originally have come from the Balkans, towards the end of Troy I it probably gradually became regionalized under the influence of a native Anatolian metallurgy operating somewhere in Northwest Anatolia. (1980:136)

It seems valid here tentatively to make a comparable suggestion for the development of metallurgy in the southern Aegean: the initial inspiration for the working of copper (and gold) may have come from the Balkans via northern Greece, but that already during the late Neolithic period there were local developments in the south that were not yet well documented in the north.

The first of these potentially local developments in the south is the emergence of flat axes, notably from Neolithic levels at the Cave of Zas (Zachos 1990:34, nos. 2, 3) but also at Sesklo (Tsountas 1908:191–192; C. Renfrew 1972:312). To these should be added the copper axe from Neolithic Knossos (C. Renfrew 1972:312, fig. 16.2) and perhaps three of uncertain provenance discussed by Phelps (Phelps, Varouphakis, and Jones 1979:177, nos. 1–3) as well as an apparently unpublished axe from Alepotrypa cited by Phelps (Phelps, Varouphakis, and Jones 1979:175, 2). Some of these pieces are decidedly plump and might be regarded as imitating lithic prototypes. So that while it is possible that the axe form in the southern Aegean is directly derived from Balkan prototypes, a local typology for this form should not yet be excluded.

Comparable arguments can now be made for another important new form: the copper dagger. Until recently it appeared that the dagger in the Aegean was essentially an Early Bronze Age innovation, and it was usual to discount the two copper daggers from an allegedly Neolithic context at Ayia Marina in Phokis (Papathanassopoulos, ed. 1996: no. 182) as being of Early Bronze Age date (for example, C. Renfrew 1972:116). The situation is transformed, however, by the discovery of four copper daggers from what is described as "a secure Final Neolithic context" in the Alepotrypa Cave (Papathanassopoulos, ed. 1996:228). The two illustrated pieces (ibid.: no. 44) were hammered from a thick sheet of copper; they were not cast like those (of copper more frequently than of bronze) from the Early Bronze Age, or apparently the two daggers from Ayia Marina. These two simple daggers lack any midrib: one has the remains of a tang; the other, five rivet holes for hafting.

Of course, one should not overlook the circumstance that the dagger is an established feature, also of the Balkan Copper Age (Vajsov 1993), where the finds are comparably early, although they fall less within the Gumelnitsa focal area of Chernykh's Balkano-Carpathian metallurgical province and rather more in the North Balkan focal area to the north and west, notably Hungary. As noted above, what is regarded as a dagger point was also found in the Chalcolithic levels at Beycesultan; an Anatolian, as well as a Balkan, origin could be argued for this form. On the other hand, the two illustrated examples from Alepotrypa (Papathanassopoulos, ed. 1996: no. 44) are both very "Aegean" in form, as seen from the standpoint of the succeeding Early Bronze Age examples, for which they would make excellent prototypes. It may be permissible to think of them as a local innovation based upon the existing technology of the smelting and casting of copper, along with extensive cold working and annealing.

The third feature of the Aegean Neolithic metallurgical assemblage, which has a very "Aegean" look, is the group of silver objects from the Alepotrypa Cave (Papathanassopoulos, ed. 1996:227): two pairs of earrings, a pendant, an amygdaloid bead, and 168 tiny perforated discs with a small annular bead. These items, discovered by speleologists working in the cave prior to its subsequent excavation, cannot be regarded as well stratified. Although the scarcity of Early Bronze Age finds and the abundance of Final Neolithic materials in the cave may not be a convincing argument, the undoubtedly Copper Age form of the pendant (1996: no. 43) certainly is. It belongs to the same family as the pair in gold from Aravissos cited earlier (Papathanassopoulos, ed. 1996: no. 302) and in a general sense with that from Sesklo (C. Renfrew 1972: fig. 16.2). And it is close to the long series of such artifacts, occasionally of silver as well as of gold, from the Balkans (Makkay 1991). But it should be emphasized that the Balkan finds are predominantly of gold. Silver is not known from the Aegean Neolithic, whereas gold, as we have seen, is well attested. But in the succeeding Early Bronze Age it is silver rather than gold that is widely seen, most notably in the Cyclades. The Alepotrypa necklace makes a very suitable prototype for one of the earliest of these finds, the necklace from the transitional EBA I/EBA II Kampos phase grave at Louros in Naxos (Papathanassopoulos 1962: pl. 67). It seems perfectly possible that silver working may have developed independently in the southern Aegean, where there were appropriate metal sources within the context of an already well-established metallurgy of copper and gold.

CONCLUSIONS: SITAGROI AND THE ORIGINS OF COPPER METALLURGY IN EUROPE (CR)

The finds from Sitagroi certainly confirm stratigraphically, from a site within the Aegean basin, the chronological priority of the Balkan Copper Age over the Aegean Bronze Age. This chronology, in turn, confirms the metallurgical priority and indeed the autonomy of the southeast European Copper Age (C. Renfrew 1969) based on the currently available evidence. The markedly local character of the gold finds from the Varna Cemetery in Bulgaria strongly confirms this view, and the recent, more modest finds of gold from the Aegean Final Neolithic complement the picture already established for copper.

Copper was known and used at Sitagroi from phase II, around 5000 BC, and was melted, cast, and worked during phase III in the later fifth millennium, when gold was also known. The copper probably came from sources fairly close by in northern Greece, where it was, at least in some cases, smelted from oxide ores. But the knowledge of the relevant techniques probably came to the Aegean from the north, along with other features so clearly evident at Sitagroi, especially during phase III, where the pottery and figurines are markedly of Balkan inspiration. The flow of ideas and commodities was certainly not all one way, however, as testified, for example, by the abundance of ornaments recovered in the Balkans and the middle Danube valley carved from the shell of the Aegean mollusk *Spondylus gaederopus*. Tin bronze, however, is not securely attested at the site until phase V, the developed Early Bronze Age.

These ideas are now widely, but not universally, accepted. Muhly, however, retains an almost mystical attachment to the diffusionist principle enunciated by Wertime (1964:1266) and reiterated by him at the International Congress in Belgrade in 1971 after the Sitagroi findings were made known (C. Renfrew 1973c):

One must doubt that the tangled web of discovery comprehending the art of reducing oxide and then sulfide ores, the recognition of silver, lead, iron, tin and possibly arsenic and antimony as distinctive new metallic substances, and the technique of alloying tin with bronze, could have been spun twice in human history. (Wertime 1973:485–486)

As Muhly puts it:

> The emphasis here is on the origins of metallurgy and on what can now be said with profit regarding the first use of metals and the ways in which metallurgy first began in the Old World, from the British Isles to Japan. I want to make it clear from the outset that I still believe that all these developments are, in ways however indirect, somehow related. I believe that the discovery whereby a hard, intractable rock is turned into a soft pliable and malleable metal, was a unique discovery, not one miraculously repeated in much the same way at different times in different parts of the world. (1988:3)

The word "miraculous" is introduced into the discussion by Muhly himself, and it is not clear from his writings what categories of archaeological data might shake his unswerving faith in the diffusionist principle. There is possibly a clash here between what used to be called the "two cultures." Although Muhly has worked with professional metallurgists, perhaps he relies so heavily upon a humanistic background as to ignore the Popperian principle that in the world of science, theories or hypotheses should in principle be testable and hence refutable (Popper 1959; Bell 1994).

For the basic principles of copper metallurgy to be discovered once, twice, or several times in different social contexts, each with a developing pyrotechnology, need not require some miraculous intervention. Indeed, the paper by Chapman and Tylecote (1983) at least raises the possibility that some of the basic techniques might have been invented several times at different places during the southeast European Copper Age (and of course beyond). As Chernykh observes:

> The phenomenon of the earliest European metallurgy evidently cannot be explained in terms of a guiding western Asiatic influence. The difference between the main forms of tools and weapons in each region was considerable, and in mining and metallurgical productive power during the fifth to fourth

millennium BC, the balance was significantly in favor of Europe. (1992:51)

The important issues here are not matters of faith, or of abstract principles of diffusion, or of independent innovation. The real problem is to investigate in what economic, social, and technological conditions important discoveries are made and significant innovations widely adopted.

We need to understand more clearly why it was that the principles of copper metallurgy were understood in the Aegean for at least two millennia before the great upsurge in production that we recognize in the Early Bronze II period, with its international spirit. In each instance it is not simply the invention that is significant, but the social and other circumstances that led to its widespread adoption or to its failure to catch on (C. Renfrew 1978b). Nakou (1995) has persuasively argued that two related factors at the onset of the Early Bronze Age may have favored the development of metallurgy and the metals trade and their clear documentation in the archaeological record. In the first place, the development of a dispersed settlement pattern, with the exploitation of areas of land beyond the alluvial plains, will have favored mutual reliance through economic interactions and probably through ritual interactions. It is in this context that the inception of the first Aegean installations for formal burial may have been constructed at the beginning of the Bronze Age (or earlier in the case of the Kephala Cemetery on Kea).

Metal objects would clearly play an important role among these economic interactions, and perhaps in the practice of ritual. Certainly it is with the inception of formal burial in constructed tombs that we find the deliberate inhumation of grave goods, sometimes with metal objects prominent among them. Were it not for this new taphonomic circumstance, our knowledge of Early Bronze Age metallurgy in the Aegean might be as scanty as it is for the Neolithic period, or as scanty as it was in the Balkans until the funerary depositions at Varna amplified the information gleaned from the settlements.

Until we better understand the social and economic conditions in which early metallurgy emerged in each region where it is found, we shall be condemned to endure continuing debates about its seemingly miraculous conception.

Appendix 8.1.
The Finds: Metal Objects
Colin Renfrew and Elizabeth A. Slater

Finds are presented in this order: phase, followed by SF number (in numerical sequence), context (square and level), reference to figures (8.1–8.5), plates (8.1–8.11), tables (8.1–8.4), and appendix 8.3; description (the initials "ES" indicate specific observations made by Elizabeth Slater), measurements, and citation to earlier publication.

PHASE II

234 ZA 50; table 8.1
Small copper fragment.
References: McGeehan-Liritzis and Gale 1988: table 5, inventory no. 2

2999 ZG 34; plate 8.1a; table 8.2
Long flat piece of copper, corroded, rectangular section.
ES: Fragment of metal with both ends broken, thin cross section, extensive internal corrosion.
L: 1.2 cm; width: 0.4 cm
References: Branigan 1974: no. 3405; McGeehan-Liritzis and Gale 1988: table 4, inventory no. 17; Renfrew 1973a: pl. 126, 3:127.

5335 ZA 55s
Small copper bead, two fragments; one fragment shows part of perforation.
L: 0.2 to 0.3 cm

5336 ZA 52s; figure 8.1a; plate 8.1b
Copper bead, complete, well made, narrow cylindrical type.
Th: 0.2 cm; Diam: 0.3 cm

PHASE III

781 ZA 47s; figure 8.1b; plate 8.2c
Small copper disk, half-size fragment, possibly half-made bead.
ES: Small, round piece of copper, very thin and extensively corroded. It has a small hole in the center and may have been a copper bead. No element other than copper was found on analysis.
Th: 0.1 cm; Diam: 0.3 cm

782 ZA 47s; figure 8.1c; tables 8.1, 8.3; appendix 8.3
Small lump of copper, with black, and yellow coloration.
ES: Small pieces of copper corrosion product found in the soil near SF 781. The two main elements found on analysis were copper and zinc.
L: 0.6 cm
References: McGeehan-Liritzis and Gale 1988: tables 3, 5, inventory no. 3

783 ZA 47s; figure 8.1d; plate 8.3a
Small, rough narrow cylindrical type copper bead.
ES: Similar to 782, left unsampled.
Th: 0.2 cm; Diam: 0.4 cm

880 MM 43; figure 8.1f; plate 8.2a; tables 8.1–8.3
Copper roll-headed pin, corroded, circular section.
L: 8.0 cm; Diam: 0.3 to 0.8 cm
References: Branigan 1974: no. 1543; McGeehan-Liritzis and Gale 1988: tables 3 and 5, inventory no. 8; Renfrew 1970: pl. XLIII, upper right; 1973a: pl. 126, 1:127.
ES: Tip removed from a pin; the metal had been cold worked and annealed.

1238 MM 43; figure 8.1g; plates 8.2b, 8.9a; tables 8.2–8.4; appendix 8.3
Copper awl or fishhook, rectangular section.
ES: Section taken from a pin; cold-worked and annealed microstructure shown in plate 8.9a.
L: 4.3 cm; Diam: 0.2 cm
References: McGeehan-Liritzis and Gale 1988: tables 3, 4, inventory no. 7; Renfrew 1970: pl. XLIII, upper left; Renfrew 1973a: pl. 126, 2:127.

3439 MMc 60; plate 8.9b; table 8.2.
Copper fragments.
ES: Copper fragments in soil, one with an uncorroded center; dendritic microstructure is shown in plate 8.9b.
L: 1.3 cm
References: McGeehan-Liritzis and Gale 1988: table 4, inventory no. 4

4803 ZB 125r; figure 8.1:e; plate 8.4
Gold bead, narrow cylindrical type, made by joining gold wire; join very crude.

ES: Gold bead; internal diameter 0.28 cm, external diameter 0.52 cm, height 0.35 cm. It was examined under a microscope, and there was evidence of working by tooling, with groove marks on the outer surface running parallel to the top. The bore was almost uniform, and the inner surface showed no working marks. The bead was probably made from a flat piece of metal beaten around an inner core. The ends had been cut diagonally and had tooling marks near their edges showing that an attempt had been made to weld them together. Not sampled for analysis.
Th: 0.2 cm; Diam: 0.4 cm
References: Branigan 1974: no. 3112; Papathanasso-poulos, ed. 1996: no. 300; Renfrew 1973a: pl. 124:126.

5334   ZA 44s; plate 8.2d; table 8.2
Copper (?) bead, in fragments.
ES: Copper bead, cold-worked microstructure, with some internal corrosion.
References: McGeehan-Liritzis and Gale 1988: table 4, inventory no. 19.

5340   ZB 125r; plate 8.3b; table 8.2
Wide cylindrical-type copper bead, with part missing.
ES: Copper bead; cold worked and annealed.
Th: 0.4 cm; Diam: 0.3 cm
References: Branigan 1974: no. 4803; McGeehan-Liritzis and Gale 1988: table 4, inventory no. 18

5621   ZB 115r; table 8.2
Two small pieces of corroded copper.
ES: External and internal corrosion, "as cast" dendritic microstructure.
References: McGeehan-Liritzis and Gale 1988: table 4, inventory no. 20

5622   ZB 119r; plates 8.2e, 8.9c; table 8.2
Small piece of corroded metal.
ES: Cold-worked and annealed microstructure shown in plate 8.9c.
References: McGeehan-Liritzis and Gale 1988: table 4, inventory no. 21

5623   ZB 126r; plate 8.2f; table 8.2
Thin piece of irregularly shaped copper.
ES: Dendritic microstructure with extensive internal corrosion.

PHASE IV

30   ZA 23; figure 8.2a; plate 8.5b; table 8.2
Copper pin, quadrangular section, tapering to a point at one end and evidence of narrowing at the other.

ES: Pin of quadrangular cross section; it had been heavily cold worked and was extensively corroded.
L: 3.3 cm; Diam: 1.5 cm
References: McGeehan-Liritzis and Gale 1988: table 4, inventory no. 26

335   SL 9; figure 8.2b; plate 8.5c
Copper fishhook, circular section, complete; curves to a point, other end flat and wide for attachment.
L: 6.0 cm; Diam: 2.5 cm
ES: Complete copper hook, left unsampled.

3229   ZHt 17; figure 8.2c; plates 8.5a, 8.9d; tables 8.2, 8.3; appendix 8.3
Copper pin; thick, curved, roll-headed, probably quadrangular section.
ES: Roll-headed pin covered in corrosion product; cold-worked and annealed microstructure shown in plate 8.9d.
L: 2.5 cm; Diam: 0.4–0.7 cm
References: McGeehan-Liritzis and Gale 1988: tables 3, 4, inventory no. 9.
Note: McGeehan-Liritzis and Gale wrongly equate this with Branigan 1974: no. 1543 (880).

5341   ZB 56r; figure 8.2d; table 8.2
Copper ring (possibly two), fragments, very fine wire.
ES: Copper; the sample was completely corroded and thus the analysis results may not be reliable.
L: 0.75 cm; Diam: 0.45 cm

5624   ZB 43r; table 8.2
Piece of corroded metal (bronze?), ball shaped.
ES: Covered in a layer of green corrosion product, difficult to sample by cutting a cross section; material was removed for analysis by drilling and thus there was no section for microstructural study.
References: McGeehan-Liritzis and Gale 1988: table 4, inventory no. 25

5625   ZB 46r; plate 8.9e; table 8.2
Piece of metal (bronze?), circular cross-section, irregularly shaped.
ES: Cold-worked microstructure shown in plate 8.9e.
References: McGeehan-Liritzis and Gale 1988: table 4, inventory no. 24.

5626   ZB 68r; table 8.2
Piece of irregularly shaped copper.
ES: Dendritic "as cast" microstructure.
References: McGeehan-Liritzis and Gale 1988: table 4, inventory no. 23

PHASE VA

3017   ROc 49; figure 8.3a; plate 8.8; tables 8.2, 8.3; appendix 8.3
Copper pin, broken at end, quadrangular section.
ES: Pin of quadrangular cross section with one broken end; sample taken from sharp end was cold worked with possible intent to sharpen and harden it.
L: 3.9 cm; Diam: 2.5 cm
References: McGeehan-Liritzis and Gale 1988: tables 3, 4, inventory no. 31

3313   PO/B 38; figure 8.3:e; plate 8.6:b; table 8.2
Copper point, corroded, quadrangular section, bent at one end.
ES: Curved awl with thick corrosion product on the surface apart from a compact layer of patina on the sharp end; cold worked and annealed microstructure; some porosity and inter-granular corrosion.
L: 9.0 cm; Diam: 0.3 cm
References: McGeehan-Liritzis and Gale 1988: table 4, inventory no. 27

3356   PO 163
Copper (bronze?) fragment, possibly part of pin or awl.
L: 1.0 cm; Diam: 0.35 cm
ES: Copper fragment of circular cross section with a loose green layer of corrosion product; completely corroded in the center with a hole through the center; too corroded for analysis or microstructural study.

PHASE VB

317   PO 6; figure 8.3d; table 8.2
Bronze awl, circular section.
ES: Irregularly shaped piece of metal; dendritic microstructure; extensive internal corrosion.
L: 2.7 cm
References: McGeehan-Liritzis and Gale 1988: table 4, inventory no. 32

1095   QN 8
Copper fragments

2084   PO/D 34; plate 8.9f; tables 8.2, 8.4
Lump of copper fragments.
ES: Irregularly shaped piece of metal covered with green corrosion product; "as cast" dendritic microstructure with some porosity between the dendrites, shown in plate 8.9f.
L: 1.4 cm
References: McGeehan-Liritzis and Gale 1988: table 4, inventory no. 15

3005   ROc 30; figure 8.3b; plate 8.7; tables 8.18.3; appendix 8.3
Copper awl, fragment, quadrangular section, wider and flatter at one end.
ES: Fragment of quadrangular cross section, possibly from an awl; both ends broken; extensive internal corrosion.
L: 2.1 cm; Diam: 0.4–0.6 cm
References: McGeehan-Liritzis and Gale 1988: tables 3, 5, inventory no. 11

5337   ZB 10r; figure 8.3h; plate 8.6e; table 8.2
Copper fishhook, broken at attachment end, circular section.
ES: Hook of circular cross-section; cold worked and annealed.
L: 4.8 cm; Diam: 0.2 cm
References: McGeehan-Liritzis and Gale 1988: table 4, inventory no. 30

5339   ZB 6r; figure 8.3c; table 8.2
Metal, bronze (?) fragment, circular section, probably part of awl or pin.
ES: Fragment of circular cross-section with both ends broken, possibly a piece of an awl or pin; cold worked and annealed.
L: 1.2 cm; Diam: 0.3 cm
References: McGeehan-Liritzis and Gale 1988: table 4, inventory no. 28

5608   ZB 10r
Copper fragment (?), circular in section.
L: 0.7 cm; Diam: 0.4 cm

PHASE V

331   SL 5; figure 8.3i; plate 8.6f; tables 8.2, 8.4
Copper awl, quadrangular section; curved at one end, widens out at other, then narrows to a blunt point.
ES: Awl covered in green corrosion product; cold worked and annealed.
L: 6.7 cm; Diam: 0.15–0.3 cm
References: McGeehan-Liritzis and Gale 1988: table 4, inventory no. 10

1041   QN 7; figure 8.3g; plate 8.6a; tables 8.2, 8.3; appendix 8.3
Large copper nail, broken at both ends, quadrangular section.
ES: Portion of a nail, 0.4 cm diameter; the interior had been cold worked and annealed, and there was further cold working at the edge.
L: 7.0 cm; Diam: 0.6 cm
References: McGeehan-Liritzis and Gale 1988: tables 3, 4, inventory no. 12

2057 PO/D 25; figure 8.3f; plate 8.6c; tables 8.1, 8.3; appendix 8.3
Copper awl, very rough and corroded; circular section, thickens at pointed end.
ES: Slightly curved cylinder of circular cross section with rough corroded surface and almost completely corroded interior, thus composition and microstructure studies yielded little information. A small particle of charcoal was adhering to the top surface.
L: 5.8 cm; Diam: 0.8 cm
References: McGeehan-Liritzis and Gale 1988: tables 3, 5, inventory no. 14

2086 PO/D 29; figure 8.3j; plate 8.6d; tables 8.2, 8.3; appendix 8.3
Copper awl, quadrangular section; narrows to point at one end, squared off at other.
ES: Awl of quadrangular cross section; cold worked microstructure; extensive internal corrosion.
L: 5.6 cm; Diam: 0.3 cm
References: McGeehan-Liritzis and Gale 1988: tables 3, 4, inventory no. 13

5627 ZB 37r; plate 8.9g; table 8.2
Small piece of corroded copper.
ES: Corroded on the surface with some internal corrosion, "as cast" dendritic structure shown in plate 8.9g; it did not appear to have been formed into a specific object.
References: McGeehan-Liritzis and Gale 1988: table 4, inventory no. 29

Appendix 8.2.
The Finds: Crucible Fragments and Sherds with Indications of Metal Working

Colin Renfrew

The data are organized by phase, small find number (not all of the sherds were numbered), context, reference to figure, plate, and table; description, measurements, and reference to earlier publication.

PHASE III

No SF no. MM 61
Sherd, partly vitrified; copper deposit on outside.
L: 5.1 cm; W: 3.5 cm; Th: 1.1 cm

No SF no. MMb 61
Crucible rim sherd, fine paste with large grit, vitrified; copper deposit on inside.
L: 3.4 cm; W: 3.1 cm; Th: 0.8 cm

No SF no. MMc 60
Sherd, fine fabric with small grit, vitrified; copper deposit on broken edge.
L: 4.9 cm; W: 4.5 cm; Th: 0.9 cm

No SF no. MM 53
Sherd, fine fabric, vitrified on one side with slight copper deposit.
L: 7.7 cm; W: 4.3 cm; Th: 1.0 cm

No SF no. MM 43
Rim sherd, medium coarse fabric, slightly vitrified; copper deposit on inside.
L: 3.9 cm; W: 3.7 cm; Th: 1.2 cm

No SF no. MM 21
Sherd, smooth outside, partly vitrified; slight copper deposit over vitrification.
L: 3.7 cm; W: 3.5 cm; Th: 1.0 cm

No SF no. MM 20
"Rim" of vessel, baked clay with large grit, lower part clay, upper part vitrified with copper and brown deposit extending down each side.
L: 5.7 cm; W: 4.8 cm; Th: 0.8 cm

No SF no. MM 20
Sherd, fine paste with large grit, vitrified at one corner with copper deposit extending over one side.
L: 4.4 cm; W: 3.3 cm; Th: 0.7–1.4 cm

No SF no. MM 20
Sherd of carinated vessel, fairly fine fabric; copper deposit over outside.
L: 4.2 cm; W: 1.9 cm; Th: 0.9–1.6 cm

No SF no. MM 20
Rim sherd of thick-walled crucible, coarse fabric with large grit, not vitrified; copper deposit inside.
L: 4.5 cm; W: 3.4 cm; Th: 1.6 cm

No SF no. MM 20
Sherd, gray paste with large grit; copper deposit on one side and broken edge.
L: 3.0 cm; W: 2.8 cm; Th: 0.8 cm

No SF no. MM 20
Rim (?) sherd, coarse fabric; copper deposit over top and both sides.
L: 3.4 cm; W: 3.2 cm; Th: 0.8 cm

No SF no. MM 20
Rim sherd of thick-walled crucible, coarse fabric; copper deposit on inside only.
L: 3.4 cm; W: 3.2 cm; Th: 1.3–1.8 cm

No SF no. MM 11
Sherd, fine fabric, vitrified, groove down one side, slight copper deposit on one corner.
L: 4.8 cm; W: 4.0 cm; Th: 1.3 cm

No SF no. ZG 29
Sherd, possibly rim; copper deposit over one side and all broken edges.
L: 6.2 cm; W: 4.0 cm; Th: 0.8 cm

No SF no. ZG 29
Sherd, vitrified; copper deposit on one side.
L: 3.8 cm; W: 1.9 cm; Th: 1.2 cm

No SF no. ZG 17
Sherd, fine fabric, a little vitrified; copper deposit on one broken edge.
L: 4.2 cm; W: 3.0 cm; Th: 1.2 cm

No SF no. ZJ 24
Sherd, partly vitrified; copper deposit on one corner and also over broken edge.
L: 4.3 cm; W: 3.0 cm; Th: 0.9 cm

No SF no. ZJ 24
Crucible rim sherd, very little curvature, partly vit-
rified at rim; copper deposit on inside and over rim.
L: 3.2 cm; W: 3.5 cm; Th: 0.8 cm

No SF no. ZA 46
Sherd, vitrified; copper deposit on one side and on
broken edge.
L: 2.3 cm; W: 1.7 cm; Th: 0.6 cm

No SF no. ZA 46
Crucible sherd; copper deposit on one side and on
broken edge.
L: 4.3 cm; W: 3.8 cm; Th: 0.8 cm

No SF no. ZB 126
Small sherd, vitrified on one side with traces of
copper deposit.
L: 2.1 cm; W: 1.8 cm; Th: 1.4 cm

No SF no. ZB 125
Sherd, partly vitrified; copper deposit on outside
and on broken edge.
L: 4.2 cm; W: 4.1 cm; Th: 1.4 cm

No SF no. ZB 112
Crucible rim sherd, flattened and thickened,
slightly vitrified; copper deposit on one side and
on broken edge.
L: 6.5 cm; W: 5.8 cm; Th: 1.1–1.9 cm

No SF no. ZB 112
Sherd, joined to previous one, probably sherds of
graphite painted stand reused after breakage; copper deposit.
L: 5.3 cm; W: 5.3 cm; Th: 1.1–1.9 cm

3596 ZG 30
Sherd with two incised grooves; copper deposit on
other side and also on broken edge.
L: 5.0 cm; W: 2.0 cm; Th: 1.0 cm

4906 MM 40; figure 8.4d; plate 8.11b
Crucible (?) sherd, coarse fabric with large grit;
copper deposit on inside only.
L: 4.5 cm; W: 4.4 cm; Th: 1.1 cm
References: Renfrew 1973a: pl. 126, 2:127.

5561 MM 50; figure 8.4e
Rim sherd, medium fabric with fine grit, vitrified;
copper deposit on top of rim and down one side.
L: 2.9 cm; W: 3.8 cm; Th: 1.2 cm

5562 MM 27; figure 8.4b; plate 8.11c
Rim sherd, fine fabric; copper (?) deposit on inside
only.
L: 3.4 cm; W: 3.7 cm; Th: 1.0 cm

5563 MM 41; figure 8.4f
Rim sherd, coarse fabric, vitrified; copper deposit
inside.
L: 2.5 cm; W: 2.7 cm; Th: 1.0 cm

5564 MM 20; figure 8.4c; plate 8.11a
Rim sherd of thick-walled crucible; copper deposit
on inside upper edge; deposit stops 2.3 cm below
rim as if splashing copper oxides were deposited.
L: 4.9 cm; W: 6.3 cm; Th: 1.0–1.8 cm
References: Renfrew 1973a: pl. 126, 3:127.

5565 ZG 29; figure 8.4a
Sherd of thickened barley-sugar rim, from large
flat plate, possibly lid to oven or crucible, partly
vitrified; copper deposit on one side and over rim.
L: 7.2 cm; W: 4.7 cm; Th: 1.3 cm

5566 MMb 60; figure 8.4g; plate 8.11d
Crucible rim sherd, fine fabric; copper deposit on
inside.
L: 3.5 cm; W: 3.4 cm; Th: 0.6 cm

5567 ZG 16; figure 8.4h
Crucible rim sherd, large grit; copper and red
deposit on inside.
L: 2.5 cm; W: 2.2 cm; Th: 1.1 cm

5584 MM 20; figure 8.4i; plate 8.10
Base and one side with rim of thick-walled, round-
based crucible, very coarse fabric with large grit;
trace of copper deposit on rim.
L: 6.0 cm; W: 9.0 cm; Th: 1.7 cm
References: Renfrew 1973a: pl. 127, 1:127.

5628 ZG 22; table 8.4
Sherd, partly vitrified; copper deposit down one
broken edge.
L: 5.3 cm; W: 4.0 cm; Th: 1.0 cm
References: McGeehan-Liritzis and Gale 1988:
table 4, inventory no. 6

PHASE IV

No SF no. ZHt 16
Crucible rim sherd, fine fabric, partly vitrified;
copper deposit on top of rim.
L: 4.4 cm; W: 3.0 cm; Th: 1.0 cm

No SF no. ZHt 14
Crucible (?) rim sherd, slightly curved, partly vitrified; copper deposit on outside and on broken
edge.
L: 3.5 cm; W: 4.4 cm; Th: 1.0 cm

No SF no. ZE 65
Crucible sherd, coarse fabric; copper deposit on
inside
L: 2.9 cm; W: 3.0 cm; Th: 0.9 cm

3686 ZE 83
Sherd, vitrified on lower part; lumpy copper
deposit on one side and on broken edge.
L: 6.5 cm; W: 2.8 cm; Th: 0.8 cm

Appendix 8.3.
Origin of Metals from Sitagroi as Determined by Lead Isotope Analysis

Zofia Anna Stos

BACKGROUND

Ten metal artifacts from Sitagroi were analyzed for their lead isotope (LI) compositions nearly twenty years ago to establish their origin (McGeehan-Liritzis and Gale 1988). This method of scientific investigation can be used for identification of the geographical sources of minerals used for metal extraction by comparing the LI "fingerprints" of known ore deposits with those of the metal artifacts (Gale and Stos-Gale 2000). Because this method of provenance identification of metal is purely comparative, the correct results rely chiefly on the available database of LI ratios for specific ore deposits. The research into sources of Bronze Age Aegean metals started around 1980, and the metals from Sitagroi were analyzed in the early stage of this project. The lead isotope database of the relevant ore deposits was at that time very small (a few hundred data) and represented ores mostly from Greece, Turkey, and Cyprus. Understandably, the conclusions as to the origin of metals from Sitagroi presented in that early paper were equivocal.

In the last twenty years the LI database of ore deposits and metal artifacts related to the Aegean Bronze Age analyzed at Oxford, Mainz, and other laboratories across the world increased to over 6200 samples. Therefore, it seems an opportune time to reevaluate the LI data for metals from Sitagroi in view of this vastly increased body of information.

The ten artifacts distribute as follows (based on Preface table 3): Chalcolithic phase III: three pieces; EBA phase IV: a pin; EBA phase V: three artifacts, including one pin from EBA phase Va, and two artifacts from EBA phase Vb (see table 8.3.1).[1]

ORE DEPOSITS IN THE NORTHERN AEGEAN

One can say that the settlement of Sitagroi is surrounded by copper and lead-silver ore deposits that could have been exploited in the Bronze Age. Most of the occurrences in these deposits have been surveyed for archaeometallurgical remains, and at least some ores and slags have been analyzed for their LI compositions. To the southwest there are large mines on the Chalkidiki Peninsula; the main exploitation there was for lead and silver, but there is also a small occurrence of copper (Wagner et al. 1986). Thasos Island, just to the south, also has been known for copper and gold mining (Wagner and Weisgerber 1988). To the north there are the Rhodope Mountains divided between Bulgaria and Greece with considerable lead and copper deposits on both sides of the border (Stos-Gale, Gale, and Annetts 1996; Stos-Gale et al. 1998a). To the northeast, near the coast of the Black Sea, there are more copper deposits near the Bulgarian resort of Burgas (Stos-Gale et al. 1998a). To the east, across the northern Aegean, there is a cluster of multimetallic mines on the Troad Peninsula (Pernicka et al. 1984). The existence of ore deposits known to modern geologists is not usually a guarantee that they have been exploited in the distant past. However, a good indication of ancient metallurgical activities is a presence of metallic slags near the mines. In all the above-mentioned mining regions there are numerous slag heaps. So far none of them have been convincingly dated to the Chalcolithic or Early Bronze Age period, but it is quite usual for later activities to destroy the earlier industrial evidence; therefore it is necessary to consider the possibility of their earlier exploitation.

Evidence of Chalcolithic–EBA Exploitation of the Ore Deposits in the Aegean and Surrounding Regions

One of the methods of identifying the chronology of the exploitation of specific ore deposits is through the numerous LI analyses of artifacts from well-dated sites. If a source of metal was exploited in a certain archaeological period, then the metal artifacts from this period will consistently show LI ratios ("fingerprints") identical with the ores from this mineral deposit. LI analyses of 100 copper artifacts from the Chalcolithic Varna Cemetery and some thirty more from various contemporary sites in southeast Bulgaria show clearly that the copper in the region of Burgas (Varly Briag and Zidarovo), as well as some outcrops of ore in the eastern Rhodope, were exploited at that time (Gale et al. in press). Numerous analyses of EBA (and some Chalcolithic) metal artifacts from the Aegean (Stos-Gale 1992, 1993, 2001) indicate that the most common source of metals was the Cycladic islands (Kythnos, Seriphos, and Siphnos) and Lavrion in Attica (Stos-Gale 1998). Since the Chalcolithic period, metals from the Anatolian Taurus Mountains and copper deposits from the Wadi Arabah (Timna in Israel and Feinan in Jordan; Hauptmann et al. 1992) were reaching the Aegean, as were some metals from Iran and unknown mines, situated perhaps to the north of the Black Sea. Cypriote copper is not very common in the EBA Aegean (LI for Cyprus published in Gale et al. 1997 and Stos-Gale et al. 1998b).

THE ORIGIN OF COPPER ARTIFACTS BASED ON THEIR LI COMPOSITIONS

The lead isotope ratios of these metals were quite varied, suggesting that they did not originate from one ore deposit. In particular, the three pieces dated to the Chalcolithic period were not consistent with any LI ore data known at the time of publication. Today we can compare these metals with quite extensive data sets for the Chalcolithic and EBA metals from the Balkans (including Pernicka et al. 1993), Greece, and Aegean Turkey (figure 8.3.1). The data used for the comparisons have been published in the Archaeometry Isotope Laboratory database series (Stos-Gale et al. 1995, 1998a; Stos-Gale, Gale, and Annetts 1996; Gale et al. 1997) and in various articles (for example, Pernicka et al. 1984, 1993; Seeliger et al. 1985).

The LI data for the ten metals from Sitagroi were compared with over 2000 data for ores from all the mining regions mentioned above and others farther afield (western Mediterranean). The ore and metal artifact are regarded as identical if the Euclidean distance calculated for all three LI ratios for the ore sample and the artifact are within the limit of the analytical error. The results of calculations can be checked visually on two lead isotope diagrams. The data for copper artifacts from Sitagroi published in 1988 (McGeehan-Liritzis and Gale) are listed in table 8.3.2 together with the names of ore deposits containing copper ores with matching LI "fingerprints."

The lead isotope data for metals from Sitagroi are compared on figure 8.3.1 with the Chalcolithic Bulgarian and EBA metals from Troy I–II, Thermi I–II, and Poliochni, and ores from southeast Bulgaria, and slags and ores from the Cycladic island of Kythnos. For the sake of clarity, this lead isotope plot does not include all of the ore sources used for comparisons, but during the process of source identification of metals, many plots are made as a matter of course. The ore data for the Taurus Mountains used for the calculations of Euclidean distances and LI diagrams were from Hirao, Enomoto, and Tachikawa (1995) and Yener et al. (1991).

Table 8.3.1 Metal Artifacts Analyzed for Their Isotope Composition*

SF no.	Context	Published number	Description	Phase / chronology
	MM 20	5	Slag	III (Chalcolithic)
SF 782	ZA 47S	3	Slag?/piece	III (Chalcolithic)
SF 1238	MM 43	7	Wire/pin	III (Chalcolithic)
SF 3229	ZHt 17	9	Pin	IV ("EB 1")
SF 2086	PO/D 29	13	Awl?	Vb ("EB 3")
SF 3005	ROc 30	11	Fragment of metal	Vb ("EB 3")
SF 3017	ROc 49	31	Pin	Va ("EB 2")
SF 3005	ROc 30	33	Fragment of metal	Vb ("EB 3")
SF 2057	PO/D 25	14	Unidentified object	Vb ("EB 3")
SF1041	QN 7	12	Nail fragment	Vb ("EB 3")

*As listed in McGeehan-Liritzis and Gale 1988; see also table 8.3.

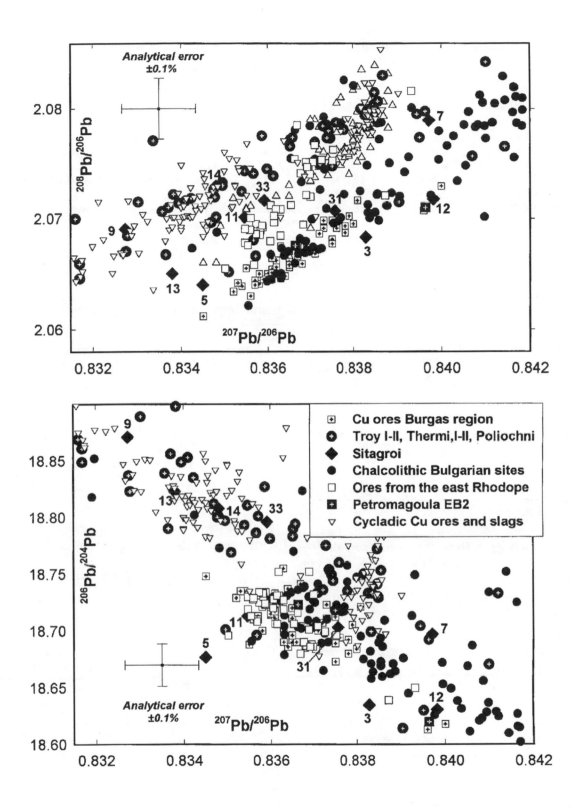

Figure 8.3.1. Lead isotope compositions of copper metals from Sitagroi compared with Bulgarian and Aegean copper ores, Aegean EBA, and Chalcolithic Bulgarian copper artifacts. Analytical error ± 0.1%

Table 8.3.2. Lead Isotope Ratios of Metals and the Interpretation of Their Origin

Pub. no.	Chronology	$^{208}Pb/$ ^{206}Pb	$^{207}Pb/$ ^{206}Pb	$^{206}Pb/$ ^{204}Pb	Isotopically consistent with ores from
5	III Chalcolithic	2.06402	0.83449	18.677	Burgas – Varly Briag
3	III Chalcolithic	2.06830	0.83829	18.635	Burgas – Zidarovo
7	III Chalcolithic	2.07892	0.83972	18.697	Taurus – Aladag
9	IV ("EB 1")	2.06902	0.83274	18.871	Cyclades – Seriphos-Kephala
13	Vb ("EB 3")	2.06504	0.83380	18.823	Lavrion
11	Vb ("EB 3")	2.07010	0.83546	18.713	Southeast Rhodope – Essimi-Kirki
31	Va ("EB 2")	2.07068	0.83756	18.703	Burgas – Zidarovo-Yurta
33	Vb ("EB 2")	2.07160	0.83592	18.796	Cyclades – Seriphos-Kephala
14	Vb ("EB 3")	2.07291	0.83480	18.808	Cyclades – Kythnos
12	Vb ("EB 3")	2.07174	0.83982	18.631	Burgas – Zidarovo-Yurta

Source: McGeehan-Liritzis and Gale 1988

Table 8.3.3. Summary of the Origin of the Earliest Aegean Copper and Silver Artifacts

Site/Origin	Kythnos	Siphnos	Seriphos	Lavrion	Taurus	Rhodope/ Burgas	Black Sea
Sitagroi	—	—	—	—	1	2	—
Sesklo	—	—	—	2	—	—	—
Alepotrypa Cave	—	—	—	3 (Ag)	—	—	—
Dhimini	—	—	—	—	1	—	1
Plakari, Euboea	—	1	—	—	—	—	—
Cyclopa Cave, Giali	1	—	—	—	—	—	—
Ftelia, Mykonos	2	—	2	—	2	—	—
Tharounia Cave, Euboea	2	—	—	—	—	—	—
Kephala-Kea	—	1	1	1	—	—	—

Chalcolithic

Two Chalcolithic pieces from Sitagroi show an origin consistent with the ores from a large mining district in southeast Bulgaria near the resort of Burgas (Zidarovo and Varly Briag). Both these pieces were identified by McGeehan and Gale (1988) as "slags?" but if their chemical analyses are correct, they both seem to be pieces of corroded arsenic copper (Cu 93 and 96.3%; McGeehan and Gale 1988: table 5:218). Copper slag is an iron silicate, typically 35% SiO_2 and 20% Fe_2O_3, with about 30% of CaO and a few percent of Al_2O_3 and MGO, with usually less than 5% of copper disseminated as metal prills and copper compounds.

The copper minerals in Zidarovo and Varly Briag have been extensively exploited in the twentieth century, and on the ground it is very difficult to find any traces of ancient mining. However, a considerable number of Chalcolithic artifacts from the Varna Cemetery located a short distance to the north of these mines is isotopically fully consistent with these ores, proving their early exploitation (see figure 8.3.1).

The third Chalcolithic object, a pin or a wire, is not consistent with an origin from any of the Aegean or Balkan ores. This artifact is isotopically identical with the copper ores from the Aladag Mountains in the Taurus range in southwest Turkey. Table 8.3.3 shows a summary of the origin of all Late Neolithic/Chalcolithic copper artifacts analyzed for their lead isotope compositions in the Isotrace Laboratory, Oxford. From this summary it is clear that while the majority of the earliest Aegean copper artifacts in this group originate in the Cyclades, the copper metal from the Taurus Mountains and from the south coast of the Black Sea was also present on these sites. However, metal from the region of Burgas occurs only in Sitagroi.

Among the group of later copper artifacts from Sitagroi, there are also two pieces consistent with

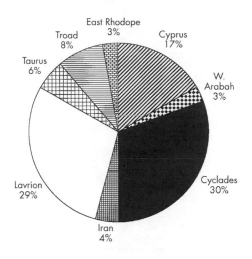

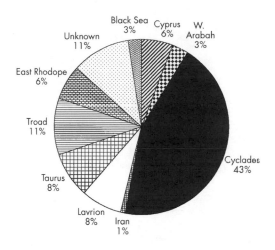

Figure 8.3.2. Pattern of the origin of Early Helladic metals (91 artifacts).

Figure 8.3.3. Pattern of the origin from EBA Aegean Island sites (220 artifacts).

an origin from the Burgas copper mines: an EB 2 pin (#31: SF 3017, ROc 49) and an EB 3 nail (#12: SF1041, QN 7). The only other EBA Aegean artifacts so far analyzed that also originate from these mines are two EB 2 awls from Petromagoula (McGeehan-Liritzis and Gale 1988: table 2: 203, nos. 36, 39; table 3:213). The other five artifacts from Sitagroi are fully consistent with an origin from the Aegean and conform fully to the overall pattern of copper sources used on the Early Bronze Age sites throughout the Aegean. Figures 8.3.2 and 8.3.3 show typical patterns of the sources of metals from various sites across the Aegean, including artifacts from the Cycladic islands, Manika (Stos-Gale, Sampson, and Mangou 1999), Kos, Thermi, Poliochni, Rhodes, Lithares, Lerna, and Tsoungiza.

Summary

In summary, the LI analyses of these few metals from Sitagroi reflect quite well the position of this site on the crossroads of the Balkans and the Aegean. It is certainly not the full picture of metal sources used on this site, but even this small sample shows that Sitagroi was an interface between these two cultural regions.

Note

[1] Note that at an earlier stage two samples (numbers 11 and 33) have in error been designated with the same Small Find number (SF 3005) and context.

9.

Items of Adornment

Marianna Nikolaidou

Adornment at Neolithic/Chalcolithic and Early Bronze Age Sitagroi is attested by both direct and indirect evidence. As direct evidence I consider categories whose ornamental character can be recognized with relative certainty: bead, bracelet/annulet, pendant, pin, plaque, and ring. These artifacts form the core of the present chapter. Indirect evidence is provided by iconographic elements on contemporary figurines that can be interpreted as jewelry; possible tools for use in ornamentation, such as stamp seals, scarification (?) needles, and color palettes; and ambiguous pieces that may have been used as ornaments include miniature figurines and elaborated bone objects. The figurines have been published by Gimbutas (volume 1, chapter 9), while the other items are treated in detail in the respective chapters of this volume dealing with artifacts of bone (chapter 2), stone (chapter 5), textiles (chapter 6), special clay objects (chapter 10), and *paralipomena* (chapter 11). Thus some artifacts are examined from several points of view, and illustrative material may be duplicated.

We should keep in mind that ornaments retrieved archaeologically are only those made of durable materials. Other, more ephemeral forms of body decoration may also have been employed, including paint or tattoos, horn, feathers, elaborate fabrics, flowers, and the like (compare Karali-Yannacopoulos 1992; Kenoyer 1991:82). At Sitagroi, some clues to such perishable ornamental forms are provided by indirect evidence.

The ornament assemblage at hand is discussed in the light of craftwork and consumption at Sitagroi itself as well as of ornamentation in the wider northern Aegean/southern Balkan area. I examine the artifacts in terms of form and style, involving choice of raw material, craftsmanship, and typology of the end products; temporal and spatial distribution, with reference to the site stratigraphy and archaeological contexts; possible uses and functions, as inferred from the formal features of the objects themselves, prehistoric iconographic and burial evidence, and ethnographic examples; and regional and interregional relations, with special emphasis on recently published material from sites closely comparable to Sitagroi in time and space. Comparable sites include Dikili Tash and Dhimitra in the Drama Plain (Karali-Yannacopoulos 1992, 1997, respectively), Paradeisos in Thrace (Reese 1987), Makriyalos in Pieria (Besios and Pappa 1995, 1996; Pappa 1995), Dhimini in Thessaly (Tsuneki 1989), and Servia in west Macedonia (Mould, Ridley, and Wardle 2000)

Technological questions are covered briefly in this text; they are treated extensively in the appendixes that follow this chapter. Appendix 9.1 consists of N. Shackleton's original study on the worked shell from Sitagroi, including items of adornment. In appendix 9.2, Miller discusses in detail the manufacturing process, based on her recent microscopic and experimental analyses conducted for all the main types of non-metal ornaments from the site. The technology of the metal ornaments is presented by C. Renfrew and Slater in chapter 8. The artifacts are catalogued in appendix 9.3.

DIRECT EVIDENCE

The data are presented in detail in appendix 9.3, the catalog, which is organized by phases (I–V and unstratified, or X) and provides the unique SF number, followed by context, numerical count (for the bead groups), raw material, description of form and surface treatment, and measurements. The following sections refer consistently to the catalog, in which the artifactual information has been tabulated for more convenient treatment.

The terms I use to describe the different items of adornment are adopted from Beck (1973), Kenoyer (1991:82), and Barge (1982:33–35). A bead is defined as any round object perforated along its major rotational axis, generally worn on a cord or wire, or sewn onto clothing. A pendant is any object that is eccentrically perforated or scored at one end and is hung or attached to a cord or wire or sewn onto clothing; contrary to beads, pendants cannot rotate and, once suspended, they will stay in one position. A bangle is any circlet made of a continuous homogeneous material that can be worn on the arm, wrist, or ankle, while a bracelet or anklet is any circlet made of components such as beads, chain, or cord. Many of the Sitagroi examples are so small they may have been worn as annulets (ring-shaped pendants). The fragmentary preservation of other examples does not allow us to determine whether the original piece was a bangle or bracelet. Therefore, all circlets have been grouped under the collective term "bracelet/annulet," and any available information on the original form is given in the catalog descriptions. Pins are pointed objects of slender proportions and careful surface treatment that may have had a decorative function aside from the practical use as piercers and fasteners. Plaques are pendant-like objects of bone, with a thin, flat, elongated rectangular body and more than one perforation on one or both narrow sides or along the body. Finally, there is a small "ring" made of thin wire.[1] These types of ornaments are common in Macedonia during the Neolithic and the Bronze Age. Because basic forms continued practically unchanged from one period to the other (compare Heurtley 1939: figs. 7e–f [Early Neolithic], 35a–c, g, j, q [Late Neolithic], 66 and 67 l–s, oo–pp [Early Bronze Age]; Karali-Yannacopoulos 1997:209–210), the abundant Neolithic/Chalcolithic material from Sitagroi can help us study the Early Bronze Age as well.

QUANTITY AND TEMPORAL DISTRIBUTION

A total of 931 ornaments belong to the groupings listed above; the overall frequency of each item is

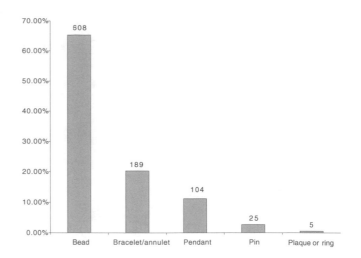

Figure 9.1. Overall frequency of the different items of adornment at Sitagroi.

given in figure 9.1. For graphic clarity, the few plaques and the ring are grouped together as "plaque/ring."

The great majority of ornaments were retrieved from the Middle Neolithic/Chalcolithic horizons (phases I–III): 823 items, or 88% of the total assemblage. In contrast, the Early Bronze Age strata (phases IV–V)[2] yielded just about 11% of the total: ninety-nine items. There are also nine pieces—six bracelet/annulets and three pendants—of unknown phase (designated X in the catalog). They are not included in those tabulations where the data are controlled by phase.

The distribution of the different items of adornment through time (phases I–V) is presented in table 9.1. There is a marked increase from phase I to II and a second, even stronger jump from phase II to III; quantities drop strikingly from phase III to IV and decrease further from phase IV to V. The sharp contrast between the overall recovery from the two main periods of the settlement, Neolithic/Chalcolithic versus Early Bronze Age, lends itself to different explanations. For one thing, it is consistent with a widely attested preference for ornamentation in the material culture of Neolithic/Chalcolithic Macedonian communities versus their Early Bronze Age successors (see Nikolaidou 1997: 188–189). Other, site-specific factors may also be at play, such as the different durations of the two periods at Sitagroi, the former representing almost two

Table 9.1. Percentage Frequencies of Ornamental Items over Total Phase Recovery

Type	Phase					
	I	II	III	IV	V	Total
Bead	36	142	388	31	11	608
	80.00	73.96	66.21	50.00	29.73	65.94
Bracelet/	4	32	123	17	7	183
annulet	8.89	16.67	20.99	27.42	18.92	19.85
Pendant	3	13	69	11	5	101
	6.67	6.77	11.77	17.74	13.51	10.95
Pin	1	4	4	2	14	25
	2.22	2.08	0.68	3.23	37.84	2.71
Plaque	1	1	2	0	0	4
	2.22	0.52	0.34	0.00	0.00	0.43
Ring	0	0	0	1	0	1
	0.00	0.00	0.00	1.61	0.00	0.11
Phase	45	192	586	62	37	922
totals	4.88	20.82	63.56	6.72	4.01	

millennia of life and the latter covering about 1300 years (volume 1 [C. Renfrew 1986e]:173, table 7.3). Although more soil was excavated in Sitagroi's Early Bronze Age deposits (440 m^3 as compared with 300 m^3 of Neolithic/Chalcolithic date; see Preface table 2), these deposits were not extensively water-sieved, as were the Neolithic/Chalcolithic horizons which proved so prolific in small finds such as ornaments.[3] It is indicative that in the small sounding ZB, where all the soil was water-sieved (volume 1 [C. Renfrew 1986c]:21–22), many more items were retrieved from the Early Bronze Age layers than from all other contemporary units together.[4] We may reasonably assume that the number of Early Bronze Age ornaments would have been larger had water sieving been employed more extensively.

RAW MATERIALS

The Sitagroi ornaments are made of bone, clay, metal, shell, and stone. According to Miller (appendix 9.2), two beads were manufactured of either clay or stone and thirteen others are of either shell or stone. These fifteen pieces are excluded from those tabulations where the data are controlled by raw material.

The distribution of the different raw materials through time (phases I–V) is shown in figure 9.2. Each material is discussed below in order of its overall frequency.

Shell

There is strong preference for shell; it represents 54% of the total ornament assemblage. It was especially popular in phase II (75% of this phase's total), extensively used in phase III, and less prevalent in phase IV. Marine shells were chosen almost exclusively,[5] including bivalves: *Spondylus gaederopus* (spiny oyster), *Glycymeris* (*Petunculus*) *violascens* (dog-cockle), *Mytilus galloprovincialis* (Mediterranean mussel), *Cerastoderma* (*Cardium*) *edule* (cockle), and *Donax trunculus* (clam); gastropods: *Luria lurida* (cowry), *Murex trunculus* (rock murex), and *Neritea neritina*, *Columbella*; plus *Dentalium vulgare* (tusk shell). All of these would have been brought from the coast, some 25 km away from the village. Surprisingly, riverine mollusca, abundant in the nearby Angitis stream, were hardly used for adornment although they were otherwise worked and apparently played an important dietary role[6] (see appendix 9.1; compare Karali-Yannacopoulos 1997:200–204). *Unio pictorum* (freshwater mussel), the single riverine species processed into ornaments, is represented by two examples only, both pendants from phase III (SF 3147, 5602). The selective use of readily available riverine mollusks for subsistence or "utilitarian" purposes, as opposed to the exploitation of seashell mainly for items of adornment,[7] cannot be explained by practical considerations. Rather, the choice of seashells for adornment was an aesthetic preference. Also, they may have had a symbolic

Total recovery of raw material (%)

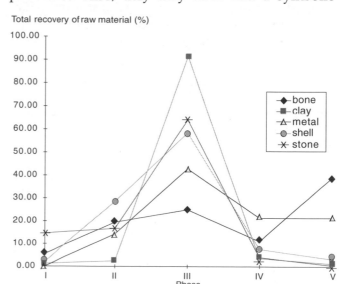

Figure 9.2. Fluctuation curves of raw materials through time (percentages over total recovery of each raw material).

value, even an exotic aura (Elster and Nikolaidou in press), since they were brought from the coast, an area not immediately accessible and perhaps never visited by villagers.

The temporal distribution of the shell used for various ornamental categories is presented in appendix 9.2 (tables 9.2.2, 9.2.4). In table 9.2, all pendants consisting of whole, modified shells are tabulated by species.

Species is more difficult to recognize in the tiny shell beads, but Miller (appendix 9.2) believes that most of them were manufactured of *Spondylus*. Where species information is available, it has been recorded in the catalog.

As is evident from the tables, *Spondylus* and, to a lesser degree, *Glycymeris* were used in significant quantities to manufacture items that required some special skills, namely the bracelet/annulets and beads. *Spondylus gaederopus* (discussed in detail in the appendixes) lives in the littoral zone, attached by its lower spiny valve to the rocks, which makes it difficult to remove. According to Miller (appendix 9.2), the *Spondylus* found at Sitagroi had probably been collected live. The same has been inferred at Dhimini (Tsuneki 1989:14) and possibly at Franchthi, too (J. Shackleton 1988:50–52).

Large *Glycymeris* lie deeply buried in sand offshore and also would have been difficult to collect live (J. Shackleton 1983) unless picked up on the beach, as N. Shackleton assumes (appendix 9.1). *Dentalia* left unmodified in its natural form, which grows into a handy bead-shape, was another favorite. Found in both deep and shallow waters, *Dentalia* would have been beachcombed or collected easily, as has also been suggested for the material from the Franchthi cave (J. Shackleton 1988:51–52).

The rest of the Sitagroi species come from a variety of habitats, ranging from soft sandy beds in shallow beaches and estuarine waters, to rocky or sandy seascapes deeper offshore (J. Shackleton 1988:50–53). N. Shackleton reasonably suggests that the few examples tabulated at Sitagroi would have been beachcombed occasionally, and it is interesting that all of them have a simple suspension hole that may even have been formed naturally.

Preference for marine shells as ornaments, especially *Spondylus*, has been observed in all excavated sites of Late and Final Neolithic/Chalcolithic in northern Greece. Local and long-distance trade and exchange linkages were in operation especially during the Chalcolithic (Sitagroi phase III) when Aegean communities were active in the procurement, manufacture, use and circulation of *Spondylus* items all over the Balkans and up to Central Europe (Grammenos 1997b:297–299; Greenfield 1991; Perlès 1992; C. Renfrew 1973d:186–187; Séfériadès 1995; N. Shackleton and Renfrew 1970; Tsuneki 1989; Vencl 1959; Willms 1985). At Sitagroi, 441 out of 494 dated shell ornaments come from the three Neolithic/Chalcolithic phases together; phase III alone yielded 290 pieces, or 58% of the total shell recovery (figure 9.2).

Quantities drop so sharply (see figure 9.2) in the Early Bronze Age phases IV (thirty-seven pieces) and V (sixteen pieces) that it is questionable whether shell procurement for ornaments continued at all into this period. It may be that we are dealing with material either contaminated from earlier strata (see appendix 9.1) or picked up as curios by Early Bronze Age inhabitants from Neolithic/Chalcolithic debris (compare C. Renfrew 1987). On the other hand, we must take into account the different methods of recovery applied to distinct chronological horizons, as mentioned earlier. Moreover, the occurrence of shell and other ornaments in securely stratified Early Bronze Age contexts, sometimes on house floors, suggests to me that, whatever the circumstance of acquisition (contemporary manufacture or heirloom), these objects were in use. Still, the sharp numerical decrease from phase III is undeniable and, aside from recovery biases, could also reflect new

Table 9.2. Numerical Distribution of Shell Species Used for Pendants, Controlled by Phase

Shell species	I	II	III	IV	V	X*	Total
Cardium	0	1	1	2	0	0	4
Columbella	0	1	1	0	0	0	2
Cypraea	0	0	0	1	1	0	2
Glycymeris	1	6	53	3	2	1	66
Murex	0	1	1	1	0	0	3
Neritea	0	0	4	0	0	0	4
Spondylus	0	0	1	0	0	1	2
Unio	0	0	2	0	0	0	2
Unidentifiable	0	0	1	0	0	0	1
Phase total	1	9	64	7	3	2	86

* Phase X indicates unphased, or mixed contexts.

patterns of raw material management and/or use of the end products (compare Nikolaidou 1997). That the Early Bronze Age villagers at Sitagroi chose differently than their predecessors is also suggested by the limited occurrence of another commodity valued in the Neolithic/Chalcolithic, honey-brown flint, which was still imported but in considerably lower quantities (Tringham 1984; this volume, chapter 3).

Stone

Although not nearly as abundant as shell in terms of overall recovery, stone is the second most used raw material for adornment. Soft and easily workable stones chosen include metamorphic steatites or soapstones (2–2.5 hardness in Mohs' scale) that can take a high polish; marble; and limestone (about 3 Mohs' hardness) (Moorey 1994:37). It is likely that limestone and marble came from local or regional sources (see chapters 4 and 5). An extensive limestone area stretches over the center of the Drama Plain, and soft white limestone was exposed as bedrock on the tell itself (volume 1 [Davidson 1986]:29, figure 3.2). On the other hand, Perlès has argued (1992:124) that the sources of the steatite, soapstone, and schist used for ornaments in Neolithic Greece were probably restricted to certain regions. Dixon (chapter 4) indicated a likely non-local origin (west Serbo-Macedonia or east Thrace) for the stones used for a few ornaments, including SF 113 (pendant) of phase I and SF 299 (pendant) of phase II. The majority of stone artifacts (65%) were recovered from phase III contexts (see figure 9.2).

Clay

In phase III, clay (seldom used for ornaments in phases I and II) suddenly becomes relatively popular (see figure 9.2), representing more than 90% of all clay ornaments excavated at the site. However, this raw material (18% of the total recovery) is hardly used in the EBA (see figure 9.2).

Bone

Both domestic and wild animal bones were recovered (see volume 1 [Bökönyi 1986]:68; this volume, chapter 2 and bone catalog, appendix 2.1). In most cases, species are not easy to distinguish because of the small size of the objects. Of the identifiable pieces from all phases (not all are illustrated), seven come from domesticates: pig (perforated astragali SF 4802 and SF 3770 of phase III [plate 2.20c, d]; pins SF 1307, 1557 of phase V), cattle (SF 834, plaque of phase III [figure 2.7d; plate 2.17a]), goat/sheep (SF 376, pin of phase III), and dog (SF 5089 and 5124 [perforated teeth] of phases V and IV [plate 9.22]). Seven are from wild animals: boar (SF 5116, 5288a [figure 2.7c; plate 2.17b], pendants of phase III), red deer (SF 4641, pendant of phase IV), and turtle shell (SF 2722 and 5094, pendants of phase IV; bead SF 2276 and pendant SF 66 of phase V). Despite the limited use of bone throughout the site's sequence, it may be worth contrasting the concentration of fourteen ornaments in phase V with the absence or rarer appearance of similar items in the previous phases. The lack of interest in bone by the Middle Neolithic ornament makers is remarkable given that the same material was systematically used for tools and other implements already in phase I and with increasing rates in phases II and III (see this volume, chapter 2).

Metal

At Sitagroi, metal (see chapter 8) first appears in the ornamental repertoire in phase II. It was continually used thereafter, although the finds are so sporadic that numerical differences between phases are of no interpretative significance.

With the exception of the gold bead SF 4803 of phase III, the rest of the fourteen metal ornaments recovered are made of copper, as are nearly all other metal artifacts from the site. There is a strong possibility that copper comes from local ores, several of which are known in the area of Alexandroupolis, in Chalkidiki, and in the Pangaion Mountains. However, a source in the larger mines further north (Ai Bunar in Bulgaria, Rudna Glava in Yugoslavia) cannot be excluded (see this volume, chapter 8). The not-so-distant mines of Pangaion and Thassos were extensively used throughout antiquity as gold sources (Koukouli-Chrysanthaki 1992).

The gold bead from Sitagroi (figure 8.1e; plate 8.4) fits well within the small but steadily increasing assemblage of gold ornaments from the Neolithic Aegean, which includes a bead from Dhimitra, a small hoard of pendants and strips from Aravissos Pellas, pendants from Sesklo and

Platomagoules in Thessaly, and a ring and a strip from the Zas Cave in Naxos. To these we can also add the typologically comparable large hoard of silver beads and earrings from the Alepotrypa Cave in southern Peloponnese (Zachos 1996a). All these artifacts are ultimately related to the pioneering gold metallurgy of the Balkans, best known from the lavish finds at Varna, Durankulak, and other sites farther north (see chapter 8 and appendix 8.3 for discussion).

Summary of Raw Material Use

The distributions of raw materials through time and across artifact categories reflect a range of choices regarding the exploitation of natural resources for ornamental purposes. A correlation of the raw materials and the different kinds of ornamental items is presented in table 9.3. In the temporal dimension (table 9.2), we see the continuous preference for shell, the sudden popularity of clay in phase III and of bone in phase V, the early appearance of metal in phase II, the early relative frequency of stone in phase I, and an impressive peak of the same in phase III. As table 9.4 shows, it is only for beads that all five raw materials have been used. Shell is primarily used for beads and bracelet/annulets (with a more or less balanced frequency between these two categories). The almost exclusive use of clay and stone for beads is striking. Much less pronounced numerically, but still distinctive, is the clustering of bone in pins, and of metal in beads and pins.

END PRODUCTS

Although simple in form, the ornaments from Sitagroi are carefully manufactured; crafters devoted time and care to produce them (compare Karali-Yannacopoulos 1997:210). The occurrence of unfinished preforms of annulets and beads (see appendix 9.2) testifies to on-site production. Techniques of manufacture were relatively uncomplicated, based more on special knowledge and dexterity than on sophisticated tools and installations.

As explained in the appendixes, shell, stone, and bone were chipped and ground into shape, then drilled through, ground smooth, and finally pol-

Table 9.3. Distribution of Raw Materials across the Categories of Ornamental Items

	Bead	Bracelet/ annulet	Pendant	Pin	Plaque	Ring	Total
Bone	3	0	10	19	4	0	36
	0.51	0.00	9.90	76.00	100.00	0.00	3.97
Clay	163	0	2	0	0	0	165
	27.49	0.00	1.98	0.00	0.00	0.00	18.19
Metal	7	0	0	6	0	1	14
	1.18	0.00	0.00	24.00	0.00	100.00	1.54
Shell	228	180	86	0	0	0	494
	38.45	98.36	85.15	0.00	0.00	0.00	54.47
Stone	192	3	3	0	0	0	198
	32.38	1.64	2.97	0.00	0.00	0.00	21.83
Total N	593	183	101	25	4	1	907
Total %	65.38	20.18	11.14	2.76	0.00	0.00	

NOTE: Excluded are items of undeterminable phase and material.

Table 9.4. Numerical Representation of Bead Types by Phase

Bead Type	I	II	III	IV	V	Total
Cylinder, narrow	28	76	151	11	3	269
Cylinder, wide	4	27	30	4	1	66
Cylinder, tubular	0	2	4	2	0	8
Cylinder, disc	0	0	1	1	1	3
Cylinder	0	0	11	0	0	11
Pinched	1	1	123	1	0	126
Dentalium tubular	0	24	38	8	0	70
Irregular	0	7	14	3	2	26
Biconical	3	0	2	1	1	7
Barrel	0	1	5	0	1	7
Segmented	0	0	3	0	1	4
"Button"	0	0	2	0	0	2
Spherical	0	0	2	0	0	2
Miscellaneous	0	4	2	0	1	7
Phase total	36	142	388	31	11	608

ished. Clay beads and pendants were molded and baked like other ceramic objects. Metal ornaments might have utilized the bread and/or pottery ovens in operation on the site (volume 1, chapter 1 [C. Renfrew 1986c]; this volume, chapters 5 and 8). Several of the chipped stone (this volume, chapter 3) and ground stone (this volume, chapter 5) implements found at Sitagroi could have belonged to the toolkit of the ornament makers: small hammerstones and anvils, sandstone querns, and pointed flakes that could have been drill bits appropriate to perforate beads and pendants (compare Tosi and Vidale 1990). The study of ornament industries in the Neolithic and Chalcolithic civilizations of the Indus Valley and in modern India has shown that such relatively simple techniques were not only highly effective in the massive production of tiny and finely worked objects, but also persisted essentially unchanged over millennia, even until today (Kenoyer 1986; Possehl 1981).

Bracelet/Annulet

QUANTITY, RAW MATERIAL, AND TEMPORAL DISTRIBUTION. Some 189 bracelet/annulets were recorded. Of these, 186 pieces were made of thick shell; only three fragmentary examples were made of stone. (Table 9.3 does not include the artifacts from unknown contexts; thus the numbers do not match. The numbers will also differ in table 9.2.2.) The concurrence of shell and stone bangles is common in Macedonian sites (see below), including Servia, Nea Nikomedeia, Vassilika, Olynthos, and Dhimitra. Farther north, stone and shell bangles were found together at the cemetery of Durankulak near Varna (Todorova and Vajsov 1993: fig. 222). Shell, clay, and limestone annulets all come from Divostin in Serbia (McPherron 1988:330, fig. 11.5, m–t).

The three fragmentary stone artifacts were made of marble. The earliest one (SF 3681; figure 9.3; plate 9.1b) dates to phase I and is thus contemporary with examples from Middle Neolithic Servia (Mould, Ridley, and Wardle 2000: fig. 4.22, pl. 4.11a). SF 5321 (figure 9.4; plate 9.1a) comes from the Late Neolithic (phase II), when stone bangles are also known from Olynthos (Heurtley 1939: fig. 34m), Vassilika C–II (Aslanis 1992:216, pl. 68, 10), and Dhimitra II (Grammenos 1991: pl. 31, 5). SF 4204 dates to the Final Neolithic/Chalcolithic (phase III), as do the marble band-shaped bangles from the cemetery at Durankulak (Todorova and Vajsov 1993: fig. 222, 3–4). Stone bangles were also found at Neolithic Nea Nikomedeia (Rodden and Wardle, forthcoming), Ayio Gala at Chios (Hood 1981:68-69, figs. 44, 330-33, pl. 11), and RachmaniRachmani in Thessaly (Hood 1981:68).

Of the shell bracelets, 170 pieces were manufactured of *Spondylus*, and sixteen of *Glycymeris* (compare appendix 9.3, table 9.3.2). The earliest examples (SF 2518 [plate 9.2b], 3556, 2681, 5271), all of *Spondylus*, come from phase I. Two pieces of *Spondylus* from Dikili Tash (Karali-Yannacopoulos 1992: table 15), several of both *Glycymeris* and *Spondylus* from Servia (Mould, Ridley, and Wardle 2000: fig. 4.43, pl. 4.28a, b, d, e), and *Glycymeris* examples from Nea Nikomedeia (Reese 1987:122) date to the same period. At Sitagroi the analyses of

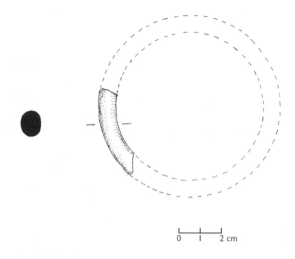

Figure 9.3. Marble bracelet/annulet: phase I, SF 3681, plate 9.1b.

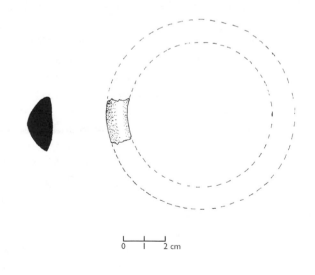

Figure 9.4. Marble bracelet/annulet: phase II, SF 5321, plate 9.1a.

N. Shackleton and Miller (appendixes 9.1, 9.2) have shown an interesting differentiation in the treatment of *Spondylus* and *Glycymeris* through time and across the range of ornamental items. The crucial phases are II and III. In phase II the two species were chosen interchangeably for bracelets/annulets, although a taste for *Spondylus* is already apparent in a ratio of 22:9 pieces. In phase III the number of *Spondylus* increases dramatically to 117 bracelets/annulets versus only five of large *Glycymeris*. At the same time, quantities of *Spondylus* beads decrease, whereas smaller *Glycymeris* valves are extensively used as pendants (fifty-three out of a total of sixty-four shell specimens in this phase: see table 9.3).

Indeed, the Late and Final Neolithic/Chalcolithic were the periods when shell bracelets/annulets, mostly of *Spondylus*, were widespread all over the Aegean and the Balkans. In the Drama Plain, eighty-three *Spondylus* items were found at Dikili Tash (Karali-Yannacopoulos 1992: 163–164, table 15, 163–164, pls. 166, 207g) and at least thirty others at Dhimitra (Karali 1991; Karali-Yannacopoulos 1997: 209). Elsewhere in Macedonia they occur at Servia (Mould, Ridley, and Wardle 2000: 278–281, fig. 4.43, pl. 4.28c), many at Makriyalos in Pieria (Besios and Pappa 1996:219; Pappa 1995: 32, top), several at Vassilika C-II (of *Spondylus* or *Glycymeris*: Grammenos 1991: pl. 33.41, 44, 53, 56, 58, 60-61, 69, pl. 34.33), Olynthos (Heurtley 1939: fig. 35I), and at Paradeisos in Thrace (Reese 1987:127-128, figs. 11–12). In Thessaly a group of 100 comes from Dhimini, and others from Sesklo, Phthiotic Thebes, Ayia Sofia-Magoula, Tsangli, and Pyrasos, as well as from Halai in Boeotia (Karali-Yannacopoulos 1992:164; Reese 1987:128; Tsuneki 1989:16, fn. 30). Examples have also been reported from the Theopetra Cave but without an exact date (Kyparissi-Apostolika 1996:68 and personal communication 1998). Farther south they are known at Franchthi Cave (J. Shackleton 1988:51–53, appendix E), Alepotrypa Cave at Diros (Papathanassopoulos 1996: 84, 229 cat. no. 46), Leonidion (Karali-Yannacopoulos 1997:164), and Saliagos (N. Shackleton 1968:127, pl. 49). In the Balkans, *Spondylus* annulets come from a plethora of sites, including Anza (Gimbutas 1976c:247–250, 254–255, fig. 215, and pl. 27), Durankulak (Avramova 1991:46–47), Gradeshnitsa, Goljamo Delčevo, and Vinča, to mention only locations where the Aegean origin of the shell has

been confirmed by oxygen isotope analysis (N. Shackleton and Renfrew 1970; Willms 1985:341–343).

The site of Sitagroi has produced the largest known group of Neolithic/Chalcolithic shell bracelets/annulets in the Aegean, and this important recovery may well be due, at least in part, to the extensive use of both dry and wet sieving in the excavation.[8] In contrast, the Early Bronze Age strata yielded only one *Glycymeris* and twenty-three *Spondylus* fragments. Quantities also dropped significantly at Dikili Tash (Karali-Yannacopoulos 1992: table 15), while elsewhere only sporadic examples have been reported from Myrtos in Crete (N. Shackleton 1972:325), Troy II (Hood 1981:69), and Kastanas (Karali-Yannacopoulos 1992:164). Thus the question whether shell bracelets/annulets were made at all during the Early Bronze Age concerns a region far broader than the settlement of Sitagroi. The fragmentary preservation of most Sitagroi EBA examples is emphasized by N. Shackleton (appendix 9.1) and Miller (appendix 9.2) as negative evidence, but the bulk of the Neolithic/Chalcolithic material was of a similar condition. As a counterpoint, I would note the identification by Miller of a phase V worked bangle preform (SF 5606: appendix 9.2; plate 9.2.1c) along with the discovery of wholly preserved *Spondylus* bangles in contemporary contexts at Dikili Tash (Karali-Yannacopoulos 1992: pl. 207h). These finds lend support to the possibility of bangle manufacture and circulation by the villagers of the Drama Plain during the Early Bronze Age, although conceivably not on the same scale as before.

A final note about the choice of raw material for bracelets/annulets at Sitagroi and prehistoric Macedonia in general concerns the absence of metal specimens, despite the presence of other metal ornaments at these same sites. Copper and/or gold bracelets do come from other regions that also produced shell and stone examples, including Pefkakia and Ayia Marina in Thessaly (Zachos 1996a:167), Durankulak (Avramova 1991:44) and Varna (Ivanov 1991:11) in Bulgaria.

FORM, STYLE, AND MODES OF WEARING. The fragments of white stone annulets from Sitagroi belong to bangles of circular (figure 9.3) and triangular (figure 9.4) sections with smoothed surfaces. They are similar to the ones from Olynthos, Vassilika, and Dhimitra mentioned above, while the one example from Servia has a ridged surface (Heurtley 1939:65, fig. 60).

Among the shell specimens, many fragments can be reconstructed as bangles, elliptical in shape, with sections varying from curvilinear to rectangular at different points of the circumference (see the idealized construction by N. Shackleton in figure 9.5 and compare SF 816 of phase III: plate 9.3). Other segments have single or double perforations drilled at one preserved end (SF 1201, 1299, 1592 of phase III [plate 9.2f–h], and SF 4263 of phase II), perhaps in order to be connected with other similar elements in link-type bracelets. In many cases the selected valves bear colorful areas in pink, orange, red, purple, gray, and brown, which would have offered a pleasing chromatic effect against the main cream-white of the shell body.

The size of the circlets, from small to fairly large, is primarily related to the particular species and original dimensions of the unmodified shell, ultimately reduced to an ornament. Beyond the limitations of the raw material, there is remarkable standardization of the final forms, reflecting the makers' skill and/or taste (see appendixes 9.1, 9.2). Thus larger specimens of *Spondylus* were systematically sought after. The thinner upper valve of the mollusk was preferred for annulets; the width and thickness of the band at the point most distant from the hinge were closely controlled, and the hinge itself was given a distinct rectangular shape. Similar choices have been observed at Dhimitra (Karali-Yannacopoulos 1997:209), Dikili Tash (Karali-Yannacopoulos 1992:163), and Dhimini (Tsuneki 1989).

The careful and consistent crafting of shell bangles has long been considered evidence for specialized ornament production in the Neolithic/ Chalcolithic Aegean, an issue discussed fully in the appendixes. At Sitagroi, Miller has recognized preforms at various stages of manufacture (plate 9.2.1). This observation lends support to the hypothesis of Sitagroi as a production center. Other sites reporting unfinished pieces and debris include Dhimini (Tsuneki 1989), Dikili Tash (Karali-Yannacopoulos 1992:160), Dhimitra (Karali-Yannacopoulos 1997: 209–210), and Makriyalos (Besios and Pappa 1996:219). However, at no site is there yet conclu-

sive evidence for workshop installations or discard areas of debris, with the possible exception of House N at Dhimini (Tsuneki 1989:13). More than 50% of the finished annulets from that site, as well as worked preforms, were accumulated in this building; stone tools potentially useful for annulet manufacture were also found (Tsuneki 1989:13).

Differences in the size and form of the bracelets/annulets from Sitagroi and related sites have led to various opinions about their modes of wearing (see plates 9.3–9.7). Several *Spondylus* bangles, ranging in interior diameter from 6.5 to 8.7 cm (examples from phase III: SF 816 [plates 9.3, 9.7q], SF 3877 [plate 9.4], SF 3486, 3485, 3484 [plate 9.5a–c]; compare Karali-Yannacopoulos 1992:163 for Dikili Tash) are large enough to have been worn around an adult's wrist, arm, or ankle, as is demonstrated

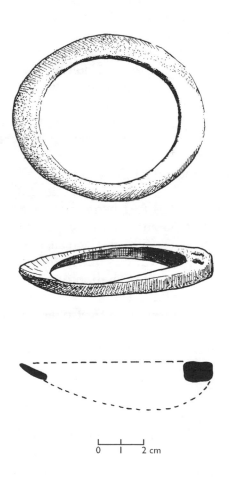

Figure 9.5. Idealized reconstruction of a *Spondylus* bracelet/annulet (by N. Shackleton).

339

by examples from Balkan (Marangou 1991:327) and Harappan (Kenoyer 1991:90–91) cemeteries. But most of the bangles, especially those made of *Glycymeris,* are too small to have been used as such by adults: 3.5 cm is N. Shackleton's estimate of the average inside diameter of the Sitagroi pieces; and 4.5 to 5 cm is the common diameter range at Dhimitra (Karali-Yannacopoulos 1997:209), Nea Nikomedeia (Reese 1987:122), Emporio, and Ayio Gala (Hood 1982:652, fig. 292). For this reason most scholars prefer to interpret them as annulets or ring-pendants. Several examples (for example, Sitagroi SF 2605 of phase II; SF 3427a, b of phase III [plate 9.6]) indeed bear natural or opened perforations at the hinge, which could have served for suspension.

Smaller circlets may have been produced as children's bangles (Karali-Yannacopoulos 1992:163) or else given to a person at an early age and never removed, as is the case nowadays with the jade bangles presented to Chinese girls as charms. According to Marangou (1991:332, fig. 4b, pl. I.4), very small circlets may have been hair ornaments, as is probably depicted on a Neolithic figurine from Dikili Tash wearing a circular element on her head. Archaeological evidence for such a fashion comes from Harappan sites (Kenoyer 1991:91) and from tombs 626 and 1036 at Durankulak, where shell bangles found in the area of the skull apparently had been attached to the head and/or to the ears (Todorova and Vajsov 1993: figs. 220–221).

The perforated fragments mentioned earlier in this section as potential parts of link-type bracelets suggest other possibilities. Such shapes could have been produced in various dimensions fit for different ages, so that consideration of adult ornaments need not be confined to the few surviving bangles of appropriate size. SF 3877 of phase III (plate 9.4) preserves more than half of the arc with a perforation at one end, intended perhaps to mend a broken bangle (compare J. Shackleton 1983, for Servia) or to attach more circlets together in a fashion known, for example, from the necropolis of Cernica in Romania (compare Karali-Yannacopoulos 1992:164, for Dikili Tash). It may also be that perforated segments did not belong to bangle/bracelets at all but were decorative plaques attached to the arm, wrist, or hair (compare Karali-Yannacopoulos 1997:209, for Dhimitra), sewn onto garments (compare Dumitrescu 1980:23, pls. XII:10, XV:11, for Rast), or connected into a diadem (compare Todorova and Vajsov 1993: pl. 107, for Durankulak).

ON-SITE USE AND DISCARD. The circulation of shell circlets as trade, exchange, or prestige items around the Neolithic Aegean and northward to Europe has been extensively discussed by many scholars (Greenfield 1991; C. Renfrew 1973d; Séfériadès 1995; Willms 1985) and need not be dealt with here. Instead I will consider the manipulation of these ornaments within the Aegean communities, including Sitagroi, which manufactured or at least had more immediate access to the raw material.

Our main clue is the fragmentary condition of most bracelet/annulets (see particularly plate 9.7 or 9.5), a common phenomenon in all northern Aegean sites. At Sitagroi, from phase III we have only one possibly complete example of *Spondylus* (SF 3829) and three more of *Glycymeris* (SF 3427a–b: plate 9.6; SF 5257). Nine *Spondylus* fragments were burnt (SF 780a–c, 3491, 3493, of phase III; SF 5140, 5141a of phase IV; SF 2244, unphased, plate 9.2.1 i), as were also several from Dhimitra (Karali-Yannacopoulos 1997:202) and Servia (the latter, though, probably due to a fire; see Mould, Ridley, and Wardle 2000:278). A large number of burnt fragments were found at Dhimini, and this has been interpreted variously. According to Tsuneki (1989), they broke and were discarded during manufacture which, as replication experiments show, must indeed have been laborious enough to cause accidental breakage (see appendix 9.2). However, this scenario cannot account for the marks of burning, since the crafting process does not seem to have involved fire. Halstead (1993), on the other hand, argues for deliberate destruction by privileged families of the community in the context of emergent social ranking. Breakage of the valuable shell ornaments would restrict their intrasite circulation, allowing for a limited accumulation of complete ornaments in "elite" hands to be forwarded to peer families inland in return for food, marital mates, and labor.

Although one may find it difficult to project such hierarchy back to the Late and Final Neolithic/Chalcolithic (compare Sherratt 1984), I find Halstead's social interpretation of the broken circlets an attractive working hypothesis that could be extended to other sites, including ours. However, from architectural and contexual information, Neolithic/ Chalcolithic Sitagroi is not comparable to that from Dhimini (but see chapter 12).

Breakages are sometimes due to recovery contingencies and post-excavation treatment of the material,[9] but Miller examined most fragments and found that a number of finished circlets had been smashed in prehistory[10] (see appendix 9.2). Several assemblages of phase III are of interest in this regard (see volume 1 [C. Renfrew 1986b: 217–218; this volume, chapter 12: tables 12.4, 12.5; illustrations in this chapter are referenced; see appendix 9.3 for the balance). First, there is a group of over a dozen fragments in layer MM 61 (SF 3486, 3485, 3484, 3489, 3431, 3505 [plate 9.5 a–f]; SF 3487a; SF 3487b [plate 9.7p]; SF 3490–3493, 3500), among which two in the same layer are burnt (SF 3491, 3493); and nine more were found slightly below in layer MM 63 (SF 3405, 3504, 3533, 3815-16, 4494, 4501, 4506, 4508). Seven further examples come from the water-sieved unit ZA 47, representing debris between construction episodes (see chapter 12). Among these, three are burnt (SF 780a–c), one is a fragment (SF 487), and one is a reworked fragment (SF 784; plate 9.2.1). Finally, there was a concentration of fifteen pieces in layers 15–31 of sounding ZG, where several indications of architectural features were seen through the sequence (volume 1 [C. Renfrew 1986b]:221). Fourteen fragments belong to finished items (SF 5587, 2944, 4746, 2961a–b, 2963, 2965, 2970, 2980, 2982, 2989, 4418), one of which is a preform (SF 2962, plate 9.2.1f). Could these contexts echo a privileged manipulation of the (presumably) cherished shell circlets by some outstanding persons in the village?

Other ways of treating valuable ornaments are illustrated by the use and discard of shell bangles in the admittedly geographically distant Harappan and contemporary traditional cultures of the Indus Valley (Kenoyer 1991:96–97). Depictions of bangles on Harappan figurines and bangles deposited as burial goods in contemporary cemeteries suggest that these ornaments were associated with mature women in prehistory, perhaps as a symbol of an age- or status-based group. They are worn today by men as amulets, by children for protection and beauty, and by women throughout life for adornment and to ensure the well-being of their families. Being highly personalized, a woman's shell bangles are broken upon her husband's death.

Beads

Beads, 608 of them in total, make up the majority of ornaments (66%), which is not surprising since many beads are usually needed for a single piece of jewelry. They come in a variety of sizes and shapes: cylindrical, spherical, biconical, rectangular, rayed, and irregular (figure 9.6).

TYPOLOGY AND CHRONOLOGY. I have classified the Sitagroi beads into fourteen morphological types, listed below in order of their numerical frequency, controlled by phase (table 9.4) and raw material (table 9.5).

In this typology, the terms referring to shape (cylinder, barrel, biconical, and so forth) are adopted from Beck's (1973) reference book on the classification of beads and pendants. The predominant shape is the straight cylinder, which I have further divided into five varieties. The main distinction (after Barge

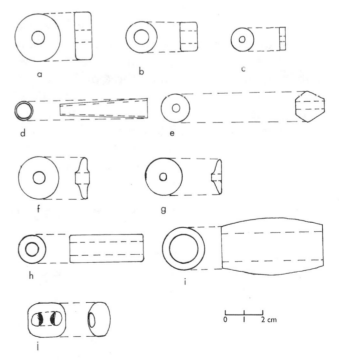

Figure 9.6. Sections of the main bead types: (a, b) Wide cylinder; (c) narrow discoid; (d) *Dentalium* tubular; (e) biconical; (f, g) pinched; (h) tubular; (i) barrel; (j) "button."

Table 9.5. Numerical Representation of Bead Types by Raw Material

Bead type	Raw material					
	Bone	Clay	Metal	Shell	Stone	Total
Cylinder, narrow	0	21	3	81	152	257
Cylinder, wide	0	3	1	48	13	65
Cylinder, tubular	0	2	0	3	3	8
Cylinder, disc	0	0	1	1	0	2
Cylinder	0	0	0	1	9	10
Pinched	0	126	0	0	0	126
Dentalium tubular	0	0	0	70	0	70
Irregular	0	0	0	19	7	26
Biconical	0	5	0	0	2	7
Barrel	0	2	0	4	1	7
Segmented	0	2	0	0	2	4
"Button"	0	0	0	2	0	2
Spherical	0	2	0	0	0	2
Miscellaneous	3	0	2	1	1	7
Phase total	3	163	7	230	190	593

1982) is between narrow and wide cylinders, measured lengthwise (that is, oriented the way the beads are positioned when strung).[11] Narrow or "shorter" beads are smaller than or equal to the diameter in length; wide or "long" beads are those larger than or equal to the diameter in length. Moreover I have separated as "discs" those narrow beads whose length is equal to or less than one-third of the diameter, and as "tubular" those wide beads whose length is equal to or more than three times their diameter. Without further specification, "cylinders" are classed as those pieces for which neither length nor diameter is available. Most cylindrical beads, as well as those belonging to other types, are rather small, with the exception of the *Dentalia* and some tubular and barrel pieces measuring up to 2 or 3 cm in length.

Each bead type is discussed below, with its archaeological comparanda. Because their numbers are very low, discoid and tubular beads have been grouped together with the narrow and wide cylinders, respectively.

CYLINDRICAL, NARROW/DISCOID BEADS. These small beads range in length from 0.1 to 0.8 cm (mean: 0.38 cm), in diameter 0.2 to 1.4 cm (mean: 0.54 cm), and hole diameter 0.015 to 0.35 cm (mean: 0.16 cm) (see appendix 9.3, plate 9.3.3). Figure 9.7d shows a narrow clay cylinder (SF 5076a), and figure 9.7b a shell

disc (SF 5076b), both from the bead group SF 5076 of phase III. A few pieces, including the gold bead SF 4803 (figure 8.3e; plate 8.1), belong to the annular version, that is, a cylinder with the hole diameter wide enough to give it a ringlike shape. The few metal beads all have simple narrow cylindrical and annular forms produced by coiling small strips of copper and gold (see chapter 8; SF 5336 [figure 8.3a; plate 8.2b] of phase II; SF 783 [figure 8.3d; plate 8.11a] and SF 5340 [plate 8.11b], both of phase II).

Preference for narrow cylindrical beads is already apparent in the small group of phase I. Their number increases sharply from phase I to II and then almost doubles from phase II to III.

Stone was clearly preferred, comprising more than 60% of the assemblage. These stone beads are remarkably standardized in their dimensions, being most likely the products of a few knowledgeable craftsmen, as Miller argues in appendix 9.2. The shell examples, mostly of *Spondylus*, but also of *Cerastoderma* (*Cardium*) *edule*, likewise exhibit uniformity that points to skilled manufacturers. The thick right valve of *Spondylus* was systematically used for this purpose (see appendix 9.2). Such beads were often found in groups, a characteristic example of which is SF 5212 of phase III (plate 9.8), consisting of thirty-six stone and nine narrow shell cylinders, together with sporadic pieces of other types and/or materials. By contrast, I have observed that clay examples usually are isolated or occur in small numbers and exhibit greater variation in their dimensions and form (compare, for example SF 1274 and SF 5058a, plate 9.9d and e, respectively, both of phase III). This is one more point in favor of Miller's view (appendix 9.2): we are dealing with nonspecialized artifacts that

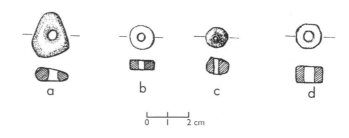

Figure 9.7. Assorted beads from the phase III group SF 5076: (a) stone irregular; (b) *Spondylus* discoid; (c) clay pinched; (d) clay narrow cylindrical.

would be easy to make from soft clay, even by untrained hands.

Discoid, annular, and narrow cylindrical beads are very common in many sites during the Middle and especially the Late Neolithic/Chalcolithic. Examples comparable to the Sitagroi finds in dimensions and/or raw materials come from Dikili Tash (Karali-Yannacopoulos 1992:162, pl. 207d; Papathanassopoulos, ed. 1996: 335, cat. no. 286; Zachos 1996a: 167), Dhimitra (with, among others, 30 copper pieces: Karali-Yannacopoulos 1997:205–206, pl. 56.6; Zachos 1996a:167), Servia (Mould, Ridley, and Wardle 2000:174–176 [fig. 4.21, pl. 4.11b], 264–265 [fig. 4.38, pl. 4.26a], 277–278 [fig. 4.42]), Achilleion (Gimbutas 1989b:252, fig. 8.2), Sesklo (Papathanassopoulos, ed. 1996: 335, cat. no. 287), and Franchthi (J. Shackleton 1988:53). An impressive group of 168 silver discoid and four annular beads was found in the FN hoard from the Diros Cave (Papathanassopoulos 1996: 227, cat. no. 41; Zachos 1996a:167). Similar shapes in copper and/or gold are known from Selevac (Glumac and Tringham 1990:554, pl. 15.3; Tringham and Stevanović 1990:3 48), Varna (Ivanov 1991: 10), and Durankulak (Avramova 1991:45). Two stone pieces are published from Early Bronze Age Poliochni (Bernabó-Brea 1976: Tav. CLXXXVII:17 and 15, respectively).

CYLINDER, WIDE/TUBULAR BEADS. The length of these cylinders ranges from 0.4 to 3 cm (mean: 1.27 cm), and diameter from 0.2 to 0.8 cm (mean: 0.49 cm). One of the longest pieces is the clay tube SF 533 of phase IV (figure 9.8; plate 9.9g). The manufacture of these larger beads in shell or stone[12] could be challenging in the stage of perforation (see appendix 9.2), which makes the careful crafting all the more remarkable (see for example, the wide shell cylinder SF 3823 of phase III [plates 9.10, 9.11b]).

Long cylinders of different materials come from Dhimitra (Karali-Yannacopoulos 1997:207), and one marble example comes from Dikili Tash (Karali-Yannacopoulos 1992:162). Beads manufactured on hollow bone shafts are reported from Nea Nikomedeia, (Rodden and Wardle, forthcoming). Stone beads were found in Servia (Mould, Ridley, and Wardle 2000:174–176, fig. 4.2:l) and Early Bronze Age Thermi (Lamb 1936: fig. 46, no. 4). Eight *Spondylus* pieces come from Dhimini (Tsuneki 1989:8).

PINCHED BEADS. These clay beads are variously hand-shaped as cones (SF 5210, phase III; figure 9.9; plate 9.12), discs, or flattened spheres (SF 5076a, phase III; figure 9.7c), always with a slightly raised ("pinched")[13] top. They are of small dimensions: 0.4 to 0.7 cm in diameter (most pieces measuring 0.5–0.55 cm), and 0.2 to 0.4 cm in length. The type became numerous in phase III, perhaps as a substitute for more elaborate (and presumably less accessible) ornaments in materials harder to work. Irregularities in their shape, finish, and firing suggest to Miller (appendix 9.2) that such beads were occasionally made by different amateurs. As a possible exception I mention SF 5210 (figure 9.9; plate 9.12), a group of twenty-two beads that seem to have been modeled by the same careful hand, being all of the same form and dimensions and bearing fingerprints (see also appendix 9.2).

DENTALIUM TUBULAR BEADS. *Dentalia*, with their hollow cylindrical form, offer attractive, ready-to-use beads. Shape varies according to the portion of the shell used: whole shells are slightly curved and taper to one end, whereas fragments are more or less straight-sided cylinder segments (for examples, see SF 5203 of phase II, an assemblage of twenty-two *Dentalia*; plate 9.13). Dimensions likewise depend on the natural form, which in general allows long beads; at Sitagroi many pieces measure 1.5–2 cm.

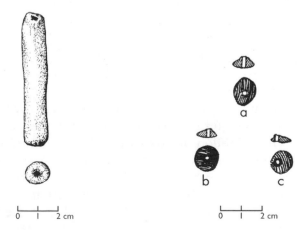

(Left): Figure 9.8. Tubular clay bead, phase IV: SF 533, plate 9.9g. *(Right): Figure 9.9.* Striated and pinched clay beads, phase III: SF 5210, plate 9.12.

Dentalium beads were popular during the Middle and Late Neolithic at Dikili Tash (Karali-Yannacopoulos 1992: pl. 207f), Dhimitra (Karali-Yannacopoulos 1997:208), Paradeisos (Reese 1987: 130–131, figs. 13–14), and Franchthi (J. Shackleton 1988:51–52). *Dentalia* of Mediterranean origin are known also in the Balkans, for example at Anza (Gimbutas 1976c: pl. 28) and Durankulak (Avramova 1991:44; Todorova and Vajsov 1993: pl. 108). In the Bronze Age, *Dentalia* are reported from various Early Cycladic tombs in Naxos, Paros, and Syros, as well as from Early and Middle Minoan layers at Knossos, Kommos, and Myrtos (Reese 1987:130).

IRREGULAR BEADS. These are either made on fragments of *Spondylus* (SF 796, phase III; figure 9.10) or on small blocks of stone in roughly geometric forms, such as wedge-shaped (SF 5076c, phase III; figure 9.7a), squarish, and pyramidal. At least some of the irregular beads are probably unfinished preforms (SF 5262 of phase II; see appendix 9.2, plate 9.2.2).

BICONICAL BEADS. Although very few in number, biconical beads come in various sizes and forms. Such variability is not surprising, given that these beads were mainly hand-shaped in malleable clay.[14] There is an unusually large bead (SF 1628) of phase I with slightly concave profiles (figure 9.11; plate 9.9a); another (SF 1219) of phase III (figure 9.12; plate 9.11c) exhibits convex surfaces and a length equal to the diameter. Additionally, one piece in the group, SF 5058 of phase IV (figure 9.13; plate 9.9f), with its length just falling short of its diameter, consists of two symmetrical truncated cones; while a bead from the clay group SF 5077a of phase III (figure 9.14; plate 9.9c) is highly asymmetric.

Only two beads from Sitagroi bear surface decoration: SF 1628 of phase I (figure 9.11) is graphite painted, and SF 1219 of phase III is decorated with incised spirals (figure 9.12). In both cases, the technique of decoration borrows from the repertoire of contemporary ceramics, namely the use of graphite in the fabric of phase I Lustre Ware (volume 1 [Keighley 1986]:346) and in the phase III Incised Ware (volume 1 [R. Evans 1986]:402), both discussed in chapter 7.

Biconical objects of clay or stone like the ones under consideration have often been interpreted as beads, whorls, or buttons (at Kritsana: Heurtley 1939: fig. 67:1–q, s; Poliochni: Bernabó-Brea 1964: 655; 1976: Tav. CLXIX:5; Thermi: Lamb 1936:161, fig. 46:5, 9). At Sitagroi, SF 1219 of phase III (figure 9.12; plate 9.11c) was initially recorded as a biconical spindle whorl. This uncertainty has to do with the fact that cones and bicones are standard forms for spindle whorls in the prehistoric Aegean and southeast Europe (see chapter 6). However, the small size of the bicones treated here make them

Figure 9.10. Two irregular *Spondylus* beads, phase III: SF 796.

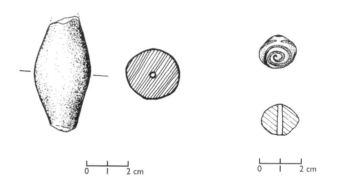

(Left): Figure 9.11. Biconical clay bead, phase I: SF 1628, plate 9.9a. *(Right): Figure 9.12.* Biconical clay bead with incised decoration, phase III: SF 1219, plate 9.11c.

(Left): Figure 9.13. Biconical clay bead, phase IV: SF 5058, plate 9.9e, f. *(Right): Figure 9.14.* Biconical asymmetric bead in clay, phase III: SF 5077(a), plate 9.9c.

344

dysfunctional for spinning (Tringham and Ste-vanović 1990:348); our beads measure an average 1.27 cm in length and 0.83 cm in diameter, versus an average 2.8 cm in length and 3.9 cm in diameter of the biconical spindle whorls from the site (see chapter 6).

BARREL BEADS. These are long beads (0.6–1.8 cm length, always longer than the diameter), of elliptical or spindle-shaped profile. The small group includes some of the finest examples of bead workmanship at Sitagroi: SF 5080b of phase III (plate 9.14b) and SF 1587 of phase V (figure 9.15; plate 9.14c), both of *Spondylus*. Shell and stone, although harder to handle in such a form (see appendix 9.2), seem to have been preferred and worked more carefully than the conveniently plastic clay (note the asymmetric contours of the clay bead SF 3833 of phase III, plate 9.9b).

Sporadic examples of barrel beads in various materials and dimensions are known from Dhimitra (Karali-Yannacopoulos 1997:207), Dikili Tash (Karali-Yannacopoulos 1992:162; Papathanassopoulos, ed. 1996: fig. 289), Servia (Heurtley 1939: fig. 34n; Mould, Ridley, and Wardle 2000:174, 175: fig. 4.21 [SF 259, 515, both described as tubular]), Dhimini (Papathanassopoulos, ed. 1996: fig. 289), Achilleion (Gimbutas 1989b:252, fig. 8.2:5), Franchthi (J. Shackleton 1988: 53), Diros (a unique silver piece: Zachos 1996a: 167, fig. 41), and Thermi (Lamb 1936: fig. 46, no. 1).

SEGMENTED BEADS. These are narrow tubes of about 1 cm in length, with grooves across their longitudinal axis. Figure 9.16 shows a pair in stone (SF 5223c) from phase III; figure 9.17 illustrates an example in clay (SF 5040) from phase V. Segmented pieces in bone, clay, shell, and stone with the grooves running parallel to the axis occur at Dhimitra (Karali-Yannacopoulos 1997:207). From Early Bronze Age Ayios Mamas, in central Macedonia, come bone beads with horizontal grooving and barrel-shaped instead of straight cylindrical profiles (Heurtley 1939: fig. 66).

"BUTTONS". The two *Spondylus* "buttons" found at Sitagroi, both from phase III, have a rectangular body that becomes conical at the upper part where a V-shaped hole is pierced (SF 5223b: figure 9.18;

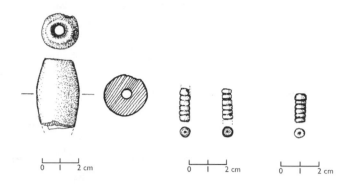

(Left): Figure 9.15. *Spondylus* barrel bead, phase V: SF 1587, plate 9.14c. (Middle): Figure 9.16. Segmented stone beads, phase III: SF 5223(c). (Right): Figure 9.17. Segmented clay bead, phase V: SF 5040.

(Left): Figure 9.18. *Spondylus* "button," phase III: SF 5223b, plate 9.14a. (Right): Figure 9.19. *Spondylus* "button," phase III: SF 5212c, plate 9.8.

plate 9.14a; SF 5212b: figure 9.19, plate 9.8). "Buttons," forming a distinctive Neolithic/Chalcolithic class of shell objects, are known from Dhimitra (Karali-Yannacopoulos 1997:205, pl. 55:4), Makriyalos (Pappa 1995:32, middle photo, second from left in lower row), Dhimini (an impressive group of 141, presumably the products of a specialized workshop [Tsuneki 1989:8]), and Varna (Tsuneki 1989:15, fn. 24). It is not clear, however, whether these rectangular and other studlike forms (Hood 1982:677, pl. 142: 60–61; Reese 1987:128; Pappa 1995:32, middle photo, left in upper row) that we conventionally call "buttons" were indeed beads or meant for fastening garments (see chapter 6), or used both ways.

MISCELLANEOUS BEADS. This miscellaneous group comprises seven beads of different shapes, each occurring only once: a star of *Spondylus* from phase III (SF 4793), a half fragment of a marble oval from phase II (SF 5205b), a pig astragalus from phase III

(SF 4802), a bone platelet from phase II with one wavy and three straight edges (SF 3674), a thin rectangular block of turtle shell from phase V (SF 2276), fragments of (at least) two copper beads of unidentifiable form (SF 5335 from phase II, SF 5334 from phase III), and two spherical beads from phase III.

THE STAR (SF 4793). A piece of excellent workmanship, this bead consists of four pointed branches that project from a discoid body (figure 9.20; plate 9.11a). I have not found parallels among the ornaments from other sites, but comparable are two clay four-pronged discs, cataloged with spindle whorls, one from Sitagroi itself (SF 159; figure 6.16) and the second from Sesklo (Papaefthymiou-Papanthimou 1989:112, cat. no. 101, pls. 17c, 18a). It is unlikely that our star bead was also a whorl, even though spinning and weaving tools of shell are known both in the prehistoric Aegean (at Poliochni: Bernabó-Brea 1976: Tav. CLXXVIII:11) and from Mesopotamia (Moorey 1994:136). The projections would have affected its use as a spindle whorl, and its relatively small size (width 3.2 cm, thickness 0.6 cm, hole diameter 0.35 cm) speaks against such a purpose when compared with the dimensions of the clay Sitagroi whorl SF 159 (width 4.8 cm, thickness 1.9 cm, hole diameter 0.7 cm). We may also note the exceptionally careful finish of the surface, which would not be best served by constant friction with thread during spinning.

THE ASTRAGALUS BEADS (SF 4802, 3770). Perforated knucklebones are a common kind of simple ornament, although usually perforated eccentrically in the fashion of pendants (see section below). Our beads (SF 4802: figure 9.22, plate 2.20c; SF 3770: plate 2.20d) may be compared to centrally perforated phalanges of caprovids from Ezero (Georgiev et al. 1979:196, fig. 122).

The Platelet and the Turtle Block. These small cut-outs of bone (SF 3674: figure 9.21; SF 2276) resemble, in terms of technique, discoid and ingot-shaped inlays (*piastrine*) of shell and alabaster from Poliochni (Bernabó-Brea 1964:671, 673; 1976: Tav. CLXXIX:3 and 25, CLXXVIII:1), shell platelets from Tsangli (Bernabó-Brea 1964:671), and a square piece from Makriyalos (Pappa 1995:32, middle photo, third from left in upper row).

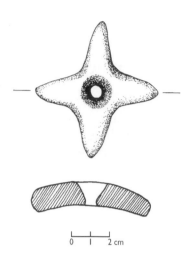

Figure 9.20. Star-shaped *Spondylus* bead, phase II: SF 4793, plate 9.11a.

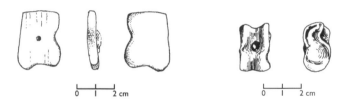

(Left): Figure 9.21. Bone bead, phase II: SF 3674.
(Right): Figure 9.22. Pig astragalus bead,
phase III: SF 4802, plate 2.20c.

POSSIBLE MODES OF WEARING: CONTEXTUAL. Beads are known worldwide as a very versatile type of ornament: elements of the same or different materials and shapes are strung together (and with pendants) to form necklaces, chains, diadems, bracelets, and anklets. They are plaited in the making of belts, hairbands, and other accessories. They are sewn, embroidered, and woven onto textiles and also attached on footware, bags, and headgear (see Dubin 1995:39–99; Seiler-Baldinger 1994:114–121, 138).

The bead assemblages (see contextual information below) from Sitagroi and comparable sites show that prehistoric makers and users were attracted by the interplay of colors, materials, and forms. Characteristic groupings from phase III include: SF 5212a–c (from ZA 44s), an assortment of fifty-six beads (plate

9.8) including pinched and spherical pieces of clay; narrow and wide cylindrical pieces made of shell, mother of pearl, and stone; a shell "button" (figure 9.19); and a stone tubular bead with colors ranging from white to buff, gray, mottled green, and red. SF 5213a–c (ZA44s) consists of thirty-four beads. Among these are pinched beads in buff/gray clay; cylinders and barrels of white, buff, and gray shell; and cylindrical, tubular, and irregular pieces of white and gray marble. SF 5223a–c (from ZA 48s), comprises eighteen beads. These include pinched shapes of gray clay, tubes of buff/white *Dentalia*, cylindrical beads, a "button" (figure 9.18; plate 9.14a) of buff *Spondylus*, and cylindrical and segmented beads (figure 9.16) of stone in various shades and mottled gray. From Neolithic Servia comes a similar group of beads of turquoise malachite and colorful marbles in black, veined gray, red, white, and buff (Mould, Ridley, and Wardle 2000:173–175), while a necklace consisting of cat claws, dog and pig teeth, and grooved bone beads was found at Ayios Mamas (Heurtley 1939: fig. 66).

We also have groups of beads of the same type and color. SF 5210, from ZA 44s, phase III (plate 9.12) comprises twenty-five pinched beads in gray and buff. Two similar groups come from ZA 52/52s of phase II: SF 5208 consists of ten orange stone cylinders, and SF 5202 comprises twenty-seven narrow *Spondylus* cylinders in white/buff. A group of twenty-two buff *Dentalia*, SF 5203 (also from ZA 52/52s), was reconstructed in the field as a chain (plate 9.13:b), which would be comparable with those found in contemporary tombs at Durankulak (Todorova and Vajsov 1993: pls. 108, 110; compare Barge 1982: fig. 24:1–2).

In terms of context, many of the bead groups at Sitagroi were found in close proximity. Among the most prolific were units ZA 52/52s of phase II (see chapter 12, table 12.2) and ZA 44s (table 12.3), 45s, and 47s of phase III.

Phase II
ZA 52/52s yielded eight bead groups:

- SF 5202, SF 5203 (plate 9.13), and SF 5208, mentioned above

- SF 5204 (ten stone beads in gray, green, black, and buff)

- SF 5205a–c (twenty-six beads of white/buff shell, three of gray stone)

- SF 5206 (seven beads of white/buff shell)

- SF 5207 (four beads of gray clay)

- SF 5209 (five shell or stone beads in white)

- SF 5262 (six white shell beads) (plate 9.2.2)

- ZA 52/52s also contained one copper example: SF 5336 (figure 8.1a; plate 8.1b).

Phase III
ZA 44s contained four bead groups: SF 5210 (figure 9.9; plate 9.12), SF 5212a–c (figure 9.19; plate 9.8), SF 5213 (mentioned above), and SF 5211 (ten white/ buff *Dentalia*).

ZA 45s produced various clusters:

- SF 5214 (ten white *Dentalia*)

- SF 5216 (twelve narrow cylinders of gray clay)

- SF 5218–20a (twenty-six pinched beads in gray/buff)

- three pairs of cylindrical beads in shell (SF 5215, SF 5220b) and stone (SF 5220c), a set of four stone cylinders (SF 5217) in white, buff, brown, red, orange, and green.

ZA 47s included the following groups:

- SF 786 (nine pinched, gray/buff)

- SF 790 (fifteen narrow cylinders in green/gray stone)

- SF 791 (five narrow and one wide cylinder in green/gray stone)

- SF 792 (seven narrow cylinders in gray clay and/or stone)

- SF 793 (fifteen narrow cylinders in white/buff shell)

- SF 1102 (seven *Dentalia* in buff/gray)

- various beads found isolated, in pairs, or three- to four-piece sets: in assorted colors, cylinders of shell (SF 499, 523), stone (SF 788a–b, 789, 794), clay (SF 787), and copper (SF 781, 783); pinched beads (SF 522); segmented clay beads (SF 785);

Dentalium beads (SF 795); irregular *Spondylus* beads (SF 796: figure 9.10); a conical or biconical bead of shell or stone (SF 797); and a pig astragalus bead (SF 4802: figure 9.22, plate 2.20c).

Such concentrations allow us to envisage richly beaded body parts and/or garments, as illustrated also by Sitagroi figurines (volume 1 [Gimbutas 1986]: 229; Marangou 1991). Both figurine iconography and patterns on fine ware pottery suggest the use of elaborate textiles at the site (chapter 6). We may further assume that at least some of this cloth was beaded, because such a fashion is amply attested for the Neolithic and Bronze Age all over southeast Europe, the Aegean, and Asia Minor (Barber 1991:130 ff.). At Sitagroi, garments seem to have been especially ornate during the Late/Final Neolithic (see volume 1, chapter 9 [Gimbutas 1986]), when beads also exhibit the greatest variation of shape, color, and material and cluster in attractive assortments.

Nevertheless, isolated beads or small groups of them, frequent at Sitagroi and elsewhere, are usually dismissed as stray finds or the poor remains of destroyed ornaments. At Harappan cemeteries, however, they have been interpreted otherwise. The position of small bead groups and pendants at the pelvis, lower back, or neck of skeletons, and marks caused by the stringing cord, imply the amuletic function of these inconspicuous ornaments, probably over several generations (Kenoyer 1991: 94). Although it has not been possible to identify distinct wear traces on the Sitagroi beads and pendants (see appendix 9.2), we should be alert to various interesting and alternate possibilities regarding the use of these tiny ornamental items.

Pendants

Sitagroi pendants come in various shapes and seem to have been made intermittently. The only exceptions are the simply perforated objects of natural shell or bone which, easy and fast to produce, were popular in every phase. There are ninety such pendants, eighty-six in shell and four in bone, which account for almost 90% of a total of 104 pieces (figure 9.1; table 9.3). This is the only type that exhibits a degree of morphological standardization, while in every other case we are dealing with versions of basic geometric forms in different sizes, materials, and techniques. Stylistic variability may imply flexibility in function, too, despite the common but eccentric perforation(s) that dictated our grouping all these items as "pendants."

The various forms are presented below in order of overall frequency, with their archaeological comparanda: perforated, ring-shaped, discoid, elongated, elliptical, polygonal, prism-shaped, triangular, and miscellaneous pendants. Style and use are discussed where pertinent.

SIMPLY PERFORATED. Perforated shells and skeletal parts of animals, wild and domestic, were used for ornamentation already in the Paleolithic (Taborin 1993) and have attracted fascination ever since, often being invested with magical power and symbolic value. The production of these simple pendants required only the drilling or grinding of a suspension hole with little to no further modification[15] of the raw material. Three kinds of faunal elements were used for this purpose at Sitagroi: shell, teeth, and bone.

PERFORATED SHELL. The majority of this grouping is comprised of intact and nicely shaped valves of medium and small-sized mollusks. The length ranges from 0.7 to 5.6 cm (mean about 2.5 cm); the width ranges from 0.7 to 5.1 cm (mean 1.9 cm). They are perforated at or near the umbo, either purposefully or by nature (Karali-Yannacopoulos 1997: 208; J. Shackleton 1988:49). As seen in table 9.2, the species most favored by far is *Glycymeris* (for example, plate 9.15a–c), accounting for 75% of perforated shells. The great bulk of *Glycymeris* pendants come from phase III (for example, SF 2971, 2981 [plate 9.15a, c]; SF 80 [plate 9.16], SF 778c, b [plate 9.17a–b]), reflecting a shift in the exploitation of large *Glycymeris* for bracelets/annulets in phase II to smaller specimens as pendants during the Final Neolithic/Chalcolithic (but see a *Glycymeris* pendant, SF 2887, of phase II in plate 9.15b). Quantities of *Glycymeris* were also found at Dikili Tash, Dhimitra, Paradeisos, Knossos, Phaistos, and Early Minoan Myrtos in Crete, while they occur sporadically at the Kitsos Cave, Saliagos, Ayio Gala, Anza, and Troy (Reese 1987:121–124, figs. 1–5).

Other bivalves used occasionally for pendants are *Cardium* (SF 2889, phase II; plate 9.18), *Mytilus* (SF 2886, phase II; plate 9.19b), *Donax*, and two valves of the riverine *Unio*. Several *Cardium* shells have also been found at Dikili Tash (Karali-Yanna-copoulos 1992: pl. 207e), Dhimitra (Karali-Yanna-copoulos 1997:208), Nea Nikomedeia (Rodden and Wardle, forthcoming), Servia (Heurtley 1939: fig. 7f, 35g; Mould, Ridley, and Wardle 2000: 283, fig. 4.44), and Neolithic Knossos (Reese 1987:119–124). Examples also come from Paradeisos, Tsangli, and Ayia Sofia-Magoula in Thessaly, Neolithic Ayio Gala and Early Bronze Age Emporio in Chios (Reese 1987: 124–125), Kitsos Cave (Papathanassopoulos, ed. 1996: fig. 293, left), and Ezero in Bulgaria (Georgiev et al. 1979: fig. 203a). The repertoire of perforated shells at Sitagroi also includes a few examples of the marine gastropods *Murex*, *Neritea*, *Cypraea*, and *Columbella*. All bear a single perforation at the top of the spiral,[16] except the *Cypraea* SF 832 of phase IV (plate 9.20), with a pair of holes at the apex. A few *Murex* shells were found at Paradeisos and at Lerna (Reese 1987:130); *Neritea* was a favorite species for ornaments at Franchthi (J. Shackleton 1988: 52) and was used occasionally for beads at Dhimi-tra (Karali-Yannacopoulos 1997:208); one *Cypraea* comes from Kitsos Cave (Papathanassopoulos, ed. 1996: fig. 293, right) and another from Poliochni (Bernabó-Brea 1976: Tav. CLXXIX:26).

In phase III, *Cardium* SF 387, *Neritea* SF 779 (plate 9.21) and both *Unio* pieces SF 3147 and SF 5602 (of which I examined SF 5602 at the Drama Museum) bear large and irregular holes on the body, which suggest that the shell was initially pierced for food extraction (compare appendix 9.1) and possibly used for suspension afterward. The double use of *Cardia* for alimentation and ornamentation has also been observed at Dikili Tash (Karali-Yannacopoulos 1992:162) and Nea Nikomedeia (Rodden and Wardle, forthcoming).

Perforated shells classified here as pendants are often described in the literature as beads (Karali-Yannacopoulos 1992, for several of the Dikili Tash specimens). They could have been used in either way, depending on whether they were hung singly or in groups. At Selevac, a large group of various pierced seashells was found next to a clay figurine; the shells, together with a miniature stone figurine

found nearby, were presumably strung into a necklace that adorned the clay figure (Milojković 1990:400, pls. 1.1–2; Russell 1990:535). Groups of perforated *Cardia* from Nea Nikomedeia and Servia have likewise been interpreted as remains of necklaces, as could also be the case with certain phase III groupings at Sitagroi: SF 5251a–l (from ZA 44s) includes eleven *Glycymeris* valves of the same size and one *Neritea*; another, SF 5255a–e (from ZA 45s), is made up of four *Glycymeris* of the same size and one *Columbella* spiral; and SF 778a–f (from ZA 47s) consists of four *Glycymeris* and one *Neritea*. As has been noted above, all three find contexts were also rich in beads, found singly or in groups.

PERFORATED TEETH. There are only a few examples of perforated teeth, including two boar tusks from phase III (SF 5116, SF 5288 [figure 2.7c; plate 2.17b]) and one canine tooth of a dog from phase IV (SF 5124 [plate 9.22a]). Many perforated teeth were found at Early Bronze Age Ezero (Georgiev et al. 1979: fig. 202a), while teeth and claws of domestic and wild animals occur sporadically in Late Neolithic/Chalcolithic and Early Bronze Age layers at Dikili Tash (Karali-Yannacopoulos 1992:161, pl. 207b left and right, respectively), Servia (Heurtley 1939: fig. 7e), Olynthos (Heurtley 1939: fig. 35j), Ayios Mamas (Heurtley 1939: fig. 66), Sesklo (Papathanassopoulos, ed. 1996: fig. 291), Emporio (Hood 1982:675, pl. 142:55–56), Thermi (Lamb 1936: pl. XXVII:40), Poliochni (Bernabó-Brea 1964:602, 1976: pls. XC:9–11 and CLXXVIII:5), and Selevac (Russell 1990:534, fig. 14.9a, pl. 14.7c). Perforated animal teeth are known in many ancient and ethnographic cultures as trophies, amulets, or symbols of prowess and virility (Barge 1982:83). Such symbolism has been proposed for the teeth and claws from Emporio, Thermi, and Poliochni.

OTHER PERFORATED BONE. Five miscellaneous pieces of bone (see also chapter 2) were also made into pendants: a pig astragalus from phase III (SF 3770: plate 2.20d), a fragment of red deer antler from phase IV (SF 4641); two pieces of turtle shell from phases IV (SF 5094) and V (SF 66); and a fragment of unidentifiable species from phase V (SF 5089: plate 2.16d). Antler pendants are known from Selevac (Russell 1990:534, pl. 14.7a) and Ezero (Georgiev et al. 1979:

figs. 122b, 202b, upper). Perforated and otherwise worked astragali were popular in ancient cultures of the Mediterranean, the Balkans, and the Near East (Amandry 1984:350–355; Gilmour 1997). Examples with multiple peforations and/or ground edges and sides were used as tokens or game pieces, and in magical, oracular, funerary and other ceremonies. Pieces with a single perforation and little or no other modification, like our example, apparently served as pendants or amulets and are known, among other Aegean sites, from the Corycian and Kitsos caves (Amandry 1984:355, fig. 10). The gold effigy of an astragalus from the cemetery of Varna bears eloquent evidence to the fascination exerted by this evocative natural form (Poplin 1991).

RING-SHAPED PENDANTS. This type comes in two distinct variations: shell ovals and stone circlets. The shell oval pendant is produced by grinding out the central part of a *Murex* whorl to an "ellipse" that incorporates both apices of the spiral. We have two examples, remarkably similar to each other in form and dimensions, considering that one comes from phase II (SF 415, plate 9.23b) and the other from phase IV (SF 4748). Being too bulky to be worn around the finger (SF 4748 measures 3.5 cm long, 2.6 cm wide, and 0.4 cm thick), they were probably suspended as annulets.

I have not found exact comparanda for *Murex* worked in this way, but the idea of reducing the body of shell or bone to a "ring" has found various other applications: a bone annulet from Dhimitra, comparable in dimensions (Karali-Yannacopoulos 1997:205); a Middle Neolithic bone pendant from Achilleion very similar in form to the Sitagroi shells (Gimbutas 1989b:252, fig. 8.5); a *Spondylus* annulet or pendant from Anza (published as a "ring," Gimbutas 1976c:247, fig. 213:15); two semicircular objects (pendants?) of *Glycymeris* from Kitsos Cave (Reese 1987:122); and a bone circlet from Ezero (Georgiev et al. 1979: fig. 202, lowest group of objects, on the upper far right).

SF 113 of phase I (figure 9.23a; plate 9.11d) is a stone circlet fragment of green stone. It is carefully shaped out of a thin and flattened block and well polished, with a small protuberance carved on the outer perimeter of the preserved segment. Too bulky for a finger ring (preserved dimensions: 30 x 11 x 0.5 cm), it could have been worn as a pendant. Two small indentations cut on either side of the small protuberance presumably facilitated suspension by securing a thread or cord that would be wound around the ornament.

In its annular form this artifact resembles the well-known ring or idol pendants that occur in various materials throughout the Aegean and southwest Europe (Hood 1982: 664–665, fig. 295.17, pls. 138, 139; Ivanov 1991:11; Karali-Yannacopoulos 1996:165; Papathanassopoulos, ed. 1996: figs. 43, 290, 298, 299, 302; Zachos 1996a:167). However, the protuberance of the Sitagroi example is too minute in relation to the more or less pronounced "heads" of those ornaments (but compare a complete bone piece from Goljamo Delčevo with a small perforated protrusion as a head [Todorova 1982: Abb. 59:6]). The fragmentary condition of our find does not allow further comparisons.

DISCOID PENDANTS. There are two examples cut from thick *Spondylus* valves. SF 2995 of phase III (plate 9.24a) is an oval with a central V-shaped perforation piercing down to the base. SF 4804, an unphased piece (plate 9.24b), is circular, with a single, slightly eccentric hole that runs through the body. Both look like "buttons" but are considerably larger than the standard, bead-size objects of that category (4 cm diameter for SF 4808, 4.4 x 3.2 cm for SF 2995). Therefore, they would have been suspended or, more likely, attached as platelets on some surface (leather or textile), the discoid form and centrally placed perforation being quite suitable for such a function.

Artifacts of similar form, and perhaps also use, include a *Spondylus* disc from Dhimitra (2.82 cm in diameter; Karali-Yannacopoulos 1997:205) and bone discs from Ezero (Georgiev et al. 1979: fig. 202, third group of objects; the size of these is not given, nor can it be assessed from the published photograph). Unspecified perforated ornaments of *Spondylus* from various other sites (Reese 1987:128–129) may also belong to this type of pendant.

ELONGATED PENDANTS. Two phase II artifacts are rectangular in form with one narrow edge curved, and bear a perforation at one of the narrow sides. They are thin, with one surface flat, the other

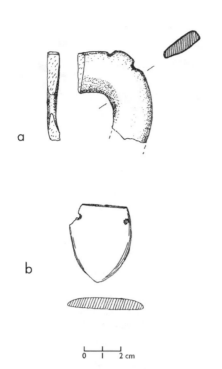

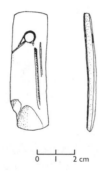

Figure 9.23. (a) Ring-shaped stone pendant, phase I: SF 113; plate 9.11d; (b) pectoral (breast plate), phase II: SF 2301.

Figure 9.24. Elongated bone pendant, phase II: SF 2839, figure 2.7b.

slightly convex. SF 2839 (figures 2.7b, 9.24), made of bone, looks very much like the plaques discussed below, except for the single, eccentric hole. Similar bone objects were found at Ezero (Georgiev et al. 1979: fig. 202, third group of objects, far left) and Achilleion (Gimbutas 1989b:252, fig. 8.4); a shell example comes from Emporio (Hood 1982:676, pl. 142:59).

SF 299, made of stone, closely resembles the so-called whetstone pendants, a characteristic group

of perforated objects in the shape of small adzes or whetstones. They have been reported from various sites: Paradimi (Bakalakis and Sakellariou 1981: Taf. 18b:7); Rast (Dumitrescu 1980:23, pl. XII:11); Ayios Mamas (Heurtley 1939: fig. 65k, l); Armenochori (Heurtley 1939: fig. 65p, with one perforation at each end); Ezero (Georgiev et al. 1979: fig. 203b, upper row, third from the left, and lower row, first from the left); Poliochni (one of clay with unfinished hole, Bernabó-Brea 1976: Tav. CLXXXVII:20); and Thermi (Lamb 1936: pl. XXVI:30.43). These and other perforated small effigies of tools have been interpreted as either small utensils with some practical purpose or "amulets" (Lamb 1936:192; Marangou 1992:182–214). The two uses need not be mutually exclusive.

LEAF-SHAPED PENDANTS. The single phase II example (SF 2301; figure 9.23b) is a leaf-shaped plaque of gray marble with one end pointed and the other worked straight; two small perforations are drilled (one incompletely) on either side near the flat (upper?) edge. It can be described as a chest decoration or "pectoral," a term used in the literature for ornaments that share a flat and wide form and double or multiple perforations at their perimeter. Sizes vary and shapes range from crescents to discs, ovals, shield-forms, and rhomboids. They are manufactured in shell, stone, or clay, sometimes with rich decoration. For comparanda, see Dikili Tash (Karali-Yannacopoulos 1992:161); Servia (Mould, Ridley, and Wardle 2000: 179, fig. 4.23 [SF 770, 773]) and Rodochori Cave in west Macedonia (Rodden 1964b: 117, pl. 8A–B); Achilleion (Gimbutas 1989a, 1989b: pl. 8.3:1); Sesklo (Papathanassopoulos, ed. 1996: fig. 285); Thermi (Lamb 1936: pl. XXIV:31.61); and several Chalcolithic sites in Bulgaria (for example, Todorova and Vajsov 1993: fig. 223:1–4). All these artifacts could have shared a common mode of frontal attachment on the chest, pelvis, or forehead, since the flat shape and often large size (7.3 x 5.8 cm for the Sitagroi example) would render free suspension rather uncomfortable. They could be connected horizontally or vertically to chains or strands of beads (compare reconstructions by Barge 1982: fig. 24:16–17), hung independently by means of a heavy cord, or wire fastened to their perforations (Rodden 1964a:117, pl. 8A), or sewn onto garments.

POLYGONAL PENDANTS. SF 1108 of phase III (figure 9.25a; plate 9.25), made of clay, is well modeled into a composite rhomboid/trapezoidal shape and decorated with a simple painted linear pattern. For comparison, see two stone pieces from Ezero, one trapezoidal and the other irregular polygonal (Georgiev et al. 1979: fig. 203b, lower row, second and third from left).

PRISM-SHAPED PENDANTS. SF 1483 of phase III (figure 9.25b) is made of clay and is stem-like and square in section and carefully fired. The fragment preserves part of a perforation (string hole?).

TRIANGULAR PENDANTS. SF 4774, an unphased piece (plate 11.3c), is a reworked sherd with rounded edges that give it a teardrop shape. Simple sherds worked into ornaments (beads or bead preforms) are also known from Selevac (Tringham and Stevanović 1990:348). Triangular pendants in shell, bone, or stone were found at Dhimitra (Karali-Yannacopoulos 1997: 205); Achilleion (Gimbutas 1989b: 253, fig. 8.5:3); Selevac (Russell 1990:534, pl. 14.7d); Ezero (Georgiev et al. 1979: fig. 202b); and Ayio Gala (Hood 1982: pl. 11, no. 318).

MISCELLANEOUS. Three items are grouped as miscellany. SF 2530 of phase I (plate 9.19a) consists of the upper part of a *Mytilus* valve that has been broken or cut into an irregular polygonal shape with worked edges, perforated at the hinge. SF 1001 of phase V (plate 9.26) is a *Cypraea* shell, ground to produce a large oval opening on the body whorl. SF 2722 of phase IV is an oblong segment of turtle shell with one end rounded, the other straightened and provided with a group of delicate, horizontal grooves around which a suspension thread could be wound, comparable to a marble pendant from Dikili Tash (Karali-Yannacopoulos 1992: pl. 207b, right).

On a contextual note, it is worth mentioning the recovery of four pendants from phase IV, ZE 61, a floor associated with a long burned house (volume 1 [C. Renfrew 1986b]:210–211). This small group includes two perforated *Cardia* (SF 5593–94), one perforated deer antler (SF 4641), and the miscellaneous turtle shell (SF 2722).

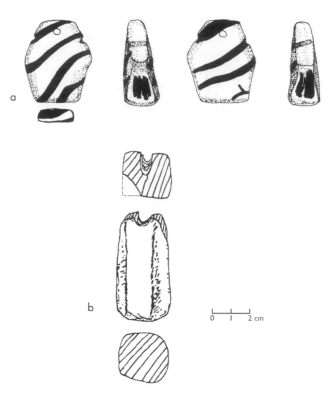

Figure 9.25. Clay pendants, phase III: (a) polygonal with painted decoration: SF 1108; plate 9.25; (b) prismatic, SF 1483.

Pins

CHRONOLOGY AND USE. Of the twenty-five pins found at Sitagroi, nineteen are made of bone (see also chapter 2) and six of metal (table 9.3; see also chapter 8). There is a notable preference for these items in the Early Bronze Age, contrary to the higher frequencies of other ornament types in the Neolithic/Chalcolithic (table 9.1). Phase V, especially, has produced more than half of the bone pins (eleven pieces) as well as three metal ones (see chapter 8), while two others date to phase IV. Neolithic/Chalcolithic examples are rarer: one metal and four bone items come from phases I and II, respectively. Three bone and one metal example come from phase III.

Ethnographic (for example, Seiler-Baldinger 1994) and archaeological (Marcus 1993) evidence shows that pins would be fastened on clothes, hair, or headdresses. For example, they could be used to fix ornaments such as shell circlets and pendants

(Marangou 1991:332), of which Neolithic/Chalcolithic Sitagroi has produced various examples.

The concentration of the Sitagroi pins in phase Vb can be related to new dress fashions toward the end of the Early Bronze Age. A weightier texture is indicated by the adoption of heavier spindle whorls, appropriate for wool or flax, and the warp-weighted loom operating with large pyramidal weights (Barber 1991:171–172; this volume, chapter 6). Heavier garments might require more frequent attachments. Similar innovations in attire have been suggested for the Early Iron Age in Macedonia, based on the sudden frequency and typological richness of pins at Kastanas during that period (Hochstetter 1987:74, Taf. 14–15).

Most pins come from the Bin Complex, a context rich in weaving equipment (volume 1 [C. Renfrew 1986b]:188; this volume, chapters 2, 5, 6, 12). Certainly, earlier than phase Vb the exploitation of animals for secondary products, including wool, was well advanced (volume 1 [Bökönyi 1986]:80; compare Sherratt 1981).

BONE PINS. Bone pins are made from whole or split sections of long bones, such as metapodials (SF 1307, SF 1557, of phase V). In most cases, it was not possible to identify animal species; however, of those examples that could be identified, caprovine bone was most frequent (see tables 2.9, 2.10). Raw material for bone pins, as for most items of worked bone at Sitagroi, would be easily available, often right from the kitchen debris. The technique of manufacture was the same followed for the pointed bone tools: fracturing or grooving and splitting to obtain the desirable bone section, retouching and smoothing the sharp edges, scraping and grinding into shape, finishing by further grinding on an abrasive substance, and perhaps polishing. The shaft of many bone pins is described as smooth and shiny. Microscopic use-wear analysis might well show whether polishing was the result of careful manufacture or friction.

All items included here as pins are graceful and carefully made, which I take as evidence for their ornamental quality (Barge 1982:56). Other pointed implements at the site are also well worked. Therefore, the decorative aspect of the assumed pins cannot be based on good workmanship alone; they could have been tools, a means of fastening, orna-

ments, or all of the above. Further data are offered by shape and size.

Shape is fairly consistent throughout our sample. A slender shaft tapers to a sharp tip, its thicker part formed in three different ways: (1) the natural joint of the bone, or part of it, is included as the "head" (compare Lamb 1936: pl. XXVII:29, from Thermi); (2) the top of the shaft is flattened (for example, SF 1048 of phase V; figure 9.26), forming an elliptical, diamond-shaped, or pointed form (for example, SF 4112 of phase I [figures 2.5a, 9.27; plate 2.5a]; for comparanda, see Bernabó-Brea 1976: Tav. LXXXIX:4, 12, 14–15, from Poliochni; Heurtley 1939: fig. 35b, from Servia; Hood 1982:670, pl. 141:35 from Emporio; Lamb 1936: pl. XXVII:20, 29, from Thermi); or (3) the shaft broadens gradually throughout its length toward the upper end with no distinct "head" (compare Bernabó-Brea 1976: Tav. LXXXIX:4, from Poliochni; Georgiev et al. 1979: fig. 203b, from Ezero; Lamb 1936: pl. XXVII:19, 21–23, from Thermi).

The head of SF 376 (phase III), consisting of the natural joint, bears fine grooves, in a trefoil-shaped pattern, that are probably refinements of the bone's natural grooves. This is one of the examples from Sitagroi of a bone pin with a decorated head (see figure 2.18c–e), comparable to a variety of examples

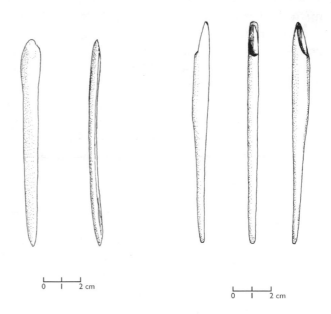

(Left): Figure 9.26. Bone pin from the Bin Complex, phase Vb: SF 1048, figure 2.5b. *(Right): Figure 9.27.* Bone pin, phase I: SF 4112, plate 2.5a (see also figure 2.5a).

with elaborate tops from other sites such as Vardino and Servia (Heurtley 1939: fig/ 35a and c, respectively), Tell Goljamo Delčevo (Todorova 1982:Abb. 54.10), Thermi (Lamb 1936:199-200 pl. XXVII:1–13,17), and Poliochni (Bernabó-Brea 1976: Tav. LXXXIX:1–15, CLXXVIII:8, CLXXIX:1–22). Yet even the simpler versions of the pronounced head indicate an attempt at formal elaboration, meaningful only if the upper part of the object was meant to be visible.

Length ranges widely from 2.6 to 11.7 cm, but more than half the examples are close to a mean value of about 7.2 cm. Width and thickness are more consistent; almost all of the fully preserved examples are 1 or 2 mm wide at the tip, although width at the top varies from 0.5 to 1.2 cm, depending on how pronounced the head of the pin is. Thickness, at approximately the middle of the shaft, is between 0.4 and 0.5 cm. From this, we can deduce that pins were long enough to have held together different portions of fabric or hair, and they could have been inserted more than once for better fastening. They were sufficiently sharp-tipped to penetrate dense and soft materials such as tightly woven cloth, leather, and bark (see Stratouli 1993:496–507). The shaft was appropriately slender in order to be inserted securely into such surfaces for a good part of its length, and sufficient length would allow the head of the pin, often much thicker and wider than the shaft, to stick out as decoration. SF 1048 of phase V (figure 9.26), a wholly preserved example with an unusually blunt tip (4 mm) and broad shaft (9 cm thick), might have pierced a fabric of looser structure, including loosely woven or knit cloth, mats, and basketry (compare Stratouli 1993:496–507). The item is long enough (10.9 cm) to have been inserted, for example, in a straw hat (compare Seiler-Baldinger 1994: pl. 4).

METAL PINS. Contrary to their bone counterparts, metal pins were products of a specialized and probably socially controlled craft (see chapter 8). Three are made of copper: SF 880 of phase III (figure 8.1f; plate 8.2a), and SF 30 (figure 8.2a; plate 8.5b) and SF 3229 (figure 8.2c; plates 8.5a, 8.9d), both from phase IV. Two could be of copper or bronze: SF 3356 (not illustrated) and SF 3017 (figure 8.3a; plate 8.8), both of phase V. SF 5339, also from phase V, is of bronze (figure 8.3c). The metal pins consist of cast rod, circular or quadrangular in section, which has been subjected to both hot and cold working into the desired shape (chapter 8). Despite their meager quantity and often fragmentary preservation, we should note the similarity with bone pins in those available dimensions that would provide clues for function: thickness in approximately the middle of the shaft ranges from 0.3 to 0.5 cm, and tip width is 0.5 to1 mm for the two wholly preserved examples (one from phase III, SF 880 [figure 8.1f; plate 8.2a], the other from phase IV, SF 30 [figure 8.2a; plate 8.5 b).

A significant difference between bone and metal pins lies in the form of the head, which is more elaborate in the latter group. The two examples of metal pins with intact head (SF 880, of phase III [figure 8.1f; plate 8.2a]; SF 3229 from phase IV [figure 8.2c; plates 8.5a, 8.9d) are topped by an inverted spiral finial, made of a hammered strip. Metal pins with spiral finials, single or double, are widely found at Varna (Ivanov 1991:11), Emporio (Hood 1982: fig. 295:5, pl. 138:5), Poliochni (Bernabó-Brea 1976: fig. 320 and Tav. LXXXVI:5, CLXXV:1, and CLXXVI: 17, respectively); and Thermi (Lamb 1936:166–167, figs. 48b:32.15 and 30.13, pl. XXV: 30.13, 32.15, 32.46). They are attested at Troy and other sites in Anatolia, and east to Mesopotamia and the Caucasus, as well as in the Balkans and central Europe (Bernabó-Brea 1964: 592; Lamb 1936:167).

The other four Sitagroi pieces preserve only part of the shaft, smoothly tapering toward the tip. Their heads may have been in any of the ornate forms known for contemporary metal pins: spiral, rounded, flattened, square, oval, pyramidal, biconical, lenticular, domed, combinations of several elements, or even animal and flower finials (Bernabó-Brea 1964:593; 1976: Tav. LXXXVI:1, LXXXVII:2, 3, 5–8, CLXXVII:28, from Poliochni; Georgiev et al. 1979: fig. 107k, from Ezero; Hood 1981: pl. 138:1–4 from Emporio, 1982:658–659, from Troy and the Cyclades; Lamb 1936: fig. 48a–b, pl. XXV, from Thermi; Zachos 1996a:167, from the Zas Cave in Naxos).

It is equally possible, however, that our pins belonged to the simple, straight-shafted type with a minimally distinct or no head (compare Bernabó-Brea 1976: Tav. LXXXVII:1, 12, from Poliochni; Georgiev et al. 1979: fig. 107, from Ezero; Heurtley 1939: 203, fig. 67:oo, pp, from Kritsana and Vardino, respectively; Lamb 1936: fig. 48a, second from left, and 48b, last in the right, from Thermi). For instance, SF 30 of phase IV (figure 8.2a; plate 8.5b) shows evidence of narrowing toward the end opposite of the tip and is thus comparable to the simple types from Kritsana and Vardino as well as to our bone piece SF 654 of phase V mentioned earlier.

Plaques

Plaques are thin, elongated sections of bone (see also chapter 2, figure 2.7c, d; plate 2.17), flattened on one surface, slightly curved on the other. SF 834 of phase III (figure 9.28; plate 2.17a) and SF 1705 of phase II (plate 9.27b) have been made of ribs, the former of cattle. In these cases at least, the slightly curved shape of the object follows the original natural form. The number, size, and position of perforations vary, with a thickness range between 0.5 and 0.7 cm; Sitagroi plaques are slightly thicker than the ones from Dikili Tash (0.35–0.5 cm; Karali-Yannacopoulos 1992:160–161). In both sites, these items were nicely cut and shaped and very well polished (see especially the color photographs in Papathanassopoulos, ed. 1996: fig. 297a–c).

The Sitagroi plaques date to the Middle, Late, and Final Neolithic/Chalcolithic, as do all known pieces from other Aegean and Balkan sites, and this type of ornament stops abruptly at the end of the period (Karali-Yannacopoulos 1996:338). Comparanda in bone, besides the finds from Dikili Tash, come from Kitsos Cave (Papathanassopoulos, ed. 1996: fig. 297d); Selevac (Russell 1990: fig. 14.9b); and Goljamo Delčevo (Todorova 1982: Abb. 59B: 17). Thin plaques in various shapes and perforated at the edges were also produced in beaten gold. Such are principally known from Varna (Ivanov 1991:10), while a few Aegean examples were found at Zas Cave in Naxos and Aravissos near Pella (Papathanassopoulos, ed. 1996: figs. 304 and 301, respectively).

Plaques were not examined for wear traces at Sitagroi, but their form suggests a use as decorative attachments on objects or on cloth, leather, and similar materials. The adornment of garments with plaques and platelets is amply attested by Neolithic and Bronze Age finds in the Aegean and the Balkans (Barber 1991:172 ff.), among others by the gold strips from the cemetery of Varna. Plaques could otherwise have been suspended as pendants (compare Karali-Yannacopoulos 1992:160), alone or connected with strands of beads (Barge 1982: fig. 24, 17). Differences in the shape of the artifacts, and in

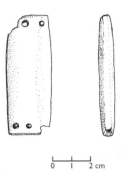

Figure 9.28. Bone plaque, phase III: SF 834, plate 9.27a (see also figure 2.7d and plate 2.17a).

the number and size of the perforations, perhaps indicate different modes of application on various media. It also seems likely that the plaques from Sitagroi and elsewhere were worn in ways overlapping with those of other flat ornaments, namely the "pectorals" or thin perforated "bracelets" examined in previous sections.

The Ring

Made of fine, circular copper wire, the little "ring" (SF 5341: figure 8.2d; see discussion in chapter 8) from Sitagroi phase IV is too small (0.75 x 0.45 cm) to have been worn around an adult finger. Therefore, it either belonged to a child or functioned as a hairring, the annular type bead, small pendant, or part of an earring. Other small ornaments of metal wire (copper, gold, silver, or lead) in various shapes and dimensions are known from the cemeteries of Durankulak (Avramova 1991:45) and Varna (Ivanov 1991:10); the Diros and Aravissos hoards, probably also funerary (Papathanassopoulos, ed. 1996: figs. 42 and 300, respectively; Zachos 1996a:167); and from the Early Bronze Age settlements at Saratsé in Macedonia (Heurtley 1939: fig. 67qq) and Poliochni Green/Red (Bernabó-Brea 1976: Tav. CLXXVII:26, 31, 33, 36, respectively).

The finds from Durankulak reveal age- and gender-specific associations for these ornaments; that is, they are items of different type and/or material that accompany male, female, and juvenile skeletons in distinct ways (Avramova 1991: table 1). Although such patterns are often limited to a single site or region, they may illuminate the presence of similar ornaments in sites such as Sitagroi, where contextual clues for use are lacking. It is worth considering them together with the iconographic evidence provided by figurines, which is presented immediately below.

INDIRECT EVIDENCE FOR ADORNMENT

Figurines

Figurines from the Neolithic/Chalcolithic and Early Bronze Age northern Aegean and the Balkans bear iconographic elements that can be interpreted as ornaments: chains, belts, necklaces, beaded strands, pendants, hair decorations, and appliqués (Marangou 1991, 1992). Several such statuettes came to light at Sitagroi itself (figure 9.29, and volume 1 [Gimbutas 1986b]:229–230), predominantly from the Neolithic/Chalcolithic strata but also a few from the Early Bronze Age. The latter, however, have also been attributed to the Neolithic on stylistic grounds and interpreted as heirlooms (volume 1 [Gimbutas 1986]:225). Even if we dismiss these pieces as inherited from an earlier tradition, figurines of Early Bronze Age manufacture from Dikili Tash, Skala Sotiros on Thassos, Troy, and Thermi do exhibit comparable decorative elements (Marangou 1992: 176–177). Interestingly, the position of ornamental motifs on figurines corresponds closely to the arrangement of burial goods in Balkan cemeteries, such as Varna and Cernica. Combined iconographic and funerary evidence thus permit us to reconstruct the fashions in which the ornaments excavated at Sitagroi and related sites would have been placed on the body, hair, garments, and accessories.

This evidence provides a picture of recognizable ornamental styles, resulting from the arrangement of different components in specific patterns (Kenoyer 1991:86). It is particularly interesting that the main ornament combinations depicted on figurines correspond to the associations of ornamental items (noted in chapter 12) in the excavated units at Sitagroi. A summary below lists the comparanda from Marangou's reports (1991, 1992) of Neolithic and EBA figurines from Greece.

1. Multiple bracelets (Marangou 1991: figs. 2a, c, 4d): compare with phase III, tables 12.2, 12.3, 12.4.

2. Multiple necklaces and pendants (figure 9.29: a–c; also volume 1, figure 9.87; Marangou 1992:

figs. 71c, 81), necklaces and belts (figure 9.29:b–c; also volume 1: figures 9.4, 9.5, 9.47, 9.87, 9.102; Marangou 1991: figs. 3a, d, 4a, d): compare concentrations of bead groups plus pendants in ZA 44, ZA 45, ZA 47 (see chapter 12, table 12.5).

3. Bracelets, necklaces, beaded belts, appliqués and pendants in various arrangements (see volume 1: figure 9.21; Marangou 1991: fig. 4d): compare with phase II ZA 52 (chapter 12, table 12.2), and phase III 47 (see chapter 12, table 12.5. We should also note the repeated occurrence of (mostly *Spondylus*) bracelet/annulets with (mostly *Glycymeris*) pendants in (among other units) MM 63 and 68 (see chapter 12, table 12.4). Bracelets were found together with plaques in KM 20 and ZA 48.

4. An annulet and/or pin? on the coiffure of the Dikili Tash figurine (Marangou 1991: fig. 4a) compares with the occurrence of pins with bracelet/annulets and/or pendants (see chapter 12, tables 12.2, 12.5, and 12.7).

The ornate statuettes from Sitagroi, its neighbors in the Drama Plain, and other culturally related sites reveal a vivid concern with adornment and with the active involvement of local people in the production, circulation, and use of ornaments (Marangou 1997:238–239, 252). Interestingly, the decorated figurines seem to be almost exclusively female, while male representation is limited to the type of idol with belt and appliqué that is characteristic in east Macedonia (Marangou 1991:332, fig. 4c, from Dikili Tash). We must be careful in accepting figurine ornamentation as representative of what people actually wore, but adornment in these prehistoric communities was arguably invested with gender-specific values (Nikolaidou 1997:187). The predilection for the embellishment of the female figure is counterbalanced by numerous cases of males being lavishly provided with finery in the Balkan cemeteries. In those burial sites, jewelry often cuts across sex and age boundaries, being rather dependent upon family rank (compare Willms 1985). It seems, therefore, that social realities were represented differently in the symbolic domains of anthropomorphic imagery and funerary ritual.

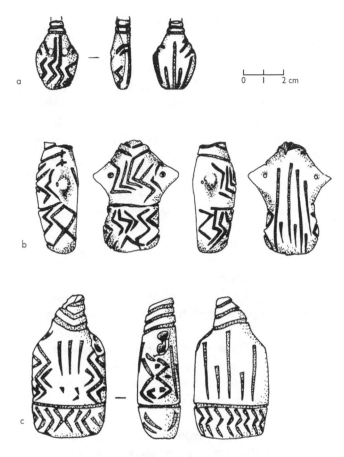

0 | 2 cm

Figure 9.29: Examples of schematic figurines from contexts of phase I (a), phase II (b), and phase IV (c) with incisions depicting ornaments and/or garments: (a) SF 53 (volume 1: figure 9.1 [19]); (b) SF 4429 (volume 1: figure 9.2 [26]); (c) SF 3920 (volume 1: figure 9.13 [23]).

TOOLS OF ORNAMENTATION

Linear and curvilinear motifs on the faces and bodies of idols from Sitagroi, Dikili Tash, and Paradeisos probably represent body paint and/or tattoos (volume 1: figures 9.27, 9.37; Marangou 1992:190, figs. 7a, 71g). Often the incised patterns were filled with color: white paste (for example, volume 1: figures 9.2, 9.4–9.6, 9.12, 9.25, 9.45–46, 9.56, 9.58, 9.83, 9.87, 9.120, 9.127, 9.131), red ochre (volume 1, figures 9.3, 9.35), or both red and white (SF 4253 of phase II; SF 4429 of phase II; volume 1: figures 9.57, 9.95, 9.106, 9.22, 9.48, 9.74). Other painted and incised elements may depict tailored and decorated garments (volume 1 [Gimbutas 1986]:230–237). Such ornamental designs may have been executed

by means of stamp cylinders and pintaderas (C. Renfrew 1987:341–353); both forms have been found at Sitagroi (see chapter 10). The incised patterns on these artifacts, including groups of zigzag lines, S- and V-shaped elements, groups of straight lines, crosses, spirals, and dotted and circular patterns, are very similar to the designs on the bodies of figurines from the site (volume 1 [Gimbutas 1986]: 240–247).

Stamps and pintaderas come from Neolithic/ Chalcolithic deposits, except for one that, although of Neolithic/Chalcolithic style, was found in Early Bronze Age strata. Whether it may actually have been used in this later period or, as C. Renfrew suggests (see chapter 10), it was mixed with Early Bronze Age debris, is as intriguing a question as the occurrence of Neolithic/Chalcolithic-looking *Spondylus* ornaments or figurines in the Early Bronze Age horizons. However, the presence of similar stamp cylinders in Early and Middle Helladic sites (Younger 1991:36), a *Spondylus* pintadera with linear incised patterns from Poliochni (Bernabó-Brea 1976: Tav. LXXXVI:g), the ornate figurines of the northern Aegean, and the evidence for tattoos on Cycladic figurines (Marangou 1992:190; Papaefthymiou-Papanthimou 1997:66–73) all provide clues for an ongoing vivid concern with body decoration.

We should, moreover, mention the little *Spondylus* and stone pestles, probably used for grinding pigments, found in Early Bronze Age contexts at Emporio, Thermi, Poliochni, Troy, Ayios Kosmas, Kitsos Cave, Peloponnese, Cyclades, EM Crete, and Anatolia (Hood 1982:675–676. At Sitagroi, evidence for the preparation of pigments for textiles, the body, and/or pottery is not altogether lacking. The two obvious candidates are a *Unio* valve (SF 2888 from phase III, cataloged in appendix 9.1; plate 9.1.1) and a small clay bowl (SF 2791, from phase IV: see chapter 7), with remains of red ochre in their interiors. Such containers are widely found in Old World prehistory, often in magic, funerary, and other ritual associations (Papaefthymiou-Papanthimou 1997). Other color palettes may be recognized in the so-called dimple bases, that is, rectangular clay plaques with one finished, flat surface and the other side with several roundish indentations (see chapter 11: SF 1112 [plate 11.27b], 1472 [plate 11.27d], 1488, 1572 [plate 11.27c], 3677 [plate 11.27a]). Admittedly, only SF 1472 bears

357

traces of color, in this case, graphite paint. These dimple bases can be alternatively interpreted as floors or as abbreviated depictions of house models. Other objects, although devoid of color indications, are reminiscent of tray-shaped color containers from elsewhere (Gimbutas 1989b: 257, from Achilleion; Marangou 1992:152, from Cyclades; Mould, Ridley, and Wardle 2000: 155–157, fig. 4.15, from Servia): one is illustrated, a flat block of polished stone (SF 2232, plate 5.17a).

Finally, it is not unlikely that many of the sharp-pointed tools found in the site (see chapters 2, 8) may have been used, among other things, as scarification needles (compare Barge 1982).

CONCLUDING REMARKS

In this chapter I have presented adornment at prehistoric Sitagroi in the light of temporal distribution, raw materials, typology, possible uses, and find contexts. The excavated items and their archaeological comparanda, iconographic material, and ethnographic support constitute a rich body of evidence as to the multiple values of ornamentation: aesthetic, economic, and conceptual. It seems appropriate to summarize the social and symbolic implications of our corpus, some of which have been treated at length elsewhere (Elster and Nikolaidou in press; Nikolaidou 1997).

First, the technological choices involved in the crafts of adornment seem to have been influenced by cultural attitudes about right and wrong ways to make and use things that reach far beyond practical solutions. We have noted the preference for "exotic" substances such as marine shell, metal, various stones, and bone from hunted animals; their processing into standardized ornament forms; and specific fashions of wearing and manipulating the end products. The manufacture, use, and disposal of ornaments undoubtedly involved stylistic and semantic elaboration that may have served social goals.

It is not known whether Sitagroi groups traveled to obtain raw materials not locally available or whether these were traded or exchanged with others, directly or down the line. Whatever the case, access to resources and geographical space would have required the formation of economic exchange and kinship bonds between communities in the region or farther afield.

Extracting the natural substances required planning, physical and technical skills, as well as proper tools and facilities. The distance between the sources and the villages of their destination, even if covered with relative ease (for instance, the 25–30 km from Sitagroi to the coast), may still have been an important social and conceptual factor differentiating the communities living in different landscapes (Broodbank 1993). It is likely that the efforts and knowledge invested in acquisition would have increased the value of the desired commodities and would also have carried an aura of prestige for those who took part.

We can speculate about the division of labor and social relations of ornament production. The available evidence about village layout and organization suggests that at Sitagroi we are dealing with part-time specialized household crafts (appendix 9.2; Miller 1996), perhaps with specialists in certain raw materials (lapidaries, potters, bone-workers, coppersmiths, and so forth). Space, time, resources, labor, and knowledge would have been negotiated among individuals, households, or even neighboring communities.

The networks through which technical expertise, and perhaps also associated ritual and mythical knowledge, were transmitted is a topic worth exploring. So too is the question of craft-dependent prestige—that is, whether "exotic" versus "domestic" raw materials and the relative difficulty of processing each were differently evaluated, such that the artisans working with "prestige" substances (seashell, metal) and more complicated techniques (such as stone- versus clay-working) enjoyed higher esteem. It is in any case possible that the fancier ornaments, more demanding to produce, are those that feature prominently in exchange networks. For example, within the Drama Plain, shell ornaments were apparently circulated in return for such essential goods as foodstuffs or woven goods (Elster 1995; Yannouli 1997:123–125). Routes through the Balkan Peninsula by river or mountain pass carried these same manufactured materials far from their loci of production, to be incorporated into new cultural contexts (Willms 1985). It might well be that the experiences and ideas encoded in the productive strategy would in turn partly determine the importance of the end products (Kenoyer 1991:82–84; C. Renfrew 1969; Zachos 1996a).

At the Sitagroi mound, the picture we derive from the excavated contexts is one of neighboring households participating in ornamentation, although conceivably in varying degrees and functions. It is interesting, on the one hand, that in the Neolithic/Chalcolithic especially, but also in the Early Bronze Age, valuable ornaments of *Spondylus* or metal are not spatially restricted. On the other hand, a remarkable feature of phases II and III is the differential combination of ornaments recovered from the investigated sectors of the mound (see chapter 12).

Aside from recovery contingencies and the different amounts of earth removed in each sector (Preface table 2), I believe that we can detect elements of personal or familial differentiation in the various ornamental patterns excavated as well as depicted on figurines from the site. It is possible that distinct aspects of individual or social personae were encoded in the ways that such material symbolism was selected and displayed. For example, comparative evidence worldwide suggests gender-specific symbolism of certain shell species ("male" *Dentalia* versus "female" *Cypraea* [Karali-Yannacopoulos 1996:165]) or items such as the "feminine" hip-belt (Barber 1994; volume 1 [Gimbutas 1986]:233). If, as I have previously suggested (Nikolaidou 1997:187–188), finery depicted on figurines represents bridal wealth, then femininity would have been evoked in terms of age, sexual availability, group affiliation, and family prestige.

Social distinctions could refer both to craftwork and/or access to finished ornaments. For example, the metal pin (SF 880: figure 8.1b; plate 8.2a) from MM 43 in phase III, found together with a copper awl (figure 8.1g) and a crucible (figure 8.4; see chapter 12: table 12.3), may well have been manufactured on the spot, since there is remarkable evidence of metallurgical activity in levels MM 16 to 50 (see chapter 8). The close association of spinning and weaving equipment and with pointed bone tools (sewing utensils?) in the phase Vb Bin Complex (see chapters 2, 5, 6, and 12: table 12.7) offers clues to the practical and decorative manipulation of cloth (see this volume, chapters 2, 6).

Another discriminating line may be drawn between the rich ornament assemblages in certain excavated units and isolated finds in others, which resonates with the selective depiction of adornment on only some figurines (chapter 11). Could the contrast between decorated and nondecorated bodies be a visual reminder of emergent social and ritual divisions (Halstead 1995:18)? If the seeds of inequality indeed lie in the control of access to special knowledge and goods (Bender 1985), then we might be able to see the production and use of adornment in the context of power strategies within the household and beyond.

At the same time, observed innovations may be accounted for by both practical and ideological considerations. Thus, the sudden popularity of clay in phase III may well be an easy and cheap response to an increased demand for ornamentation, as Miller suggests (appendix 9.2). But the prominent role of clay in a wide spectrum of formal and symbolic elaboration in this period (figurines and miniatures, social ceramics, decorated pottery, seals, and other items of notation) suggests that this material was also imbued with conceptual value. In the Early Bronze Age, the remarkable numerical decrease of ornaments all over Macedonia need not merely reflect a lack of cultural sophistication in the region, as has often been assumed (for example, volume 1 [Sherratt 1986]:448–449). Alternative factors at play would include valuable raw materials becoming scarce and therefore recycled until they were exhausted; jewelry "worn out" by successive generations as family heirlooms; few ornaments actually produced and used as isolated amulets; items closely attached to their wearer being deposited in burials that have not been preserved, or destroyed on a person's death (Kenoyer 1991:92–95); or, simply, investment in media of symbolic expression other than adornment, which may not be traceable archaeologically.

The items of adornment from Sitagroi have survived in scant numbers or fragmentary condition, ambiguous and incomplete in their contextual associations. Nevertheless, they can be evaluated as key elements in procurement and exchange networks; points of reference in the community's narratives and worldviews; vehicles for culturally important knowledge; and marks of social integration but also differentiation. In this way, the ornate human body becomes a powerful and multivalent symbol (Marcus 1993; Sorensen 1991). Here the element of visibility, inherent in the socialized milieu of manufacture and display of the end products, would obviously play a decisive part. In prehistoric Sitagroi we can reasonably assume close interaction among houses closely packed on the limited area of the mound (Elster 1997), and thus plenty of opportunities to see and be seen. The Bin Complex, in particular, can be studied as a context (see chapter 12) where performance of everyday activities (storage, craft, discard) on a scale wider than the household would as well have provided a full field for ornaments as symbolic expression.

ACKNOWLEDGMENTS

Warm thanks are due to Dr. John Schoenfelder, Department of Anthropology and the Cotsen Institute of Archaeology at UCLA, for his help with the electronic processing of the data.

NOTES

[1] In the catalog of chapter 8, Renfrew and Slater list this piece together with more metal fragments, possibly belonging to another similar ring. I include here only the identifiable ring.

[2] Because the number of the Early Bronze Age ornaments is relatively small, I treat all phase V pieces together, without differentiating between Va and Vb (volume 1 [C. Renfrew 1986e]:173, table 7.3). I only refer to each subphase in relation to specific find contexts of interest.

[3] Similar biases resulting from selective application of wet sieving have been observed in a general sense (see Preface) as well as specifically for the chipped stone tools from the site (see chapter 3).

[4] In the catalogs (appendixes 9.2 and 9.4), artifacts recovered during water sieving (a 3-cm mesh) are denoted by an "s" (for example: SF 499 ZA 47s); an "r" reflects recovery from the 3-mm mesh flotation of ZB (for example: SF 5144a ZB 117r); see also volume 1 (C. Renfrew 1986c): 21, 22.

[5] Species terminology follows Reese (1987:120) and J. Shackleton (1988:50–52).

[6] For example, a closed floor deposit was revealed in level ZA 41 which contained a large number of mussel shells, probably food remains (volume1 [C. Renfrew 1986b]:180).

[7] Although the succulent meat of the edible *Spondylus* and *Glycymeris* (J. Shackleton 1988:45) may well have been eaten first (see Bar-Yosef Mayer 1997:100–101), there was still no unworked marine shell reported from rubbish pits, midden, or elsewhere in any phase. Besides, there are relatively few marine shells that had been ground or shaped to be used as implements (see this volume, appendix 9.1).

[8] Large quantities are also reported from the recently excavated site of Makriyalos (Besios and Pappa 1996; Pappa 1995).

[9] Miller observed that many pieces in the Philippi and Drama museums displayed fresh breakages, possibly caused during excavation.

[10] Miller kindly informed me that many pieces with ancient breakages from the same excavation unit do seem to have belonged to a single ornament but do not join. They often have different dimensions, length and/or width, possibly coming from different parts of the bracelet/annulet. Such fragments have been cataloged separately.

[11] A division into narrow and wide had already been used for the cylindrical beads in the original file records of the Sitagroi excavation, but on the basis of length alone. There, "narrow cylindrical" referred to beads ranging in length from 0 to 2 mm and "wide cylindrical" to those measuring between 2 and 7 mm in length. The problem was that in most cases (especially for beads found in groups) only diameter had been recorded in detail, while we have the length range of the cataloged group but not exact measurements for each single bead. Since my own typological and quantitative analysis relied on the counting of each single bead separately, it was not always helpful to work with the original classifications. Instead I regrouped the material according to Barge's more versatile length-to-diameter ratio, incorporating in my typology all available notebook data. When bead description has been modified, I provide the length range of the old, notebook type in order to facilitate comparison between the excavation documents and the published entries. For example, SF 1274 of phase III, a cylindrical bead of 1.1 mm diameter, was initially recorded as wide. It is now classified as narrow cylindrical, because the 0.2 to 0.7 cm length range of the notebook "wide" group is smaller than the diameter of this particular bead.

[12] Miller, however, believes (see appendix 9.2) that the larger stone beads were probably unfinished preforms for the standard narrow cylindrical type. SF 3054 of phase IV (plate 9.9h), with partly rough surface, may be such a case.

[13] This term was originally used in the excavation notebooks.

[14] Two hollow fragments of phase III (SF 797, 5077b) of shell or stone in the shape of domed cones, perforated at the top, may also have belonged to biconical beads and have been included in the group, although all other bicones at Sitagroi are made of clay.

[15] Edge working has been observed in the two *Mytilus* pendants SF 2530 (plate 9.19a) and 2889 (plate 9.19b), but the overall form of the valve remains unaltered.

[16] D. Reese (1987:129) believes that the *Murex* shells from Sitagroi were beach-worn and not intentionally perforated.

Appendix 9.1.
Preliminary Report on the Molluscan Remains at Sitagroi

Nicholas J. Shackleton

It is obvious from a cursory examination that the marine molluscan remains at Sitagroi do not represent food refuse. Most of the shell fragments are worked, and it seems reasonable to group the few unworked examples with the worked ones, treating them as art objects, or material for fabricating art objects (plate 9.1.1), rather than as faunal remains. By contrast, it seems likely that the freshwater shells found do represent food refuse (plate 9.1.2), and these are considered in the section concerned with faunal remains.

Spondylus, *Glycymeris*, and *Mytilus* are all present in important quantities and are considered separately. The distribution of these three species among the phases of occupation of the site has raised some interesting problems and is discussed in detail (see table 9.1.1). For the rest, the situation is as commonly observed in Mediterranean sites: the species represented on the whole are those that any tourist today would pick up on the beach and take home.

PHASE DISTRIBUTION: *SPONDYLUS*, *MYTILUS*, *GLYCYMERIS*

The distribution of the three significant marine molluscan genera throughout the phases of Sitagroi's occupation poses certain fascinating problems. The evidence is conflicting. The basic information stems from two sources: the total listing in the small finds catalog (see appendix 9.2) and the distribution of species among phases from the water-sieving experiment. This list includes all *Spondylus* annulet fragments, all worked *Mytilus* fragments, and all worked *Glycymeris* fragments (see table 9.1.1). It excludes beads.

Table 9.1.1. Species by Phase

| Shell type | Phase | | | | | | |
	I	II	III	IV	V	X*	Total
Spondylus	3	19	113	11	6	20	172
Mytilus	1	29	5	1	1	4	41
Glycymeris	1	15	60	3	2	6	87
Phase total	5	63	178	15	9	30	300

* X indicates unphased or mixed contexts.

Distribution among Phases in the Water-Sieving Experiment

This list is of all identifiable fragments in levels of clearly ascertained phase, as shown in table 9.1.2; for clarity the layers showing interphase contamination are ignored. The number of fragments with evidence of working are shown in table 9.1.2 in parentheses.

The water-sieving data on *Glycymeris* are not useful because it was not possible to distinguish between the larger group, used for annulets, and the smaller group, used pierced for suspension.

It seems likely that in phase I, the rare fragments of *Spondylus* and *Glycymeris* have no significance; they almost certainly represent some form of

Table 9.1.2. Distribution by Phase from the Water-Sieving Experiment

| Shell type | Phase | | | | | |
	I	II	III	IV	V	Total
Spondylus	2 (0)	83 (8)	82 (21)	9 (2)	11 (1)	187 (32)
Mytilus	40 (0)	151 (16)	105 (2)	2 (0)	2 (1)	300 (19)
Phase total	42 (0)	234 (24)	187 (23)	11 (2)	13 (2)	487 (51)

Note: Worked pieces in parentheses.

contamination. Indeed, the overall impression gained from an examination of the remains is that there was essentially no interest in products from the sea among the inhabitants at that time. The matter might have rested there, but when the results of the water-sieving experiment were analyzed, the data showed that there were large numbers of *Mytilus* fragments in phase I.

A possible explanation for these might be misidentification: the fragments are small, and not a single umbo fragment was detected. However, if this were the case, one must ask what, in fact, was represented. One could postulate confusion with *Unio*, which has a similar shell structure, but quite apart from our confidence in S. Payne's identifications, it would be rather remarkable that so few *Mytilus* fragments were reported from phase IV, when *Unio* was, in fact, more abundant. An alternative hypothesis would be contamination from above, but here the difficulty is that within phase I deposits, a layer almost devoid of *Mytilus* separates the bulk of the reported fragments from the overlying phase II. I am unable to put forward any explanation for this enigma and can only point out that these data are a product of the water-sieving experiment, and only another similar experiment could be expected to shed light on the problem.

In phases IV and V, there is again a distinct lack of marine material; the finds could be due to contamination or to the very occasional use of shell at these times.

The interesting comparison from our point of view is between phases II and III. From the find lists, one would have deduced that working with *Mytilus* was a feature of the phase II occupation, while working with *Spondylus* developed in phase III. The ratio of *Mytilus* to *Spondylus* changes from 1.5 to 0.05. However, when we examine the reports of these species in the water-sieving experiment, we find the ratio changing only from 2 to 1.2. Thus macroscopic collection indicates a factor of 30 change, and sieving less than a factor of 2.

I have made the comparison in terms of the ratio of *Mytilus* to *Spondylus* to avoid confusion with regard to volume of excavated material and other factors, but there are two separate questions posed. First, was *Mytilus* worked in phase II only, or was it also worked in phase III? Second, was *Spondylus* already being worked in phase II, or was

the fabrication of *Spondylus* annulets confined to phase III?

With regard to *Mytilus*, a fruitful approach is to examine the dimensions of the fragments found in deposits of each phase (see table 9.1.3). The standard deviation among the lengths in phase II is 0.9 cm, so that the fragments in other phases are significantly smaller. There is no indication that the shells were smaller; this is certainly a matter only of greater fragmentation. This increase in fragmentation outside phase II deposits constitutes evidence that the phase II examples are those most nearly in situ, and that those found in deposits from other phases were also made in phase II times.

This finding constitutes a useful comment on the information provided by the water-sieving experiment. Although it is quite obvious that the representation of very small objects can only be assessed realistically by this kind of procedure, a crude count of fragments of larger objects, taking no account of the size of the fragments, can be highly misleading.

With regard to *Spondylus*, the mean length of phase II fragments is 4.1 cm, of phase III fragments 4.9 cm, and of phase IV fragments 4.0 cm. Again, the phase with the greatest abundance also contains the largest pieces, although the difference is not particularly striking. Since *Glycymeris* annulets were certainly made in phase II times, it seems possible that *Spondylus* and *Glycymeris* were used indiscriminately in phase II and that a strong preference for *Spondylus* became established in phase III. This immediately raises interesting questions as to the relative representation of *Glycymeris* and *Spondylus* in inland sites, and whether these can be related either to the age of the sites or to the origin of the material on different parts of the coast (see appendix 9.3 for a discussion of habitat).

Table 9.1.3. Mean Length (cm) of *Mytilus* Fragments by Phase

Phase	No. of *Mytilus* examined	Mean length (cm)
I	1	2.1
II	16	4.0
III	4	2.5
IV	1	0.5
V	1	1.5

In considering the question of *Spondylus* utilization, it should be pointed out that *Spondylus* was used for making beads as well as annulets, and that *Spondylus* beads are abundant in both phases II and III. Indeed, the recovery of beads was about equal to the recovery of all other *Spondylus* fragments, in the water-sieved levels. This indicates that the abundance of unworked *Spondylus* in phase II (plate 9.1.3) cannot be taken as evidence that it was used for annulets. Conversely, the fact that it was a popular raw material during phase II, when *Glycymeris* annulets were certainly made, makes it highly unlikely that its suitability for annulet making would pass unnoticed. (Not having examined the beads, I cannot say whether at least some of the "narrow cylindrical" group could have been made from *Glycymeris* shell, but see appendix 9.3).

SPONDYLUS ANNULETS

It is now likely that sites in the plain of Drama may have been distribution points of much of the *Spondylus* found in Neolithic Europe (Shackleton and Renfrew 1970). At the same time, the isotope techniques used in the above-cited work are not susceptible to much refinement, although it is possible that work on the technology of the objects could contribute to a close delineation of trade routes. For this reason, I present some measurements of those dimensions that could prove to be of value in comparing assemblages from different sites. It is unfortunate that circumstances prevented me from seeing all the excavated material; after I left the site, a substantial amount of the phase III deposit was excavated, with a concomitant increase in the number of *Spondylus* fragments reported.

The procedure involved in the manufacture of *Spondylus* annulets is as follows. First, the outer surface of the shell is ground on a flat surface until the bowl shape gives way to a ring. Next, the rough inner edges produced are smoothed using a "file" through the hole. Finally the surfaces are all ground, the outer natural surface wholly or partly removed, and the shape refined. I am grateful to Rene Treuil for allowing me to see some of the material from the nearby site of Dikili Tash, where one piece has been reduced to the ring shape but had undergone no finishing or thinning at all; this was most helpful in clarifying the order of procedure.

It will be clear that some dimensions are a function of the size of the original shell, which is only in the control of the maker to the extent that he can select the most appropriate shells. Other dimensions depend on his skill or taste. In this respect, the most important variable is the width of the band at the opposite side of the ring to the hinge of the shell; this is the only dimension that depends entirely on the maker. It is remarkable how closely controlled this dimension is.

Dimensions of *Spondylus* Annulet Fragments

The measurements used are tabulated below. It might be noted that they are based on a number of fragments varying from approximately one-quarter to half of the complete ring. The external diameter of most pieces was estimated by tracing the outline of the annulet on graph paper and estimating the diameter of the ring that would make a plausible fit to the section. Only a few pieces were long enough to estimate the large and small diameters. The mean diameter is approximately 54 mm, and the shape of an average annulet would have been approximately 58 x 50 mm. The average inside diameter is approximately 35 mm; it is obvious that the term "bracelet" is a misnomer for these objects.

Shape of *Spondylus* Annulets

The ultimate shape of the annulets (see figure 9.5) owes much to the structure of the shell. At the hinge end of the shell, where an adequate thickness of material is present, the ring is kept stout and given a more or less rectangular section about 12 mm x 9 mm. Moving away from the hinge, the cross section thins out and twists toward the outer edge. Here, the form is a band inclined at about 30° to the plane of the annulet (dictated by the shape of the shell). The band is just under 3 mm thick on average; some are as thin as 2 mm, and a few as thick as 3.5 mm. The two thickest (SF 1710: 4.7 mm [plate 9.7n]; SF 816: 4.2 mm [plates 9.3, 9.7q]) are obviously unfinished, there being no working on the inner surface. We surmise that these were broken during manufacture.

The width of the band at the point farthest from the hinge is the dimension most in the control of the maker (or least controlled by the shell itself). SF 1710, one of the definitely unfinished examples, measures 14.5 mm, and SF 898 (plate 9.7b) is an exceptionally narrow fragment at 6.5 mm. For the rest, the average is 9.9 mm, and the variability is less than for the other dimensions measured. Seventy percent lie within 10% either side of the average value, whereas for other dimensions the range covered by 70% of the examples is between 15% and 20% either side of the average. This suggests that if any dimension is to be useful as an aid in discriminating among *Spondylus* shell annulets on the basis of technology of manufacture, it is the width of the band at the point most distant from the hinge. It will be interesting, therefore, to discover to what extent variation in the dimensions can be found by investigating other sites.

The thickness of the band at this point is also under the control of the maker. Notably, the thinnest piece measured is a phase II occurrence; whether there is any significance in this observation one can only tell by examining more material.

GLYCYMERIS SPECIES

Many of the annulet fragments that at first glance would be ascribed to *Spondylus* are in reality made from the very different *Glycymeris* shell. Probably many of the alleged *Spondylus* pieces in public collections are of the same genus (about 30% of the collection from Vinča at the Birmingham Museum and Art Gallery are *Glycymeris*; I am grateful to Dr. Joan Taylor for allowing me to examine these specimens in detail).

Plate 9.6 illustrates two annulet examples (SF 3427a, 3427b) of the smaller *Glycymeris* species, neither of which has been artificially modified apart from holes for suspension (not clearly shown in the photograph) in the umbos. The characteristic hinge-teeth and the denticulate margin are clearly visible. In the left-hand example, traces of both these features are visible, while the muscle-attachment scars may be picked out in the right-hand example. Even examples from which the external morphology of these characteristics has been completely ground away retain a characteristic growth-structure reflecting the existence of these features throughout development and are visible to the naked eye.

The inside diameter of the rings is not easy to estimate reliably: 50 mm, about the same as the *Spondylus* annulets, is a rough average. They are cer-

tainly examples of the larger *Glycymeris* species, either *G. pectunculus* or *G. pilosus*. The form of the annulets resembles those made of *Spondylus*, although they are generally more slender and fragile. The material from this site is not plentiful enough to enable us to present useful average dimensions.

It seems that the smaller *Glycymeris*, perhaps *G. violescans*, was also used at this site; examples pierced for suspension are quite common. Curiously enough, these are the most common in phase III (pierced examples as well as the same smaller, unmodified species), while the larger species used for annulets are most prevalent in phase II (again this is true for unmodified examples as well as for annulet fragments). The water-sieving experiment is of no help here, as it was not possible to distinguish between the species.

THE (MARINE) MUSSEL *MYTILUS GALLOPROVINCIALIS*

A total of sixteen pieces (plate 9.1.4) plus a pendant have been found (table 9.1.4). Every single fragment is worked.

The distribution suggests that these mussels were only worked during phase II. One thinks at

Table 9.1.4. Listing of Worked *Mytilus Galloprovincialis* Pieces by Phase and Location

Phase	Small Find	Level	Plates
I	2530	JL 104	9.19a
II	2880	KM 9	9.1.4k
II?	2878	KL 2	9.1.4i
II	2879	ZA 57	9.1.4j
II	2874	KM 17	9.1.4e
II	2872	ZA 52	NA
II	2885	KM 17	9.1.4p
II	2870	KL 103	9.1.5, 9.1.4a
II	2875	KM 20	9.1.4f
III	2876	ML 105	9.1.4g
II	2871	KM 18	9.1.4b
III	2873	MM 27	9.1.4d
II	2877	ZA 52	9.1.4h
II	2881	KL 110	9.1.4l
II	2882	KL 117	9.1.4m
II	2883	KL 114	9.1.4n
I	2884	KL 151	9.1.4o

once of the "Saliagos spoons," made at about the same time, although the shape worked here is different (Evans and Renfrew 1968:68, 69). The pieces are from the same shape as the unbroken SF 2870 (plate 9.1.5), that is to say, a roughly triangular shape. It will be recalled that the Saliagos examples had been ground on a flat surface so that the shape of the shell was only slightly modified. Here the working is across the shell, and the shape is considerably modified as the end distant from the umbo (where the shell is thinnest and least pearly) is straightened off. As in the Saliagos case, we cannot suggest any use for these objects.

Unlike the *Spondylus* annulets, there is no means of telling whether these objects were fabricated on the site or imported ready-made, because we have no way of recognizing an unfinished example or one broken during manufacture. At any rate, the selection of shells with a reasonably thick pearly layer was presumably made elsewhere, since no fragments of unsuitable shells were found.

OTHER MOLLUSCAN SPECIES

Fourteen examples of cockles (*Cerastoderma*), including three in phase IV, were removed. These do not seem to have any direct significance, although they help to confirm the absence of shell working after phase III.

Five other species seem to be devoid of significance: *Ostrea edulis* (oyster; three specimens; see plate 9.1.6), *Nerithea neritina* (two specimens), *Murex trunculus* (four beach-worn specimens), *Cerithium vulgatum* (two specimens), and *Arca noae* (one specimen). It is worth mentioning that none of these occurred in phase I. It may be that there was essentially no contact with the sea at this time.

COWRY

Finally, there are two cowry shells: *Luria lurida*, SF 832, phase IV (plate 9.20), with two holes ground in it, and SF 1001 (plate 9.26) from phase V, with a ground hole.

Appendix 9.2.
Catalog of Worked Shell
Nicholas J. Shackleton

PHASE I

88   JL 4
Spondylus fragment
L: 4.4; W: 2.3; Th: 0.97

2884   KL 151, plate 9.1.4o
Mytilus fragment; one worked edge
L: 2.2

PHASE II

965   KM 18; plate 9.1.6
Oyster disc with evidence of grinding
L: 4.4; W: 4.3; Th: 0.5

2320   KL 108; plate 9.1.3
Spondylus lower valve fragment; not worked
L: 5.5; W: 6.0; Th: 1.8

2870   KL 103; plates 9.1.5, 9.1.4a
Mytilus fragment; worked into triangular shape
L: 5.0

2871   KM 18; plate 9.1.4b
Mytilus fragment; worked edge
L: 4.5

2872   ZA 52; plate 9.1.4c
Mytilus fragment; worked edge
L: 3.5

2874   KM 17; plate 9.1.4e
Mytilus fragment; worked edges
L: 4.0

2875   KM 20; plate 9.1.4f
Mytilus fragment; yellowish in color; one edge worked
L: 3.8

2877   ZA 52; plate 9.1.4h
Mytilus fragment; edges worked
L: 5.3

2878   KL 2; plate 9.1.4i
Mytilus fragment; one edge worked
L: 4.2

2879   ZA 57; plate 9.1.4j
Mytilus fragment; reddish/yellowish in color; one edge worked
L: 5.0

2880   KM 9; plate 9.1.4k
Mytilus fragment; disc; black to red surface discoloration; edge worked
L: 4.5

2881   KL 110; plate 9.1.4 l
Mytilus fragment; red exterior; possibly smoothed; two edges worked
L: 3.8

2882   KL 117; plate 9.1.4m
Mytilus fragment; red exterior; two edges worked
L: 4.5

2883   KL 114; plate 9.1.4n
Mytilus fragment; red exterior; possibly smoothed; two edges worked
L: 2.0

2885   KM 17; plate 9.1.4p
Mytilus fragment; red; two edges worked
L: 4.6

2892   KL 102
Glycymeris; modified; use-wear along one edge
D: 5.0

4003   ZG 41
Mytilus fragment; possibly worked; purplish coloration
L: 4.2; W: 3.6

5264(a) ZA 52s
Unio fragment
L: 1.5–2.0

5264(b) ZA 52s
Mytilus fragment
L: 0.4–3.5

5264(c) ZA 52s
Mytilus fragment
L: 0.4–3.5

5264(d) ZA 52s
Mytilus fragment
L: 0.4–3.5

5264(e) ZA 52s
Unio fragment
L: 1.5–2.0

5264(f) ZA 52s
Cardium fragment
L: 1.0–1.4

5264(g) ZA 52s
Cardium fragment
L: 1.0–1.4

5264(h) ZA 52s
Mytilus fragment
L: 0.4–3.5

5264(i) ZA 52s
Mytilus fragment
L: 0.4–3.5

5267(a) ZA 55s
Mytilus fragment, worked
L: 3.0

5267(b) ZA 55s
Mytilus fragment, worked
L: 3.7

5269(a) ZA 58s
Spondylus fragment
L: 0.2–2.3

5269(b) ZA 58s
Spondylus fragment
L: 0.2–2.3

5269(c) ZA 58s
Spondylus fragment
L: 0.2–2.3

5270(a) ZA 58s
Mytilus fragment; worked
L: 2.5

5270(b) ZA 58s
Unio fragment; worked
L: 1.7

5596 ML 15
Glycymeris; modified, worked
D: 3.8

5598 KL 117
Unio; modified, worked
L: 5.6

5599 KL 107
Unio; modified, worked
L: 5.5

PHASE III

1908 MM 54
Unidentified shell fragment; brown encrustation; polished interior
L: 7.0; W: 1.8; Th: 0.4

2873 MM 27; plate 9.1.4d
Mytilus fragment; reddish in color; one edge worked
L: 3.8

2876 ML 105; plate 9.1.4g
Mytilus fragment; reddish in color; two edges worked
L: 3.0

2888 ZA 38; plate 9.1.1
Unio fragment; use-wear along edge; evidence of red pigment on interior surface
L: 5.3; W: 3.0

3836 MMb 65
Unidentified shell
L: 2.8; W: 0.7; Th: 0.7

3897(b) MMd 68
Spondylus fragment; worked
L: 2.5; W: 0.7; Th: 0.3

5144(a) ZB 117r
Mytilus fragment; worked
L: 1.2

5144(b) ZB 117r
Mytilus fragment; worked
L: 1.2

5147 ZB 120r
Unio; modified, worked
L: 2.2

5148 ZB 121r
Unio; modified, worked
L: 4.3

5149 ZB 122r
Unio; modified, worked
L: 3.8

5155(a) ZB 128r
Mytilus fragment; worked
L: 2.2

5252(a) ZA 44s; plate 9.1.2a
Unio; modified, worked
D: 0.9–2.1

5252(b) ZA 44s; plate 9.1.2b
Unio; modified, worked
D: 0.9–2.1

5252(c) ZA 44s; plate 9.1.2c
Unio; modified, worked
D: 0.9–2.1

5252(d) ZA 44s
Unio; modified, worked
D: 0.9–2.1

5252(e) ZA 44s
Unio; modified, worked.
D: 0.9–2.1

5256(a) ZA 45s
Unio; modified, worked
L: 2.0–3.2

5256(b) ZA 45s
Unio; modified, worked
L: 2.0–3.2

5258(a) ZA 47s
Unio; modified, worked
L: 2.8

5258(b) ZA 47s
Unio; modified, worked
L: 3.8

5260 ZA 48s
Unio; modified, worked
L: 2.4

5597(a) MM 20
Unio; modified, worked.
L: 4.1–5.9

5597(b) MM 20
Unio; modified, worked
L: 4.1–5.9

5597(c) MM 20
Unio; modified, worked
L: 4.1–5.9

5597(d) MM 20
Unio; modified, worked
L: 4.1–5.9

5600 MM 27
Unio; modified, worked
L: 5.3

5601 MM 19
Unio; modified, worked
L: 3.8

5603 MM 40
Unio; modified, worked
L: 3.3

5604 ZA 47
Ostrea; modified, worked
L: 6.2

5610 MM 60
Unio; modified, worked
D: 4.3

PHASE IV

5135 ZB 52r
Mytilus; modified, worked
L: 0.5

5136(a) ZB 62r
Unio; modified, worked
L: 2.6–4.2

5136(b) ZB 62r
Unio; modified, worked
L: 2.6–4.2

5136(c) ZB 62r
Unio; modified, worked
L: 2.6–4.2

5136(d) ZB 62r
Unio; modified, worked
L: 2.6–4.2

5137 ZB 64r
Unio; modified, worked
L: 4.0

5140 ZB 101r
Spondylus bracelet fragment; burned
L: 0.7

5141(a) ZB 102r
Spondylus bracelet fragment; burned
L: 1.5

5141(b) ZB 102r
Unio; modified, worked
L: 4.3

5590 ZA 32
Glycymeris; modified, perforated
D: 3.6

5593 ZE 61
Cardium; modified, perforated
D: 3.6

5594 ZE 61
Cardium; modified, perforated
D: 2.5

5595 ZE 61
Cardium; modified, worked
D: 1.8

PHASE V

5125 ZB 10r
Unio; modified, worked
L: 2.7

5127 ZB 22r
Mytilus fragment; worked
L: 1.8

5128 ZB 37r
Unio; modified, worked
L: 0.9

5129(b) ZB 37r
Unio; modified, worked
L: 4.0

5130 ZB 40r
Unio; modified, worked
L: 4.7

MIXED CONTEXTS

3527 MMc
Spondylus bracelet fragment
L: 5.1; W: 1.3; Th: 0.6

5368 ZA
Glycymeris
L: 3.5

Appendix 9.3.
Technical Aspects of Ornament Production at Sitagroi

Michele Miller

This study of the production of ornaments at Sitagroi is part of a larger research project exploring the production, consumption, and distribution of pre-Bronze Age personal ornaments in the Aegean (Miller 1997). There has been little previous comprehensive study of any aspect of Aegean pre-Bronze Age ornaments, and the production of these objects has been rather ignored. Partly this deficiency results from the tendency scholars have to concentrate on the stylistic forms of these "prestige" objects, while focusing production studies on more "utilitarian" goods. Yet another reason is it can be difficult to recognize evidence for the manufacture of ornaments on the finished objects themselves, while debitage from production is often not identified or collected during excavations. To counteract this, I have recently concentrated on the production of ornaments in the Aegean (Miller 1996), including this detailed examination of ornament production at Sitagroi. Here I wish to acknowledge the useful preliminary report on the molluscan remains at Sitagroi by N. J. Shackleton (appendixes 9.1, 9.2), upon which I have drawn in preparing this further appendix.

My goal is to clarify the manufacture processes for the dominant classes of ornaments found at Sitagroi using archaeological, ethnographic, and experimental evidence. I examine evidence to determine whether the ornaments were locally produced at Sitagroi and discuss the production process, as well as explore the possible changes in production technology over time, especially in the transition from Neolithic to the Early Bronze Age.

SHELL ANNULET PRODUCTION

The production of shell annulets has received more attention than that of any other Aegean Neolithic ornament. Thus it has been suggested that several sites in Thessaly and Macedonia, where considerable quantities of shell annulets were found (including Sitagroi), were specialized production centers where large numbers of the annulets were manufactured specifically for export trade (Tsuneki 1989:16; C. Renfrew 1973d:187). No significant study of the shell artifacts and debris at these Macedonian sites has yet been completed in order to evaluate such claims, whereas studies in other areas of Greece have provided more debate than answers (see Tsuneki 1987, 1989; Halstead 1993). Clearly, further analysis of the manufacture of shell annulets is necessary to resolve these questions.

Raw Materials and Procurement

Marine shells were heavily utilized for ornament manufacture at Sitagroi. As Shackleton has noted (appendix 9.1), considering Sitagroi's distance from the sea, it is unlikely that any of the shells found at the site were brought there as food, but rather almost all seem to have been utilized as material for ornaments and tools.

The shell of the bivalve, *Spondylus gaederopus*, was undoubtedly the most important for ornament manufacture, although the shell of a large species of *Glycymeris* was also used for the manufacture of annulets. The hard, thick shell of the *Spondylus* is valuable material for both beads and pendants and is distinctly suitable for the many large shell annulets found at the site. Although *Spondylus gaederopus* is a Mediterranean species and was almost certainly available in local waters, the procurement of *Spondylus* shells suitable for ornament manufacture took considerable effort. It is unlikely that such shells were collected "dead" on the beach. None of the *Spondylus* shell artifacts or debris that I have observed at Sitagroi show signs of beach-wear, although admittedly such wear would be difficult to detect in the worked objects in which most of the outer surface of the shell has been ground away. Additionally, in experiments replicating the manufacture of *Spondylus* annulets and beads, I have noted that beach-collected shells are drier and more fragile than those recently collected "live," and therefore they tend to break in the manufacture process. Thus, beach-collected shells would not have been useful for ornament manufacture. Finally, it is unlikely that enough shells of the large size necessary for ornament production would have been available from beachcombing alone.

The procurement from the sea of large *Spondylus* shells must have been a laborious undertaking. For one thing, the mollusks firmly attach themselves by the right valve to a rock or coral, "where they remain for life and are able to move only one valve, the upper, during life" (Webb 1948:185). Thus, unlike many mobile mollusks, such as the predatory *Murex*, the *Spondylus* is rarely pulled up in fishing nets. Rather, it is likely that *Spondylus* collectors had to dive for their prey, first spotting the shells often hidden by marine growth such as sponges or algae (Tornaritis 1987:138) and then prying or cutting them from the rocks to which they were cemented. It is difficult to determine how deep the *Spondylus* collectors needed to dive. Today, live *Spondylus* of the size utilized in prehistoric ornament production are difficult to find, and *Spondylus* of any size are primarily found in deeper waters. In fact, Tornaritis notes that, "recently they have been almost extinct from Cyprus waters" (Tornaritis 1987:138) and my conversations with Greek divers and shell collectors indicate that they are increasingly rare in most of the coastal waters of the Aegean. Furthermore, those that can be found are rather small and thin-shelled, not nearly the size

utilized in prehistoric ornament production (Evi Theodorou, molluscologist, Goulandris Museum of Natural History, personal communication, 1994/1995). It is likely, however, that the scarcity of *Spondylus* is a recent event, brought on by pollution and over-fishing in the Mediterranean. I have occasionally found large shells of this species on coastal archaeological sites of both prehistoric and historic periods, and therefore we cannot assume that in the past large *Spondylus* shells were equally as infrequent.

Manufacturing Technique

I have based my evaluation of the production of shell annulets at Sitagroi on archaeological, ethnographic, and experimental evidence. The archaeological evidence results from my examination of the unfinished annulets (plate 9.3.1), shell debris, and wear traces found on finished and unfinished annulets. For instance, wear marks and debris indicate that both grinding and chipping were used to reduce the shell, but I have not observed any evidence for the cutting or sawing of shells in the manufacture of annulets. I have also been able to examine the unfinished annulets and reconstruct the relative sequence of steps in annulet manufacture. My observations of the archaeological evidence was confirmed by similar conclusions reached in research at other Greek Neolithic sites (Tsuneki 1987, 1989).

Interestingly, bangle "bracelets"[1] of marine shell are manufactured in many parts of the world, which provides us with valuable ethnographic and ethnohistoric comparanda for the manufacture process of the Sitagroi annulets. In many cases, large bivalves such as various species of *Spondylus* and *Glycymeris* were employed for this purpose. For instance, shell annulets were produced in great numbers by the Trincheras culture in the Sonora region of northern Mexico and by the Hohokam of Arizona. These two societies manufactured almost identical shell annulets out of a large species of *Glycymeris*, but employed different manufacturing techniques (McGuire and Howard 1987:120; Haury 1976:306; Woodward 1936:121). The Trincheras annulet production technique involves the sawing and removal of the shell core (Woodward 1936:119–

120) and thus is not an appropriate model for the manufacture of the Sitagroi shell annulets. The manufacture technique employed by the Hohokam, on the other hand, probably closely resembles the process in the production of Greek Neolithic shell annulets. In Hohokam annulet manufacture,

> the highest part of the convex surface of a *Glycymeris* valve, preferred for bracelet production, was worn down on an abrasive surface until a small hole could be punched through it. The diameter of the opening was then expanded by chipping. If the valve wall became too thick for successful chipping, more grinding thinned the shell and provided the edge that made further chipping easy. Roughed out in this way the shell circle could then be finished by rasping and reaming. (Haury 1976:306)

The manufacturing sequence employed by the Hohokam provides valuable clues to the production of Sitagroi annulets.

Shell bracelets similar to those from Sitagroi are also known from Neolithic and Chalcolithic sites in northern India. There, researchers had the advantage of comparisons with the work of native craftsmen who continue to make shell bracelets in the traditional method. An ethnographic study conducted by Mark Kenoyer (1983) reveals a technology only moderately modified by new tools. First, the gastropod *Turbinella pyrum* (conch) is hollowed out and cut to form a circlet using several types of specialized metal saws and chisels. Next, the interior of the bangle is ground down using a rasp, much like a cylindrical piece of sandstone, constructed by coating a wooden rod with a mixture of coarse sand and insect resin. The rasp is held in a stationary position, and the bangles are run up and down against it. Flat sandstone slabs are still used for grinding the exterior of the bangles. Finally, the finished bangles are polished by being dipped in an acetic acid solution, although in an earlier tradition polishing was accomplished using fine brick dust as an abrasive (Kenoyer 1983:335). Although these bracelets are manufactured from gastropods, not bivalves, and although the technique includes sawing as well as grinding, comparisons to this present-day shell bangle production provides evidence for the tools and labor in the manufacture of Greek shell annulets.

I also conducted several experiments to replicate the manufacture of the *Spondylus* annulets, to better understand the sequence of production steps and the types of tools utilized in annulet manufacture. To some extent, the experiments enabled me to predict the amount of time and effort expended in annulet manufacture, although this varied according to the size and species of shell used.[?] Based on archaeological, ethnographic, and experimental evidence, I have determined the manufacturing process of the Sitagroi *Spondylus* shell annulets to be as described in the following.

STEP 1: In the first step, the ventral margin of one valve (almost always the left) is ground down on a grinding stone to smooth its irregular surface. At the same time, any remaining spines on the exterior surface of the shell are either broken off or ground down.

STEP 2: Next, the rough outer surface of the valve is ground down, and the overall thickness of the shell is reduced. Sometimes the hinge teeth are also partly ground down at this stage. Both sandstone and igneous grinding stones were used in experiments. The latter was initially more successful at grinding the shell. Those found at Sitagroi were mostly made of slabby schist (see chapters 4, 5). The addition of quartz sand and water increased the efficiency of grinding. Experimentally, it took about one-half to one hour to grind away traces of the outer spines, resulting in a shell with a smooth rounded outer surface, with the area near the umbo somewhat flattened. As grinding proceeds, the outer surface of the shell is flattened further until a small hole opens in the center of the valve. Depending on the thickness and condition of the shell, it could take from one to several hours to open a small hole in the shell solely by grinding.

STEP 3: In the third step, this small hole is enlarged by chipping with a hammerstone while supporting the shell against an anvil. Although the hammerstone is tapped against the interior of the shell, large flakes of shell will fall away from the shell exterior.

STEP 4: Once the area of the shell around the central hole is thinned by chipping, the hole is enlarged and ground down using a small handheld grinding stone as a rasp or reamer. The hole is thus reamed until a thicker, harder area of the shell is reached, and then this area is also chipped. Chipping is always faster than grinding as a means of enlarging the hole, but also is more risky. Frequently, a fracture will form in the shell when it is tapped by the hammerstone. The only way to prevent the shell from breaking is by carefully grinding (and thus thinning) the area on the shell exterior to be chipped by grinding while carefully supporting this area against another stone. Chipping and grinding are thus continuously alternated, with about twenty minutes of grinding followed by five to ten minutes of chipping, until the valve takes on the shape of a circular or oval ring, with smooth, even, inner walls.

STEP 5: Finally, any remaining hinge teeth, ears, and other projections are ground down on the grindstone to form a smooth, even annulet. Experimentally, the entire manufacturing process took from five to ten hours, depending on the thickness of the original shell, although it is possible that an experienced shell-worker could reduce this time by half. Ideally the finished annulet will be oval in shape, with few of the original features of the shell still visible. In actuality, however, the overall form of the annulet reflects the shape of the shell from which it was formed, and the reduction of shell features varies depending on the thickness of the shell. For instance, while the hinge teeth are always ground away on a finished annulet, often the hinge sockets are still visible, as further grinding may cause the annulet to become dangerously thin and apt to break. In addition, the naturally smooth interior layer of the shell is not usually ground away except at the area near the hinge, while the outer surface of the shell is always ground, although often retaining traces of the natural reddish coloring of the shell.

The Organization of Shell Annulet Production at Sitagroi

Now that the manufacturing process of shell annulets has been determined, we can begin to evaluate the hypothesis that Sitagroi was a center for the production of these important artifacts. First, we must determine if all stages of shell annulet manufacture occurred at Sitagroi. Of a total of 169 annulets that I was able to examine,[3] only twelve (7%) seem to be unfinished (table 9.3.1). Although this may seem a small proportion of unfinished products for a "production center," it is possible that excavated areas did not include the primary shell ornament workshop, or, as is more likely, the area where shell wasters and debris were dumped was outside the main habitation. It is encouraging, however, that annulets were found at Sitagroi in most stages of manufacture, indicating that annulets were likely manufactured at the site from start to finish.

Table 9.3.1. Manufacturing Stage of Sitagroi Annulets*

Manufacturing step		Count	Cumulative count	%	Cumulative %
1:	Edges ground and spines removed	2	2	1.18	1.18
1.5:	Edges and exterior lightly ground	4	6	2.37	3.55
2:	Exterior ground and hinge teeth ground	1	7	0.59	4.14
2.5:	Ground to create hole	1	8	0.59	4.73
4:	Hole enlarged by chipping and grinding	4	12	2.37	7.10
5:	Finished annulet	152	164	89.90	97.00
5/6:	Finished (and reworked?)	1	165	0.59	97.60
6:	Finished and reworked annulet fragment	2	167	1.18	98.80
0?:	Fragment or debris	1	168	0.59	99.40
Unidentified		1	169	0.59	100.00

* Manufacturing stages are represented by 169 shell annulets examined from Sitagroi.

In determining how the production of these objects was organized, we must consider whether the manufacture of annulets was specialized.

Opinions abound on the definition of craft specialization and are too numerous to review here (but see Miller 1996). Several scholars, however, have pointed to similar evidence to evaluate the presence of craft specialization in prehistory. This includes direct evidence, which involves the recognition of actual production loci or workshops, as well as indirect evidence, such as an increase in the standardization of finished products, the high skill of producers, the efficiency of manufacturing techniques, and an increase in the volume of finished products (Costin 1991; Brumfiel and Earle 1987).

I have found little evidence for shell ornament workshops at Sitagroi. Although shell annulets were found in greater quantity in some trenches than others, these slight concentrations seem to relate to the greater volume of overall material removed from these locations. In addition, any concentrations are only in finished shell annulets, while the few unfinished annulets were found in scattered contexts. Concentrations of finished objects more likely reflect their post-manufacturing function rather than where they were manufactured. Likewise, any concentrations of shell debitage cannot be used to indicate shell production loci, as studies have shown that the debris from craft production in sedentary communities was almost always swept up and discarded away from workshops and active residences (Murray 1980). Since direct evidence for shell annulet manufacture is lacking at Sitagroi, I will briefly examine the indirect evidence for the organization of production.

STANDARDIZATION. Unfortunately, the annulets found at Sitagroi are primarily fragments, and thus it is not possible to determine if the size of finished annulets became more standardized over time. An important consideration concerning the size of shell annulets, however, is that the dimensions of the finished ornament were primarily dictated by the dimensions of the unmodified shell used to create it. In other words, large valves produced large annulets, while small valves created small annulets. Thus, the primary means of standardizing the size of the final product was in the selection of the original shells. This selection involved several decisions made by annulet manufacturers, including the choice of type of material (the preferred species of mollusk), the selection of a certain size of shell, and the decision to use a particular valve (right or left) to manufacture the annulets. The Sitagroi shell workers seemed to have considered all these parameters.

In the selection of suitable species of shell, of course, the annulet producers would have been limited by the intended function of the annulets. It seems that large annulets were preferred, presumably to fit over the wrists as bracelets. Only a few Aegean bivalves are large enough to meet this requirement, and fewer still may have been readily available in local waters. Both *Spondylus gaederopus* and the larger species of *Glycymeris* (*G. pectunculus* or *G. pilosus*) are large and locally available, and both these species were used for Sitagroi annulets. However, while it seems that slightly fewer *Glycymeris* shell were used in annulet manufacture in phase II than in phase III, the use of *Spondylus* shell for annulet manufacture appears to have increased dramatically between these two periods (see table 9.3.2).[4] It does not seem that this increasing reliance on *Spondylus* relates to the lesser availability of *Glycymeris* shells, as *Glycymeris* were commonly perforated (probably for use as pendants) in this later period (see table 9.3.4). Rather, it seems likely that *Spondylus* shells were preferred by prehistoric craftsmen for the manufacture of annulets of larger, but standardized, dimensions, as *Glycymeris* shells are generally smaller and more delicate than those of *Spondylus*. In fact, several of the *Glycymeris* annulets found at Sitagroi appear to be too small to fit on adult wrists.

A further parameter that could be controlled by the shell-workers is the choice of which valve to use for the annulet. Ninety-seven (57.4%) annulets found at Sitagroi can be positively identified as being made from the thinner left (upper) valve of the *Spondylus* shell. A further fifty-six (33.1%) of the remaining annulets are probably also made from this valve, although the fragments do not include the hinge by which absolute identification is possible. Only sixteen (9.5%) of the annulets seem to be made from the thicker right (lower) valve. These annulets are distinctly thicker than those made from the left valve[5] and must have been much more difficult to manufacture. When not used in annulet manufacture, the heavy right valves were not discarded, however; rather they were utilized for the manufacture of shell beads and pendants. Therefore, there seems to have been a conscious selection by Sitagroi shell-workers of specific valves for specific products.

OUTPUT VOLUME. It is difficult to estimate the total volume of shell annulets produced at Sitagroi. Although 186 annulets were recorded in the Sitagroi excavations, it is impossible to equate this with total production output. Among other scenarios, finished annulets may have been removed from the site for regional or long-distance exchange. A measure of the volume of *Spondylus* debris found at the site (see appendix 9.1) unfortunately cannot be used to indicate the volume of *Spondylus* annulet production, as debris resulting from annulet manufacture is not distinguishable from that left from bead/pendant manufacture. Moreover, much of the debris from shell ornament production is in the form of minute flakes and ground shell remains that were not recovered in excavation.

TIME, EFFICIENCY, AND PRODUCER PROFICIENCY. The detailed explication of the shell annulet manufacturing process presented in this chapter reveals the elaborate compromise between decreasing the time and effort and increasing the success rate of finished product in the production of shell annulets at Sitagroi. An annulet can be manufactured by grind-

ing alone, but this would take an excessive amount of time and labor. Increasing the amount of chipping would, however, probably result in more breaks and discards. Only an experienced shell craftsperson would be able to determine the optimal proportion of grinding and chipping to produce the annulets in a reasonable time without costly breaks and discards. Like the knapping of chert and obsidian, the chipping of shell required an experienced hand to create predictable results.

BEAD PRODUCTION

Beads were manufactured from a variety of materials, each of which is considered separately.

Shell Beads

About a third of the beads from Sitagroi were manufactured from marine mollusk shell. The greatest majority of these beads were manufactured from *Spondylus gaederopus* shell. As discussed above, annulets were primarily manufactured from the left valve, leaving the thick lower valve available for bead manufacture. In fact, the larger shell beads could only have been made from the extremely thick lower valves of *Spondylus*. Another shell used at Sitagroi was the common cockle, *Cerastoderma edule (glaucum)*. Unfinished short beads of both shells were found at Sitagroi: SF 5262 (unfinished *Spondylus* beads; plate 9.3.2), 5154, and 5065a (unfinished *Cerastoderma edule* beads). These allow us to reconstruct the manufacturing technique, which would have been similar for all species of shell. The manufacturing sequence is as follows.

STEP 1: In the first step, a bead blank is chipped from the shell. It would have been far easier to chip a blank from the thin cockle shell than from the thick, heavy *Spondylus* valve. From the variety of forms of the unfinished beads found at Sitagroi, we can detect that in both cases, little care was taken to chip a circular blank.

STEP 2: At this point, the faces of the bead blanks were ground flat. A flat grindstone and perhaps quartzite sand and water would have been all that was necessary for grinding the shell beads. These were undoubtedly the same grindstones as those

Table 9.3.2. Shells Used in Annulet Production by Phase

Raw material	I	II	III	III–IV	IV	V	X*	Total
Glycymeris								
No.	0	7	5	0	1	0	0	13
Row %	0	53.8	38.5	0	7.7	0	0	100
Column %	0	24.1	4.46	0	9.1	0	0	7.7
Spondylus								
No.	3	21	107	2	10	7	5	155
Row %	1.9	13.5	69.0	1.3	6.5	4.5	3.2	100
Column %	100	72.4	95.5	100	90.9	100	100	91.7
Unknown								
No.	0	1	0	0	0	0	0	1
Row %	0	100	0	0	0	0	0	100
Column %	0	3.5	0	0	0	0	0	0.6
Total								
No.	3	29	112	2	11	7	5	169
Row %	1.8	17.2	66.3	1.2	6.5	4.1	3.0	100

* X indicates unphased or mixed contexts.

employed in annulet manufacture. In the case of the cockle blanks, care was taken to grind away the ribbing from the exterior of the shell, as well as to flatten the natural curve of the shell. No such precautions were necessary for the *Spondylus* blanks, which were most often removed from the center of the valve; thus the faces of many of these blanks seem to be only lightly ground.

STEP 3: Finally, the blanks are perforated by drilling, almost always from both faces of the blank. For the thin "disc" beads of cockle and *Spondylus* shell, this would have been a relatively simple and rapid step. For longer beads, drilling would have been more laborious and time consuming, with the added difficulty of ensuring that the perforation from one face met that drilled from the other face. The pattern of score-marks in the perforations indicates that an oscillatory motion was used in drilling. This was probably achieved using a bow drill fashioned with a chert drill tip. The unfinished beads found at Sitagroi also indicate that drilling was a risky procedure, often resulting in the fracturing of the blank.

STEP 4: The sides of the perforated blanks were then ground to a circle. Short or disc beads were strung together on some thin fiber or reed and ground on a flat abrasive stone until they were circular. Longer beads were ground individually, sometimes given a biconical or barrel-shaped profile.

STEP 5: With a little more abrasion, and perhaps the addition of finer sands, the beads were given a fine polish. Many of the finely polished translucent shell beads are barely distinguishable from polished marble.

The bead manufacture process described here is well-known in ethnography, where it is sometimes referred to as the "heishi" technique (Francis 1989: 31). The primary distinction of this bead-manufacturing process is the stringing and grinding of the bead edges together, most often in a grooved grindstone made for this specific purpose. One advantage of such a method is that the time to manufacture each bead is reduced. Experiments show that the time to produce a single bead using this technique is only about thirty minutes, depending on the number of beads produced at a time and the type of material. Larger beads ground individually would have taken quite a bit longer. A second advantage of this technique is that the edges of a group of beads are ground together to a uniform diameter. In fact, the shell beads from Sitagroi do exhibit a remarkable uniformity in diameter. The average diameter of the 101 finished shell beads (all species) from Sitagroi is 5.1 mm, with a range from 3.2 to 8.7 mm and a standard deviation (SD) of 1.1. With further analysis it may be possible to distinguish groups of shell beads that were ground in unison.

Stone Beads

Most stone beads were manufactured from soft stones (soapstone, steatite) with a hardness under 4 on the Mohs' scale. The process for the production of stone beads was similar to that used for shell. That stone beads were also produced from this "heishi" process was determined by analyzing manufacturing traces, as well as by studying several unfinished stone beads. Additional evidence is the remarkable standardization in diameters of Sitagroi stone beads. Except for several unusually large, probably unfinished beads, all of the stone beads I studied are of a single type: of exceptionally uniform diameter, ranging from 3.1–5.4mm, with a mean of 4.3 mm and a standard deviation of only 0.54. Among the majority of stone beads, not only were the diameters highly uniform, but their thicknesses varied little as well.[6] An explanation for this phenomenon may be that bead blanks were chipped from prepared ground slabs of soft stone, instead of grinding the faces of the beads individually. The highly uniform dimensions of stone beads hints at some sort of standardization in the organization of stone bead production. It may also suggest that stone bead manufacture was limited to a few individuals who shared manufacturing techniques and perhaps even tools. For instance, the use of the same grooved abrading stone would have ensured that the edges of all beads would be ground to uniform diameters even when ground in different groups.

Fired Steatite Beads

The production of one type of stone bead found at Sitagroi, fired steatite beads, is of particular interest. These beads are characterized by small size, a straight or cylindrical profile (edge form), and very clear, dense scoring on most surfaces, resulting from the grinding stages of production. Most distinctively, these beads are manufactured from a dark soapstone[7] that has been purposely heated to the point that it has turned white. Heating stone is common in the production of beads and has a history dating back to the Paleolithic period. For example, Randy White has recently discovered that many of the ornaments and small figurines from the European Upper Paleolithic have been deliberately heated, probably in order to alter both the color of the stone and make it smoother to the touch (Bisson and White 1996; personal communication, 1996). An analogy to this process occurs in the modern Indus Valley, where in the early stages of bead production unworked nodules of agate are heated to ease the chipping of the bead blank (Kenoyer 1991:50; Possehl 1981:41–42), while in later stages of production, bead blanks and finished beads are fired repeatedly, until the deep red color of high quality carnelian is achieved (Kenoyer 1991: 52–53). The use of heating to improve bead color in India seems to date back to at least the Harappan period (Kenoyer 1986); further, there is a considerable bibliography on heat treatment of stone artifacts (see Leudtke 1992).

Softstone beads found in the Neolithic levels of Sitagroi exhibit a remarkable degree of size uniformity. This characteristic is heightened in the fired steatite beads, which not only show a great degree of standardization within the Sitagroi assemblage, but also show a surprising similarity of size and form throughout Greece. A total of 525 fired steatite beads have been identified from Late Neolithic levels at five sites other than Sitagroi, which range geographically from the southern tip of the Argolid (Franchthi) all the way to eastern Macedonia (Dikili Tash and Sitagroi), including much of the area in between (see table 9.3.3). In fact, as these small beads seem to have been recovered only at sites and in units that had been screened, it is probable that their actual distribution was much greater, and perhaps they were ubiquitous to almost every permanent Greek settlement of the Late Neolithic period.

Even more striking than this broad distribution pattern is the evidence that the fired steatite beads found over this wide area are remarkably uniform

Table 9.3.3. Distribution of Fired Steatite Beads

Site	Region	Number of beads
Franchthi Cave	S. Argolid	98
Kitsos Cave	Attica	132?
Halai	Phokis	250
Dhimini	Thessaly	18+
Sitagroi	E. Macedonia	25
Dilkili Tash	E. Macedonia	2

in size, form, and production method. Box plots reveal a similarity in diameter (D), thickness (TH), and perforation diameter (PD) in fired steatite beads from Sitagroi, Franchthi Cave, and Dikili Tash (figures 9.3.1–9.3.3). Further statistical testing confirms this. A t-test was used to test the null hypothesis of no significant difference between bead diameter, thickness, or perforation diameter at Franchthi, Sitagroi, and Halai. The results of these tests[8] indicated that there was no significant difference between these dimensions of the fired steatite beads from Franchthi Cave and Sitagroi (that is, the null hypothesis, Ho, could not be rejected at 0.05 confidence interval).

This similarity between the fired steatite beads from the two sites is of great interest, since they are almost 400 km apart. The most plausible explanation for this phenomenon is that the fired steatite beads found at both sites are from a single population, and thus were probably made at the same manufacturing site. We might be able to extend this hypothesis to suggest that all the fired steatite beads found at Greek mainland sites were made at the same production center, for if several production loci were involved we would not expect a uniformity in beads from such distant sites as Franchthi and Sitagroi. It is possible, then, that this one production center supplied all the fired steatite beads to all of the Late Neolithic sites in mainland Greece. Although the number of such beads I have observed is only 525 in total, it is likely that they originally numbered in the thousands, if not tens of thousands. Thus we are talking about the mass production of these small, distinctive beads.

Although no unfinished fired steatite beads or bead manufacturing debris has been identified, it is still possible to determine the approximate production process by noting the evidence on the finished

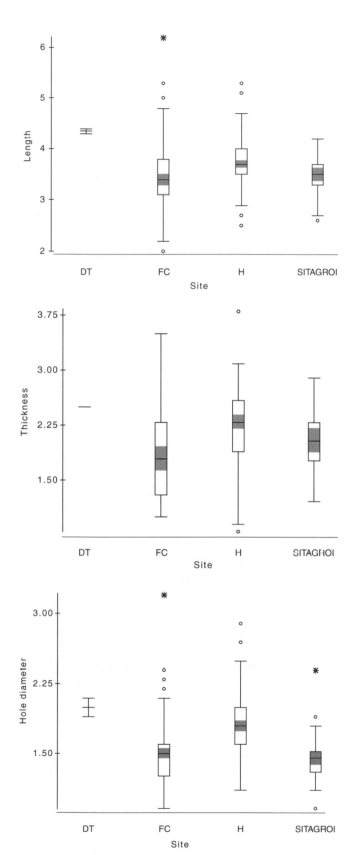

beads. It is clear, for instance, that initial stages of production were not very different from that of other small beads. Small nodules of steatite were chipped and ground to suitably flat, if irregular bead blanks. The center of each blank was then drilled, most probably using a bow drill with a flint drill bit. As indicated by the bead profiles and edge scoring, these irregular, unfinished beads were then strung together, and ground as a group, forming beads of a regular, circular form, much as the other softstone beads found at Sitagroi. However, these unmodified score marks and the extremely straight edge of the beads also indicate that, unlike the other small stone beads, the fired steatite beads were not further polished or finished off. Instead, the beads were fired.

Without locating the exact steatite used for these beads, it is difficult to determine exactly what firing temperature was achieved to turn them the distinctive white color. Preliminary experiments with the firing of common types of steatite, however, indicate that the stone must be fired at very high temperatures, perhaps as high as 1000° to 1200° Celsius to achieve this notable white coloring and distinct glossy outer layer. At lower temperatures, around 500–600°, the color of steatite is actually deepened, such that gray-green soapstone turns a dark black. Obviously a kiln would be needed to reach these high temperatures, a further indication that not only great effort and labor were devoted to the manufacture of these beads, but special equipment as well.

One obvious question is why such effort was employed to fire these beads; what was the advantage of firing? One possibility is, of course, the white color. As surveys of traditional bead-working indicate, even where colored beads are available, white is often chosen as the primary color for beaded

(Top left): Figure 9.3.1. Box plots: Diameter (length) of opaque white beads from four Greek Late Neolithic sites: Dikili Tash (DT), Franchthi Cave (FC), Halai (H), and Sitagroi.
(Middle): Figure 9.3.2. Box plots: Thickness of opaque white beads from four Greek Late Neolithic sites: Dikili Tash, Franchthi Cave, Halai, and Sitagroi.
(Bottom left): Figure 9.3.3. Box plots: Perforation diameter of opaque white beads from four Greek Late Neolithic sites: Dikili Tash, Franchthi Cave, Halai, and Sitagroi.

costumes. Often white was employed as the background color to accentuate designs made from color beads. White is also more easily seen against a dark hide or leather background. White may also have been worn especially for certain ceremonies, when the symbolism of the color was paramount.

In fact, white is the most common color in Aegean Neolithic ornaments. This includes many ornaments of shell, stone such as marble, as well as the fired steatite beads. However, marble and shell are both much harder and more difficult to work than steatite; by firing this originally soft, dark stone the Late Neolithic bead manufacturers were thus able to work a softer material and still achieve the desired white color.

The second desirable result of firing steatite is its subsequent increase in hardness. Whereas many of the unfired steatite beads of the Greek Neolithic that I observed showed pronounced use-wear, including deep grooves from stringing (plate 9.3.3), none of the fired steatite beads showed any signs of wear. This may imply that these beads were sewn or strung onto objects that would be heavily used, or were considered so very important that harder, more solid beads were desirable.

Whatever the final use of the fired steatite beads, it is clear that they were made in large numbers, that manufacturing techniques required considerable time, skill, effort, and special equipment, and that bead manufacture was concentrated in very few, if not a single production center. Note that these are all characteristics of specialized craft manufacture.

One last important detail about the trade in fired steatite beads that still deserves greater attention is exactly where they were produced. One might expect that production centers would be close to the source of the raw material, steatite, but unfortunately these sources have not yet been found. Production loci are also often identified by manufacturing debris and unfinished products. While the manufacturing debris from steatite bead production might be difficult to identify, it is interesting that no unfinished fired steatite beads have been found in Greece.

While the lack of evidence for fired steatite bead manufacture in Greece cannot prove that the beads were not of indigenous manufacture, espe-

cially considering the low rate of recovery of these small objects, some other evidence may point to an origin outside mainland Greece. One intriguing clue is the abundance of these beads found outside the Aegean. This includes very similar white beads of fired steatite, also with cylindrical profiles and heavy scoring, found at Neolithic sites in the Levant, such as a bead recently found at the Yarmoukian (Pottery Neolithic) site of Sha'ar Hagolan in the Jordan Valley of Israel (dating to the mid-sixth millennium BC), and as far as India, dating to at least the Harappan period and perhaps earlier. It is doubtful that all these beads were made in the same production center—and even visually there appears to be a difference in size among them—but the similarities among fired steatite beads from these regions is certainly worthy of further study.

Clay Beads

Clay was the most common material utilized in bead manufacture at Sitagroi (table 9.3.4). The explanation for this preference is simple. First, clay sources were undoubtedly local, and material suitable for bead manufacture could be easily obtained. For the most part, the clay used in bead production was quite fine, with minute mica and black sand inclusions, and appears similar to the fabric of the local prehistoric pottery of the plain of Drama.[9] Secondly, the plastic qualities of clay allow the production of a variety of bead forms without the tedious grinding or risky drilling required in stone or shell bead production. While many different shapes of beads were found at Sitagroi, the most popular bead type also appears to be the easiest to produce. These are flattened disc or short beads of somewhat irregular circular or elliptical plan and basically oblate section (so-called pinched beads). Almost 150 of these were found at Sitagroi. The production sequence for these beads is as follows.

STEP 1: In the first step, a minute ball of clay, often of less than a few millimeters, was produced by rolling the clay between thumb and finger. The clay was probably quite wet and plastic at this stage.

STEP 2: The ball was flattened by applying pressure between the thumb and finger. Very little care was taken to produce a smooth outer surface of the

Table 9.3.4. Beads and Pendants of Various
Materials by Phase

Raw material	I	II	III	IV	IV–V	V	X*	Total
Stone	8	19	62	4	0	0	0	93
Shell	3	75	76	7	2	5	1	169
Bone	2	2	2	0	0	0	0	6
Clay	17	11	172	5	0	2	0	207
Metal	0	1	3	0	0	0	0	4
Clay or stone	5	0	12	0	0	0	0	17
Shell or stone	0	4	17	1	0	0	0	22
Phase total	35	112	344	17	2	7	1	518

*X indicates unphased or mixed contexts.

bead, or a regular plan. Some beads were flattened to a disc, while others are almost barrel-shaped in section. One bead was never flattened at all. Often fingerprints were left on the outer surface of the clay from flattening the blank.

STEP 3: The flat disc was then pierced by a thin twig or flower stem to create a small perforation. Most often this twig was removed and probably reused, thus leaving a small ridge of clay around both sides of the resultant hole.

STEP 4: The finished beads were dried and then fired. As in the forming, little care seems to have been taken with the firing of these ornaments. Often the process produced a gray or black bead, a color not purposefully selected as other beads were only partly smudged.

The manufacture of these beads seems to have taken little time or effort. Forming each bead would have taken only seconds, while firing seems to have been haphazard and uneven. It is possible that the beads were fired in open kitchen hearths, rather than in kilns, as some beads were burnt while others seemed to have been hardly fired at all, and consequently were crumbly and highly fractured. If done in kilns, firing might have been undertaken concurrently with the firing of pottery and other terra-cotta objects. The final products, although all vaguely similar in form, vary considerably in overall size, circularity, section, amount of ridging around the perforation, and final color after firing. Thus, there seems to be little standardization of the manufacture of these clay beads, and inconsequen-

tial time, effort, or skill needed for production. It is thus probable that the producers of these flattened clay beads were not specialists, but that various Sitagroi inhabitants produced these beads, perhaps each for personal or family use. Although I cannot conclude how many clay bead producers were active at Sitagroi, we have evidence that may one day provide the answer; with the assistance of forensic experts, it may be possible to determine how many hands were responsible for the fingerprints that cover these beads.

Other clay beads seem to have been given more care in manufacture. For instance, other short beads were also made by hand-molding, but these were not as carelessly flattened, but were formed with straighter sides and regular barrel profiles. The manufacturers of these clay beads seem to have taken care not to leave a ridge around the perforation. This could have been achieved by leaving the stick in the perforation until it burnt away during firing or by forming the beads when the clay was in a drier state. In some cases a flat, slightly raised area ringing the perforation is visible, revealing how the manufacturers smoothed over the ridge that was formed when the stick was poked through the clay. Fingerprints are rare on these more carefully formed beads, and in some cases there are signs of further surface treatment, including burnishing and perhaps application of a slip. One bead of phase I (SF 1628) was "graphite-painted," much like the local pottery of that period (see figure 9.11; plate 9.9a). Some of the larger beads seem to have been manufactured by rolling a long rope of clay from which blanks of the appropriate thickness were cut and then perforated. Other large beads were molded to more unusual forms, such as biconical or concave in section. None of the clay beads found at Sitagroi, however, were truly complex in form, and all would have been rather simple to manufacture.

PENDANTS

The majority of pendants[10] are simple forms of shell and stone that could easily have been manufactured at Sitagroi, although we have no direct evidence for their production. One exquisite four-pointed star-shaped pendant (SF 4793: see figure 9.20, plate 9.11a) and two small "buttons" (SF 5223b [figure 9.18; plate 9.14a]; 5212c [figure 9.19; plate 9.8]), all probably of *Spondylus* shell, if made at the site, showcase the considerable skills of the Sitagroi shell-workers.

CONCLUSIONS

It is interesting to compare the production of the different ornament types and speculate on how ornament production was organized at Sitagroi. For instance, it is probable that the same craftspeople produced both the shell annulets and the shell beads. Although the exact manufacturing process for each product differs, there are so many similarities in the tools and skills needed for both classes of ornaments that it would be strange if these were not manufactured by the same people. In addition, the selection of primarily left valves for annulet production and right valves for bead and pendant production indicate that these activities were highly coordinated (compare Tsuneki 1989). The similarities in shell and stone bead production processes suggest that these, too, could have been manufactured by the same craftpeople. The extreme standardization in size of stone beads may indicate, however, that the production of these ornaments was limited to only a few individuals who shared tools and the "template" for stone bead dimensions.

The production of clay beads differs completely from that of shell and stone, and it is probable that these crafts were not practiced by the same people. Unlike the production of shell and stone ornaments, the manufacture of clay beads took relatively little time and effort, However, the use of the same clays and occasional surface treatment (such as graphite paint) as found in local pottery, as well as the treatment of the clay, indicating some knowledge of the plastic qualities of the material, suggest that the manufacturers of the larger and better-made clay beads may also have been the Sitagroi potters. In this case we can suppose that clay bead production was a supplementary activity for these potters.

Another major aspect of ornament production at Sitagroi that deserves closer attention is the change in production over time, as Shackleton noted for the data at his disposal. His observations can now be confirmed and elaborated by the addition of subsequent material; the results of this analysis are tabulated in tables 9.3.4 and 9.3.5.

There seems to be very little ornament production at all during the first phase of occupation at the site, with only a few beads of clay and stone found in the levels of this phase (this relative paucity of ornaments remains even if we account for the smaller volume of soil excavated for this phase).[11] As first pointed out by Shackleton (appendix 9.1), it is particularly apparent that ornaments were not manufactured from marine shell during this phase, and it seems that Sitagroi inhabitants did not exploit the coastal environment until phase II, when we note an overall blossoming of ornament production at Sitagroi. Interestingly, during this phase clay bead production remains an inconsequential activity, but by phase III clay beads have become the dominant ornament class. This may

Table 9.3.5. Modified Whole Shells Used as Ornaments by Phase

Shell species	II	III	III?	IV	IV?	V	X*	Total
Cockle	1	1	0	1	0	0	0	3
Columbella	0	1	0	0	0	0	0	1
Dentalia	23	42	1	9	1	0	0	76
Glycymeris	4	50	0	1	0	2	1	58
Cowry	0	0	0	0	0	1	0	1
Neritea	0	3	0	0	0	0	0	3
Donax	1	0	0	0	0	0	0	1
Murex	1	0	0	1	0	0	0	2
Phase total	30	97	1	12	1	3	1	145

* X indicates unphased or mixed contexts.

reflect an increased demand for ornaments, and thus an increased emphasis on clay beads which could be produced much more rapidly and easily than those of shell and stone. Overall, it is apparent that ornaments of almost all types are produced in the greatest numbers in phase III, when ornament quantities almost triple from the previous period.

Yet the developments from phase II to III do not only indicate an increase in ornament production activities, but also suggests significant changes in the organization of ornament production. One important change is in the exploitation of *Spondylus* shell. While the numbers of beads manufactured from *Spondylus* shell seem to decrease from phase II to III, the quantity of annulets produced from this shell increased significantly during this period. This is associated with an apparent increase in preference for the utilization of *Spondylus* shell over *Glycymeris* shell for annulet manufacture during phase III (table 9.3.2). At the same time, during the later phase, more whole *Glycymeris* shells are perforated at the umbo and perhaps worn as pendants (table 9.3.5). Altogether, these changes indicate an increasing standardization in shell exploitation, with *Spondylus* selected primarily for annulet production and *Glycymeris* modified in other ways. Such standardization may be associated with increased specialization in shell ornament production. At the same time, the explosion in clay bead manufacture may reflect an increasing demand for ornamentation in the Sitagroi community, wherein the limited and controlled supply of the more difficult to produce shell and stone beads was supplemented by expedient clay bead production. There appears to be a dramatic drop-off in ornament production at Sitagroi after the Neolithic period; the quantity of ornaments found in levels of EBA phases IV and V is almost inconsequential. Although one could thus conclude that ornament production practically ceased in the Bronze Age, a substantial problem is that the later soils were not water-sieved. Thus, instead of indicating a genuine change in ornament production at Sitagroi, these numbers indicate the importance of sieving for the recovery of these and other small finds.

This study of ornament production at Sitagroi adds important dimensions to the analysis of a largely ignored class of artifacts. It is worth noting again that it is primarily because fine water-sieving was employed in several areas of the Sitagroi excavation that we have the physical remains—minute objects and fine debris—that have facilitated the study of ornament production at the site. I therefore express the hope that the studies offered in this volume will encourage further analysis of these "small finds" as well as promote the more careful recovery of the evidence we need for continued research in prehistoric ornamentation.

NOTES

1 Bangles are circlets of a single material that can be worn around a human appendage (arm or leg). Ethnography points to the use of many such bangles as bracelets, and I have retained the word here when such use has been attested. Since we cannot know for certain how the Sitagroi ornaments were worn, I prefer to identify them by the descriptive terms annulet or circlet.

2 As discussed above, today it is difficult to obtain fresh *Spondylus gaederopus* shells of suitable size for annulet manufacture. I conducted initial experiments using large specimens found on beaches or near archaeological sites. These older shells consistently broke during the chipping stages of manufacture. I then conducted experiments with the fresh shells of *Spondylus princeps*, a species of *Spondylus* from the Gulf of Mexico that achieves a large size similar to *S. gaederopus* but has different coloring and pattern of spines. Experiments using *S. princeps* were successful, but due to differences in the structure of these shells, I have considered the times of experiments only approximate.

3 Note that numbers of ornaments in this appendix refer to those finds I was able to personally analyze in the autumn of 1994. Unfortunately, a considerable amount of mixing and attrition of finds and labels occurred in the thirty years since the material was first excavated and registered, especially as the finds from Sitagroi had recently been moved from the museum at Philippi, where they had first been stored, to a new museum in Drama. It is, in fact, a testimony to the organization of the project and the patience of the editors of this volume that I was able to identify the majority of ornaments.

4 Note that the numbers in table 9.3.2 do not correspond to those in Shackleton's table 9.1.1 (appendix 9.1). Table 9.3.2 lists the shell species used only for annulet fragments, while Shackleton's table includes all *Spondylus* annulet fragments and all worked *Glycymeris* fragments. Elsewhere in my study I have recorded the "modified whole shell" (see table 9.3.5) which comprises a total of 58 *Glycymeris* shells. Only two of these (both of phase II) are possibly unfinished annulets; both have ground holes at the umbo and ground ventral edges and may thus be in the initial stage of annulet manufacture. All the other *Glycymeris* recorded as modified whole shell (most of phase III) have natural or partly ground holes at the umbo and were probably used as pendants. Any additional discrepancies between Shackleton's

data and my own is due to the 20-year span between our two studies, and the attrition in data.

[5] Average thickness of annulets from left valve at the hinge: 11.0 mm (n = 49; SD = 3.5)

Average thickness of annulets from right valve at the hinge: 29.5 mm (n = 16; SD = 13.0)

Average thickness of annulets from left valve at ventral margin: 3.6 mm (n = 61; SD = 1.9)

Average thickness of annulets from right valve at ventral margin: 22.7 mm (n = 3; SD = 4.8)

[6] The thickness of finished stone beads ranges from 0.7 to 3.3 mm, with a mean of 1.8, and standard deviation of 0.5 mm.

[7] A general term for a softstone, otherwise known as talc or steatite.

[8] Results of Pooled T-Test: Fired Steatite Bead Diameters from Sitagroi and Franchthi Cave:

Individual alpha level: 0.05

Ho: $\mu1-\mu2 = 0$ Ha: $\mu1-\mu2 \neq 0$ TH - TH :

Test Ho: $\mu(TH)-\mu(TH) = 0$ vs. Ha: $\mu(TH)-\mu(TH) \neq 0$

Difference between Means = -0.3548, t-Statistic = -4.704 w/218 df

Reject Ho at Alpha = 0.05; $p \leq 0.0001$

[9] I thank Zoi Tsirtsoni for this information.

[10] I define bead-pendants (beads) as pendants with a central hole and circular plan. All other ornaments with suspension hole are defined as non-bead pendants (pendants).

[11] The approximate volumes of soil excavated (in cu. m) for each phase are as follows. I: 60; II: 110; III: 130; IV: 90; V: 350 (see table 8.1 in volume 1:222).

Appendix 9.4
Catalog of Items of Adornment

Marianna Nikolaidou

Under phase headings, the catalog is ordered by type of artifact (bead, pendant, bracelet/amulet, pin, plaque, ring), and includes the following information (if available or applicable): small find number and context; published illustrations; quantity; shape; raw material (bone or shell species); description; surface: texture, color, and/or decoration; technical information; measurements. All beads and pendants are perforated.

An "r" after the ZB context and level number indicates recovery in the special water-sieving project of Sebastian Payne (1975); and "s" (after the ZB context and level number) refers to the sieving project undertaken on the mound.

Comments followed by initials MM, NS, ZT, and TW refer to Michele Miller, Nicholas Shackleton, Zoi Tsirtsoni, and Thomas Wake. The species identification of shell artifacts was made by Nicholas Shackleton. Graphs of assorted beads have been subdivided alphabetically in order of raw material. Within each subgroup they are ordered by type. Measurements are in centimeters.

- *Beads:* Small find number and context; quantity; shape; raw material; surface: texture, color and/or decoration; technical information if available; measurements if available. All beads are perforated.

- *Pendants:* Small find number and context; raw material or shell species; description; surface: texture, color and/or decoration; measurements, if available. All pendants are perforated.

- *Bracelet/annulet:* Small find number and context; raw material or shell species; description; surface: texture, color and/or decoration; technical information if available; measurements.

- *Pins:* Small find number and context; raw material or bone species; description; surface: texture, color and/or decoration; measurements.

- *Plaques:* Small find number and context; bone species; description; measurements.

- *Rings:* Small find number and context; one artifact has been so classified and description follows the usual system.

PHASE I

Beads

- 1628   ML 45; figure 9.11; plate 9.9a
  1 biconical; clay; surface: matt, dark gray/buff; decoration: graphite-painted (MM, ZT)
  L: 2.7; D: 1.3; HD: 0.015

- 5225(a) ZA 63s
  2 cylinders, narrow (1 fragmentary); shell; surface: buff/white
  D: 0.2–0.5
  1 cylinder, wide; shell; surface: naturally grooved, buff
  D: 0.6

- 5225(b) ZA 63s
  12 cylinders, narrow (1 fragmentary); stone; surface: 1 red, 11 gray
  D: 0.3–0.6
  2 biconical (1 fragmentary); stone; surface: dark gray
  D: 0.7

- 5226(a) ZA 64s
  1 pinched; clay; surface: gray
  D: 0.4–0.5

- 5226(b) ZA 64s
  2 cylinders, wide (fragmentary); shell; surface: white/buff

- 5226(c) ZA 64s
  4 cylinders, narrow; stone; surface: 3 gray, 1 red
  D: 0.3–0.4

5227 ZA 65s
2 cylinders, narrow; clay or stone (MM); surface: 1 red, 1 orange
D: 0.35–0.45

5343 ZA 61s
8 cylinders, narrow (1 fragmentary); stone; surface: 7 green/gray, 1 red
D: 0.3–0.4
1 cylinder, wide; stone; surface: dark gray
D: 0.6

Pendants

113 JL 12; figure 9.23a; plate 9.11d
Ring-shaped fragment; stone; wedge-like in section, small protuberance carved on outer perimeter of circlet; surface: smooth, shiny, green; interior: matt
L: 3.0; W: 1.1; Th: 0.5

1441 ZA 60
Glycymeris; perforated; ground perforation; surface: some brown color preserved
L: 2.0; D: 2.1; H: 0.7

2530 JL 104; plate 9.19a
Mytilus fragment; perforated; biconically drilled perforation; edges worked
L: 3.4; W: 2.9; H: 0.2

Bracelets/Annulets

2518 JL 102; plate 9.2b
Spondylus fragment; perforated
L: 6.3; W: 5.65; Th. 0.15

3556 KL 151
Spondylus fragment; surface: polished, some orange color with gray encrustation
L: 5.3; W: 1.1; Th: 1.1

3681 KLb 133; figure 9.3; plate 9.1b
Marble fragment; surface: white with dark encrustation
L: 4.3; W: 1.1

5271 ZA 65s
Spondylus fragment
L: 3.2

Pins

4112 KLb 137; figures 2.5a, 9.27; plate 2.5a
Bone; split, straight-sided, upper part is flat and relatively broad, narrows toward top; surface: highly polished, yellow
L: 11.7; W: 0.2–1.0; Th: 0.4

Plaques

923 ZA 77; plate 9.27c
Bone fragment; rectangular, perforation near one end; surface: polished
L: 4.3; W: 1.3; Th: 0.7

PHASE II

Beads

3674 ZG 35; figure 9.21
1 miscellaneous: platelet of roughly rectangular shape with one undulating and three straight sides; bone; small, drilled perforation; surface: yellowish, incisions on one face
L: 3.1; W: 2.3; Th: 0.5; HD: 0.015

4793 ZA 51; figure 9.20; plate 9.11a
1 miscellaneous: "star-shaped," with four pointed branches projecting from a discoid body; *Spondylus* (MM); surface: white
W: 3.2; Th: 0.6; HD: 0.3

5081 ZB 131r
2 cylinder, narrow; stone; surface: 1 green, 1 white
D: 0.4

5082 ZB 131r
1 cylinder, narrow; shell (MM); surface: white
L: 0.2; D: 0.6

5202 ZA 52s
19 cylinders, narrow; *Spondylus*; surface: white/buff, some naturally grooved;
D: 0.3–0.6
8 cylinders, wide; *Spondylus*; surface: buff, naturally grooved;
D: 0.5–0.7

5203 ZA 52s; plate 9.13
22 *Dentalium* tubular; surface: white/buff
L: 0.3–1.9; D: 0.1–0.4

5204 ZA 52s
10 cylinders, narrow; stone; surface: 6 gray, 2 green, 1 black, 1 buff
D: 0.3–0.5

5205(a) ZA 52s
14 cylinders, narrow (fragmentary); shell; surface: white/buff
11 cylinders, wide; shell; surface: 7 buff, 3 white, 1 gray
1 *Dentalium* tubular; surface: white/buff
L: 0.7; D: 0.15

5205(b) ZA 52s
1 cylinder, tubular (fragmentary); stone; surface: dark gray
L: 1.15; D: 0.4

1 irregular fragment; marble; surface: white
W: 0.65
1 miscellaneous: oval fragment; marble; surface:
white
D: 0.18

5206 ZA 52s
4 cylinder, narrow; shell; surface: white
D: 0.35–0.4
3 cylinder, wide; shell; surface: white/buff
D: 0.4–0.7

5207 ZA 52s
2 cylinders, wide; clay (MM); surface: dark gray
D: 0.4
1 pinched; clay; surface: gray
D: 0.4–0.7
1 barrel; clay (MM); concave sides; surface: dark
gray
D: 0.7

5208 ZA 52s
10 cylinders, narrow; soft stone (MM); surface: dark
orange
D: 0.35–0.45

5209 ZA 52s
5 cylinders, narrow; shell or stone (MM); surface:
white
D: 0.35

5221(a) ZA 55s
4 cylinder, narrow; shell; surface: white.
D: 0.3–1.9
2 cylinders, wide (1 fragmentary); shell; surface: 1
white, 1 buff
D: 0.5
1 *Dentalium* tubular; surface: white.
L: 0.7; D: 0.6

5221(b) ZA 55s
3 cylinder, narrow; stone; surface: dark gray
D: 0.4–0.5
1 cylinder, wide; stone; surface: green/gray
D: 0.6
1 cylinder, tubular; stone; surface: dark gray
L: 1.15; D: 0.4

5224 ZA 58s
3 cylinders, narrow; shell; surface: white/buff
D: 0.35–0.55

5262 ZA 52s; plate 9.2.2
6 irregular (2 fragmentary); *Spondylus*; surface: naturally grooved, buff; unfinished (MM)
D: 0.8–0.11

5335 ZA 55s
1 miscellaneous: 2 fragments, 1 perforated; copper
L: 0.2–0.3; D: 0.3–0.5

5336 ZA 52s; figure 8.3a; plate 8.2b
1 cylinder, narrow; copper; slightly asymmetric,
well made (see chapter 8)
L: 0.2; D: 0.3; HD: 0.015

Pendants

299 KL 2
Elongated; stone; thin, rectangular form with one
narrow edge curved and perforated, one surface
flat, the other slightly convex; surface: matt, light
gray/brown with shiny flakes
L: 5.8; W: 2.6; Th: 0.9–1.2

415 KL 2; plate 9.23b
Ring-shaped; *Murex* (TW); central part of the whorl
has been ground to an oval form that incorporates
both apices of the spiral; surface: polished and/or
beach worn
L: 4.0

2301 KL 106; figure 9.23b
Leaf-shaped plaque ("pectoral"); marble; convex in
section, with one end pointed and the other cut
straight; two small perforations (one of them
incompletely drilled) on either side near the flat
(upper?) edge.
L: 7.3; W: 5.8; Th: 1.1

2839 KL 111; figure 9.24
Elongated; bone; thin rectangular form, one narrow
edge straight and with drilled perforation, the other
slightly curved and partly broken; one surface flat,
the other slightly convex; surface: top and edges
smoothed
L: 6.3; W: 2.1; Th: 0.5; HD: 0.5

2886 KM 17; plate 9.19b
Perforated *Mytilus*; edges worked; surface: reddish
L: 5.3

2887 KL 106; plate 9.15b
Perforated *Glycymeris*; possibly drilled at umbo
D: 4.8

2889 KM 16; plate 9.18
Perforated *Cardium*; perforation at umbo produced
by surface grinding
D: 3.2

5265(a) ZA 52s
Perforated *Glycymeris*
D: 1.5–3.0

5265(b) ZA 52s
Perforated *Glycymeris*
D: 1.5–3.0

5265(c) ZA 52s
Perforated *Columbella*
D: 0.9

5265(d) ZA 52s
Perforated *Glycymeris*
D: 1.5–3.0

5268 ZA 55s
Perforated *Glycymeris*
D: 1.5

5589 ZA 50
Perforated *Glycymeris*
D: 2.2

Bracelets/Annulets

248 ZA 52
Spondylus fragment; surface: polished, whitish
L: 4.7; W: 3.4; Th: 1.5

250 ZA 52
Spondylus fragment; surface: white with natural red markings
L: 6.2; W: 0.7; Th: 0.1

288 KL 2
Spondylus fragment
L: 3.2; W: 1.0; Th: 0.3

408(a) KM 2
Spondylus fragment; surface: heavy grain observable
L: 5.2; W: 0.1

408(b) KM 2
Spondylus fragment; surface: pink marking
L: 4.0; W: 0.8

453 KL 2
Spondylus fragment; surface: pink/cream
L: 2.2; W: 1.5

454 KM 2
Spondylus fragment; surface: rose with darker red markings
L: 4.8; W: 0.9

724 ML 17
Glycymeris fragment; ground edge
L: 4.6; W: 1.1; Th: 0.4

910 ZA 57
Glycymeris fragment
L: 4.8; W: 0.6; Th: 0.3

912 ZA 57
Glycymeris fragment
L: 4.1; W: 0.7; Th: 0.4

976(a) KM 20
Spondylus fragment; surface: black encrustation
L: 3.6; W: 1.7; Th: 1.0

976(b) KM 20; plate 9.2c
Spondylus fragment; surface: black encrustation
L: 6.7

1444 KM 2
Glycymeris fragment; surface: polished, amber-white with gray encrustation
L: 4.5; W: 1.2; Th: 0.4

2305 KL 106
Glycymeris fragment; surface: brown veins
L: 4.0; W: 0.5; Th: 0.3

2364 KL 113; plate 9.2.1g
Spondylus fragment; partially ground, worked preform (MM)
L: 4.9; W: 3.8; Th: 0.5

2605 KL 114
Glycymeris fragment; perforation at umbo
L: 4.0

2611 KL 114
Glycymeris fragment
L: 5.2; W: 1.1; Th: 0.5

2631 KL 116
Spondylus fragment
L: 4.8; W: 1.0

2663 KL 117
Glycymeris fragment
D: 4.5–5.0

3659 ZG 39; plate 9.2.1b
Spondylus valve fragment; worked preform (MM)
L: 5.0

3734 ZG 34; plate 9.2.1h
Spondylus valve; fragmentary preserved hinge; surface: red lines near edge; worked preform in an advanced stage of manufacture (MM)
L: 5.7; W: 4.0; Th: 1.3

4227 ZE 96
Spondylus fragment; surface: some red color preserved
L: 4.7; W: 1.2; Th: 0.5

4263 ZJ 44
Spondylus fragment; unfinished with two perforations incompletely drilled
L: 6.3; W: 3.0; Th: 1.6

4502 KL 115
Spondylus fragment
L: 3.5; W: 1.6; Th: 0.9

4747 ZG 42
Spondylus fragment
L: 6.4; W: 1.5; Th: 1.5

5190 ZB 131r
Spondylus fragment
L: 2.0

5263(a) ZA 52s
Spondylus fragment
L: 3.0

5263(b) ZA 52s
Spondylus fragment
L: 3.5

5266 ZA 55s
Spondylus fragment
L: 2.5

5321 ZA 52s; figure 9.4; plate 9.1a
Marble fragment; triangular in section
L: 2.6; Th: 1.8; D: 7.0

5345 ZA 53s
Glycymeris valve fragment
L: 3.1; W: 1.2; Th: 0.2

5605 ML 10; plate 9.2.1a
Spondylus fragment; worked preform (MM)
L: 6.4; W: 2.5

Pins

247 ZA 52
Bone; slender shaft, broadens toward head; surface: polished
L: 7.4; W: 0.1–0.8

472 ZA 52
Bone; slender, straight shaft; surface: polished
L: 5.8; W: 0.2–0.6

3752 ZE 93
Bone; breakage at head; slender, straight shaft, broadens toward head; surface: light brown
L: 6.9; D: 0.3–0.7

4555 KL 117
Bone; both ends broken; slender shaft, slightly tapering toward tip; surface: smooth, gray/yellow
L: 6.7; W: 0.4–0.7

Plaques

1705 KM 20; plate 9.27d
Rib; both ends broken; flattened, top and edges worked; large perforation in the center, and remains of a smaller one on broken edge
L: 3.7; W: 1.8; Th: 0.5; HD: 0.9

PHASE III

Beads

499 ZA 47s
1 cylinder, narrow; shell (MM); surface: white
D: 0.5

522 ZA 47s
1 pinched fragment; clay; surface: striated, gray
D: 0.4

523 ZA 47s
1 cylinder, narrow (fragmentary); *Spondylus* (MM); surface: white/red
D: 0.7

781 ZA 47s
1 cylinder, disc (fragmentary); copper; probably half-made bead (see chapter 8)
L: 0.1; D: 0.3

783 ZA 47s; figure 8.1d; plate 8.3a
1 cylinder, narrow; copper; unperforated (see chapter 8)
L: 0.2; D: 0.4

785 ZA 47s
1 segmented; clay (MM); surface: dark gray
L: 0.8; D: 0.4

786 ZA 47s
9 pinched (1 fragmentary); clay; surface: striated, 8 gray, 1 buff
H: 0.3; D: 0.7

787 ZA 47s
1 cylinder, narrow; clay; surface: buff
L: 0.8; D: 1.3

788(a) ZA 47s
2 cylinders, narrow; marble; surface: white
L: 0.2–0.5; D: 0.5–1.2

788(b) ZA 47s
1 cylinder, narrow; shell or stone (MM)

789 ZA 47s
4 cylinders, narrow; stone; surface: red/orange
D: 0.35–0.5

790 ZA 47s
15 cylinders, narrow; stone; surface: green/gray
D: 0.3–0.4

791 ZA 47s
5 cylinders, narrow; stone; surface: 4 green/gray, 1 mottled green/yellow.
L: 0.4; D: 0.3–0.5
1 cylinder, wide; stone; surface: green.
L: 0.4; D: 0.4

792 ZA 47s
7 cylinders; soft stone, 3 maybe clay or stone (MM); surface: dark gray
L: 0.3; D: 0.2–0.4

793 ZA 47s
15 cylinders, narrow (4 fragmentary); shell; surface: white/buff
D: 0.3–0.4
1 cylinder, wide; shell; surface: buff
D: 0.5

794 ZA 47s
1 cylinder, narrow; stone; surface: brown

D: 0.35
1 cylinder, wide; stone; surface: brown/gray
D: 0.4

795 ZA 47s
1 *Dentalium* tubular; surface: buff
L: 0.6; D: 0.3

796 ZA 47s; figure 9.10
2 irregular; *Spondylus*; roughly triangular; surface: naturally grooved, buff
L: 0.8–0.95; W: 0.45–0.5; Th: 0.2–0.35; HD: 0.015

797 ZA 47s
1 biconical (?) fragment; shell or stone (MM); preserved part is a hollow, domed cone, perforated at the top; surface: buff
H: 0.4; D: 0.7

1102 ZA 47s
7 *Dentalium* tubular fragments; surface: buff/gray
L: 0.6–2.0; D: 0.15–0.3

1219 ML 112; figure 9.12; plate 9.11c
1 biconical; clay; decoration: incised spirals
H: 1.7; D: 1.7; HD: 0.15

1274 MM 51; plate 9.9d
1 cylinder, narrow; clay; surface: dark gray
L: 1.2; D: 1.1

2292 ZA 46
1 pinched fragment; clay; surface: striated, gray
H: 0.2; D: 0.5

3415 MM 60
1 cylinder, narrow; shell or marble (MM); surface: very smooth, white
L: 0.7; D: 1.0

3823 MMb 63; plates 9.10, 9.11b
1 cylinder, wide; shell (MM); surface: gray/buff veined
L: 1.3; D: 0.55

3828 MMb 63
1 cylinder, wide; shell; surface: pale cream
L: 1.3; D: 0.6

3833 MMc 65; plate 9.9b
1 barrel; clay; surface: matt, dark gray/buff
L: 1.4; D: 0.65

4802 ZA 47s; figure 9.22; plate 2.20c
1 miscellaneous: pig astragalus
L: 2.5; W: 1.7; Th: 1.4; HD: 0.5

4803 ZB 125r
1 cylinder, narrow; gold; annular shape made of thin band, oblong in section, with joining ends (see chapter 8)
L: 0.35; Th: 0.15; D: 0.52; HD: 0.35

5063 ZB 110r
1 spherical; clay; roughly modeled; surface: gray
D: 0.5

5064 ZB 111r
2 cylinders, narrow; stone; surface: 1 gray, 1 mottled green/yellow
D: 0.4

5065(a) ZB 112r
1 cylinder, narrow; *Cerastoderma edule* (MM); surface: buff; unfinished (MM)
D: 0.5
1 *Dentalium* tubular; surface: white
L: 0.5; D: 0.3

5065(b) ZB 112r
2 cylinders, narrow; stone; surface: 1 buff, 1 green/gray
D: 0.5

5066(a) ZB 113r
1 cylinder, tubular; *Cerastoderma edule* (MM); surface: white.
L: 1.0; D: 0.3

5066(b) ZB 113r
2 cylinders, narrow; stone; surface: 1 light buff, 1 mottled.
D: 0.4–0.45

5067(a) ZB 116r
1 cylinder, narrow; clay; surface: gray
D: 0.5
1 pinched; clay; surface: gray

5067(b) ZB 116r
1 *Dentalium* tubular; surface: white.
L: 1.2; D: 0.3

5067(c) ZB 116r
2 cylinders, narrow; stone; surface: 1 dark gray, 1 red
D: 0.4

5068(a) ZB 117r
1 cylinder, wide (fragmentary); shell; surface: buff

5068(b) ZB 117r
1 cylinder, narrow; stone; surface: dark gray
D: 0.4
1 cylinder, wide; stone; surface: light gray
D: 0.8

5069(a) ZB 118r
2 pinched; clay; surface: 1 buff, 1 gray
1 barrel; clay; surface: dark gray
L: 0.6; D: 0.3

5069(b) ZB 118r
1 cylinder, tubular; shell; surface: white
L: 1.0; D: 0.2

5069(c) ZB 118r
2 cylinders, narrow; stone; surface: 1 white marble, 1 dark gray
D: 0.4–0.8

5070(a) ZB 119r
1 pinched; clay; surface: buff

5070(b) ZB 119r
1 *Dentalium* tubular; surface: yellow/white
L: 0.9; D: 0.3

5070(c) ZB 119r
2 cylinders, narrow; stone; surface: 1 gray, 1 red.
D: 0.35–0.4

5071 ZB 120r
2 cylinders, narrow; stone; surface: 1 gray, 1 white
D: 0.4–0.5
1 cylinder, wide; stone; surface: dark gray
L: 0.6; D: 0.25

5072 ZB 121r
1cylinder, narrow; soft stone; surface: mottled green
D: 0.45
1 irregular fragment; soft stone; roughly trapezoidal; surface: green/brown
W: 0.9

5073 ZB 122r
1 cylinder, narrow; shell; surface: buff
D: 0.3
2 *Dentalium* tubular; surface: white
L: 1.3; D: 0.1–0.3

5074(a) ZB 123r
1 cylinder, narrow; clay; surface: dark gray
D: 0.3
1 cylinder, wide; clay; surface: dark gray
D: 0.5
1 pinched; clay; surface: gray

5074(b) ZB 123r
1 barrel; *Spondylus* (MM); surface: buff
L: 0.6; D: 0.45

5075 ZB 124r
1 cylinder, narrow; soft stone; surface: mottled yellow/green
D: 0.4

5076(a) ZB 125r; figure 9.7
1 cylinder, narrow; clay; somewhat irregularly modeled; surface: gray; figure 9.6d
L: 0.4; D: 0.75; HD: 0.25
6 pinched; clay; surface: 4 buff, 2 gray; figure 9.6c
H: 0.4; D: 0.55; HD: 0.015

5076(b) ZB 125r; figure 9.7
1 cylinder, wide (fragmentary); *Spondylus* (MM); surface: buff
D: 0.5

1 cylinder, tubular; *Spondylus* (MM); surface: white
L: 2.4; D: 0.3
1 cylinder, disc; *Spondylus* (MM); surface: buff; figure 9.6b
L: 0.2; D: 0.6; HD: 0.015

5076(c) ZB 125r; figure 9.7
1 cylinder, wide; stone; surface: light gray
D: 0.55
1 cylinder, tubular; stone; surface: dark gray
L: 0.7; D: 0.3
1 irregular; stone; wedge-shaped, eccentric perforation; surface: light buff; figure 9.6a
L: 1.1; W: 0.8; Th: 0.2–0.35; HD: 0.25

5077(a) ZB 126r; figure 9.4; plate 9.9
3 pinched; clay; surface: 1 buff, 2 gray
1 biconical; clay; asymmetric, with one cone higher and narrower, "ridge" modeled around diameter; surface: gray; figure 9.13; plate 9.9c.
H: 1.0; D: 0.4; HD: 0.02

5077(b) ZB 126r
1 biconical (?) fragment; shell; preserved part is a hollow, domed cone, perforated at the top; surface: buff
D: 0.5

5077(c) ZB 126r
4 cylinders, narrow; stone; surface: mottled green/white/yellow
D: 0.4–0.5
1 cylinder, wide; stone; surface: dark gray
L: 1.2; D: 0.5

5078 ZB 127r
1 pinched; clay; surface: buff

5079(a) ZB 128r
3 pinched; clay; surface: 2 gray, 1 buff

5079(b) ZB 128r
1 irregular fragment; stone; roughly cylindrical; surface: green/gray
D: 0.6

5080(a) ZB 130r
1 cylinder, narrow; clay; surface: gray.
D: 0.45

5080(b) ZB 130r; plate 9.14b
1 barrel; *Spondylus* (MM); surface: white
L: 1.0; D: 0.65

5154 ZB 126r
1 irregular; *Cerastoderma edule* (MM); surface: buff; unfinished (MM)
D: 1.0

5210 ZA 44s; figure 9.9; plate 9.12
25 pinched; clay; surface: striated, 22 gray, 3 buff
H: 0.2–0.25; D: 0.55; HD: 0.055

5211   ZA 44s
10 *Dentalium* tubular; surface: white/buff
L: 0.25–1.5; D: 0.15–0.3

5212(a) ZA 44s; figure 9.19; plate 9.8
7 pinched; clay; surface: 4 buff, 3 gray
1 spherical; clay; roughly modeled; surface: gray
D: 0.5

5212(b) ZA 44s; plate 9.8
8 cylinders, narrow; 7 shell, 1 mother-of-pearl; surface: 7 white (shell), 1 buff
D: 0.2–0.5
2 cylinders, wide; shell; surface: 1 grooved, buff, 1 gray/buff
L: 0.7; D: 0.5 (gray/buff bead)
1 "button"; probably *Spondylus* (MM); rectangular pyramidal, V-shaped perforation through the top; surface: light buff; figure 9.19
H: 0.45; W: 0.8; HD: 0.25

5212(c) ZA 44s; plate 9.8
36 cylinders, narrow; stone; surface: 11 gray, 8 mottled, 7 green/gray, 4 white marble, 4 red, 2 white
D: 0.2–0.7
1 cylinder, wide; marble; surface: white
D: 0.8

5213(a) ZA 44s
22 pinched (21 fragmentary); clay; surface; 20 gray (1 complete), 2 buff

5213(b) ZA 44s
1 cylinder, narrow (fragmentary); shell; surface: white
5 cylinders, wide (fragmentary); shell; surface: 4 white/buff, 1 naturally grooved, buff
L: 1.3; D: 0.55 (grooved bead)
1 barrel fragment; shell; surface: naturally grooved, gray
L: 1.4; D: 0.55

5213(c) ZA 44s
1 cylinder, wide (fragmentary); marble; surface: white
L: 0.8, D: 0.7
2 cylinders; stone; surface: 1 gray, 1 white marble
D: 0.45–0.9
2 irregular fragments; marble; surface: white
D: 0.8–0.9

5214   ZA 45s
10 *Dentalium* tubular; surface: white
L: 0.2–2.2; D: 0.1–0.45

5215   ZA 45s
2 cylinders, narrow; 1 *Spondylus*, 1 *Cerastoderma edule* (MM); surface: 1 white, 1 buff
D: 0.3–0.6

5216   ZA 45s
12 cylinders, narrow; clay (MM); surface: gray
D: 0.3–0.4

5217   ZA 45s
4 cylinders, narrow; stone; surface: 2 brown, 1 red, 1 white
D: 0.3–0.4

5218   ZA 45s
8 pinched; clay; surface: gray

5219   ZA 45s
4 pinched; clay; surface: buff

5220(a) ZA 45s
14 pinched; clay; surface: 11 gray, 3 buff
D: 0.5–0.6

5220(b) ZA 45s
2 cylinders, wide; 1 *Spondylus*, 1 unidentifiable species (MM); surface: 1 white, 1 orange

5220(c) ZA 45s
1 cylinder, narrow (fragmentary); stone; surface: green
D: 0.5
1 cylinder, wide; marble or shell (MM); surface: white
D: 0.6

5222(a) ZA 46s
13 pinched (9 fragmentary); clay; surface: gray

5222(b) ZA 46s
1 *Dentalium* tubular; surface: buff
L: 0.7; D: 0.2
1 cylinder, wide (fragmentary); shell; surface: white

5222(c) ZA 46s
3 cylinders, narrow; stone; surface: gray
D: 0.2–0.35
1 irregular fragment; marble; roughly trapezoidal; surface: white
W: 0.9

5223(a) ZA 48s; figure 9.18; plate 9.14a
1 pinched; clay; surface: gray

5223(b) ZA 48s
2 cylinders, narrow; shell; surface: 1 white, 1 buff
D: 0.3–0.5
3 cylinders, wide (1 fragmentary); shell; surface: naturally grooved, buff
D: 0.5–0.6
4 *Dentalium* tubular; surface: buff/white
L: 0.6–1.0; D: 0.2–0.3
1 "button"; *Spondylus*; rectangular pyramidal, V-shaped perforation through the top; surface: naturally grooved, buff; figure 9.18; plate 9.14a
H: 0.6; W: 0.8; HD: 0.025

5223(c) ZA 48s; figure 9.16
3 cylinders, narrow; stone; surface: 2 gray, 1 mottled gray/white
D: 0.35–0.45
2 cylinders, wide; stone; surface: 1 light gray, 1 dark gray
D: 0.5–0.6
2 segmented; stone; surface: 1 gray, 1 buff; figure 9.15
L: 0.9; D: 0.25; HD: 0.05

5254 ZA 44s
1 irregular fragment; *Spondylus*; surface: buff
W: 0.6

5261 ZA 48s
1 irregular fragment; *Spondylus*; surface: buff
W: 0.7

5334 ZA 44s
1 miscellaneous fragment; copper? (see chapter 8)

5340 ZB 125r; plate 8.3b
1 cylinder, wide (fragmentary); copper (see chapter 8)
L: 0.4; D: 0.3

5574 ZB 118r
2 irregular; *Spondylus*; surface: buff
W: 0.8

5575 ZB 112r
1 irregular fragment; *Spondylus*; surface: buff
W: 0.8

Pendants

80 ML 2; plate 9.16
Perforated *Glycymeris*; surface: rose color with encrustation
D: 3.2; H: 1.10

379 MM 20
Perforated *Glycymeris*
D: 1.7–1.8; H: 0.6

387 MM 21
Perforated *Cardium*; crude perforation
D: 5.0; H: 2.0

778(a) ZA 47s
Perforated *Neritea*
L: 1.8; H: 0.7

778(b) ZA 47s; plate 9.17b
Perforated *Glycymeris*
D: 2.2; H: 0.8

778(c) ZA 47s; plate 9.17a
Perforated *Glycymeris*
D: 1.5; H: 0.5

778(d) ZA 47s
Perforated *Glycymeris*
D: 0.7; H: 0.3

778(e) ZA 47s
Perforated *Glycymeris*
D: 1.4; H: 0.8

778(f) ZA 47s
Perforated shell fragment
L: 0.6; H: 0.3

779 ZA 47s; plate 9.21
Neritea; perforated near edge with large irregular hole (for food extraction and suspension?)
L: 1.4; W: 1.2; Th: 0.7

1108 ML 107; figure 9.25a; plate 9.25
Polygonal; clay; composite rhomboid/trapezoidal form, well-modeled, with finished edges; surface: smooth, red; decoration: wavy stripes painted diagonally across the body; core: rough, light gray
H: 4.3; W: 3.4; Th: 1.8; HD: 0.35

1483 MM 12; figure 9.25b
Clay fragment; prismatic, square in section with rounded base, perforated at broken end; surface: smooth, buff/charcoal; core: coarse, red; medium temper; well-fired
H: 3.9; W: 1.9

2894 MM 43
Perforated *Glycymeris*; ground perforation
D: 2.4

2895 MM 49
Perforated *Glycymeris*; ground perforation
D: 3.4

2896 ZA 47
Perforated *Glycymeris*; ground perforation
D: 2.2

2897 MM 27
Perforated *Glycymeris*; ground perforation; surface: pinkish
D: 2.8

2898 MM 50
Perforated *Glycymeris*; ground perforation
D: 2.0

2899 ZA 43
Perforated *Glycymeris*; ground perforation
D: 2.2

2971 ZG 26; plate 9.15c
Perforated *Glycymeris*
D: 4.0; W: 3.8; Th: 0.5

2978 ZG 27
Perforated *Glycymeris*; ground perforation
D: 1.8

2981   ZG 28; plate 9.15c
Perforated *Glycymeris*; ground perforation; surface: reddish/tan
D: 5.1

2995   ZG 31; plate 9.24a
Discoid; *Spondylus*; oval form, V-shaped eccentric perforation drilled down to the base
L: 4.4; W: 3.2; Th: 2.1

3120   ML 152
Perforated *Glycymeris*; ground perforation; surface: pinkish/yellow
D: 2.2

3146   ML 152
Perforated *Glycymeris*; ground perforation; surface: pale cream
D: 2.0

3147   ML 152
Perforated *Unio* fragment; large irregular perforation on the body, possibly for food extraction
D: 3.1–5.0; Th:1.0

3407   MM 48
Perforated *Glycymeris*; ground perforation; surface: faint trace of natural color
L: 1.7

3471   MMt 60
Perforated *Glycymeris*; surface: pink coloration
D: 2.3

3503   MMb 63
Perforated *Murex trunculus*; surface: pale pink
H: 5.5; W: 4.1; Th: 3.0

3506   MMb 63
Perforated *Glycymeris* fragment; surface: pink coloration
L: 1.9; W: 1.5

3770   ML 158; plate 2.20d
Perforated pig astragalus
H: 2.7; W: 1.7; Th: 1.4

3801   MMd 65
Perforated *Glycymeris*; surface: tan
D: 1.8

3840   MMd 66
Perforated *Glycymeris*
D: 2.4; H: 0.8

3864   MMd 66
Perforated *Glycymeris*; surface: cream/orange
D: 2.8–3.0

5116   ZB 117r
Lower canine of wild pig

5143(a) ZB 115r
Perforated *Glycymeris*
D: 0.9–2.0

5143(b) ZB 115r
Perforated *Glycymeris*
D: 1.3

5143(c) ZB 115r
Perforated *Glycymeris*
D: 2.0

5145(a) ZB 118r
Perforated *Glycymeris*
D: 0.9–2.0

5145(b) ZB 118r
Perforated *Glycymeris*
D: 1.3

5145(c) ZB 118r
Perforated *Glycymeris*
D: 2.0

5146   ZB 119r
Perforated *Glycymeris*
L: 0.9

5152(a) ZB 125r
Perforated *Glycymeris*
D: 0.9

5152(b) ZB 125r
Perforated *Glycymeris*
D: 1.3

5152(c) ZB 125r
Perforated *Glycymeris*
D: 1.9

5152(d) ZB 125r
Perforated *Glycymeris*
D: 2.1

5155(b) ZB 128r
Perforated *Glycymeris* fragment
D: 1.8

5251(a) ZA 44s
Perforated *Glycymeris*
D: 0.8–2.2

5251(b) ZA 44s
Perforated *Glycymeris*
D: 0.8–2.2

5251(c) ZA 44s
Perforated *Glycymeris*
D: 0.8–2.2

5251(d) ZA 44s
Perforated *Glycymeris*
D: 0.8–2.2

5251(e) ZA 44s
Perforated *Glycymeris*
D: 0.8–2.2

5251(f) ZA 44s
Perforated *Glycymeris*
D: 0.8–2.2

5251(g) ZA 44s
Perforated *Glycymeris*
D: 0.8–2.2

5251(h) ZA 44s
Perforated *Glycymeris*
D: 0.8–2.2

5251(i) ZA 44s
Perforated *Glycymeris*
D: 0.8–2.2

5251(j) ZA 44s
Perforated *Glycymeris*
D: 0.8–2.2

525 (k) ZA 44s
Perforated *Glycymeris*
D: 0.8–2.2

5251(l) ZA 44s
Perforated *Neritea*
D: 1.1

5255(a) ZA 45s
Perforated *Glycymeris*
D: 0.9–2.1

5255(b) ZA 45s
Perforated *Glycymeris*
D: 0.9–2.1

5255(c) ZA 45s
Perforated *Glycymeris*
D: 0.9–2.1

5255(d) ZA 45s
Perforated *Neritea*
D: 1.1

5255(e) ZA 45s
Perforated *Columbella* shell (M. M)
D: 0.7

5288(a) ZA 48s; figure2.7c; plate 2.17b
Perforated lower canine of wild pig fragment

5580   MM 66s
Perforated *Glycymeris*
D: 1.7

5581   MMd 68
Perforated *Glycymeris*
D: 2.1

5582   ZG 30
Perforated *Glycymeris*
D: 3.6

5591   MM 49
Perforated *Glycymeris*
D: 3.0

5602   MM 19
Perforated *Unio*; large, irregular perforation on
body, possibly for food extraction
L: 5.6

Bracelets/Annulets

50   ML 2
Spondylus fragment
L: 6.1; W: 1.3; Th: 0.4

162   MM 11
Glycymeris fragment; formed from hinge area
L: 5.9; W: 1.4; Th: 0.5

206   ZA 38; plate 9.2d
Spondylus fragment
L: 5.7; W: 1.9; Th: 0.7

212   ZA 40
Spondylus fragment; surface: amber-white, with
gray encrustation
L: 4.7; W: 1.1; Th: 0.9

213   ZA 41; plate 9.7t
Spondylus fragment; surface: red color preserved
L: 6.7; W: 1.6; Th: 0.9

260   ML 2
Spondylus fragment
L: 5.8; W: 1.3; Th: 0.9

399   ML 5
Spondylus fragment; surface: natural red
L: 6.1; W: 1.3; Th: 0.8

400   MM 27; plate 9.7u
Spondylus fragment; surface: natural red
L: 7.3; W: 1.1; Th: 0.9

420   ZE 88
Spondylus fragment

487   ZA 47s; plate 9.2a
Spondylus fragment; surface: polished, creamy
white-brown
L: 5.8; W: 2.6; Th: 0.8

505   ZA 41; plate 9.2.1e
Spondylus valve (half-fragment); surface: whitish,
natural purple stains; worked preform (MM)
L: 7.6; W: 3.5; Th: 1.3

548   MM 11
Spondylus fragment; surface: natural red
L: 3.0; W: 0.8; Th: 0.8

780(a) ZA 47s
Spondylus fragment; burned
W: 1.2; Th: 0.1

780(b) ZA 47s
Spondylus fragment; burned
W: 0.1; Th: 0.4

780(c) ZA 47s
Spondylus fragment; burned
W: 1.0; Th: 0.9

780(d) ZA 47s
Spondylus fragment
W: 0.9; Th: 0.4

780(e) ZA 47s
Spondylus fragment
W: 0.9; Th: 0.2

784 ZA 47s; plate 9.2.1j
Spondylus fragment; irregular; edges: smoothed;
upper surface: white with gray and pink; probably
reworked for secondary use after breakage (MM)
L: 2.6; W: 0.6-0.9; Th: 0.4

816 ML 107; plates 9.3, 9.7q
Spondylus fragment; surface: white with natural red;
worked perform (NS)
L: 7.3; W: 1.2; Th: 0.8

817 ML 107
Spondylus fragment
L: 4.5; W: 2.2; Th: 0.9

892 MM 43; plate 9.7h
Spondylus fragment; surface: natural red
L: 4.3; W: 1.0; Th: 0.6

898 MM 43; plate 9.7b
Spondylus fragment; surface: natural red
L: 4.8; W: 0.7; Th: 0.6

1201 ML 110; plate 9.2g
Spondylus fragment; two perforations drilled near
one broken end
L: 3.5; W: 3.0; Th: 0.7

1202 ML 110
Spondylus fragment
L: 4.6; W: 1.8; Th: 0.7

1203 ML 110; plate 9.7i
Spondylus fragment
L: 5.8; W: 1.4; Th: 0.5

1205 ML 110; plate 9.7g
Spondylus fragment
L: 6.7; W: 1.1; Th: 0.3

1227 MM 49; plate 9.7c
Spondylus fragment
L: 5.3; W: 1.0; Th: 0.3

1233 MM 49; plate 9.7d
Spondylus fragment; surface: red
L: 5.7; W: 1.0; Th: 0.7

1234 MM 49; plate 9.7a
Spondylus fragment; surface: red
L: 4.5; W: 1.0; Th: 0.3

1243 MM 50; plate 9.7j
Spondylus fragment; surface: red
L: 5.1; W: 1.2; Th: 0.5

1256 MM 50; plate 9.7e
Spondylus fragment; surface: red
L: 6.2; W: 0.6; Th: 1.0

1259 MM 50; plate 9.7r
Spondylus fragment
L: 5.7; W: 1.2; Th: 1.0

1279 MM 52; plate 9.7s
Spondylus fragment; surface: red; possible carving
L: 6.3; W: 1.2; Th: 1.0

1287 MM 52; plate 9.7k
Spondylus fragment; surface: red
L: 3.9; W: 1.0; Th: 0.3

1299 ML 115; plate 9.2f
Spondylus (MM); fragment; carefully worked, perfo-
ration near one end
L: 3.0; W: 2.1; Th: 0.5

1300 ML 115; plate 9.7v
Spondylus fragment
L: 5.7; W: 1.1; Th: 0.8

1403 MM 36
Spondylus fragment
L: 5.0; W: 2.0; Th: 0.6

1445 MM 40; plate 9.7 l
Spondylus fragment; surface: red
L: 5.0; W: 0.3; Th: 1.2

1446 MM 40
Spondylus fragment; surface: red
L: 3.5; W: 1.1; Th: 0.7

1480 MM 50
Spondylus fragment
L: 4.0; W: 1.2; Th: 0.9

1536/ MM 54; plates 9.7f, m
1537 *Spondylus*; two joined fragments (1536, 1537); surface: natural (?) red stains
L: 5.9; W: 0.9; Th: 0.25–0.8

1566 MM 53; plate 9.7o
Spondylus fragment
L: 4.5; W: 1.3; Th: 0.8

1592 MM 50; plate 9.2h
Spondylus fragment; drilled perforation at one end
L: 4.7; W: 2.8; Th: 0.7

1710 ML 115; plate 9.7:n
Spondylus fragment; surface: red; worked perform
(NS)
L: 5.5; W: 1.4; Th: 0.4

1727 ML 107
Spondylus fragment
L: 3.9; W: 3.3; Th: 0.7

2893 MM 40
Glycymeris fragment; surface: ground, polished, and
smoothed
L: 4.0; W: 0.9; Th: 0.3

2944 ZG 17
Spondylus fragment; surface: red
L: 6.7; W: 1.2; Th: 0.8

2961(a) ZG 23
Spondylus fragment; surface: pale cream
L: 4.0; W: 1.2

2961(b) ZG 23
Spondylus fragment; surface: dark cream
L: 2.1; W: 1.4

2962 ZG 23; plate 9.2.1f
Spondylus valve; almost complete; surface: red
spots; worked preform (MM)
L: 6.0; W: 2.1

2963 ZG 23
Spondylus fragment
L: 4.3; W: 2.2; Th: 1.0

2965 ZG 24
Spondylus fragment
L: 7.3; W: 1.2; Th: 0.6

2970 ZG 26
Spondylus fragment
L: 9.3; W: 2.4; Th: 0.9

2980 ZG 28
Spondylus fragment; hinge present; surface: pale
gray
L: 6.0; W: 1.3; Th: 0.9

2982 ZG 28
Spondylus fragment; surface: cream with pink
L: 2.6; W: 1.2; Th: 0.2

2989 ZG 30
Spondylus fragment; surface: polished; brown/pale
orange with pink
L: 5.7; W: 1.1; Th: 0.3

3112 ML 151
Spondylus fragment; surface: red
L: 2.9; W: 1.0; Th: 0.4

3405 MMd 63
Spondylus fragment

3427(a) MMa 60; plate 9.6a
Glycymeris; pierced umbo, ground to produce
bracelet/annulet (?)
D: 5.0

3427(b) MMa 60; plate 9.6b
Glycymeris; pierced umbo, ground to produce
bracelet/annulet (?)
D: 5.4

3431 MMb 61; plate 9.5e
Spondylus fragment; hinge preserved
L: 6.0; W: 1.5; Th: 0.8

3460 MMt 60
Spondylus fragment; surface: pink
L: 3.2

3484 MMc 61; plate 9.5c
Spondylus fragment; hinge preserved; surface:
cream with pink
D: 7.5; Th: 1.0

3485 MMc 61; plate 9.5b
Spondylus fragment; hinge preserved; surface: some
pink coloration
D: 8.7; Th: 1.0

3486 MMc 61; plate 9.5a
Spondylus fragment; surface: cream, pink
L: 8.0; Th: 1.1

3487(a) MMc 61
Spondylus fragment; hinge preserved
L: 4.2; W: 1.3

3487(b) MMc 61; plate 9.7p
Spondylus fragment; hinge preserved; surface: pink
L: 5.5; W: 1.5

3489 MMc 61; plate 9.5d
Spondylus fragment; surface: cream
L: 6.0; Th: 1.4

3490 MMc 61
Spondylus (MM) fragment
L: 4.4; W: 1.0; Th: 0.5

3491 MMc 61
Spondylus fragment; burned
L: 1.3; Th: 0.8

3492 MMa 61
Spondylus fragment
L: 4.5; W: 2.2; Th: 0.9

3493 MMc 61
Spondylus fragment; hinge (?) preserved; burned
L: 1.3; W: 1.1

3497 MMc 61
Spondylus fragment
L: 5.0; W: 1.3; Th: 0.7

3500 MMc 61s
Spondylus fragment
L: 3.2; W: 2.4; Th: 1.7

3504 MMd 63
Spondylus fragment
L: 4.8; W: 1.3; Th: 0.7

3505 MMc 61; plate 9.5f
Spondylus fragment; hinge preserved; surface: red
D: 6.3; W: 1.3; Th: 0.8

3533 MMc 63
Spondylus fragment
L: 6.4; W: 2.1; Th: 0.8

3540 MMd 65
Spondylus fragment; surface: pink
L: 3.7; W: 1.0; Th: 0.9

3800 MMd 65
Spondylus fragment; surface: pink
L: 4.6; W: 2.1; Th: 1.1

3815   MMa 63s
Spondylus fragment; surface: pale cream with pink
L: 4.3; W: 1.1; Th: 0.3

3816   MMa 63
Spondylus fragment; hinge preserved; surface: pink
D: 7.0; Th: 0.8

3829   MMc 65
Spondylus
L: 3.0

3839   MMd 66
Spondylus fragment; hinge preserved; surface: pale cream with pink
L: 6.8; W: 2.8; Th: 1.2

3860   MMd 66
Spondylus fragment; surface: pink
L: 3.1; W: 0.9; Th: 0.2

3868   MMb 65
Spondylus fragment; hinge preserved
L: 6.2; W: 0.7; Th: 0.7

3871   MMb 65
Spondylus fragment
L: 5.4; W: 1.1; Th: 0.5

3877   MMd 68; plate 9.4
Spondylus fragment; perforation drilled at one end
D: 7.3; W: 2.5; Th: 0.8

3879   MMb 66
Spondylus fragment; surface: pink
D: 6.2; W: 0.9; Th: 0.6

3897(a) MMd 68
Spondylus fragment; hinge preserved
D: 5.4; W: 0.9; Th: 0.8

4204   ZE 87
Marble; fragmentary; surface: white
L: 6.4; W: 3.3; Th: 1.2

4205   ZE 88
Spondylus fragment; hinge preserved; surface: beige
D: 5.0; W: 0.6

4206   ZE 88
Spondylus fragment; hinge preserved; surface: yellow-cream
L: 4.7; W: 1.4; Th: 0.7

4418   ZG 30
Spondylus fragment; surface: smoothed, white
L: 2.6; W: 1.0; Th: 0.4

4494   MMa 63
Spondylus fragment; surface: cream with pink
L: 5.0; W: 0.8; Th: 0.7

4496   ZE 85
Spondylus fragment; surface: black discoloration
L: 5.7; Th: 0.7

4497   ZE 87
Spondylus fragment; surface: white encrustation
L: 6.6; W: 1.2; Th: 0.5

4501   MMd 63
Spondylus fragment; surface: pale cream
L: 3.4; W: 0.8; Th: 0.7

4505   MMd 68
Spondylus fragment; surface: cream
L: 4.7; W: 0.6; Th: 0.5

4506   MMc 63
Spondylus fragment; hinge preserved; surface: pale cream
L: 6.0; W: 2.3; Th: 0.8

4508   MMc 63
Spondylus fragment; surface: smoothed and worked, white
L: 3.5; W: 1.1; Th: 0.6

4746   ZG 18
Spondylus fragment
L: 6.1; W: 0.7; Th: 0.7

4874   MM 16
Spondylus fragment
L: 5.5

4885   MM 41
Spondylus fragment
L: 4.8

5139   ZB 112r
Spondylus fragment; burned
L: 2.2

5150   ZB 123r
Spondylus fragment
L: 6.2

5151 (a–c)ZB 124r
Spondylus; 3 fragments joined (MM)
L: 1.6–2.5

5153(a) ZB 125r
Spondylus fragment
L: 3.0

5153(b) ZB 125r
Spondylus fragment
L: 4.5

5153(c) ZB 125r
Spondylus fragment
L: 6.0

5156   ZB 129r
Spondylus fragment
L: 5.3

5157(a) ZB 130r
Spondylus fragment
L: 5.2

5157(b) ZB 130r
Spondylus fragment
L: 6.9

5253(a) ZA 44s
Spondylus fragment
D: 1.2–3.1

5253(b) ZA 44s
Spondylus fragment
D: 1.2–3.1

5253(c) ZA 44s
Spondylus fragment
D: 1.2–3.1

5253(d) ZA 44s
Spondylus fragment
D: 1.2–3.1

5253(e) ZA 44s
Spondylus fragment
D: 1.2–3.1

5253(f) ZA 44s
Spondylus fragment
D: 1.2–3.1

5257　ZA 45s
Glycymeris; perforated
L: 2.7; W: 0.9; Th: 0.1

5259　ZA 48s
Spondylus fragment
L: 1.3

5435　MM 43
Spondylus fragment
L: 5.8; W: 1.0; Th: 0.5

5587　ZG 15
Spondylus fragment
L: 6.7

5607　MM 12; plate 9.2.1d
Spondylus valve; fragmentary; worked preform
(MM)
L: 5.6

Pins

376　MM 20
Sheep/goat metapodial; slender shaft, broadens in
upper part; surface: smooth, brown; decoration:
head includes epiphysis worked (?) into cloverleaf
pattern
L: 6.5; Th: 1.0

807　MM 27
Bone; slender shaft, broadens in upper part, tapers
slightly and irregularly toward tip; surface: brown
with lime deposits
L: 8.1; W: 0.3–1.2; Th: 0.3–0.7

880　MM 43
Copper; broken at tip, lower part of shaft has been
curved; circular in section; decoration: spiral finial
(see chapter 8)
L: 8.0; D: 0.3–0.8

1523　MM 42
Bone; flattened; surface: polished
L: 10.5; W: 0.9; Th: 0.3

Plaques

834　MM 38; figures 2.7d, 9.28; plates 2.17a, 9.27a
Cattle rib; slightly broken at two corners; rectangular in section; two perforations and traces of a third
preserved at each end
L: 6.7; W: 2.6; Th: 0.9

5288(b) ZA 48s; plates 2.17b, 9.27b
Bone fragment; two perforations at preserved end,
traces of another at the broken one
L: 5.6; W: 1.6; Th: 0.5

PHASE IV

Beads

533　ZA 32; figure 9.8; plate 9.9g
1 cylinder, tubular; clay; surface: smooth, buff/light
yellow-brown
L: 3.0; D: 0.7; HD: 0.1

2741　ZE 65
1 *Dentalium* tubular; surface: white
L: 1.6; D: 0.4

3054　ROc 671; plate 9.9h
1 cylinder, tubular; stone; surface: gray/brown
L: 2.2; D: 0.8

5045　ZB 48r
1 cylinder, narrow; stone; surface: gray/brown
D: 0.45

5046　ZB 49r
1 cylinder, wide; shell; surface: white
D: 0.3

5047　ZB 52r
1 cylinder, disc; shell or stone (M. M); surface: white
L: 0.1–0.2; D: 8.0

5048　ZB 53r
1 cylinder, narrow; soft stone (MM); surface: dark
gray
D: 0.5

5049(a) ZB 56r
1 cylinder, wide; shell; surface: naturally grooved,
buff
D: 0.55

5049(b) ZB 56r
1 cylinder, narrow; stone; surface: brown/gray
D: 0.4

5050(a) ZB 57r
1 cylinder, narrow (fragmentary); clay; surface: gray
L: 0.2–0.7; D: 1.4

5050(b) ZB 57r
2 Dentalium tubular; surface: buff/gray.
L: 0.6–1.5; D: 0.2–0.3

5051   ZB 57s
1 Dentalium tubular; surface: white
L: 1.2; D: 0.3

5052   ZB 58r
1 pinched; clay; surface: gray

5053   ZB 60r
1 irregular; shell (MM); roughly polygonal; surface: light buff
W: 0.5

5054   ZB 61r
1 cylinder, narrow; shell or stone (MM); surface: white
D: 0.4

5055   ZB 64r
1 Dentalium tubular; surface: white
L: 0.9; D: 0.4

5056   ZB 70r
1 Dentalium tubular; surface: light buff
L: 1.2; D: 0.35

5057   ZB 102r
1 Dentalium tubular; surface: light buff
L: 2.0; D: 0.3

5058(a) ZB 104r; plate 9.9e
1 cylinder, narrow; clay; surface: dark gray
D: 0.35

5058(b) ZB 104r; figure 9.13; plate 9.9f
1 biconical; clay; convex profile; surface: dark gray
L: 0.55; D: 0.75; HD: 0.15

5059   ZB105r
1 Dentalium tubular; surface: light buff
L: 1.6; D: 0.3

5060   ZB 107r
1 cylinder, narrow; clay; surface: dark gray
D: 0.6

5061   ZB 108r
1 cylinder, narrow; shell or stone (MM); surface: buff
D: 0.3
1 cylinder, wide; shell or stone (MM); surface: buff.
D: 0.5

5062   ZB 109r
3 cylinders, narrow; stone; surface: 1 white marble, 2 dark mottled.
D: 0.4-0.5
1 cylinder, wide; stone; surface: orange/gray
D: 0.4

5133   ZB 48r
1 irregular fragment; Spondylus; surface: buff
D: 0.8

5134   ZB 50r
1 irregular fragment; Spondylus; surface: buff/gray
D: 0.8

Pendants

832   MM 34; plate 9.20
Cypraea; pair of perforations at the apex; surface: some white encrustation
L: 3.2; W: 1.9

2722   ZE 61
Miscellaneous: oblong segment of turtle shell with one end rounded, the other straightened; surface: orange, fine parallel incisions near straight end, possibly for suspension
L: 4.0; W: 1.3; Th: 0.3

3705   ZE 80
Perforated Glycymeris; surface: pale cream
L: 3.1

4641   ZE 61
Perforated fragment; red deer antler; irregularly oblong; perforation near one long edge
L: 7.3; W: 1.7; Th: 1.0

4748   ZE 63; plate 9.23a
Ring-shaped; Murex (TW); central part of the whorl has been ground to an oval form that incorporates both apices of the spiral; surface: polished and/or beach worn
L: 3.6; W: 2.5; Th: 0.4

5094   ZB 47s
Perforated turtle shell

5124   ZB 101r; plate 9.22a
Perforated dog canine tooth

5138   ZB 109r
Perforated Glycymeris
D: 2.0

5590   ZA 32
Perforated Glycymeris
D: 3.6

5593   ZE 61
Perforated Cardium
D: 3.6

5594   ZE 61
        Perforated *Cardium*
        D: 2.5

Bracelets/Annulets

290   ZD 7
        Glycymeris fragment
        L: 7.0; W: 1.0; Th: 0.5

826   MM 30
        Spondylus fragment; surface: red coloration
        L: 6.8; W: 1.1; Th. 1.3

896   MM 34
        Spondylus fragment; surface: some red coloration
        L: 5.3; W: 1.0; Th: 0.5

2735   ZE 64
        Spondylus fragment
        L: 3.4

2788   ZE 81
        Spondylus fragment; surface: pinkish coloration;
        carefully smoothed and polished
        L: 5.8; W: 1.0; Th: 0.7

2890   MM 10
        Spondylus fragment
        L: 2.5; W: 1.4; Th: 0.4

3211   ZHt 10
        Spondylus fragment
        L: 3.9; W: 2.5; Th: 0.7

3263   ZHt 26
        Spondylus fragment; surface: pinkish coloration
        L: 4.4; W: 0.9; Th: 0.6

3266   ZH
        Spondylus fragment (listed in volume 1:209)

3267   ZH
        Spondylus fragment (listed in volume 1:209)

3271   ZH
        Spondylus fragment (listed in volume 1:209)

3274   ZH
        Spondylus fragment (listed in volume 1:209)

3527   MMc 1
        Spondylus fragment
        L: 5.1; W: 1.3; Th: 0.6

4495   ZJ 17
        Spondylus fragment; surface: pale cream and pink
        with white encrustation
        L: 6.6; W: 1.0; Th: 1.3

4749   ZE 35
        Spondylus fragment
        L: 4.6; W: 0.7; Th: 0.7

5140   ZB101r
        Spondylus fragment; burned
        L: 0.7

5141(a) ZB 102r
        Spondylus fragment; burned
        L: 1.5

Pins (see chapter 8 for metal artifacts)

30   ZA 23
        Copper; rectangular in section, tapering toward
        both ends
        L: 3.3; D: 1.5

3229   ZHt 17; figure 8.2c; plates 8.5a, 8.9d; tables 8.2, 8.3
        Copper; fragmentary; irregularly oval in section,
        preserved upper part curves slightly into an S and
        thickens gradually to an inverted spiral finial
        L: 2.5; D: 0.4-0.7; Th: 0.25

Ring

5341   ZB 56r; figure 8.2d; table 8.2
        Copper, very fine wire; circlet is complete but has
        been squeezed into an elliptical, asymmetric shape
        L: 0.75; W: 0.45

PHASE V

Beads

1587   PO 65; figure 9.15; plate 9.14c
        1 barrel; *Spondylus*; surface: naturally grooved,
        buff/gray
        L: 1.8; D: 1.2; HD: 0.3

2276   POb 37
        1 miscellaneous: thin block of turtle shell; almost
        rectangular, slightly curved, small perforation
        drilled through from back
        L: 2.3; W: 1.4; Th: 0.3

5039   ZB 9r
        1 cylinder, narrow; shell or stone (MM); surface:
        buff
        D: 0.2

5040   ZB 16r; figure 9.17
        1 segmented; clay; surface: brown
        L: 0.8; D: 0.3

5041   ZB 25s
        1 cylinder, narrow; shell (MM); surface: white
        D: 0.45

5042   ZB 36r
        1 biconical; clay; convex profiles; surface: buff/gray
        D: 0.6

5043   ZB 37s
        1 cylinder, disc; shell (MM); surface: white
        L: 0.1–0.2; D: 7.5

5044(a) ZB 45r
        1 cylinder, wide; shell; surface: naturally grooved,
        buff
        D: 0.5

5044(b) ZB 45r
1 cylinder, narrow; marble; surface: white
D: 0.6

5576 ZB 37s
1 irregular fragment; *Spondylus*; surface: white
D: 0.9

5577 ZB 10r
1 irregular fragment; *Spondylus*; surface: buff
D: 0.8

Pendants

66 ZA 17
Perforated turtle shell
L: 4.0

667 PO 8
Perforated *Glycymeris* fragment; burned
L: 2.2; W: 0.9

1001 PN 5; plate 9.26
Miscellaneous: *Cypraea* shell, ground to produce a large oval opening on the body whorl
L: 1.7; W: 1.2; Th: 0.8

5089 ZB 37r; plate 9.22b
Perforated tooth
L: 7.0; D: 5.0

5126 ZB 11r
Perforated *Glycymeris*
D: 0.8

Bracelets/Annulets

37 ZA 14
Spondylus fragment; surface: red coloration
L: 3.7; W: 1.0; Th: 0.7

43 PO 2
Spondylus fragment
L: 6.6; W: 1.0; Th: 0.8

489 QO 2
Spondylus fragment; surface: creamy white with encrustation and weathering
L: 3.0; W: 2.5; Th: 2.3

2891 ZA 13
Spondylus fragment
L: 4.3; W: 1.3; Th: 0.9

4599 PNd 80
Spondylus fragment; surface: cream with gray coloration; from the Burnt House
L: 5.0; W: 1.0; Th: 0.5

5129(c) ZB 37s
Spondylus fragment
L: 4.7

5606 PO 4; plate 9.2.1c
Spondylus valve fragment; worked preform (MM)
L: 6.0

Pins

654 PO 7
Bone; head is broken; slender, straight shaft; surface: smoothed, dark brown with slight white deposits
L: 5.0; D: 0.4

655 PO 7
Bone; head is fractured; slender shaft, with one side slightly concave; surface: pale brown with slight, light gray deposits
L: 7.0; W: 0.1–0.5

665 PO 8
Bone; slender, straight shaft, tapers toward blunted tip; surface: smooth, pale brown/yellow
L: 5.5; W: 0.1–0.5; Th: 0.4

1048 QN 7; figure 9.26
Bone; flat, straight shaft, broadens slightly at head; surface: bright/light brown, some polishing, some deposits on underside
L: 10.9; W: 0.3–1.0; Th: 0.5

1307 PN 10
Pig fibula; head is broken; slender shaft, broadens at head, sharp tip; surface: shiny, yellow/brown
L: 5.6; W: 0.2–0.7; Th: 0.4

1557 QN 7
Pig fibula; slender, straight shaft tapering smoothly, broad head; surface: brown with lime deposits at basal end
L: 8.1; W: 0.2–0.9; Th: 0.3

1568 PO 9
Bone; slightly broken at tip; very slender, smoothly tapering shaft, broad head includes epiphysis; surface: some polishing, mottled brown-gray
L: 6.6; W: 0.1–1.21; Th: 0.05–0.6

1804 PO 23
Bone; slender shaft, flattened head includes epiphysis; surface: polished along the shaft; well-made
L: 7.6; W: 0.2–1.3; D: 0.5

2044 QO/D 9
Bone; slender shaft, rounded tip; surface: polished, brown/yellow
L: 2.6; W: 0.5; Th: 0.3

2076 PN/E 50
Bone; slender shaft, smoothly tapering toward tip, rounded head; surface: polished, dark brown
L: 5.7; W: 0.2–0.7; Th: 0.5

3017 ROc 49; figure 8.3a; plate 8.8; tables 8.2, 8.3
Copper; broken at tip; quadrangular in section
L: 3.9; D: 2.5

3356 PO 163
Copper or bronze; fragmentary, heavily corroded;
circular in section
L: 1.0; D: 0.35

3357 PO 164
Bone; slender shaft, sharp tip; surface: polished;
carefully made
L: 4.6; W: 0.1–0.5

5339 ZB 6r; figure 8.3c; table 8.2
Bronze (?); fragmentary; circular in section
L: 1.2; D: 0.3

MIXED CONTEXTS

Pendants

4774 OGc 1; plate 11.3c
Triangular; clay; sherd reworked into a teardrop
shape, with rounded edges; surface: red
L: 3.3; W: 2.0; Th: 0.9

4804 Surface; plate 9.24b
Discoid; *Spondylus*; circular form, single slightly
eccentric perforation drilled through
D: 3.9; Th: 1.3; HD: 0.7

5592 Unknown context
Glycymeris
D: 2.7

Bracelets/Annulets

686 Surface
Spondylus fragment
L: 5.2; W: 0.9; Th: 0.9

1643 Surface; plate 9.2e
Spondylus fragment; surface: gray veining with gray
encrustation
L: 4.0; W: 2.8; Th: 0.7

2226 OGc 1
Spondylus fragment
L: 4.9; W: 1.2; Th: 0.7

2227 OGc 1
Spondylus fragment; surface: white with red colora-
tion
L: 7.3; W: 1.2; Th: 0.7

2244 PGc 1; plate 9.2.1i
Spondylus fragment; unfinished perforation; burned
L: 3.6; W: 1.0; Th: 0.6

2766 ZE
Glycymeris fragment; surface: pinkish
L: 2.9; W: 2.5

10.

Special Clay Objects: Cylinders, Stamp Seals, Counters, Biconoids, and Spheres [1]

Colin Renfrew

Five decorated clay cylinders were found during the excavations at Sitagroi. They are of particular interest because their form resembles that of cylinder seals from the ancient Near East, although these are generally of stone. Decorated clay objects from Romania, Yugoslavia, and other southeast European countries, notably the much discussed Tărtăria tablets (Vlassa 1963; C. Renfrew 1966; Hood 1967), have sometimes been compared with possible Near Eastern prototypes, with the implication that those of the Balkans may reflect direct Near Eastern influence (Falkenstein 1965; Popovitch 1965). That view is not advocated here, but it is appropriate to describe such objects with some care so that the evidence may be properly assessed. Along with the cylinders were found a clay stamp seal or pintadera, a number of small circular or conical clay disks that might have been used as counters, some small spheres, and several biconoids usually interpreted as slingshots.

Parts of this assemblage were discussed earlier in a Festschrift in honor of the late Marija Gimbutas, co-organizer of the Sitagroi excavations (C. Renfrew 1987). Fortunately, the stratigraphic context of each cylinder is clear. Both SF 516 (figure 10.1a; plate 10.1) and SF 446 (figure 10.1b; plate 10.2) were found in square KM, the former recognized in the workroom with pottery from layer 7 (from pottery bag 48), and the latter recognized and recorded in situ. Cylinder SF 3684 (figure 10.1c; plate 10.3) was recognized after washing the contents of bone bag 79 from the small sounding ZG, layer 43, which was some 80 cm below the uppermost layer (layer 34) of phase II in this sounding. Cylinder SF 1443 (figure 10.2a; plate 10.4) was recovered with the sieved residue from layer 50 in the deep stratigraphic sounding, square ZA; this was the uppermost layer in that trench assigned to phase II.

Cylinder SF 1145 (figure 10.2b; plate 10.5) came from a very much later context of phase Vb, found with pottery from layer PN 5. This layer is associated with the Bin Complex which overlay the Long House in square PN, and there is no doubt about the context. Because this cylinder is typologically so close to the others, which unequivocally belong to phase II, the question arises as to whether it was made at the same time as these and represents a "throw-up"—that is, found out of context in phase Vb and originally made in phase II. From the stratigraphic point of view this is perfectly possible. The piece may have been picked up as a curiosity from anywhere on the mound and then brought to the top of the magoula. There were a few sherds and other objects found in phase V levels also clearly assignable to earlier phases on typological grounds. The stratigraphy permits such a view but does not suggest it. Nevertheless, typological similarity between this and the other cylinders is so close that I prefer this conclusion.

Unfortunately, none of the cylinders were found in association with recognizable structures, whether inside or outside them. Though in common with many of the artifacts from phases I and II (and other phases also) at Sitagroi, they lack a clear functional context.

THE DATE OF THE SITAGROI CYLINDERS

The stratigraphic position of the first four cylinders lies securely within phase II, and as discussed above it is possible, although not demonstrated,

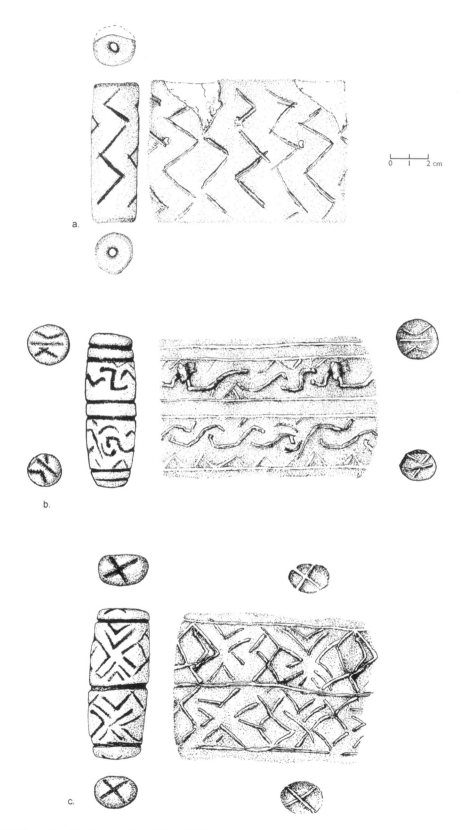

Figure 10.1. Incised cylinders of phase II: (a) SF 516, plate 10.1; (b) SF 446, plate 10.2; (c) SF 3684, plate 10.3.

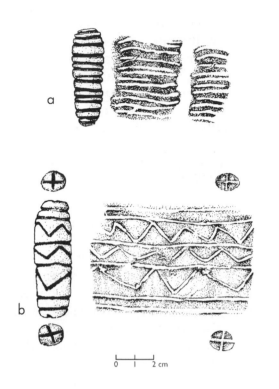

Figure 10.2. Clay cylinders: (a) Phase II, SF 1443, plate 10.4; (b) phase Vb, SF 1145, plate 10.5.

that the fifth cylinder was also made at this time. As we shall see in a later section, these finds situate quite easily within the context of phase II (or phase III) at Sitagroi and within that of the Balkan Late Neolithic and Copper Age in general.

The first point to stress is that phase II is securely stratified between two phases whose pottery bears unmistakable associations in the Balkans. Sitagroi phase I, whose levels are below those of phase II, may be equated securely, on the basis of the pottery, with the Veselinovo culture of Bulgaria (Karanovo III), as well as with the earlier levels at Paradimi in Thrace. Both may be regarded within the Balkan culture succession as contemporary with the earlier phase of the Vinča culture, Vinča-Tordoš (see volume 1 [Keighley 1986]:345–392).

Sitagroi phase III, whose levels lie above those of phase II, has many features, including abundant graphite-painted ware (see volume 1 [R. Evans 1986]:393–428), that link it with the Gumelnitsa culture of Bulgaria and Romania (Karanovo V–VI). Comparisons for the Sitagroi phase III figurines point in the same direction (see volume 1 [Gimbutas 1986]: 225–301).

It should be stressed that in Aegean terms, it is Sitagroi phase V that may be equated with the Aegean Early Bronze Age, as I initially suggested (C. Renfrew 1970b) and as Sherratt's more detailed study has now amply documented (see volume 1 [Sherratt 1986]:429–476). The conclusion is that Sitagroi IV is the approximate equivalent of Aegean Early Bronze 1, and Sitagroi phases Va and Vb is the equivalent of Aegean Early Bronze 2 and 3.

In view of the controversy that surrounded the question of chronological equivalences between the Aegean and the Balkans, it is important to assert that the observations made so far do not rely in any way on radiocarbon determinations nor on long-distance comparisons with faraway lands. Rather, they are based on the systematic comparison of the Sitagroi finds, especially the pottery (and the figurines), with relevant finds from neighboring areas in the northern Aegean and the southern Balkans.

Turning now to the radiocarbon evidence, the position at Sitagroi is fortunately very clear (C. Renfrew 1971; volume 1 [C. Renfrew 1986e]: 173, table 7.2; see also Preface table 1). We have a good sequence of twenty-nine radiocarbon dates from the site, undertaken mainly by the Berlin and British Museum laboratories. All but one of them lie within a reasonable order in relation to the stratigraphy. One date, for a phase I level (Bln 885), is 1500 years earlier than the others for that phase and must be regarded as misleading, whether because the material dated was old at the time of burial or for technical reasons. In general, the sequence is a satisfying one, and the radiocarbon dates for the successive phases, allowing for the usual standard errors, harmonize with the stratigraphic succession. The four dates for phase II, also taking into account those for phases I and III, suggest a duration in radiocarbon years for phase II from about 4300 bc to about 3800 bc (uncalibrated). Applying the tree-ring radiocarbon calibration, whether that of Clark (1975) or the others now available, gives from about 5200 BC to 4600 BC in calendar years as the approximate duration for phase II.

This sequence harmonizes completely with the broad equivalences suggested earlier, placing Sitagroi phase II as contemporary with the earlier part of the Balkan Copper Age—for instance, Karanovo phase V and phase C of the Vinča culture (early Vinča-Pločnik). Within the Aegean, Sitagroi II is seen as the contemporary of the Saliagos culture of the Cyclades (Evans and Renfrew 1968:144), and falls in terms of the Thessalian sequence between the developed Sesklo culture and classic Dhimini. Indeed, the implied equation with the Arapi phase of the early Dhimini culture has already been argued purely on typological grounds (see volume 1 [R. Evans 1986]:393–427). Sitagroi phase II thus ends at least a millennium before the beginning of the Aegean Early Bronze Age.

THE SITAGROI CYLINDERS AND THE MOST ANCIENT EAST

When the tell mound at Vinča was first excavated, the most obvious and convenient suggestion for the early origins of copper metallurgy on the Danube and for the variety of plastic forms found in the Vinča culture was direct contact with the proto-urban communities of the Aegean Early Bronze Age, most notably Troy. This was the position argued by Childe and later supported by much more detailed analyses by D. and M. Garašanin, and V. Milojčić. It is not necessary here to cover these familiar arguments again (surveyed, for instance, in C. Renfrew 1969).

Although much of the evidence on which such comparisons were based has been effectively called into question, there are one or two intriguing discoveries in the Balkans for which parallels may be found in the predynastic period in the Near East, and in some cases also in the Aegean Early Bronze Age, which are so plausible that they continue to excite comment and speculation. Prominent among these are the Tărtăria tablets (Makkay 1975; Charvat 1975) and certain finds from Tordoš in Romania (Hood 1973). The Sitagroi cylinders could very easily fit into the same framework of discussion, as briefly noted by Hood (1973:193) and as argued much more comprehensively by Makkay, who concluded:

> It is evident that the Sitagroi cylinders (and their South-East European parallels) must be regarded as imitations of Near Eastern forerunners. In evaluating the Near Eastern origin of the South-East European cylinder industry, the comparison, interpretation and secure dating of the Sita-

groi cylinders would be of the utmost importance. It would appear that at present we have no grounds for speaking of a local origin or local inspiration. The manufacture of the first European cylinders in South-East Europe was strongly influenced by Near Eastern and Anatolian traditions. South-East European Late Neolithic cultures were introduced to the cylinder tradition of the East, and thereupon made it their own. (1984:53)

These observations are all the more notable because they occur within a meticulous and comprehensive study of the stamp seals of southeast Europe which shows definitively that, prior to the period of the clay cylinders when stamp seals are also found (i.e., the Late Neolithic/Copper Age), there was an earlier phase of stamp seal production in the Early Neolithic period. All authorities are agreed that these Early Neolithic Greek and Balkan stamp seals owe much of their inspiration to the stamp seals of Anatolia, such as those of Çatalhöyük, which may in turn be related to those of the Early Neolithic Levant. It is accepted that the early spread of farming from the Near East to the Balkans resulted in the transmission of cultural traits, of which the stamp seals are the most obvious.

Makkay correctly points out, however, that after the Early Neolithic period (represented, for instance, in Bulgaria by the Karanovo I and II phases), such artifacts are less commonly found. There is, however, a noted resurgence in the Late Neolithic and Copper Age (represented in Bulgaria by Karanovo phases V and VI). He justly pointed to the Middle or Late Neolithic period in Bulgaria (represented by Karanovo phases III and IV), where such artifacts are not seen. On the grounds of this apparent hiatus, he suggests that the re-emergence of stamp seals in the Copper Age, and with it the first appearance of decorated clay cylinders, is the result of contacts with the Near East in the Uruk, Jemdet Nasr, and Early Dynastic phases.

It should be noted that the Jemdet Nasr period may conventionally be dated from ca. 3100 to 2900 BC. Although there has been a tendency to push the chronology earlier in light of calibrated radiocarbon dating as applied to the Near East, there can be little question of situating the Jemdet Nasr period before 4500 BC. The suggestion advocated by Makkay and others thus comes into immediate conflict with the radiocarbon chronology and the Sitagroi stratigraphic evidence.

The view of Makkay, Hood, and Charvat is, of course, perfectly in harmony with the conclusion that the Tărtăria tablets (from a context claimed as belonging to the Vinča-Tordoš culture) are either direct imports from or directly inspired by Mesopotamia of the protoliterate period. They quite reasonably bring into the discussion two cylinders from Troy. The first of these (Schmidt 1902: no. 8869; Schliemann 1881: nos. 500, 501; 1970: no. 206) is a decorated clay cylinder, reputedly from Early Bronze Age levels at Troy. It is significant in the present discussion, first because it is made of clay, which in general the well-known cylinder seals of the Near East are not. It can thus be regarded as typologically intermediate. Second, it is relevant to the argument to offer a point of comparison of the right date, that is, contemporary with Early Dynastic Mesopotamia, and very much closer geographically to the finds in Sitagroi and the Balkans.

The second find from Troy (Schmidt 1902: no. 8868; Schliemann 1881: nos. 502, 503) is of green stone and reputedly dates from the Troy II period in the Early Bronze Age. Both of these finds are used by Hood (1973) in his interesting and well-documented discussion that illustrates an impressed plaque from Tordoš, reputedly from a Copper Age context, that bears the impression of what he identifies as a Mesopotamian cylinder seal.

Along with these two finds from Troy is the green stone cylinder found in an Early Cycladic grave on Amorgos in the Cyclades (C. Renfrew 1967: pl. 4, no. 19). Originally I dated this artifact toward the end of the Early Cycladic period, but would now set it earlier, within the time span of the Kampos group. The find certainly confirms that decorated cylinders of broadly Near Eastern type were known in the Aegean during the Early Bronze Age, as does an additional find from Poliochni (C. Renfrew 1972: pl. 23, 3a). The points made in the relatively recent literature about these objects certainly merit close attention because they are no longer based on the vague comparisons and generalized parallels on which some of the earlier arguments were founded. The Tărtăria tablets, the

Sitagroi cylinders, and the Tordoš plaque are much more specific instances, which do indeed find provoking parallels in the early Near East.

THE SITAGROI CYLINDERS AND THE BALKANS

Here I wish to show that, despite the comparisons just cited, we need not accept the view of Makkay (1975:27) that these finds provide primary and convincing evidence for the way Mesopotamian influences penetrated southeast Europe and in particular reached the site of Tărtăria.

The chronological arguments are already familiar. No one denies that there were contacts between the Aegean and Near East during the Early Bronze Age, that is, in the third millennium BC. The Poliochni ivory cylinder must be regarded as a direct import from the Near East. The same may be true of the Amorgos cylinder and the stone cylinder from Troy II. The clay cylinder from Troy is more difficult to explain. On the view offered here, it must either be a local imitation in clay following a Near Eastern prototype (a view with which Makkay and Hood would presumably agree), or it might be a southeast European product, probably of earlier manufacture, in the same manner as is cylinder SF 1145 (figure 10.2b) from Sitagroi. The latter was likewise found in levels of the Aegean Early Bronze Age, probably a little later than Troy II.

The Tărtăria tablets are probably to be regarded as correctly located stratigraphically by their excavator and thus as indeed belonging to the Vinča-Tordoš culture. In the case of the impressed plaque from Tordoš illustrated by Hood (1973: pl. 3), it is difficult to be categorical. The main point here is surely that the find is entirely without stratigraphic context of any kind: "A rumour has begun to circulate in Romania and Hungary that this plaque is really part of a mediaeval oven tile" (Hood 1973: 190). Stylistically, the find does not appear to me to be at home in the Late Neolithic or Chalcolithic of the Balkans. And while I would not allow a rather subjective impression of this kind to contradict a firm stratigraphic attribution, without a sound context this must surely be regarded as a very doubtful piece indeed.

At this point it should be emphasized that the Sitagroi cylinders do fit into a perfectly acceptable context within the contemporary cultures of north Greece and the Balkans. A very comparable clay cylinder (unperforated) has been published by Detev (1965:68, fig. 6, 3) from the tell mound at Bikovo in Bulgaria (Makkay 1984: no. 21); in the same figure Detev illustrates an object of uncertain shape whose decoration closely resembles our cylinders from Sitagroi. There is also a clay cylinder from Tordoš in Romania (Makkay 1984: no. 265, and fig. XXV, 6).

The repertoire is greatly extended by a series of interesting clay cylinders from the appropriate period at the important site of Maliq in eastern Albania. Four of these, assigned to Maliq phase IIA, were illustrated in the original publication by Prendi (1966: pl. X, f) along with a number of stamp seals. Four cylinders are illustrated in a later paper by Prendi (1967: pl. XX, 12–15), of which number 15 appears to be the same as one of those in the 1966 publication. Most of the Maliq pieces appear to be perforated in the same manner as Sitagroi SF 516 (figure 10.1a; plate 10.1).

The site of Maliq shows a striking series of parallels with other Balkan sites, including Sitagroi, especially in phases IIa and IIb, which Prendi terms Eneolithic (that is, Copper Age). It is not clear whether all the clay cylinders from Maliq fall within phase IIa or whether they also occur in IIb at that site. One might anticipate the former, because some of the new ceramic forms of Maliq phase IIb (Prendi 1966: pl. XI) find parallels at Sitagroi for the first time in phase IV. The concentration of clay cyl-

inders at Maliq is certainly notable, especially because they do not seem to be a common find in Bulgaria, Romania, or Yugoslavia.

There are close parallels to the Sitagroi cylinders much nearer home. In the first place, there is a squat, perforated cylinder from the site of Dikili Tash in the plain of Drama (Zervos 1962: fig. 582). Secondly, our site survey in and near the plain of Drama produced several relevant pieces (see appendix 13.1). One of these, Dhoxaton 2 from Dhoxaton Tepe in the plain of Drama (figure 10.3; see also appendix 13.1; C. Renfrew 1987:360, fig. 6) is an approximately cylindrical object, 8.8 cm long, bearing incised decoration, including some running spirals. It probably may be assigned to the time span of Sitagroi phases II and III and indicates that such objects occur at other sites in the plain of Drama. A decorated clay object from the site of Dhimitra (Dhimitra 5; see figure 10.4) near the plain of Drama (see appendix 13.1; C. Renfrew 1987:362, fig. 7) extends the discussion. It is of comparable length to the cylinders (5.6 cm), but rectanguloid rather than cylindrical, and bears an excised decoration with a spiral on one surface. These richly decorated objects from within and near the plain of Drama may be set within the larger context of the Balkan Copper Age. There is no suggestion that any one of the Sitagroi cylinders is an import (although they have not in fact been the object of petrological examination with questions regarding raw material source in mind).

The site of Dhoxaton in the plain of Drama produced, in the course of our surface survey, another

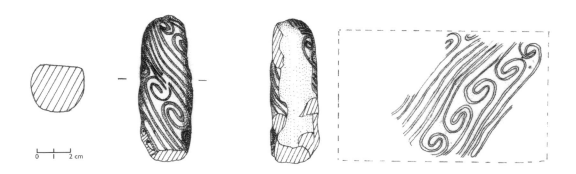

Figure 10.3. Dhoxaton Tepe cylindrical artifact with incised curving lines and running spirals, Dhoxaton 2.

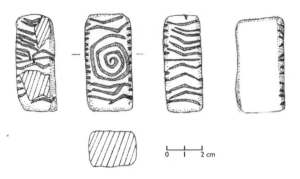

Figure 10.4. Dhimitra excised block, Dhimitra 5.

class of object that was not well documented at Sitagroi (see appendix 13.1; Dhoxaton 1: figure 10.5). This is an almost flat, rectangular, clay plaque, decorated with incised zigzags filled with angled lines on all four sides and connecting parallel lines on the upper surface.

Although the Dhoxaton pieces may be thicker than the Bulgarian comparanda, they immediately call to mind clay plaques from Yassatepe and Vinča (C. Renfrew 1969: pl. 1; Detev 1965: fig. 7). Once again the function of these objects is not known. But like some of the others that we have been dis-

cussing, they are richly decorated with incised lines, cut with considerable care. As in a number of other cases, they show a repeated meander motif, in this case rectilinear.

These somewhat disparate examples, taken from Sitagroi and other sites in the plain of Drama, and each with comparanda in the Copper Age of the Balkans, help to establish a wider context for the decorated clay cylinder seals of Sitagroi.

The most telling argument for the distinction between the Sitagroi clay cylinders and the Near Eastern cylinder seals, is of course, chronological. But other arguments should be given due attention. Seal impressions are not found in the Balkans. And the Sitagroi cylinders differ from the alleged Near Eastern counterparts in that the southeast European cylinders are perforated—specifically Sitagroi SF 516 (figure 10.1a), the cylinder from Dikili Tash, and those from Maliq.

The chronological case can be made without the benefit of radiocarbon dating. The four cylinders from Sitagroi phase II belong— like those of Maliq in Albania, Dikili Tash in the plain of Drama, Bikovo in Bulgaria, and Tordoš in Romania—to the

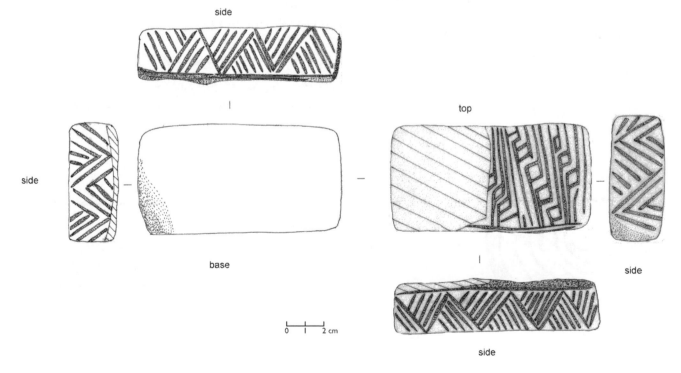

Figure 10.5. Dhoxaton Tepe incised clay, Dhoxaton 1.

Balkan Copper Age. The clay cylinder from Sitagroi phase Vb, whatever its ultimate origin, was found in an Aegean Early Bronze Age context like the clay cylinder from Troy, the stone cylinders from Troy II and Amorgos, and the ivory cylinder from Poliochni. There is no way that these two broad chronological "horizons" may be conflated.

A FUNCTIONAL CONTEXT

Very frequently when the case of external origin (diffusion) or indigenous origin (independent invention) is being discussed, the latter case is advanced by showing that the innovation in question fulfills a useful function in the context where it is found and might thus be presumed to have evolved locally. Such a point is often made in relation to the local origins of copper metallurgy, whether the material utility or the social worth of the new material is being emphasized.

In the case of the clay cylinders, such an argument is difficult to advance because their function is simply not known. Makkay (1984:53) is critical of the suggestion that they may have functioned as "roll cylinders," used for impressing their decoration upon a soft surface such as clay, since impressions from such cylinders have not been found in the Balkans. It is possible, indeed likely, that these cylinders, like the stamp seals, may instead have been used to impress a decoration on some object whose constituent material could not be preserved. This could be the case for a whole range of materi-

als, for only if these designs had been stamped upon wet clay and subsequently fired would we have expected to find clear evidence of such use.

The clay cylinders and stamp seals do not, however, stand alone. There is a whole range of terracotta objects from this period (Sitagroi II and III) whose use is not understood. Many of them are quite elaborately incised. Without attempting a specific interpretation, it is appropriate, I believe, to follow the lead of Marija Gimbutas (1976a) in thinking in terms of ideograms, symbolic design, and ritual.

The notion of ideograms has been developed in considerable detail by Winn (1973), who has shown that the Tărtăria tablets and other artifacts with incised signs belong quite naturally within the context of the Vinča culture and its neighbors. This is not to assert that the Vinča signs reflect sentence writing, pictographic writing, or the use of phonemes (Gimbutas 1976a:78). So it is scarcely necessary to ask obtusely with Milojčić, "Oder haben die Sumerer in Rumänien schreiben gelernt?" (quoted by Makkay 1975:21 n. 53). Such a question simply illustrates the limitations of extreme diffusionist thought. But Winn has argued that these signs do nonetheless form a coherent graphic system, and Gimbutas has further developed this idea in relation to figurines and other symbolic objects.

THE "STAMP SEAL"

The "stamp seal" (SF 861; figure 10.6; plate 10.6) from Sitagroi belongs within the same general

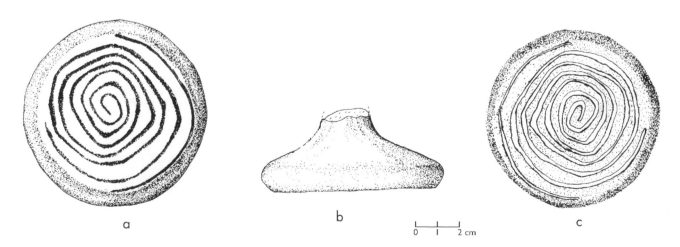

Figure 10.6. "Stamp seal" from phase III: SF 861 (plate 10.6): (a) enlargement; (b) side view; (c) imprint.

context. This form is common throughout much of the Balkans, and numerous examples are illustrated by Makkay (1984: figs. XVII–XX) in his useful survey. Most of them belong to his phase C (that is, Copper Age), and indeed the spiral seems to have been less a feature of the earlier Neolithic than the square-meander pattern with its rectilinear character. The form of the Sitagroi stamp seal finds close parallels in a number of finds from Thessaly, notably from Sesklo (Pini 1975:589, no. 715; Papathanassopoulos, ed. 1996:332, no. 279) and Macedonia, including Kalambaki in the plain of Drama (Pini 1975:354, no. 450; Papathanassopoulos, ed. 1996: 332, no. 277). The Greek stamp seals have been reviewed by Pilali-Papasteriou (1992) and Onassoglou (1996). There is an interesting parallel from the site of Drama on the Kalnitsa River, a tributary of the lower Tundzha River (also of the Maritsa River) in southern Bulgaria (Fol et al. 1989:76, fig. 24; also Lichardus et al. 1996: Taf. 3, nos. 5, 7).

It is necessary to question Makkay's suggestion that the Copper Age (his period C) stamp seals of the Balkans have an external derivation. He is right to make the point that they are much less common in his period B (Middle Neolithic) than in the preceding period A (Early Neolithic) or the succeeding period C. It does indeed seem generally the case that profuse decoration was not a feature of period B, whether on pottery or other media: the finds of Karanovo phase III, for instance, are decidedly sober in appearance. But there seems no need to postulate a hiatus; this is certainly not the view of Bulgarian scholars. Features of quite early Neolithic aspect may well overlap chronologically at some sites, such as Porodin, with others that we think of as Middle or Late Neolithic in character. The suggestion that there was some degree of continuity in the use of stamp seals in the Balkans between periods A and C seems far more economical.

But what were they used for? Whatever it was, it was not to stamp clay in the way that the seals of Bronze Age Greece and Crete were later used, for we lack the corresponding impressions. Various suggestions have been made, including the stamping of the skin (using pigment) for decorative purposes and the decoration of textiles. The red ochre in the incisions of Sitagroi cylinder SF 516 (figure 10.1a) might support this view. It is not necessary to resolve this problem here. We may simply remark that the Sitagroi cylinders may have functioned within a broadly similar context of use.

The suggestion is not irrelevant to the question of the clay cylinders, whose circular section evidently facilitates rotation. That is also, after all, the reason for the circular form of Near Eastern cylinder seals. But if these were not used to impress a design, they might have been made circular to allow them to roll. While their designs are continuous, rendering them ineffective as circular dice, they might nonetheless have functioned as gaming pieces. The combination of shape and decoration makes this possible. Several small clay balls found at Sitagroi may also have been gaming pieces.

DISCUSSION OF CLAY COUNTERS AND OTHER CLAY OBJECTS

Three categories of baked clay (that is, terra-cotta) beyond those already discussed have been selected from the Sitagroi finds for special discussion. The reasons for doing so are, in effect, external to the site at Sitagroi itself and the nature of the finds. For just as the cylinders from Sitagroi are valuable in illuminating the long-standing debate on potential "influences" from the preliterate period of Mesopotamia, so these objects must be considered in the light of a larger debate. That debate is based largely on the work of Denise Schmandt-Besserat (1992a, 1992b) and her claim that terra-cotta counters were used in western Asia from the Early Neolithic period onward as part of a complex accounting system that preceded the emergence of writing in those areas.

It should be stressed at once that these two themes of potential influence from western Asia refer to different time periods there. Each theory is to be discussed on its own merits, but the two should not be hastily conflated. The first issue, discussed above, is the theory of Makkay (1984) and others (including Vlassa [1963], Falkenstein [1965], Popovitch [1965], and Hood [1967]) that the clay cylinders, and in particular the signs seen in the Chalcolithic Balkans (Winn 1973), were related to and derive from the cultures of western Asia

411

(mainly Mesopotamia) in the Uruk, Jemdet Nasr, and Early Dynastic phases. As argued above, there are problems with this theory, and the Balkan contexts, such as Sitagroi II, may well be earlier than those of the alleged western Asiatic prototypes.

The chronological context of the features discussed by Schmandt-Besserat is much earlier, or at least it begins much earlier. The thrust of her argument is that the terra-cotta counters she describes were used in the areas in question from the early period of farming (about 8000 BC) onward. As we shall see, it cannot be denied that there are similarities between the terra-cotta spheres described here and the spherical counters ("spheres") of her Type 2 (Schmandt-Besserat 1996:131). The "counters" described here are of much the same form as the "equilateral" and "flat" cones that constitute types I,4 and I,6, respectively, of the Cones that constitute her Type 1 (Schmandt-Besserat 1996:128–129). The third class selected, which has been regarded by the Sitagroi excavators as "slingstones," or more accurately as "baked clay slingshots," visually resembles the biconoids that constitute Schmandt-Besserat's Type 9 (Schmandt-Besserat 1996:147). There are differences, however, as discussed below.

It is easy to see how a case might be made for thinking that the system Schmandt-Besserat describes for Mesopotamia and more widely in western Asia might be claimed for a much larger area, including Greece and the Balkans. It could be suggested that this was some wider diaspora already of the Early Neolithic (accompanying the early spread of the pintaderas so carefully documented by Makkay [1984]). That, of course, is a matter to be judged on the basis of the evidence. But it is pertinent, before taking the superficial analogy among these artifacts too far, to note two objections of a general nature.

The first of these is that the accounting system Schmandt-Besserat describes is really a *system* involving the simultaneous use of a considerable range of shapes among the counters which contrives "to endow each token shape, such as the cone, sphere or disc with a specific meaning. . . . Each token stood for one concept" (Schmandt-Besserat 1992a:161). It is readily seen that there is a restricted repertoire of forms at Sitagroi, so that the putative counters from the site could not be said to effectively constitute a system in this sense.

Second, there is the geographical situation, because tokens as described by Schmandt-Besserat are not found in Central Anatolia:

> In Turkey, tokens are limited to five sites located in the Taurus Mountains, like Gritille and Çayönü Tepesi, and along the Mediterranean Coast, like Can Hasan, Suberde and Beldibi. There is no evidence for the use of clay counters, however, at Çatal Höyük or Hacilar, suggesting that the token system never reached Central Anatolia. (Schmandt-Besserat 1992a:35)

I was not able to locate a specific reference in either of her major volumes (Schmandt-Besserat 1992a, 1992b) to a publication for Can Hasan and presume that the coastal location indicated (Schmandt-Besserat 1996:26, map 1, no. 13) refers to a different site from the one by that name excavated by David French. Moreover, the distribution of clay envelopes (Schmandt-Besserat 1992a:44, map 2) is a much more restricted one than that of counters, corresponding rather to the subsequent distribution of clay tablets (Schmandt-Besserat 1992a:56, map 3). This situation perhaps suggests that the complete functioning system, as she describes, had a more restricted distribution that was not shared by those Anatolian coastal sites. These are matters to keep in mind before making any sweeping claims for a system of counting on the basis of the discovery of a few, simple form, terra-cotta objects at southeast European sites. Each of the three forms in question (flat cones, spheres, and slingshots [biconoids]) may have had its own function quite outside the kind of counting or accounting system that Schmandt-Besserat envisaged for the Near East.

Counters (Cones, Equilateral, or Flat)

Several clay objects were found at Sitagroi. They are flat on the lower surface, in the form of a low cone on the upper surface, and decorated with a number of circular, dot-like incisions. Three of these "flat cones" (to use the descriptive terminology of Schmandt-Besserat) are illustrated in figure 10.7. SF 5199a (figure 10.7c) is from a phase II context (ZA 54); SF 105 (figure 10.7a) is also from a phase II context (KL layer 4); and SF 407 (figure 10.7b), from a mixed upper layer of KM, also possibly originates in a phase II context.

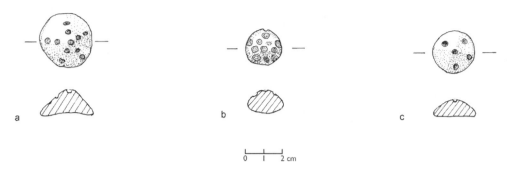

Figure 10.7. Clay "counters," phase II (a, c); unphased (b): (a) SF 105; (b) 407; (c) SF 5199a.

The function of these small objects, between 2.0 and 2.8 cm in diameter, is not known. A possible analogy is offered by the miniature loaves seen on a little model table from the site, which supports what seem to be model loaves of bread (figure 11.49; see also Theocharis 1975: fig. 130),whose form resembles that of the counters. However, an equally plausible suggestion is that these were gaming pieces or counters.

Spheres

Four complete spheres and two fragments were found with a regularly punctated surface, which makes them somewhat reminiscent of golf balls: SF 691 (figure 10.8a; plate 10.7e; diameter 2.5 cm, from phase V); SF 3607 (figure 10.8b, from an unstratified context); SF 3603 (plate 10.7d, incomplete, diameter 4.3 cm, from phase III); and SF 3826 (incomplete, diameter 3.6 cm, from phase III). The remaining two and SF 3607 cited above (plate 10.7c; diameter 2.6 cm) are also unstratified: SF 55 (plate 10.7a; diameter 2.9 cm); SF 81 (plate 10.7b). It is possible that they are contemporary with other plain spheres, one of which dates from phase II, eleven from phase III, one from phase IV, and seven from phase V. It is uncertain whether SF 691 (plate 10.7e) was actually *manufactured* in phase V, but this is perfectly possible. Treuil has published a comparable punctated sphere from Dikili Tash (1992; p.121and pls.148f and 201a) and notes the similarity of form and surface treatment. These punctated spheres could be claimed as the equivalent of Type 2.5 of Schmandt-Besserat (1996:131), but the form is a general one, and no connection need be assumed.

As noted above, the plain spheres (plates 10.8–10.9) are more numerous, with twenty from stratified contexts (phase III: plate 10.9) and three from unstratified. Most are between 2 and 3 cm in diameter, but three (SF 3562a–3562c; plate 10.8e, g, h), found together in a phase V context, are a little smaller. Tsountas (1908:345) refers to clay spheres from Sesklo and Mesiani Magoula in Thessaly, but the dimensions are not precisely given. He is inclined to class them with the biconoids.

The "Slingshots" or "Sling-bullets"

"Slingshot" (ellipsoidal) or "sling-bullet" (biconical) objects were found in phase I (five examples; plate 10.10a, c, e) and are common in phase II (fourteen cases; plates 10.10b, d; 10.11a–h), with four occurrences in phase III strata (plates 10.12a–c; 10.13a), two in phase IV, and four in phase V (plate 10.13b). Their greatest abundance, therefore, was in phase II. In general they are plump: the maximum diameter is generally greater than half the length. Most, but not all, exceed 4.0 cm in length and are thus distinctly larger than the majority of the biconoid counters of Schmandt-Besserat's Type 9 (Schmandt-Besserat 1996:147) or the small (1 cm

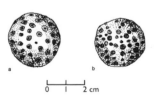

Figure 10.8. "Golf balls," phase V (a); unphased (b): (a) SF 691, plate 10.7e; (b) SF 3607, plate 10.7c.

long) "olive-shaped sling-bolts" reported from Servia (Mould et al. 2000:266; 268: fig. 4.39, SF 1066 A–C). Their weights, when available (see appendix 10.2), often exceed 20 g.

As with other minor baked clay objects, there are rather few published comparanda from east Macedonia except for several from Dikili Tash (Treuil 1992: p. 120 and pls. 148b, c and 200g). From trench I at Vassilika, some 15 km southeast of Thessaloniki, comes a closely similar object (Grammenos 1984: pls. 63,4 and 156) described as a slingshot (*pessos sphendonas*), while a similar piece from unit 15 of trench II at Vassilika (Grammenos 1984:153, pl. 60,39) is similarly documented. These pieces were published by Grammenos (1991: pls. 37,4 and 34,39). Examples from Late Neolithic Olynthos and Kapoutzedes in Macedonia, designated as sling-bullets, are cited by Heurtley (1939:78).

In Thessaly published finds are more numerous: 110 clay slingshots were found at Sesklo (Tsountas 1908:344), and the form is compared with stone examples from Sesklo and Dhimini (Tsountas 1908:329, figs. 252, 253), which compare well in appearance with the Sitagroi examples. Wace and Thompson (1912) cite sling-bullets from Rachmani, Mesiani Magoula, Sesklo, Dhimini, Tsangli, Tsani, Zerelia, and Chaeronia. A hoard of 131 such items was found at Rachmani.

CONCLUSION

The overall conclusion must be that these three classes of object, like the clay cylinders of Sitagroi, belong in a north Aegean and indeed essentially Balkan context. Just as the arguments of Falkenstein (1965) and Vlassa (1963) for a Near Eastern origin for the celebrated Tărtăria tablets are to be rejected, so, too, should be any comparable argument for the Sitagroi cylinders. As I have argued, it would be imprudent to extend to the north Aegean and the Balkans the interesting case made by Schmandt-Besserat (1996) for the clay tokens of the Near East with their postulated accounting system. There are not yet good arguments to suggest a link between the two.

NOTE

[1] Catalogs in appendixes 10.1 and 10.2 are organized as follows: Phase; type (cylinder, stamp, counter for appendix 10.1 and sphere, biconoid for appendix 10.2); SF number (in numerical sequence); context; reference to illustration; description; measurements (L or H, W, D, Ht in cm; weights in grams); and bibliographic reference. Complete information was not always available.

Appendix 10.1.

Catalog of Cylinders, Stamps, and Counters

Colin Renfrew

PHASE II

Cylinders

446   KM 13; figure 10.1b; plate 10.2
Brown clay cylinder of fine paste, lightly burnished and well fired. The incised decoration is divided into upper and lower zones by a double line at the middle. The upper zone is defined by a double line at the top, the lower by a single line at the bottom. The decoration within each zone consists of a series of S-shaped incisions with an incomplete border of zigzags above and below. The cylinder is unperforated, and each end is decorated with a single diametric line flanked on each side by a V-shape formed by two incisions.
L: 3.9; D: 1.3
Illustrated: Pini 1975: no. 636; Makkay 1984: no. 231; Renfrew 1987:344 (fig. 2), 343 (pl. B); Theocharis 1973: fig. 238, right

516   KM 7; figure 10.1a, plate 10.1
Brown clay cylinder, with a porous surface decorated with incisions. It is perforated along its length. The decoration consists of zigzag lines. Each is formed by five or six separate oblique incisions, which together form a zigzag along the main axis. The ends are undecorated. Note that traces of red ochre remain in the incisions.
L: 3.5; D: 1.2; HD: 0.3
Illustrated: Pini 1975: no. 633; Makkay 1984: no. 228; Renfrew 1987:341 (fig. 1), 342 (pl. A); Theocharis 1973: fig. 238, left

1443   ZA 50; figure 10.2a; plate 10.4
Irregularly shaped oblong of approximately cylindrical form, of gray-brown clay. The decoration is of rather crude, deep incised parallel lines. The cylinder is unperforated, and the ends are tapering and undecorated.
L: 5.0; D: 1.3–1.5
Illustrated: Renfrew 1987:349 (fig. 4), 350 (pl. D)

3684   ZG 43; figure 10.1c; plate 10.3
Gray-brown clay cylinder, with slightly flattened section. The incised decoration is divided into two zones by a central line, and each zone is defined at the end of the cylinder by a further line. Within each zone the decoration consists of a series of short, straight, incised lines, all set at about 45° to the axis of the cylinder so as to intersect at right angles, forming V-shapes and crosses. The cylinder is unperforated, and each end is decorated by two incisions, forming a cross.
L: 3.8; D: 1.2–1.5
Illustrated: Pini 1975: no. 635; Gimbutas 1976: fig. 5, 8; Makkay 1984: no. 230; Renfrew 1987:347 (fig. 3), 348 (pl. C); Theocharis 1975: fig. 238, center;

Counters

105   KL 4; figure 10.7a
Flat cone of smooth, matt-surfaced, light brown clay. The flat underside is slightly concave. The conical surface has a pattern of excised dots, 1–2 mm deep, cut at the apex and in two concentric circles, each of five holes, so as to form five lines radiating from the apex.
D: 2.8; Th: 1.4
Illustrated: Renfrew 1987:367, fig. 9

407   KM 2 (superficial levels, underlain by material of phase II); figure 10.7b
Hemispherical form of baked clay with red matt surface. The underside is lightly convex; the surface bears decoration of excised dots about 2 mm deep. One of these is at the apex, with four in a circle below, and a further five in an outer circle.
D: 2.0; Th: 1.2
Illustrated: Renfrew 1987:367, fig. 9

445   KM 10
Clay disk. Incomplete (missing approximately one third) with lightly concave base and slightly convex upper surface. The decoration takes the form of

four roughly circular excisions about 4 mm in diameter, grouped at the center.
D: 3.4; Th: 0.6

5199(a) ZA 52; figure 10.7c

5199(b, c)
These three are approximately conical, of a flattened, bun shape. 5199a has a small incised dot about 2 mm deep at the apex, and four further excised dots below (see Renfrew 1987:367, fig. 9 [5199a])
D: 2.3; H 0.8 (the dimensions of 5199b and c are not recorded.)

PHASE III

Stamp or "Pintadera"

861 MM layer 41; figure 10.6; plate 10.6
Circular baked clay object with one flat surface. Approximately conical form, rising toward what may have been a finial or knob handle, now broken. The color is light brown, the surface smoothed and slightly porous. The flat underside bears incised decoration consisting of a spiral with six rotations, partially enclosed by an incised semicircle.
D: 3.9; H: 1.6 (broken)
Illustrated: Renfrew 1987:365, fig. 8

PHASE VB

Cylinder

1145 PN layer 5; figure 10.2b; plate 10.5
Brown to dark gray baked clay cylinder. Incised decoration in three zones of zigzags separated by single horizontal lines. The zigzags run horizontally (at right angles to the axis of the cylinder) and are regularly formed by short, straight, intersecting incised lines. The cylinder is unperforated, and each end is decorated by two incisions, forming a cross.
L: 6.0; D: 1.5–1.7
Illustrated: Pini 1975: no. 634; Makkay 1984: no. 229; Renfrew 1987:351 (fig. 5), 352 (pl. E)

Appendix 10.2.
Catalog of Spheres and Biconoids

Colin Renfrew

PHASE I

Biconoids

117   KL 15; plate 10.10e
Biconical; surface: buff, pink
L: 5.6; W: 3.0

2543   JL 105
Biconical; one end broken off

2694   KLb 129; plate 10.10c
Biconical; fragmentary; surface: pink/green; clay of
poor quality
L: 4.4; W: 2.8

4103   KLb 132; plate 10.10a
Biconical; surface: buff
L: 5.6; W: 3.1; Wt: 48.0

PHASE II

Spheres

4800   KL 2
Half fragment; irregularly oval; surface: coarse, red,
markings on apparently broken side
D: 4.9; W: 2.6

Biconoids

107   ML 6
Biconical; surface: orange/black
L: 5.0; W: 2.5; Wt: 24.0

411   KM 2
Biconical; partly broken; poorly baked
L: 4.9; W: 2.5; Wt: 27.5

417   KL 2
Biconical
L: 4.6; W: 2.6; Wt: 29.0

922   ZA 54s; plate 10.11g
Biconical; surface: matt
L: 4.2; W: 2.3; Wt: 22.0

964   KM 18; plate 10.11b
Biconical; surface: buff with black patches
L: 4.8; W: 2.8; Wt: 35.0

2613   KL 114; plate 10.11e
Biconical; surface: tan, black with fire spots; coarse
temper; may have been used unbaked and fired by
chance
L: 4.3; W: 2.2; Wt: 22.0

2635   KL 115; plate 10.11h
Biconical; one side chipped
L: 3.4; W: 2.3; Wt: 13.0

2638   KL 117; plate 10.11a
Biconical
L: 6.2; W: 3.2; Wt: 46.0

2643   KL 117; plate 10.11f
Biconical; surface: brown/gray
L: 3.6; W: 2.2; Wt: 13.5

2660   KL 117
Conical; surface: tan; gritty clay
L: 2.0; W: 2.2

2677   KLb 118; plate 10.11c
Biconical
L: 5.5; W: 2.8; Wt: 34.5

2678   KLb 119s; plate 10.10d
Biconical; decoration: two crescent-like incisions on
one side
L: 4.0; W: 2.0; Wt: 14.5

2680   KLb 120; plate 10.10b
Biconical; surface: orange
L: 5.8; W: 2.8; Wt: 35.5

4226   ZE 97; plate 10.11d
Ellipsoidal; surface: orange with large pieces of grit
L: 5.3; W: 3.0; Wt: 40.0

PHASE III

Spheres

153   MM 8; plate 10.8b
Surface: smooth
D: 2.7; Wt: 19.0

157   MM 11; plate 10.9e
Surface: smooth
D: 3.4

383 MM 21; plate 10.9b
Surface: smooth
D: 2.3

385 MM 21; plate 10.9a
Surface: coarse, light gray/brown
D: 4.3

723 ML 100; plate 10.9c
Irregularly spherical; surface: dark patches
D: 3.0; Wt: 24.0

837 MM 27; plate 10.9f
Surface: smooth, matt, dark gray
D: 2.1

881 MM 43; plate 10.9d
Surface: smooth, light gray with red/light brown
patches; core: dark gray.
D: 2.8

3603 ZG 32; plate 10.7d
Half fragment; surface: matt, gray; core: gray with
organic inclusions. Decorated with evenly spaced
punctations, producing a "golf ball" effect.
D: 4.3

3826 MMc 65
Half fragment; surface: matt, pale tan, indented.
Decorated with evenly spaced punctations, produc-
ing a "golf ball" effect.
D: 3.6; W: 1.7; Wt: 20

3880 MMd 68; plate 10.9j
Fragment; surface: smooth, matt, gray; core: tan
D: 3.0

5192 ZA 44s; plate 10.9h
Surface: smooth
D: 2.1; Wt: 10.0

5193 ZA 44s; plate 10.9i
Surface: smooth
D: 2.2; Wt: 11.0

5198 ZA 48s; plate 10.9g
Surface: smooth
D: 2.5

Biconoids

394 ML 5; plate 10.12b
Biconical; broken; surface: reddish
L: 4.2; W: 3.4

531 ZA 42; plate 10.12c
Biconical; two fragments joined; surface: dark, matt
L: 6.0; W: 3.5; Wt: 62.0

1278 MM 51; plate 10.12a
Biconical; surface: reddish, black discoloration on
one side
L: 5.3; W: 3.2; Wt: 45.5

2779 ZE 72; plate 10.13a
Biconical; surface: reddish with dark discoloration
L: 5.2; W: 3.1; Wt: 48.5

PHASE V

Spheres

691 QN 5; figure 10.8a; plate 10.7e
Decorated with evenly spaced punctations, produc-
ing a "golf ball" effect
D: 2.5

2011 ROc 7; plate 10.8a
Somewhat spherical with one edge flattened and
another pointed. Surface: smooth, gray with white
deposit
H: 4.0; D: 3.9; Wt: 72.5

2083 POd 34; plate 10.8f
Somewhat cylindrical; surface: smooth, gray with
reddish tinge
D: 1.5; Th: 1.2; Wt: 3.2

2090 PO (level not indicated); plate 10.8d
Irregularly oval; surface: coarse, dark brown, some
discoloration
D: 2.5; W: 1.6; Wt: 9.0

2401 PNf 53; plate 10.8c
Fragment; surface: coarse, red; unbaked
D: 2.9

3562a POd 32, plate 10.8h
Irregularly spherical; surface: light brown; partially
baked
D: 1.5–2.0; Wt: 7.0

3562b POd 32; plate 10.8e
Irregularly spherical; surface: light brown; partially
baked
D: 1.7–2.3; Wt: 9.0

3562c POd 32; plate 10.8g
Irregularly spherical; surface: light brown; partially
baked
D: 1.4-1.6; Wt: 3.0

Biconoids

20 ZA 2; plate 10.13b
Biconical
L: 4.1; W: 2.3; Wt: 21.0

3765 PN extension
Biconical; surface: buff encrustation, very dark
gray/black
L: 4.5; W: 2.4; Wt: 23.0

4301 PNb 104
Conical; broken; surface: orange
L: 2.5; W: 2.6

4354 PN/PO balk
      Ellipsoidal; surface: buff, gray
      L: 4.6; W: 2.9

4768 POb 1
      Biconical; surface: reddish/gray
      L: 4.5; W: 2.0; Wt: 13.5

UNPHASED/MIXED CONTEXTS

Spheres

55   Surface; plate 10.7a
      Surface: rough, porous, brown, with punctations
      that give a "golf ball" effect
      D: 2.9

81   Surface; plate 10.7b
      Fragment; surface: rough, porous, reddish/brown,
      with punctations that give a "golf ball" effect
      D: 1.9

3607 Surface; figure 10.8b; plate 10.7c
      Decorated with evenly spaced punctations that give
      a "golf ball" effect
      D: 2.6; Wt: 1.8

4764 OJb 1
      Surface: matt, gray
      D: 2.5; Wt: 13.5

Biconoids

435   IL surface
      Biconical; friable; unbaked clay
      L: 4.6; W: 2.8

5558 Unknown
      Ellipsoidal
      L: 4.6; W: 2.9; Wt: 48.0

5559 Unknown
      Biconical (?) fragment; preserved end pointed
      L: 3.0; W: 2.7

11.

Paralipómena and Other Plastic Forms

Ernestine S. Elster and Marianna Nikolaidou

INTRODUCTION

This chapter presents clay objects that were recorded separately from the bulk of excavated ceramics because of their unique shape or decoration. It does not include the entire array of special clay artifacts retrieved at the site, since in this volume, chapter 6 covers spindle whorls, loom weights, and other spinning and weaving tools; chapter 9 treats beads, pendants, and other items of adornment; and chapter 10 covers seals, pintaderas, slingshots, spheres, and counters. In addition, the figurines, tripods, plastic vessels, and similar objects were treated earlier (see volume 1: chapters 9 [Gimbutas 1986] and 10 [Elster 1986]). Many of these objects are *paralipómena* ("things left out") or were illustrated but referred to only briefly and might have been included in the first volume but for the fact that volume 1 was exceedingly full. Others make up distinct formal and/or functional groups that are fully presented here for the first time. Each category—objects of utility, pottery, plastic forms, and miniatures and models—contains several distinct types or subtypes, including ladles, plugs, sieve fragments, pottery profiles, worked and reshaped sherds, fragments of vessels, handles, lids, figurine parts, and enigmatic objects, such as miniature furniture and house forms.

This heterogeneous grouping of miscellanea points to a whole spectrum of activities at the Sitagroi village. We have tried to maximize the information to be drawn from items occurring with low frequency rather than publishing just a listing. When the different classes of artifacts are considered together, interesting functional categories of material culture may be reconstructed which illuminate both mundane and ritual aspects of life in the prehistoric household.

The catalog (appendix 11.1) and distribution tables are based on the inventory card data and study notebooks. The information follows the structure used throughout this volume: artifacts are sorted by phase and category, in numerical order by small find (SF) number, followed by context, type/subtype, description, comments, and lastly, measurements (in cm). In the following sections we discuss the artifacts with reference to the line drawings and plates, reflect on their role at the site, and refer to comparanda from volume 1, from the site of Dikili Tash in the Drama Plain (Treuil 1992), from Dhimitra, just west of the plain itself (Grammenos, ed. 1997), and related cultures in the Aegean and the Balkans. It certainly comes as no surprise to find again what we already learned from volume 1, that there are many similarities among the Neolithic/Chalcolithic and Early Bronze Age (EBA) sites of the Drama Plain and those of the same time period farther north. Excavation reports are famously uneven, and especially so in terms of miscellaneous objects, although the miniatures and models have found a more systematic reportage.

Categorization of the material into classes and types relies both on formal and inferred functional criteria. The artifact classes are presented in a sequence that leads from what appears to be repeatedly made or used domestic equipment to items of a more pronounced symbolic and/or ritual quality that exhibit formal and/or symbolic elaboration. Formal and perhaps semantic elaboration is observable on individual items across categories. As archaeologists we try to put things in order so that we may more systematically describe their form and propose how they functioned. However, our interpretations are ambiguous at best.

Objects of Utility, Pottery, and Plastic Forms
Ernestine S. Elster

OBJECTS OF UTILITY

Objects of utility include ladles, reshaped and reworked sherds of discoid and other forms, lids, plugs or stoppers, and sieve fragments, plus ambiguous artifacts.

Ladles

Sixteen ladles from various phases have been recorded with more than half recovered from phase III. Two handle fragments (SF 186 [figure 11.1; plate 11.1a]; SF 3418 [plate 11.1:b; and volume 1: plate XCI: bottom right: 1, 2]) represent handled spoons or ladles with bowls more generous than a single serving requires. For example, the bowls are roughly 7 cm across with a depth of about 3.5 cm; including the handle they might have reached about 20 cm in length. Interestingly, red ochre pigment was observed inside the SF 3418 bowl and in SF 1486 (not illustrated; see appendix 11.1), although identification has never been confirmed. Excellent comparanda are published from Achilleion (Gimbutas, Winn, and Shimabuku 1989: 364, pl. 7.22:2), Dikili Tash (Marangou 1992: 33–143, pls. 157–163, 204b–g, 205a–g; Karanovo (Hiller and Nikolov 1997: Taf. 69:2), and Servia (Ridley et al. 2000: 266, 267, 273, fig. 4.41: SF 642, SF 285).

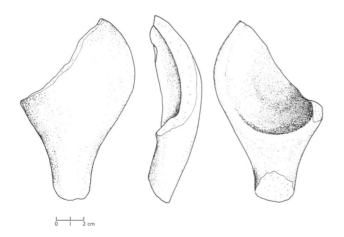

Figure 11.1. Ladle, phase III: SF 186, plate 11.1a.

Another handle was attached to the fragment of a flatter bowl (plate 11.2); it is burnished and carefully formed with just the edge of a bowl or pan remaining. The handle wings out or widens at its termination much like examples from Dikili Tash (Treuil 1992: pls. 162d; 205f, left) and Thermi (Lamb 1936: fig. 45:10). The Thermi ladles are perforated as if for hanging, whereas the one from Sitagroi is not.

Some of these ladles were serving pieces of particular significance, with handles terminating in a sculptured, abstract human head (Treuil 1992: pls. 159, 204b, c, 205a–c). SF 1486 from phase III (not illustrated) bears graphite-painted decoration on the bowl exterior. Whether or not they were set aside for particular functions, to be used with special food and/or people, the dimension of the bowls allows us to infer their role in serving, processing, and/or measuring liquids or dry substances.

Reworked and Reshaped Sherds

This grouping consists of over two dozen sherds, all having been reworked into unique (plate 11.3b) as well as geometric forms (triangles: plate 11.3a, d; discs: plate 11.4). The majority of the sherds are from phase V, followed by phase III. A small number are from unphased contexts. Although these artifacts were originally part of a vessel of some type, their current reworked form sets them apart from the original pottery. The majority were made on undecorated sherds.

Discs

Discs are flat sherds shaped into a circular form that ranges between 4.0 and 5.3 cm in diameter and 1.0 to 2.0 cm thick; the faces are unworked and reflect the color or lack thereof of the original fragment. The edges have been ground, but whether or not these edges were utilized in some way is not known. All the discs illustrated (plate 11.4) are from sherds of a single color or of different colors on each face. Painted sherds are reshaped (see catalog, phase III: SF 3534), some as whorls (chapter 6). At the site of Obre II in Bosnia (Gimbutas 1974), excavators reported several pottery discs that show the beginnings of perforations but are not finished (Sterud and Sterud 1974: pl. XXIV:5, 6). Intuitively, it seems that production of these discs would not have been difficult: a sherd is selected and reduced to a circular form by chipping away the irregular edge against a solid surface, perhaps with a small axe (chapter 5); once circular, the edge is ground smooth. Potentially these discs may have been used as counters, gaming pieces, lids for small mouth jars, or perhaps worked further into spindle whorls.

Distinct Forms

Distinct from the discs are sherds of triangular or unique shape that are produced as above but exhibit both smoothed surfaces and edges. Three are illustrated: two triangles from phase III (SF 4575 [plate 11.3a] and SF 4909, with black decoration on a red background [plate 11.3d]) and one unique shape from a mixed context (SF 3720, ZL 1 [plate 11.3b]). The two triangular, flat sherds are similar in size and are comparable to a Selevac artifact described as a "pot polisher" (Tringham 1990:672, pl. 10.6b). These have been carefully prepared; it is possible they were employed in polishing or burnishing pottery, but they also could have been used as gaming pieces or counters.

The final worked sherd illustrated (SF 504; plate 11.5) is a vessel fragment from phase II with three holes drilled, one below and two on each side of the broad handle which sweeps up and could have been part of a jar, mug, or bowl. Another fragment of a handle with perforations is SF 4108 (phase I, not illustrated; see appendix 11.1). It has been tabulated with the worked sherds because of the drilled holes, but it is also possible that the edges were ground. A glance at the pottery chapters 11, 12, and 13 of volume 1 provides many parallels for this fragment of *paralipómena*.

Lids, Plugs, Oven Stoppers

Six artifacts have been identified as lids, including three illustrated in volume 1 (see plate LXXXVI:11–13; SF 856, 1200, and 1296). All lids (circular, oval, or square with central knob-handles) were recovered from phases prior to the EBA. Most of the plugs, however, were recovered from contexts in the EBA and include two carefully shaped, well-modeled and fired rounded cones (SF 4306: figure 11.2; illustrated in volume 1: plate XXXII:10), one of which has

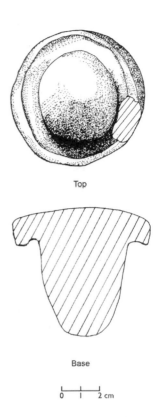

Top

Base

0   2 cm

Figure 11.2. Plug from the Burnt House, phase Va: SF 4306.

a broad base (SF 3657; plate 11.6). SF 4306 does indeed resemble a miniature "bowler hat"; it was recovered from the phase Va Burnt House and thus functioned in a domestic context, ambiguous at best.

It is likely that the hemispherical lumps of clay, found from the EBA, were also plugs (plates 11.7, 11.8). Although four were published earlier (volume 1: plate CI:8–11), we illustrate them again (and two others) and provide different views: SF 309 (plates 11.7a, 11.8a); SF 1301 (plate 11.7b); SF 1087 (plates 11.7c, 11.8c); SF 5560 (plates 11.7d, 11.8b); SF 1351 (plate 11.7e); and SF 1646 (plate 11.7f). They are roughly shaped, of coarse fabric, and poorly fired but with a ridge circling the object which provides the argument for their use. In appearance they are quite similar and range in diameter from 7.0 to 11.0 cm (plates 11.7, 11.8). They could have been used, if unfired, to stop a jar or jug. There are many vessels with openings of the right dimension (see volume 1, chapter 13 [Sherratt 1986]). However, because the inventory cards note that several are "crudely or poorly baked, baked at base," another interpretation is that these lumps of unfired clay were plugged into a hole at the side of an oven and used to control the firing. During that process, they were partially baked. It should be noted, however, that these artifacts are smaller than the diameter of the "draft hole" (14 cm) of the single "oven" with this feature (Oven 2 in the Burnt House; see volume 1 [C. Renfrew 1986b]:191). So again their use is ambiguous.

Perforated Fragments

These fragmentary *paralipómena* may be compared to examples of partially or completely preserved "sieves" published in volume 1, from phase I (figure 11.7:5 [plate LXXVII, bottom: 6], figure 11.7:8 [plate LXXVII, bottom: 3], figure 11.8:12); phase II (figure 11.10:15); phase III (figure 12.10:6 [plate XCIII, top left]); and phase IV (plate CI:7). A drawing of the latter is illustrated in this volume (SF 2737, ZE 64; figure 11.3), as is a small curved "sieve" fragment from phase III (SF 1135; figure 11.4) with four rows of regularly placed holes. SF 2737 (figure 11.3), described as "shoe-shaped" on the inventory card, is a match of two fragments: one separated from the mass of pottery in the context of ZE 64 and given a small find number, and the other subsequently plucked from the wash table for the match. As preserved, it is 11.2 cm high and 6.5 cm at its widest point, with

holes all over the body, but none on the "base," although the finished form is unclear.

Perforated pottery has been regarded as auxiliary to food preparation, and the name "sieve" implies that something was put inside which required ventilation (aromatic herbs) or straining (cheese making). Ada Kalogirou (1995:5) examined perforated sherds from Greek Neolithic sites, and after reviewing the literature she suggested that because these sieves are few in number, the original containers were not in high demand and were probably used only occasionally for very specific or seasonal tasks. She further reports that, based on ethnography, they might have been used for sprouting corn, producing brine from burned goat and sheep dung, or burning coal for the emission of smoke. One could also add to that list the burning of roots, aromatic leaves, herbs, or sprouts. Their use must have been diverse at Sitagroi, as the original vessels differ so much in size. Other fragments of rough pottery covered with perforations have been published from Poliochni (Brea 1964:626, Tav. CXXXIV: a, c, f) and Obre II (Sterud and Sterud 1974:199, pl. XXIV:8).

SF 1527 (QO 8, phase V) was recorded as a "crucible fragment." Although we have no line drawing or plate, earlier published crucible fragments were recovered from phase III (see chapter 8; also, volume 1: plate XCIII, top right: 4–6).

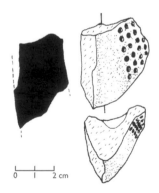

Figure 11.4. Perforated fragment, phase III ("sieve"): SF 1135.

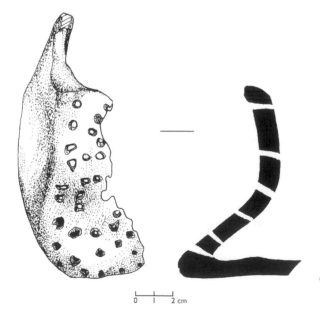

(Left): Figure 11.3. Perforated fragment ("sieve"), phase IV: SF 2737.

POTTERY

Over fifty artifacts are associated with this grouping, including complete vessels and fragments of recognizable shape (small and medium-sized open bowls with flat or concave bases including half of a double vessel with legs), incised flat handles (a distinctive group, occasionally referred to as "plaque handles"), and various sherds.

Pots

Pots are rightly considered *paralipómena* for, although fairly small, they could have been published in volume 1 with the specific chapters on pottery. The distinctive graphite decoration of Chalcolithic phase III ceramic artifacts, which Robert Evans described as "the most characteristic [pottery] of the Dikili Tash phase" (volume 1 [R. Evans 1986]:397) appears as swirling spirals on a black, brown, or red burnished surface. SF 185 from a phase III context (figure 11.5) is a small square bowl (6.5 cm on a side) with a centered shallow depression (2.5 cm deep) and the remains of a horizontal handle extending from one side. It exhibits such a pattern on the red-burnished sides, and under the

bowl are the stubs of a pair of legs. These stubs may represent half of the original artifact, with the "handle" actually connecting the double bowls. With another pair of stubby legs, it would have stood upright. A double bowl with a linking bridge is not unusual for phase III (volume 1: figure 10.9:10), but it does suggest a special role in the ceramic inventory or symbolic repertoire of any household. It may have held incense, or it may have been used in ceremonies or events. The graphite decoration is a signature for phase III ceramics and is often repeated among the artifacts earlier illustrated (see volume 1: figures 12.2–12.6). Such artifacts illustrated here include three sherds representing pedestaled bowls: two are from phase III (SF 189 [figure 11.6] and SF 87 [figure 11.8]), and the other sherd is from an unknown context but is likely attributable to either phase II or III (SF 775; figure 11.7). All of these pedestaled bowls were modeled with open bowls bearing incised decoration, similar to those published earlier (see volume 1: figure 11.10:1–6) and may also be compared to similar shapes from Karanovo (Hiller and Nikolov 1997: Taf. 10:26; 11:13, 17; 16:13).

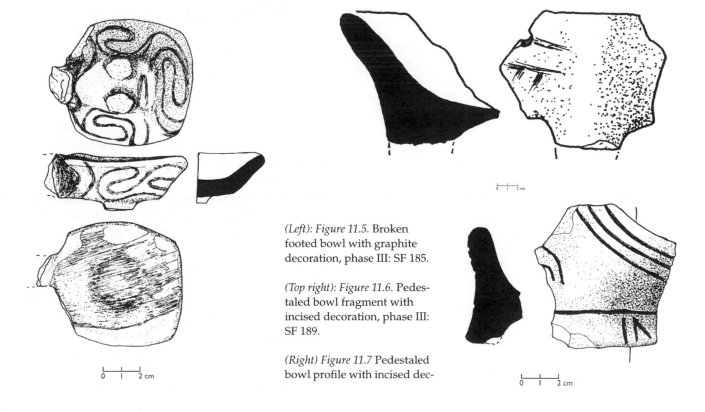

(Left): Figure 11.5. Broken footed bowl with graphite decoration, phase III: SF 185.

(Top right): Figure 11.6. Pedestaled bowl fragment with incised decoration, phase III: SF 189.

(Right) Figure 11.7 Pedestaled bowl profile with incised dec-

A small, low, fractured, rectangular, open bowl (SF 47, MM30; figure 11.9; plate 11.9) can be compared to an earlier published "coarse rectangular bowl" (volume 1: plate XCV:3). Its various features reflect Middle Neolithic and Chalcolithic vessels, such as a Kritsana-like rim and low height (volume 1: figure 12.13:3, 4); and the square opening (volume 1: figures 11.16:10, 12.10:2).

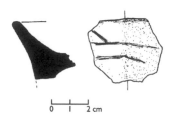

Figure 11.8. Pedestaled bowl profile with incised decoration, phase III: SF 87.

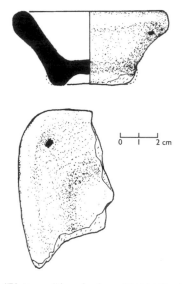

Figure 11.9. "Kritsana" bowl, phase III: SF 47, plate 11.9.

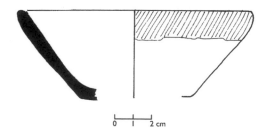

Figure 11.10. Open bowl, unphased (II–III?): SF 1414.

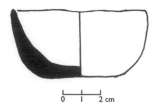

Figure 11.11. Rounded bowl, phase IV: SF 50.

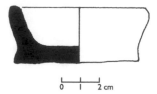

Figure 11.12. Shallow bowl with protruding base, phase III: SF 71.

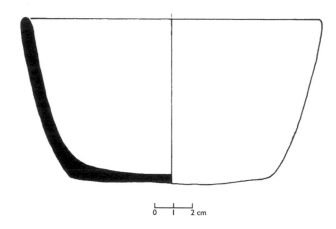

Figure 11.13. Open bowl with flat base from the Bin Complex, phase Vb: SF 153.

Another low, open bowl from an unknown context (SF 1414; figure 11.10) is flat-based with straight, flaring sides, quite similar to published vessels from phase II (volume 1: figure 11.17:9) and from phase III (volume 1: figure 12.14:1). Phase IV provided us with a small, flat-based bowl with straight sides but a rounded, open top (SF 50; figure 11.11), which is similar in profile to a slightly larger, deeper version published earlier (volume 1: figure 13.5:2).

A shallow, thick-walled bowl with a protruding base (SF 71; figure 11.12) like the base of an EBA urn published earlier (volume 1: figure 13.22:8) comes from phase III.

A deep, open bowl with a flat base (SF 153, QO 7; figure 11.13) was recovered from phase Vb contexts. The open shape is easily comparable to several that appear in the distribution sheet of EBA pottery published earlier (volume 1: figure 13.2) and is midway in size between two other similarly shaped bowls from the EBA (volume 1: figure 13.24: 3, 11). It is of interest that none of these pots were described as highly burnished or slipped or painted and therefore are probably all part of the kitchen repertoire of the various time periods that they represent at Sitagroi.

Lastly, there are two finds (not illustrated; see appendix 11.1) that contain traces of red ochre: SF 2791, a partial bowl from phase IV, and SF 4778, a body fragment from phase Va. These ceramics are otherwise undecorated, and it seems they were used as containers for pigment. The most obvious use of the pigment would be to fill the incisions of those wares. However, that type is most common in phase III, while the fragments above contain red ochre are from phase IV and Va, suggesting perhaps another use of pigment.

Incised Flat Pieces

These fragments are also referred to as "plaques" (as in the catalog, appendix 11.1) because of the incised designs on the surface of fairly flat, rectangular-like forms (plates 11.10, 11.11). The designs are composed of combinations and repeating sets of lines: multiple curves (plates 11.10b–e, 11.11c), straight lines (plate 11.11a, b; figure 11.14), angled lines (plate 11.11d), sometimes with incisions forming a centered oval or diamond (plate 11.10a, b, f) and zigzags (plate 11.10g, h). All of these fragments exhibit three finished edges and one broken edge that seems to have been the point of connection (legs, handles?) with a bowl, pan, or perhaps a stand. If part of a stand, these pieces would then have been the sides or legs of a flat-topped form as is represented by the corner fragments (volume 1: figures 10.1:5, 6, 10.9:1–5).

Two attributes divide these artifacts into separate groupings: the presence (plate 11.10a–e, h) or absence (plates 11.10f, g, 11.11a–d) of an opening centered along the fractured edge, and a straight (plate 11.11a, b, d; figure 11.14) or waisted form (plates 11.10, 11.11c). If they are horizontal handles, there is a similarity to an earlier published artifact with a centered opening from phase Vb (volume 1: figure 13.27:21). The straight form bears similarities

to fragments from the sides of social ceramics (see volume 1, chapter 10 [Elster 1986]), to "cult objects" from Karanovo (Hiller and Nikolov 1997: Taf. 100:3), and to some of the incised designs on earlier published figurines (see volume 1, chapter 9 [Gimbutas 1986]). The width of the finished edge is remarkably similar: 5.0 cm to 7.4 cm. We have thickness measurements for a few with a range of 0.7 to 1.3 cm. None of these incised flat pieces is longer than 7.4 cm. The waisted artifacts were recovered from Middle Neolithic and EBA contexts; the straight ones are from phases II and III.

Graphite designs cover the outside of one rectangular arm and the flat, square-like top/face of an unusual fragment, shaped like an inverted U (SF 5024; figure 11.15). It could be the broad handle of a vessel, attached so that the painted arm and face

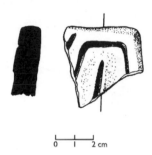

Figure 11.14. Incised flat piece ("plaque"?), unphased: SF 86.

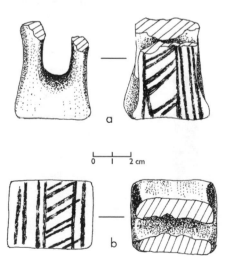

Figure 11.15. V-shaped handle (?) fragment with graphite decoration, unphased (III?): SF 5024; (a) two side views; (b) top and bottom view.

would be observable, with the underarm unpainted. Although this fragment comes from an unknown context, the design of multiple straight and paired angled lines is very much at home among the graphite-painted decoration of phase III (volume 1 [R. Evans 1986]:415–418).

The final pieces in this section consist of two body sherds: SF 85 (figure 11.16) is from an unknown context, and SF 4778 (not illustrated) is from phase V. Both bear button-like protuberances. They may be compared to an earlier published example from phase III (volume 1: figure 12.11:3) and to those from Karanovo (Hiller and Nikolov 1997: Taf. 17:30, 21:10). Phase IV yielded a base (?) fragment incised with paired, rounded lines in antithetical position (SF 1402: figure 11.17; plate 11.12). The incised face is rounded; its obverse is flat. Although the design seems familiar, there are no exact parallels.

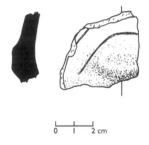

Figure 11.16. Incised body fragment with "omphalos," unphased: SF 85.

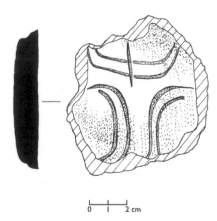

Figure 11.17. Incised fragment (base?), phase IV: SF 1402, plate 11.12.

PLASTIC FORMS

Artifacts in this class all possess a plastic or three-dimensional quality. Much of the material can be related to figurines and social ceramics published in volume 1, chapters 9 and 10. The fragments of figurines include schematically depicted body parts: leg, foot, thigh, torso, head, trunk, and phallus. They are presented below in order of similarity.

1. SF 416a, b (KL 21; plate 11.13a, b) from phase I: two upper leg pieces (not a pair), fractured at the "waist"; comparable to earlier published artifacts from Sitagroi (volume 1: figure 9.103, cat. no. 3) and one from Achilleion (Gimbutas 1989a:243, no. 134, fig. 7.144).

2. SF 233 (ZA 49; figure 11.18; plate 11.13c) from phase III: the top section of a similar figurine leg broken off at "thigh" and "waist"; comparable to the rounded part of SF 416 (above) and earlier published fragments (volume 1: figure 9.109, cat. no. 58). The latter is incised, but the finish of those above are reported as smooth.

3. SF 237 (ZA 51; figure 11.19) from phase II: the form of a foot, fractured at the ankle and similar to many single feet recovered from the site, especially an earlier published fragment (volume 1: plate LXXII:13).

4. SF 5579 (ROc 59; plate 11.14): a leg that differs from those above because it is much larger and of a coarser paste. It was probably not part of a figurine but perhaps represents one leg of a multilegged stand or coarse vessel like others published earlier (volume 1: figure 9.105, cat. no. 53; plate LXXIX: bottom, 1–4); also comparable to examples from Dhoxaton in the Drama Plain

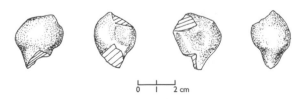

Figure 11.18. Fragment of upper leg of a figurine, phase III: SF 233, plate 11.13c.

(volume 1: figure 10.9:11), and from Selevac (Tringham 1990:677, pl. 10.13, left).

5. SF not recorded (ZG 25; plate 11.15) from phase III: a protome, appearing like a framed abstraction of a head, with schematic features and a neck that widens at the break where the protome joined the vessel. Although these heads are similar to those on ladles from Dikili Tash (see above), the widening neck of this example indicates that it was connected to a rim, not a ladle. This artifact is very similar to earlier published zoomorphic protomes from Sitagroi which are modeled to emerge from the rim of an open plastic vessel (volume 1: figure 10.1:2 [plate LXX: 1]; figure 10.7:1 [plate LXXIV: 2]) and from Selevac as well (Tringham 1990:346, fig. 7.10:22a).

6. SF 462 (QN 2; figure 11.20) from phase V: an undecorated, very schematic figurine; upper torso only, with waist delineated, a fracture at the base; reminiscent of earlier published schematic artifacts from Sitagroi (volume 1: figure 9.164, cat. no. 208) and from Selevac (Tringham 1990:679, pl. 11.3:b).

7. SF 1738 (surface; figure 11.21): either the flat rectangular base (broken at waist) or the abstract head (fractured at neck) of a figurine. It is somewhat enigmatic but may be compared to an earlier published Sitagroi artifact (volume 1: figure 9.122, cat. no. 140) which is a smaller figurine torso with more features delineated but similar nevertheless.

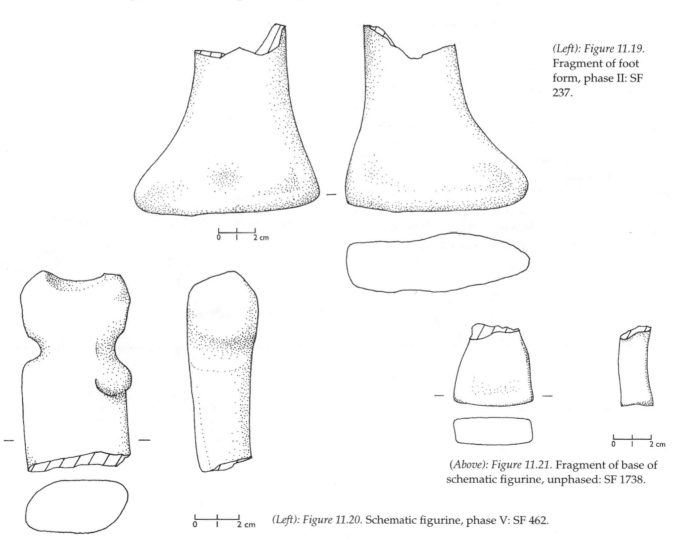

(Left): Figure 11.19. Fragment of foot form, phase II: SF 237.

(Above): Figure 11.21. Fragment of base of schematic figurine, unphased: SF 1738.

(Left): Figure 11.20. Schematic figurine, phase V: SF 462.

8. SF 2805 (PN/B 100; figure 11.22) from phase V: the schematic head of a figure broken at the neck, comparable in size and form to earlier published artifacts from Sitagroi (volume 1: figure 9.136 [cat. no. 212]; 9.164 [cat. no. 208]), Karanovo (Hiller and Nikolov 1997: Taf. 114 III, top right), and Selevac (Tringham 1990:682–683, pls. 11.7a, 11.10c).

9. SF 1123 (MM 16; figure 11.23): broken animal body with head, forelegs, and hind quarter missing. These were published earlier and identified by Marija Gimbutas as "torsos of bulls" (volume 1: figures 9.151 [cat. no. 177], 9.152 [cat. no. 176]; 9.153 [cat. no. 179], and 9.156 [cat. no. 182]) and are comparable to those published from Servia (Phelps 2000:194, fig. 4.27: SF 360) and Selevac (Tringham 1990:684, pl. 11.12a–d).

10. SF 1264 (ML 13; figure 11.24; plate 11.16) from phase III: identified as a phallus (?).

In summary, the following utilitarian and/or symbolic functions may be suggested for the miscellaneous clay artifacts: food preparation including measuring, processing and serving (small and large pots, bowls, sieves, ladles); combustion equipment (plugs and oven stoppers, "crucibles," incense burners); pottery preparation (discoid or other forms of sherds for polishing or burnishing pot surfaces); lighting or other equipment for burning incense, smoking leaves, herbs (sieves, tripods, stands); presentation artifacts (double-bowl, deco-

rated handle, pedestal stands, lids and ladles, plastic vessels, elaborated ladles, vessels with protomes, incised "plaques"); symbols of ritual, belief, and/or gaming (figurine fragments, discs, geometric sherds).

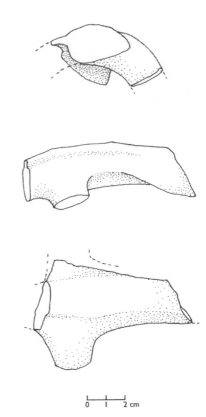

Figure 11.23. Fragment of animal torso, phase III: SF 1123.

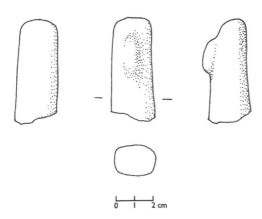

Figure 11.22. Fragment of schematic head, phase V: SF 2805.

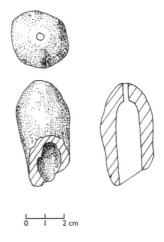

Figure 11.24. Fragment of phallus (?), phase III: SF 1264, plate 11.16.

Miniatures and Models
Marianna Nikolaidou

A minimum of sixty-nine clay miniatures and models were recorded at prehistoric Sitagroi. Of these, fifteen were published earlier (including furniture: volume 1: figures 9.49 [cat. no. 12], 9.79 [cat. no. 5], 9.80 [cat. no. 10], 9.83 [cat. no. 9], 9.84 [cat. no. 11], 9.85 [cat. no. 8]; and pots: volume 1: figures 11.10:12 [pot 22], 11.16:7–9 [pots 163, unnumbered, and 169, respectively], 11.19:1 [pot 165], and 13.27:4–7 [pots 362, 51, unnumbered, 114, respectively]). The number fifteen is a minimum because it includes only the whole miniatures illustrated in volume 1. It is possible that others, whole or fragmentary, were also retrieved among the pottery but not recorded separately. Although not cataloged again in this chapter, they have been counted in the quantitative analysis and discussion. Five more miniature vessels were illustrated (volume 1: plate XCV:5–9) and listed in the concordance of figures to plates. These have been included in appendix 11.1 because additional unpublished information existed about them. Furthermore, the items cataloged by Gimbutas as "stools or thrones" (see volume 1, cat. nos. 5, 8–10) have been here tabulated as stools, the "throne" (cat. no. 11) as a chair. The remaining forty-nine pieces are fully described in our catalog (appendix 11.1). The assemblage consists of the following items: axeheads, miniatures of furniture and vessels, models of a house and an oven, and the so-called dimple bases, that is, clay slabs with indentations on one surface. The latter are considered as possibly connected to the house model, because their indented surface is similar to the underside of the house's base.

TEMPORAL DISTRIBUTION

Fifty-three miniatures and models come from Neolithic levels documented first in phase II; twelve are from Early Bronze Age strata, while four are of uncertain phase. The numerical yield of different items from each phase is grouped in table 11.1. Table 11.2 presents the various types of miniature furniture and vessels in the two most significant phases, II and III.

The temporal distribution of miniatures and models harmonizes with developments in many other artifact categories at Sitagroi, especially the closely related figurine corpus (see volume 1 [Gimbutas 1986]:225). It is thus not surprising to find the greatest number and widest repertoire of artifacts in Phase III, versus their extreme scarcity during the Early Bronze Age. At the same time, it is worth noting a sharper thematic focus in phase II, favoring miniature furniture and, among the vessels, bowls and pedestaled bowls. Although our sample is very small for the time span it covers, we may still entertain the possibility that quantitative and qualitative change over time reflects meaningful choices rather than a mere accident of archaeological recovery.

Table 11.1. Distribution of Miniatures and Models by Phase

| Miniature | Phase | | | | | |
	II	III	IV	V	X	Total
Furniture	12	8	1	0	1	22
Vessel	9	16	1	7	1	34
Model	0	2	0	0	0	2
"Dimple base"	0	3	1	0	1	5
Axehead	0	3	1	1	1	6
Total	21	32	4	8	4	69

Table 11.2. Distribution of the Different Types of Miniature Furniture and Vessels in Phases II and III

| Phase | Furniture | | | Vessel | | | | | Total |
	Chair	Stool	Table	"Amphoriskos"	Bowl	Jar	Pedestaled bowl	Urn	
II	3	6	3	0	6	0	3	0	21
III	1	4	3	2	7	2	2	3	24
Total	4	10	6	2	13	2	5	3	45

THE ARTIFACTS

Artifacts that appear to be miniature copies of what was made of clay or other materials in larger size (Tringham 1990:347) are widespread in the Aegean and the Balkans during the Neolithic and Early Bronze Age (see Marangou 1992 for full discussion and references). Interpretations as to their role in society range widely: toys, ritual offerings, amulets or devices for initiation and magic, design models for craftsmen, didactic devices, elements of a communication code, full-sized functioning artifacts, or a combination thereof (Hourmouziadis 1994; Marangou 1992, 1996, 1997; Tringham 1990:347–348). In the following sections I assess the creation and uses of such micrographic (see Marangou 1997) images at Sitagroi from two aspects: (a) the form, style, and find context of the artifacts themselves; (b) the general efflorescence of ceramic arts at the site, which is manifest in figurines (see volume 1, chapter 9 [Gimbutas 1986]), pottery (volume 1, chapters 11–13 [Keighley 1986, R. Evans 1986, Sherratt 1986]), "social ceramics" (volume 1, chapter 10 [Elster 1986]), ornate spindle whorls (this volume, chapter 6), and seals, stamps and "counters" (this volume, chapter 10). As discussed below, these different classes of artifact present common elements of form, iconography, and application.

Miniature Furniture

Most pieces of miniature furniture (stools, chairs, and tables) come from phase II, which may be significant in relation to the frequency of seated (or "throned") figurines (see volume 1, chapter 9 [Gimbutas 1986]), tripods, and seals in the same period.

STOOLS. The descriptive term "stool" is preferred here to the heavily interpretive "throne" that Gimbutas used for some of these artifacts and which she connected with an assumed "Pregnant Goddess" (volume 1 [Gimbutas 1986]:251). Stools represent the most common type of miniature furniture, especially if we include those examples fused with seated figurines (volume 1: figures 9.56, 9.57, 9.59, 9.81; plate LV:1, 2), which demonstrate one use of the objects. Artifacts with a flat upper surface could have represented stools or tables; in fact, the two terms are often fused in the literature (for example, Marangou 1997). Shape is quite standardized: usu-

ally four, sometimes three (SF 2508 [volume 1: figure 9.85; this volume: plate 11.17b) or six (SF 1492 [figure 11.25; plate 11.18g], SF 4615 [figure 11.26]) cylindrical or conical legs spread obliquely to support a flat or slightly concave upper surface (seat?) of rectangular form. In SF 245 (figure 11.27; plate 11.18h), SF 427 (figure 11.28), SF 827 (figure 11.29; plate 11.17:e), SF 1662 (figure 11.30; plate 11.17c), and SF 5174 (figure 11.31; plate 11.17a), one side is raised to a very subtle ridge. In SF 3212 (volume 1: figure 9.84 [cat. no. 11]), this ridge is more pronounced and forms a low triangular "back support" (see volume 1 [Gimbutas 1986]:290) which recalls much more accentuated examples from elsewhere (for example, Gimbutas 1989c: color plate 9 [seated "Snake Goddesses" from Early Cucuteni Moldavia]). Although carefully modeled, most Sitagroi stools are plain. Only SF 427 (figure 11.28) preserves red ochre, while SF 2666 (volume 1: figure 9.83; this volume, plate 11.17d) bears simple white-infilled incisions at its four corners; red paint is also preserved on the legs of a stool fused with a figurine (volume 1 [Gimbutas 1986]: 251, cat. no. 14).

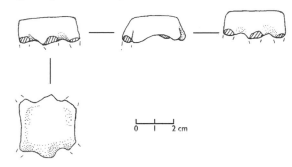

Figure 11.25. Miniature stool or table, phase III, multiple views: SF 1492, plate 11.18g.

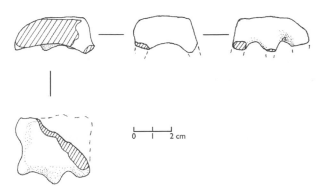

Figure 11.26. Miniature stool or table, phase III, multiple views: SF 4615.

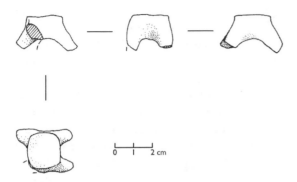

Figure 11.27. Miniature stool, phase II, multiple views: SF 245, plate 11.18h.

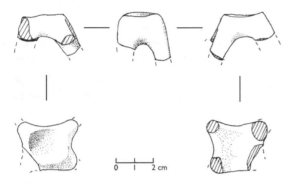

Figure 11.28. Miniature stool, phase II, multiple views: SF 427.

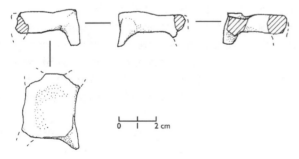

Figure 11.29. Miniature stool, phase III, multiple views: SF 827, plate 11.17e.

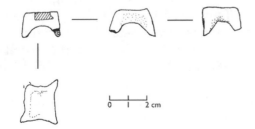

Figure 11.30. Miniature stool, phase II, multiple views: SF 1662, plate 11.17c.

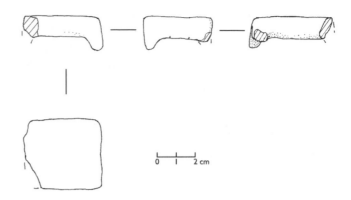

Figure 11.31. Miniature stool or table, phase III, multiple views: SF 5174, plate 11.17a.

CHAIRS. Chairs look quite similar to stools in the lower part, but the seat is deeper and more spacious. In addition, they have a raised back that is distinctly, although variously, modeled. In SF 144 (figure 11.32; plate 11.18d) the back is broken, but its trace is preserved; in SF 901 (figure 11.33; plate 11.18f) the back is simply formed by a thin semicircular strip of clay; whereas in SF 1257 (figure 11.34; plate 11.18a) the back rises with rounded openings and incised decoration, probably imitating woodworking. This miniature is larger than all other chairs and stools in the corpus, with a comfortable seat that could accommodate many of the figurines from the site. Figure 11.34c illustrates a reconstruction on the basis of finds from the Balkans; a chair of very similar form (save only one circular opening at the back) with a figurine actually seated on it comes from a Chalcolithic site in Bulgaria (Gimbutas 1989c: 143, fig. 220), while several other such pieces belonged to an assemblage of miniatures and figurines from Ovčarovo (Gimbutas 1989c: fig. 112). The association of this particular type of chair with figurines on both Bulgarian sites, as well as with what has been interpreted as presentation tables, painted tablets, and musical drums in the Ovčarovo "tableau" (Gimbutas 1989c:71) suggests a special, ritualistic (?) character for such elaborate pieces of furniture. This may also be inferred from the full-size chair with high "horned" back from the sanctuary at Sabatinovka, where a large number of figurines were also found (Gimbutas 1989c: 132–133, fig. 215). It is interesting to compare the small radiating incisions defining the outlines on the Sitagroi miniature chair with those around the arms and torso of a figurine from the site (volume 1: figure 9.48), both artifacts dating to Phase III; and with those around the leg/body corners of a (phase II?) tripod from Dhoxaton (volume 1: figure 10.5:16)

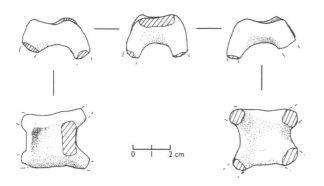

Figure 11.32. Miniature chair, phase II, multiple views: SF 144, plate 11.18d.

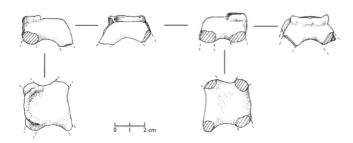

Figure 11.33. Miniature chair, phase II, multiple views: SF 901, plate 11.18f.

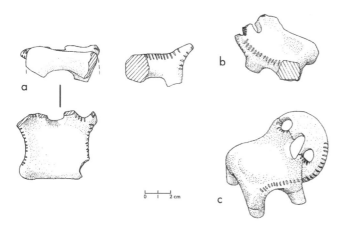

Figure 11.34. Miniature decorated chair, phase III: SF 1257, plate 11.18a; (a, b) fragments of chair; (c) reconstruction of chair.

TABLES. Tables are four-legged, rectangular or square. A raised border around all four sides implies that, if actual tables served as the prototype, those were perhaps used for presentation rather than for eating. Accordingly, the miniatures might have had a role in the display of token items, similar perhaps to the tables bearing lidded vessels from the Ovčarovo "tableau" (although those do not have a ridge: Gimbutas 1989c: fig. 112). SF 1451 (figure 11.35) and SF 5177 (figure 11.36) have a central concavity, possibly to contain something; SF 2600, with a central concavity and figurine protomes at the border, has indeed been interpreted as a ritual basin (volume 1: 290 [cat. no. 12], 249 [figure 9.49]).

Special function is moreover suggested by the elaborate upper surface and/or borders of all tables: they are covered with incised or painted chevrons, netting, zigzags, X motifs, and groups of horizontal, vertical, or radiating lines. The singular existence of rich decoration on these (among the miniature pieces of furniture) arguably underlines their significance in the micrographic assemblage or as representations of actual ornate prototypes. Interestingly, all the ornamental motifs are paralleled with signs of the Neolithic "proto-script" (Gimbutas 1991: fig. 8.2; Masson 1984; Winn 1981), which links the miniature tables with figurines, tripods, spindle whorls, and seals bearing the same elements. In some cases even the combinations of signs are similar across different artifacts: compare, for example, the profusion of chevrons in SF 3836 of phase II (figure 11.37; plate 11.18b) with matching designs on the "Bird Goddess" figurines (volume 1: figures 9.2, 9.3 [phase III], 9.13, 9.32, 9.36 [phase II]), on spindle whorls SF 1254 (this volume: figure 6.11c; plate 6.2b), and SF 1458, SF 1543 (figure 6.7d; plate 6.2c), SF 5035 (figure 6.6d; plate 6.2g), all from phase III, and on seal SF 3684 (figure 10.1c) from phase II. The multiple rows of zigzags on SF 78 of phase II (figure 11.38; plate 11.18e) correspond to those on contemporary seal SF 516 (figure 10.1a). Finally, the "netting" on the top surface of SF 5177 (figure 11.36) and SF 78 (figure 11.38) recalls similar patterns on tripods and spindle whorls but especially resembles "inscribed" artifacts from the Balkans (volume 1: figure 9.55 [clay disk from Ploskata Mogila near Plovdiv]; Masson 1984: figs. 4–5

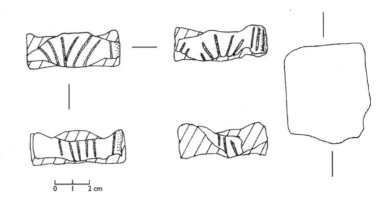

Figure 11.35. Miniature table with incisions, phase III, multiple views: SF 1451.

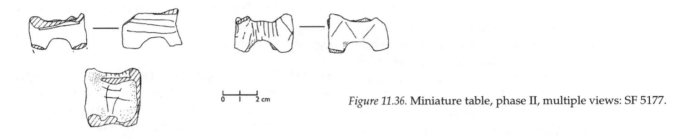

Figure 11.36. Miniature table, phase II, multiple views: SF 5177.

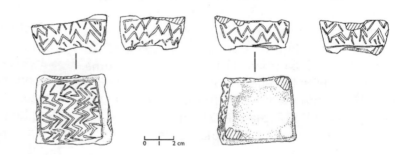

Figure 11.37. Miniature table, phase III, multiple views: SF 3836, plate 11.18b.

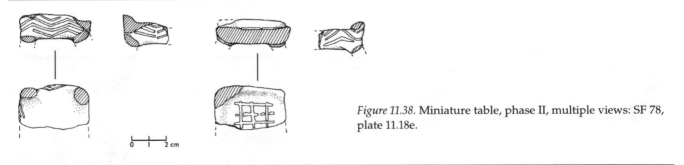

Figure 11.38. Miniature table, phase II, multiple views: SF 78, plate 11.18e.

[marks on sherds from Vinča and related sites], and plate IIb [clay plaque from Tangîru in Romania]). Besides decoration, formal features including legs, raised border, and (in two cases) central concavity may also serve to connect the miniature tables with tripods and other types of special vessels with legs at Sitagroi (see volume 1, chapters 10–12).

Miniature Vessels

Pots with a rim diameter less than 10 cm are so defined (compare Tringham 1990:348). They include bowls, cups, jars, jugs, urns, and pedestaled bowls, all closely corresponding to the actual ceramic types in each period (see specific references in catalog). These miniature forms are suitable for holding or presenting small portions of food, drink, seeds, herbs, and the like. They also could have been children's toys. In the finer examples, these functions may also have involved aesthetics, symbolism, and social values (compare volume 1, chapter 13).

BOWLS. Bowls are the most common shape, numbering fifteen in a total of thirty-four miniature vessels. They are followed by pedestaled bowls (six pieces) and cups or beakers (four pieces), while other types are unique. Common to all are thick walls and rim. With the exception of a deep rounded bowl from phase V (see volume 1: figure 13.27: 7, pot 114), all other specimens come from phases II and III. Many shape variations (see volume 1, chapters 11–12, and this volume, figures 7.11–7.15) are represented. These include open, everted: SF 46 (figure 11.39; also volume 1: figure 11.16: 8), SF 68 (figure 11.40, plate 11.19:b), SF 76 (figure 11.41), SF 83 (plate 11.19c), pot 163 (volume 1: figure 11.16:7); biconical: pot 169 (volume 1: figure 11.16: 9); rounded: SF 59 (figure 11.42), SF 205 (plate 11.20b), SF 317 (plate 11.21), and pot 165; and Kritsana-type shapes: SF 197 (plate 11.20a).

CUPS, JARS, AND URNS. All four cups come from the Early Bronze Age when such drinking vessels were common (see volume 1, chapter 13). One of them is footed (pot 51 illustrated in volume 1: figure 13.27:5). Of the two phase III jars, SF 58 (figure 11.44; plate 11.20d) has a globular profile and tiny ring handles, whereas SF 88 (plate 11.22a) has a sinuous profile with a cylindrical neck and an incised design circling the neck and shoulder. "Amphoriskos" SF 61 (figure 11.45; plate 11.20c) has a wide biconical body and lug handles, while SF 322 (plate 11.22b), also biconical but less accentuated, exhibits thick handles set from neck to body. Two urns (SF 60 [figure 11.46; plate 11.22c] and SF 178 [heavily reconstructed; figure 11.47]) are of very similar form, with cylindrical base, biconical body, no handles, and high neck; the third has a cylindrical base rising to a wider but straight-sided body (SF 115; figure 11.43; plate 11.22d).

DECORATION AND SIZE. The forms are well represented among full-size fine wares (see appendix 11.1). Miniatures themselves are mostly plain monochrome; several are smoothed (bowls 163, 165, 169, 205 [plate 11.20b]; jar SF 58 [figure 11.44; plate 11.20d]; "amphoriskos" SF 61 [figure 11.45; plate 11.20c]); and some are coarse (for example, bowl SF 115 [figure 11,43; plate 11.22d]). Surface elaboration is an exception: one straight-sided bowl (illustrated in volume 1: figure 11.16:8) belongs to the red-crusted ware diagnostic of phase II (volume 1 [Keighley 1986]: 358); SF 317 (plate 11.21) of phase II, a deep hemispherical bowl with incised spirals, recalls in both form and decoration a common type of contemporary incised ware (volume 1 [Keighley 1986]:360); jar SF 88 (plate 11.22a) bears simple

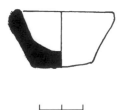

Figure 11.39. Miniature bowl, phase III: SF 46.

Figure 11.40. Miniature bowl, phase III: SF 68, plate 11.19b.

(Above): Figure 11.41. Miniature bowl, phase II: SF 76.

(Right): Figure 11.42. Miniature bowl, phase III: SF 59.

Figure 11.43. Miniature urn or bowl, phase III: SF 115, plate 11.22d.

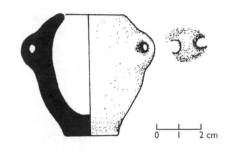

Figure 11.44. Miniature jar, phase III. SF 58,

Figure 11.45. Miniature "amphoriskos," phase III: SF 61, plate 11.20c.

Figure 11.46. Miniature urn, phase III: SF 60, plate 11.22c.

Figure 11.47 Miniature urn from the Bin Complex, phase Vb: SF 178.

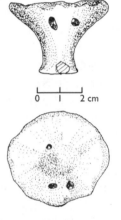

Figure 11.48. Miniature pedestaled bowl, phase III: SF 384, plate 11.23a.

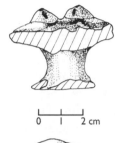

Figure 11.49. Miniature pedestaled platter holding five rounded elements, phase II: SF 5377, plates 11.23b, 11.24.

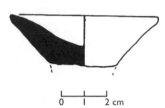

Figure 11.50. Fragment of miniature pedestaled bowl with everted profile, phase III: SF 10, plate 11.19a.

incised decoration of zigzags, although full-sized vessels of such form are mostly known in painted wares (volume 1: figures 12.5:1, 3; 12.9).

Size varies, perhaps corresponding to a variety of uses. Most pieces range in rim diameter from 3.0 to 4.5 cm and in height from 2.0 to 3.5 cm, and could have been used as small containers of spices, ornaments, drugs, or other special commodities (compare Tringham and Stevanović 1990:347–348). Some larger pieces are even more likely to have held substances: bowls SF 317 and pot in volume 1: figure 11.16:8 (D: 6.0 cm x H: 6.5 cm and D: 7.5 cm x H: 5.1 cm, respectively); also jars SF 58 and SF 88 (D: 2.8 cm x H: 5.4 cm, D: 2.6 cm x H: 5.2 cm, respectively). On the other end of the scale we have microminiatures, with rim diameter and/or height smaller than the average: bowls SF 76 and pots 163, 205; cups 362, 51 (volume 1: figure 13.27:4, 5, respectively). These may have belonged to "tab-

leaux" together with furniture and figurines of analogous size, as Balkan parallels illustrate (see Marangou 1992). In Mesopotamia during Neolithic and early city periods, tiny vessels of various types served as counting tokens (Schmandt-Besserat 1992: 23, 24, and 228, chart 13).

PEDESTALED BOWLS OR PLATTERS. Pedestaled bowls constitute an interesting small group, quite homogeneous in form through phases II and III. They consist of an open, shallow container, conical or discoid according to depth, raised on a cylindrical foot with a round base. But dimensions vary. Very small examples, measuring 3.0 to 4.5 cm in bowl rim diameter and up to 3.5 cm in height, include SF 84 (plate 11.23c), SF 384 (figure 11.48; plate 11.23a), and SF 5377 (figure 11.49; plates 11.23b, 11.24). By contrast, SF 338 (figure 11.51; plate 11.25), decorated with incisions, is larger, more comparable with others

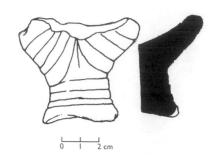

Figure 11.51. Miniature pedestaled bowl, phase III:
SF 338, plate 11.25.

from phase II, with rim diameter up to 6.0 cm and height around 5.0 cm. (Another example is pot 22 in volume 1: figure 11.10:12). Across these two groups, bowl depth ranges from a few mm (in the flattened "platter," SF 5377) to 1.5 to 2 cm for the deeper receptacles, such as SF 338 exhibits. The pedestal can be rather short and thick (SF 338, 5377) or slender (SF 84). The surface is usually monochrome, even coarse, but there are two elaborate examples: SF 338 bears incised arcs arranged in two groups circling the bowl, which recall somewhat the rendition of skirt folds on a figurine (volume 1: figure 9.10). More outstanding is SF 5377 (figure 11.49; plate 11.24), because the top, covered with red ochre, holds an array of what appear to be five round breads or cakes (first illustrated in Theocharis 1973: fig. 130, but see also chapter 10 for discussion of similar forms as counters). The above differences in such a small group of miniatures perhaps reflect the considerable variability of full-sized elevated bowls at Sitagroi in terms of form, clay body, surface treatment, and decorative techniques (see volume 1: figure 11.10:1–5, 6–8, 10, 11, 13). We can only speculate whether stylistic variation in both the actual and miniature pedestaled vessels relates to functional difference, too. One use at least, presentation or serving, is charmingly illustrated by the "cake stand" (SF 5377), which probably reproduced a full-sized prototype.

Models

THE HOUSE. The house (SF 755: plates 11.26, 11.27e; also illustrated in volume 1: figure 8.20a, plates XL:1a-d, XCV: 4; Theocharis 1973: fig. 290) belongs to a characteristic group of unroofed models of buildings, presumably representing house interiors, that are known in the Aegean and the Balkans particularly during the Late Neolithic (Marangou 1992; Toufexis 1996:161–162). While earlier house models had a roof and richly decorated outer walls (for example, Papathanassopoulos 1996: figs. 14, 17, cat. nos 262–264), the unroofed examples clearly emphasize the furnishings within: all models are variously equipped with ovens, platforms, and other domestic features (for example, Gimbutas 1991: fig. 3–53 from Ovčarovo I, with references; Gallis 1985, from Plateia Magoula Zarkou) which correspond closely to excavated house remains (Elster 1997; Todorova 1982). The Sitagroi find is "furnished" with a domed oven and adjoining platforms of the same type as the oven model SF 813 from an associated excavation layer (plate 11.28). The house consists of one space only, probably a summarized depiction (compare Gallis 1985 and 1996:65), although buildings with two or more rooms are common in the period (see volume 1 [C. Renfrew 1986b]:175–222; elsewhere: Andreou, Fotiadis, and Kotsakis 1996; contributions in Papathanassopoulos, ed. 1996:41–76; Gimbutas 1991; Todorova 1982). The thick walls suggest the massive wattle-and-daub structures of contemporary architecture (Elster 1997; Tringham and Stevanović 1990:352–357, 389–396), as do also groups of incised irregular lines on the outer surfaces (compare Gallis 1985:20–24; Toufexis 1996: 162, fig. 43; and the Ovčarovo model with chevrons or groups of lines [Gimbutas 1991: figs. 3–53]). The size of the model (13.3. x 12.3 x 5.6.cm) would conceivably have allowed the insertion of microminiature figurines, pots, and/or furniture in "tableaux" like those from Plateia Magoula Zarkou (Gallis 1985) or elsewhere in the Balkans (Marangou 1992: refs.). Several miniature vessels, furniture, and many figurines were indeed recovered together with the house model in the archaeological episode described as the Hearth and Debris levels (see chapter 12; and volume 1 [C. Renfrew 1986b]:212–217).

The peculiar indented underside of the model floor ("dimple base"; see plate 11.27e) is puzzling. The regularity of the size and arrangement of the circular depressions, large and small, may be taken as evidence for meaningful design, possibly along the lines of gaming, recording, or calculation. It brings to mind a grid, interpreted as "calendar," incised on the bottom of an oven model from Chalcolithic Slatino in Bulgaria (Bailey 1993:209 fig. 3).

THE OVEN. The oven, SF 813 (plate 11.28; also illustrated in volume 1: figure 8.20b, plate XL:2a–b; Theocharis 1973: fig. 131), is a finely modeled and finished representation consisting of a domed structure on a raised platform with an additional platform in front. This type of oven was used for baking bread and processing cereal grains (Bailey 1993:206, with refs.). It is well attested archaeologically and by various representations, independent of or incorporated into house models such as the Dikili Tash types (Marangou 1996: cat. no. 267). Excavated examples from Obre show that the dome consisted of a frame built of twigs (Gimbutas 1991: fig. 3.11) over which plaster was applied in thick successive layers (Todorova 1982:42). At Sitagroi the platform of such an oven was found in the Early Bronze Age Burnt House; it is almost circular in form and raised from the floor (Elster 1997:26; Renfrew 1970:131–134; see also volume 1 [C. Renfrew 1986b]:191, 199, figure 8.12, plate XXVI). The floor of another similar structure was revealed and sectioned in layer ML 151 of phase III; it had a base of large stones over which successive layers of pebbles and clay were spread and then finished with a layer of clay (volume 1 [C. Renfrew 1986b]:214, plate XXXVIII). Interestingly, this oven was located in the same area but in levels earlier than the Hearth and Debris horizon, where the oven model was found (layer MM 27).

Details of structure are not indicated in the Sitagroi model; a broken protuberance on top of the dome could have formed a "knob" such as we see on two Tisza models from Hungary (Gimbutas 1989c: fig. 228). On the other hand, the frontal platform is clearly shown on the Sitagroi model, as a ridge rising above the rest of the platform to enclose a small area in front of the opening. We can imagine tiny miniatures standing on it, in imitation of actual oven furnishings including tools and pottery (Gimbutas 1991: fig. 2.6 [from Achilleion], fig. 3.10 [from Obre]) or even figurines (Gimbutas 1989c:132–133, fig. 215 [shrine at Sabatinovka]) or breads (figure 11.49; plates 11.23b, 11.24). Gimbutas

infers (volume 1 [Gimbutas 1986]:262) that many of the Sitagroi figurines were placed on benches/altars attached to "sacred" ovens, of which the model oven on its platform offers a depiction. Ritual associations are certainly possible, although by no means the only explanation for the presence of this domestic effigy.

Dimple Bases

These enigmatic objects (plate 11.27a–d), five examples of which were recovered, are rectangular slabs that have one surface indented with circular and/or oval depressions. The surface is generally well smoothed and the edges finished (with the exception of SF 1488; see appendix 11.1). The characteristic indented form obviously links them to the house model, as does also their chronology and context. Three slabs date to phase III: SF 1472 (plate 11.27d) and SF 1488 belonged to the Hearth and Debris levels together with the house, while SF 3677 (plate 11.27a) comes from the lower levels in the same area, MM/ML. Of the remaining two examples, SF 1112 (plate 11.27b) comes from square MM also, in layers of phase IV although it can be placed stylistically in phase III, as were seals (see chapter 10) and figurines (see volume 1, chapter 9), both recovered in EBA contexts. The unphased SF 1572 (plate 11.27c) was found in square LM, again in proximity to MM.

Nevertheless, it does not necessarily follow that "dimple bases" also belonged to structural representations. For one thing, it is not known whether their "dimpled" surface was meant as the upper or underside, the latter being the case with the house model. The thickness of the finished slabs measures just about half the height of the house (the walls of which are modeled in one piece with its base) and are therefore too low to represent walls. We can of course envisage them as independent models of house floors, shorthand renditions of the whole structure, on which miniatures could be arranged in domestic scenes, but this would be a case without recognized parallels.

On the other hand, differences in size and in the dimensions and regularity of depressions among the "dimple bases" imply that originally the objects (now fragmentary) may not have been meant as identical in form and/or use. SF 1112 (plate 11.27b) has the greatest similarity to the house model (plate

11.27e), with the same arrangement of depressions in two different sizes and with incisions on the sides (compare plate 11.27b and e, respectively). SF 1472 (plate 11.27d), however, bears graphite paint on its unusually large oval indentations, thus possibly qualifying as a palette for pigment preparation (see chapter 9), unless the paint is decorative, which is not known. SF 1572 (plate 11.27c), with its two preserved rows of small, very closely arranged, and neat, circular indentations, brings especially to mind a gaming or calculation board (compare Bailey 1993). We should also note here the formal similarity between "dimple bases," especially SF 1572, and the "golf balls" from Sitagroi, small clay spheres with indented surfaces that may have been counters (see chapter 10). Although we are not in the position to say what exactly "dimple bases" were used for, the existing evidence allows us to consider these artifacts in the context of play, decoration, or notation (compare C. Renfrew 1987).

Axeheads

All clay axeheads are models of shaft-hole axes (figures 11.52–11.55; plate 11.29), with the exception of perhaps SF 5024, cataloged but not drawn (see appendix 11.1). This type of edged stone tool was recovered at Sitagroi (see figures 5.14–5.18) more commonly in the Early Bronze Age (see chapter 5). Interestingly, only one clay axehead came from Early Bronze Age deposits (SF 3207: phase IV; figure 11.52; plate 11.29c). Three out of a total of five models belong to phase III (SF 375 [figure 11.53; plate 11.29b]; SF 3416 [figure 11.54; plate 11.29a];

and SF 5024 [not illustrated]). The clay replicas thus provide evidence that shaft-hole axes were indeed used in phase III, but perhaps not preserved as a result of circulation and/or disposal strategies (compare Voytek 1990; Wickham-Jones 1985).

Depictions of tools in clay or other materials are quite common in the Neolithic and Early Bronze Age, but those are mostly miniature pendants/amulets (see Marangou 1992). The clay axeheads from Sitagroi are modeled at a larger scale, rather too massive for suspension, although their "shaft-hole" could in principle be used for threading. Wear analysis around the holes and edges was not undertaken, nor were the items weighed. The size, of the clay axehead reaches about 50% to 60% that of stone axes (see chapter 5), as can be estimated by comparing sufficiently preserved fragments from both groups. These dimensions suggest a possible use as craftsmen's models for the manufacture of the actual tools. Given the skill and time required to produce a stone shaft-hole axe (for example, Wickham-Jones 1985) and the high quality of such artifacts at Sitagroi (see chapter 5), instructive models may have been necessary to facilitate work. In turn we should note the careful modeling of the clay axeheads themselves; again wear analysis might have indicated whether these items were actually hafted.

No portrayals of other, more common tool types such as flat axes were found at Sitagroi. This fact perhaps reflects a special material and/or symbolic value attributed to shaft-hole axes, technologically the most sophisticated and efficient of

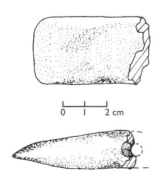

Figure 11.52. Clay axehead, phase IV: SF 3207, plate 11.29c.

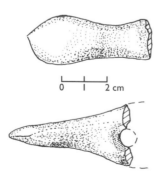

Figure 11.53. Clay axehead, phase III: SF 375, plate 11.29b.

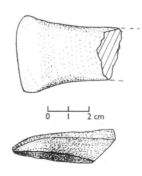

Figure 11.54. Clay axehead, phase III: SF 3416, plate 11.29a.

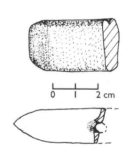

Figure 11.55. Clay axehead, unphased: SF 337, plate 11.29d.

polished stone tools (Voytek 1990:451). Accordingly, symbolic significance was conceivably attached to the clay models themselves, besides any practical utility that they may have had in the technological or other processes. For instance, they may have functioned as charms, insignia of master stoneworkers (Marangou 1996:149), or ritual substitutes in play (C. Renfrew 1987) and in dramatic performances (see volume 1, chapter 9). Similar phenomena are known in other prehistoric cultures. In Minoan Crete, for example, depictions of the double axe, a new and advanced bronze implement that was introduced in the Early Bronze Age, count among the most numerous and prominently ritualistic tool representations (Mavriyiannaki 1983: 195–228). By analogy we might speak of the clay axes from Sitagroi as meaningful reproductions of a tool with manifold importance in that society (chapter 5, figures 5.14–5.18).

DISCUSSION

Among plastic representations in the prehistoric Drama Plain and its neighboring cultures, the miniatures and models from Sitagroi constitute an assemblage of particular importance. Because of their thematic variety, relatively good numerical representation of types, long-term temporal distribution, and careful stratigraphic documentation, we can make a contextual assessment of the finds. Although full exploration of the interpretive potential of these artifacts lies beyond the scope of this chapter (but see chapter 12), some key points can be highlighted. And while the comparative material is still too fragmentary to allow a regional study of the production, use, and circulation (?) of miniatures and models, such a study should be possible in the future with the forthcoming publication of important assemblages, such as the one from Dikili Tash.

The first point concerns the relationship between miniatures/models and material reality. It is reasonable to assume that the models from Sitagroi reproduce full-size artifacts and facilities, but not always in one-to-one correspondence. Instead, there are *pars pro toto* renditions (house model, perhaps some "dimple bases"); simplified versions of the original forms (oven model, plain miniature copies of decorated vessels); or pieces bearing ochre and

rich decoration that were possibly intrinsic to the miniature and not a feature of the prototype—as indeed may be implied by the use of symbolic motifs that occur across different classes of special clay objects. The chair, SF 1257 (plate 11.18a; figure 11.34), perhaps combines elements of actual elaborate furniture (high openwork back) with ornamental details (radiations) characteristic of ceramic arts. Selective representation of the prototype could have been due to a number of factors, including aesthetics, function, ritual, symbolism, or others that remain obscure to us. Likewise, thematic choice may have been value-laden, celebrating the creation and socioeconomic functions of the household (compare Elster 1997; Toufexis 1996; Tringham and Krstić 1990): building (house model, perhaps "dimple bases"); food processing (house, oven); craftwork (furniture, axes, vessels); serving, presentation, hospitality (vessels, tables, stools, and chairs); notation, play ("dimple bases"?); and/or ceremony in which some or all the different categories were represented.

Archaeological context offers interesting clues as to how the "microcosm" (compare Marangou 1997) of miniatures and models might have been tied to activities at prehistoric Sitagroi. Two patterns are apparent, which harmonize with discoveries in other sites of the Drama Plain and beyond (see Marangou 1996, 1997). The first is the concurrence of various pieces, of the same or different types, in a single excavation unit and/or building episode. Second, we find a strong presence in these same contexts of figurines, jewelry, weaving equipment, tools, and working materials. Most prolific were the Hearth and Debris levels of phase III, which feature an outdoor hearth possibly associated with a house (MM16–50, ML 103–115: volume 1 [C. Renfrew 1986b]:212–217). The majority of miniatures dating to this phase, a group of fourteen, was recovered there: stools SF 827 and SF 1492, chair SF 1257, bowls SF 46 and SF 205, jar SF 58, "amphoriskos" SF 61, urn SF 115, pedestaled bowl SF 384, house SF 755, oven SF 813, "dimple bases" SF 1472, SF 1488, and axehead SF 375.

The same levels also yielded twenty-five figurines, various social ceramics (stands, pedestal, tripods, twenty-four plastic vessels), jewelry, ceramic utensils, many ground and polished stone tools (among them fourteen axes), evidence for metallurgy, items of notation (balls, a pintadera), pottery (including ten bowls), one stone vessel, ample evidence for spinning/weaving (eighteen impressions and thirty-nine spindle whorls), and many bone tools (fourteen points and other types). Despite poor architectural preservation, the rich record of artifacts from this habitation episode offers vivid glimpses of complex household life at Neolithic Sitagroi (see chapter 12)— a domesticated mode of existence (compare Hodder 1990)—important aspects of which were captured in and symbolically promoted by the miniatures and models.

Other important contexts include the following (see volume 1, chapters 7, 8; this volume, chapter 12):

- ZA 52, phase II (floor 16: water-sieved), yielded two miniature stools (SF 245, 5180 [volume 1 [Gimbutas 1986]:290, cat. no. 11] and table SF 5177. Recovery also included many figurines and other plastic forms, social ceramics (a pedestal and a tripod), considerable jewelry of different kinds, a counter, and various stone and bone tools.

- ZA 41, phase III (floor 15), yielded a pedestaled bowl (SF 10), shell bracelets, ground and polished stone items, pottery, and one mat impression.

- The phase III midden beneath floor 15 of ZA 42–47 (ZA 47 water-sieved) yielded bowls SF 59, SF 68, urn SF 60, pedestaled bowl SF 338, and stool SF 5174. Also recovered were twenty-one figurines and other plastic forms, social ceramics (including five plastic vessels and five stands), many jewelry items, chipped, ground and polished stone, many bone tools including twelve points, spinning and weaving equipment, a copper fragment and crucible fragments, a ball and "slingstones", and pottery vessels of good quality.

- ZHt 24, phase IV, revealed levels with a floor and wall and yielded a miniature cup (SF 3254), one bracelet, one figurine, one stand, one elaborate bone piece, many ground stone tools, many whorls, and bone tools.

- Bin Complex (QO 7 and QO/B 9), phase Vb, yielded a miniature cup (see volume 1: figure 13.27:5, pot 51) and urn SF 178. This complex also produced a considerable amount of weaving equipment, pendants and especially pins, many axes and various ground stone tools, chipped stone, ceramic utensils, elaborate stone and bone items, a few figurines, stands and tripods, and a cylinder stamp.

It remains to look further for the people who participated in the activities implied by the artifacts, and their relation to the miniatures and models, as producers, users and spectators.

Appendix 11.1.
Catalog of *Paralipómena* and Other Plastic Forms

Ernestine S. Elster and Marianna Nikolaidou

Entries are grouped under phases I through V, followed by unphased entries; subsequently each artifact can be found under the four categories (objects of utility, pottery, plastic forms, and miniatures and models) in numerical sequence of the small find number, followed by context, reference to illustration, and description.

PHASE I

Objects of Utility

137 KL 20
Perforated fragment ("sieve"); seventeen holes pierced on the body wall; surface: black

4100 KLb 131
Reworked sherd; discoid, oval-shaped; surface: black/green
L: 4.9; W: 4.0; Th: 1.0

4108 KLb 134
Reworked sherd; pierced handle; elongated; surface: dark
L: 6.1; W: 2.8

Pottery

2828 JL 105; plate 11.10f
"Plaque" fragment; surface: light orange/gray; decoration: incised pattern of crossing semicircles in the center, flanked by wavy lines and arcs
L: 6.1; W: 5.7; Th: 1.6

Plastic Form

416 KL 21; plate 11.13a, b
Figurine legs, two pieces; elongated, narrowing to one end, broken at the other end which is roundish; surface: black
L: 3.6; W: 1.2; Th: 0.35

2534 JL 104
Phallic (?)-shaped fragment
L: 6.7; D: 2.2

PHASE II

Objects of Utility

110 ML 12
Reworked sherd; disc; slightly hollow

504 KM 9; plate 11.5
Reworked sherd; handle fragment with three small drilled holes; surface: burnished
L: 7.5; W: 7.8

519 ZA 52
Lid: circular, with central knob-handle broken off; top surface: smooth, light brown; underside: flat, smooth, shiny, black; core: coarse, light brown
D: 6.4; Th: 1.3

528 ZA 54
Reworked sherd; disc fragment; surface: smooth, light tan/gray
L: 8.5; W: 5.4; Th: 1.2

2835 KL 113
Ladle fragment; surface: tan/gray; interior: coarse, with marks of working stick; decoration: incised spiral on base, grooves on side
L: 5.5; W: 5.0; Th: 1.9

Pottery

242 ZA 52; plate 11.10d
"Plaque" fragment; perforated; surface: pink-gray; decoration: two groups of incised concentric arcs, antithetically arranged
L: 8.5; W: 7.4

461 KM 2; plate 11.11c
"Plaque" fragment; surface: coarse, reddish-brown; decoration: incised arcs with white infills; fine paste and temper; well-fired
L: 3.7; W: 3.2; Th: 1.2

743 KM 18; plate 11.10b
"Plaque" fragment; perforated; surface: burnished, brown; decoration: four groups of incised concentric arcs (one in each corner) and hatched diamond in the center; fine paste; coarse temper; well-fired
L: 7.8; W: 6.5; Th: 0.7

1498   LL 6; plate 11.11b
        "Plaque" fragment; surface: smooth, light brown;
        decoration: incised lozenges and diagonal lines
        with white infill; fine paste and temper
        L: 4.6; W: 5.2; Th: 0.6

1726   ML 8
        "Plaque" fragment; upper surface: smooth, red-
        brown; underside: black/dark gray; decoration:
        incised linear pattern; core: black/red
        L: 8.8; W: 8.2; Th: 1.4

2279   KL 105
        "Plaque" (corner fragment); surface: smooth, red;
        decoration: incised rectangular design; traces of
        organic temper
        L: 4.2; W: 3.2; Th: 1.1

2280   KL 113; plate 11.10a
        "Plaque" fragment; perforated; decoration: incised
        diamond pattern within linear border
        L: 7.0; W: 6.7; Th: 0.7

2281   KL 113; plate 11.10c
        "Plaque" fragment; surface: red, burnished; decora-
        tion: incised arcs and parallel lines with white infill;
        coarse temper
        L: 8.4; W: 6.0–11.8; Th: 0.5

2354   KL 111
        "Plaque" fragment; surface: smoothed, gray/
        brown; decoration: incised diamond pattern (?)
        within linear border (compare SF 2280)
        L: 3.9; W: 5.5; Th: 1.6

2636   KL 109
        "Plaque" corner fragment; surface: dark gray/
        brown; coarse paste with grit
        L: 5.1; W: 3.9; Th: 1.8

2815   KL 114
        Pedestaled bowl fragment (compare volume 1: fig-
        ure 11.10:1–6); surface: orange/gray; decoration:
        incised curvilinear and rectilinear patterns with
        white infill
        H: 8.8; W: 5.5

Plastic Forms

237   ZA 51; figure 11.19
        Foot fragment of some large incised vessel (com-
        pare volume 1: figure 10.8:15, 17, 22); trapezoidal in
        shape, strongly tapering toward upper, broken end;
        surface: brown, smoothing marks preserved;
        medium paste and temper; well fired
        H: 9.7; W: 5.6–10.0; Th: 1.1–3.1

2243   KL 106
        Fragment probably from a tripod (compare volume
        1: figure 10.5:13); triangular in section; surface:
        black; decoration: circular incision with white infill
        L: 5.76; W: 2.52 Th: 2.99

2284   KL 113
        Fragment, possibly from a large incised vessel
        (compare volume 1: figure 10.9:11–12 from
        Dhoxaton); oval in section, slightly tapering toward
        rounded end; surface: smooth, red/buff; decora-
        tion: incised horizontal lines; coarse temper
        H: 5.1; W: 3.8; Th: 1.6

2640   KL 117
        Fragment of an open vessel (compare volume 1: fig-
        ure 10.6:2, 13–14); surface: burnished, beige; core:
        gray; decoration: series of incised small triangles
        L: 2.2; W: 3.2; Th: 1.9

5357   ZA 54/33
        Foot of large incised vessel (see figure 11.19 and
        compare volume 1: figure 10.8:15, 17, 22); trapezoi-
        dal, tapering toward upper end; surface: pink/buff;
        decoration: incised
        H: 4.5; W: 3.2

Miniatures/Models

76   Context unknown; figure 11.41
        Bowl: everted form with slightly incurved rim and
        flat base (compare volume 1: figure 11.19:2)
        D. base: 1.4; D. mouth: 3.0; H: 1.4

78   ML 7; figure 11.38; plate 11.18e
        Table fragment: traces of only two legs are pre-
        served; rectangular, with rounded corners and
        curved border; surface: course, porous, brown; dec-
        oration: incised lattice pattern with traces of white
        infill on upper surface, group of zigzag lines
        around the border exterior.
        L: 4.1; W: 2.5; H: 0.9

84   LL 10; plate 11.23c
        Pedestaled bowl: partly broken at base; tall foot,
        very shallow conical receptacle; surface: coarse,
        porous, brown; medium paste and temper; well
        fired
        D. base: 2.0; D. top: 3.0; H: 3.0

144   KL 2; figure 11.32; plate 11.18d
        Chair fragment: four legs, partly missing; traces of
        raised back, concave seat; surface: coarse, porous,
        brown; fine paste and temper; well-fired
        L: 3.2; W: 2.8; H: 2.8

245   ZA 52; figure 11.27; plate 11.18h
        Stool fragment: four legs, partly missing; flat seat
        with rounded corners; surface: light pinkish-gray
        L: 2.9; W: 2.1; H: 1.8

317   ML 11; plate 11.21
        Bowl fragment: deep hemispherical form, traces of
        one handle; decoration: incised spirals around the
        body
        D. base: 4.0; D. rim: 6.0; H: 6.5

427   KM 6; figure 11.28
Stool fragment: four legs, partly missing; slightly concave seat somewhat raised on one side; surface: matt, gray, traces of red ochre
L: 3.0; W: 2.4; H: 2.5

901   ZA 53; figure 11.33; plate 11.18f
Chair fragment: four legs (missing), semicircular strip forms raised back; surface: matt, light gray/brown, some black coloration on the seat
L: 3.4; W: 2.8; H: 1.9

1662   ZA 51s; figure 11.30; plate 11.17c
Stool fragment: four legs, one of them missing; seat is slightly raised on the back; surface: matt, light brown, black coloration in places
L: 2.1; W: 2.1; H: 1.5

5177   ZA 52s; figure 11.36
Table fragment: four legs, partly missing; square with central concavity; decoration: incised small lattice pattern on top surface, groups of horizontal, vertical and zigzag lines on each of the three preserved exterior border sides, respectively
L: 3.4; W: 3.2; H: 2.1

5377   KM 2; figure 11.49; plates 11.23b, 11.24
Pedestaled, partly broken at base; short, thick foot, flattened platter with five attached rounded elements; surface: traces of red ochre
D. base: 3.0; D. rim: 4.5; H: 3.4

PHASE III

Objects of Utility

No SF no.   ZB 121r; plate 11.2
Ladle/pan fragment; the whole handle and part of the vessel wall preserved; handle is widening to a trapezoid at its free end

49   ML 3
Ladle fragment; surface: coarse, brown, with traces of burnishing; fine paste; coarse temper; well fired
L: 3.2; W: 3.4; Th: 1.0

185   MM 19; figure 11.5
Footed bowl fragment: handle missing; stubs of a pair of legs are preserved under the bowl; surface: burnished, red; decoration: graphite-painted spirals on the exterior surface; medium/fine paste; medium temper
L: 7.6; W: 6.5; H: 2.5

186   MM 19; figure 11.1; plate 11.1a; volume 1: plate XCI, bottom right: 2)
Ladle fragment; surface: dark gray/black, red ochre (?) on interior of bowl; medium paste; medium/coarse temper
L: 12.6; W: 7.8; H: 2.8

226   ZA 45
Lid fragment; surface: dark gray; decoration: incised rectangular pattern
D: 7.5; Th: 1.0

397   ML 5
Lid: square, with central knob-handle; top surface: smooth, concave, light brown; underside: coarse, light brown; sides: smooth; well-fired
L: 7.1; W: 6.2; Th: 1.0

820   ML 107
Ladle; handle missing; surface: coarse, porous, brown, with traces of burnishing; fine paste and temper; well-fired
L: 5.5; W: 1.0

856   MM 40; volume 1: plate LXXXVI:11
Lid: square, with central knob-handle partly broken; surface: smooth, matte, light brown; core: coarse, light brown; well-fired
L: 7.0; W: 6.8; Th: 3.4

1135   ML 107; figure 11.4
Perforated fragment ("sieve"); four rows of holes preserved
L: 4.3; W: 2.9; Th: 2.1

1150   MM 40
Ladle fragment; surface: smooth, light brown/dark gray; core: coarse, light brown
L: 3.0; W: 3.0

1200   MM 40; volume 1: plate LXXXVI:13
Lid: square, with central knob-handle (partly broken); surface: burnished, brown; decoration: graphite painted network pattern
L: 7.4; W: 5.5; Th: 3.3

1296   MM 53; volume 1: plate LXXXVI:12
Lid: square, with central knob-handle (broken off); surface: burnished, dark; decoration: incised parallel lines forming rectangular pattern
L: 7.0; W: 7.0; Th: 1.9

1412   MM 19
Ladle fragment; surface: coarse, matte, black; core: reddish
L: 7.0; W: 5.8

1486   MM 50
Ladle fragment; spouted (?) bowl, perforated handle; surface: smooth, dark gray, patch of red ochre preserved; interior: coarse, black; decoration: graphite-painted on the exterior
L: 7.4; W: 3.3; Th: 0.3

3418   MM 60b s; plate 11.1b; volume 1: plate XCI, bottom right:1)
Ladle fragment; surface: orange
L: 7.2; W: 7.4; Th: 3.5

3534 MMd 65
Reworked (?) sherd; rounded edges; decoration: black on red linear pattern, Gumelnitza style
L: 9.1; W: 5.7; Th: 1.1

3719 ZE 86; plate 11.4d
Reworked sherd; disc, traces of ground edges; surface: matte, brick-red
D: 5.9

4210 ZE 90
Plug; surface: gray
H: 3.3; D. cone: 2.8; D. base: 1.7

4575 ZG 28; plate 11.3a
Reworked sherd; roughly triangular; surface: orange
L: 4.9; W: 3.9; Th: 0.8

4909 MM 41; plate 11.3d
Worked sherd: triangular; decoration: black on red diagonal lines
L: 4.7; W: 4.1

4911 MM 45; plate 11.4a
Worked sherd: discoid.
D: 5.7

5619 ML 109
Worked sherd: rounded; decoration: graphite-painted lines.
D: 10.0

Pottery

47 MM 30; figure 11.9; plate 11.9
Bowl: square, with everted thickened rim (Kritsana type), ring-footed
D. base: 4.2; D. mouth: 7.5; H: 3.9

71 MM 50; figure 11.12
Bowl: shallow, straight-sided, with protruding base and thick walls
D. base: 6.6; D. mouth: 7.0; H: 3.0

87 ML 109; figure 11.8
Pedestaled bowl corner fragment; decoration: incised lozenges, curvilinear and straight lines
H: 7.6; W: 7.4; Th: 1.0–2.0

189 ZA 47s; figure 11.6
Pedestaled bowl corner fragment (compare volume 1: figure 11.10:4,5 from phase II); decoration: incised linear pattern
H: 3.3; W: 3.9; Th: 0.5–1.8

4812 ZG 28; plate 11.11d
"Plaque" fragment; surface: matte, gray; decoration: incised groups of diagonal lines
L: 6.0; W: 4.3; Th: 1.0

5159 ZA 44s; plate 11.11a
"Plaque" fragment; surface: coarse, buff/gray; decoration: panels filled with incised vertical lines alternating with plain ones, in "checkerboard" pattern
L: 6.4; W: 6.5; Th: 1.7

5572 ML 101
"Plaque" (corner fragment); decoration: incised parallel lines
L: 3.9; W: 2.7; Th: 1.2

5573 ZA 47
"Plaque" (corner fragment); decoration: incised parallel lines
L: 3.6; W: 2.6; Th: 1.2

5583 ZA 42
Body fragment; red clay; decoration: Gumelnitza style; black on red spirals (?) on the interior, panels with wavy lines and network on the exterior. All these patterns imitate, or closely resemble. weaving motifs
L: 10.0; W: 7.5; Th: 0.65–1.15

5613 ZJ 33
"Plaque" fragment; perforated; decoration: incised groups of arcs arranged in different directions
L: 6.8; W: 6.9

5618 ZG 25
"Plaque" (corner fragment); decoration: incised arcs
L: 4.6; W: 3.7

Plastic Forms

No SF no. ZG 25; plate 11.15
Protome fragment; abstract head with neck widening at its broken joint to a vessel

233 ZA 49; figure 11.18
Top section of figurine leg: pear-shaped fragment (compare volume 1: figure 9.91); broken at both ends
H: 3.1

732 MM 12
Protome handle; surface: red/black

1123 MM 16; figure 11.23
Animal torso fragment (compare volume 1: figures 9.150–9.153); surface: coarse, porous, brown; medium paste and temper; well-fired
L: 8.0; W: 2.3–5.7; H: 3.5

1264 ML 113; figure 11.24; plate 11.16
Phallus (?); one end broken, the other end rounded and carefully perforated; surface: smooth, light brown/gray with small shiny specks; core: coarse
L: 5.2; D: 2.8; HD: 0.3

1642   MM 27
Rectangular block; broken on two sides, finished on the other two; traces of a big protuberance in one of the corners; surface: smooth, light brown
L: 6.6; W: 4.6; Th: 2.2

2993   ZG 30
Fragment, possibly from a large incised vessel (compare volume 1: figure 10.8:21); conical, strongly tapering toward rounded end; groove down one broken side
H: 6.8; W: 6.1; Th: 3.5

5162   ZA 44s
Leg/foot fragment of some large incised vessel (compare volume 1: figure 10.8:13–20); anthropomorphic; surface: red/brown
L: 4.2; W: 3.1; Th: 1.8

5167   ZA 44s
Fragment of a tripod (compare volume 1: figure 10.5:6–7); conical; surface: coarse, dark gray; decoration: incised groups of vertical and diagonal lines
H: 2.5; W: 1.6

5169   ZA 44s
Fragment of some large incised vessel (compare volume 1: figure 10.8:21); conical; surface: buff
H: 3.0; D: 2.3

5172   ZA 45s
Fragment of some large incised vessel (compare volume 1: figure 10.8:21); conical, strongly tapering toward pointed lower end; surface: buff
H: 1.9; W: 0.8

5379   MM 21
Stand fragment (compare volume 1: figure 10.9:5); angled, L-shaped in section; dark fabric

5380   MM 18
Y-shaped fragment; two arms broken, the third (vertical) arm is tapering toward rounded end, traces of a fourth arm (for attachment to vessel?); surface: red ochre and white encrustation
L: 5.4; W: 4.3; Th: 2.2

Miniatures/Models

10   ZA 41; figure 11.50; plate 11.19a
Pedestaled bowl fragment: only the conical receptacle is preserved
D. base: 3.1; D. rim: 6.5; H: 2.2

46   ML 107; figure 11.39
Bowl: open, straight-sided, with flat-base (compare volume 1: figure 11.16:8)
D. base: 2.9; D. mouth: 4.2; H: 2.5

58   MM 43; figure 11.44; plate 11.20d; volume 1: plate XCV:9
Jar fragment: two-handled, with oval-shaped body; partly preserved; surface: smooth
D. base: 2.5; D. rim: 2.8; H: 5.4

59   ZA 47; figure 11.42
Bowl: part of upper body is missing; cylindrical form
D. base: 2.9; D. rim: 3.6; H: 2.0

60   ZA 47; figure 11.46; plate 11.22c
Urn: upper part of neck is missing; globular body, cylindrical foot/base and tall neck (compare volume 1: figure 12.10:5)
D. base: 1.4; D. body: 2.5; H: 3.5

61   MM 43; figure 11.45; plate 11.20c; volume 1: plate XCV:8
"Amphoriskos": neck and handles missing; globular body, traces of horizontal lug handles; surface: smooth " (compare volume 1: figure 12.12:6)
D. base: 1.0; D. body: 3.0; H: 2.5

68   ZA 47; figure 11.40; plate 11.19b
Bowl: everted form with rounded base (compare volume 1: figures 11.16:7, 12.13:3)
D. base: 2.0; D. rim: 3.6; H: 2.4

83   MM 12; plate 11.19c
Bowl: everted form with incurved rim and flat base (compare volume 1: figure 11.19:2)
D. base: 2.6; D. rim: 4.6; H: 2.2

88   MM 52; plate 11.22a; volume 1: plate XCV:5
Jar: two-handled, globular body, cylindrical neck with oval mouth, flat base; decoration: incised zig-zag lines around the upper body and neck (compare volume 1: figures 12.5:1, 3; 12.9:3)
D. base: 2.0; D. rim: 2.6; H: 5.2

115   MM 50; figure 11.43; plate 11.22d; volume 1: plate XCV:6
Urn or bowl: deep, asymmetric biconical form on cylindrical foot; surface: coarse (compare volume 1: figure 12.11:1)
D. base: 1.1; D. rim: 1.6; H: 3.6

197   ZG 19; plate 11.20a
Bowl of Kritsana type; one lug-handle below rim (compare volume 1: figure 12.13:5)
D. base: 2.2; D. rim: 4.0; H: 2.8

205   MM 20; plate 11.20b; volume 1: plate XCV:7
Bowl: cylindrical form; surface: smooth
D. base: 2.4; D. rim: 2.2; H: 1.4

322   ZB 125; plate 11.22b
"Amphoriskos": neck missing; biconical body, vertical angular handles, flat base
D. base: 1.0; D. body: 2.2; H: 3.0

338   ZA 47; figure 11.51; plate 11.25
Pedestaled bowl: breakages at base and bowl rim; concave base, short thick foot, rounded open receptacle with thick walls; decoration: incised lines around foot and two antithetical groups of concentric semicircles on bowl exterior
D. base: 4.1; D. rim: 6.0; H: 5.0

375   MM 20; figure 11.53; plate 11.29b
Axehead: fragmentary; breakage at hafting hole; rounded edges; surface: burnished, brown; fine paste and temper; well-fired
L: 5.4; W: 2.0; Th: 1.6

384   MM 21; figure 11.48; plate 11.23a
Pedestaled bowl: base is missing; cylindrical foot; conical receptacle pierced with three small irregular perforations at its base; surface: matt, red
D. foot: 1.8; D. rim: 4.6; H: 3.3

755   MM 16; plates 11.26, 11.27e; volume 1: figure 8.20a; plate LX:1a, d
House model fragment: about one-fourth is missing; originally unroofed, rectangular structure with thick walls that curve at the interior corners; open interior is furnished with domed oven on a platform that occupies the whole length of one wall; floor underside has the form of "dimple base," with sixteen large circular indentations arranged in four rows and smaller circular depressions in between; surface: buff; decoration: groups of lines, intersecting but in no apparent arrangement, on outer wall
L: 13.3; W: 12.3; Th: 5.6

813   MM 27; plate 11.28; volume 1: plate XL:2a–b
Oven model: domed elliptical structure on platform that extends on both sides; raised step along the oven's door opening; ventilation equipment (?) was indicated by protuberance (now broken) on top of the dome; surface: burnished, brown; fine paste and temper; well-fired
L: 6.0; W: 2.6; H: 2.5

827   MM 31; figure 11.29; plate 11.17e
Stool fragment: four legs, almost completely missing; seat has slightly raised back; surface: coarse, porous, brown
L: 3.2; W: 2.2 H: 1.8

1257   MM 50; figure 11.34; plate 11.18a
Chair fragment: four legs, partly missing; tall back with three large oval openings, two oval and a larger irregular; surface: smooth, reddish/brown; decoration: nail incisions along the edges of the seat and the back; medium paste and temper
L: 4.5; W: 3.0; H: 3.0

1451   ZA 40; figure 11.35
Table fragment: four legs missing; breakages at border; rectangular with central concavity; surface: matt, red; ends: coarse where broken; decoration: incised linear patterns around border exterior
L: 5.5; W: 4.8; H: 1.9

1472   MM 20; plate 11.27d
"Dimple base" fragment; two oval and two or three circular indentations preserved; surface: burnished, dark brown to black; decoration: graphite paint on indentations
L: 11.2; W: 5.9; Th: 2.7

1488   MM 19
"Dimple base" fragment; irregular indentations, ovalish and roundish, of various sizes; edges: rough, unfinished, light gray; surface: smooth, gray/light red; core: coarse, red
L: 11.5; W: 9.0; Th: 2.9

1492   MM 50; figure 11.25; plate 11.18g
Stool fragment: three legs partly preserved on each long side; flat seat; surface: matt, red; core: dark gray
L: 3.1; W: 2.5; H: 1.5

2997   ZG 32
Urn: biconical body, cylindrical tall neck; surface: light/dark brown (compare volume 1: figure 12.5:5, but with handles and spout)
D. base: 2.0; D. body: 3.6; H: 2.8

3416   MMb 60; figure 11.54; plate 11.29a
Axehead fragment: breakage above hafting hole; edges rounded; surface: matt; core: grayish
L: 8.0; W: 3.5; Th: 1.6

3677   ML 151; plate 11.27a
"Dimple base" fragment; two oval indentations and traces of a third one preserved
L: 6.2; W: 6.3; Th: 4.0

3836   MMc 65; figure 11.37; plate 11.18b
Table: four legs, largely missing; roughly square, flat; surface: matt, gray; decoration: groups of incised chevrons on top surface and around border exterior
L: 5.2; W: 4.4; H: 2.5

4615   MM 68; figure 11.26
Stool fragment; four out of original six (?) legs are partly preserved on the long sides, three on the complete side, and one on the other side
L: 4.1; W: 3.3 H: 1.7

5024   ZB 129r
Axehead fragment

5174   ZA 47s
Stool fragment; two legs partly preserved
L: 4.3; W: 3.7; H: 1.8

5615   ZJ 32
Table fragment; decoration: graphite-painted linear pattern on upper surface
L: 6.0; W: 4.5; H: 1.0

PHASE IV

Objects of Utility

2737   ZE 64; figure 11.3a; volume 1: plate CI:7
Perforated fragment ("sieve"): two fragments joined; shoe-shaped; surface: matt, gray; core: gray
L: 13.1; W: 5.8; H: 4.0

3036   ROc 61
Elongated handle fragment, probably from a scoop or ladle; diamond-shaped in section, central ridge that bifurcates toward the broken base; surface: burnished, black
L: 3.7; W: 1.6; Th: 1.3

5015   ZB 101r
Reworked sherd; triangular; surface: red
L: 3.8; W: 4.5

Pottery

50   MM; figure 11.11
Bowl: rounded profile (compare volume 1: figure 13.5:2)
D. base: 4.0; D. mouth: 7.0; H: 3.5

1402   MM 30; plate 11.12
Base (?) fragment (compare volume 1: figure 13.10:1–3 and plate XXXIII): surface: matt, dark; decoration: incised pairs of antithetical rounded lines
L: 7.9; W: 7.2; Th: 2.3

2791   ZE 81
Bowl: base and part of the body preserved; straight-sided (compare volume 1: figures 13.25:1, 13.27:2); surface: burnished, dark gray, red ochre on the interior
L: 5.5; W: 5.5; Th: 0.5

5381   MM 29
Handle fragment: U-shaped, angular, round in section (compare volume 1: figure 13.27:20); decoration: black-on-red

Plastic Forms

527   MM 8
Corner fragment from a tripod or another open elevated vessel (compare volume 1: figure 10.6:12); cylindrical, hollow at three-fourths of its height, from base to top; surface: finished, smooth, gray/red; decoration: shallow vertical grooves; core: coarse, red
H: 2.3; D: 0.8

4595   ZHt 26
Fragment of a stand, including part of the leg (compare volume 1: figure 10.9:5, 9); angular, L-shaped in section; surface: buff; decoration: groups of incised horizontal and vertical lines
L: 4.9; W: 2.2; Th: 1.5

5579   ROc 5; plate 11.14
Leg fragment of a large incised vessel or stand (compare volume 1: figure 10.8:4, 8); oval in section, cylindrical, tapering toward lower end; surface: buff, traces of painting on one side; core: black; very friable fabric
H: 8.7; W: 4.7; Th: 2.5

Miniatures/Models

1112   MM 9; plate 11.27b
"Dimple base" fragment: two rows of large circular indentations preserved, several smaller depressions in between; surface: smooth, red; sides: incised; core: coarse, red
L: 13.0; W: 8.2; D. indentations: 0.9–3.4

3207   ZHt 6; figure 11.52; plate 11.29c
Axehead fragment: break at hafting hole; surface: black/light brown
L: 5.4; W: 2.9; Th: 1.7

3254   ZHt 24
Cup: straight-sided, with flat base; surface: buff/brown (compare volume 1: figure 13.27:4)
D: 3.3; H: 2.2

PHASE V

Objects of Utility

309   PO 3; plates 11.7a, 11.8a; volume 1: plate CI:8
Plug/oven stopper: nearly flat base, slight ridge; surface: coarse, dark gray
D: 9.1; H: 4.9

351   PN 2
Ladle: break at handle, bowl incomplete; surface: gray/black
L: 7.0; W: 5.2; Th: 0.8

493 QN 4; plate 11.4f
Reworked sherd; disc; surface: black
D: 4.2; Th: 0.7

731 QO 7
Ladle fragment; exterior surface: smooth, matt, black; interior surface: smooth, matt, dark gray; core: coarse, black
L: 4.5; W: 5.0; Th: 0.6

1087 QN 8; plates 11.7c, 11.8c; volume 1: plate CI:10
Plug/oven stopper; top broken off; slightly tapered, flat base; surface: coarse, light gray
D: 8.8–10.1; H: 5.2

1301 PN 7; plate 11.7b; volume 1: plate CI:9
Pug/oven stopper; broken into two halves, burned at base; roughly conical, hint of ridge; surface: coarse, brick brown/dark gray
D: 8.9; H: 4.1

1351 PN 25; plate 11.7e; volume 1: plate CI:11
Plug/oven stopper; nearly flat base, some ridging; surface: coarse, gray/brown; crudely baked
D: 10.9; H: 6.0

1527 QO8
"Crucible" (for the form, compare volume 1: plate XCIII, top right: 4–6 from phase III)

1646 PN 12; plate 11.7f
Plug/oven stopper; ridged; poorly baked
D: 7.0; H: 6.0

1652 PO 10; plate 11.4e
Reworked sherd; disc; top surface and sides: coarse, red, underside: black
D: 4.3; Th: 1.8

1667 PO 21
Reworked sherd; disc fragment; top surface: smooth, shiny, red; broken edge and disc edges: coarse black with narrow layer of red on top and bottom; underside: coarse, red
D: 3.8; Th: 0.9

1723 SL 8; plate 11.4g
Reworked sherd; disc; surface: matt, brown; core: coarse, brown
D: 4.5; Th: 1.4

2066 POb 35; plate 11.4b
Reworked sherd; pot base ground into a disc; surface: brown/dark gray, charcoal burns on side where circular ridge is discernible
D: 5.7; Th: 1.0

2261 PNf 53
Ladle: two fragments joined, handle missing; oval-shaped, deep bowl; part of the rim is cut lower than rest
L: 6.4; W: 4.3; Th: 1.8–2.5

3339 POb 49
Ladle: handle missing; surface: light brown
L: 2.6; W: 3.0; Th: 1.6

3401 POd 33; plate 11.4c
Reworked sherd; disc of irregular contour; possibly still in stage of manufacture
D: 5.4; Th: 2.3

3657 PN ext; plate 11.6
Plug; slightly curved base
D: 9.2; H: 6.8

4306 PNf 264; figure 11.2; volume 1: plate XXXII:10
Plug; surface: very smooth, reddish; burnt
D. base: 9.8; D. cone: 6.0; H: 9.2

4439 PN ext; plate 11.4h
Reworked sherd; disc; surface: brown; underside: black; perhaps intended to become a spindle whorl
D: 5.5; Th: 0.9

4463 PNb 104
Reworked (?) sherd: roughly triangular, ridged (?); surface: smooth on two sides, coarse on the third
L: 7.8; W: 6.6; Th: 3.2

4466 POc 67
Elongated handle, probably from a ladle or scoop; rectangular in section, rounded and perforated at the end, widening toward broken base; surface: green/gray
L: 7.8; W: 3.1; Th: 1.5

4750 PO 159
Reworked sherd; disc; broken into several pieces; surface: matte, pinkish/gray, with straw impressions
D: 20.7; Th: 2.5

5009 ZB 22
Reworked sherd; discoid, oval-shaped; surface: black
L: 5.0; W: 2.8; Th: 0.4

5013 ZB 3s
Reworked sherd

5586 PNe 68
Reworked sherd; disc; flat; surface: brown/black
D: 17.0 Th: 1.4

Pottery

153 QO 7; figure 11.13
Bowl: deep, straight-sided, with flat base
H: 8.7; D. base: 10.7; D. mouth: 15.5

544 PO 7; plate 11.10h
"Plaque" fragment; perforated; surface: light brown/gray; decoration: groups of incised zigzag lines with white infill
L: 6.6; W: 6.4; Th: 1.8

1350 PN 25s
"Plaque" fragment: edges broken; perforated; surface: matt, red-brown/light gray; core: coarse, light gray
HD: 1.5; L: 5.1; W: 3.3; Th: 1.5

1661 Context unknown
Bowl (?): rim fragment; decoration: incised band of alternating, straight and zigzag lines on the interior, just below the rim edge (compare volume 1: figures 13.13:2, 13.3:1–4, 8).

1695 QN 50; plate 11.10g
"Plaque" fragment: perforated; surface: coarse, porous, brown; decoration: incised zigzag lines; fine paste and temper; well-fired
L: 4.8; W: 5.0; Th: 1.1

3215 ZHt 12
"Plaque" fragment: angular, with bifurcated U-shaped end; decoration: incised groups of horizontal and vertical lines
L: 6.0; W: 4.8; Th: 2.3

4479b ROc 23
Handle: perforated lug, U-shaped (compare volume 1: figure 13.27:21); surface: black with buff encrustation
L: 2.8; W: 1.6–0.7

4778 PNcn 82
Body fragment; surface: plain; decoration: large, low-relief "button"; red ochre on the interior
L: 9.4 Th: 1.5

5395 PO 164
"Plaque" fragment; perforated; surface: buff; decoration: incised curved and straight lines
L: 5.5; W: 4.7; Th: 1.0

Plastic Forms

462 QN 2; figure 11.20
Figurine fragment: highly schematic, oblong, "waisted," slightly concave at its finished end, with one roundish protuberance just below the "waisted" middle part
H: 9.3; W: 4.7; Th: 2.6

467 ZA 15
Irregularly spherical object; surface: partially coarse and partially smooth, black/light red
L: 2.9; D: 1.8

1682 PO 9
Probably base fragment of a stand (compare volume 1: plate LXXIV:4); surface: smooth, black, core: coarse, red/light gray; decoration: graphite-painted linear pattern
L: 6.2; W: 2.5; Th: 1.5

1741 ZA 15 Hearth I
Fragment; rectangular, one edge rounded, the other three broken; surface: unburnished, light red-red/black; edges: gray/light red
L: 6.7; W: 5.3; Th: 2.5

2269a ROc 4
Fragment of an elevated vessel, probably a tripod (compare volume 1: figure 10.6:16); triangular in section; surface: matte, reddish; core: red/dark gray; coarse temper
L: 2.9; W: 1.4; Th: 0.9

2269b ROc 4
Fragment of an elevated vessel, probably a tripod (compare volume 1: figure 10.6:16); triangular in section; surface: matt, reddish; core: red/dark gray; coarse temper
L: 2.4; W: 1.2; Th: 0.8

2805 PNb 100; figure 11.22
Schematic head fragment: stem-like, squarish in section, with long oval projection near preserved, rounded end; surface: smooth, light brown/gray, with gray/green staining speckles of mica and pyrite and traces of black paint; medium fine clay
H: 5.3; W: 2.3; Th: 1.7

3353 PO 159
Figurine leg (?) (compare volume 1: figure 9.103); broken at both ends; pear-shaped, elongated, with depression on the rounded side; surface: brown-gray; temper exhibits large grit inclusions
L: 3.15; W: 2.2; Th: 1.5

5005 ZB 9s
Block: irregularly polygonal, flat; fractured at one edge; surface: red
L: 3.1; W: 2.9

Miniatures/Models

178 QOb 9; figure 11.47
Urn fragment: tall cylindrical neck (compare SF 30, phase III)
D. rim: 1.3

362 QO 3
Bowl fragment

1599 ZA 14
Unidentifiable fragment; surface: smooth, matt, black/red-light brown, some yellow and white coloration; core: coarse, red
D: 2.6; H: 3.9

3344 POcd 128
Axehead fragment
L: 5.1; W: 3.5; Th: 1.6

UNPHASED/MIXED CONTEXTS

Objects of Utility

138   Unknown
Perforated fragment ("sieve"): at least seven pierced holes on the body wall

1574   LM 5
Reworked sherd; disc fragment; surface: coarse, porous, brown; medium coarse paste and temper; well-fired
L: 9.0; Th: 1.8

2819   Surface
Ladle fragment: handle almost wholly preserved; most of the bowl missing; handle is pointed at the end; surface: red
L: 2.5; W: 2.6; Th: 1.8

3720   ZL 1; plate 11.3b
Reworked sherd; polygonal; surface: matt, brick-red; edges: ground
L: 3.9; W: 2.9; Th: 1.1

5560   Context unknown; plates 11.7d, 11.8b
Plug/oven stopper; ridged; poorly baked
D: 8.0; H: 6.0

Pottery

85   Context unknown; figure 11.16
Body fragment with button-like protuberance; decoration: two incised lines preserved, one of them U-shaped
H: 3.4; W: 4.0

86   Context unknown; figure 11.14
"Plaque" (corner fragment); decoration: incised linear pattern
L: 4.3; W: 4.1; Th: 1.3

775   Context unknown; figure 11.7
Pedestaled bowl; corner fragment; decoration: incised linear pattern
H: 3.4; W: 3.8; Th: 0.5–1.2

1414   Context unknown; figure 11.10
Bowl: open, straight-sided
H: 4.7; D. rim: 12.2; D. base: 6.0

2289   JL surface; plate 11.10e
"Plaque" fragment: perforated; surface: burnished, buff; decoration: incised groups of concentric arcs, arranged in different directions; organic temper; well-fired
L: 7.8; W: 6.6; Th: 0.7

5024   Context unknown; figure 11.15
Handle (?) fragment: U-shaped strap, with rectangular arms and a plaque-like top; decoration: on the arms painted pattern of vertical and diagonal lines on the outside of one arm and on the top
L: 5.1; W: 4.5; Th: 1.1

Plastic Forms

497   Surface
Fragment of some large incised vessel (compare volume 1: figures 10.8:23, 10.9:12; also plate LXXIII:3); conical; surface: gray/pink; decoration: groups of incised circles around leg; evidence of organic temper
H: 5.8; D: 2.9–4.4

1738   Surface; figure 11.21
Trapezoidal fragment: slightly waisted near fractured narrowing end; probably the flat base or abstract head of a figurine (compare volume 1: figure 9.122, cat. no. 140: 275)
H: 4.3; W: 2.9–4.3; Th: 1.8

Miniatures/Models

74   TL 2
Stool fragment: one leg preserved, traces of at least two others; surface: gray
L: 2.8; W:1.5; H: 1.7

337   SM 2; figure 11.55; plate 11.29d
Axehead fragment: break at hafting hole; rounded edges; surface: matt, light gray with brown patches
L: 4.0; W: 2.3; Th: 1.6

1572   LM 5; plate 11.27c
"Dimple base" fragment: two rows of circular indentations preserved; surface: smooth, light gray; core: coarse, light gray
L: 7.2; W: 4.4; Th: 1.5; D. indentations: 1.5

2286   JL surface
Pedestaled bowl fragment; surface: gray/brown
D: 4.3; H: 2.8

12.

Contextual Commentary, Phases I–V

Marianna Nikolaidou and Ernestine S. Elster

This chapter is the culmination of a process started in the first volume and completed here with volume 2, the final report. In chapters 7 and 8 of the first volume, each phase was defined in terms of stratigraphy and chronology, with excavation units further described in relation to structural content (architectural features: floors, walls, hearths, ovens, and/or building debris) and artifact recovery. The aim of this chapter is to expand on that work through an augmentation of the structural data by placing all the artifacts (as reported in both volumes and in the ZA excavation notebooks [on temporary file in the McDonald Institute, Cambridge, England]) back into those excavation units. Placing the artifacts back into place allows for an assessment of the various activities and the actors involved and provides a contextual companion to the important and rich chronological, stratigraphical, and typological record of Sitagroi mound. The results of the analysis are tabulated in tables 12.1 through 12.7, controlled by phase, building episode, context, and unit in descending order. The structural/contextual features relevant to each unit are extrapolated from Colin Renfrew's (CR) narrative describing the excavation, stratigraphy, and features (volume 1, chapter 8 [C. Renfrew 1986b]).

The picture presented here is not one without limitations, due to the following factors (discussed in turn below): the sampling strategy undertaken for this analysis; the inconsistent (but necessary) cataloging of artifacts; the nature of the artifacts themselves; the differing excavation techniques; and the inevitable occasional disturbance of the stratigraphy of the mound.

Admittedly, the finds under study here form only a limited part of the total recovery, and the respective units represent merely a portion of the excavated area on the site. Our sampling strategy was to select only those units with both structural

features and many finds. If either the quality of a unit (in terms of context; see CR discussion in volume 1, chapter 8) or the quantity of the material remains was minimal, it was not included (but see appendix 12.1 for additional units). Nevertheless the units discussed here are valuable as complementary to the important stratigraphic and chronological results, presented earlier (volume 1, chapters 7–8 [C. Renfrew 1986b, 1986e]) and provide further insight into the spatial and material correlates of human activity in each episode of the mound's long history.

The representation of the various classes of artifacts tabulated in tables 12.1 through 12.7 was affected by the way in which they were cataloged. For example, the pottery reported in both volumes is recontextualized in this discussion, but the bulk of sherds could not conveniently be tabulated because many but not all of these were counted and weighed to establish the phasing for the various strata excavated on the mound (see volume 1, chapter 7 [C. Renfrew 1986e]). Furthermore, with some exceptions, small find numbers were not assigned to chipped stone finds, and thus we could use only those artifacts identified in chapter 3 (as well as some finds described in volume 1, chapter 8 [C. Renfrew 1986b]).

When evaluating the relative counts of different classes of artifacts, it must be noted that preservation of artifact classes differs. For example, ceramic artifacts break easily and leave many sherds, whereas stone grinding tools have a longer use-life and do not leave a quantitative record as does pottery. Therefore, this analysis is careful not to infer function solely on the amount of specific finds.

During the excavation, different approaches were used that have impacted the types of artifacts presented in this chapter. For example, both troweling and dry- versus water-sieving affect the recovery of small items; thus very high concentrations of beads, chipped stone, or miniatures were recovered from water-sieved units (see particularly ZA 52 of phase II, the ZA layers of phase III, and ZB) as opposed to a rather flat overall distribution pattern.

The volume of earth moved was 740 m³ (see Preface table 2), but each phase was not represented equally (see volume 1, chapter 8 [C. Renfrew 1986b]). Thus phase III Chalcolithic strata account for close to 20% by volume (and much of that from MM/ML units), while the EBA levels amount to almost 50%, and much of that is from the four squares of PO, PN, QN, and QO in the Main Area where the three EBA building episodes were excavated. Therefore, differences in the frequency of artifacts through space and time (tables 12.1–12.7) have to be assessed with these constraints in mind.

Lastly, the contextual focus is not equally sharp throughout the site: in some fortunate cases we have floor deposits, with at least some objects in situ, in recognizable rooms associated with structures securely dated and relatively well understood; the Burnt House is the most illustrative example. Most contextual evidence of the Middle Neolithic/Chalcolithic (MN/C), however, cannot be clearly tied to a specific building or time frame, but rather consists of either patchy floors or other building features with an ambiguous structural association. Or, as is the case of the phase III MM/ML Hearth and Debris levels and Lower Layers (tables 12.3–12.4), there are subsequent floors presumably within a restricted time range of successive building episodes. In such contexts we are possibly not dealing with the original use-setting of many of the recovered artifacts: broken pots, incomplete items (a large part of the assemblage) dumped together in discard (?) areas, and debris fallen onto floors call our attention to fragmentation, secondary use, and purposeful and/or accidental deposition.

Sometimes classes of artifacts were found to cluster stylistically in specific phases of the MN/C and were considered as *fossiles directeurs*, as for example, the phase II tripods (see volume 1, chapter 10 [Elster 1986]) or figurines (see volume 1, chapter 9 [Gimbutas 1986]), with both types recovered only occasionally from Early Bronze Age (EBA) layers. This kind of inconsistency is always

part of excavation and may mean that a particular object was considered an heirloom and was curated from an earlier time (see Lillios 1999), or was thrown up in plowing or by rodent activity, or simply cannot be accounted for. In any case, we do not reject any part of the material record; ambiguity accompanies us at all times.

It seemed fitting to partner the presentation of the site's rich archaeological record with a contextual companion to chapters 1 through 11 of this volume but also, in retrospect, to chapters 8 through 13 of volume 1 dealing, respectively, with architecture (C. Renfrew 1986b), figurines (Gimbutas 1986), social ceramics (Elster 1986), and pottery (Keighley 1986; R. Evans 1986; Sherratt 1986). The artifacts analyzed are organized into the groupings established in volume 1 and in this volume;[1] to these we add the rich vegetational history (volume 1, chapter 4 (Turner and Greig 1986; Rackham 1986), archaeobotanical (see chapter 1), and faunal remains (volume 1, chapter 5 (Bökönyi 1986). To conclude with this introduction, readers are invited to open the doors of the Sitagroi households and glimpse prehistoric people weaving their material, social, and symbolic existence around the artifacts and features that have come down to us in all their quantity and sometimes mysterious variability.

PHASE I

The exposure of Phase I levels, although limited (see volume 1 [C. Renfrew 1986b]:176, 218–221), sets the stage for the actors and actions that will come into sharper focus during the continuing Middle Neolithic phase II and ensuing Chalcolithic phase III. In particular, two closely associated units of the deep soundings ZA 61 and 62, floors 17 and 18 (see stratigraphic section, volume 1 [C. Renfrew 1986b]:178, figure 8.2), the contents of which were both water-sieved, provide us with an evocative group of two dozen artifacts (table 12.1). These include an interesting concentration of eleven bowl fragments from ZA 62, in various forms and fabrics (notably the fine Gray Lustre Ware), reflecting the links with the Veselinovo culture. Other artifacts with comparanda in the Balkan Neolithic as well as in Drama Plain sites (see chapter 13) include a tripod fragment and an animal figurine. Beads for adornment were also recovered and, from ZA 63 contiguous with floor 18, a most important recovery—the first clear impression of a woven fabric in the Aegean (SF 1439, see chapter 6). A few cattle bones come from both floors, and a dog/wolf mandible from floor 18. Combining these with other phase I units across the mound (see Preface table 3 and appendix 12.1), we are informed about the lives of these first settlers: farmers, builders, craftsmen and women, traders, and middlemen/women involved in exchanges of value, with a developed symbolic system and links with contemporary Drama region settlements and with other sites north across the Rhodope Mountains.

Table 12.1. Phase I: Deep Sounding ZA 61, Floor 17 and ZA 63, Floor 18

| | Context | | |
| Category | Floor 17 | Floor 18 | Total |
Item	ZA 61	ZA 63	
Adornment: Bead	9		9
Pottery: Bowl		11	11
Presentation: Elab. bone	1		1
Sculpture: Figurine		1	1
Social ceramic: Tripod	1		1
Spinning/weaving: Impression		1	1
Total	11	13	24

PHASE II

In the deep sounding of ZA, the deposits of phase II were mainly fill (volume 1 [C. Renfrew 1986b]: 176), but layer ZA 52 (all water sieved) exposed postholes of floor 16 (volume 1 [C. Renfrew 1986b]: 178 [figure 8.2], 181) and offers a rich and characteristic material record of a Middle Neolithic household (table 12.2). Flotation provided a sample of more than 900 seeds (see this volume, chapter 1), representing cereals (most important), pulses, and a few wild fruit. Faunal recovery included skeletal parts of caprovids (six), cattle (three), and pig (four). An impressive number of small artifacts such as beads (see chapter 9), chipped stone (see figure 3.6), and figurines (see volume 1 [Gimbutas 1986], chapter 9) were retrieved.

Table 12.2. Phase II: Deep Sounding ZAs 52, Floor 16

| Category | Floor 16 |
Item	ZA 52 (sieved)
Adornment	
Bead	119
Bracelet/annulet	5
Pendant	4
Pin	2
Chipped stone	
Blade	22
Borer	2
Core	2
Point	6
Scraper	5
Ground/polished stone	
Axe	1
Grinder	1
Other processing tool	1
Quern	2
Rubber	1
Notation	
Counter	1
Pottery	
Bowl	5
Jar	2
Lid	1
Pedestal bowl	4
Plaque-handle	1
Presentation	
Misc. elaborated	3
Sculpture	
Figurine	13
Miniature/model	3
Misc. plastic form	2
Social ceramic	
Pedestal	1
Tripod	1
Worked bone	
Flattened	3
Misc. worked	2
Pointed	7
Spatulate	1
Total	223

There are remarkable clusters of objects that belong to either the same or different types and categories; for example, sets of beads, bracelets, and pendants (see chapter 9); figurines and miniatures/

models; high-quality pottery, especially bowls of elaborate forms and/or painted decoration; chipped stone; and worked bone. Many categories of evidence seem interlinked. For instance, the processing stone tools and (sickle?) blades partner with the rich botanical record; faunal remains and items of worked bone belong to the same species; bone items with flattened ends might have been used for working the hides of those same animals; while stone scrapers and blades could also have been used to process animal parts and to manufacture bone tools. Stone and bone implements with sharp points, relatively well represented, may have produced the perforated ornaments and incised figurines, social ceramics, and plaque-handle. Scrapers, borers, querns, and rubbers may also have been, in addition to their function as food processors, tools for the manufacture of shell, stone, and bone ornaments, as well as of the stone presentation artifacts.

Along with traditional technologies, these villagers were developing new and sophisticated patterns of life. It is certainly worth noting the variety and high numerical representation of innovative artifacts that were arguably invested with special values, ranging from ornaments to sculpture, notation, elaborated pieces, social ceramics, presentation artifacts, and fine vessels. Items such as the *Spondylus* ornaments, a metal bead, painted pottery, and possibly chipped stone attest to networks of exchange, social and perhaps also ritual links within and outside the Drama Plain. The profusion of such material symbols in a single excavated layer of limited extent may be interpreted in two ways. First, it may indicate that certain contexts within the settlement served as foci for conceptual and social elaboration; however, this must remain a hypothesis only, since there are no other watersieved floor contexts for comparison from this phase. Or, perhaps more likely, it may be evidence that Middle Neolithic households at Sitagroi invested richly in aesthetics, symbolism, and socioeconomic affiliations. The chronological/stratigraphic system established for ZA phase II (see Preface table 3) can be related to other units (volume 1 [C. Renfrew 1986b]:218–219) across the mound (see appendix 12.1), and thus we may consider ZA as reflective of all the phase II units, which presage the Chalcolithic florescence of phase III.

PHASE III

The finds of phase III are numerous and of great interest (tables 12.1–12.3). Our first phase III case (table 12.3) is represented by MM 16 and 18–20 of the Hearth and Debris levels (see volume 1 [C. Renfrew 1986b]:214–217, figure 8.19) which revealed postholes, the remains of a floor with a baked hearth (MM 18–20), and a burnt wall (MM 16). This floor was probably not inside a house, although it was possibly associated with one because the structure was open on one side. J. Renfrew's report on the grains, seeds, and fruits (chapter 1) and eightyfour faunal elements indicate animal and plant husbandry, hunting, scavenging, collecting, food preparation (on the hearth?), and consumption. The consistency of the samples is characteristic of a phase III diet; the seeds are almost all wheat, while the faunal elements represent primarily cattle (twenty-two), sheep (twenty), goat (six), pig (eleven), dog/wolf (seven), red deer (ten), fallow deer (three), hare (four), and brown bear (one).

Several of the seventy-three artifacts highlight a variety of household tasks and crafts: there are grinders for processing food and other substances, axes for felling trees or carpentry, bone items for working on hides, fibers, cloth, or pottery, storage jars, serving or measuring ladles, spindle whorls, and mat impressions. Crucible fragments associated with metallurgy (see chapter 8) and fine ceramics, especially the graphite-painted and Black-on-Red wares, provide evidence for innovative technologies (see chapter 7) of (presumably) prestige value, widespread among associated Drama Plain and Balkan cultures. A bracelet of *Spondylus* (likely from the North Aegean Sea, about a 25 km distance) and stone axes of raw materials (likely from west Macedonia or east Thrace; see chapter 4) reflect the circulation of raw materials and finished products (perhaps also of middlemen/women, specialists, and skills) to and from the site. Sophisticated vessels for serving and presentation, social ceramics, decorated spindle whorls, figurines and miniatures, and ornaments further evoke the social and symbolic frameworks of action: people offering and receiving hospitality, crafting goods for exchange and display, embellishing themselves and their utensils, creating artistic

Table 12.3. Phase III: Debris and Hearth Levels (MM 16, 18–20, and Probably Earlier: MM 17, 21–50)

Category/Item	MM 18	MM 19	MM 20	MM 16	MM 17	MM 21	MM 23	MM 27	MM 31	MM 36	MM 38	MM 40	MM 41/42	MM 43	MM 44	MM 4547	MM 48	MM 49	MM 50	Total
Adornment																				
Bracelet/annulet				1				1	1			3	1	3				3	5	18
Pendant		1	1			1		1						1			1	2	1	9
Pin			1					1					1	1						4
Plaque											1									1
Ceramic utensil																				
Ladle		3										1							1	5
Worked sherd													1			1				2
Chipped stone																				
Blade		1																1		2
Composite																		2		2
Core														1						1
Scraper												1	1					1		3
Ground/ polished stone																				
Axe		1		2		1		4	1			3	1	1				1	1	16
Chisel														1						1
Grinder				1								1			1	1			1	5
Quern								1								2				3
Rubber			1															1		2
Sphere						1			1											2
Metallurgy																				
Awl														1						1
Crucible/sherd			9			1		1				1	1	1					1	15
Notation																				
Ball						2		1						1						4
Pintadera													1							1
Pottery																				
Bowl		1	1					1				1		1			1	1	1	8
Lid												2								2
Urn						1														1
Presentation																				
Vessel																		1		1
Sculpture																				
Figurine	1		3	4		1		6			1	2	1	3		2		2	3	29
Miniature/ model		1	3	1		1		1	1					2					4	14
Misc. plastic form								1												1
Social ceramic																				
Pedestal				1																1
Plastic vessel	1	4		5		2		4			1	4	5	1		1		1	2	31
Stand		1		1		1								1		1				5
Tripod		1		1				1			1	1		1						6
Spinning/ weaving																				
Impression		3	2			1	1	6				2	2	2					1	20
Loom weight										1										1

Continued on next page

Table 12.3. Phase III: Debris and Hearth Levels (MM 16, 18–20, and Probably Earlier: MM 17, 21–50)

Category/Item	MM 18	MM 19	MM 20	MM 16	MM 17	MM 21	MM 23	MM 27	MM 31	MM 36	MM 38	MM 40	MM 41/42	MM 43	MM 44	MM 4547	MM 48	MM 49	MM 50	Total
Worked bone																				
Flattened						2				1		3	1							7
Misc. worked		1	2	2		2		4		1		3	5	2			2		1	25
Pointed				1		2						1	1	2			3		5	15
Rounded																		1		1
Shaft-holed												1	1							2
Spatulate				1																1
Total	3	19	25	25	1	24	1	38	1	7	4	32	28	34	1	8	7	14	35	307

representations, sharing knowledge and rituals with near and distant neighbors. The picture of village life is complemented by the other contexts of phase III.

The other levels, MM 17, 21–50 (volume 1 [C. Renfrew 1986b]:215–217) of the Hearth and Debris episode (table 12.3) and the Lower Habitation levels, MM 51–53, 60–68 (table 12.4) in the same area (see volume 1 [C. Renfrew 1986b]:217–218), produced rich phase III material assemblages, likely spanning earlier occupation. MM 52 is within about 40 cm, in absolute height, of ZA layer 41, floor 15 (volume 1 [C. Renfrew 1986b]:218).

Artifacts from the deep sounding square ZA, layers 41–47 (see volume 1 [C. Renfrew 1986b]:180–181) are tabulated in table 12.5. ZA 41 is an important closed destruction deposit associated with floor 15, a domestic area (volume 1 [C. Renfrew 1986b]:176). ZA layers 42 through 45[2] include the midden deposit beneath floor 15; ZA 46 through 47 have been added to ZA 42–45 for two reasons: first, on the stratigraphic section of the trench (volume 1 [C. Renfrew 1986b]:178, figure 8.2), levels 46 through 47 seem directly connected to the midden above, and there is at least one posthole that looks associated with level 47. Second, units ZA 46 and 47 offer further examples (along with ZA 44 and 45) of the value of water-sieving for retrieving small artifacts.

The counts of various categories of artifacts vary in the three tables, reflecting in part the differences in the amount of soil removed and/or in the retrieval strategies used in the units tabulated, that is, water- versus dry-sieving. For example, one class of artifact missing from one of the tables (table 12.5) is ceramic utensil; otherwise, each grouping is present in the phase III tabulations although in varying intensity. Comparable distributions imply that common practices of producing, acquiring, and manipulating material culture linked the households of Chalcolithic Sitagroi in space and time. This suggests a shared involvement in specialized technologies including high-quality pottery, crafting of shell and stone ornaments, intensive spinning and weaving (and basketry?), stone tool production, and metallurgy.

In regard to the latter, the retrieval of metal ornaments in ZA contexts and the recovery of two crucible sherds near or on an oven floor in layer ZJ 24 (see volume 1 [C. Renfrew 1986b]:221; this volume, chapter 8) is noted but not tabulated in table 12.5. Furthermore, there appears to be an overall concern for the elaboration of form and (arguably) content, reflected in the high concentrations of ornaments, sculpture, distinct ceremonial (?) pottery types, decorated spindle whorls, and items of notation and presentation. Both whole and fragmentary valuables such as *Spondylus* bracelets, special ceramics, figurines, prized tools, and the like may have circulated among affiliated persons and groups. Once their use-cycle was complete, perhaps these artifacts were deposited carefully in the loci of continuing habitation.

PHASE IV

Phase IV areas of burned flooring were exposed in a 2 x 2 m sounding, ZH, which was subsequently extended to an area measuring 12 m north-south x 8 m east-west, immediately north of square MM (see volume 1 [C. Renfrew 1986b]:207–209, figure 8.16). In this area, burned floors and walls belonging to

Table 12.4. Phase III: Lower Habitation Levels of the Hearth and Debris Episode (MM 51–53, 60–68)

Category/Item	MM 51	MM 52	MM 53	MM 60	MM 61	MM 63	MM 64	MM 65	MM 66	MM 67	MM 68	Total
Adornment												
Bead	1			1		2		1				5
Bracelet/annulet		2	1	3	14	9		5	3		3	40
Pendant				1		2		1	3		1	8
Ceramic utensil												
Ladle				1								1
Worked sherd								1				1
Chipped stone												
Scraper			1									1
Ground/polished stone												
Adze					2	1						3
Axe		1		1	1	1		1				5
Grinder					2			1				3
Quern			1	1	1			1	1			5
Rubber					1							1
Metallurgy												
Copper				1								1
Crucible/sherd			1	2	2							5
Notation												
Ball								1			1	2
Sling-shot	1											1
Pottery												
Amphora								1			1	2
Jar				1								1
Lid			1				1					2
Presentation												
Elaborated				1								1
Sculpture												
Figurine		3	1		3	1			1			9
Miniature/model		1		1				1			1	4
Social ceramic												
Plastic vessel	1	1		1	2				3			8
Tripod		2										2
Spinning/weaving												
Impression		1	1		3	1						6
Whorl	2	1	2	5	2			1		1		14
Worked bone												
Flattened					3	2		1				6
Misc. Worked		2		5		4		1	4		2	18
Pointed	1	4	1	3	3	1		3	1			17
Rounded				1								1
Shaft-holed					1							1
Spatulate				1								1
Total	6	18	10	30	40	24	1	20	16	1	9	175

Table 12.5. Phase III: Deep Sounding ZA 41–47*

| Category | Floor 15 | Modern deposit below floor 15 | | | Modern deposit above floor 15 | | | |
Item	ZA 41	ZA 42	ZA 43	ZA 44	ZA 45	ZA 46	ZA 47	Total
Adornment								
Bead				127	58	20	81	286
Bracelet/annulet	2			6	1		7	16
Pendant			1	12	5		8	26
Chipped stone								
Blade	1	2		4	1	2	5	15
Borer					1		3	4
Composite				1				1
Core		1		2		1	2	6
Point				2			3	5
Scraper		1	1	2				4
Ground/polished stone								
Axe				1			1	2
Grinder	2	1						3
Pounder		1						1
Quern	4	1		1	1			7
Rubber				1				1
Metallurgy								
Copper							1	1
Crucible/sherd						2		2
Notation								
Ball				2				2
Sling-shot		1						1
Pottery								
Amphora	3			2	1			6
Bowl			1	2	1			4
Jar				1				1
Lid					1			1
Plaque-handle				1			1	2
Pyxis	1							1
Sculpture								
Figurine				7	2		9	18
Miniature/model	1						5	6
Misc. plastic form				2			1	3
Social ceramic								
Pedestal							1	1
Plastic vessel		1		3	1			5
Stand		4			1			5
Tripod				1				1
Spinning/weaving								
Impression	1	2	1				1	5
Loom weight		1						1
Whorl		1		2		1	2	6
Worked bone								
Flattened		1				1	3	5
Misc. worked		1		1		2		4
Pointed		1	1	5			5	12
Spatulate							2	2
Total	15	20	5	188	74	29	141	472

*A domestic area associated with floor 15.

Table 12.6. Phase IV: Sounding ZH Extended to Examine Burned House Floors and Walls*

Item	ZH 6	ZH 13	ZH 19	ZH 22	ZH 23	ZH 24/28	ZH 14	ZH 24	ZH 26	ZH 27	ZH 28	ZH 12	ZH 17	ZH 18	ZH 20	ZH 21	Total
Adornment																	
Bracelet/annulet									1								1
Pin													1				1
Stone pendant	1																1
Chipped stone																	
Arrowhead								1									1
Blade											1						1
Blade/flake						14											14
Core															1	1	2
Scraper								1									1
Ground/polished stone																	
Adze		1															1
Axe					1						1						2
Quern															1		1
Rubber					1			1									2
Metallurgy																	
Crucible	1						1										2
Pin		1		1													2
Pottery																	
Bowl		1	2		1			1	1				1	1	1	1	10
Cup		1															1
Jar					1												1
Jug					1												1
Plaque-handle												1					1
Urn			1						2	1			1				5
Presentation																	
Misc. elaborated								1									1
Sculpture																	
Figurine								1									1
Miniature/model								1									1
Social ceramic																	
Stand									1								1
Tripod			1														1
Spinning/weaving																	
Loom weight											1						1
Whorl		1		3	2			7		2			1	1	1		18
Worked bone																	
Flattened			1						2							2	5
Misc. worked			1	3				1	3								8
Pointed		2		2				2	1				1		1		9
Total	2	7	6	8	8	14	1	17	11	3	3	1	5	2	4	5	97

*Units encountered in sequence: ZH 12, 17, 18, 20–21; ZH 13, 19, 22, 23; ZH 6; and ZH 14, 24, 26–28.

two long houses were uncovered, located next and parallel to each other. Ninety-four items were tabulated from here (table 12.6). Not all levels, however, are clearly associated with structural features: ZH 14, 15, 24, and 26–28 are the most representative, while ZH 13, 19, 22, and 23 are overlying layers perhaps containing associated material; ZH 12, 17-18, and 20–21 lie over a higher floor. Remains of comparable houses with evidence of burning were also excavated in the stratigraphic trench ZA (see volume 1 [C. Renfrew 1986b]:177), in square ROc (see volume 1 [C. Renfrew 1986b]:203-207), and in area SL with sounding ZE (the former [SL] dated to late phase IV or early phase Va [see volume 1 [C. Renfrew 1986b]:209, 210]), suggesting the onset of a pattern of EBA village layout. The artifact record also presents similarities across contexts. An important common feature is the dramatic decrease in symbolic items we consider so characteristic of the earlier Middle Neolithic/Chalcolithic, although *Spondylus* bracelets, sculpture, items of notation and presentation, and social ceramics do occur occasionally throughout the sequence.

Such finds have been traditionally interpreted as disturbances from earlier, MN/C strata (for example, see volume 1, chapter 9 catalog; and this volume, chapter 10). However, their presence in stratified domestic assemblages suggests that these objects also had a meaningful place in the Early Bronze Age households of phase IV—perhaps, as suggested earlier, as heirlooms (see Lillios 1999), that is, material reminders of continuity linking the inhabitants with the land and the ancestral (?) households on top of which they chose to build and rebuild their own dwellings (compare Chapman 2000; Elster 1997; Nikolaidou 1997).

Technologies also reflect earlier material culture. For example, there is evidence for metallurgy (metal pins from ZH 17 and ZA 23, crucible fragments recovered from both ZH and ZE squares), interesting concentrations of spindle whorls, chipped stone, and worked bone, although the typology of the objects, especially the whorls, does change (see chapter 6). An axe from ZH 23 and a pendant from the associated surface layer ZH 6 were made of stone from likely sources in west Macedonia or Thrace (see chapter 4), an indication

of continuity in trade and exchange networks established during the MN/C.

The few ornaments, especially the exotic ones of metal, stone, and *Spondylus*, imply an ongoing interest in aesthetics and symbolism, although admittedly on a different scale than previously. The important innovations reported for phase IV pottery (volume 1, chapter 13 [Sherratt 1986]) are seen in the contexts discussed here: jugs, cups, and a range of bowls and scoops, echoing new habits of food serving, drinking, and hospitality. These sometimes appear in "sets" (in ZH 13, 19, 23 and ZA 26 and 30), and when made of fine clay with a high burnish or decoration, such vessels were perhaps valued presentation pieces as well as receptacles. The characteristic large storage pots of the period, as well as jars and urns, also occur; ZE 76 is especially interesting since excavation exposed two jars filled with acorns and a unique sample of more than 60,000 grains (chapter 1). These were obviously staple materials for the family meals; more acorns and scoops were found in associated levels ZE 79 and 66. This example illustrates, in part, the differing tastes of phase IV villagers: a preference for barley over wheat, heavy use of acorns, and, importantly, the cultivation of grapes (see chapter 1).

Dietary differences from the Chalcolithic are also evident in the phase IV faunal record, with pig doubling at the expense of cattle, which is half as important in comparison with the MN/C patterns of husbandry; and wild game is highest for all phases (see volume 1 [Bökönyi 1986]:68–69). Specifically for square ZH contexts, the percentages of the various taxa (of a total of sixty-eight elements) distribute as follows: cattle (16%), caprovine (12%), pig (28%), dog/wolf (10%), and wild (4%); for the latter, the emphasis is on red, fallow, and roe deer. Perhaps the decrease in the dietary importance of caprovines is linked to the exploitation of their secondary products such as wool (see volume 1, chapters 5 [Bökönyi 1986] and 13 [Sherratt 1986]; this volume, chapter 6). This is reflected, among other cases, in the finds from a burned household in ROc 73: four loom weights, probably used for weaving woolen fabrics on an upright loom, and a deep, roughly burnished bowl appropriate for holding and/or processing liquids, soups, or perhaps stews made with grains and meat.

We are thus dealing, at the onset of the Early Bronze Age, with a spectrum of archaeologically tangible permutations in culinary habits, patterns of land and animal management, associated artifacts (pottery, spinning/weaving implements, stone and bone tools), and, by inference, mechanisms of trade and exchange. The social and symbolic logic linking these phenomena together still remains to be fully explored. In this context, other developments, more elusive to us, should also come into play: the changing experiences of self and the world around, different aesthetics and values, a rearrangement of roles, and new channels of expression and social reproduction.

PHASE V

The layers of phase V (volume 1 [C. Renfrew 1986b]: 192 [figure 8.5], 194 [figure 8.8]), closest to the mound surface, were well investigated, while the recovery from the stratigraphic section ZA (volume 1 [C. Renfrew 1986b]:176, 178, figure 8.2) provides us with an important reflection of those horizontal exposures. There seems to have been a regular village layout, with long houses built next to each other and similarly aligned, implying close contacts (perhaps also kinship bonds) among the inhabitants. Thick successions of floor layers (repairs or rebuilding) and superimposed (even similarly oriented) structures indicate familial links through time as well. Habitation in square ROc, for example, spanning almost two millennia (phases IV through Vb), vividly echoes a powerful attachment of people to their land and ancestors (compare Chapman 2000; Elster 1997; Tringham and Krstić 1990). We can infer the same for the three building episodes revealed in the excavation of the Main Area (squares PN, PO, QN, and QO) on top of the mound (see volume 1 [C. Renfrew 1986b]:184–185). The Burnt House, Long House, and Bin Complex were published with care in volume 1; additionally, the contents of the Burnt House, a well-equipped EBA phase Va dwelling, has been earlier described and analyzed (this volume, chapter 5, figure 5.35; Renfrew 1970; 1986b:190–203; Elster 1997) and will not be reexamined here.

The Phase Vb Long House (see plan in volume 1 [C. Renfrew 1986b]:195, figure 8.9) was a wattle-and-daub structure of apsidal plan, 15.5 x 5.5 m (but the southern end was not delineated), exposed in squares PO and PN. The "house" revealed no recognizable interior divisions. During excavation, and for stratigraphic control, the grid was modified to PO/A–PO/D and PN/A–PN/F (see volume 1 [C. Renfrew 1986b]:184). It had been partly built over the Burnt House and was partly underlying the Bin Complex. During excavation, a "layer cake" complex of clay floors could be identified (for section drawing, see volume 1 [C. Renfrew 1986b]: 193, figures 8.6, 8.7). Renfrew observed (volume 1 [C. Renfrew 1986b]:189) that the Long House and the Bin Complex presented opposite recoveries: the Long House offered clear information on structure and few finds (see appendix 12.1), while the Bin Complex (for early exposure, see volume 1 [C. Renfrew 1986b]:192, figure 8.5) revealed numerous features and finds but no evidence of house structure.

Thus, we concentrate on the Bin Complex of phase Vb (table 12.7), with a rich exposure of large bins of plaster or clay associated with patchy remains of flooring, postholes, hearth, a processing platform, and pits. Although domestic in nature, this area was not clearly associated with a single structure: the various features possibly belonged to several now-perished houses (volume 1 [C. Renfrew 1986b]:187). Thus, our focus shifts from the individual household to the neighborhood and village community.

Many features of the Bin Complex merit attention because it is partly situated over the Long House (itself built over the Burnt House), with associated Bin Complex floors and pits often cutting through earlier layers of habitation. The stratigraphic units associated with the Bin Complex are PO 7–9, PN 5–7, QO 7–9, and QN 6–8. Two fragments of decorated bowls dated to phase Va, but found in layers PO 9 (Bin Complex) and PN 92 (Long House) (volume 1: figure 13.13:3 and 6, respectively), might have been cherished curios or heirlooms. The structural features of bins and hearths suggest practices of food storage, preparation, production, and consumption encompassing more than one household; communal meals and

Table 12.7. Phase Vb: Stratigraphic Units of the Bin Complex in the Main Area of Sitagroi Mound

Item	PN 5	PN 6	PN 7	PO 7	PO 8	PO 9	QN 6	QN 7	QN 8	QO 7	QO 8	QO 9	Total
Adornment													
Pendant	1				1								2
Pin				2	1	1		3				1	8
Ceramic utensil													
Ladle										1			1
oven stopper			1						1				2
Chipped stone													
Blade						1	1				6		8
Sickle blade								2					2
Ground/polished stone													
Axe					3	1		1		1	1	1	8
Grinder							1	2			2	2	7
Grooved											1		1
Hammer stone					1			1					2
Other processing tool											1		1
Pestle									1				1
Pounder						1	2				1		4
Quern		1				5		1					7
Rubber						1					1		2
Sphere										1			1
Metallurgy													
Awl								1					1
Copper									1				1
Crucible											1		1
Slag											2		2
Notation													
Cylinder	1												1
Pottery													
Amphora				1									1
Bowl				5	15	2				1	4		27
Cup					2	2		1		1	9		15
Jar		1			2						1		4
Lid				1	2								3
Plaque-handle				1									1
Urn				1	6						3		10
Presentation													
Misc. elaborated											1		1
Mace head	1												1
Stone vessel				1									1
Sculpture													
Figurine					1						1		2
Miniature/model										1		1	2
Social ceramic													
Stand						1							1
Tripod					1					1			2
Spinning/weaving													
Anchor/hook	1		3	1	2	2		2	2		4		17
Loom weight			1	1				4	1		1		8

Continued on next page

Table 12.7. Phase Vb: Stratigraphic Units of the Bin Complex in the Main Area of Sitagroi Mound

Item	PN 5	PN 6	PN 7	PO 7	PO 8	PO 9	QN 6	QN 7	QN 8	QO 7	QO 8	QO 9	Total
Spool				1	4					1	3		9
Whorl	1	1	3		10	7	3	8	7	4	23	2	69
Worked bone													
Flattened							1				2		3
Pointed									3		3		6
Spatulate											1		1
Total	5	3	8	15	51	24	10	24	16	12	72	7	247

feasting are plausible possibilities. This idea seems supported by the large numbers of organic remains, including 175 elements of domestic and wild fauna (see volume 1, chapter 5 [Bökönyi 1986]), and more than twenty botanical samples (this volume, chapter 1), many of which consist of hundreds or thousands of seeds, acorns, and fruit pips. Also characteristic are the groupings of artifacts associated with the above activities: bowls, drinking cups, jars or urns with big lids in PO 7–9 and QO 8 (in the latter seeds were found within pots), chipped stone blades, axes, and various ground stone processors in PO 8 and 9, QN 7, and QO 8 and 9. Ceramic shapes and distinct elements, such as handles, cords, and cordon impressions, appear remarkably standardized, albeit in a range of sizes and with varying details of treatment (see volume 1 [Sherratt 1986]:466–473, figures 13.20–13.27 [cups, urns, jugs, bowls, etc.]). Besides the practical advantages (see volume 1, chapter 13 [Sherratt 1986]), overall similarity of form possibly implies socially and symbolically prescribed (but not absolutely binding) ways for dealing with the food apparatus (compare Miller 1985). We may detect analogous stylistic codes in other categories of artifacts, such as the pins (this volume, chapters 2 and 9) or the large typological groups of spindle whorls (chapter 6). The wealth of material recovery from the Bin Complex has already been noted (volume 1, chapter 8 [C. Renfrew 1986b]; this volume, chapter 5 and various other chapters). The 245 artifacts recorded illuminate multiple aspects of life, both practical and elaborate: farming; food processing; tool-making crafts, notably weaving and metallurgy; trade (axes made of likely nonlocal raw materials in PO 7, 8; QO 8, 9; QN 7,8); adornment and fashion; presentation and/or display (see appendix 5.2 for the mace head, SF 1127, from PN 5); and hospitality (note the cups and a decorated jar from PO 8). Symbolic manipulation is further suggested by figurines, social ceramics, a decorated cylinder, all artifacts (not surprisingly) reflecting earlier phases.

If more than one family participated in the facilities of the Bin Complex (as is implied by the structural features), it would be interesting to consider the elements of visibility, collaboration, or competition involved in the performance of activities. Notable are the special items (of earlier date or contemporary manufacture) found, although isolated, in all other excavated contexts of phase V (see appendix 12.1). Could such material symbols be interpreted as common reference points of the community? We may further wonder whether the deposition of the rich cultural material among the installations of the Bin Complex had as its sole purpose the disposal of unwanted refuse (in itself a modern notion; compare Chapman 2000) or was rather structured in socially (perhaps ritually; compare Brük 1999) meaningful ways.

Such a contextually informed database can serve as a starting point for another look at an ever stimulating site following current questions of archaeological thinking. We could, for example, focus on an entire culture or people of a single time period (and their activities) instead of on abstract processes; or, we could investigate the household as a basic unit of social reproduction; or, we could study material symbolism and performance. These issues have been touched upon in various chapters of this volume, but can be fruitfully pursued further using the data analyzed here and comparable materials from other published sites in the region and beyond.

NOTES

[1] These are listed alphabetically: adornment (metal artifacts and bone pins discussed in chapter 9 are tabulated in this grouping); ceramic utensils (chapter 11); chipped stone (chapter 3); ground/polished stone (chapters 4, 5); metal/metallurgy (chapter 8); notation, including pintaderas, balls, and "slingshots" (chapter 10); pottery (volume 1, chapters 11–13 [Keighley 1986; R. Evans 1986; Sherratt 1986]); presentation, including elaborate bone pieces (chapter 2), mace heads and marble vessels (chapters 4, 5); plastic representation, including figurines (volume 1, chapter 9 [Gimbutas 1986]), miniatures and models (chapter 11), and miscellaneous plastic forms (chapter 11); social ceramics (volume 1, chapter 10 [Elster 1986]; this volume, chapter 11); spinning/weaving tools (chapter 6); and worked bone (chapter 2).

[2] An unexpected find exposed in the middle of layer ZA 43 (see volume 1:180) was particularly ambiguous: a human skull, with no associated bones. Human remains were not recovered from other strata, nor is this a common find in related sites of northeast Greece or the Balkans.

Appendix 12.1.
Additional Contextual Units
Marianna Nikolaidou

This appendix is organized as follows for each phase (I–V): square/sounding (reference, illustration), level, floor, and description/comments.

PHASE I

Square ZA (volume 1:178 [figure 8.2], 181)
Levels
61: Floor 17
62/63: Floor 18
67: Floor 20 (with wall on northeast side): a sample of 163 einkorn seeds; artifacts: one chipped stone blade, one axe, two bowls, and a sieve
68: Floor 19 with postholes, hearth; artifacts: one bead, one *Spondylus* bracelet, two chipped stone blades, one scraper, three processors (quern, rubber, pounder), one jar fragment, and one foot of open bowl.
69: Floor 20 and wall (ZA 70) preserved in parts up to 30 cm

Square KL (volume 1:219, 220 [figure 8.21])
Levels 120–122: Wooden beam, bones; artifacts: one slingshot, and three bone tools including two flattened end and one pointed end.

ML Sounding (volume 1:219–220)
Level 45: Destruction deposit associated with oven; artifacts: one bead, one axe, two bowls

Total Other Phase I Artifacts: 23

PHASE II

Square KM (volume 1:219)
Levels 9, 16, 19, 22: Hearth remains, baked levels; artifacts: one pendant, one worked sherd, two axes, one quern, two rubbers, one burnished and two bichrome-painted bowls, one miniature vessel, three tripods, three bone tools including one pointed and one miscellaneous.

ML Sounding (volume 1:219, 220)
Level 15: Hearth feature; artifacts: two bone tools

Total Other Phase II Artifacts: 19

PHASE IV

Square ROc (volume 1:203–207, figure 8.14, 8.15)
Levels
59–67: A sequence of hearths.
65: Hearth or oven composed of broken sherds.
61: Faunal elements: three cattle, two caprovids, three pig, three dog/wolf, two red deer; artifacts: one bead, two stone cores, one ladle, one plastic vessel, two spindle whorls, four pointed and three miscellaneous worked stone tools.
73: Destruction deposit of burnt house; clay daub, posthole, traces of wall, hearth near balk; faunal remains: one red deer metacarpus; artifacts: four loom weights, one bowl

Total Other Phase IV ROc Faunal Elements: 14
Total Other Phase IV ROc Artifacts: 19

Square SL (volume 1:209–210, 211, figure 8.17)
Levels
5: Ridge-backed hearth; one metal awl.
14: Better-preserved hearth, burnt wall and flooring of long house comparable to house in ZE; one barley seed, fourteen acorns; artifacts: one jar, three loom weights, one spindle whorl.

Sounding ZE (part of square SF) (volume 1:210–212)
Levels
50–55, 61–65: Clay floors, postholes; 100 acorns, two seeds (emmer, barley); faunal elements: seven cattle, eight caprovids, ten pig, three dog/wolf, eleven red deer, four fallow deer, ten roe deer, one marten, one beaver; artifacts: one bead, one bracelet, five pendants, one clay sieve, one stone core, one scraper, four axes (one shaft-holed), two processors, one crucible fragment, one urn, one loom weight, three whorls, two bone points, eight bone tools (one flattened, five miscellanea, two points).
76: Fire destruction; two pithoi including carbonized grains (61,514 seeds), carbonized acorns found in a depression with an urn close by.

79   (Level associated with ZE 76): Artifacts: a clay scoop, one stone scraper.

66:    Destruction levels of house; burnt wall and flooring; burnt acorns and one scoop, associated with finds in ZE 76; one stone blade.

59, 66–79: Destruction levels; faunal elements: five cattle, five caprovids, ten pig, two dog/wolf, eleven red deer, six fallow deer, one roe deer; artifacts: twenty-four blades, one borer, three axes (one shaft-holed), one grinder, one "clay slingshots," one loom weight, four spindle whorls, two bone tools (one point, one miscellaneous).

Total Other Phase IV SL and ZE Faunal Elements: 95
Total Other Phase IV SL and ZE Artifacts: 80

PHASE Va:
CONTEMPORARY WITH THE BURNT HOUSE

Square ZA (volume 1:178–179, figure 8.2)
Levels
11–13:   Floor 4, postholes; artifacts: one quern.
15–19:   Floor 5; hearth; faunal elements: one sheep horn, three pig (tooth, scapula, humerus); artifacts: one notation ball, one stand.
Floor 6: Hearth; faunal element: one dog/wolf tooth; artifacts: two spindle whorls.

Floor 7: Faunal elements: one sheep metacarpal, one goat metatarsal, two pig teeth; artifacts: one bone point.

Square ROc (volume 1:203)
Levels
49–52:   Succession of floors contemporary with Burnt House; faunal element: one sheep metacarpal; artifacts: one metal pin, one axe, one spindle whorl.
41:    Postholes indicating corner of house, cut by two other superimposed structures; faunal elements: two teeth (one pig, one dog/wolf), one scapula and one femur of dog/wolf.

Total Phase Va Faunal Elements: 14
Total Phase Va Artifacts: 9

LONG HOUSE (BETWEEN Va AND Vb)

Square PO (volume 1:189–190, figure 8.9)
Level 23: House floor with hearth, bins; artifacts: one bone pin, two chipped stone blades, two querns and one rubber, one jar fragment, one hook/anchor, two spindle whorls, one flattened bone tool.

Squares PO and PN
Levels PO/A 45–47, PO/B 33–36, PO/C 25–29, PO/D 25–32, PN 29, PN/A 91–93, PN/B 100–101, PN/C 80–83, PN/D 70–75, PN/E 60–62, PN/F 51–54: Faunal elements: cattle (three), sheep (four), pig (two), fallow deer (20), beaver (one), fox (one); artifacts: two utensils (ladle, worked sherd), two blades, six processors (querns, grinder, rubber, hollowed stone, miscellaneous), two metal awls, four notation balls, one bowl, one mace head in the shape of a lioness head (SF 2409: plate 5.42), one figurine (?) fragment, one hook/anchor, five spools, sixteen spindle whorls, three bone tools (points, flattened); one-handled cups are also reported but not illustrated (volume 1:189).

Total Long House Faunal Elements: 13
Total Long House Artifacts: 55

PHASE Vb

Square ZA (volume 1:24, table 2.1)
Levels
4:    Floor 1; faunal element: one goat metacarpus; artifacts: one hook/anchor, one spindle whorl, one flattened bone tool.
6:    Floor 2
7:    Floor 3; artifact: one spindle whorl.

Square ROc Layers 2–40 (volume 1:203, 204 [figure 8.14], 206 [figure 8.15])
Levels
13–30:   Floors (with associated pits, ditches) comparable to the layer cake complex of the Long House.
7:    Faunal elements: one sheep scapula, one deer or beaver radius; artifacts: one grinder, one hook/anchor, two spindle whorls, one flattened bone tool.
8:    Artifacts: three sickle blades, two axes
9:    Artifacts: two hook/anchors
19:    Faunal element: one pig astragalus; artifact: one spindle whorl
21:    Artifacts: one whetstone, one hook/anchor, two spindle whorls
22:    Artifact: one spindle whorl
23:    Faunal element: one sheep astragalus; artifacts: one grinder, one U-shaped ceramic handle.
24:    Artifact: one axe
26:    Artifact: one pestle
30:    Artifact: one metal awl

Total Other Phase Vb Faunal Elements: 5
Total Other Phase Vb Artifacts: 27

13.

Prehistoric Sites in the Plain of Drama

Colin Renfrew and David Hardy

The excavations at Sitagroi had as their aim the investigation of several important themes in the prehistory of southeast Europe. Sitagroi was chosen for excavation both because of the long time span evidently covered by the site (as documented by preliminary site survey) and because of the cultural connections between both the Aegean and the Balkans as indicated by a preliminary study of the surface finds. These finds and the indications resulting mainly from surface survey (for example, French 1964) clearly indicated the richness and variety of the material of the late Neolithic period from east Macedonia in general and from the plain of Drama in particular.

Part of our intention was to set the Sitagroi finds within their context, both locally and within a wider framework. Before excavations began, the major known sites in east Macedonia and Thrace were visited, including Paradimi to the east and Dhimitra to the west. During the course of the excavations, the then-known sites within the plain of Drama were visited, several new sites were identified, as were several more again during Donald Davidson's geomorphological survey. It was therefore decided to establish the survey, reported on herein, upon a more official basis. With the support of the Ephor of Antiquities, Dr. Haido Koukouli-Chrysanthaki, a permit was obtained for a site survey.

The survey was accomplished primarily by David Hardy, accompanied by the archaeological phylax for the plain of Drama, Mr. Demetrios Chariskos. They were accompanied on weekends and other occasions by members of the excavation team. With the permission of the Greek Archaeological Service, surface materials were systematically collected, washed, studied, and recorded in the excavation workroom at Sitagroi. After being marked and cataloged, the finds were deposited in

the Philippi Museum in the Sitagroi excavation storeroom. Currently all materials relevant to the prehistory of the plain of Drama are curated in the Kavalla and Philippi Museums and in the newly dedicated Archaeological Museum of Drama.

OBJECTIVES

The objectives of this survey were to locate and study as many of the prehistoric sites of the plain of Drama as possible (see Preface figure 1 and figure 13.1) and collect surface materials as well. The most prominent *toumbas*, shallow tell mounds of accumulated archaeological deposits, are often set on a low natural hill whose contour is accentuated by the subsequent cultural accumulation, as at the toumba of Sitagroi. The Macedonian toumba is the precise counterpart of the Thessalian *maghoula*, the Bulgarian *moghila*, and the sometimes more modest analogue of the Turkish *hüyük*. The strategy followed was to visit all such features rising above the plain, as well as other likely localities near springs or on suitable positions on the foothills around the plain, to determine if they were indeed archaeological sites. This effort was thus a site-maximizing survey of the kind pioneered in Greece by Wace and Thompson (1912) and Heurtley (1939) and carried further in central and north Greece by French (1964, 1967), in south Greece by Hope Simpson (1979) and his colleagues, and more recently in eastern Thessaly by Gallis (1989, 1990).

It should be clearly understood, however, that this project was not an area-intensive site survey involving complete field walking of selected areas, like that carried out, for instance, on the island of Melos (Renfrew and Wagstaff 1982). Such an inspection, which is much more demanding in terms of labor, has the different objective of obtaining a representative sample of the settlement pattern. It is generally carried out after the initial exploratory phase of recognizing some of the major sites and after establishing the basic material culture sequence. Our survey was at the initial exploratory stage, and its primary task was to identify, and surface collect, as many of the Drama Plain sites as time allowed. These surface collections (see figures 13.1.2–13.1.19), admittedly an incomplete snapshot of what any of the given mounds represented, were nevertheless firmly compared with materials from the five phases of the Sitagroi sequence. We could rely confidently on that sequence from the Middle Neolithic through the Early Bronze Age; only for the later period of occupation, the later Bronze Age (which might include material possibly of early Iron Age), were the Sitagroi finds not an adequate basis of comparison. Two of the important results of our survey were to document the apparent completeness of the Sitagroi repertoire for the earlier periods, and to supplement it with finds from sites such as Platania and Nikiphoros for the later Bronze Age.

It was hoped that this preliminary survey, which now could be usefully followed up by more intensive work like that of the Melos survey, would give a valid introductory picture, albeit incomplete, of settlement in the plain of Drama. Brian Blouet's study of the plain, published earlier (volume 1:133–143), noted site size and location and presented a tentative reconstruction of the settlement pattern in the plain over time. He prefaced his report with, "every statement about settlement pattern should carry the qualifying phrase, 'from the evidence available it would seem'" (volume 1:133). Indeed, the importance of the geomorphology, settlement pattern study, and site-catchment analysis was appreciated from the outset. We learned that the plain of Drama has changed considerably since early prehistoric times, and no site survey can begin an overall interpretation without fully appreciating this. These issues, some of them also discussed by Higgs and Vita-Finzi (volume 1:144–146; see also Vita-Finzi 1969), affected the goals of Donald Davidson's field research (volume 1:15–40); his discussion of the actual formation of the toumba of Sitagroi (see also Davidson 1973) has a direct bearing upon that of the other mounds in the area. The palynological work of Judith Turner and James Greig, previously reported (volume 1:41–54;

see also Greig and Turner 1974) presents the vegetational background to early settlement in the area. With this evidence of settlement and environment in this well-defined local region, the documentation of subsistence and economy from the excavations at Sitagroi could be better interpreted. Thus, the faunal remains examined by Sándor Bökönyi (volume 1:63–132) and the plant remains investigated by Jane Renfrew (this volume, chapter 1) and by Oliver Rackham (volume 1:55–62) can be more effectively interpreted in terms of the regional environment exploited, rather than as representing a single site location.

An understanding of the range of material culture and its variability within the single well-defined regional unit (the plain of Drama), rather than of a single site, offers an important and much better basis for articulating that culture vis-à-vis neighboring regions. Features found at Sitagroi are seen again at early sites such as Mylopotamos or Chorla, and in phase III at such important locations as Dikili Tash and Dhoxaton. This allows comparison with relevant nearby sites such as Akropotamos or Dhimitra, as well as more distant locations in Thrace, west Macedonia, and indeed Thessaly. The site survey thus allowed the Sitagroi material to be interpreted more coherently than would be possible in isolation.

HISTORY OF RESEARCH

The plain of Drama survey did not begin in terra incognita. Indeed, prehistoric archaeological research in Macedonia was developed intensively during the First World War, when the first discoveries in the plain of Drama were made at Dikili Tash and Drama itself (Welch 1919). Initially, the main focus of research was in west and central Macedonia, culminating in Heurtley's publication of *Prehistoric Macedonia* (1939). Work in east Macedonia and Thrace was first carried out energetically by Professor George Bakalakis, the excavator of the important site of Paradimi in Thrace (Bakalakis 1961, 1962; Bakalakis and Sakellariou 1981). Our own early survey work owes much to his encouragement. Immediately prior to the Second World War came the excavations at Polystylon, the first to take place on the plain of Drama (Mylonas and

Bakalakis 1938) and at Akropotamos (Mylonas 1941). Thus, the main ceramic styles of Sitagroi had earlier been recognized in the study of the materials from these Drama Plain excavations or surface collections. During the war there was naturally a lull.

In 1954, Schachermeyr visited the site of Galepsos, later writing about the characteristic Black-on-Red ware found there (Schachermeyr 1955:108–111), and in 1961 a program of excavations was begun at the important site of Dikili Tash near Philippi. The site was discovered by Blegen (Welch 1919) and was apparently first dug by the French School in 1921 (Mylonas 1941:565, n. 18; Heurtley 1939: xvi, n. 4). From 1961 it was dug by both Greek and French workers (Theocharis and Rhomiopoulou 1961; Deshayes 1970a, 1970b; Treuil 1992). A standard in the publication of material from site surveys was set by French (1961; 1967), who published a systematic consideration of the east Macedonian material (French 1964). Theocharis and Rhomiopoulou likewise recorded another important site, Dhimitra, for the first time (1961:81). Koukouli-Chrysanthaki (1970; Koukouli 1967, 1969) has subsequently published useful notes on a number of sites. More recently, Grammenos (1975, 1991), in two valuable publications, has reviewed the prehistoric settlement of east Macedonia, for which we were happy to make available notes from our own site survey (see also Andreou, Fotiadis, and Kotsakis 1996:586–591). The topographic details given below in some cases draw on Grammenos's descriptions. In what follows (see Site Register, appendix 13.1), attention focuses first on the plain of Drama itself, where our principal collecting effort was directed. Relevant sites in adjoining areas are mentioned, but as mentioned earlier, our survey was not in any sense systematic, although it did allow the opportunity for a first-hand comparison with Drama area materials to Sitagroi phases and to specific illustrated artifacts.

THE PLAIN OF DRAMA

The nature of the plain of Drama has been described by Davidson in volume 1, chapter 3. Its principal feature—the plain itself—was formed by the progressive subsidence of the graben floor and is drained by the Angitis River through the gorge at the west. To the north are the steep slopes of Mount Falakron and then the Nevrokopi basin; to the south Mount Pangaion divides the plain from the coast. The path to the west is not a difficult one. The road now, and no doubt in ancient times, passes through Alistrati, which at a height of over 300 m overlooks the plain, approximately 50 to 80 m above sea level. To the southeast the plain is divided from Kavalla and the sea by a ridge of hills traversed by a pass at an elevation of about 200 m. To these two principal lines of communication must be added a third to the northeast, where the road rises nearly 300 m before descending to the Nestos River at Paranestion.

The area of the site survey was the Drama basin, the area drained by the Angitis River above its gorge at the west, through which it passes to meet the Strymon (Strouma) River. Parts of this area lie within the modern administrative *nomoi* of Serres and Kavalla, as well as of Drama. The geomorphology of the plain itself (see volume 1: fig. 3.2) and the sites recorded during the survey are listed and located on the map accompanying this chapter (figure 13.1).

Sherds were in general collected from the surface of each site; table 13.1 gives an approximate indication of their abundance for each phase. It should be noted that the phases represented by incised and/or painted pottery or other ceramic fragments (phases II and III) are more easily recognized on the basis of small surface collections. The data, as recorded, may thus reflect some inevitable bias toward these periods.

We did not collect sherds from Dikili Tash, and the indications in table 13.1 are based primarily on the published reports by the excavator, the late professor Jean Deshayes, to whom we are indebted for kindly showing us his finds in 1968 and 1969 and for additional useful information. The periods listed are those defined from the Sitagroi sequence (see Preface table 3) as set out in volume 1 (chapters 2 and 7 [C. Renfrew 1986a, 1986e]). The term "later Bronze Age" indicates material later than that found stratified at Sitagroi. In this sense, Sitagroi phases Va and Vb may be regarded as "earlier Bronze Age."

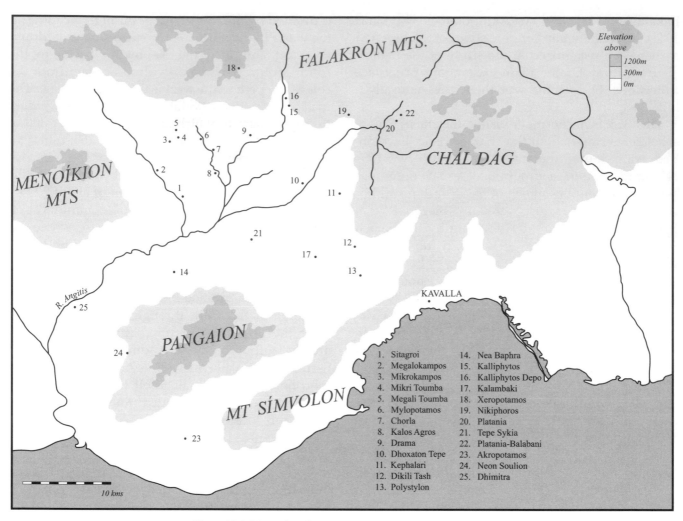

Figure 13.1. Map of prehistoric sites in the plain of Drama.

Map legend:

1.	Sitagroi	14.	Nea Baphra
2.	Megalokampos	15.	Kalliphytos
3.	Mikrokampos	16.	Kalliphytos Depo
4.	Mikri Toumba	17.	Kalambaki
5.	Megali Toumba	18.	Xeropotamos
6.	Mylopotamos	19.	Nikiphoros
7.	Chorla	20.	Platania
8.	Kalos Agros	21.	Tepe Sykia
9.	Drama	22.	Platania-Balabani
10.	Dhoxaton Tepe	23.	Akropotamos
11.	Kephalari	24.	Neon Soulion
12.	Dikili Tash	25.	Dhimitra
13.	Polystylon		

Sherd collection offers a series of time-slices within a particular region which we think provides clues to local site "shaping," vis-à-vis economy, ideology, and even politics. In any case, we cannot be sure that patterns of datable artifacts collected from the surface today are representative of patterns that obtained in the past. Still, the occurrence of certain types (the artifact distribution)—even though we have no knowledge of direct connection—brings us to propose that, based on the similarity of pottery and other ceramic forms, the sites in the Drama Plain were in contact with one another.

What, then, was the nature of this interaction? This would probably depend on the political and economic organization in place in the Drama Plain, the Serres Basin, and outside. Although some sites exhibit long-term settlement, others do not (see table 13.1); yet there are no clear reasons for the difference. Perhaps the long-lasting settlements used a land-use strategy, a sophisticated idea but surely one not beyond a group of people whose cognitive abilities allowed them to plan for and execute near- and long-distance trading partnerships. If there was conflict (and we have not yet recognized the evidence), it seems to have been managed. Just considering the various ecological niches occupied by the two dozen sites, and the data collected during our survey that make the "connections," it seems reasonable to propose that certain kinds of interchange took place, more or less intense over time:

Table 13.1. Synoptic View of the Occurrence of Surface Materials from 20 Sites in the Plain of Drama Compared to Diagnostics from Sitagroi Phases I–V

Site	Sitagroi Phase					Later Bronze Age
	I	II	III	IV	V	
1. Sitagroi	XX	XX	XX	XX	XX	—
2. Megalokampos	—	XX	XX	—	—	T
3. Mikrokampos	—	—	—	—	—	X
4. Mikri Toumba	—	X	—	T	?	—
5. Megali Toumba	—	—	—	—	—	X
6. Mylopotamos	—	X	XX	T	X	T
7. Chorla	XX	XX	T	—	?	—
8. Kalos Agros	—		?	—	—	X
9. Drama	X	X	XX	T	—	—
10. Dhoxaton	—	X	XX	—	—	—
11. Kephalari	—	X	—	?	—	—
12. Dikili Tash	X	XX	XX	X	X	X
13. Polystylon	?	X	T	?	?	—
14. Nea Baphra	X	X	X	—	—	—
15. Kalliphytos	—	—	—	—	—	X
16. Kalliphytos Depo	—	T	X	T	?	X
17. Kalambaki	—	—	—	—	—	X
18. Xeropotamos	—	—	—	—	—	X
19. Nikiphoros	—	—	—	—	—	X
20. Platania	—	—	—	—	—	X

XX = Abundantly represented
X = Represented
T = Trace only (one to five sherds)
? = Doubtful, represented by only one or two sherds, or sherds of uncertain phase

exchange of surpluses and information, establishment of social relationships, and the establishment, development, and maintenance of long- and near-distance trading partnerships.

The main value of this documentation today must, however, be one of record—and a record that can no longer be re-created. At the time this survey was conducted more than 30 years ago, our purpose was to discover hitherto unknown sites and reassess those previously recognized. That enterprise had its utility and formed the basis for the discussion of settlement patterns already found in Volume 1. In addition, it formed a foundation for the further survey activities in the area subsequently conducted by other scholars, notably Grammenos (1975, 1991). At the time, these were sites that could readily be revisited, once they were properly recorded.

Today, however, these observations have an additional value: a number of the sites have disappeared, and others are in much damaged condition. Several of them were being plowed at the time of the visits recorded here, and in successive seasons they have been further eroded and damaged. Others that were not at that time under the plow have subsequently been brought within the boundaries of cultivated land. This means that the various finds reported here, mainly potsherds but also the various special objects documented, form a valuable sampling record that in some cases can no longer be repeated.

Some of these sites would still merit excavation today. At the time of its discovery, we felt that Chorla (appendix 13.1, site 7) would amply repay excavation, because the finds were predominantly of Sitagroi phase II, which might offer an unparalleled opportunity to investigate a large areal extent of a settlement from that early period. That may well remain true to the present day. However, in some cases it would be difficult to repeat the observations made here. For that reason it seemed appropriate to publish data from these sites in this volume.

Appendix 13.1.
Site Register and Selected Materials
from the Drama Survey

Colin Renfrew

The topographic detail and site descriptions are based primarily on the field notes of Dr. David Hardy (cited below as DAH) who, in the company of Mr. Chariskos, undertook the sherd collections at most of the sites listed. Each site is numbered in this register, and these numbers signify their location on the map (figure 13.1). Map references are to sheets G.10 ("Drama"), G.11 ("Lekani"), D.10 ("Rhodolivos"), and D.11 ("Kavalla") of the British War Office (1944) 1:100,000 map series. Large-scale Greek maps were not available at the time of the survey, and the convenient grid on the British maps of 1944 facilitates precise topographic reference. For each site, under "material," periods of probable occupation are noted, and illustrations of significant finds are referenced along with comparanda to Sitagroi artifacts from volumes 1 and 2. A few unusual artifacts were assigned numbers; these were discussed in volume 1, chapter 10 (Elster 1986), and in this volume, chapter 10). The profiles for fourteen survey sites are shown in figure 13.1.1.

SITES OF THE DRAMA PLAIN

1. *Sitagroi* (also known as Photolivos or Toumba Alistratiou): The site (figures 13.1 and 13.1.1) lies on the left bank of the Angitis River 2 km south of the road from Drama and Sitagroi to Alistrati. It is reached by cart track from this road near the Angitis bridge (or by cart track north from the village of Photolivos). The site lies within the administrative *nomos* of Serres and the *koinotita* of Alistrati. The site is described in detail in volume 1, chapter 3 (Davidson 1986).

   References: Map "Drama" 822870; French 1964; Garašanin and Dehn 1963; C. Renfrew 1970a, 1970b, 1970c, 1973b, 1975a; Grammenos 1991: no. 25.

Material: The finds of phases I through V are fully described in volume 1 and in preceding chapters in this volume.

2. *Megalokampos*: The site lies on the left bank of the Angitis River some 2 km northwest of the village of Megalokampos. The site is a low tell mound about 200 m long along its major (north-south) axis (figure 13.1.1), and cut by the river on the west side. The geomorphology of the site is shown in volume 1: figure 3.5.

   References: Map "Drama" 785925; discovered by Colin Renfrew (cited as ACR) in 1966; sherds collected in 1969; Grammenos 1975, 1991: no. 42.

   Material: Sitagroi phases II, III, Va.

3. *Mikrokampos* (also known as Gerani or Monastiraki): The site is located approximately 1 km north of the village of Mikrokampos (along the Prosotsani road), lying immediately to the east of the road. It is a low ellipsoidal toumba (height 3.5 m), about 110 m north-south and 75 m east-west (figure 13.1.1). The site is surmounted by two trees and a small church—hence the name Monastiraki.

   References: Map "Drama" 815940; sherds collected by DAH, 1969 and 1970; Grammenos 1975: no. 41.

   Material: Later Bronze Age, Classical.

4. *Mikri Toumba*: The site is reached by the dirt road from Megali Toumba 1.2 km to the south (figure 13.1: nos. 4, 5). After a dirt road intersection, it lies immediately to the west of the road. It is difficult to detect, being merely a gentle rise in the ground level (figure 13.1.1). It is a very low, roughly circular mound (about 1.5 m high and 110 m wide).

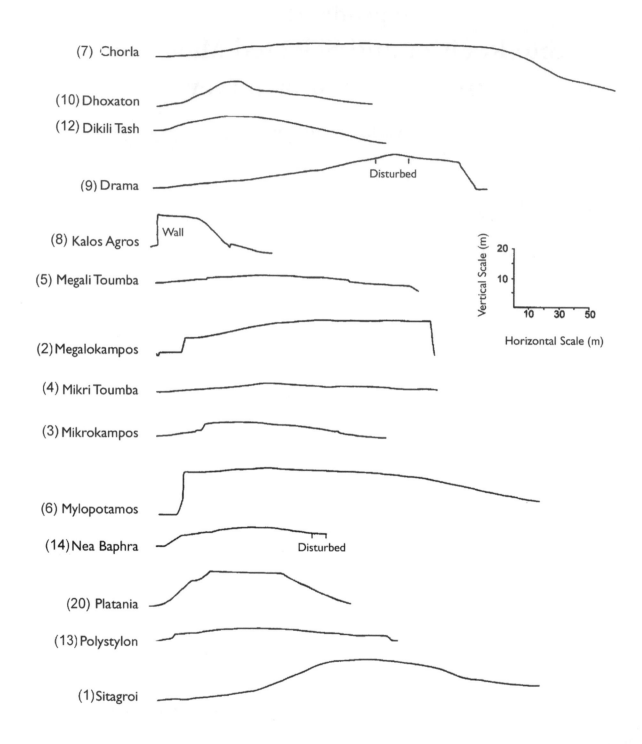

Figure 13.1.1. Site survey profiles (numbers refer to site locations on map, figure 13.1).

References: Map "Drama" 829940; Rhomiopou-lou 1965:451; sherds collected by DAH, 1969 and 1970; Grammenos 1991: no. 26.

Material: Sitagroi phases II, IV, and possibly V.

5. *Megali Toumba*: The toumba is best approached from the main Drama to Prosotsani road, turning south along a dirt road, immediately opposite the road leading north to Petrousa. The mound is approximately 2 km south of this turning. It is easily recognizable as a low toumba, although only 2 m high (figure 13.1.1). It is about 150 m long (north-south) and 125 m wide (east-west).

References: Map "Drama" 828952; first noted by ACR in 1966; surface collected by DAH in 1969 and 1970; Grammenos 1975: no. 11.

Material: Later Bronze Age: one fragment of shaft-hole axe-hammer (figure 13.1.2a)

6. *Mylopotamos*: The road from the village of Mylo-potamos turns west through its small triangular

plateia and crosses the river. As the road turns south, the mound is immediately to its west, situated in the angle of the perennial river (Bunar-bashi). The mound is large, about 250 m north-south and 200 m east-west. Because of the configuration of the plain, it appears higher than it really is; the mound section on its east side is cut by the road, showing it to be about 3 m high (figure 13.1.1). There is a spring southwest of the mound.

References: Map "Drama" 863937; French 1964:31; surface collected by DAH in 1969 and 1970; Grammenos 1991: no. 33.

Material: Sitagroi phases II through V: a sherd of smoothed red fabric with stabbed and incised decoration (figure 13.1.3c) comparable to a Sitagroi phase Va example (see volume 1 (Sherratt 1986): 459, figure 13.13:2); fragments of two shaft-hole axe-hammers (figure 13.1.2b, c), of which the former is comparable to a Sitagroi phase IV axe-hammer fragment (see discussion in this volume, chapter 5 and figure 5.14); also Later Bronze Age, Classical.

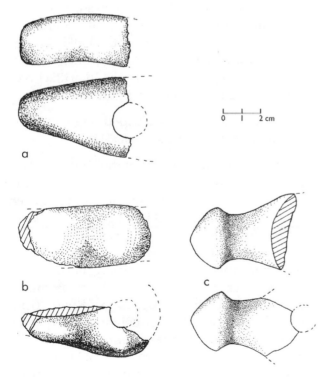

Figure 13.1.2. Axe hammers: (a) Megali Toumba; (b, c) Mylo-potamos.

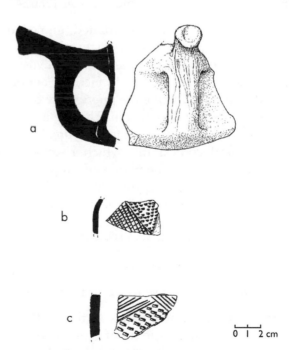

Figure 13.1.3. Survey sherds, phases II (a), and Va (b, c). (a) Fragment of bowl with prong handle, from Chorla; (b) fragment of incised and impressed decoration on black burnished surface, from Chorla; (c) stabbed, incised decoration on red surface, from Mylopotamos.

7. *Chorla* (also known as Zoodochos Pigis): The site is visible to the south of the Drama-Sitagroi road and is reached by turning south along the dirt road opposite the road leading north to Mylopotamos. The toumba measures approximately 200 m north-south by 180 m east-west and stands some 4 m high (figure 13.1.1).

References: Map "Drama" 885925; discovered in 1966 by Jane M. Renfrew; surface collected in 1969 and 1970; Grammenos 1975, 1991: no. 47.

Material: Sitagroi phases I and II: includes a Smooth Ware bowl rim sherd with prong handle (figure13.1.3a) comparable to Sitagroi Phase II prong handle (volume 1 [Keighley 1986]:375, figure 11.6:10); an incised and impressed black-burnished sherd (figure 13.1.3b) which may be compared to phase Va examples (volume 1 [Sherratt 1986]:459, figure 13.13:2, 8); fragment of an incised plaque of baked clay, buff exterior with incisions on both sides (figure 13.1.4f).

In addition: Chorla #s 5, 8–12, all tripod fragments, published in volume 1 (Elster 1986:343).

8. *Kalos Agros*: The site is situated immediately behind the Kalos Agros village school on the road between Drama and Photolivos; the grounds of the school are, in fact, cut out of the site (figure 13.1.1). Like the previous two sites, it lies on the River Bunarbashi. The site is covered by trees making it difficult to measure. In form it is a natural conical hill which rises approximately 10 m above the plain and drops about 15 m to the river. It is roughly 100 m in diameter at the bottom and 30 m in diameter at the top.

References: Map "Drama" 878898; Koukouli-Chrysanthaki 1970: 402; surface collected by DAH 1969 and 1970; Grammenos 1975, 1991: no. 16.

Material: Sitagroi phase III; Later Bronze Age.

9. *Drama*: Located immediately to the south of the town of Drama, the site is north of the road leading to Nea Amisos. It lies south of the town cemetery of Drama. No clear sign of a toumba is now visible (figure 13.1.1). Sherds are found over a wide area, some 500 x 500 m on a slope.

References: Map "Drama" 915938; Welch 1919: 50; French 1961: 107 (the site was not specifically located in these references); surface collected by ACR in 1966 and 1968; Grammenos 1975, 1991: no. 48.

Material: Sitagroi phases I, II, III: profile of a black-topped bowl (figure 13.1.4a); two corner/leg fragments of graphite-painted "offering stands": one pierced with two holes at corner (figure 13.1.5), the other of a fine, well-fired fabric (figure 13.1.4b) decorated with brown paint on black with burnishing and graphite painting, both comparable to phase III examples (see volume 1 [Elster 1986]:322, figure 10.1:6); two star-shaped whorls (figure 13.1.4d, e), with incising comparable to phase II and III examples in this volume, chapter 6 (but not the four-pronged shape); graphite-coated askos-like form (figure 13.1.4c). Also collected were three baked clay figurine fragments: figure 13.1.6a, with brown surface and red core (compare with volume 1 [Gimbutas 1986]:280, figure 9.145 [149]); figure 13.1.6b, an incised upper torso on well-fired reddish-brown clay, with beaked head, long-neck, torso and neck incised, comparable to phase III artifact (see volume 1 [Gimbutas 1986]:241, figs. 9.31 [103]); and figure 13.1.6c, an incised body fragment comparable to a phase III artifact (volume 1 [Gimbutas 1986]:266, figure 9.86 [152]).

In addition: Drama #13, a tripod fragment, published in volume 1 (Elster 1986:344).

10. *Dhoxaton Tepe*: To the west of the Drama-Kalambaki road and north of the drainage canal (the Xeropotamos River), this site lies approximately 1 km north of Kalambaki village. The site is not visible from the road, being screened by trees, and is reached by a dirt road lined with trees that runs eastward immediately north of the bridge over the canal. This is a prominent toumba, near the Xeropotamos River, rising today to nearly 10 m in height (although this may in part be a natural prominence, as at Sitagroi). This prominent rise is some 40 m in diameter, but sherds are found over a much wider area (see figure 13.1.1).

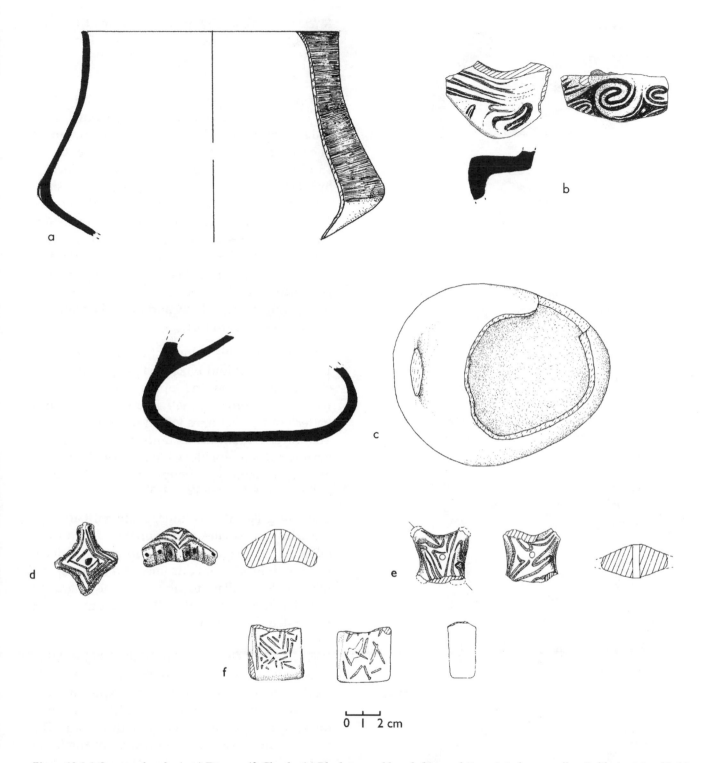

Figure 13.1.4. Survey sherds: (a–e) Drama, (f) Chorla. (a) Black-topped bowl; (b) graphite-painted corner/leg "of fering stand"; (c) graphite-painted askos-like form; (d, e) incised whorls; (f) fragment of incised, baked clay plaque.

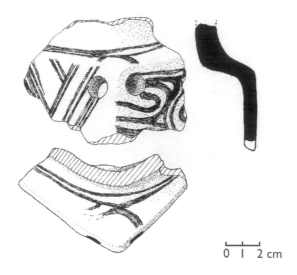

Figure 13.1.5. Graphite-painted corner/leg fragment of "offering stand" from Drama.

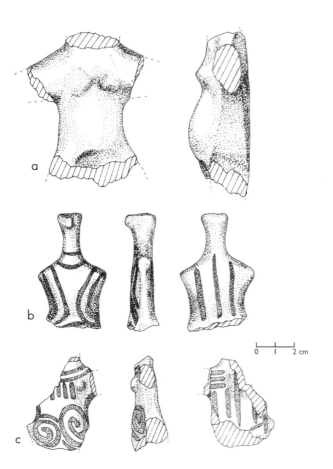

Figure 13.1.6. Figurine fragments from Drama.

References: Map "Drama": 964846; Koukouli 1967:429; 1969:355 (termed Kalambak-Tepe), and pl. 363; surface collected by ACR 1969; Grammenos 1975, 1991: no. 8.

Material: Sitagroi phase II, including some I/II: an orange-red burnished carinated bowl with roll rim (figure 13.1.7b); a bowl and leg fragment of coarse red-burnished and incised ware (figure 13.1.7a); and phase III: lower body of incised female figurine of gray clay (figure 13.1.8a), similar to a phase III figurine (volume 1 [Gimbutas 1986]:236, figure 9. 21); a red clay body of an animal figurine, possibly a pig (figure 13.1.8b), very comparable in shape to another phase III example (volume 1 [Gimbutas 1986]:261, figure 9.75 [215]); and a hollow, red clay torso figurine fragment, with enlarged belly and incised decoration below waist (figure 13.1.8c).

Dhoxaton 1 (see this volume chapter 10 and figure 10.5): a rectanguloid block or "plaque" of baked clay decorated on the upper flat surface (of which approximately half is damaged) with a pattern of parallel lines joined to form lozenges. The lower flat surface is undecorated. The four narrow sides of the block have herringbone decoration formed of groups of parallel lines, obliquely set. L: 10.9; W: 5.8; Th: 2.9

Dhoxaton 2 (see this volume, chapter 10 and figure 10.3): a small, approximately cylindrical (although damaged) artifact, its surface decorated with incised oblique lines and running spirals. It is similar to the Sitagroi engraved cylinders (see figures 10.1, 10.2) although it is not perforated. L: 8.8; D 3.5

11. *Kephalari*: The site lies 1 km east of Agios Athanasios. It is reached from the Drama-Kavalla road by taking the road toward Kephalari, and then taking the first turn left (north) and turning off to the right (east) along a dirt road. The mound can be seen just southwest of the army installations in the foothills. The site is a low, wide-spreading toumba whose bounds were difficult to distinguish: some 260 m east-west and 250 m north-south (figure 13.1.1). It is cut by

a small gorge at the west, and sherds were found both in this section and to the west.

References: Map "Lekani" 022850; 467; sherds collected by DAH 1970; Theocharis 1971: no. 9; Grammenos 1975, 1991: no. 19.

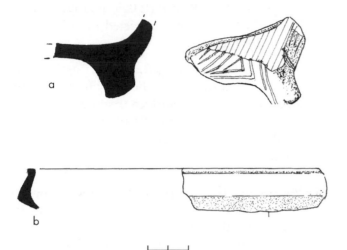

Figure 13.1.7. Phase II sherds from Dhoxaton Tepe: (a) Red burnished and incised bowl and leg fragment; (b) orange-red, burnished, carinated, rolled-rim bowl fragment.

Material: Sitagroi phase II and probably phase IV; Classical. Of special interest is the figurine fragment ("pobble") with incised spirals (figure 13.1.9a) comparable to phase III examples of this shape (volume 1 [Gimbutas 1986]:253, figure 9.60 [156]; 269: figure 9.98 [155]).

12. *Dikili Tash*: The site lies immediately to the south of the old road from Kavalla to Drama, 1 km northeast of the new road, and 2 km southeast of Krinides. The excavation house of the French school lies immediately to the south. The site is a large toumba (230 m long) on a natural eminence (see figure 13.1.1), beside a perennial spring.

References: Map "Lekani" 065775: Welch 1919; Theocharis and Rhomiopoulou 1961; French 1961; Daux 1962, 1968; Deshayes 1970a, 1970b, 1972, 1973; Theocharis 1971, 1973; Séfériadès 1983; Treuil 1992; Koukouli- Chrysanthaki 1993; Grammenos 1991: no. 24.

Material: The finds from the Greek and especially the French excavations have been summarized in the preliminary reports cited above.

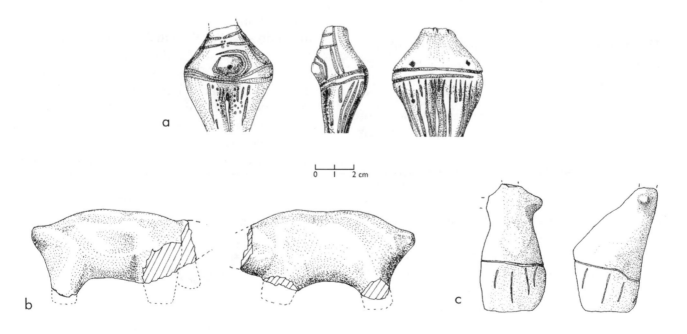

Figure 13.1.8. Figurines from Dhoxaton Tepe.

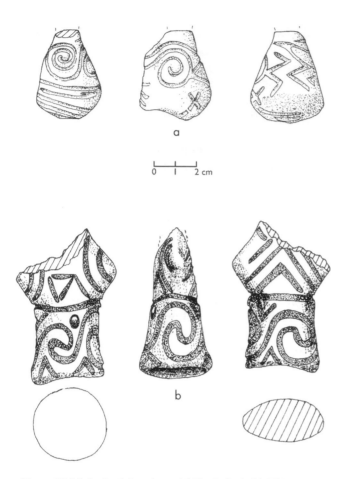

Figure 13.1.9. Incised figurines: (a) Kephalari; (b) Dhimitra.

These document a major settlement of the period of Sitagroi phase III, as did the reports by Welch (1919) and French (1961) on the material collected by Blegen. Material of phases II and V has also been published, together with some of the earlier part (probably) of the later Bronze Age (see Deshayes 1970b: figs. 22, 30, 39, 40). During our visit to the excavation storage, we were shown material relating to Sitagroi phase IV by Professor Deshayes (see Deshayes 1970b: fig. 18). The material from this site, published by the French School (Treuil 1992), will not be further described here. It should be noted, however, that the pot published in Theocharis (1973) as figure 231 is (like figure 232 also) wrongly assigned, and was in fact found at Sitagroi (see volume 1: plates. XVI:3, XLI:1).

13. *Polystylon*: This site, situated to the west of the Drama-Kavalla road and north of the village of Polystylon, lies beside a small river. The toumba is low and difficult to define, measuring some 180 m southeast to northwest. Cultivation prevented further measurements (see figure 13.1.1).

References: Map "Kavalla": 065749; Mylonas and Bakalakis 1938; sherds collected in 1970; Grammenos 1991: no. 27.

Material: Sitagroi phases II, III, and possibly I, IV, and Va: illustrated is a bowl with channeling (figure13.1.10), with surface treatment comparable to bowl from phase IV (volume 1 [Sherratt 1986]:450, figure 13.4:2); also medieval material noted.

14. *Nea Baphra*: The site is located in the village, on the right of the road from Kavalla to Serres: the church and the village school are on top of it. It is a low mound measuring nearly 200 x 150 m (see figure 13.1.1).

References: Map "Rhodolivos": 813768; Theocharis 1971: no. 14; sherds collected by DAH 1970; Grammenos 1975, 1991: no. 20.

Material: Sitagroi phases I, II, and III.

15. *Kalliphytos*: This site is almost at the north end of the main street of the village and approximately 100 m to the east of it (behind the houses along the main street). The site is difficult to delimit, the settlement area lying on a long ridge-plateau running roughly north-south from the foot of the mountains, and cut to the east by a streambed. The plateau is wide at the area of settlement (some 350 m from the gully to edge

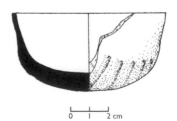

Figure 13.1.10. Polystylon channeled bowl.

482

of the village). The site is neither a toumba nor a defensible hill site.

References: Map "Drama": 988963; not hitherto published (although the name "Kalliphytos" has been used to designate site 16 below). Discovered by Drs. D. A. Davidson and A. Sherratt in 1969 and visited in 1970 by DAH.

Material: Later Bronze Age.

16. *Kalliphytos Depo*: The site lies 500 m to the west of the village, which one leaves by a steep cobbled road after passing the church on the right. The road swings south along the side of a long spur extending south from the mountains, at the end of which is the site. It is bounded on the west by a large winter torrent (Xeropotamos Kalliphytos) and on the east by a smaller dry river. The spur holds a series of flat shelves and terraces. The sherd material extends over a considerable area and is concentrated on the southern part of the spur itself. What may be stone walls are seen about 1.5 m below the top of the "acropolis" on its west side. The "acropolis" itself is quite small, only 100 m north-south x 90 m east-west, but sherd material extends over a wider area. The term *depo* is Turkish for *dexameni* (cistern), indicating that this location supplied Drama with water.

References: Map "Drama": 977963; note that this site has previously been termed "Kalliphytos": it should not be confused with number 15 above. Garašanin and Dehn 1963; Koukouli 1967: 429; sherds collected by DAH 1970; Grammenos 1975, 1991: no. 18.

Material: Sitagroi phases II, III, IV, perhaps phase V; Later Bronze Age.

17. *Kalambaki* (also known as Kalambak Tepe, not to be confused with number 10 above): About 1 km southeast of Kalambaki village; a low mound.

References: Map "Drama": circa 975820; Koukouli 1967:428; Theocharis 1971: no. 8; sherds collected in 1969; Grammenos 1975, 1991: no. 18.

Material: Later Bronze Age.

18. *Xeropotamos*: Immediately to the east of the village, the site is a large, flat-topped, tree-covered natural hill, not a toumba. It ranks as a foothill site. Sherds are found over a wide area.

References: Map "Drama": 900990; discovered by Andrew Sherratt in 1969; sherds collected by DAH in 1970; Grammenos 1975, 1991: no. 43. This is apparently not the site noted by Koukouli (1969: 355).

Material: Later Bronze Age.

19. *Nikiphoros*: The site is plainly visible from the road from Drama to Nikiphoros, some 600 m before entering the village. It is a prominent natural hill, reached from this point by a dirt road leading to the north, which crosses the railway line. The site is on the left, half a kilometer away. This is a hilltop (foothill) site, and sherds are found over much of the summit and on the slopes.

References: Map "Lekani": 051951; discovered by ACR 1960; sherds collected by DAH 1970; Grammenos 1975: no. 40.

Material: Later Bronze Age (figures 13.1.11, 13.1.12).

20. *Platania* (also known as Kale): A dirt road turns right (east) from the main road from Drama to Paranestion, about 1 km before this road is intersected by the Platania-Paranestion road. The site lies about 3 km west of Platania, on the west side of the railway line. The site is a prominent hill rising some 11 m from the surrounding land, and with steep sides to a summit forming a plateau measuring 100 m east-west x 30 m north-south (see figure 13.1.1). The plateau is fortified by a stone wall, now ruinous, of irregular stones up to about 50 cm in length (Koukouli 1967: pl. 316a).

References: Map "Lekani": approximately 140950; Koukouli 1967: 428; discovered independently (and subsequently) by ACR in 1969; sherds collected in 1970; Grammenos 1975: no. 38.

Material: Later Bronze Age.

OTHER SITES

Two further sites in the Drama area were visited in the course of our survey, but insufficient sherds were collected to allow confident attribution to phase. The available information is listed here, but in view of the incomplete record they are not included in table 13.1.

21. *Tepe Sykia* (Kalambaki): Our field notes are incomplete for this site and can be supplemented by the information supplied to Dr. Grammenos by Mr. Chariskos: the site is listed as number 44 in his list (Grammenos 1975). The prehistoric potsherds collected include two suggestive of phase IV or V. It was visited by Andrew Sherratt in 1970.

    Reference: Map "Drama": approximately 910840. Grammenos 1975, 1991: no. 44.

22. *Platania-Balabani*: Precise location is not clear from field notes; see site 39 ("Platania II") in the list of Grammenos (1975). Prehistoric sherds of Neolithic and early Bronze Age date were recovered when the site was visited by Mrs. Cressida

Ridley in 1970 in the company of the local schoolmaster Mr. Chatzopoulos.

Reference: Map "Lekani": about 155975. Grammenos 1975: no. 39.

Another two sites mentioned by Grammenos (1975) should be noted. The first of these, his number 33, "Mylopotamos, Mylopotamos village," may be identical with our number 6 above, which we believe to be the site reported by French (1964). The second is Grammenos's number 17 (Theocharis 1971: no. 7), as the prehistoric settlement at Ano Symvoli (Banitsa). We were not able to locate a settlement in this area, but the reported occurrence of black-topped ware here is suggestive of Sitagroi phase II.

No doubt there are many other sites that remain to be found in the Drama area as here defined, both on the plain and in the surrounding foothills. The survey reported here, as usefully supplemented by the work of Grammenos, simply gives a preliminary outline, which more intensive work in the future must correct and supplement.

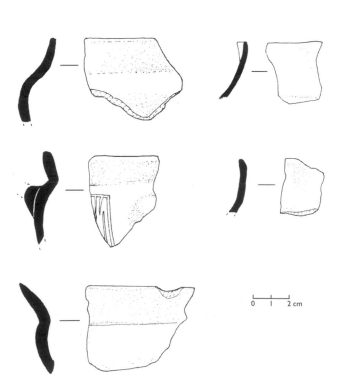

Figure 13.1.11. Later Bronze Age material from Nikiphoros.

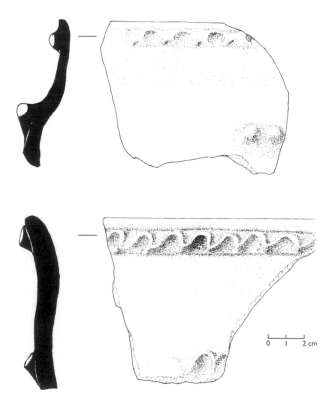

Figure 13.1.12. Later Bronze Age material from Nikiphoros.

PREHISTORIC SITES OUTSIDE THE PLAIN OF DRAMA

During the course of the excavation, several other sites were visited for purposes of material comparison. These were all located within eastern Macedonia although outside the immediate area of the plain of Drama (see figure 13.1).

23. *Akropotamos*: Situated at the confluence of two valleys east of Galepsos, well south of the Amphipolis-Kavalla road.

References: Mylonas and Bakalakis 1938; Mylonas 1941; Grammenos 1975, 1991: no. 23.

Material: Material related to phases II and III at Sitagroi was collected. The following painted wares of phase II are present: Brown-on-Cream (including part of a ladle, figure 13.1.13a), Matte Brown-on-White neck pieces from two jars (figures 13.1.13b, c), Brown-on-Buff (including a pointed leg, figure 13.1.14c). Other painted styles collected but not present at Sitagroi are: matt orange-on-buff, matt red-on-red, matt black-on-white (figure 13.1.15a), matt red-on-cream (neck pieces from two jars, one illustrated, figure 13.1.13f), sherds with trichrome decoration of dark red and black on pale orange (figure 13.1.13d, e) and a polychrome rim (figure 13.1.14a), and red crusting on mushroom brown burnish (figure 13.1.15b). Other phase II related wares are represented by a sherd of Incised ware and another of Black-Topped ware. Phase III is represented mainly by Black-on-Red ware, although a few sherds of graphite-decorated pottery were also collected. The shapes of Black-on-Red vessels appear to be very similar to those found at Sitagroi. although the decoration is different as the individual design elements are larger and the negative circle is very common. The corner/side fragment of an incised red tripod (figure 13.1.14b) is comparable to a phase II example (volume 1 [Elster 1986]:323, figure 10.2:5).

24. *Neon Soulion*: The site rests on a large outlier of limestone in the center of village.

References: Grammenos 1975, 1991: no. 14.

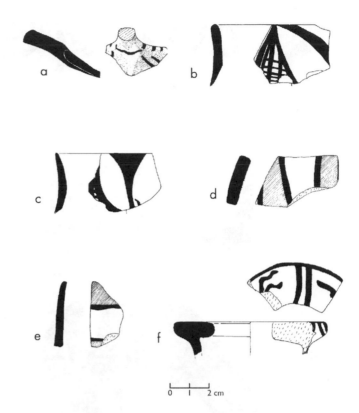

Figure 13.1.13. Akropotamos sherds with painted decoration: bichrome (a–c, f), polychrome (d, e). (a) Brown-on-Cream; (b, c) Brown Painted with White Slip; (d, e) Black, Red, and Orange; (f) Matte Red-on-Cream.

Material: Some Black-Burnished sherds of phases I/II and a single sherd of Buff-on-Cream comparable to phase II and a Brown-on-Buff pithos rim (figure 13.1.16). Also some graphite and plain wares from phase III and some phase V material.

25. *Dhimitra*: Situated on a natural gravel ridge above the bank of the River Angista, the site is 1.5 km southeast of the village of Dhimitra.

References: French 1964; Grammenos 1975; 1991: no. 31; Grammenos, ed. 1997.

Material: Finds related to Sitagroi phases II and III are plentiful. Also a small amount of Vb pottery was found. Comparanda include two ceramic stand fragments with Black-on-Red painted decoration (figure 13.1.17a, b); the former is comparable to those forms decorated in graphite paint from phase III (volume 1 [Elster

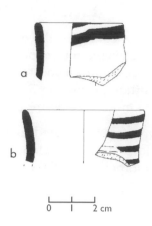

Figure 13.1.15. Sherds from Akropotamos comparable with Sitagroi phases I and II: (a) Matte Black-on-White; (b) Red Crusting on Mushroom Brown Burnish.

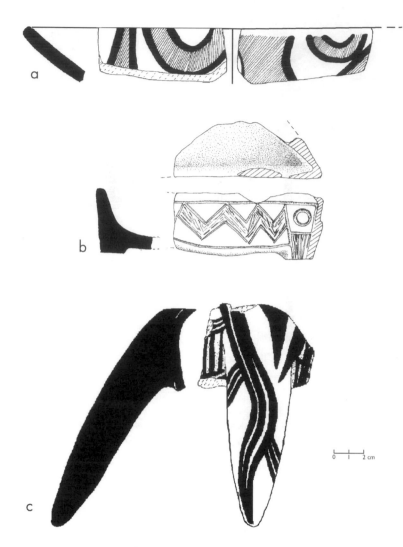

Figure 13.1.14. Akropotamos finds: (a) Polychrome rim; (b) incised tripod corner/leg fragment; (c) Brown-on-Buff painted leg.

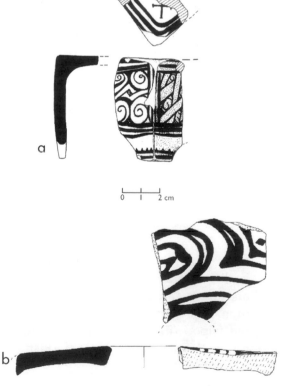

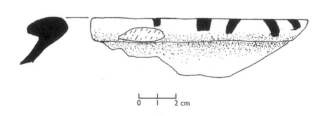

Figure 13.1.16. Neon Soulion Brown-on-Buff pithos rim.

Figure 13.1.17. Dhimitra Black-on-Red stand fragments.

1986]:330, figure 10.93). A fragment of an incised clay figurine of well-fired brown ware (figure 13.1.9b) is comparable to a phase II figurine (volume 1 [Gimbutas 1986]:227, figure 9.2 [26]); and Dhimitra 5 (see this volume, chapter 10 and figure 10.4), an oblong baked clay block of rectanguloid form (L: 5.6; W: 2.8; Th: 2.0), with the incised decoration on one of the narrow sides comparable to the phase II Sitagroi cylinder (see chapter 10 and plate 10.4). The decoration of the other two sides is composed of vertical irregular lines with a centered spiral on the broadest surface.

Published earlier was Dhimitra #1, a tripod fragment (see volume 1 [Elster 1986]:343).

26. *Aghia Pneuma*: The site (not included in figure 13.1) is located toward Serres; no further information obtained.

References: Grammenos 1975, 1991: no. 2.

Material: These finds are very rich in painted styles related to Sitagroi phase II. Sherds illustrated are a Red-on-Brown handle (figure 13.1.18a) similar to strap handles of phase II (volume 1 [Keighley 1986]:384, figure 11.15:3–5); a sherd of Gray Lustre Rippled Ware (figure

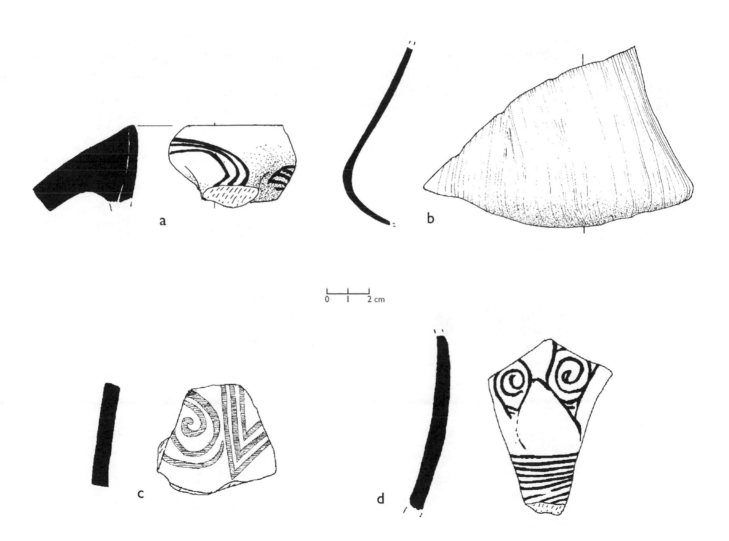

Figure 13.1.18. Aghia Pneuma sherds: (a) Red-on-Brown handle; (b) Rippled Ware; (c) White-on-Red; (d) Thin-Red on Orange-Red.

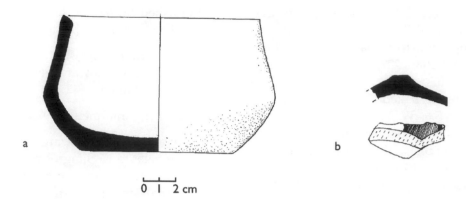

Figure 13.1.19. Aghia Pneuma finds: (a) Red Crusted bowl; (b) trichrome sherd.

13.1.18b); a sherd of White-on-Red ware (figure 13.1.18c) present only in small quantities at Sitagroi; and a carinated Red Crusted bowl (figure 13.1.19a). Painted wares not found at Sitagroi (but see those from Akropotamos [figures 13.1.13d, e, 13.1.14a]) are represented by a trichrome sherd of dark red, black and white (figure 13:1.19b) and a sherd of thin red-on-orange-red (figure 13.1.18d).

14.

Concluding Observations

Colin Renfrew and Ernestine S. Elster

With the publication of this second volume, fifteen years after that of volume 1 and more than thirty years after the completion of fieldwork at Sitagroi, the project may be regarded as concluded. That the process should have taken so long to complete is regrettable, and it might be worth considering the circumstances that so often lead excavators to take an inordinately long time to fulfill their obligations to publish. Indeed, in Greece as elsewhere, it is not uncommon for death to intervene before the original excavators see the final publication of the enterprise. One reason contributing to this, to which we can testify, is that excavators frequently underestimate the very considerable effort of time and labor (and hence of expenditure) that has to be undertaken in the course of preparing an excavation for adequate publication. Moreover, it is sometimes more difficult to obtain funding for the post-excavation process than for the active fieldwork phase. For that reason, we are particularly grateful to those, listed in the Preface and Acknowledgements, who have supported this enterprise. We regret that the task has taken so long but are content that it is now complete.

At this point, however, it may be permissible to take a more positive note and to review some of the features of the project that now seem particularly important. There are others, moreover, that will certainly prove a stimulus to further study.

One of the main motivating forces for the original excavation was the need to clarify the chronological relationships operating within southeast Europe in the Neolithic, Chalcolithic, and Bronze Age periods. The excavation was undertaken during the early days of what came to be called "the second radiocarbon revolution," when the tree-ring calibration of radiocarbon was calling into question the radiocarbon time scale. Indeed, that early, uncalibrated radiocarbon time scale had been criticized as too long (i.e., too early) by scholars such as the late Vladimir Milojčić, who strenuously resisted any suggestion that appropriate calibration would situate the corrected dates yet earlier. For that reason much emphasis was placed during the first year of the excavation on obtaining a secure stratigraphy. Indeed, the deep sounding, trench ZA, was excavated from top to bottom during that first season, under the energetic supervision of the late Cressida Ridley. The ceramics from ZA were the subject of quantitative study during that first year by Jenifer Marriott Keighley. On the basis of the stratigraphy and of this ceramic study, the site was divided into a succession of phases. Radiocarbon samples were taken for each phase, and very consistent radiocarbon determinations were obtained from the Berlin and British Museum laboratories. It was possible to show that the site of Sitagroi, both in its stratigraphic sequence and in its radiocarbon determinations, unequivocally supported the revised view of chronology and confirmed the overthrow of the old equation between early Troy and the Vinča culture which had formed the classical basis for dating since the early work of V. Gordon Childe.

This firm and clear stratigraphic framework has made Sitagroi one of the key sites for understanding the culture sequence and chronology of southeast Europe (see Johnson 1999). The basic conclusions, reached shortly after the excavations and set out in detail in Sitagroi, volume 1 (1986), have been supported by further work in the region, not least by the publication of the excavations (directed by the late Jean Deshayes) at the nearby site of Dikili Tash (Treuil 1992).

The present volume now completes the inventory of the cultural materials from the successive phases at Sitagroi. It may be claimed that we now have the most comprehensive documentation available from any long sequence of the Greek Neolithic, unless the admirably detailed reports from the Franchthi Project be given pride of place, which might well be appropriate (for example, see Jacobsen 1993). Yet while the Franchthi volumes have a number of strengths that remain unrivalled in any Aegean publication, one of the strong points of the Sitagroi publication is now its completeness. All the categories of cultural material that were recovered during the excavations are considered here, and every class of "small find" is dealt with. In this respect, we have tried to follow up the admirable initiative shown by Wace and Thompson (1912) in *Prehistoric Thessaly* and by W. A. Heurtley (1939) in *Prehistoric Macedonia*. These, and Winifred Lamb's *Thermi in Lesbos* (1936) were the exemplars to which we worked during the excavation seasons, and to some extent they remain such today.

One aspect of the project dealt with only in summary in volume 1 was the survey of sites in the plain of Drama, carried out largely through the initiative of David Hardy. That data, which in 1986 formed the basis for Brian Blouet's chapter on the "Development of the Settlement Pattern" (volume 1 [Blouet 1986]:133–144), were not discussed in detail. The site list and the material were, however, available to Demetrios Grammenos in the course of his surveys, so that the relevant sites were included in his doctoral dissertation (Grammenos 1984) and were published in full several years later (Grammenos 1991). Fortunately, therefore, our delay in publishing this material has not withheld the necessary information about site location. Further details are now given here (see chapter 13) about the location of the sites in question. Diagnostic sherd materials and other objects that had been selected for documentation are illustrated here (figures 13.1.2–13.1.19). Recent inspection shows that a number of these sites have been damaged or destroyed in the thirty years since the initial survey. This documentation thus provides information that may not otherwise be available.

The environmental evidence was in general reported on fully in volume 1. An important feature of the present report, however, is the chapter "Grains, Seeds, and Fruits from Prehistoric Sitagroi" by Jane Renfrew. The sample plant remains available were abundant because flotation and water sieving were systematically used for samples from every level at Sitagroi. Results allow a phase-by-phase comparison for the development of the exploitation of food plants, a companion, in a sense, to the discussion of the faunal remains by the late Sándor Bökönyi in volume 1 [Bökönyi 1986]. The appearance of wild and then domesticated grapes is of particular importance. It should be noted that further interesting information about the faunal remains, including the microfauna, would have been available from the residues of the sieving experiment (conducted in Square ZB by Sebastian Payne) had the detailed analysis of the residues been undertaken. At the same time, the totality of "small finds" is much the richer for Payne's careful recovery procedures which are responsible for nearly all the artifacts from Trench ZB as listed in the inventories.

The lithic materials are described here in detail, with Ruth Tringham's comprehensive study of the chipped stone tools and Ernestine S. Elster's chapter on the ground and polished tools. Of particular interest also is John Dixon's contribution on the lithic petrology. Dixon was a member of the original project team, as the excavation's petrologist, and took relevant lithic samples during the excavation. At that time there were few comparative materials for him to use. Here, at least, the report is better for the lapse of time, as the lithic petrology of northern Greece is now much better understood than it was thirty years ago, partly through Dixon's own research over the intervening period.

One of the most important chapters in the present report is Elster's discussion of the finds relating to spinning and weaving and the cognitive inferences she makes about the connection among three classes of artifact during phase III: painted pottery, faunal remains, and decorated whorls. These latter were particularly abundant at Sitagroi, and we were especially fortunate in finding, in levels of phase I, an impression of a textile on the base of a pot which remains the earliest documented textile find (or rather textile impression) from the Aegean. Of course, spindle whorls and occasional finds of loom weights and other relevant materials do occur widely at sites in the Neolithic Aegean. Here, however, there is an unusual profusion. This may in due course help to clarify why such finds are frequent in some phases and not in others, and why there is considerable regional variation: indeed, the crafts of spinning and weaving, once they came to be widely practiced in the Aegean, were never abandoned and are practiced to this day in rural Greece.

The pottery from Sitagroi was comprehensively published in volume 1, and the study by Elizabeth Gardner now fills out the information on technical aspects. The development of the techniques of pyrotechnology is of particular interest since Sitagroi remains one of the earliest—perhaps in fact still the earliest—site in the Aegean with explicit evidence for metalworking, in the form of crucibles and copper waste as well as copper artifacts. The first evidence comes in Sitagroi phase II, and is particularly strong in phase III, a period when the relationships with the cultures of Bulgaria and Romania (Gumelnitsa, Karanovo V and VI, and so on) are noticeably clear. Thus while recent finds from Greece (reviewed by Zachos 1996a) document the widespread use of metal during the Neolithic period, it would still seem that the basic techniques of Copper Age metallurgy (see chapter 8) are likely to have been learned from the north. Sitagroi remains a key location for this process. Colin Renfrew and Elizabeth Slater present a full discussion of these issues in their chapter on metallurgy, which is amplified by the most recent work on provenience on the basis of lead isotope analysis.

Some of the most important materials dealing with what may be termed the "cognitive dimension" at Sitagroi were comprehensively surveyed by our late colleague Marija Gimbutas in her chapter on "Mythical Imagery in Sitagroi Society" in volume 1 (Gimbutas 1986). These materials are now supplemented and completed in three substantial studies by Colin Renfrew, Ernestine S. Elster, and Marianna Nikolaidou. The first (see chapter 10) reviews the engraved clay seals of various shapes and forms, some holding a role perhaps in measurement, marking, and/or metrology. The second (see chapter 11) deals with the clay models and

other terra-cotta finds, while the third (see chapter 9) offers a pioneering review of objects of adornment, including those of marine shell.

Inevitably the publication today of an excavation whose fieldwork was completed in 1970 must, by current archaeological standards, manifest a number of limitations. Nevertheless, we have sought to document what we did, what we found, and what we inferred. We have sought also to illustrate a broad sample of finds, so that these may be compared with those of other sites, in the Aegean and beyond. Indeed, this complete publication of the project provides us and other scholars with abundant scope for further work. Perhaps we may be forgiven for claiming Sitagroi as the most completely published site-based project in the Aegean today. And because the material culture is accessible—that is, each class of artifact is reported on and virtually every individual artifact located in time and space in the separate catalogs—Sitagroi offers us an unparalleled opportunity to study the cognitive system that underlies the engagement of the Sitagroi settlers with their material world. Indeed, material culture is used knowingly by these settlers and in furtherance of concepts and categories, some of which were noted earlier in the separate chapters. Here we briefly touch on the way these categories lead us to talk comfortably about cognitive archaeology at Sitagroi; furthermore, since what is important in the cognitive field is also social, so we advance as well a social archaeology of Sitagroi.

This work was advanced by Nikolaidou and Elster (see chapter 12) with a careful study of the description of the excavation units (as described in volume 1, chapter 8 [C. Renfrew 1986b]) from each phase in order to identify structural units/architectural features such as floors, walls, hearths, ovens, and the like, and then to recombine, as far as possible, all of the materials recovered in the context of those units. An expanded summary of this large task is offered in chapter 12 as "Contextual Commentary." Originally the limited goal was to offer a functional assessment of the units based on the contextual data. What we realized—and this had been stated earlier in volume 1 (chapter 8 [C. Renfrew 1986b])—is that most contextual evidence before the EBA levels cannot be clearly tied to a specific building, but rather consists of either patchy floors, hearth residue, fallen wall debris, and other building features with an ambiguous structural association, or successive floors presumably within a restricted time range of successive building episodes. But shortcomings notwithstanding, interesting Middle Neolithic/Chalcolithic intersections of architecture and a wide spectrum of prehistoric artifacts are noted, ranging from objects of utility to crafted goods, to items of display and representation. This network of artifacts, viewed within spatial and functional settings, seems to represent the "household" or "workshop," offering us a picture, a glimpse, of what prehistoric villagers made, used, valued, traded, and/or exchanged in a series of historic "moments," moments that varied over time and space.

It is especially fascinating to study, examine, and discuss the cognitive aspects of the Sitagroi villagers' engagement with material culture. For example, the notion of "value" can be applied to several classes of artifact or commodities. Such a notion is cognitive in that one commodity leads to a consideration of its relation to others, and how much each is worth. Thus we can build from issues of "commodity" and "value" and to the notion of "economy" and eventually reach for an understanding of the social dynamics at Sitagroi.

To be more specific, at this site, and commencing at a particular time, the material evidence shows, for example, that honey-brown flint, likely native to a region some 300 km distant, resonated in the minds of the Sitagroi villagers as a commodity of value. According to Ruth Tringham (chapter 3), the assemblage of lithics included other locally available raw materials of almost equal utility. Yet the data show that at the very outset of settlement, in phase I, ca. 5400 BC, the settlers established (or continued) a line of trade or exchange for this commodity which was maintained at differing levels of intensity over 3000 years. This observation gives us some insight into the significance of social interaction—in this case action at a distance, generated by at least some of the Sitagroi villagers with an impressive network of contacts. This is just one small part of the cognitive system at work at Sitagroi, of course, but it is an extremely clear one. We

can see the concept that Madara flint is valuable and worth having; this leads to a mental construct of who gets it and how it is procured—probably by down-the-line trade and/or exchange—and to a consideration of what commodity is given in exchange. We propose that the mental construct inherent in the Sitagroi villagers' maintenance of a line of trade to obtain Madara flint is an important cognitive aspect in the archaeological investigation of this site. It concerns the capacity to plan and execute tasks, organize activities, and cope with social relations.

If the aim of cognitive/social archaeology is to get under the surface of things, to understand the concepts and categories that underlie the workings of material culture and the people in that culture, we believe the excavations at Sitagroi provide a relevant and impressive body of data. That is, because so much of the Sitagroi material is context-rich, it offers great opportunities for researchers to further analyze how the inhabitants of Sitagroi engaged with the material world, and by a range of symbolic means, how they interacted with one another also (see Renfrew 2001). Through their actions and the cognitive constructs by means of which they coped with their world, they left a material record that should be susceptible of further analysis today. Indeed, in an earlier publication, the contextual information provided by the Burnt House excavation was reconsidered in order to understand the crafts and technologies used there and to propose the kinds of roles played by the men, women, and children involved in the building's construction and use (Elster 1997:20–35). These may be regarded as initial steps toward a cognitive archaeology for Sitagroi, steps that we hope the publication of this volume will encourage others to follow.

With the publication of this volume, the way now lies open for further field seasons at the site. Any future work at Sitagroi will be affected by the fact that a large part of the mound was purchased at the outset of the excavation and transferred to the Greek state and to the care of the Archaeological Service. This parcel of land measures 130 m east-west x 40 m north-south; the southeast corner of square SL (Preface figure 2) lies at the southeast corner of the area purchased. This portion of the mound was taken out of cultivation and remains in good condition today. By contrast, the other parts of the mound that remained in cultivation have suffered some loss of soil, and the surface, at the time of visiting in 2000, had been reduced by at least 50 cm.

Were we to undertake such fieldwork ourselves, we would be inclined to continue excavating in squares PO, QO, PN and QN, as well as ROc. This would offer a sufficiently large area to recover house plans such as those obtained from periods Vb and Va (the Burnt House). Of course, an alternative strategy would be to excavate down to the level of the Burnt House over the entire top of the mound, and to seek traces of contemporary conflagration in adjacent buildings.

Naturally it would be interesting to excavate a large area to a considerable depth. In doing so, it would be particularly profitable to study with care the levels below phase IV, since the transition from phase III to phase IV was not well documented during our excavations. It remains unclear whether there was a hiatus in occupation at that time—although an examination of the pertinent ZA levels in Bökönyi's faunal report indicates that rather than a hiatus, continued occupation may have taken place.

Much of the interest in returning to Sitagroi, however, would be in seeking a detailed comparison with the finds from other sites in the plain of Drama and beyond. How far do the distributions in the different styles of graphite ware extend? What is the distribution of the characteristic black-on-red ware, also of phase III? Similar questions could be asked for the various ceramic fabrics of phase II. How many of these ceramics were made locally? Could ceramic petrology, or the application of trace element analysis, give a specific answer to these questions?

So far as we are aware, there is still no clear evidence from the plain of Drama of Neolithic occupation prior to phase I at Sitagroi. Was the plain unoccupied until that point? Do the strong affinities of phase I with the Veselinovo culture of Bulgaria indicate that the first settlement came from the north?

It was, of course, in phase II that the first figurines were found, along with the first painted pottery. To what extent do these features relate more with the cultures of Thessaly than with those to the north? We also still lack a clear understanding of the prosperity and flamboyance of the material culture of phase III in contrast with the more restrained cultural materials of phase IV. This was the end of what our late colleague Marija Gimbutas was inclined to term "Old Europe"—the flourishing Chalcolithic of the Aegean and the Balkans. What processes promoted the changes, seen so widely at that time?

The answers to some of these questions may perhaps be open to inference from the materials, which are now published, taken together with those from other sites and regions. But others will require further fieldwork. It may reasonably be claimed that the basic structure of the toumba at Sitagroi is now well understood. It would therefore be possible to initiate an excavation with a well-defined series of questions and to devise specific strategies by which some of these may be answered.

Whoever undertakes further fieldwork at the mound is likely to receive warm cooperation from the citizens of the modern village of Sitagroi, just as we did thirty years ago. Some of those who worked with us on the site remain our personal friends today. There is, moreover, strong local interest in the site, encouraged by the excellent display of the finds which are now housed in the new Archaeological Museum at Drama, organized by the Ephor of Antiquities, Dr. Haido Koukouli-Chrysanthaki— the same energetic archaeologist who, as an Epimeletria of Antiquities, contributed so much to the progress of our enterprises in the years from 1968 to 1970. As the inaugural exhibition program states, "The Museum . . . marks the beginning of a major effort to systematize archaeological research and promote the cultural identity of the area" (Koukouli-Chrysanthaki et al. 2000).

With the completion of what might be described as the first phase in the study of the mound at Sitagroi, the way lies open for the second phase to begin.

Bibliography

ABBREVIATIONS

Books

Achilleion:
Gimbutas, M., S. Winn, and D. Shimabuku
  1989   *Achilleion, A Neolithic Settlement in Thessaly, Greece 6400–5600 B.C.* Monumenta Archaeologica 14. Los Angeles: UCLA Institute of Archaeology.

Dikili Tash:
Treuil, R., ed.
  1992   *Dikili Tash: Village préhistorique de Macédoine orientale I: Fouilles de Jean Deshayes (1961–1975).* BCH Supplément 24. Athens: École française d'Athènes.

Divostin:
McPherron, A., and D. Srejović, eds.
  1988   *Divostin and the Neolithic of Central Serbia.* Ethnology Monograph 10. Pittsburgh: Department of Anthropology, University of Pittsburgh.

Neolithic Macedonia:
Gimbutas, M.
  1976c *Neolithic Macedonia as Reflected by Excavation at Anza, Southeast Yugoslavia.* Monumenta Archaeologica 1. Los Angeles: UCLA Institute of Archaeology.

Neolithiki Makedonia:
Grammenos, D., ed.
  1997   *Neolithiki Makedonia.* Ypourgeio Politismou, Dimosieymata tou Arkaiolologikou Deltion Ar. 56. Athens: Ekdosi tou Tameiou Arkaiologikon Poron kai Apallotrioseon.

Obre:
Gimbutas, M., ed.
  1974   *Obre and Its Place in Old Europe.* Wissenschaftliche Mitteilungen des Bosnisch-Herzegowinishen Landesmuseums, IV/A. Sarajevo.

Selevac:
Tringham, R., and D. Krstić
  1990   *Selevac: A Neolithic Village in Yugoslavia.* Monumenta Archaeologica 15. Los Angeles: UCLA Institute of Archaeology.

Servia I:
Ridley, C., K. A. Wardle, and C. A. Mould, eds.
  2000   *Servia I: Anglo-Hellenic Rescue Excavations 1971–73, Directed by Katerina Rhomiopoulou and Cressida Ridley.* BSA Supplementary Volume 32. Athens: BSA.

Sitagroi 1:
Renfrew, C., Gimbutas M., and Elster E. S., eds.
  1986   *Excavations at Sitagroi, A Prehistoric Village in Northeast Greece.* Vol. 1. Monumenta Archaeologica 13. Los Angeles: UCLA Institute of Archaeology.

TEXNH:
Laffineur, R., and P. P. Betancourt, eds.
  1997   *Craftsmen, Craftswomen, and Craftsmanship in the Aegean Bronze Age.* Proceedings of the 6th International Aegean Conference, Philadelphia, Temple University, 18–20 April 1996. Aegaeum 16. Liège: Université de Liège; Austin: University of Texas, Program in Aegean Scripts and Prehistory.

Periodicals

AEMθ   *Archaiologikó Ergo sti Makedonía kai Thráki.* Thessaloniki: Aristotelio University, Greek Archaeological Service and Ministry of Culture.
AA   *American Antiquity.* Washington, DC.
AD   *Archaiologikon Deltion.* Athens.
AJA   *American Journal of Archaeology.* New York.
Am. Anth. *American Anthropologist.* Washington, DC.
AS   *Anatolian Studies.* London: British Institute of Archaeology at Ankara.
BAR   British Archaeological Reports.
BCH   *Bulletin de Correspondance Hellénique.* Paris.
BRGK   *Bericht der römisch-germanischen Kommission.* Frankfurt am Main.

BSA   *Annual of the British School of Archaeology at Athens*. London.

IAI   *Izvestiia na Arheologicheskiia Institut*. Sofia.

JRGZ   *Jahrbuch des römish-germanischen Zentralmuseums*. Mainz.

PPS   *Proceedings of the Prehistoric Society*. London.

PZ   *Prähistorische Zeitschrift*. Berlin.

ZNM   *Zbornik Narodnog Muzeja*. Belgrade.

REFERENCES

Adovasio, J. M.
1975–1977   The Textile and Basketry Impressions from Jarmo. *Paléorient* 3:223–230.
1977   *Basketry Technology: A Guide to Identification and Analysis*. Chicago: Aldine Publishing Company.
1983   Notes on the Textile and Basketry Impressions from Jarmo. In *Prehistoric Archaeology along the Zagros Flanks*, edited by L. S. Braidwood, R. J. Braidwood, B. Howe, C. A. Reed, and P. J. Watson, pp. 425–426. The University of Chicago Oriental Institute Publications, Vol. 15. Chicago: The Oriental Institute of the University of Chicago.

Adovasio, J. M., D. C. Hyland, and O. Soffer
1997   Textiles and Cordage: A Preliminary Assessment. In *Pavlov I—Northwest*, edited by J. Svoboda, pp. 403–424. Brno: Academy of Sciences of the Czech Republic, Institute of Archaeology.

Adovasio, J. M., D. C. Hyland, O. Soffer, J. S. Illingworth, B. Klíma, and J. Svoboda
1998   Perishable Industries from Dolní Vestonice I: New Insights into the Nature and Origin of the Gravettian. Paper presented at the Masaryk Conference, Brno, Czech Republic.

Adovasio, J. M., and R. F. Maslowski
1988   Textile Impressions on Ceramic Vessels at Divostin. In *Divostin*, pp. 345–354.

Adovasio, J. M., O. Soffer, D. Dirkmaat, C. Pedler, D. Pedler, D. Thomas, and R. Buyce
1992   Flotation Samples from Mezhirich, Ukranian Republic: A Micro View of Macro Issues. Paper presented at the 57th Annual Meeting of the Society for American Archaeology, Pittsburgh, Pennsylvania.

Adovasio, J. M., O. Soffer, D. C. Hyland, B. Klíma, and J. Svoboda
1999   Textil, Kosíkárství a Síitê v Mladém Paleolitu Moravy. *Archeologické Rozhledy* 51:58–94.

Adovasio, J. M., O. Soffer, and B. Klíma
1996   Upper Palaeolithic Fibre Technology: Interlaced Woven Finds from Pavlov I, Czech Republic, ca. 26,000 years ago. *Antiquity* 70:526–534.

Amandry, P.
1984   Os et Coquilles. In *L'Antre corycien*, II, pp. 347–380. BCH Supplément IX.

Anderson-Gerfaud, P.
1982   Comment préciser l'utilisation agricole des outils préhistoriques? *Cahiers de l'Euphrates* 3:149–164.

Andreou, S., M. Fotiadis, and K. Kotsakis.
1996   Review of Aegean Prehistory V: The Neolithic and Bronze Age of Northern Greece. *AJA* 100 (3):537–597.

Angelov, N.
1958   Die Siedlung bei Hotnica. *Studia in Honorem D. Dečev*. Sofia: Bulgarian Academy of Sciences.

Arnaudov, N.
1936   Über prähistorische und subrezente pflanzenreste aus Bugarien. *Trihove na Bulgarskoto Prirohomspitatelo Hrishectvo*, A XVII. Sofia.
1937–1938   Untersuchung über pflanzenreste aus den Ausgrabungen bei Sadowetz in Bulgarien. *Annuaire de l'Université de Sofia, Faculté Physico-Mathématique* XXIV, livre 3, Sciences Naturelle. Sofia.
1939   Pflanzenreste aus einer prähistorischen Seidlung in Südbulgarien. *Österr. Bot. Zeitschr.* 88:53-57.
1940–1941   Über die Neuendeckten Prähistorichen pflanzenreste aus Süd bulgarien. *Jahrbuch der Universität sveti Climent Ochridski in Sofia Physico-Mathematischen Faculté*, XXXVII, Band 3, Naturwissenschaft. Sofia.
1948–1949   Prehistoricki Rasteli Materiali. *Annuaire de l'Université de Sofia, Faculté de Sciences*, tome 45, livre 3, Sciences Naturelle. Sofia.

Aschmann, H.
1949   A Metate Maker of Baja, California. *Am Anth.* 51: 682–686.

Aslanis, J.
1985   *Die frühbronzezeitlichen Funde und Befunde. Kastanas: Ausgrabungen in einem Siedlungshügel der Bronze- und Eisenzeit Makedoniens, 1975–1979*. Prähistorische Archäologie in Südosteuropa 4. Berlin: Volker Spiess.
1992   *I proistoria tis Makedonias I. I Neolithiki epochi*. Athens: Kardamitsa.

Aspinall, A., and S. W. Feather
1972   Neutron Activation Analysis of Prehistoric Flint-Mine Production. *Archaeometry* 14 (1):41–54.

Avramova, M.

1991 Gold and Copper Jewelry from the Chalcolithic Cemeteries near the Village of Durankulak, Varna District. In *Découverte du métal*, edited by J. P. Mohen and C. Éluère, pp. 43–47. Paris: Picard.

Bačkalov, A.

1979 *Bone and Antler Objects in the Pre-Neolithic and Neolithic of Serbia*. Fontes Archeologiae Yugoslaviae, tome II. Belgrade: Savez Arheoloskih Drustava Jugoslavije.

Bailey, D. W.

1993 Chronotypic Tension in Bulgarian Prehistory: 6500–3500 BC. *World Archaeology* 25 (2):204–222.

Bakalakis, G.

1961 *Archaiologikes Erevnes sti Thraki*. Thessaloniki: Demosieumata tis Thrakikis Estias Thessalonikis.

1962 Archaiologikai erevnai en Thraki. *AD* 17:258–261.

Bakalakis, G., and A. Sakellariou

1981 *Paradimi*. Internationale Interakademische Kommission für die Erforschung der Vorgeschichte des Balkans. Monographien Band 2. Heidelberger Akademie der Wissenschaften. Mainz am Rhein: Philipp von Zabern.

Balfanz, K.

1995 Bronzezeitliche Spinnwirtel aus Troia. *Studia Troica* 5:117–144. Eberhard Karls Universität, Tübingen, and University of Cincinnati; Mainz: Verlag Philipp von Zabern.

Barber, E.

1991 *Prehistoric Textiles: The Development of Cloth in the Neolithic and Bronze Ages with Special Reference to the Aegean*. Princeton: Princeton University Press.

1994 *Women's Work: The First 20,000 Years*. New York: W.W. Norton & Co.

1997 Minoan Women and the Challenges of Weaving for Home, Trade, and Shrine. In *TEXNH*, pp. 515–520.

Barge, H.

1982 *Les Parures du Néolithique ancien au début de l'âge des Métaux en Languedoc*. Paris: Centre national de la recherche scientifique.

Bar-Yosef Mayer, D. E.

1997 Neolithic Shell Bead Production in Sinai. *Journal of Archaeological Science* 24:97–111.

Barta, J.

1960 Zur Problematik der Hohlensiedlungen in der Slowakischen Karpaten. *Acta Archaeologica Carpathica* II (1–2):1–39.

Beck, H.

1973 *Classification and Nomenclature of Beads and Pendants*. York: Liberty Cap Books.

Behm-Blancke, G.

1963 Bandkeramische Erntgeräte. *Alt-Thuringen* 6:105–174.

Bell, J. A.

1994 *Reconstructing Prehistory: Scientific Method in Archaeology*. Philadelphia: Temple University Press.

Benac, A.

1973 *Obre I and II*. Wissenschaftliche Mitteilungen des Bosnisch-Herzegowinischen Landesmuseums, III/A. Sarajevo.

Bender, B.

1985 Prehistoric developments in the American Mid-continent and in Brittany, Northwest France. In *Prehistoric Hunter-Gatherers: The Emergence of Cultural Complexity*, edited by T. D. Price and J. A. Brown, pp. 21–57. Orlando: Academic Press.

Bernabó-Brea, L.

1964 *Poliochni: Città preistorica nell' isola di Lemnos*, Vol. I. Rome: Monografie della scuola archeologica di Atene.

1976 *Poliochni: Città preistorica nell' isola di Lemnos*, Vol. II. Rome: Monografie della scuola archeologica di Atene.

Bertsch, K., and F. Bertsch

1949 *Geschichte unserer Kulturflanzen*. 2nd ed. Stuttgart.

Besios, M., and M. Pappa

1995 O neolithikos oikismos ston Makryialo Pierias. *Archaiologika Analekta ex Athinon* 23–28:13–30.

1996 Neolithikos oikismos Makrygialou, 1993. *AEMθ* 7:215–222.

Bibikova, V. I.

1973 Kostnye ostatkie l'va eneolitičeskih poselenii tach Severozapadnogo Pričernomorja (Bone Remains of Lion from an Eneolithic Settlement of the North-Western Black Sea Area). *Vestnik Zool.* 1: 57–63. Kiev.

Biskowski, M.

1990 Groundstone Tools at Otumba. Paper presented at the 55th Annual meetings of the Society for American Archaeology, at the symposium "The Aztec City-State of Otumba: A Case Study in City-State Political and Economic Evolution," Las Vegas, 1990.

1997 The Adaptive Origins of Prehispanic Markets in Central Mexico: The Role of Maize-Grinding Tools and Related Staple Products in Early State Economies. Ph.D. dissertation, Department of Anthropology, UCLA.

2000 Maize Preparation and the Aztec Subsistence Economy. *Ancient Mesoamerica*, 2:293–306.

In press   Patterns in the Consumption of Metates at Teotihuacan: A Preliminary Assessment. In *Socioeconomics at Teotihuacan*, edited by J. Sheehy. Boulder: University of Colorado Press.

Bisson, M., and R. White
1996   L'imagerie féminine du Paléolithique: Étude des figurines de Grimaldi—Response. *Culture* 16 (2): 61–64. Montreal.

Blitzer, H.
1995   Minoan implements and industries. In *Kommos I: The Kommos Region and Houses of the Minoan Town*, edited by J. S. Shaw and M. Shaw, pp. 403–535. Princeton: Princeton University Press.

Blouet, B.
1986   Development of the Settlement Pattern. In *Sitagroi* 1:133–143.

Bognar-Kutzian, I.
1976   On the Origins of Early Copper Processing in Europe. In *To Illustrate the Monument: Essays on Archaeology Presented to Stuart Piggott*, edited by J. V. S. Megaw, pp. 70–76. London: Thames and Hudson.

Bökönyi, S.
1986   Faunal Remains. In *Sitagroi 1*, pp. 63–132.

Bökönyi, S., and L. Bartosiewicz
1997   Tierknockenfunde. In *Karanovo, Die Ausgrabungen im Südsektor 1984–1992*, Band I.1, edited by S. Hiller and V. Nikolov, pp. 385–423. Archäologisches Institut der Universät Salzburg and Archäologisches Institut mit Museum der Bulgarischen Akademie der Wissenschaften, Sofia. Salzburg and Sofia: Verlag Ferdinand Berger.

Bolviken, E., E. Helskog, K. Helskog, I. M. Holm-Olsen, L. Solheim, and R. Bertelsen
1982   Correspondence Analysis: An Alternative to Principal Components. *World Archaeology* 14:41–60.

Bradley, R., and M. Edmonds
1993   *Interpreting the Axe Trade: Production and Exchange in Neolithic Britain*. New Studies in Archaeology. Cambridge: Cambridge University Press.

Branigan, K.
1974   *Aegean Metalworking of the Early and Middle Bronze Age*. Oxford: Oxford University Press.

Brea, B.
1964   *Poliochni, Citta preistorica nell'isola di Lemnos*. Monografie della Scuola archeologica di Atene e delle Missioni Italiane in Oriente 1–2 (1964–1976).

British Naval Intelligence Division
1944   *Greece*, Vol. III: *Regional Geography*. B.R. 516B, Geographical Handbook Series. London.

Brük, J.
1999   Ritual and Rationality: Some Problems of Interpretation in European Archaeology. *European Journal of Archaeology* 2 (3):313–344.

Brumfiel, E. M.
1994   Ethnic Groups and Political Development in Ancient Mexico. In *Factional Competition and Political Development in the New World*, edited by E. M. Brumfiel and J. W. Fox, pp. 89–102. Cambridge: Cambridge University Press,

Brumfiel, E. M., and T. K. Earle
1987   Specialization, Exchange, and Complex Societies: An Introduction. In *Specialization, Exchange, and Complex Societies*, edited by E. M. Brumfiel and T. K. Earle, pp. 1–9, Cambridge: Cambridge University Press.

Broodbank, C.
1993   Ulysses without Sails: Trade, Distance, Knowledge and Power in the Early Cyclades. *World Archaeology* 24 (3):315–331.

Burke, B.
1998   From Minos to Midas: The Organization of Textile Production in the Aegean and in Anatolia. Ph.D. dissertation, University of California, Los Angeles.

Burnham, H. B.
1965   Çatal Hüyük—The Textiles and Twined Fabrics. *Anatolian Studies* 15:169–174.

Butzer, K.
1982   *Archaeology as Human Ecology*. Cambridge: Cambridge University Press.

Campana, D. V.
1989   *Natufian and Protoneolithic Bone Tools: The Manufacture and Use of Bone Implements in the Zagros and the Levant*. BAR International Series 494. Oxford: British Archaeological Reports.

Campbell, J.
1964   *Honour, Family, and Patronage, A Study of Institutions and Moral Values in a Greek Mountain Community*. Oxford: Clarendon Press.

Carington Smith, J.
1975   Spinning, Weaving and Textile Manufacture in Prehistoric Greece. Ph.D. dissertation, University of Tasmania.
1977   Cloth and Mat Impressions. In *Keos* I: *Kephala, A Late Neolithic Settlement and Cemetery*, pp. 114–125, edited by J. E. Coleman. Princeton: American School of Classical Studies.
2000   The Spinning and Weaving Implements. In *Servia I*, pp. 98–137.

Chapman, J.
1981 *The Vinča Culture of South-East Europe: Studies in Chronology, Economy and Society*. BAR International Series 119 (I). Oxford: British Archaeological Reports.
1990 The Neolithic in the Morava-Danube Confluence Area: A Regional Assessment of Settlement Pattern. In *Selevac*, pp. 13–43.
2000 *Fragmentation in Archaeology: People, Places, and Broken Objects in the Prehistory of South Eastern Europe*. London: Routledge.

Chapman, J. C., and R. F. Tylecote
1983 Early Copper in the Balkans. *PPS* 49:371–376.

Charvat, P.
1975 Tartarijske tabulky jako Komunikacni problem (Tărtăria Tablets as a Problem of Communication). *Archeologicke rozhledy* 27:182–187.

Chernykh, E.
1978a *Gornoe delo i metallurgiya v drevneishei Bolgarii*. Sofia: Bulgarian Academy of Sciences.
1978b Aibunar: A Balkan Copper Mine of the Fourth Millennium BC. *PPS* 44:203–18.
1991 Ancient Gold in the Circumpontic Area. In *Découverte du métal*, edited by J. P. Mohen and C. Éluère, pp. 387–396. Paris: Picard.
1992 *Early Metallurgy in the USSR*. Cambridge: Cambridge University Press.

Cheynier, A.
1967 *Comment Vivait l'Homme des Cavernes*. Paris: Robert Arnoux.

Chinas, B.
1973 *The Isthmus Zapotecs: Women's Roles in Cultural Context*. New York: Holt, Rinehart & Winston.

Choyke, A. M.
1998 Bronze Age Red Deer: Case Studies from the Great Hungarian Plain. In *Man and the Animal World: Studies in Archaeozoology, Archaeology, Anthropology, and Palaeolinguistics, in Memoriam Sándor Bökönyi*, edited by P. Anreiter, L. Bartosiewicz, E. Jerem, and W. Meid, pp. 157–178. Budapest: Archaeolingua.

Christenson, A. L.
1987 The Prehistoric Tool Kit. In *Prehistoric Stone Technology on Northern Black Mesa*, edited by W. J. Parry and A. L. Christenson, pp. 43–93. Carbondale: Center for Archaeological Investigations, Southern Illinois University, Carbondale.

Christidou, R.
1997 Dimitra. Bone-working. In *Neolithiki Makedonia*, pp. 128–199.
1999 Outils en os néolithiques du nord de la Grèce: Étude technologique. Ph.D. dissertation, Université de Paris X-Nanterre.

Clark, J. G. D.
1952 *Prehistoric Europe: The Economic Basis*. Stanford: Stanford University Press.

Clark, J. E.
1986 From Mountain to Molehill: A Critical Review of Teotihuacan's Obsidian Industry. In *Economic Aspects of Prehispanic Highland Mexico*, edited by B. L. Isaac, pp. 23–74. Research in Economic Anthropology, Supplement 2. Greenwich, CT: JAI Press.

Clark, R. M.
1975 A Calibration Curve for Radiocarbon Dates. *Antiquity* 49:251–266.

Coghlan, H. H.
1962 *Notes on the Prehistoric Metallurgy of Copper and Bronze in the Old World*. Oxford: Pitt Rivers Museum.

Coleman, J.
1977 *Keos I: Kephala, A Late Neolithic Settlement and Cemetery*. Princeton: American School of Classical Studies.

Comsa, E.
1967 Über die Verbreitung und Herkunft einiger von den jüngsteinzeitliche Menschen auf dem Gebiet verwendeten Werkstoffe. *A Móra Ferenc Múzeum Évkönyve* 1966–67:25–33.
1971 Silexul de tip Banaţean. *Apulum* IX:15–19.
1991a L'utilisation du cuivre en Roumanie pendant le Néolithique Moyen. In *Découverte du métal*, edited by J. P. Mohen and C. Éluère, pp. 77–85. Paris: Picard.
1991b L'utilisation de l'or pendant le Néolithique dans le territoire de la Roumanie. In *Découverte du métal*, edited by J. P. Mohen and C. Éluère, pp. 85–93. Paris: Picard.

Cook, S.
1970 Price and Output Variability in Peasant-Artisan Stoneworking Industry in Oaxaca, Mexico: An Analytical Essay in Economic Anthropology. *Am. Anth.* 72:776–801.
1982 *Zapotec Stoneworkers: The Dynamics of Rural Simple Commodity Production in Modern Mexican Capitalism*. Washington, DC: University Press of America.

Cooke, S. R., R. B. Nielsen, and R. V. Nielsen
1978 Slags and Other Metallurgical Products. In *Excavations at Nichoria in Southeast Greece. Vol. I, Site, Environs and Techniques*, edited by G. Rapp and

S. E. Aschenbrenner, pp. 182–224. Minneapolis: University of Minneapolis Press.

Costin, C.

1991 Craft Specialization: Issues in Defining, Documenting, and Explaining the Organization of Production. In *Archaeological Method and Theory*, Vol. 3, edited by M. B. Schiffer, pp. 1–56. Tucson: University of Arizona Press.

1993 Textiles, Women, and Political Economy in Late Prehispanic Peru. In *Research in Economic Anthropology* 14:3–28.

Crabtree, D.

1968 Mesoamerican Polyhedral Cores and Prismatic Blades. *Am. Anth.* 33 (4):446–478.

Craddock, P. T.

1995 *Early Metal Mining and Production.* Edinburgh: Edinburgh University Press.

Daux, G.

1962 Chronique des fouilles et découvertes archéologiques en Grèce en 1961. *BCH* 86:912–933.

1968 Chronique des fouilles et découvertes archéologiques en Grèce en 1967. *BCH* 92:1062–1077.

Davidson, D. A.

1973 Particle Size and Phosphate Analysis: Evidence for the Evolution of a Tell. *Archaeometry* 15:143–152.

1986 Geomorphological Studies, with a contribution by Barry Thomas. In *Sitagroi 1*, pp. 25–40.

Demoule J. P.

1994 Problèmes chrono-culturels du néolithique de Grèce du nord. In *La Thessalie. Quinze années de recherches archéologiques, 1975–1990. Bilans et perspectives. Actes du colloque international, Lyon, 17 avril 1990*, edited by K. Gallis, pp. 79–90. Athens: Greek Ministry of Culture.

Demoule, J. P., and M. Lichardus-Itten

1993 Fouilles Franco-Bulgares du site Néolithique ancien de Kovačevo (Bulgarie du Sud-ouest). *BCH* 118 (II):561–618.

Demoule J. P., and C. Perlès

1993 The Greek Neolithic: A New Review. *Journal of World Prehistory* 7 (4):355–416.

Dennell, R. W.

1978 *Early Farming in South Bulgaria from the 6th to the 3rd Millennium BC.* BAR International Series Supplement 45.

Deshayes, J.

1970a Dikili Tash. *BCH* 94:799–808.

1970b Les fouilles de Dikili Tash et l'archéologie Yougoslave. *ZNM* 6:21–41.

1972 Dikili Tash and the Origins of the Troadic Culture. *Archaeology* 25:198–205.

1973 Dikili Tash. *BCH* 97:464–473.

1974 Fours Néolithiques de Dikili Tash. *Mélanges helléniques offerts à Georges Daux*, pp. 67–91. Paris.

Detev, P.

1965 Modeli za ukrasa ot kamenno-mednata epocha. *Archeologiya* (Sofia) 7 (4):65–73.

Dibble, C. E., and A. J. O. Anderson

1961 *Florentine Codex: The General History of the Things of New Spain: Book 10—The People. Fray Bernardo de Sahagun.* Monographs of the School of American Research and the Museum of New Mexico, No. 14, Pt. XI. Santa Fe.

Dierckx, H. M.

1992 Aspects of Minoan Culture, Technology, and Economy: The Bronze Age Stone Industry of Crete. Ph.D. dissertation, University of Pennsylvania, Philadelphia.

Dimadis, E., and S. Zachos

1986 1:200,000 Geological Map of the Rhodope Region. I.G.M.E. (Institute of Geology and Mining Research), Athens, Greece.

Dimitriadis, S., and K. Skourtopoulou

2001 Characterization of Lithic Materials by Petrographic and SEM Techniques: Towards Suggestions on Chipped Stone Provenance from Neolithic Sites of Northern Greece. In *Archaeometry Issues in Greek Prehistory and Antiquity*, edited by Y. Bassiakos, E. Aloupi, and Y. Facorellis, pp. 779–790. Athens: Hellenic Society for Archaeometry and the Society of Messenian Archaeological Studies.

Dixon, J. E., and S. Dimitriadis, eds.

1984 Metamorphosed Ophiolitic Rocks from the Serbo-Macedonian Massif, near Lake Volvi, North-east Greece. In *The Geological Evolution of the Eastern Mediterranean*, edited by J. E. Dixon and A. H. F. Robertson, pp. 603-618. Geological Society Special Publication 17. London Geological Society; Palo Alto, CA: Blackwell Scientific Publications.

Dixon, J. E., and A. H. F. Robertson, eds.

1984 *The Geological Evolution of the Eastern Mediterranean.* Geological Society Special Publication 17. London Geological Society; Palo Alto, CA: Blackwell Scientific Publications.

Doumas, C.

1998 Metallurgy and the So-Called Battle Axe: The Tool of a Trade? In *Mensch und Umvelt in der Bronzezeit Europas*, edited by B. Hänsel, pp. 157–162. Kiel: Octker-Voges Verlag.

Driver, H. E.
1961 *Indians of North America*. Chicago: University of Chicago Press.

Dubin, L. S.
1995 *The History of Beads: From 30,000 B.C. to the Present*. New York: H. N. Abrams.

Dumitrescu, V.
1966 New Discoveries at Gumelnitza. *Archaeology* 19 (3):162–172.

1980 *The Neolithic Settlement at Rast (South-west Oltenia, Romania)*. BAR International Series 72. Oxford: British Archaeological Reports.

Dzieduszycka-Machnikowa, A., and J. Lech
1976 *Neolityczne Zespoly Pracowniane w Kopalni Krzemienia w Saspowie*. Warsaw: Ossolineum.

Efstratiou, N.
1992 Proneolithika evrimata apo tin Aigaiaki Thraki. *AEMΘ* 6:643–651.

Efstratiou, N., and M. Fotiadis
1998 I Erevna s'ena proistoriko latomeio pyritoliou sti Thraki-ta prota apotelesmata. *AEMΘ* 12:31–40.

Efstratiou, N., M. P. Fumanal, C. Ferrer, D. Urem Kotsos, A. Curci, A. Tagliacozzo, G. Stratouli, S. M. Valamoti, M. Ntinou, E. Badal, M. Madella, K. Skourtopoulou
1997 Excavations at the Neolithic Settlement of Makri, Thrace, Greece (1988–1996): A Preliminary Report. *Saguntum (Plav)* 3:11–62.

Elster, E. S.
1976 The Chipped Stone Industry of Anzabegovo. In *Neolithic Macedonia*, pp. 257–278.

1986 Tripods, Plastic Vessels, and Stands: A Fragmentary Collection of Social Ceramics. In *Sitagroi 1*, pp. 303–344.

1992 An Archaeologist's Perspective on Prehistoric Textile Production: The Case of Sitagroi. In *I Dráma kai i Perioxi tis Istoría kai Politismós*, pp. 29–46. Drama.

1995 Textile Production at Sitagroi and Beyond: Spinners and Weavers, Exchange and Interchange. Paper presented at the panel "The Archaeology of Tools and Technology: Craftsmen and Craftswomen, Producers and Consumers," 97th Annual Meeting of the Archaeological Institute of America, San Diego, 27–29 December.

1997 Construction and Use of the Early Bronze Age Burnt House at Sitagroi: Craft and Technology. In *TEXNH*, pp. 19–36, pls. II-VIII.

Elster, E. S., and M. Nikolaidou
In press Shell Artifacts from Sitagroi, Northeast Greece, Symbolic Implications of Gathering in an Early Agricultural Society. In *From the Jomon to Starr Carr: Prehistoric Foragers of Temperate Eurasia*, edited by L. Janik, S. Kaner, A. Matsui, and P. Rowley-Conwy. British Archaeological Reports International Series.

Evans, A.
1921 *The Palace of Minos: A Comparative Account of the Successive Stages of the Early Cretan Civilization as Illustrated by the Discoveries at Knossos*, Vol. 1. London: Macmillan.

Evans, J., and C. Renfrew
1992 *Excavations at Saliagos near Antiparos*. BSA. London: Thames and Hudson.

Evans, J. D., and C. Renfrew
1968 *Excavations at Saliagos near Antiparos*. Supplementary Volume 5. London: Thames and Hudson.

Evans, R. K.
1986 The Pottery of Phase III. In *Sitagroi 1*, pp. 393–428.

Falkenstein, A.
1965 Zu den Tontafeln aus Tartaria. *Germania* 43:269–273.

Fol A., R. Katincharov, J. Lichardus, F. Bertemes, and I. K. Iliev
1989 Bericht über die bulgarisch-deutschen Ausgrabungen in Drama (1983–1988). *BRGK* 70:5–127.

Forbes, R. J.
1950 *Metallurgy in Antiquity*. Studies in Ancient Technology. Leiden: E.J. Brill.

Foster, C.
1997 Preliminary Report on the Examination of Palaeo-Ethnobotanical Remains from Dimitra, N. Greece. In *Neolithiki Makedonia*, pp. 217–219.

Fotiadis, M.
1984 *Natural and Human Ecology in the Serres Basin*. Ph.D. Dissertation, University of Michigan, Ann Arbor. Ann Arbor: University Microfilms International.

1997 Dimitra, Eastern Macedonia: Reconstructing the Economic Model of a Neolithic Community's Natural Environment. In *Neolithiki Makedonia*, pp. 63–79.

Francis, P., Jr.
1989 The Manufacture of Beads from Shell. *In Proceedings of the 1986 Shell Bead Conference, Selected Papers*, edited by C. F. Hayes III, L. Ceci, and C. C. Bodner, pp. 25-36. Rochester, NY: Research Division of the Rochester Museum and Science Center.

French, D. H.
1961 Late Chalcolithic Pottery in North West Turkey and the Aegean. *AS* 11:99–142.

1964 Prehistoric Pottery from Macedonia and Thrace. *PZ* 42:30–48.

1967   Index of Prehistoric Sites in Central Macedonia. Athens: British School, unpublished manuscript.

Frierman, J.

1969   The Balkan Graphite Ware. *PPS* 35:42–44.

Frierman, J. D., E. Elster, and E. Gardner

1971   Ceramic Firing Temperature: A Simplified Method and Its Application to Archaeological Problems. Paper presented to the Archaeological Institute of America, San Francisco.

Fytikas, M. F., P. Innocenti, R. Manettis, A. Mazzuoli, A. Peccerillo, and L. Villari

1984   Tertiary to Quaternary Volcanism in the Aegean Region. In *The Geological Evolution of the Eastern Mediterranean*, edited by J. E. Dixon and A. H. F. Robertson, pp. 687-699. Geological Society Special Publication 17. Palo Alto, CA: Blackwell Scientific Publications.

Gabori, M.

1950   Quelques problèmes du commerce de l'obsidienne à l'âge préhistorique. *Archaeologiai Ertesito* 77:50–53.

Gale, N., and A. Stos-Gale

2000   Lead Isotope Analyses Applied to Provenance Studies. In *Modern Analytical Methods in Art and Archaeology*, edited by E. Ciliberto and G. Spoto, pp. 503–584. Chemical Analyses Series 155. New York: John Wiley and Sons.

Gale, N. H., Z. A. Stos-Gale, P. Lilov, M. Dimitrov, and T. Todorov

1991   Recent Studies of Eneolithic Copper Ores and Artefacts in Bulgaria. In *Découverte du métal*, edited by J. P. Mohen and C. Éluère, pp. 49–75. Paris: Picard.

Gale, N. H., Z. A. Stos-Gale, G. Maliotis, and N. Annetts

1997   Lead Isotope Data from the Isotrace Laboratory, Oxford: Archaeometry Data Base 4, Ores from Cyprus. *Archaeometry* 39 (1):237–246.

Gale, N. H., Z. A. Stos-Gale, A. Raduncheva, I. Ivanov, P. Lilov, T. Todorov, and I. Panayotov

In press   Early Metallurgy in Bulgaria. In *Early Metallurgy*, edited by P. Craddock. Special Publication, British Museum, London.

Gallis, K.

1987   Die stratigraphische Einordnung der Larisa Kultur: eine Richtigstellung. *PZ* 62:147–163.

1985   A Late Neolithic Foundation Offering from Thessaly. *Antiquity* 59:20-24.

1989   Atlas Proistorikon Oikismon tis Anat. Thessalikis Pediadas. *Thessaliko Imerologio*, tomos 16:6–32 (including map).

1990   Atlas Proistorikon Oikismon tis Anat. Thessalikis Pediadas. *Thessaliko Imerologio*, tomos 17:31–48; tomos 18:47–96.

1994   Results of Recent Excavations and Topographical Work in Neolithic Thessaly. In *La Thessalie, Quinze années de recherches archéologiques, 1975–1990. Bilans et perspectives. Actes du Colloque International, Lyon, 17–22 Avril 1990*, Vol. A, edited by K. Gallis, pp. 57–60. Athens: Greek Ministry of Culture.

1996   Central and Western Thessaly. In *Neolithic Culture in Greece*, edited by G. A. Papathanassopoulos, pp. 61–66. Athens: N. P. Goulandris Foundation, Museum of Cycladic Art.

Garašanin, M.

1958   Neolithikum und Bronzezeit in Serbien und Makedonien. *BRG* 39:1–130.

Garašanin, M. V., and Dehn, W.

1963   Thrakisch-makedonische Wohnhügelfunde in der Sammlung des vorgeschichtlichen Seminars zu Marburg/Lahn. *JRGZ* 10:1–33.

Gardner, E. J.

1979   Graphite Painted Pottery. *Archaeology* 32 (4):18–23.

Georgiev, G.

1958   Über einige Produktionwerkzeuge aus dem Neolithikum und Äneolithikum in Bulgarien. In *Studia in honorem D. Dečev*, pp. 369–375. Sofia: Bulgarian Academy of Sciences.

Georgiev, G., and N. Angelov

1957   Razkopi na selishtnata mogila do Ruse prez 1950–1953 godina. *IAI* 21:41–127.

Georgiev, G., N. Y. Merpert, R. V. Katincharov, and D. G. Dimitrov

1979   *Ezero: Ranobronzovoto Selishte*. Sofia: Arkheologicheski Institut, Bulgarian Academy of Sciences.

Ghirshman, R.

1938   *Fouilles de Sialk* I:38–40. Paris: Geuthner.

Gilmour, G. H.

1997   The Nature and Function of Astragalus Bones from Archaeological Contexts in the Levant and Eastern Mediterranean. *Oxford Journal of Archaeology* 16 (2):167–175.

Gimbutas, M.

1974   Chronology of Obre I and Obre II. In *Obre*, pp. 15–35.

1976a   Ideograms and Symbolic Design of Ritual Objects of Old Europe. In *To Illustrate the Monuments, Essays on Archaeology Presented to Stuart Piggott*, edited by J. V. S. Megaw, pp. 77–98. London: Thames and Hudson.

1976b   *Neolithic Macedonia as Reflected by Excavation at Anza, Southeast Yugoslavia*. Monumenta Archaeologica 1. Los Angeles: UCLA Institute of Archaeology.

1976c Ornaments and Other Small Finds. In *Neolithic Macedonia*, pp. 244–256.

1982 *The Goddesses and Gods of Old Europe*. Berkeley: UC Press; London: Thames and Hudson.

1986 Mythical Imagery of the Sitagroi Society; and Figurine Catalog. In *Sitagroi* 1, pp. 225–301.

1989a Figurines and Cult Equipment: Their Role in the Reconstruction of Neolithic Religion, and Appendix C, Catalog. In *Achilleion*, pp. 171–225, 228–250, and pp. 343–364 (pls. 7.1–7.22).

1989b Ornaments and Miscellaneous Objects. In *Achilleion*, pp. 251–258.

1989c *The Language of the Goddess*. San Francisco: Harper Collins.

1991 *The Civilization of the Goddess: The World of Old Europe*. San Francisco: Harper Collins.

Gimbutas, M., S. Winn, and D. Shimabuku, eds.

1989 *Achilleion, A Neolithic Settlement in Thessaly, Greece 6400–5600 B.C.* Monumenta Archaeologica 14. Los Angeles: UCLA Institute of Archaeology.

Glumac, P. D., and J. Todd

1991 Fifth Millennium BC Evidence for Metallurgical Processing of Copper and Copper Alloys in Southeast Europe. In *Materials Issues in Art and Archaeology* II, edited by P. B. Vandiver, J. Druzik, and G. S. Wheeler, pp. 637–642. Materials Research Society Symposia Proceedings 185. Pittsburgh: Materials Research Society.

Glumac, P., and R. Tringham.

1990 The Exploitation of Copper Minerals. In *Selevac*, pp. 549–565.

Gould, R.

1978 Beyond Analogy in Ethnoarchaeology. In *Explorations in Ethnoarchaeology*, edited by R. Gould, pp. 249–294. Albuquerque: University of New Mexico Press.

Gould, R., D. Koster, and A. Sontz

1971 The Lithic Assemblages of the Western Desert Aborigines. *AA* 36 (2):149–169.

Graburn, N., M. Lee, and J.-L. Rousselot

1996 *Catalogue Raisonnée of the Alaska Commercial Company Collection*. Phoebe Apperson Hearst Museum of Anthropology. Berkeley: University of California Press.

Grammenos, D.

1975 Apo tous proistorikos oikismos tis Anatolikis Makedonias. *AD* 30A:193–234.

1984 Neolithikes Erevnes stin Kentriki kai Anatoliki Makedonia, Thessaloniki. Doctoral dissertation, Section of History and Archaeology, Aristotelian University of Thessaloniki.

1991 *Neolithikes Erevnes stin Kentrike kai Anatoliki Makedonia*. Athens: Library of the Athens Archaeological Society.

1997a Meros I. Dimitra Proistorikos Oikismos Konta stis Serres. In *Neolithiki Makedonia*, pp. 25-227.

1997b Meros II. Neolithika themata apo ti Madedonia kai tin evryteri tis periochi. In *Neolithiki Makedonia*, pp. 267–316.

Grammenos, D., ed.

1997 *Neolithiki Makedonia*. Ypourgeio Politismou, Dimosieymata tou Arkaiolologikou Deltion Ar. 56. Athens: Ekdosi tou Tameiou Arkhaiologikon Poron ke Apallotrioseon.

Greenfield, H. J.

1991 A Kula Ring in Prehistoric Europe? A Consideration of Local and Interregional Exchange during the Late Neolithic of the Central Balkans. In *Between Bands and States*, edited by S. A. Gregg, pp. 287–308. Southern Illinois University, Center for Archaeological Investigation, Occasional Paper 9. Carbondale: Southern Illinois University.

Greeves, T. A. P.

1982 Review of *Gornoe delo i metallurgiya v drevneishei Bolgarii*, by E. Chernykh. *PPS* 48:538–544.

Greig, J. R. A., and J. Turner

1974 Some Pollen Diagrams from Greece and Their Archaeological Significance. *Journal of Archaeological Science* 1:177–194.

Gupta, H. O., O. Prakash, and J. Singh

1989 Influence of Endosperm Texture on Milling, Chemical Composition and Nutritive Quality in Maize. *Plant Foods for Human Nutrition* 39:235–243.

Hague, P. F.

1993 The Structural and Volcanic Evolution of Tertiary Basins along the Southern Margin of the Rhodope Massif, Northeastern Greece. Ph.D. dissertation, University of Southampton, U.K.

Halstead, P.

1981 Counting Sheep in Neolithic and Bronze Age Greece. In *Patterns of the Past: Studies in Honour of David Clarke*, edited by I. Hodder, G. Isaac, and N. Hammond, pp. 307–335. Cambridge: Cambridge University Press.

1993 *Spondylus* Shell Ornaments from Late Neolithic Dhimini, Greece: Specialized Manufacture or Unequal Accumulation? *Antiquity* 67:503–609.

1995 From Sharing to Hoarding: The Neolithic Foundations of Aegean Bronze Age Society. In *Politeia:*

Society and State in the Aegean Bronze Age. Proceedings of the 5th International Aegean Conference, University of Heidelberg, Archäologisches Institut, 10–13 April 1994, edited by R. Laffineur and W. D. Niemeier, 11–22. Aegaeum 13. Université de Liège: Histoire de l'art et archéologie de la Grèce antique, and University of Texas at Austin: Program in Aegean Scripts and Prehistory.

Halstead, P., and G. Jones
1987　Bioarchaeological Remains from Kalythies Cave. In *Neolithiki Periodes sta Dodecanese*, edited by A. Sampson, pp. 135–152. Athens: Ministry of Culture.

Hansen, J. M.
1991　*The Palaeoethnobotany of the Franchthi Cave. Excavations at Franchthi Cave, Greece*, Fasc. 7. Bloomington: Indiana University Press.

Hauptmann, A., F. Begemann, R. Heitkemper, E. Pernicka, and S. Schmitt-Strecker
1992　Early Copper Produced in Feinan, Wadi Araba, Jordan: The Composition of Ores and Copper. *Archeomaterials* 6 (1):1–33.

Haury, E. W.
1976　*The Hohokam, Desert Farmers and Craftsmen: Excavations at Snaketown 1964–65*. Tucson: University of Arizona Press.

Hayden, B.
1987　Traditional Metate Manufacturing in Guatemala Using Chipped Stone Tools. In *Lithic Studies among the Contemporary Highland Maya*, edited by B. Hayden, pp. 8–119. Tucson: University of Arizona Press.

Hayden, B., ed.
1979　*Lithic Use-Wear Analysis*. New York: Academic Press.

Hayden, B., and A. Cannon
1984　*The Structure of Material Systems: Ethnoarchaeology in the Maya Highlands*. Society for American Archaeology Papers 3. Washington, DC.

Heider, K.
1967　Archaeological Assumptions and Ethnographical Facts: A Cautionary Tale from New Guinea. *Southwestern Journal of Anthropology* 23:52–64.

Hellström, P.
1987　Small Finds. In *Paradeisos, A Late Neolithic Settlement in Aegean Thrace*, edited by P. Hellström, pp. 83–88. Memoir 7. Stockholm: Medelhausmuseet.

Hellström, P., ed.
1987　*Paradeisos, A Late Neolithic Settlement in Aegean Thrace*. Stockholm: Medelhausmuseet.

Helms, M. W.
1993　*Craft and the Kingly Ideal: Art, Trade, and Power*. Austin: University of Texas Press.

Heurtley, W. A.
1939　*Prehistoric Macedonia*. Cambridge: Cambridge University Press.

Higgs, E. S., and C. Vita-Finzi
1972　Prehistoric Economies: A Territorial Approach. In *Papers in Economic Prehistory*, edited by E. S. Higgs, pp. 27–36. Cambridge: Cambridge University Press.
1986　Appendix D: Site Catchment Analysis. In *Sitagroi 1*, pp. 144–146.

Hiller, S., and V. Nikolov
1997　*Karanovo, Die Ausgrabungen im Südsektor 1984–1992*, Band I.1 (Text), I.2 (Tafeln). Archäologisches Institut der Universät Salzburg and Archäologisches Institut mit Museum der Bulgarischen Akademie der Wissenschaften, Sofia. Salzburg and Sofia: Verlag Ferdinand Berger.

Hirao, Y., J. Enomoto, and H. Tachikawa
1995　Lead Isotope Ratios of Copper, Zinc and Lead Minerals in Turkey in Relation to the Provenance Study of Artifacts. In *Essays on Ancient Anatolia and Its Surrounding Civilisations*, edited by H. I. H. Prince Takahito Mikasa, pp. 89–114. Wiesbaden: Harrassowitz.

Hochstetter, A.
1987　*Die Kleinfunde. Kastanas: Ausgrabungen in einem Siedlungshügel der Bronze- und Eisenzeit Makedoniens, 1975–1979*. Prähistorische Archäologie in Südosteuropa 6. Berlin: Volker Spiess.

Hodder, I.
1990　*The Domestication of Europe: Structure and Contingency in Neolithic Societies*. Oxford: Basil Blackwell.

Hoffman, M.
1974　*The Warp-Weighted loom. Studies in the History and Technology of an Ancient Implement*. Oslo: Universitets Forlaget.

Hoglinger, P.
1997　Neolithisches Bein- und Geweihgerät. In *Karanovo, Die Ausgrabungen im Südsektor 1984–1992*. Band I.1, edited by S. Hiller and V. Nikolov, pp. 157–196. Archäologisches Institut der Universät Salzburg and Archäologisches Institut mit Museum der Bulgarischen Akademie der Wissenschaften, Sofia. Salzburg and Sofia: Verlag Ferdinand Berger.

Hood, M. S. F.
1967　The Tărtăria Tablets. *Antiquity* 41:99–113.

1973 An Early Oriental Seal Impression from Romania? *World Archaeology* 5:187–197.

Hood, S.

1981 *Excavations in Chios (1938–53). Prehistoric Emporio and Ayio Gala*, I. BSA Supplementary Volume 15. London.

1982 *Excavations in Chios (1938–53). Prehistoric Emporio and Ayio Gala*, II. BSA Supplementary Volume 16. London.

Hook, D. R., I. C. Freestone, N. D. Meeks, P. T. Craddock, and A. Moreno Onorato

1991 The Early Production of Copper Alloys in South East Spain. In *Archaeometry '90*, edited by E. Pernicka and G. Wagner. Basel.

Hoops, J.

1905 *Waldbaume and Kulturpflanzen in Germanischen Alternum.* Strasbourg: K. J. Trübner.

Hope Simpson, R., and O. T. P. K. Dickinson

1979 *A Gazetteer of Aegean Civilisation in the Bronze Age, 1: The Mainland and Islands.* SIMA 52. Göteborg: Paul Åstrom.

Hopf, M.

1958 Neolithische Getreidefunde aus Bosnien und der Herzegovina untersuchungsbericht. *Zemaljski musej u Bosni i Hercegovini Glasnik Arheologija*, n.s., XIII:97–103. Sarajevo.

1961a Untersuchungs bericht über Kornfunde aus Vršnik. *Zbornik na Shitpskiot Naroden Musei* II (1960–1961). Stip.

1961b Pflanzen aus Bosnien und der Herzegowina. In *Zuchter* 31:239–247.

1962 Bericht über die Untersuchung von Samen und Holzkohlenresten von der Argissa-Maghula aus den präkeramischen bis mittelbronzezeitlichen Schichten. In *Das prekeramische Neolithicum sowie die Tier- und Pflanzenreste)*, edited by V. Milojcić, J. Boessneck, and M. Hopf, pp. 101–110. Die Deutschen Ausgrabungen auf der Argissa-Maghula in Thessalien 1. Beiträge zur ur-und-frühgeschichtlen Archäologie des Mittelmeer-Kulturraumes Band 2 . Bonn.

1964 Nutzpflanzen von Lernäischen Golf. *JRGZ* 11. Mainz.

1967 Untersuchungsbericht ber die botanischen Reste aus der Neolithischen Ansiedlung in Gornja Tuzla. *Glasnik Zemaljksi Musej, Sarajevo*, XXI/XXII:169–171.

1971 Plant Remains from the Athenian Agora: Neolithic to Byzantine. In *The Athenian Agora: The Neolithic and Bronze Ages*, edited by S. A. Immerwahr, pp. 267–269. Princeton, NJ: American School of Classical Studies at Athens.

1973 Frühe Kulturpflanzen aus Bulgarien. *JRGZ* 20:1–55.

1974 Pflanzenreste aus Seidlungen der Vinča-Kultur in Jugoslawien. *JRGZ* 21:1–11.

Horsfall, G. A.

1987 Design Theory and Grinding Stones. *In Lithic Studies among the Contemporary Highland Maya*, edited by B. Hayden, pp. 332–377. Tucson: University of Arizona Press.

Hourmouziadis, G. C.

1994 *Ta Neolithika eidolia.* Proistorika Anagnosmata 4. Thessaloniki: Vanias.

Hurley, W.

1979 *Prehistoric Cordage.* Aldine Manuals on Archaeology 3. Taraxacum: Washington, DC.

Ioannou, G.

1987 *Paramithia tou Laoumas.* Athens.

Isaac, B. L.

1986 Introduction. In *Economic Aspects of Prehispanic Highland Mexico. Research in Economic Anthropology*, Supplement 2, edited by B. L. Isaac, pp. 1–19. Greenwich, CT: JAI Press.

Ivanov, I. S.

1991 Les objects métalliques de la nécropole chalcolithique de Varna. In *Découverte du métal*, edited by J. P. Mohen and C. Éluère, pp. 9–11. Paris: Picard.

Jacobsen, T. W., ed.

1993 *Excavations at Franchthi Cave, Greece*, Fasc. 8. Bloomington: Indiana University Press.

de Jesus, P. S.

1980 *The Development of Prehistoric Mining and Metallurgy in Anatolia.* BAR International Series 74. Oxford: British Archaeological Reports.

Johnson, J.

1987 Decorated Pottery. In *Paradeisos, A Late Neolithic Settlement in Aegean Thrace*, edited by P. Hellström, pp. 39–76. Stockholm: Medelhausmuseet.

Johnson M.

1999 Chronology of Greece and South-East Europe in the Final Neolithic and Early Bronze Age. *PPS* 65:319–336.

Jones, C. E., J. Tarney, J. A. Baker, and F. Gerouki

1992 Tertiary Granitoids of Rhodope, Northern Greece: Magmatism Related to Extensional Collapse of the Hellenide Orogen? *Tectonophysics* 210: 2195–2314.

Jovanović, B.

1971 *Metalurgija Eneolitskog Perioda Jugoslavije.* Belgrade: Arheološki Institut.

1982 *Rudna Glava.* Bor-Belgrade: Muzej Rudarstva i Metalurgije/Arheološki Institut.

1986 Early Metallurgy in Yugoslavia. In *The Beginning of the Use of Metals and Alloys*, edited by R. Maddin, pp. 69–79. Cambridge, MA: MIT Press.

1991 La métallurgie énéolithique du cuivre dans les Balkans. In *Découverte du métal*, edited by J. P. Mohen and C. Éluère, pp. 93–103. Paris: Picard.

Kaczanowska, M., and J. Kozlowski

1990 Chipped Stone Industry of the Vinča Culture. In *Vinča and Its World*, edited by D. Srejović and N. Tasić, pp. 35–47. Belgrade: Serbian Academy of Sciences and Arts.

Kahlenberg, M. H.

1977 *Textile Traditions of Indonesia.* Los Angeles: Los Angeles County Museum of Art.

Kalogirou, A.

1995 Greek Neolithic "Cheese Pots": A Reevaluation of the Evidence. Paper given at the 60th Annual SAA Meetings, Minneapolis.

Kancev, K. [see also Kunchev, K.]

1972 The Tools from the Occupation Site of Ezero, District of Sliven, as a Source for the Study of the Economics of Early Bronze Age Society. In *Thracia*, pp. 57–77. Kongres po trakologiia, Serdicae. Sofia: Acadmeiae Litterarum Bulgarilae.

Karali, L.

1991 Parure en coquillage du site de Dimitra en Macédoine protohistorique. In *Thalassa: L'Égée préhistorique at la mer. Actes de la troisième rencontre Égéenne internationale de l'Université de Liège, 23–25 avril 1990*, edited by R. Laffineur and L. Basch, pp. 315–322. Aegaeum 7. Liège: Université de Liège.

Karali-Yannacopoulous, L.

1992 La parure. In *Dikili Tash*, pp. 159–164.

1996 Shell, Stone and Bone jewellery. In *Neolithic Culture in Greece*, edited by G. A. Papathanassopoulos, pp. 165–166. Athens: N. P. Goulandris Foundation, Museum of Cycladic Art.

1997 Dimitra, matériel malacologique. In *Neolithiki Makedonia*, pp. 200–211.

Karimali, L.

1995 *The Neolithic Mode of Production and Exchange Reconsidered: Lithic Production and Exchange Patterns in Thessaly, Greece, during the Transitional Late Neolithic- Bronze Age Period.* Ph.D. dissertation, Boston University. Ann Arbor, MI: University Microfilms International.

Katz, S. H., M. L. Hediger, and L. A. Valleroy

1974 Traditional Maize Processing Techniques in the New World: Traditional Alkali Processing Enhances the Nutritional Quality of Maize. *Science* 184:765–773.

Keeley, L.

1980 *Experimental Determination of Stone Tool Uses.* Chicago: University of Chicago Press.

1996 *War before Civilization.* New York: Oxford University Press.

Keighley, J. M.

1986 The Pottery of Phases I and II. In *Sitagroi 1*, pp. 345–390.

Kenoyer, M. J.

1983 *Shell Working Industries of the Indus Civilization: An Archaeological and Ethnographic Perspective.* Ph.D. dissertation, Department of South and Southeast Asian Studies, University of California, Berkeley. Ann Arbor, MI: University Microfilms International.

1986 The Indus Bead Industry: Contributions to Bead Technology. *Ornament* 10 (1):18–23.

1991 Ornament Styles of the Indus Valley Tradition: Evidence from Recent Excavations at Harappa, Pakistan. *Paléorient* 17 (2):79–98.

Kilikoglou, V, Y. Bassiakos, A. P. Grimanis, K. Souvatzis, B. Pilali-Papasteriou, and A. Papanthimou-Papaefthimou

1996 Carpathian Obsidian in Macedonia, Greece. *Journal of Archaeological Science* 23 (3):343–349.

Killen, J.

1964 The Wool Industry of Crete in the Late Bronze Age. *BSA* 59:1–15.

Kingery, W. D., and J. D. Frierman

1974 The Firing Temperature of a Karanovo Sherd and Inferences about South-East European Refractory Technology. *PPS* 40:204–205.

Kohl, G., and H. Quitta

Berlin radiocarbon measurements II. *Radiocarbon* 8:27-45.

Kolocotroni, C.N.

1992 The Origin and Emplacement of the Vrontou Granite, Serres, Greece. Ph.D. dissertation, University of Edinburgh, U.K.

Körber-Grohne, U.

1991 The Determination of Fibre Plants in Textiles, Cordage and Wickerwork. In *New Light on Early Farming*, edited by J. Renfrew, pp. 93–104. Edinburgh: Edinburgh University Press.

Koukouli, H.
1967 Archaiotites kai mnimeia Anatolikis Makedonias. *AD* 22B:417–432.
1969 Archaiotites kai mnimeia Anatolikis Makedonias. *AD* 24B:346–357.

Koukouli-Chrysanthaki, H.
1970 Archaiotites kai mnimeia Anatolikis Makedonias. *AD* 25B:397–404.
1992 *Protoistoriki Thassos: ta nekrotafeia tou oikismou Kastri.* Dimosieumata tou Archaiologikou Deltion 45. Athens: Ypourgeio Politismou, Tameio Archaiologikon Poron.
1993 Dikili Tash. *To Ergon tis Archaiologikis Etaireias*: 68-75.

Koukouli-Chrysanthaki, H., I. Aslanis,
F. Konstantopoulou, and M. Valla
1997 Anaskafi ston proistoriko oikismo Promahonas-Topolnica kata to 1995. *AEMΘ* 9:435–440.

Koukouli-Chrysanthaki, H., E. Tsouri, K. Trakosopoulou,
K. Peristeri, K. Trandalidou, V. Poulios, N. Zikos,
X. Savvopoulou, A. Emery-Barbiet, M. Magafa, and
P. Tsombos
2000 *Archaeological Museum of Drama.* Exhibition program. Drama: Ministry of Culture, 18th Directorate of Prehistoric and Classical Antiquities.

Kourtessi-Philippakis, C.
1997 Les industries lithiques taillées de Dimitra. In *Neolithiki Makedonia*, pp. 212–216.

Kozlowski, J.
1982 La Néolithisation de la zone balkano-danubienne du point de vue des industries lithiques. In *Origin of the Chipped Stone Industries of the Early Farming Cultures of the Balkans*, pp. 130–170. Prace Archeologiczne 33. Warsaw: Panstwowe Wydawn, Naukowe.

Kozlowski, J., and M. Kaczanowska
1986 *Gomolava, Chipped Stone Industries of the Vinča Culture.* Krakow.

Kozlowski, J., and S. Kozlowski, eds.
1987 *Chipped Stone Industries of the Early Farming Cultures of Europe.* Warsaw: University of Warsaw Press.

Kramer, C.
1982 *Village Ethnoarchaeology: Rural Iran in Archaeological Perspective.* Studies in Archaeology. New York: Academic Press.

Krause, V. M., H. V. Kuhnlein, C. Y. Lopez-Palacios,
K. L. Tucker, M. Ruz, and N. W. Solomons
1993 Preparation Effects on Tortilla Mineral Content in Guatemala. *Archivos Latinoamericanos de Nutrición* 43:73–77.

Kroll, H.
1979 Kulturpflanzen aus Dhimini. In *Festschrift Maria Hopf*, edited by U. Körber-Grohne. Archaeo-Physica 8. Köln: Reinland Verlag GMBH.
1983 *Die Pflanzenfunde. Kastanas: Ausgrabungen in einem Seidlungshügel der Bronze- und Eisenzeit Makedoniens 1975-1979.* Prähistorische Archäologie in Südosteuropa 2. Berlin: Volker Spiess.
1984 Bronze Age and Iron Age Agriculture in Kastanas, Macedonia. In *Plants and Ancient Man*, edited by W. van Zeist and W. A. Casparie. Rotterdam and Boston: A. A. Balkema.
1991 Südosteuropa. In *Progress in Old World Palaeoethnobotany, A Retrospective View on the Occasion of 20 Years of the International Work Group for Palaeoethnobotany*, edited by W. van Zeist, K. Wasylikova, and K-E. Behre. Rotterdam and Brookfield: A. A. Balkema.

Kronberg, P.
1969 Gliederung, Petrographie und Tektogenese des Rhodopen-Kristallins im Simvolon und Ost-Pangäon (Griechisch-Makedonien). *Geotektonische Forschungen* 31:1–49.

Kuhnlein, H. V., and D. H. Calloway
1979 Adventitious Mineral Elements in Hopi Indian Diets. *Journal of Food Science* 44:282–285.

Kunchev, K. [see also Kancev, K.]
1972 Opiti za klasifickatsiya na kremenite stragali ot eneolitni selishta v severoistochna Bulgariya. *IAI* 33:31–37.
1983 Neolithic tools in Bulgaria. In *Ancient Bulgaria*, edited by A. G. Poulter, pp.135–153. Nottingham: University of Nottingham.

Kyparissi-Apostolika, N.
1996 The Theopetra Cave. In *Neolithic Culture in Greece*, ed. G. A. Papathanassopoulos, pp. 67-68. Athens: N. P. Goulandris Foundation, Museum of Cycladic Art.

Kyriacopoulos, K.
1987 Geochronological-Geochemical-Mineralogical Study of Tertiary Plutonic Rocks of the Rhodope Massif and their Isotopic Characters. Ph.D. dissertation, University of Athens (in Greek).

Lamb, W.
1936 *Excavations at Thermi on Lesbos.* Cambridge: Cambridge University Press.

Larje, R.
1987 Animal Bones. In *Paradeisos, A Late Neolithic Settlement in Aegean Thrace*, edited by P. Hellström, pp. 89–118. Memoir 7. Stockholm: Medelhausmuseet.

LeMoine, G. M.
1994 Use Wear on Bone and Antler Tools from the Mackenzie Delta, Northwest Territories. *American Antiquity* 59 (2):316–333.

Leroi-Gourhan, A.
1982 The Archaeology of Lascaux Cave. *Scientific American* 246 (6):80–88.

Leroi-Gourhan, A., and J. Allain
1979 *Lascaux Inconnu*. Paris: CNRS.

Lewis, O.
1949 Husbands and Wives in a Mexican village: A Study of Role Conflict. *Am. Anth.* 51:602–611.

Lichardus, J., A. Fol, L. Getov, F. Bertemes, R. Echt, R. Katincharov, and I. K. Iliev
1996 Bericht über die bulgarisch-deutschen Ausgrabungen in Drama (1989–1995). *BRGK* 77:5–153.

Lillios, K.
1997 Amphibolite Tools of the Portuguese Copper Age (3000–2000 B.C.): A Geoarchaeological Approach to Prehistoric Economics and Symbolism. *Geoarchaeology: An International Journal* 12 (2):137–163.

1999 Objects of Memory: The Ethnography and Archaeology of Heirlooms. *Journal of Archaeological Method and Theory* 6 (3):235–262.

Lloyd, S., and J. Mellaart
1962 *Beycesultan*, Vol. I. London: British Institute of Archaeology at Ankara.

Logothetis, B. C.
1970 *The Development of the Vine and Viticulture in Greece Based on Archaeological Findings in the Area* (in Greek with an English summary). Thessaloniki: Thessaloniki University.

Leudtke, B. E.
1992 An Archaeologist's Guide to Chert and Flint. *Archaeological Research Tools* 7:91–96. Los Angeles: UCLA Institute of Archaeology.

Lyneis, M. M.
1988 Antler and Bone Artifacts from Divostin. In *Divostin*, pp. 301–319.

Maddin, R., T. S. Wheeler, and J. D. Muhly
1980 Distinguishing Artifacts Made of Native Copper. *Journal of Archaeological Sciences* 7:211–225.

Maddin, R., T. Stech, and J. D. Muhly
1991 Çayönü Tepesi. In *Découverte du métal*, edited by J. P. Mohen and C. Éluère, pp. 357–374. Paris: Picard.

Madsen, T.
1988 Multivariate Statistics and Archaeology. In *Multivariate Archaeology: Numerical Approaches in Scan-dinavian Archaeology*, edited by T. Madsen, pp. 7–27. Aarhus: Aarhus University Press.

Maggi, R., E. Starnini, and B. Voytek
1997 The Bone Tools from Arene Candide: Bernabó Brea Excavations. In *Arene Candide: A Functional and Environmental Assessment of the Holocene Sequence (Excavations Bernabó Brea-Cardini 1940–1950)*, edited by R. Maggi, pp. 514–554. Rome: il Calamo.

Makkay, J.
1975 Some Stratigraphical and Chronological Problems of the Tărtăria Tablets. *Mitteilungen des Archäologischen Instituts der Ungarischen Akademie der Wissenschaften* 5:13–31.

1984 *Early Stamp Seals in South-East Europe*. Budapest: Akadémiai Kiadó.

1991 The Most Ancient Gold and Silver in Central and South-East Europe. In *Découverte du métal*, edited by J. P. Mohen and C. Éluère, pp. 119–124. Paris: Picard.

Malamidou, D.
1997 Anaskafi ston proistoriko oikismo "Kryoneri" N. Kerdyllion. *AEMΘ* 509–538.

Manganas, A., and M. Economou
1988 On the Chemical Composition of Chromite Ores from the Ophiolitic Complex of Soufli, N.E. Greece. *Ofioliti* 13:15–27.

Manolakkakis, L.
1987 L'industrie lithique de Sitagroi III: Étude technologique du débitage. Unpublished M.A. thesis, University of Paris 1.

1994 L'industrie lithique taillée du chalcolithique des Balkans. Unpublished Ph.D. dissertation, University of Paris 1.

1996 Production lithique et émergence de la hiérarchie sociale: L'industrie lithique de l'Énéolithique en Bulgarie. *Bulletin de la Société préhistorique française* 93 (1):119–123.

Marangou, C.
1991 Figurines Néolithiques parées de Macédoine orientale (néolithique récent, Grèce du nord). In *Actes du XIIe Congrès internationale des sciences préhistoriques et protohistoriques, Bratislava, 1–7 septembre 1991*, Vol. 2, edited by J. Pavuk, pp. 327–334.

1992 *Eidolia: Figurines et miniatures du néolithique récent et du bronze ancien en Grèce*. BAR International Series 576. Oxford: British Archaeological Reports.

1996 Figurines and Models. In *Neolithic Culture in Greece*, edited by G. A. Papathanassopoulos, pp.

161–162. Athens: N. P. Goulandris Foundation, Museum of Cycladic Art.

1997 Neolithic Micrography: Miniature Modeling at Dimitra. In *Neolithiki Makedonia*, pp. 227–265.

Maratos, G.

1960 The Ophiolites of the Soufli Area. *Geological and Geophysical Research* 6 (2):83–178. (Greek text; English summary).

Marcus, M. I.

1993 Incorporating the Body: Adornment, Gender, and Social Identity in Ancient Iran. *Cambridge Archaeological Journal* 3 (2):157–178.

Masson, E.

1984 L' "écriture" dans les civilisations danubiennes Néolithiques. *Kadmos* 23 (2):89–123.

Mavriyiannaki, C.

1983 La double hache dans le monde hellénique à l'âge du Bronze. *Revue Archéologique* 2:195–228.

Mbofung, C. M. F., and R. Ndjouenkeu

1990 Influence of Milling Method and Peanut Extract on In-Vitro Iron Availability from Maize and Sorghum Flour Gruels. *Journal of Food Science* 55: 1657–1659, 1675.

McBryde, F. W.

1947 *Cultural and Historical Geography of Southwest Guatemala*. Smithsonian Institution, Institute of Social Anthropology 4. Washington, DC.

McGeehan-Liritzis, V., and N. H. Gale

1988 Chemical and Lead Isotope Analyses of Greek Late Neolithic and Early Bronze Age Metals. *Archaeometry* 30 (2):199–225.

McGuire, R. H., and Howard, A.V.

1987 The Structure and Organization of Hohokam Shell Exchange. *The Kiva* 52 (2):113–146.

McPherron, A.

1988 Miscellaneous Small Artifacts. In *Divostin*, pp. 325–336.

McPherron, A., and J. Gunn

1988 Quantitative Analysis of Excavated Materials at Divostin. In *Divostin*, pp. 359–379.

Melena, J.

1975 *Studies on Some Mycenaean Inscriptions from Knossos Dealing with Textiles*. *Minos*, Supplementary Vol. 5. Salamanca: Universidad de Salamanca.

Mellaart, J.

1970 *Excavations at Haçilar* I. Occasional Publication of the British Institute of Archaeology, Ankara. Edinburgh: Edinburgh University Press.

Miller, D.

1985 *Artefacts as Categories: A Study of Ceramic Variability in Central India*. Cambridge: Cambridge University Press.

Miller, M.

1996 The Manufacture of Cockle Shell Beads at Early Neolithic Franchthi Cave, Greece: A Case of Craft Specialisation. *Journal of Mediterranean Archaeology* 9 (1):7–37.

1997 Jewels of Shell and Stone, Clay and Bone: The Production, Function, and Distribution of Aegean Stone Age Ornaments. UMI Microform: 9735158.

Millon, R.

1973 *Urbanization at Teotihuacan, Mexico*. Vol. 1: *The Teotihuacan Map*. Part I: *Text*. Austin: University of Texas Press.

Millon, R., R. B. Drewitt, and G. L. Cowgill

1973 *Urbanization at Teotihuacan, Mexico*, Vol. 1: *The Teotihuacan Map*. Part 2: *Maps*. Austin: University of Texas Press.

Milojčić, V.

1949 *Chronologie der jüngeren Steinzeit Mittel- und Südosteuropas*. Berlin: Gebruder Mann.

Milojković, J.

1990 The Anthropomorphic and Zoomorphic Figurines. In *Selevac*, pp. 397–439.

Moesta, H.

1989 Zur Metallurgie des Meissels von Drama. In Bericht über die bulgarisch-deutschen Ausgrabungen in Drama (1983–1988), by A. Fol et al. *BRGK* 70:107–127.

Molleson, J.

1994 The Eloquent Bones of Abu Hureyra. *Scientific American* (August 1994):70–75.

Moore, A.

1975 The Excavation of Tell Abu Hureyra in Syria. *PPS* 41:50–77.

Moorey, P. R. S.

1994 *Ancient Mesopotamian Materials and Industries: The Archaeological Evidence*. Oxford and New York: Clarendon Press.

Mould, C. A., C. Ridley, and K. G. Wardle

2000 Additional Clay and Shell Small Finds. In *Servia I*, pp. 264–290.

Movius, H., N. David, and H. Bricker

1968 The Analysis of Certain Major Classes of Upper Palaeolithic Tools. *Bulletin of the American School of Prehistoric Research* 26.

Muhly, J. D.

1988 The Beginnings of Metallurgy in the Old World. In *The Beginning of the Use of Metals and Alloys*, edited by R. Maddin, pp. 1–20. Cambridge, MA: MIT Press.

Murdock, G., and C. Provost
1973 Factors in the Division of Labor by Sex. *Ethnology* 12:23–35.

Murra, J.
1962 Cloth and Its Function in the Inca State. *Am. Anth.* 64 (4):710–728.

Murray, P.
1980 Discard Location: The Ethnographic Data. *AA* 45 (3):490–502.

Mylonas, G. E.
1929 *Excavations at Olynthos 1: The Neolithic Settlement.* John Hopkins University Studies in Archaeology 6. Baltimore.
1941 The Site of Akropotamos and the Neolithic Period of Macedonia. *AJA* 45:557–76.

Mylonas, G., and G. Bakalakis
1938 Anaskaphai neolithikon synoikismon Akropotamou kai Polystylou. *Praktika tis Archaiologikes Etaireias*: 103–111.

Nachev, I., G. Kovnurko, and K. Kunchev
1981 Kremachnite skali v Balgariya i tyakhnata eksploatatsiya. *Interdisciplinarni Issledovaniya* 7–8:41–58.

Nachev, I. K., and K. Kunchev
1984 Aptian and Quaternary Flint in Northeast Bulgaria. In *III Seminar in Petroarchaeology*, pp. 65–82. Plovdiv: University of Plovdiv "Paisii Hilendarski."

Nadel, D., A. Danin, E. Werker, T. Schick, M. E. Kislev, and K. Stewart
1994 19,000-Year-Old Twisted Fibers from Ohalo II. *Current Anthropology* 35 (4):451–457.

Nakou, G.
1995 The Cutting Edge: A New Look at Early Aegean Metallurgy. *Journal of Mediterranean Archaeology* 8 (2):1–32.

Nandris, J.
1977 A Re-consideration of the Southeast European Sources of Archaeological Obsidian. *Bulletin of the University of London Institute of Archaeology* 12:71–94.

Naroll, R.
1962 Floor Area and Settlement Population. *AA* 27 (4): 587–589.

Nelson, G. C.
1966 *Ceramics.* New York: Holt, Rinehart, and Winston.

Nikolaidou, M.
1997 Ornament Production and Use at Sitagroi, Northeast Greece: Symbolic and Social Implications of an Early Bronze Age Technology. In *TEXNH*, pp. 177–196.

In press Technotropikes epiloges tis Neolithikis kosmimatopoiias: To anthropino prosopo mias proistorikis technologias. In *I proistoriki erevna stin Ellada kai oi prooptikes tis: theoritikoi kai methodologikoi provlimatismoi*, edited by G. Hourmouziadis et al. *Archaiologiko symposio sti mnimi tou D. R. Theocharis, Thessaloniki-Kastoria, 26–28 Noemvriou 1998.*

O'Dell, B. L., A. R. de Boland, and S. R. Koityonann
1972 Distribution of Phytate and Nutritionally Important Elements among the Morphological Components of Cereal Grains. *Journal of Agriculture and Food Chemistry* 20:718–721.

Odell, G.
1977 The Application of Microwear Analysis to an Entire Prehistoric Settlement. Ph.D. dissertation, Harvard University.

Onassoglou, A.
1996 Seals. In *Neolithic Culture of Greece*, edited by G. Papathanassopoulos, pp. 163-164. Athens: N. P. Goulandris Foundation, Museum of Cycladic Art.

Papaefthymiou-Papanthimou, A.
1989 Oi anaskafes tou D. R. Theochari sto neolithiko oikismo tou Sesklou: Pilina mikroantikeimena. Manuscript on file. Thessaloniki: Department of Archaeology, University of Thessaloniki.
1992 Weaving Implements from Sesklo. *Praktika*, pp. 78–84. Athens.
1997 *Teletourgikos kallopismos sto proistoriko Aigaio.* Thessaloniki: Vanias.

Papaefthymiou-Papanthimou, A., and A. Pilali-Papasteriou
1998 I Yfantiki ston Proistoriko Oikismo tou Archondiko. In *Mneias Charin Tomos sti Mneme Marias Siganidou*, edited by M. Lilimbaki-Akamati and K. Tsakalou-Tzanavari. Thessaloniki: Ypourgeio Politismou.

Papathanassopoulos, G. A.
1962 Kykladika Naxou. *AD* 17: Meletai: 104–151.
1996 Neolithic Diros: The Alepotrypa Cave. In *Neolithic Culture in Greece*, edited by G. A. Papathanassopoulos, pp. 80–84. Athens: N. P. Goulandris Foundation, Museum of Cycladic Art.

Papathanassopoulos, G. A., ed.
1996 *Neolithic Culture in Greece.* Athens: N. P. Goulandris Foundation, Museum of Cycladic Art.

Pappa, M.
1995 O proistorikos oikismos tou Makrygialou. In *Pydna*, edited by M. Besios and M. Pappa, pp. 15–35. Katerini: Pieriki Anaptyxiaki.

Păunescu, A.
1970   Evoluția uneltelor și armelor de piatră cioplită desco-
        perite pe teritoriul României. Biblioteca Arheoligica
        15. Bucharest: Editura Academiei RSR.

Payne, S.
1972   Partial Recovery and Sample Bias: The Results of
        Some Sieving Experiments. In *Papers in Economic
        Prehistory*, edited by E. Higgs, pp. 49–64. Cam-
        bridge: Cambridge University Press.
1973   Kill-off Patterns in Sheep and Goats: The Mandi-
        bles from Asvan Kale. *Anatolian Studies* 23:281–
        304.
1975   Partial Recovery and Sample Bias. In *Archaeologi-
        cal Studies*, edited by A. T. Clason, pp. 7–17.
        Amsterdam: Elsevier.

Pedersen, B., and B. O. Eggum
1983a   The Influence of Milling on the Nutritive Value of
        Flour from Cereal Grains, 3: Barley. *Qualitas Plan-
        tarum: Plant Foods for Human Nutrition* 33:99–112.
1983b   The Influence of Milling on the Nutritive Value of
        Flour from Cereal Grains, 4: Rice. *Qualitas Plan-
        tarum: Plant Foods for Human Nutrition* 33:267–
        278.
1983c   The Influence of Milling on the Nutritive Value of
        Flour from Cereal Grains, 5: Maize. *Qualitas Plan-
        tarum: Plant Foods for Human Nutrition* 33:299–311.

Pedersen, B., K. E. Bach Knudsen, and B. O. Eggum
1989   Nutritive Value of Cereal Products with Empha-
        sis on the Effect of Milling. In *Nutritional Value of
        Cereal Products, Beans and Starches*, edited by G. H.
        Bourne, pp. 1–91. World Review of Nutrition and
        Dietetics 60. Basel: Karger.

Peristeri, K.
1994   Anaskafiki erevna sto neolithiko oikismo tou
        Arkadikou Dramas (1991–92). *I Drama ke I periohi
        tis. Istoria ke politismos*, B' Epistimoniki Synantisi,
        Drama 18–22 May 1994, pp. 103–110.

Perlès, C.
1987   *Les industries lithiques taillées de la grotte de Franch-
        thi (Grèce)*. Excavations at the Franchthi Cave,
        Greece, Fasc. 3, 5. Bloomington: Indiana Univer-
        sity Press.
1990   L'outillage de pierre taillée néolithique en Grèce:
        Approvionnement et exploitation des matières
        premières. *BCH* 114 (1):1–42.
1992   Systems of Exchange and Organization of Pro-
        duction in Neolithic Greece. *Journal of Mediterra-
        nean Archaeology* 5 (2):115–164.
1994   Technologie des industries lithiques thessal-
        iennes: Problèmes méthodologiques et perspec-

tives socio-economiques. In *La Thessalie, quinze
        années de recherches archéologiques, 1975–1990,
        Bilans et perspectives. Actes du Colloque Interna-
        tional, Lyon, 17–22 Avril 1990*, Vol. A, edited by K.
        Gallis, pp. 71–78. Athens: Greek Ministry of Cul-
        ture.

Perlès, C., and P. Vaughan
1983   Pièces lustrées, travail des plantes et moissons à
        Franchthi, Grèce, Xème–IVème mill. B.C.). In
        *Traces d'utilisation sur les outils néolithiques du
        Proche-Orient*, edited by M.-C. Cauvin, pp. 209–
        224. Lyon: Maison de l'Orient.

Perlès, C., and Vitelli, K. D.
1994   Technologie et fonction des premières produc-
        tions céramiques de Grèce. In *Terre cuite et société.
        la céramique, document technique, economique, cul-
        turel*, XIV Rencontres internationales d'archéolo-
        gie et d'histoire d'Antibes. Editions APDCA,
        Juan-les-Pins, 1994, pp. 225–241.
1999   Craft Specialization in the Neolithic of Greece. In
        Neolithic Society in Greece, edited by P. Halstead,
        pp. 96–107. Sheffield Studies in Aegean Archaeol-
        ogy 2. Sheffield: Sheffield Academic Press.

Pernicka, E., F. Begemann, S. Schmitt-Strecker, and
G. A. Wagner
1993   Eneolithic and Early Bronze age Copper Artifacts
        from the Balkans and Their Relation to Serbian
        Copper Ores. *PZ* 68:1–57.

Pernicka, E., T. C. Seeliger, G. A. Wagner, F. Begemann,
S. Schmitt-Strecker, C. Eibner, Ö. Öztunali, and I. Baranyi
1984   Archeometallurgische untersuchungen in Nord-
        westanatolien. *JRGZ* 31:533–599.

Petkov, N.
1964   Four de potier du site énéolithique près du vil-
        lage Galabovci, arrondissement de Sofia. *Arche-
        ologiya* (Sofia) 6:48–59.

Pétrequin, P.
1993   North Wind, South Wind, Neolithic Technical
        Choices in the Jura Mountains, 3700–2400 BC. In
        *Technological Choices: Transformation in Material Cul-
        tures Since the Neolithic*, edited by P. Lemonnier, pp.
        36–76. London and New York: Routledge.

Phelps, W.
2000   The Figurines. In *Servia I*, pp. 192–206.

Phelps, W. W., G. J. Varouphakis, and R. E. Jones
1979   Five Copper Axes from Greece. *BSA* 74:175–184.

Pilali-Papasteriou, A.
1992   Oi sphragides apo to Sesklo kai ta provlemata tis
        thessalikes sphragidoglyphias. In *Diethnes
        Synedrio yia tin Archaia Thessalia*. Athens.

Pini, I.
1975   *Corpus der Minoischen und Mykenischen Siegel V, 2: Kleinere Griechische Sammlungen.* Berlin: Mann.

Poplin, F.
1991   Reflexions sur l'astragale d'or de Varna: Les pieds fourchus et la métallisation de l'animal. In *Découverte du métal*, edited by J. P. Mohen and C. Éluère, pp. 31–42. Paris: Picard.

Popovitch, V.
1965   Une Civilisation Égéo-orientale sur le moyen Danube. *Revue archéologique* 2:1.

Popper, K. R.
1959   *The Logic of Scientific Discovery.* New York: Basic Books.

Possehl, G. L.
1981   Cambay Beadmaking: An Ancient Craft in Modern India. *Expedition* 23 (4):39–47.

Prendi, F.
1966   La civilisation préhistorique de Maliq. *Studia Albanica* 3:255–280.
1967   Le néolithique et l'énéolithique en Albanie. *Iliria* 6:49–99.

Prinz, B.
1988   The Ground Stone Industry from Divostin. In *Divostin*, pp. 255–285.

Rackham, O.
1986   Charcoal. In *Sitagroi 1*, pp. 55–62.

Radovanovic, I., M. Kaczanowska, J. Kozlowski, M. Pawlikowski, and B. Voytek
1984   *The Chipped Stone Industry from Vinča.* Belgrade: University of Belgrade.

Rapp, G., E. Henrickson, M. Miller, and S. Aschenbrenner
1980   Trace Element Fingerprinting as a Guide to the Geographic Sources of Native Copper. *Journal of Metals* 32:35–45.

Rappaport, R.
1968   *Pigs for the Ancestors.* New Haven and London: Yale University Press.

Rasson, J.
1988   Loom Weights. In *Divostin*, pp. 337–338.

Rathje, W. L.
1972   Praise the Gods and Pass the Metates: A Hypothesis of Development of Lowland Rainforest Civilizations in Mesoamerica. In *Contemporary Archaeology*, edited by M. Leone, pp. 365–392. Carbondale: Southern Illinois University Press.

Reese, D. S.
1987   Marine and Fresh-water Molluscs. In *Paradeisos: A Late Neolithic Settlement in Aegean Thrace*, edited by P. Hellström, pp. 119–134. Memoir 7. Stockholm: Medelhausmuseet.

Reinhold, J. G., H. Hedayati, A. Lahimgaradeh, and K. Nasr
1973   Zinc, Calcium, Phosphorus and Nitrogen Balance of Iranian Villagers Following a Change from Phytate-Rich to Phytate-Poor Diet. *Ecology of Food and Nutrition* 2:157–162.

Reinhold, J. G., and J. S. Garcia-Lopez
1979   Fiber of the Maize Tortilla. *American Journal of Clinical Nutrition* 32:1326–1329.

Reinhold, J. G., J. S. Garcia-Lopez, and P. Garzon
1981   Binding of Iron by Fiber of Wheat and Maize. *American Journal of Clinical Nutrition* 34:1384–1391.

Renfrew, C.
1966   The Tărtăria Tablets. *Nestor* (December): 469–470.
1967   Cycladic Metallurgy and the Aegean Early Bronze Age. *AJA* 71:2–26.
1969   The Autonomy of the South-East European Copper Age. *PPS* 35:12–47.
1970a   The Burnt House at Sitagroi. *Antiquity* 44:131–134.
1970b   The Tree-Ring Calibration of Radiocarbon: An Archaeological Evaluation. *PPS* 36:280–311.
1970c   The Place of the Vinča Culture in European Prehistory. *ZNM* 6:45–57.
1971   Sitagroi, Radiocarbon and the Prehistory of South-East Europe. *Antiquity* 41:276–288.
1972   *The Emergence of Civilisation: The Cyclades and the Aegean in the Third Millennium BC.* London: Methuen.
1973a   *Before Civilisation.* New York: Alfred Knopf.
1973b   Excavations at Sitagroi-Photolivos 1969. *AD* 25:405–406.
1973c   Sitagroi and the Independent Invention of Metallurgy in Europe. In *Actes du VIIIe Congrès International des Sciences Préhistoriques et Protohistoriques, Beograd 1971*, Belgrade, UISPP, Vol. 2:473–481.
1973d   Trade and Craft Specialisation. In *Neolithic Greece*, edited by D. Theocharis, pp. 179–200, pls. 117–120. Athens: National Bank of Greece.
1975a   Activities at Sitagroi 1970. *AD* 26:419–420.
1975b   Trade as Action at a Distance: A Question of Integration and Communication. In *Ancient Civilisation and Trade*, edited by J. A. Sabloff and C. C. Lamberg-Karlovsky, pp. 3–60. Albuquerque: University of New Mexico Press.
1977   Alternative Models for Exchange and Spatial Distribution. In *Exchange Systems in Prehistory*, edited by T. K. Earle and J. E. Ericson, pp. 71–90. New York: Academic Press.

1978a Varna and the Social Context of Early Metallurgy. *Antiquity* 52:199–203.

1978b The Anatomy of Innovation. In *Social Organization and Settlement*, edited by D. Green, C. Haselgrove, and M. Spriggs, pp. 89–117. BAR International Series 47 (i). Oxford: British Archaeological Reports.

1986a Development of the Project. In *Sitagroi 1*, pp. 15–24.

1986b The Excavated Areas. In *Sitagroi 1*, pp. 175–222.

1986c Northeastern Greece: The Archaeological Problem. In *Sitagroi 1*, pp. 3–13.

1986d Sitagroi in European Prehistory. In *Sitagroi 1*, pp. 477–486.

1986e The Sitagroi Sequence. In *Sitagroi 1*, pp. 147–174.

1986f Varna and the Emergence of Wealth in Prehistoric Europe. In *The Social Life of Things*, edited by A. Appadurai, pp. 141–168. Cambridge: Cambridge University Press.

1987 Old Europe or Ancient East? The Clay Cylinders of Sitagroi. In *Proto-Indo-European: The Study of a Linguistic Problem. Studies in Honor of Marija Gimbutas*, edited by S. N. Skomal and E. C. Polomé, pp. 339–374. Washington, DC: Institute for the Study of Man.

2001 Symbol Before Concept: Material Engagement and the Early Development of Society. In *Archaeological Theory Today*, edited by I. Hodder, pp. 122–140. Cambridge: Polityn Press; Malden, MA: Blackwell.

Renfrew, C., J. R. Cann, and J. E. Dixon

1965 Obsidian in the Aegean. *BSA* 60:225–247.

Renfrew, C., Gimbutas M., and Elster E. S., eds.

1986 *Excavations at Sitagroi, A Prehistoric Village in Northeast Greece*, Vol. 1. Monumenta Archaeologica 13. Los Angeles:UCLA Institute of Archaeology.

Renfrew, C., and J. M. Wagstaff

1982 *An Island Polity: The Archaeology of Exploitation on Melos*. Cambridge: Cambridge University Press.

Renfrew, J. M.

1966 A Report on Recent Finds of Carbonized Cereals and Seeds from Prehistoric Thessaly. *Thessalika* 5: 21–36.

1968 Appendix 1: The Cereal Remains. In *Excavations at Saliagos near Antiparos*, edited by J. D. Evans and C. Renfrew, pp. 139–141. BSA. London: Thames and Hudson.

1969 Palaeoethnobotany and the Neolithic Cultures of Greece and Bulgaria. Ph.D. dissertation, University of Cambridge.

1971 Recent Finds of *Vitis* from Neolithic Contexts in S. E. Europe. *Acct Mushroom Agriculture Prague* 6 (1–2).

1972 The Plant Remains (Appendix V). In *Myrtos, An Early Bronze Age Settlement in Crete*, edited by P. M. Warren. BSA Supplementary Volume 7:315–317. Athens.

1973a Agriculture. In *Neolithic Greece*, edited by D. Theocharis, pp. 147–164. Athens: National Bank of Greece.

1973b *Palaeoethnobotany: The Prehistoric Food Plants of the Near East and Europe*. London: Methuen; New York: Columbia University Press,

1973c Plant Remains: An Interim Report. In *Excavations in the Franchthi Cave, 1969-1971*, Pt. 1, edited by T. W. Jacobsen. *Hesperia* 42 (1):45–88.

1976a Report on the Carbonized Grains and Seeds from Obre I, Kakanj and Obre II. In *Obre*, pp. 47–53.

1976b Carbonized Seeds from Anza. In *Neolithic Macedonia*, pp. 300–312. Monumenta Archaeologica 1. Los Angeles: UCLA Institute of Archaeology.

1977 Appendix 3: The Seeds from Area K. In *Keos 1: Kephala, A Late Neolithic Settlement and Cemetery*, edited by J. Coleman, pp. 127–128. Princeton: American School of Classical Studies.

1989 Carbonized Grains and Seeds. In *Achilleion*, pp. 307–310.

1995 Palaeoethnobotanical Finds of *Vitis* from Greece. In *The Origins and Ancient History of Wine*, edited by P. E. McGovan, S. J. Fleming, and S. H. Katz, pp. 255–268. University of Pennsylvania Museum and Gordon and Breach Publishers.

1997 Plant Husbandry at Prehistoric Dimitra. In *Neolithiki Makedonia*, pp. 220–226.

Rhomiopoulou, K.

1965 Proistorikos oikismos Lafroudas. *AD* 20:461.

Ridley, C., K. A. Wardle, and C. A. Mould, eds.

2000 *Servia I: Anglo-Hellenic Rescue Excavations 1971–73, Directed by Katerina Rhomiopoulou and Cressida Ridley*. BSA Supplementary Volume 32. Athens: BSA.

Rimantiene, R.

1979 *Sventoji: Narvos Kulturos Gyvenietes*. Vilnius: Mokslas.

Rodden, R. J.

1962 Excavations at the Early Neolithic Site at Nea Nikomedeia, Greek Macedonia. *PPS* 28:267–288.

1964a A European Link with Chatal Huyuk: Uncovering 7th Millennium Settlement, Pt. II. *Illustrated London News* 18 (April): 604–607.

1964b Recent Discoveries from Macedonia: An Interim Report. *Balkan Studies* 5:109–124.

1965   An Early Neolithic Village in Greece. *Scientific American* 212 (4):83–92.

Rodden, R., and K.A. Wardle, eds.

ND   *Nea Nikomedeia: The Excavation of an Early Neolithic Village in Northern Greece 1961–1964*, Vol. II. BSA Supplementary vol. London: British School of Athens. Forthcoming.

Runnels, C. N.

1981   A Diachronic Study and Economic Analysis of Millstones from the Argolid, Greece. Ph.D. dissertation, Department of Anthropology, Indiana University.

1985   Trade and the Demand for Millstones in Southern Greece. In *Prehistoric Production and Exchange: The Aegean and Eastern Mediterranean*, edited by A. B. Knapp and T. Stech, pp. 30–43. Monograph 24. Los Angeles: UCLA Institute of Archaeology.

Runnings, A. L., D. Bentley, and C. E. Gustafson

1989   Use-Wear on Bone Tools: A Technique for Study under the Scanning Electron Microscope. In *Bone Modification*, edited by R. Bonnichsen and M. Sorg, pp. 259–266. Orono: Center for the Study of the First Americans, University of Maine.

Russell, N.

1982   Experimentation as an Aid to the Study of Manufacture and Utilization Patterns of Bone Artifacts. Paper presented at the 47th Annual Meeting of the Society for American Archaeology, Minneapolis.

1990   The Bone Tools. In *Selevac*, pp. 521–548.

1992   More than Calories and Protein: The Social Significance of Meat. Paper presented at the meetings of the American Anthropological Association, San Francisco.

Sackett, J. S.

1966   Quantitative Analysis of Upper Paleolithic Stone Tools. *Am. Anth.* 68, Ser. 2, Pt. 2:356–394.

Sampson, A.

1988   *Neolithiki katoikisi sto Giali tis Nisyrou*. Athens: Euboike Archaiophilos Etaireia.

Sanders, W. T., and R. S. Santley

1983   A Tale of Three Cities: Energetics and Urbanization in Pre-Hispanic Central Mexico. In *Prehistoric Settlement Patterns: Essays in Honor of Gordon R. Willey*, edited by E. Z. Vogt and R. M. Leventhal, pp. 243–291. Albuquerque: University of New Mexico Press; Cambridge, MA: Peabody Museum of Archaeology and Ethnology, Harvard University.

Sarpaki, A.

1995   Toumba Balomenou, Chaeronia: Plant Remains from the Early and Middle Neolithic Levels. In

Res Archaeobotanicae. International Work Group Palaeoethnobotany, Proceedings of the 9th Symposium, Kiel 1992, edited by H. Kroll and P. Pasternak.

Schachermeyr, F.

1955   *Die ältesten Kulturen Griechenlands*. Stuttgart: W. Kohlhammer.

Schenk, P. F.

1970   Geologie des westlichen Pangaion in Griechisch-Ostmakedonien. *Beihefte der geologisches Jahrbuch* 88:81–132.

Schick, T.

1986   Perishable Remains from the Nahal Hemar Cave. *Journal of the Israel Prehistoric Society* 19:84–86.

Schiffer, M.

1987   *Formation Processes of the Archaeological Record*. Albuquerque: University of New Mexico Press.

Schliemann, H.

1881   *Ilios, The City and Country of the Trojans*. London.

1970   *Troy and Its Remains* (1881). Translated by P. Smith. New York: Arno Press.

Schmandt-Besserat, D.

1992a   *Before Writing. 1: From Counting to Cuneiform*. Austin: University of Texas Press.

1992b   *Before Writing, II: A Catalog of Near Eastern Tokens*. Austin: University of Texas Press.

1996   *How Writing Came About*. Austin: University of Texas Press.

Schmidt, H.

1902   *Heinrich Schliemann's Sammlung Trojanischer Altertümer*. Berlin: Reimer.

Schneider, J.

1987   The Anthropology of Cloth. In *Annual Review of Anthropology* 16:409–448.

Schröter, C.

1895   Über die Pflanzenreste der Neolithisehn Landseidlung von Butmir in Bosnien. In *Die neolithische Station von Butmir bei Sarajevo in Bosnien (1895–1898)*, edited by M. Hoernes, W. Radimsk, F. Fiala, and C. Schröter. Vienna: A. Holzhausen.

Seeliger, T. C., E. Pernicka, G. A. Wagner, F. Begemann, S. Schmitt-Strecker, C. Eibner, Ö. Öztunali, and I. Baranyi

1985   Archäometallurgische Untersuchungen in Nord- und Ostanatolien. *JRGZ* 32:597–659.

Séfériadès, M.

1983   Dikili Tash: Introduction à la préhistoire de la Macédoine orientale. *BCH* 107:635–677.

1992a   Le métal. In *Dikili Tash*, pp. 113–119.

1992b   L'os et le bois de cervide. In *Dikili Tash*, pp. 99–112.

1992c   L'outillage. In *Dikili Tash*, pp. 59–83.

1995 Préhistoire: Le commerce des *Spondyles*, de la Mer Égée à la Manche. *Archéologia* 309:42–50.

Séfériadès, M., with V. Anagnostopoulos

1992 La pierre polie. In *Dikili Tash*, pp. 84–99.

Seiler-Baldinger, A. M.

1994 *Textiles: A Classification of Techniques*. Washington, DC: Smithsonian Institution Press.

Selmeczi, L.

1969 Das Wohnhaus der Körös-gruppe von Tiszajenö neuere angabau zu den haustypen des Frühneolithikums. *A Móra Ferenc Múzeum Évkönyve*, 2: 17–22. Szeged.

Semenov, S. A.

1964 *Prehistoric Technology*. 3rd ed. Trans. by M. W. Thompson. Bath, England: Adams and Dart.

Shackleton, J.

1983 An Approach to Determining Prehistoric Shellfish Collecting Patterns. In *Animals and Archaeology 2: Shell Middens, Fishes and Birds*, edited by C. Grigson and J. Clutton-Brock, pp. 77–85. BAR International Series 183. Oxford: British Archaeological Reports.

1988 *Marine Molluscan Remains from Franchthi Cave*. Excavations at Franchthi Cave, Greece, Fasc. 4. Bloomington and Indianapolis: Indiana University Press.

Shackleton, N.

1968 Worked Shell. In *Excavations at Saliagos near Antiparos*, edited by J. D. Evans and C. Renfrew, pp. 68–69. BSA Supplementary Volume 5. Oxford: Thames and Hudson.

1972 The Shells. In *Myrtos, An Early Bronze Age Settlement in Crete*, edited by P. Warren, pp. 321–325. BSA Supplementary Volume 7. Oxford: Thames and Hudson.

Shackleton, N., and C. Renfrew

1970 Neolithic Trade Routes Re-aligned by Oxygen Isotope Analysis. *Nature* 228 (5276):1062–1065.

Shepard, A. B.

1965 *Ceramics for the Archaeologist*. Washington, DC: Carnegie Institution.

Shepherd, W.

1972 *Flint*. London: Faber and Faber.

Sherratt, A.

1972 Socio-economic and Demographic Models for the Neolithic and Bronze Ages of Europe. In *Models in Archaeology*, edited by D. Clarke, pp. 477–541. London: Methuen.

1976 Resources, Technology and Trade: An Essay in Early European Metallurgy. In *Problems in Eco-nomic and Social Archaeology*, edited by G. Sieveking, I. Longworth, and D. Wilson, pp. 557–581. London: Duckworth.

1981 Plough and Pastoralism: Aspects of the Secondary Products Revolution. In *Pattern of the Past: Studies in Honour of David Clarke*, edited by I. Hodder, G. Isaac, and N. Hammond, pp. 261–305. Cambridge: Cambridge University Press.

1983 The Secondary Exploitation of Animals in the Old World. *World Archaeology* 15:287–316.

1984 Social Evolution: Europe in the Later Neolithic and Copper Ages. In *European Social Evolution: Archaeological Perspectives*, edited by J. Bintliff, pp. 123–134. Bradford: University of Bradford.

1986 The Pottery of Phases IV and V. In *Sitagroi 1*, pp. 429–473.

Skourtopoulou, K.

1998 The Chipped Stone Industries of Makri: Domestic Contexts of Tool Production and Use. *Saguntum (Plav)* 31:40–45.

Smith, A, B., and C. Poggenpoel

1988 The Technology of Bone Tool Fabrication in the South-Western Cape, South Africa. In *World Archaeology*, edited by J. Graham-Campbell, pp. 103–115. Routledge.

Smith, M. L.

1999 The Role of Ordinary Goods in Premodern Exchange. *Journal of Archaeological Method and Theory* 6:109–135.

Snow, P., and K. O'Dea

1981 Factors Affecting the Rate of Hydrolysis of Starch in Food. *American Journal of Clinical Nutrition* 34: 2721–2727.

Soffer, O., J. M. Adovasio, and D. C. Hyland

2000 The "Venus" Figurines: Textiles, Basketry, Gender, and Status in the Upper Paleolithic. *Current Anthropology* 41 (4):511–538

Soffer, O., J. M. Adovasio, D. C. Hyland, B Klíma, and J. Svoboda

1998a Perishable Industries from Dolní Vestonice I: New Insights into the Nature and Origin of the Gravettian. Paper presented at the 63rd annual meeting of the Society for American Archaeology, Seattle, Washington.

1998b Perishable Technologies and the Genesis of the Eastern Gravettian. *Anthropologie* 36 (1–2):43–68.

Solomons, N. W., and R. J. Cousins

1984 Zinc. In *Absorption and Malabsorption of Mineral Nutrients*, edited by N. W. Solomons and I. H. Rosenberg. New York: A. R. Liss.

Sorensen, M.-L. Stig
1991 The Construction of Gender Through Appearance. In *The Archaeology of Gender. Proceedings of the 22nd Annual Conference of the Archaeological Association of the University of Calgary,* edited by D. Walde and N. D. Willows, pp. 121–129. Calgary: University of Calgary, Archaeological Association.

Spears, C. S.
1990 Macrocrystalline Stone Artifacts. In *Selevac,* pp. 495–520.

Spector, J. D.
1991 What This Awl Means: Toward a Feminist Archaeology. In *Engendering Archaeology: Women and Prehistory,* edited by J. M. Gero and M. W. Conkey, pp. 388–406. Cambridge, MA: Basil Blackwell, Inc.

Spink, M.
1982 *Metates as Socioeconomic Indicators during the Classic Period at Copan, Honduras.* Ph.D. dissertation, Department of Anthropology, Pennsylvania State University. Ann Arbor: University Microfilms International.

Steele, D. G., and B. W. Baker
1993 Multiple Predation: A Definitive Human Hunting Strategy. In *From Bones to Behavior,* edited by J. Hudson, pp. 9–37. Carbondale: Center for Archaeological Investigations, Southern Illinois University at Carbondale.

Sterud, E. L., and A. K. Sterud
1974 A Quantitative Analyses of the Material Remains. In *Obre,* pp. 155–279.

Stocks, D. A.
1993 Making Stone Vessels in Ancient Mesopotamia and Egypt. *Antiquity,* 67 (256):596–603.

Stos-Gale, Z. A.
1992 The Origin of Metal Objects from the Early Bronze Age Site of Thermi on Lesbos. *Oxford Journal of Archaeology* 11 (2):155–178.
1993 Lead Isotope Provenance Studies of the Early Minoan Weapons. In *Trade and Exchange in Prehistoric Europe,* edited by C. Scarre and F. Healy, pp. 115–129. Oxford: Oxbow Books.
1998 The Role of Kythnos and Other Cycladic Islands in the Origins of Early Minoan Metallurgy. In *Kea-Kythnos: History and Archaeology: Proceeding of the Kea-Kythnos Conference, Kea, June 1994,* edited by L. Mendoni and A. Mazarakis, pp. 717–736. Paris and Athens: Diffusion de Boccard.
2001 Minoan Foreign Relations and Copper Metallurgy in MMIII–LMIII Crete. In *The Social Context of Technological Change,* edited by A. Shortland, pp. 195–210. Oxford: Oxbow Books.

Stos-Gale, Z. A., N. H. Gale, and N. Annetts
1996 Lead Isotope Analyses of Ores from the Aegean. *Archaeometry* 38 (2):381–390.

Stos-Gale, Z. A., N. H. Gale, J. Houghton, and R. Speakman
1995 Lead Isotope Analyses of Ores from the Western Mediterranean. *Archaeometry* 37 (2):407–415.

Stos-Gale, Z. A., N. H. Gale, N. Annetts, T. Todorov, P. Lilov, A. Raduncheva, and I. Panayotov
1998a Lead Isotope Data from the Isotrace Laboratory, Oxford: Archaeometry Database 5, Ores from Bulgaria. *Archaeometry* 40 (1):217–226.
1998b A Preliminary Survey of the Cypriot Slag Heaps and Their Contribution to the Reconstruction of Copper Production on Cyprus. In *Metallurgica Antiqua, in Honour of Hans-Gert Bachmann and Robert Maddin,* edited by T. Rehren, A. Hauptmann, and J. Muhly, pp. 235–262. Bochum: Deutches Bergbau Museum.

Stos-Gale, Z. A., A. Sampson, and E. Mangou
1999 Analyses of Metal Artifacts from the Early Helladic Cemetery of Manika on Euboea. *Aegean Archaeology* 3:49–62. Warsaw: Art and Archaeology.

Stratouli, G.
1993 Osteina Ergalei. In *Skoteini, Tharrounia: The Cave, the Settlement and the Cemetery,* edited by A. Sampson, pp. 496–526. Athens: Eleftheroudakis.

Sugaya, C.
1993 The Stone Axes of Tharrounia. In *Skoteini, Tharrounia: The Cave, the Settlement and the Cemetery,* edited by A. Sampson, pp. 442–447. Athens: Eleftheroudakis.

Taborin, Y.
1993 *La parure en coquillage au Paléolithique.* Gallia Préhistoire XXIXe Supplément. Paris: Centre nationale de la recherche scientifique.

Theocharis, D.
1971 *The Prehistory of Eastern Macedonia and Thrace.* Ancient Greek Cities 9. Athens: Centre of Ekistics.
1973 *Neolithic Greece.* Athens: National Bank of Greece.

Theocharis, D., and K. Rhomiopoulou
1961 Anaskaphi Ntikili Tas. *Praktika tis en Athinais Archaiologikis Etairias:* 81–87 (pls. 42–46).

Todorova, H.
1978 *The Eneolithic Period in Bulgaria in the Fifth Millennium B.C.* BAR International Series 49. Oxford: British Archaeological Reports.

1982 *Kupferzeitliche Siedlungen in Nordostbulgarien.* Munich: Verlag C. H. Beck.

1991 Die Kupferzeit Bulgariens. In *Die Kupferzeit als historische Epoche*, edited by J. Lichardus, pp. 89–94. Saarbrücker Beiträge zur Altertumskunde 55. Bonn: Rudolf Habelt GMBH.

Todorova, H., and I. Vajsov

1993 *Novokamennata epocha v Bălgarija.* Sofia: Verlag Nauka I Izkustvo.

Tornaritis, G.

1987 *Mediterranean Sea Shells.* Nicosia: Proodos Printing and Publishing Co.

Torrence, R.

1986 *Production and Exchange of Stone Tools.* Cambridge: Cambridge University Press.

Tosi, M., and M. Vidale

1990 4th Millennium BC Lapis Lazuli Working at Mehrgahr, Pakistan. *Paléorient* 16 (2):89–99.

Toufexis, G.

1996 House Models. In *Neolithic Culture in Greece*, edited by G. A. Papathanassopoulos, pp. 146–151. Athens: N. P. Goulandris Foundation, Museum of Cycladic Art.

Touloumis, K., and K. Peristeri

1991 Anaskafi ston Arkadiko Dramas 1991: Prokatarktikes paratiriseis gia tin organosi ke ti xrisi tou xorou me vasei ti diakrisi esoterikon ke eksoterikon xoron. In *AEMΘ* 5:359–369.

Trandalidou, K.

1998 Agriculture, Animal Husbandry, Hunting and Fishing. In *Neolithic Culture in Greece*, edited by G. A. Papathanassopoulos, pp. 95–102. Athens: N. P. Goulandris Foundation, Museum of Cycladic Art.

Treuil, R., ed.

1992 *Dikili Tash: Village préhistorique de Macédoine orientale I: Fouilles de Jean Deshayes (1961–1975).* BCH Supplément 24. Athens: École Française d' Athènes.

Triantafyllos, D.

1986 Proskinites Rodopis. *To Ergon tis Arkhaiologikis Etaireias* (1986):50.

Tringham, R.

1968 A Preliminary Study of the Early Neolithic and Latest Mesolithic Blade Industries in Southeast and Central Europe. In *Studies in Ancient Europe*, edited by J. Coles and D. Simpson, pp. 45–70. Leicester: Leicester University Press.

1971 *Hunters, Fishers and Farmers of Eastern Europe, 6000-3000 BC.* London: Hutchinson University Press.

1978 Experimentation, Ethnoarchaeology and the Leapfrogs in Archaeological Methodology. In *Explorations in Ethnoarchaeology*, edited by R. Gould, pp. 169–199. Albuquerque: University of New Mexico Press.

1984 Analysis of the Flaked Stone Assemblage from Sitagroi. In *Third Seminar on Petroarchaeology, Plovdiv–Bulgaria: Reports*, edited by K. S. Kunchev, I. K. Nachev, and N. T. Tcholakov, pp. 257–269. Plovdiv: Bulgarian Academy of Sciences Institute of Archaeology.

1988 Microwear Analysis of the Chipped Stone Assemblage from Divostin. In *Divostin*, pp. 203–224.

1991 In Anbetracht der Vinča-Pločnik-Phase der Vinča-Kultur: Die Manipulierung der Zeit. In *Die Kupferzeit als historische Epoche*, edited by J. Lichardus, pp. 271–286. Saarbrücker Beiträge zur Altertumskunde 55. Bonn: Rudolf Habelt GMBH.

1992 Life after Selevac. *Balcanica* 23:133–145.

Tringham, R., G. Cooper, G. Odell, B. Voytek, and A. Whitman

1974 Experimentation in the Formation of Edge-Damage: A New Approach to Lithic Analysis. *Journal of Field Archaeology* 1 (1–2):171–196.

Tringham, R., and Krstić, D.

1990 Conclusion: Selevac in the Wider Context of European Prehistory. In *Selevac*, pp. 437–494.

Tringham, R., and M. Stevanović

1990 The Nonceramic Uses of Clay. In *Selevac*, pp. 323–396.

Tsountas, C.

1908 *Ai Proistorikai Akropoleis Diminiou kai Sesklou.* Athens: Bibliothêkê tês en Athenais Archaeologikês Hetairias.

Tsuneki, A.

1987 A Reconsideration of *Spondylus* Shell Rings from Agia Sofia Magoula, Greece. *Bulletin of the Ancient Orient Museum* 9:1–15.

1989 The Manufacture of *Spondylus* Shell Objects at Neolithic Dhimini, Greece. *Orient* 25:1–21.

Tylecote, R. F.

1962 *Metallurgy in Archaeology.* London: E. Arnold.

Vajsov, I.

1993 Die frühesten Metalldolche Südost- und Mitteleuropas. *PZ* 68:103–145.

Valamoti, S.

1997a Arhaivotanika katalipa apo ton iskismo tou Arhontikou: Anakafiki periodos Septemvriou 1993. *AEMΘ* 7:155–158.

1997b Plant Remains from Neolithic Makri. *Saguntum (Plav)* 31:47–51.

1998 Agrotikes drastiriotites kai diatrofi sto neolithiko oikismo tou Arkadikou: Mia prokatarktiki eksétasi ton arhaiovotanikon dedoménon. *I Dráma kai i Perioxi tis Istoría kai Politismós* 2. Drama.

van Zeist, W.

1975 Preliminary report on the Botany of Gomolava. *Journal of Archaeological Science* 2:315–325.

Vaughan, P., C. Jarrige, and P. Anderson-Gerfaud

1987 Sickles and Harvesting Motions in Baluchistan (Pakistan). In *La main et l'outil manches et emmanchements préhistoriques*, edited by D. Stordeur, pp. 311–318. Lyon: G. S. Maison de l'Orient.

Vencl, S.

1959 Spondylové Sperky v Podunajském Neolitu. *Archeologické Rozheldy* 11:599–742.

1971 Soucasny stav pozvani postmesolitickych industru v Ceskoslovensku. In *Z badan nad krzemieniarstwem Neoliticznym i Eneoliticznym*, edited by J. Kozlowski, pp. 74–99. Krakow.

Vita-Finzi, C.

1969 *The Mediterranean Valleys.* Cambridge: Cambridge University Press.

Vlassa, N.

1963 Chronology of the Neolithic in Transylvania, in the Light of the Tărtăria Settlement's Stratigraphy. *Dacia* 7:485–494.

Vogt, E. Z.

1970 *The Zinacantecos of Mexico.* New York: Holt, Rinehart & Winston.

Voytek, B.

1985 *The Exploitation of Lithic Resources in Neolithic Southeast Europe.* Ph.D. dissertation, University of California, Berkeley. Ann Arbor: University Microfilms International.

1990 The Use of Stone Resources. In *Selevac*, pp. 437–494.

Wace, A. J. B., and M. S. Thompson

1912 *Prehistoric Thessaly.* Cambridge: Cambridge University Press.

Wagner, G. A., and G. Weisgerber

1988 Antike Edel- und Buntmetallgewinnung auf Thasos. *Der Anschnitt* 6. Bochum: Deutchen Bergbau Museum.

Wagner, G. A., E. Pernicka, M. Vavelidis, I. Baranyi, and I. Bassiakos

1986 Archaeometallurgische Untersuchungen auf Chalkidiki. *Der Anschnitt* 38 (5–6):166–186. Bochum: Deutchen Bergbau Museum.

Walton, P.

1989 *Textiles, Cordage, and Raw Fibre from 16–22 Coppergate.* York Archaeological Trust, Vol. 17, Fasc. 5. London: CBA.

Wardle, K., ed.

1996 *Nea Nikomedeia: The Excavation of an Early Neolithic Village in Northern Greece, 1961–1964, Directed by R. J. Rodden.* BSA Supplementary Volume 25. London: British School at Athens.

Webb, W. F.

1948 *Handbook for Shell Collectors.* Rev. ed. Lee Publications.

Weide, D.

1976 Source Areas of Lithic Materials. In *Neolithic Macedonia*, pp. 279–282.

Weinberg, S. S.

1965 *The Stone Age in the Aegean.* Cambridge: Cambridge University Press.

Welch, F. B.

1919 Macedonia—Prehistoric Pottery. *BSA* 23:44-50.

Wertime, T. A.

1964 Man's First Encounter with Metallurgy. *Science* 146 (3649):1257–1267.

1973 How Metallurgy Began: A Study in Diffusion and Multiple Innovation. In *Actes du VIIIe Congrès international des sciences préhistoriques et protohistoriques, Beograd 1971*, Belgrade, UISPP, Vol. 2:481–492.

Weisshaar, H.-J.

1980 Ägäische Tonanker. *Mitteilungen des deutschen archäologischen Instituts zu Athen* 95:33–49. Berlin.

1989 *Die deutschen Ausgrabungen auf der Pevkakia-Magula in Thessalien I: Das späte Neolithikum und das Chalkolithikum.* Bonn: Rudolf Habelt Verlag.

Weisberger, G., ed.

1980 *5000 Jahre Feuersteinbergbau.* Bochum: Deutschen Bergbau Museum.

Wickham-Jones, C. R.

1985 The Importance of Craftsmen: Stone. In *Symbols of Power at the Time of Stonehenge*, edited by D. V. Clarke, T. G. Gowie, and A. Foxon. Edinburgh: National Museum of Antiquities of Scotland.

Wiener, A., and J. Schneider

1989 *Cloth and Human Experience.* Washington: Smithsonian Institution Press.

Willms, C.

1985 Neolithischer *Spondylus* schmuck: Hundert Jahre Forschung. *Germania* 63 (2):331–343.

Winn, S. M. M.

1973 The Signs of the Vinča Culture, An Internal Analysis: Their Role, Chronology and Independence from Mesopotamia. Ph.D. dissertation, University of California at Los Angeles.

1981 *Pre-Writing in Southern Europe: The Sign System of the Vinča Culture, ca. 4000.* Calgary: Western Publishers.

Winn, S., and D. Shimabuku

1989a Architecture and Sequence of Building Remains. In *Achilleion*, pp. 32–74.

1989b Bone and Ground Stone Tools. In *Achilleion*, pp. 259–272.

Woodward, Λ.

1936 A Shell Bracelet Manufactory. *AA* 2:117–125.

Yannouli, E.

1994 Aspects of Animal Use in Prehistoric Macedonia, Northern Greece. Ph.D. dissertation, Department of Archaeology, University of Cambridge.

1997 Dimitra, A Neolithic and Early Bronze Age Site in Northern Greece: The Faunal Remains. In *Neolithiki Makedonia*, pp. 101–127.

Yener, K. A., E. Geçkinli, and H. Özbal

1996 A Brief Survey of Anatolian Metallurgy prior to 500 BC. In *Archaeometry 1994*, edited by S. Demirci, O. M. Özer, and G. D. Summers. Ankara: Tübitak.

Yener, K. A., E. V. Sayre, H. Özbal, E. C. Joel, I. L. Barnes, and R. H. Brill

1991 Stable Lead Isotope Studies of Central Taurus Ore Sources and Related Artefacts from Eastern Mediterranean Chalcolithic and Bronze Age Sites. *Journal of Archaeological Science* 18 (5):541–577.

Yerkes, R., and N. Kardulias

1993 Recent Developments in the Analysis of Lithic Artifacts. *Journal of Archaeological Research* 1 (2): 89–120.

Younger, J.

1991 Seals? from Middle Helladic Greece. *Hydra* 8:35–54.

Zachos, K. L.

1990 The Neolithic Period in Naxos. In *Cycladic Culture: Naxos in the Third Millennium BC*, edited by L. Marangou, pp. 29–38. Athens: N. P. Goulandris Foundation.

1996a Metal Jewelry. In *Neolithic Culture in Greece*, edited by G. A. Papathanassopoulos, pp. 166–167. Athens: N. P. Goulandris Foundation, Museum of Cycladic Art.

1996b Metallurgy. In *Neolithic Culture in Greece*, edited by G. A. Papathanassopoulos, pp. 140–145. Athens: N. P. Goulandris Foundation, Museum of Cycladic Art.

Zervos, C.

1962 *Naissance de la Civilisations en Grèce*. Paris: Editions Cahiers d'Art.

Plates

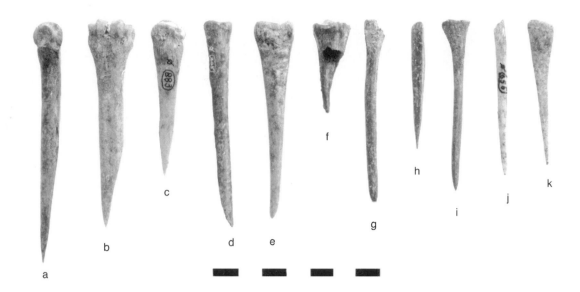

Plate 2.1. Pointed tools on metapodials: (a) phase II, SF 3750, distal metapodial, split, figure 2.2b; (b) phase III, SF 207, distal metapodial, not split; (c) phase III, SF 883, split proximal metapodial, base modified; (d) phase III, SF 205, split proximal metapodial, base modified; (e) phase IV, SF 25, split proximal metapodial, base modified, figure 2.2d; (f) phase II, SF 3133, proximal metapodial, not split, roe deer, figure 2.2a, plate 2.3c; (g) phase IV, SF 4731, split proximal metapodial, base modified; (h) phase III, SF 3843; (i) phase V, SF 1804, split proximal metapodial, base modified; (j) phase V, SF 655; (k) phase V, SF 4432, split metapodial, base modified.

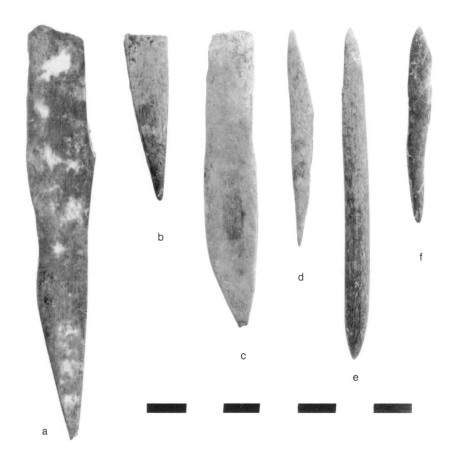

Plate 2.2. Pointed tools on ribs (a–d, f) and metapodial (e): (a) phase IV, SF 3687; (b) phase II, SF 440; (c) phase II, SF 3776, figure 2.3b; (d) phase V, SF 1081, double point, figure 2.5c; (e) phase IV, SF 1528, double point, figure 2.5b; (f) phase V, SF 1854.

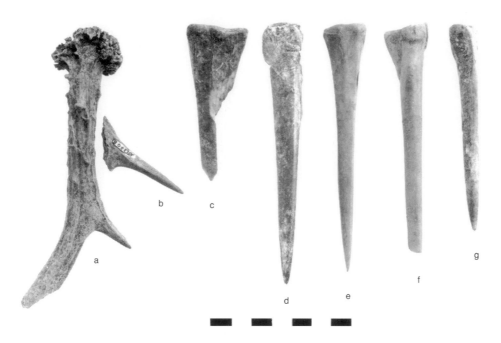

Plate 2.3. Pointed tools on antler (a, b), and deer metapodial (c–g): (a) phase I, SF 3711, figure 2.12a; (b) phase I, SF 3708; (c) phase II, SF 3133, figure 2.2a, plate 2.1f; (d) phase IV, SF 122, figure 2.2c; (e) phase III, SF 1194, figure 2.3c; (f) phase IV, SF 3709, figure 2.3d; (g) phase III, SF 3124.

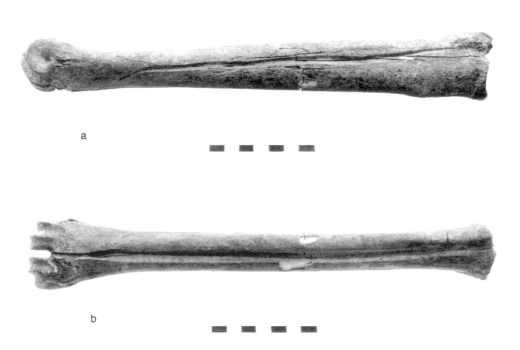

Plate 2.4. Two views of deer metapodial preform from the EBA Burnt House, phase Va, SF 4567: (a) vascular groove; (b) prepared groove, curving slightly.

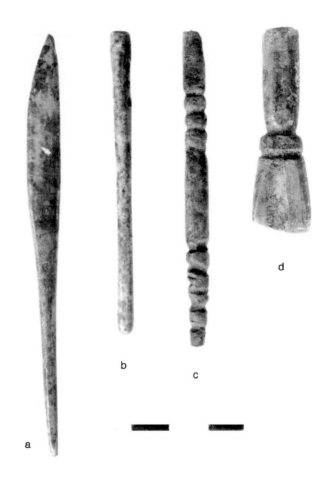

Plate 2.5. Elaborated bones, phase I: (a) SF 4112, double point, smooth, carved rib, figure 2.5a; (b) SF 916, rod, carefully formed and smoothed, figure 2.7a; (c) SF 3706, rod with sets of encircling grooves at each end, figure 2.18b; (d) SF 106, carved, smoothed broken handle, probably of spoon or spatula, figure 2.18a.

Plate 2.6. Antler, split beam segments with chisel-like ends (a-c) and a cut tine (d): (a) phase II, SF 246, figure 2.8a; (b) phase II, SF 5405, figure 2.9a; (c) phase IV, SF 4645, figure 2.8b; (d) phase IV, SF 874.

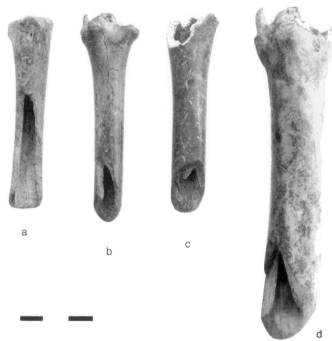

Plate 2.7. Chisel/bevel ended tools: sheep/goat proximal metacarpal (a), tibia (b, c), and red deer (d): (a) phase IV, SF 5427, figure 2.10a; (b) phase V, SF 4581, figure 2.10b; (c) phase V, SF 3779; (d) phase V, SF 5410, figure 2.10c.

a

b

c

d

Plate 2.8. Socketed antler tine, phase V: SF 310, figure 2.11a; note the worked point.

Plate 2.9. Antler tine, phase III: SF 2916, figure 2.11a.

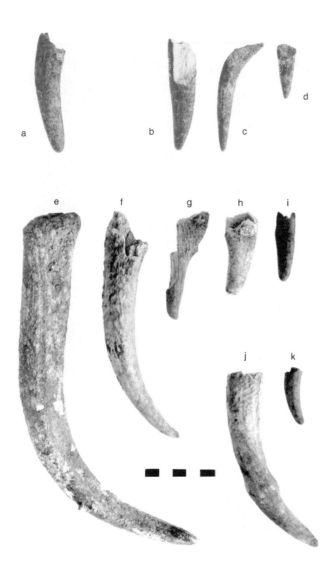

Plate 2.10. Antler tines, mostly waste: (a) phase I, SF 111, figure 2.9b; (b) phase II, SF 108, (c) phase II, SF 1752; (d) phase II, SF 434; (e) phase III, SF 1249, figure 2.11b, note cut-and-break marks; (f) phase III, SF 3132; (g) phase III, SF 3756; (h) phase III, SF 765; (i) phase III, SF 3452; (j) phase IV, SF 4732, note the pathological bump; (k) phase IV, SF 102.

Plate 2.11. Antler beam segments: (a) phase II, SF 447, "punch"?, figure 2.9c; (b) phase II, SF 4745, figure 2.8; note cut marks on the wider end of (b), and one end of (a) flattened and the other beveled.

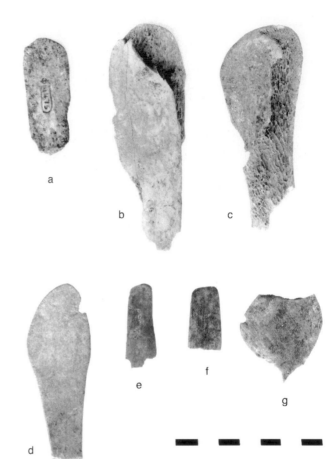

Plate 2.12. Fragments of spatulate shapes: antler (a, d), unsplit rib with beveled ends (b, c); antler (?) handle fragments (e, f), broken scoop (g): (a) phase V, SF 4475, figure 2.13c; (b) phase V, SF 1558, figure 2.13d; (c) phase V, SF 4829; (d) phase III, SF 501, figure 2.13d; (e) phase II, SF 4554; (f) phase I, SF 5352; (g) phase I, SF 5414.

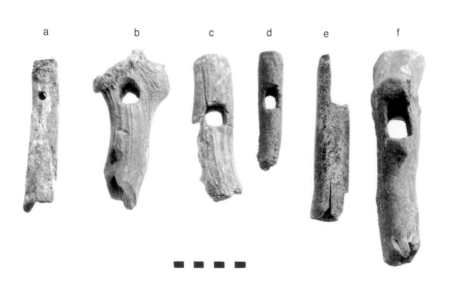

Plate 2.13. Antler beams, perforated (a) and socketed (b–f): (a) phase II, SF 4522, figure 2.14; (b) phase III, SF 521, figure 2.16; (c) phase III, SF 815; (d) phase III, SF 1422; (e) phase III, SF 4632; (f) phase III, SF 871, figure 2.15.

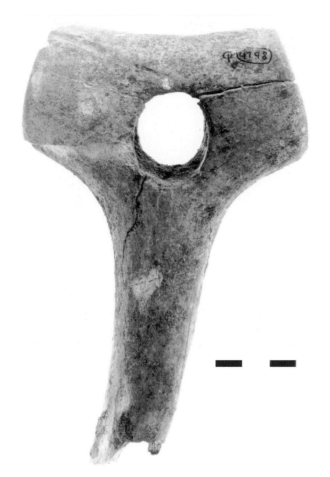

Plate 2.14. Socketed antler, phase III: SF 4798, figure 2.17.

Plate 2.15. Carved antlers, phase III: (a) SF 4848, unfinished ladle or spoon, figure 2.12b; (b) SF 4543, grooved and shaped long bone or rib, figure 2.18e.

a

b

Plate 2.16. Elaborated ribs, split, thinned, grooved, smoothed, phase III: (a) SF 3111, figure 2.18d; (b) SF 3449, figure 2.18c.

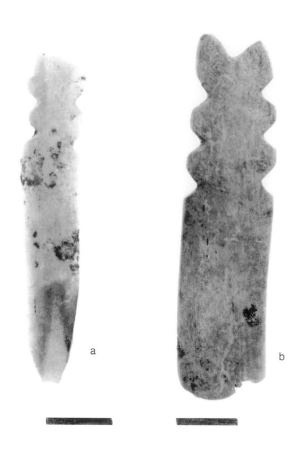

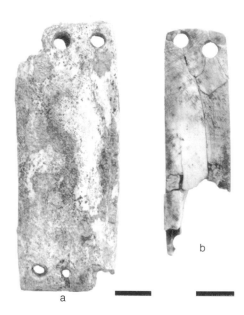

Plate 2.17. "Plaques," perforated and shaped rib of cattle (a) and unidentifiable taxa (b), phase III: (a) SF 834, figure 2.7d; (b) SF 5288, figure 2.7c.

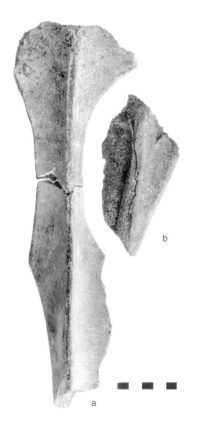

Plate 2.18. Worked scapulae, phase IV: (a) SF 4617, two pieces, figure 2.19; (b) SF 4660, figure 2.13a.

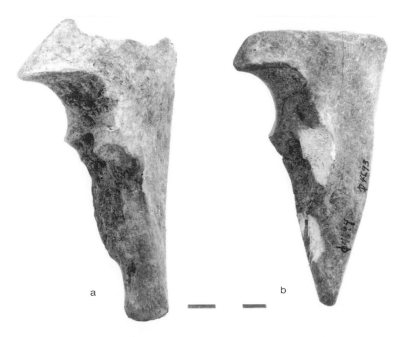

Plate 2.19. Worked ulnae: (a) phase IV, chisel/bevel end, SF 4520; (b) phase III, rounded point, SF 4693, figure 2.20a.

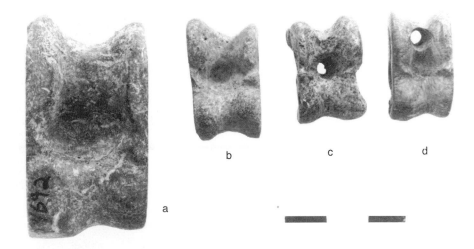

Plate 2.20. Astragali, from phase III, ground on the sides (a, b, d) and perforated (c, d): (a) SF 4698, red deer or cattle, figure 2.20b; (b) SF 4654; (c) SF 4802, figure 9.22; (d) SF 3770.

a

b

Plate 2.21. Worked rib (a) and long bone (b), phase V:
(a) SF 3331, polisher (?); (b) SF 5088, polisher (?)

Plate 2.22. Two views of a section of antler, broken,
shafted with considerable grinding and shaping;
phase III, SF 2945.

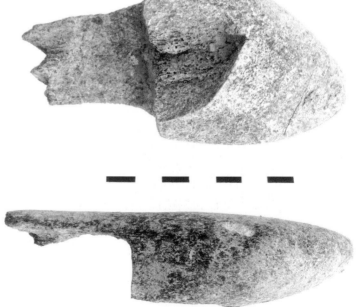

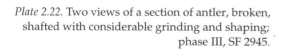

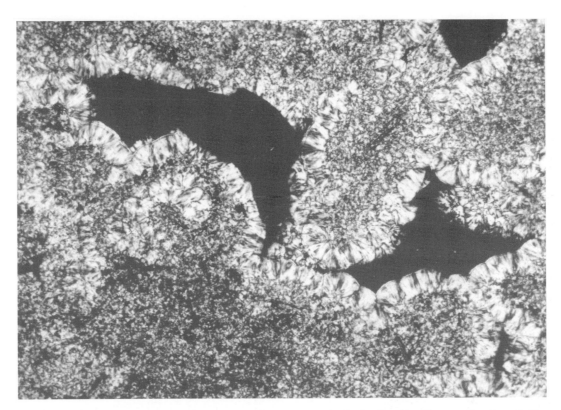

Plate 3.1.1. Chalcedony spheroids lining internal cavities in silicified volcanic tuff; crossed polars; field width 2.3 mm.

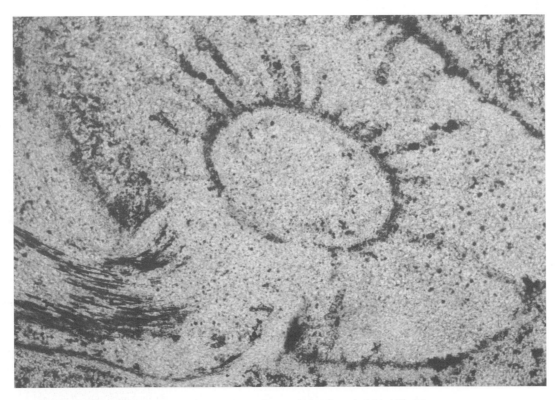

Plate 3.1.2. Plant remnant in silicified volcanic tuff; parallel polars; field width 2.3 mm.

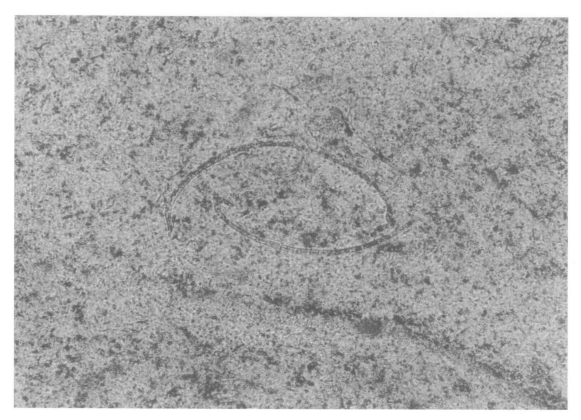

Plate 3.1.3. Ostracoid shell in silicified volcanic tuff; parallel polars; field width 0.83 mm.

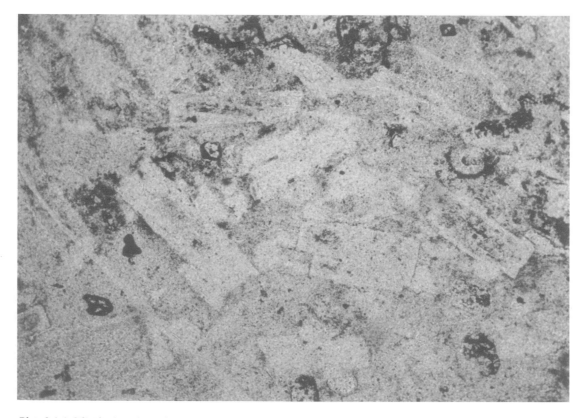

Plate 3.1.4. Silicified acidic volcanic rock with porphyritic texture; parallel polars; field width 2.3 mm.

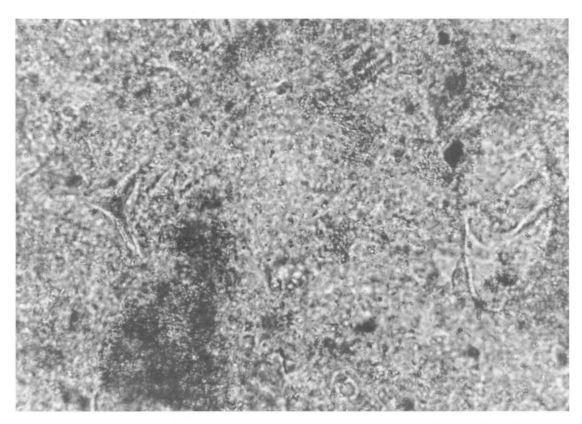

Plate 3.1.5. Silicified pelagic limestone: a sponge spicule (right) and a Foraminifer (left); parallel polars; fi eld width 0.4 mm.

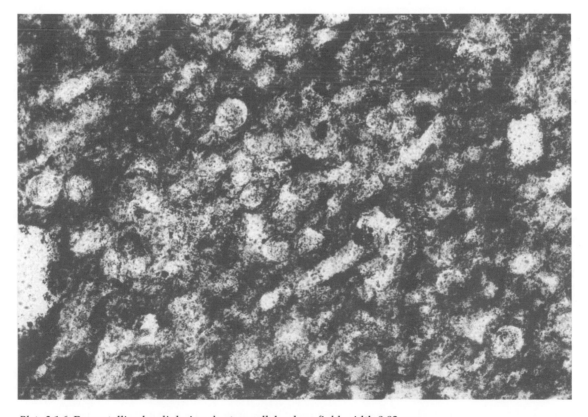

Plate 3.1.6. Recrystallized radiolarian chert; parallel polars; fi eld width 0.83 mm.

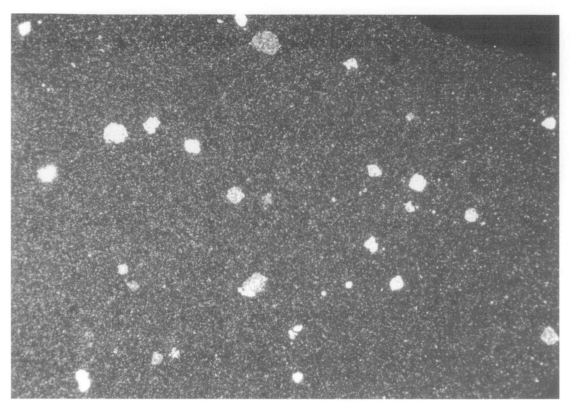

Plate 3.1.7. Microgranular flint with single crystal dolomite rhombohedrons dispersed in it; crossed polars; field width 2.3 mm.

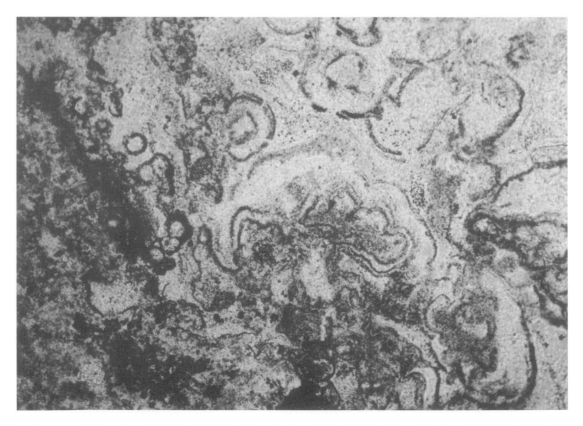

Plate 3.1.8. Convoluted structures (inorganic or inherited from algae or fungal hyphae) in a pure silica rock; parallel polars; field width 2.3 mm.

Plate 5.1. Axes, various sizes, phase I: (a) SF 970, polished dark green, figure 5.6; (b) SF 919, dark gray/green; (c) SF 984, mottled light gray.

a

b

c

Plate 5.2. Celts, phase II: (a) SF 714, fragment, white crystal in pale green matrix; (b) SF 987, axe/ wedge (?), polished, fine-grained, dark gray/green.

a

b

Plate 5.3. Axes, phase II: (a) SF 5350, polished blue/gray; (b) SF 926, polished, medium-grained, mottled white/gray/green/yellow, figure 5.9; (c) SF 471, mottled, fine-grained dark green/black; (d) SF 2309, fine-grained deep green, figure 5.10; (e) SF 478, mottled gray/pink/white; (f) SF 951, coarse-grained pale green with white patches, figure 5.2; (g) SF 956, chisel, fine-grained dark gray, figure 5.4; (h) SF 904, fine-grained deep green; (i) SF 2335, dark green.

Plate 5.4. Axes, phase II (a), phase III (b–d): (a) SF 393, grainy, mottled olive green/ blue, figure 5.1 and plate 5.5b; (b) SF 259, fine-grained dark gray; (c) SF 1635, fragment, polished blue/green; (d) SF 176, fine-grained bottle green.

Plate 5.5. Axes/adzes, phase III: (a) SF 3824, fragment, greenish; (b) SF 393, grainy, mottled olive green/blue, figure 5.1 and plate 5.4a; (c) SF 818, coarse, white flecked with gray, figure 5.5.

Plate 5.6. Axes, medium size (a–f), chisels (g, h), phase III: (a) SF 1269, fine-grained dark gray/green; (b) SF 1563, light brown with white patches; (c) SF 2968, waxy green/brown; (d) SF 811, gritty gray/green; (e) SF 1588, mottled gray/white, figure 5.11; (f) SF 821, matt white with gray patches; (g) SF 891, grooved, polished, mottled gray with green, figure 5.20; (h) SF 5320, fragment, gray.

Plate 5.7. Small axes, phase III (a–e), phase IV (f): (a) SF 1506, polished dark/light green, figure 5.12; (b) SF 1235, fine-grained gray/green; (c) SF 846, mottled gray with brown; (d) SF 842, fine-grained light to medium blue/green, figure 5.3; (e) SF 3450, adze, polished yellow/green, figure 5.13; (f) SF 1277, matt mottled green with white.

Plate 5.8. Small axes, phase V: (a) SF 1011, matt blue/green; (b) SF 1561, fine-grained blue/dark gray; (c) SF 692, matt, mottled white with gray; (d) SF 21, fine-grained, polished, dark blue; (e) SF 656, smooth, polished, black/gray; (f) SF 2217, fine-grained, dark blue/gray (note pointed working [?] edge).

Plate 5.9. Axes/chisels (?), phase IV: (a) SF 2725, fine- to medium-grained, polished green/black; (b) SF 2769, fine-grained, highly polished gray/green; (c) SF 2752, polished gray/green; (d) SF 3925, white/gray flecked with green; (e) SF 2717, coarse, polished gray/green, figure 5.21.

Plate 5.10. Axes, medium-sized, phase V: (a) SF 2249, polished, dark gray/brown; (b) SF 2013, polished, dark gray/brown; (c) SF 2034, fine-grained, polished, dark blue/gray; (d) SF 3012, polished, dark blue/gray; (e) SF 1060, polished, smooth, mottled dark gray with light brown patches, plate 5.12b.

Plate 5.11. Axe fragments, phase II (a, c), phase V (b), unphased (d, e): (a) SF 294, fine-grained, polished, green; (b) SF 486, polished, black/pink; (c) SF 54, matt, polished, fine-grained, light green with light brown patches; (d) SF 1104, polished, mottled, gray/black/dark green; (e) SF 3433, medium-grained, polished, gray/green.

Plate 5.12. Axe fragments, phase V: (a) SF 2232, fragment, medium-grained, light green; (b) SF 1060, polished, smooth, mottled dark gray with light brown patches, plate 5.10e; (c) SF 1308, fragment; one side: polished, smooth, black; obverse: rough (note pitting, from fire [?]).

Plate 5.13. Shaft-hole axeheads, unphased: (a) SF 2248, brown with patches of light brown and veined in dark green; (b) SF 2851, smooth, polished, green/gray/blue, figure 5.16.

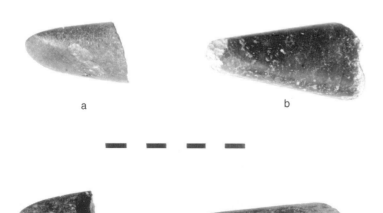

Plate 5.14. Shaft-hole axehead bit fragments, phase V (c) unphased (a, b, d): (a) SF 1719, polished gray/blue/black, figure 5.22; (b) SF 3434, polished yellow/greenish, figure 5.18; (c) SF 1654, matt, dark green with light green flecks; (d) bit, SF 60, cracked but smooth, polished gray/green with brownish end, figure 5.17.

Plate 5.15. Shaft-hole axehead, unfinished, phase V: SF 1650, polished, dark blue with white striations, fine-grained, figure 5.19.

Plate 5.16. Milling pair, phase II: (a) SF 1154, flat oval grinder; (b) SF 1159, grainy schist quern.

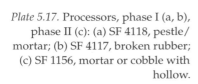

Plate 5.17. Processors, phase I (a, b), phase II (c): (a) SF 4118, pestle/ mortar; (b) SF 4117, broken rubber; (c) SF 1156, mortar or cobble with hollow.

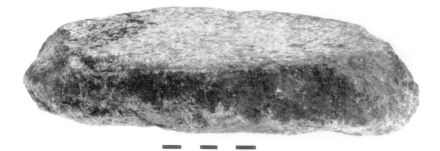

Plate 5.18. Flat quern, phase II: SF 436, split cobble.

Plate 5.19. Small quern from Burnt House, phase Va: SF 4309.

Plate 5.20. Broken quern from the Burnt House, phase Va: SF 4310.

Plate 5.21. Flat quern, three fragments joined from the Burnt House, phase Va: SF 4751.

Plate 5.22. Flat quern, phase V: SF 2247.

Plate 5.23. Saddle quern, phase III: SF 1175.

Plate 5.24. Saddle quern from the Burnt House, phase Va: SF 4687.

Plate 5.25. Mortar/hollowed stone, phase III: SF 1281.

Plate 5.26. Mortar/quern, broken, from the Burnt House, phase Va: SF 4606.

Plate 5.27. Broken quern with double grinding surfaces, phase III: SF 1183.

Plate 5.28. Quern with double grinding surfaces, phase III: SF 1155.

Plate 5.29. Broken saddle quern, phase II: SF 139.

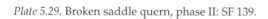

Plate 5.30. Broken saddle quern from the Burnt House, phase Va: SF 4600.

Plate 5.31. Broken saddle quern with elevated rim, phase II: SF 1157.

Plate 5.32. Flat rubbers from the Burnt House, phase II (b, c) and phase Va (a): (a) SF 4308, with break at one end; (b) SF 1154, with fracture at one end, plate 5.16a; (c) SF 1166, oval, rounded.

a   b   c

a   b

Plate 5.33. Round grinder/rubbers, phase II (b), phase III (a): (a) SF 3122, smooth surfaced; (b) SF 431, quite flat with pecking around edges.

Plate 5.34. Oval, heavy grinder from the Burnt House, phase Va: SF 4601.

Plate 5.35. Pestles (?), phase I (a) and phase V (b): (a) SF 4118, plate 5.17a; (b) SF 4792, broken.

Plate 5.36. Impactor with centered depression, phase II: SF 2679.

Plate 5.37. Impactor/grinders, phase II: (a) SF 4407, oval; (b) SF 3831, flattened sphere.

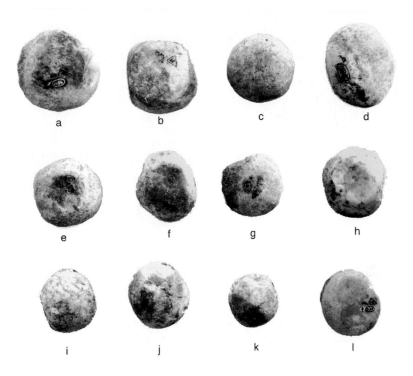

Plate 5.38. Flattened pebble/cobbles, phase III: (a) SF 1136; (b) SF 3447; (c) SF 845; (d) SF 1185; (e) SF 899; (f) SF 1167; (g) SF 1212; (h) SF 3142; (i) SF 5314; (j) SF 2992; (k) SF 839; (l) SF 3129.

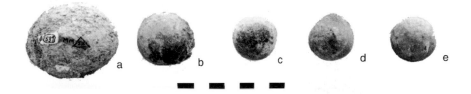

Plate 5.39. Flattened pebble/cobbles, phase III: (a) SF 1539; (b) SF 2943; (c) SF 381; (d) SF 3104; (e) SF 749.

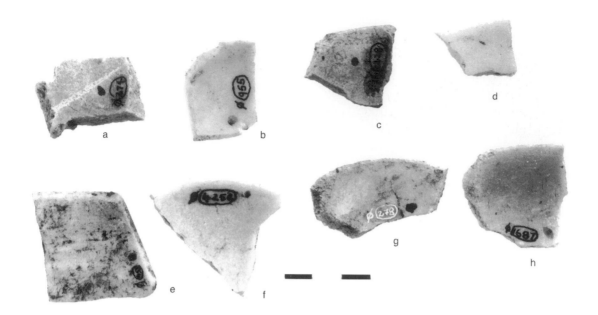

Plate 5.40. Bowl fragments, phase II (b, d–h), phase III (c), unphased (a): (a) SF 274, figure 5.31; (b) SF 955, figure 5.25; (c) SF 1228, figure 5.24; (d) SF 4266, figure 5.30; (e) SF 452, figure 5.23; (f) SF 4254, figure 5.28; (g) SF 278, figure 5.29; (h) SF 1687, figure 5.26.

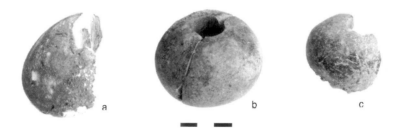

Plate 5.41. Mace heads. (a) Phase V; (b) unphased; (c) phase III: (a) SF 3670, figure 5.33; (b) SF 1344, figure 5.32; (c) SF 830, figure 5.34.

Plate 5.42. Scepter from the Long House: SF 2409.

Plate 6.1. Incised whorls, phase III: (a) SF 5195, figure 6.8d; (b) SF 808, figure 6.8e; (c) SF 2925, figure 6.14d; (d) SF 1437, figure 6.12c; (e) SF 4211, figure 6.5a; (f) SF 2990, figure 6.5c; (g) SF 1266, figure 6.6e; (h) SF 1222, figure 6.11a.

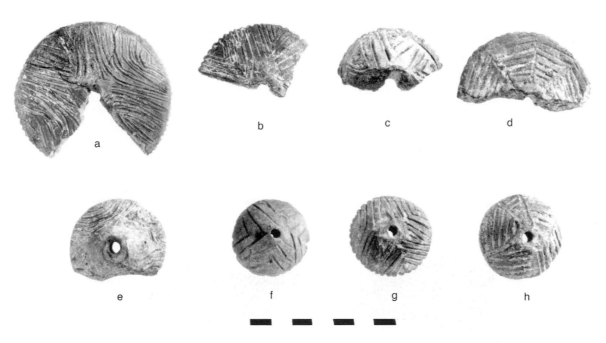

Plate 6.2. Incised whorls, phase III: (a) SF 1684, figure 6.11d; (b) SF1254, figure 6.11c; (c) SF 1543, figure 6.7d; (d) SF 1440, figure 6.11e; (e) SF 1267, figure 6.7e; (f) SF 3478, figure 6.6a; (g) SF 5035, figure 6.6d; (h) SF 841, figure 6.6c.

Plate 6.3. Incised whorls, phase III: (a) SF 739, figure 6.13b; (b) SF 737, figure 6.9d; (c) SF 183, figure 6.7a; (d) SF 3488, figure 6.6b; (e) SF 1423, figure 6.12a; (f) SF 862, figure 6.13a; (g) SF 3588, figure 6.12d; (h) SF 2933, figure 6.14b.

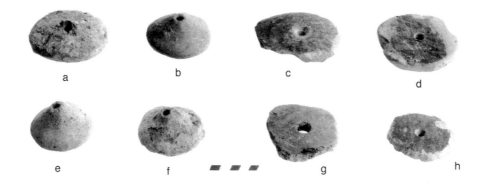

Plate 6.4. Whorls, phase III (a, b, d–h), phase V (c); flat (a), shallow cones (b, e, f); recycled sherds (c, d, g, h): (a) SF 2946; (b) SF 3589; (c) SF 22, figure 6.15c; (d) SF 392, figure 6.15b; (e) SF 2991; (f) SF 3128; (g) SF 3743, figure 6.15a; (h) SF 1540.

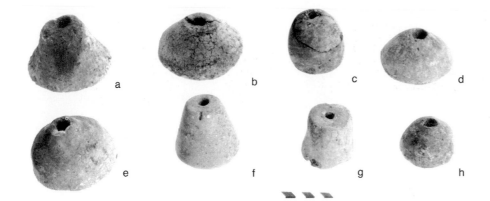

Plate 6.5. Whorls, flat-based with variously shaped faces: phase IV (a, b, e, f); phase V (c, d, g, h): (a) SF 2742, figure 6.3c; (b) SF 3252, figure 6.3d; (c) SF 3304; (d) SF 658; (e) SF 2765; (f) SF 3206; (g) SF 364; (h) SF 1049.

Plate 6.6. Whorls, all biconical, and (d) incised, phase V: (a) SF 3354; (b) SF 4435; (c) SF 1013; (d) SF 1014; (e) SF 1359; (f) SF 1651; (g) SF 608; (h) SF 2043.

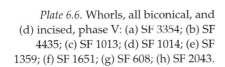

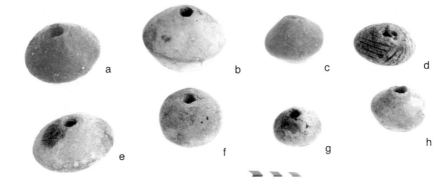

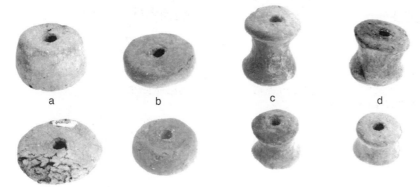

Plate 6.7. Whorls, phase V, truncated (a, f), flat (b, e); spools (c, d, g, h): (a) SF 1065, figure 6.4g; (b) SF 2024; (c) SF 1317; (d) SF 1653; (e) SF 1610; (f) SF 2014; (g) SF 2068; (h) SF 373.

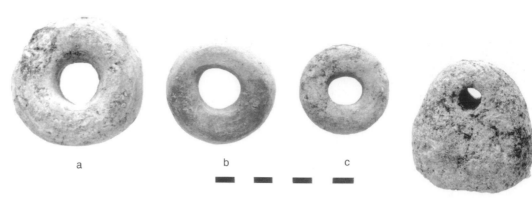

Plate 6.8. Weights, phase III, round (a, b, c) and bag shape (d): (a) SF 5017, figure 6.23; (b) SF 1520; (c) SF 220; (d) SF 492, figure 6.20.

a

b

c

d

a

b

d

c

Plate 6.9. Weights, various shapes, phase IV: (a) SF 3060, cone or bell, figure 6.21; cylinders (b, c): (b) SF 3057; (c) SF 3058; bag (d): SF 3059.

Plate 6.10. Weights, phase IV: (a) SF 2703, cylindrical; (b) SF 1043, pyramidal, plates 6.11b, 6.21c.

a

b

Plate 6.11. Weights, pyramidal (a–d), phase V: (a) SF 1042, plate 6.12b; (b) SF 1043, plates 6.10b, 6.12c; (c) SF 1058; (d) SF 1050; hook fragments: (e) SF 1670; (f) SF 1674.

Plate 6.12. Weights, pyramidal (a–e), phase V: (a) SF 1028, figure 6.18; (b) SF 1042, plate 6.11a; (c) SF 1043, plates 6.10b, 6.11b; (d) SF 495, figure 6.22a; (e) SF 3622, stone, figure 6.22b; round, rough clay (f, g): (f) SF 357; (g) SF 372, figure 6.19b.

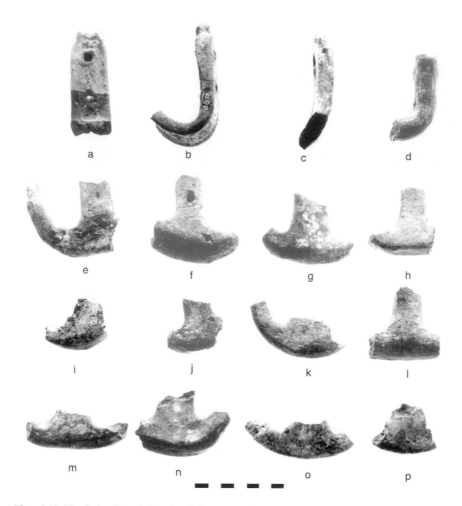

Plate 6.13. Hook (a–d) and "anchor" fragments (e–p), phase V: (a) SF 529, figure 6.24b; (b) SF 538, figure 6.26; (c) SF 539, figure 6.25; (d) SF 57, figure 6.24a; (e) SF 1080, figure 6.28b; (f) SF 2448, figure 6.30; (g) SF 1681, figure 6.29a; (h) SF 1649; (i) SF 1728; (j) SF 5447, figure 6.29b; (k) SF 1552; (l) SF 1336; (m) SF 4404; (n) SF 1334, figure 6.28a; (o) SF 1361; (p) SF 4779.

Plate 6.14. Mat impression, close coiling, phase III: SF 1542.

Plate 6.15. Mat impression, twill plaiting, 2 x 2 interval, phase III: SF 1724.

Plate 6.16. Mat impression, twill plaiting, 2 x 2 interval, Phase III: SF 5611.

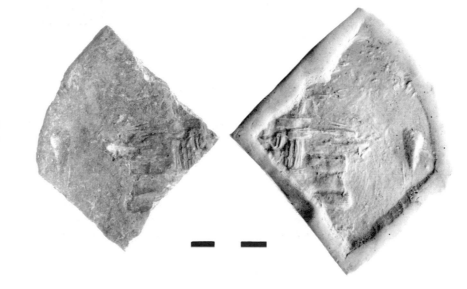

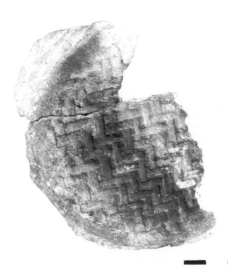

Plate 6.17. Mat impression, twill plaiting, 2 x 2 interval, phase I: SF 1410.

Plate 6.18. Mat impression, twill plaiting, 2 x 2 interval, with selvage, phase II: SF 1639.

Plate 6.19. Cloth impression, faced plain weave, phase I: SF 1439.

Plate 7.1. Low-fired ceramics: (a) gray lustre, (b) red-on-buff, (c) black burnished rippled, (d) gray lustre channeled, (e) red slipped, (f) fine black burnished, (g) brown-on-cream, (h) white-on-red, (i) brown-on-buff, (j) brown-on-red, (k) orange burnished, (l) orange-on-orange.

Plate 7.2. High-fired ceramics (types: a, b, e–g; forms: c, d): (a) incised with white infill, (b) graphite painted, (c) lamp, (d) pithos with grooves, (e) incised, (f) grooved, (g) pointillé.

Plate 7.2.1. Rim sherd with curving graphite lines on brown body, SF 60, MM19.

Plate 7.2.2. Body sherd with linear design of parallel and angled graphite paint, SF 7, ZA 32.

a

b

Plate 8.1. Metal artifacts, phase II: (a) SF 2999, flat piece of copper; (b) SF 5336, copper bead, figure 8.1a.

Plate 8.2. Metal artifacts, phase III: (a) SF 880, copper roll-headed pin, figure 8.1f; (b) SF 1238, copper awl or fishhook, figure 8.1g, plate 8.9a; (c) SF 781, small copper disc, figure 8.1b; (d) SF 5334, copper (?) bead in fragments; (e) SF 5622, small piece of corroded metal, plate 8.9c; (f) SF 5623, thin piece of irregularly shaped copper.

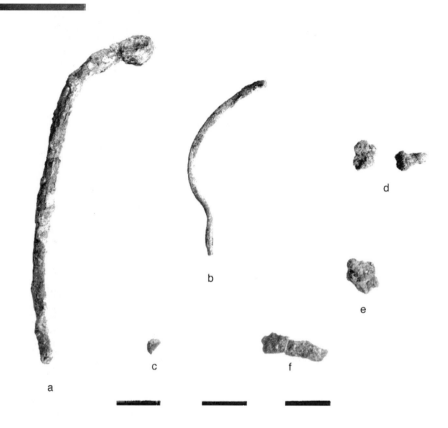

d

b

c

f

e

a

a

b

Plate 8.3. Copper beads, phase III: (a) SF 783, figure 8.1d; (b) SF 5340.

Plate 8.4. Gold bead, two views, phase III: SF 4803, figure 8.1c.

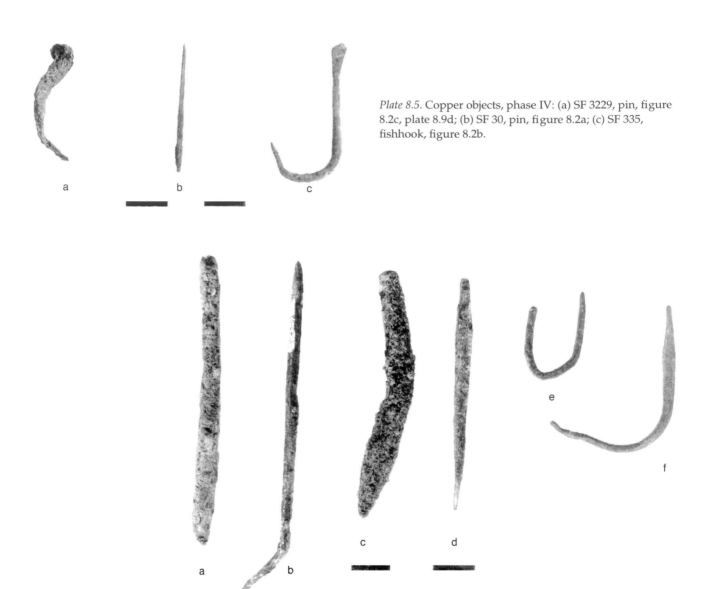

Plate 8.5. Copper objects, phase IV: (a) SF 3229, pin, figure 8.2c, plate 8.9d; (b) SF 30, pin, figure 8.2a; (c) SF 335, fishhook, figure 8.2b.

Plate 8.6. Copper objects, phases Va (b), Vb (a, c–e), and V (f): (a) SF 1041, large nail, figure 8.3g; (b) SF 3313, point, figure 8.3e; (c) SF 2057, awl, figure 8.3f; (d) SF 2086, awl, figure 8.3j; (e) SF 5337, fishhook, figure 8.3b; (f) SF 331, awl, figure 8.3i.

Plate 8.7. Copper awl, phase Vb: SF 3005, figure 8.3b.

Plate 8.8. Copper pin, phase Va: SF 3017, figure 8.3a.

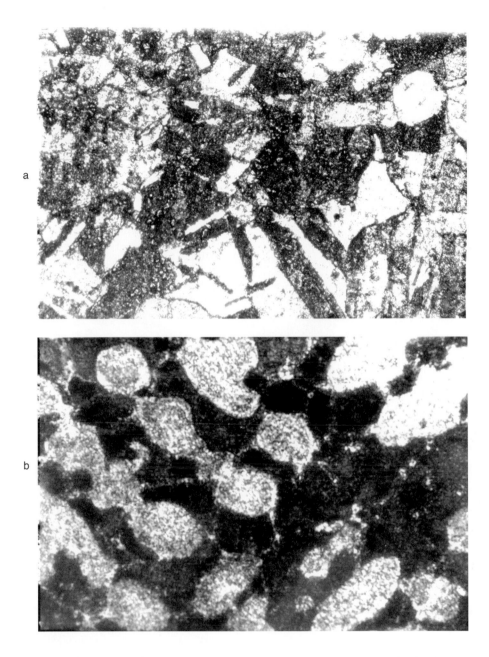

Plate 8.9. Metal microstructures, phase III: (a) SF 1238, copper awl or fishhook, magnification 180 X, showing cold-worked and annealed microstructure; figure 8.1g, plate 8.2b; (b) SF 3439, copper fragments, magnification 240 X, showing dendritic microstructure.

Plate 8.9. Metal microstructures (continued): (c) phase III, SF 5622, small piece of corroded metal, magnification 300 X, showing cold-worked and annealed microstructure; plate 8.2e; (d) phase IV, SF 3229, copper pin, magnification 240 X, showing cold-worked and annealed microstructure; figure 8.2c, plate 8.5a.

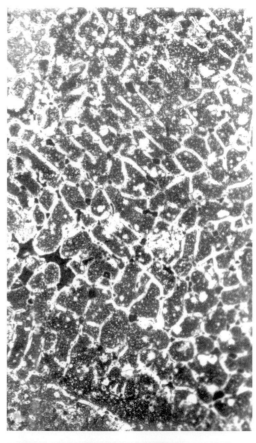

Plate 8.9. Metal microstructures (continued): (e) phase IV, SF 5625, piece of metal (bronze?), magnification 120 X, showing cold-worked microstructure; (f) phase Vb, SF 2084, lump of copper fragments, magnification 120 X, showing as-cast dendritic microstructure; (g) phase V, SF 5627, small piece of corroded copper, magnification 120 X, showing as-cast dendritic microstructure.

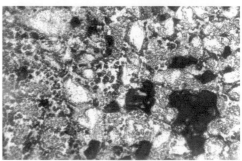

Plate 8.10. Crucible fragment with trace of copper deposit on rim, phase III: SF 5584, figure 8.4i.

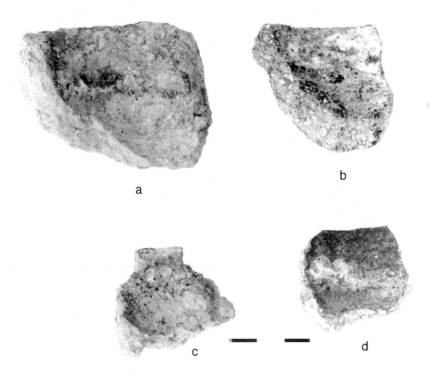

Plate 8.11. Crucible fragments (rim sherds) with copper deposits, phase III: (a) SF 5564, figure 8.4c; (b) SF 4906, figure 8.4d; (c) SF 5562, figure 8.4b; (d) SF 5566, figure 8.4g.

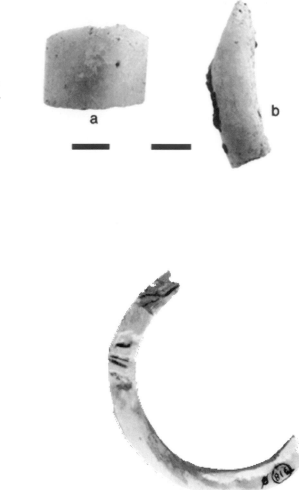

Plate 9.1. Fragments of two marble bangles: (a) phase II, SF 5321, figure 9.4; (b) phase I, SF 3681, figure 9.3.

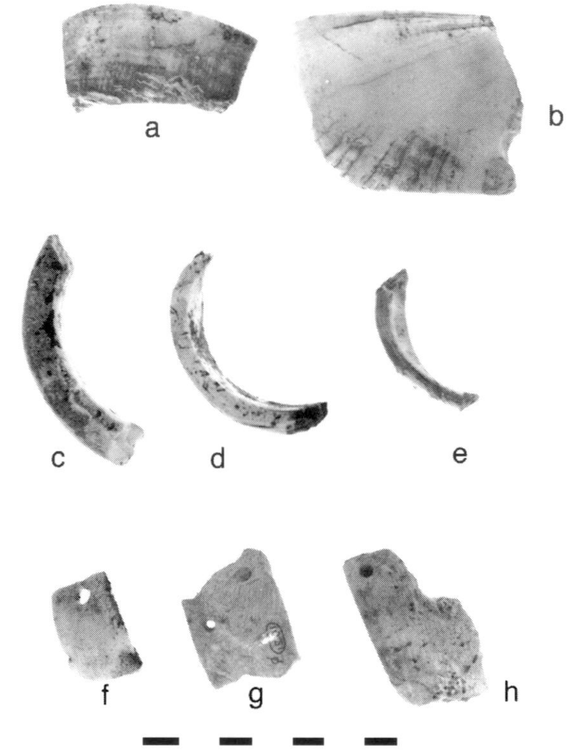

Plate 9.2. Fragments of *Spondylus* bracelet/annulets: (a) phase III, SF 487; (b) phase I, SF 2518; (c) phase II, SF 976b; (d) phase III, SF 206; (e) unphased, SF 1643; (f) phase III, SF 1299; (g) phase III, SF 1201; (h) phase III, SF 1592.

Plate 9.3. Worked preform of a *Spondylus* bangle, phase III: SF 816, plate 9.7q.

Plate 9.4. Large segment of perforated *Spondylus* bracelet or bangle, phase III: SF 3877.

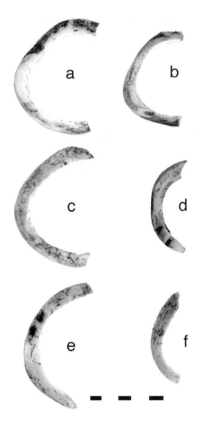

Plate 9.5. Group of fragmentary bangles or bracelets, MM 61, phase III: (a) SF 3486; (b) SF 3485; (c) SF 3484; (d) SF 3489; (e) SF 3431; (f) SF 3505.

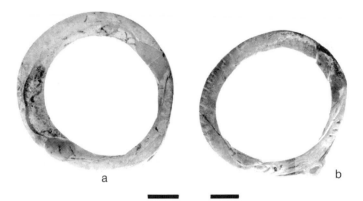

Plate 9.6. Glycymeris bracelet/annulets, phase III: SF 3427 (a, b).

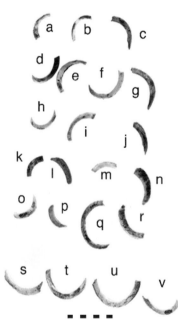

Plate 9.7. Fragments of *Spondylus* bracelet/annulets, MM/ML hearth and debris levels (a–e, g–j, l, n, q–r, u–v); MM/ML lower levels (k, o–p, s); and ZA floor 15 (t), phase III: (a) SF 1234; (b) SF 898; (c) SF 1227; (d) SF 1233; (e) SF 1256; (f) SF 1536; (g) SF 1205; (h) SF 892; (i) SF 1203; (j) SF 1243; (k) SF 1287; (l) SF 1445; (m) SF 1537; (n) SF 1710; (o) SF 1566; (p) SF 3487b; (q) SF 816; (r) SF 1259; (s) SF 1279; (t) SF 213; (u) SF 400; (v) SF 1300.

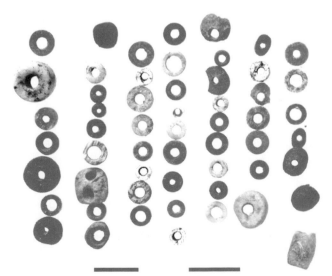

Plate 9.8. Grouped assorted beads from ZA 44s, phase III: clay, SF 5212a; shell, SF 5212b; and stone SF 5212c; figure 9.19.

Plate 9.9. Assorted beads of clay (a–g) and stone (h): (a) biconical, phase I, SF 1628, figure 9.11; (b) barrel, phase III, SF 3833; (c) biconical, phase III, SF 5077a, figure 9.14; (d) narrow cylindrical, phase III, SF 1274; (e) narrow cylindrical, phase IV, SF 5058; (f) biconical, phase IV, SF 5058, figure 9.13; (g) tubular, phase IV, SF 533, figure 9.8; (h) tubular, SF 3054, phase IV.

Plate 9.10. Wide cylindrical shell bead, phase III: SF 3823, also plate 9.11b.

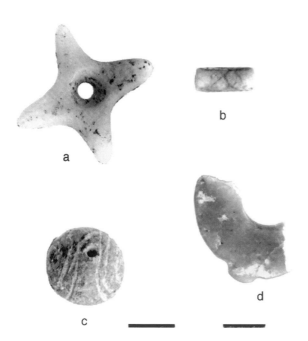

Plate 9.11. An assortment of elaborated beads (a–c) and a pendant (d): (a) *Spondylus* "star," phase II, SF 4793, figure 9.20; (b) shell, cylinder, phase III, SF 3823, plate 9.10; (c) decorated clay biconical, phase III, SF 1219, figure 9.12; (d) stone ring-shaped, phase I, SF 113, figure 9.23a.

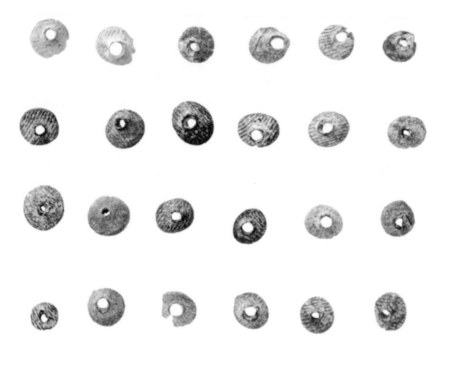

Plate 9.12. Grouped striated, pinched clay beads from ZA 44s, phase III: SF 5210, figure 9.9.

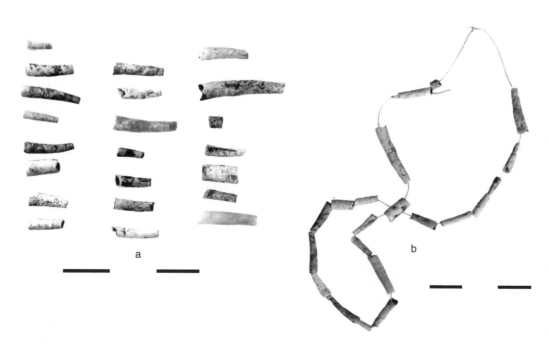

Plate 9.13. Group of *Dentalium* beads from ZA 52s, phase II, SF 5203; (a) as found; (b) reconstructed as a chain.

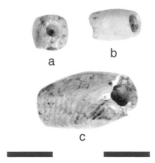

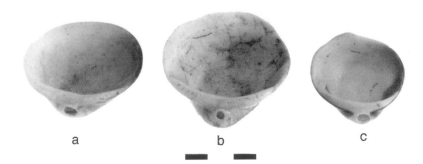

Plate 9.14. Elaborate *Spondylus* beads:
(a) phase III, SF 5223b, "button," figure
9.18; (b) phase III, SF 5080b, barrel-
shaped; (c) phase V, SF 1587, barrel-
shaped, figure 9.15.

Plate 9.15. Glycymeris pendants: (a) phase III, SF 2971; (b) phase II, SF 2887;
(c) phase III, SF 2981.

Plate 9.16 Glycymeris pendant, phase III:
SF 80.

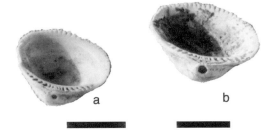

Plate 9.17. Glycymeris pendants, phase III:
(a) SF 778c; (b) SF 778b.

Plate 9.18. Cardium pendant, phase II: SF 2889.

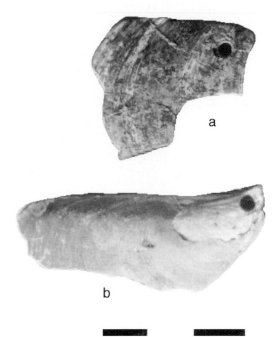

Plate 9.19. *Mytilus* pendants, worked and perforated: (a) phase I, SF 2530, miscellaneously worked; (b) phase II, SF 2886.

Plate 9.20. *Cypraea* pendant, phase IV: SF 832.

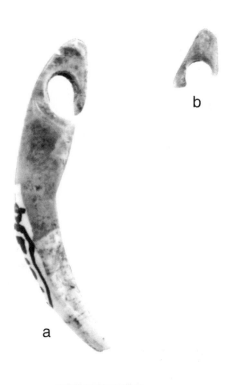

Plate 9.21. *Neritea* shell bearing a large hole for possible food extraction and/or suspension, phase III: SF 779.

Plate 9.22. Fragment of perforated animal pendant: (a) phase IV, SF 5124, canine tooth of a dog; (b) phase V, SF 5089, unidentifiable fragment.

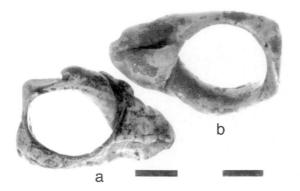

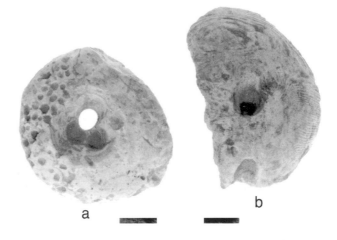

Plate 9.23. Murex ring-shaped pendants: (a) phase IV, SF 415; (b) phase II, SF 4748.

Plate 9.24. Spondylus discoid pendants: (a) phase III, SF 2995; (b) unphased, SF 4804.

Plate 9.25. Clay polygonal pendant with painted decoration, phase III: SF 1108, figure 9.25.

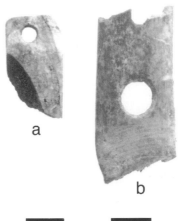

Plate 9.26. Cypraea pendant, phase V: SF 1001.

Plate 9.27. Bone plaques: (a) phase I, SF 923; (b) phase II, SF 1705.

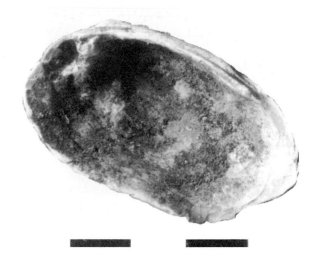

Plate 9.1.1. Worked *Unio* valve with remains of red ochre in the interior, phase III: SF 2888.

a

b

c

Plate 9.1.2. Worked *Unio* valves, phase III: SF 5252a–c.

Plate 9.1.3. Unworked *Spondylus* fragment, phase II: SF 2320.

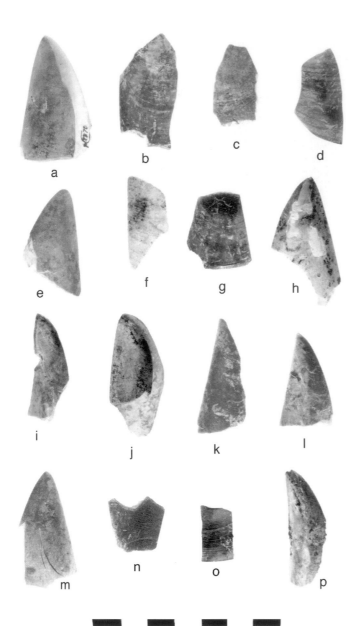

Plate 9.1.4. Worked *Mytilus* fragments: phase I (o); phase II (a–c, e, h, m); phase III (d, f, g); (a) SF 2870; (b) SF 2871; (c) SF 2573; (d) SF 2873; (e) SF 2874; (f) SF 2875; (g) SF 2876; (h) SF 2877; (i) SF 2878; (j) SF 2879; (k) SF 2880; (l) SF 2881; (m) SF 2882; (n) SF 2883; (o) SF 2884; (p) SF 288.

Plate 9.1.5. Worked *Mytilus* "triangle," phase II: SF 2870, plate 9.1.4a.

Plate 9.1.6. Worked oyster valve (*Ostrea edulis*), phase II: SF 965.

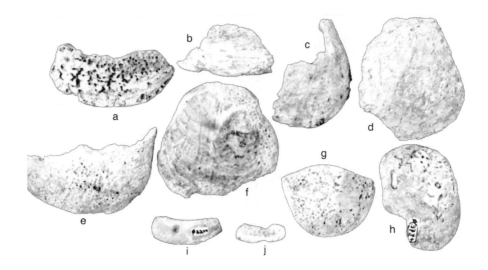

Plate 9.2.1. Bracelet/annulets made from *Spondylus* valves: phase II (a, c, g, h); phase III (d–f, j); unphased (i). (a) SF 5605; (b) SF 3659; (c) SF 5606; (d) SF 5607; (e) SF 505; (f) SF 2962; (g) SF 2364; (h) SF 3734; (i) SF 2244; (j) SF 784.

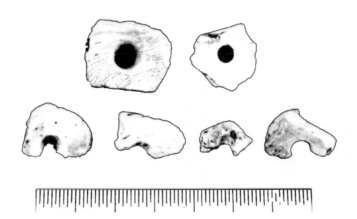

Plate 9.2.2. Spondylus bead fragments, phase II: SF 5262.

Plate 9.2.3. Small fired steatite beads: Length, 0.1 to 0.8 cm (mean 0.38); diameter, 0.2 to 1.4 cm (mean 0.54); hole diameter, 0.015 to 0.35 cm (mean 0.16).

a

b

Plate 10.1. Incised cylinder, phase II, SF 516; (a) cylinder and roll-out, (b) enlarged roll-out, figure 10.1a.

a

b

Plate 10.2. Incised cylinder, phase II, SF 446; (a) cylinder and roll-out, (b) enlarged roll-out, figure 10.1b.

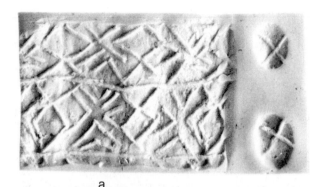

a

Plate 10.3. Incised cylinder, phase II,
SF 3684; (a) cylinder and roll-out,
(b) enlarged roll-out, figure 10.1c.

b

Plate 10.4. Incised cylinder and roll-out,
phase II: SF 1443, figure 10.2a.

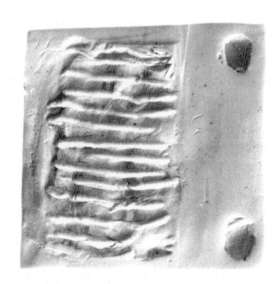

Plate 10.5. Incised cylinder and roll-out from the Bin Complex, phase Vb: SF 1145, figure 10.2b.

a

b

Plate 10.6. "Stamp seal," two views, phase III, SF 861: (a) side view, (b) left: enlargement of incised base, and right: imprint; figure 10.6.

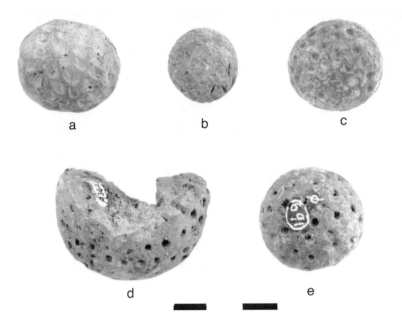

Plate 10.7. Clay spheres or "golf balls," unphased (a–c), phase III (d), and phase Vb (e): (a) SF 55; (b) SF 81; (c) SF 3607, figure 10.8b; (d) SF 3603; (e) SF 691, figure 10.8a.

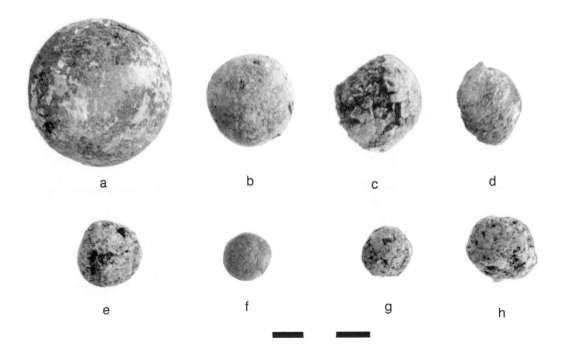

Plate 10.8. Plain spheres of various sizes, phase III (b) and phase V (a, c–h): (a) SF 2011; (b) SF 153; (c) SF 2401; (d) SF 2090; (e) SF 3562b; (f) SF 2083; (g) SF 3562c; (h) SF 3562a.

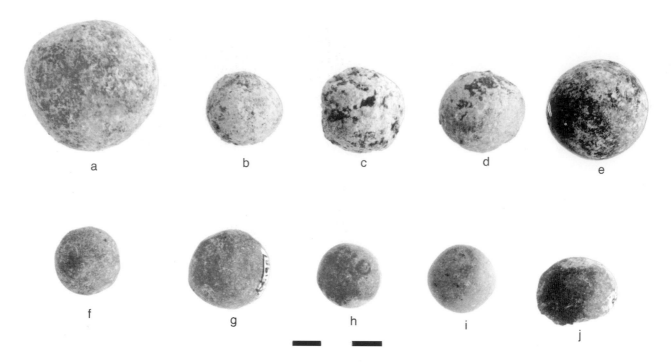

Plate 10.9. Plain spheres, phase III: (a) SF 385; (b) SF 383; (c) SF 723; (d) SF 881; (e) SF 157; (f) SF 837; (g) SF 5198; (h) SF 5192; (i) SF 5193; (j) SF 3880.

Plate 10.10. Clay biconoids, phase I (a, c, e), phase II (b, d): (a) SF 4103; (b) SF 2680; (c) SF 2694; (d) SF 2678; (e) SF 117.

Plate 10.11. Clay biconoids, phase II: (a) SF 2638;
(b) SF 964; (c) SF 2677; (d) SF 4226; (e) SF 2613;
(f) SF 2643; (g) SF 922; (h) SF 2635.

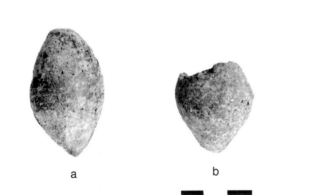

Plate 10.12. Clay biconoids, phase III:
(a) SF 1278; (b) SF 394; (c) SF 531.

Plate 10.13. Clay biconoids: (a) phase III, SF 2779;
(b) phase Vb, SF 20.

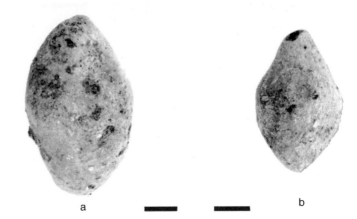

Plate 11.1. Ladle fragments, phase III: (a) SF 186, bowl section, figure 11.1; (b) SF 3418; handle fragment.

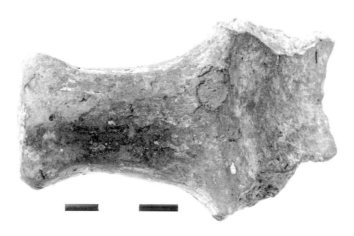

Plate 11.2. Handle section of pan, phase III: SF unknown.

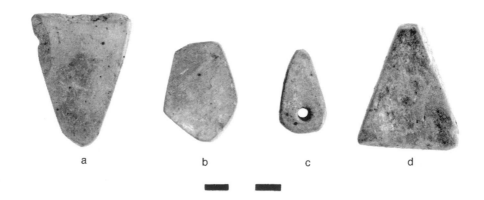

Plate 11.3. Sherds worked into various shapes, phase III (a, d), unphased (b, c): (a) SF 4575, triangle; (b) SF 3720, polygonal; (c) SF 4774, pendant; (d) SF 4909, triangle.

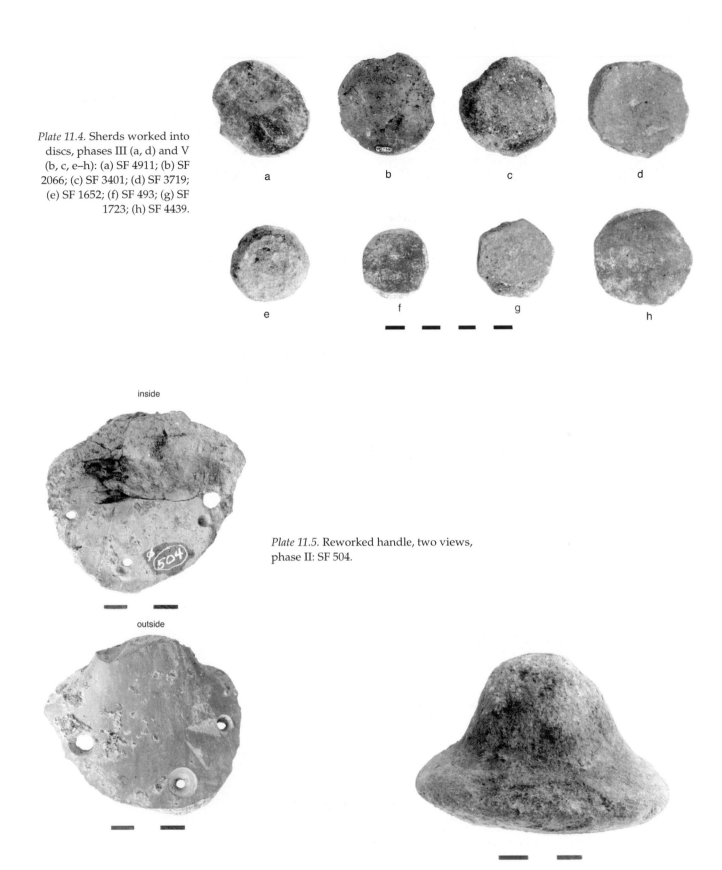

Plate 11.4. Sherds worked into discs, phases III (a, d) and V (b, c, e–h): (a) SF 4911; (b) SF 2066; (c) SF 3401; (d) SF 3719; (e) SF 1652; (f) SF 493; (g) SF 1723; (h) SF 4439.

a

b

c

d

e

f

g

h

inside

Plate 11.5. Reworked handle, two views, phase II: SF 504.

outside

Plate 11.6. Clay plug or lid, phase V: SF 3657.

Plate 11.7. Oven (?) stoppers, phase V: (a) SF 309; (b) SF 1301; (c) SF 1087; (d) SF 5560; (e) SF 1351; (f) SF 1646.

Plate 11.8. Oven (?) stoppers, phase V (a, c) and unphased (b): (a) SF 309, figure 11.7a; (b) SF 5560, plate 11.7d; (c) SF 1087, figure 11.7c.

Plate 11.9. "Kritsana" bowl fragment, phase III: SF 47, figure 11.9.

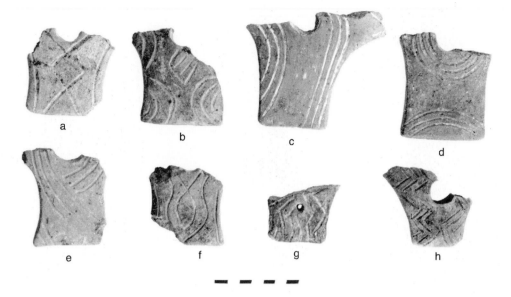

Plate 11.10. Incised flat pieces (handles?), phases I (f), II (a–d), and V (g, h) and unphased (e): (a) SF 2280; (b) SF 743; (c) SF 2281; (d) SF 242; (e) SF 2289; (f) SF 2828; (g) SF 1695; (h) SF 544.

Plate 11.11. Incised flat pieces ("plaques"), phases II (b, c) and III (a, d): (a) SF 5159; (b) SF 1498; (c) SF 461; (d) SF 4812.

Plate 11.12. Phase IV, incised fragment: SF 1402, figure 11.17.

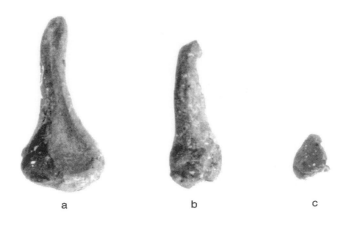

Plate 11.13. Figurine leg sections (a, b): phase I, SF 416; upper leg fragment (c): phase III, SF 233, figure 11.18.

a b c

Plate 11.14. Leg of a stand or vessel, phase IV: SF 5579.

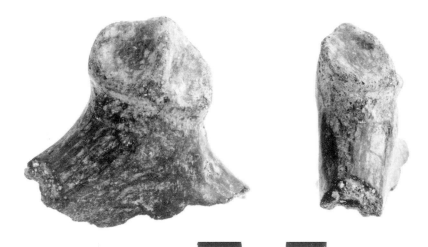

Plate 11.15. Protome attached to vessel, phase III: SF unknown.

Plate 11.16. Phallus, phase III: SF 1264, figure 11.24.

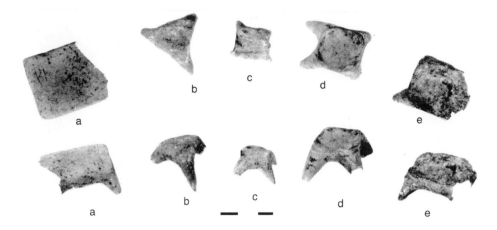

Plate 11.17. Miniature stools or table, two views; phase II (b–d); phase III (a, e): (a) SF 5174, figure 11.31; (b) SF 2508; (c) SF 1662, figure 11.30; (d) SF 2666; (e) SF 827, figure 11.29.

Plate 11.18. Miniature furniture, phase II (c–f, h); phase III (a, b, g): (a) chair, SF 1257, figure 11.34; (b) table, SF 3836, figure 11.37; (c) stool, SF 2666, plate 11.17d; (d) chair, SF 144, figure 11.32; (e) table, SF 78, figure 11.38; (f) chair, SF 901, figure 11.33; (g) stool, SF 1492, figure 11.25; (h) stool, SF 245, figure 11.27.

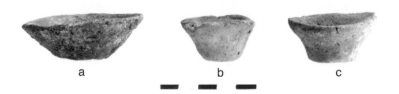

Plate 11.19. Miniature bowls with everted profile, phase III: (a) SF 10, figure 11.50; (b) SF 68, figure 11.40; (c) SF 83.

Plate 11.20. Miniature vessels, phase III: (a) bowl, SF 197; (b) bowl, SF 205; (c) "amphoriskos," SF 61, figure 11.45; (d) jar, SF 58, figure 11.44.

Plate 11.21. Miniature bowl or jug with incised decoration, phase II: SF 317.

Plate 11.22. Miniature vessels, phase III: (a) jar, SF 88; (b) "amphoriskos," SF 322; (c) urn, SF 60, figure 11.46; (d) urn or bowl, SF 115, figure 11.43.

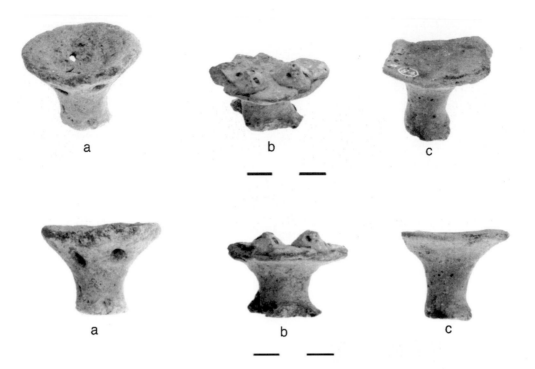

Plate 11.23. Miniature pedestaled bowls or platters, two views: (a) phase III, SF 384, figure 11.48; (b) phase II, SF 5377, figure 11.49, plate 11.24; (c) phase II, SF 84.

Plate 11.24. Miniature pedestaled platter holding three rounded elements, phase II: SF 5377, figure 11.49, plate 11.23b.

Plate 11.25. Miniature incised pedestaled bowl, phase III: SF 338, figure 11.51.

Plate 11.26. House model, phase III: SF 755, plate 11.27e.

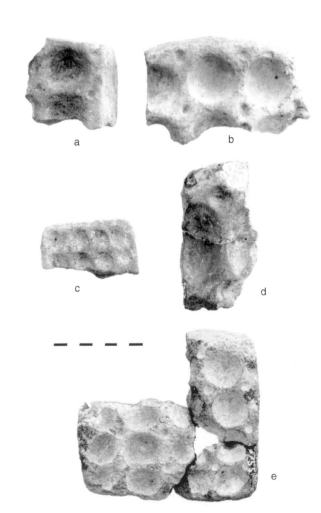

Plate 11.27. "Dimple bases," phase III: (a) SF 3677; (b) SF 1112; (c) SF 1572, unphased (III?); (d) SF 1472; (e) house model, SF 755, plate 11.26.

Plate 11.28. Oven model, phase III: SF 813.

Plate 11.29. Model clay axeheads, two views, phase III (a, b), phase IV (c), and unphased (d): (a) SF 3416, figure 11.54; (b) SF 375, figure 11.53; (c) SF 3207, figure 11.52; (d) SF 337, figure 11.55.

Site Index

Index